Islamic Art

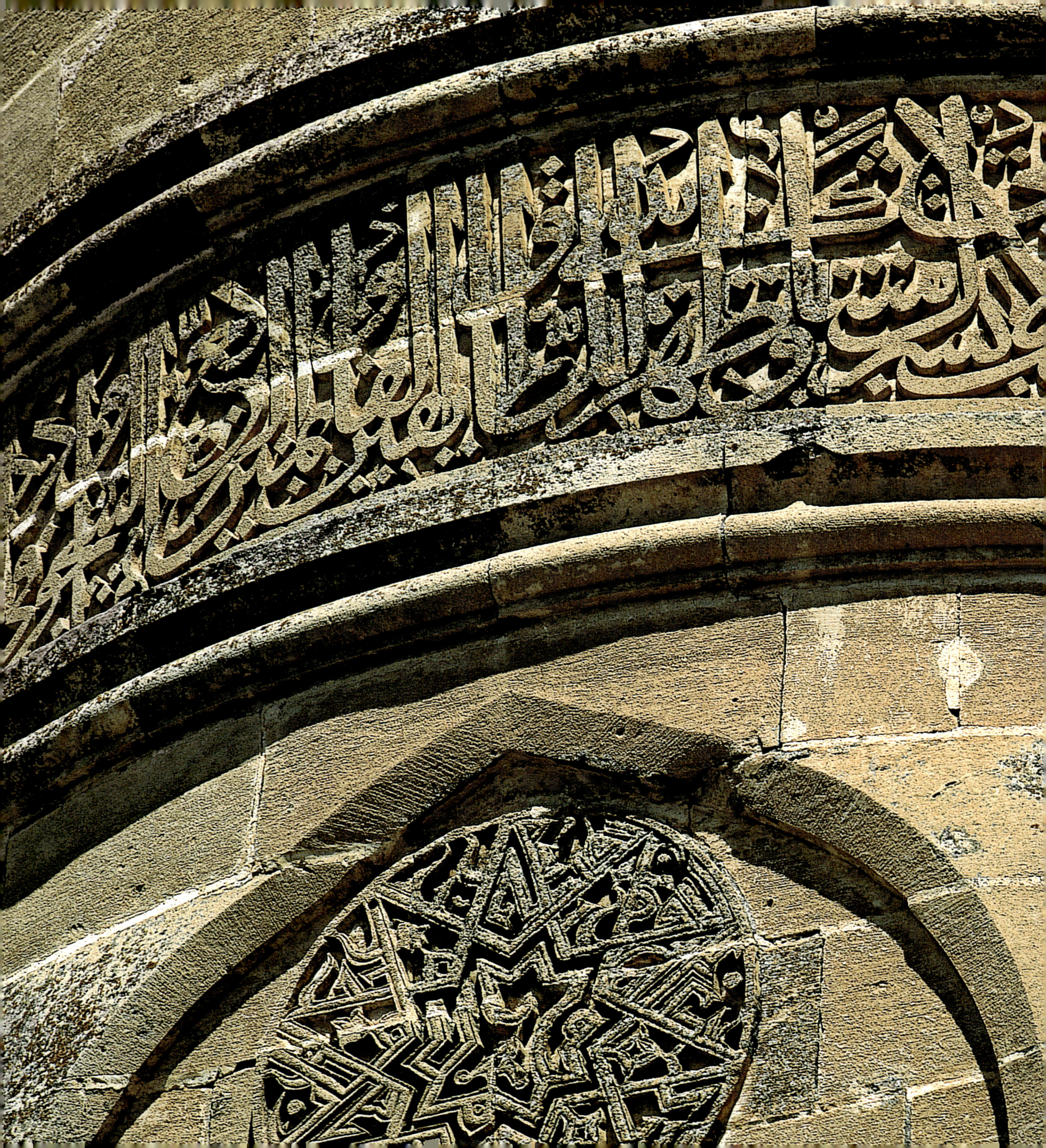

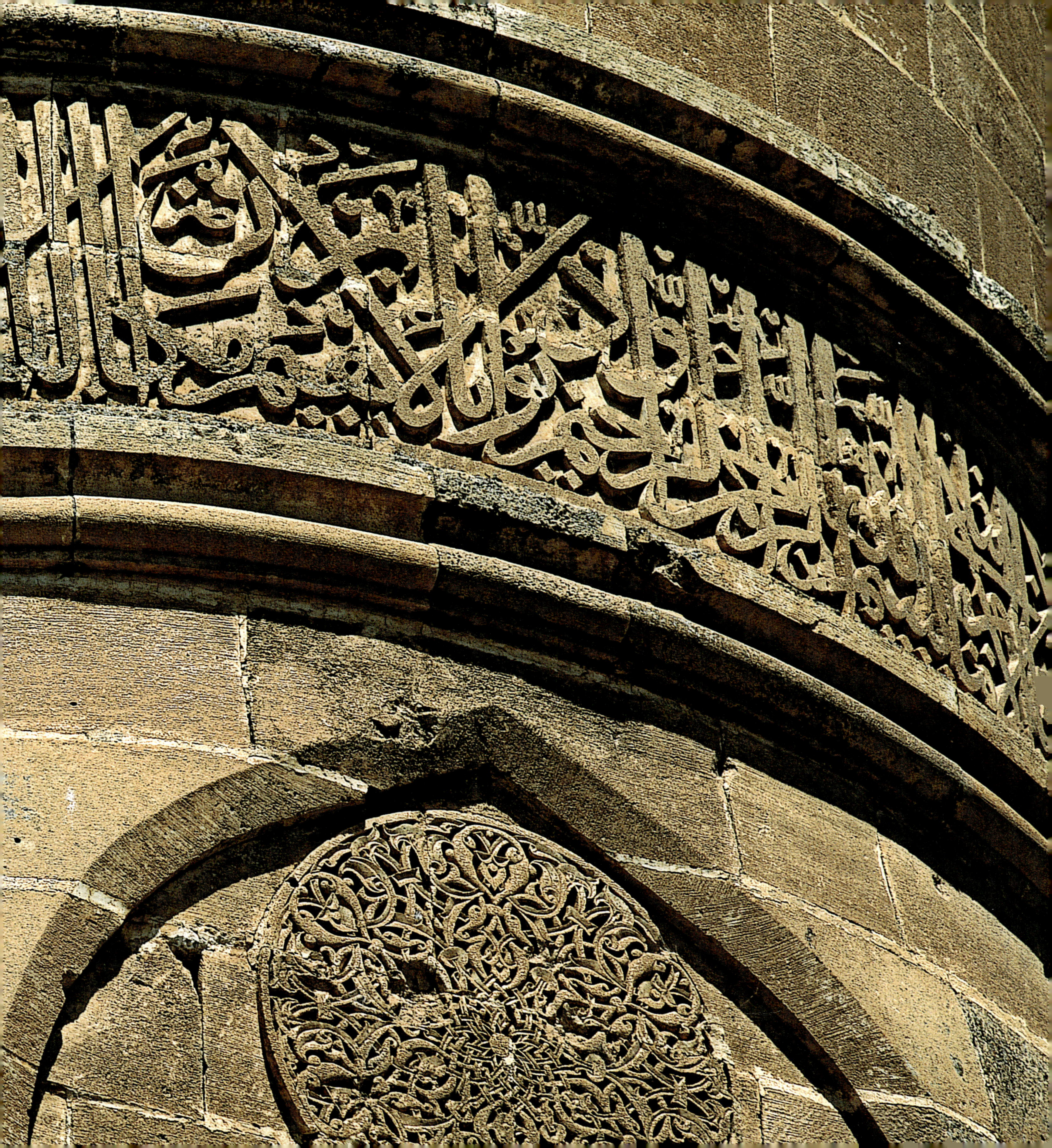

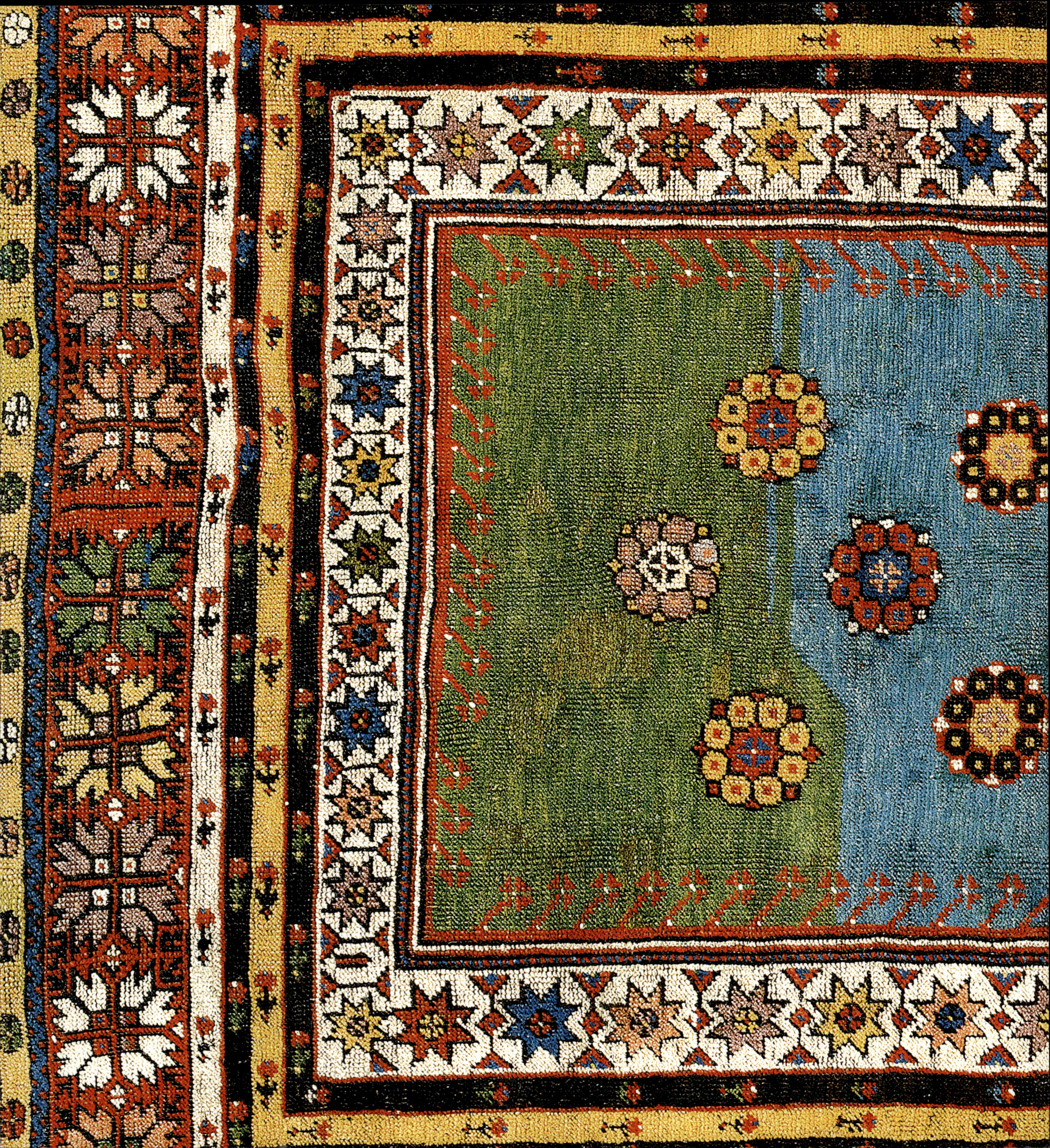

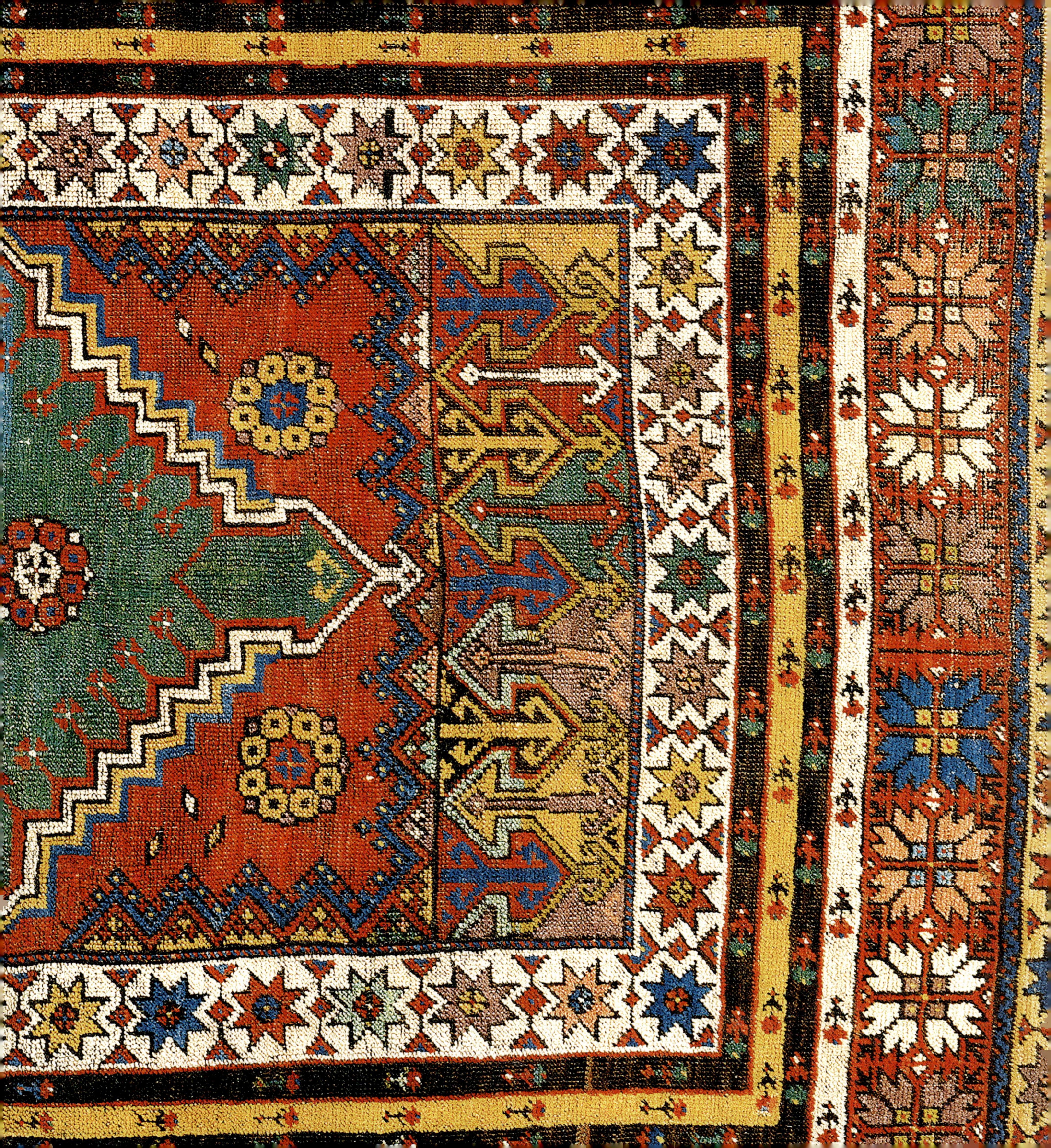

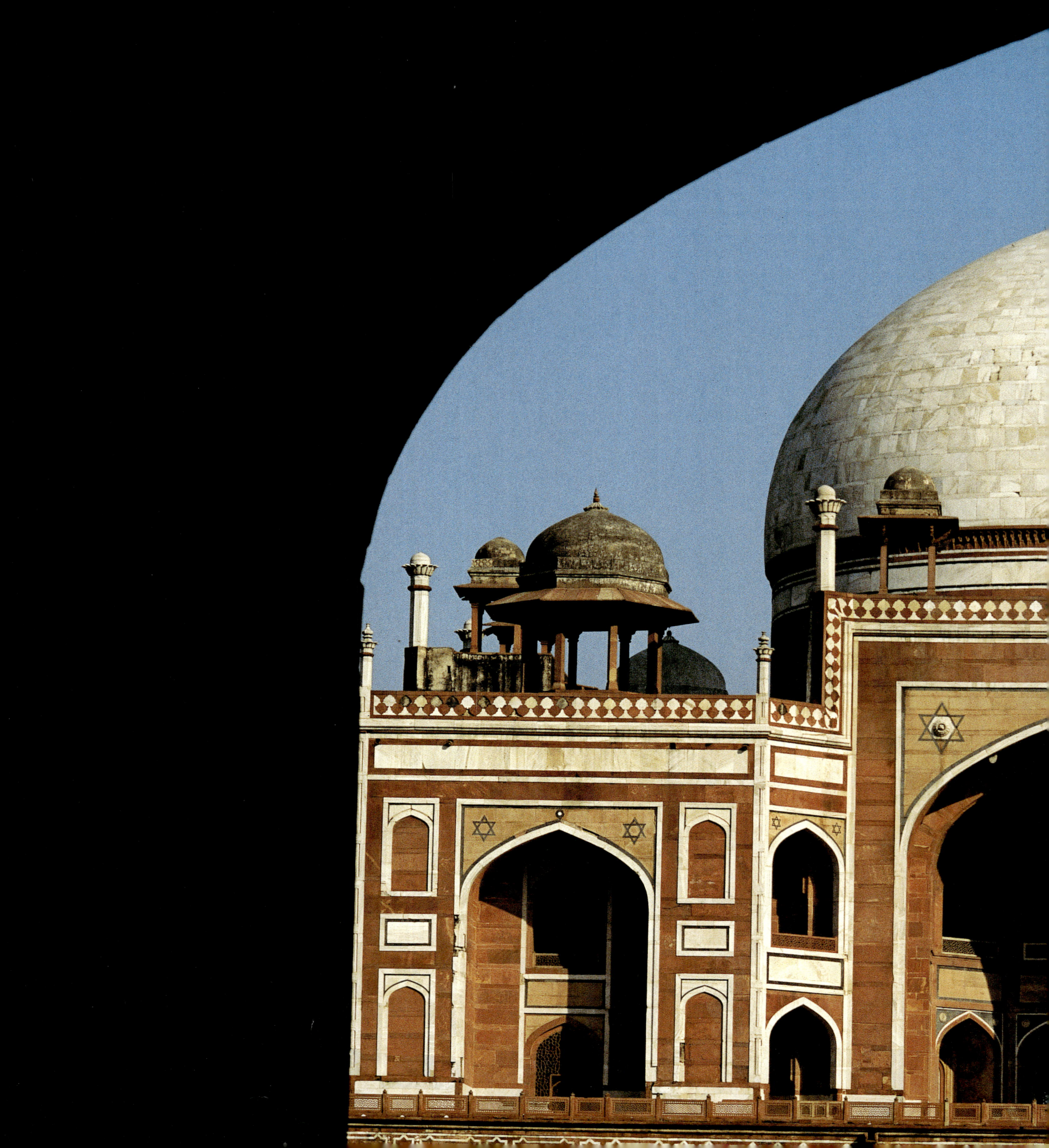

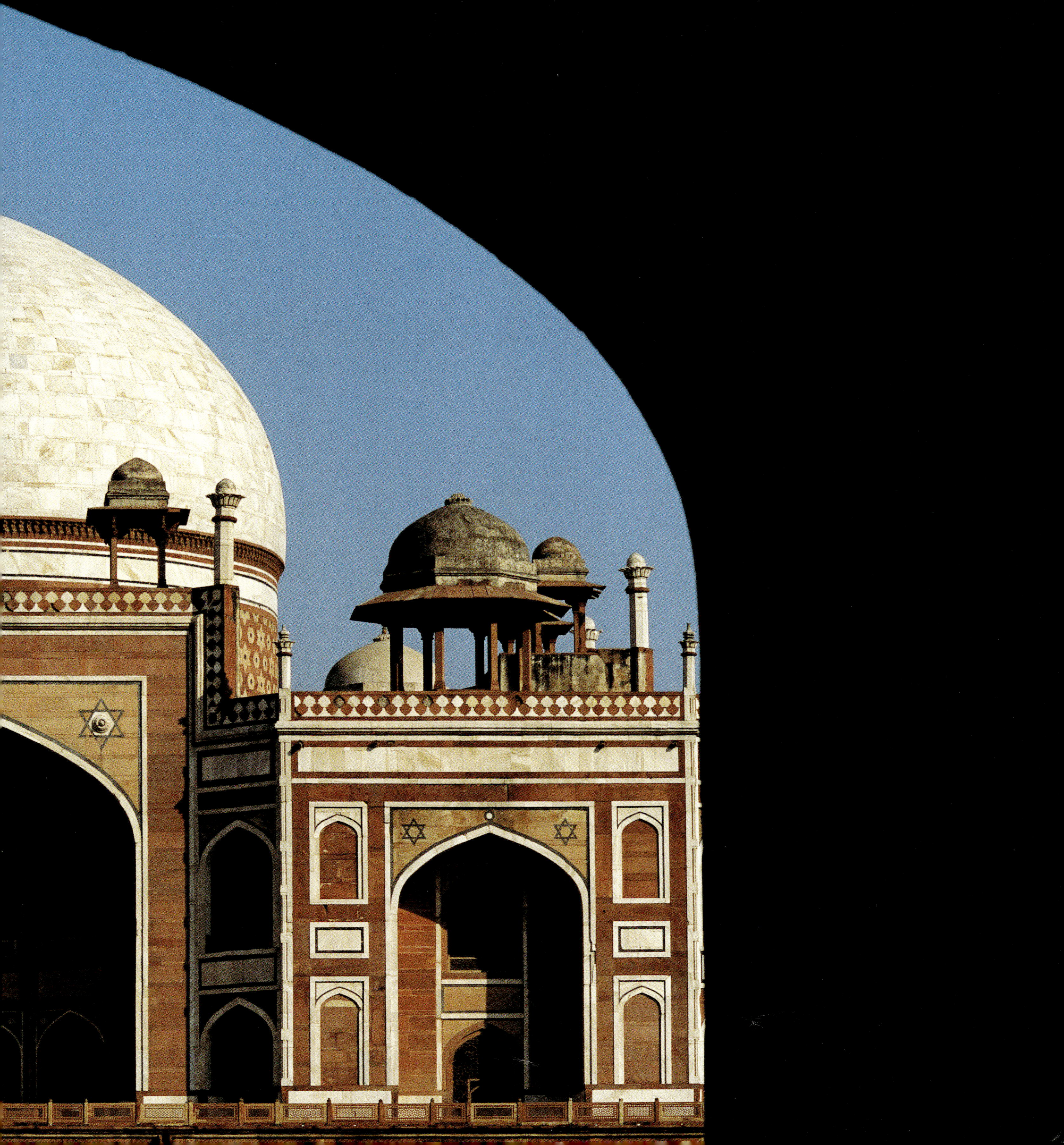

Luca Mozzati

Islamic Art

Architecture
Painting
Calligraphy
Ceramics
Glass
Carpets

PRESTEL
MUNICH • BERLIN • LONDON • NEW YORK

CONTENTS

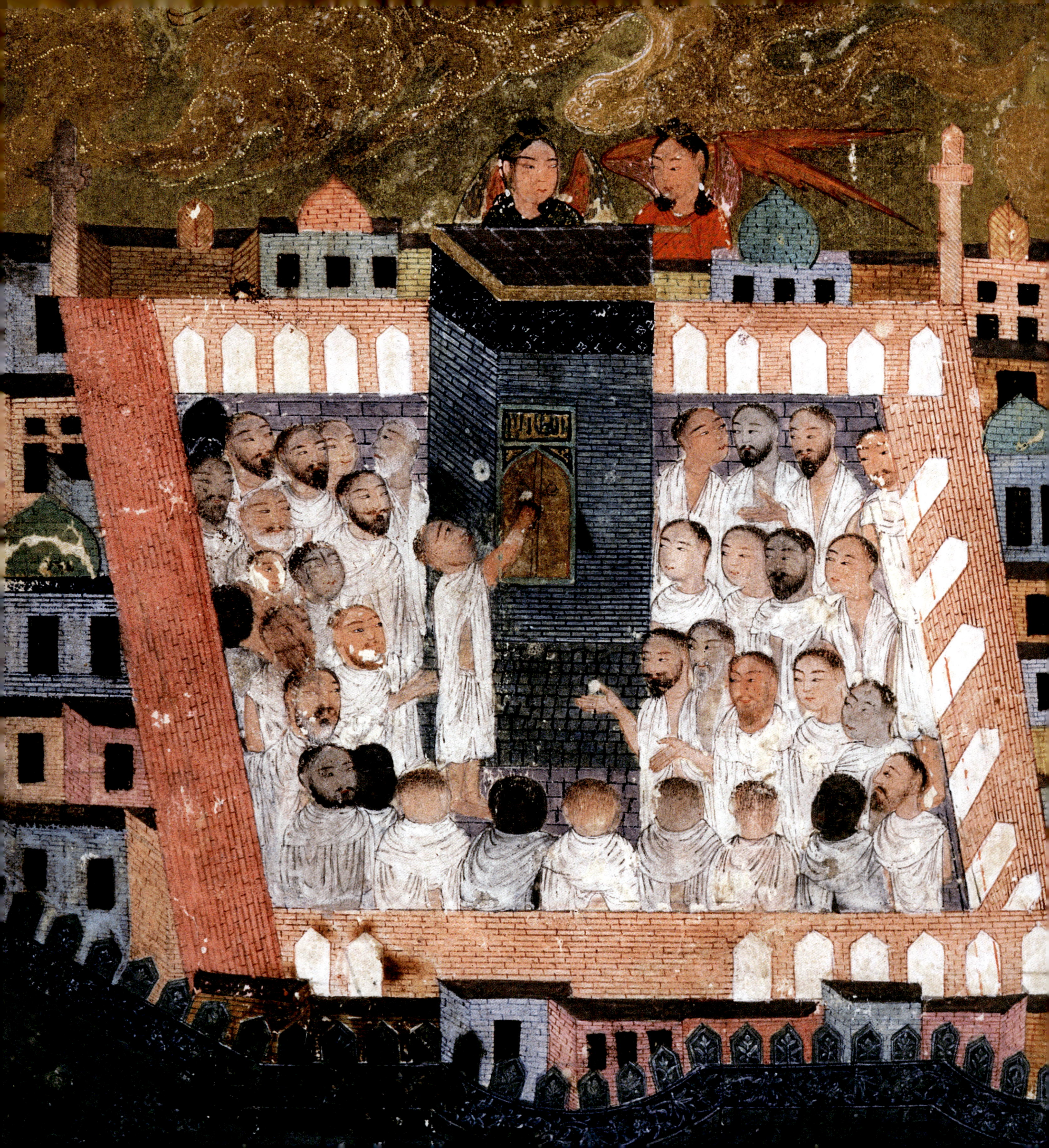

INTRODUCTION

In keeping with the true nature of things, the human should conform to the Divine, and not the Divine to the human.
(Sayyed Hossein Nasr)

"Let us suppose that we are living back, say, in the year 900. [During this period] the Islamic Middle East/North Africa was the cradle of civilisation. Not only was it the most advanced region in the world economically, standing at the centre of the global economy, but it enjoyed considerable economic growth and even per capita income growth. ... Were we to ... inquire into the causes of Islamic economic progress, we might come up with the following answer. The Middle East/North Africa was progressive because ... first, it was a pacified region in which towns sprang up and capitalists engaged in long-distance global trade. Second, Muslim merchants were not only traders but rational capitalist investors who traded, invested and speculated in global capitalist activities for profit-maximising ends. Third, a sufficiently rational set of institutions was created including a clearing system, banks engaged in currency exchange, deposits, and lending at interest, a special type of double-entry bookkeeping, partnerships and contract law, all of which presupposed a strong element of trust. Fourth, scientific thought had developed rapidly after 800. And fifth, Islam was especially important in stimulating capitalism on a global scale. Certainly no-one would have entertained the prospect of writing a book entitled *The Christian* [sic] *Ethic and the Spirit of Capitalism;* ... more likely someone would have written a book called *The Islamic Ethic and the Spirit of Capitalism,* which would definitively demonstrate why only Islam was capable of significant economic progress and why Christian Europe would be mired forever in agrarian stagnation. Or one might subscribe to the claim made by a contemporary, Said al-Andalusi (later followed by Ibn Khaldun) that Europe's occupation of a cold temperate zone meant that its people were ignorant, lacked scientific curiosity and would remain backward." (John M. Hobson, *The Eastern Origins of Western Civilizations,* Cambridge 2004, p. 272)
Islam (from *Islàm,* an Arabic word meaning 'abandonment', 'submission' to God) is a religion characterised by absolute and uncompromising monotheism, and a radical and unitary view of the world, indifferent to the historical, social, cultural and racial particularities of its adherents. Disseminated with breathtaking speed and facility throughout a world exhausted by the constant state of belligerence between the Byzantine and Persian empires and the inevitable consequences in terms of economic, social and religious upheaval, within the space of a few short decades Islam was to invade and conquer Spain and part of Southern Italy; traverse the wastes of the Sahara and convert populations in black Africa where it overlaid their local cults; and expand to the borders of distant Asia, encountering Vedic religions and Buddhism. To the north it flooded into Oxiana (today Uzbekistan), venturing farther even than the conquering armies of Alexander the Great, until it ran up against the frontiers of China.
The territory over which Islam held sway had already witnessed the Greco-Roman and Judeo-Christian civilisations in the West, followed by Greek Orthodoxy. In ancient times the East had seen the dominance of Persian and Zoroastrian cultures. It was this joint legacy that laid the foundations of Islamic artistic experience. In the domain of culture – and therefore of art too – the Islamic world assimilated the creative energies, technical skills and local customs of the conquered peoples, rejuvenating them with original concepts the like of which had never been seen before. Islam and its language, Arabic, constituted a powerful 'glue' that bound together various cultural traditions, composing a surprisingly homogeneous amalgam that informed a wide range of civilisations, as well as the spiritual and political experience of hundreds of millions of people in many nations. Sharing one and the same perspective, each gradually developed idioms of art and custom which, although stamped with a common Islamic identity, gained an individual character over time.
Aided and abetted by vigorous input from indigenous communities, these codes were complemented by contributions from new arrivals and by the constant flux of populations for religious, commercial, or even scientific reasons.
Within this Islamic mosaic, cultural, spiritual and artistic worlds coexisted, which, although characterised by specific values and legacies, were nonetheless imbued with a definably 'Islamic' identity.

The Islamic religion

The Islamic profession of faith runs: "There is no God other than God and Muhammad is his prophet." In order to become a

Note
The transliteration of names, in particular in Arabic, Persian and Turkish, is based on frequently encountered current English forms (though our selection in no way excludes other, equally valid alternatives). For the sake of simplicity, the majority of diacritics have been omitted.

Pilgrims at Mecca
1410–1411
Persian miniature from a manuscript by Jalal al-Din Iskandar (15th century)
British Library, London

Muslim (from the Arab *muslim* – plural *muslimun/muslimin* – that which is 'submitted' to God), it is enough to pronounce this before two witnesses. The term 'Allah' derives from the Arab-Semitic root *'lh* meaning 'divinity' in the generic sense, which in the Arabic *al-ilah* signifies the One and Only God. In a *sura* of the Qur'an (LV), the Supreme Being is also known as *al-Rahman,* "the Merciful," the first of "The Ninety-Nine Most Beautiful Names" of Allah. The doctrine of the omnipotence and the absolute freedom of Allah leads to a conception of the world created by and arising continuously from God.
In this sense, there can be no becoming, since everything, and therefore every event, is constituted from atoms created and destroyed in one ceaseless action by the godhead: reality as it appears to us, all that happens and is seen, both objects and events, is but pure illusion. In such a perspective, human freedom contrasts with divine omnipotence in that a man's action too is established and created by God, and therefore intended and permitted by him. Nonetheless, the concept of human responsibility does exist in the Qur'an ("Did you reject the faith after accepting it?" III, 106), and underpins the doctrine of the Last Judgement, when humankind will be judged for its actions and rewarded in paradise or punished with hell (LXXXIX, 15–30). Therefore the two aspects of divine omnipotence and human will can be seen to coexist, although this constitutes no obstacle to faith, because the chief obligation for an authentic Muslim is obedience (*Islam,* that is, 'submission') to divine law, and not theological or philosophical investigations entered into in the hope of elucidating its mysteries through intellect and reason. "The *Islam* of a man is never sure unless it is based on submission and acceptance. Whoever desires to know things whose knowledge lies beyond their capacity and whoever is not satisfied with acceptance will find that their desire distances them from a pure understanding of the true unity of Allah, from clear comprehension and correct belief, and they will oscillate between faith and scepticism, confirmation and negation, acceptance and rejection. They will be subject to rumour and will become confused and full of doubt, since they will be neither a believer who accepts nor a non-believer who has reneged." (Abu Ja'far At-Tawahi al-Misri, ninth century).
Allah has announced his will to humanity through prophets chosen among the common people, including both Jews and Christians: the first was Adam, followed by Abraham and Moses, until Jesus Christ, the last of the twenty-eight prophets cited in the Qur'an and named as "the Messiah." The cross, however, was said to be occupied by a counterpart who died in Christ's stead, while the true Jesus (whose divinity is obviously denied) will return to guide humanity resurrected and freed of corruption in the millennium preceding the Last Judgement. Muhammad, however, "the seal of the prophets," the last and most important emissary of the divine, the bearer of a message that will maintain its value unalloyed until the end of days and with whom the revelation concludes, outranks all his predecessors and invalidates all his successors,

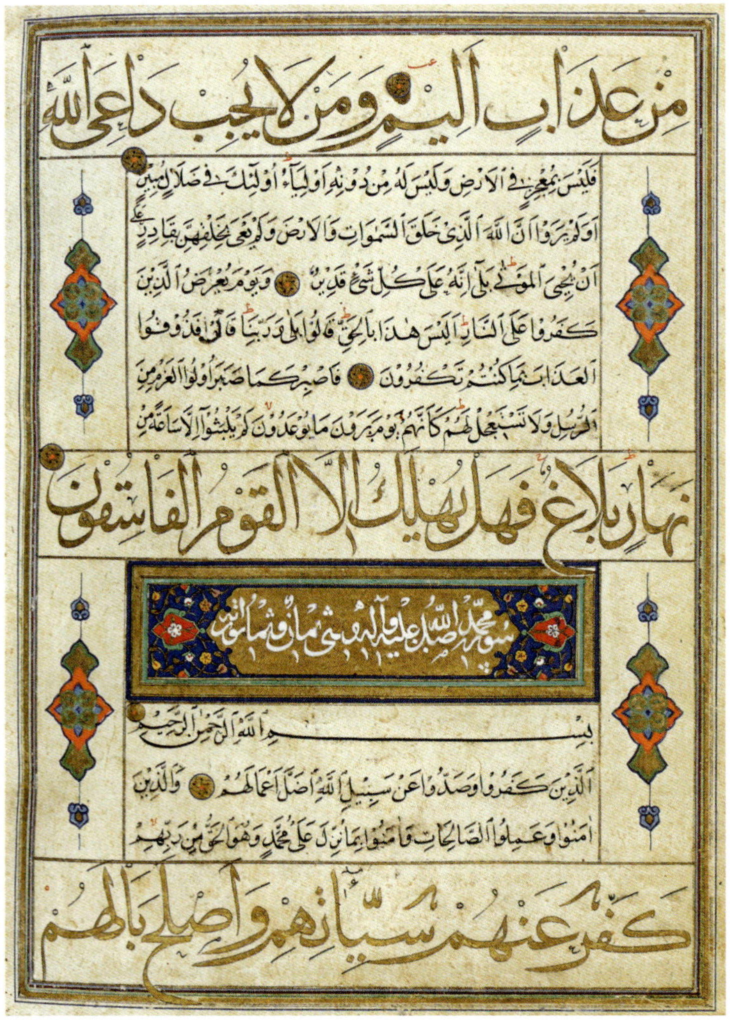

Page from a Qur'an in *naskh* script, end of sura 46 and beginning of 47
First half of the 16th century, Safavid era
Persian miniature
Russian Academy of Sciences, St Petersburg

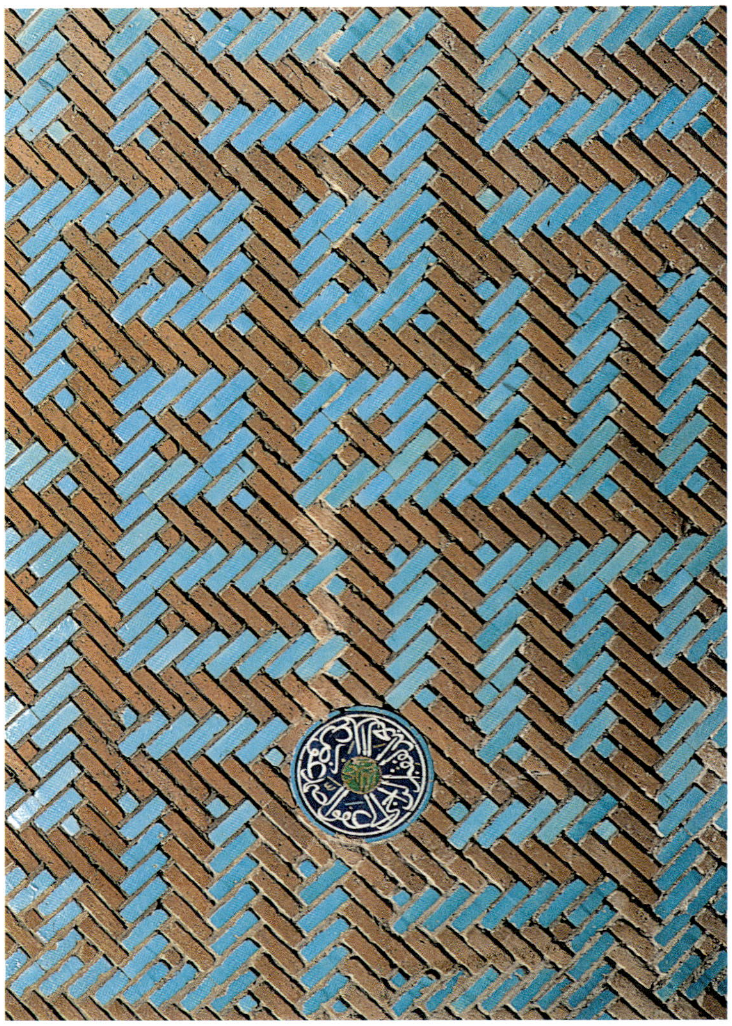

Mausoleum of Shaykh Safi, detail of the wall decoration with the repeated invocation of "Allah"
(*bannai* script)
16th century, Safavid era
Ardebil, Iran

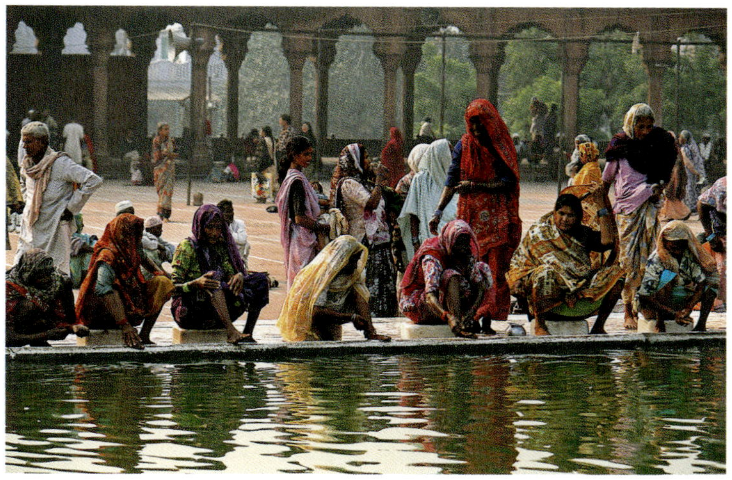

Ritual washing in the *sahn* ('courtyard') of the Friday mosque
1650–1656
Delhi, India

since "every pretension to be a prophet after him is but falsity and deceit." Islam respects earlier religions that refer to a revealed book, be they Zoroastrian, Jewish or Christian, accepting part of their message and adopting various elements, first and foremost monotheism.
As understood in Islam, the difference between the sacred and the profane is flexible: everything is sacred, since everything derives from the will of God. Thus nature cannot exist as distinct from God and no values exist that are not essentially religious. Islam then makes no distinction between the religious and the political spheres. Muhammad was at once a political and a spiritual guide, the same role being invested – at least in theory – in his successors.

The Qur'an

The mission of the prophets and of Muhammad in particular consists in communicating to humanity ethical and moral norms to enable men to regulate their existence in accordance with the divine will. These recommendations are contained in the Holy Qur'an, a book that records the revelations handed down to Muhammad, whose original text – uncreated, like God Himself – has existed with Allah from the beginning of time. "The Qur'an is the word of Allah. It came from Him as speech without it being possible to say how. He sent it down on His Messenger as revelation. Believers accept it as the absolute truth. They are certain that it is, in truth, the word of Allah. It is not created, as is the speech of human beings, and anyone who hears it and claims that it is human speech has become an unbeliever. Allah warns him and censures him and threatens him with Fire when He says, exalted is He: 'I will burn him in the Fire [*saqar*].' [Al-Muddaththir 74:26] When Allah threatens with the Fire those who say 'This is just human speech.' [Al-Muddaththir 74:25] we know for certain that it is the Word of the Creator of mankind and that it is totally unlike the speech of mankind." (Al-'Aqidah At-Tahawiyah [3], by Abu Ja'far At-Tawahi al-Misri, ninth century).
The Qur'an contains the revelation sent by Allah and dictated in Arabic by the Archangel Gabriel to Muhammad on several occasions between 610 and 632 CE. The term derives from the Arabic *'al-qur'an,* 'to recite, to read'. Initially this revelation was learned by rote and recited by the Prophet to his followers. After his death, his most devout disciples continued to recite it to the Muslim community. Unlike other revealed books (104 according to tradition) whose existence is accepted by Islam, the Qur'an is seen as perfect and inimitable, thus conferring immense prestige on the Arabic language itself. The more than 6,200 verses are organized in 114 chapters called *suras* (or *surahs*), arranged (with the exception of the opening *sura*) in order of decreasing length. The text, transmitted orally in the earliest times and transcribed on palm leaves or stone slates, was redacted in a definitive form under the third caliph, Othman (644–656 CE). It can be recited, intoned, and explained, though textual criticism as such is not permitted. The commitment to memory and faultless recitation of the Qur'an constitute the foundation stone of the education of every Muslim. Above and beyond stipulations of an explicitly religious character, the Qur'an also contains legal procedures and norms, as well as rules of behaviour covering every type of situation and touching on practically every aspect of public and private life, from the family to the structure of the state and society. These teachings have since given rise to a legislative code, the *shari'a* ('right path,' 'correct way'), that in Muslim countries has currency as law, rendering all secular statutes superfluous – at least in theory. However since the Qur'an cannot include rules for every conceivable facet of human existence, the law deriving from it has been supplemented with *hadith* (literally: 'story'), plural *ahadith*, which, based on reliable testimony, codify the recommendations and actions of Muhammad, forming together the *Sunnah* (literally: 'usual practice', 'orthodoxy').

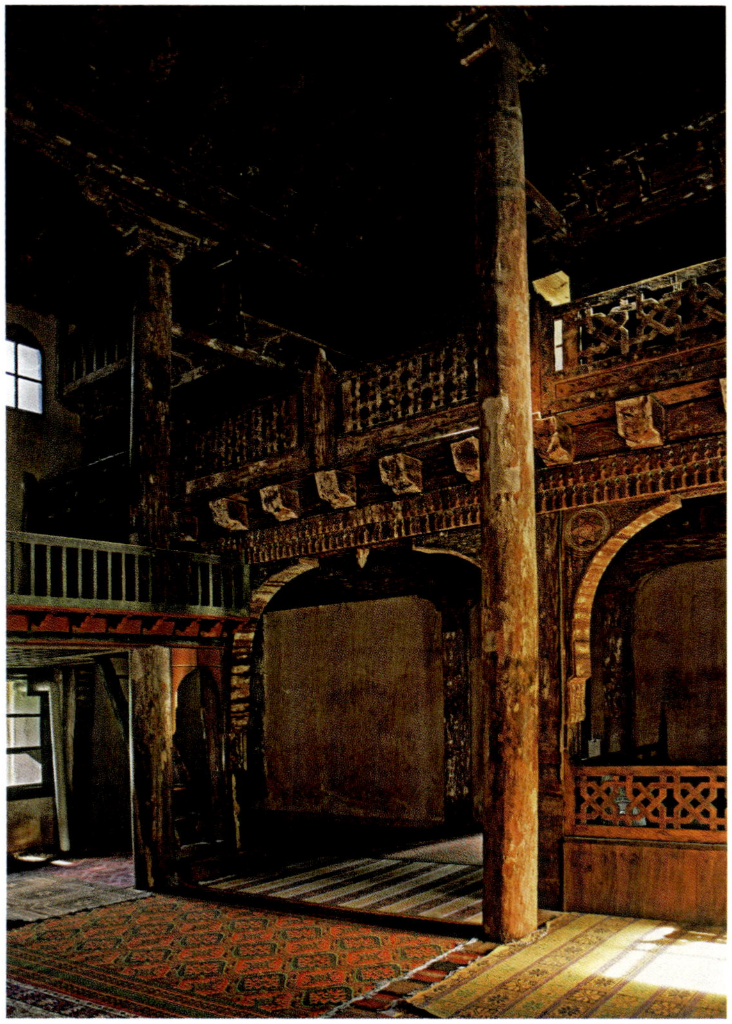

Mosque of Mahmut Bey
1336
wood
Kasaba (Kastamonu), Turkey

Legislation and law schools

Later building-blocks in the legislation were added by consensual agreement (*igma*) by the community of believers, which can rule on problems not referred to in the Qur'an or *ahadith*. Their deliberations, dating from the tenth century on, were collected and summarized in legal texts. The last and most complicated source for jurisprudence is analogical reasoning (*qiyas*), that is, practices that can be applied solely by certain scholars on the basis of traditions interpreted in the light of new events.

After independent legal interpretation was prohibited in the twelfth century, four legal schools were recognized in Sunni Islam as possessing equal authority. The Hanafi School is the most flexible and open to fresh interpretations; approximately half the Muslim community adhere to this school today. The Maliki School is conservative in character; the Shafi'i School is more systematic; and the Hanbali School is traditionalist and restrictive in the sense that it admits of nearly no sources other than the Qur'an and *ahadith*.

The Shias or Shiites follow their own school of law, the Ja'fari. In theory any Muslim is free to follow the legal current of his choice. Since in Islam, 'church', clergy and sacrament do not exist, it is the doctors of the law, the *mufti,* who resolve religious and juridical issues, handing down legal opinions or findings (*fatwa*) founded on their interpretation of jurisprudence – though these might not be accepted by adepts of other schools.

The Five Pillars of Islam

Islamic religious practice is based on five absolute obligations or pillars (*arkan*).

1. The *shahada* (public profession of faith), consisting in reciting the formula, "There is no God but God and Muhammad is the messenger of God," before appropriate witnesses. No additional ritual is necessary. Acceptance into the community is irrevocable and apostasy is punishable by death. Divergences exist between legal schools as to whether the profession of faith is sufficient to make a good Muslim or whether works are also necessary, and to what extent.

2. *Salat* covers ritual worship, the visible sign of submission to Allah. Unlike spontaneous, personal prayer (*du'ha*), recommended but not obligatory, it is composed of Qur'anic formulae and pre-established gestures and has to be performed at five specific times of day. It can be performed in any place or situation, in a group or individually, provided that the worshipper is in the required state of ritual purity. Only on Friday at the *juma* ('assembly') must the faithful recite the noon *salat* together, but separated according to sex in an accredited mosque (called Friday mosques, *masjid-e juma*), which are different from those used for everyday prayers. The service, also comprising a sermon (*hutba*), serves as an important cohesive element. Not considered a holiday as such, Friday was in fact chosen because it coincided with market day, for which the faithful already congregated, while Saturday and Sunday, sacred days in other religions, are discarded. Prayers are led by the *imam,* while the *khatib* ('preacher') delivers the homily. Both these functions are designated by the community.

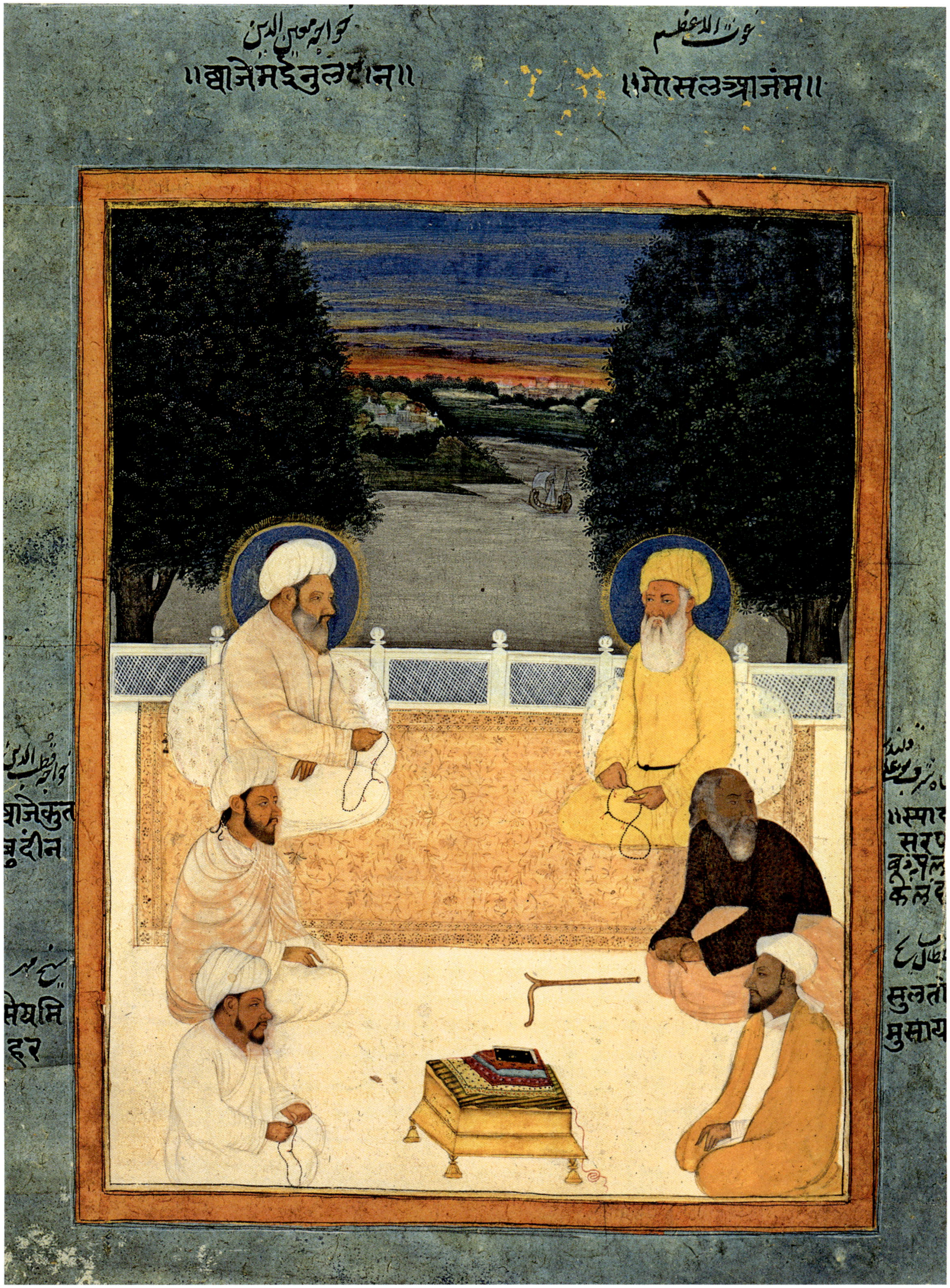

Six Sufi saints on a terrace: Khwaja Mu'in al-Din, Ghaus al-A'zam, Khwaja Qutb al-Din, Shaykh Mihr, Shah Sharaf Bu Ali Qalander, Sultan Musa Shaykh
c. 1760
Mughal miniature
British Library, London

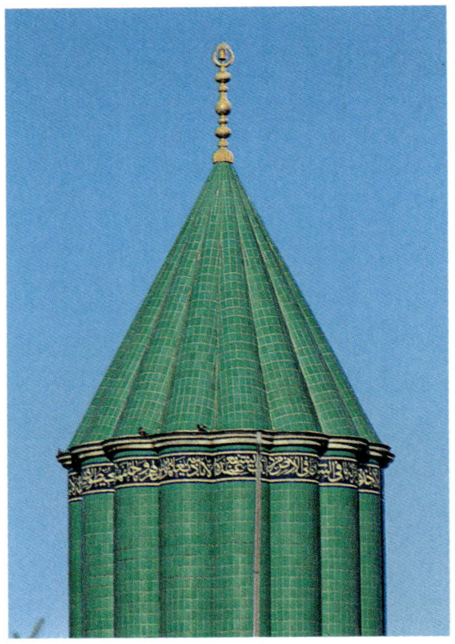

Summit of the mausoleum of the Sufi mystic Meulawa Gialalu'd ad-Din Rumi
1295, Safavid period
Konya, Turkey

Pilgrimage to the necropolis Shah-i Zinda ("of the king who lives"), mausoleum of Ulugh Sultan Begum and Emir Burundur
1385, 1390, Timurid period
Samarkand, Uzbekistan

3. The distribution of alms (*zakat*) was originally voluntary, only becoming a "tax for the poor" during the early Islamic era. Established according to specific criteria, and distinct from additional voluntary payments (*sadaqa*), it covers the religious duty of coming to the aid of a brother believer in financial straits or some other predicament. The Qur'an does not specify precise amounts or the frequency of such donations, but it emphasizes the inner benefits afforded by giving alms, particularly if they are made anonymously so as to avoid committing the sin of vanity or offending the recipient.
4. The ritual fast (*sawn*), also originally a voluntary form of renunciation, is performed in a special month, *ramadhan* (the ninth in the Muslim calendar). It is forbidden to eat, drink, smoke and have sexual relations between dawn and dusk. It concerns all adult Muslims, with the exception of the sick, pregnant women, nursing mothers, those performing heavy jobs, or travelling, who must complete their fast at some later date, even if it means splitting it up. Additional penitential fasts are particularly meritorious. Constituting a form of prayer favourably regarded by God, physical self-discipline is seen as an aid to inner purification and a spur to the renunciation of worldly things.
5. Every healthy Muslim adult with sufficient means must complete at least once in his lifetime the *hajj* (the 'great pilgrimage') to the holy sites of Islam, to Mecca, in the month set aside for it, *dhu-'l-hijja*. Having prepared himself to the required level of devotion and meditated deeply as to its meaning, the pilgrim can perform the required rituals, both individual and collective. In a tradition harking back to pre-Islamic times, the believer, having reached the Kaaba in the Great Mosque of Mecca, thus reaffirms his ties with the entire community. Of merit, but not comparable to the *hajj,* are pilgrimages to Mecca which may be undertaken during other periods of the year (*u'mra*).
Although not one of the five pillars, another fundamental duty concerns *jihad* (literally 'effort', 'engagement'), 'holy war' – a term that means both military combat and the inner struggle for self-improvement. In this manner, the world is divided into *dar al-Islam* (the sphere of Islam) and *dar al-harb* (the sphere of war) where, in theory, the Arabs would fight the enemies, the polytheists, even when they had no interest in converting them. Jews, Christians and Zoroastrians, the "People of the Book" whose monotheistic religion was of revealed character and transmitted in texts (albeit written by human hand and not dictated by God) who lived in Islamised regions were permitted to keep their faith and live in independent communities protected by law, but had to pay a poll-tax and did not enjoy rights on a par with those accorded Muslims.

Muslim mysticism

Although official interpretations tend to discourage mysticism, since the dawn of Islam numerous mystics have delved inwards – and therefore as individuals – to explore its content, rejecting over-literal interpretations of its tenets as a wasteful reduction of the immense potential of the new faith. The chief exponents of this way of thinking were ascetics

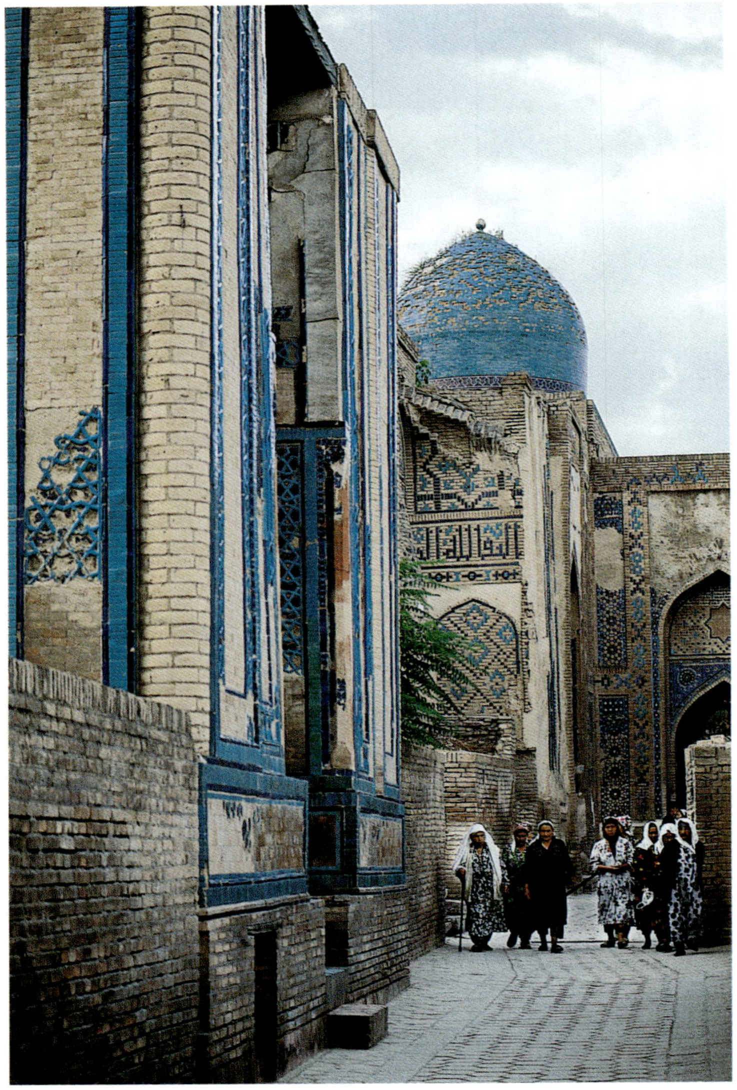

whose plain wool garments (in Arabic, *suf*) gives us the term Sufism, improperly used to refer to what are in fact highly diverse religious concepts. Contact with Neo-Platonist and Christian doctrines in countries conquered by Islam provided a formidable impulse to this primal mysticism, which, by laying the stress on the absolute unity of God, could on occasion end up despising all that is not divine, a rocky path that sometimes led to total negation. Often at odds with the doctrinal Islam of the city, these mystics, anchorites or nomads, who scorned worldly goods and experienced visions, were often followed by the populace. They were viewed as privileged mediators between man and God, and as such hugely venerated. Cults sprang up around them which, though initially heterodox, were slowly accepted throughout the Muslim world. Except for a handful of doggedly persecuted recusants, the most important currents of mysticism do not deny the value and obligatory nature of *shari'a,* thanks above all to the work of the great Persian theologian and philosopher al-Ghazali (1058–1111), who foreshadowed a moderate asceticism that bridged the gap between the dryness of certain theological speculations and a short-sighted ritualism. His interpretation was countered by more intransigent and ardent minds that chafed at rules and regulations they considered hypocritical and restrictive in comparison with the immense love for God that burned within them. The most notable, for his profoundly

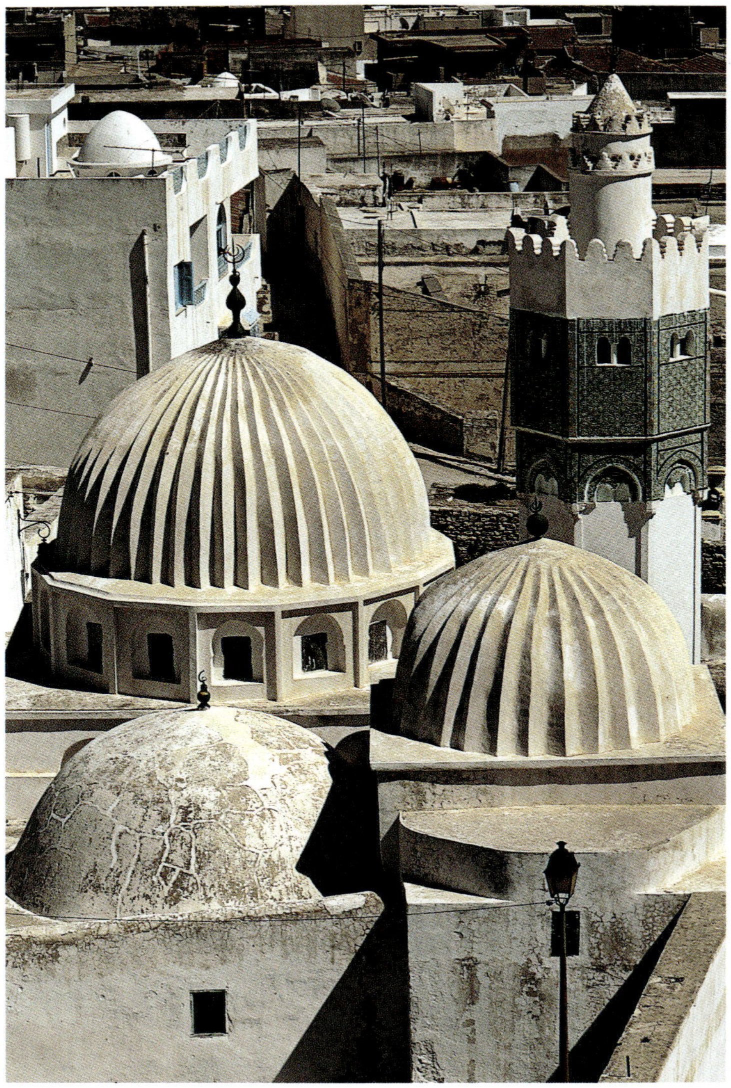

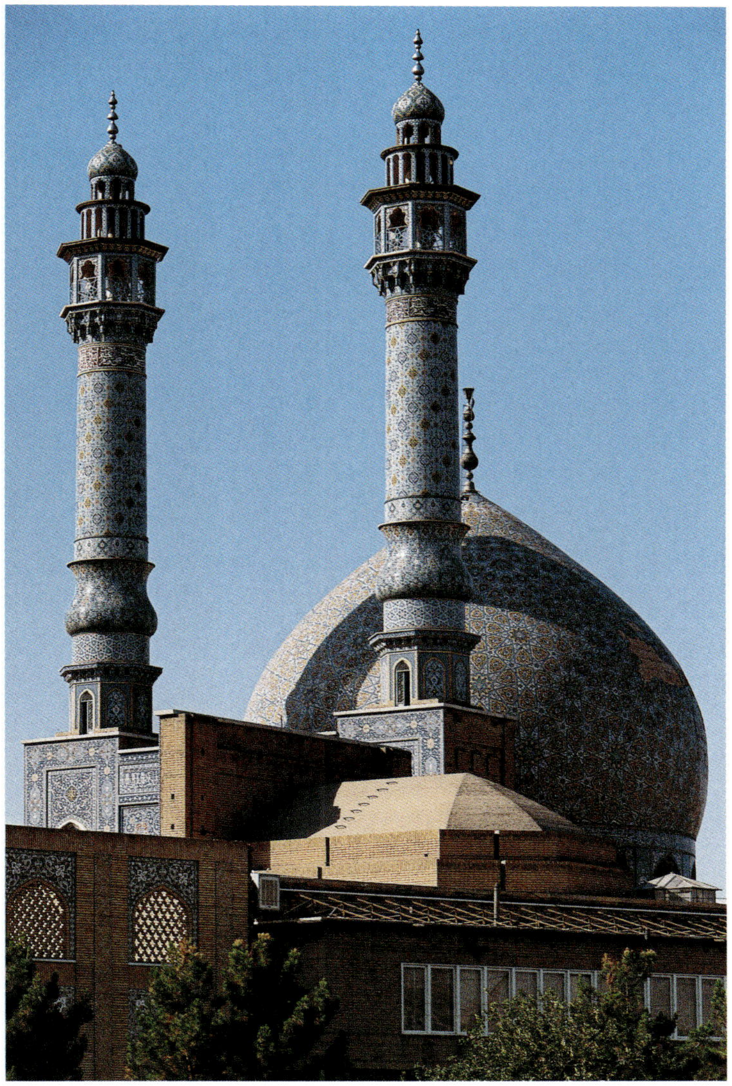

Mosque of Sidi Bou Makhlouf
16th century, subsequently altered
Le Kef, Tunisia

Sanctuary of Hazrat-e Masumeh
17th–19th century
Qom, Iran

human ability to convey aspirations to the divine in verse, is the Persian Gialalu'd ad-Din Rumi (1207–1273), founder of a religious brotherhood, the so-called "whirling dervishes" (from *darwish,* 'poor'). These dervish confraternities (*tariqa,* 'way', 'path'), which developed in the twelfth century and still flourish to this day, were a response to the mystical yearnings of a substantial proportion of the faithful. Although Islam does not look kindly on monasticism and celibacy, many Muslims have joined such associations and pursue specific communitarian practices in order to attain ecstasy in an authentic and personal communion with the divine.

The Shias and the seven branches

The Islamic religion whose doctrines and forms we have described is that professed by the vast majority of Muslims, called Sunni – that is, who subscribe to the *Sunnah.* Several other tendencies exist, however, embraced by communities of various sizes that differ to a greater or lesser extent from Sunni orthodoxy and that were sometimes of considerable influence in the past. The only one to boast a substantial following today (approximately a tenth of all Muslims) is the Shia or Shiite branch (from *shia,* 'party' of Ali), now divided into seven strands, each following different theological lines. All Shias, however, subscribe to the conviction that the role of guide (*imam*) in the Muslim community after the death of Muhammad fell to his cousin and son-in-law Ali and thenceforth to his descendants. To varying degrees, Ali and his lineage are allotted a mission of near-priestly character, denied by the Sunni, who instead advocate the free election of successors to the Prophet. The holiness of the *imam,* compounded by the influence of neo-Platonist and Gnostic doctrines, is greatly emphasized in the Isma'ili schism that alleges an unbroken chain of infallible guides. Today, however, this current claims a limited number of followers and the most substantial Shia community is that of the Imamis, whose credo became Iran's official religion in the sixteenth century. More moderate from a theological point of view, they assert that there have been twelve *imams* in all and that the last, Muhammad al-Mahdi ("the rightly guided"), remains hidden, waiting to return at the end of days to re-establish the purity of Islamic law. The differences between the Imamis and the Sunnites are of minor importance. There also exist 'doctors' of the law among the Imamis, who, when offering guidance to the faithful, take their inspiration from the sacred texts and tradition (including that of the *imam*). Nonetheless, as demonstrated by recent political events, particularly in Iran, where the Shias constitute the great majority of the population, and in Iraq, such prelates enjoy still greater prestige than Sunni doctors, since for Shias the field of theological research remains open.

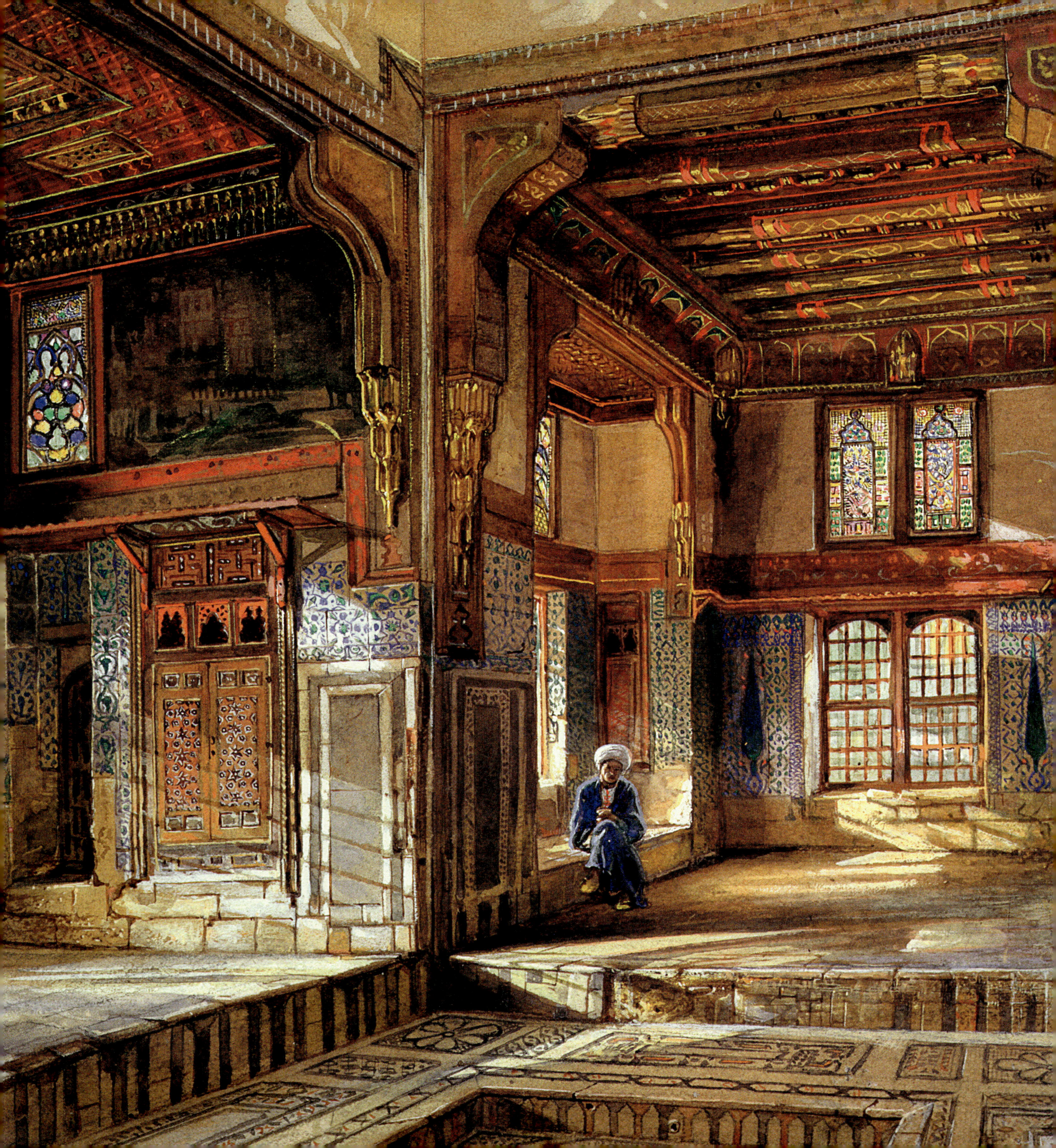

BASIC PRINCIPLES

THE INTERPRETATION OF ISLAMIC ART

p. 20
Frank Dillon (1823–1909)
The House of the Mufti Sheikh el Mahadi in Cairo, detail
1873 (Ottoman period)
Victoria & Albert Museum, London

Casket lid
14th century, Nasrid art
Bronze hinges and wood and ivory geometric inlay

Palazzo della Zisa
Open-plan room with garden and fountain
1164–1180, Sicilian art with Islamic influences
Palermo

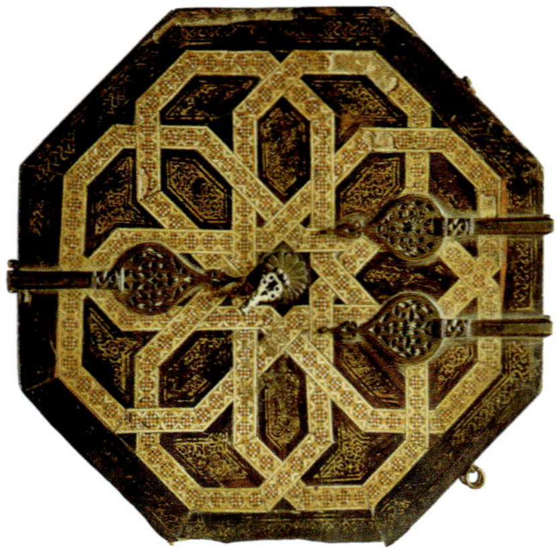

The elaboration of a theory of the arts, or, more simply, of an approach to the meaning and aesthetic value of images, has proved largely alien to Islamic culture, in and for which painting and sculpture have been rather marginal concerns. Due to the paucity of documentary evidence, particularly for the earliest centuries, authentic Muslim attitudes towards the arts remain in the realm of hypothesis. Even *a posteriori* the identification of a specifically 'Islamic' art remains problematic: for, although we speak about art produced in culturally Islamic countries, for Muslim patrons, or by Muslim artists, or else about Iranian, Maghrebi, Fatimid and Mughal art, it is not easy to extract elements or concepts indicative of a truly 'Islamic' art. Still more strikingly, is it correct to consider as 'Islamic' a Mudejar church in Spain or the Cappella Palatina or the Palazzo Zisa in Palermo – that is to say, works of Islamic character formally, but commissioned by Christians for their own use?

The paucity of original Arabic words for what are commonly termed artistic activities implies that sculpture and painting were almost non-existent among its speakers in pre-Islamic Arabia, a region where the most important religious sites, such as the Kaaba in Mecca, were composed of architecturally archaic structures, constructed, moreover by Jewish craftsmen.

The rapid conquest of the Muslim armies suddenly placed the Arabs – strangers to sophisticated figurative and architectural cultures – in contact with the awe-inspiring heritage of Byzantium, Mesopotamia and Iran. At first dazzled, the conquerors subsequently rejected some of the characteristics which were at odds with their cultural background, most notably the deployment of narrative and anthropomorphic imagery, especially for religious structures and objects. The prohibition on imagery, around which a measure of confusion exists, is in fact attested for the first time by a *hadith* in the compilation by Muhammad al-Bukhari dating to approximately 870: "In the day of the Judgement the painter will be destined to the pains of hell, and he will be asked to infuse life into the forms he modelled; but he will not be able to infuse them with life." The only incontrovertible document concerning the earlier period of Islam is the Holy Qur'an, though it is no easy task to extricate passages reflecting authentically original imperatives from those marshalled after the fact to justify subsequent theological and/or intellectual positions.

If overall instances of painting and sculpture of a figurative character remain few and far between – the exceptions being illuminated manuscript books and decorations on everyday articles – the chief peculiarity of Muslim artistic expression is the invention and deployment, especially in the field of architecture, of a highly characteristic artistic language of a geometric and floral type verging on the abstract. More than just a sumptuous decorative backdrop for large stretches of wall, this language has a specific meaning: and indeed, given the particular nature of the Islam, its meaning can only be theological.

Islam considers all worldly goods to be the fruit of human vanity. This fact is most obvious in the activity of architecture

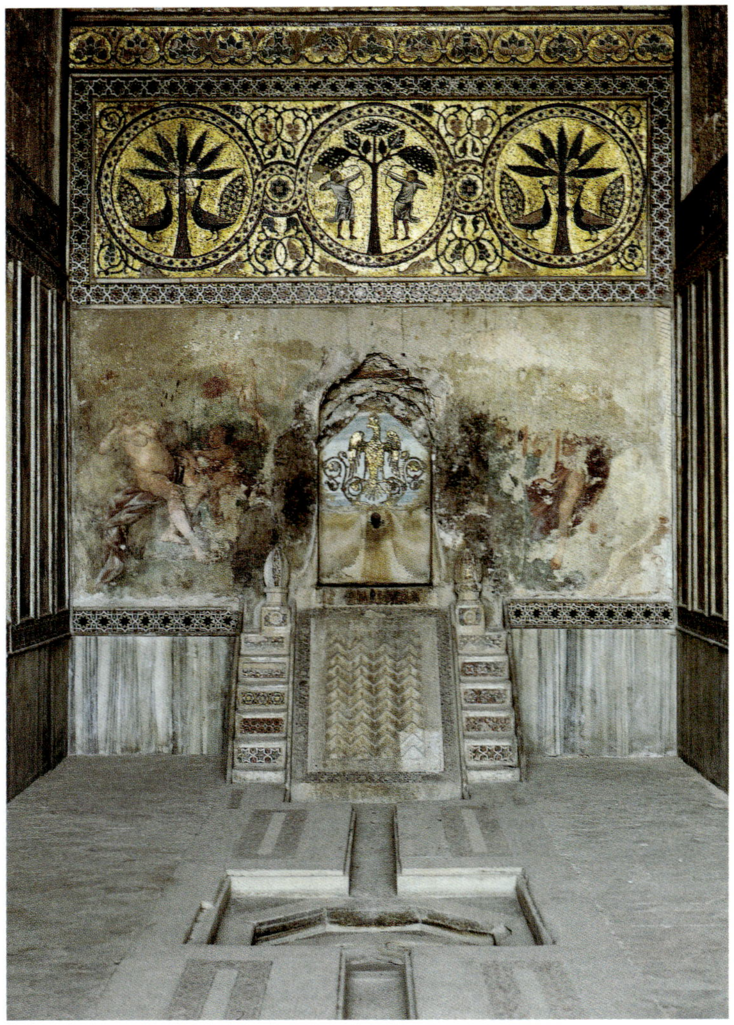

– a reproach unsurprising in a religion that sprang up in a nomadic culture. Indeed, as one *hadith* puts it: "Building is the vainest thing to eat up the wealth of a believer." And yet Muslims were and are builders par excellence. For, like any product of craftsmanship or the intellect, an edifice can have validity provided it is "rightly conceived"; that is, though it remains manufactured – and therefore transient and worthless – it can point believers in the direction of the only truth of interest to them. A visible, tangible entity, it instructs the spirit and can show how the divine permeates everything constructed (not created) by humankind.

In this sense it is possible to speak of specifically Muslim artistic expression, whose object does not consist in the reproduction of the visible world but rather in offering to the senses an entity which, though it exists as an unquestionable initial postulate, is not immediately apparent. In this context – not without a measure of pragmatism – examples of architecture and precious objects that the new conquerors had learned to appreciate and covet, were no longer a pretext for outrage and blasphemy, but instead vehicles for transmitting the religious content which an authentic Muslim culture could not dispense with.

Magnificent buildings funded by the greatest patrons and sophisticated artefacts produced by the most skilled craftsmen for demanding customers demonstrate how novel religious concepts can be translated into materials and monumental forms that express, through the language of artistic form and symbol, the spiritual ideas and the aspirations of the Islamic world. Just as the word is not able to exhaust the meaning of the symbolic, so the complexity of the symbol patently outstrips what is expressible verbally.

This means that every instance of Muslim art, and consequently architecture which is its most prominent manifestation, is substantially symbolic and lends itself to different levels of interpretation and appreciation. It is practical for the faithful in that it provides a place for worship; it is political for the great and the good, who use it to perpetuate their memory or assert their power through patronage; for the aesthete, it reveals a subtlety of thought that informs creation; and mystics and theologians, meanwhile, recognize in it an ineffable expression of the most profound tenets of the faith. The nomadic Arabs' uncompromising faith in a single and non-anthropomorphic God was compounded by their rugged spiritual universe, fashioned in the silence of the desert while crossing interminable distances beneath the stars. Even grafted onto the complex and extremely rich culture inherited from the lands they conquered, it gave rise to a recognizably Islamic, aniconic and anti-narrative conception of art which is singularly well adapted to making the invisible manifest as a life experience. In Islamic art, non-figurativeness bears the stamp of rationality, articulated in accordance with the iron logic of the laws of geometry, but counterbalanced by lyrical rhythms and the abstract if naturalistic outpourings of the arabesque.

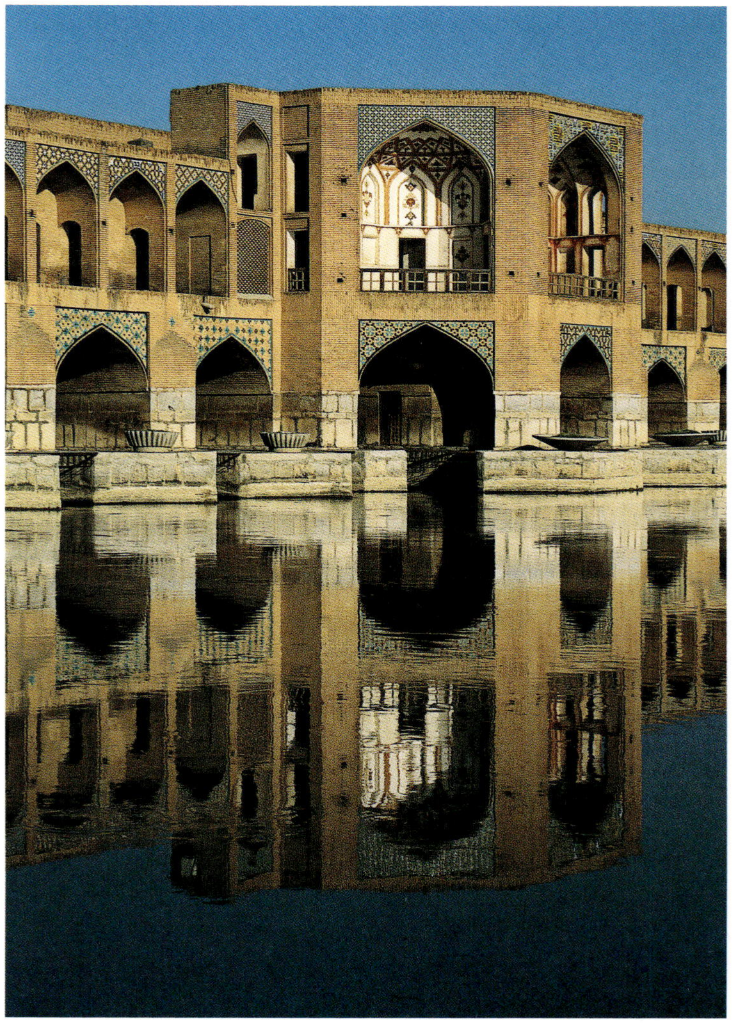

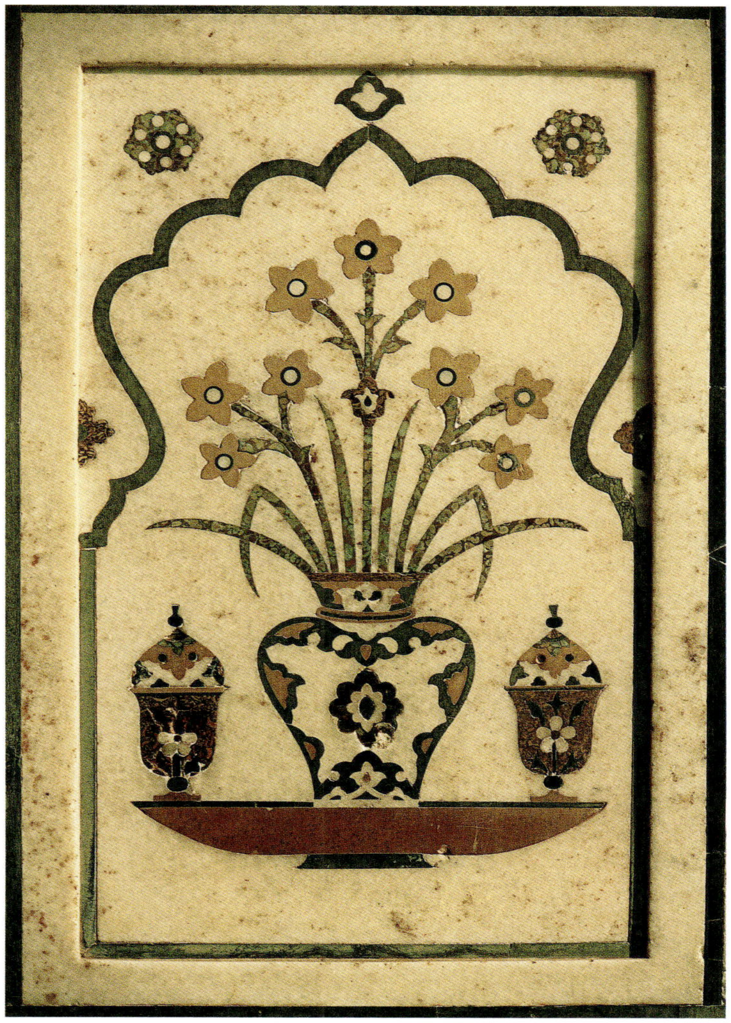

Pol-e Khaju
1641–1666, Safavid period
Isfahan, Iran

Mausoleum of Itimad ud-Dawla
Decorative panel on the façade
Inlaid marble
1622–1628, Mughal period
Agra, India

These two ingredients formed a wellspring for various idioms, or alphabets, in which the Word directly "descended" from God could be inscribed. The resulting aesthetic presents remarkable similarities with Pythagorean number philosophy and views the visible world as a mirror of the authentic dimension of the reality beyond. Of Platonist ancestry, this conception is of course deployed in a universe dominated by the sacred, where rational enquiry can but serve as a path to the divine.
In Islamic art order and beauty are not mere adornments: they presuppose and are meant to demonstrate the existence of God.

Geometry and the spirit

"Geometry is one of the gates that lead us to the essence of the spirit that lies at the root of every form of knowledge." The fundamental article of the Muslim creed, *la ilaha illa 'llah* ("There is no God other than God"), is equivalent to asserting "there are no parts other than the whole," or "there are no infinite dimensions, but *one* dimension." Geometry, a discipline to which the Islamic mind applied itself with extraordinary pertinacity, expresses this concept through the point, that simplest of all geometrical entities. The point is a primal concept, intuitively equivalent to a geometric concept that, according to Euclidean geometry, is totally lacking in extension in any direction (length, area, volume). Related to the straight line and the plane (the two other fundamental geometric entities of Euclidean geometry), it is possessed of no characteristics save for its position. From the point of view of the Muslim religion, this 'metaphysically' absolute and infinite point represents God, His motion determining or generating a space which did not exist prior to or outside Him. It is He who breathes life into dimensions so they can be measured and experienced as the world in which we live. In the quest for the universal principle that governs their existence, the study of the laws of geometry that preside over cosmic relationships, life forms and the creations of humanity can be ascribed to the unfathomable and indivisible initial unity that, from a religious point of view, corresponds to the unknowable mystery of the divine. But how exactly is geometry enlisted in the service of such concepts? It is not necessary, for instance, for the 'generating point' of a form to be explicitly and identifiably present in the form. It is a mental supposition intended to organise the world of experience and can thus be reconstituted by replaying the process that gave rise to the form. Geometrically and symbolically, the point represents the centre (the one) that potentially contains all other forms and dimensions (the multiple). Although this point cannot be measured – that is, known – since measuring is possible only *between* two points, it exists nevertheless (fig. 1). For it to be measurable there has to be motion – i.e., an action that renders measurement possible and that is equivalent to knowledge. The moving point generates a line – equating to the projection of the point outside itself and therefore to its reduction from infinity to finitude, from potential to completed action – and it terminates in a new point related to the initial locus (fig. 2). A movement of this second point, necessarily dependent on the first inasmuch as it could never have come into being without its moving, generates a circumference, the line inscribing its radius, the arc its perimeter and the point its centre, which may remain invisible, but which *cannot not exist* (fig. 3). Inquiring into the structure of a circle, we are forced rationally to presuppose and emotionally to intuit the existence of a 'generating' central point, though it might still be impossible to measure and, therefore, to acquire knowledge of it. The circle represents a complete unity that reflects the "perfect and not perfectible" unity of the starting point. Its structure is absolutely symmetrical (all points on the circumference are equidistant from the centre) and therefore *perfect*. Having neither beginning nor end, it represents eternity. In order to construct the other geometric figures – that is, other forms of truth – one commences with the circle, which is, therefore, the intelligible principle of each and every shape. Comprised of centre, limit and surface, its essence is threefold: it postulates the existence of everything beyond it – a border *has to* separate two entities – which will only become knowable (that is, again, measurable) on projecting the circle beyond its prescribed limits. It might be said that the circle is both finite and infinite at one and the same time and that it is the measure of all things, all things originating in it and returning to it so as to become known.
Its analogy to the divine is then perfectly logical. With the same radius (that is, the repetition of the *act* that generates the initial line) a second circle can be constructed whose fulcrum is a point on the circumference of the first (fig. 4): origin and manifestation coincide since their respective centres are each to be found on the other's circumference. The implication is that the second circle has 'moved' exactly from the same space from which the first point was translated to produce the original line. Bringing the circles together at a particular point (in accordance with the "principle of reflection") and adding a third by dint of the same process, we generate three tangential circles. Joining their centres with straight lines corresponding to the radii (that is to say, to the first line fixed by the original *creative* act), we obtain an equilateral triangle, the first polygon, to which all other polygons can be reduced. By connecting tangential points on the circumferences, a new equilateral triangle is obtained whose side length is of course congruent with the radius and whose area constitutes a submultiple of its larger counterpart (fig. 5): four identical equilateral triangles thus combine to create a larger one whose sides coincide with the diameter of the circles. Exegetes interpret this triangle as representing three indispensable epistemological prerequisites: the knower, the known, the act of knowing. For some mystics, they also stand for the three primary biological functions (ingestion, digestion, and secretion). By iterating the process to add more circles and by multiplying lines between the triangles, the addition of a seventh circle creates a new unit, the hexagon, constructed from the radii of the six external circles with the original point as its centre, at which the apexes of the triangles also meet, and so on (fig. 6). By analogy, the square can be constructed by

intersecting the diameters of four circles with the tangents from the circumferences of the other two (fig. 7).

So far we have followed the process from the original point to the creation of the triangle (the symbol of human knowledge), the square (that of materiality and therefore of the earthly world) and the hexagon (symbol of the celestial realm). The solids are composed from two-dimensional figures using the same principle, redeploying Platonist symbolism that attributes symbolic values to the sequence of solids (cube-earth, tetrahedron-fire, octahedron-air, icosahedron-water, dodecahedron-aether), which was widely known in the Muslim world. The icosahedron is a regular polyhedron with twenty sides in the shape of equilateral triangles, thirty edges and twelve apexes (fig. 8). The harmonic form of the pentagon, identifiable in the icosahedron (the unshaded part in fig. 8) – similar in that to the arms of the five-pointed star (fig. 9) – is closely linked with the so-called golden section, a 'perfect' system of proportion applied in countless artistic endeavours and that occurs in the spirals of many living organisms. Given a segment (AC), a golden section is obtained when the shorter line (BC) is to the longer (AB) what the longer (AB) is to the entire segment (AC). This proportion is therefore expressed: BC: AB = AB: AC. Treating the segment as equal to a unit (AC = 1), it is possible to calculate the length of the two lines, AB and BC, as follows: AB + BC = 1 and BC = AB x AB: AC. Therefore: BC = 1–AB and 1–AB = AB2/1, which is solved as an equation of the second degree, the result being an irrational number, dubbed 'golden' for a host of special properties, 1.618034… (fig. 10). In *De Divina proportione* (1509) by the Renaissance mathematician Luca Pacioli illustrated with drawings of solids by Leonardo da Vinci, the adjective 'divine' derives from the comparison between the mathematical irrationality of the number (meaning that it cannot be expressed as a fraction) and the incomprehensibility of the divine for human reason. The golden section is seen as a universal law of harmony that establishes the correct proportions between two elements. Muslim mystics elaborated countless theories concerned with the symbolism of geometric figures, some rather obscure, others crystal clear. All, however, intuit the manifestation of divine perfection from geometrical beauty and the awareness of the completeness of creation from an understanding of its structure. It is therefore clear how geometric design underpins all Islamic art, its abstract and non-narrative forms spawning a complex system of expression in which geometric designs (but also others, *apparently* freer and floral) on buildings, books, carpets, everyday and luxury articles are not *decoration* but *ornament*. Thus they justify both the existence of the object and the validity of human creativity as a tool or instrument in approaching the node of a truth that is unknowable, but still intuitable and *necessary*. These infinite geometrical patterns, then, are all pathways that lead to God.

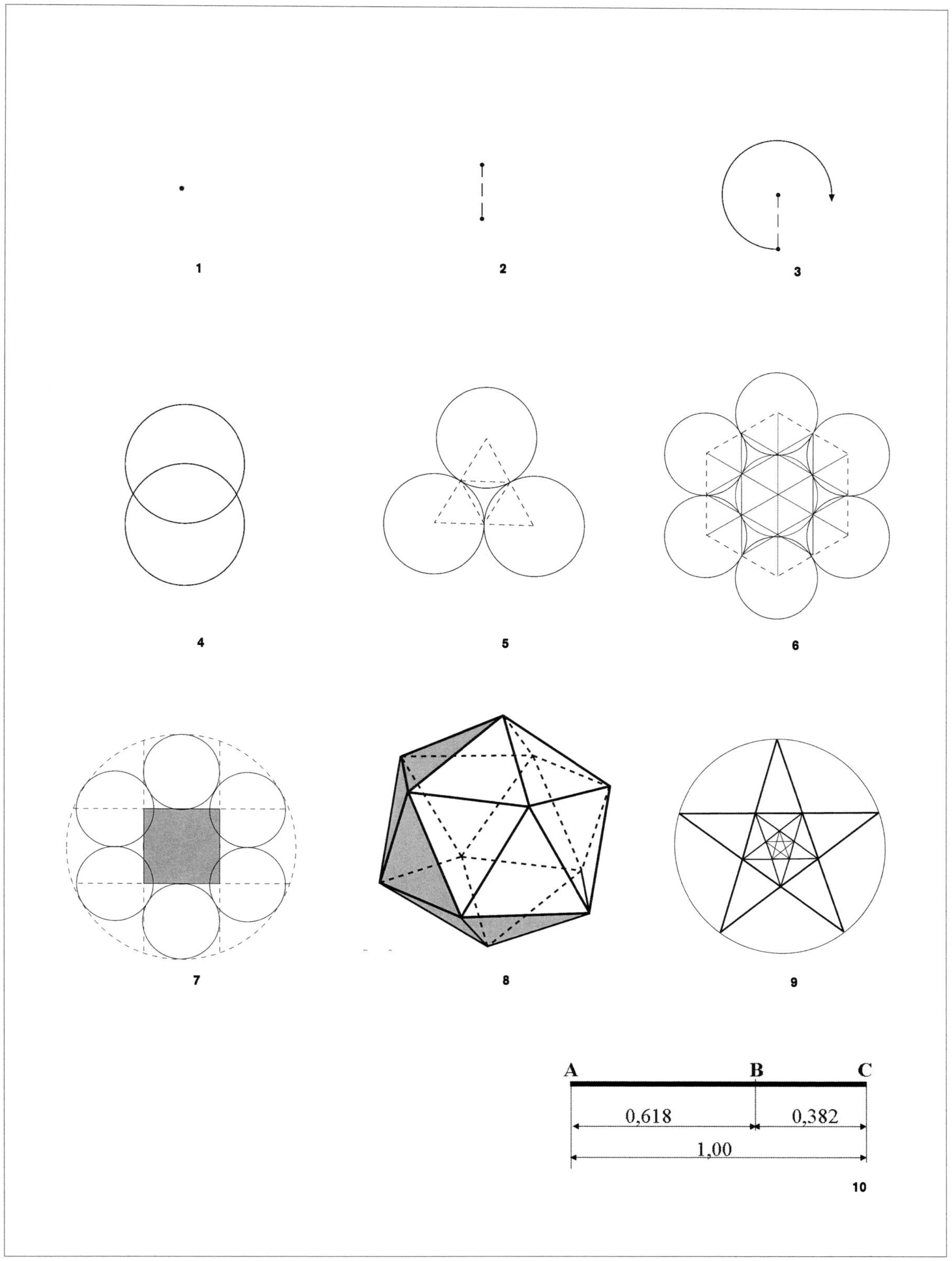

The origin of forms

Fig. 1. The point: an infinite entity that contains all potential and every dimension

Fig. 2. The point moves: it becomes measurable, one possibility among an infinitude

Fig. 3. The displacement of a second point creates a form as perfect as the original

Fig. 4. Two circles sharing a common radius

Fig. 5. Three tangent circles produce equilateral triangles from their radii

Fig. 6. Seven identical tangent circles and their attendant equilateral triangles

Fig. 7. Seven identical tangent circles and a square drawn on their diameters and the tangents perpendicular to their circumference

Fig. 8. Icosahedron

Fig. 9. Circle, five-pointed star, pentagon

Fig. 10. Golden section

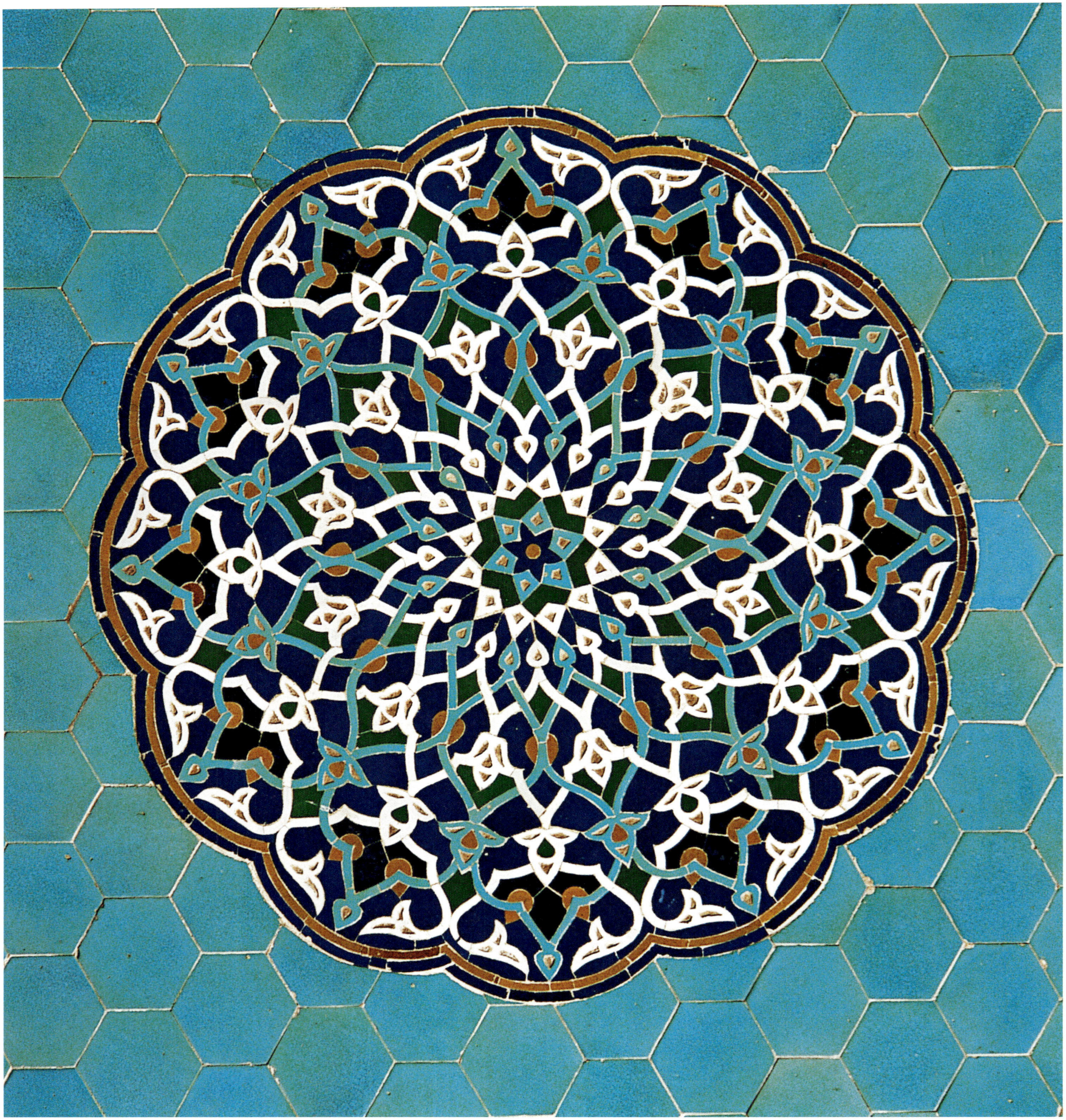

Friday mosque
Panel with floral motif
1375
Mo'arraq ceramic mosaic
Yazd, Iran

Plunged into a sea of bright greenish blue, the *mihrab* hall in the Friday mosque at Yazd boasts a series of ceramic medallions in a narrow range of white-turquoise-blue-brown shades that shimmer over a surface of hexagonal tiles of a light, watery green (unfortunately spoiled by being replaced during restoration with industrial materials). The central point is the motif that generates the entire composition: from it, in accordance with a flawless geometrical plan and through two six-pointed stars, there radiates out a rigorous and compact design underscored by a delicately floral impulse based on a rhythmical twelvefold modulation. The combination of rationality and lyricism seems intended to remind believers that in order to be receptive to the invisible concealed behind the visible, one must rely as much on the emotional as on the intellectual faculties.

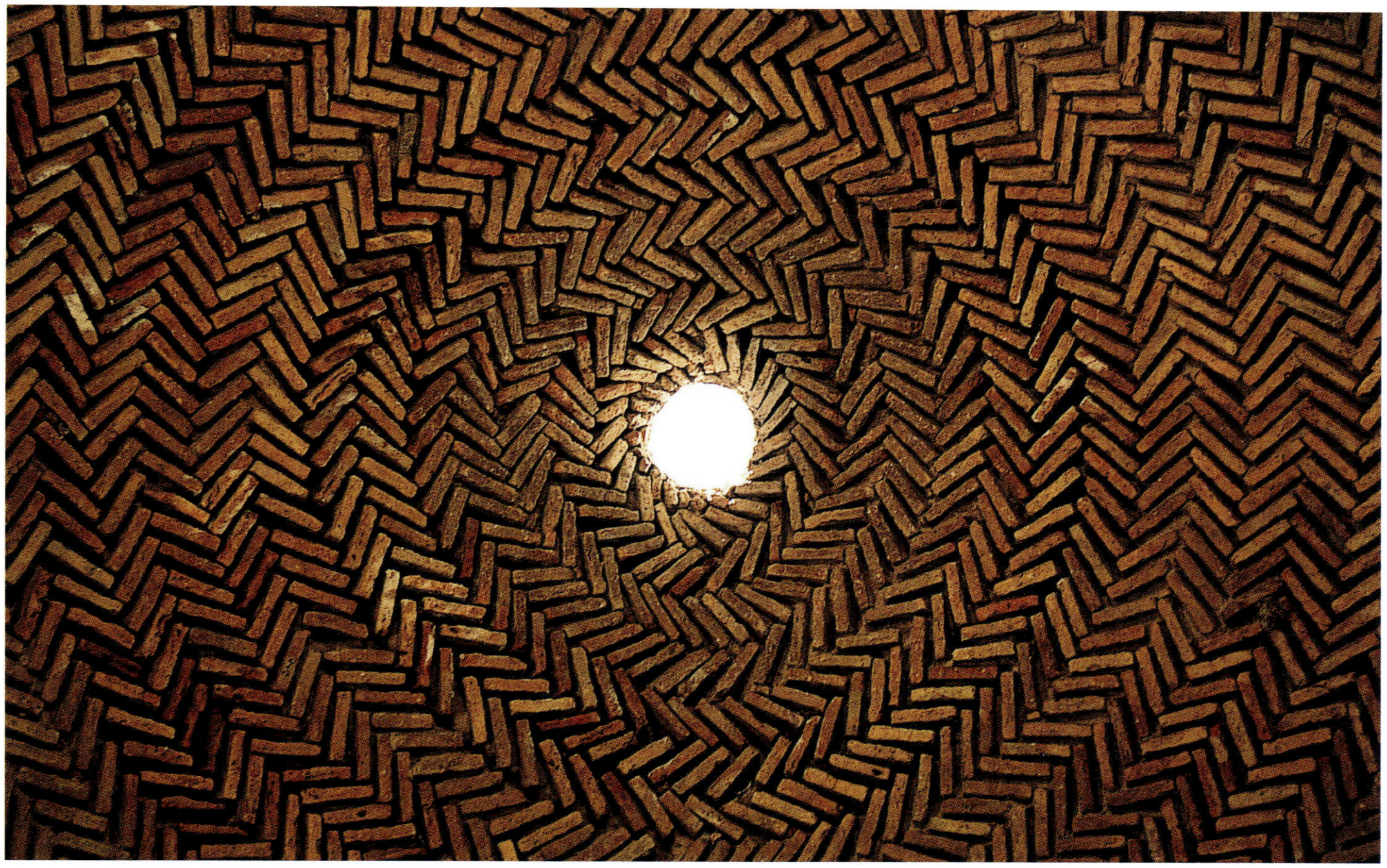

Mausoleum of Arslan Jarib
Detail of dome
998–1030, Ghaznavid period
Sangbast (Khorasan), Iran

There can be no better demonstration of how the point, immeasurable and infinite and as immaterial as light itself, constitutes the matrix of a form, here informing that humblest of materials, mud-brick. Even as they move out concentrically, the herringbone spirals of on-edge bricks held in place with very little mortar do not seek to conceal the way they were assembled, leading the eye with captivating simplicity up to an oculus which, mystical and subdued, allows light to pass down unimpeded into the space below.

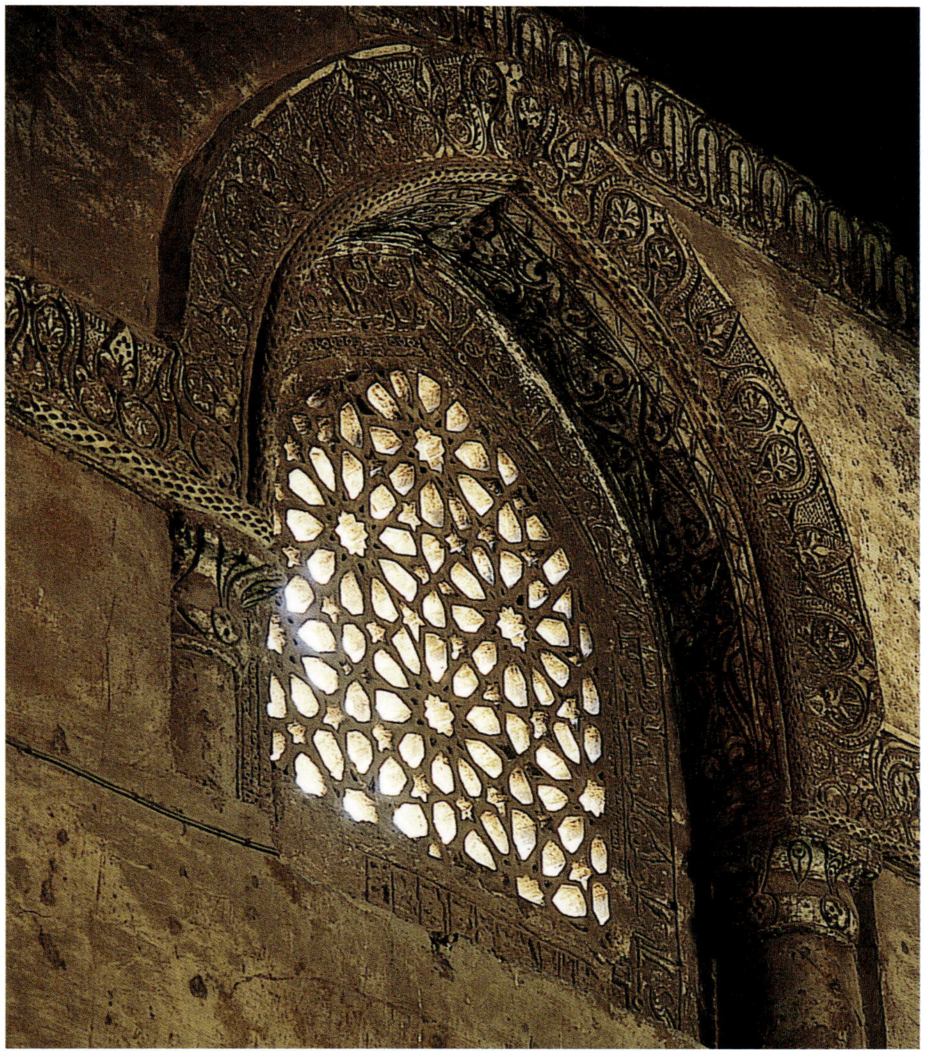

Mosque of Ibn Tulun
Window with stucco grille
876–879, Tulunid period
Cairo, Egypt

The pattern in the grille over the windows by which the prayer hall is lit confers geometrical form on rays of light that pour in to reveal the clarity of the divine design. However, this revelation of the value of light is conveyed through materials of the utmost modesty.

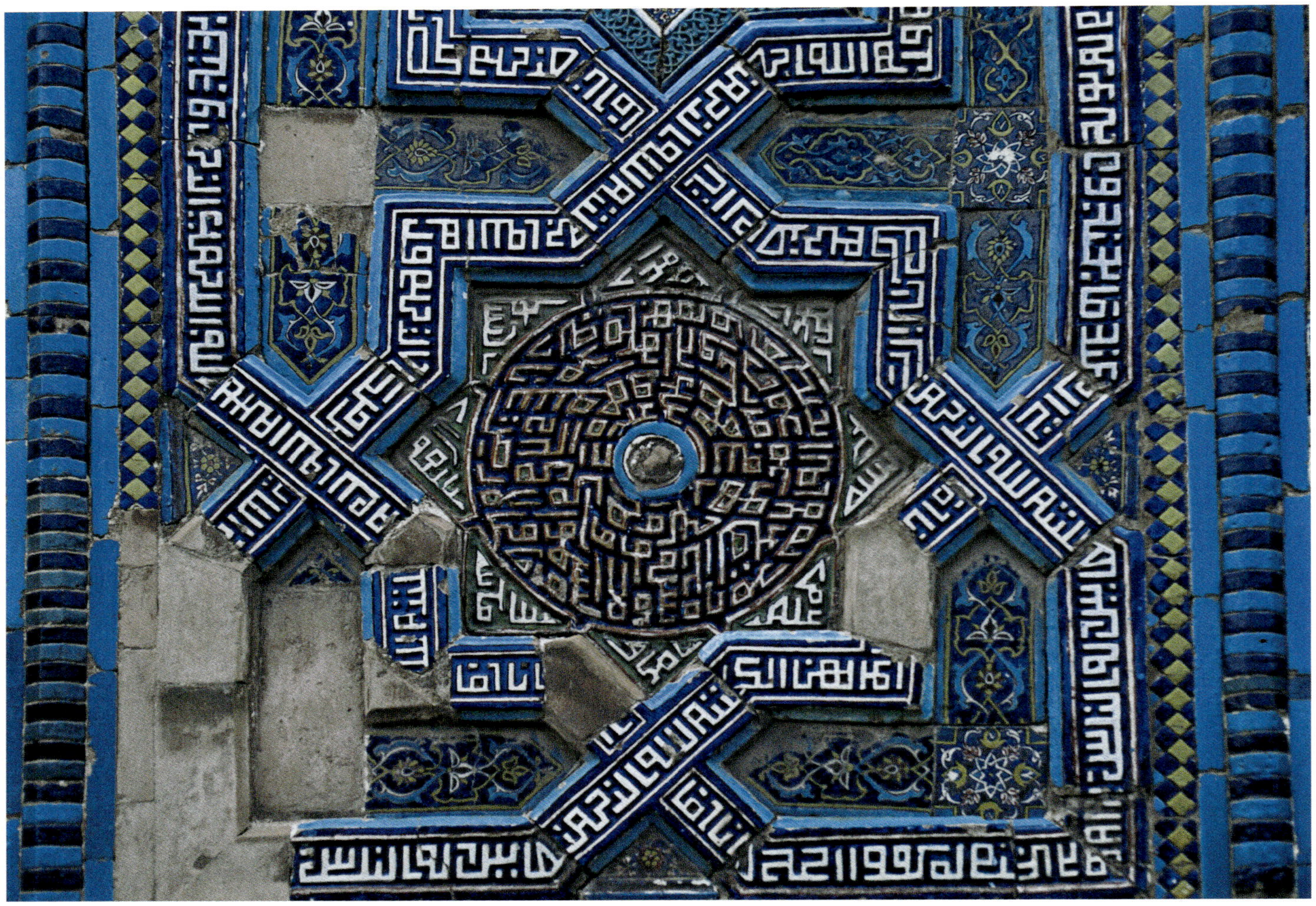

Necropolis of Shah-i Zinda, Mausoleum No. 1
Detail on the façade
c. 1385, Timurid period
Samarkand, Uzbekistan

The word too can add structure to geometrical figures that reinforce meaning, though it is tempered here by subtle, elegant plant motifs. From the central point, in relief, the script opens in concentric circles inserted into an eight-pointed star. Its perimeter – ringed by a frame over which runs a text that enhances the overall design and intersects with other geometric figures – defines in its turn a larger scheme. The visible element is, as always, but a small part of some greater totality.

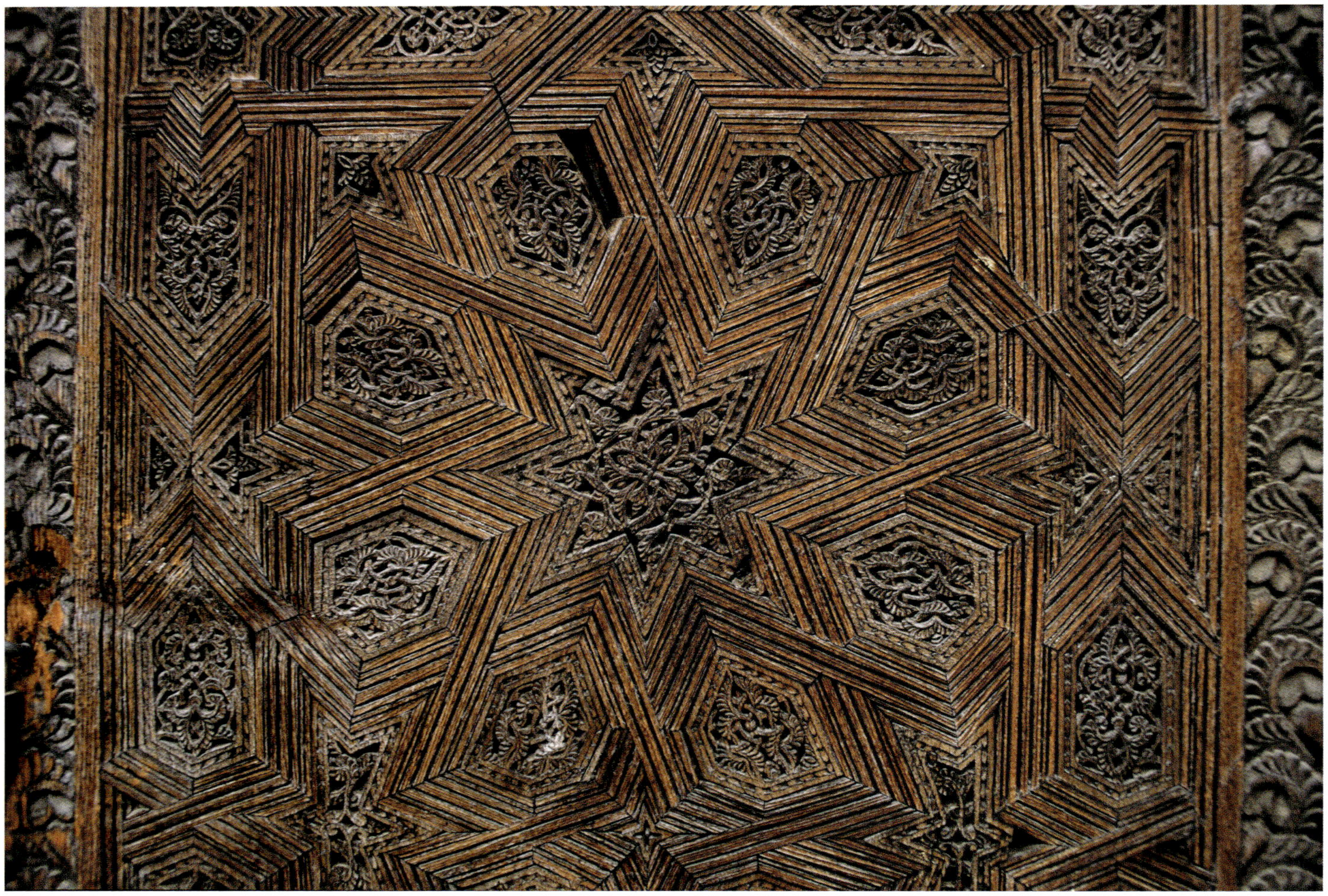

Madrasah Bu Inaniyya
Panel with a star motif
Cedar
1350–1355, Merinid period
Fez, Morocco

It is with something approaching drama that the delicate floral panels here are inserted into a geometrical surround that expands into a kind of abstract vision of the cosmos.

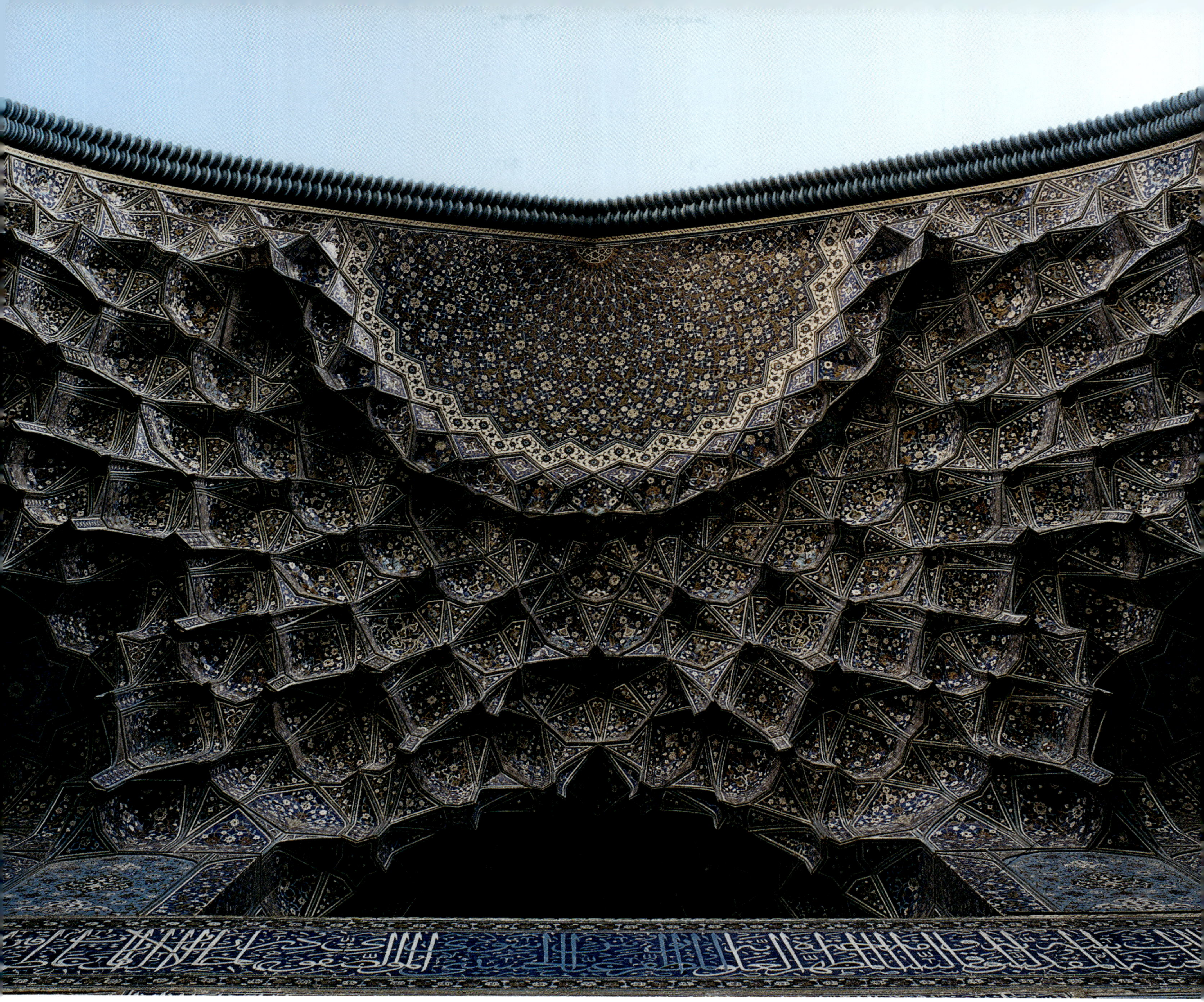

Masjid-e Shah (Mosque of the Shah)
Vaulting with *muqarnas*
1612–1638, Safavid
Isfahan, Iran

The cascade of *muqarnas* overhanging many entryways to mosques, *madrasahs,* tombs, and countless other architectural structures, sparkling with opulent yet secret cosmic harmonies, culminates in the point-like generative motif at the apex – both divine symbol and universal principle. The three-dimensional structure of the support, ascending in a series of tiers that build up towards the centre, is enlivened with 'hanging' stars interlaced with exquisite floral panels so that they seem to pulse in the boundless beauty of the cosmos.

THE FORMS OF ISLAMIC ARCHITECTURE

The territories conquered by Islam extended across a vast area in which highly evolved and diverse architectural traditions had developed to foster religions whose liturgies required extremely specialized structures. This makes it impossible to give a linear chronological and/or geographical portrait of the "development," and to some extent even of the existence of an Islamic architecture, in the sense that it can be called essentially "Muslim," not merely because of the function it fulfils (that of the faith) but because of its unmistakably recognizable characteristics. The absence of a specific architectural tradition among pre-Islamic Arabs, together with the scorn expressed by Muhammad in some *ahadith* towards building in general that was shared by a large proportion of less well-to-do Muslims, have undermined the formation of a clearly definable Islamic building practice. Moreover architects and masons, frequently not of the faith, continued to build as they had always done under earlier regimes. The idea of architecture as a discipline capable of organizing space rationally in both secular and sacred spheres is deeply rooted in Western thought, where the function of a building is in principle explicit from its outward appearance and its structure deducible from the form of its elements. Hence, a church is rarely hard to recognize; nor is a hotel, a school, a palace, a castle, a monastery, a tomb or a market, even when they have been reduced to archaeological ruins and in the absence of irrefutable documentary evidence, such as a dedication or act of foundation. Islamic architecture, although heir to the classical Greco-Roman tradition as well as to the Eastern Mesopotamian-Persian tradition, is characterized instead by a lack of concern with obviously functional design, perhaps because – without sharing their cultural and social substrata – Muslims were to take over architectural devices born in other contexts and for purposes that were alien to a religion whose 'liturgy' demanded no specific forms of building and was wary of the religions already in residence. The mosque is an answer to the practical need for a location for collective prayer, but, unlike a temple or a church, it possesses no intrinsically sacred character. It therefore does not have to be – and indeed was not before extraneous conceptions not rooted in Islam had been assimilated – designed as a model intended to communicate a determinate notion of the divine. A prime example of this 'indifference' is provided by one of the iconic architectural typologies present in nearly every Islamic country, whose origin moreover is far from clear: a building articulated around a large square or rectangular space ringed by porticoes set with four great *iwans* (vaulted zones open to each of its four sides), onto which give various inner rooms. It can easily be a *madrasah* (school), an aristocratic palace, a mosque, a *han* or *funduq* (a hotel, inn, or caravanserai in a city), or a monumental sepulchre (complete with dervish community in an annexe), a charitable institution (*külliye*), a hospital or a hostel for pilgrims. Nor is the spatial arrangement indicative of function and purpose: inside a house or palace, by and large, rooms are not assigned to night or day and the relative lack of furniture makes the use of the various spaces still more flexible. Architectural form tends, therefore, to be free from function, almost as it were a separate entity, whose theoretical significance is of scant importance and can be adapted to

Madrasah Mir-i Arab Façade
1535–1536, Uzbek period
Bukhara, Uzbekistan

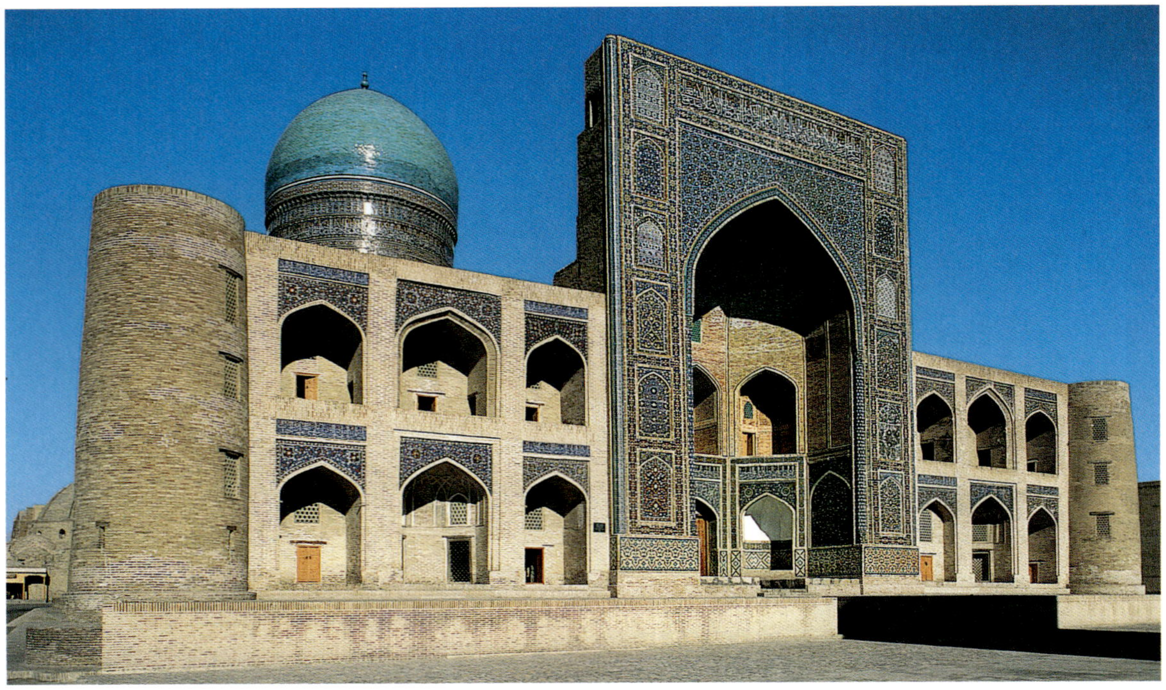

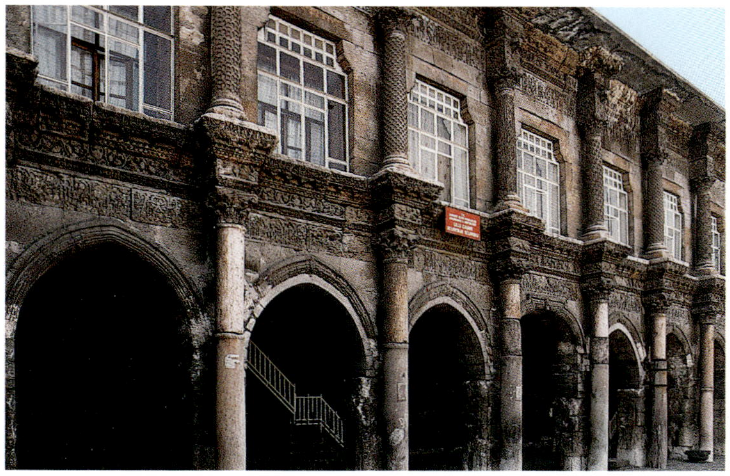

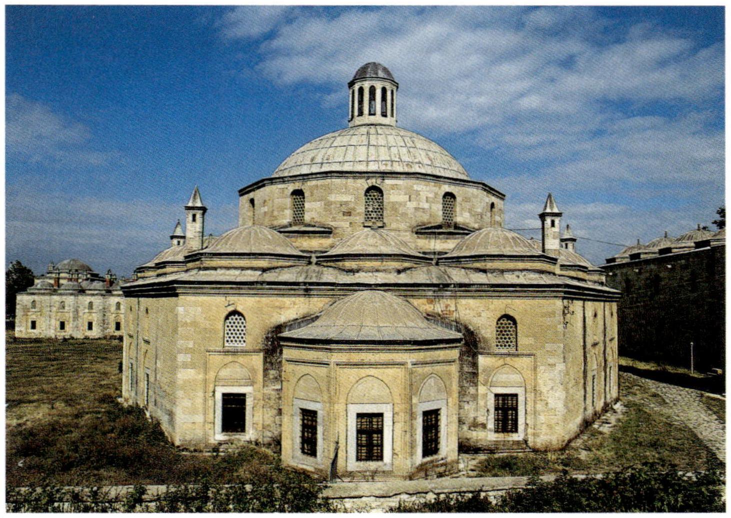

various necessities and needs depending on place and time. Architecture in Islamic lands tends to face inwards, perhaps in conformity to a typology harking back to the traditional Mediterranean house, protected by blind walls and, wherever possible, furnished with an inner courtyard. Similarly typical and going back to pre-Islamic traditions is the division of the internal space into private and public rooms, with the women housed in the most remote wing, a characteristic that recurs in other ancient civilizations.

Nor does city planning adhere to clear structures, as in the West, where the church and the palace occupied by the civilian power would dominate the urban fabric. The town spreads rather like an organic form built around poles of common interest, such as a market or religious institution, offering essential services for the inhabitants of its catchment area. Buildings of the greatest importance, such as the congregational mosque, can be all but unrecognizable among the congested weave of the city around it, as if threaded within it with disarming casualness. But elsewhere they can rise in glorious isolation, protected by row upon row of walls separating the space of prayer from the hustle and bustle of everyday existence outside. Or again it can dominate the skyline from some strategic point, as with Suleiman's mosque in Istanbul, a case in which the propaganda value of the building is of course obvious. The entrance to even a modest building endowed with any architectural dignity is stressed by sizable architectural elements that both separate and bridge two worlds: between the secular and the sacred, the collective and the private, the lowly and the princely, the urban and the rural, the built and the natural, even between the living and the dead. The gates to many passageways convey their purpose only thanks to verbal cues: hence, gateways are places adorned with epigraphs, be it for celebration, invocation or dedication. Decoration, when its function is more than to protect building elements in fragile materials, can assume a virtually 'anti-architectonic' role: it does not clearly or rationally emphasize the structural or organic nodes, the stresses and strains, as is the case in Western classical architecture, but rather seems to dissolve the building members into a luminous continuum, transforming the masses into surfaces overrun by calligraphy and geometrical patterns, turning the structure into a vehicle for a message rather than leaving it as an entity with its own independent significance. The condemnation of architecture attributed to Muhammad has encouraged a view of building as a response to a human need realized through an act of will, as a conduit for a religious message that can be the sole justification for monumental edifices. Their surfaces overrun with demonstrations of the geometric laws that govern the cosmos and life; they lead the believer, if he enquires into their principle and meaning, to the unfathomable and indivisible unity from which springs their form.

Far from being gratuitous accessories, calligraphy and geometric design are a fundamental component of Islamic architecture. Basically Islamic architecture exhibits no interest in rendering intelligible a building's superstructure; that is, in making explicit how the forces in action are controlled and balanced rationally through orders and members. It strives instead to attain effects of weightlessness, to glory in light and in infinite space, pushing its walls, pillars, and vaults to the brink of dematerialization.

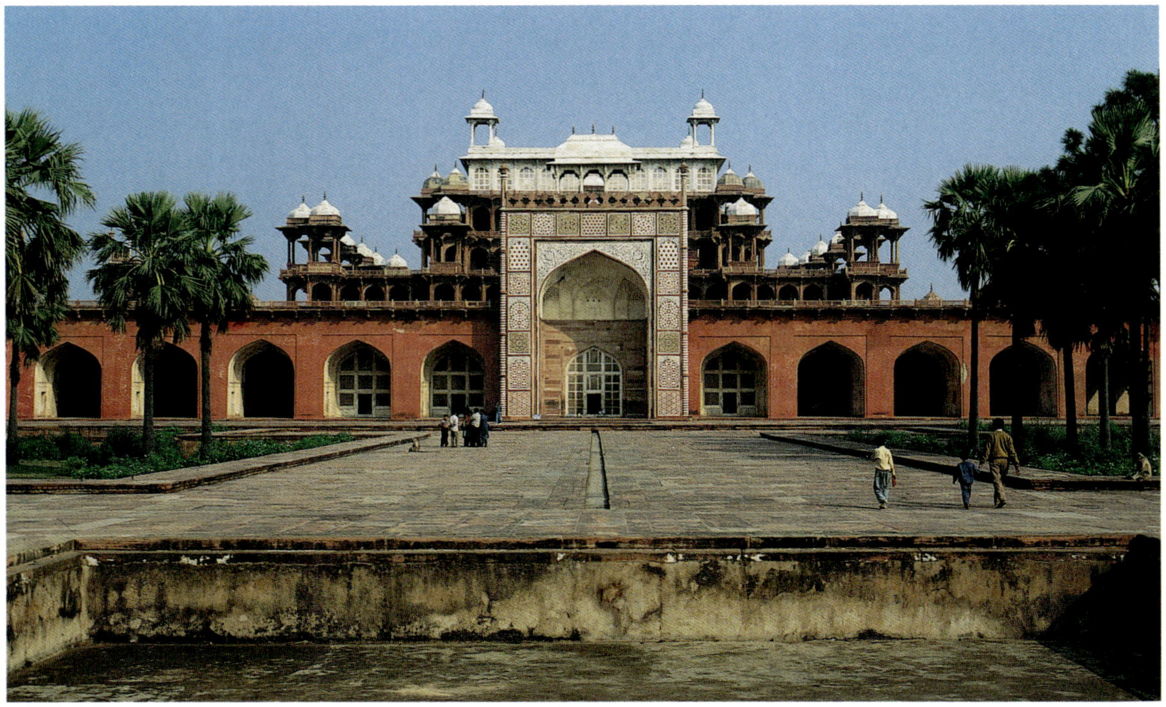

Great Mosque
Façade
11th–12th century
Seleucid period
Diyarbakir, Turkey

Hayreddin (1442–1512), the *külliye* of Bayazet II (hospital on a hexagonal plan)
1484–1488, Ottoman period
Edirne, Turkey

Mausoleum of Akbar
1605–1612
Mughal period
Sikandra, India

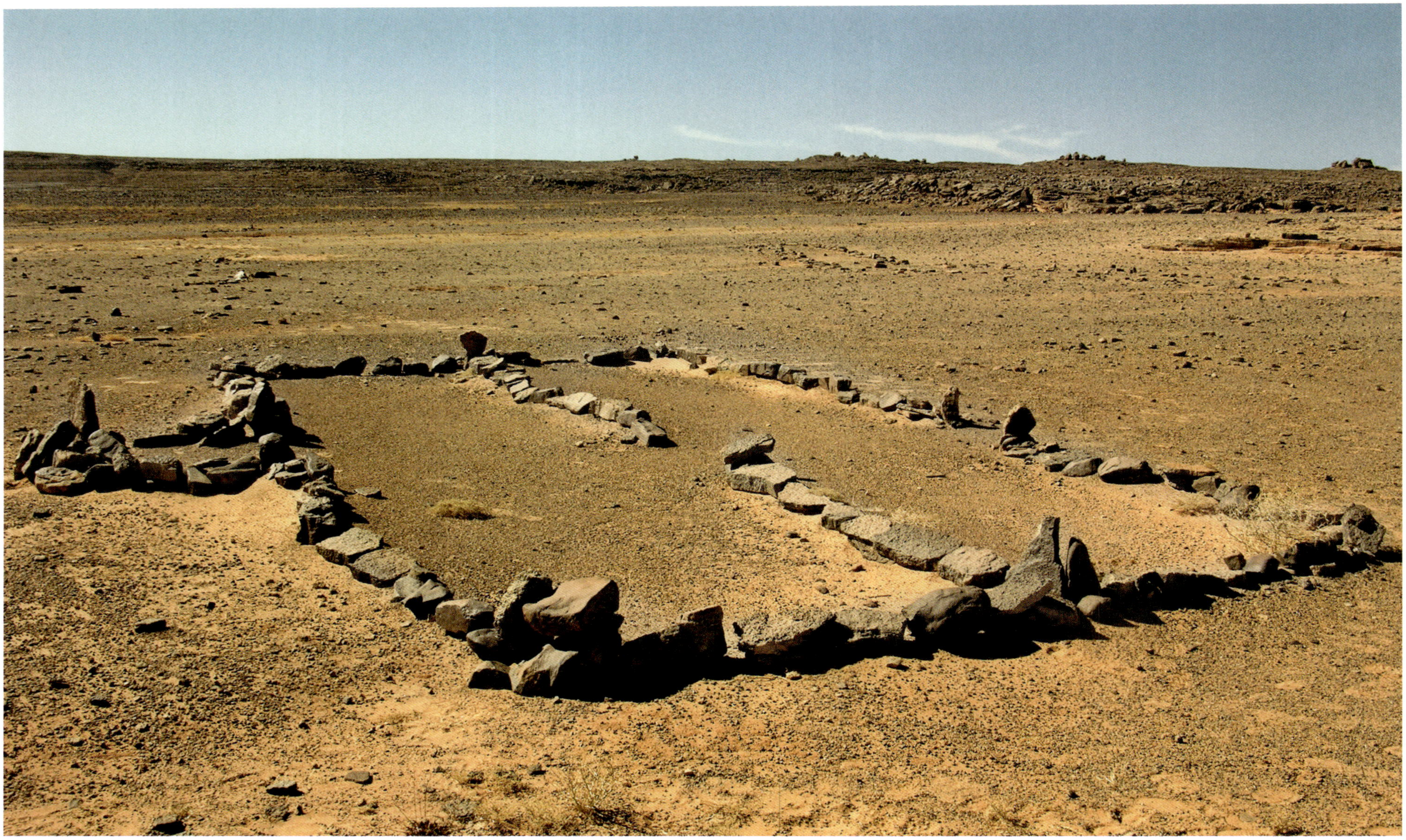

'Mosque' or prayer area constructed from a ring of stones
Period unknown
Outskirts of Djanet, Algerian Sahara

The Qur'an does not lay down rigorous norms for religious building: the term "mosque" – ultimately from the Arabic, *masjid,* 'place of prostration' – means simply a space for prayer, whose structure is undefined and is invested with no sacred value. It is possible to worship in any place, provided that the space for prayer is marked out by some object or other (a carpet, a rug, stones) and is ritually clean. Along their caravan routes the Bedouins delimited the prayer space as in a mosque: courtyard, prayer space, and *mihrab.*
Led by Muhammad himself, the first collective prayers would often take place in the middle of the desert. The Prophet's simple home was in fact the first official site of Islam, because it answered a practical and concrete need: a courtyard encircled by a wall with two areas shaded by roofs supported on palm trunks; there was no theoretical notion or aesthetic idea behind its form. It is this wonderfully simple structure that has constituted the model for all subsequent mosques.

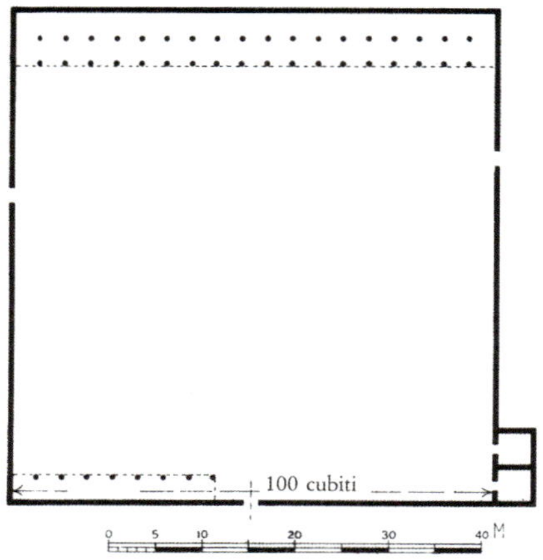

Hypothetical reconstruction of Muhammad's house
7th century
Medina, Saudi Arabia

***Khanaqah* ('Convent of the Sufi') of Sultan Barquq**
Mihrab* and *minbar
1410, Mamluk period
Cairo, Egypt

Normally recited in private, prayer became a collective duty on Fridays, when the community gathered to hear the Prophet or his delegate, the *imam*. He would stand before the faithful next to the *qibla* wall towards which prayers are directed, communicating information of various kinds, leading prayers, and pronouncing the *khutbah* (the community's act of fidelity to its guide) from a pulpit called the *minbar* that was to become the symbol of the official status of the place of collective worship. The *qibla* wall is indicated by a niche known as the *mihrab* that may be no more than a drawing on the wall; the term has the same root as *harba*, 'to fight', and is therefore the place where God is revealed, the direction in which lies the salvation of man when transformed by his battle against Satan.

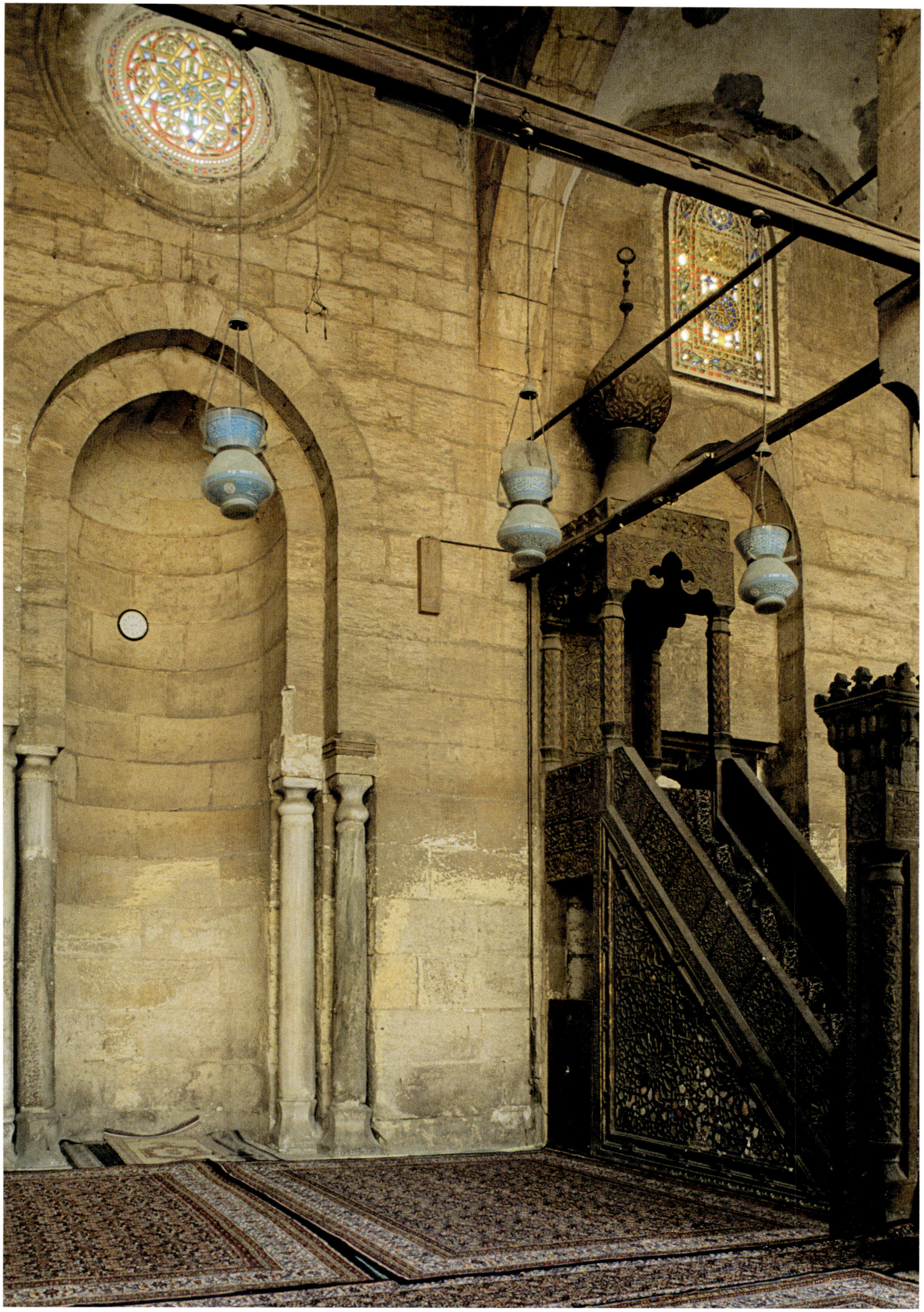

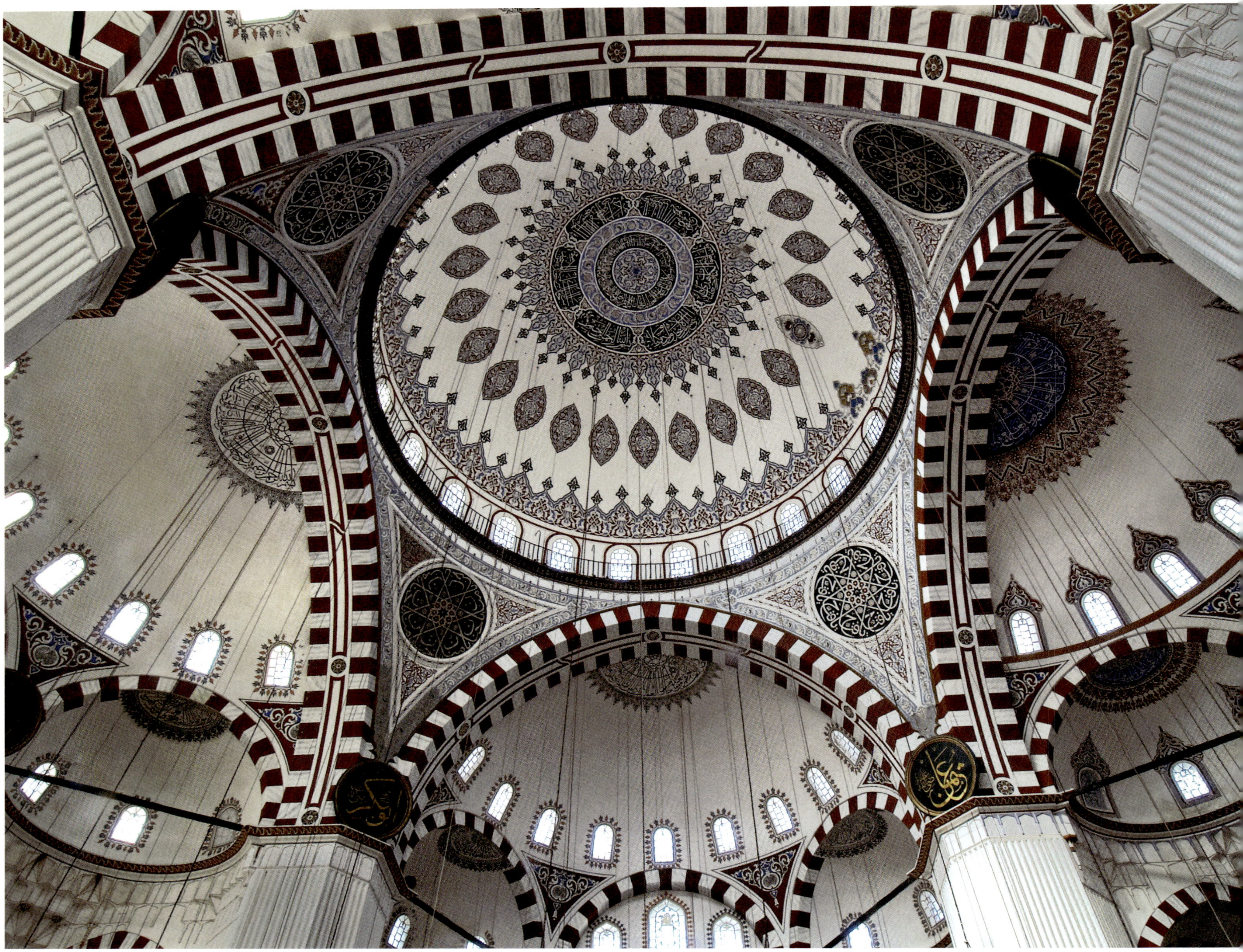

Mimar Sinan (1491–1588)
Roof of the Sehzade Mosque
1543–1548, Ottoman period
Istanbul, Turkey

In general the area dedicated to prayer (*musalla*) presents a rectangular plan, allowing worshippers to arrange themselves in rows and ranks. It can be covered by the classic flat ceiling borne on columns or pillars (hypostyle hall), with a number of domes placed on large pillars (transitional style, such as the Ulu Cami, the Great Mosque, on pillars in the Turkish tradition) or by a single cupola reinforced by half-domes. It is to this last group that the Sehzade Mosque belongs, the first great achievement of Mimar Sinan and the prelude to the most glorious period of Ottoman architecture. The conclusion of a lengthy process culminating in the study of the Byzantine church of Hagia Sophia in Istanbul, the inner space is organized according to a plan of great formal coherence topped by the central cupola.

Quwwat al-Islam Mosque, Qutb Minar ('Qubt minaret')
Begun in 1199, Sultanate period, upper section, 1368
Delhi, India

The minaret (from the Arabic, *manara* 'beacon', 'tower') is a tower of variable height and shape. From its summit the *muezzin* (Turkish, from the Arabic, *mu-adhdhin*, root *udhn,* 'ear', and therefore "to listen", "to perceive"), calls the faithful to prayer (*adhan*) five times a day at the canonical hours. During the early years of Islam, when prayers were held in private houses like Muhammad's, the call would have been made from the roof; the minaret was an innovation of a later age, perhaps to compete with the contemporary introduction of the church spire. Over time it became the object of a particular strand of architectural development that gave rise to several regional schools. More than just a place from which the call to prayer could be made, it increasingly assumed a symbolic value as a 'beacon' of Islam, perhaps taking its cue from the ancient Roman lighthouses strung out along the Palestine shoreline.
The Qutb Minar is one of the most ambitious minarets ever constructed: originally with four floors (the top two were added during repairs for lightning damage) and a height of seventy-two metres it was the tallest of its time.

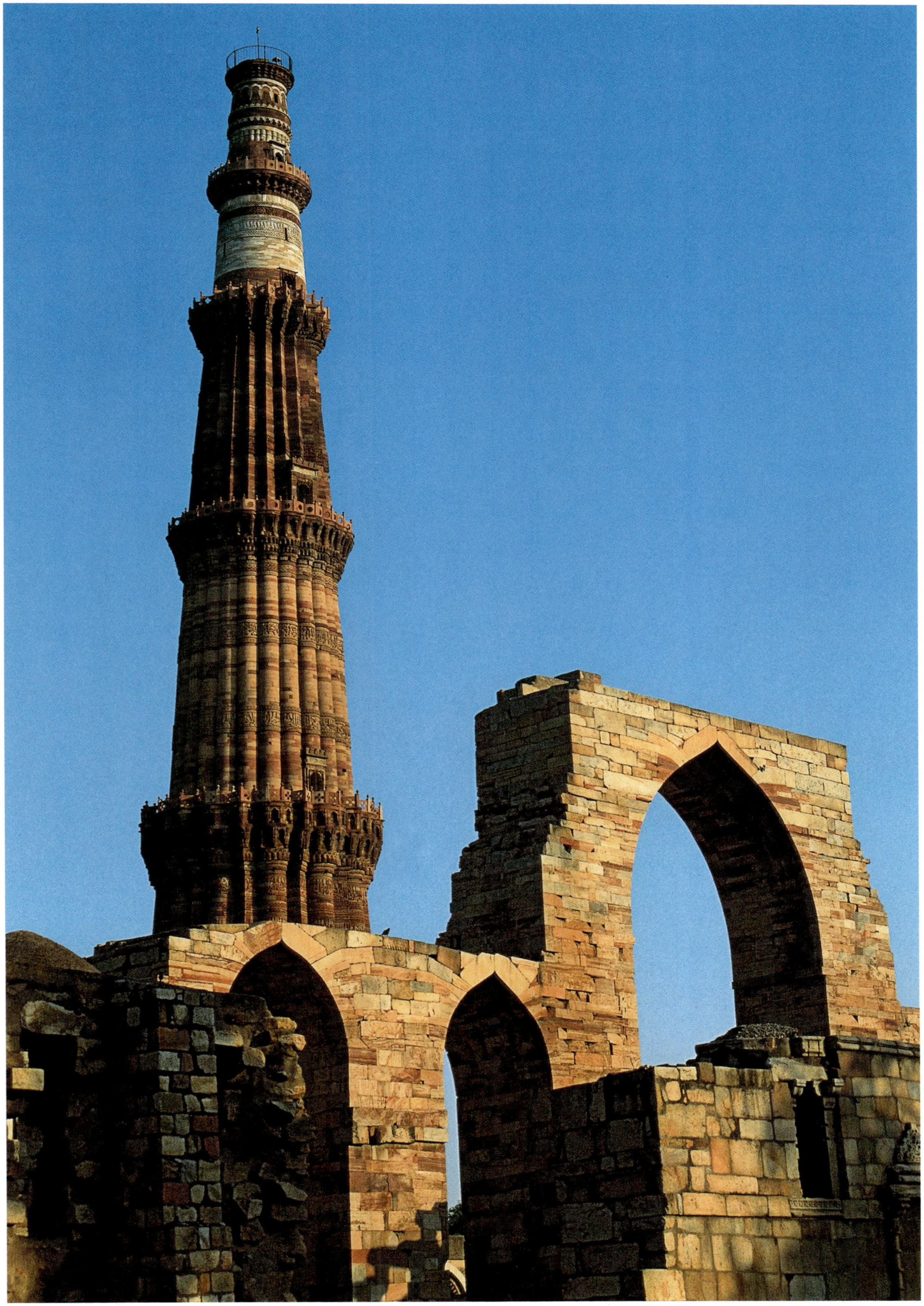

Çifte Minareli Medrese
('Madrasah with double minaret')
1235, Seljuq era
Erzurum, Turkey

The Arabic term *madrasahh* (from *darasa* 'to study') means 'school' and covers every type of educational institution. The madrasah as a building appeared relatively late, since for a long time instruction took place at the mosque or in the teacher's house. Over time, though, schools grew up around the most celebrated masters. After the conflict between the Shias and the Sunni, the latter, to exert control over education, started erecting dedicated teaching institutions. The first purpose-built madrasahs for university education were erected in Persia in the eleventh century under the Seljuqs. The Çifte Minareli has two floors, with four *iwans,* two minarets and the tomb of the founder in front of its entrance.

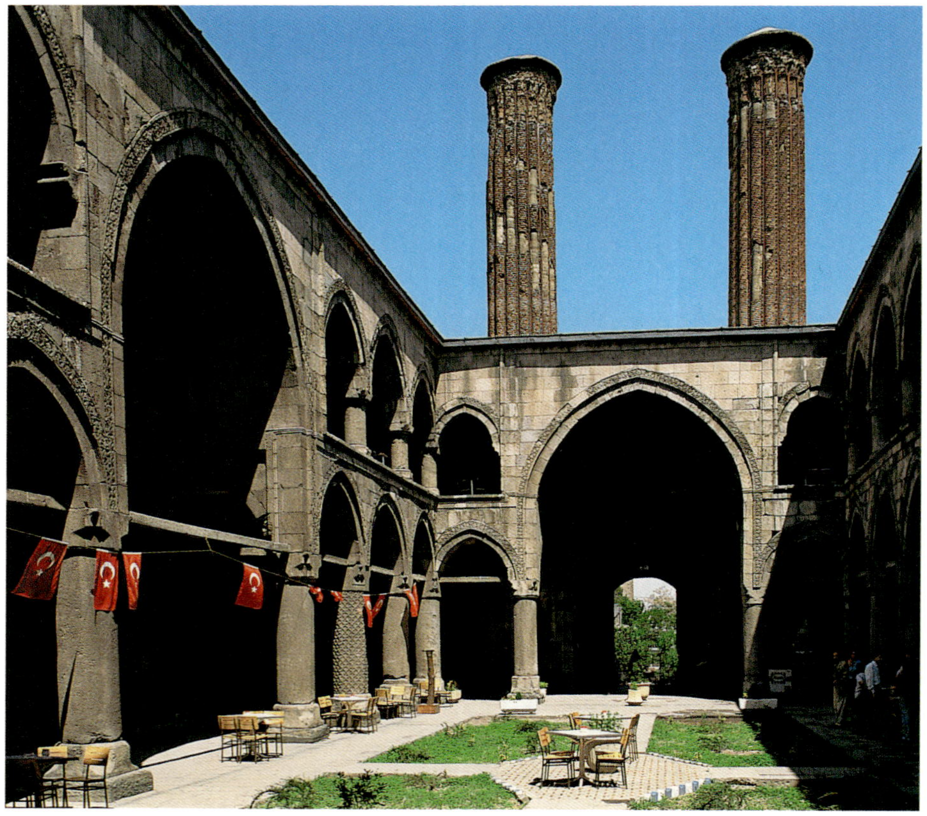

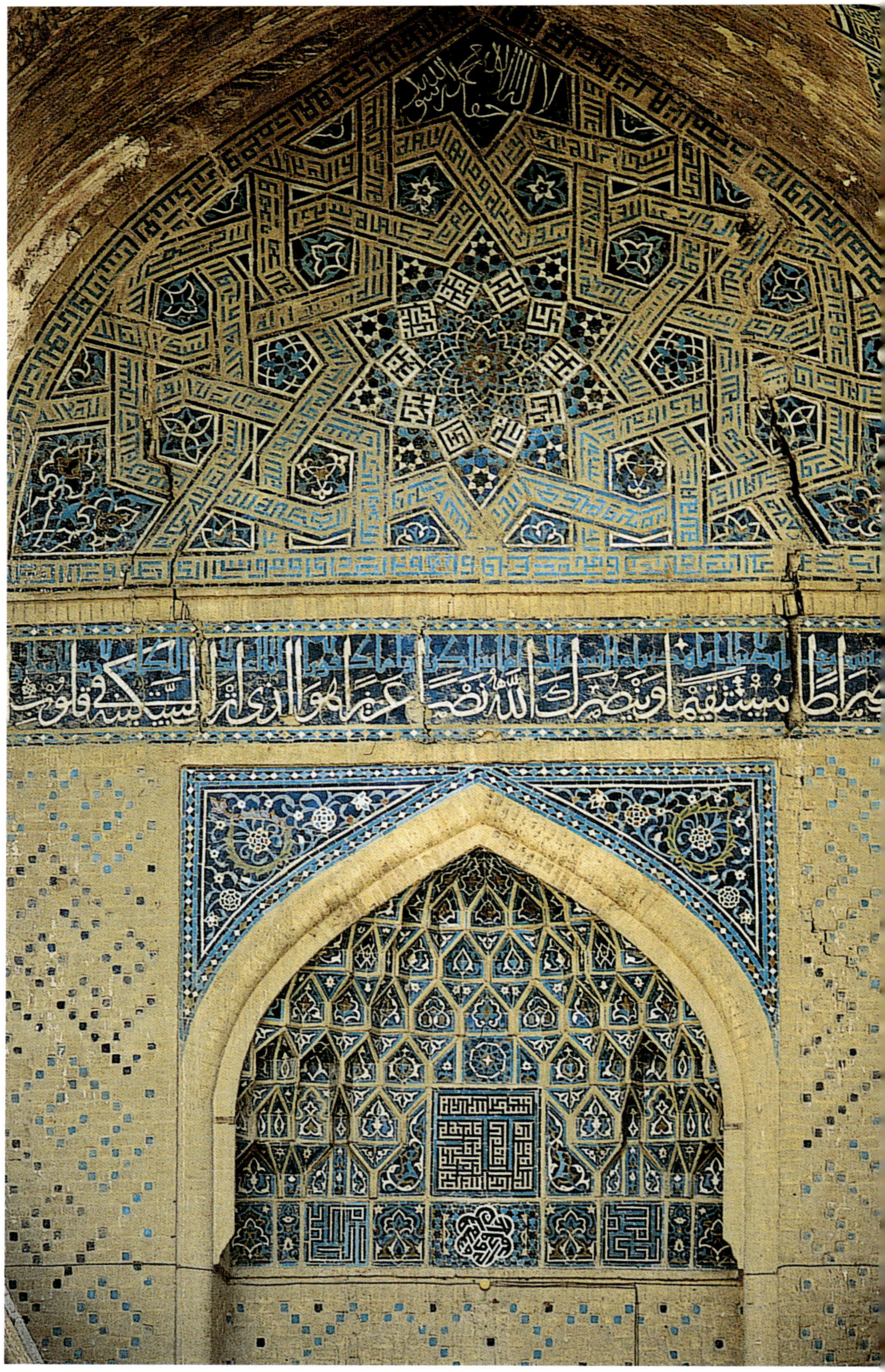

Madrasah of the Imam Iyeh
Iwan* with *mihrab
c. 1340, Ilkhanid period
Isfahan, Iran

The typology of the madrasah, often arranged around an open-air courtyard with four *iwans* dedicated to the four official schools of jurisprudence, most likely derives from the traditional house plan in the Khorasan – a region straddling Iran, Turkmenistan and Afghanistan – or from the Persian mosques inspired by it.

Madrasah el-Attarin
Courtyard
1323–1325, Merinid period
Fez, Morocco

The entrance to a madrasah is often framed by a monumental doorway overarched by an *iwan,* at times flanked by a pair of minarets, while the external wall is usually closed off so as to protect students from the outside world, although this rule was soon very often disregarded. Of modest dimensions and generally spread out over two floors, the students' chambers give onto the inner courtyard. The classic madrasah also comprises a prayer hall, a fountain at the centre of the court, a library, washrooms etc., and occasionally the tomb of the founder; apart from the prayer hall it does not differ in any obvious way from an urban caravanserai. The Merinid madrasah, of which el-Attarin is a magnificent example, adds accents of refined and intimate fantasy to these traditional structures, incorporating materials such as cedar, stucco and ceramic with consummate grace, as in the most splendid private dwelling.

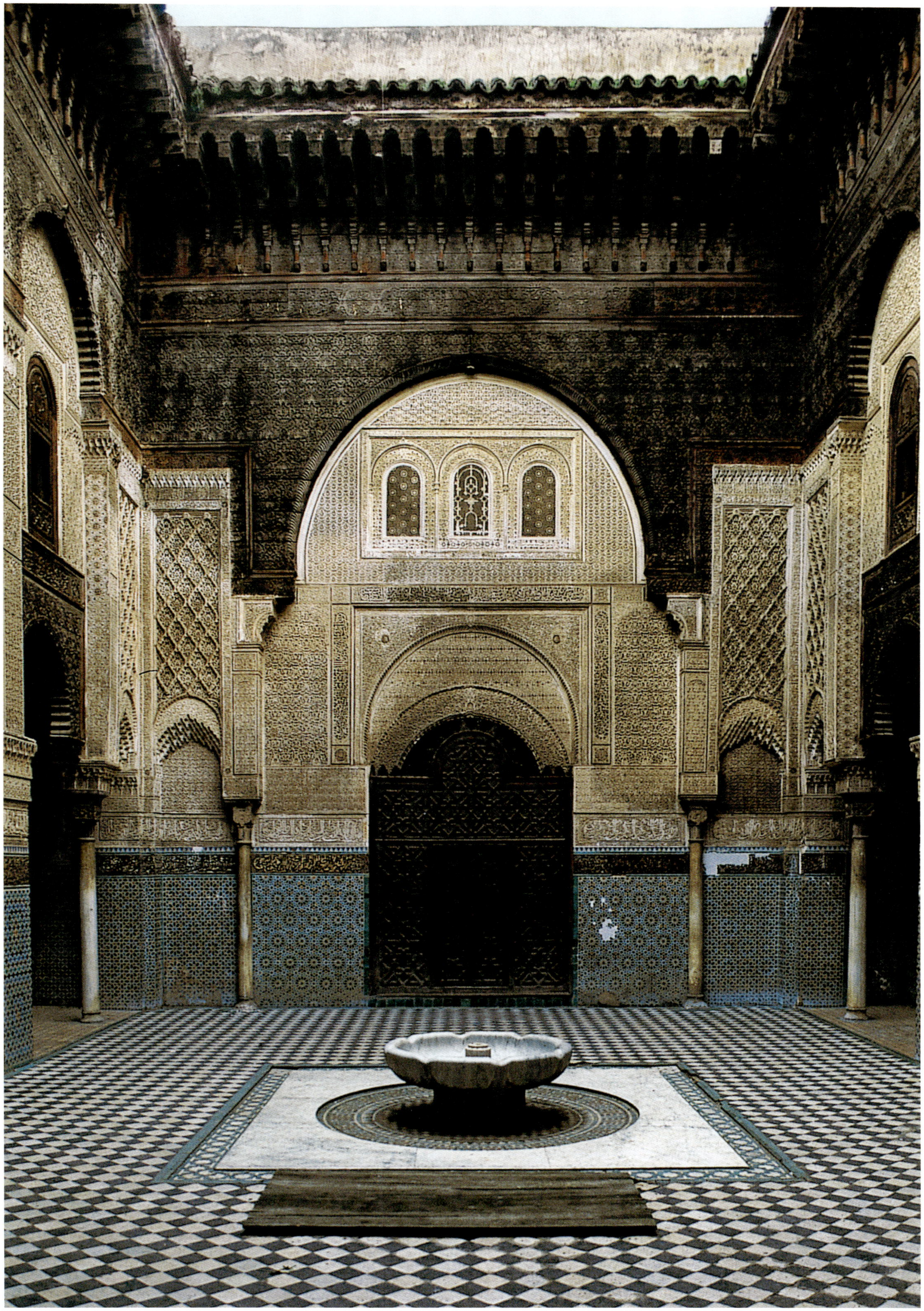

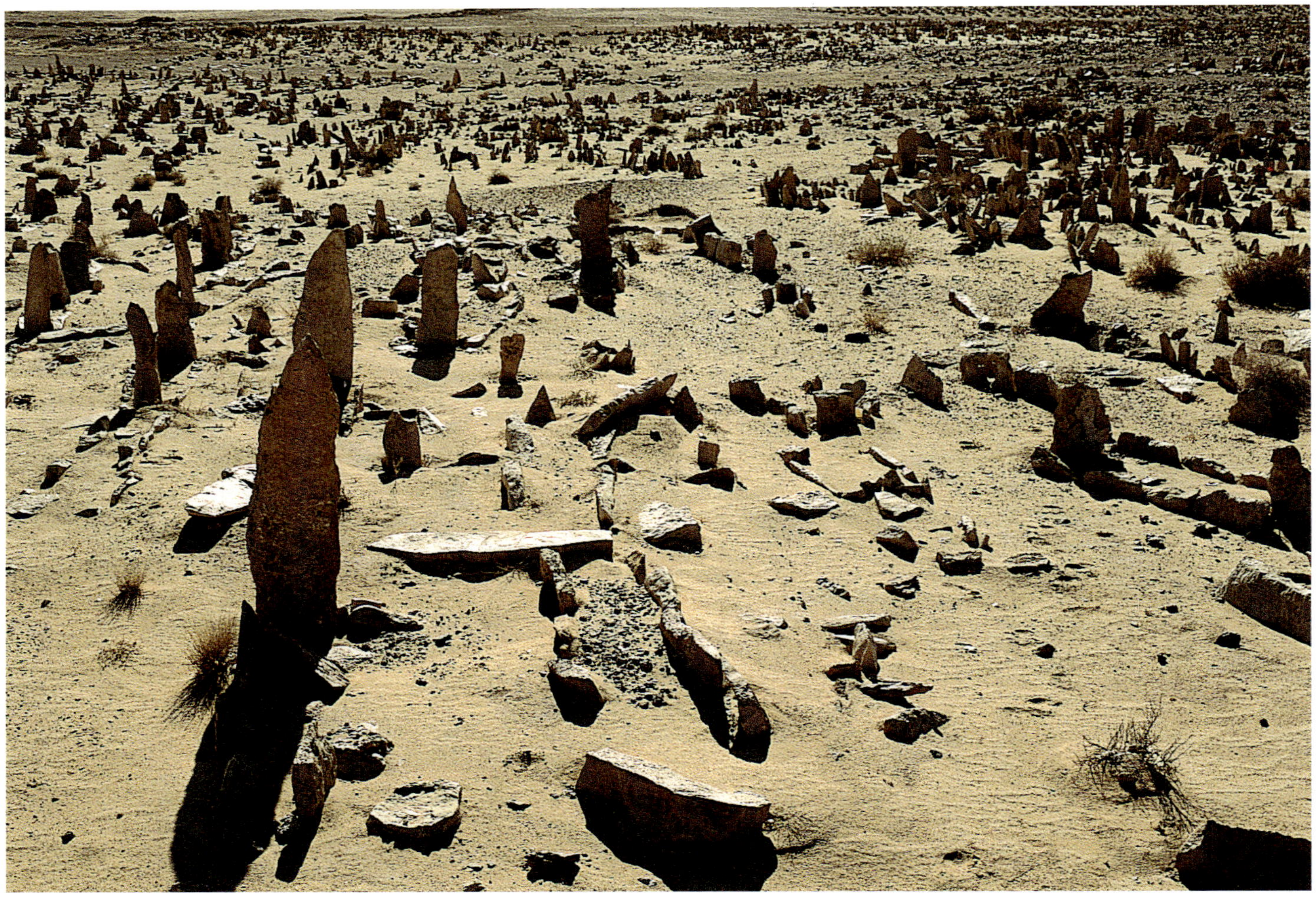

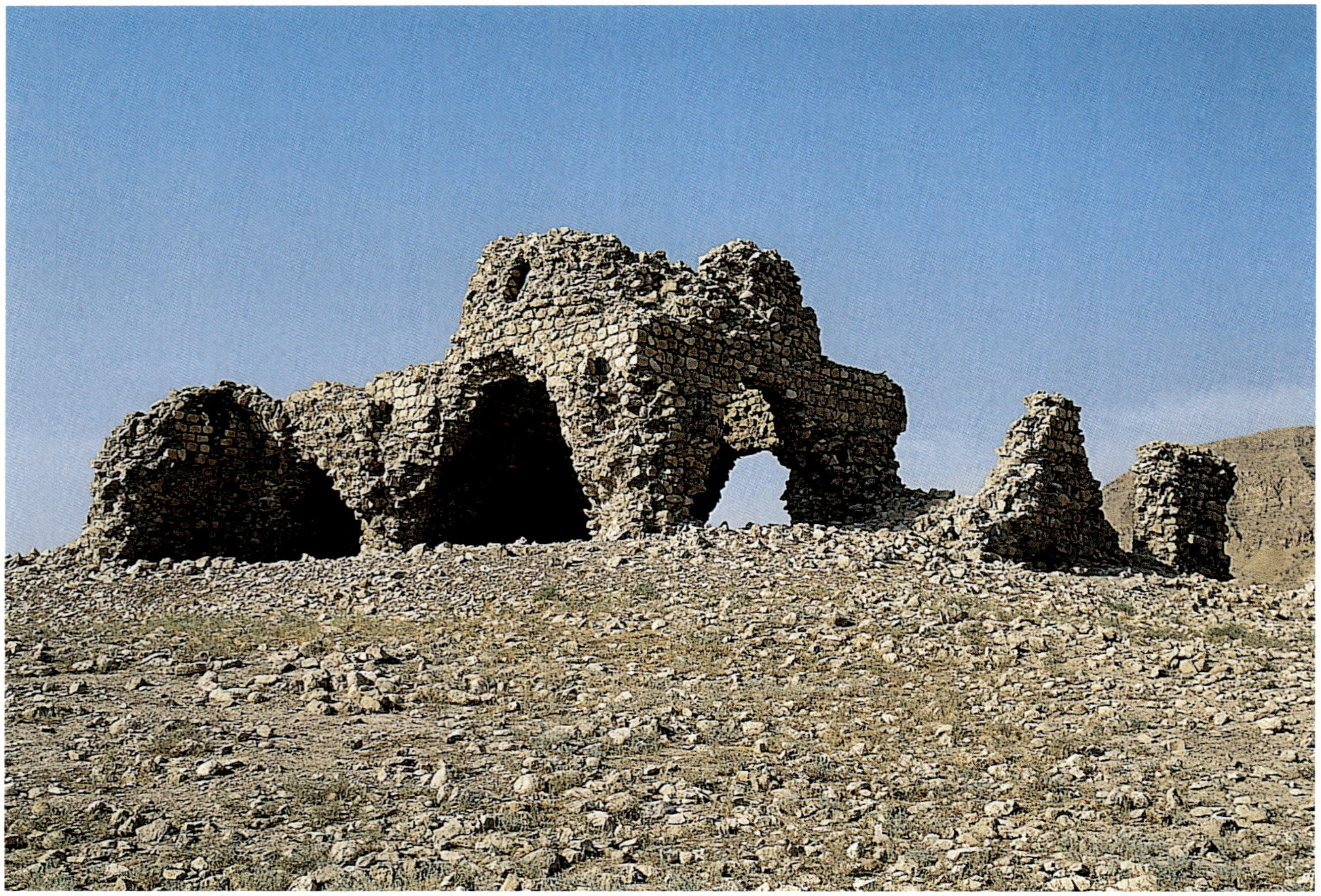

Ancient cemetery
Unknown date
Ghadames, Libya

Exploring the history of tombs in the Muslim world is a paradoxical affair. Although Muhammad prohibited the erection of structures of any type at burial places, Muslim monumental tombs constitute the greatest architectural creation outside the religious sphere. Theoretically, as among nomadic peoples, a tomb should be a simple trench marked with a tombstone or stele. Personal ambition and the emulation of funerary complexes in conquered territories, however, together with various contrivances gleaned from passages on paradise in the Qur'an and *ahadith* as well as from poetic literature, were marshalled when circumventing this prohibition, to the point that tombs became lawful.

Zoroastrian fire temple
4th–5th century
Sassanid era, outskirts of Jar (Jiyar), Iran

In its account of paradise, the Qur'an lays great stress on the presence of shade. So, with a flexibility typical of Muslim pragmatism, a burial place was permitted to have a structure if it offered shade without being enclosed; a model was found in the Sassanid fire temple, a simple, canopied structure open on all four sides. The transition from square base with a roof to a circular dome was moreover a frequent metaphor for the shift from the earthly to the cosmic dimension.

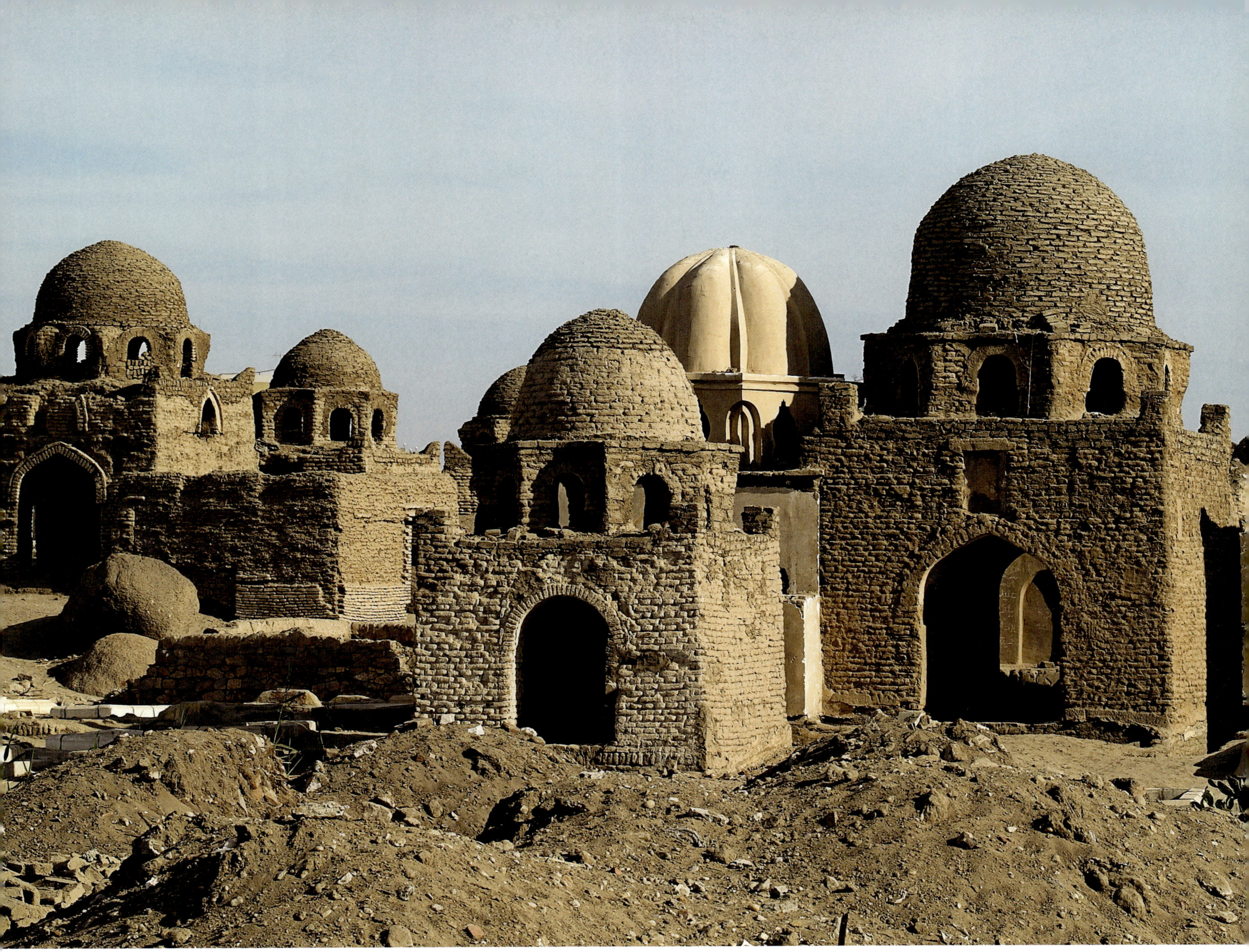

Mausoleums
Beginning of the 11th century, Fatimid era
Aswan, Egypt

In the cemetery at Aswan approximately sixty intriguing mausoleums survive, many occupied by women; they were places of great veneration dating to the Fatimid era. Although the practice is theoretically rejected by Islam, it remains extremely widespread, particularly in Shiite regions, where a more general reverence for martyrs persists. Its traditional structure derives from the fire temple: a square base with open sides and crowned with a dome. The casket itself, made of marble or other materials and placed on the ground, is not a sarcophagus but a cenotaph, the deceased being interred in a white sheet, the face turned towards Mecca. The dome crowning the upper part of such funerary monuments is an obvious image of heaven, an effect often reinforced by the colours chosen and by star motifs. Thanks to the ever-present implications of Islamic geometrical symbolism, the choice of plan – circular, square, hexagonal, octagonal (modelled on the *martyria* of the Christian baptistery), or star-shaped – can also be loaded with significance.

Medina and *Kasbah*
9th century
Sousse, Tunisia

The Muslim city can be founded *ex novo,* and thus correspond to a rational city plan invested with high symbolic value, as in the case of Baghdad; it may rise spontaneously; or else it may take over a previously occupied site. It often developed around a trading hub or a halt on an important caravan artery; it tends to be centred on a market, either open-air or housed in a purpose-built structure, and on the headquarters of religious institutions. In short, then, cities are commercial emporia, small or large, bustling with life and awash with merchandise, places of production and shops, meeting places crammed with people buying and selling. In Arabic lands, within the *intra muros* city proper stand the medina (from the Arabic, *madina,* 'city'), dense with *suqs* (in Arabic; *bazaar* in Turkish, 'market'), dominated, particularly in the Maghreb and in Spain, by the *kasbah* (from the Arab *qasaba,* 'citadel'), the fortified citadel. Other elements invariably present include the congregational mosque (*jami masjid*) and the palace (*saray*) occupied by the ruler.

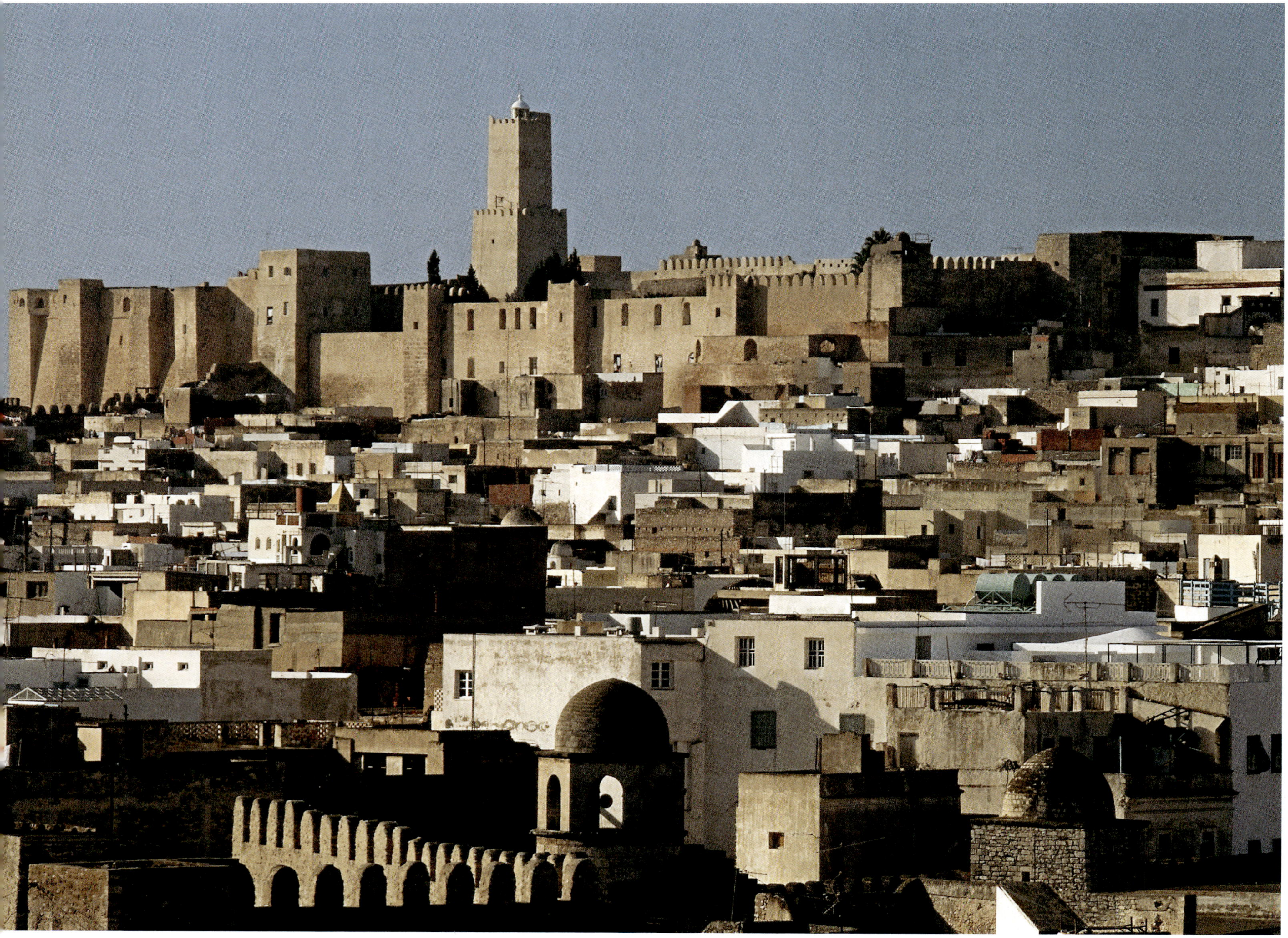

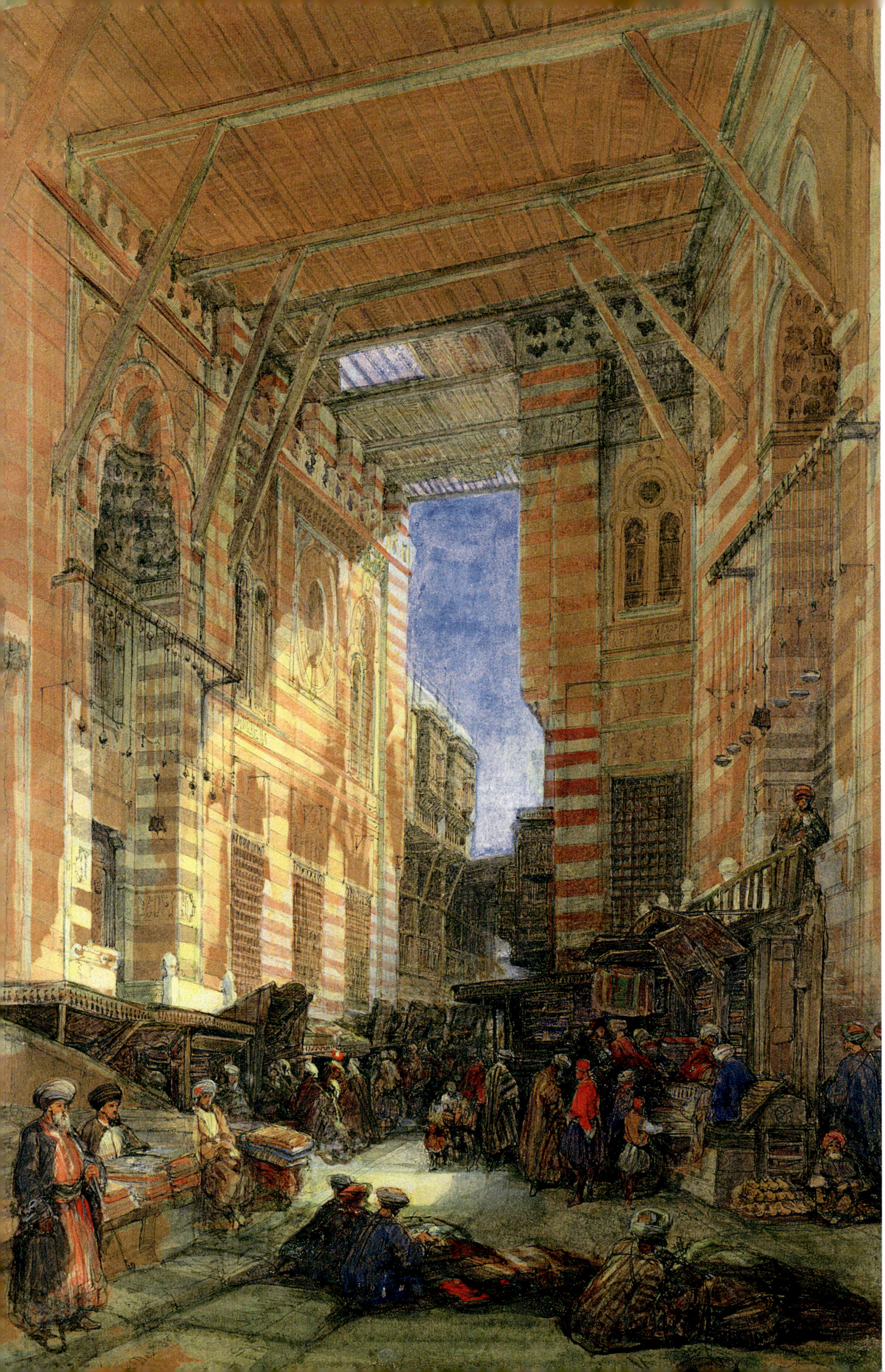

David Roberts (1796–1864)
The Silk Vendors' Bazaar in Cairo
1838–1839
Lithograph, hand-painted with watercolour

In Muslim cities the sacred and the profane mix inextricably and seamlessly: roads, markets and mosques, interlinked poles of city life, spring up together; even buildings of major importance are unrecognizable from the outside and in theory continuous façades can only be distinguished by monumental entryways. The mosque stands next to the market in order to fulfil the obligation of religious observance without losing too much trading time, without which the inhabitants would not earn enough to give alms or endow pious foundations. Save in larger cities laid out in a regular plan inherited from the metropolises of the ancient world, the winding and narrow streets finish in a dead end at the last dwelling in a given area.

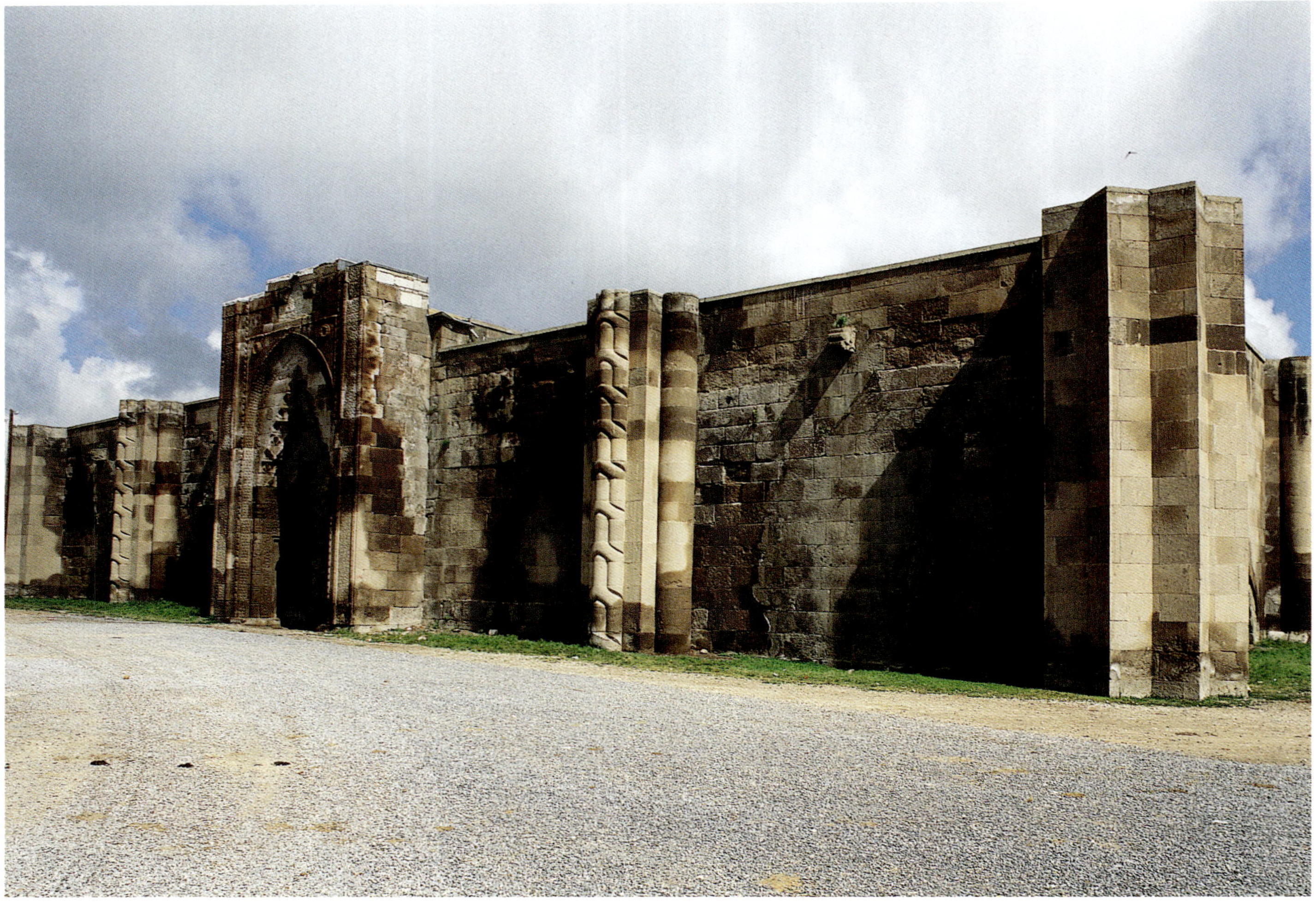

Karatay Han
1246, Seljuq period
Outskirts of Kayseri, Turkey

The all-conquering Muslims inherited a network of military and trading routes and commercial nerve centres of primary importance that they maintained in perfect working order and indeed expanded by removing frontiers. Along these thoroughfares, at regular intervals, hundreds of caravanserais were built (250 are listed for Seljuq in Turkey alone); they were financed by officials from the higher echelons of the civil service.

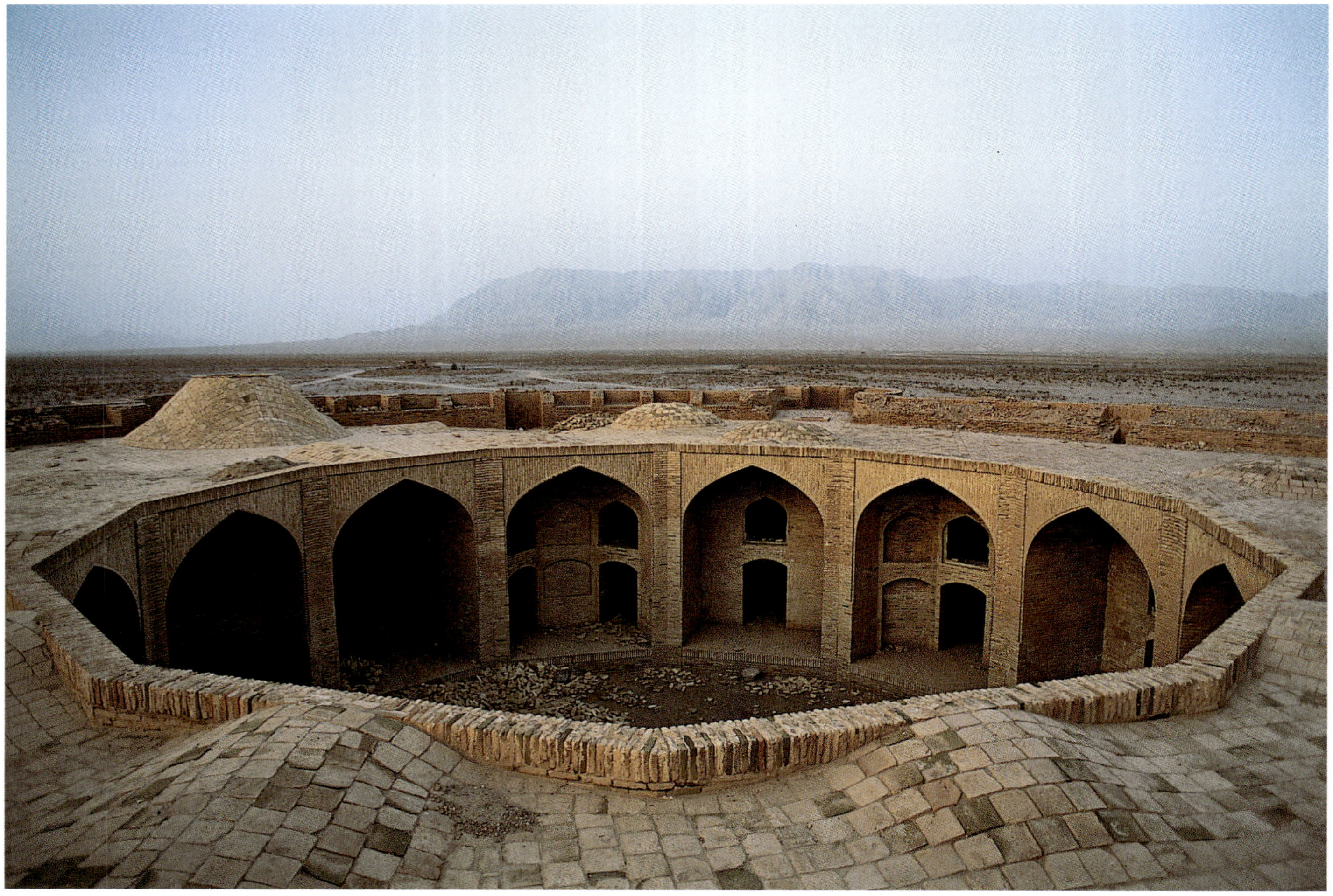

Robat-e Zeid ad-Din Han
17th–18th century, Safavid period
Outskirts of Yazd, Iran

With various forms, on occasion conforming to a geometric plan (as illustrated here, a dodecagon), and erected using various materials depending on the resources available and on the local climate, caravanserais shared certain specific structural characteristics: a walled and fortified enclosure with a single monumental entryway opening into a courtyard with covered spaces. They all offered similar facilities: shelter, water and food for the traveller and animals, storerooms, physicians (sometimes) and veterinary surgeons (always), together with a prayer hall. Lodging, permitted for up to three days, was free.

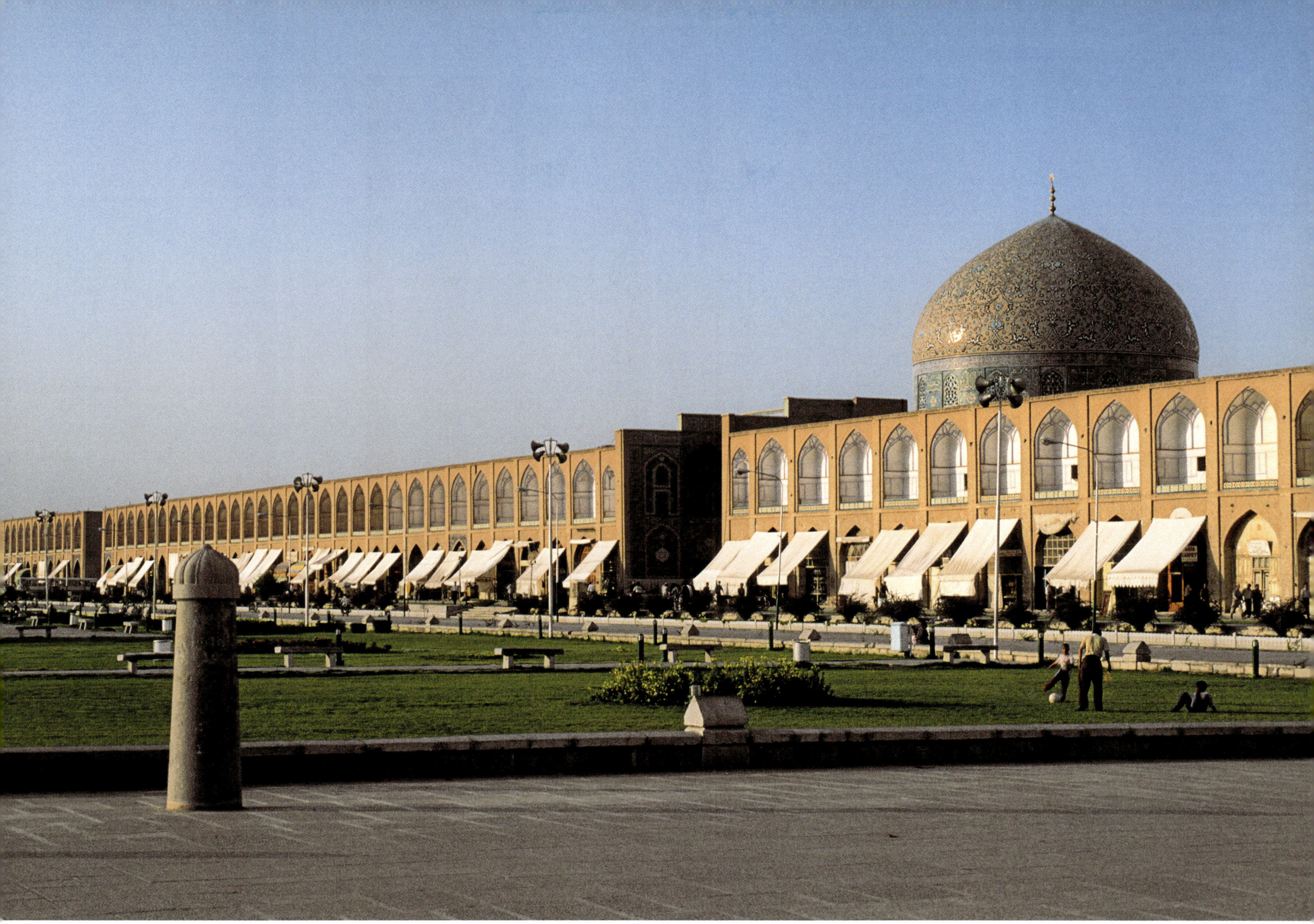

Meydan-e Shah ('Public square of the Shah')
with the stores of the bazaar
and the Mosque of Sheikh Lutf Allah
c. 1617, Safavid period
Isfahan, Iran

The immense Meydan-e Shah forms the main focus of Isfahan's urban fabric; at the time of its construction, it was used for parades, processions and above all for polo, a game for which some elements remain, such as the stone marker post in the foreground. The perimeter is formed by a two-storey curtain wall: round the first runs a continuous parade of shops, while the upper tier represents a kind of proscenium of purely decorative value. The focal point is provided by the spectacular entrance to the Mosque of the Shah, which stands opposite the long roofed bazaar which extends to the Friday mosque. In the middle of the western side stands the seat of government, the Ali Qapu, with, before it, the Sheikh Lutf Allah Mosque (in the photo), the private oratory of the court, which, as such, has no need of a minaret.

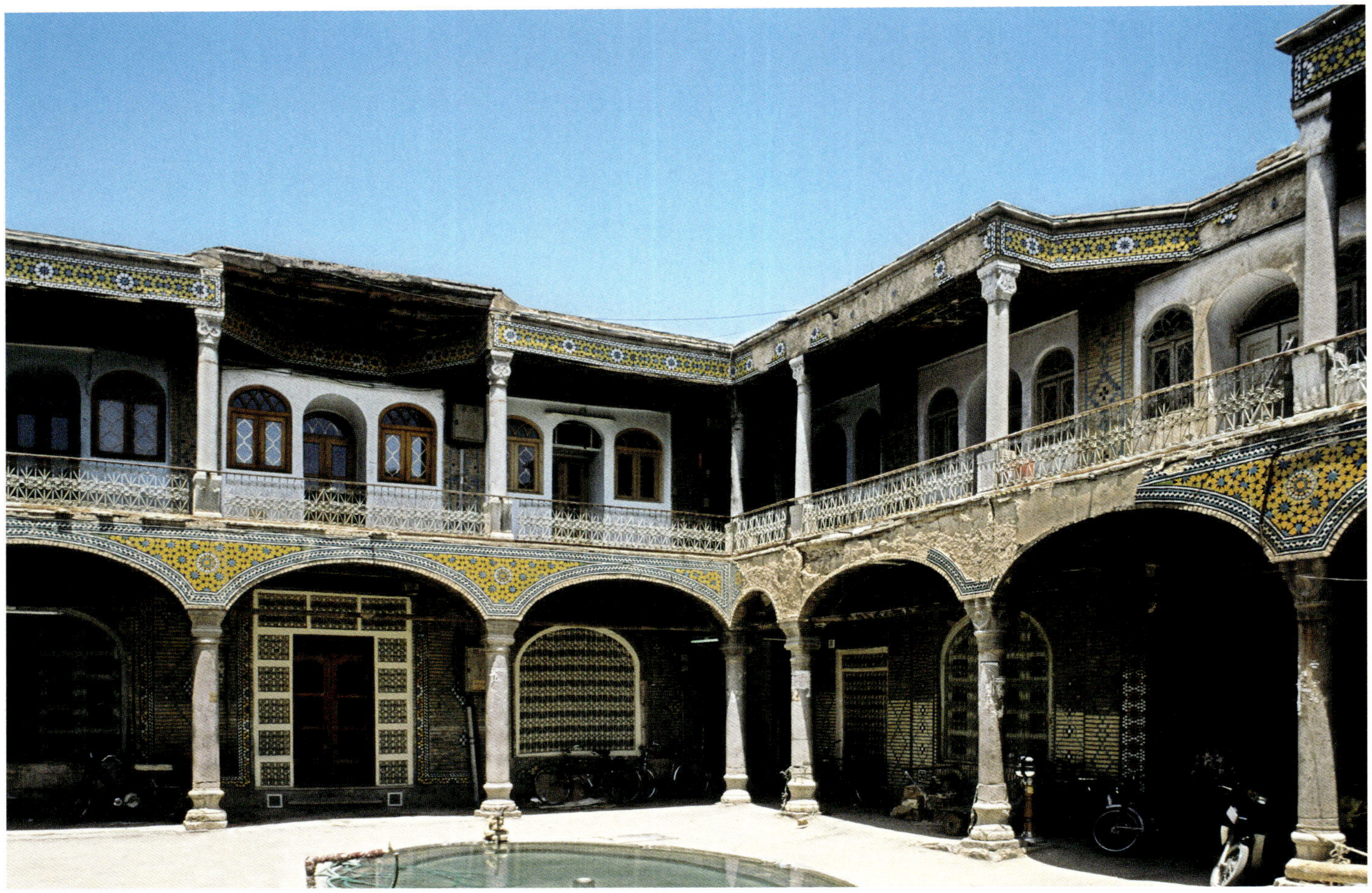

Caravanserai
19th century, Qajar period
Isfahan, Iran

In sizable agglomerations, particularly in cities where the focus was trade, numerous structures catered for travellers and merchants; these urban caravanserais – *funduq* in Arabic and *han* in Turkish – offered various levels of service and, therefore, naturally enough, of tariffs. Broadly comprised of a multi-storey complex set around a wide rectangular court with a fountain, it was designed specially for loading and unloading merchandise that could be left in the open or stored in warehouses or, in the case of valuable goods awaiting transfer to market, in guarded units. The number, dimensions and quality of these various structures afford an accurate idea of the prosperity of the society concerned.

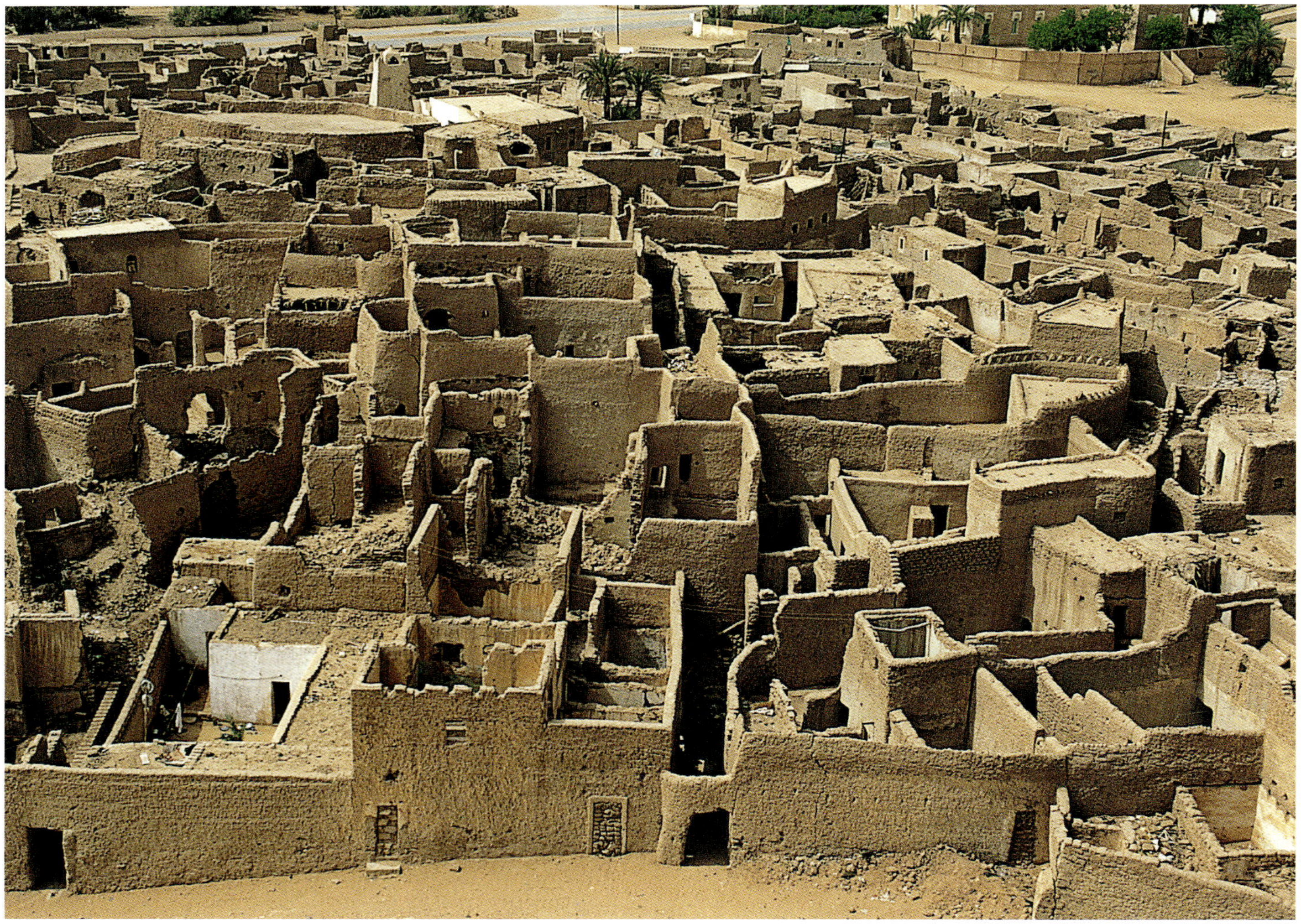

Houses and alleyways in the centre of the old city of Ghat
c. 18th–19th century
Libya

In the typical Muslim city, dwellings only rarely gave directly onto a thoroughfare, being hidden away down winding alleys. Grouped in zones round a religious foundation and inhabited by people of similar origin, profession and denomination, these groups would develop a strong sense of solidarity and reciprocal duty. Divisions were not based on social status: members of different classes would live side by side, sharing the same market, mosque, *hammam,* and services of every kind, thereby constituting administratively and fiscally homogenous units.

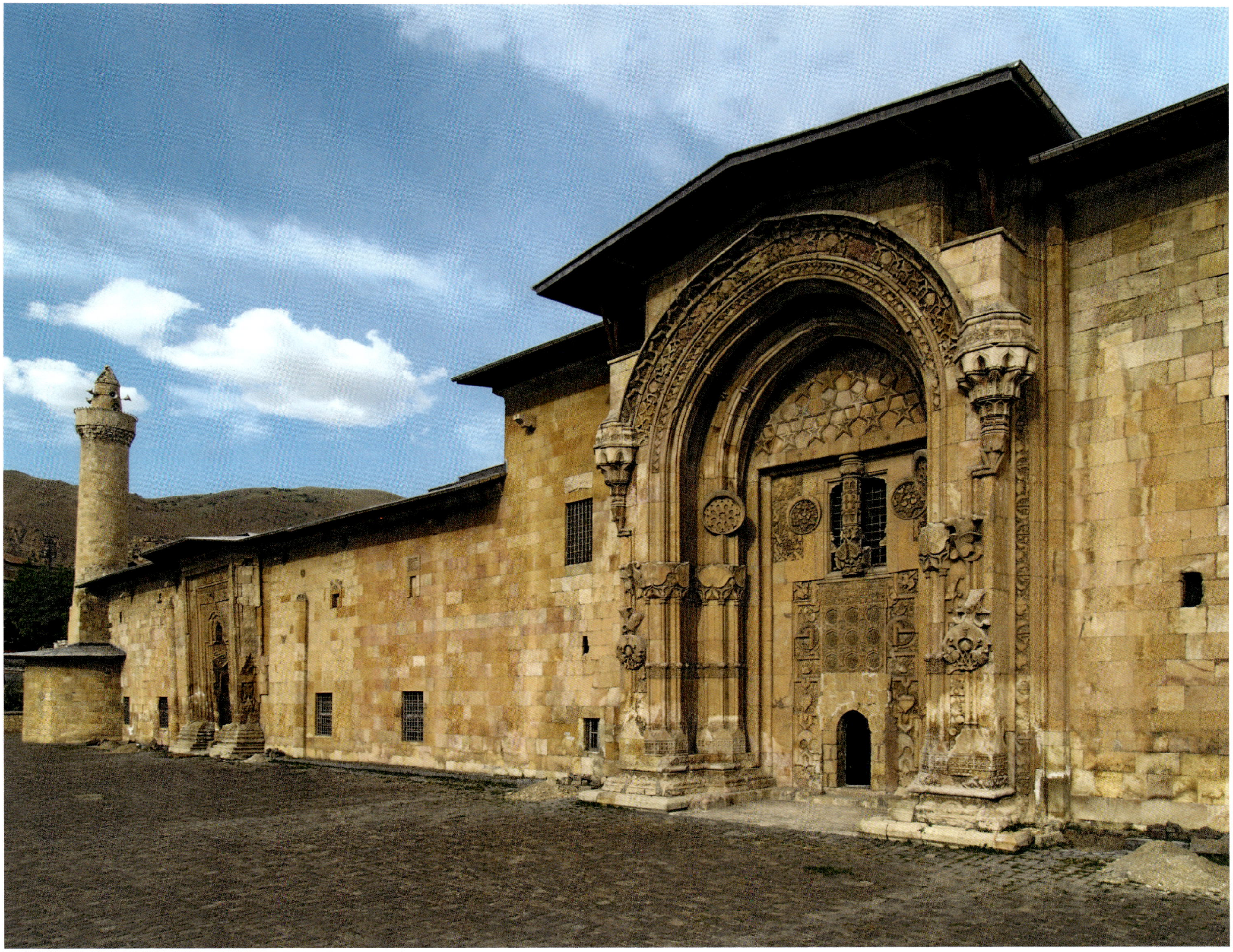

Hospital (façade) and
Great Mosque (secondary entrance)
1228–1229, Seljuq period
Divriği, Turkey

The first hospital in the Muslim world was set up in Damascus in 707 for lepers who were treated at the expense of the caliph. Within a short space of time every city had numerous health institutions, including some for mental patients, soon located next to other welfare structures of charitable character. The majority of these hospitals tended to be lay institutions, financed by governors and staffed by qualified scientific personnel. Grander examples were endowed with regularly updated libraries, meeting rooms, accommodation for the employees, and madrasahs for students.
The Seljuq hospital at Divriği is remarkable for the extraordinary architectural decoration of its monumental portal, in which echoes of Gothic imported by the Crusaders from the West are in evidence. The structure to the left, with a smaller portal and a minaret, is the Ulu Cami (Great Mosque).

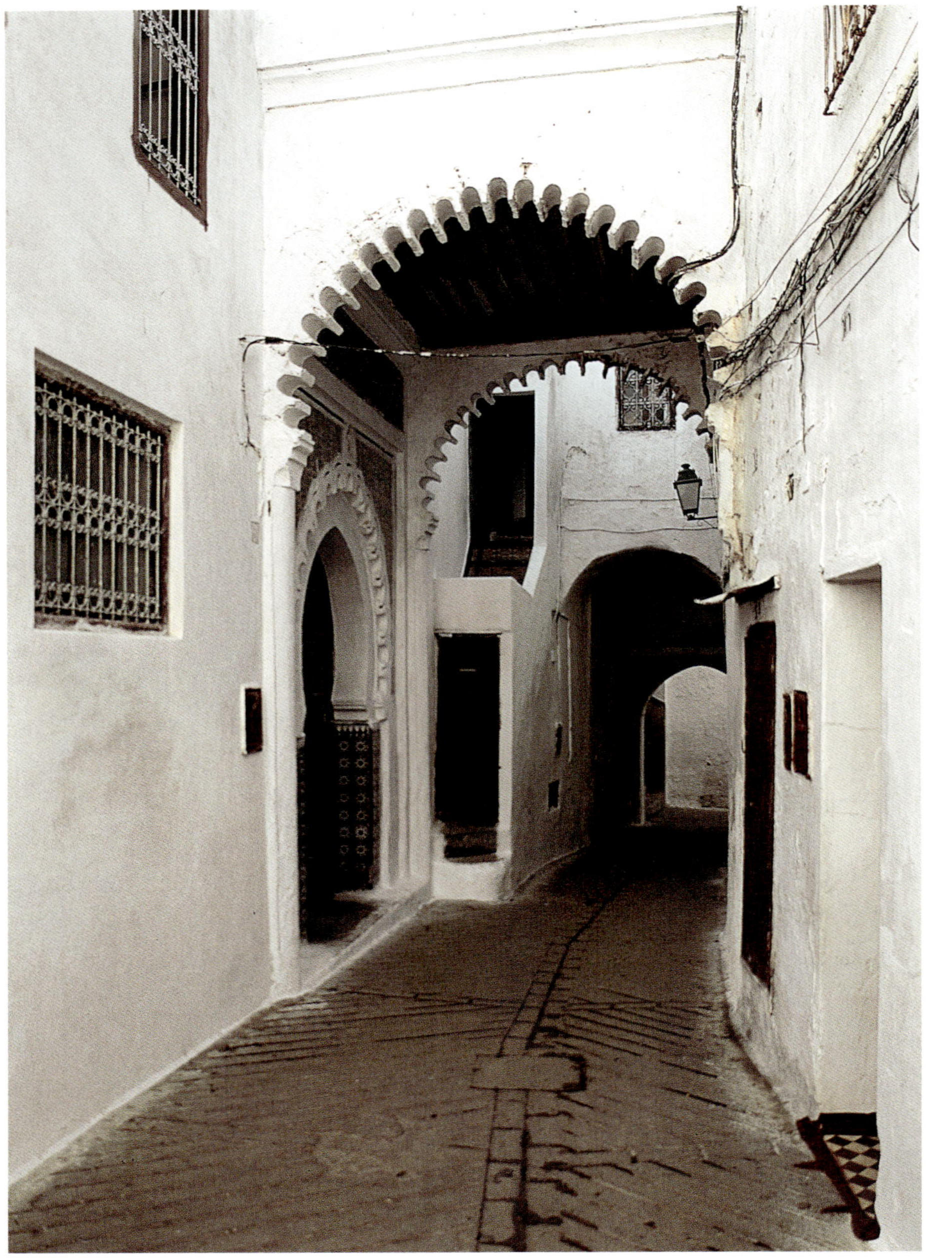

Street in the Medina at Tétouan
18th–19th century, Morocco

Despite the diversity of the solutions arrived at in different contexts, in the Muslim world domestic life was organized with the chief aim of ensuring absolute privacy for the family. Often reinforced through influences from local culture, this attitude is deeply rooted in the precepts of the faith. Public life, in many countries reserved solely for the menfolk, took place in the open, in the *suq,* mosque and coffee-house. The houses of Tétouan, a city subjected to Western influence, are fitted with windows streetside.

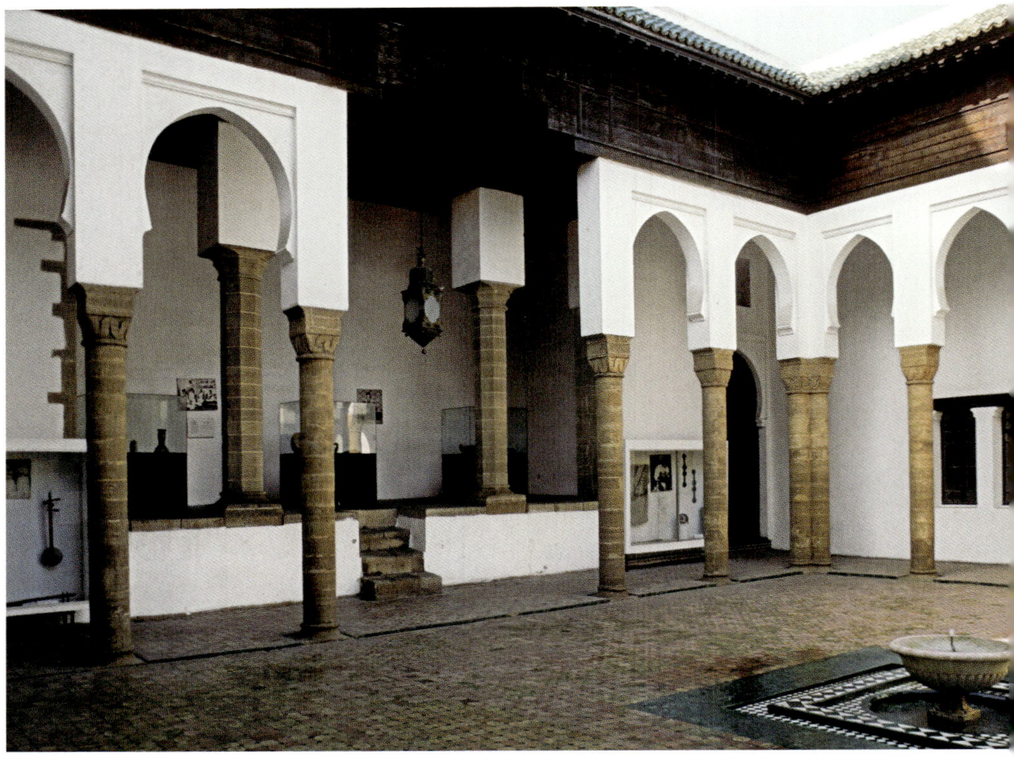

The Palace of Mulay Isma'il, courtyard
17th century, Alawid period
Rabat, Morocco

The Muslim house is a jealous guardian of what Islamic society considers one of its most precious attributes: the family. In this connection, one of the most striking social features of Muslim culture is the separation between public and private life that is observed throughout the dwelling. The Arabic term for a house, *sakan,* is related to *sakina* 'peaceful', 'sacred', while *harim,* 'woman', is linked to *haram,* meaning "holy place." By extension, therefore, the whole house is *haram,* protecting the sacrosanct nature of she who manages a home. The room next to the harem (the space reserved for the women) is assigned to the husband. Where possible the house, accessible by means of a single entrance, is set about a courtyard, a shared space concealed from prying eyes, perhaps provided with a fountain, and, in noble residences such as the one in the picture, arcades, *iwans,* watercourses and a garden, in an obvious image of paradise within the microcosm of the domestic space.

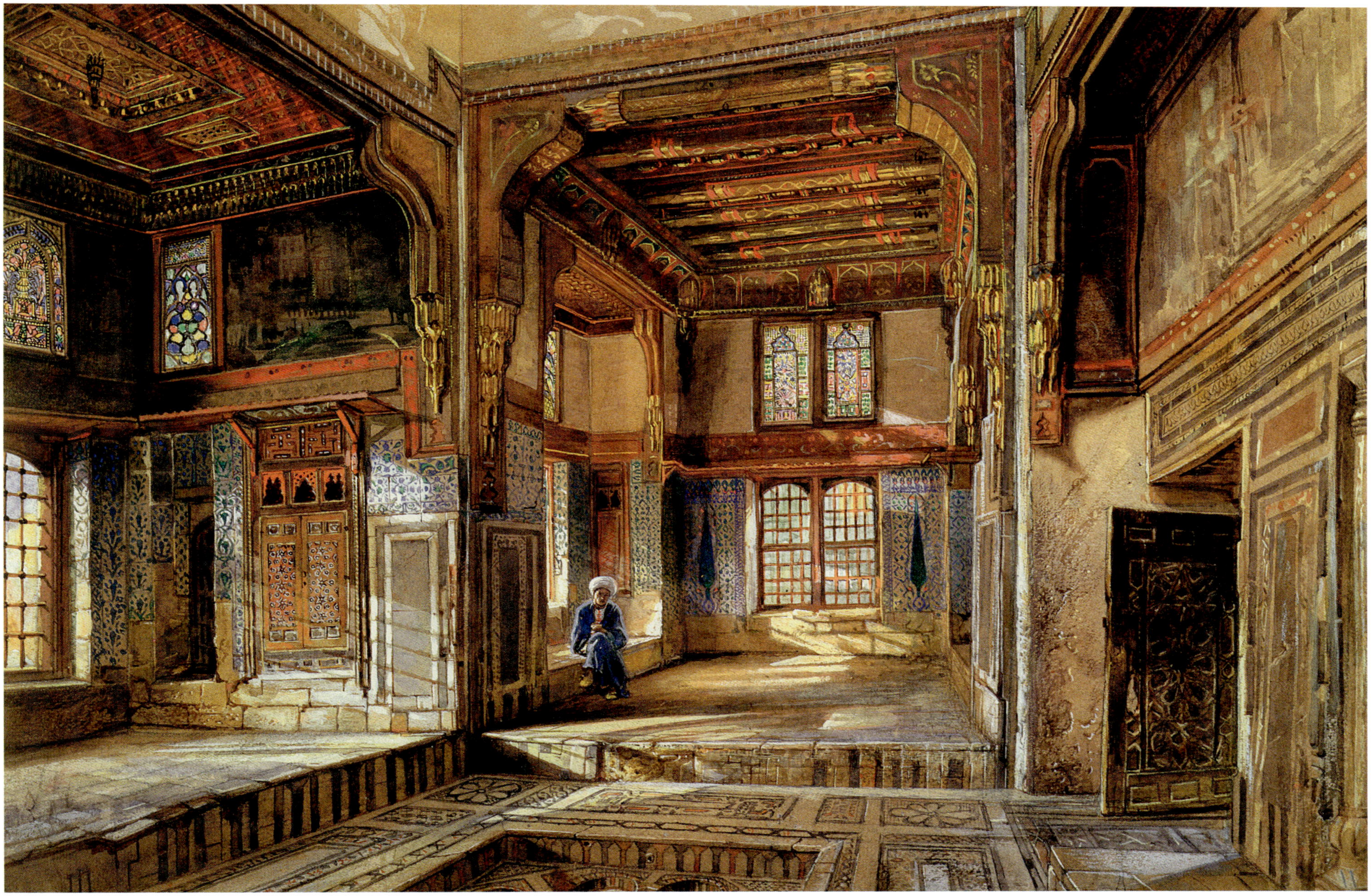

Frank Dillon (1823–1909)
The House of the Mufti Sheikh el Mahadi in Cairo
1873, Ottoman period
Victoria & Albert Museum, London

On the whole, unlike in Western architecture, the subdivision and arrangement of the interior spaces does not correspond to functional demands, but is instead adapted to social custom, as much regarding visitors as its occupiers. In order to be as flexible as possible and to fulfil various functions depending on the situation and requirements, the structure of the rooms tends to lack differentiation. The habit of eating and sleeping on the floor on carpets and cushions, common in many Muslim populations, renders a good deal of furniture superfluous. In the elegant house illustrated the rooms, all virtually identical and opulently decorated, open onto a central space redolent of a covered courtyard flanked by four *iwans* and fitted with an archetypal pool.

Scene in a hammam
c. 1595
From the *Shahnameh* ("The Book of the King"), by Firdusi (11th century)
British Library, London

All over the Muslim world, *hammams* (from the Arabic 'to heat', here meaning a thermal bath) are places to relax and meet up comparable to that of the thermal baths of Antiquity. Women in particular found that the freedom from male interference they enjoyed there made the *hammam* an important focus for their social life. Functionally speaking the system and plan derives from Roman models: a heating chamber feeds hot air through pipes laid beneath the paving into the installations, as well as through special terracotta conduits running through the walls. The miniature (top) shows an ox outside the *hammam* drawing water from a well. An entryway, below left, leads to the changing-rooms, a traditional place for conversation (above left). To the right can be seen the massage parlour, vaulted by the classic glazed canopy.

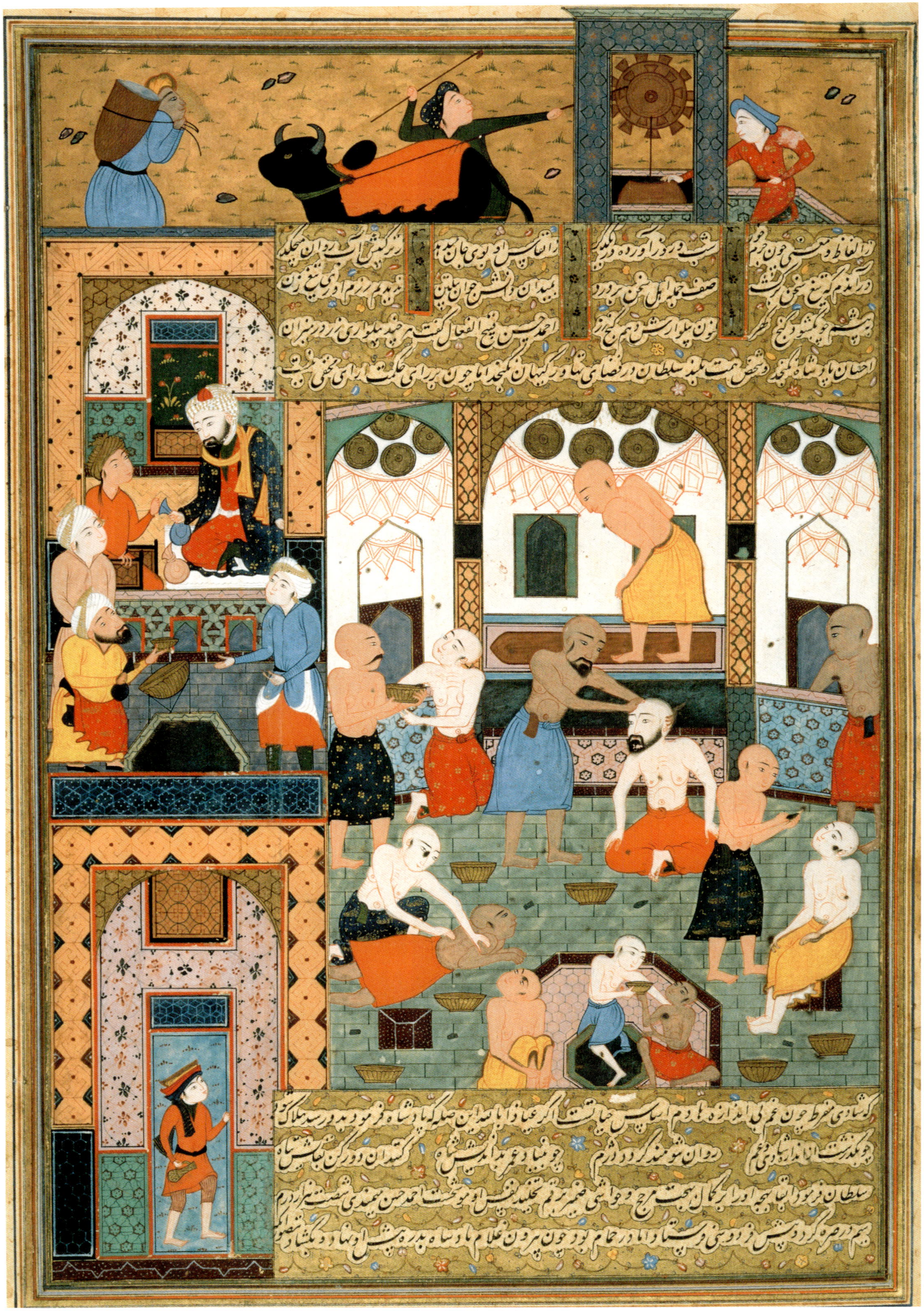

Mimar Sinan (1491–1588), side view of the baths of Haseki Hürrem Sultan
1556–1557, Ottoman period
Istanbul, Turkey

Haseki Hürrem Sultan, known in the West as Roxelana, was Suleiman's first wife and distinguished for her prodigal patronage that paved the way for a new role for women in high society. The structure of the *hammam* here is symmetrical, with the area dedicated to men on one side faced by an identical one for women on the other, the warmest room being located in the middle so that both sexes might benefit equally from the heating system. This double plan also allowed men and women to frequent the baths at any hour of the day, obviating the need for separate timetables.

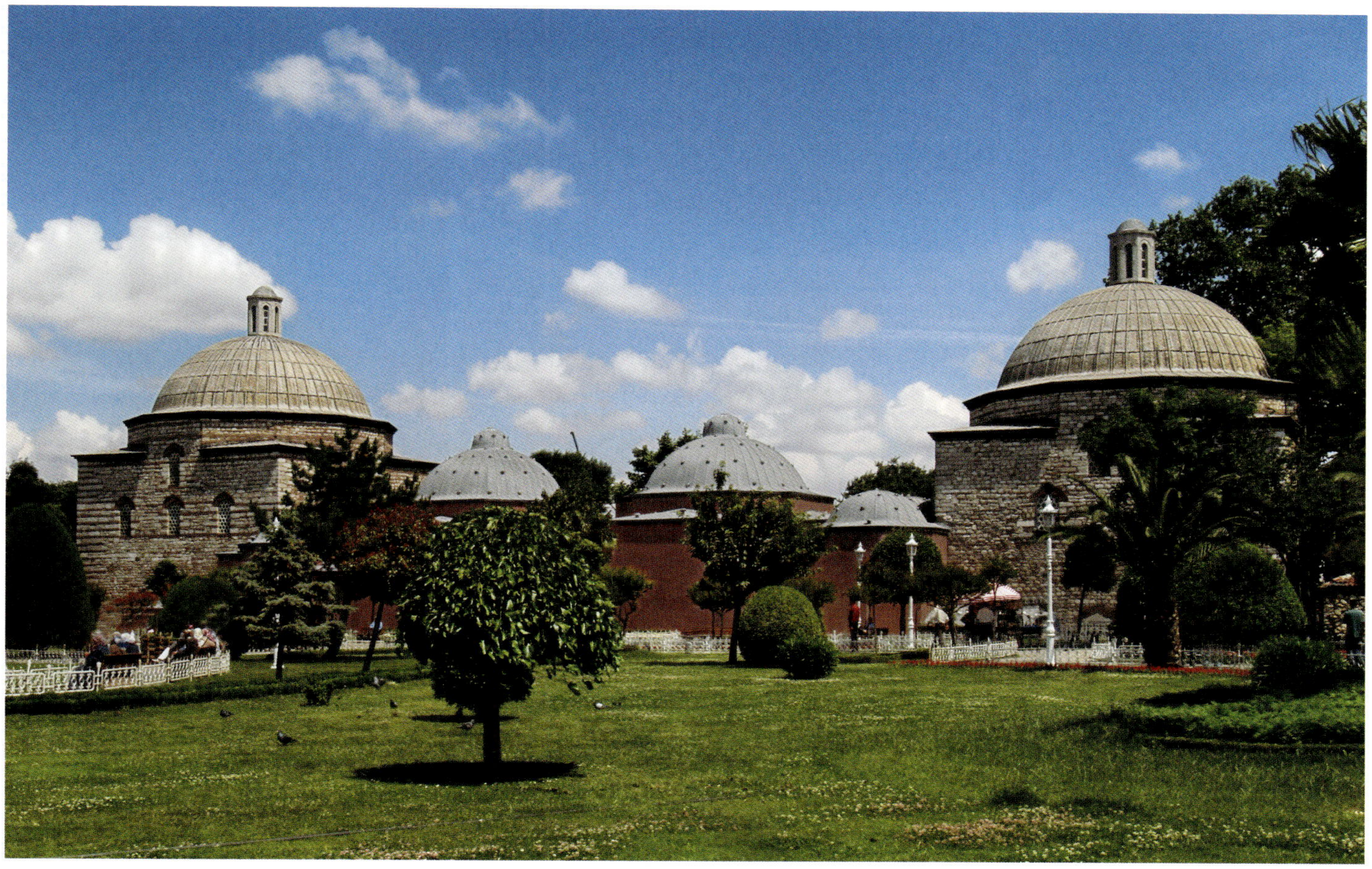

Bañuelo in the Albaicin Changing-room
11th century
Granada, Spain

The most important social and architectural space is the changing-room: a hall, generally domed, provided with a fountain in the centre and furnished with benches with cushions and partitions. The changing-room is a place for leisure, social interaction, and conversation, illuminated by skylights, sometimes in the shape of a star, on the cupola. Heated halls culminate in the 'sauna' where temperatures can soar. Although sometimes extremely large, *hammams* do not have the monumental character of the thermal baths of Antiquity.

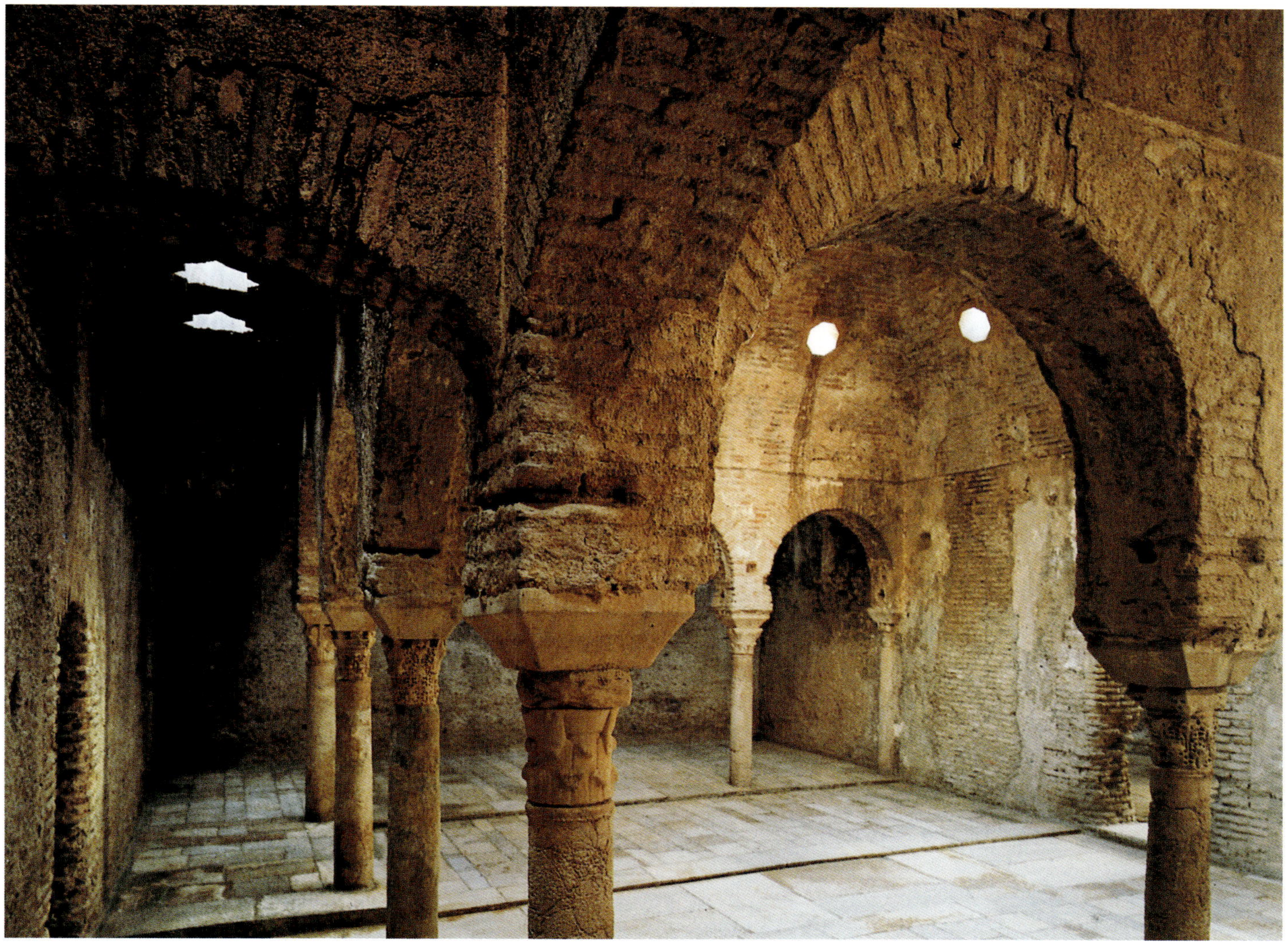

The Garden of Paradise
1398
Persian miniature from an anthology of mystic poetry, Behbahan school
Museum of Turkish and Islamic Arts, Istanbul

The vogue for the garden and its constant presence all over the Muslim world, in the private domestic space, in the courtyards of mosques – often planted with fruit-trees – and even, in portable form, on rugs, harks back to the original cultural heritage of nomadic peoples and is deeply rooted in their ancestral ways of life. For anyone accustomed to crossing deserts and living in the midst of a hostile natural environment, paradise is necessarily represented by its polar opposite: a carpet of grass studded with sweet-smelling flowers, shady and fresh, through which run inexhaustible streams bordered by leafy trees laden with seasonal fruits, cheered by birdsong and the dance of the *urì* or *huri,* the eternal virgins who will attend those who, on the day of judgement, are to be admitted to paradise. According to tradition these girls are capable of conceiving and giving birth. The women-elect enter a female equivalent, the *ghulam.*
The Muslim garden, an idealised embodiment of the yearned-for oasis, is at once sensual delight and heavenly metaphor, created by God since its sublimation of sensual pleasure provides a glimpse of the bliss that awaits the faithful in paradise. At the same time a real and an ideal place, it exists as an indispensable corollary to daily life.

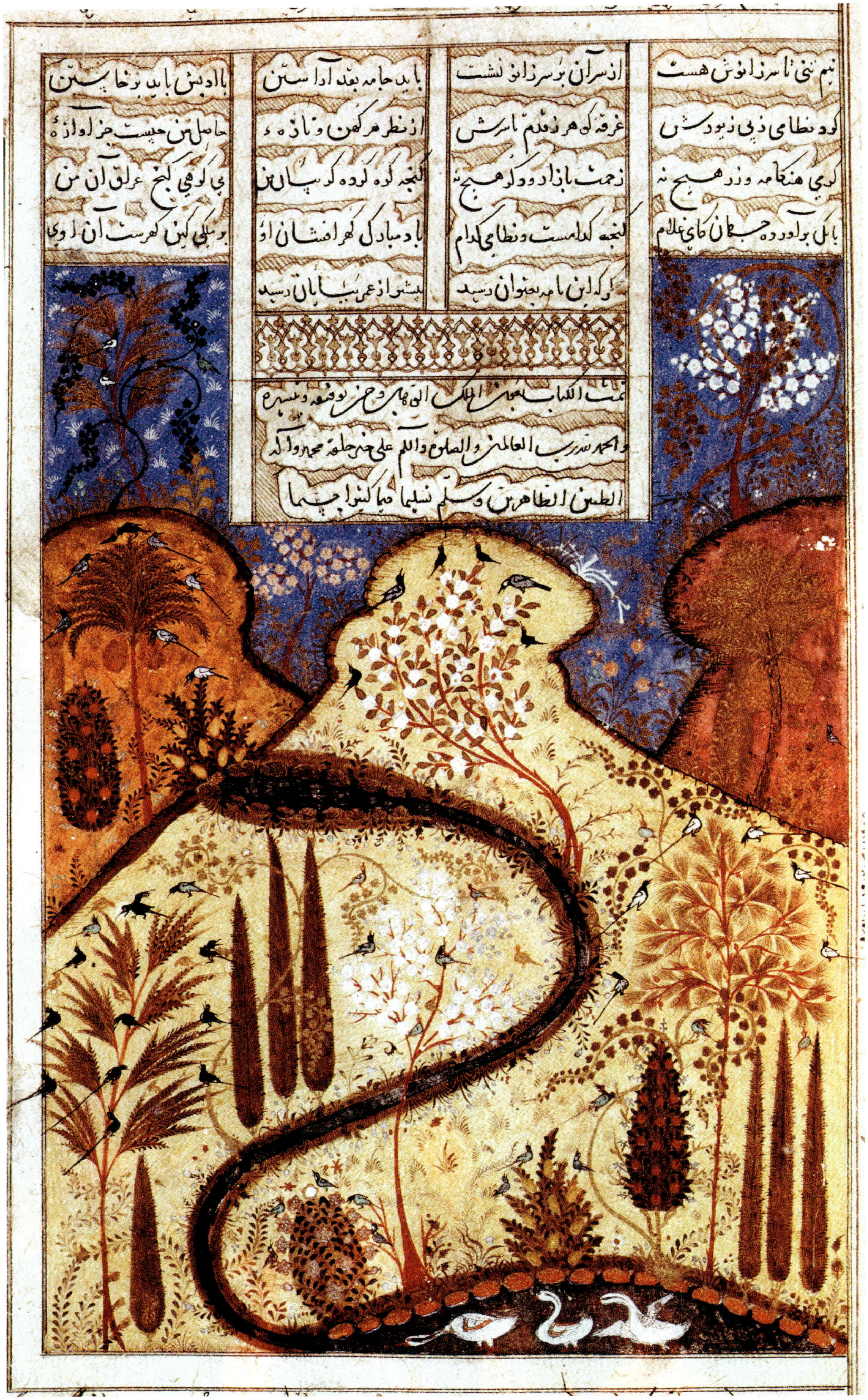

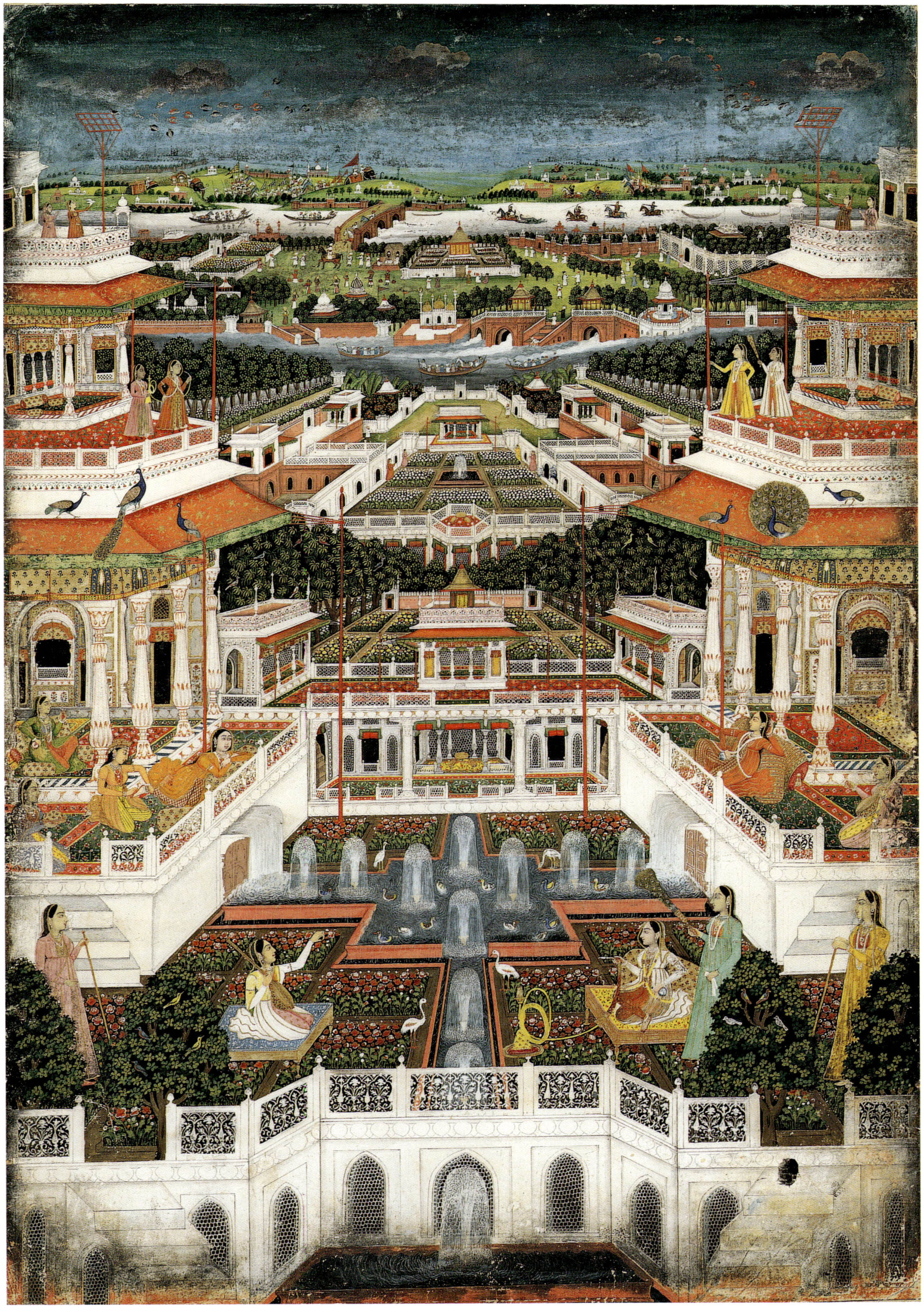

Garden in a harem
18th century miniature, Mughal period
Copenhagen, David Collection

If wild and savage nature is a dangerous place, then its contrary, the garden – as it is an image of divine creation reserved for true believers – has to be artificial, perfect and, as such, geometrical. This form is inherited from the Persian garden (Persian, *pairidaeza,* from whence 'paradise', in Arabic *firdaus*), typically subdivided into four regular areas with the same number of water channels (the "four rivers of paradise") that converge at the centre in a pool or fountain perhaps occupied by another square or circular shrine. These are complemented by structures such as pavilions and kiosks – and even palaces – standing like tents in an encampment.

CALLIGRAPHY: THE FORM OF THE DIVINE WORD

Islam is a religion that descends directly from God, whose revelation is faithfully transcribed in the Qur'an (Koran). The written word, the irreplaceable instrument for the correct understanding and spread of Islam, thus possesses exceptional value and has become the object of both aesthetic research and mystical speculation. A *hadith* recalls how on the point of death Muhammad commanded: "Bring me something to write with, so that I can put down in writing that which will preserve you from error when I am gone."
In Islamic culture, writing, and therefore the book, occupies a place of prime importance. This was reinforced subsequently by the circumspection with which, from pre-Islamic times, Arabs, fearing its magical power, had always regarded manifestations of figurative art, especially anthropomorphic and zoomorphic sculpture.
After Muhammad's death in 632 CE, it became necessary to transmit the Qur'an in an incontrovertible written form and to systematize the various divergent oral traditions. The need for such a compilation was made still more urgent after many who had known the words of the Prophet's revelation by heart were killed at the battle of Aqraba (633 CE). It was the third caliph, 'Uthman, who completed this delicate task around 650 CE. The primitive Arabic alphabet was of Semitic origin, derived in part from Aramaic and in part from Nabataean. It was thus improved upon, both syntactically and aesthetically, to such an extent that before long it was possible to speak of a calligraphic art of fundamentally Islamic expression, at a time when contemporary art and architecture were still very much subject to Sassanid and Classical-Byzantine culture. In the course of the seventh century two main styles of writing developed: a cursive style, round and flowing, and a more geometrical, square, severe and concise form, known as Kufic (from the city of Kufa in Iraq), which was widespread in the earliest times, and which was adopted for writing the Qur'an. For religious reasons, and above all for linguistic clarity, long vowels were first indicated with dots in various colours and later on, towards the end of the century, with diacritical marks in the strict sense, in order to distinguish letters written in a similar manner. Later still, in the course of the eighth century, the alphabet was enriched with additional signs standing for short vowels and other indications. The complete script comprising all necessary signs for reading is, in fact, very rarely used, thus rendering the interpretation of the text problematic; it is composed from a corpus of twenty-eight consonants and three long and three short vowels, which in general are not indicated.
As with the majority of alphabets, the script proceeds from right to left and a book begins with what Westerners would view as the final page. Other characteristics that can also render the process of reading challenging include the absence of capital letters; lack of headings; various devices employed to lengthen or shorten words in order to complete the line correctly; and the absence of punctuation marks (obviated in modern Arabic), which are often replaced by literary formulae. Calligraphy, then, is an articulate and fully-fledged form of art based on a precise code and complex geometric principles and ornaments, and to enjoy it to the full, it is of course necessary to be able to read the language. From the compositional point of view, it is comparable to music, with metrical, rhythmic and harmonic values. For readers in a position to appreciate all these qualities, it affords aesthetic and spiritual emotions of great intensity, shedding light on the meaning of earthly existence as well as providing a glimpse of the mystery of the divine through its sheer

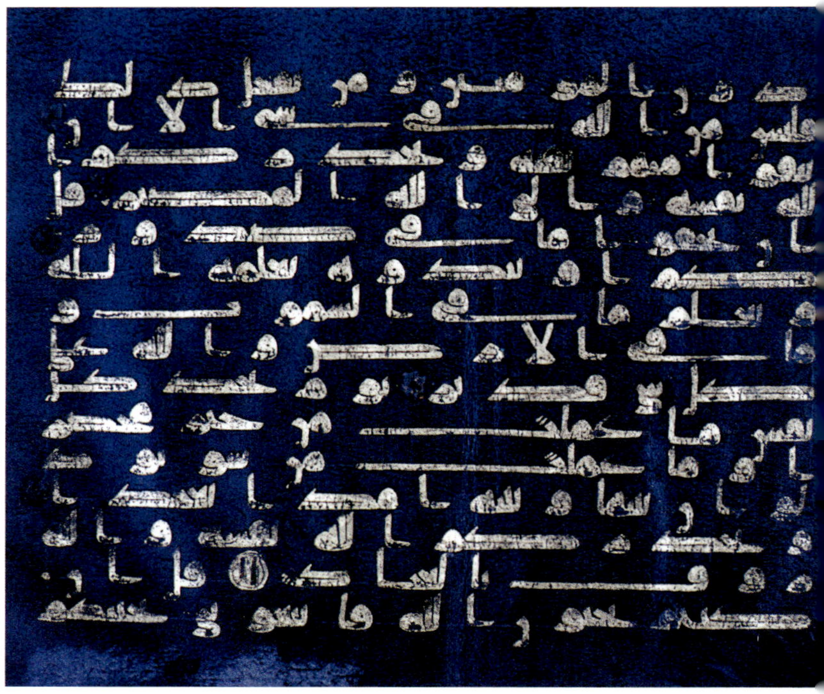

Page from a Qur'an in Kufic script without diacritical marks
9th century, 'Abbasid period
Blue parchment
Teheran, Iran

beauty. The word, of and by itself, *is,* since it has been divinely revealed. When written with due care and attention, it is transformed into the love of God, a manifestation of mankind's aspiration to the divine and a justification of our yearning for beauty. The word becomes a kind of message both coded and symbolic, both cryptic and introductory, decipherable in all its ramifications only by the greatest mystics, but always pleasing in its cadences, in the rhythms it unfolds over page or wall, always *beautiful* and, as such, never less than meaningful.

A script is therefore a system of extremely flexible signs, perfectly adapted to the task of transmitting its content. The shape of the grapheme allows for further interpretation and meaning, as can be readily appreciated in any page of calligraphy even by readers who know no Arabic, since the aesthetic value is distinct from the meaning of the text. The penmanship of a poem is, for instance, as important as the meaning of the verse. The letter as image corresponds to three stipulations, obeys three types of rule: phonetic, semantic, and aesthetic. In some interpretations, particularly in those adumbrated by Sufi mystics, the relationships between horizontal and vertical elements symbolize the overlap between the values of the external, tangible and material world and those of the inner world, hidden and transcendent.

The first letter of the alphabet, *alif,* constitutes the modular unit from which the others are constructed, since all can be inscribed in a circle of its diameter. Its length is determined by a series of square dots, called *noqta,* corresponding to the mark left by the *qalam,* the classic writing instrument cut from a stalk of reed. Its width is always a dot whose length varyies, depending on the script style concerned, from three to twelve 'points'. Its most salient characteristics are axiality, linearity, equilibrium and upright strokes. Since the sign is analogous in form to the digit '1', it has been taken as a symbol of oneness and of the divine essence. Due to its position at the beginning of the alphabet, some exegetes compare it to Adam (in which

ب م د ا

The Arabic letters
alif*, *dal*, *mim*, and *ba

case, the associated diacritics specifying its value are identified with Eve). Pursuing this interpretation – and as a further indication of the complexity of the symbolic values inherent in Arabic calligraphy – the three letters composing the name ADM (Adam), *alif* ('a'), *dal* ('d') and *mim* ('m') represent the three fundamental positions assumed in prayer of standing, kneeling and prostration. The second letter of the alphabet is *ba* ('b'), which is regarded as being of particular importance because it is the initial letter of the Basmala (or *Bismillah*) – that is, the invocation *Bi-smi 'ilahi al-rahmani al-rahimi* ("In the name of God, the Compassionate, the Merciful"), with which all *suras* in the Qur'an begin, save one. It is also the first horizontal letter and its shape recurs, together with different diacritics, in other letters. In the eyes of some interpreters even the diacritic dot below the letter is invested with extraordinary value. In their view, since the Qur'an contains all the revealed books, and the first *sura* the whole of the Qur'an, and the *Basmala* the whole first *sura,* the entire meaning of the *Basmala* can be seen as being condensed into this diacritic dot that imparts value to the letter (in an obvious parallel with the infinite and/or immeasurable point of geometry). The interpretation of the intrinsic values of the letters of the alphabet can be pursued along arduous paths accessible only to mystics and sages, though none of this prevents the message being clear to anyone who can read the text.

Everything is (in) the word. The highest aspiration of the artist can only be to bestow a glorious form on this tool that God employs in His communication with man, while for the patron the supreme attainment is to muster every means at his disposal to render the message convincing to all.

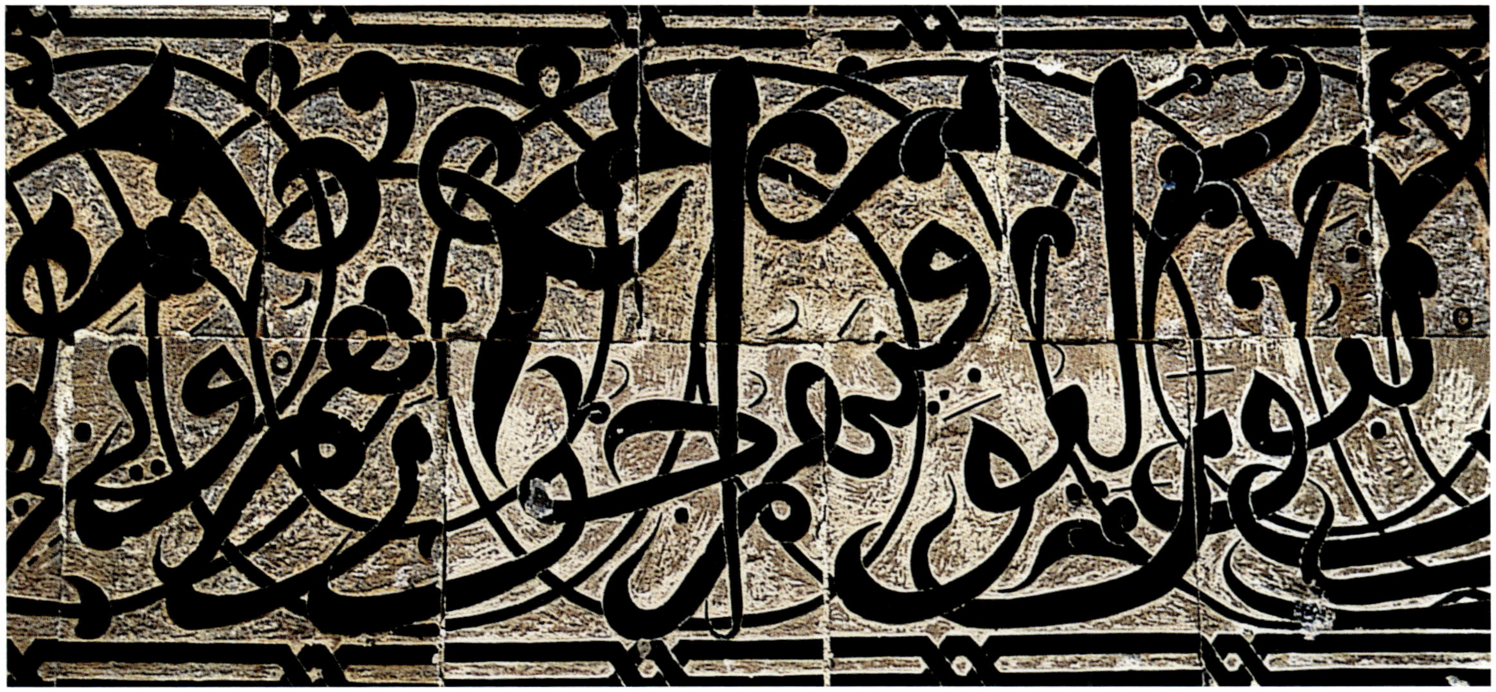

Madrasah el-Attarin
Detail of the inscription on the walls of the courtyard
1323–1325, Merinid period
Fez, Morocco

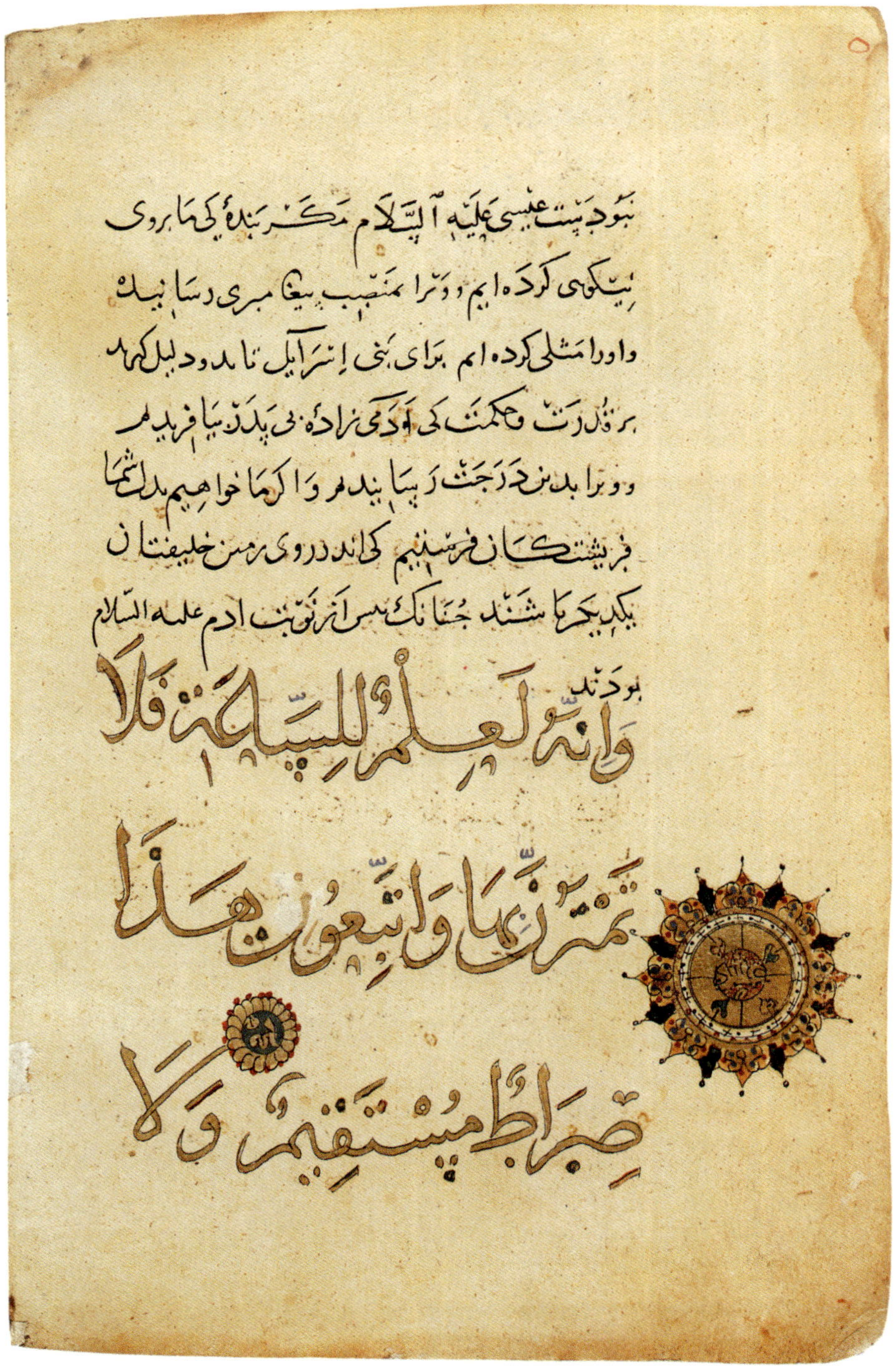

Qur'anic commentary on sura XL
1151, Persian copy of 1232–1233
Russian Academy of Sciences, St Petersburg

Two different scripts are used in the text in order to make the Qur'an immediately distinguishable from its commentary. The Arabic text is executed in a peerless large *thulth* script, in liquid gold highlighted by a thin red line. In *thulth* (literally 'third') the consonants with uprights are a third as high as the verticals, creating an elegant cursive style with ample curves. The Persian translation and the commentary are executed by contrast in a wonderful large *naskh irani* script. The *naskh* is the most widely used cursive, characterized by thin, rolling lines, though the variant here is Iranian. Various diacritics and other signs are also in evidence.

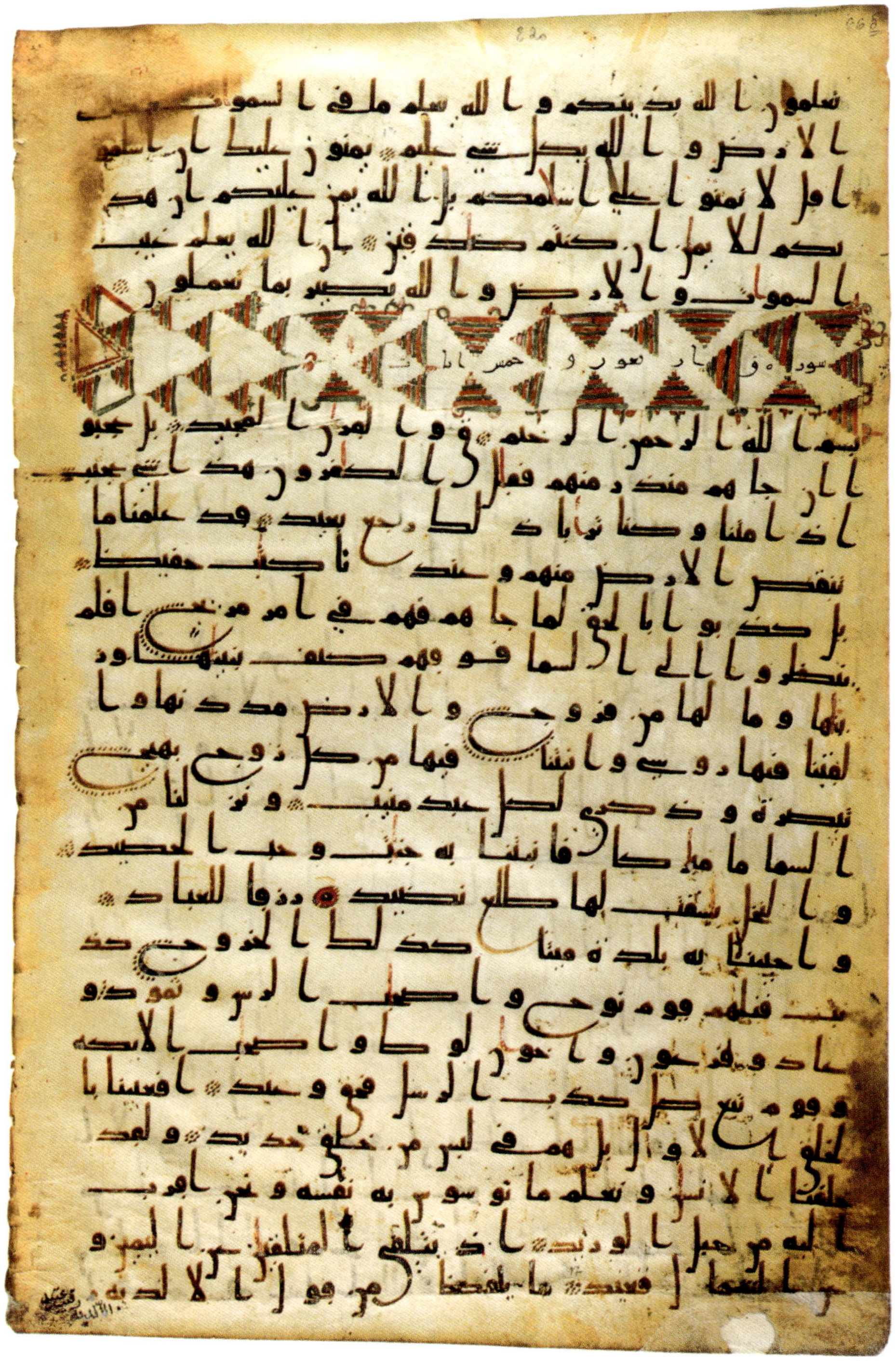

Fragment of a Qur'an on parchment
Late 7th–early 8th century
Russian Academy of Sciences, St Petersburg

The calligraphy in this precious and rare fragment constitutes a prime example of archaic Kufic from Hijaz, the region of Arabia where both Mecca and Medina are located. The *suras* are subdivided with an ornamental motif composed of triangles in finely drawn red and green strokes. The title of the *sura* and the number of *ayat* ('verses'; from which the term *ayatollah,* composed of *ayat* and *allah*) are inscribed in small black characters within the decoration. Black diacritical signs are present, but not actual vowel indications. The signs in short diagonal lines indicate the end of a verse. The *alifs* in red were spelling corrections inserted at a later juncture. The addition of the titles of the suras and the decoration here already represents an evolved state of Qur'anic script: initially these spaces were left blank as they did not constitute a text dictated by God, but human interpolations which, therefore, do not form part of the revelation.

Casket with hunting scenes
1049, period of Taifa rule
Wood with gilt leather and ivory insets
from Cuenca, Spain

The Kufic inscription records the genealogy of the heir to the throne for whom this valuable object was made. The calligraphy harmonizes wonderfully with the abstract, zoomorphic and phytomorphic decorative pattern.

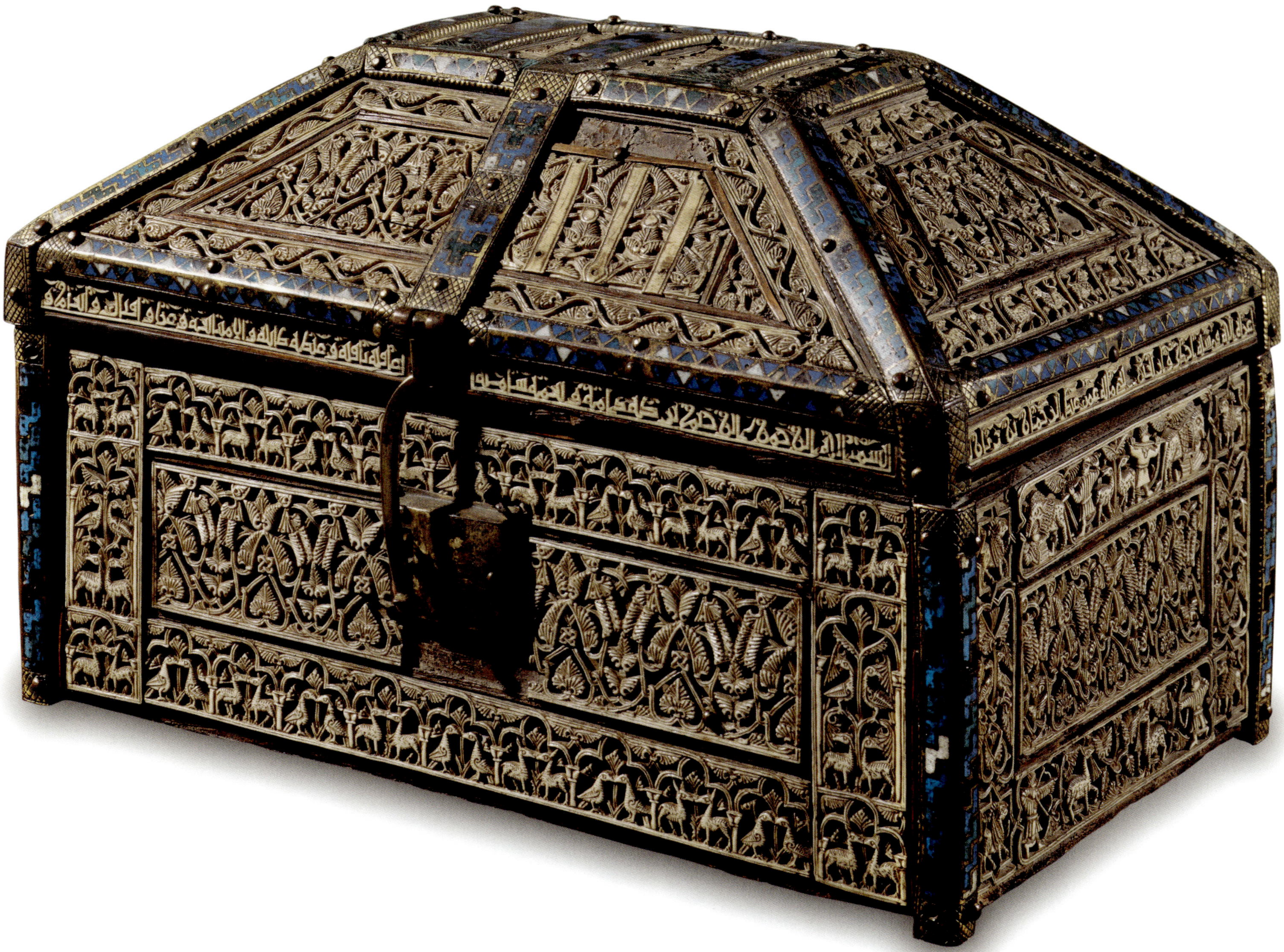

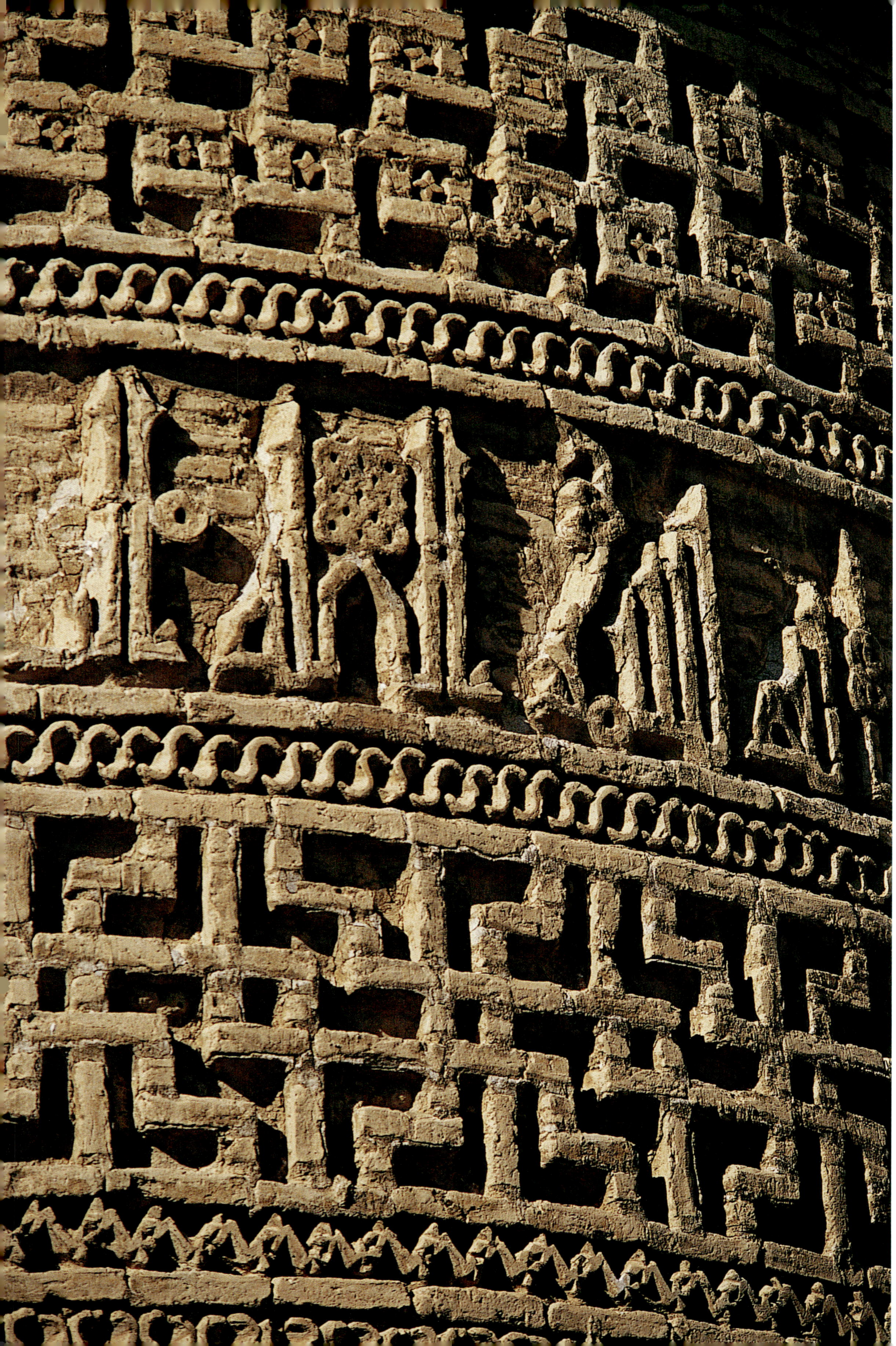

Mausoleum Pir-e Alamdar
Detail
1021–1026, Seleucid period
Damghan, Iran

Calligraphy extends triumphantly over the exterior surfaces of many major edifices, playing a fundamental artistic role. The extraordinary malleability, low cost, and longevity of stucco and clay made them the most widely employed materials in the Islamic world, deployed to no less glorious and lively effect in epigraphy. Among the profusion of geometrical motifs, here simply hollowed out following an outline made by the lines of header bricks, the calligrapher has cleverly inserted an epigraphic band, which, contrasting in the sunlight with the darker zones, confers a sense of dynamism on to what is an intrinsically humble material. Joyously and energetically unfurled, these forms convey, indeed trumpet, their message, offering believers constant succour in their infinite praise of the Creator. Simultaneously, they may admire the magnanimity of the man who built the funerary tower or recite a prayer in his name, thereby earning the spiritual benefit (*baraka*) afforded on visiting such an illustrious forbear.

Minaret of Shaykh Hasan Chupani
Detail
1419, Timurid period
Shushtar, Iran

Bannai (from the Persian for 'builder') script constitutes a highly schematic and strictly linear extension of the most geometric form of Kufic created deliberately to stand out prominently on the immense stretches of drums, walls and vaults over which square or rectangular glossy glazed bricks are arranged as lettering in various formats. Here tile bricks in wonderful turquoise shades repeat the invocation *"Allah akbar"* ("God is Great") *ad infinitum* along the topmost reaches of the minaret: this impressive effect is carefully calculated, making heaven visible in the material world, as if outward appearances were formed purely from the exaltation of the greatness of God. The most representative creations of great Islamic architecture are imbued with a strong sense of lyricism, which, in this region of southern Iran, harks back to the Elamites of the second millennium BCE who employed azure ceramics to line their ziggurats, so emphasizing the transformation of matter, made sacred by the faith.

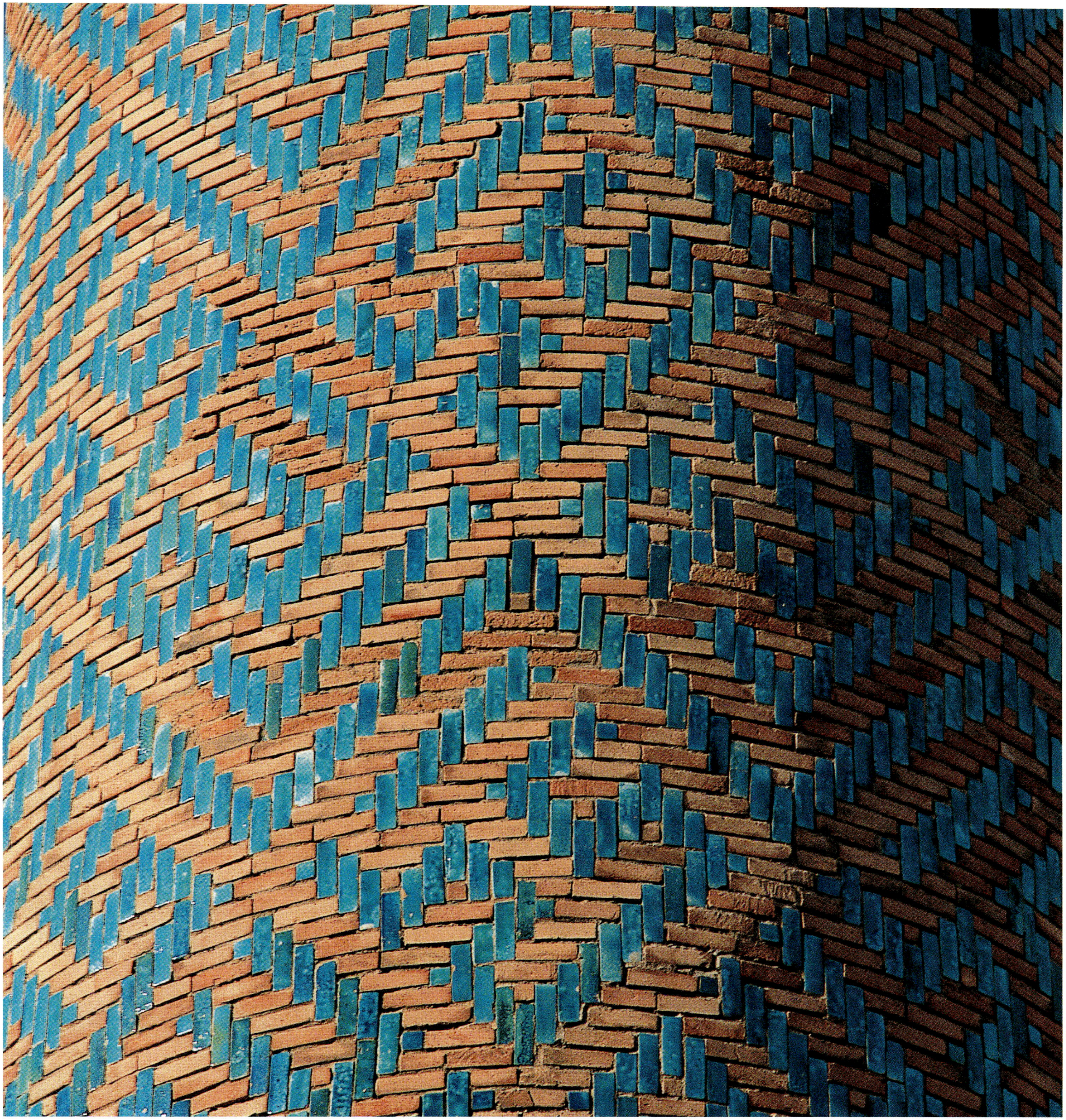

Friday mosque
Prayer hall with epigraphy in the name of Ali
1375, Muzaffarid period
Kerman, Iran

In the Persian domain, geometrical calligraphy often attained summits of artistic and expressive excellence. It also displays an exceptional aptitude for synthesis, reaching its most conclusively confident manifestations under the Ilkhanids and Muzaffarids, as in this splendid example of the prayer hall in the Friday mosque at Kerman. Under Shia dominion, the name of Ali, the fourth Rightly Guided Caliph became an object of great veneration. Here his name is repeated nine times: three in white, three in blue and three in a deep ultramarine, radiating from an ochre-tinged six-pointed star at the centre out into a hexagon of controlled dynamism. The spaces between one hexagon and its neighbour, adorned with sturdy floral motifs, are composed of equilateral triangles in glazed ceramic of terracotta colour with a fine geometrical and vegetal interlace pattern.

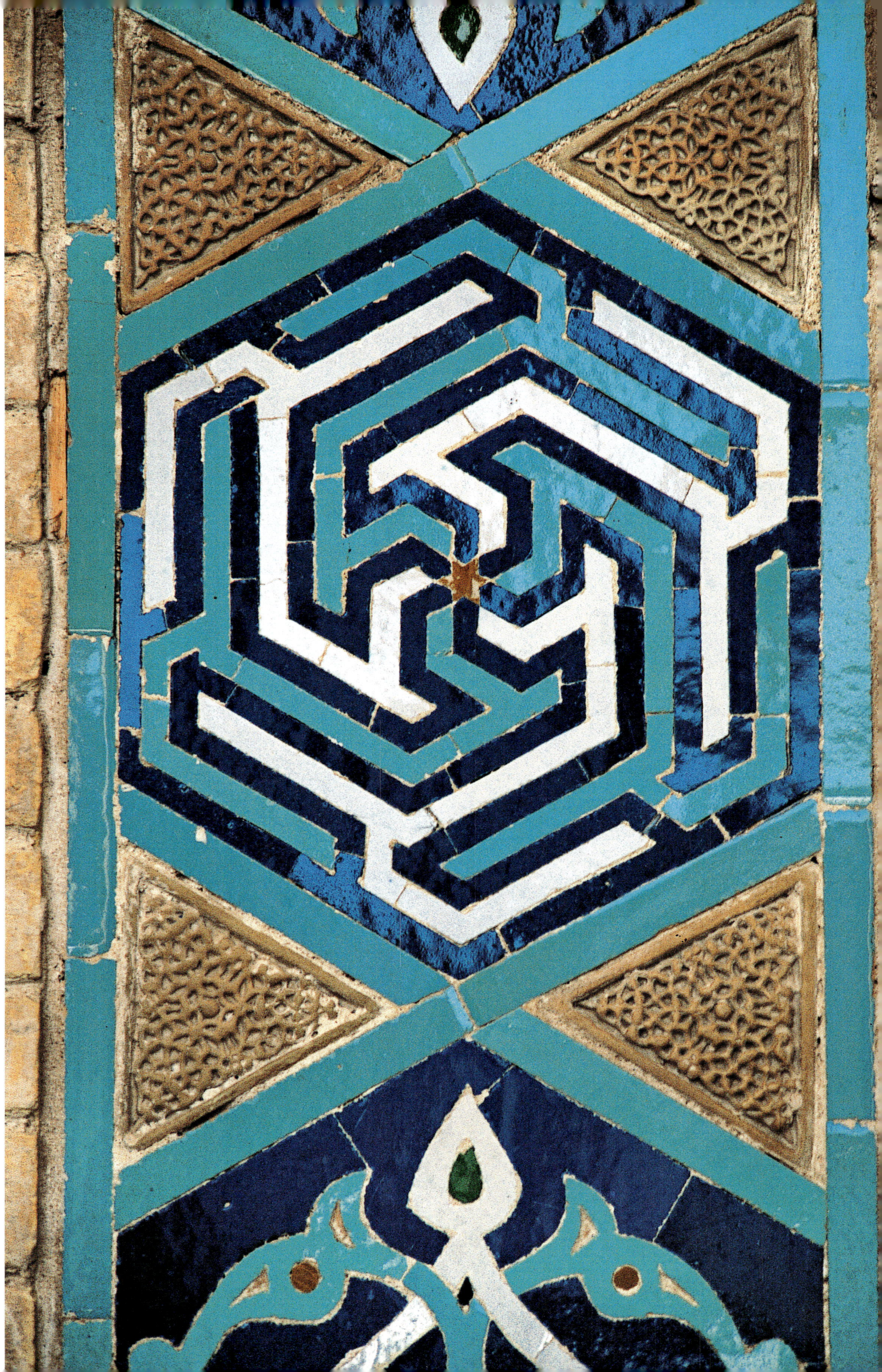

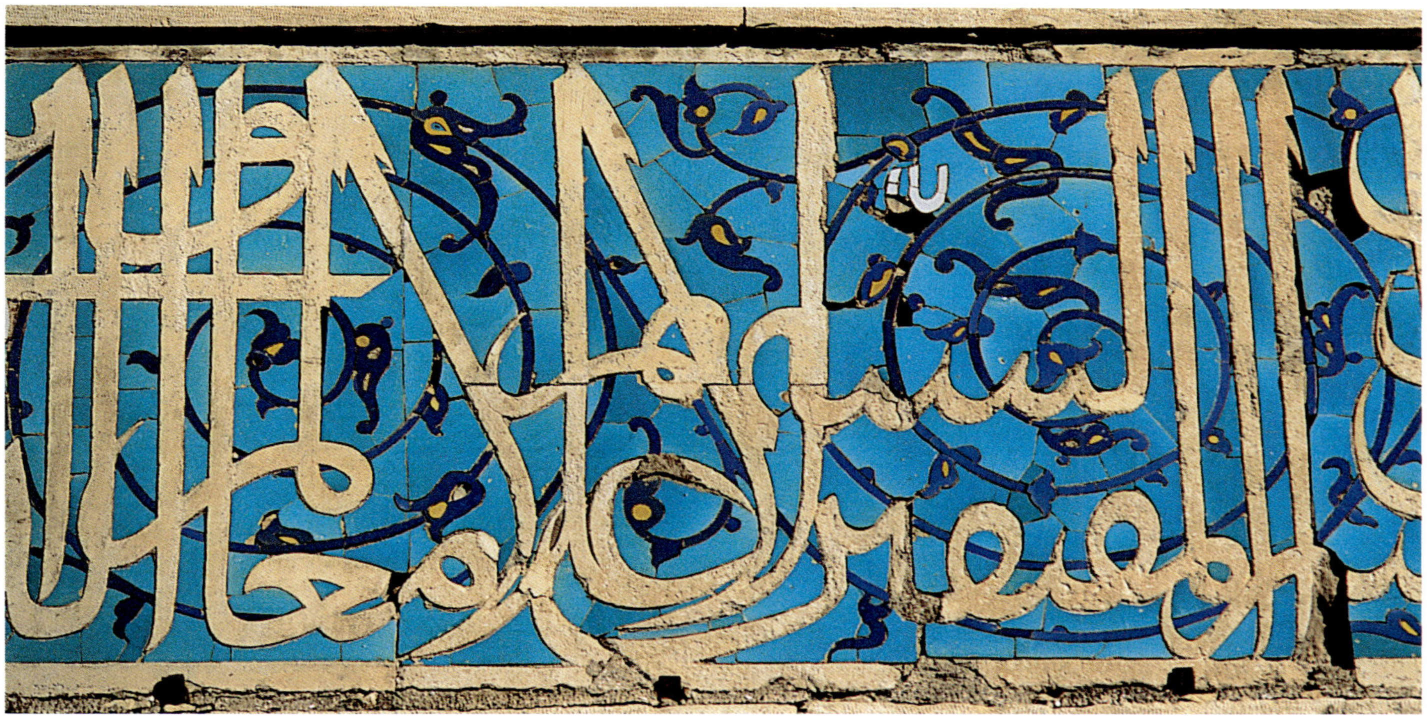

Friday mosque
Detail of calligraphy along a wall
14th century, Ilkhanid period
Shiraz, Iran

This intricate outpouring of script and arabesque derives its immense energy from the close collaboration between the rhythmic dynamism of the phrases as they scroll off towards the left and the breathtaking accents of the verticals, beneath which runs a plant motif in subdued tones that seems to unwind in the opposite direction. Giving rise to a sort of silent spiritual music, it is enlivened by the relationship between the meaning and its translation into loosely interlacing signs in what looks like an infinite to-and-fro between word and 'decoration', between geometric and 'natural' logic. Like a painter or musician, the penman composes his work letter by letter, word by word, phrase by phrase, page by page, following coherent principles of harmony. In the same vein, the reader interprets the text between empty spaces and full ones, imparting rhythm with his voice as it shifts between explicit and implicit, between clear and obscure.

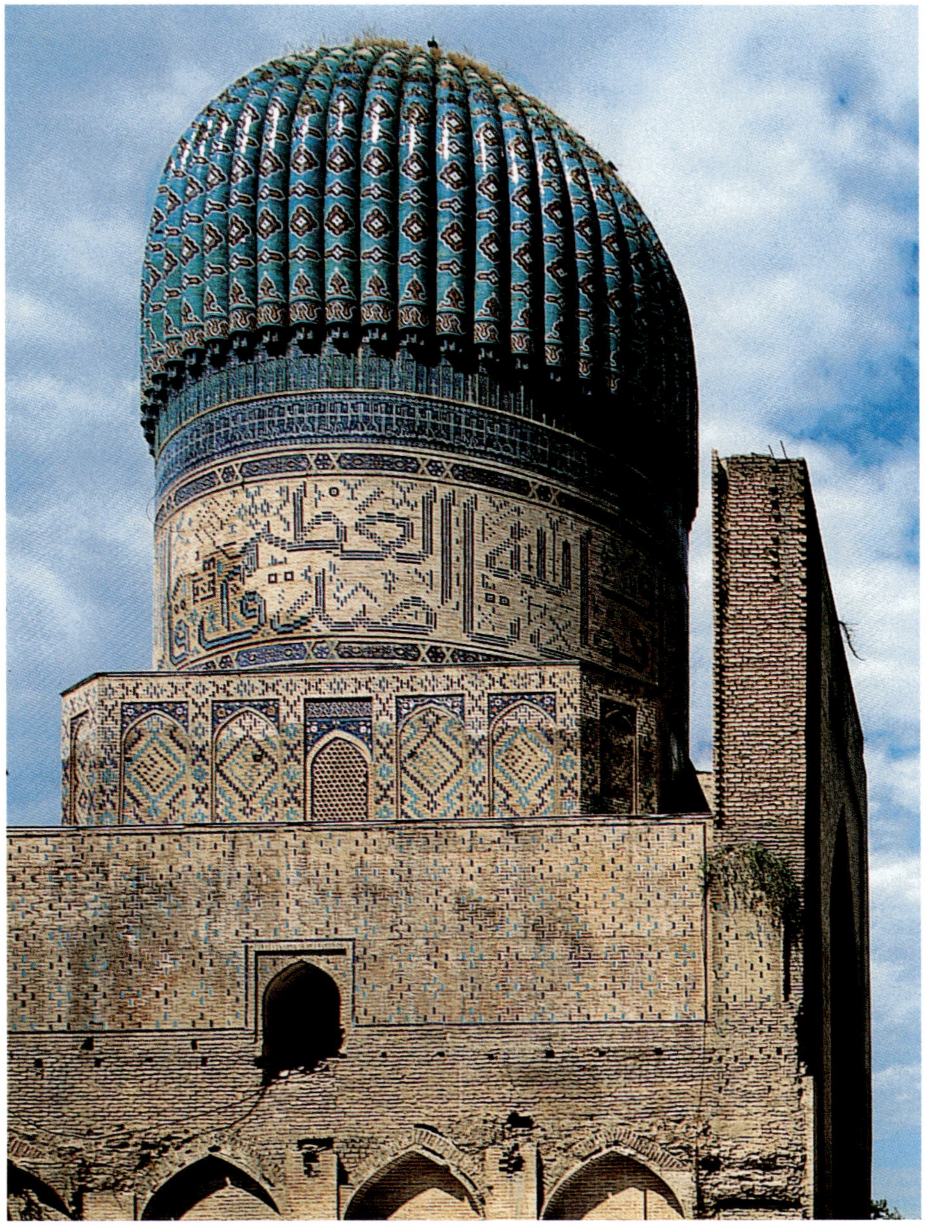

Bibi Khanum Mosque
Dome over the north *iwan*
1399–1405
Samarkand, Uzbekistan

Bannai characters developed in the Timurid period. They soon attaining colossal dimensions, covering vast swathes of walls, dome drums and minaret towers and fostering a sense of grandeur that is one of the distinguishing features of the art of the period. The awe-inspiring scale and schematic structure of the script allowed the faithful to read the message with ease even from the ground as it snakes over structures treated essentially as material supports for the divine word, while the celestial blue elevates its meaning to the level of the sublime. The characteristic geometric structure, moreover, permitted infinite combinations for more abstract decorations, as can be seen here in the blind arcade on the base below the cylindrical drum, where the words are only identifiable if read attentively, thereby exalting the significance of the truth it conceals.

THE APPLIED ARTS

The custom of making and using ceramic wares and of cladding mud-brick structures with glazed tiling had already been widespread for thousands of years among the ancients in the cradle of Islam and in the territories into which the new faith expanded. Decoration and ornament derived from the Sassanid and Coptic traditions initially elaborated motifs from late Antiquity. Of a decidedly synthetic and sometimes fantastically abstract character, they were of fundamental importance in the development of a specifically Islamic taste. This soon received a new and determinant impulse from the import of valuable Chinese porcelain of a type that potters tried to imitate and even outstrip, often with remarkable success.

The most traditional technique was slipware, in which the clay object is brushed with a coat (slip) of transparent clay diluted in water so as to obtain a whitish surface that is then used as a ground for the decor or as a undercoat for sgraffito (incising). A next stage saw the piece covered in a transparent glaze and decorated with a metal lustre. Invented during the tenth century in Cairo, this technique endowed its surface with an extraordinary metallic sheen.

It was also in Egypt that the imitation of sought-after Chinese porcelain led to the development of monochrome ware with a turquoise glaze and incised decoration. It became especially widespread in the Fatimid and Mamluk periods. However, it was mainly due to the ancient traditions of the Elamite kingdom and Mesopotamia that exceptional results were obtained in the Iranian region. Time-honoured techniques were perfected including painted and incised slip, resulting in *champlevé* ceramics in which the slip is scratched off to expose a glaze below. The greatest works date from the Seleucid era, in the twelfth to thirteenth centuries, and come from the great centres of Ravy and Kashan. These include painted *laqabi* ceramics, the highly imaginative and splendidly colourful *minai,* and *layvardina,* with their magnificent shades of lapis-lazuli. In the case of pottery for daily use, produced for an artistically aware and prosperous clientele, traditional forms were now joined by objects of remarkable formal resourcefulness; the most notable were surely the plates with brief inscriptions, for the most part of moralizing character; those from Nishapur in Iran were prime examples. This category includes a host of zoomorphic pieces that also offer a further demonstration of how imagery – disapproved of on buildings and in religious contexts generally – was embraced in the private domain.

Ivory, leather, rock crystal and enamelled and gilded glass also played a very important role. They were used in the production of luxury furnishings and especially to make hanging lamps for mosques which were characterized by inscriptions from the Qur'an and were both magnificent and symbolic in effect.

The manufacture of prestige objects in metal, designed for lavish interiors in residences belonging to the élite, has been a major factor in the history of Muslim countries. It probably reached its peak in the remarkably refined pieces forged by craftsmen between the eleventh and fifteenth centuries in the region extending from Egypt to Persia. Although these were

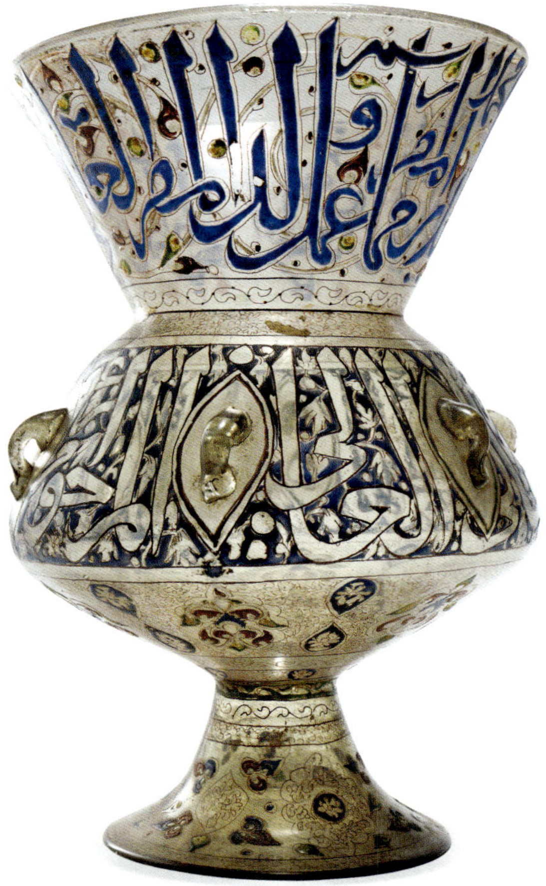

Mosque lamp with calligraphy
1337, Mamluk period
Enamelled and gilded glass
Musée Jacquemart-André, Paris

not objects designed for religious use, since Islam did not call for them, their shape and above all their decoration is strongly influenced by the Muslim aesthetic and can be immediately identified by a few telltale characteristics. The lion's share of production comes in the shape of tableware and utensils, perfume-burners and braziers, jewellery, weapons and armour, and scientific or surgical tools and instruments. There also exist, however, intricate cases for writing-sets, monumental candlesticks, and lavish fittings for wooden furniture. A particular role can be ascribed to the technique often incorrectly described as 'damaskeening' or 'damascening'. Known in fact at least since the Mycenaean age, it consists of applying thin layers of different metals in the form of inscriptions or patterns to a metal surface which has been previously worked with the burin. Authentic damascene actually consists of a more complicated technique of sword forging; Muslim craftsmen, especially in Damascus, were supreme masters of this art. The importance attributed to these objects in the domestic context is remarkable, since Islam not only discourages three-dimensional sculpture and figurative decors, but explicitly condemns – at least theoretically – the use of gold and silver plate.
Carpets and rugs are of course absolutely indispensable to the nomadic life. Woven carpets were also used to make travelling bags which could then be carried by pack animals; joined in the middle, they were also transformed into 'architectural' elements or furnishings. The tents themselves were made of rugs, from canopy to flap, or they were used to create partitions inside. They could also be laid on the floor, made up into couches, thrown over divans, or employed as actual bags to hold garments, furnishings, and in fact every type of movable property, the only things a nomad would own. The raw material, wool, came from animals that moved from pasture to pasture with the tribe, such as sheep, goats and camels, depending on region. Using techniques handed down from mother to daughter, women stained the wool with natural dyes taken from grasses, berries, flowers, wood and insects (in more recent times in conjunction with synthetic ones). Generally a female occupation, carpet-making is carried out among nomadic peoples on a simple and practical wooden foldaway loom comprising a few small poles fixed to the ground or a vertical support. Each woman employs the colours and patterns customary for her ethnic group, according to designs so individual that it is possible to pinpoint their origin exactly.
Based on the techniques with which they are woven, carpets are divided into four main groups: knotted (knotted-pile; *goli-boft*), plain woven (*kilim*), embroidered (*jijim, cicim*), and chain-stitched (*sumak, soumak*). Knotted rugs, the heaviest, most valuable and most comfortable, can readily serve as furniture. They have both weft and warp in cotton, wool or silk, around which are tied knots of various kinds and in pieces of wool and/or silk of varying lengths that are then cut. Further carpet classification depends on region, city and ethnic origin. The four chief areas of production however are the Caucasus, characterized by sturdy geometric designs; Anatolia, with repetitive geometric interlace patterns and large dimensions, as in the famous 'Holbein' and 'Lotto' rugs often depicted by these painters that were extremely popular in Europe and featured the famous Ghiordes knot (*ghorza*); Iran, whose production features lively floral and figurative motifs of great refinement, supremely expressed in the smallest of the knots, the *senneh;* and central Asia, where geometric plant motifs prevail. The border that invariably encircles the central section fulfils an apotropaic function, protecting whoever is inside it from the dangers that surround him. Unlike the soft and springy knotted carpets, the surface of the flatweave *kilims* is smooth.
Jijim carpets are composed of strips of flatweave in which coloured threads (generally thicker than those used for the plain weft) are threaded through the weft and warp to compose little designs. Unlike *kilim, sumak* carpets have both a 'right' and a 'wrong' side; the loose ends of the coloured brocade yarn forming the pattern are whipped around the warp and left to hang loose on the reverse, an effect that gives the carpet a relatively dense consistency and renders it resistant to wear and tear.

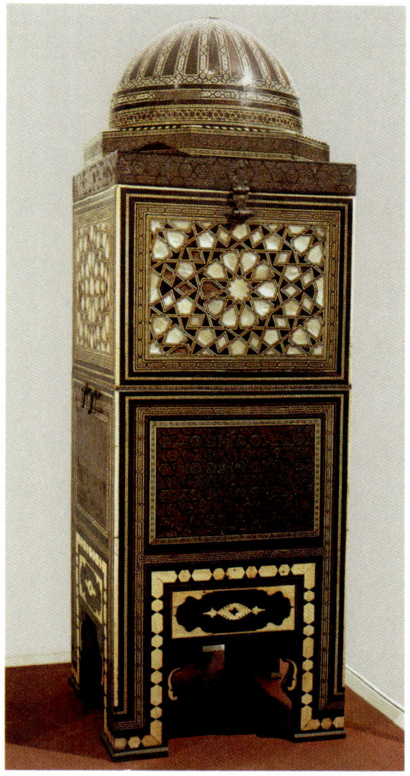

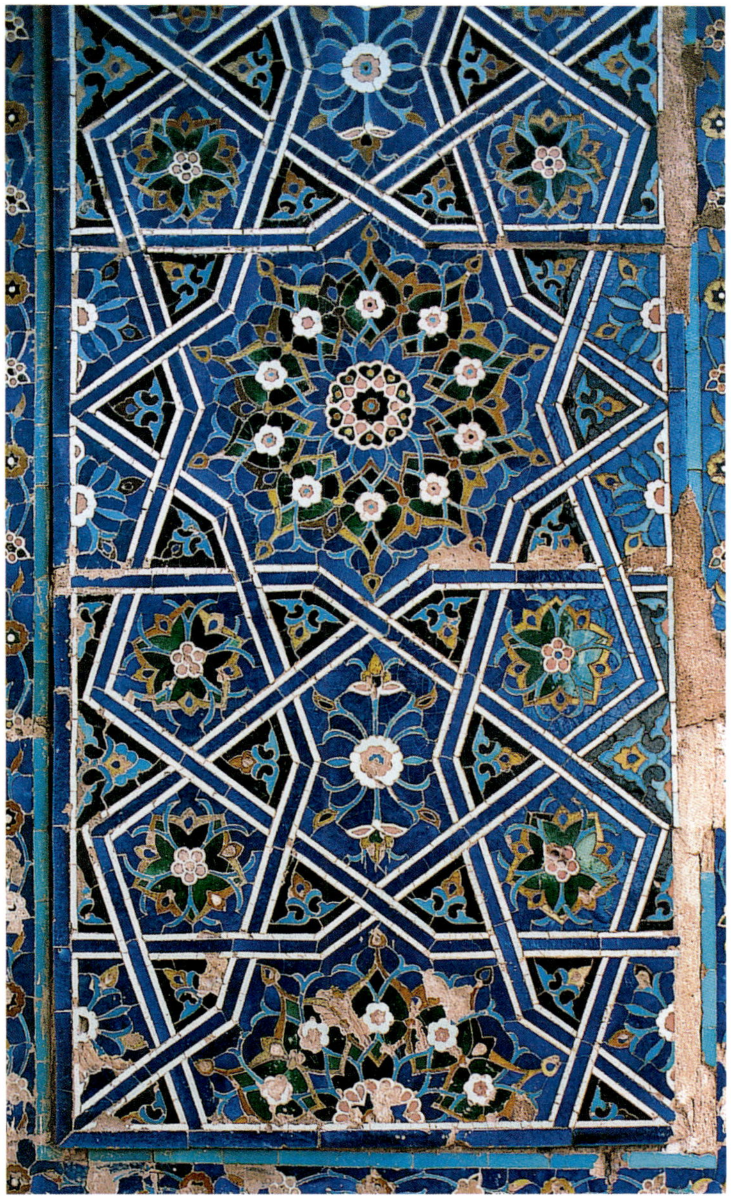

Qur'an cabinet of Selim II
1566–1575, Ottoman period
Wood with mother-of-pearl inlay
Museum of Islamic and Turkish Art, Istanbul

Necropolis of Shah-i Zinda Mausoleum of Tuman Agha Detail of façade
1405, Timurid period
Mo'arraq ceramics
Samarkand, Uzbekistan

Mosque of Rüstem Pasha
Ceramic tiling
1561–1563, Ottoman period
Istanbul, Turkey

We owe the existence of these splendid tiles to the passion of the great Grand Vizier Rüstem Pasha. He collected them and supported their production for his mosque. It was actually built after his death by his wife, Mihrimah (daughter of Suleiman and renowned patron), who made use of the materials amassed by her late husband. Their high quality derives from the fact that the majority of the ceramics were produced shortly before a rapid increase in demand led to an explosion of output, particularly at Iznik; the resulting industrial levels of production had a negative impact on quality.

Complex of Shaykh Bayazid
Detail of the entrance
12th–14th century, Ilkhanid period
Glazed ceramic
Bastam, Iran

Persia's tradition of ceramic production goes back for thousands of years and includes a dressing for the exterior surfaces of buildings constructed in unfired brick. Turquoise in a multiplicity of shades and hues has been a favourite colour since the reign of Elam (second millennium BCE), transfiguring the earthy substance of the bricks with an ethereal glow. Here, using techniques in which the ceramic craftsmen of the Ilkhanid era were supreme masters, the name of Caliph Ali unfolds in a shape similar to a swastika and is repeated *ad infinitum* with the turquoise passing through a tonal range of rare intensity.

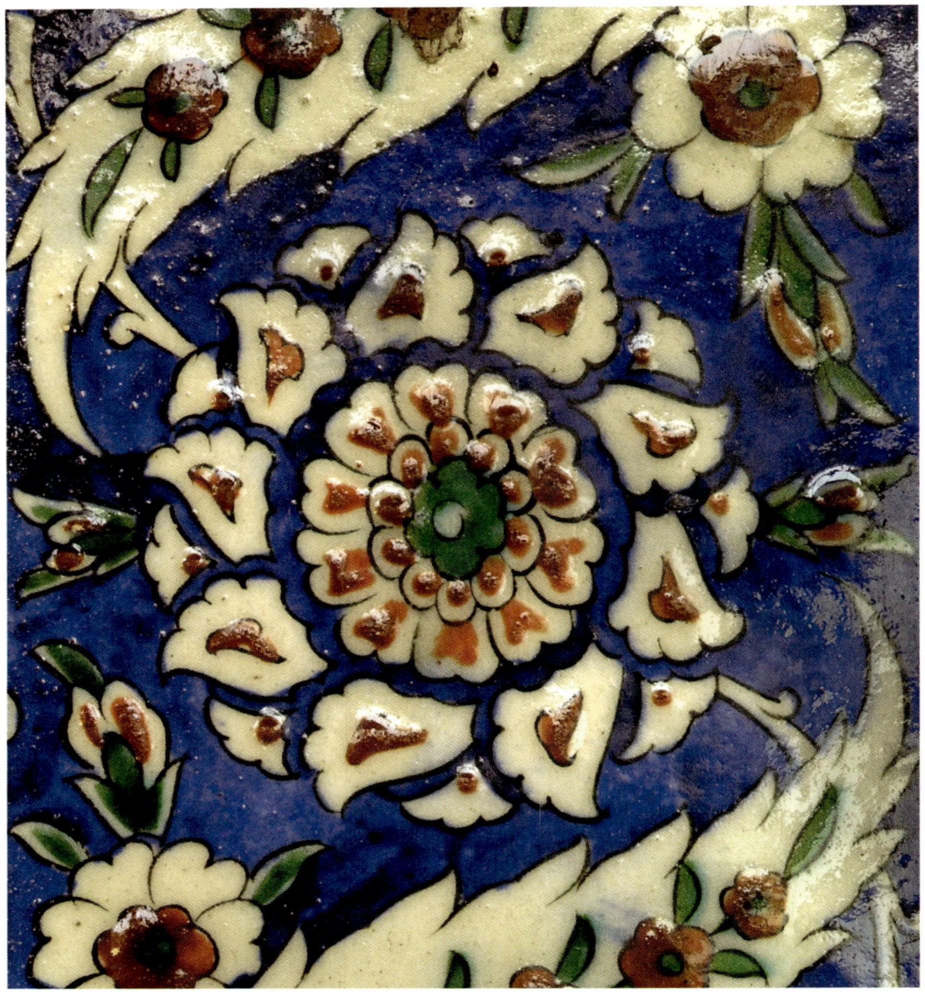

Detail of the ewer
'Baptistery of St Louis'
Late 13th century
Mamluk period
Brass with silver and gold damask
Louvre, Paris

The art of metalworking presents a precise reflection of the aspirations, lifestyle and interests of Muslim élite society as depicted in a selection of iconographic themes and described in inscriptions of dedication, benediction or morality. The use of medallions to isolate genre scenes of an aristocratic character is extremely widespread, although examples with astrological or animal motifs are also common. Complementing a background with plant trails or geometric patterns, in combination they impart a luxuriant feeling of *horror vacui*. In the detail reproduced here a huntsman is on the point of spearing his quarry. The sheets of silver and gold are hammered into the surface of the brass panel, which has been worked and treated with pine resin (the black ground) to keep the metal foil in place.

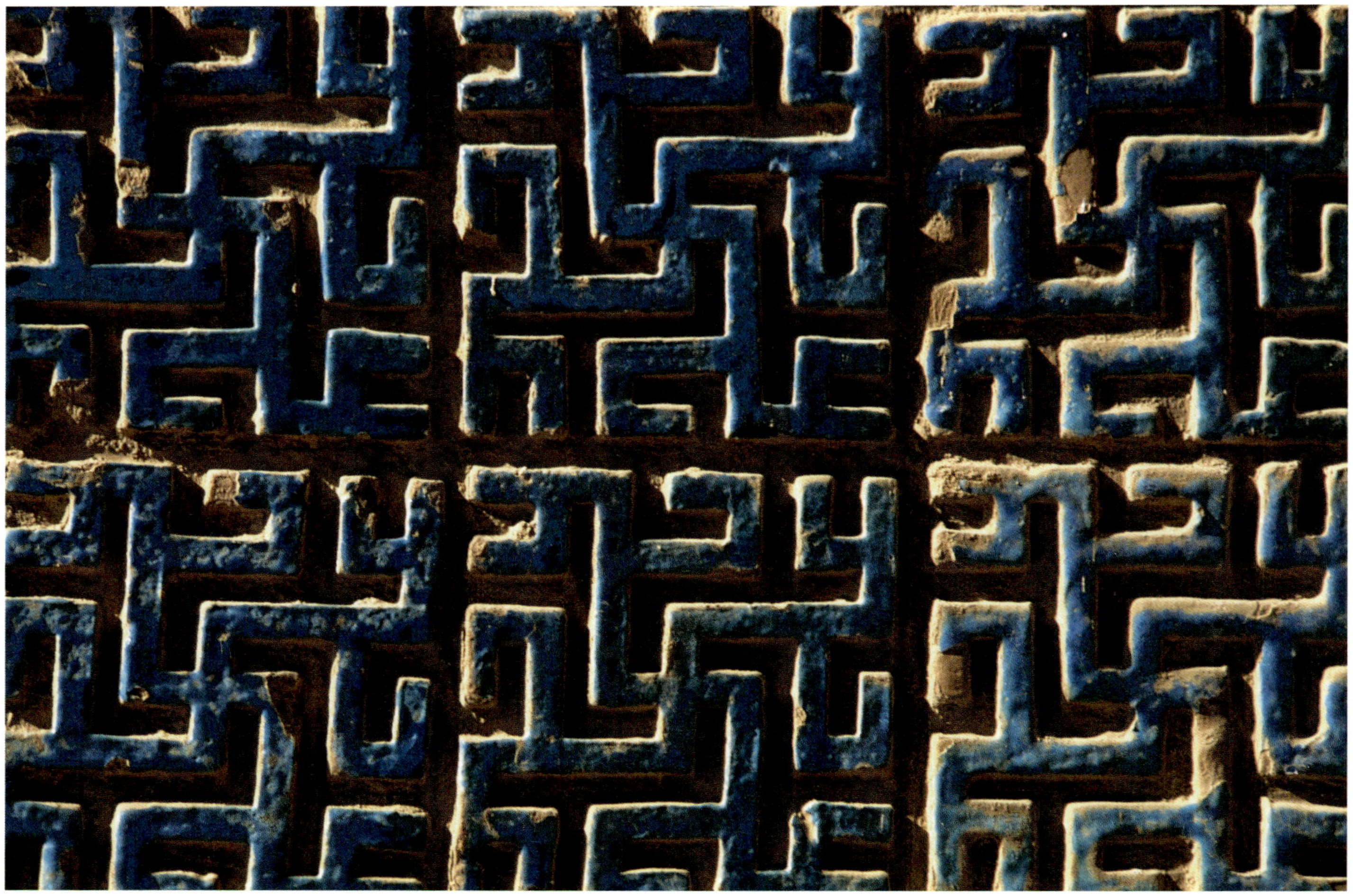

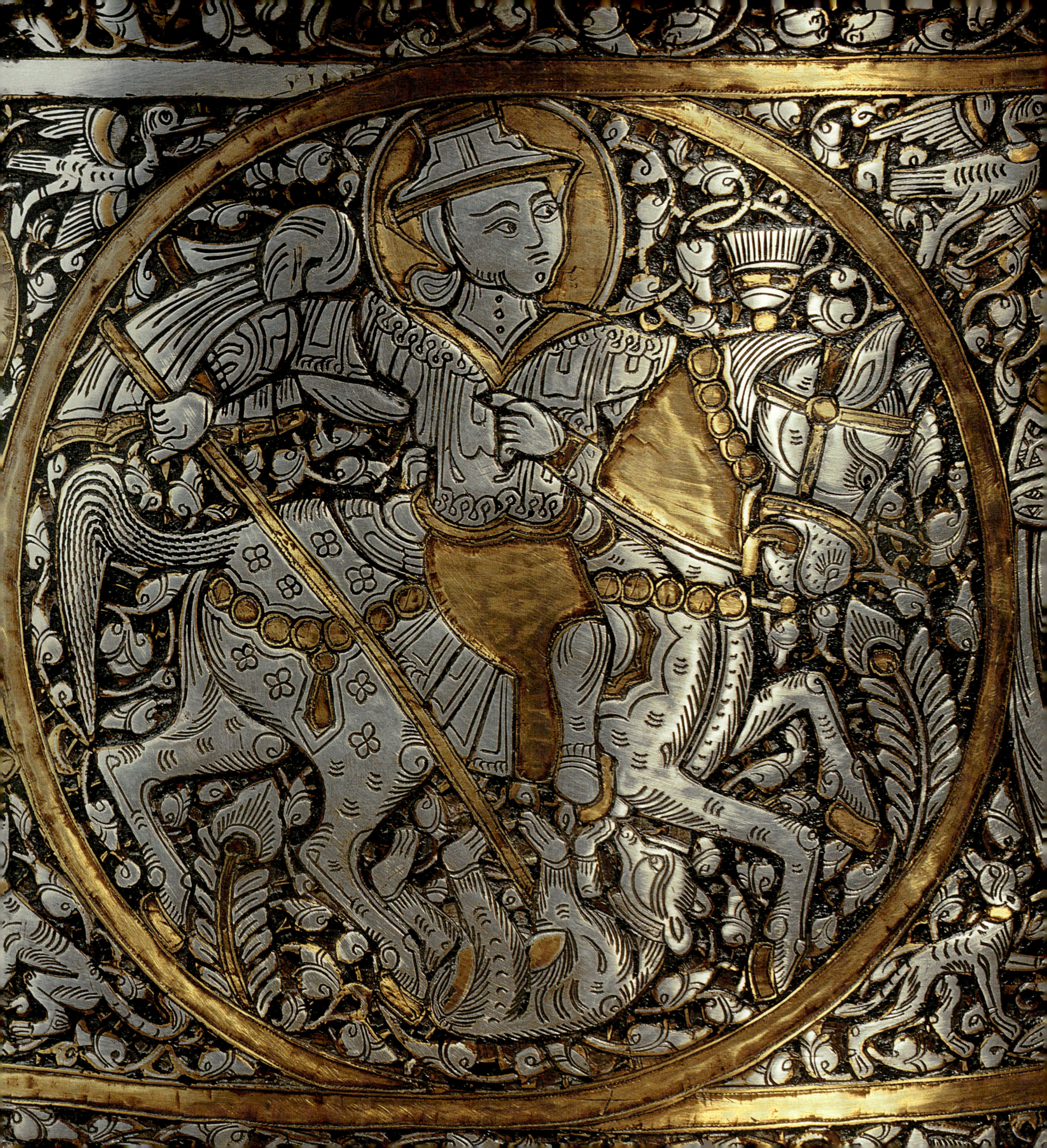

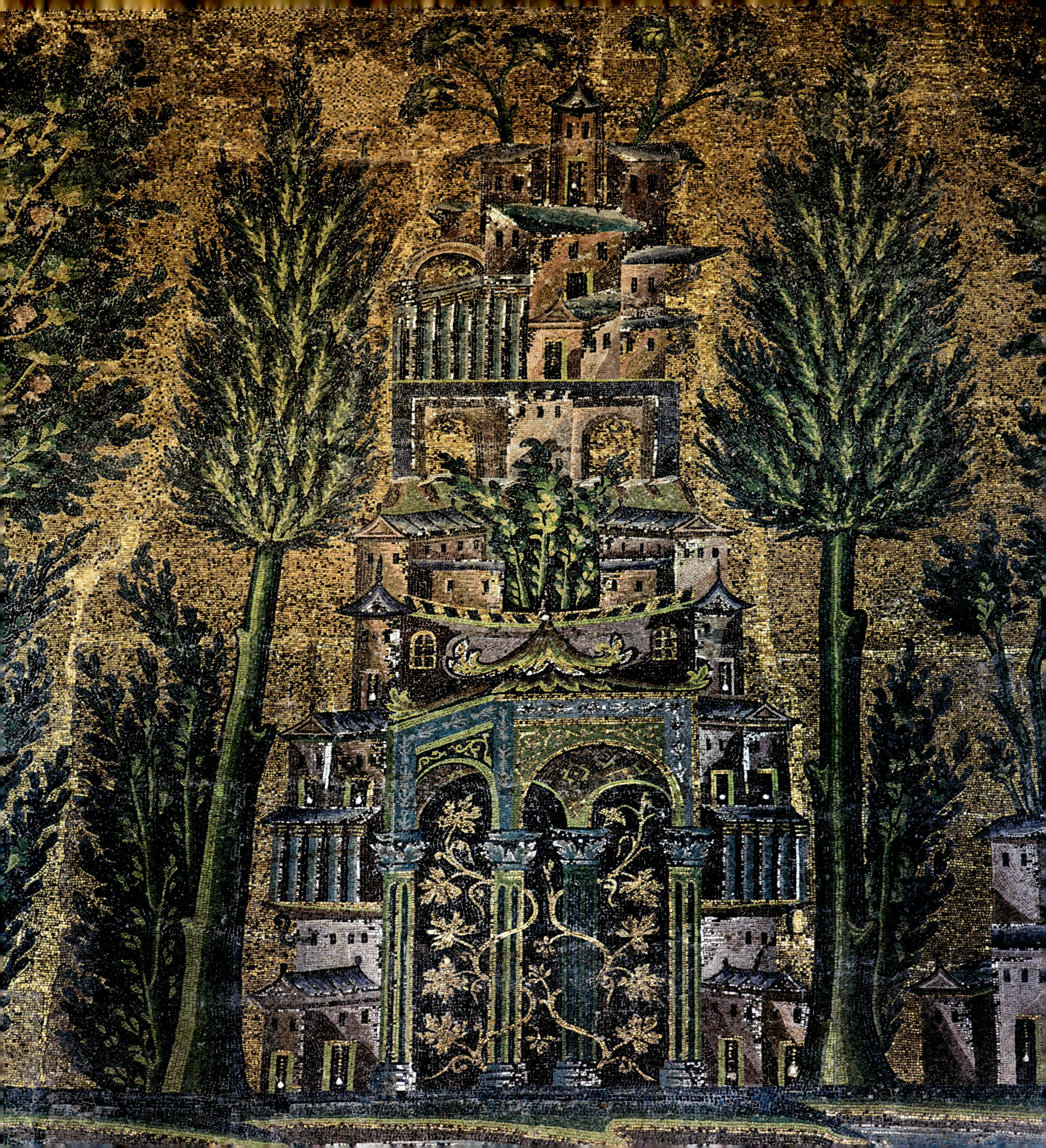

THE HISTORY OF ISLAMIC ART

THE UMAYYADS

page 64
Great Mosque
Detail of the mosaic decoration in the courtyard representing landscapes evoking paradise
706–715
Damascus, Syria

Incense burner depicting a domed audience hall decorated with geometrical motifs borne on arches hung with suspension lamps
7th–8th century
Stone
Jordan Archaeological Museum, Amman

The meteoric victories of the first caliphs brought the Arabs into contact with new cultural contexts and artistic traditions with centuries of history behind them, in which religious architecture formed an important centre of interest. Compared with such buildings, early mosques, based on Muhammad's house, inevitably appeared unsatisfactory. In the decades between 640 and 670, the mosque of Kufa was rebuilt, becoming the first to boast a full hypostyle plan. In 661, as the Umayyad dynasty (661–750) tightened its grip, Damascus was elevated to the status of a capital. In order to bolster the pride of the fledgling community in its faith and render less odious the comparisons with the architectural achievements of resident populations, it became necessary to create a place of congregation with a strong symbolic value – hence the mosque, where all could gather and reinforce their sense of group identity.
The birth of Islamic architecture came about through the efforts of Caliph Abd al-Malik, who erected the Dome of the Rock in Jerusalem, and al-Walid, who built the Great Mosque at Damascus. Both chose incontestably iconic locations for buildings which were important for a number of reasons. Proclaiming the presence of a new power, a new order and a new religion, they were couched in an architectural vocabulary familiar to the populations over which they ruled and from whom the architects and skilled workers were drawn.

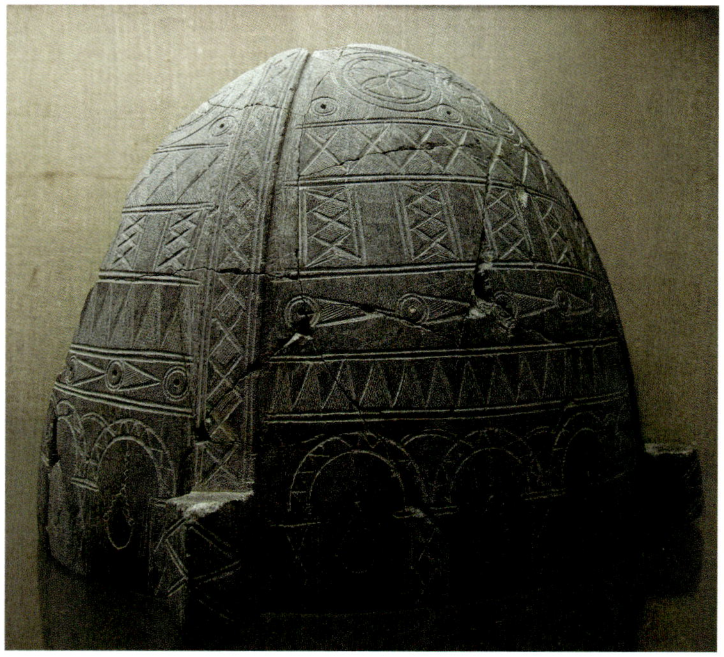

The Dome of the Rock in Jerusalem (the Qubbat as-Sakhra, also known incorrectly as the Mosque of Omar), was built between 689 and 691. It is the first major Islamic monument and above all the first one intended to make an artistic impact and provoke a response – even if, curiously enough, its exact function remains unknown (it was not planned as a mosque). The site, where the Temple of Solomon had once stood, is of unique political, religious and emotional importance for Muslims, Christians and Jews alike, who all associate it with the story of the Creation, the death of Adam and the sacrifice of Isaac. The site chosen and the iconography of the layout, with an octagonal double ambulatory set around a circular nucleus surrounding the bare rock, are perfectly adapted to the kind of ritual circumambulation undertaken in holy places such as the Ka'ba. This form of worship is probably related to the legendary nocturnal journey (*isra*) of Muhammad, recalled in Qur'an XVII, 1: "Glory be to Him who made His servant go by night from the Sacred Temple [of Mecca] to the Farther Temple [the most distant religious site, interpreted as Jerusalem]," and with the no less prodigious ascension of the Prophet (*mi'raj*) that took place from a cliff enclosed in a building, from which, according to a *hadith,* God had repaired to heaven following the Creation. In this sense, the architectural form of the dome amounts to an Islamic counterpart to the Christian *martyria* (literally 'witness'), as proved by the close formal echoes with monuments such as the sanctuary of the Ascension and the Church of the Holy Sepulchre (Anastasis) in Jerusalem.
Much of our knowledge of Umayyad architecture derives from the mosques constructed by al-Walid I (705–715), since almost nothing has survived of earlier examples or of his successors' residences *extra muros,* although wall paintings and decorative outlines in stucco which have survived are particularly intriguing. The Umayyads constructed, rebuilt or enlarged congregational mosques in Basra, Kufa and Wasit in Iraq, at al-Fustat (now engulfed by Cairo) in Egypt, and in Kairouan in Tunisia. They also converted innumerable churches to the new faith, often but not always eliminating the sacred imagery and simply adding on one wall a *mihrab* indicating the *qibla.*
The congregational mosque is the most important construction in every city, combining religious, social and political functions.

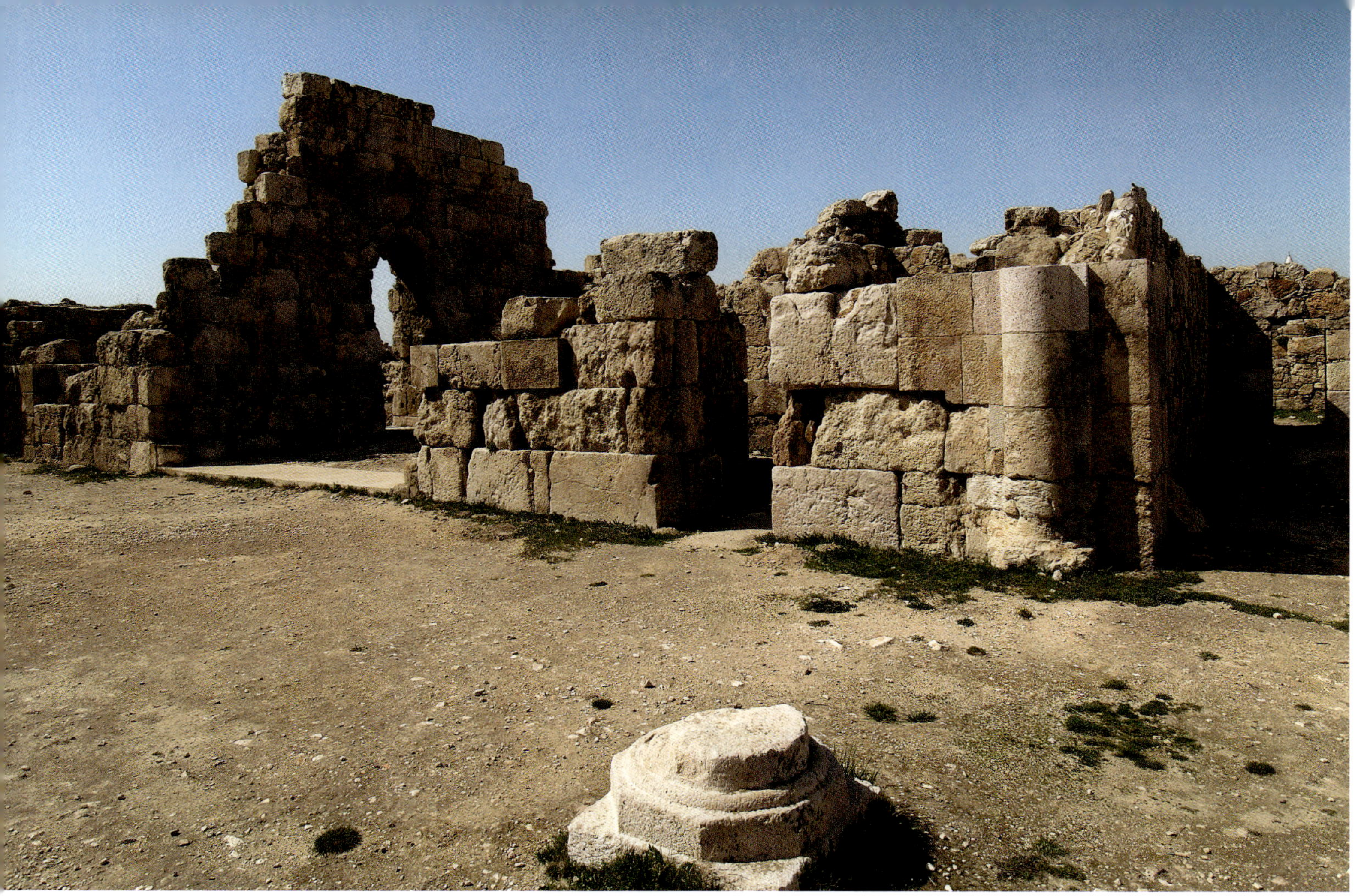

Umayyad palace
Entrance to the throne room
724–743
Amman, Jordan

Qusayr Amra
Detail of the wall decorations in the reception hall showing a dancer
711
Jordan

It was here that a wide range of activities, including school instruction, community events and the administration of justice all took place. Two important structures seem to have developed in these early mosques, although their origin remains uncertain. The first is the *maqsura,* a special enclosure reserved for the prince and generally placed in the middle of the *qibla* wall. Designed as protection against possible attack, it also served to glorify the ruler by cordoning him off from his subjects. The second seems to have been the introduction of the minaret, the most prominent architectural symbol of Islam, whose age and place of origin has been the subject of much discussion. The consensus is, however, that this structure derives from the Roman lighthouse, whose purpose it echoes on a symbolic level since it is a 'beacon' to guide true believers. Al-Walid constructed or completed the three monumental mosques at Medina (710); Jerusalem (715), where he completely rebuilt the al-Aqsa mosque; and Damascus (706–715). The Great Mosque at Damascus retains the major part of its original character, although the terrible damage wrought by the fire of 1893 and recent and ill-considered restorations have disfigured the columns of the courtyard with awkward pillars and replaced the original beaten earth pavement with a dazzlingly polished marble floor.

It was thus the Umayyads who paved the way for a true Islamic artistic tradition, particularly in the field of architecture, creating the typologies on which later realizations rely. The magnificent openwork marble lattices in the mosque at Damascus; the mosaics in the residence of Khirbat al-Mafjar; and the layout of the Dome of the Rock proudly proclaim the might and pageantry of the new faith. Geometry occupies an important position because it provides a cognitive framework for the activities of mankind and generates models for the mosaics and inscriptions that occupied the furnishings, furniture and surfaces of their buildings. On the other hand, some forms of artistic expression that blossomed during their reign, such as luxury bronzes of erotic character and large-scale wall paintings with secular themes, and figurative mosaics and monumental sculptures, disappeared with the collapse of the dynasty. They were seen as having originated among the subject populations and were condemned as being alien to the Islamic moral code as it became more narrowly defined over the following decades.

It is especially hard to arrive at a precise analysis of the changes affecting luxury items; their production differs only marginally from earlier Byzantine, Sassanid and Coptic examples, which makes specifically Islamic pieces hard to identify. Moreover, the objects most characteristic of Islamic crafts – carpets, cloth, objects in metal, glass and books with illuminations and calligraphy – are extremely rare. A turning-point, however, occurred when Abd al-Malik abandoned figurative coinage derived from Sassanid and Byzantine models, replacing it by issues on which the word is the sole feature.

Umayyad art was eclectic, experimental and propagandist: eclectic in the sense that it succeeded in linking the rational and naturalistic language derived from Hellenistic-Byzantine sources in the West with the representational and symbolic art of Mesopotamia, Iran and Central Asia; experimental in that it was confronted with a remarkable variety of models and content, which it reinvented in a most original, creative and uninhibited manner; and propagandistic, in that it produced superlative works with the intention of broadcasting and exalting the power and magnificence of the Arabic and Islamic Umayyad state and of its caliphs.

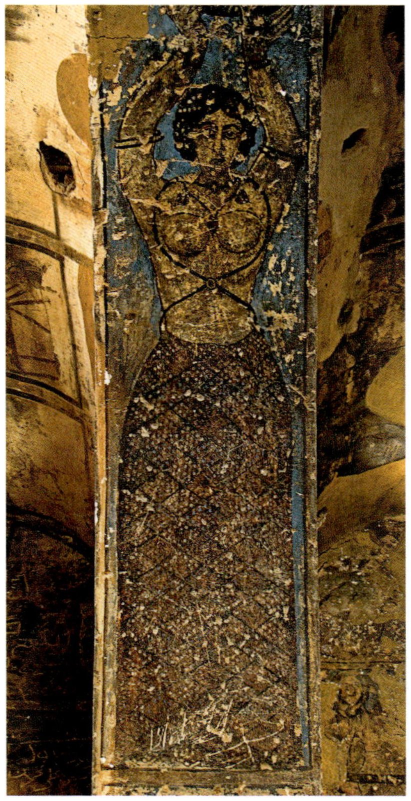

Dome of the Rock and al-Aqsa Mosque on the terrace of the Temple of Solomon
689–691 and subsequent alterations
715 and subsequent alterations
Jerusalem

"Al-Walid … saw that Syria was a country long occupied by the Christians and he noted the fine churches still belonging to them, so charming and beautiful and renowned for their splendour … Therefore, he strove to build for the Muslims a mosque without equal and a wonder of the world … Abd al-Malik, seeing the majesty of the *martyrium* at the Holy Sepulchre and its magnificence, was seized by the fear that it would dazzle the minds of the Muslims, and therefore erected over the Rock the Dome that one sees today." (Al-Muqaddasi, 10th century).
The building, crowned by a centred cupola built of wood, rises regally upon the immense artificial platform known as al-Haram al-Sharif ('the noble sanctuary'), corresponding to the so-called Mount of Solomon's Temple and dating back to the time the temple was extended and reconstructed under Herod the Great in 20 CE. The diameter of the octagonal base measures some sixty metres, that of the cupola approximately twenty. The geometric design underlying the structure can be interpreted in the light of the analysis in the preceding chapter. The entire levelled terrace acted as a precinct for the contemporary mosque of al-Aqsa, although later alterations have transformed the structure to such an extent that it is impossible to picture how it looked originally.

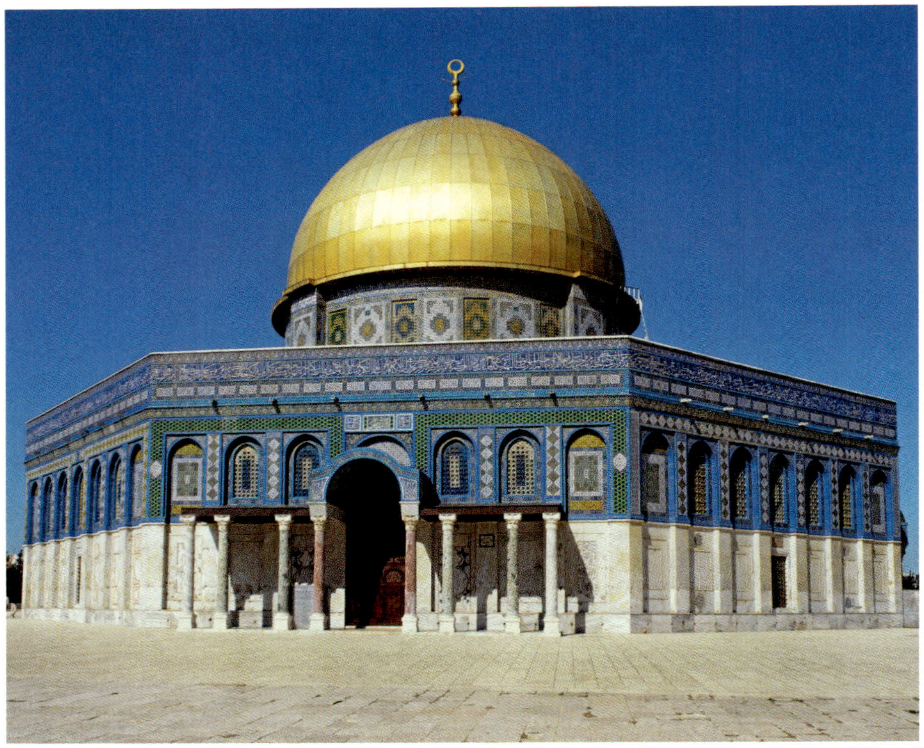

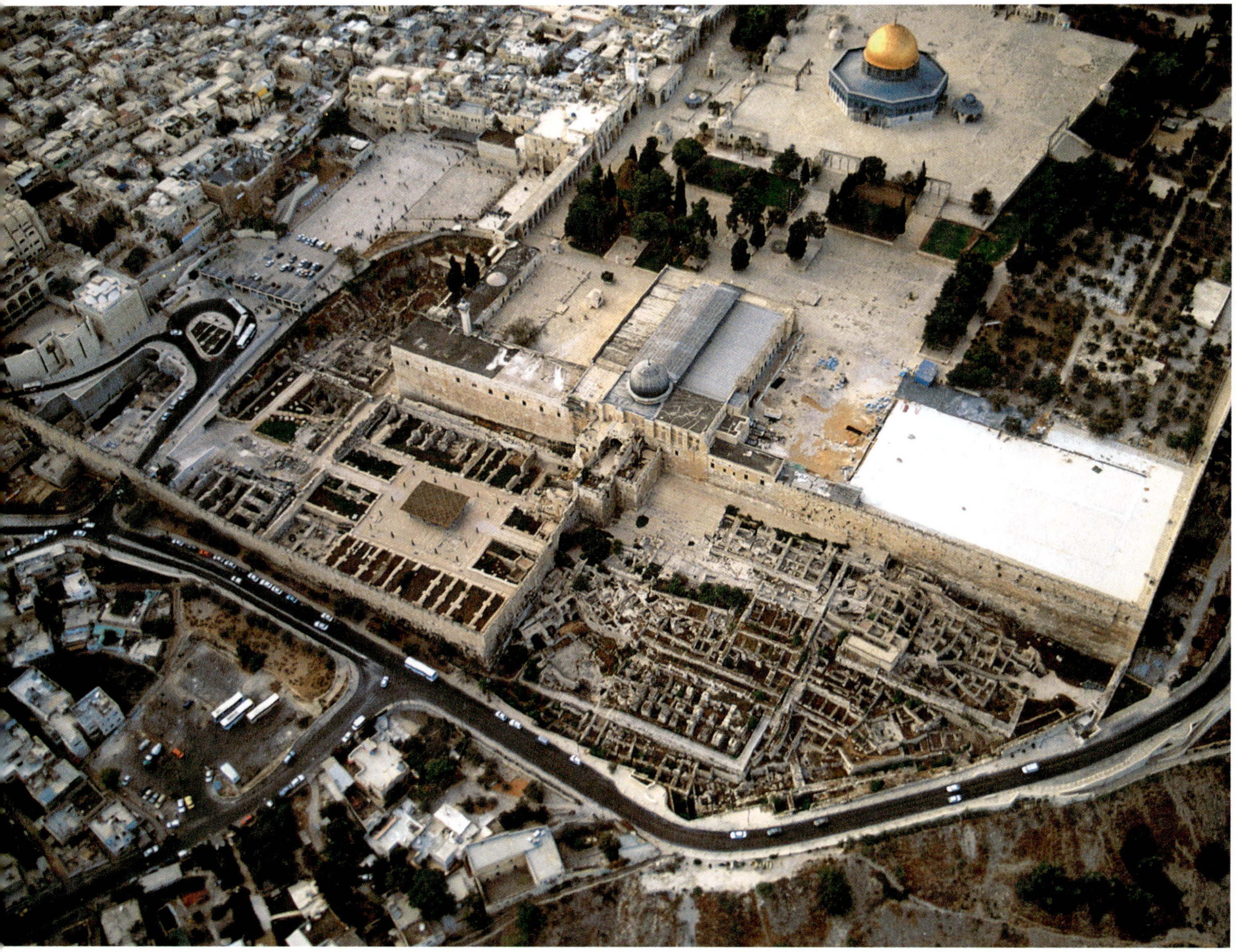

Dome of the Rock Interior
689–691
Jerusalem

Resembling a colossal ciborium, the structure is derived from the Byzantine architectural and decorative style, modified by Sassanid influences which are particularly noticeable in the mosaics in the middle gallery showing jewels and crowns. These motifs should be seen as an allusion to the treasures seized from the defeated emperors that were stored in the Ka'ba in Mecca, of which the Dome represents a kind of symbolic double. Amidst the luxuriant growth of plants, script assumes a new and specifically Islamic role, imposing itself as a necessary element in the iconography: the inscription is 240 metres long and provides the key to reading the monument. The fundamental principles of Islam are boldly asserted, as is the role of Muhammad as the last of the prophets, although a special place is also reserved for Jesus and Mary. The epigraphy concludes with an explicit invitation to the "people of the book" to acknowledge Islam as the final revelation, superior to both Christianity and Judaism.

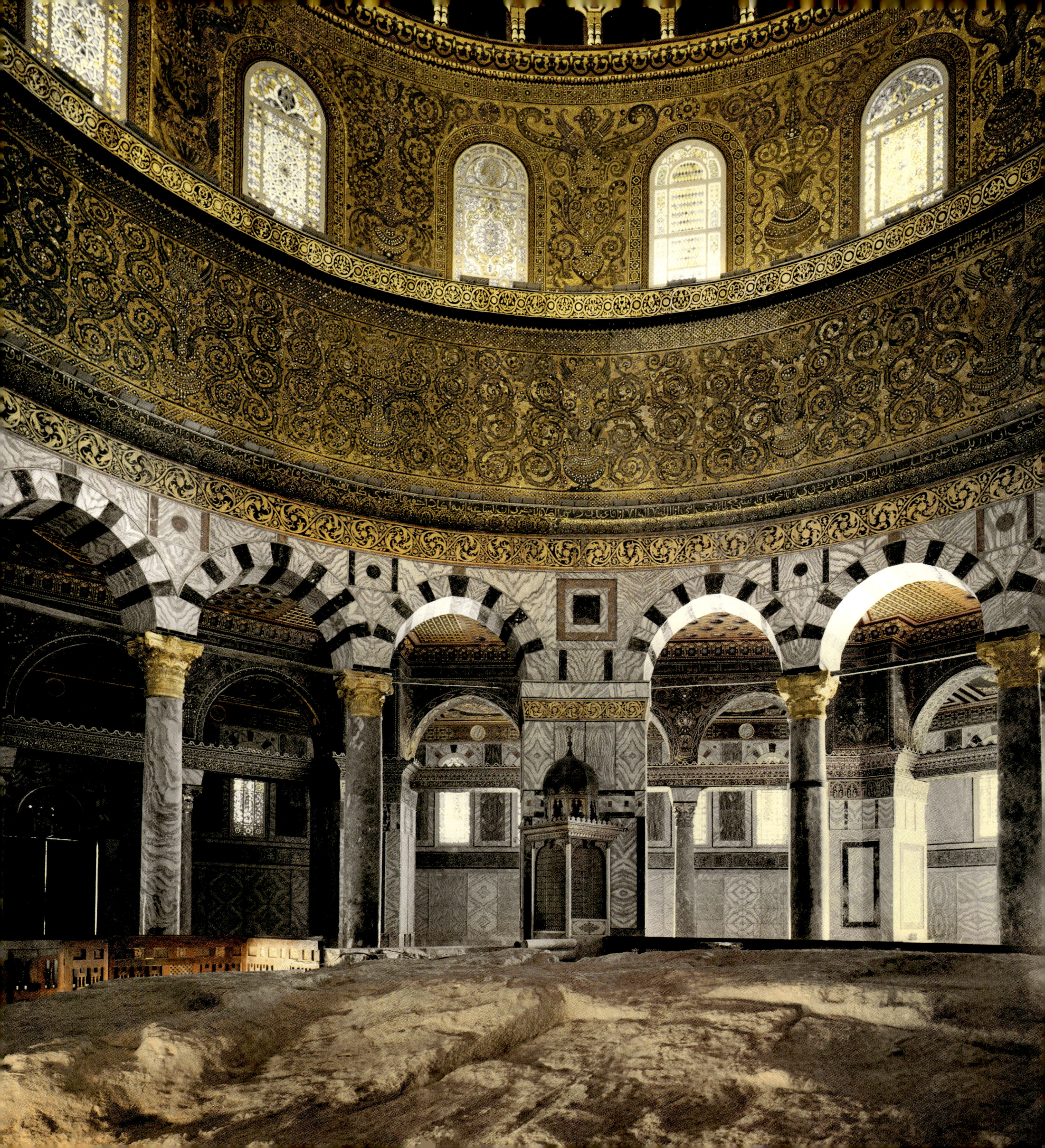

Great Mosque
Façade
706–715 and subsequent alterations
Damascus, Syria

The central nave emerges at the centre of the long façade of the mosque, standing perpendicular to the other sides. The dome towering above, called the 'Eagle', is only documented from the twelfth century, and is hence probably a modification from the Seljuq era, although what can be seen currently dates to a clumsy programme of restoration undertaken after the disastrous fire of 1893; at that juncture the radical decision was taken to integrate landscapes dominated by huge trees into the non-figurative mosaics. The architectonic design is clearly Byzantine: a triumphal arch topped by a tympanum and opening into a grand triple-arched atrium overhung by a smaller open gallery, a solution rather similar to that adopted in the Hagia Sophia basilica in what was then Constantinople, as well as in other late Antique and Byzantine churches of the period.

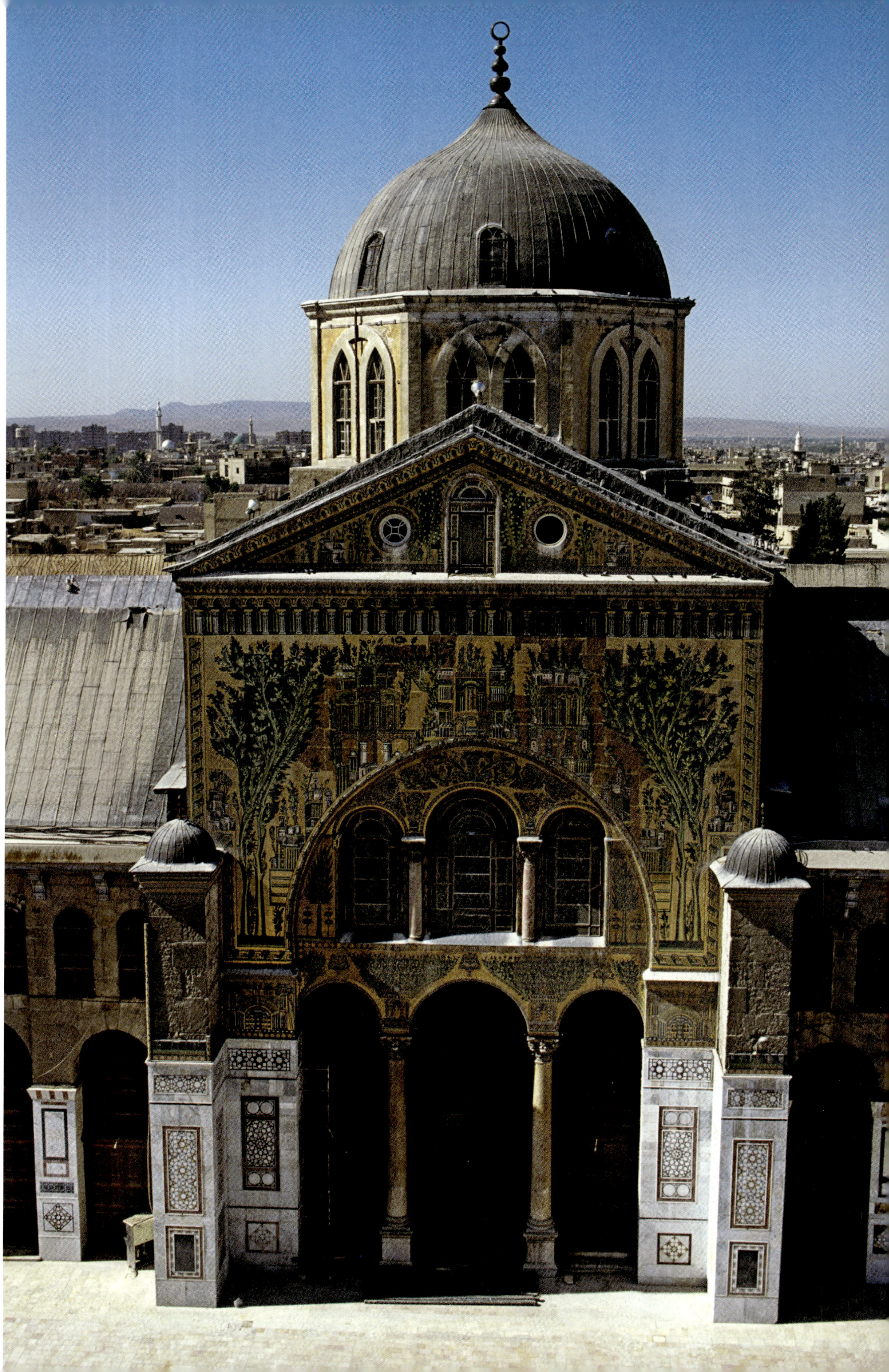

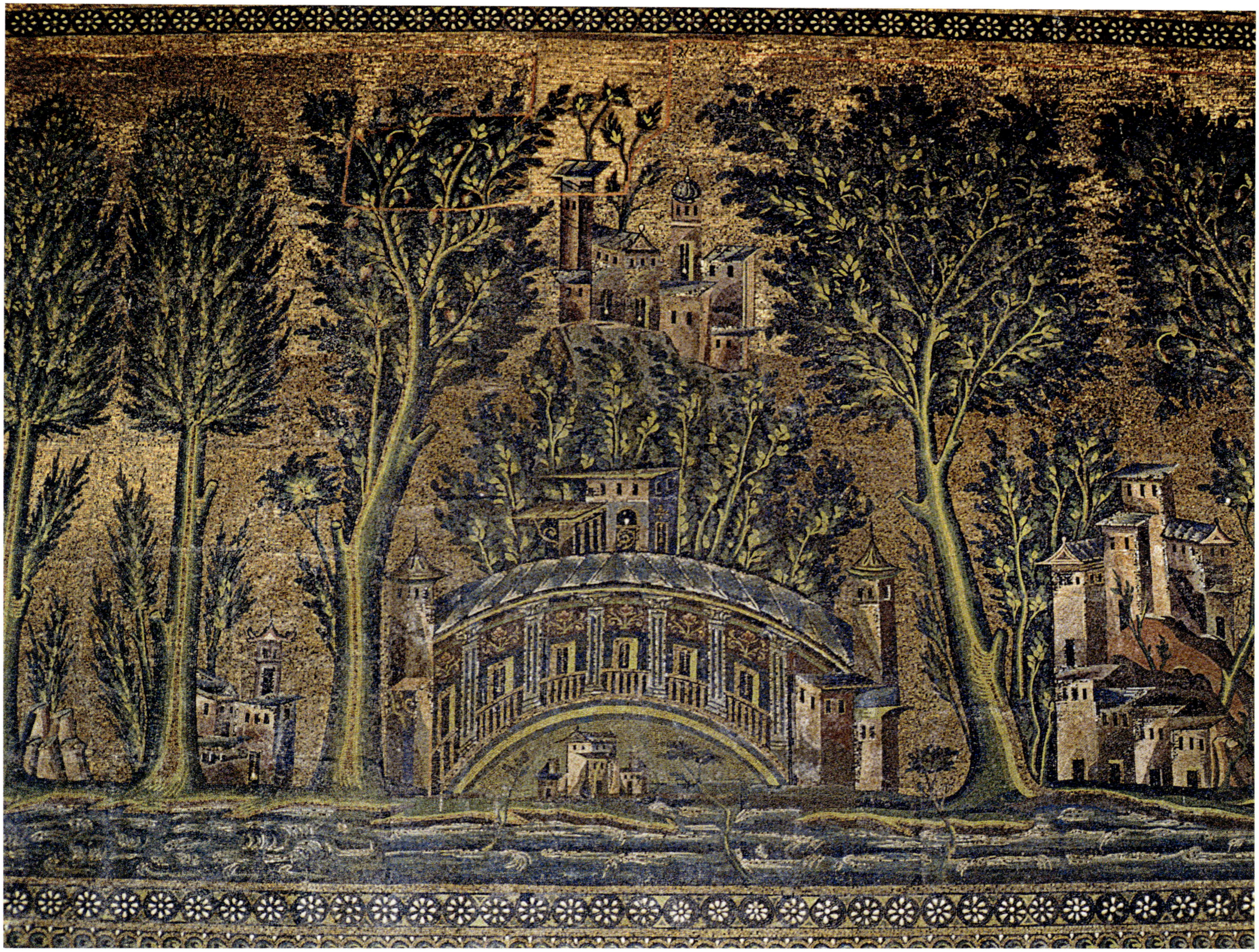

Great Mosque
Detail of the mosaic decor in the courtyard
706–715
Damascus, Syria

“For magnificence it is the greatest mosque in the world, and nothing equals it for artistic quality and wondrous beauty … It is adorned with a cloth of gold called mosaic, of divers colours and of extraordinary beauty. The Cathedral Mosque, known as the Umayyad Mosque, is the most magnificent mosque in the world, the finest in construction and noblest in beauty, grace and perfection; it is matchless and unequalled.” (Ibn Battuta, *Travels in Asia and Africa, 1325–1354,* transl. and ed. by H. A. R. Gibb, London 1929).
The mosaics, executed by expert Byzantine craftsmen, take their inspiration from the Islamic conception of paradise, where believers are greeted by cool babbling streams and luxurious apartments standing in the shade of enormous evergreen trees. This representation alludes at the same time to the Umayyad *pax* – an obvious reference to the *pax augusta* of the Roman age and its attendant imperial ideology – and might also be seen as portraying various cities in the Muslim empire. The iconographic models for the background derive from Roman and Byzantine compositions, frequently found in the region and transformed here, after the figures teeming in the originals were painstakingly expunged, into a silent backdrop.

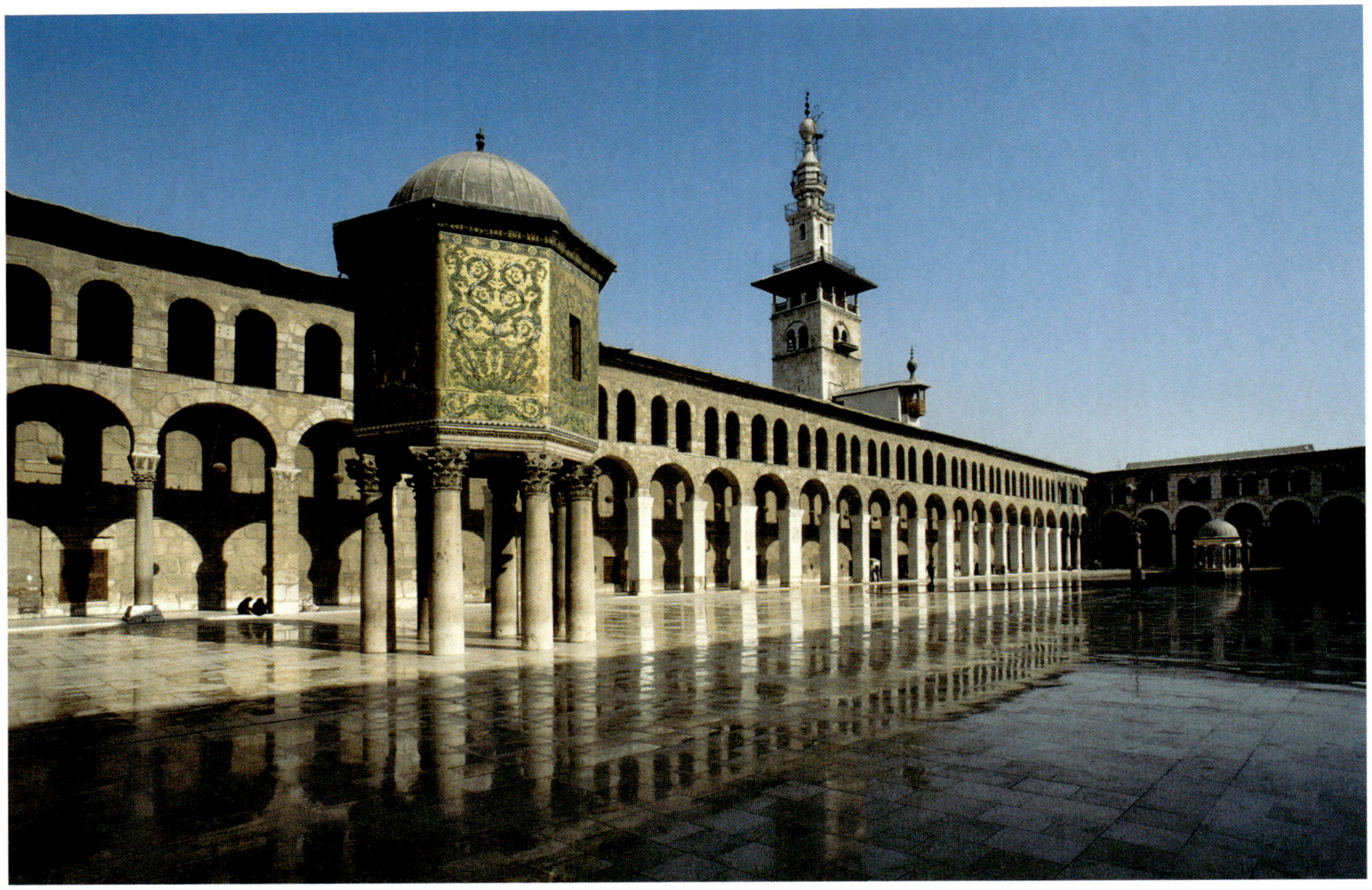

Great Mosque
Courtyard overlooked by the north minaret
706–715
Damascus, Syria

The classic formula for the hall mosque preceded by a courtyard is in truth the outcome of the conversion into an Islamic place of worship of the former basilica of St John the Baptist (supposedly containing his tomb) inserted within the *temenos* of the Roman temple dedicated to Jupiter Damascenus. In early times, after the conquest, Christian liturgy and Muslim prayer cohabited within the basilica that was partially converted into a mosque. The perimeter is a quadrilateral measuring 157 x 100 metres, with square towers at the corners functioning as minarets. The monumental entryways to the east and west are those of the Roman *temenos*, while that to the north in line with the *mihrab* and crowned by a minaret (of which solely the severe lower part is Umayyad) dates from the eighth century CE. The courtyard (122 x 50 metres) is encircled by a portico, originally composed of rows of columns alternating with pillars, at one time clad in mosaics symbolising paradise but now unfortunately disfigured by recent restoration.

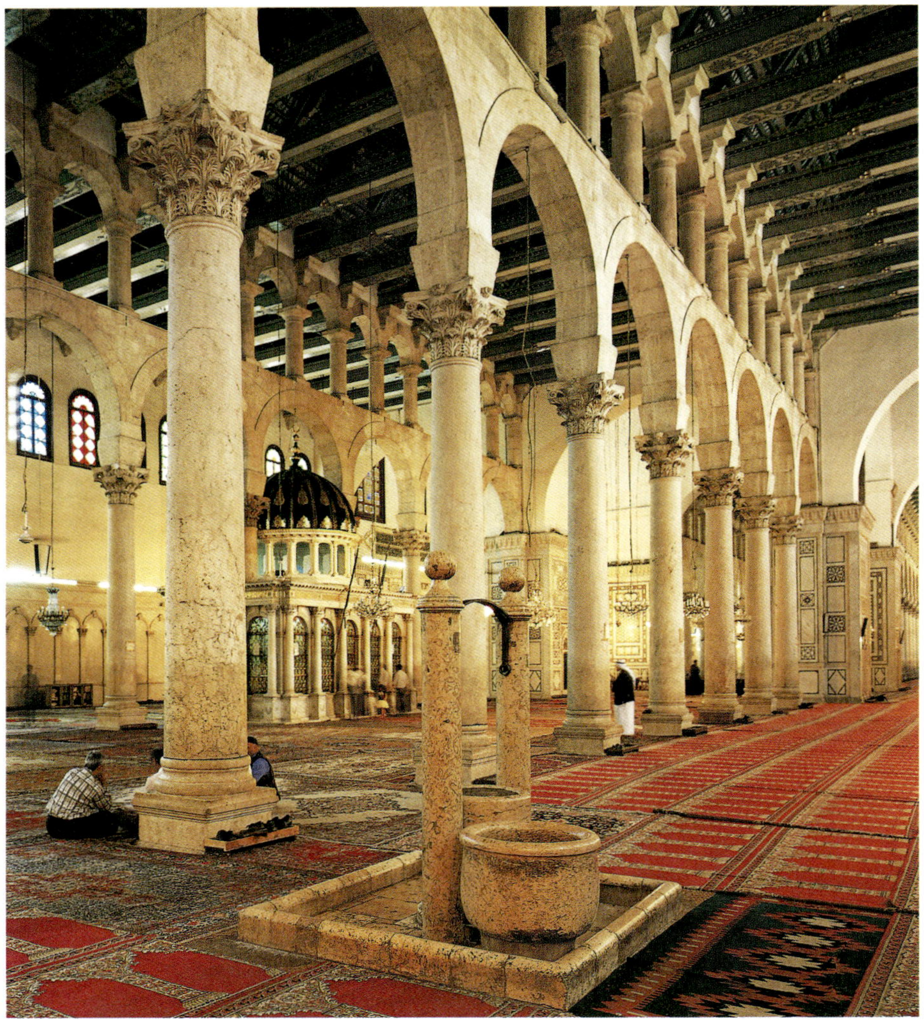

Great Mosque
Prayer hall
706–715
Damascus, Syria

The three naves parallel to the *qibla* wall are marked out by magnificent monolithic *spolia* columns which are all identical and over six metres high. They are crowned with Corinthian capitals (probably Roman) bearing vaguely horseshoe-shaped arches surmounted by a second arcade of smaller dimensions. The (restored) ceiling with timber trusses would have originally been painted. A solemn, regal atmosphere reigns in the colossal hall, emphasized by the fact that the perspective down the central nave running perpendicular to the others is immediately blocked off by the *qibla* wall. The sense of depth and progression that animated the Christian basilica is inverted, negated even: the plan takes up instead with the conception of the Roman civil basilica which was also entered from the longer side. In this mosque, although owing so much to Classical and Byzantine models, it is clear that the structure is meant to be a unified place of prayer and not an itinerary staged from door to altar as in a church.

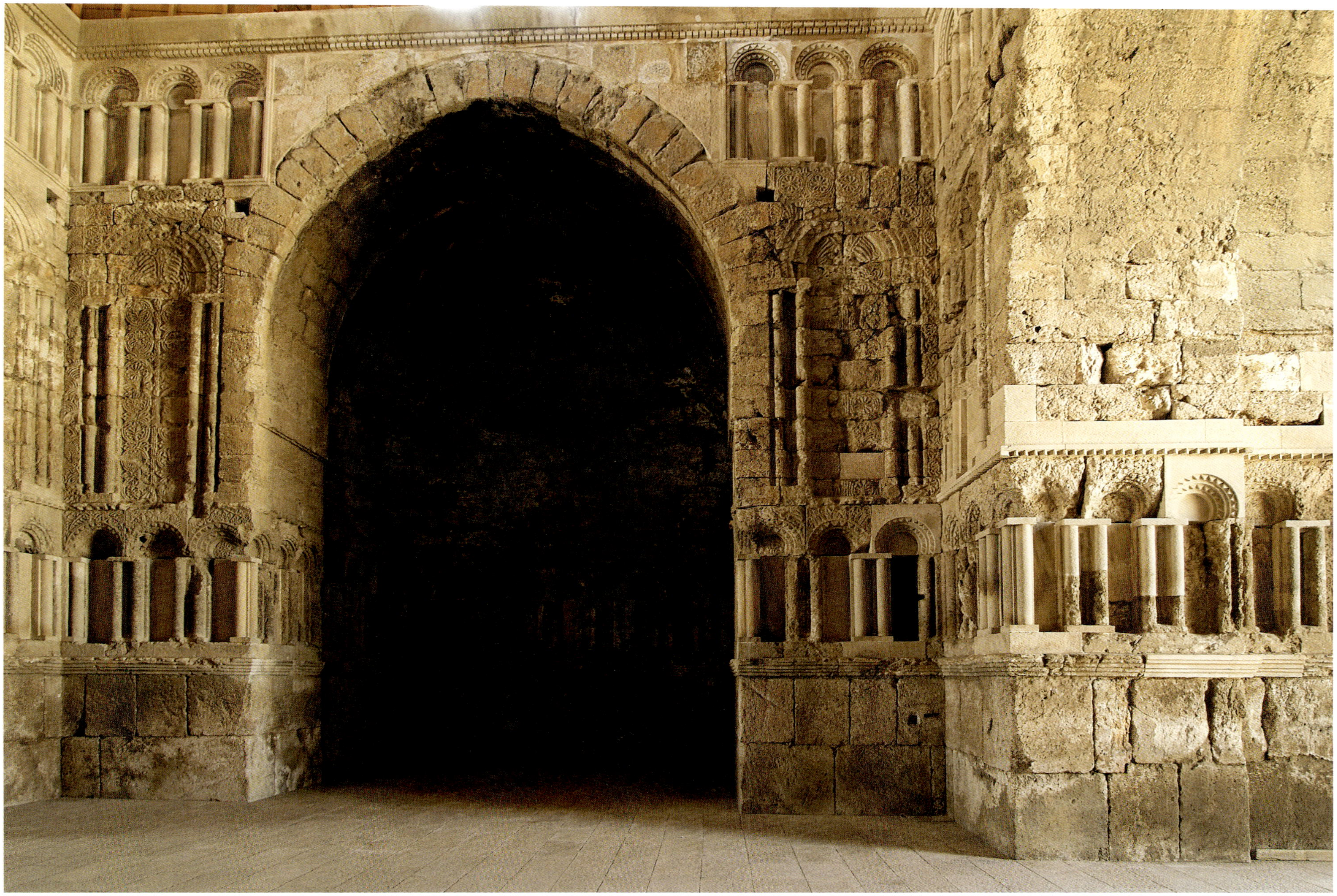

Umayyad Palace
Vestibule
724–743
Amman, Jordan

Once they had established their capital at Damascus, the Umayyads set about rebuilding the citadel of Amman and converting it into a headquarters for the governor. The upper terracing was divided into three sections encircled by walls and dominated by the audience hall. The latter also acted as a monumental entrance to the vast palace complex facing the mosque. The carved decoration extends over three orders. A cornice separates the bottom plinth from a row of blind niches flanked by double engaged colonnettes spanned by a dentillated arch. A second cornice separates the lower order from a broader blind arcade, likewise flanked by miniature columns and decorated with medallions of palmettes and rosettes. A third, smaller range of blind niches runs over the lower orders and crowns the wall. Elements derived from Sassanid building are much in evidence, as much in the cruciform plan with its four *iwans* as in the decoration. Initially, the timber roofing would have been parabolic in form.

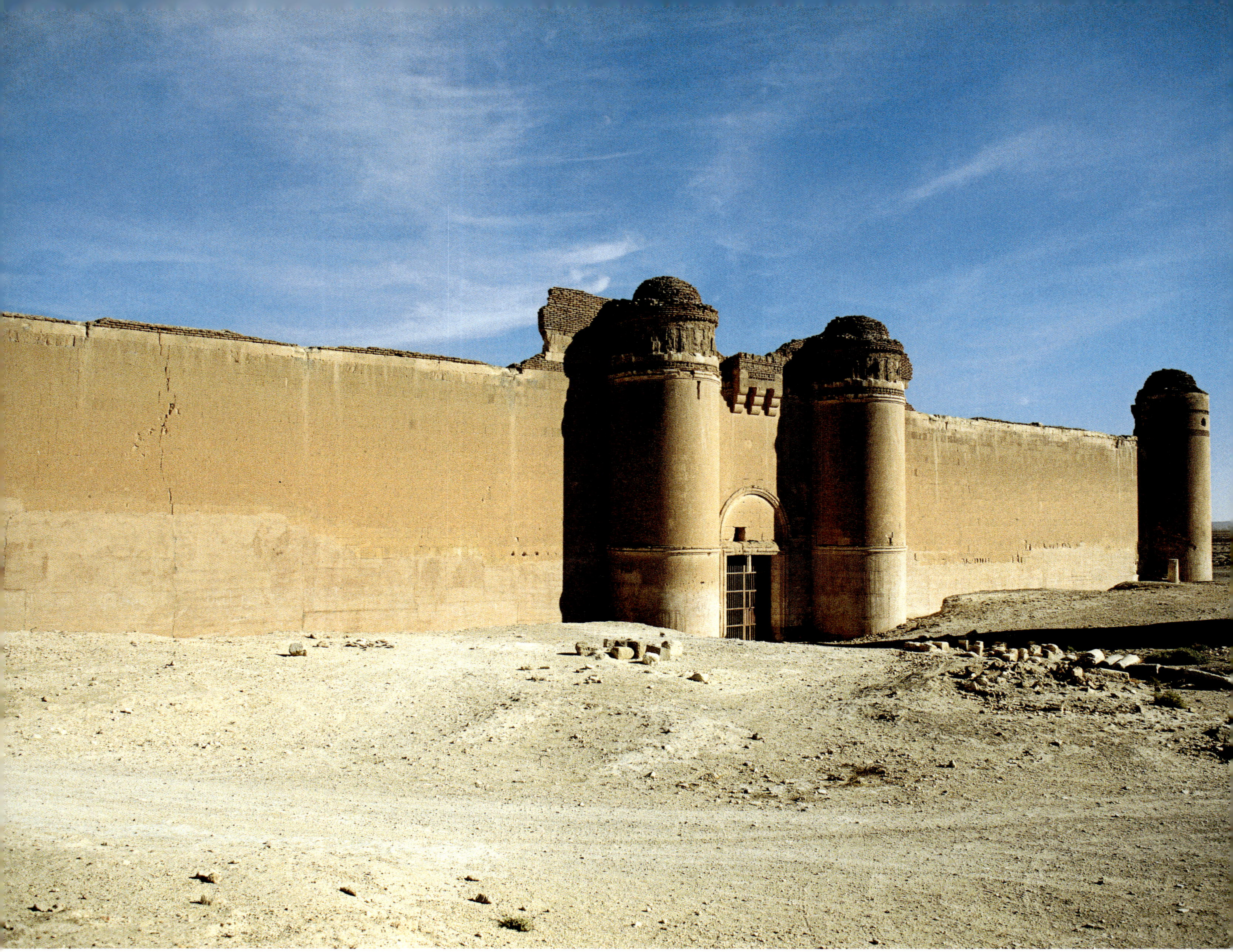

Qasr al-Heyr ash-Sharqi
728–729
Syria

The so-called Umayyad desert castles were costly and luxurious complexes of fortified appearance. They stemmed from a particular historical contingency which arose due to the coincidence of a number of factors. Apart from the difficulty of expropriating or constructing ostentatious dwellings in the urban centre which might have offended the religious sensibilities of the masses, there was the necessity of maintaining links with nomadic populations often reluctant to enter the city; and the need to administer the expanses of agricultural land essential to the economy of the time, a role formerly carried out by the same Roman villas from which Umayyad patrons and craftsman alike took their cue. The castles rose in general over two floors around a central courtyard and with various spaces to ensure the nobles remained comfortable during their sojourn: a mosque, a reception hall, a heating plant (sometimes built outside the castle), latrines, miscellaneous utility rooms and warehouses. All these were analogous to those found in numerous Sassanid palaces, which, together with the Roman and Byzantine forts, constituted the prototype.

Qasr al-Kharrana
705–710
Jordan

The castle has no properly military function and was in fact designed as a meeting-place for Umayyad princes and chiefs of local groups. Probably constructed for al-Walid, the square plan with semicircular towers at the corners recalls Roman and Byzantine forts constructed on the *limes* to keep the desert tribes at bay, with additional fortified towers halfway down the sides. The entrance is formed by a large tower fanning out into a tall archway with the gate in the centre. The slender openings in the walls, at one time thought to be arrow-loops, in fact serve to let light into the interior.

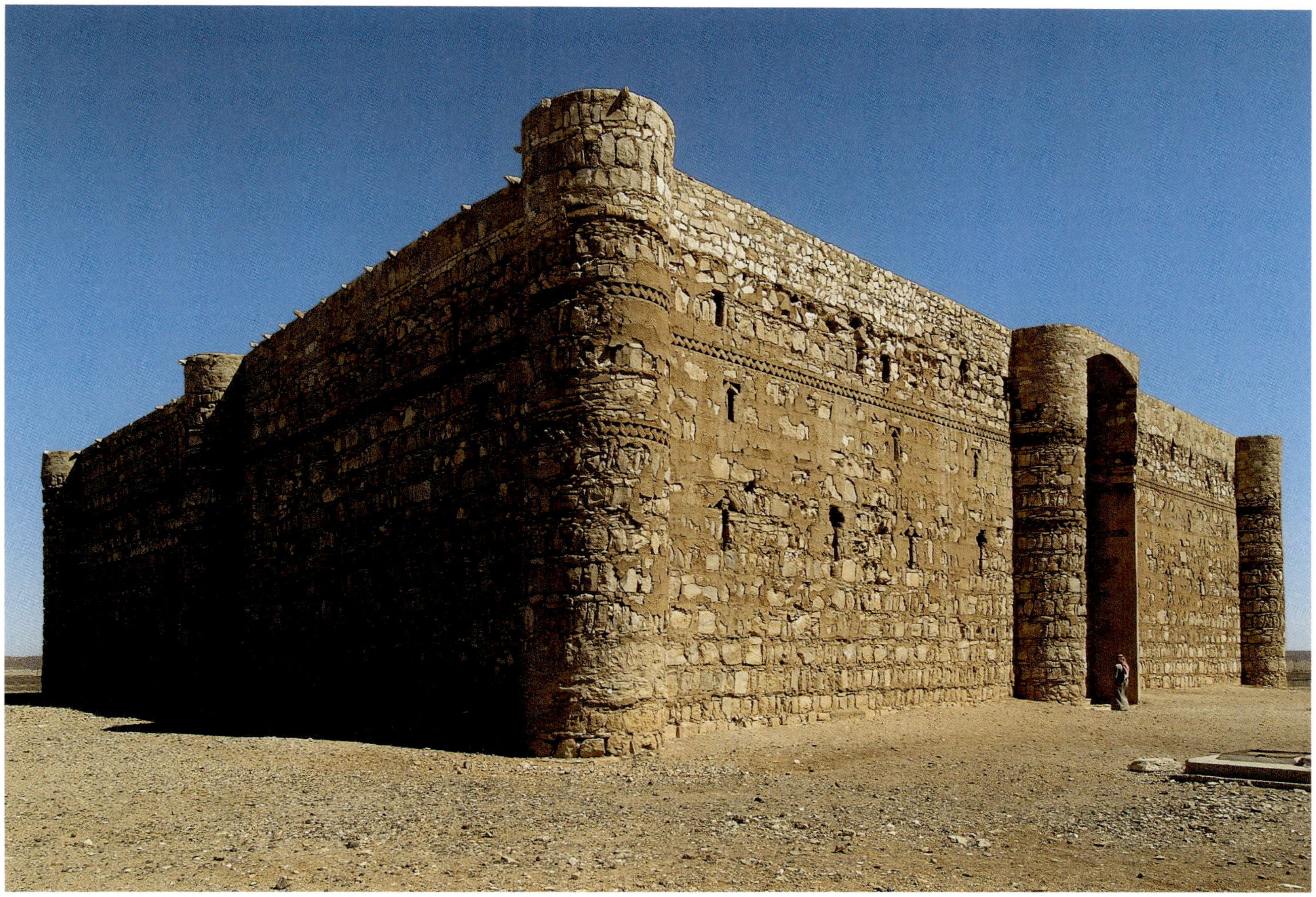

Al-Kharrana Qasr
Western ceremonial hall
705–710
Jordan

The interior is structured over two floors disposed around a central court. The lower storey was occupied by warehouses while the architecturally more elaborate upper floor housed the offices. The similarities to Sassanid palaces, notably in the triple engaged columns and in the types of roofing cover, are striking.

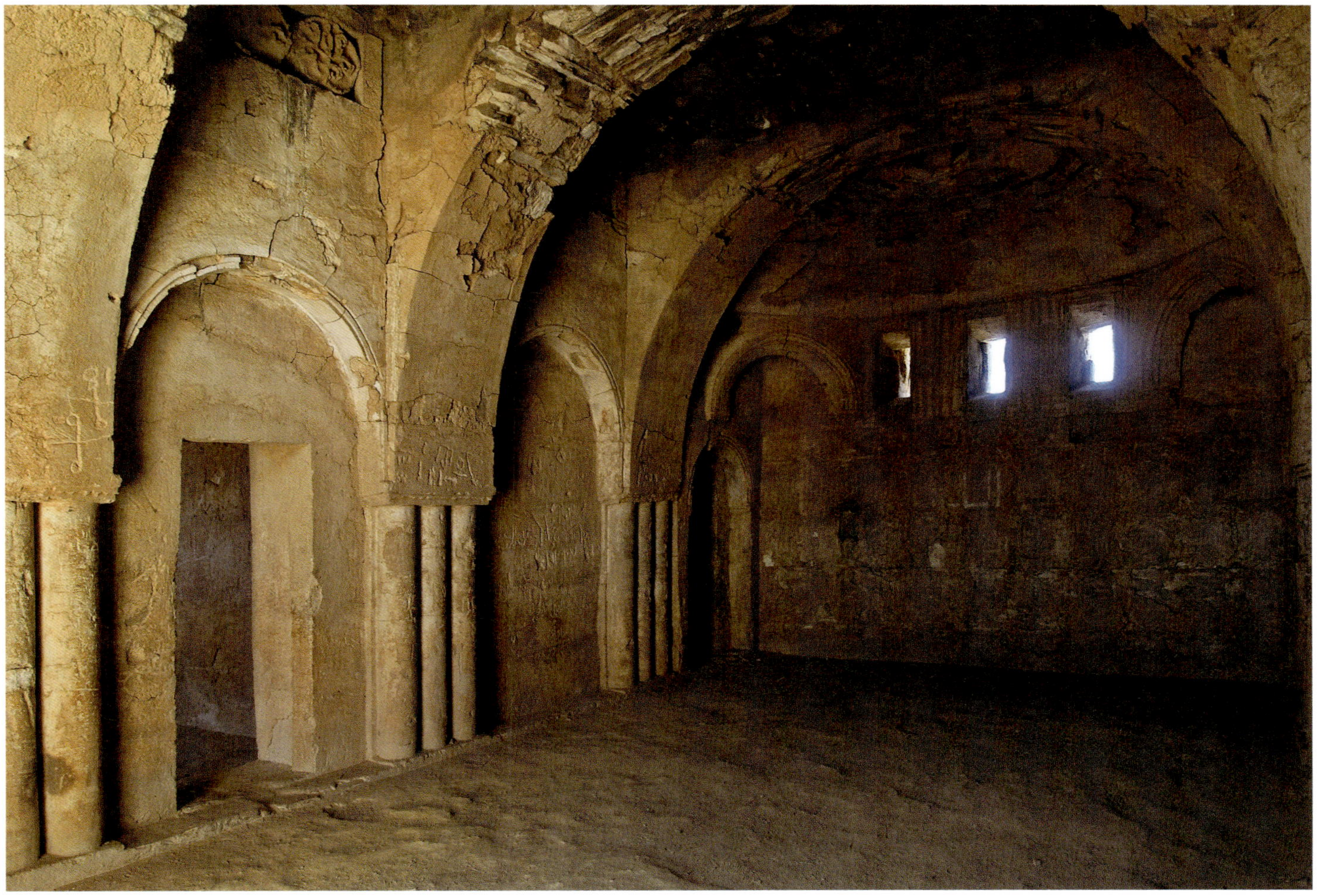

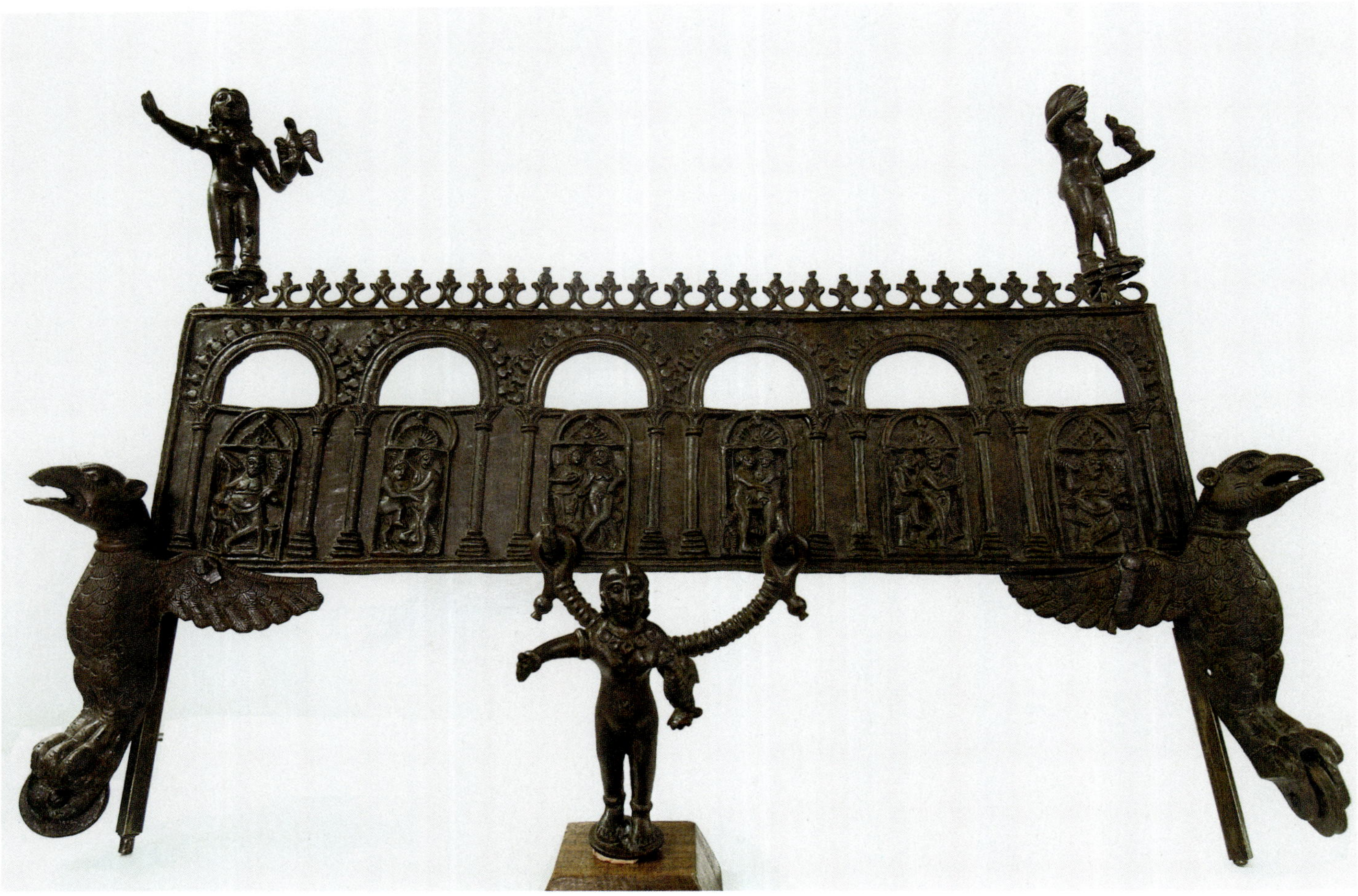

Fragment of a brazier
First half of the 8th century
Bronze and iron
From the palace of al-Fudayn (Mafraq)
Jordan Archaeological Museum, Amman

This fragment constituted one of four sides of a brazier of refined manufacture depicting explicitly erotic scenes with couples engaged in various coital positions beneath an arcade. The tone and subject are analogous to those in licentious paintings found in baths in extramural residences, though here more attention is paid to anatomical details which are clearly lifted from late Hellenistic and Roman art. Though reinterpreted by artisans unacquainted with such a refined idiom, the subjects must have whetted the appetite of more than one wealthy patron. The eagles supporting this section, mounted on wheels so it can be pushed about, as well as the smaller nude female figures hark back to oriental imagery with roots back in the Urartu kingdom in around the ninth century BCE.

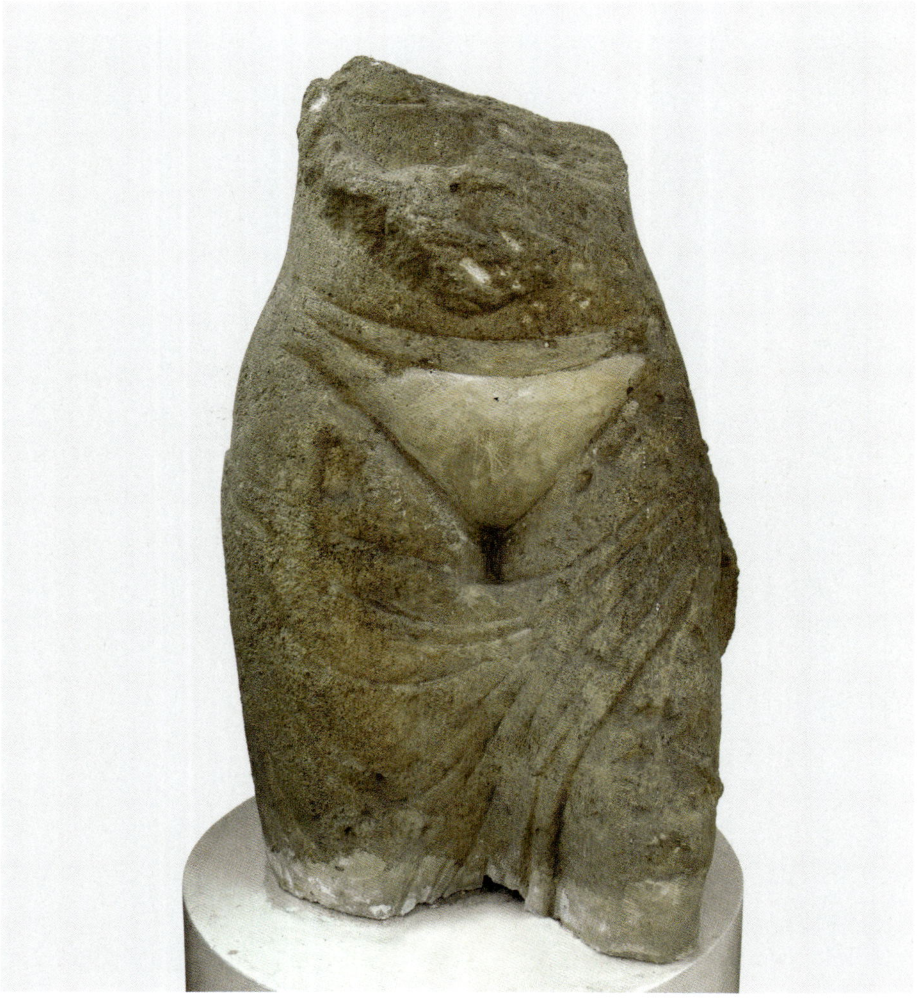

Fragment of a female statue
743–744
From the Qasr al-Mushatta
Jordan Archaeological Museum, Amman

The Qasr al-Mushatta Palace must have surely been one of the most exquisite of its time, as is demonstrated by the extraordinary external wall (today in Berlin) lined entirely in low-reliefs. Known only from vestiges that remain difficult to reconstruct, the interior decoration must also have been fabulous judging by this fragment from a large-sized statue representing a naked dancing-girl similar to those painted on the walls of the Qusayr Amra, which at one time were vibrant with colour. It constitutes a precious testimony of the more guilty pleasures of Umayyad aristocracy, prudently hidden from the eyes of the religiously-minded masses. The ponderous forms and awkward execution, however, are more reminiscent of Sassanid sculpture than of Hellenistic or Byzantine models.

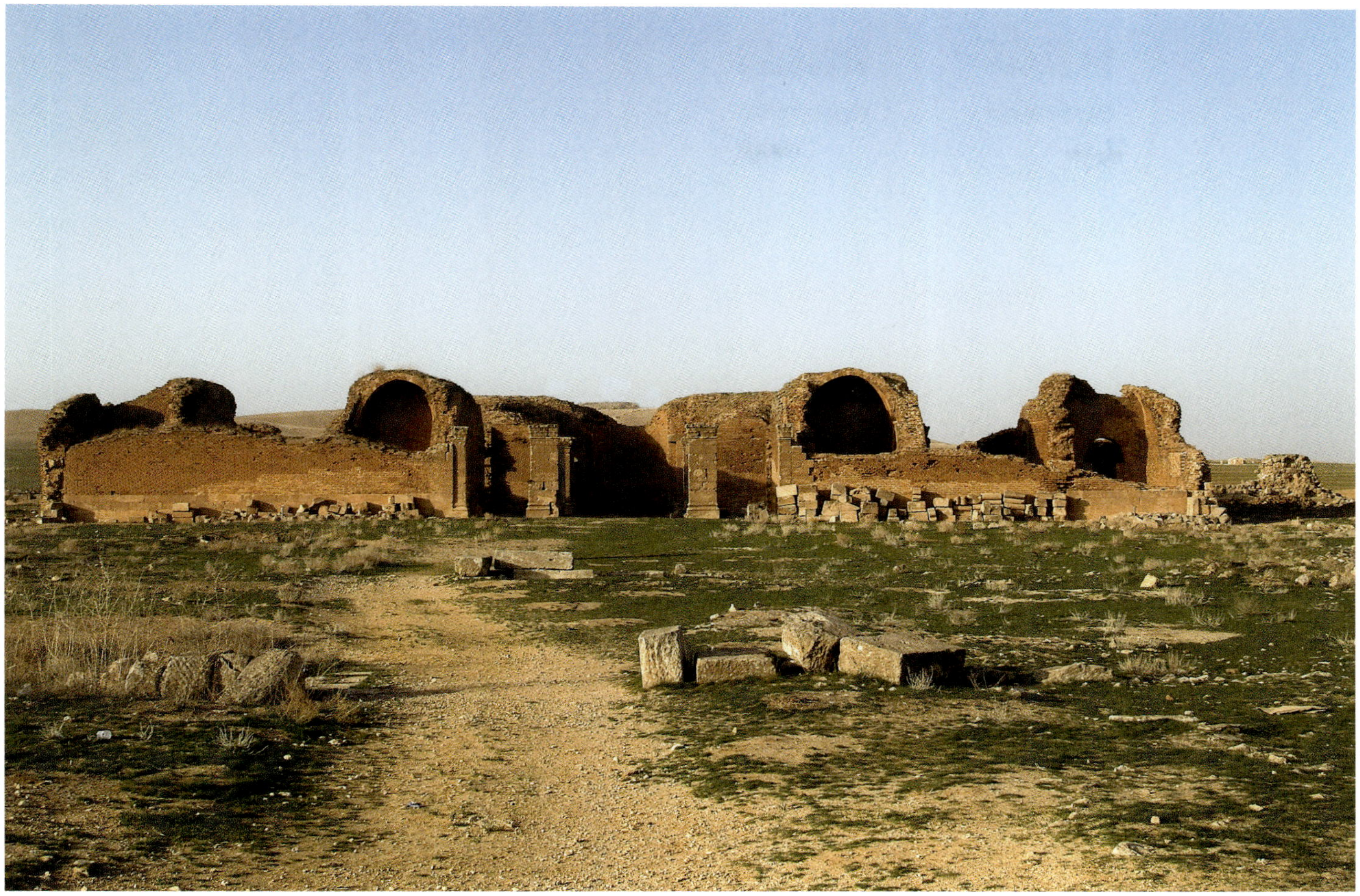

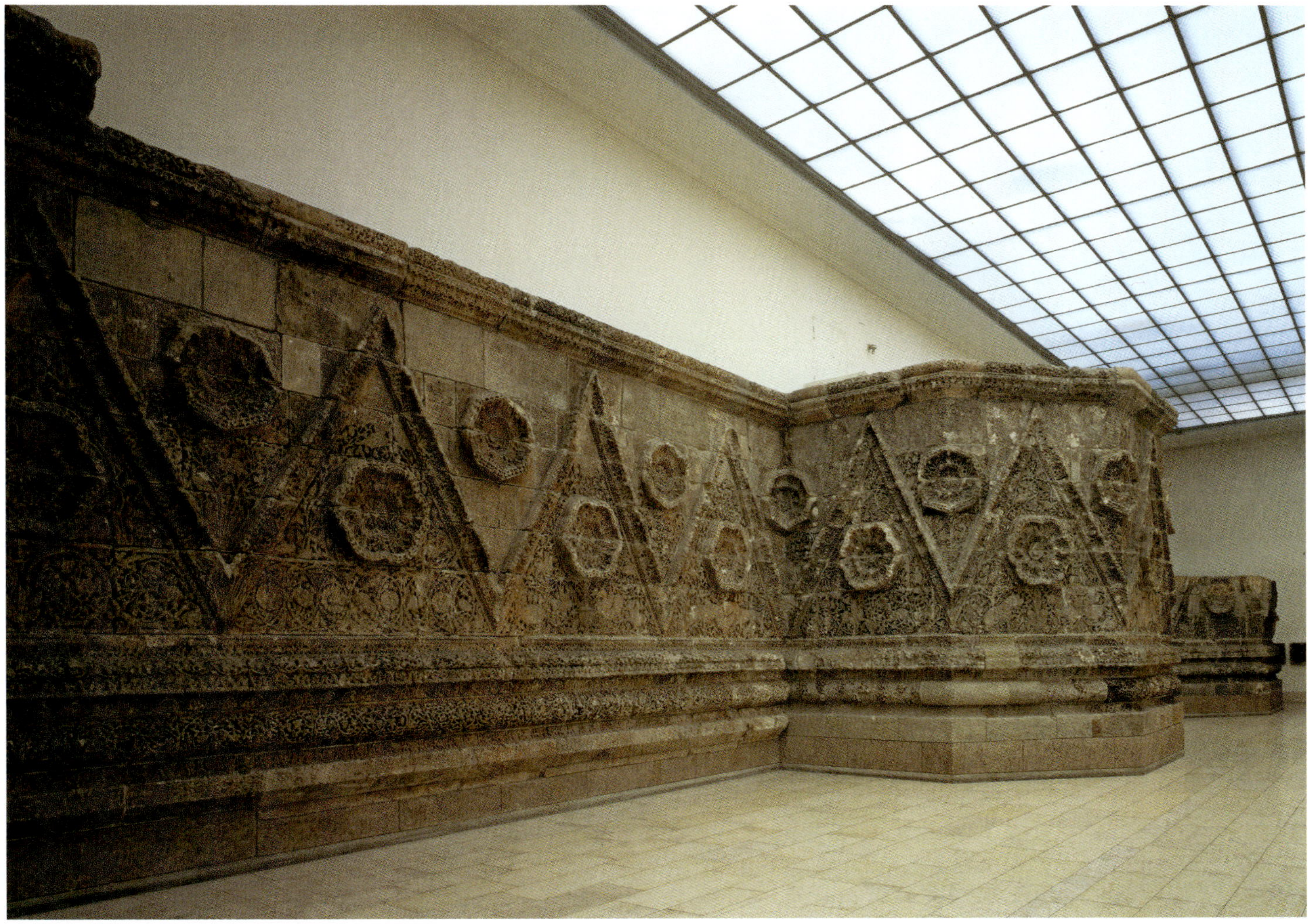

Qasr al-Mushatta
Façade
743–744
Jordan

The vast palace was encircled by a square perimeter wall with sides measuring 144 metres. At the centre stands the monumental triple-nave audience hall, spanned by a great vault of Sassanid type, with three arches to the front, together with a throne room with triple apses, a small mosque and apartments that were never finished. The plan, construction methods and details show the influence of a combination of styles: Byzantine, in the use of stone for the external walls, and Sassanid, in the use of brick for the internal walls and vaulting. Apparently designed to accommodate a large number of people, perhaps an entire court, it was also perfectly adapted to the celebration of grand ceremonies with spectacular processions.

Qasr al-Mushatta
Part of the outer wall
743–744
Museum für Islamische Kunst, Berlin

Standing some four metres high, the retaining wall in front of the entrance was adorned by a sumptuous carved decor of animals and, above all, of plants, unfurling over a single order emblazoned with enormous zigzagging triangles. In past times the surface was worked as delicately as embroidery so that it shone vibrantly in the bright sunshine. Mediating between the plain below, the upper undecorated reaches of masonry, and the infinite sky beyond, it must have been pervaded by a feeling of *horror vacui*.
Presented by Sultan Abdulhamid to Kaiser Wilhelm II as a gift in 1903, the wall was taken apart stone by stone and transported to Berlin. The interior decoration was enriched with animal motifs: rows of partridges and mountain goats on the dome bases, winged horses in the spandrels, and a veritable menagerie of monkeys, rabbits and animals similar to pigs, carved according to models recalling those of Iran.

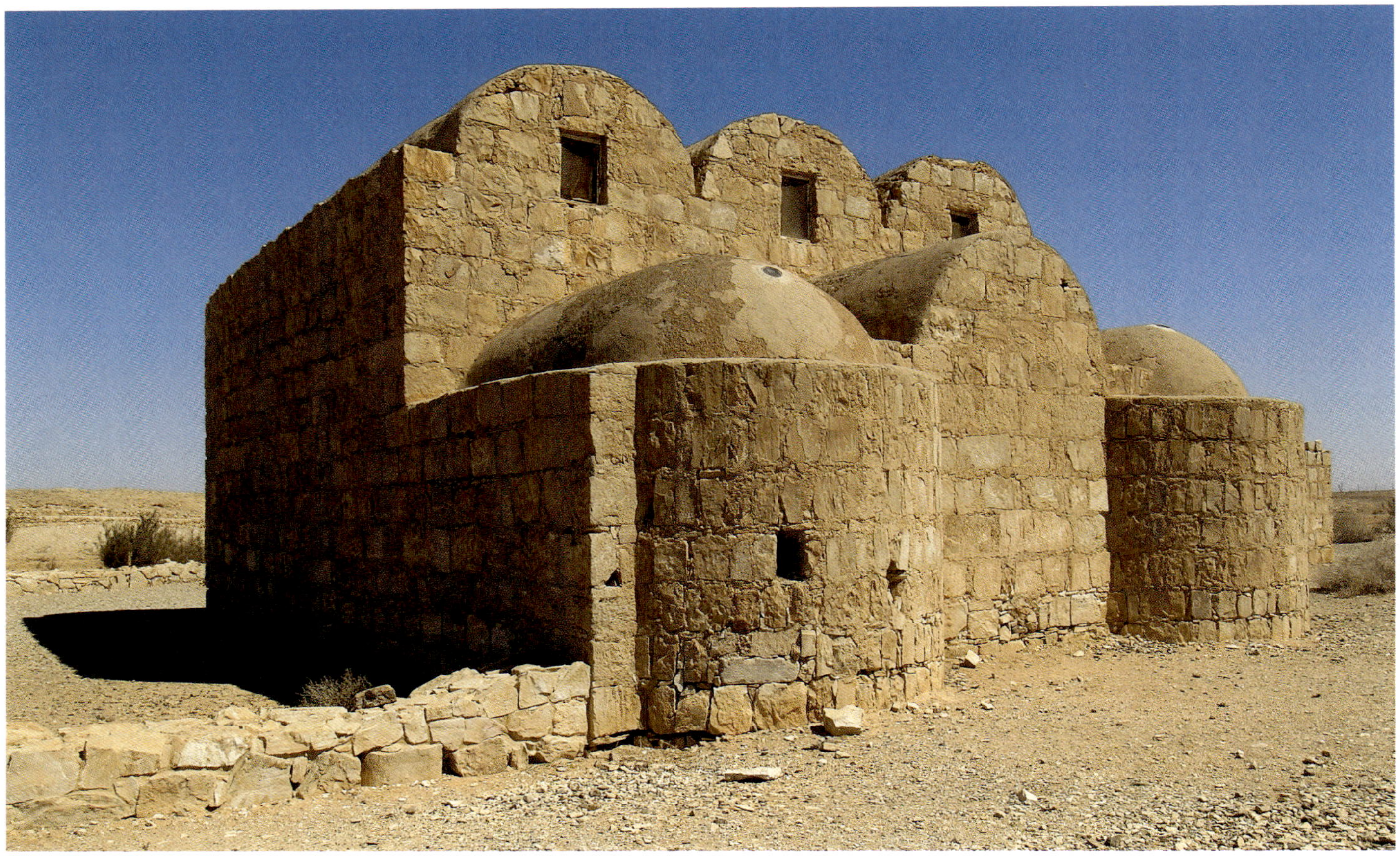

Qusayr Amra
711
Jordan

Built for Caliph al-Walid, this relatively small complex comprises an audience hall leading to modest but elegant *thermae* based on Roman models. The most interesting feature is the paintings that cover virtually every surface in the ceremonial halls and the baths, where the scenes take on an erotic character. By constrast the dome of the *calidarium* is decorated with subjects of an astronomical nature derived from classical Roman art.

Khirbat al-Mafjar
Mosaic pavement in the audience hall
724–744
Jericho, Palestine

With its sixteen pillars topped by a small central dome and geometric panelling of the highest quality, the mosaic pavement in the large centrally planned bath-hall is the largest example to have come down to us from Antiquity. This urban complex also comprised a mosque and a sumptuous residence. Richly decorated with stucco, the mosaic in the apse of the great hall in the centre of the complex still survives. Exquisitely executed in a style reminiscent of woven fabric, the mosaic pavement presents a scene showing a pair of gazelles nibbling at the leaves of a tree, while on the other side a lion brings down one of their companions. This depiction is usually interpreted as an allegory of Umayyad power, juxtaposing the delights of life under their rule with the fury of the caliph when engaged in battle against his enemies. Taking a cue from the poets of the time, it is possible, however – indeed not unreasonable – to assume that the scene can also be read as an erotic allegory.

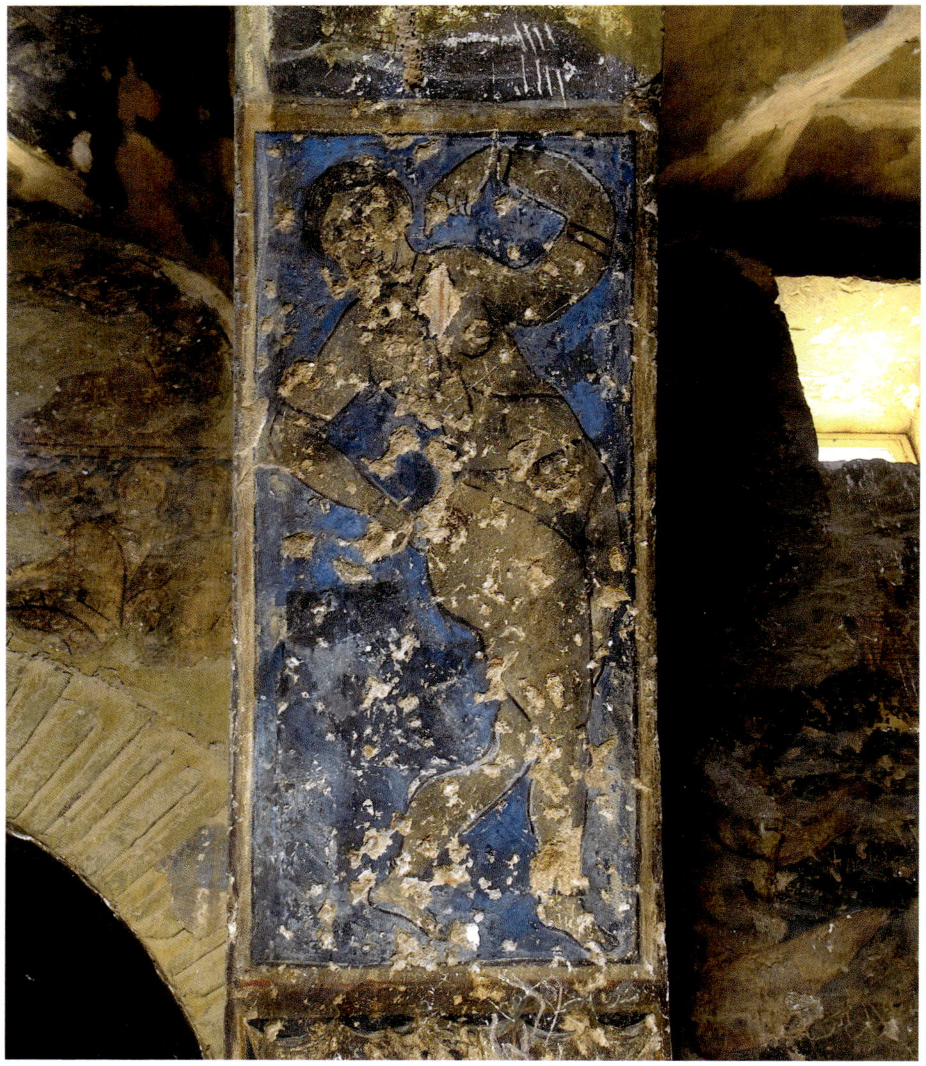

Qusayr Amra
Detail of the wall decorations in the reception hall representing a dancer
711
Jordan

Extolling the merits of the caliph, the paintings show the great and good of the sublunary realm rendering him homage: the Byzantine emperor; Roderick, the ruler of Visigothic Spain; Chosroes (Khusraw), emperor of Persia; and Negus, emperor of Abyssinia. Other scenes offer a tantalizing snapshot of court life: hunting scenes of Hellenistic character; scantily clad dancing-girls of Iranian or Indian derivation; in the apse the prince redolent of a Byzantine Christ; young gymnasts performing exercises; craftsmen at their trades; and animals playing music.

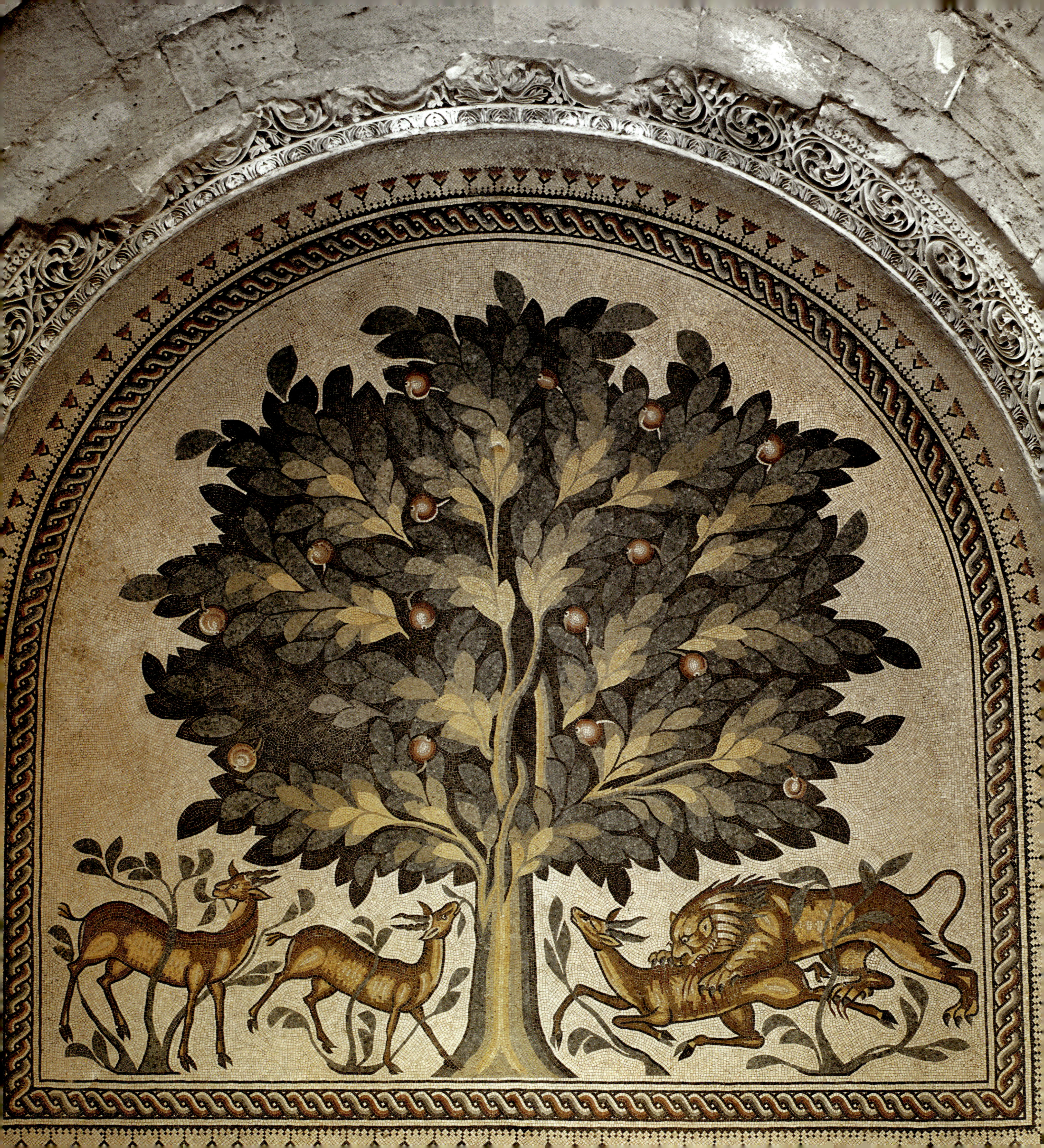

THE 'ABBASIDS: EMPIRE OF THE CALIPHATE

The 'Abbasids, who came to prominence in 750 after overthrowing the Umayyads, transformed the nature of the caliphate from elective to dynastic. This new mode of governance was signalled by the foundation of Baghdad, a capital in keeping with the new political equilibrium that controlled major communication routes: the urban fabric of this cosmopolitan linchpin of Islamic civilization was to outgrow Constantinople, expanding to become the largest city in the world at the time. To obviate a problem that had already eroded the Umayyads' power base, the 'Abbasids recognized all Muslims as equals. They abolished the privileges of the Arabs, recruiting an army of slaves and mercenaries devoted to the dynasty; they also undermined the military power of the tribes and centralized the administration and government, handing over the provinces to trusted governors whom they replaced frequently.

This explicitly imperial program was publicly enshrined in ceremonies, arts and architecture that deliberately imitated Byzantine and Sassanid models and elevated the caliph to a position of remote kingship. In keeping with Umayyad tradition, the mosque became a focus of generous patronage and a symbol of the caliph's power that was rooted in an amalgam of religion and politics. The caliphs assumed pompous-sounding titles reflecting what was thought of as their messianic mission, proclaiming themselves the "shadow of God on earth" and intervening in decisions relating to doctrinal discussions. The palaces in which they lived and the cities they founded attest to their majesty, making them appear more as the successors of the 'infidel' emperors than mentors of the faithful. This thorny dilemma was tackled by various religious and philosophical schools which, in proposing

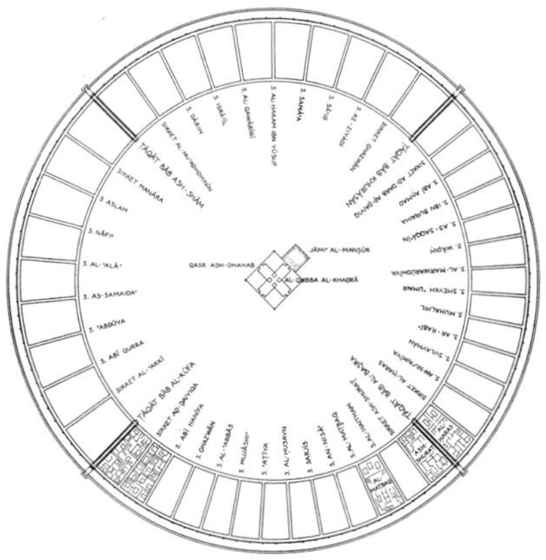

Plan of Baghdad
hypothetical reconstruction
after K. A. C. Creswell

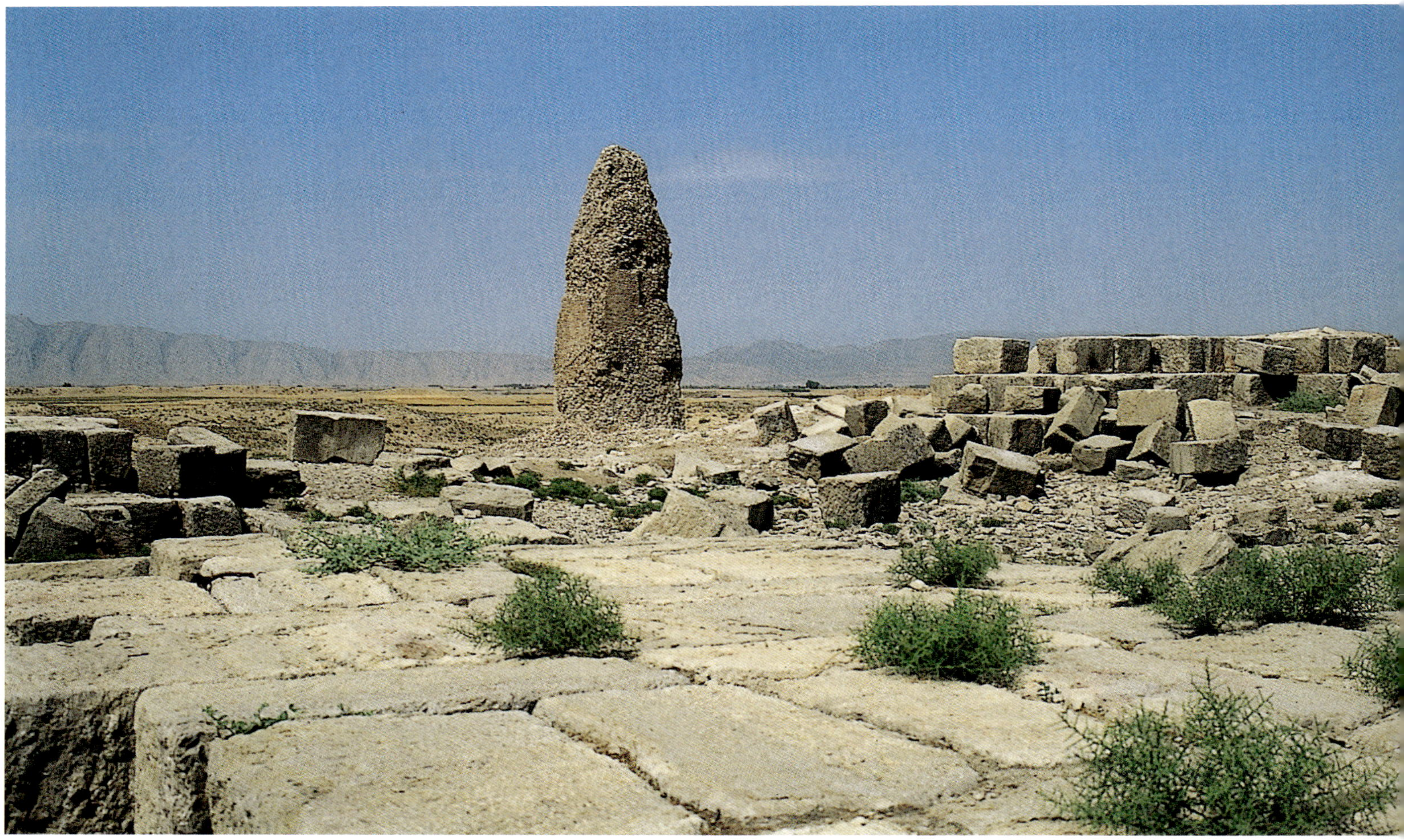

The tower at the centre of the circular city of Khurra
c. 224, Sassanid period
Firuzabad, Iran

various interpretations of the Qu'ranic revelation, undercut the absolutism of the 'Abbasid caliphate and evolved a vision of an independent Islam often in opposition to the power of the state under the aegis of spiritual masters.

Founded in Persia on the banks of the Tigris on the famous site of Baghdad by the caliph al-Mansur in 762, the new Islamic metropolis of legendary splendour that had taken the place of Umayyad Damascus was known as Madinat as-Salam, that is, 'City of Peace', an allusion to the 'Abbasid *pax* that had put an end to the bloody internecine strife for the succession that had ravaged the Islamic world. In studied imitation of Parthian and Sassanid models, the city plan represented the universal order as projected on earth. Encircled by a ring of perfectly circular walls fortified by 113 towers, it was entered through four symmetrically disposed entrances each crowned by a dome on which, it seems, was placed a rotating sculpture. Each faced one of the most important regions in the Islamic world instead of the cardinal points – an explicit reference to the new world order. Proceeding through a series of concentric rings comprising the districts in which the population was split up into the various ethnic, tribal and economic groups of the empire, the visitor then reached a vast central esplanade occupied by government buildings. The symbolic axle of this many-spoked wheel was of course the caliphal complex, including a classic columnated mosque and a palace of unknown structure: the sources speak of a generous reception room and audience hall roofed with a vast green dome (a symbol of paradise), on which stood an equestrian statue.

'Abbasid architecture is characterized by a predilection for the colossal bequeathed by the Sassanids. Although it has completely vanished from Baghdad, it is well-documented at Samarra, a city founded by decree in 836 by the caliph al-Mutasim. Concerned about the risk involved in quartering a personal army of 70,000 Turkic slaves in the mother city, he had ordained the construction of a new capital a hundred or so kilometres upstream. Of this vast ensemble, approximately thirty-five kilometres long and with a width of some two to five kilometres, only a few under-researched vestiges remain. It must have been a fabulous site, characterized by immense blocks with mosques and gigantic palaces encircled by high walls, preceded by gardens and defended by monumental gates, arranged in a regular plan of intersecting perpendicular axes.

Known as the *asba* ('seventh'), the city of Kufa was also planned along symbolic lines. Within a disposition of seven circles the 'centre' is constituted by the seventh, while the peripheral rings are occupied by the rest of the city. The spaces left between these circular perimeters were set aside for refuse. Further new districts sprang up in twelve external circles. This general disposition can readily be converted into seven hexagons, a model still highly regarded in modern city-planning for its practical and social as well as symbolic value.

The forms of social organization and conceptions of the cosmos conveyed by the Greco-Roman model of the grid city and the circular oriental model are radically different: the former is the projection of a static universe lacking a visible focus and is therefore the expression of a sedentary life, while the latter manifests a more dynamic conception of the universe, whose sole point of reference is an idealized fulcrum, according to a symbolic typology frequently found in populations of nomadic ancestry.

Absolute rulers over an empire that exceeded the borders of that of Alexander the Great, the caliphs and the wealthier 'Abbasid élite had at their disposal practically unlimited funds and proved enthusiastic patrons of all the arts. They lived a life of luxury that is hard to imagine. Beside objects in metal and precious stones, pride of place was allotted to textiles, among which were sumptuous capes and carpets, an essential complement to their gorgeous furnishings. The production of the necessary materials, from clothes to dyes; their transport; and the trade in finished products, constituted key elements in the economy of the time. They were also the object of some brazen cases of industrial espionage, the prime example being the fraudulent import of the silkworm – a *sine qua non* for the production of the most sought-after raw material of all – that was purloined from China and packed off to Persia. Silk-embroidered tapestries and drapes, often decorated with threads of gold and generally adorned with stylized animals – on occasion facing head-on in the Sassanid taste or arranged in rows or circles – are documented from several pieces exported to the West and wrapped round precious relics of martyrs. Ceramic production also soared – fostered by a condemnation of objects in precious metals (a prohibition readily ignored, it should be said, by the members of the court) and by competition from Chinese products. Apart from superb polychrome examples, decorated with figurative scenes which tended to reflect the local cultural background and remained closely linked to the region in which they were produced, there also arose a more identifiably Islamic style. This was particularly in evidence in whiteware adorned with simple calligraphy, the most active centre for which was in Nishapur (northern Iran). The eleventh and twelfth centuries saw the development of the greatest centre of Iraqi production at Raqqa, with objects sporting the most elegant calligraphic designs beneath a green or blue transparent glaze. Sassanid traditions persisted for a long time in the field of metalwork, however, with the re-use of explicitly imperial subject matter allied with decoration of sober geometric character that replaced the lavish depictions of hunts and banquets.

With the exception of the court art and architecture of Samarra, the age of the 'Abbasids is basically a refined and simplified version inherited from the Umayyads but viewed through a sort of austerity readily sensed in the surfaces of their buildings, their wood panelling and their stucco decoration. Meanwhile, figurative scenes become increasingly rare. In a sense, 'Abbasid art marks the end of the predominance of Hellenistic models that had characterized the lands of the Mediterranean for more than a millennium.

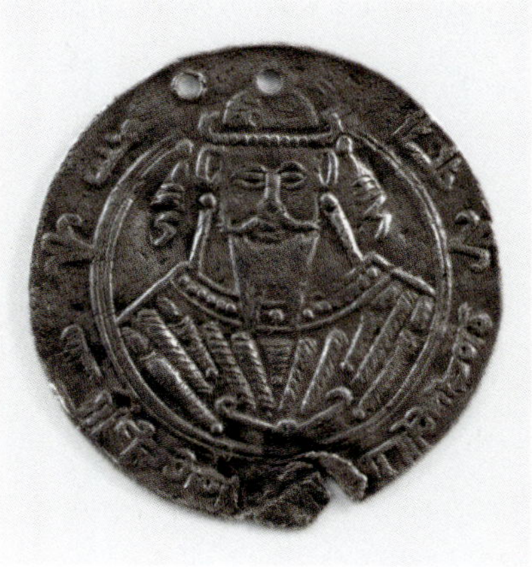

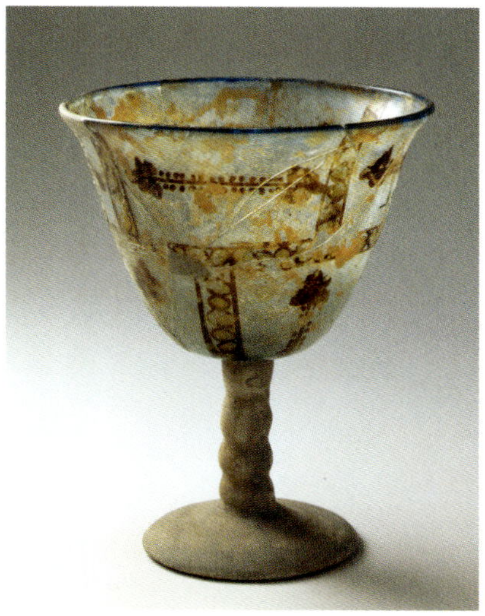

Medallion with a portrait of al-Mutawakkil
9th century
Silver
Kunsthistorisches Museum, Vienna

High-stemmed goblet
810
From Palace B at Raqqa, Syria
National Museum, Raqqa

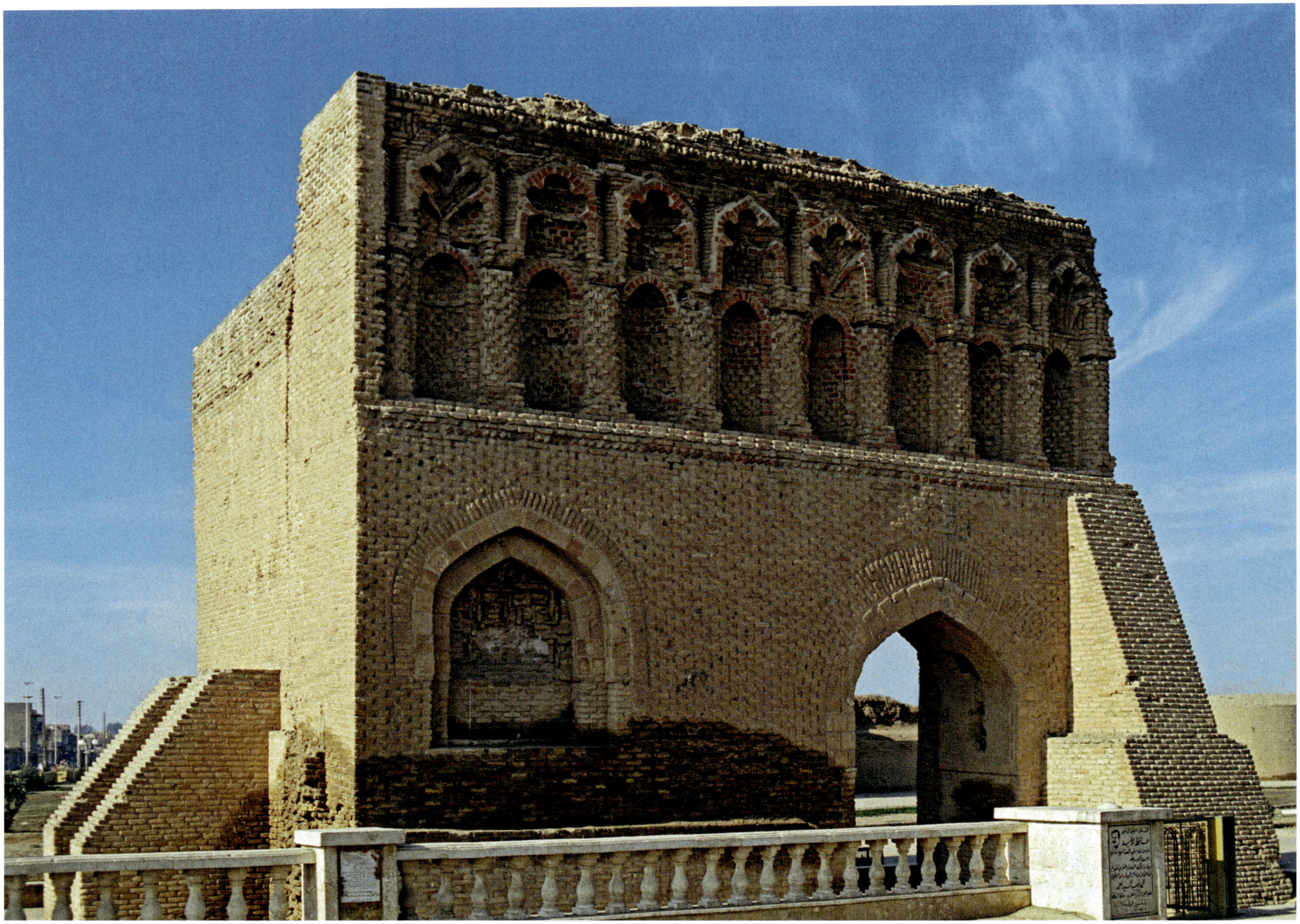

Baghdad Gate
c. 772 or 10th–11th century
Raqqa, Syria

Although badly mutilated and now far from splendidly isolated, the Baghdad Gate, built in sturdy fired bricks (the walls were made of unfired ones) is the most striking remnant of the celebrated 'Abbasid enceinte. Originally symmetrical, the structure unfolds in decorative elements, niches, semi-columns and scalloped arches, the chromatic effect being enhanced by the brickwork which is cleverly coursed to make the most of the slightest variation in sunlight. Of Mesopotamian descent, it was to have an immense impact on architectural developments throughout Persia and Central Asia. The pointed ogival arch is based on an unprecedented polycentric design. In the light of the progressive form of this arch, some scholars date the gate to a period posterior to the Palace of Ukhaidir (764–778), where the same design occurs in a less confident guise, dating it to a later stage in the history of this flourishing city (second only to Baghdad) around the tenth or eleventh century.

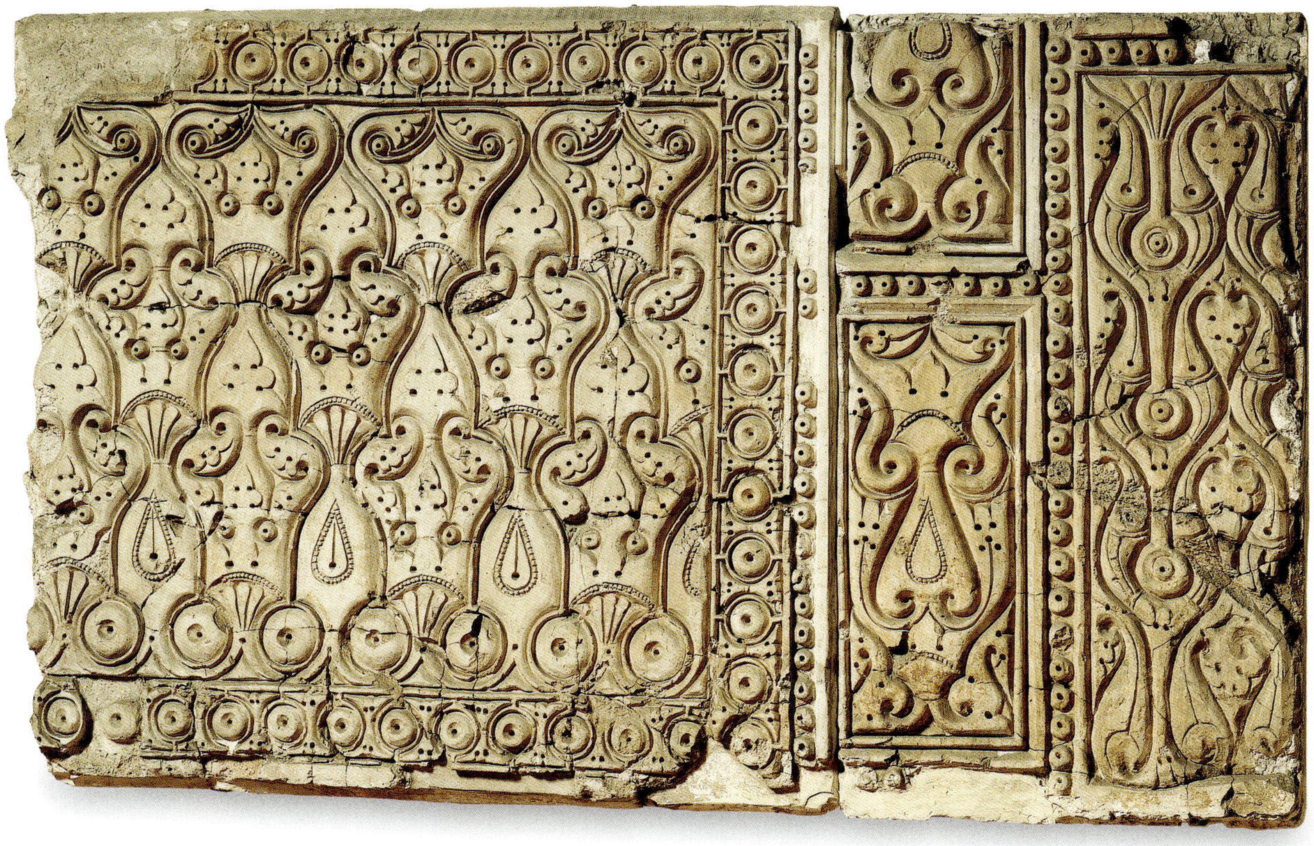

House 1, Samarra
Wall covering from Room 1
9th century
Stucco
Museum für Islamische Kunst, Berlin

House 1, Samarra
Detail of wall covering from Room 4
9th century
Stucco
Iraq Museum, Baghdad

As under the Sassanids, the problem of covering large surfaces in an aesthetic yet economical fashion was gloriously resolved by the use of stucco, plastered on the wall and worked with a stick or else prepared separately and stamped before being installed and finished at a later date, in what was a more rapid and less costly solution. The illustrated example belongs to this type, based on a vaguely vegetal motif repeated *ad infinitum:* when deployed on a large-scale, the repetition of such indefinite motifs can be imbued with a visionary, almost hypnotic magnetism typical of the Islamic concept of art.

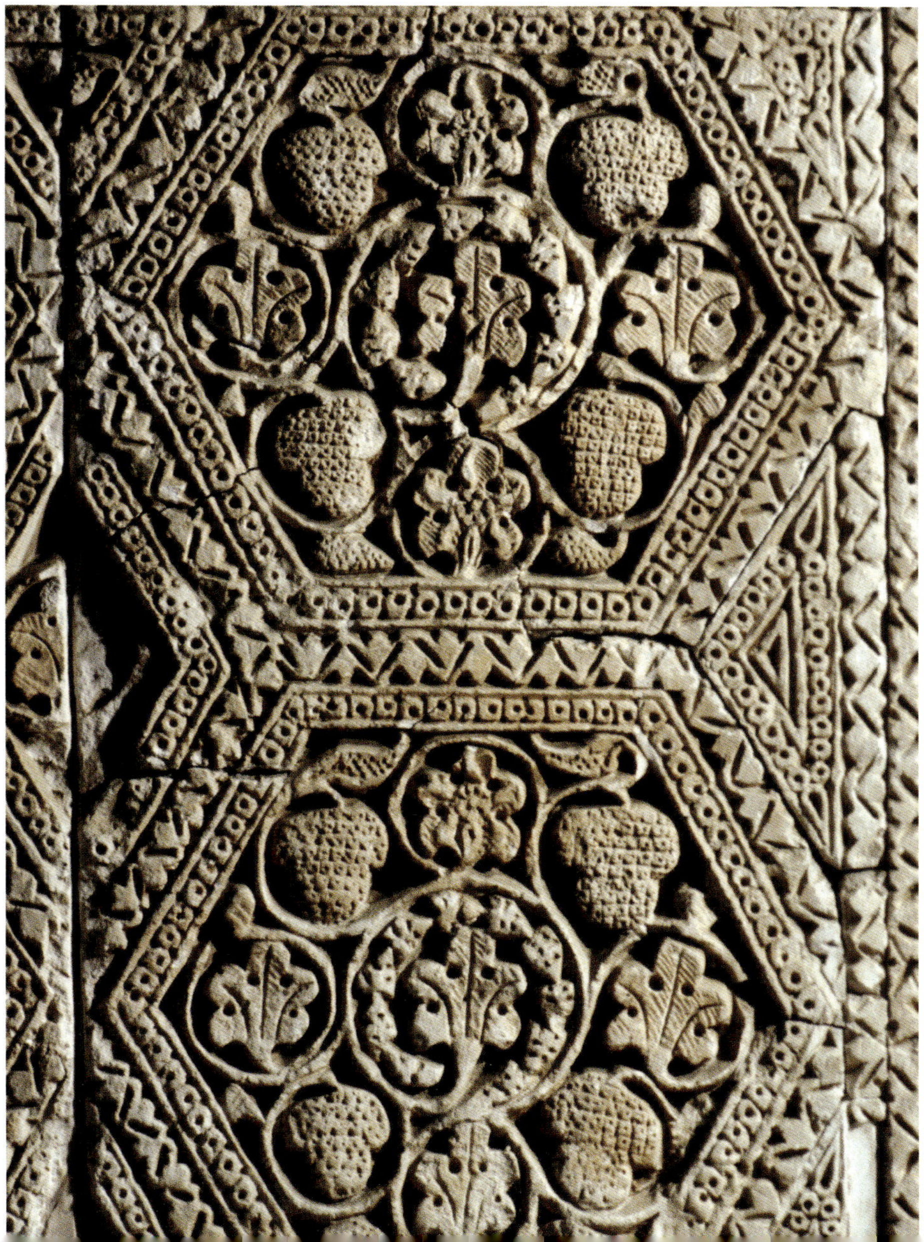

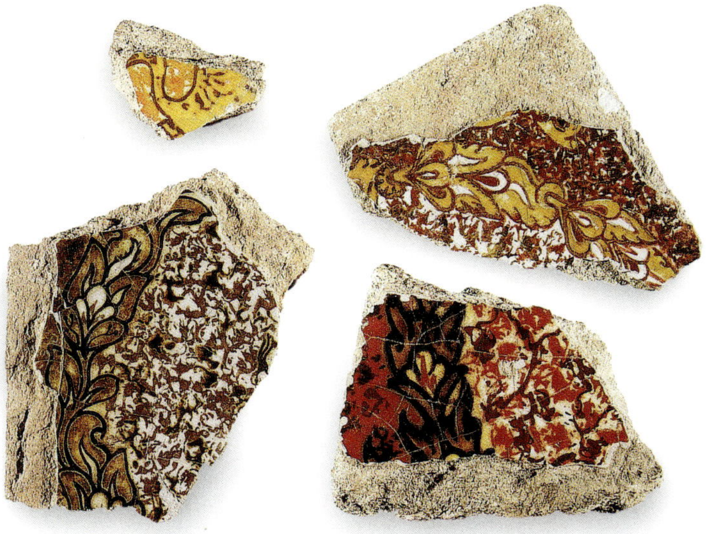

The Jawsaq al-Khaqani Palace, Samarra
Fragments from the wall decoration
836
Lustreware
British Museum, London

These fragments come from the colossal palace of al-Mutasim that stood on the banks of the Tigris. The splendid decor was composed of marble panels, stucco, wainscoting and frescoes that depicted court life in the tradition of pre-Islamic Iran and the Central Asian domain. Scant remnants survive of this wonderful decoration, including these fragments of lustre ceramic with a bird encircled by a garland in the centre. The refinement and dazzling splendour of its colouring affords tantalising glimpses into the felicity and glory that filled the palace many centuries ago.

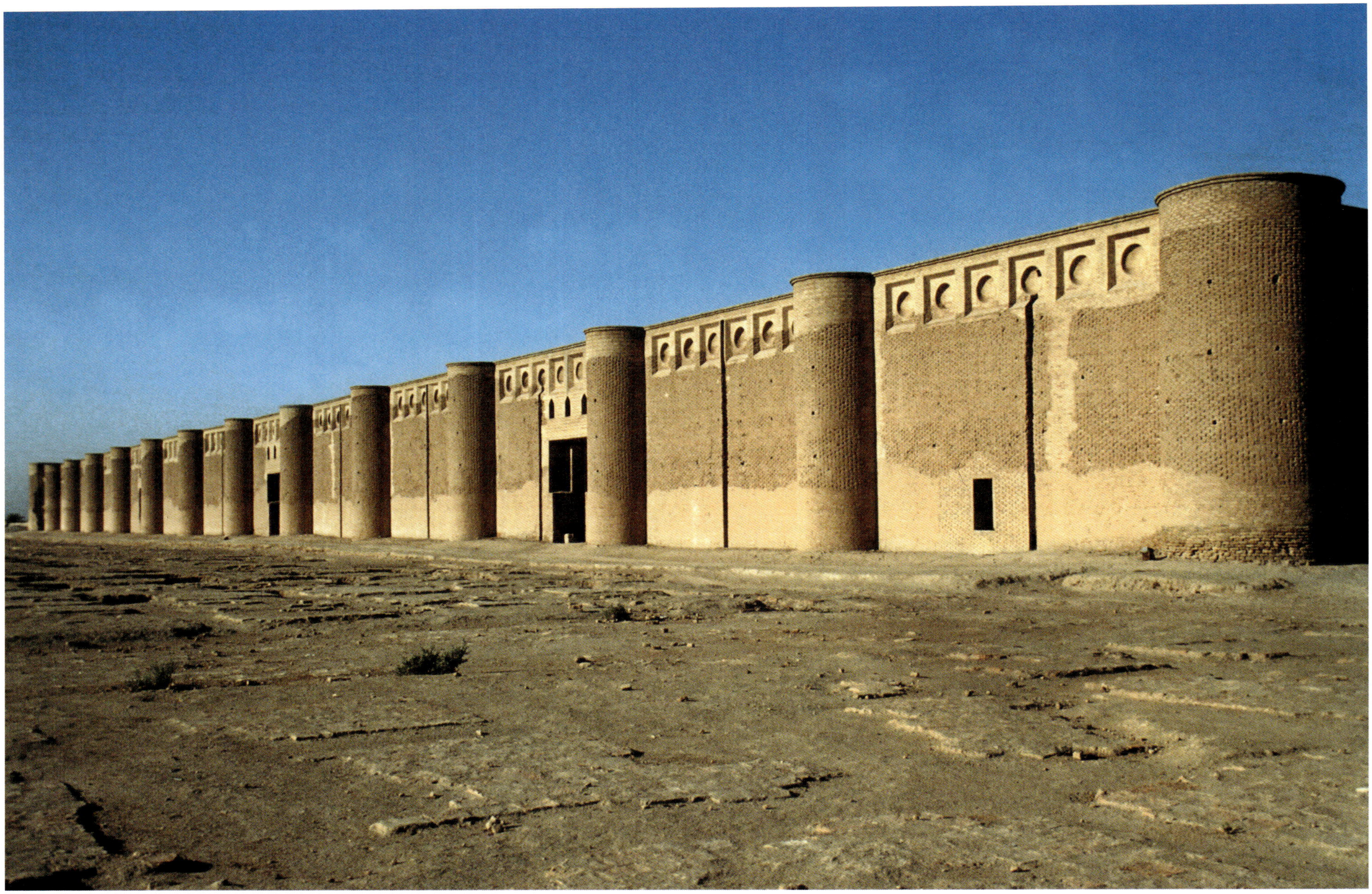

Great Mosque of al-Mutawakkil
848–852
Samarra, Iraq

Realized within the space of a few years, the Great Mosque of Caliph al-Mutawakkil is the product of a convergence between the "functional symbolism" of Islamic conception and the "sacred gigantism" of ancient Mesopotamia as expressed iconically in the ziggurat. The solemn simplicity of the classically structured mosque with prayer hall and courtyard is inflated here to colossal dimensions, without however losing touch with the ideal model at Medina. Studded with forty-four sturdy plain semicircular towers between which runs a frieze composed of square elements inserted with circles, the perimeter wall conveys a solemn and austere sensation of overwhelming power.

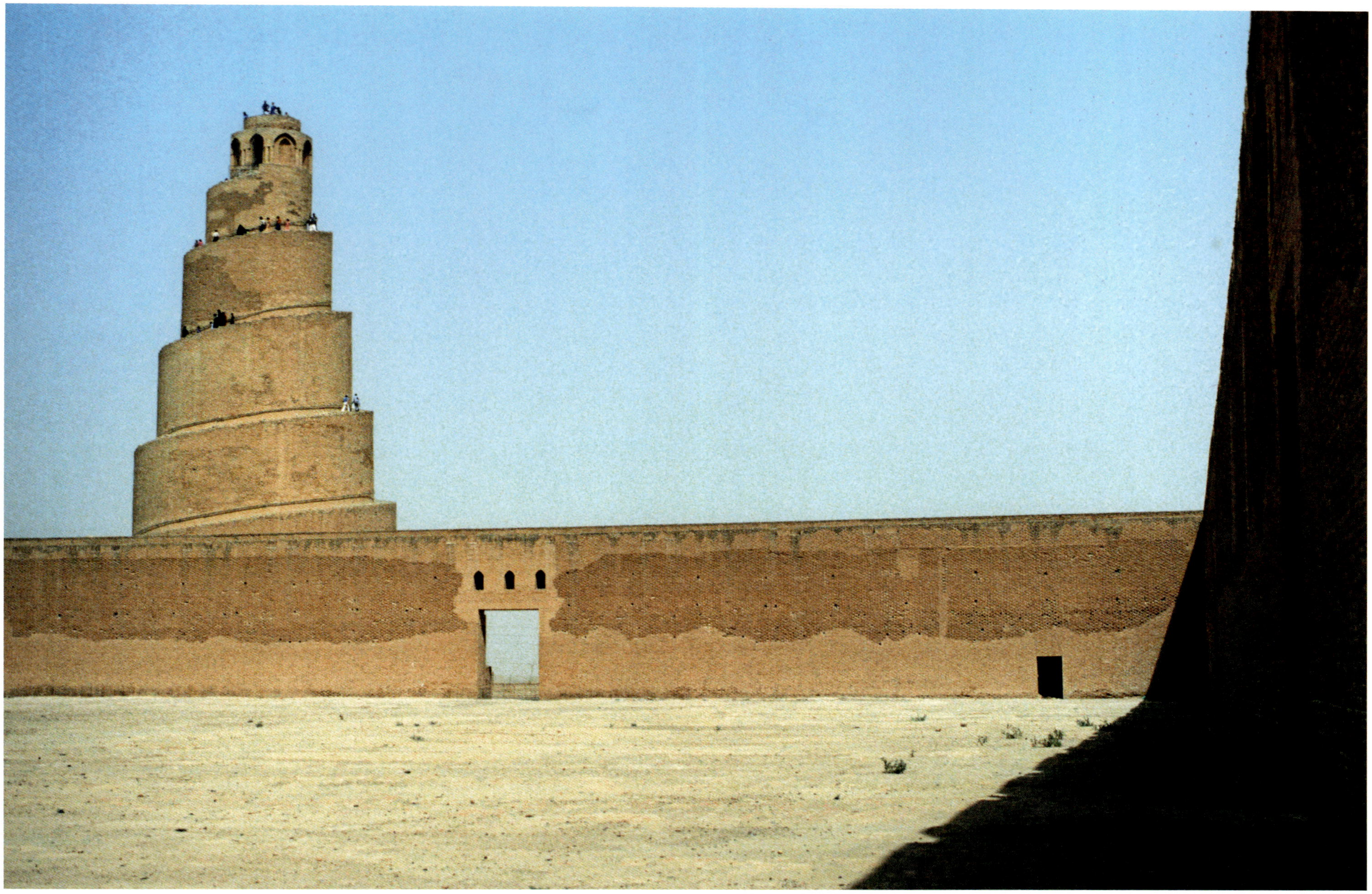

Great Mosque of al-Mutawakkil
Interior of the enceinte
848–852
Samarra, Iraq

The inner space, the largest in all Islam (240 x 156 metres), is empty today, but at one time it was decorated with glass paste mosaics and carved wooden panels. Originally the 456 supports, stuccoed clustered brick pillars painted to imitate marble and each flanked by four *spolia* columns, ran round the central courtyard that opens to the south onto the prayer hall, comprising twenty-five aisles perpendicular to the *qibla*. The flat teak ceiling rested directly on the pillars, like an image of heaven borne on an infinite forest of trees in rows, in perfect keeping with this type of mosque.

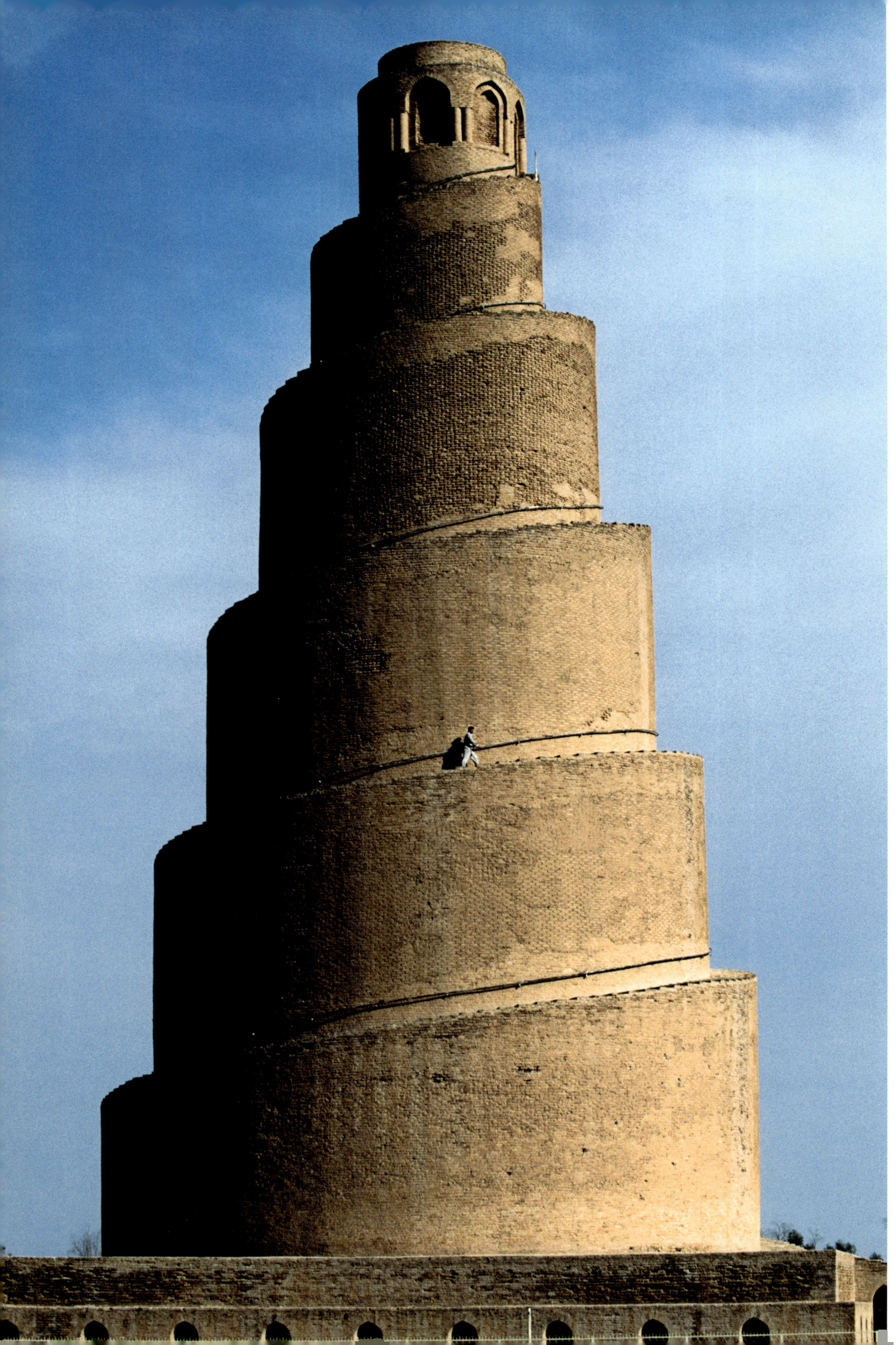

Great Mosque of al-Mutawakkil
Minaret
848–852
Samarra, Iraq

Perfectly aligned with the middle of the northern façade of the mosque, the renowned helical minaret (Manaret al-Malwiya) seems to twist up from the sterile desert dust into the flawless gleam of the sky, transfiguring the ponderous matter as it slowly ascends, dispersing it into the impalpable air. Fifty metres high on the square plinth (restored) thirty-three metres wide and three metres high on which it rests, the minaret is connected to the mosque down a (restored) sloping ramp, passing over a bridge and joining it smoothly where the spiral fuses with the square base. As the ramp climbs it narrows and becomes steeper, keeping the stages the same height and terminating before the southern niche whence a still narrower staircase ascends to the terrace at the summit, once crowned by a pavilion borne on eight wooden columns: to put it mildly, a sublime manifestation of the idea of ascension through religion. The image of the muezzin leaving the mosque, circumambulating up the seven stages of the tower to call the faithful to prayer, is without doubt one of the most glorious inventions in all Islamic art. The resemblance to ancient Mesopotamian ziggurats, so often referred to, is here carried off with unsurpassed lyricism.

Palace of Ukhaidir
764–778
Iraq

The complex presents a rectangular plan ensconced within a stout outer wall 175 x 169 metres and currently seventeen metres high. The enceinte's defensive function is emphasized by loopholes in rooms in the towers and by embrasures at the summits of the pairs of colossal blind arcades that alternate with ten burly three-quarter-circle towers on each side terminating in round towers at the corners. The median axis is signalled by a kind of flanged tower equipped with a battery of sophisticated devices to ward off the poliorcetic strategies of the time (portcullis, arrow-slits, guardroom over the entryway). Together these contrivances bestow on the wall a buoyant and unforgettable chiaroscuro, even sculptural effect. Supported on huge arches, the caponier running along the walls combines savings in material with increased robustness and in all likelihood derives from the numerous Byzantine fortifications still visible on the Syrian border.

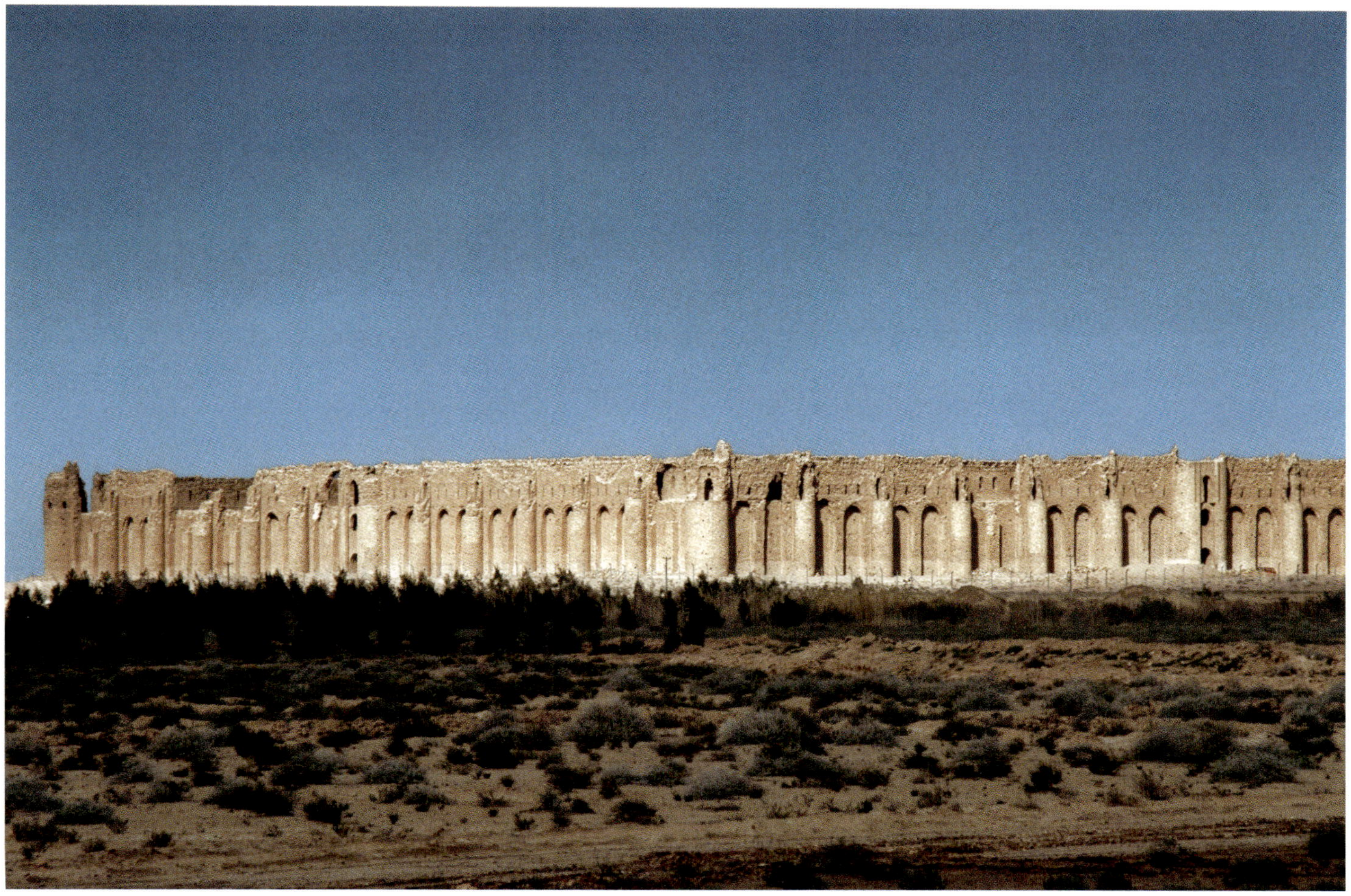

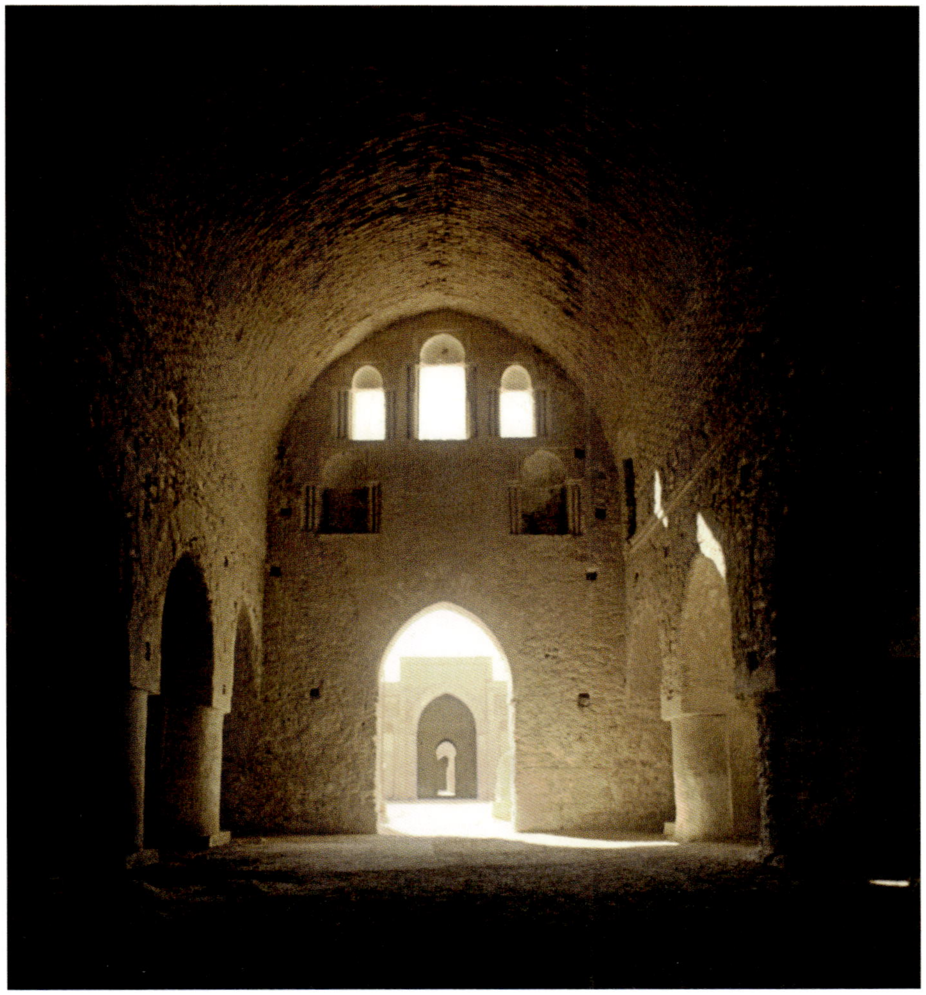

Ukhaidir Palace Hall
764–778
Iraq

This spacious and solemn space, around seven metres wide by fifteen deep and ten high, is vaulted with drop arches of brick resting on a series of stocky semi-cylindrical pillars lacking capitals to the sides which open into perpendicular recesses bolstering and relieving the mass of the wall. It is a solution that clearly recalls earlier Sassanid examples, such as the palace of Bahram V at Sarvistan, also harking back to construction techniques that deploy roughly hewn stone generously mortared and daubed in plaster in the lower section. The particularly elegant rear of the façade, with three rounded lancets and two blind windows framed by a brace of semi-columns, seems to anticipate a number of achievements of Cistercian architecture. Its present-day appearance, however, is not what would have been seen in the past: stucco decoration and furnishings, such as carpets, of which rare but splendid examples survive, used to cover every surface.

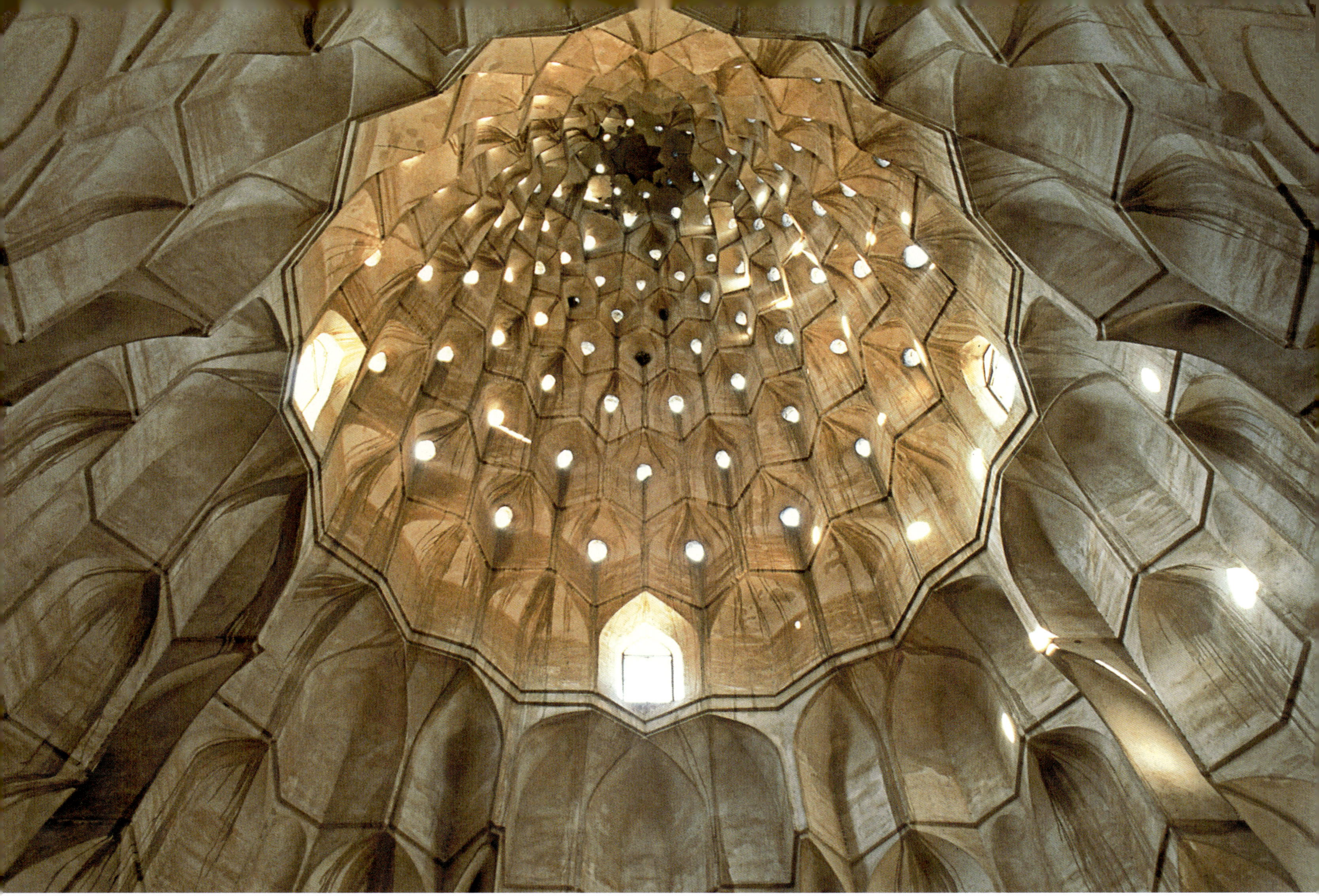

Mausoleum of Zumurrud Khatun, known as of 'Sitta Zubaida'
Interior of the cupola with *muqarnas*
1179–1225
Baghdad, Iraq

The renowned mausoleum was constructed by the caliph al-Nasir for his mother, Sitta Zubaida, in a cemetery reserved for burying people of noble birth. The interior space is an inverted reflection of the external structure, the latter boldly soaring into the sky, the former extending like a kind of infinite stairway into a dazzling, chiselled penumbra, multiplying to infinity in a stellar glow that wafts up from the unfathomable depths of the cosmos. The gossamer line of demarcation between one order of *muqarnas* and the next exalts the sense of distance until it culminates in the motif of the star plunged into mysterious half-light at the summit.

Mausoleum of Zumurrud Khatun, known as of 'Sitta Zubaida'
***Muqarnas* with cupola**
1179–1225
Baghdad, Iraq

Standing on a base of octagonal plan from which the cupola surges up in spectacular fashion with the *muqarnas* imparting vibrant dynamism, the building is perfectly at one with its function. Probably of Iraqi origin, this 'honeycombing' technique consists in subdividing the surface of corner niches in a precisely geometric fashion so as to connect the successive tiers of the cupola as it ascends. Deeply carved in an arabesque motif known as *hazarbaf,* the terracotta is laid flush with the smoothed brick. The tomb represents an elaborate architectonic solution typical of the final flourishing of the 'Abbasid caliphate, by that time under Seljuq rule. The unmistakable 'sugar-loaf' outline, in which the honey-combs are visible while the window apertures remain hidden, was invented in ninth-century Samarra.

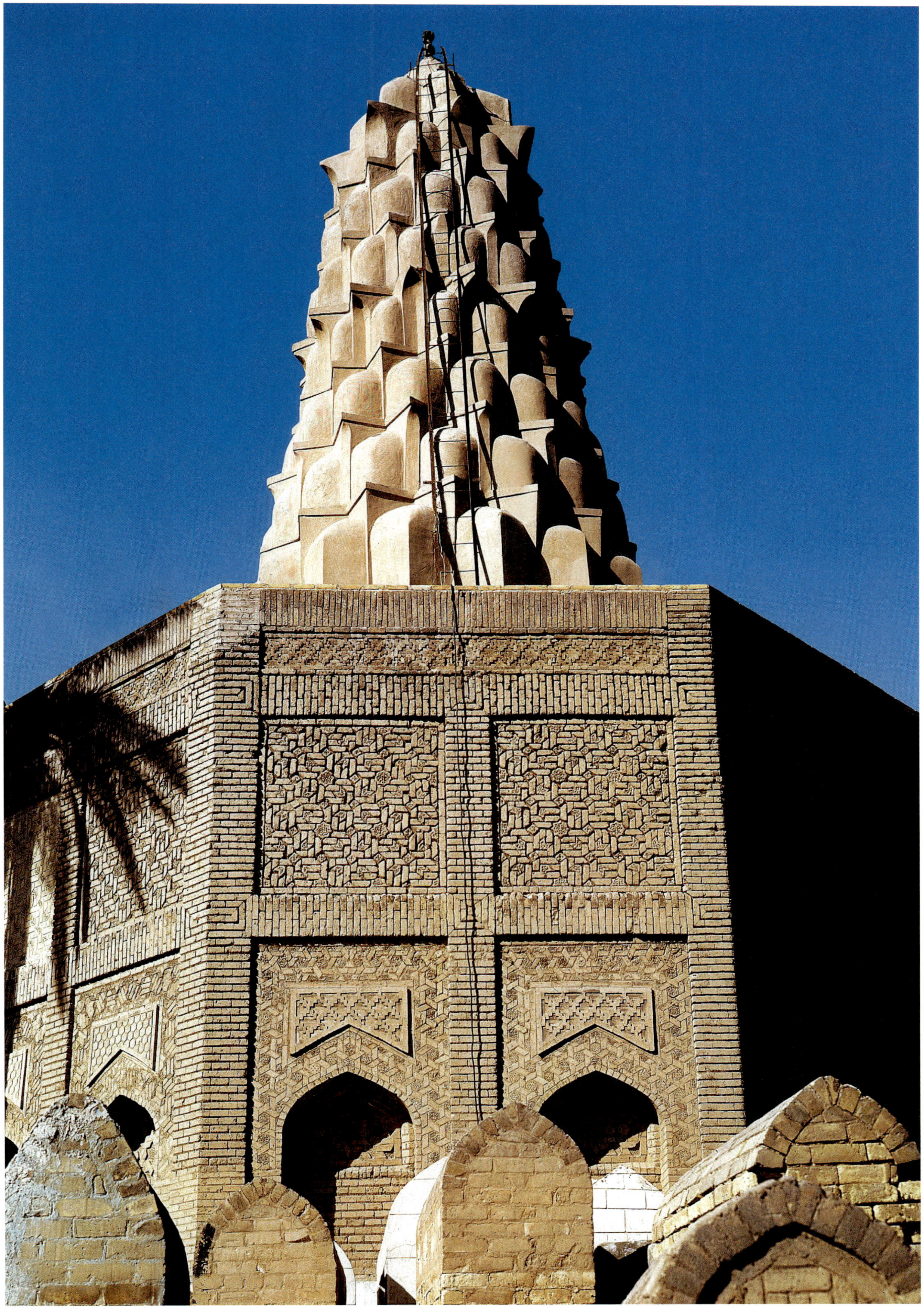

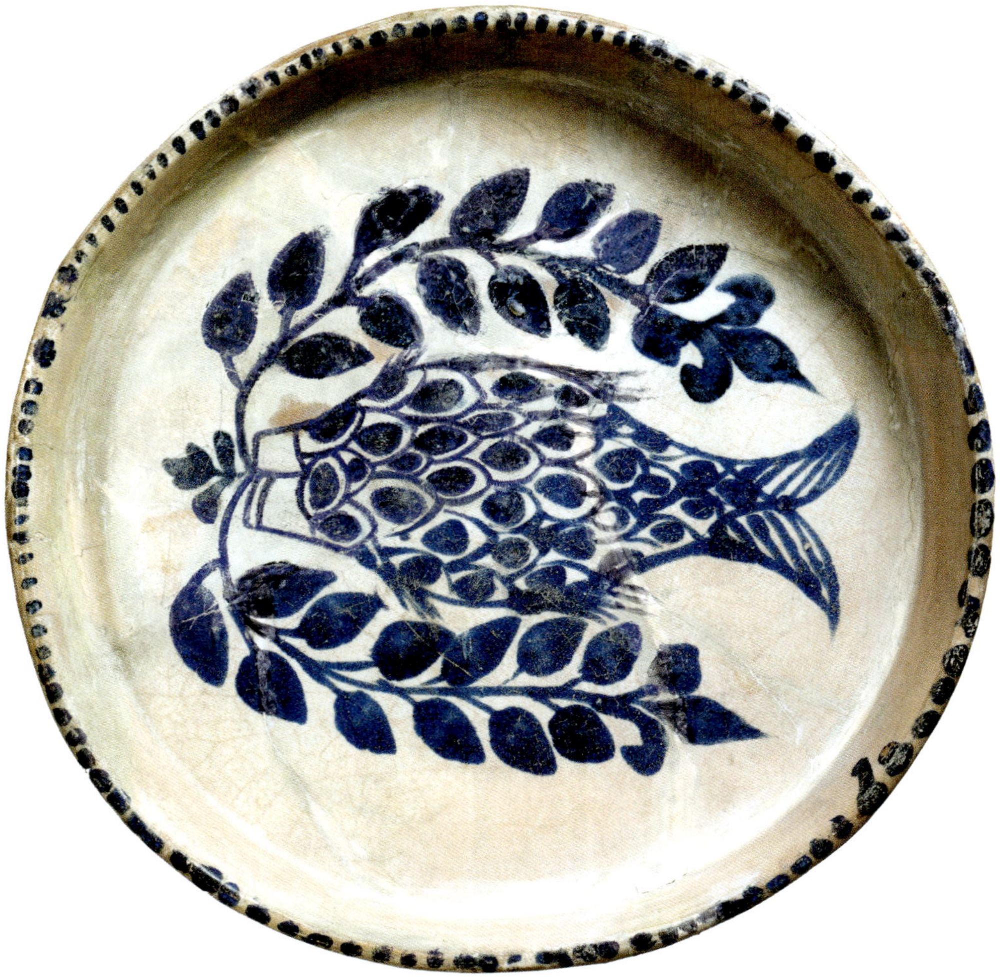

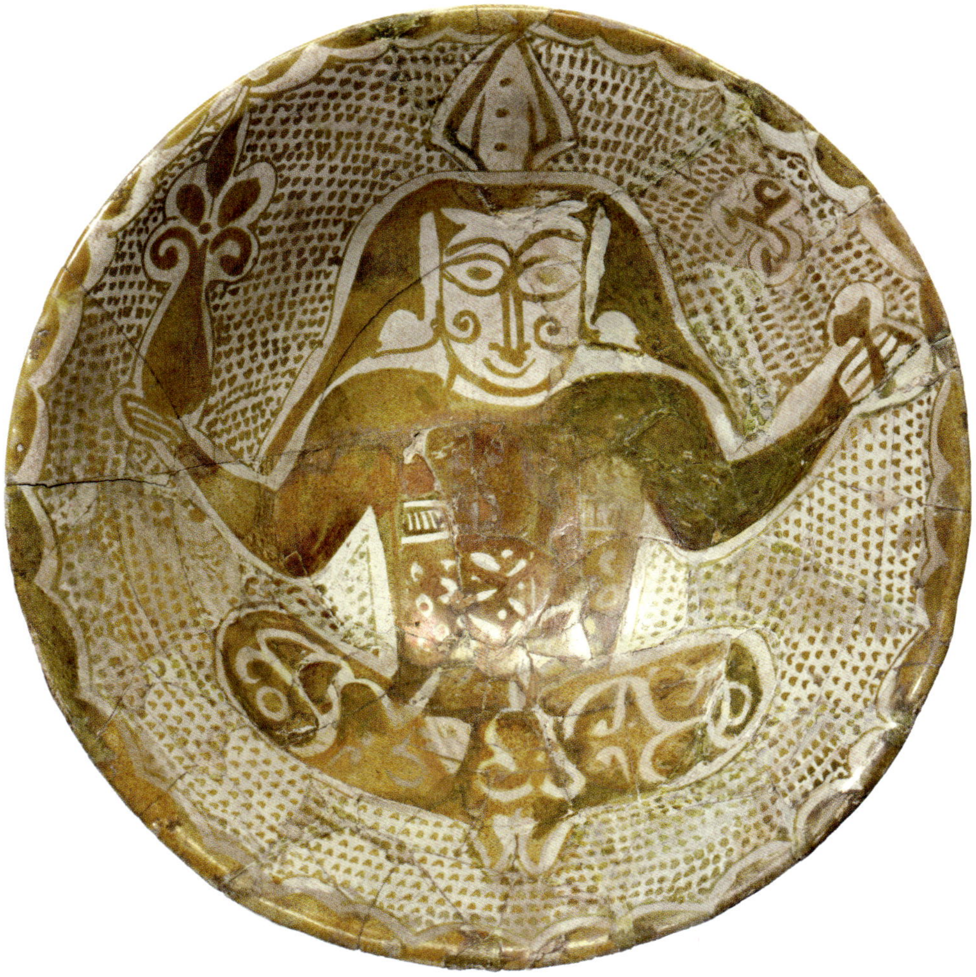

Dish
9th century
Terracotta
Ashmolean Museum, Oxford

Painted in a bold cobalt blue on a white ground, the image shows a fish with two sprigs of water weed in its mouth and is a classic example of Samarra ceramics. Next to models with modest and solemn inscriptions of a moral or religious tone, craftsmen also turned out immense numbers of wares of more 'popular' character to satisfy the demands of a constantly expanding market.

Bowl
9th century
Lustre-painted glazed terracotta
Ashmolean Museum, Oxford

Already widespread in ancient Egypt, the technique of lustre had been lost and only rediscovered in the Islamic age. It exemplifies the excellence of 'Abbasid ceramics, particularly appreciated for a metallic sheen redolent of gold, a metal banned on religious grounds. The bowl here represents a Bodhisattva, a key figure in Buddhism but quite alien to Islam. This unusual subject arose in the wake of mercenaries employed by the 'Abbasids, composed mostly of Turks, some of whom might have converted to Buddhism, a religion with which they would have become acquainted during campaigns in the Far East.

Miniature from the Maqamat (Picaresque Stories) of Damascus
c. 1240
Russian Academy of Sciences, St Petersburg

This miniature illustrates an episode from the *Maqamat,* an immensely successful collection of short stories composed in Iraq at the beginning of the twelfth century from the Arabic of al-Hariri, one of the few literary texts of which illustrated manuscripts were made. The names of the decorator and calligrapher of the copy preserved at St Petersburg, considered one of the finest of all, remain unknown. The episode shown depicts the protagonist who, after completing the ritual pilgrimage to Mecca, takes shelter from the stifling heat in his camp in the company of some wealthy companions. An old man accompanied by a youth comes up and exhorts them to be generous and give them supplies so they can continue their journey. The entire cycle is carried off in a naturalistic vein with a sure, detailed hand full of telling details and great elegance. Emblazoned with wonderfully intricate ornamental motifs, the tents are of especial interest.

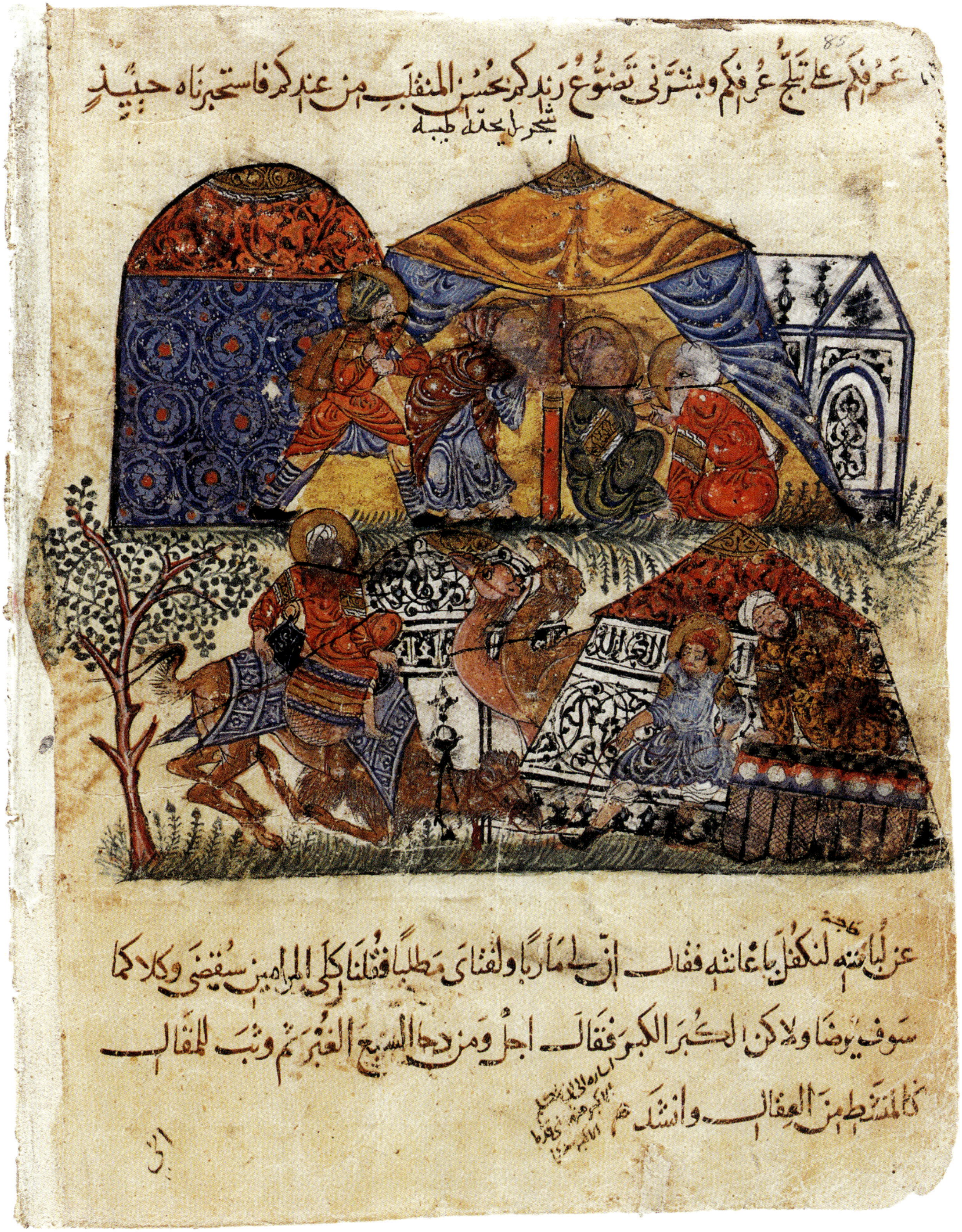

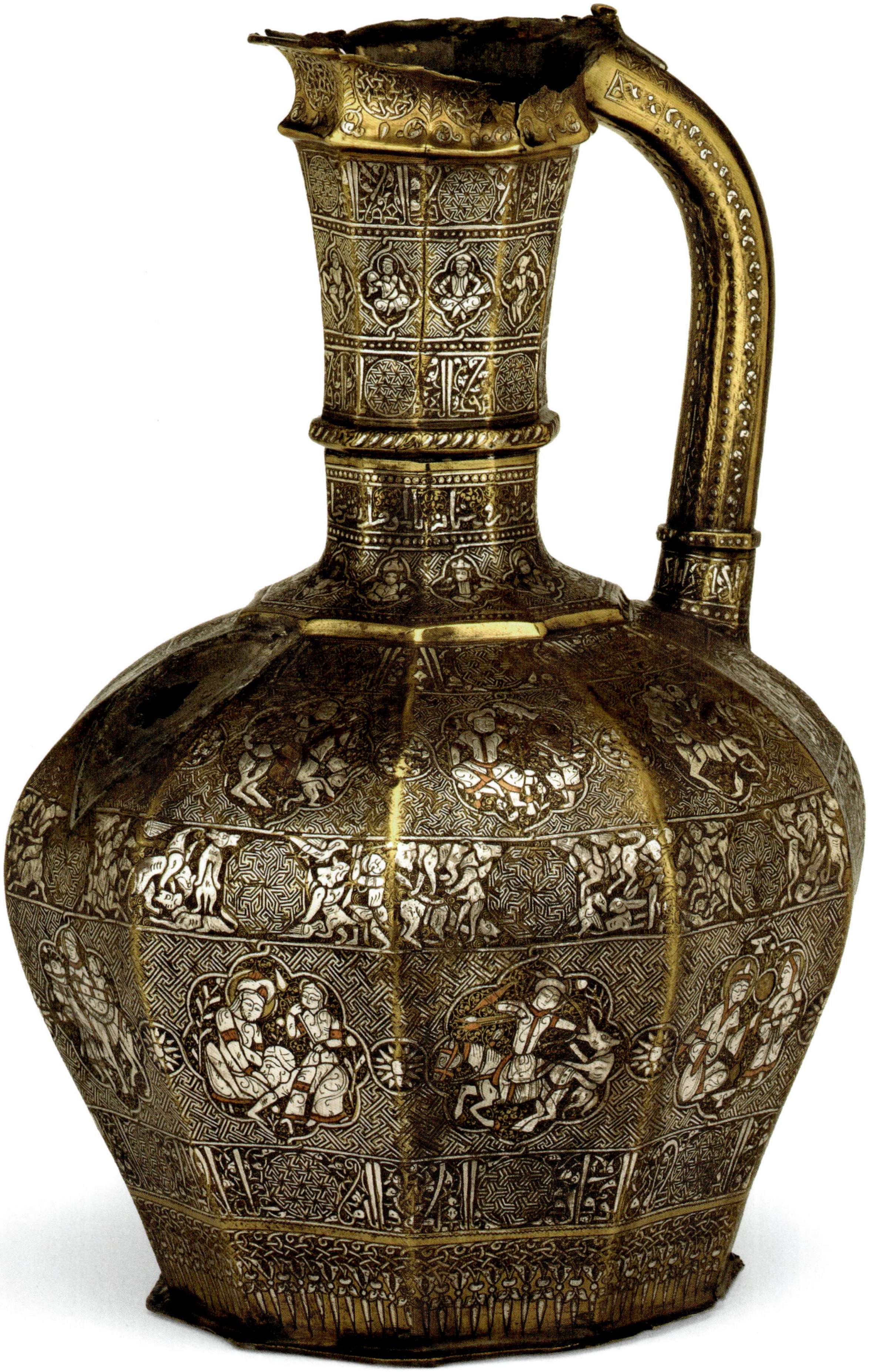

Shuja Ibn Mana (13th century)
The 'Blacas' ewer
Entire object and detail (facing)
1232
British Museum, London

Metallurgical techniques in Iraq reached an apogee with the production of the splendid silver- and copper-inlaid brassware characteristic of Mosul in the twelfth and thirteenth centuries and decorated with refined scenes of court life tailor-made to satisfy a demanding and privileged clientele. The priceless 'Blacas' ewer is signed by Shuja Ibn Mana, one of city's most consummate craftsmen, whose compositions with friezes and medallions were popular and widely imitated. Among a number of genre scenes showing camels, women at their looking-glass, hunting episodes, and musicians, one of the most telling presents a medallion with an illustration of the renowned *Shahnameh* ('Book of the King') by the Persian Firdusi. The Sassanid ruler Bahram Gur is depicted during a beat at a hunt, accompanied by the pretty Azadeh, his favourite musician strumming her harp. Showing off, Bahram fires a single arrow at a deer, transfixing its ear to its hoof. But the girl remains unimpressed and the enraged king throws her to the ground, trampling her to death under his horse's hooves.

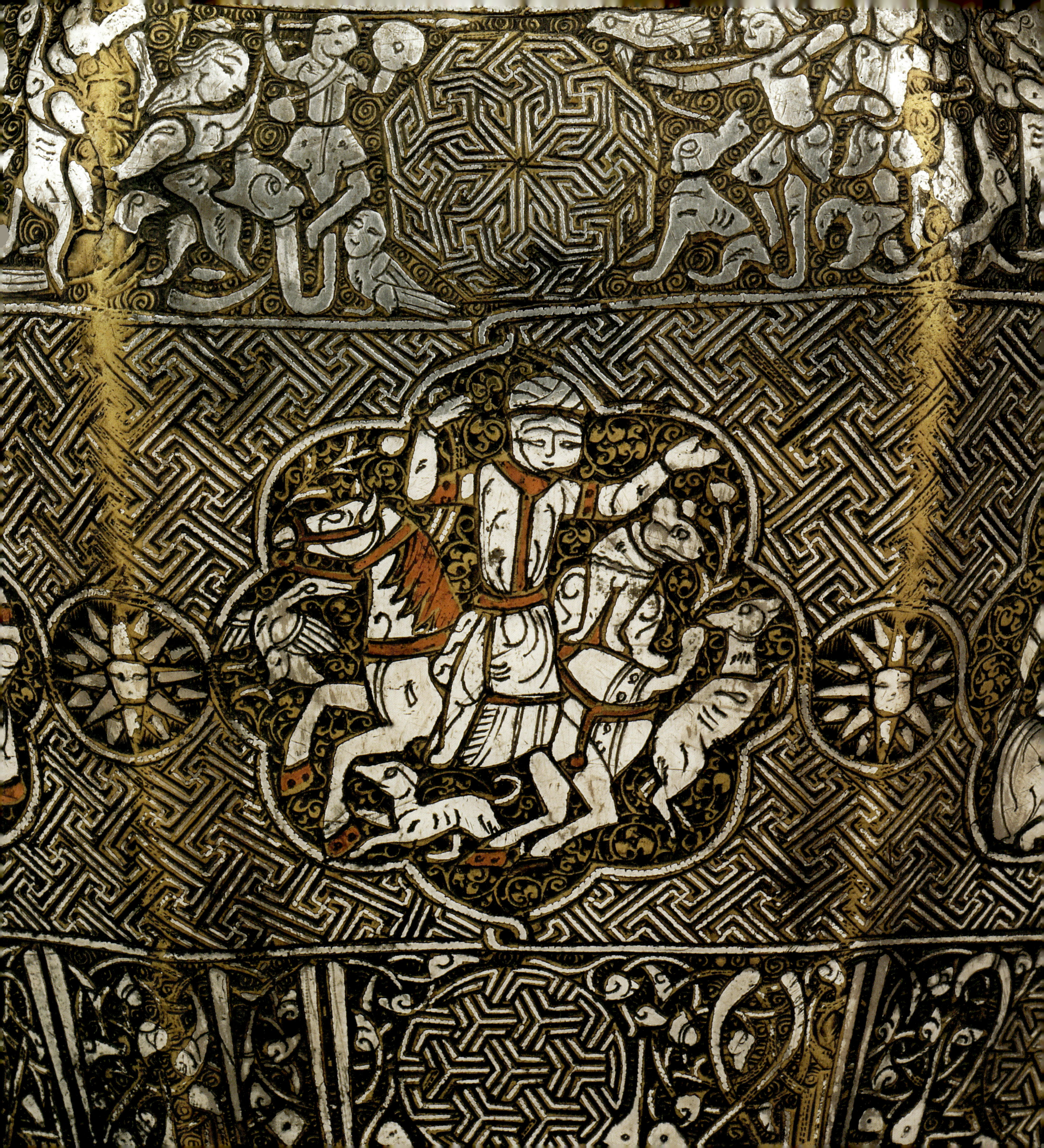

THE MEDITERRANEAN BASIN BETWEEN THE EIGHTH AND ELEVENTH CENTURIES: THE BIRTH OF REGIONAL IDENTITY

Great Mosque
Façade of prayer hall
836, 862, 14th century
and subsequent alterations
Kairouan, Tunisia

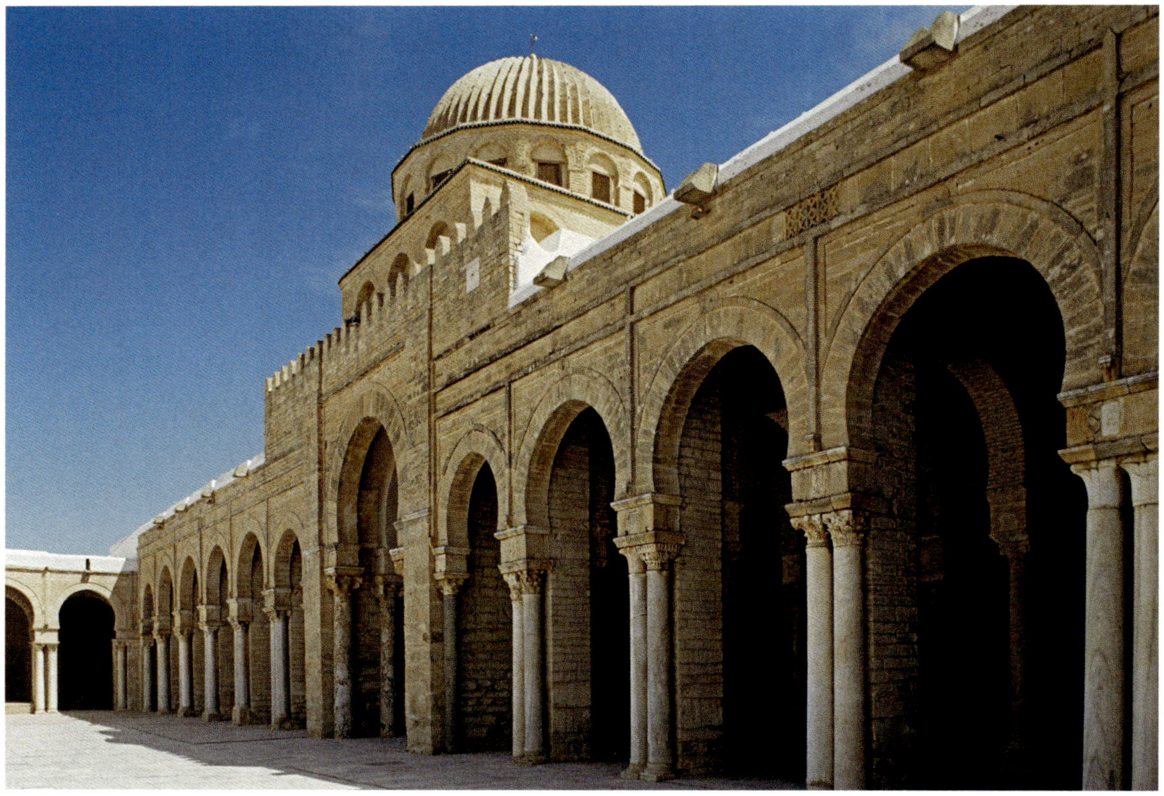

Beneath the apparent unity of the 'Abbasid caliphate bitter controversies raged regarding the significance of the caliph's role. Fuelled by frequent bids for independence, they fired the ambitions of rulers whose local autonomy permitted them to assert their independence gradually from the official central power. In the artistic field, the quality of 'Abbasid works of art set a high standard to be surpassed – or at least, as regards luxury goods, to be equalled. In the field of architecture in particular, the buildings reverted at times to earlier, local solutions. The most dramatic sign of the disintegration of the central power that had accelerated throughout the ninth century was the establishment of the powerful kingdom of al-Andalus in Spain and the subsequent proclamation of the al-Andalus caliphate in 929. This resulted from the efforts of the last survivors of the Umayyads of Damascus (756), who opposed the 'Abbasids outright since they had exterminated their family. In fact, between 868 and 905, Egypt was governed by the Tulunid dynasty, who were dependent on Baghdad only in a formal sense. The Aghlabids of Kairouan in Tunisia had already had become independent in 800; in 909, the Fatimids, an Isma'ili Shia dynasty and the self-proclaimed sole heirs of the Prophet in accordance with the law, overthrew the Aghlabids and inaugurated an explicitly anti-'Abbasid policy culminating in the conquest of Egypt in 969 and the foundation of a second caliphate with its capital at Cairo.
Meanwhile, in Asia, governors and warlords were conspiring everywhere against the tottering central power. In 945 the Buyids of Transoxiana (Uzbekistan) went so far as to occupy Baghdad, depriving the caliph of any real authority. Although the 'Abbasid dynasty was formally only defeated at the time of the Mongol invasions in 1258, the de facto dissolution of the empire between the eighth and ninth centuries had already sounded the death knell for any idea of a universal ecumenical community under the banner of Islam. In its place there arose various entities in which pre-Islamic components often weighed heavily. Apart from theoretical and often loose ties to the faith, they displayed profound differences in language, tradition, culture and interests that at times erupted into fierce conflict. The Islamic art of Ifriqiya (present-day Tunisia) owed much to the omnipresent Roman-Byzantine heritage, whose grandiose vestiges characterize the urban fabric and countryside, followed by inspiration from the Orient, in particular from the Syrian-Mesopotamian world.
Two main 'schools' grew up in the field of architecture, at Kairouan and Susa. The first boasts the Great Mosque and the Mosque of the Three Gates in Kairouan, the Great Mosque of Sfax and the mosque at Tunis – elaborately decorated buildings in which (recycled) marble columns support timber ceilings. Columns and capitals from the ancient world were reused along the lines of a Christian basilica: the capital does not support the impost of the arch directly, the abacus being surmounted by a pyramidal architrave, moulded or carved, on which the block-like impost rests. The school of Susa opted for the monumental forms of 'Abbasid architecture, with pillars instead of columns and powerful chiaroscuro effects, replacing Mesopotamian brickwork with the splendour of locally cut stone. The shapes are austere and solemn, the spaces severe and spare, and the language strongly characterized, monumental and visionary, redolent of a home-grown Romanesque. The later architecture of the Fatimids was conditioned by contrast by the monumental Tulunid

structures of Cairo, still more explicitly related to 'Abbasid models.
In the field of the applied arts these tendencies eventually merged, as in the exquisite wooden panels of the *minbar* in the Great Mosque at Kairouan (856–863) and on that in the Andalus Mosque in Fez of 980, where they obviously derive from stucco wall decorations from the Iraqi region. The Aghlabid emirate was swept up by the Shia reaction, asserted most forcefully by the turbulent inland Berber tribes from Morocco to Tunisia. The art and architecture fostered by the new masters hardly differed from those of the Aghlabids. After the foundation of Mahdia on the Tunisian coast, the perfect springboard for raids throughout the Mediterranean, the Fatimids also settled in Egypt (969) where, adjacent to the former capital of al-Fustat, they founded a new city called al-Qahira ('the victorious', today's Cairo), leaving Tunisia in the hands of the Zirid Berbers. When these again made approaches to the Sunnites the Fatimid caliph reacted by unleashing the savage nomadic tribes of the Banu Hilal (1052) on the land, occasioning such devastation that the glowing embers of Ifriqiya were extinguished forever.
In al-Andalus the Umayyad Abd al-Rahman, brought up within the great artistic tradition of Damascus, adopted certain Hispanic and Visigothic influences and turned Cordoba, capital of the new and flourishing emirate (and from 929 the self-proclaimed caliphate), into one of the most splendid cities of the era. In so doing he inaugurated an extraordinary artistic and cultural flowering that was destined to leave a mark on the art of the Iberian Peninsula and the Maghreb that endured for centuries. In the course of the tenth century the art and culture of Cordoba made headway in every field (with the exception of book production), its crowning glory in the domain of architecture being the glorious innovation of the world-renowned *mezquita.*
In nearly every artistic domain production reached amazing levels. The craftsmen excelled in luxury metal objects, wonderful woven cloths, refined ceramics and above all in exquisite works in ivory, an area that produced formal solutions harking back directly to classical Antiquity, but which, unlike the architecture, vanished when the world that created them passed into oblivion. The brilliant era of the Umayyads flowed seamlessly into the age of the Taifa ('faction') rulers that emerged from the dismemberment of the caliphate: relatively wealthy statelets that were incapable of political unity and were at risk of being overrun by Christian incursions. Their art progressed, above all in architecture, towards a gradual dissolution of buoyant forms that verge on disembodiment. This fascinating development, in the architecture of later centuries, culminates in Merinid Morocco and in the Alhambra Palace complex.
In general the artistic and architectural production of Muslim countries in the central and western Mediterranean was the expression of a society in which Arab Muslims coexisted with Islamicized Berbers and converted Hispanics, side by side with a vital and resilient Christian community (called Copts in Egypt), as well as a substantial Jewish minority. Individual characteristics in motifs from various centres of production do not preclude recognizable common features, however. The most significant consists in the adoption of a vocabulary of architecture and decoration of Classical, late Antique and Byzantine stamp. Embracing al-Andalus and the major part of North Africa (and beyond that to Sicily, where Muslim monuments have completely vanished, but have evident echoes in Norman buildings), it relegated the Mesopotamian and oriental heritage to a few closely circumscribed situations, to such an extent that the term 'Umayyad nostalgia' has been used, understood as the reclamation of the art produced in Syria during the previous century. In this sense, Islamic art in these regions forms a noteworthy chapter in the history of European art.

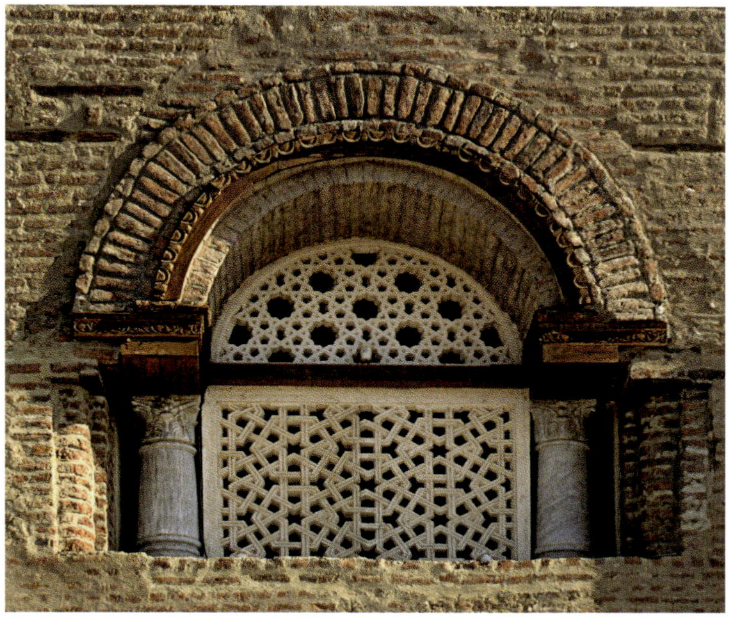

Mosque of Amr Ibn al-As
Window and fanlight
827
Cairo, Egypt

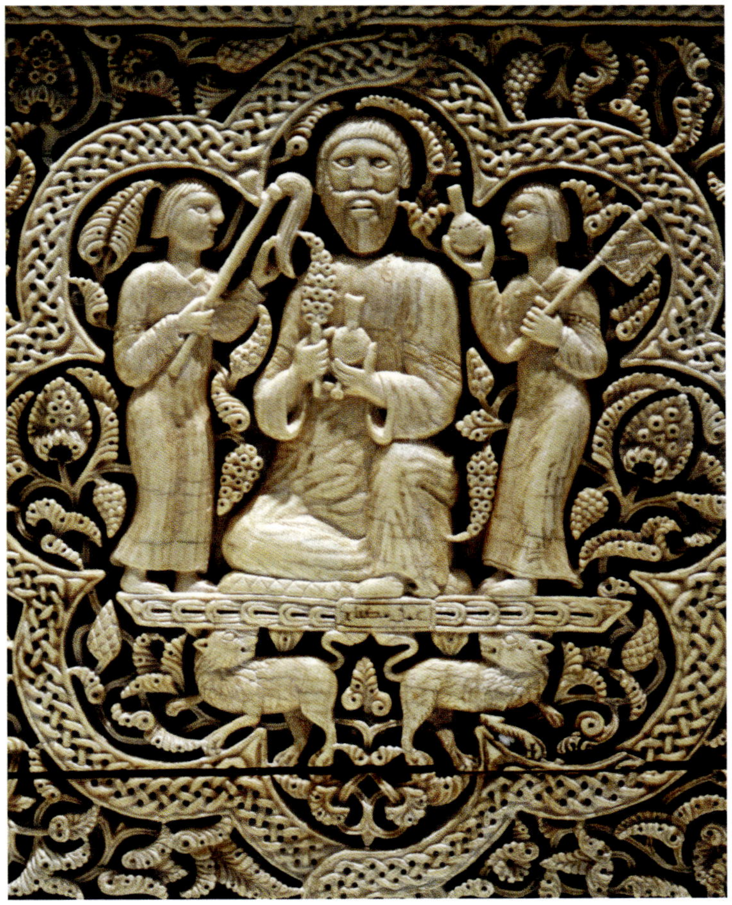

Detail of a round box
Late 10th century,
from Leire (Cordoba)
Museo de Navarra, Pamplona

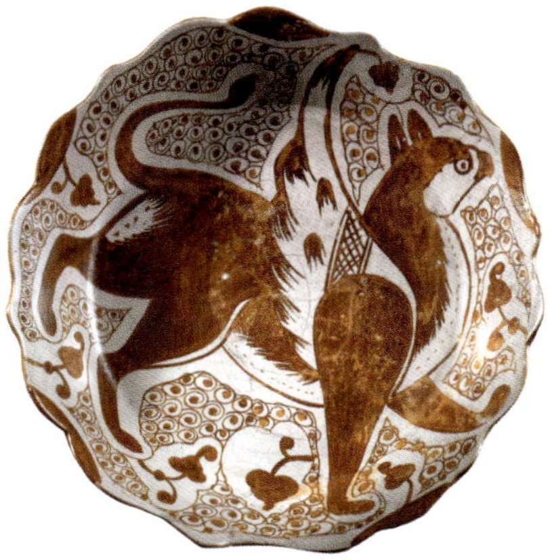

Dish with gryphon
11th century
Lustreware
Fatimid period
Museum of Islamic Art, Cairo

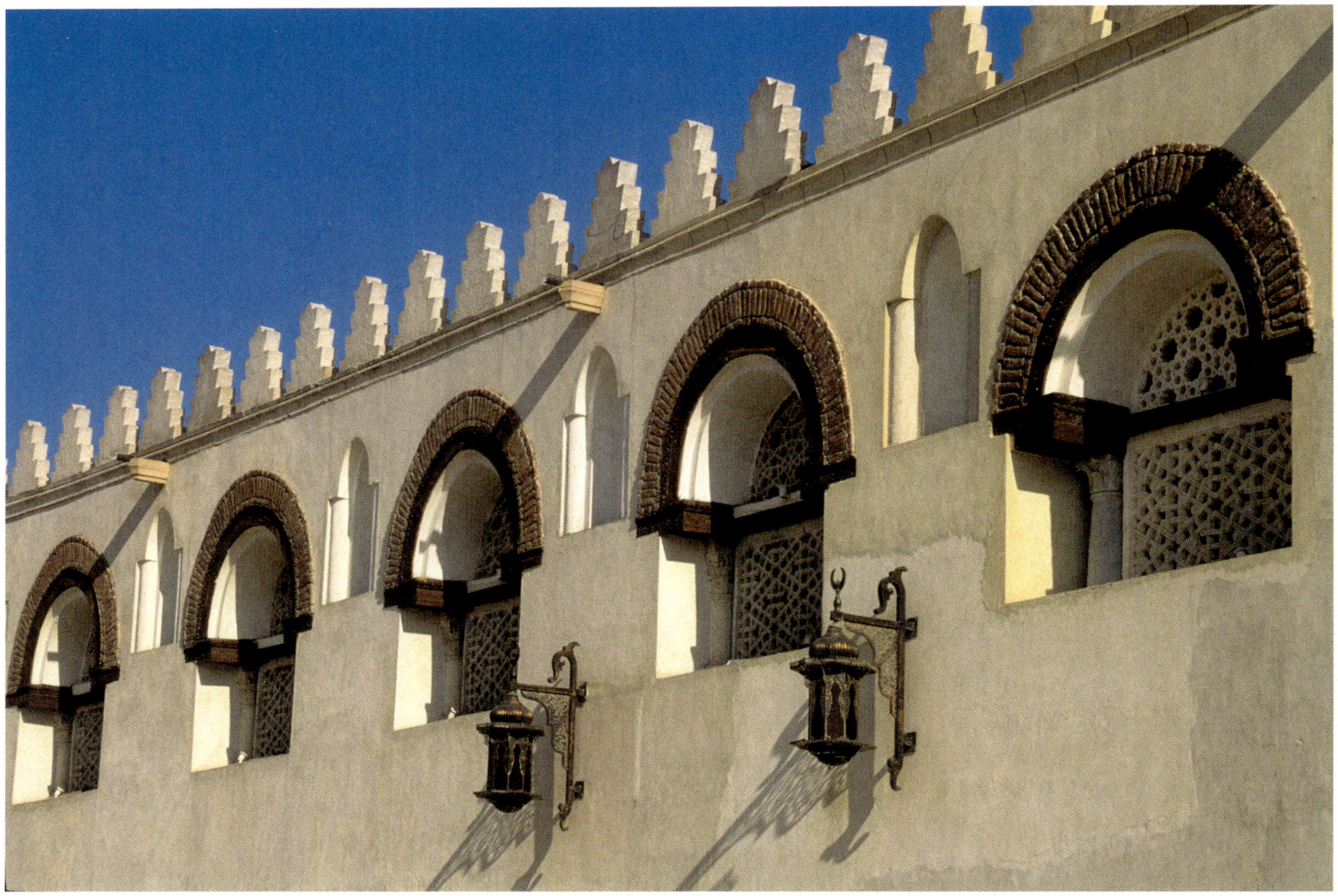

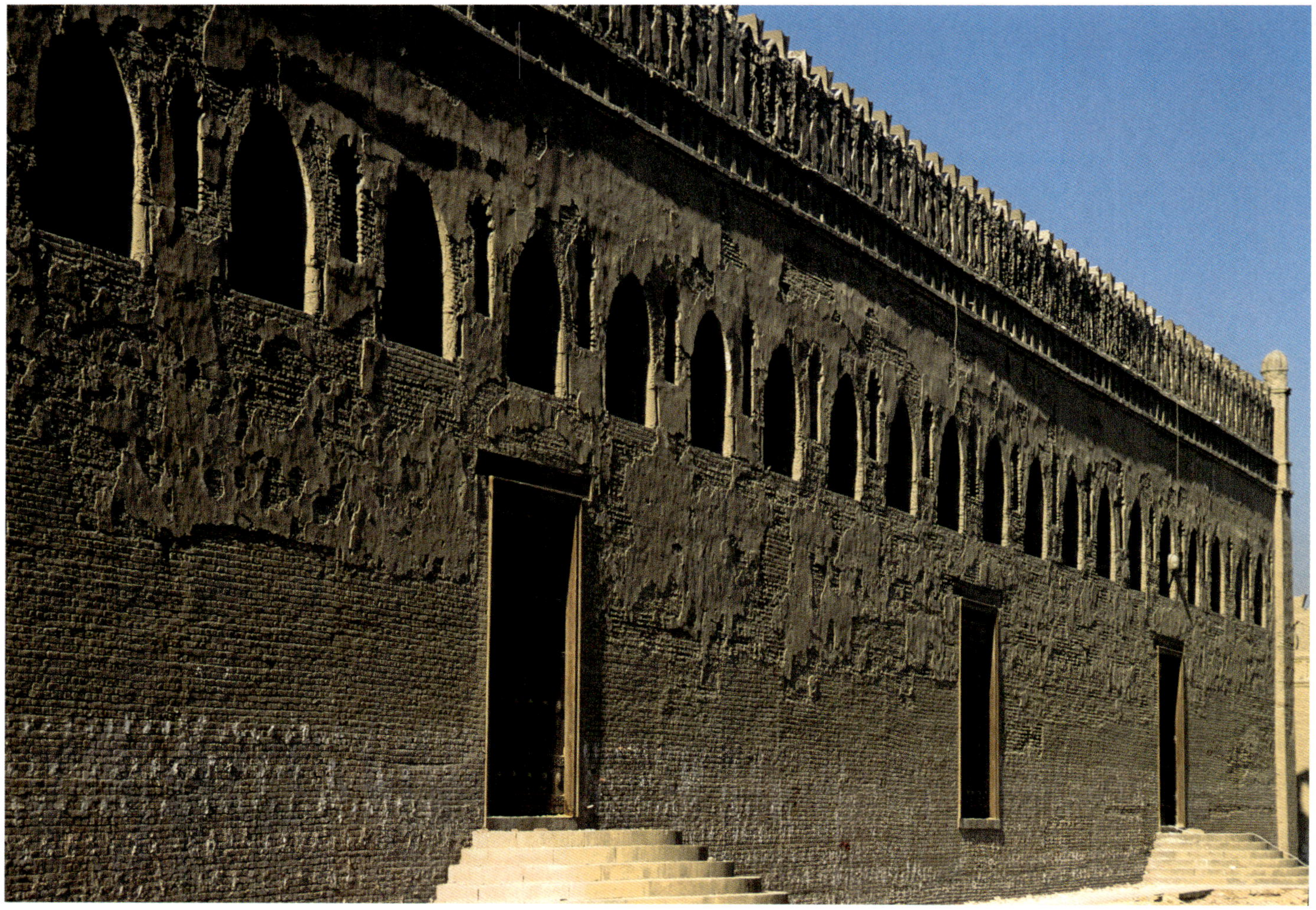

Mosque of Amr Ibn al-As
Mid 9th century
Cairo, Egypt

The first mosque to be erected in Egypt was that of al-Amr, founded in 641 at al-Fustat by the country's conqueror. The original edifice with its hypostyle hall has disappeared. The result of a radical enlargement of the erstwhile building, the oldest part of the present-day mosque remains the southeast wall. The semicircular arched windows are set with decorated wooden architraves and with stucco grilles in a geometric pattern and supported on sturdy colonnettes with capitals from earlier constructions – a solution, like the adjacent small blind niches, with a Mesopotamian flavour.

Mosque of Ibn Tulun
External wall
876–879
Cairo, Egypt

The congregational mosque for the new capital, al-Qatai, is the only Ibn Tulun monument to have survived. This gigantic pile was entirely realized in brick, like the Iraqi mosques that inspired its ground plan and elevation. The external wall is studded with drop-arched windows placed on a low springing line whose shoulders rest on stocky columns deeply engaged into the thickness of the wall. The subdued light permeating the hall enters through elaborate stucco gratings between which shell-like niches gape. The wall is crowned by a balustrade pierced by circular oculi (as at the mosque of al-Mutawakkil in Samarra), while the pediment is constituted by a bizarre, vaguely anthropomorphic openwork motif, energizing its rippling surface with a sense of dynamic release.

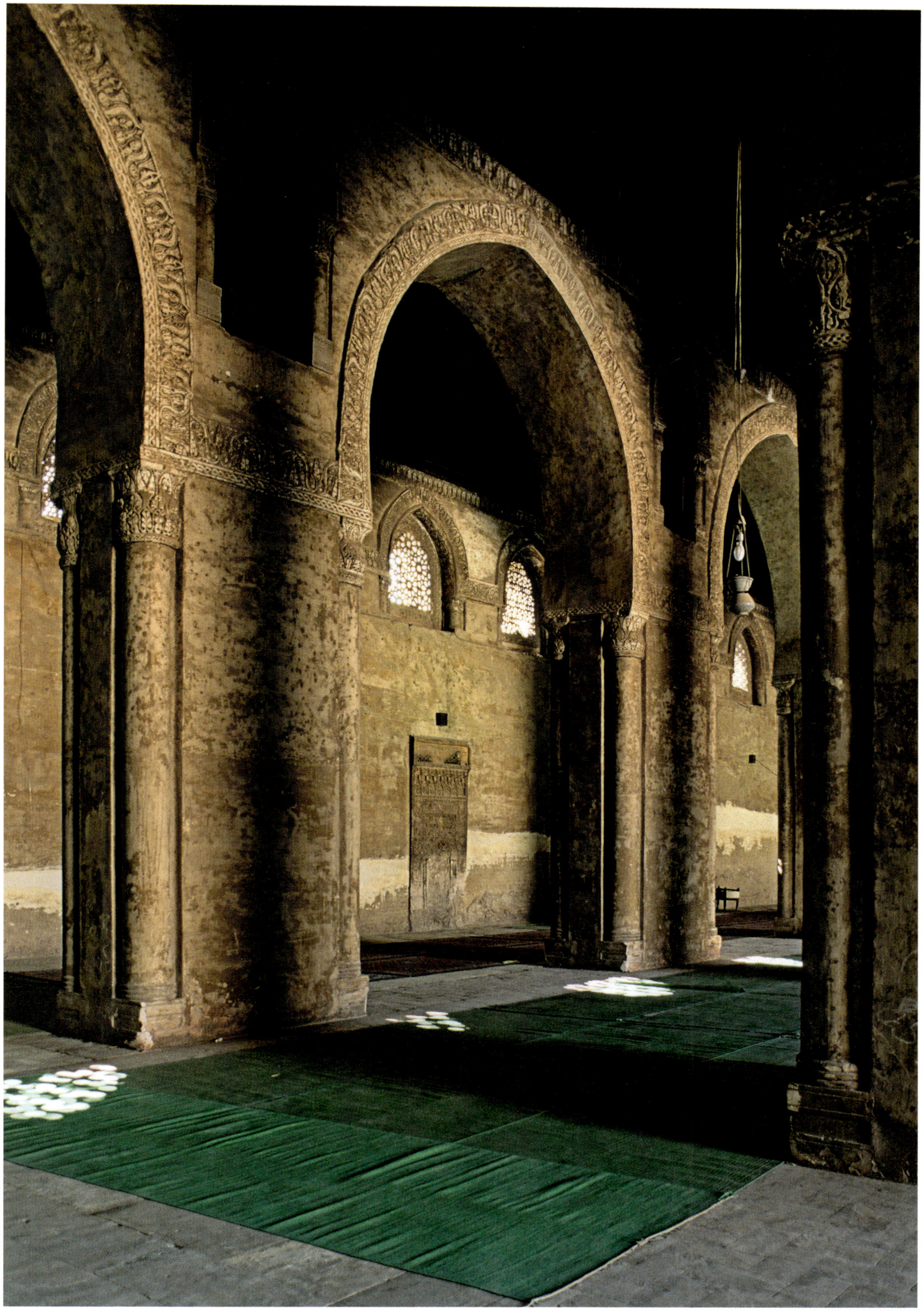

Mosque of Ibn Tulun
***Qibla* wall and adjacent aisle**
876–879
Cairo, Egypt

Many innovations were introduced here with respect to the prototypes in Samarra. Octagonal in the Great Mosque at Samarra, in Cairo the brick pillars engaged into the four corner columns are oblong, a discrepancy further pursued in the ceiling. This, instead of resting directly on the pillars, is borne on arches, which thus perform a key role (as in the Abu Dulaf Mosque in Samarra) in dividing the immense space into bays. In this manner, the space is more clearly defined and organized, rather than, as it were, intuiting the unbound and infinite. The idea of piercing the massive pillars with apertures framed by colonnettes and with a stucco frieze that, as in the capitals, freely reiterates plant motifs is analogous to certain variants in Iraq; the intrados once presented geometric and plant patterns in stucco of exquisite refinement and variety, although scant vestiges survive today. The light penetrates though the arches on the courtyard and, less directly, flickers through the stucco geometrical lattices with what is by now customary symbolism.

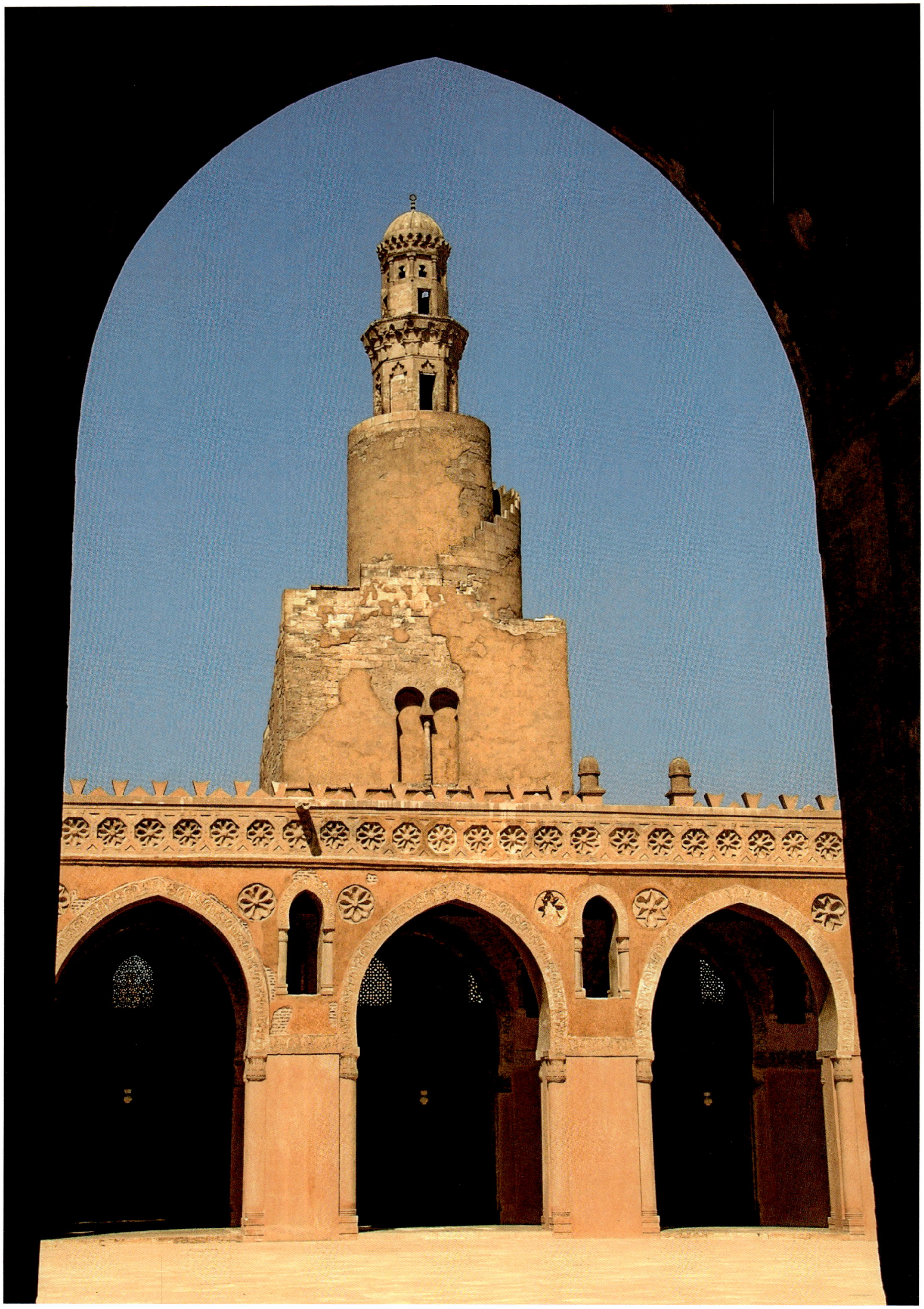

Mosque of Ibn Tulun
Courtyard and minaret
876–879, upper part 1296
Cairo, Egypt

The courtyard is framed by pointed arches verging on the horseshoe, a curve as emphasized by the continuous ornamental banding in stucco that confers lightness and harmony as well as solidity. The section of wall over the pillars is perforated by lancets that echo, with greater dynamism, the larger motif, flanked by circular rosettes disposed with nonchalant asymmetry and terminating in a frieze of rosettes in stucco. Intended to receive thousands of worshippers, the vast expanse of the courtyard is dominated by a stone minaret articulated over four tiers. The first level is rectangular, the second circular, the third and fourth an octagonal kiosk, with the whole reaching a height of some forty metres. According to the sources, Ibn Tulun erected a minaret with an external staircase, but the analogies with prototypes at Samarra, in brick and entirely circular, end there. The Mamluk Lajin restored the mosque in 1296, notably the dome in the courtyard and upper octagonal reaches of the minaret.

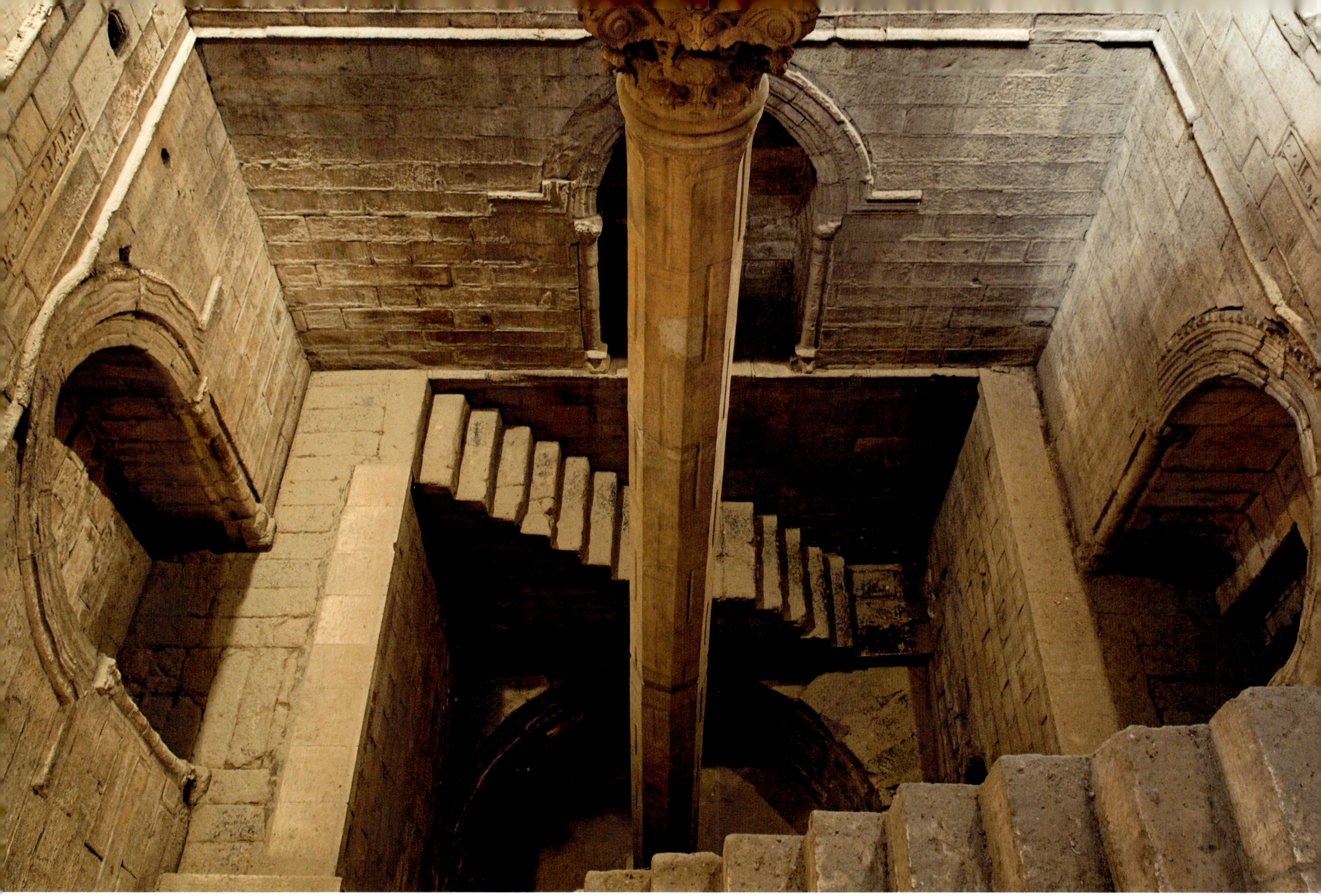

Nilometer
861
Cairo, Egypt

A nilometer serves to measure the flow of the Nile, and hence the quantity of water available for irrigation, the basis for calculating the amount of tax levied. This one was built in 861 by Caliph al-Mutawakkil to replace an earlier construction derived from the simple models of Pharaonic Egypt, at a time when the branch of the Nile situated between the island of al-Rawda and the city of al-Fustat had practically dried up. Before installing the perimeter walls, an octagonal column more than ten metres high marked with a measuring scale was fixed onto a timber plinth and attached to wooden beams embedded in the sides down the centre of a borehole ten metres square and twelve and a half metres deep. The three pointed-arched niches correspond to the channels through which the water flowed. Access was ensured down two staircases fixed to the walls and split into landings. The Kufic inscriptions constitute the most ancient example of architectural epigraphy in the country. The structure was restored in 872 by Ibn Tulun, who advertised his independence by effacing the name of the preceding 'Abbasid caliph.

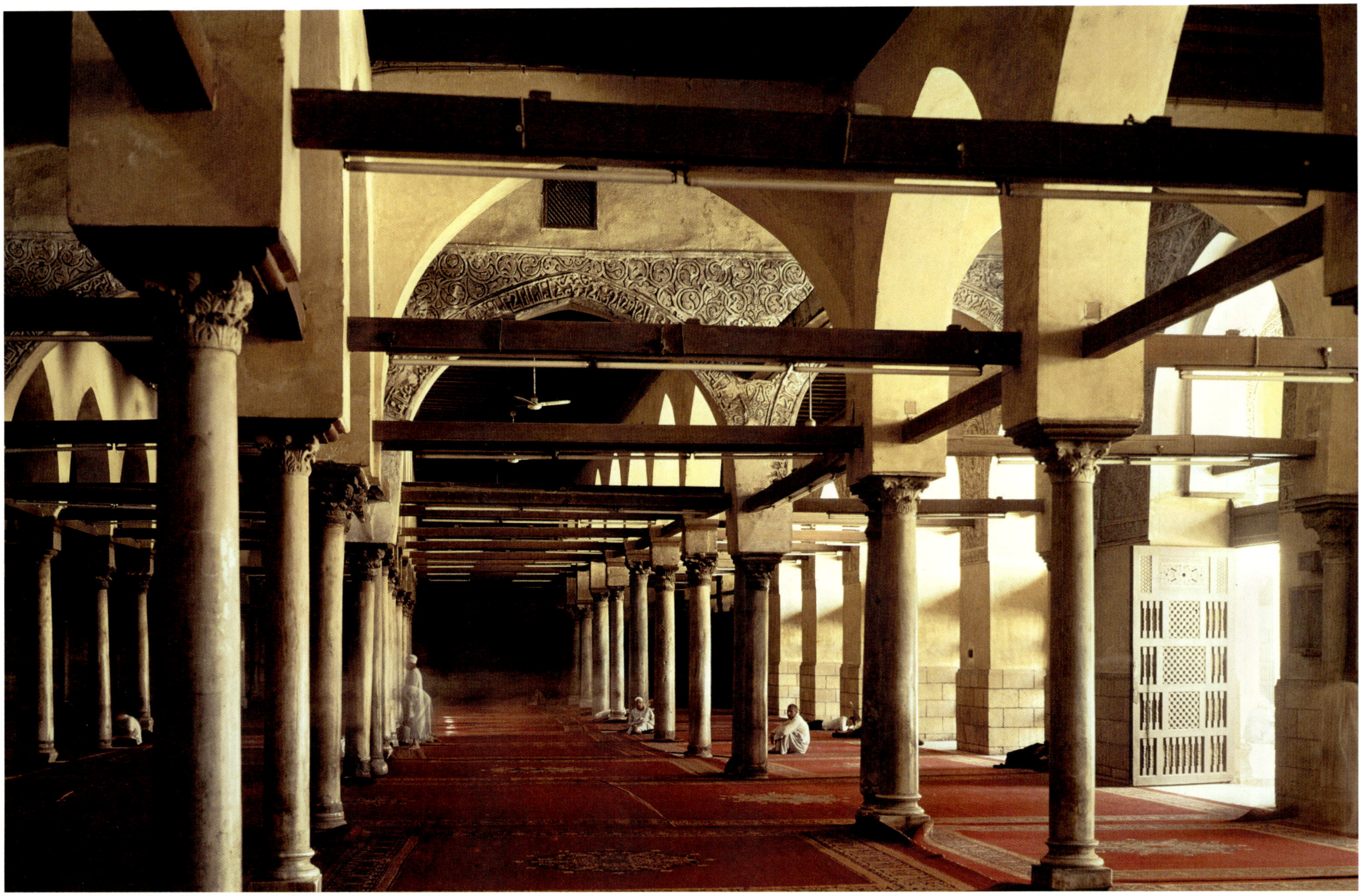

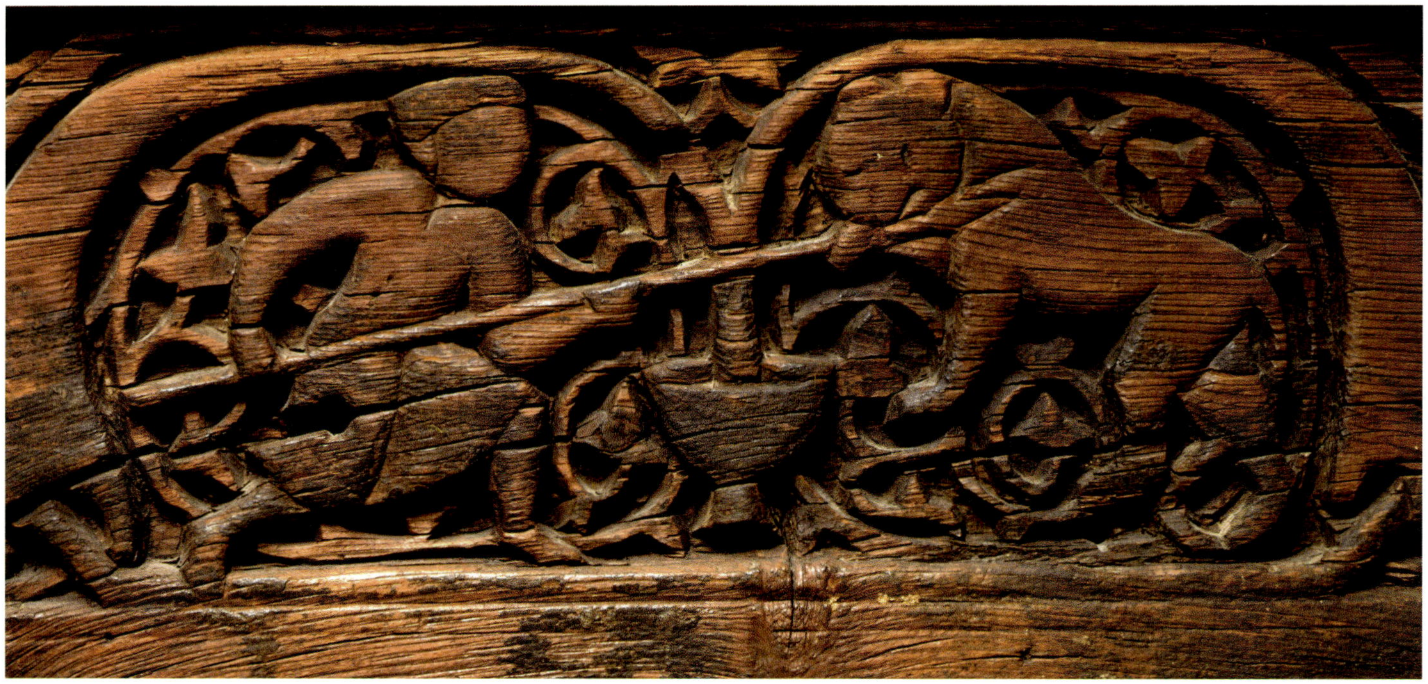

Al-Azhar Mosque
Interior
970–972 and subsequent alterations
Cairo, Egypt

As soon as they had conquered Cairo, the Shias promptly erected their own mosque, al-Azhar ('the Flourishing'), which for more than one thousand years has also fulfilled the role as the University of Islam. The hypostyle hall is articulated along five aisles parallel to the *qibla,* intersecting with a higher and broader nave at the perpendicular that is illuminated from above and leads to the *mihrab.* In place of the massive pillars of the mosque of Ibn Tulun, here elegant columns with spoliated Corinthian capitals are used, making the space airy and luminous in what is a clear break with the style of the emirs and with imperial mosques at Samarra. The window grilles, the niche of the *mihrab,* the perimeter walls and the centre aisle were once adorned with magnificent decorations in stucco. Surviving in parts, though not all date to the first phase of building, it is inspired, rather than by the inevitable models of Samarra, by a Byzantine idiom and above all by the decor in the Mosque of Ibn Tulun, here infused with a certain *horror vacui.*

Western Palace
Detail of a frieze with figures
11th century
Museum of Islamic Art, Cairo

Luckily, this architrave, over four metres long by approximately thirty centimetres high, was saved from the now-ruined Western Palace of the Shia sultan and reinstalled back to front (decorated face inwards) in the interior of the Mamluk mausoleum of Sultan Qalawun. Like an ivory carving, which it closely resembles, this wooden sculpture represents genre scenes from daily life such as hunting and animals within a series of arches that spring from the vases separating the figures. The background comprises a plant motif from which the medallion gradually emerges.

Coptic textile
11th century, Fatimid period
Museum of Islamic Art, Cairo

The Egyptian arts of weaving, dominated by Coptic craftsmen (a word derived from the Greek for 'Egyptian' and taken up to mean Egyptian Christian), flourished notably under the Fatimids, who dressed in sumptuous robes and liked to decorate their apartments with embroidered fabrics. Unlike the border, clearly of local taste, the two figures are inspired by classical art, an example the Fatimids esteemed, although here it is given a decidedly local twist.

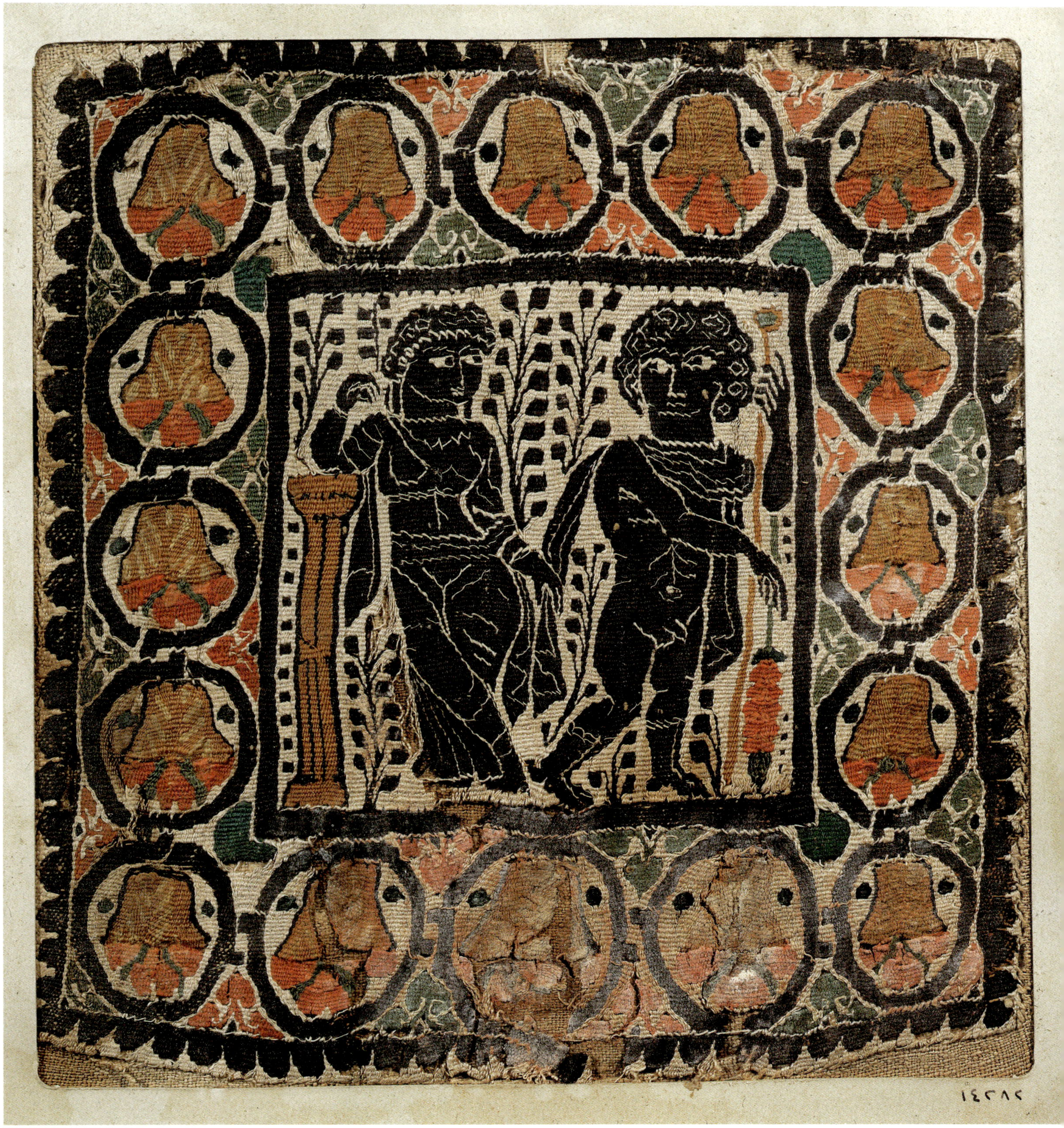

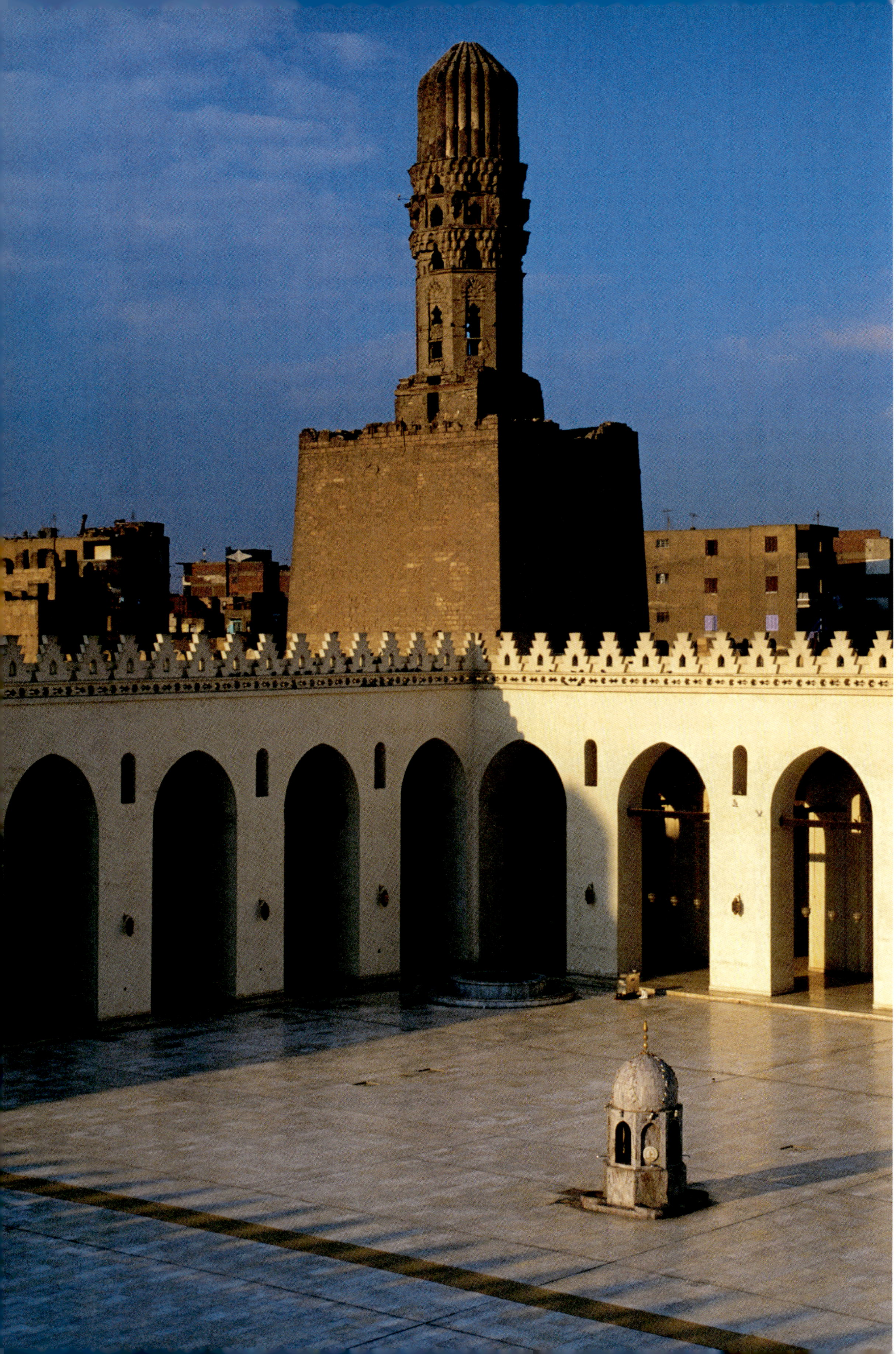

Mosque of al-Hakim
Minaret and courtyard
11th and 12th century
Cairo, Egypt

At the onset of the eleventh century Caliph al-Hakim completed the mosque begun by his father al-Aziz in 990. Destined to exalt the city of the Shia caliphate, its fortified appearance makes it appear virtually part of the enceinte, so closely does it hug the walls. The corner minarets – the discrepancies between which verge on the incomprehensible – were originally far slenderer, one cylindrical and the other octagonal, and both stand on squared plinths emblazoned with magnificent inscriptions. In 1010, for reasons that remain unclear, al-Hakim decided to have them removed, but fortunately the architect charged with the task limited himself to masking them and encircling them with a bulky and unattractive wall with a pyramidal base. Although concealing them entirely from view, this at least preserved the interior – perhaps as a mark of respect to the memory of the caliph.
The impressive upper section with drop-arched niches, scalloped windows and balconies with *muqarnas* is one of the masterworks of the architecture of the time and was probably completed in the Ayyubid period. By contrast the elevated top-piece in brick *mabkharas* is the result of a restoration in 1303. The use of shiny marble paving, buffed plaster, an inappropriate colour scheme and fitted carpets in the place of rugs during the clumsy restoration of 1981 has unfortunately compromised the appearance of the building.

Mosque of al-Hakim
Prayer hall
11th–12th century
Cairo, Egypt

The pillars with corner columns supporting arches in the prayer hall parallel to the *qibla* differ from the prototype in the mosque of Ibn Tulun in that they are totally lacking in decoration, to the point that they even do away with capitals. Very little remains of the inscribed ribbon that originally ran along beneath the ceiling (completely renovated, like the dazzling and unrealistic marble pavement). The lamps, however, do represent models similar to the originals, diffusing the light through coloured glass or holes in the brass in an explicit expression of the divine.

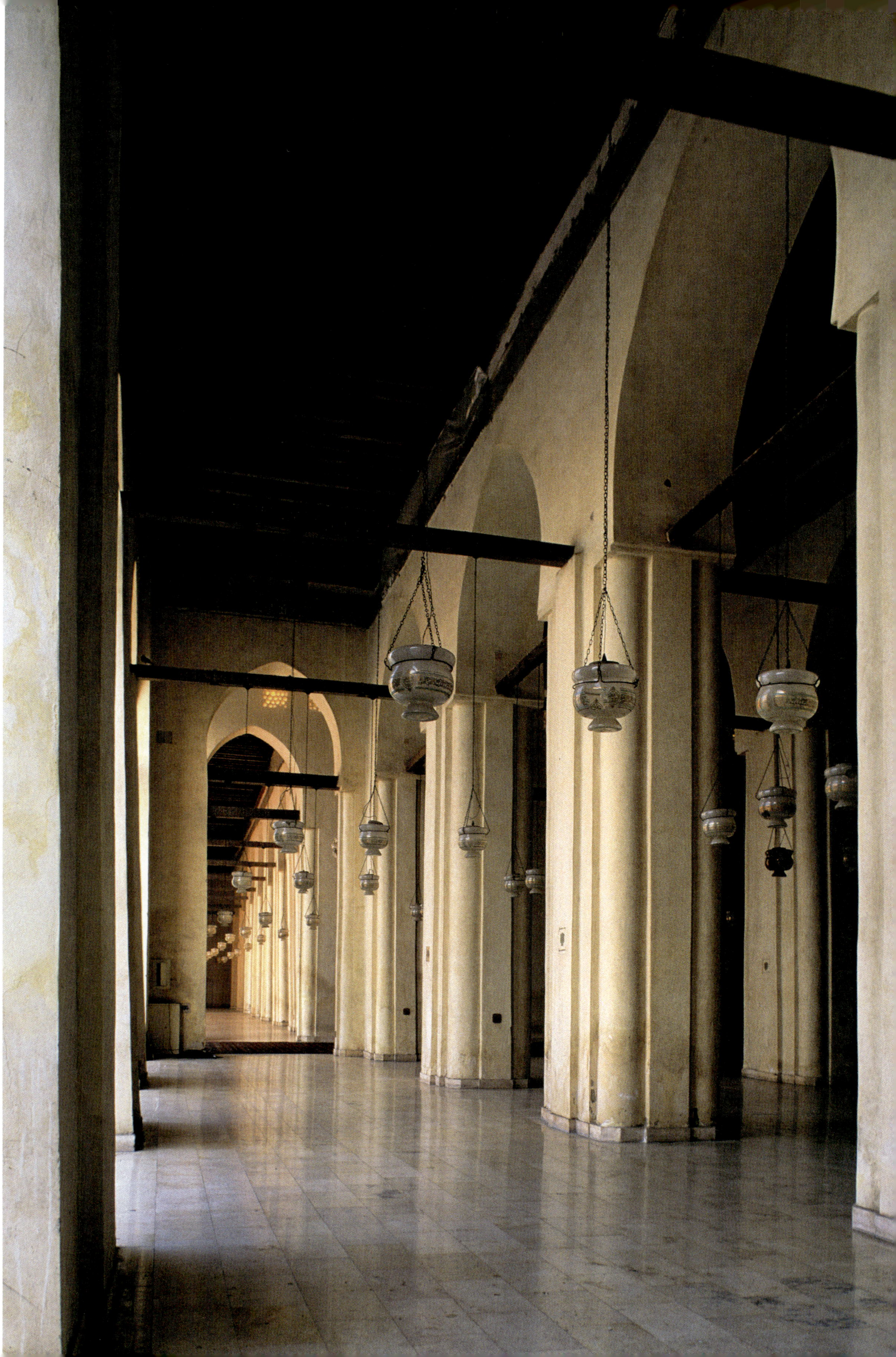

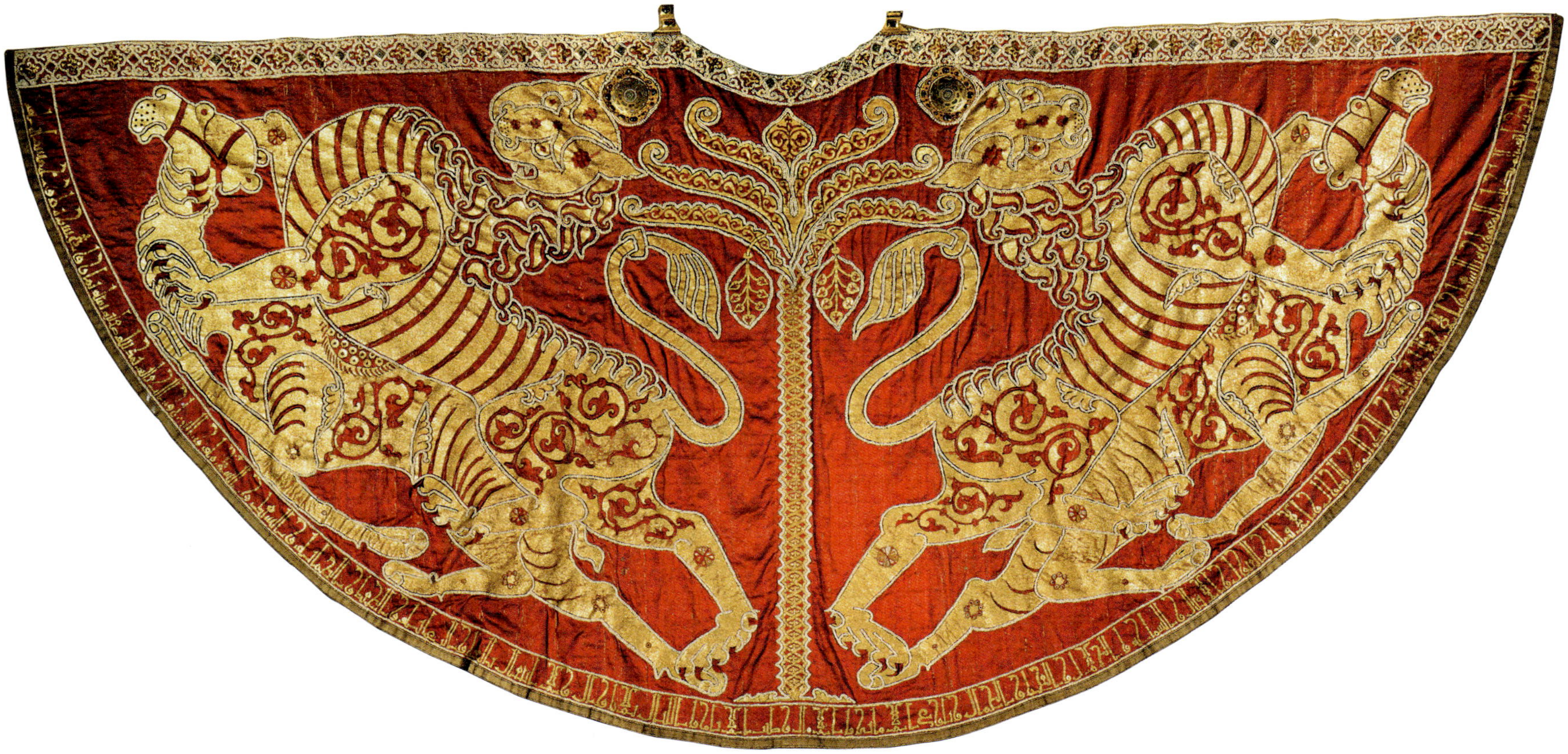

Coronation mantle of King Roger II
1133–1134
Silk
Kunsthistorisches Museum, Vienna

Although there is an almost total lack of carpets and above all of dress from the Fatimid court, their legendary beauty, praised effusively in the sources, can be ascertained from the extraordinary mantle produced in a Sicilian workshop for the Norman king, Roger (Ruggero) II. (Sicily was overrun by the Arabs from 827 and fell under Fatimid rule at the time of the Norman Conquest.) With its elegant calligraphy, the stylized depiction of this fierce hunting scene unfolds in a rhythmic counterpoise of supple lines, magnificently enhanced by bold chromatic contrasts.

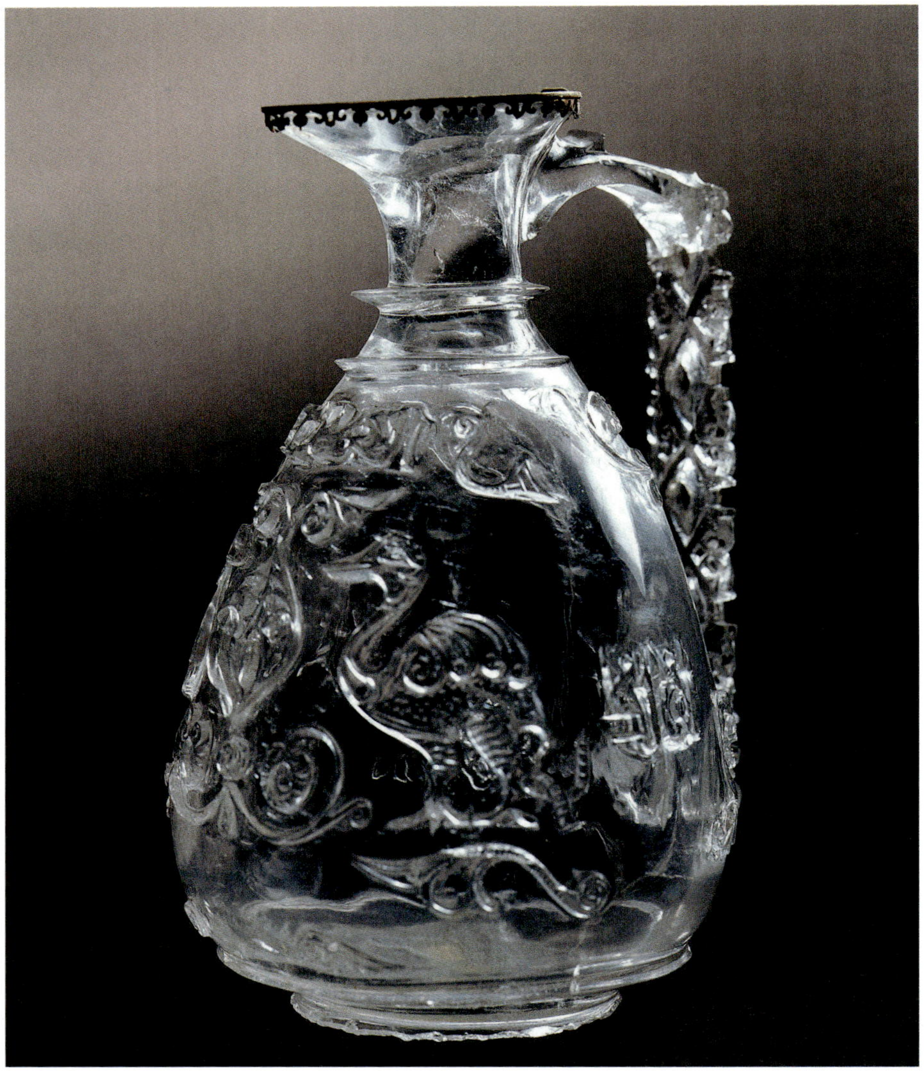

Brocca
10th century
Fatimid period
Rock crystal
Palazzo Pitti, Florence

Under the impact of the Fatimid court, during the tenth century Cairo supplanted Baghdad as the focus in the Islamic world for the production of high-quality objects. Inscribed with the caliph's name immediately beneath the neck, this water jug belongs to a group of articles in rock crystal that were widely considered as masterpieces of Cairo craftsmanship, which was then at its technical zenith. In the space of a very few years, this technique went into decline, as did the related art of the glass cameo, and the surfaces of such pieces tended subsequently to be left plain.

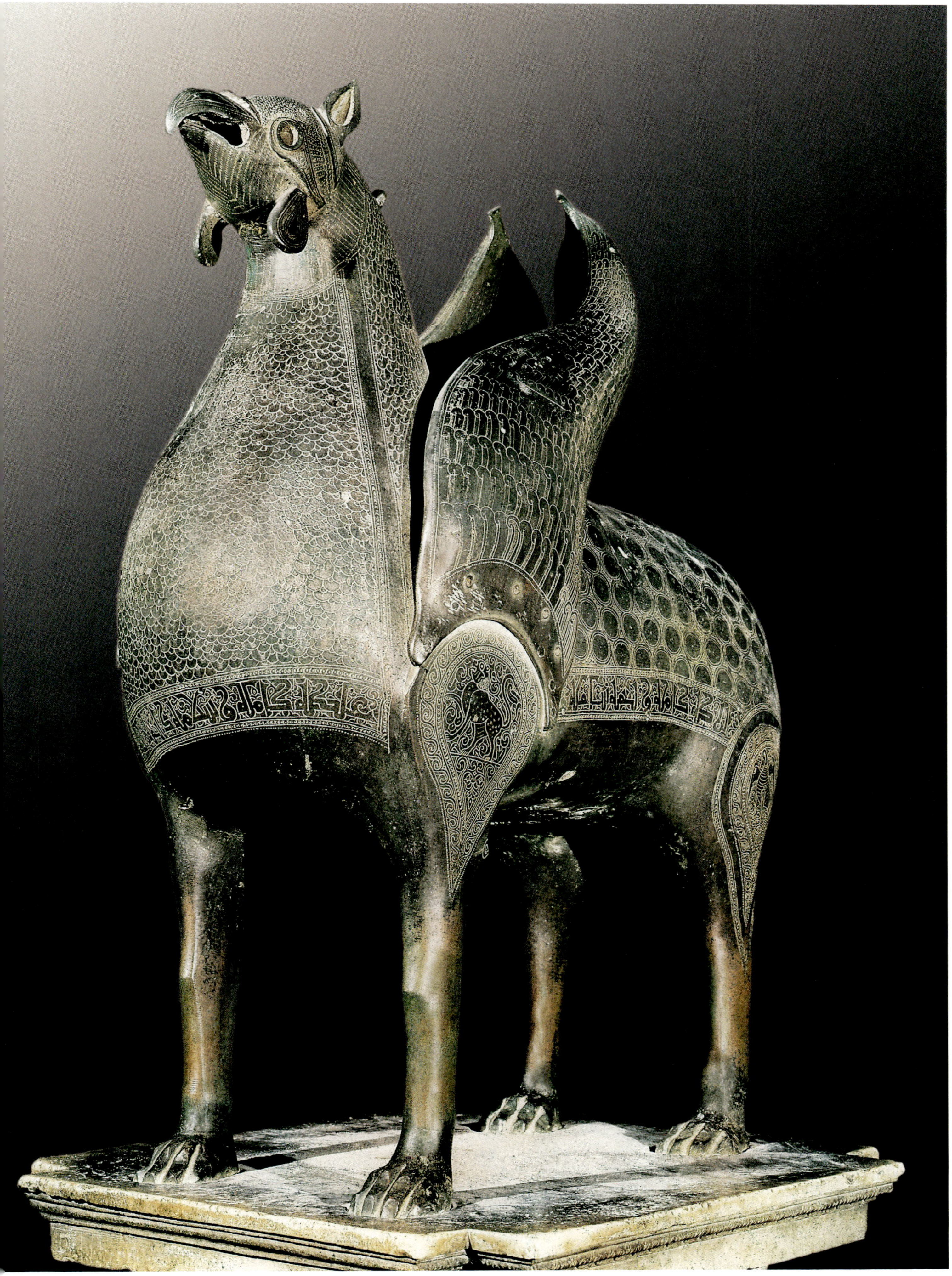

Gryphon
11th century
Bronze
Museo dell'Opera del Duomo, Cathedral, Pisa

More than one metre tall, this extraordinary piece – which probably served as a support for a candelabra or part of a fountain – was surely intended to adorn an extremely prestigious palace. Painstakingly crafted, this stylized and rather graceful object is endowed with a vibrant energy enhanced by an inlay that mimics feathers. The body is cast in a single piece, the wings and the tail (lost) being attached by rivets. The extraordinary carapacon over its back, edged with elegant Kufic calligraphy emblazoned with blessings for the owner and in the medallions on which images of animals appear, evidences the period's well-recorded enthusiasm for sophisticated fabrics. The sturdy design owes little to the art of the goldsmith, making the piece more like a sculpture than an article of furniture. It may not have been produced in Fatimid Egypt at all, and – as a proof of the extraordinary circulation of ideas and artists throughout the Islamic Mediterranean world between the tenth and eleventh centuries – origins such as Iran, Sicily, North Africa and Spain are perhaps all equally possible.

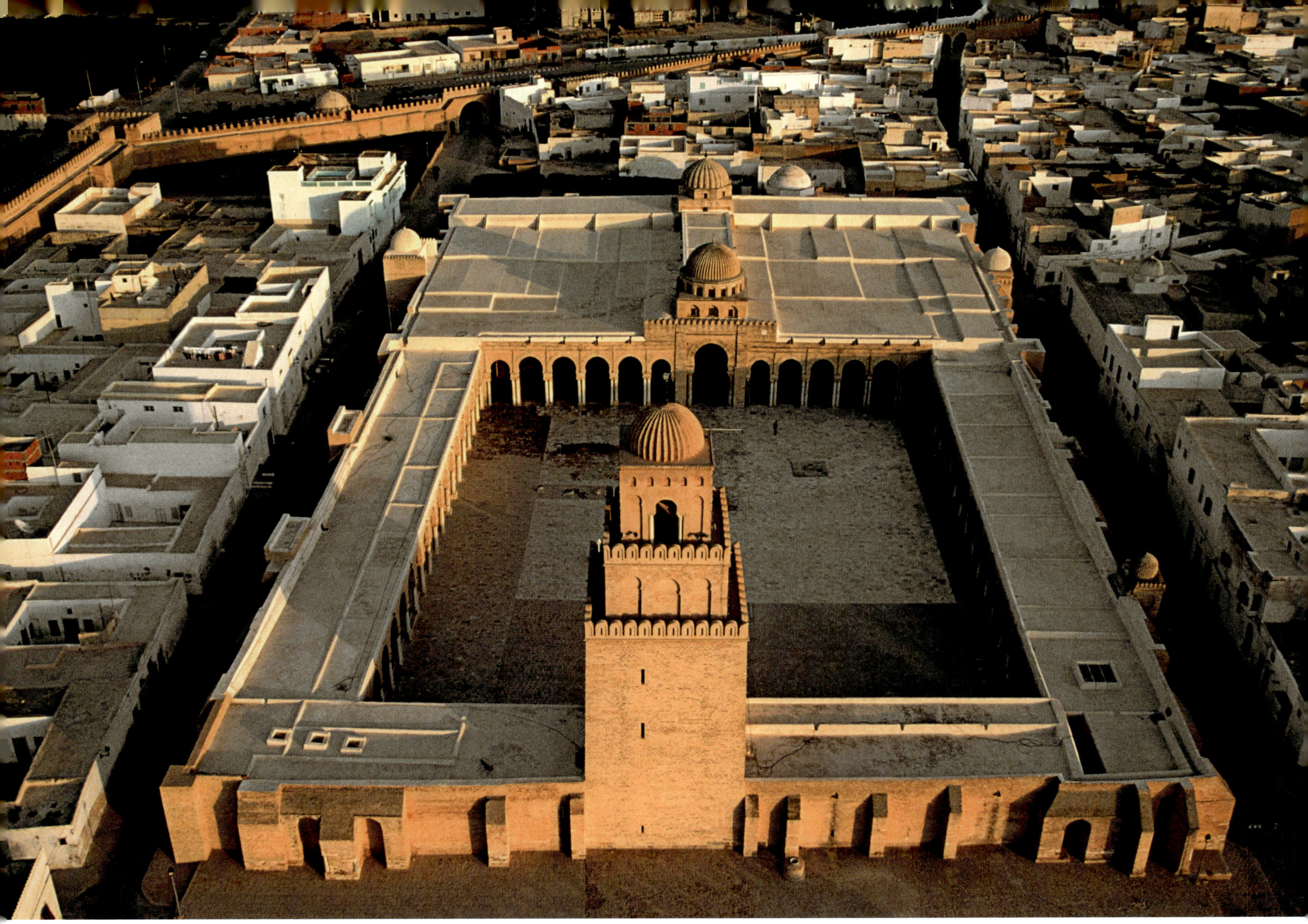

Great Mosque
836 and subsequent alterations
Kairouan, Tunisia

One of the absolute masterworks of Islam, the Great Mosque at Kairouan is not just the supreme achievement of Aghlabid dynasty architecture; it also constitutes the point of departure for all later North African architecture. Standing like an immense curtain wall, it inscribes a rectangle 125 metres long by nearly seventy-five metres wide. Supported on awkward-looking buttresses added between the thirteenth and eighteenth centuries to improve its statics, seen from a nearby road its appearance is anything but impressive. The sole remarkable elements from outside are the ribbed dome over the *mihrab,* contemporary with the first building phase, and the monumental three-stage minaret constructed in 836, a stocky, four-square form whose solemn bulk grandiloquently dominates the courtyard. The hypostyle hall presents the classic flat roof: the elevated elements arranged in a classic 'T' ground plan correspond to the central nave running between the cupola over the entrance and that over the *mihrab,* with the aisle parallel to the wall of the *qibla* lying perpendicular to the aforementioned.

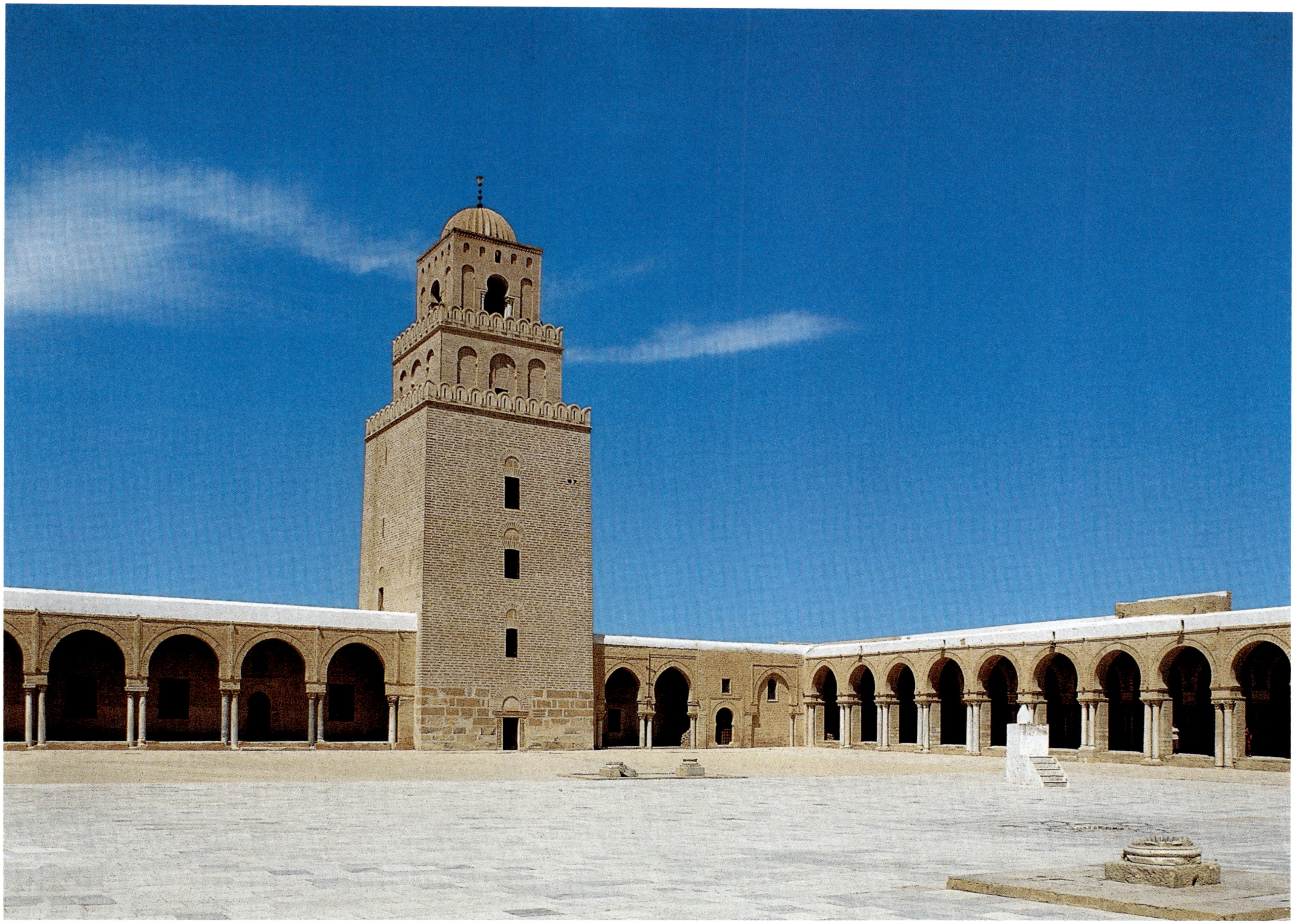

Great Mosque
Minaret and courtyard
836 and subsequent alterations
Kairouan, Tunisia

The mosque is dominated by the uncompromising square bulk of the great minaret over three tiers, one of the most fascinating Islamic monuments, constructed in 836 and characterized by the enormous thickness of the walls and its chunky, squat demeanour. Owing little to Syrian models, its form seems inspired by the Roman lighthouse at Salakta, still standing in the eleventh century and recalled in a mosaic at Ostia. Its unmistakable silhouette is visible for a considerable distance from the surrounding flat countryside. The almost square base is approximately eleven metres down each side. The total height of the three levels, of various heights and areas, exceeds thirty-one metres (excluding the pinnacle at the summit). The blind windows with horseshoe arches on the second floor are remarkable. Given its similarities with the spandrels on which the dome rests, the third level might well date to the same Hafsid campaign of restoration as the gate of Lalla Rayhana (1294), to the eastern side of the prayer hall, since it is constructed out of brick and demonstrates different techniques. The *sahn* ('courtyard') is ringed by arcades presenting a rhythmical alternation of semicircular and horseshoe arches borne on capitals and columns from Roman and Byzantine spolia. Although it is not clear whether the galleries had already been constructed at the time of Ziyadat Allah, they were certainly restored during the decline caused by the Hilalian invasions (1055) in the Hafsid period and then walled up, as demonstrated by a carved stone panel with floral motifs to be found at the southwest corner.

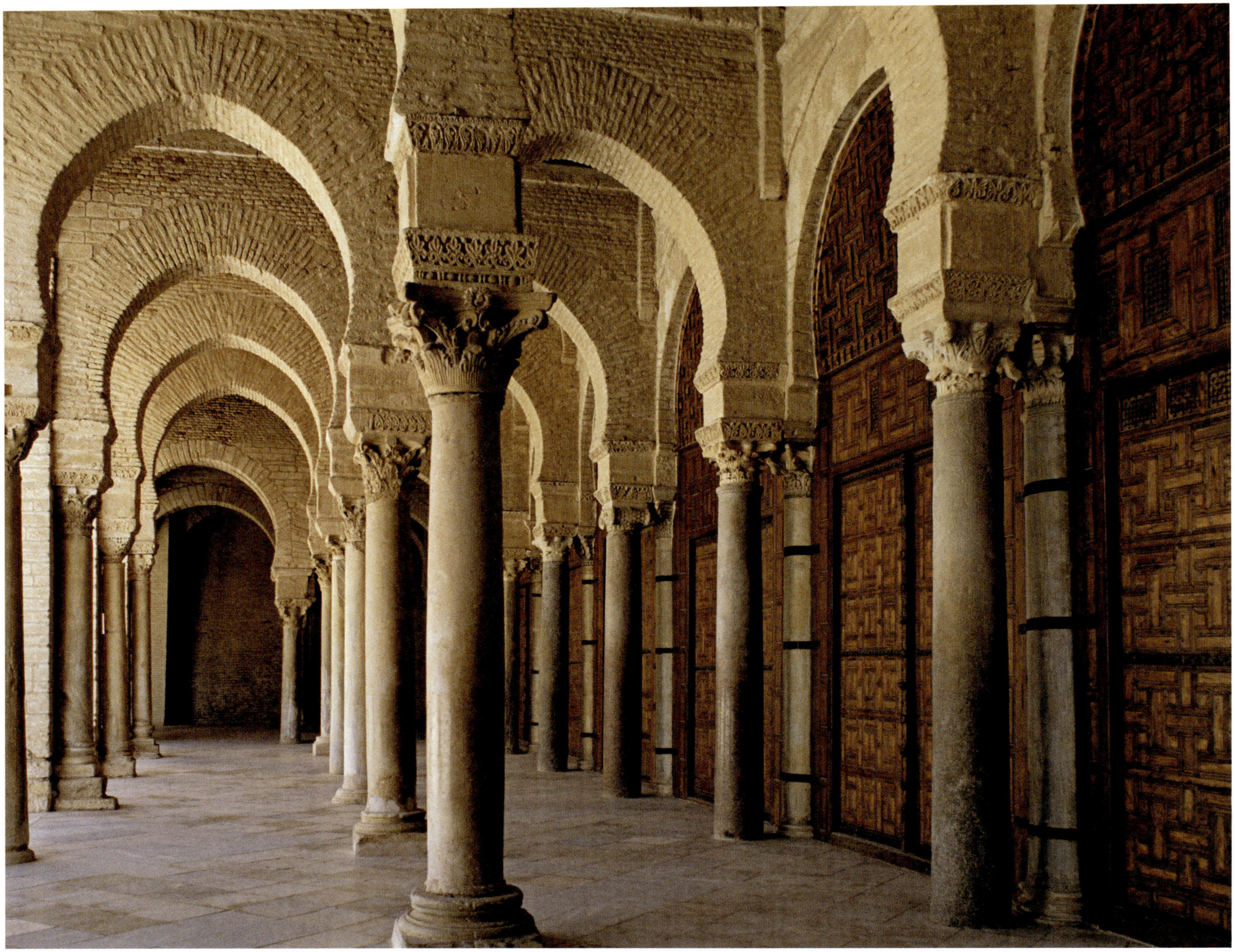

Great Mosque
Narthex facing the prayer hall
Late 9th century and subsequent alterations
Kairouan, Tunisia

The courtyard is encircled by arcades that rhythmically alternate horseshoe and round arches resting on capitals and columns with beautiful capitals from Roman and Byzantine-era spolia, probably added to the courtyard as early as the ninth century and later rearranged when repairing the damage caused during the Hilalian invasion. Surmounted by a dome, the narthex flanking the prayer hall was added by Ibrahim II (ninth century) and subsequently reworked.

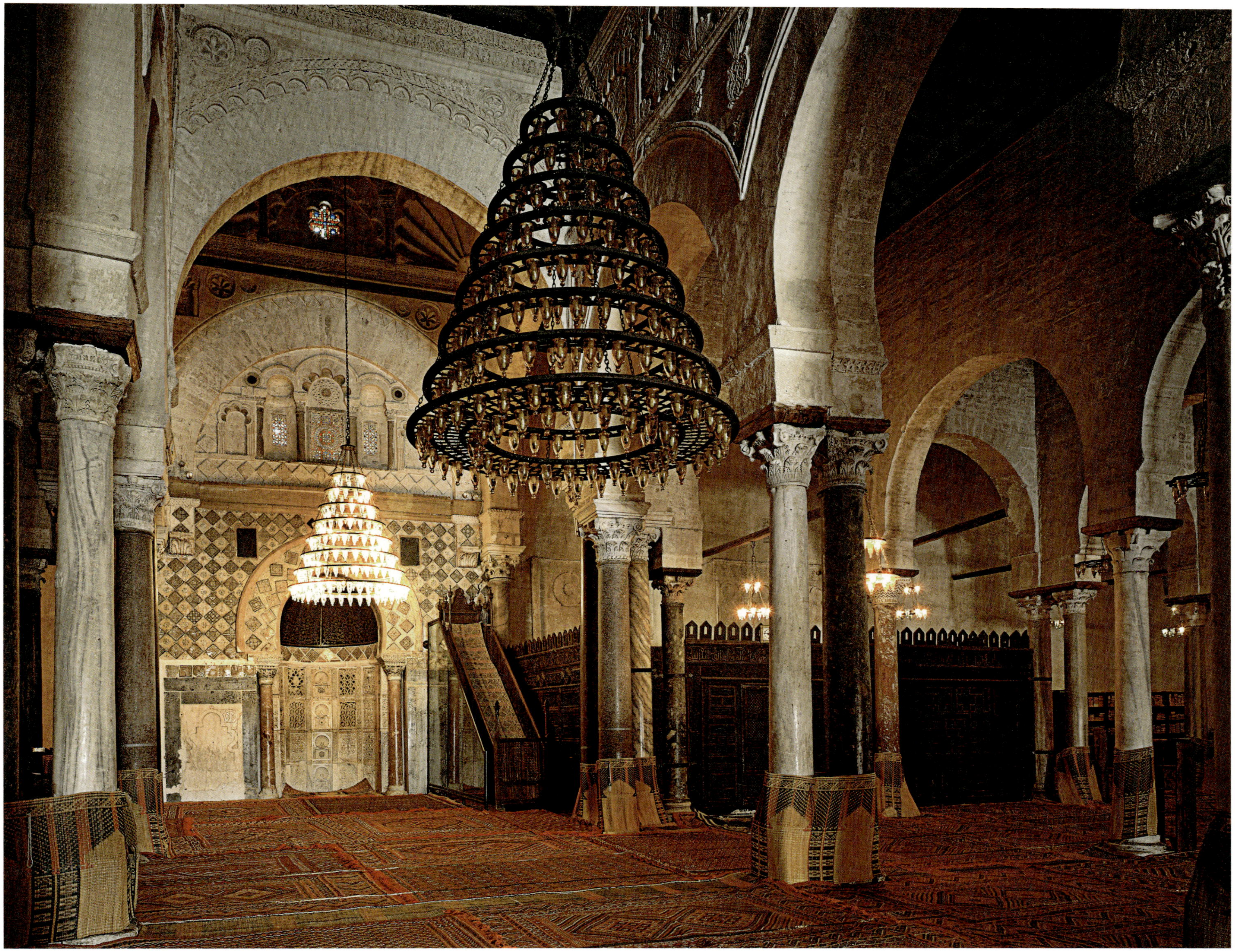

Great Mosque
***Mihrab* and *minbar* (9th century) and *maqsura* (11th century)**
Kairouan, Tunisia

The prayer hall is a perfect example of the Umayyad-type hypostyle mosque, with seventeen aisles perpendicular to the *qibla* and eight bays, the last forming in fact a continuous nave parallel to the *qibla* wall. Many of the columns and capitals come from Hadrumetum and Carthage. Save in the central nave that closes with the spectacular *mihrab,* the inner space appears unconfined, yet solid and solemn. The frame of the niche around the *mihrab* is adorned with approximately 150 lustreware tiles dating from the ninth century whose metallic shimmer produces the most beautiful shade of golden yellow. The oldest surviving securely datable examples, such tiles were imported from Baghdad by Abu Ibrahim Ahmad (856–863), who wanted to use them to decorate a palace reception hall, together with some teakwood for making lutes. He used them to build the *minbar* instead, a real jewel of Ifriqiyana art and the oldest to have survived.

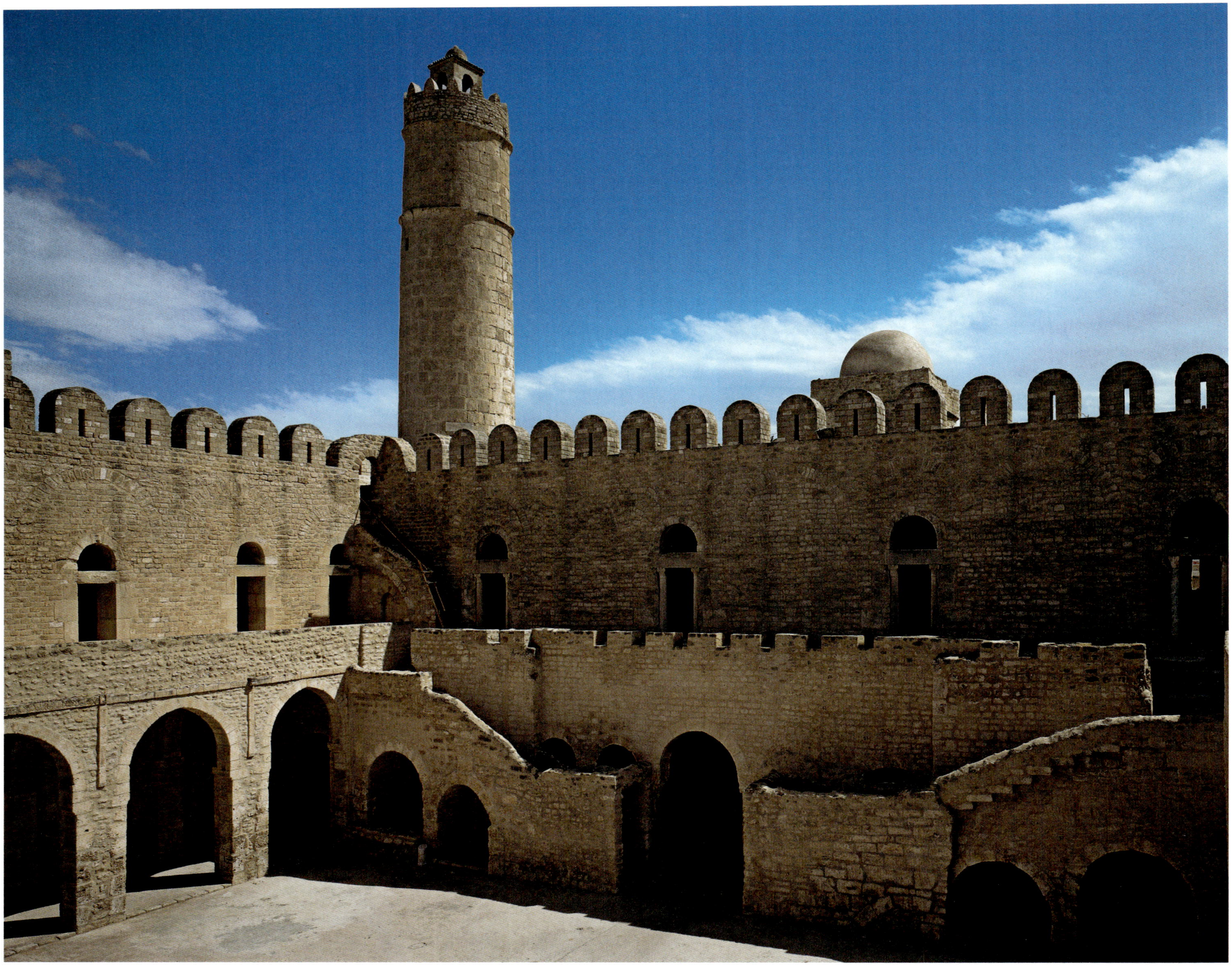

Ksar er-Ribat
821
Susa, Tunisia

The *ribat* of Susa stands before the contemporary Great Mosque, with which it formed the port's defensive system. The garrison was manned by 150 volunteers, keen to earn credit for participating in the *jihad* and who, in peacetime, dedicated themselves to devotional ascetic practices or missions, thereby earning the improper title of 'warrior monks'. The structure therefore has a twofold character, both military and religious, translated on the architectonic level by a planimetric typology with courtyards, as well as in the sobriety of the construction, the exiguity of the cells, and in the austerity of the prayer hall. The lofty tower is in fact not a minaret for the severe mosque within but fulfils a military function.

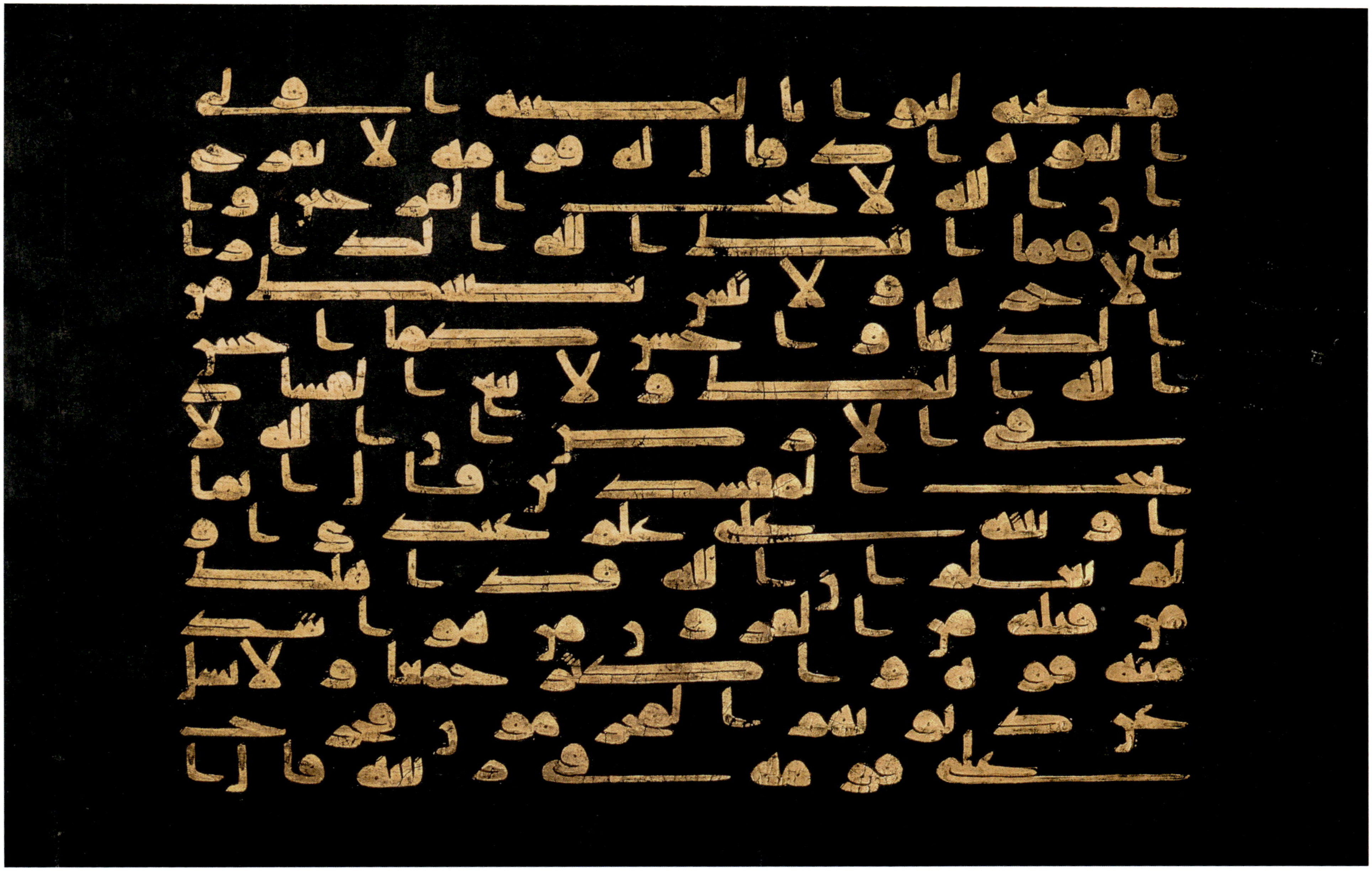

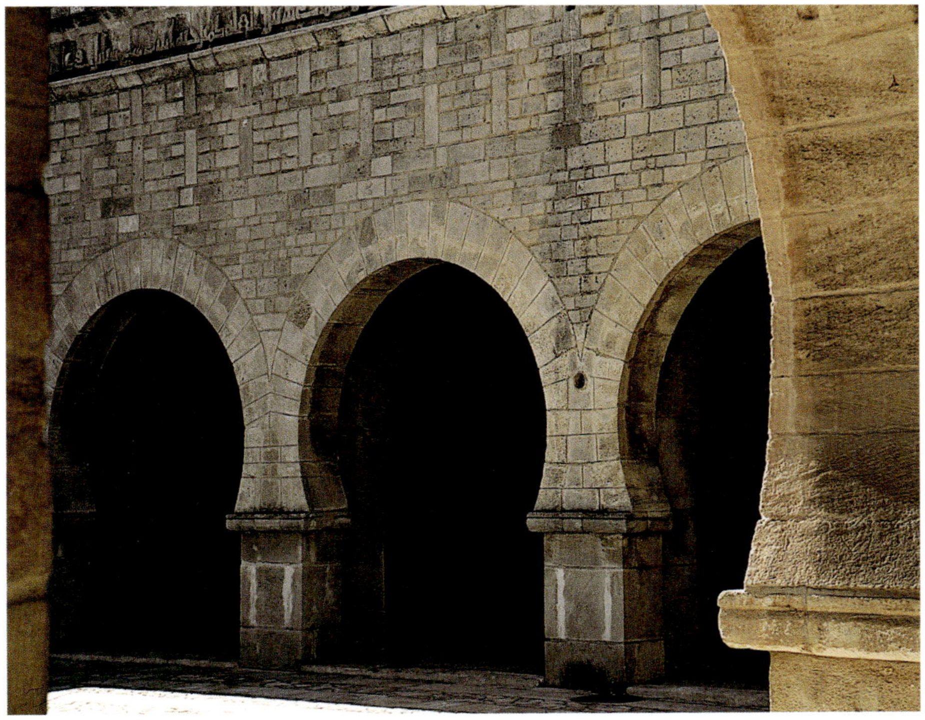

Great Mosque
Courtyard, detail
851
Susa, Tunisia

The mosque and courtyard are both imbued with the same ideals of austere beauty. Conveyed by structures pared down and cleansed of all decorative elements, here pillars have preference over columns, resulting in an absence of allusions to the Classical architecture of Rome and Byzantium. The 'school of Susa' derives its greatest aesthetic impact from the solemn rhythms arising from this impressive oscillation between matter and void.

Leaf from a Qur'an
11th (?) century
Gold on blue parchment
National Museum of Islamic Art, Raqqada

In the ninth century, Kairouan became one of the most prosperous cities in the Islamic world. The Great Mosque constituted its cultural heart and it disposed of a workshop that produced magnificent copies of the Qur'an which were subsequently exported to many places. These manuscripts include a practically unique piece whose peculiarity does not reside in its decorative inventiveness, in the quality of the calligraphy, or in the dimensions of the leaves, but in the materials out of which it is made. It was written in fact completely in letters of gold on sheets of parchment stained with a deep bluish indigo ink, with the addition of decorative elements in silver corresponding to the beginning of groups of verses. This solution was perhaps inspired by certain purple-dyed documents of especial prestige addressed by the papal chancery in Byzantium to the caliphs.

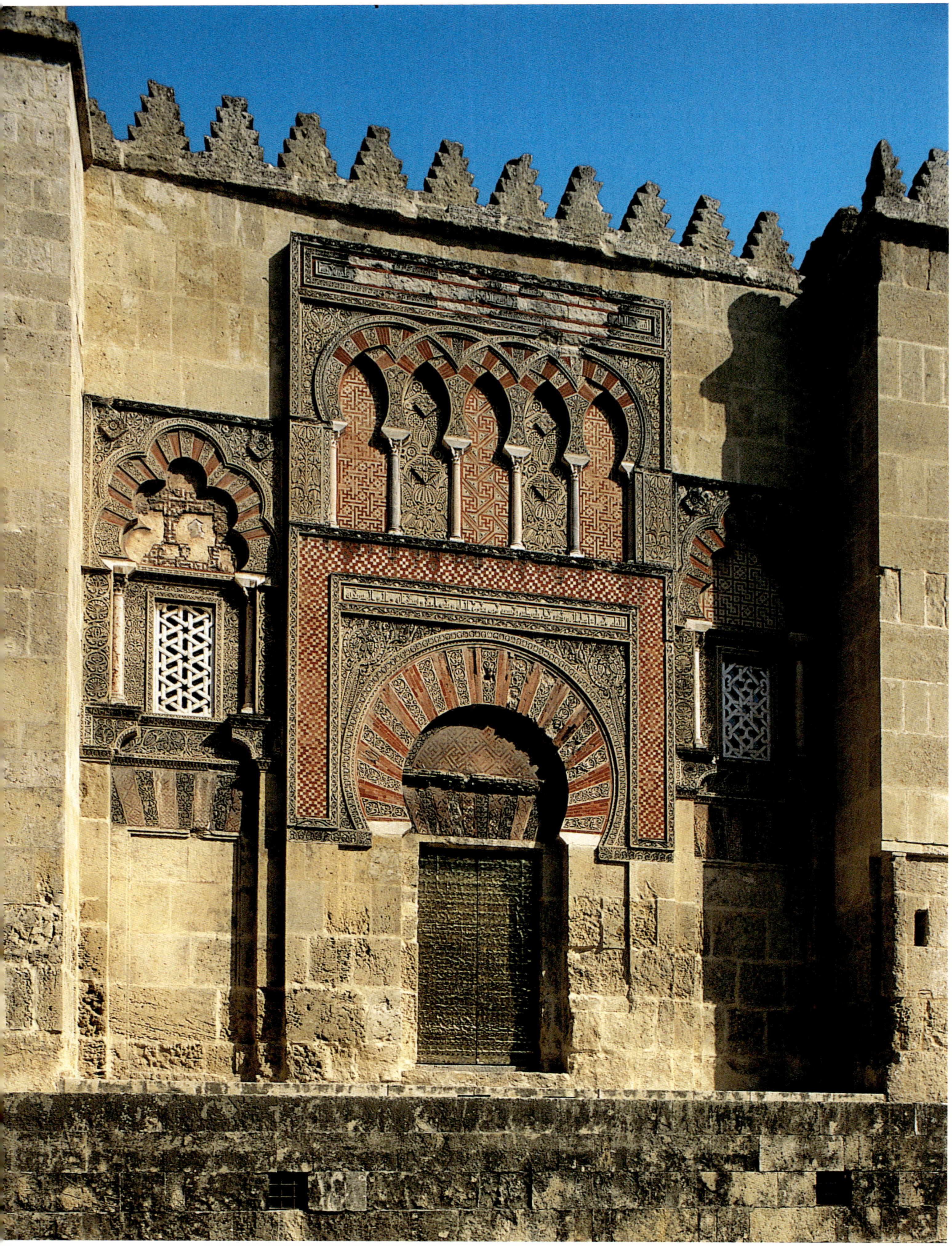

Great Mosque
South gate of al-Hakam II on the western side
786, 961–976
Cordoba, Spain

Planned by Abd al-Rahman and completed around 786, it took three successive campaigns to build the exterior of the Great Mosque. The powerful wall swells with huge buttresses between which stand open entryways employing a decorative programme that left its mark on all succeeding art in al-Andalus. The decoration is articulated over two levels: while the lower one is completely plain with neatly worked stone, referring perhaps to the condition of sublunary existence, the upper tier suddenly explodes into a grandiose arch and arcade that might allude to the unexpected glory brought by an insight into the divine attainable only through the act of prayer. The arch is bordered with the *alfiz,* an element destined to become enormously popular in al-Andalus, and is surmounted by a motif composed of four intersecting horseshoe arches, emboldening what is a visually and chromatically refined ensemble. The elegant little windows to the sides, protected by marble grating with a geometric pattern and crowned by a polyfoil arch make a graceful counterpoint for the central feature.

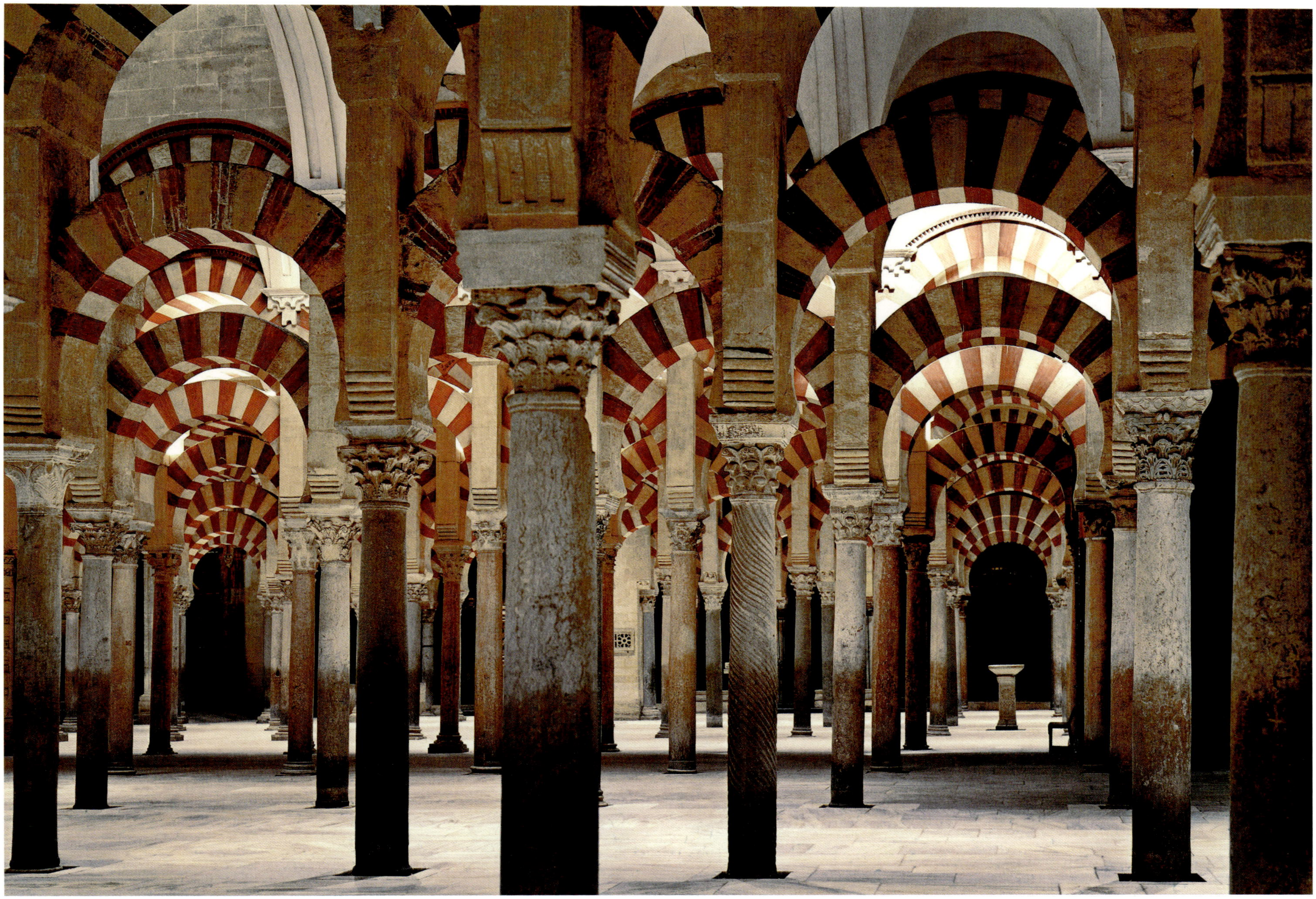

Great Mosque
Area extended by al-Mansur
987–988
Cordoba, Spain

The monument that provides the most accomplished interpretation of the classical conception of the hypostyle mosque in the Mediterranean Basin is the *mezquita* in Cordoba, inspired by the al-Aqsa at Jerusalem and by the Great Mosque in Damascus. Realized over a period of more than two centuries, the successive additions in general respected the splendid formulation of the original nucleus of Abd al-Rahman I with great coherence. A final programme of enlargement was undertaken by the minister al-Mansur, who had recourse to less valuable materials than those used in earlier eras, perhaps out of respect so as not to compete with the magnificence of the caliph's endowment. Since the available columns, many taken from Carthage, were not tall enough, two orders of archway were superposed: horseshoe arches were deployed below, acting as tie-beams, with semicircular ones above, resulting in a design of singular aesthetic effectiveness. Open to diverse readings, the space generated is therefore at once ordered and infinite, enfolded and surging upwards in what is a perfect balance between a sense of peace and harmony and an inexhaustible dynamism.

Great Mosque
Dome over the bay
preceding the *mihrab*
971–976
Cordoba, Spain

The structure of the cupola over the *mihrab* by al-Hakam II pushes the consequences of the solutions adopted in the main aisle to the extreme. Thanks to the use of mosaic the singular structural clarity of the ceiling of the nearby Capilla de la Villaviciosa seems here to melt into a glorious interlace of golden arches – forming two squares rotated through forty-five degrees, generating an octagon out of the base square – against which emerges the phantasmagorical apparition of the central dome. The exceptional quality of the handiwork, comparable to the Great Mosque in Damascus, also derives from the participation of Byzantine masters dispatched by the emperor of Constantinople, Nicephorus Phocas, with sixteen quintals of tesserae in gold and glass paste. They are responsible for the refined abstract floral motifs, pure and luminous transpositions in two dimensions of the stucco below. An inscription in Kufic provides symbolic support for a dome whose undulations, originating from a carefully calculated superimposition of geometric figures, is reinforced by eight blue ribs radiating out from a central sphere.

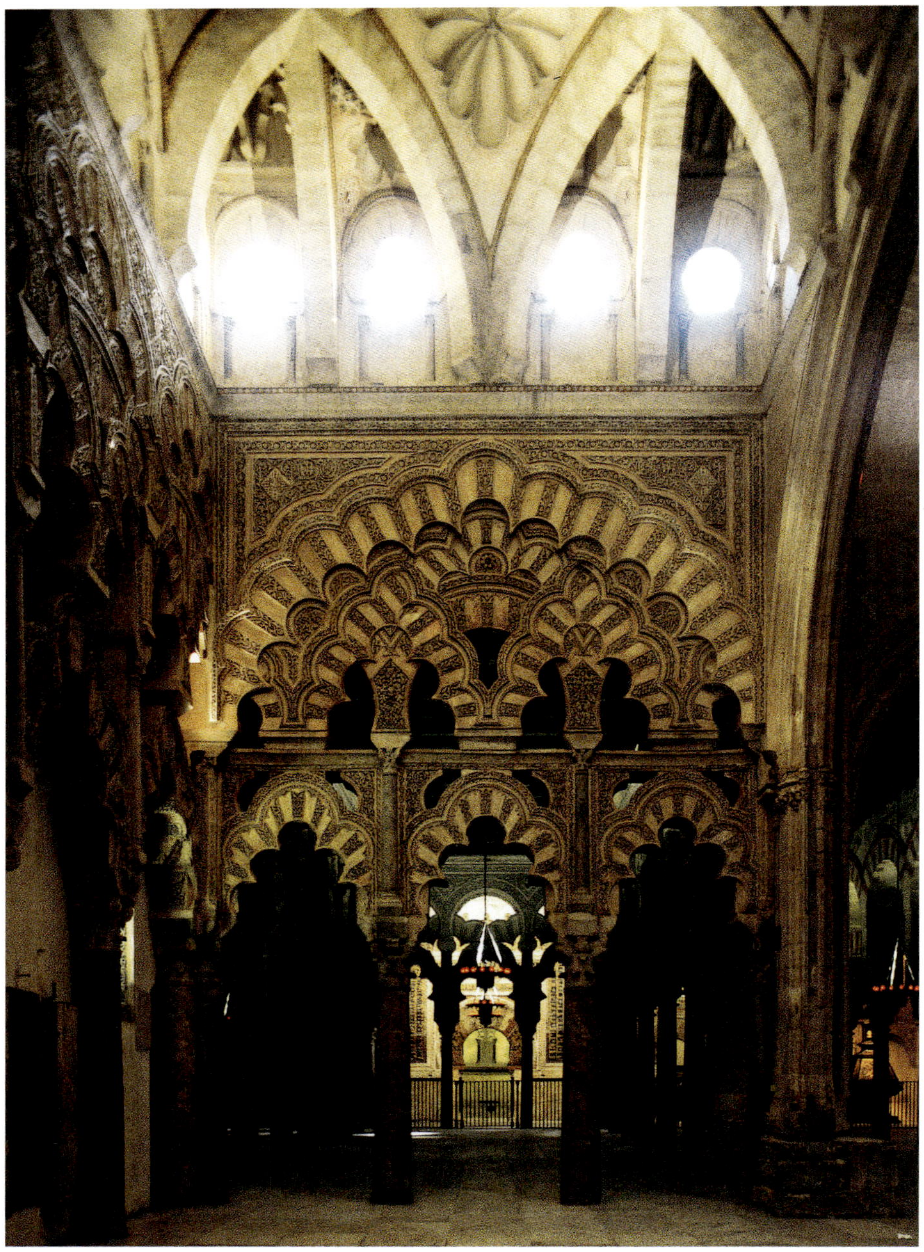

Great Mosque
Capilla de la Villaviciosa
961–976
Cordoba, Spain

Added during the enlargement undertaken by al-Hakam II (961–976), the span element in line with the *mihrab,* known as the Capilla de la Villaviciosa, upsets the architectonically rational conception of the archway, morphing what was a semicircular profile into scalloped edging. Multiplying the depth of the various planes, it dissolves the sculptural quality of the space, pre-empting, through an extraordinary crescendo, the explosion of light in the *mihrab.* The markedly theatrical statement made here seems to transgress the classical architectural rationality of Islam.

Great Mosque
Dome of the Capilla de la Villaviciosa
961–976
Cordoba, Spain

Composed of an octagon in which is inscribed an umbrella dome in twelve segments, the cupola rests on a pair of perpendicular arched braces, crossing four others at intersecting points. The twelve resultant triangles are crowned with smaller domes of great inventiveness, brilliantly lit by a particularly effective lighting system, originally through sixteen small windows with polyfoil arches borne on colonnettes.

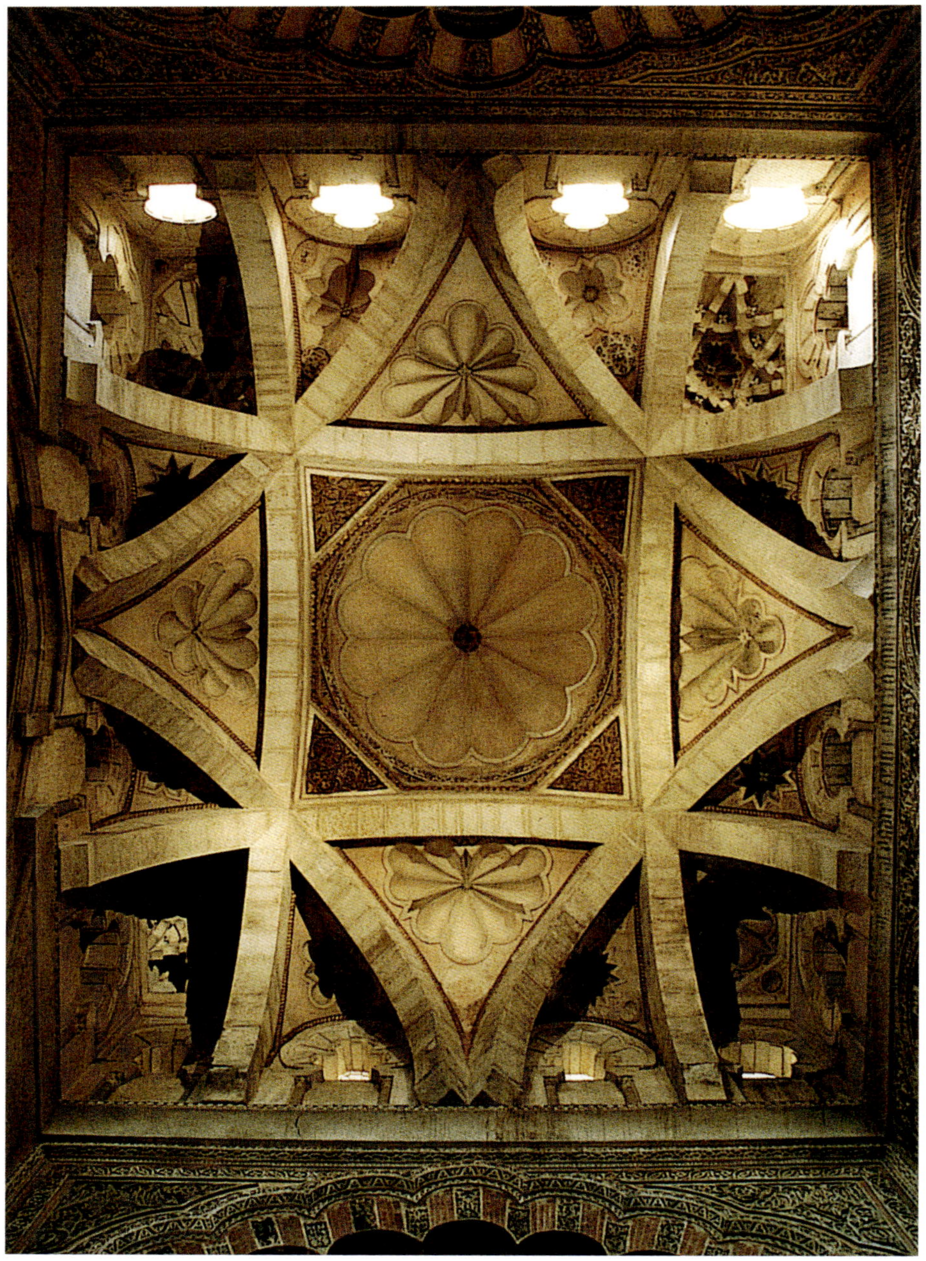

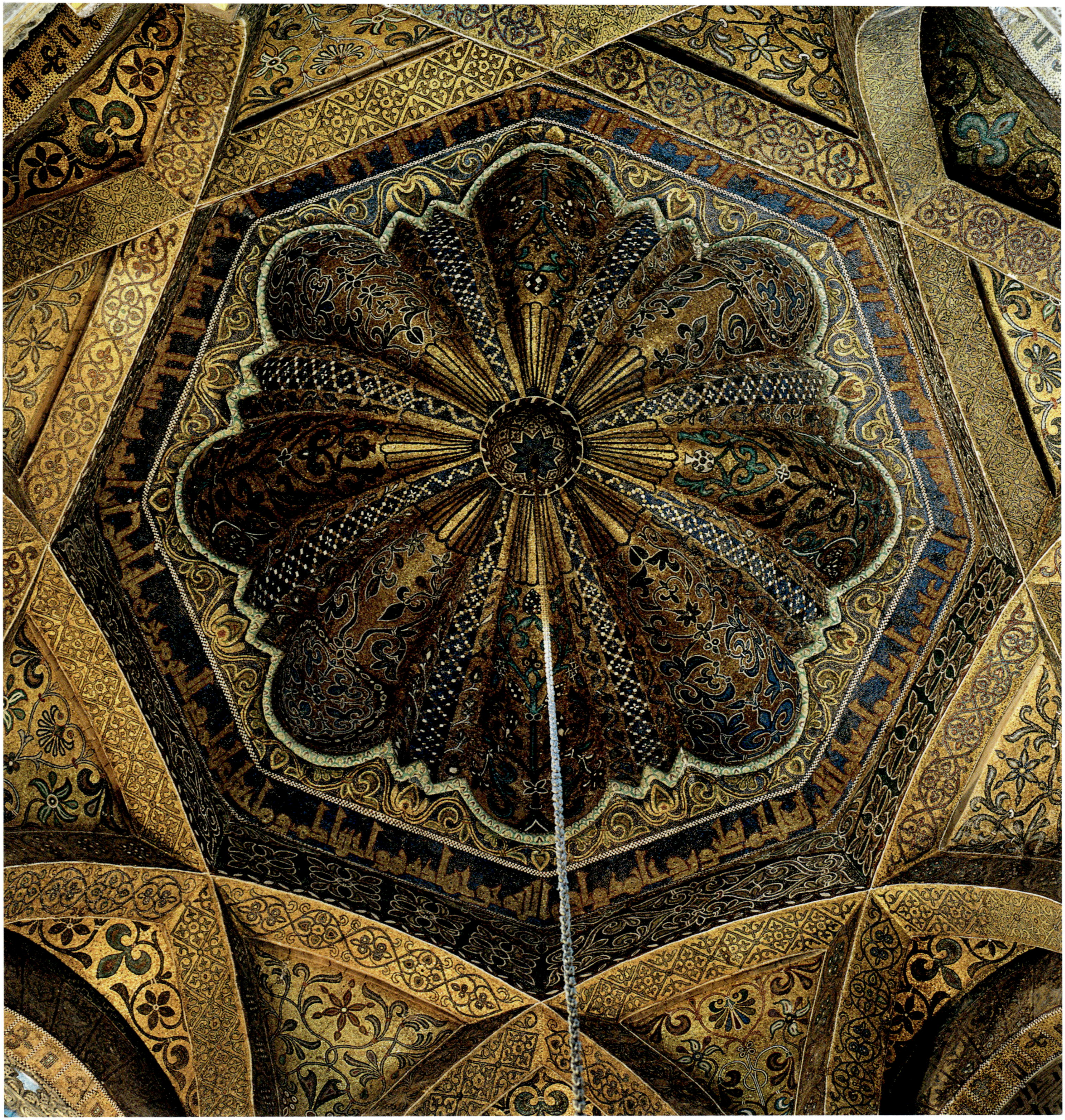

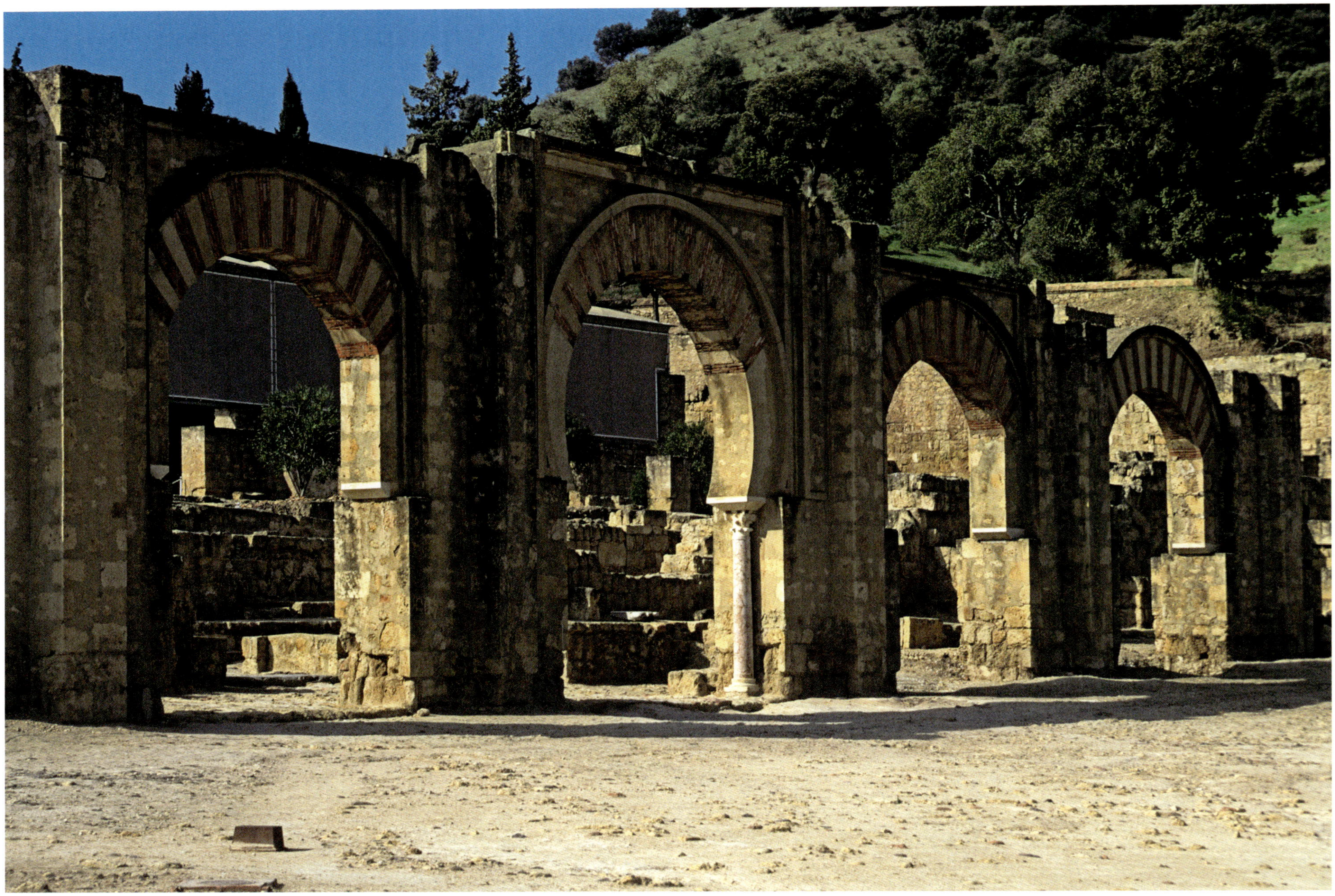

Madinat az-Zahra
Portico
Commenced in 936
Outskirts of Cordoba, Spain

Madinat az-Zahara, the new city ordained by Abd al-Rahman III but never completed and razed in the eleventh century, has for some years now been the subject of a patient restoration that strives to bring out its extraordinary architectural and urbane qualities. Of legendary refinement, the constructions are realized on successive levels of terracing, creating prospects of great variety and allowing maximum benefit to be made of a site rich in gardens, its open pavilions connected by colonnaded arcades serving as an ideal venue for promenading.

Pyx with the name al'Mughira
968
Ivory
Louvre, Paris

In al-Andalus the production of ivory objects attained unsurpassable levels of quality, comparable in terms of imagination to the architecture of the period. Surviving pieces include a number of ciboria which are either cylindrical with a convex lid, or else are in the shape of a rectangular box. They feature the names of the caliphs or court worthies for whom they were executed and thus allow for secure dating. The one illustrated comes from Madinat az-Zahra: one noteworthy characteristic consists in the way in which the plant interlace unwinds and defines with precision the space in which the human figures and animals act out various scenes. Thanks to the resourceful way in which the people, beasts and ribbons are woven into the underlying vegetal motif in the medallion and thus integrated into the space, the ensemble forms a harmonious whole that preserves it from a barbaric sense of *horror vacui* that might otherwise upset its delicate balance.

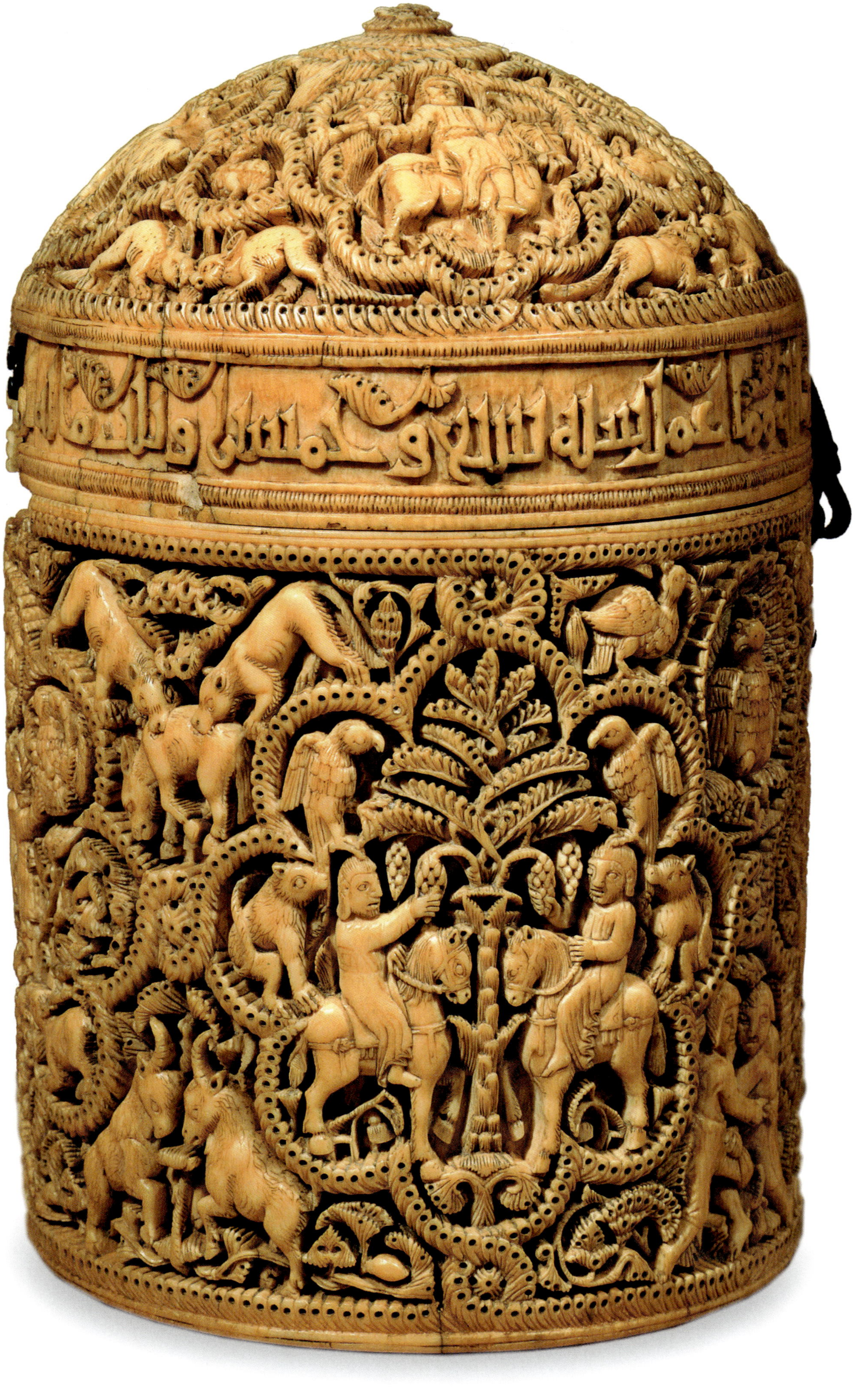

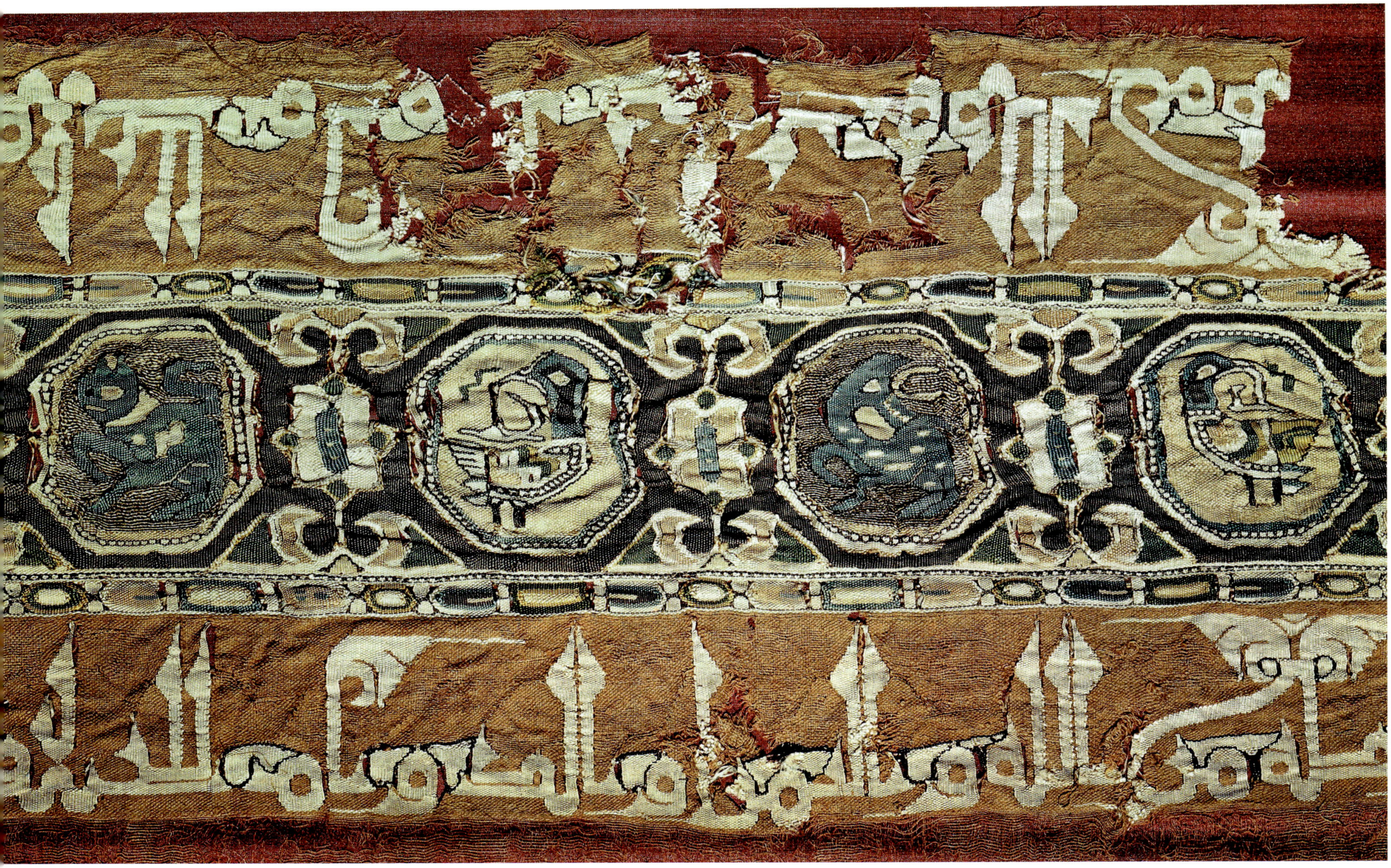

Cloth fragment
976–1013
Silk, linen and gold thread
Real Academia de la Historia, Madrid

This fragment is all that remains of a *tiraz,* a classic garment adorned with elaborate embroidery – in particular with embroidered bands containing writing – which was worn in the Umayyad realm and later under the 'Abbasids by powerful individuals, or at least by those of high rank, in both Ifriqiya and al-Andalus. The wide band in the middle unfolds into a series of octagonal medallions containing quadrupeds, birds or human figures alternating with a delicate design inspired by motifs from silverwork. It is flanked on both sides by a display of energetic calligraphy in a vaguely Kufic and elegantly foliate script. It informs us that the piece was realized for Caliph Hisham II (976–1013) and probably woven in Cordoba. 'Abbasid features, in particular those from the architectural ceramics at Samarra, are self-evident, but there are also affinities with contemporary productions from Fatimid Egypt, showing the osmosis in taste between Muslim élites in Mediterranean society.

Deer
Second half of the 10th century
Bronze
Museo Archeológico y Etnólogico, Cordoba

The passion for objects in bronze or copper alloy, particularly in the shape of predators or other animals, stems from the Sassanid world and is well-documented for the Umayyads of Damascus as well as later among the 'Abbasids. The taste for incense-burners, water jugs, bottles, and other utensils for liquids or hand-washing at table was prevalent throughout the Maghreb as well as in al-Andalus, where it became especially common until the arrival of the Almoravids with their penchant for moderation.
This red deer, found among the ruins of Madinat az-Zahra with other similar pieces, originally formed part of a garden fountain: passing through a tube under the base, the water travelled along the hollow legs and body to issue through the mouth. The massive trunk and legs lack naturalism, but the design manages to remain balanced and elegant. The surface has been worked all over with the graver to produce an iterative and schematic design of tiny saplings and eyelets inscribed in a series of tiny circles.

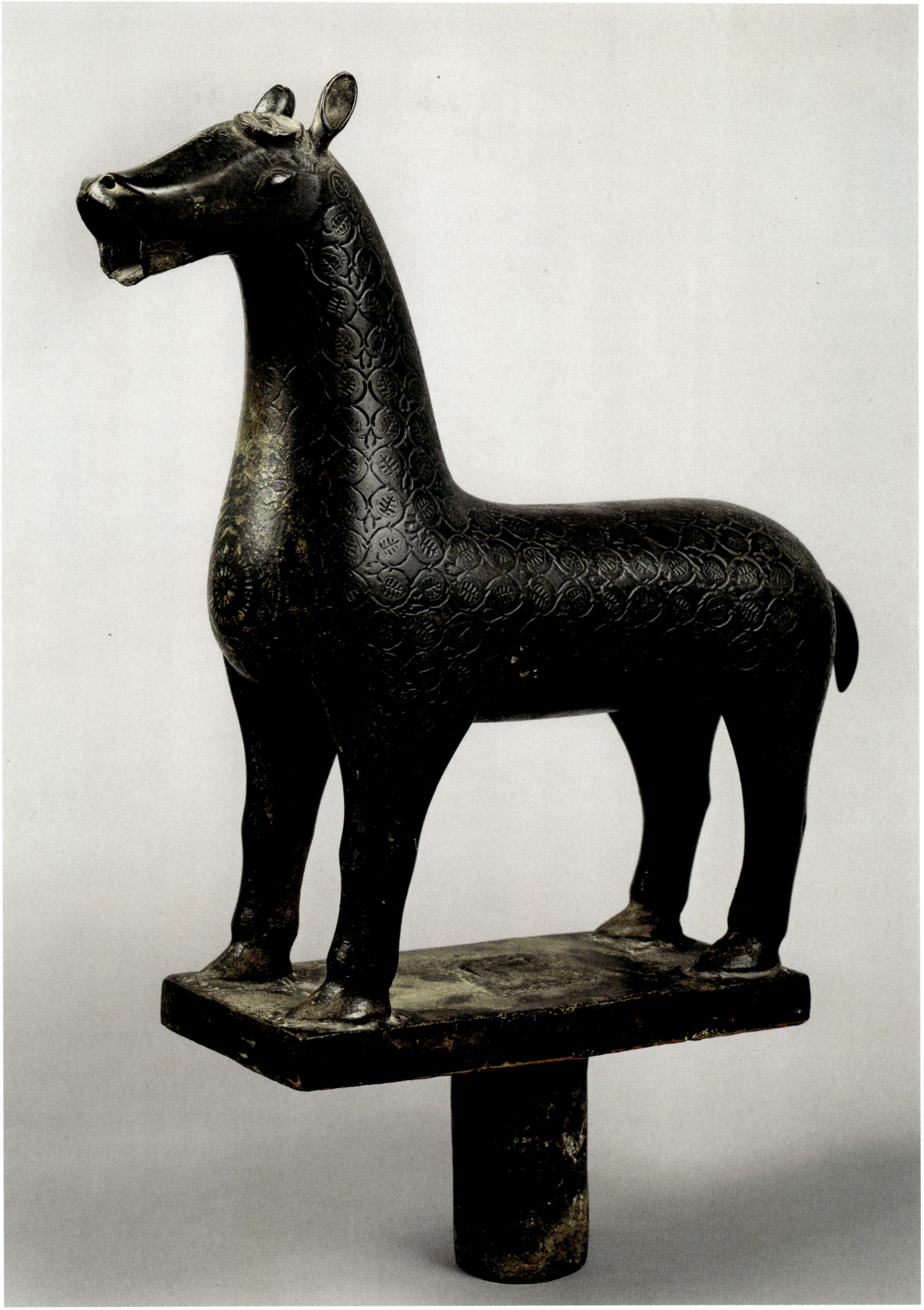

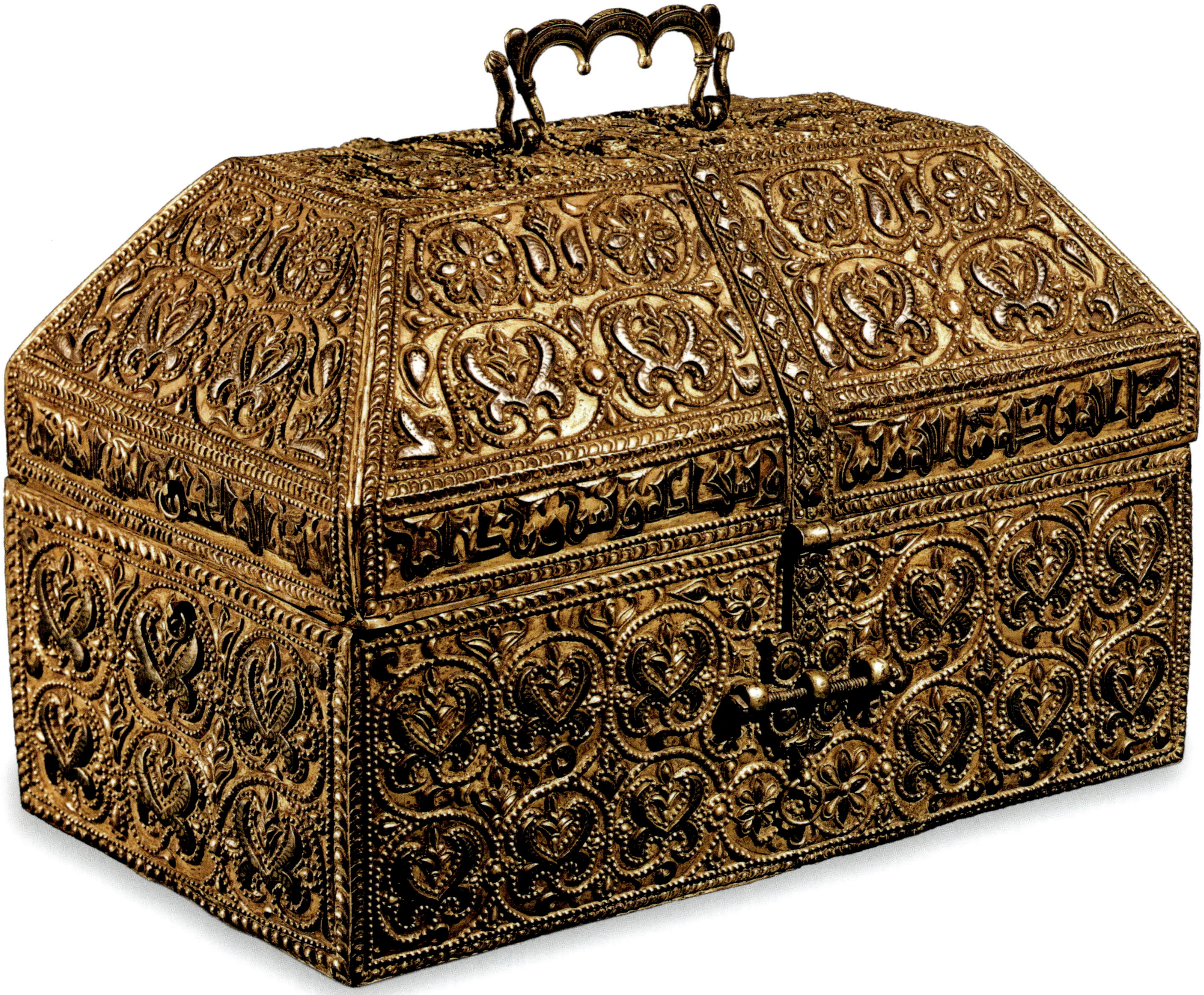

Casket decorated in niello
976
Silver and gold
Tesoro de la Catedral, Gerona

Umayyad, Fatimid and 'Abbasid sources all report how the practice of exchanging valuable objects of considerable size was widespread between members of the élite and that the more important pieces normally served as state gifts. Because of their material value, however, very few of these objects have come down to the present-day. The only surviving object in silver with gold inserts from a production much in vogue in the tenth century, the spectacular casket in Gerona, absolutely intact, demonstrates that the descriptions in the sources were not the result of poetic licence. It can be inferred from the lettering embossed into the nielloed silver sheet that runs along the side of the lid that the piece was created in 976 by the goldsmiths Badr and Tarif, who moreover left their signatures beneath the clasp. Embossed from behind, the decoration on the metal sheet echoes the much-vaunted style deployed in ivory carving (which in turn was not above re-echoing that of metal inlay). The silver inserts repeat in niello a floral motif of vaguely plant-like swirls with small golden spheres and culminating in elegant florets.

The Aljaferia
Second half of the 11th century,
Zaragoza, Spain

On the dissolution of the caliphate, emirs in various cities in al-Andalus assumed regal titles and financed prestigious architectural projects whose quality was in no way inferior to those of the caliphs. Abu Jafar Ahmad Ibn Suleiman, for example, built the Aljaferia, one of the most eloquent architectural testimonies of the period. Outwardly a powerful fortress with a moat, inside it is a sumptuous arbour, equipped with all the most up-to-date comforts and sophisticated artistic contrivances.

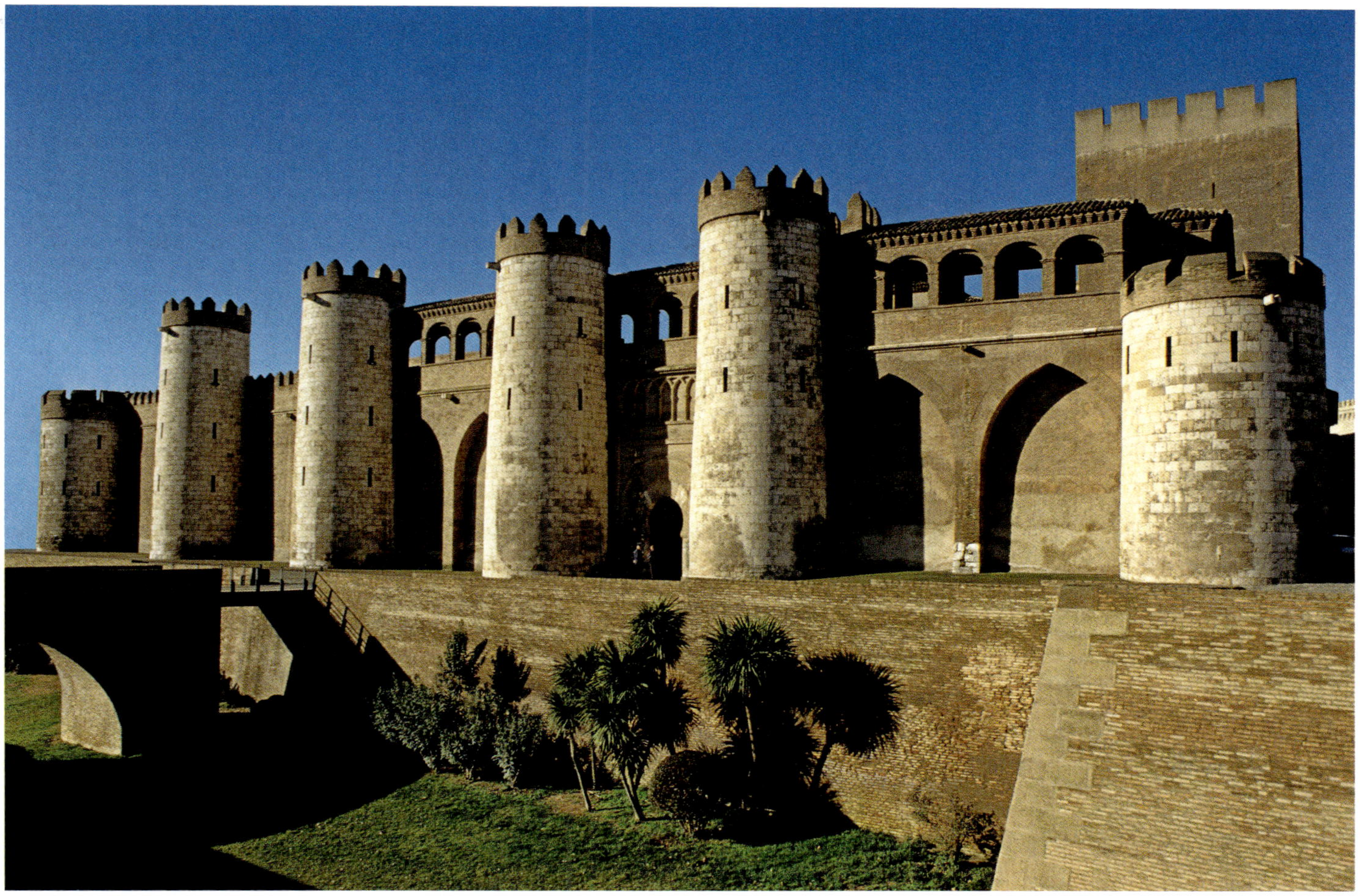

The Aljaferia
Detail in the courtyard
Second half of the 11th century,
Zaragoza, Spain

The rectangular courtyard is closed by a portico with pointed arches. It constitutes an important stage in the evolution of a motif handled here with such boundless creativity and decorative overabundance that the architectonic structure is suffocated. The ambivalence apparent in the archway into the Capilla de la Villaviciosa at Cordoba is here pushed to its extreme conclusion: decoration is fused and confused with the structure, while architectural forms morph into evanescent and elegant graphics liable at any time to wander off into the arabesque. Anticipating analogous designs in Granada and Morocco, this setting of singular refinement, in which the prince was fond of playing host to poets, must surely have been a splendid venue for hedonistic banquets complete with wine, food, verse and music.

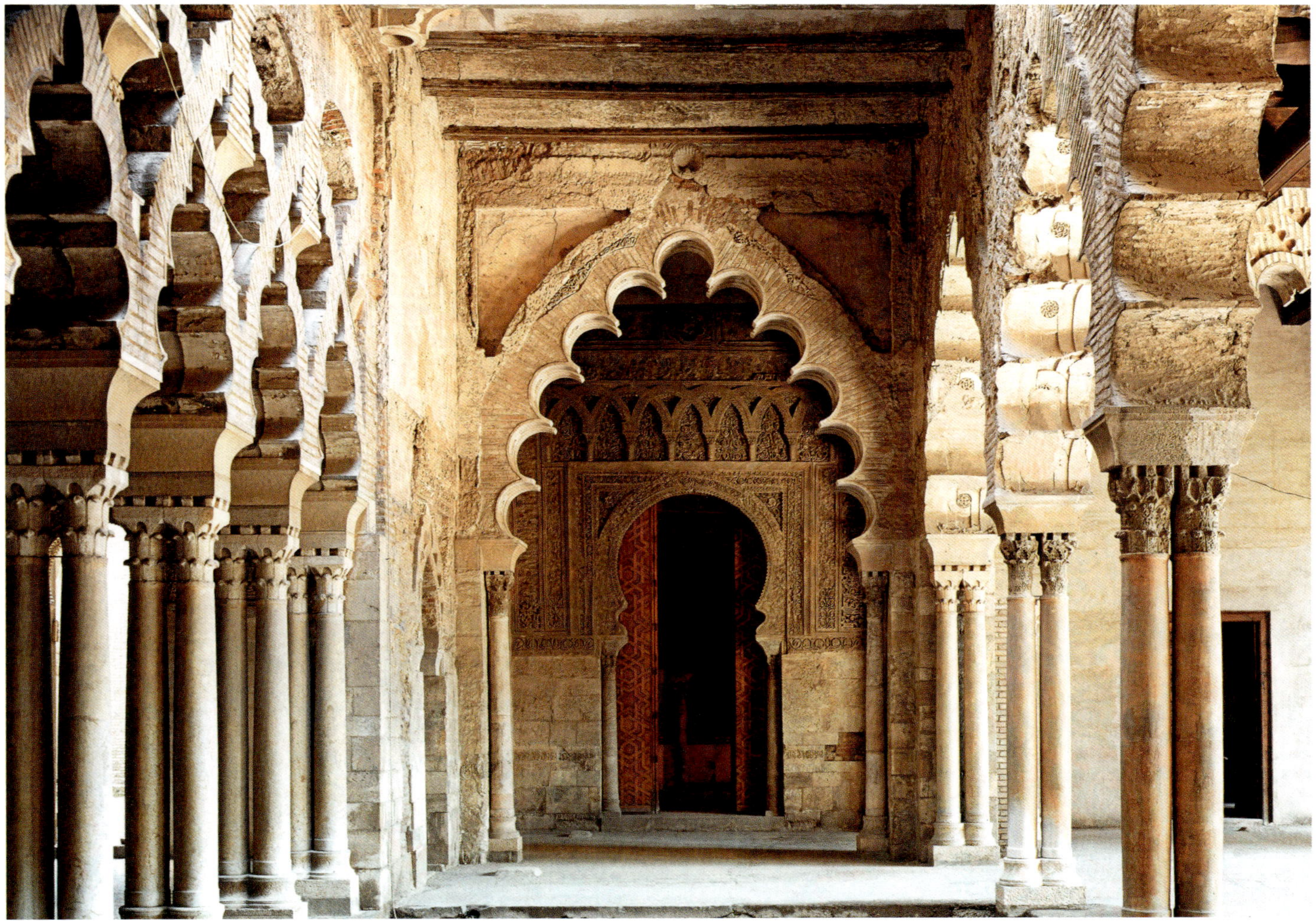

CENTRAL ASIA BETWEEN THE TENTH AND TWELFTH CENTURIES

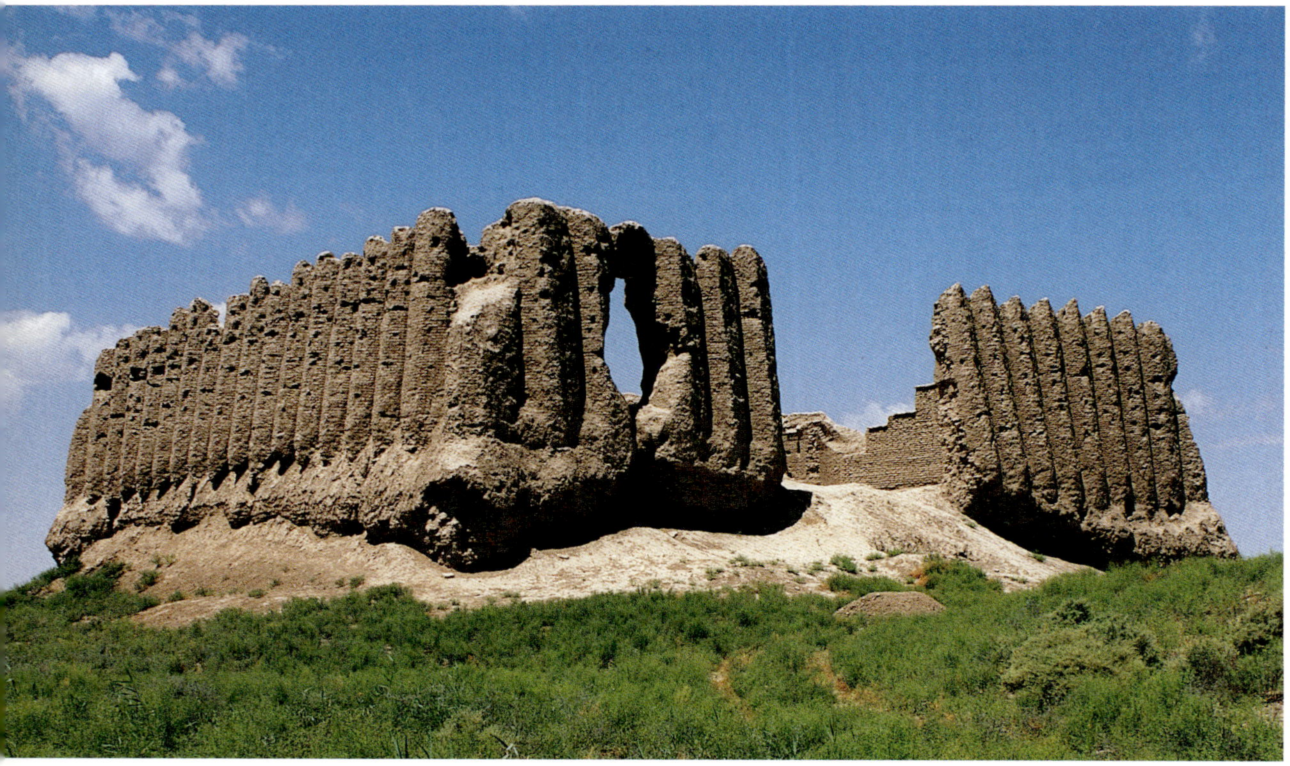

Sultan Qal'a
('Palace of the Governor')
8th or 10th century
Merv, Turkmenistan

The spread and gradual consolidation of the faith in the boundless expanses of Central Asia, where Muslim civilizations produced some of their grandest achievements, is still a relatively unfamiliar subject. Early monuments which have survived are rare and scattered over an immense and geographically and culturally diverse territory. The history of the region remained tumultuous even after the process of Islamicization, which came to a halt at the borders of the Chinese empire in the eighth century. The area under Islamic rule can be split into five main regions: southwest and western Iran, open to contact with the Mesopotamian world and with Kurdish peoples from the Near East and the Mediterranean; northwestern Iran (present-day Azerbaijan) with links to Armenian and Georgian peoples who, strongly indebted to the Byzantine world, had forged a remarkable independent tradition, particularly in the field of architecture; wild, mountainous and inaccessible northern Iran, inhabited by daunting warrior tribes; the (Greater) Khorasan and Transoxiana, regions of ancient civilization (corresponding to today's northeast Iran, northwest Afghanistan, Turkmenistan and Uzbekistan) lying along trade routes with China down which poured the invading armies from the East; and Sistan (southern Afghanistan and western Pakistan) and Afghanistan, tough, arid scenery crisscrossed by important communication routes along which Buddhism travelled from India.

These regions were all converted by a tiny number of Arabs, for the most part military men who set up their headquarters in major frontier cities. These outposts were occupied by *ghazi* – warriors of a faith that acquired an epic, 'frontier' character; numerous *ribat* are documented in the sources. They were soon followed by merchants, so that the cities became bastions in the spread of the new religion. How exactly their presence was manifested in terms of architecture is far more difficult to say, but the adoption of Islam seems to have paralleled the development of the new Persian language, a valuable indicator of cultural unity that would find in art and above all in architecture further novel and highly characteristic means of expression.

In the ninth century, the 'Abbasids' grip on power in Baghdad slackened notably and some governorships, such as the Tahirid Arabs (820–973), the Iranian Samanids (819–999), the Saffarids of the Sistan (the 867–963) and the later the Buyids of Iran (932–1062), eventually gained control over large swathes of land that lacked defined borders and were subject to frequent changes of rule. These vast territories contained relatively few notable cities, the lion's share being located in northern regions, such as Rey (near Tehran), or in the Khorasan, with Nishapur, Herat, Balkh and Merv (Marw), all situated along significant axes of trade. Of equal importance were the cities such as Bukhara and Samarkand on the frontiers of Transoxiana, the heartland of Sogdian rule in the pre-Islamic epoch, and a crossroads between the steppes and the urban world as well as between China and Persia. Over the centuries a culture of remarkable richness had sprung up in Sogdiana, taking its inspiration from the Greco-Hellenistic world bequeathed by the conquests of Alexander the Great.

In these areas cultural development was marked by the encounter and fusion of two reciprocally reinforcing influences. The first grew up from the fertile heritage of a culture of Arab-Islamic imprint which was in turn abundantly indebted to Greek civilization, especially in the philosophical, medical and scientific fields. The latter gravitated towards the Mediterranean world, where important schools of philosophy, medicine and astronomy developed. These centres witnessed the birth and career of some of the most brilliant cultural personalities of any age: al-Farabi (c. 870–950), known to the Arabs as 'the second master' after Aristotle, a philosopher of great penetration, a powerful logician, talented musician and political theorist; al-Farghani (died 861), an eminent astronomer and author of the *Elements* which remained a textbook in Europe until the seventeenth century; al-Razi (850–925/935), the most famed physician of the premodern age after Galen and the only thinker of the time to consider philosophy as a self-governing instrument and the only royal road to truth, and with the courage to deploy it in fundamentally rational readings of and commentaries on the revelation; al-Khorezmi (780–850), a noteworthy astronomer and brilliant mathematician, the inventor of the procedure of systematic calculation that now bears his name, 'algorithm'; Ibn Sina (Avicenna, 980–1037), a groundbreaking physician and profound philosopher who put the Aristotelian corpus into perspective by treating it as but one of many degrees of truth, and who considered God as an incontrovertible philosophical principle; and al-Biruni (973–1048), one of the greatest astronomers of all time. The second, Iranian tendency was prompted by the example of the towering poet Firdusi (Firdawsi, literally 'the Heavenly'), born at Tus in the Khorasan around 940 and dying around 1020. He was the author of the great national epic poem, the *Shahnameh* ('Book of the King', written in the eleventh century), which signalled the birth of modern Persian and the renaissance of Persia as a protagonist of the first rank in Islamic culture.

This is the backdrop against which the Central Asian interpretation of Islamic art, characterized by breathtaking speculation and mystical vision, unfolded. To this bubbling cauldron came ingredients added by the constant influx of immigrants that increased exponentially from the tenth century. These included Turkic peoples from the east: at first their role was that of slaves and soldiers, but they later coalesced into shifting tribal groups, some of huge size like the Ghaznavids and the Seljuqs, and redrew the history of Central Asia and of Muslim civilization generally. The civil buildings and still more tellingly the congregational mosques from the first centuries of Islam in all the major cities here have mostly disappeared, even if the most ancient surviving structures can boast some authentic masterpieces. This renders problematic any linear reconstruction of the roots of an architectural heritage that culminated in some of the most fascinating constructions of all time. Fortunately the situation proves far less drastic when it comes to contemporary objects, which have survived to the present-day in relatively high numbers, although they can only rarely be dated with certainty and it remains difficult to allocate them to a specific place of production. The greater part might date to the tenth century – in other words during the dynasties of the Samanids and the Buyids.

The most impressive articles to have survived and the most innovative experiments occurred in the field of ceramics. Production attained a *nec plus ultra* in both eastern Iran, at Nishapur and in the region of Samarkand. If the origins and early stages are unknown, it appears evident that its sources of inspiration are to be sought essentially in three areas. The first wellspring is constituted by items from the region of Iraq, in particular the much-vaunted white-glazed ceramics decorated in cobalt blue or green with geometric or vegetal patterns or with calligraphy, as well as a polychrome variant showing animal figures within medallions. The second consists in ceramics from China (attempts to imitate which were already underway in the Iraq region), most notably three-colour *sancai* pieces with dots and patches in green, tawny-yellow and violet on a white ground, a technique often combined with incising. The third stimulus derived from a reinterpretation of local Sassanid art, with subjects of imperial nature, which developed primarily at Nishapur. The influence of Sassanid court art is especially noticeable in precious metalwork objects and, although less well-documented, also in textiles, not only for rugs, carpets and wall-hangings, but also for garments.

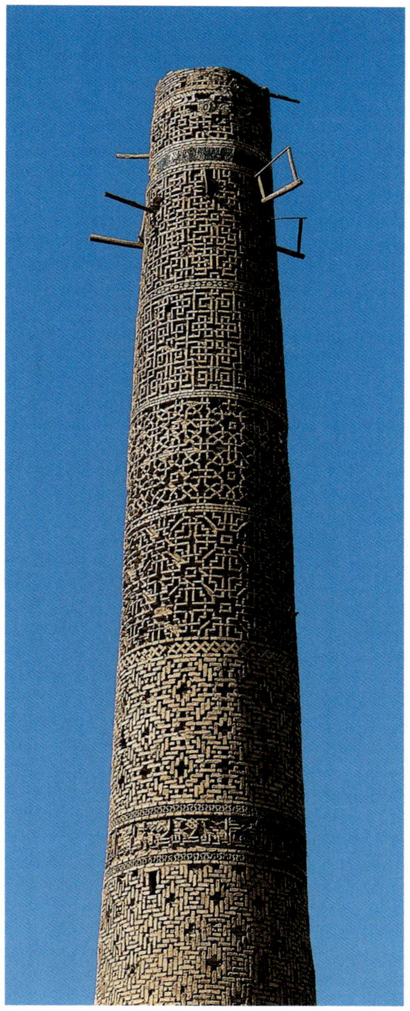

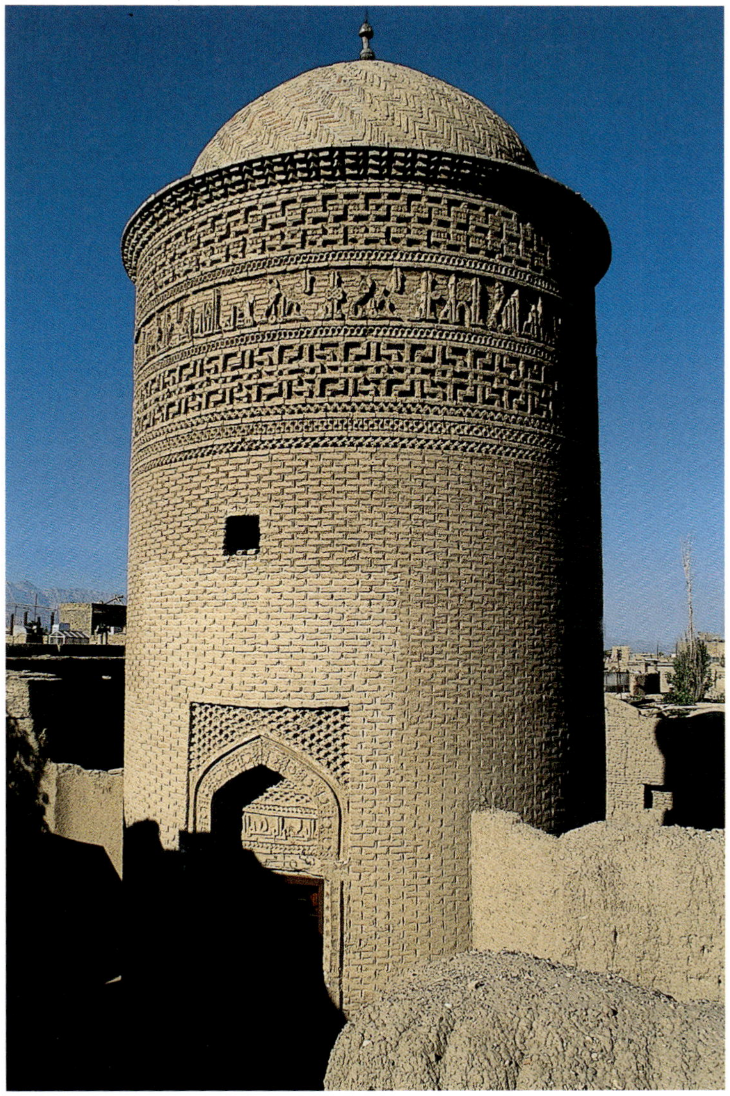

Pir-e Alamdar Mausoleum
1021–1026, Seljuq period
Damghan, Iran

Tarik Khane Mosque Minaret
1028, Seljuq period
Damghan, Iran

Mausoleum of Isma'il
c. 907
Bukhara, Uzbekistan

The level of philosophical abstraction attained in the age of the Samanids also had a secondary impact on contemporary architecture, encouraging aesthetic solutions that convey in highly intellectualized forms the complex conceptions enlightened by faith that man can intuit though lucid thinking. This small-scale mausoleum was conceived as a quivering cube drenched in light due chiefly to the peculiar manner in which the bricks (standing for the earthly world) are coursed and crowned by a hemispherical cap (the infinite universe). Of solemn simplicity, intricate but limpid, combining grandeur with buoyancy and imposing though of modest proportions, the monument is of strikingly serene geometry. Bright and vibrant in its chromatic weft and weave, uncluttered yet inexhaustibly rich, its materials emerge from the apparent uniformity of four equal sides to make a noble statement of eternity. Freighted with historical and symbolical significance, the structure of the Zoroastrian fire temple is here defined through the ineluctable geometrical and mathematical definitions of al-Khwarizmi, al-Farghani, or Ibn Sina, who confer on such illustrious and incontrovertible traditions the stamp of a truth acquired through mental alertness and an enquiring mind.

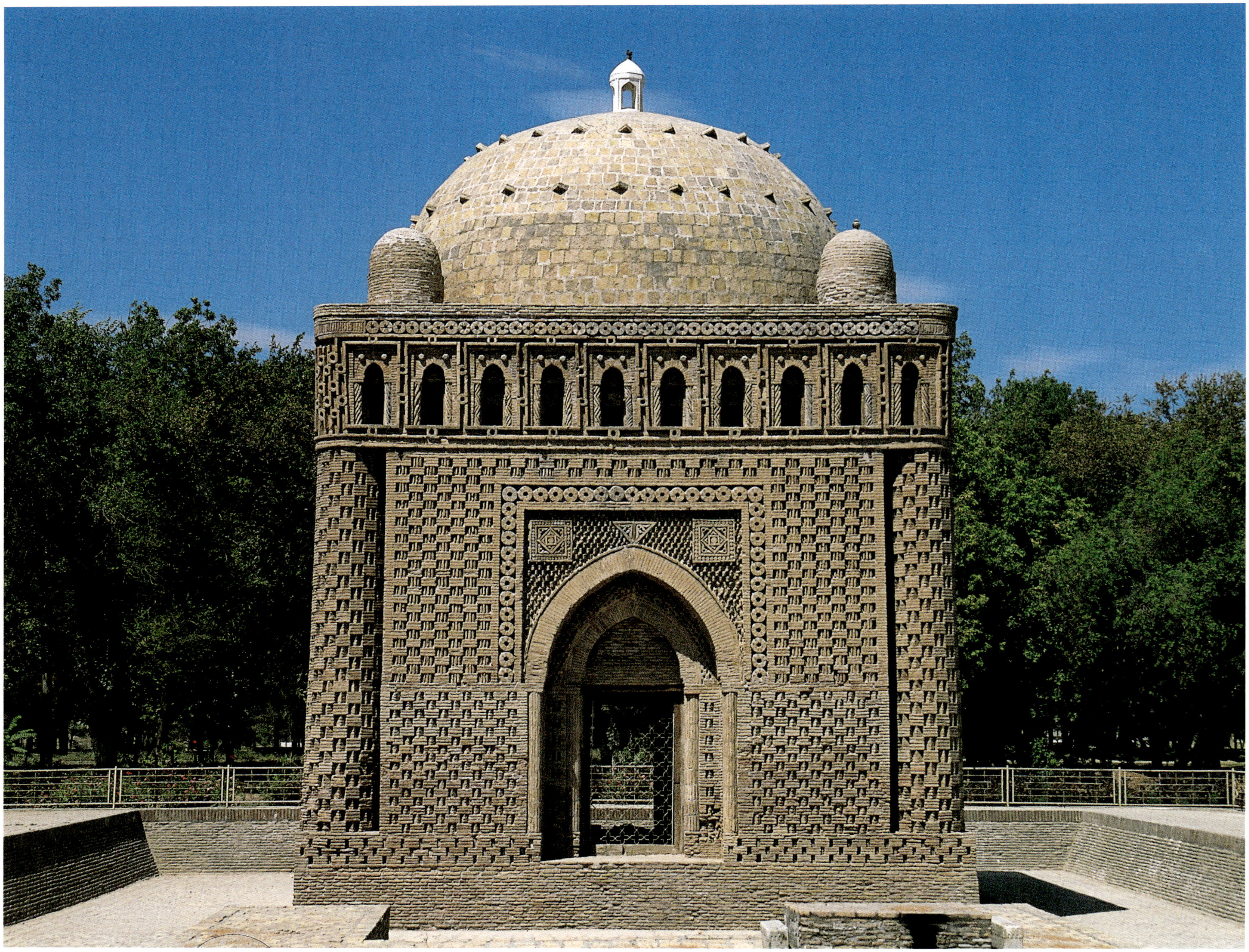

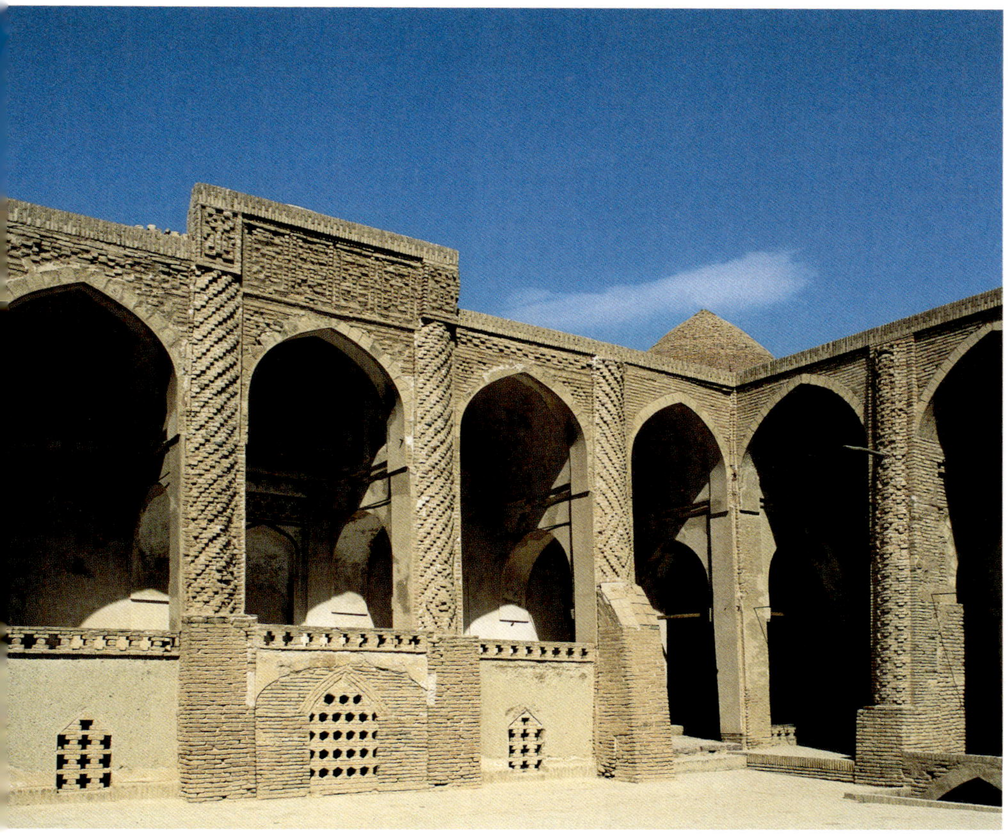

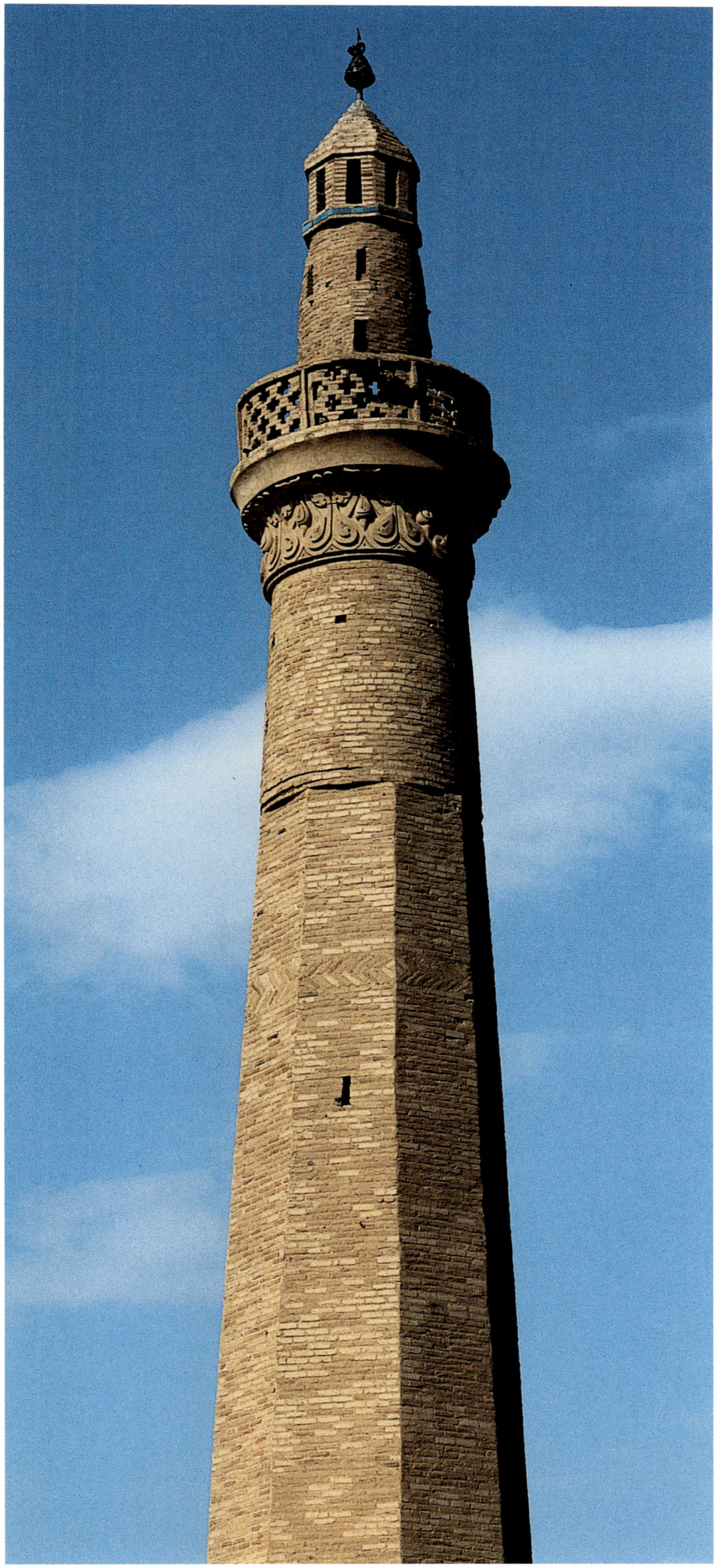

Friday mosque
Courtyard
10th century
Nayin, Iran

The oldest of the few surviving monuments in Iran all owe a great deal to the imposing 'Abbasid and Sassanid models of the past. But soon 'Mesopotamian' rigidity and the rugged materiality of Sassanid stamp were supplanted by unheralded expressive freedom. The relatively retiring Friday mosque at Nayin, following the hypostyle pattern but vaulted and gathered around a small courtyard, is a splendid example of the effort made by Persian architecture to alleviate all sense of massiveness. Contrasting with the huge shadows cast by the vaulting, the vibrant colour scheme is entirely due to a shimmering weave of arches created by a special brick bond, a rudimentary but extraordinarily expressive and effective expedient.

Friday mosque
Minaret
10th century
Nayin, Iran

The stem of the minaret, perhaps the most ancient in all Persia, is octagonal to a certain height before abruptly morphing into a tube; it is almost as if the traditional 'Abbasid predilection for polygonal forms had suddenly been jettisoned in favour of the cylinder, a form less harsh in sunlight and destined to become the most widely used in minarets in the Persian empire as well as in Central Asia. 'Abbasid craftsmen had limited their vegetal patterns to a monotonous and repetitive language, while abstract rationality characterizes the builders who had made the mausoleum of Isma'il into an image in miniature of the cosmic order charged with a restrained sense of poetry. Here they are abruptly transformed by a creative spark kindled by new populations from the boundless expanses of Asia who introduced far-reaching innovations that fed fruitfully into indigenous Persian culture.

Gunbad-e Qabus
1006–1007
Gorgan, Iran

Among the most significant productions of these intense and dramatic decades, the tomb tower of Qabus Ibn Washmgir remains unique. Surging up into the sky, the monumental shaft towers over fifty metres high, dominating the surrounding plain into whose bowels its foundations sink to a depth of more than twelve metres. Ten sturdy right-angled ribs course up the barrel, proudly projecting from a structure crowned by a conical cusp that ascends into the unfathomable depth of the cosmos – an expression of self-affirmation so obvious that it verges on hubris.
Governor of Gorgan between 976 and 1012, Qabus was a keen scholar and poet, a generous patron, a calligrapher, astrologer and linguist, a competent chess player and a brave warrior. He was murdered by nobles in his entourage exasperated at his distrustful personality. His crystal coffin may have been suspended at some breathtaking height inside the empty hull of the tower.

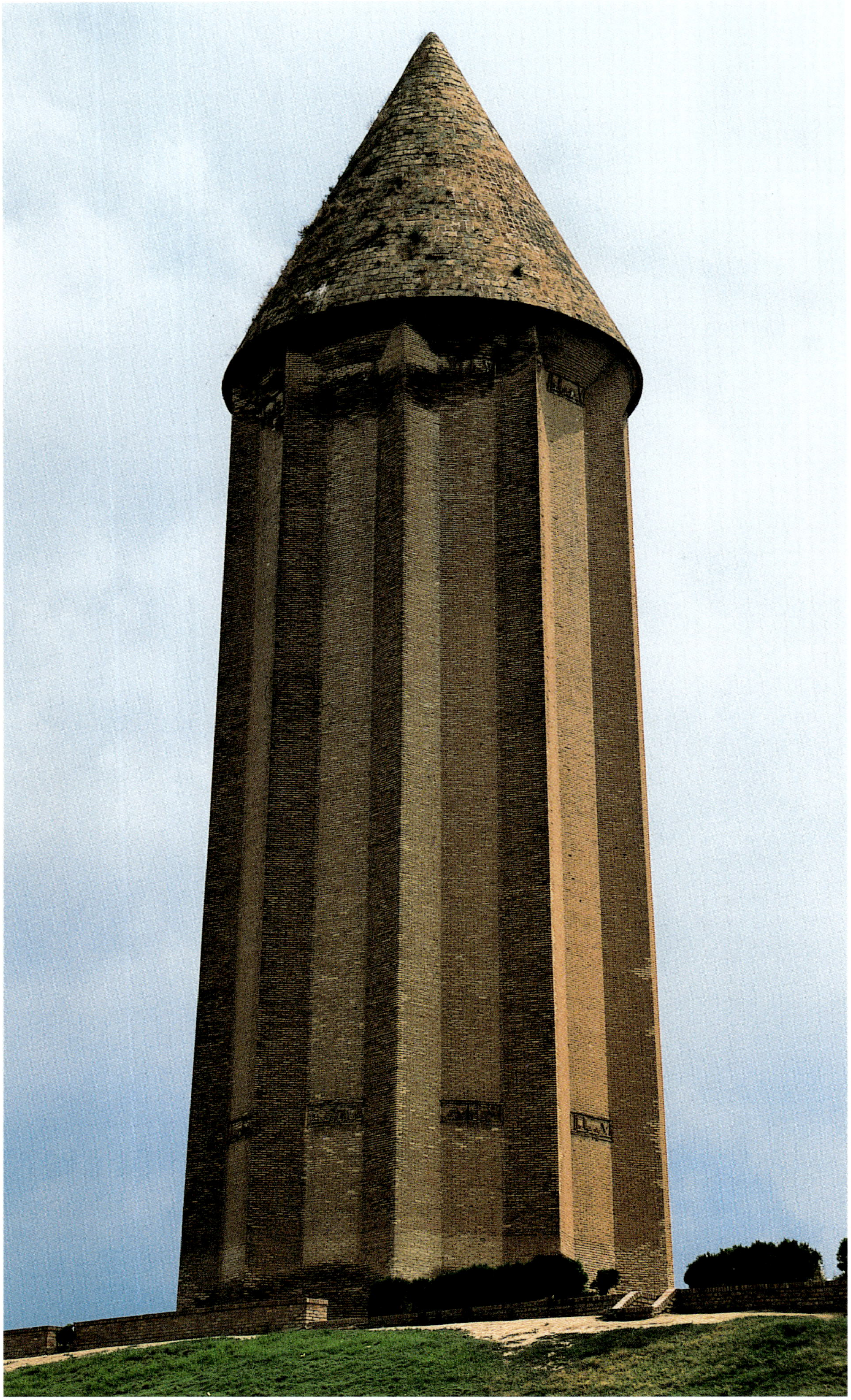

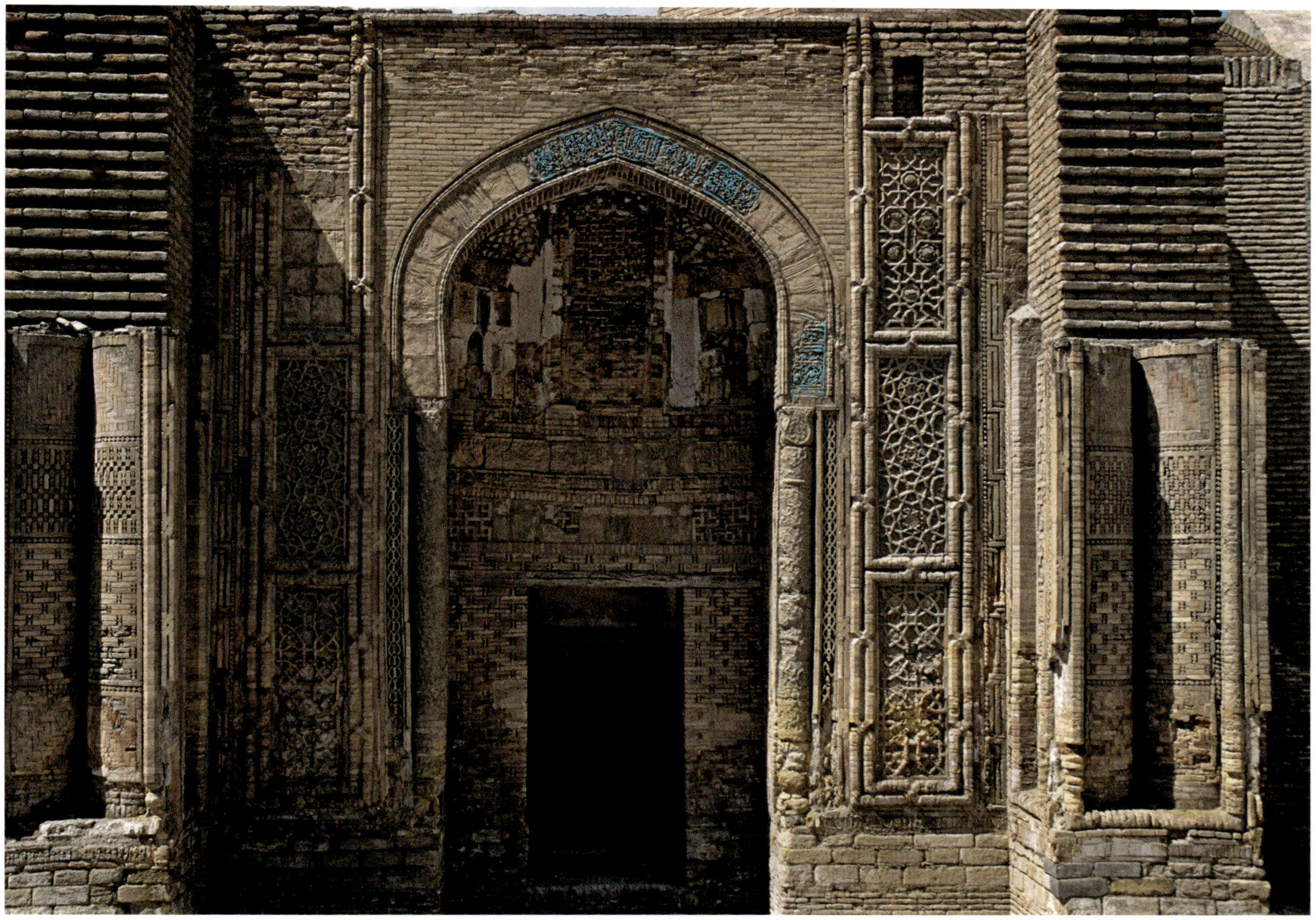

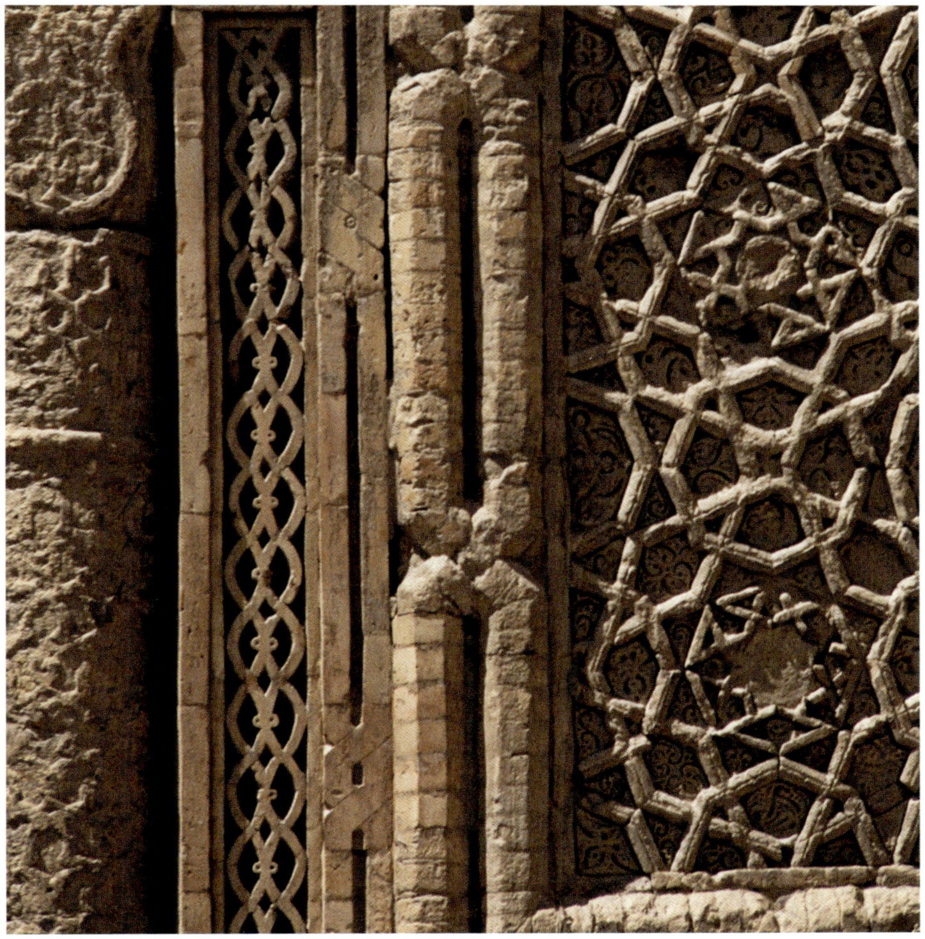

Magok-e Attari Mosque
Façade and detail
Late 12th century
Bukhara, Uzbekistan

It was during this period that the evolution of architecture began to invest increasing importance in the main gate as a planning element, so that it became a focus of various devices exploiting changes in the observer's standpoint. The effective and economic technique of realizing ornamental motifs by means of bricks laid in different bonds led to the development of increasingly lavish and detailed façades, reaching an acme of decorative intricacy with the introduction of a technique of incising and/or carving terracotta that allowed for infinite variations in pattern and calligraphic forms. Fired brick, by now an essential ingredient in architectural decoration, was used with perfect mastery of its structural and chromatic values, while the transitions between the bricks were bridged with a mortar whose divers shades of yellow and pink added effects of colour and line that were complemented by the insertion of shards of turquoise glass and examples of elegant penmanship. Similarly the introduction of majolica in the wonderful blue of the period brings out the various zones of the structure, bestowing a note of colour that was destined to enjoy a glorious future. The name of the mosque, which translates as 'scented ditch', might allude to the sub-basement plinth and the herb market that stood in its vicinity. The location had long been considered sacred: in the fifth century BCE a fire temple rose on the site and was then replaced by a Buddhist temple and later still by a place of worship of the God Moh. This fact is recalled in the name Mokh which was given to the mosque constructed at the turn of the eighth century, very shortly after the Islamic conquest of the region. One of the most ancient in all Central Asia, almost nothing else has survived. The present-day portal dates to the Qarakhanid dynasty, members of which developed the Seljuq site, completely rebuilding it during the second half of the twelfth century. This fact renders it much harder to recognize the characteristics of the medieval building, the magnificent gate being the most significant element.

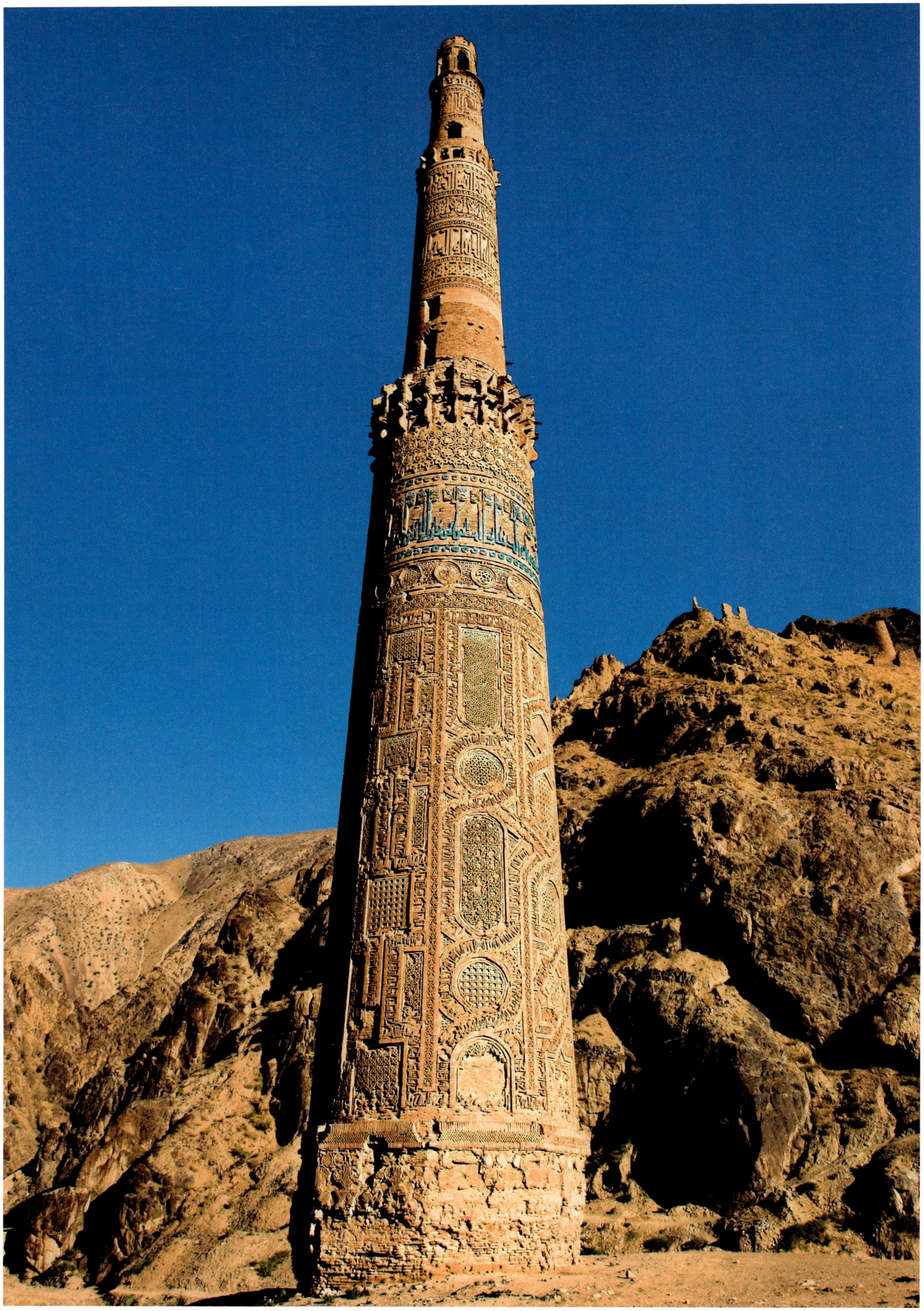

Minaret of Jam
1179–1194
Jam, Afghanistan

The tower, approximately sixty-five metres high and articulated over three levels of harmonious proportions, survives in an optimal condition, with the exception of the collapsed balconies. Today it stands in glorious isolation, although in the past it served as the minaret for the since vanished mosque of Firuzkuh. The entire height of the tower is completely covered with ornaments in stucco deeply carved into a fabulously opulent counterpoint of floral and geometric motifs. Uniquely, the inscription band in Kufic running its entire height contains a complete *sura* of remarkable length: the nineteenth, 'Mary', which records in austere tones the birth of Christ and the punishments that await evil-doers. Its purity make it a masterpiece of the mystical-rational conception of architecture that developed in the Persian ambit, a foretaste, in what is a wild and primeval setting, of mankind's assuredness as it follows the path of righteousness blazed by the Prophet.

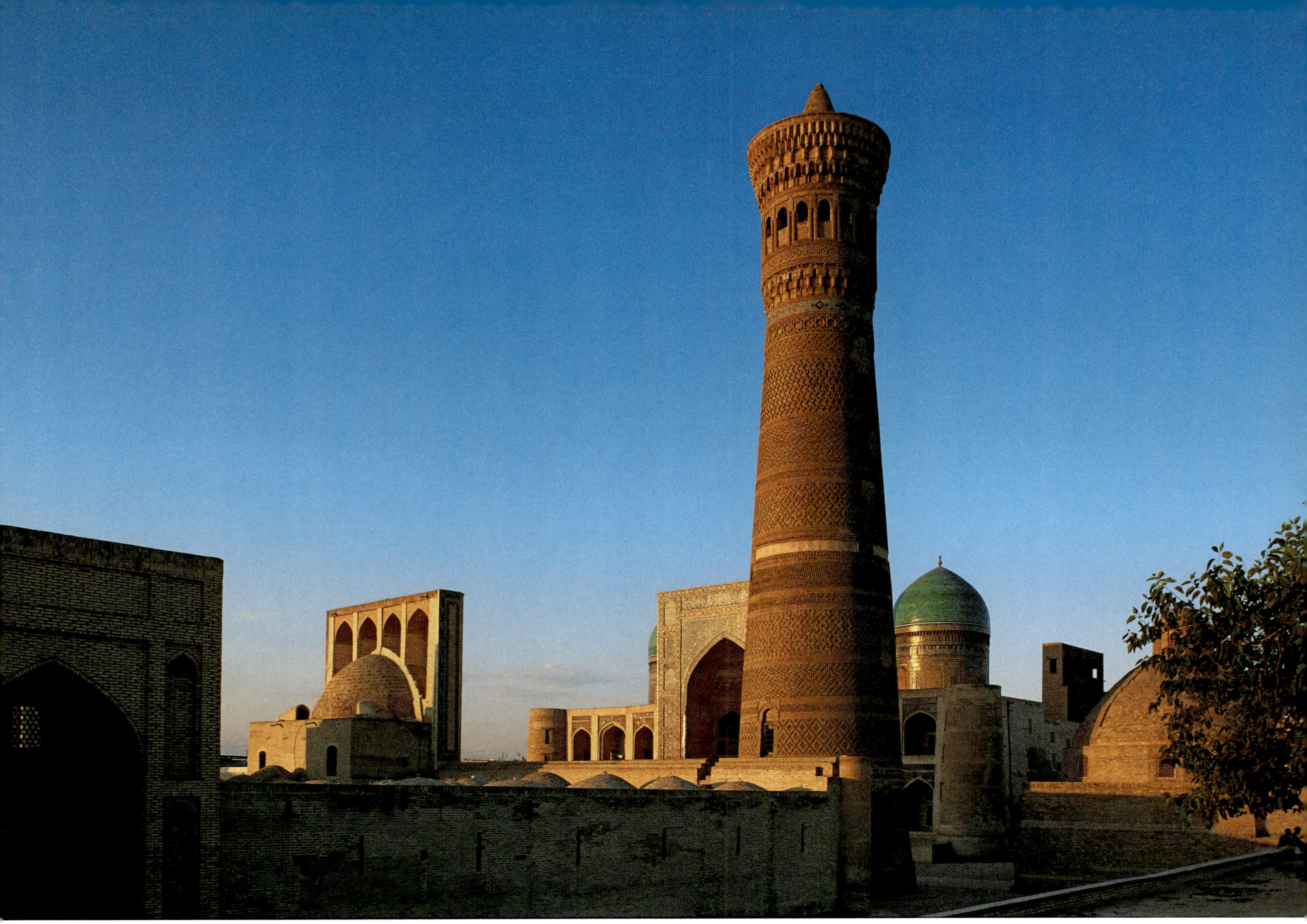

Kalyan Minar ('Great Minaret')
in front of the Mir-e Arab madrasah
1127, 1536
Bukhara, Uzbekistan

Rising to nearly fifty metres on deep foundations, the great minaret survives from the magnificent Friday mosque endowed in 1127 by the ambitious Qarakhanid Arslan Shah, who explicitly wanted it to possess the tallest minaret in the world. The massive barrel strikes out from a low polygonal base (perhaps in a throwback to 'Abbasid constructional techniques), before tapering gently upwards. Higher up, after a strip in a star pattern in marked relief, it flanges out into a sturdy system of *muqarnas* on which rests a vertical loggia. This in its turn is surmounted by a second crown of *muqarnas* that projects still further and that bore the final element of the structure (destroyed by the Soviets during a battle in 1920). According to legend, in order to consolidate the foundations, the architect mixed camel milk and bull's blood into the mortar. Yet he died a disappointed man shortly after the conclusion of the works, complaining that "my imagination soared higher than the minaret I built."

'Shroud of St Josse'
ante 961
Silk
Louvre, Paris

Although sources recall it as plentiful, very little of the extremely lavish and much-vaunted production of high-quality woven fabric from this period remains to the present-day. The most important survivor is this, the so-called 'Shroud of St Josse', which, like the majority of the woven pieces that can be ascribed to this time, represents an advance on the vocabulary of Sassanid textiles. This superb example, however – reaching the West in the guise of a precious mantle wrapped round a relic conserved in the cathedral at Caen – demonstrates how over time the Sassanid influence became less restricting. In spite of its sumptuousness and undoubted prestige, the idiom remains relatively static; not only in the elephants facing each other, but also in the line of camels that shows little propensity to move. The date is gleaned from the inscription which, as in a *tiraz*, can include the name of the caliph or some other important detail. Here the record is of a Khorasan emir who passed away in 961.

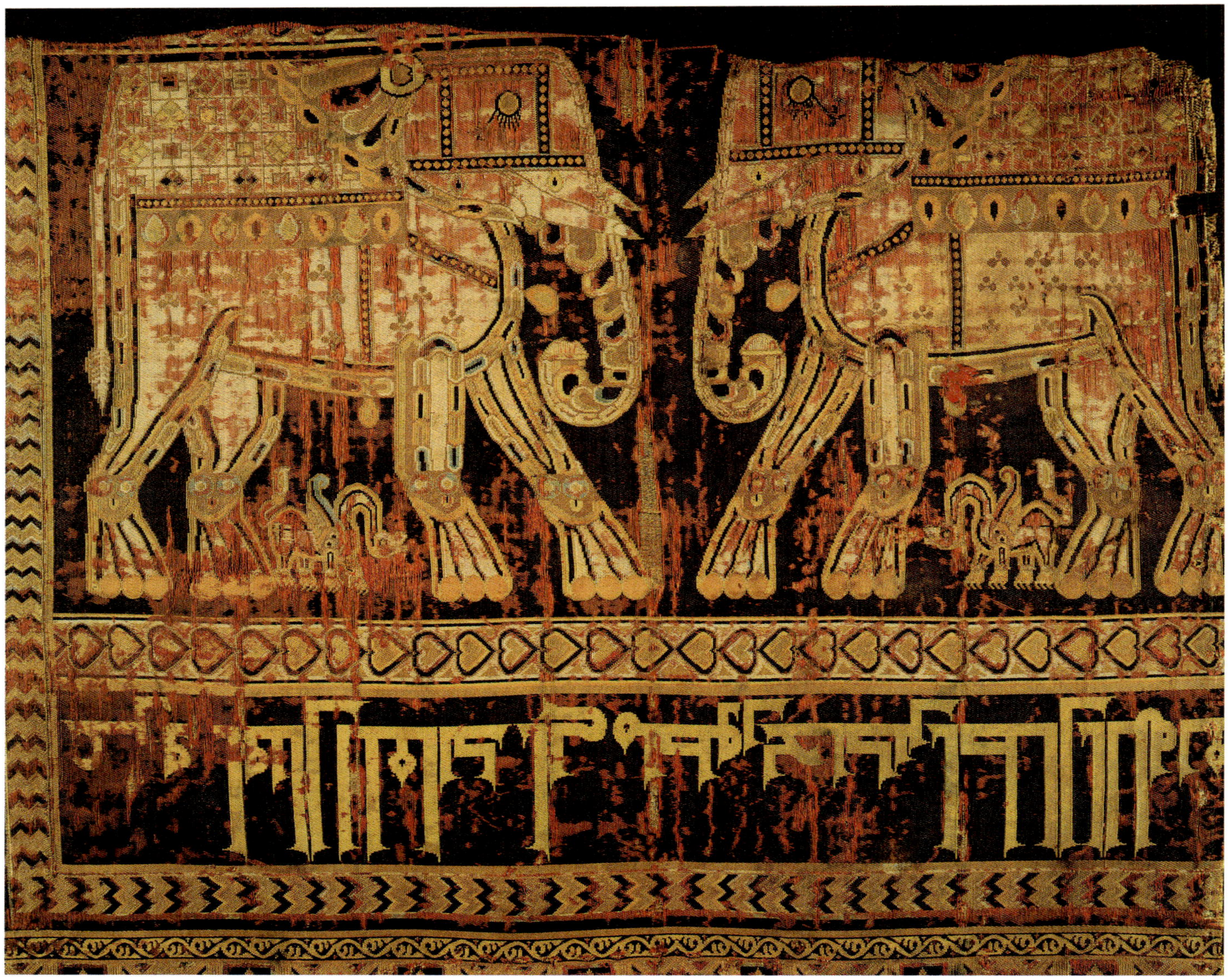

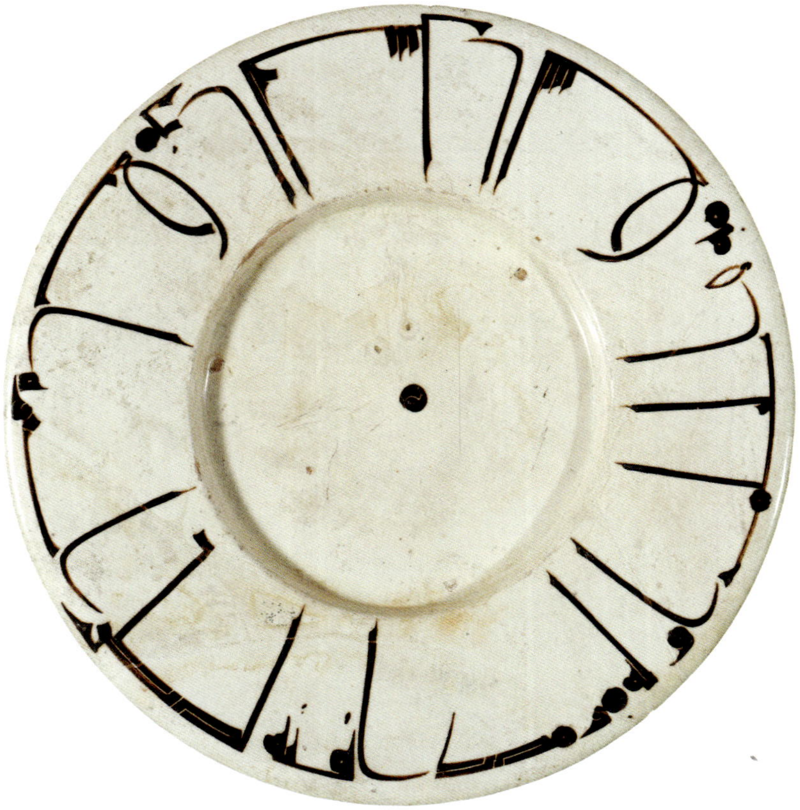

Plate with epigraphy
Ceramics
10th–11th century
Louvre, Paris

The phase during which the market demand was for items imitating foreign models did not preclude Persian craftsmen from making unprecedented advances in the area of ceramic decoration. Among the many and various types, a special place is occupied by serving plates and small basins, in general coated in a simple white slip with neat inscriptions in formal angular Kufic, rigorously in black and nearly always leaving a circular band around the rim. In essence, the texts are exhortations or proverbs analogous to the one on the object shown here that runs something like: "Magnanimity smacks of bitterness at first, but its lingering taste is as sweet as honey," or elsewhere, "good planning means no regrets," and similar aphorisms. The fact that the concern here is more with popular adages than religious quotations implies that such products were destined chiefly for a middle-class urban clientele, even if the dot in the white void at the centre could well be seen to stand for the idea of God.

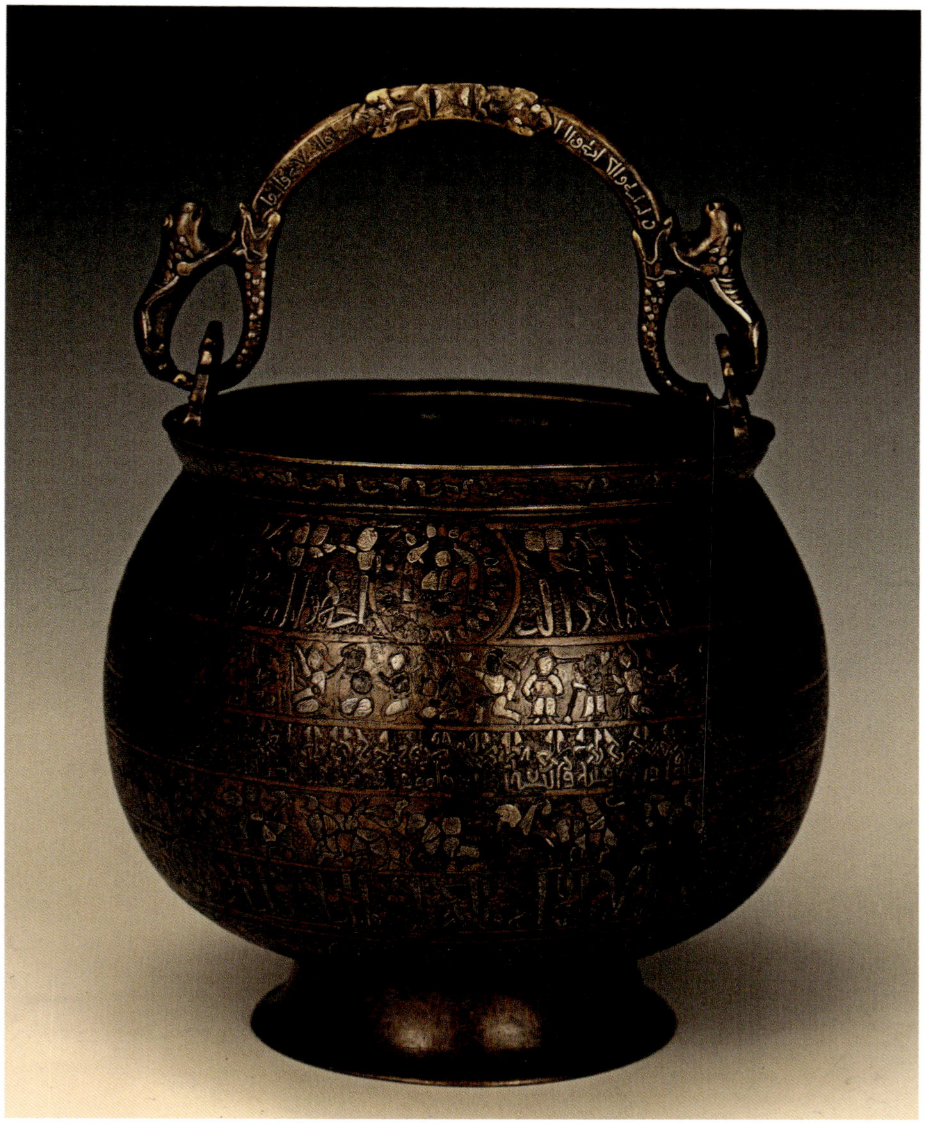

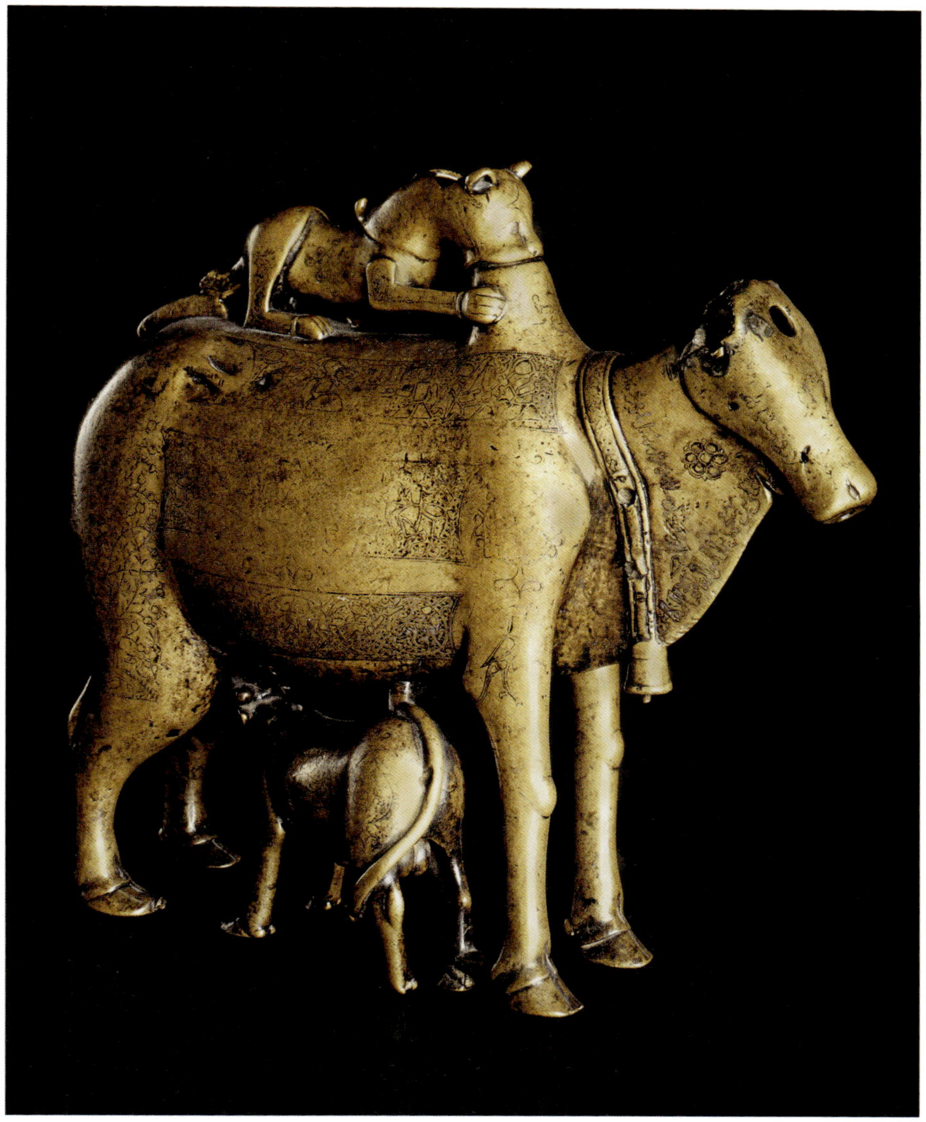

'Bobrinsky Bucket'
1163
Brass with silver and copper inlay cast
by Muhammad Ibn Abd al-Wahid
and decorated by Masud Ibn Ahmad
Hermitage, St Petersburg

The presence of a nouveau-riche 'mercantile bourgeoisie' whose demand for articles of a type different from those commonly called for at court compelled craftsmen to invent many novel classes of object. An exceptional example of the resulting output is the 'Bobrinsky Bucket', created in Herat in 1163 as a gift from a merchant not above dubbing himself "pillar of the state," "pride of traders" and even "ornament of the *hajji* and the two sanctuaries." In all probability it was a ceremonial piece, destined perhaps to be displayed publicly in the *hammam.* The superb banded decoration in copper and silver inlay alternates archways, epigraphy in various scripts (with splendid anthropomorphic terminations showing men engaged in combat) with phrases of well-wishing and scenes of figures at a banquet, men playing games, and horsemen at the hunt and in battle.

Aquamanile
1206
Brass with silver inlay
Hermitage, St Petersburg

Objects reverting to the taste for zoomorphic forms – at one time hugely popular – remain extremely rare but sometimes of excellent quality, as demonstrated by this virtually unique piece that seems to link Sassanid and 'Abbasid elements with the passion for animals typical of the inhabitants of the steppes. This brass aquamanile, that is, a water-jug for hand-washing at table, was crafted in 1206, probably for an Iranian nobleman, and takes the shape of a zebu nursing a calf while a lion bites into its hump. The lion attacking an animal is an ancient astronomical sign, documented since prehistory and famous from the reliefs at Persepolis, although it had also become a celebrated symbol of the might of Islam. The obvious disproportion between the animals suggests, however, that the emphasis is not chiefly on realism, as underscored by the silver inlay on the animals' bodies that moderates their plastic value – though this is counterbalanced by the insistence on certain naturalistic characteristics, particularly evident in the suckling calf.

THE MEDITERRANEAN BASIN BETWEEN THE ELEVENTH AND FIFTEENTH CENTURIES

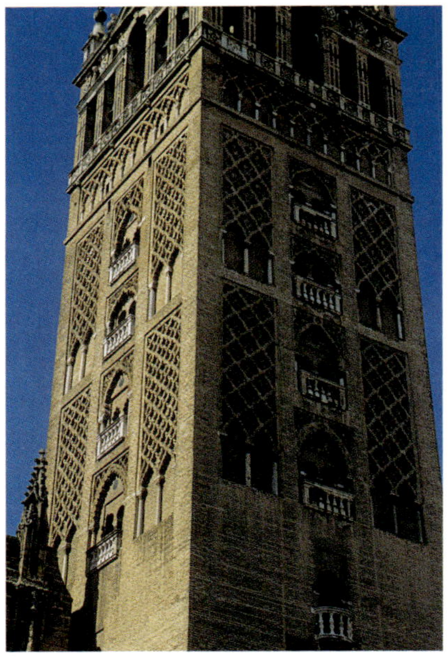

Minaret, now known as the Giralda
1184–1198 (converted into a belltower in the 16th century)
Seville, Spain

Beyond the confines of the cities, with their cosmopolitan atmosphere and open-minded culture, Islam often assumed less sophisticated forms. Among the Berber tribes of the Moroccan Atlas, these attitudes gave rise to widespread intolerance manifested in open hostility to everyone and everything that might be construed as deviant or unorthodox. When a leader emerged for the energetic and intransigent people of the desert, with their simplistic world views, they would embark on a violent conflict with the cultured civilization of the Maghreb and al-Andalus.
The holders of these values were nomadic caravans called *al-Murabitun* (from which the term Almoravid is derived), from the root '*r-b-t*', to 'fight in serried ranks'. Fanatical warriors of the *jihad,* they led austere lives in their *ribats,* viewing science with suspicion, the city with disapproval, and beauty as a threat. In the course of the eleventh century the Almoravids gradually wrested control of the Maghreb and imposed their ideology on the region. By 1074, they were helping the tottering regimes of the Taifa, which were being swallowed up by Christian invaders. The Almoravids believed their weakness lay in the pollution of authentic Islamic values by urban civilization. The following year, they invaded Andalusia, routing the Christians and recovering the Muslim realms. Creating a new empire that recognized the authority of the caliph of Baghdad, they applied the Qur'an with unbending tenacity. Before long, however, the Almoravid emirs, sworn enemies of art and fundamentally hostile to every form of cultural expression apart from religion, were inveigled by the glories of the civilization of al-Andalus. They were soon presiding over an artistic renaissance, turning their capital Marrakesh into a splendid court which welcomed some of the foremost cultural figures of the age.
In the early decades of the twelfth century, however, Almoravid power began to crumble under Christian incursions into al-Andalus and the irrepressible tribal autonomy of the Berbers. There then arose in the Atlas Mountains a new movement, known as the Almohads (from *al-Muwahhidun,* 'who believes in the unity of God'), which fought in its turn for a revival in tradition and opposed the authority of the law schools. Its leader Ibn Tumart established a socio-military structure of a Spartan type; the self-proclaimed *mahdi* reunited the tribes and attacked what he saw as the decadent and corrupt society of the Almoravids (1118) under the banner of a fanatical Messianism. His successor Abd al-Mumin (1130-1163) assumed the title of caliph, transforming the religious oligarchy into a dynastic monarchy, seizing Morocco, Algeria, Tunisia, Libya and al-Andalus (1146-1154) and forging the whole Muslim West into a single huge empire. Then, once again, the fanaticism of the new masters was gradually defused by the refined civilization against which it had fought. The Almohads too began to finance monuments and sponsor the arts, as well as attracting a scientific community that could boast Averroes, Maimonides and al-Idrisi, among others.
The power of Islam was, however, in decline: it could not stem the flow of a flourishing Christian Europe. After their victory at Las Navas de Tolosa (1212), Islam's enemies overran al-Andalus. Only the kingdom of Granada remained, while in Morocco the machinations of the Arab tribes brought the Merinids to power. In 1275, this last dynasty founded a capital at Fez el-Jedid near the splendid ancient city of Fez. Following the conquest of Algeria and Tunisia, their might reached its zenith towards the mid-fourteenth century before interference from the Wattasids and Nasrids of Granada led to its decline. In 1549, their power passed to the Sa'adi sharifs; during the second half of the seventeenth century the Alawi dynasty, the present occupants of the throne, rose to power. Art and architecture flourished in the Maghreb during the fourteenth century, when innovations from al-Andalus filtered

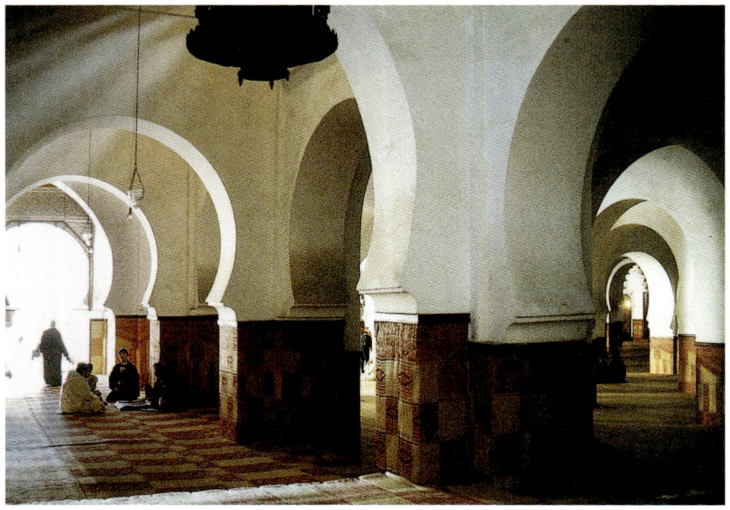

Mosque Qarawiyyn
859–1135 and subsequent alterations
Fez, Morocco

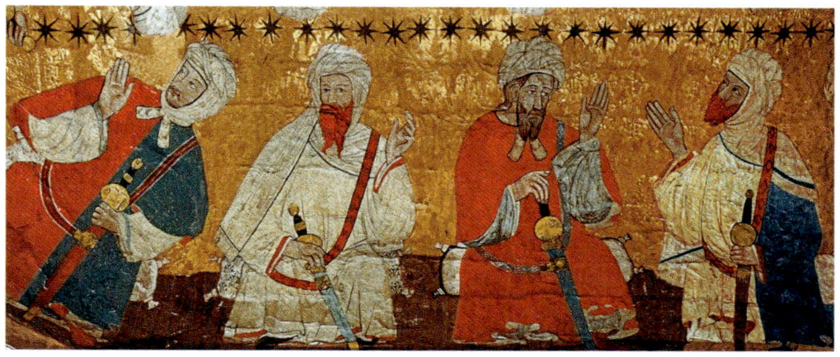

through the Almoravid and then Almohad aesthetic and precipitated a new synthesis. The highpoint of this restrained, delicate idiom can be seen in the famous madrasahs in Fez and Marrakesh. In al-Andalus, the power vacuum following the collapse of the Almohad empire allowed the dynasty of the Nasrids to annex Granada (1238). This satellite state of the kingdom of Castile lingered on for two centuries in anachronistic splendour until 1492, when it was the last place to fall in the Reconquista led by their Catholic Majesties Ferdinand and Isabella. The dynasty's highwater mark coincided with that of its allies, the Merinids, culminating in the palatial complex of the Alhambra – more a fairy-tale apparition than a monument, and a poetic if melancholic finale to a glorious artistic flowering.
The deposition of the last Fatimid caliph (1171) had brought Egypt back into the Sunni fold. It promptly passed into the hands of Saladin and the Kurdish Ayyubid dynasty. Crushing the Crusaders, they established regimes in the region comparable to those of the Seljuqs (the rulers of Anatolia in the eleventh and twelfth centuries). Considered as the family's personal property, the state was dismembered into a series of independent kingdoms, destroying whatever remained of the universality of the caliphate. In this period the arts followed the lines set down during the Fatimid era: the result, particularly in architecture, was a pared-down, implacable style enriched with reminiscences from the Seljuq age, yet receptive to elements borrowed from the Latin kingdoms of the Occident.
In 1250 the Ayyubids were driven out by their own army of Turkish slaves, known as Mamluks; in 1260 the kingdoms of Aleppo and Damascus were swept aside by the invading Mongols. The Mamluks established a military regime, devising ceremonies and developing an imperial architecture devoted to the exultation of the sultanate. Admired as mighty conquerors with military qualities and revered for their inherently religious power, the sultans were also feared as the lords of cosmic forces based on archaic Turkic beliefs. Formidable on the battlefield, the Mamluks wrest the Holy Land from the Crusaders and even defeated the Mongol hordes. On the spiritual plane they made a great show of being mainstays of (true) Islam and opponents of the Shias, elevating Sunnism to the status of a state religion, rigidly enforced with preachers, *ulama* (theological scholars) and Sufis appointed and paid for by the government. Enthusiastic and prolific patrons of religious building, they erected mosques, madrasahs and *khanaqah* beside mausoleums in their honour. Many had grandiose and elaborate domes and opulent minarets erected to perpetuate their fame. The strict and measured aesthetic of the Fatimids was engulfed by an exuberant hotchpotch of architectural elements, structural clarity being drowned out by a haphazard plethora of decorative inlay, making Cairo into the most extravagant cityscape of the time.
Their boundless appetite for luxury manifested itself in status symbols that were displayed publicly, nourished by a boom in the production of precious artefacts. Monarchs and members of the upper echelons of the military hierarchy frittered away vast sums on gorgeous furnishings and magnificent manuscripts (handbooks as well as religious and literary tomes), embellished with page upon page of elegant illumination.
Since mosques had to be lit with all due dignity, the output of glass lamps swelled – often wonderfully calligraphied with the sura of Light and the name of some illustrious patron, encouraging the rivalry between Cairo and Damascus.
Containers and scent bottles, and paintings showing scenes of aristocratic life, were enormously popular, while the passion for metalwork gave rise to sumptuous and unusual pieces, at their acme in the supreme opulence of damaskeen. Dress played a fundamental role in social life and textile production was encouraged, counteracting a crisis affecting the market for silk with developments in that for carpeting, characterized by the peerless quality of the wool and polychrome richness dominated by cherry-red and geometric designs, the production and export of which became a crucial factor in the economy.

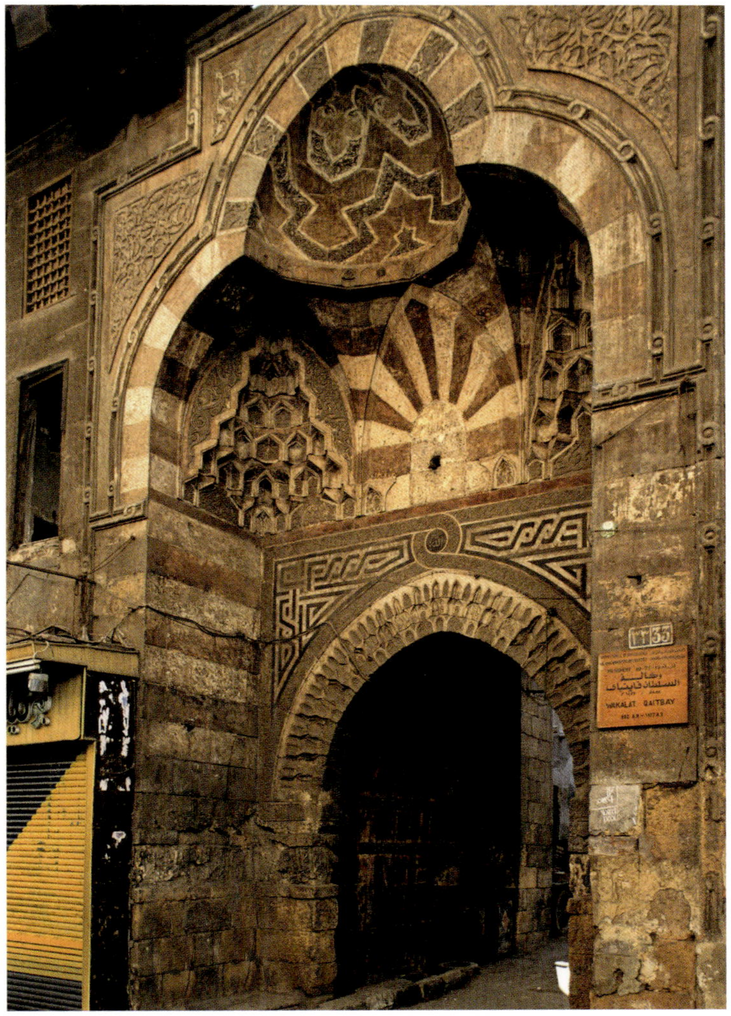

***Nasrid Sovereigns,* painting in a vault in the Hall of the King, in the Alhambra**
Mid-14th century
Granada, Spain

Complex of Sultan Qait Bay Entryway
1477
Cairo, Egypt

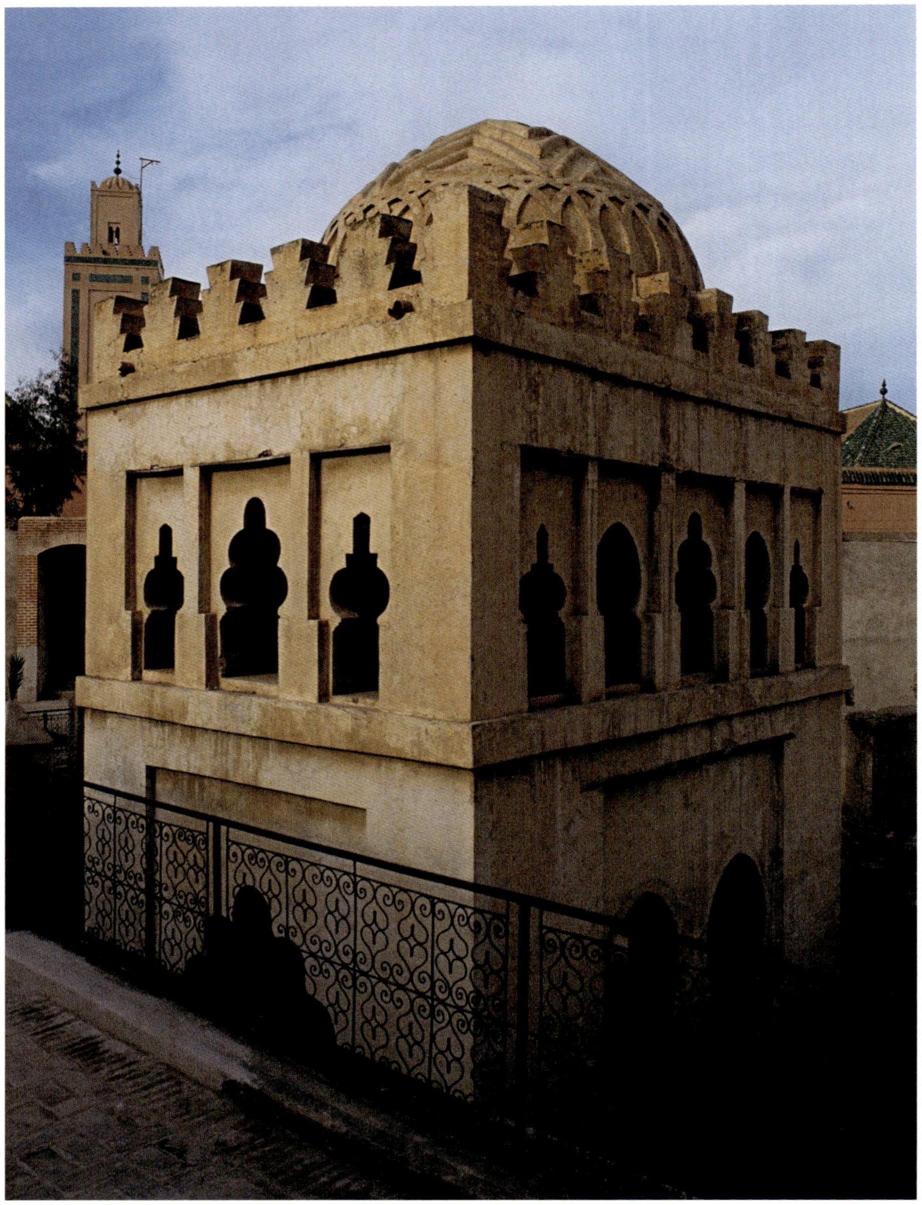

Qubba Ba'adiyyn
c. 1117
Marrakesh, Morocco

Like nearly all the religious buildings from that time, the Friday mosque in Marrakesh inaugurated by the Almoravid governor Ali Ibn Yusuf has disappeared, but what has survived is a rectangular kiosk, whose function is still shrouded in mystery. It might have been destined to shade the ablution fountain from the sun, a type of structure whose history is far from clear; a commemorative building like the Ka'ba at Mecca, whose rectangular shape it recalls; or else a princely pavilion annexed to the mosque, a parallel to the north dome of the Friday mosque at Isfahan, whose use is also anyhow unknown. Although divorced from its purpose, this small building, practically unheralded in terms of shape and dimensions, represents a high point in Almoravid art. Currently the outside presents a character of elegant sobriety, from the shifting surface peppered with refined polylobate windows with merlons of a typical Syrian flavour to the extrados of the cupola decorated with intersecting arch curves and a zigzag pattern.

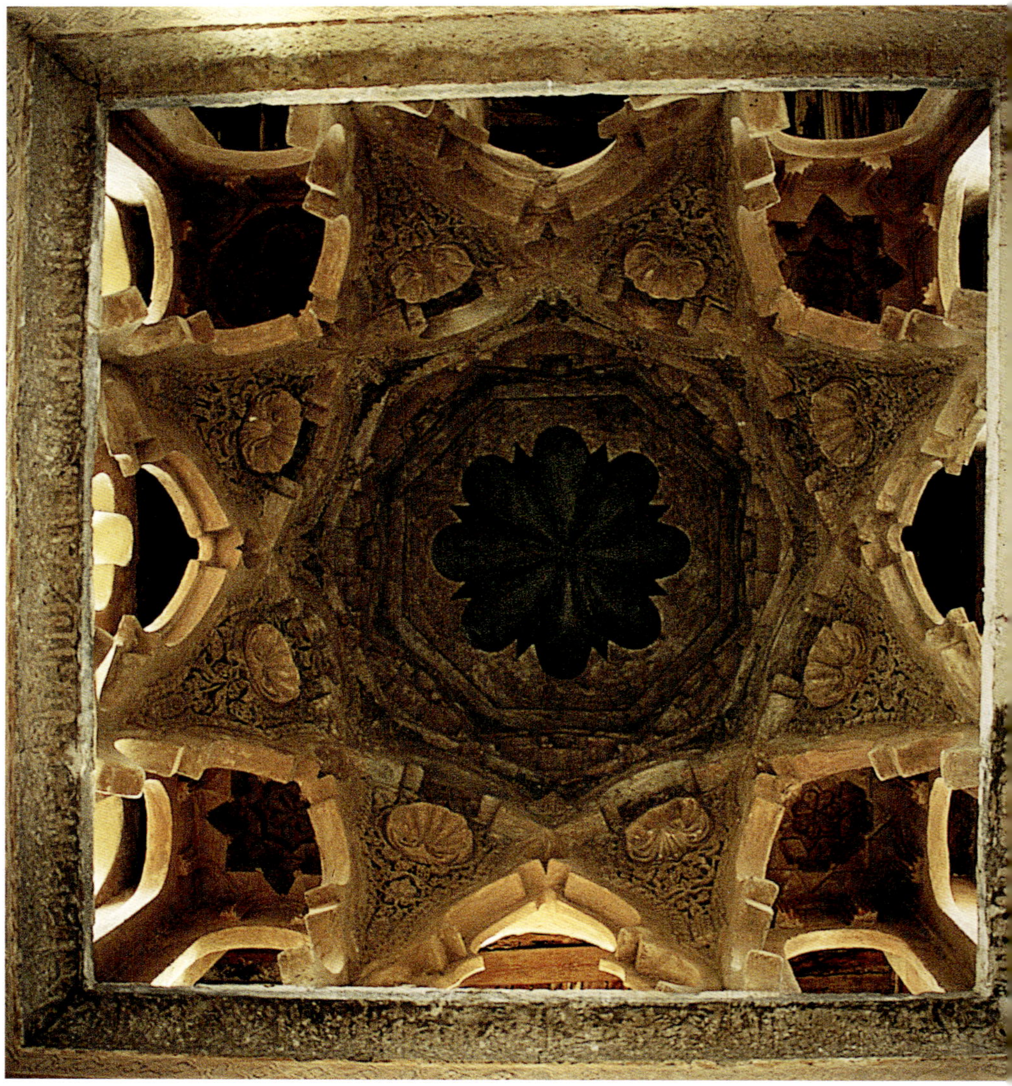

Qubba Ba'adiyyn
Dome
c. 1117
Marrakesh, Morocco

The interior of the mosque is dominated by a fantastic cupola suspended on a complex system of arches over an octagon inserted into a square base whose relatively plain archways form a diaphanous light-filled screen behind counterparts inside. At the centre, supported by a series of polylobate arches set up over the summits of those below, stands the dazzling motif of the great dome derived from a mosaic prototype in the mosque at Cordoba. Subtly choreographed, the dappled light pours in through alternating arches and external windows, at one time embellished with stucco latticework glazed with coloured glass that must have made the interior still more vibrant and conferred on the semi-darkness a spellbinding atmosphere, perhaps still further enhanced by the waters babbling from the fountain below. The evocative ensemble of intersecting arches, deriving, like the cupola, from caliphate models, is reworked here in view of 'anti-structural' experiments in vogue in the Taifa kingdoms. This approach might well have influenced the otherwise ascetic Almoravids and resulted in elaborate formal solutions that apparently anticipate the analogous Baroque inventions of Guarino Guarini, where, however, the problems of load-bearing are resolved in a structurally far more complex fashion.

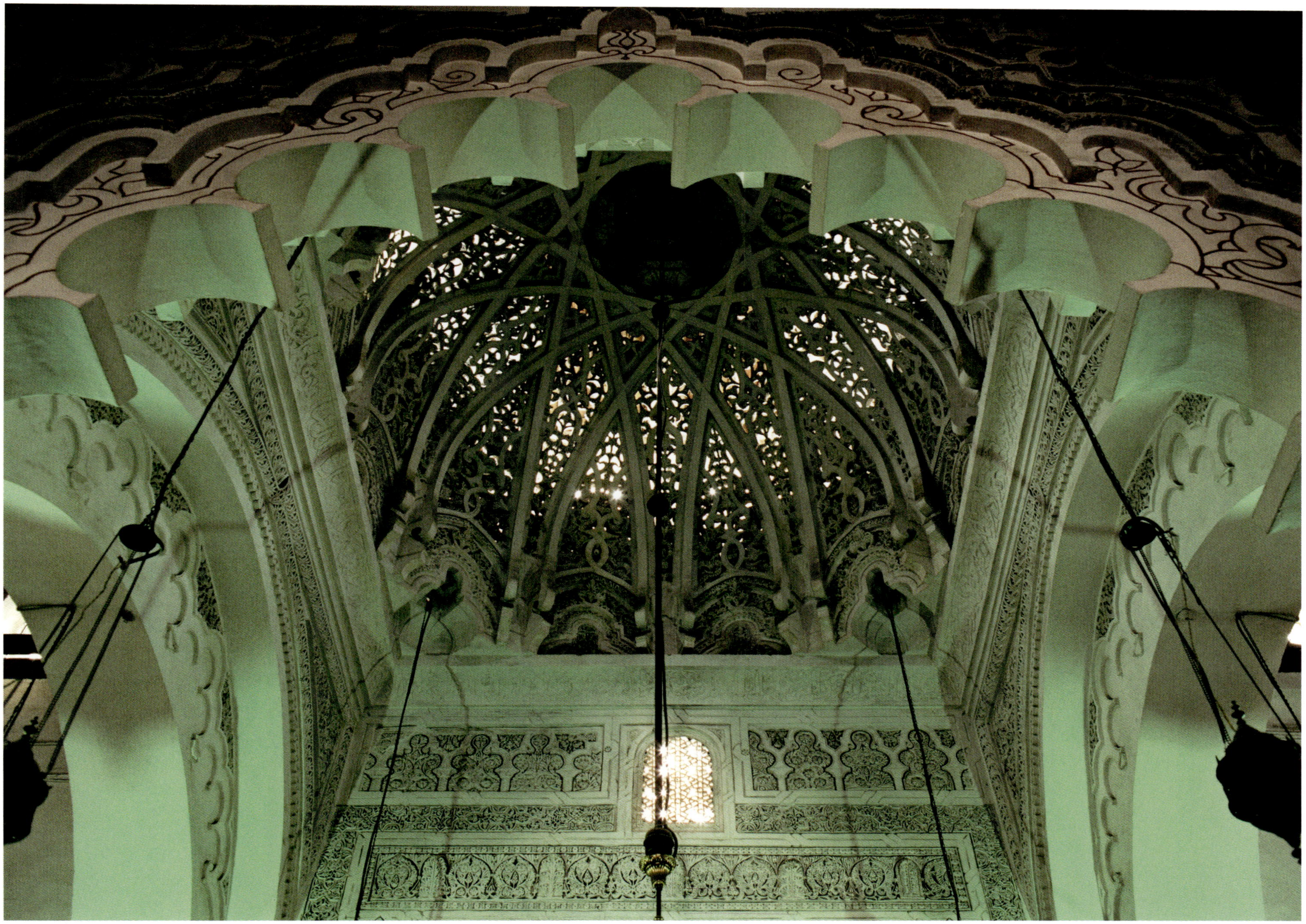

Great Mosque
Dome
Completed c. 1136
Tlemcen, Algeria

The great Almoravid mosque at Tlemcen, with its thirteen aisles perpendicular to the *qibla* and a square courtyard fronting the roofed prayer hall, as well as numerous elements relating it to the Great Mosque of Cordoba, deviates from the latter in its earnest square pillars in place of columns and the double arches that bear the trussed roof. Utterly unprecedented, however, is the solution adopted for the cupola in the *mihrab* borne on arches with lambrequins. It is demonstrably close to examples in al-Andalus, and constituted from an audacious gossamer net in stucco fretwork crimped between twenty-four slender intersecting ribs that support the windowless cap of the dome at the centre. Natural light is here subject to metaphysical illumination and to the tangible splendour of the golden mosaic in the prototype at Cordoba. The intransigent ideology of the Almoravids, expressed so well through the bracing horseshoe arches on squat cruciform pillars of austerely ascetic religiosity in the Qarawiyyn Mosque at Fez, here assumes, under the impulse of the refined art of al-Andalus, hints of feathery delicacy.

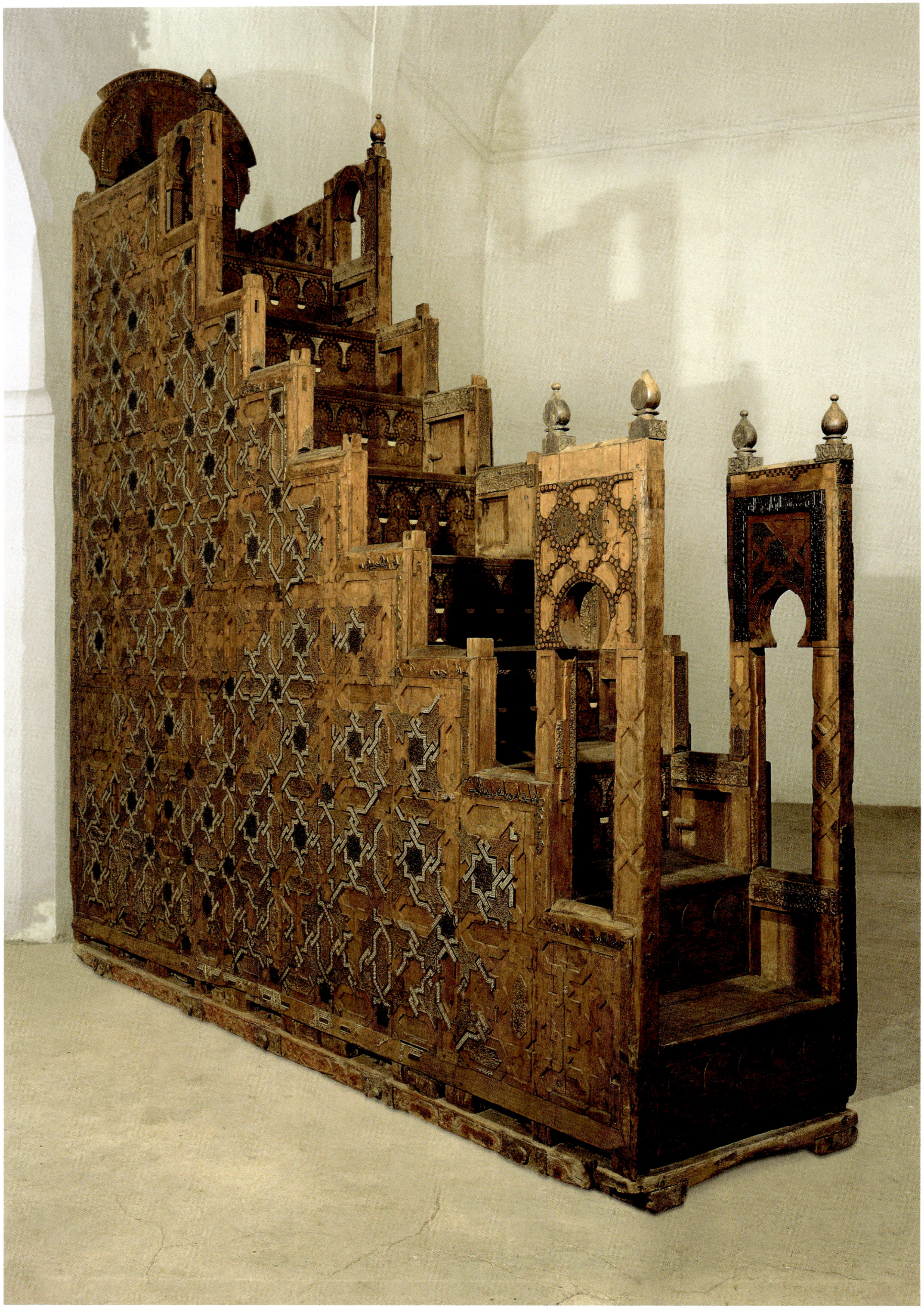

Kutubiyya Idi Marrakesh Mosque
Minbar
Begun 1137
Palace Badi, Marrakesh

In spite of their coolly austere attitudes, the Almoravids, like the Almohads after them, fostered an art of extreme richness, here exemplified by the renowned *minbar* commissioned as a kind of rival to the masterpiece in the Great Mosque at Kairouan. The minbar of the Kutubiyya Mosque is, however, mounted on wheels to allow it to be transported from the warehouse in which it was guarded into the mosque for the Friday predication. It was crafted in Cordoba, where another exceptionally famous *minbar* renowned for the quality of its polychrome inlay once existed but is now lost. The sides of the great *minbar* are skilfully clad with ivory and various woods, creating a geometrical inlay pattern of consummate equilibrium based on the eight-pointed star framed by small wooden panels in various shades, carved with plant motifs of faultless precision and unsurpassable refinement.

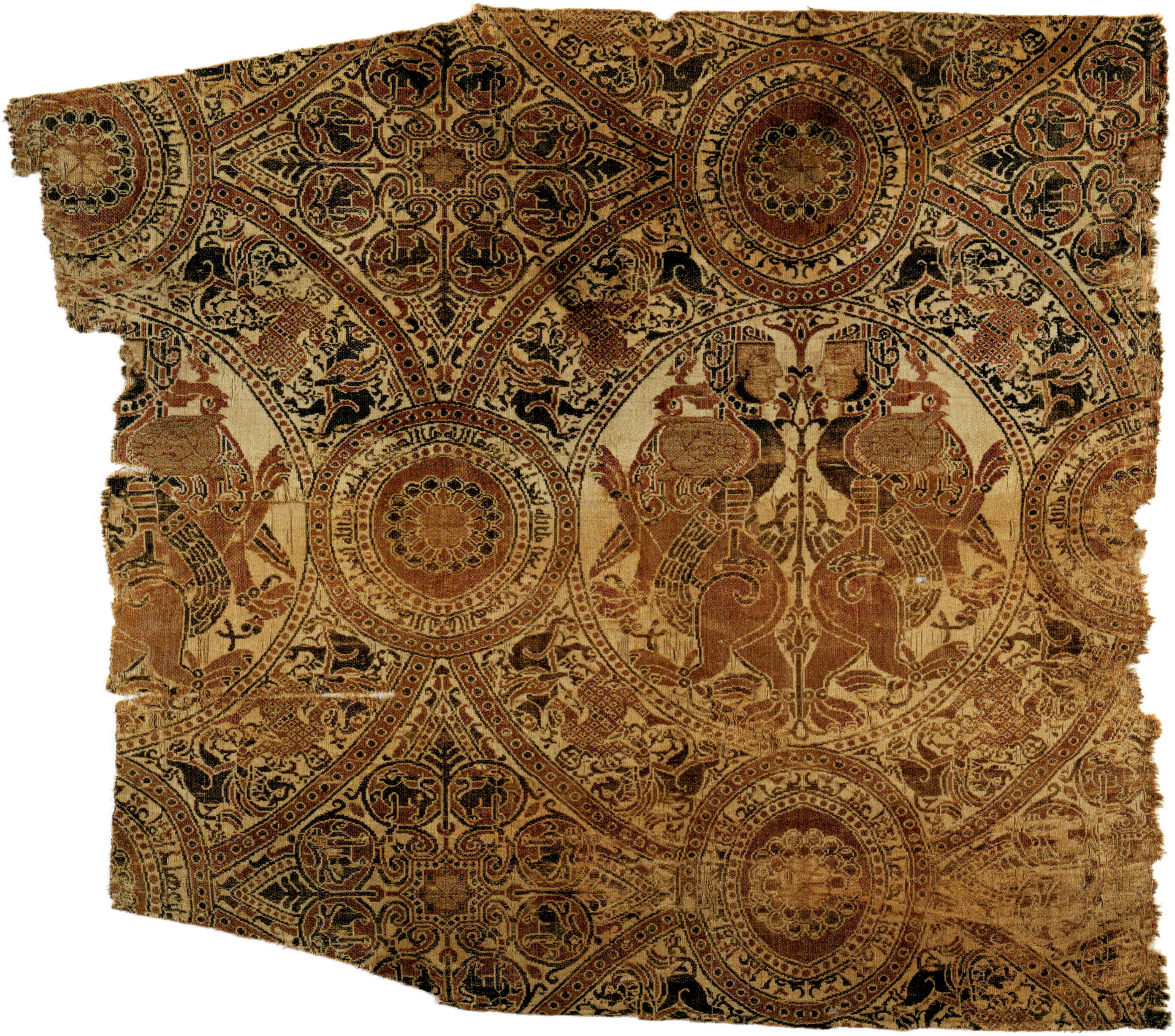

Fragment of cloth with figures of sphinx
Late 11th–beginning of the 12th century
Silk and gold
Museum of Fine Arts, Boston

This priceless fragment was rediscovered in the cathedral of Burgo de Osma inside the tomb of Bishop Pedro, who had died in 1109. The surviving part preserves one complete medallion and a fragment of a second representing two facing sphinxes with the tree of life at the centre. The border is constituted by a band with a figure of a man grasping the front paws of two gryphons standing next to him, a motif repeated four times in the same number of rings encircled by four floral roundels. An inscription cites Baghdad as the place of production and, in effect, analogies with Iraqi pieces are close, even if the piece was in fact woven in Spain, probably at Almeria. It is impossible today to establish with any certainty whether the cloth is a contemporary 'counterfeit' of the much-vaunted Baghdad output whose manufacture mark it reproduces, or whether it is more simply a copy 'in the style of'.

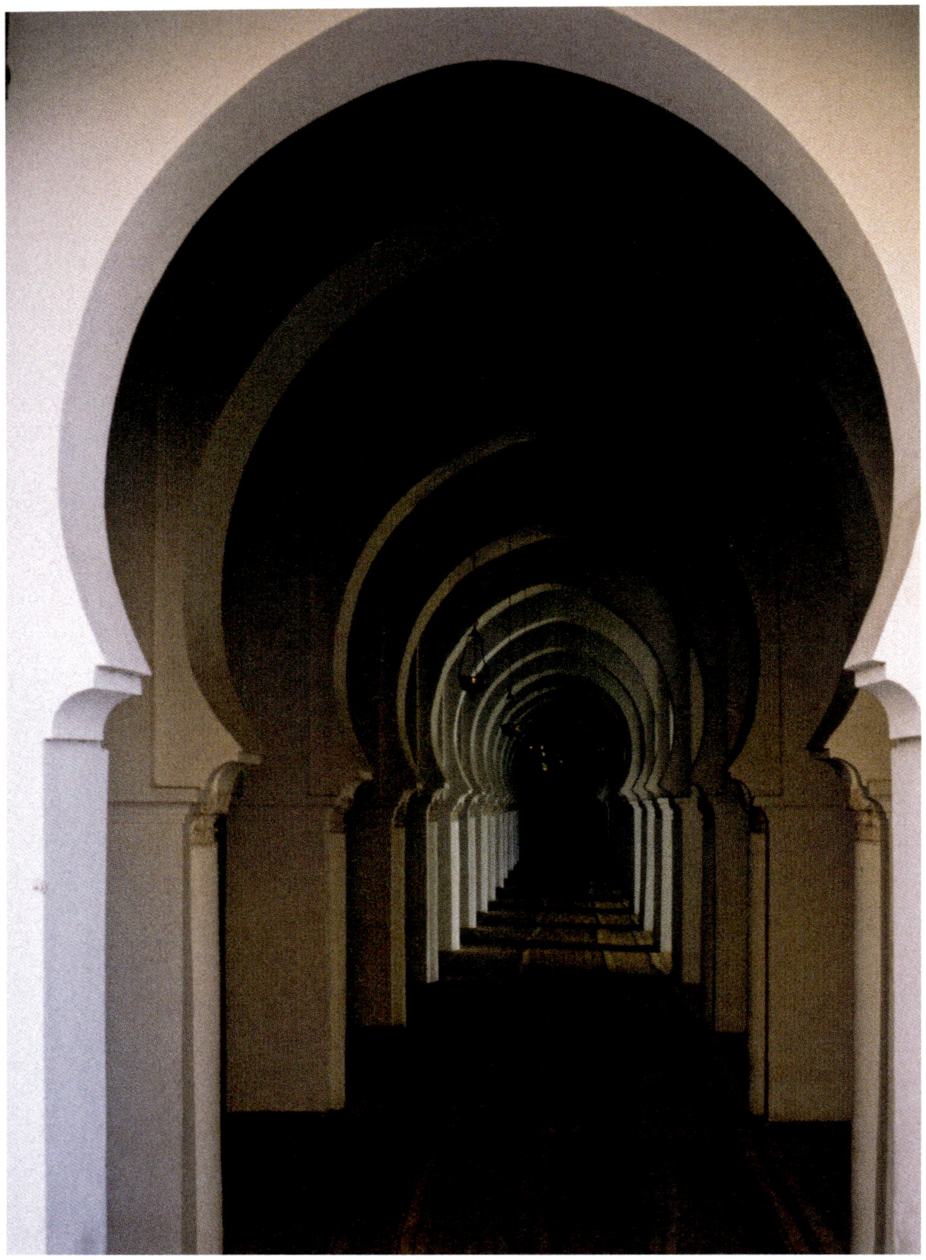

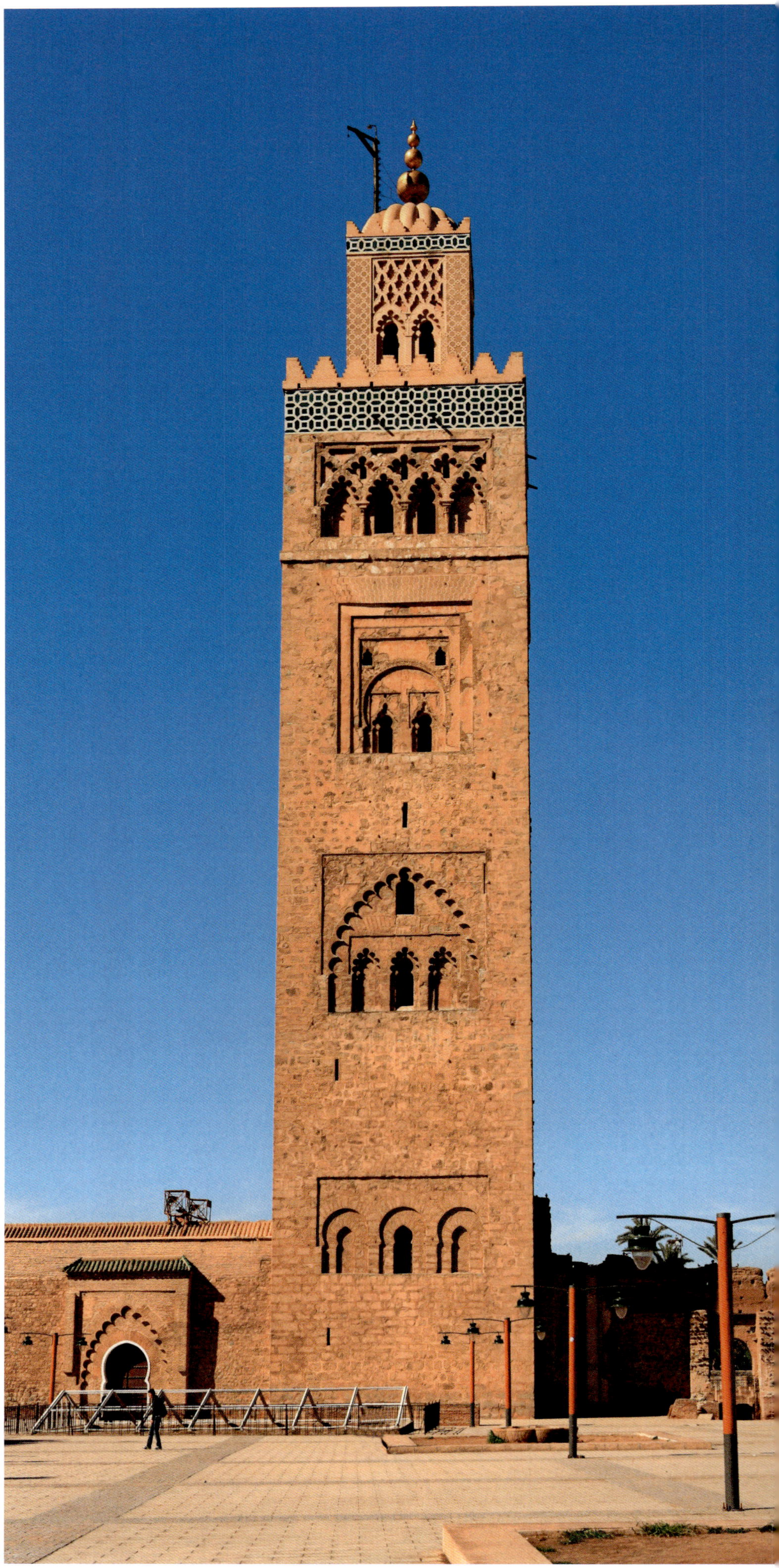

Kutubiyya Mosque
Interior
1158
Marrakesh, Morocco

On the pattern of the Qarawiyyn Mosque in Fez and the architecture from the 'school of Susa', the decor of the Kutubiyya Mosque introduces the accents of dry functionality typical of Almohad architecture, deriving from the reduction of every element to its essence. The ogival heads confer a powerful yet serene sense of thrust onto the horseshoe arches.

Kutubiyya Mosque
Minaret
Second half of the 12th century
Marrakesh, Morocco

The sturdy square minaret, approximately sixty-eight metres high on a base of twelve, formed a prototype for the extraordinary minarets of Seville (such as the famous Giralda) and for the Hassan tower in Rabat. The square shaft is barely lit by a few windows corresponding to the stairway which are therefore asymmetric and framed by vast blind arches of attractive polyfoil tracery which is particularly impressive in the shifting rays of the sun. The upper zone comprises a blind arcade whose profile unfolds and intersects to form the motif known as a *sebka,* frequently employed in later architecture. The band on the stretch of wall above was once decorated with turquoise majolica, while the aedicule at the top recapitulates, in miniature, the motifs displayed below.

Mosque of al-Hasan
Minaret
1195–1196
Rabat, Morocco

The superb, unfinished minaret of the mosque of al-Hasan, one of the most ambitious monuments ever undertaken in the Islamic world but abandoned shortly after work began due to the demise of the patron, is a digest of all the most important characteristics of mature Almohad art. If it had ever been finished, this immense mosque – of which only the first few column drums were ever erected – would have been second in size only to the Great Mosque in Samarra. The heavy-looking tower constitutes an evolution of the minaret of the Kutubiyya in Marrakesh, although here the subsidiary insertions are developed with greater coherence. The decoration progresses from a completely plain lower level, via the intermediate – a majestic arch with internal lambrequins framing a double or triple blind lancet – up to the upper reaches, where a kind of tripartite blind arcade is surmounted by a spectacular *sebka* at the peak. As the incidence of the sun alters, with each passing hour the light intensifies or tempers the crisp linearity of the architectonic motifs.

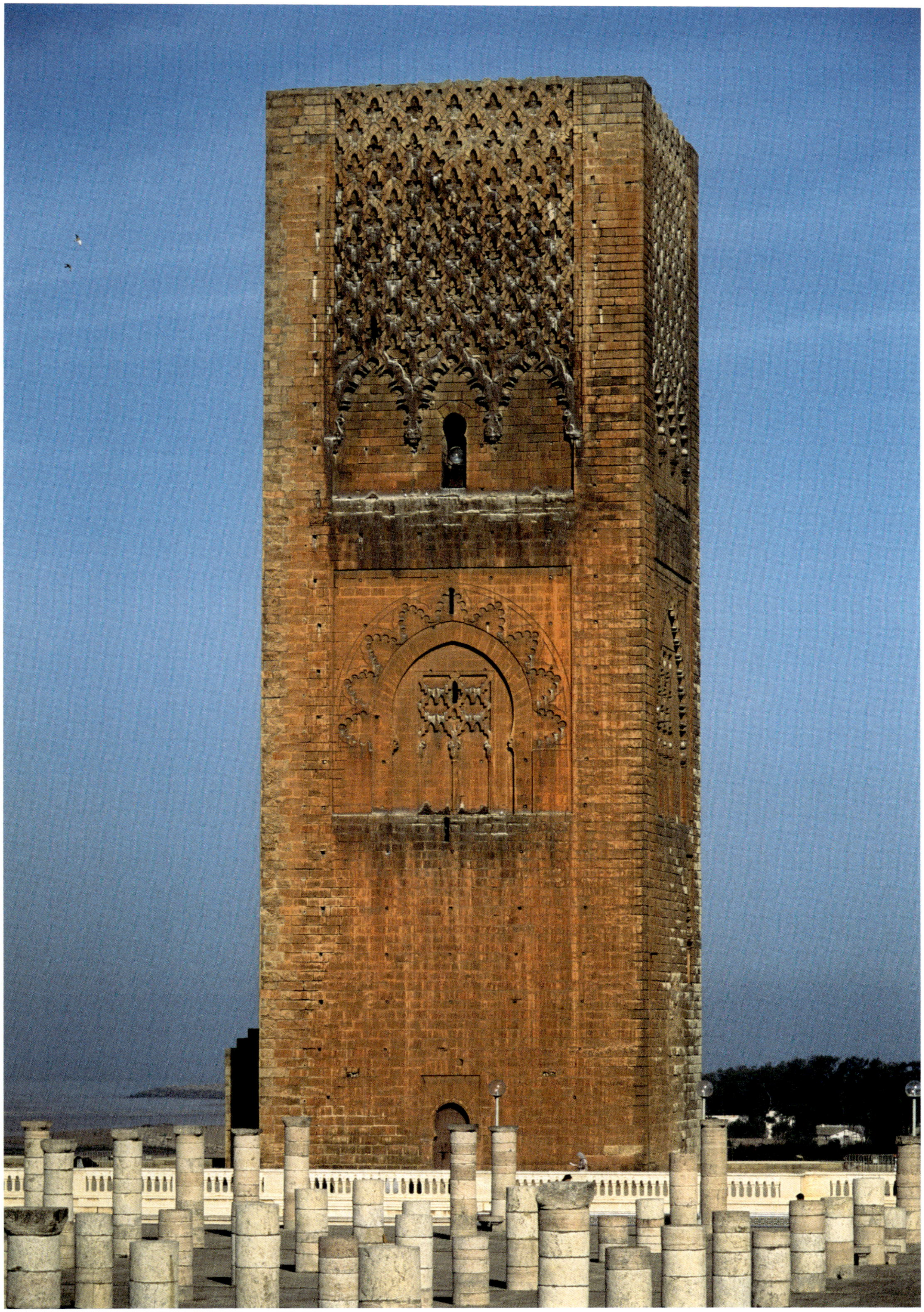

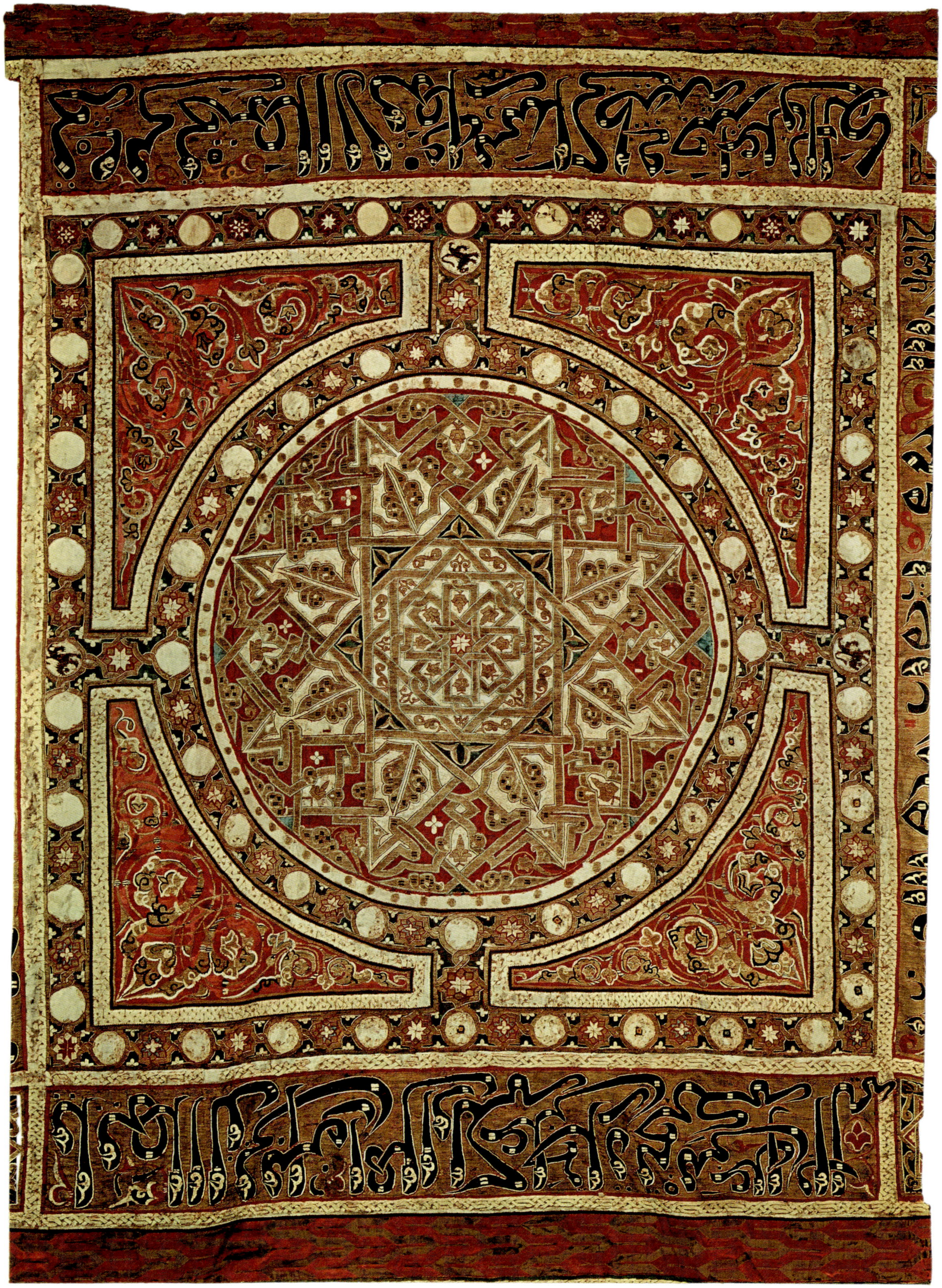

Standard
Early 13th century
Saint María la Real de Las Huelgas,
Museum de Telas Medievales, Burgos

After initially banning lavish *tiraz* and precious materials, such as silk and gold, in woven cloth, the Almohads relaxed their rigour. Towards the end of their reign luxury goods came back into vogue, enhanced by the most elegant decoration, although the representation of human figures and animals was still avoided. This parchment banner embroidered with silk and gold thread was probably captured at the disastrous battle of Las Navas de Tolosa, in which the Almohad troops were definitively routed by a coalition of Christian armies under the command of Alfonso VI of Castile. Next to the quotation from *sura* 16 (vv. 10–12), with an exaltation of *jihad* and a description of paradise that awaits believers who perish in the field, the complex geometric decoration based on the eight-pointed star and squares seems to be arranged into a kind of *mandala* which perhaps once possessed an apotropaic function, furthered by the complicated numerical relationships that seem to underpin the composition.

Page from the Bayad wa-Riyad (The Story of Bayad and Riyad)
Late 12th–early 13th century
Biblioteca Apostolica Vaticana, Rome

The only illustrated manuscript from the Maghreb of the Almohad era to have come down to the present-day is an incomplete copy of a popular love story. Lacking conclusive clues as to date and origin, of the fourteen surviving miniatures, some illustrate genre scenes set in a garden with personages cheered by musicians. The motifs are reworked from contemporary Syrian and Mesopotamian production, with the introduction of elements for the most part familiar to Andalus readers, for whom a work that, in the eyes of some, was produced in Granada or Seville, may have been destined. It is this backdrop that spawned the numerous *miradores*, lobate arches, the alternately coloured sections of wall, and the different bonds used in the building stone. Beyond offering a tantalizing glimpse into the cultural life of the ruling classes of the time – with the gorgeous detail of the girls totally absorbed in the music and holding goblets of wine (a favourite subject that recurs in Almoravid textiles) – this precious manuscript is clearly the fruit of an élite tradition whose precedents are lost in the mists of time.

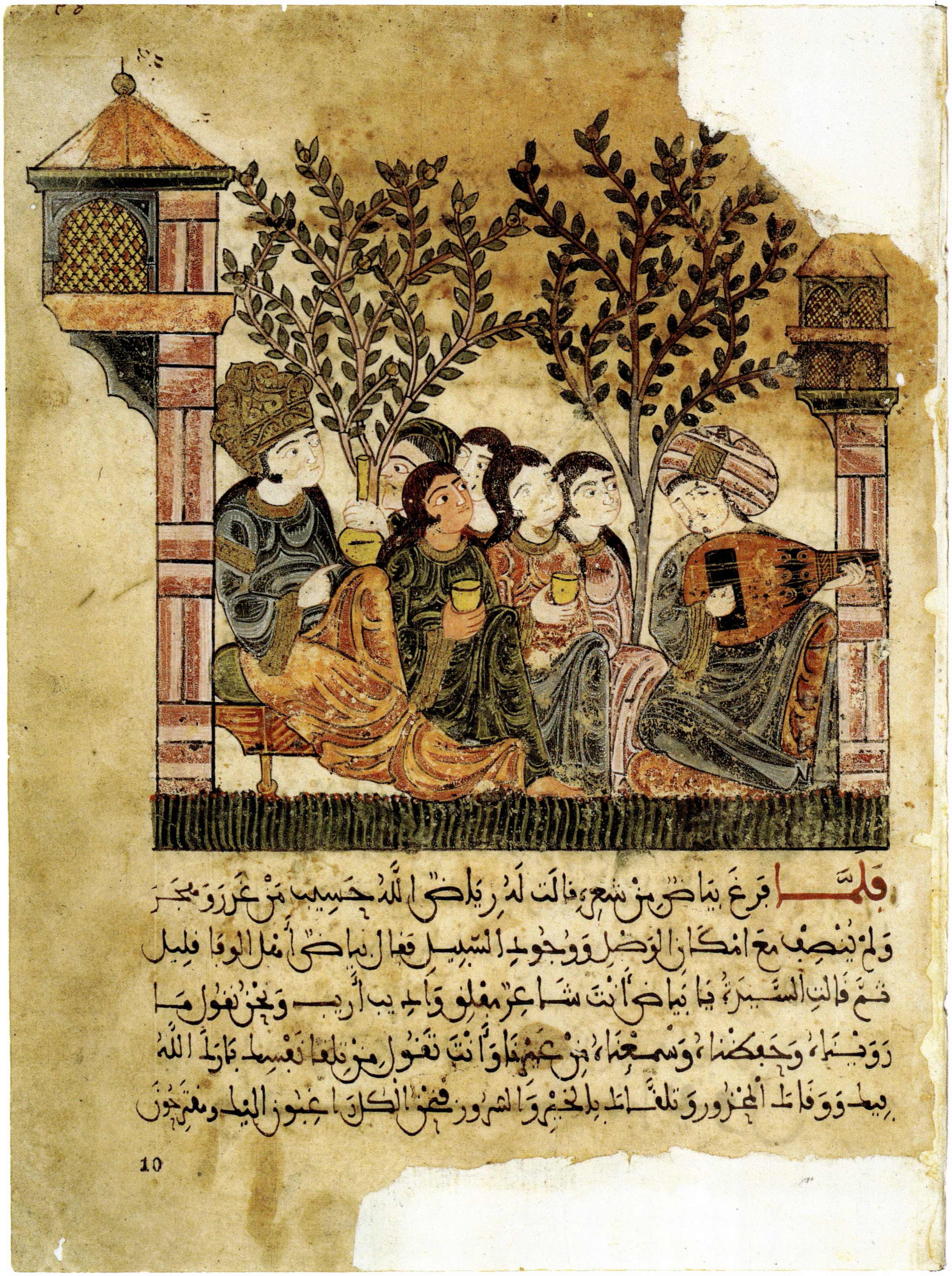

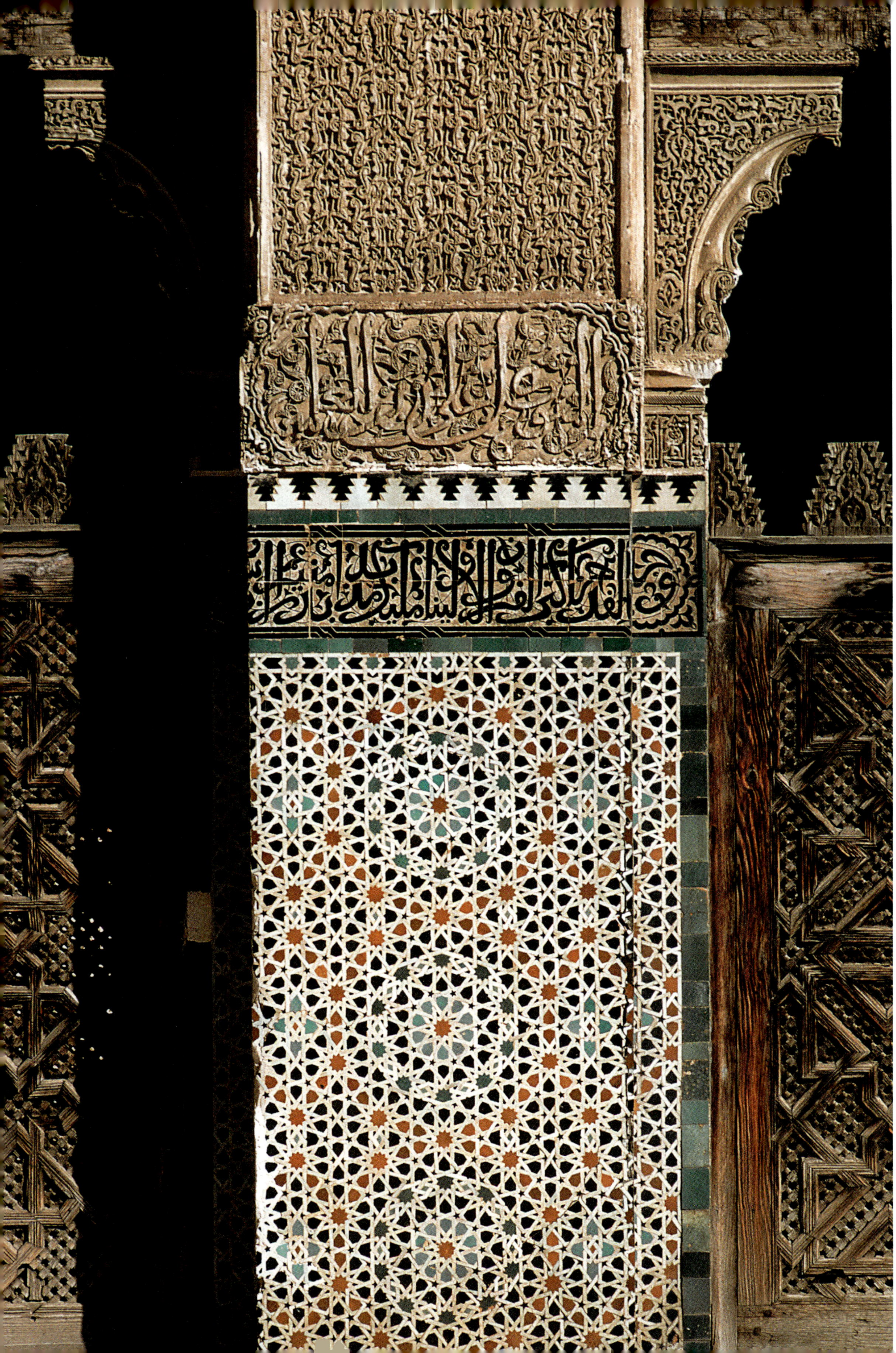

Bou Inaniyya Madrasa
Detail of courtyard
1350–1355, with major restoration between the 17th and 20th centuries
Fez, Morocco

Applied seamlessly in various materials, the refined idiom of Merinid art unfurls all over the decoration of the madrasah's courtyard: carved and at times gilded wood, colourful, scored ceramics, stone and stucco (occasionally painted) all conspire to create an uninterrupted, vibrating surface. These techniques and materials liquefy solid architectural elements creating a refreshing oasis, a calm meeting-place that is at once adjacent to yet separate from the hustle and bustle of the *suq*.

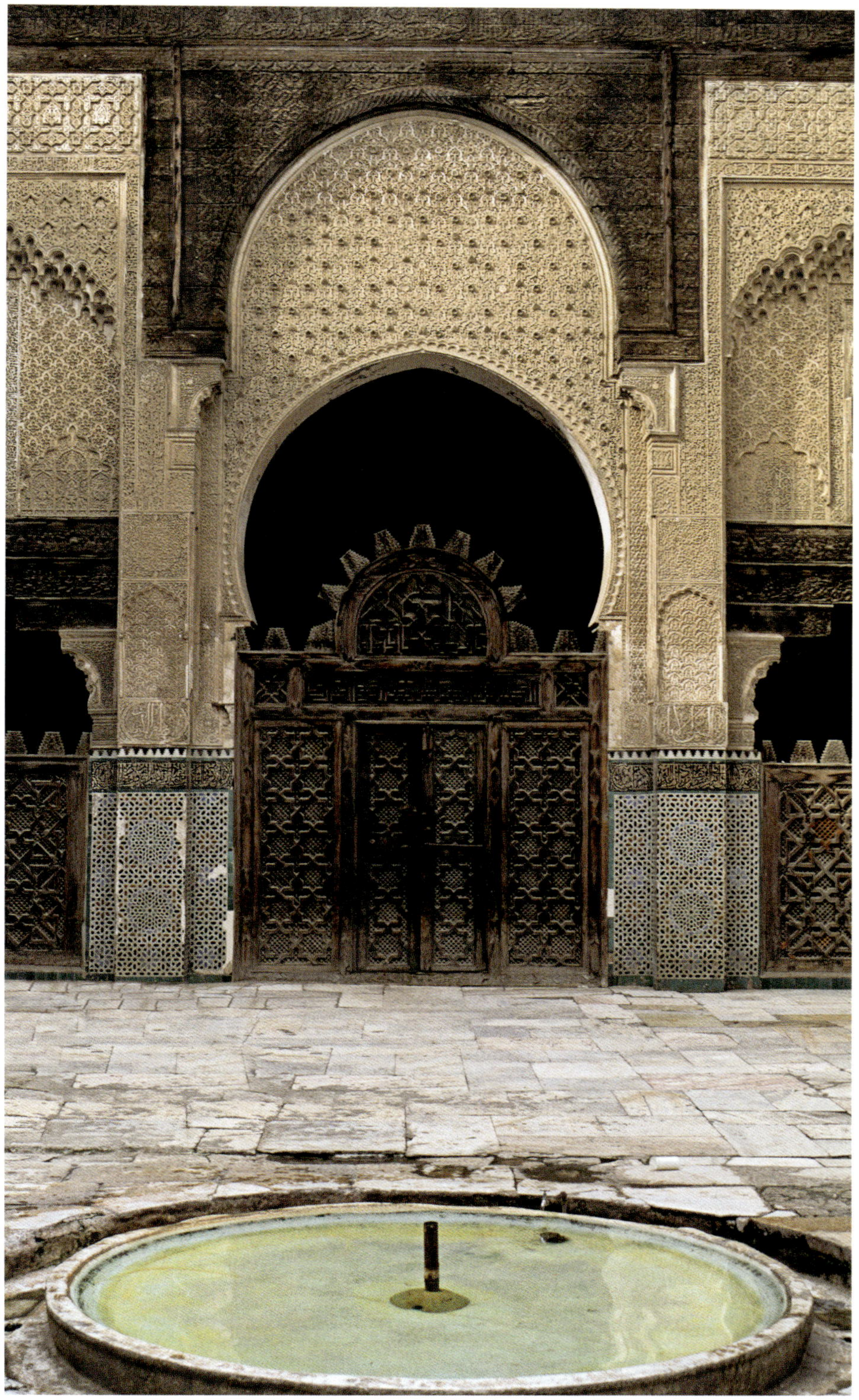

Necropolis of Chellah Gateway
1310–1339
Rabat, Morocco

On the hill outside Rabat, in an idyllic location dotted with remains of Roman villas, Abu al-Hasan decided to honour Abu Yacub Yusuf, who met his death at the battle of Algeciras, with a necropolis of a particular form, in which numerous other members of the Merinid dynasty were to be subsequently interred. The enormous complex is ringed by what looks like a formidable defensive enceinte wall, though in fact its purpose is more metaphoric. An inscription defines it as *ribat* and exalts *jihad*. It stresses the role of the dynasty in defending and proselytizing the faith, to the detriment of the populace who, encouraged by the Sufi mystics, increasingly turned in religious matters to *marabouts* (saints and hermits and, by extension, their mausoleums, to which particular powers are still attributed). The monumental entrance is flanked by towers on an octagonal plan crowned by an unusual square summit, the transition to which is ensured by a stone *muqarnas* squinch: an imaginative variation on the typically Almohad motif of the gateway.

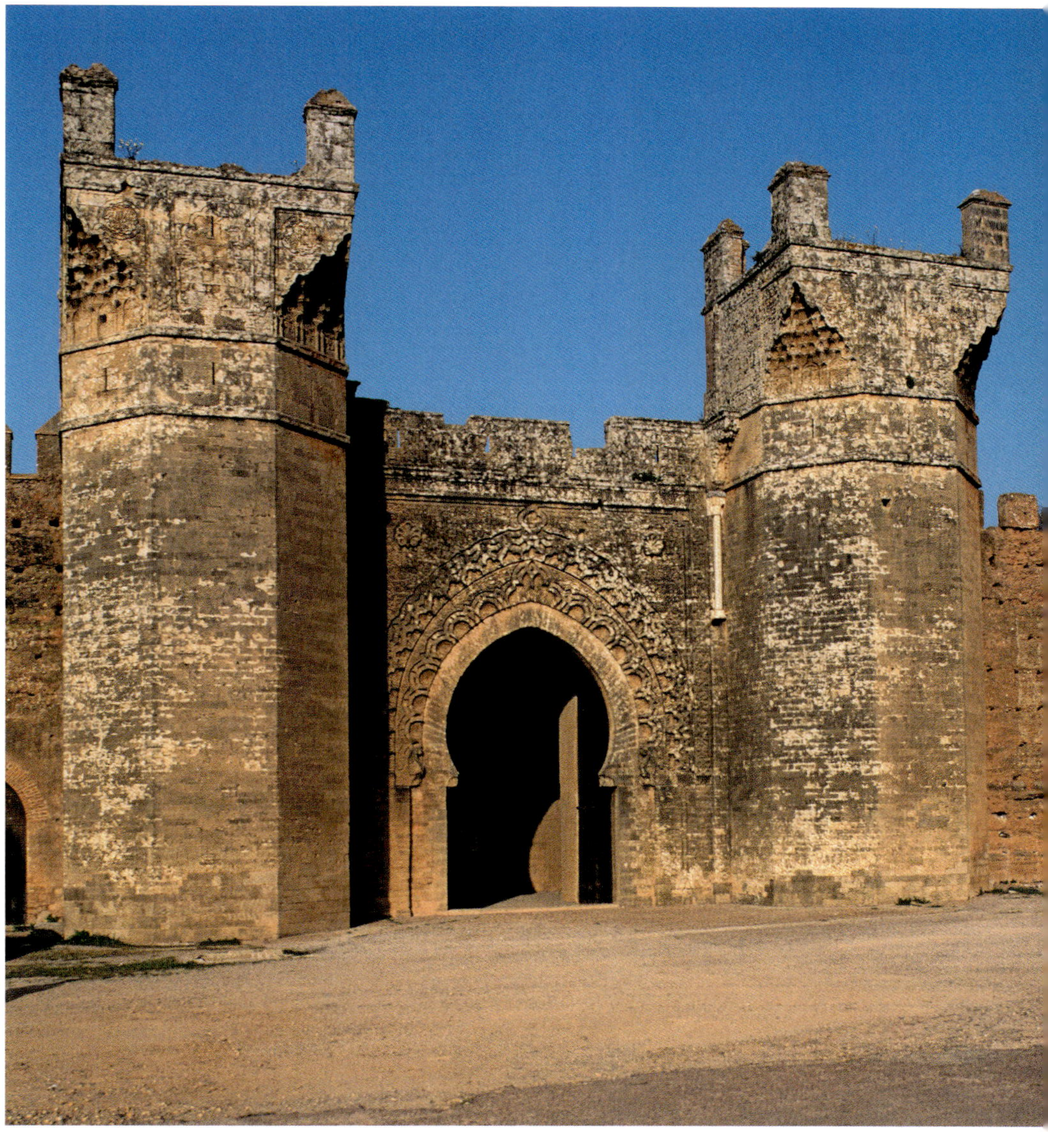

Bou Inaniyya Madrasah
1350–1355, with major restoration between the 17th and 20th centuries
Fez, Morocco

The Merinids subsidized numerous madrasahs in order to ensure the inculcation of Sunnism and to check the rising tide of Sufism which was gnawing away at the religious basis for their authority, and to train loyal bureaucrats for their civil service. Such foundations are generally laid out around a high and relatively exiguous courtyard, paved in marble with a pool for ablutions in the centre. A projecting wooden roof with eaves supported on carved and painted consoles offers shade from the blazing sun, and there are various indispensable services, cells for students, sometimes arranged over a number of floors, and a prayer hall.

Ksour of Ait Arbi
17th–18th centuries
Morocco

In the region between the southern slopes of the Atlas and the Sahara the Berbers developed an architectural typology quite independent of that created in the larger imperial cities. It was designed to ensure safety for their extended families and their property, including harvests and livestock. The minimal component of this type of settlement, which had benefitted from the subsidiary purpose of advertising the power of its occupiers, is the *ksar* (plural, *ksour*) – the fortified core of the village, constituted by a fence with square towers at the corners and a single entryway. The living spaces, warehouses, stables and well were all disposed at different points along the perimeter wall, generally leaving an area free in the centre, both as a source of fresh air and a venue for communal activities.

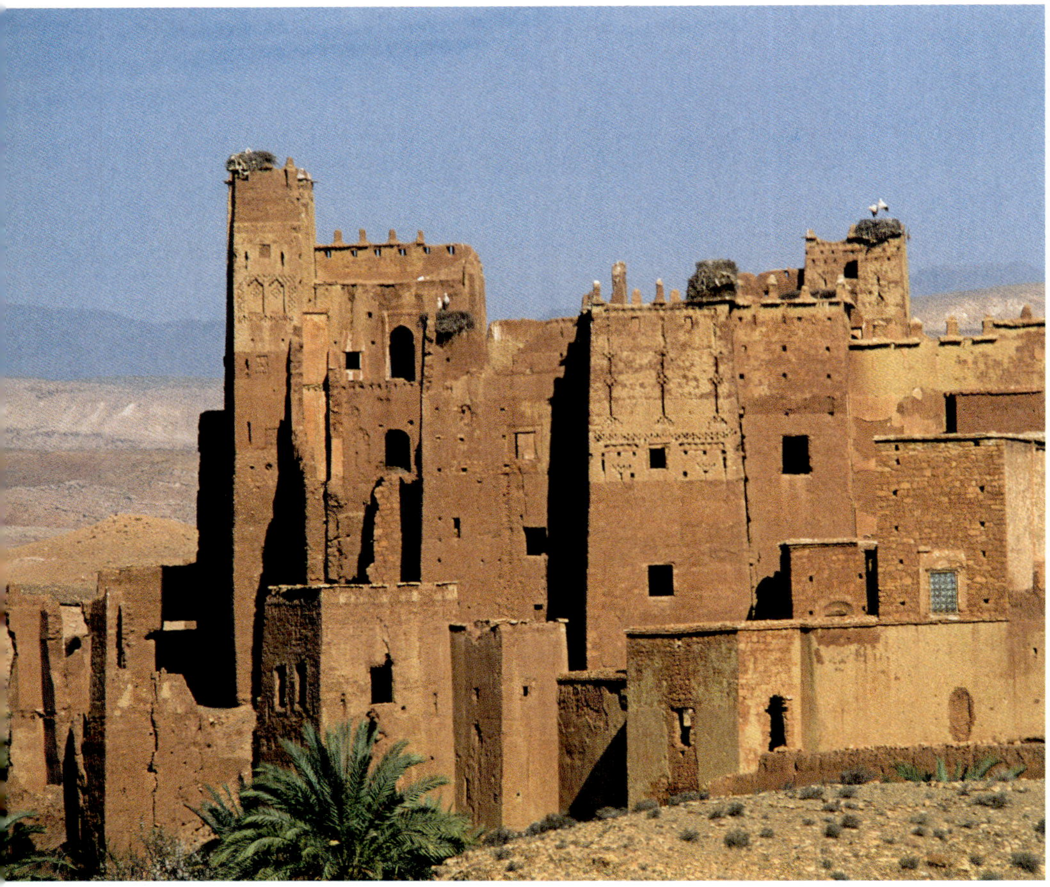

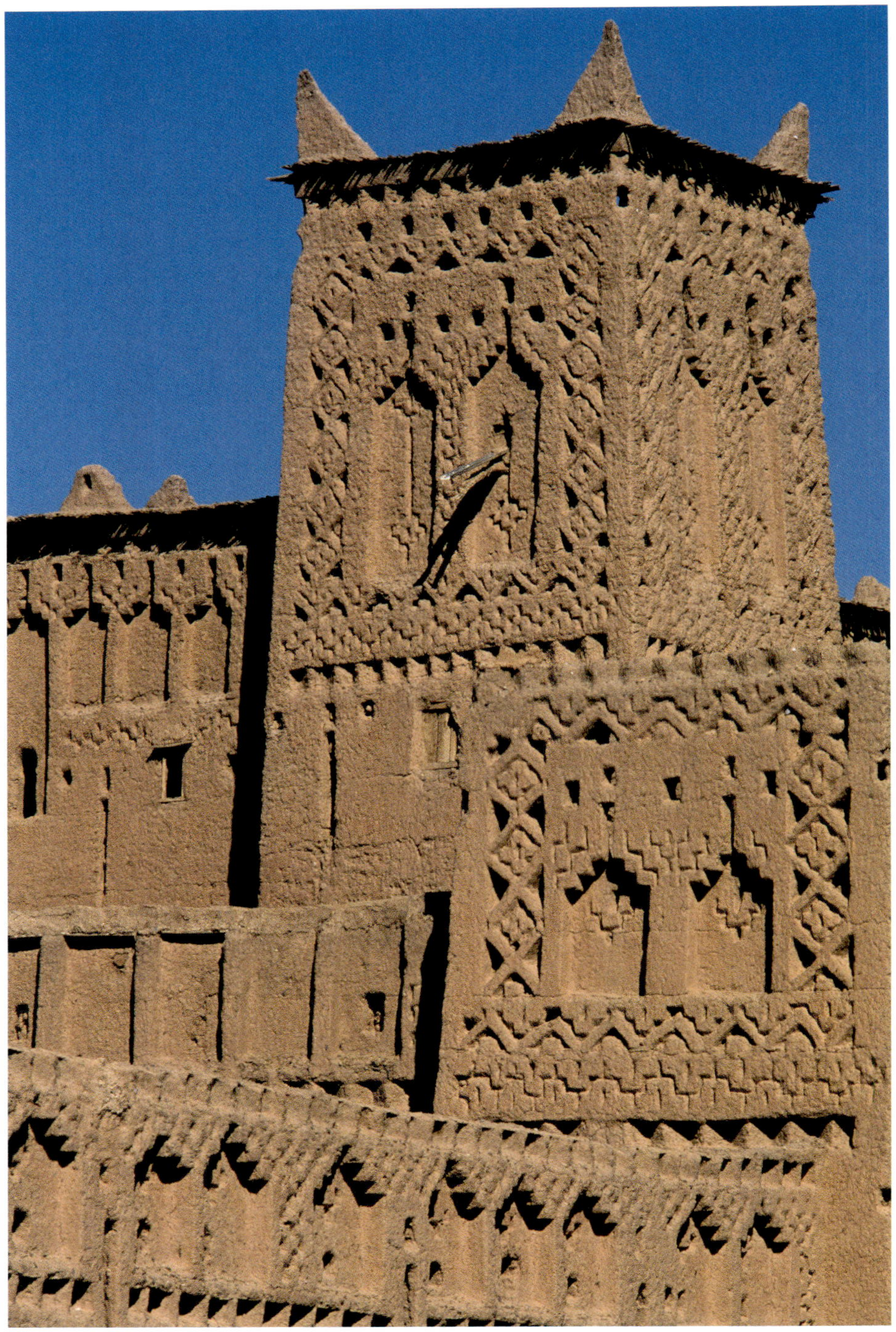

Amerhidil *kasbah*
18th century
Skoura, Morocco

Berber architecture reflects the rugged lifestyles of populations who inhabit the unforgiving terrain of the slopes of the Atlas and the desert fringe. As if in a mirage, the land is dotted about with castles with turrets and battlements adorned with apotropaic motifs of a rustic but prepossessing elegance. Derived in the main from the traditional cloth woven by these nomadic peoples, their formal language is at once restrained and naive. The decoration, for the most part confined to the upper reaches, is composed of simple geometric motifs: lozenges, crosses, *mihrabs,* trees of life, scorpions, and meanders are deployed through an effective linear stylization that animates with ingenuous spontaneity the mud walls of these large and severe strongholds.

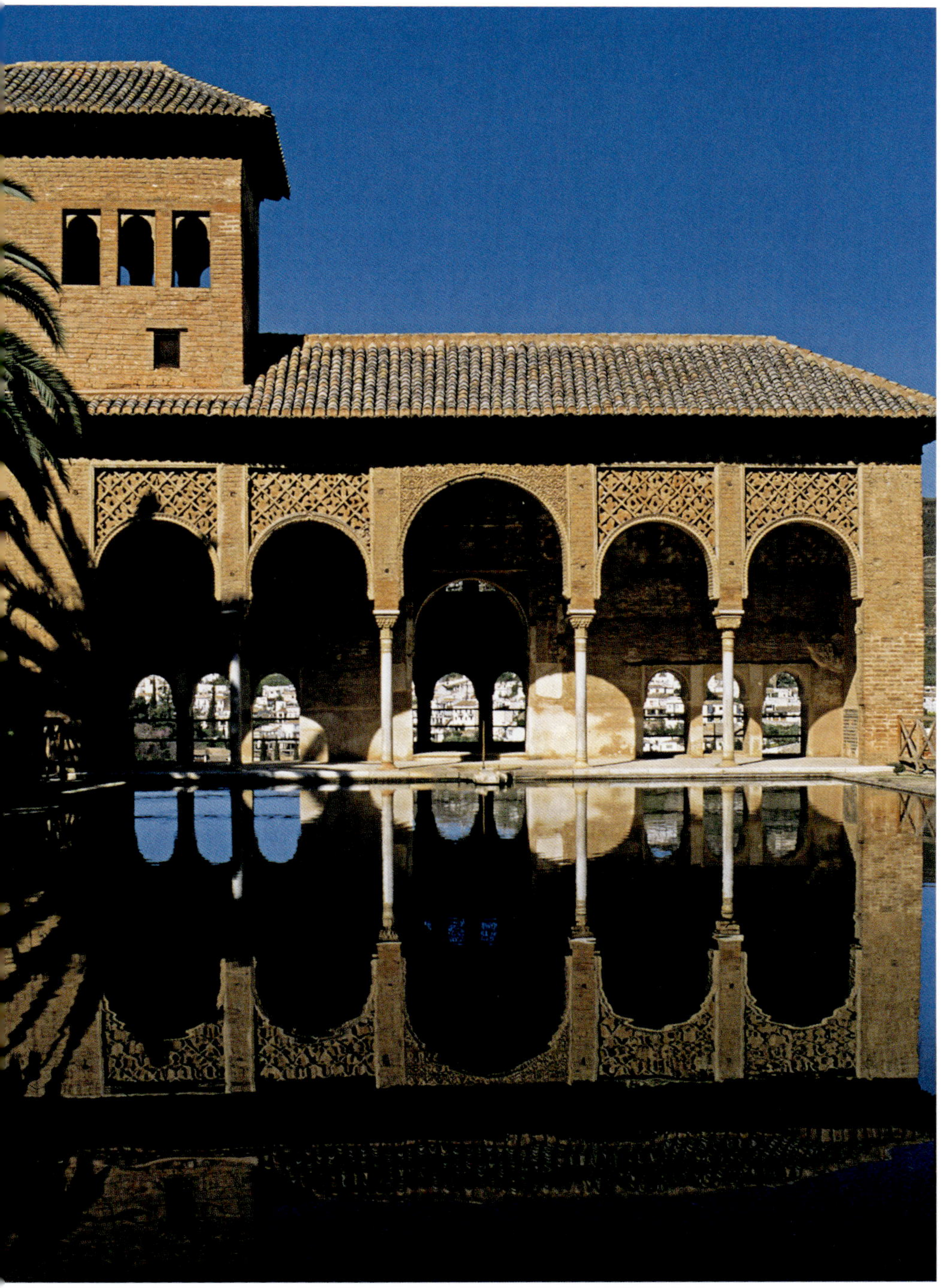

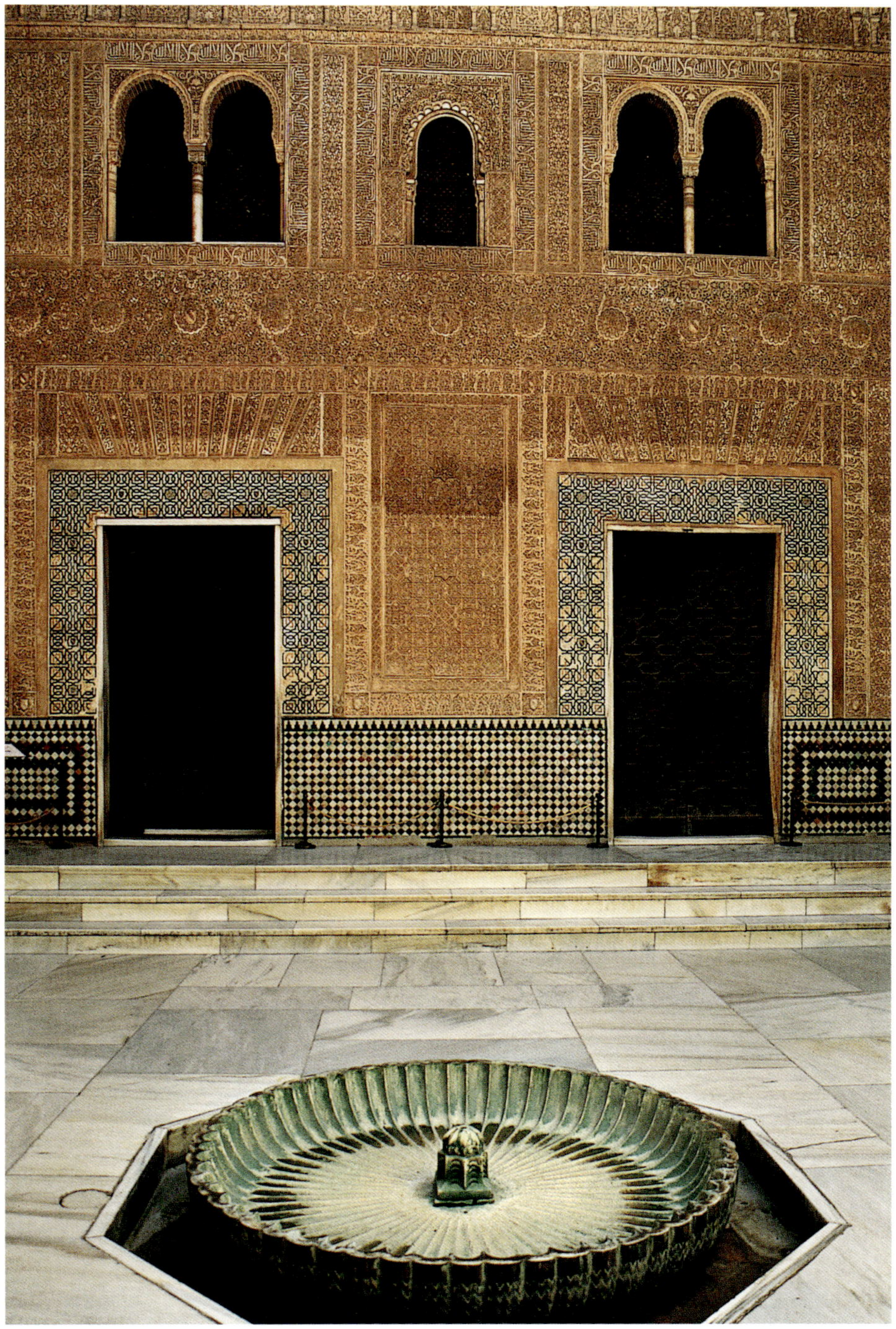

The Alhambra
Palace of the Partal
Early 14th century
Granada, Spain

Practically a self-sufficient entity, the Alhambra was the splendid residence of the court in the Nasrid era. Although the original plantings of gardens, pastures and orchards have been rearranged, abused, and decimated over the years, the complex – in which the mirror-like waters, the fountains, and enfilades framed by archways all play a key role – still speaks volumes as to the strangely unreal atmosphere of life in that bygone age.

The Alhambra
Façade of the Cuarto de Comares
1370
Granada, Spain

Overlooked by a sheltered courtyard, the façade of the Cuarto de Comares was saturated with ornaments whose magnificence today has been compromised by the removal of the stucco decoration that also lined the side walls. The elaborate coloured panels that would have conferred dazzling vitality have long since been taken down, ruining the hallowed sense of rhythm and order. On the other hand the original treatment of the space remains perceptible, the interior resembling as it were a precious casket with elaborately embroidered sides.

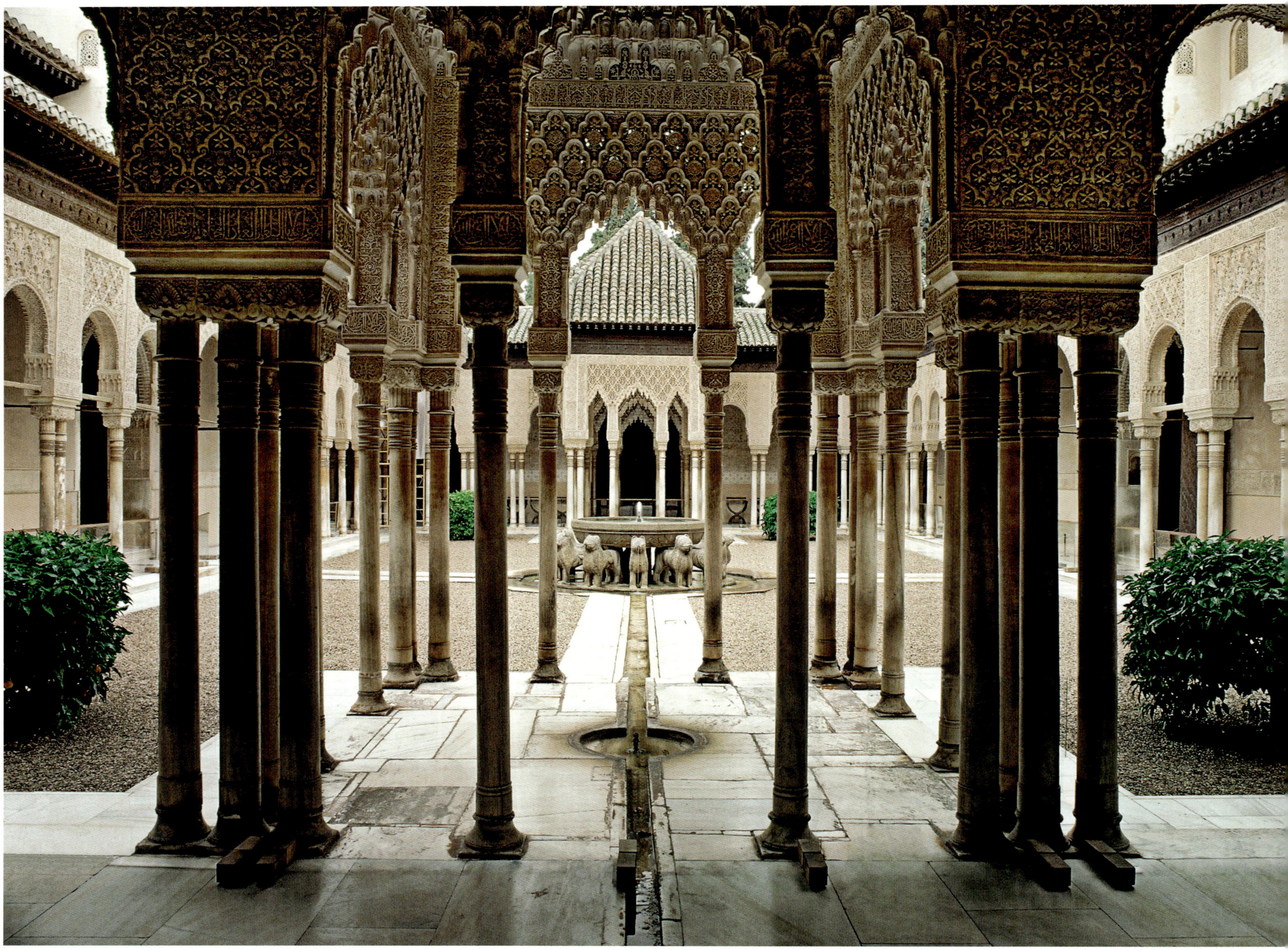

The Alhambra
Patio de Los Leones
Second half of the 14th century
Granada, Spain

The Alhambra is a vast walled complex boasting apartments, steam baths, service wings and gardens of various shapes and sizes combined with refreshing freedom and realized over a considerable period of time. The beating heart of all this poetry, the extraordinary Patio de Los Leones, provides an evanescent precipitation of its vaporous architectural ingredients. The delicately framed arches resting on colonnettes whose slenderness points up the immateriality of the walls above establish a material limit to the vibrant surface of the fretted moulded stucco. The finest qualities of the aesthetic conception of the Alhambra – that otherwise might appear trite and repetitive – reside precisely in the manner in which the structure fissures into infinite variations of light and shadow. As the daylight changes, the arches and walls become ethereal, an illusion that echoes the spiritual climate that presided over the birth of the complex, a fragile and dreamlike apparition of a glorious, eternal sunset, vulnerable and protean – like earthly existence itself.

Vase of 'Alhambra' type
1350
Museo Nacional de Arte
Hispanomusulmán, Granada

The royal enceinte at the Alhambra has yielded objects of extraordinary quality, both imported and produced locally. This latter group includes a series of ceramic vases of monumental dimensions with wing-shaped handles magnificently decorated in lustre known as 'Alhambra vases', because various examples were unearthed in the palace in the eighteenth century. Eight of these pieces have survived in a reasonable condition; together with countless fragments, they demonstrate the spread of prestigious pieces which, with an average height of well over a metre, appear to have been the largest wares in this technique. The object illustrated, from Malaga, belongs to the most recent type, characterized by a more elongated and elegant shape and nearly entirely covered with dazzling cobalt blue and gold decorations. It shows a brace of gazelles facing each other, while the calligraphy, which in earlier examples proudly strode with great angular letters over the body of the vase, is reduced here to a modest ribbon of cursive script round the belly.

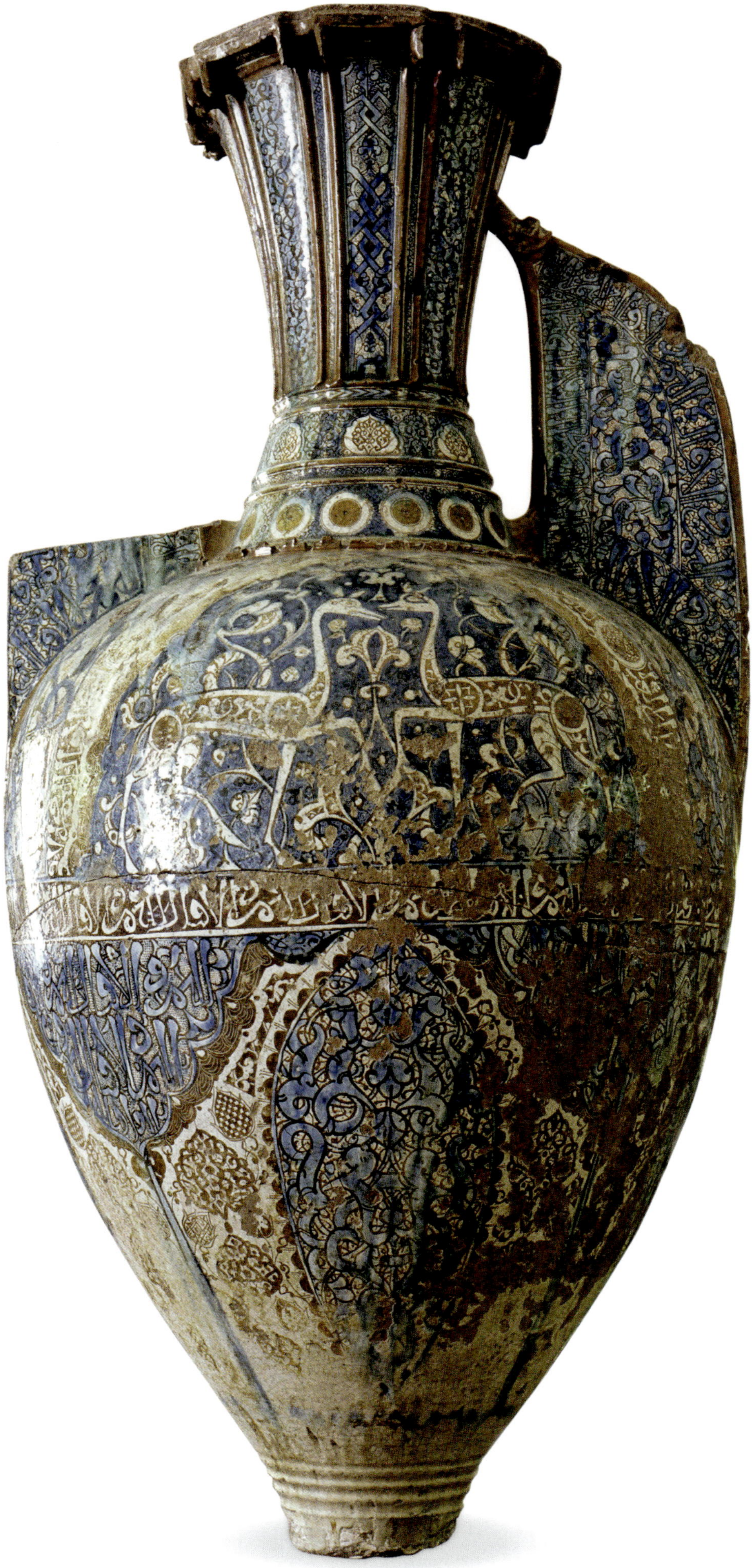

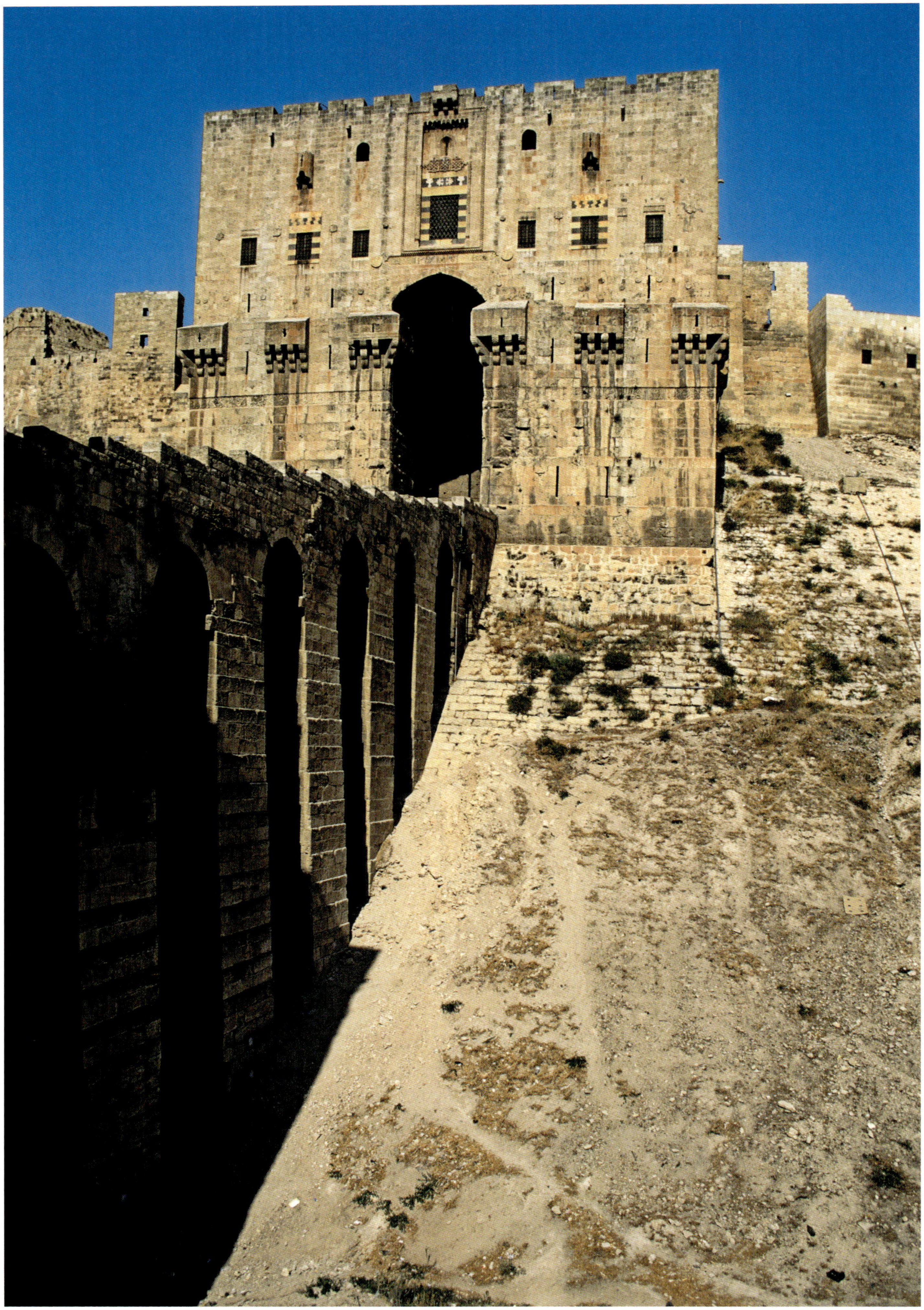

Citadel of Aleppo
Keep and access bridge
13th century
Syria

The natural features of the hillock in the middle of Aleppo had made it an ideal site for defensive structures since prehistory. After the victories of Saladin over the Crusaders its key role as a stronghold in the control of Syria was bolstered further; his son al-Malik al-Zahir Ghazi converted it into a formidable war machine bristling with the most modern developments in military technique, a process accelerated by a state of constant belligerence. The entrance was protected by a brace of powerful keeps crowned by a series of embrasures at the end of a defiant access bridge additionally guarded by a forepart tower. The latter was joined and further raised in the Mamluk period with an immense structure as identifiable by the two-colour inlay around the windows. A colossal ditch was dug all around the hill to make the slope higher and steeper. Entirely flagged with reused stone, material thrown down from the restored and upgraded walls would have had a lethal effect on anyone bold enough to try to scale them or undermine them with tunnels.

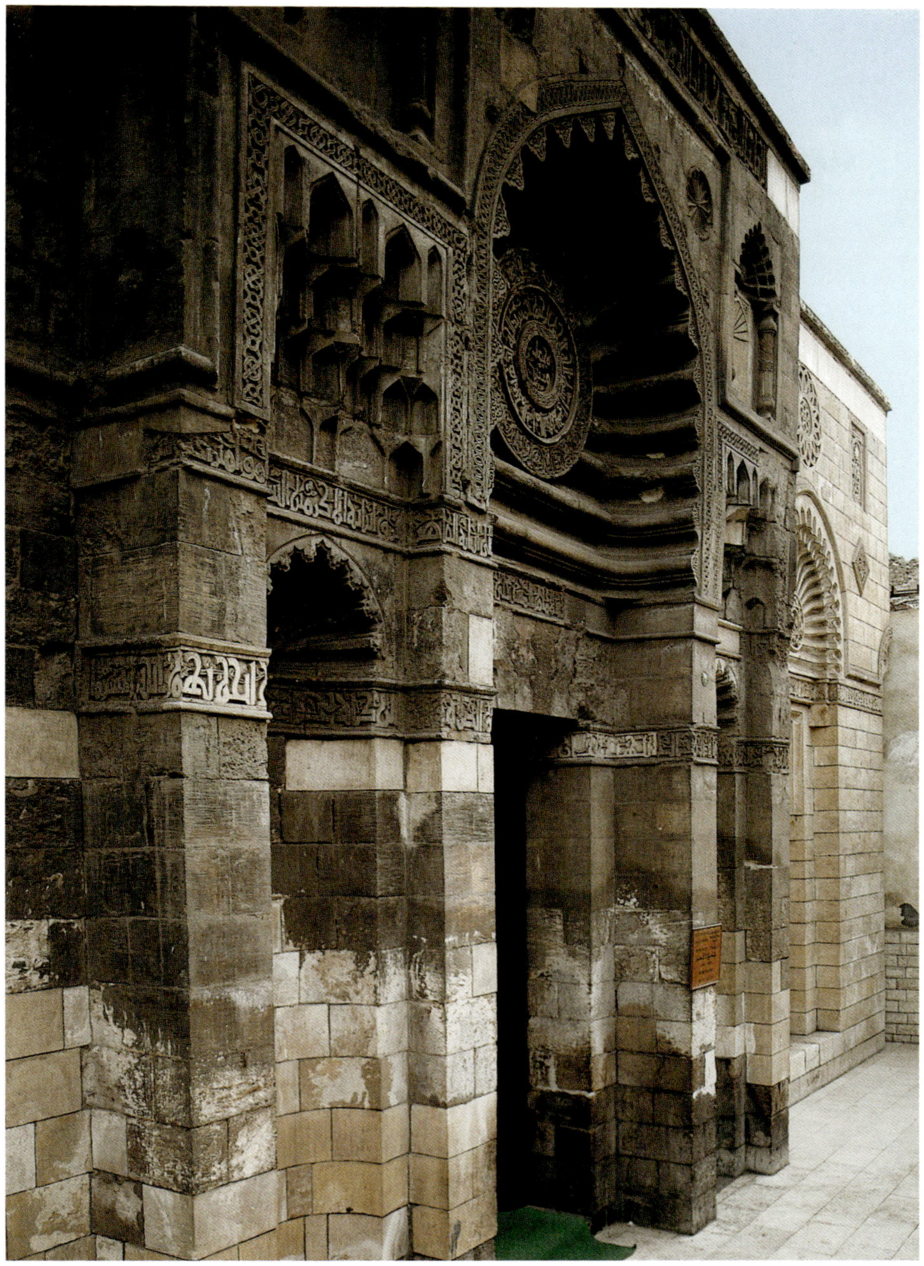

Al-Aqmar Mosque
Façade
1125
Cairo, Egypt

The little al-Aqmar Mosque of 1125 reveals obvious innovative characteristics – the walls, for instance, which can in all likelihood be ascribed to planners from Armenia. Contrary to custom, moreover, the plan is longitudinal, while the façade, placed at a slant with respect to the main range, runs parallel to the road and not to the *qibla* in what is an unusual preoccupation with urban siting. Although of modest dimensions, its powerful decorative synthesis, realized with a perfect mastery of the new Fatimid formal syntax that is enhanced by the skilful use of stonework, makes it one of most memorable sites in all Cairo. As in pre-Tulunid times, the motifs contrast with a plain background strewn with arabesques. The monumental inscription in Kufic constitutes an essential ingredient in the decorative ensemble; especially worthy of note are the arabesques at the top of the ascenders standing out against a backdrop of flourishes. Particularly effective too is the deployment of *muqarnas* in the square crown above the niches flanking the entrance and the latter's huge lunette (a throwback to Coptic precedents), where the theme of the drop arch and the shell are knit into a remarkable expression of serene authority that was destined to leave a profound mark on later architecture, a new formal conception conveyed by the volumes of the domes.

Madrasah of al-Salih Najm al-Din Ayyub
Minaret
1243
Cairo, Egypt

The minaret of the madrasah of al-Salih Najm al-Din Ayyub is the only one of its era to have survived to the present-day virtually intact. The lower reaches of the tower preserve traces of drop-arched panels with rabbetted stucco of singular energy. In the octagonal upper section a series of elegant lobate openings is surmounted by a crown of spiky *muqarnas* on which stands the sturdy crowning piece with alternating widths of chunky ribbing. The minaret is an optimal example of the dynamic equilibrium between form and decoration that was fated to be eclipsed by the pretentious and showy proliferation of Mamluk decorativeness.

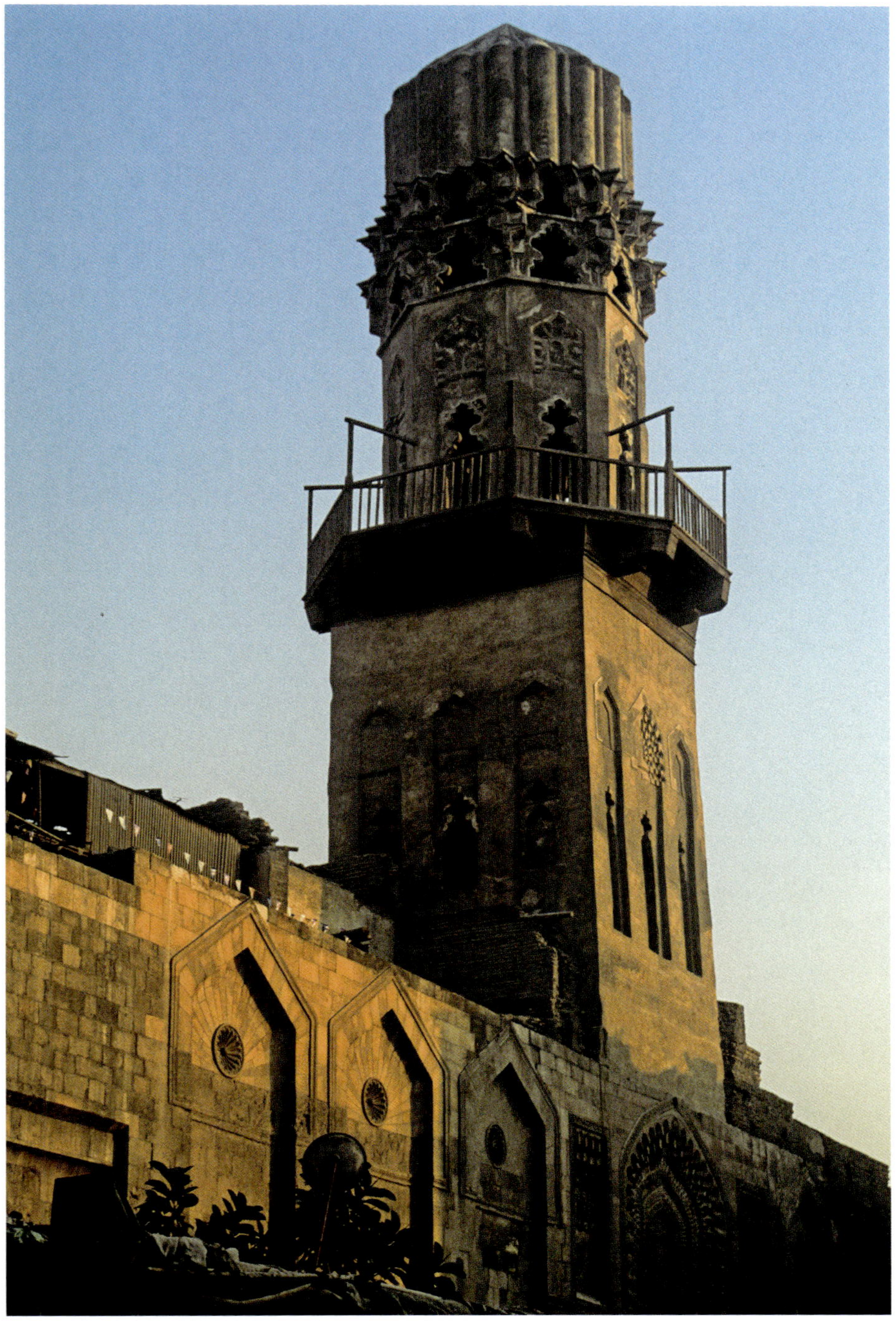

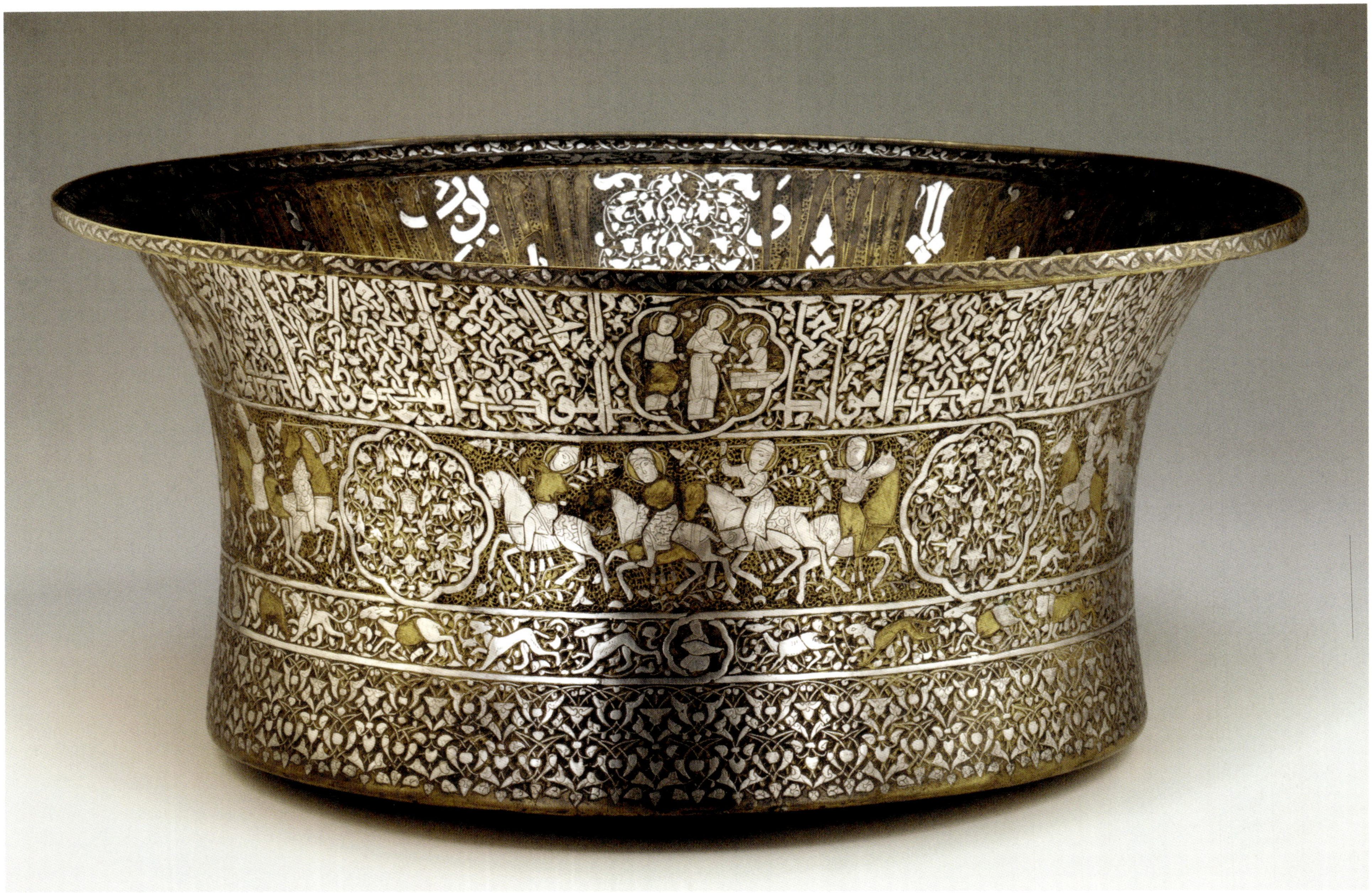

'Arenberg Basin'
1239–1249
Copper alloy with silver inlay
Smithsonian Institution, Washington

The Mongol invasions forced countless craftsmen in Asian countries to seek safety elsewhere, taking with them their technical expertise and a rich baggage of iconography. Their talent had a revitalizing impact on the art of damaskeen which materialized in products of exceptional quality made throughout the Mamluk age both for the wealthy and elegant local market and for export. Vases in bronze with silver inlay constituted moreover an acceptable substitute for those in precious metals – the cost of which naturally restricted them solely to the upper echelons of society – contributing to the runaway success of this type of ware. The 'Arenberg Basin' was made for al-Malik al-Salih Ayyub, sultan of Cairo and Damascus: the decoration is tightly organized into four bands arranged harmoniously up the curving sides. The top boasts magnificent examples of angular calligraphy, the ascenders twisting into intricate designs. In the middle, various groups of knights are separated by floral motifs, with a thin contour which passes elegantly from the band above to that below to twist into polyfoil medallions.

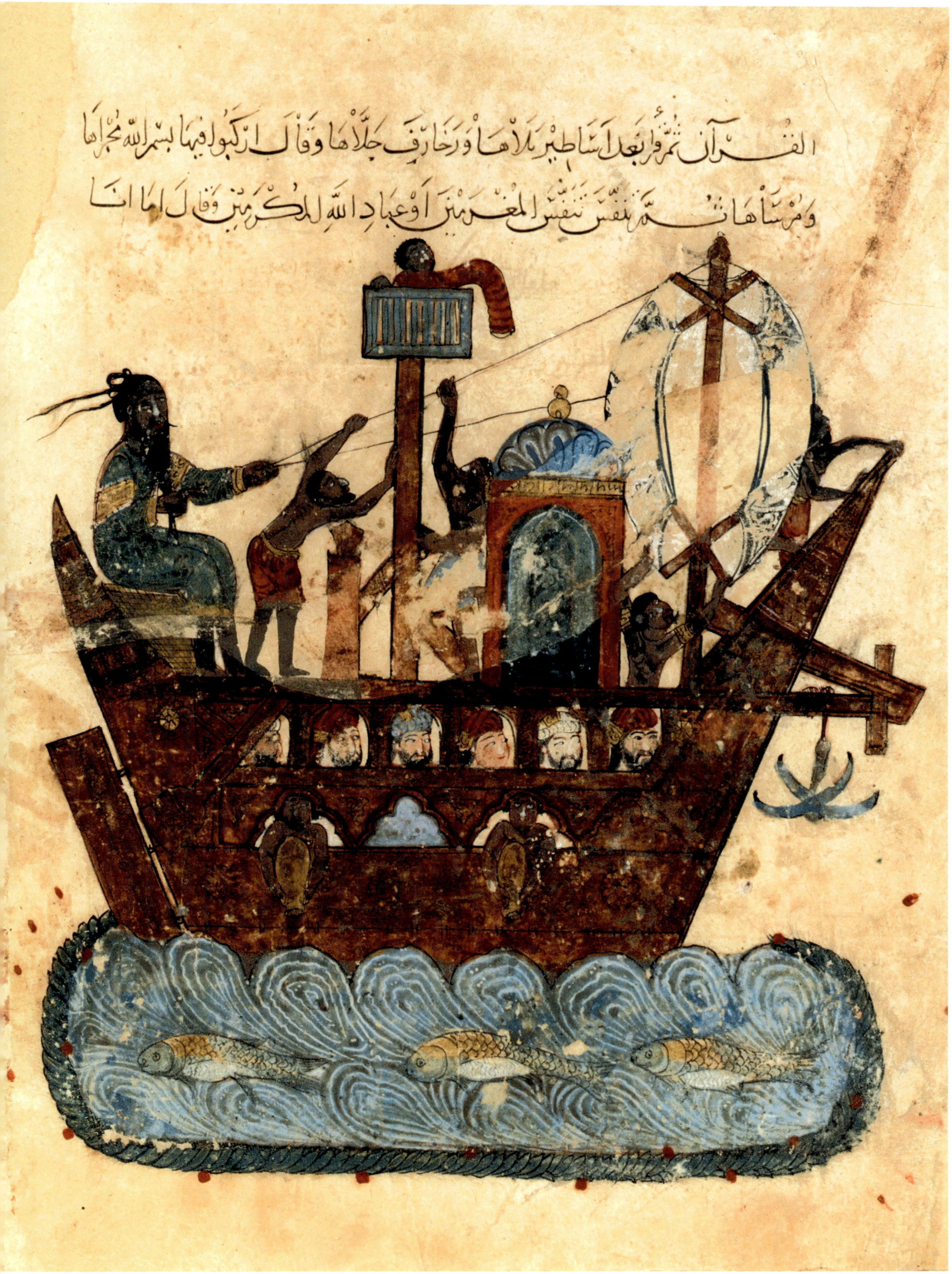

Al-Wasiti (13th century), page from a manuscript of the Maqamat (picaresque stories) of al-Hariri (12th century)
1237
Bibliothèque Nationale de France, Paris

The faithful and amusing miniatures illustrating the picaresque adventures related in the attractive short stories of al-Hariri accurately portray the many facets of Arab merchant society. Described from the inside with unbridled vivacity, they provide an incomparable snapshot that seems more reliable than any other source, literary or not. The only possible iconographic parallel is with certain priceless articles of metalwork, whose greater stylization, lack of colour and grandiose elegance, however, meant that they tended to eschew the depiction of authentic slices of life. Journeys by boat, no less than those by camel caravan, occupy an important place in the *Maqamat,* since both were integral to trade and essential to those concerned with it – such as the merchants shown here gazing out through the parapet on the bridge of the vessel. The elegantly dressed captain seated at the stern mans the rudder and handles the sails assisted by a crew of blacks, probably slaves.

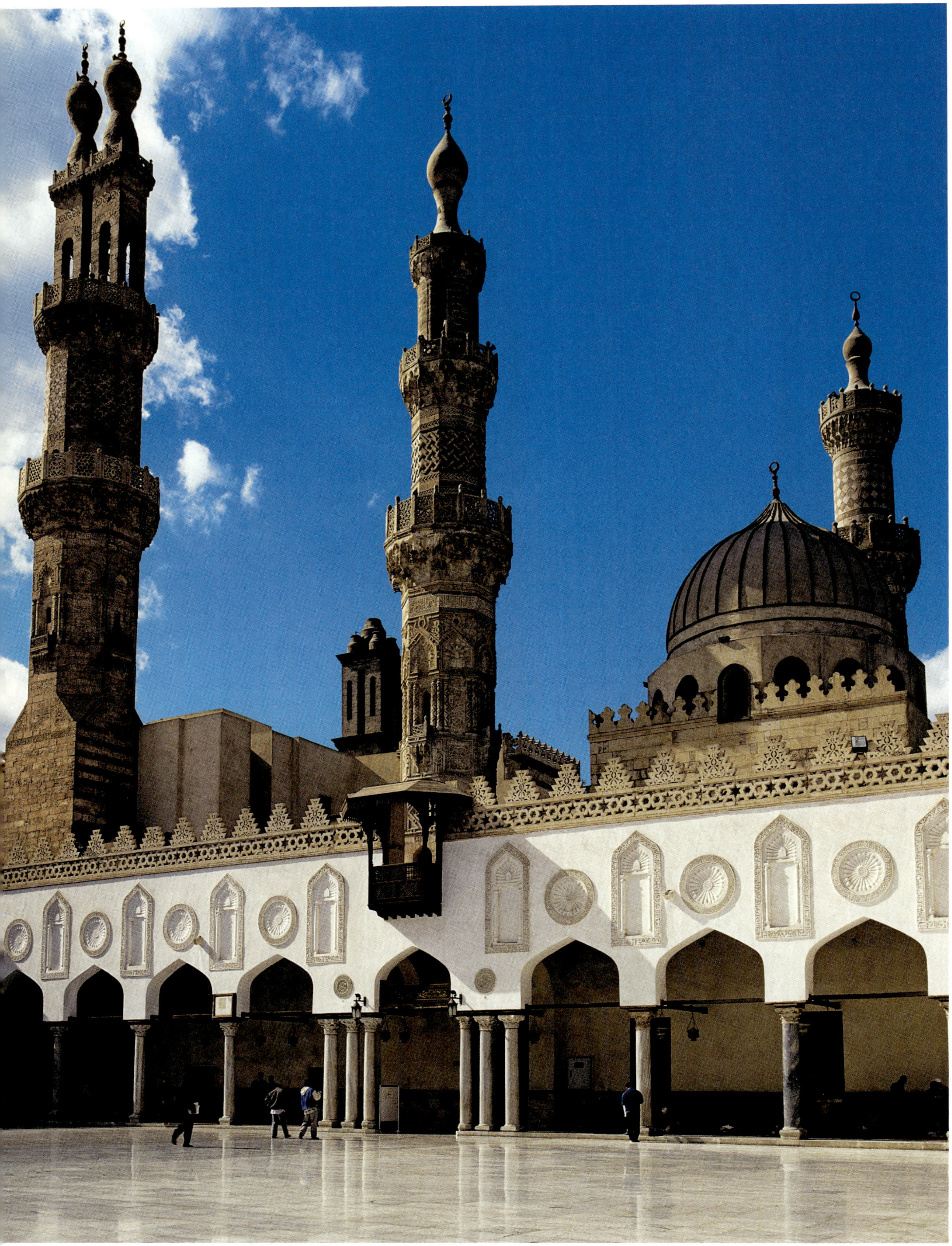

Al-Azhar Mosque
Courtyard with minarets
10th–15th centuries, Mamluk
Cairo, Egypt

The Mamluks gave Cairo its countenance of a city dominated by innumerable striking domes and minarets towering over narrow medieval lanes and displaying a proliferation of forms and fantastic profiles that sometimes verge on the eccentric. Even venerable institutions did not escape this architectural outpouring, as shown by the historic al-Azhar Mosque. The porch erected by the Fatimid caliph al-Hafiz in the first half of the thirteenth century was peppered by minarets, each characterized by details and artistic excursions that are not always flawless, but each a monument to the prestige of some grand patron.

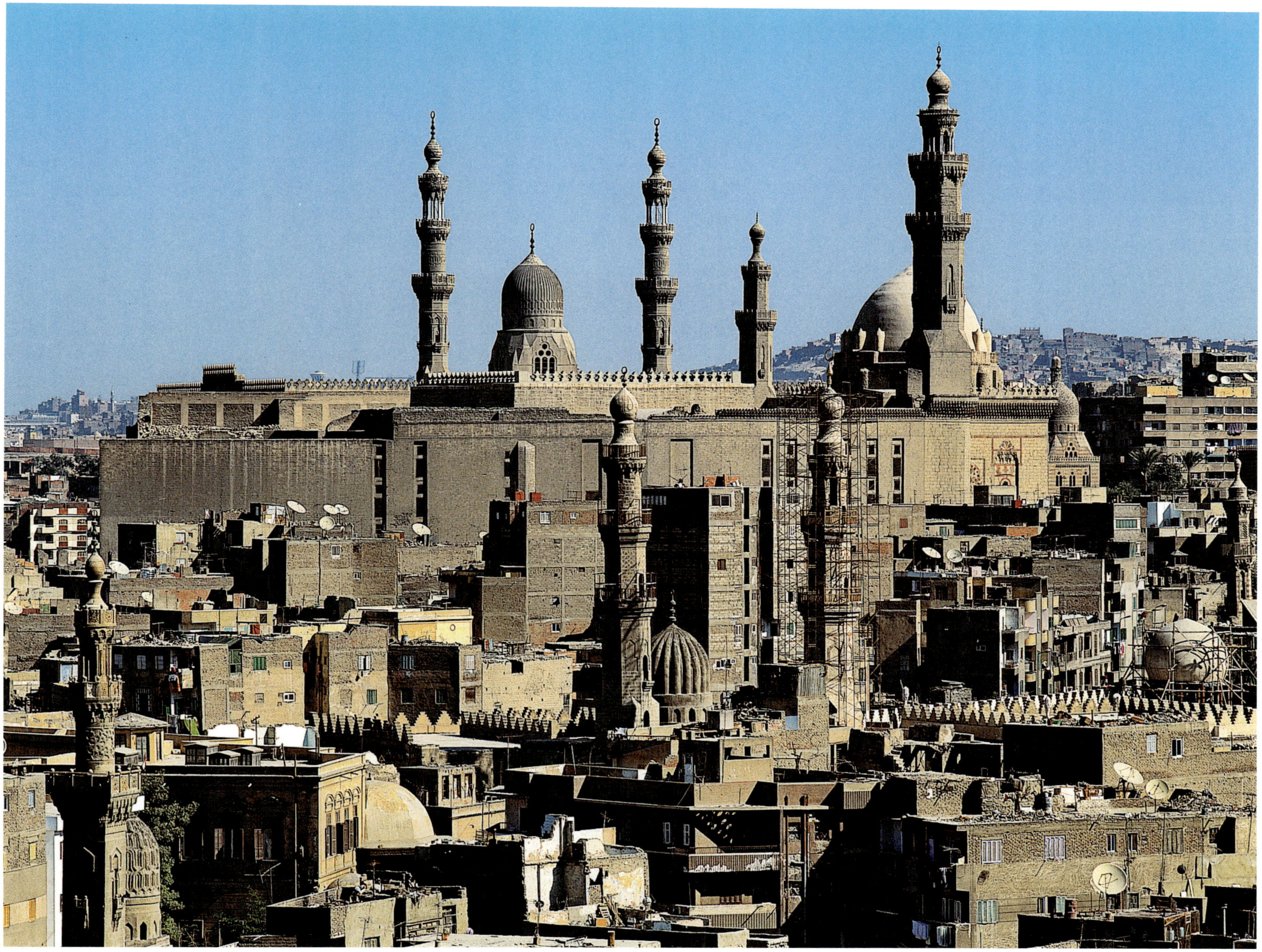

Complex of Sultan Hasan and the Rifa'i Mosque
1356–1362 (and subsequent restorations), 1869–1912
Cairo, Egypt

The towering mass of blind wall that dominates the heart of the city at the foot of the citadel is in fact a gigantic complex with four madrasahs and a Friday mosque, as well as a mausoleum in an annex commissioned by Sultan Hasan al-Nasir, together making up the largest Islamic monument in Egypt. His additions include the minaret to the right and the colossal cupola in the background. The propaganda purpose of the ensemble is manifest in the oversized external walls through which the windows of the madrasah open over four towering floors. A compact and severe block, ponderous rather than grandiose, its language is articulated into an unconvincing statement of formal power. Given its structure, the complex was used on more than one occasion as a fortress, although the cupola had to be rebuilt after damage by cannon fire. The outlandish minarets and domes of various forms visible in front of the complex are Mamluk, while the Rifa'i Mosque in the background was erected in the Mamluk style in the dying years of the Ottoman Empire.

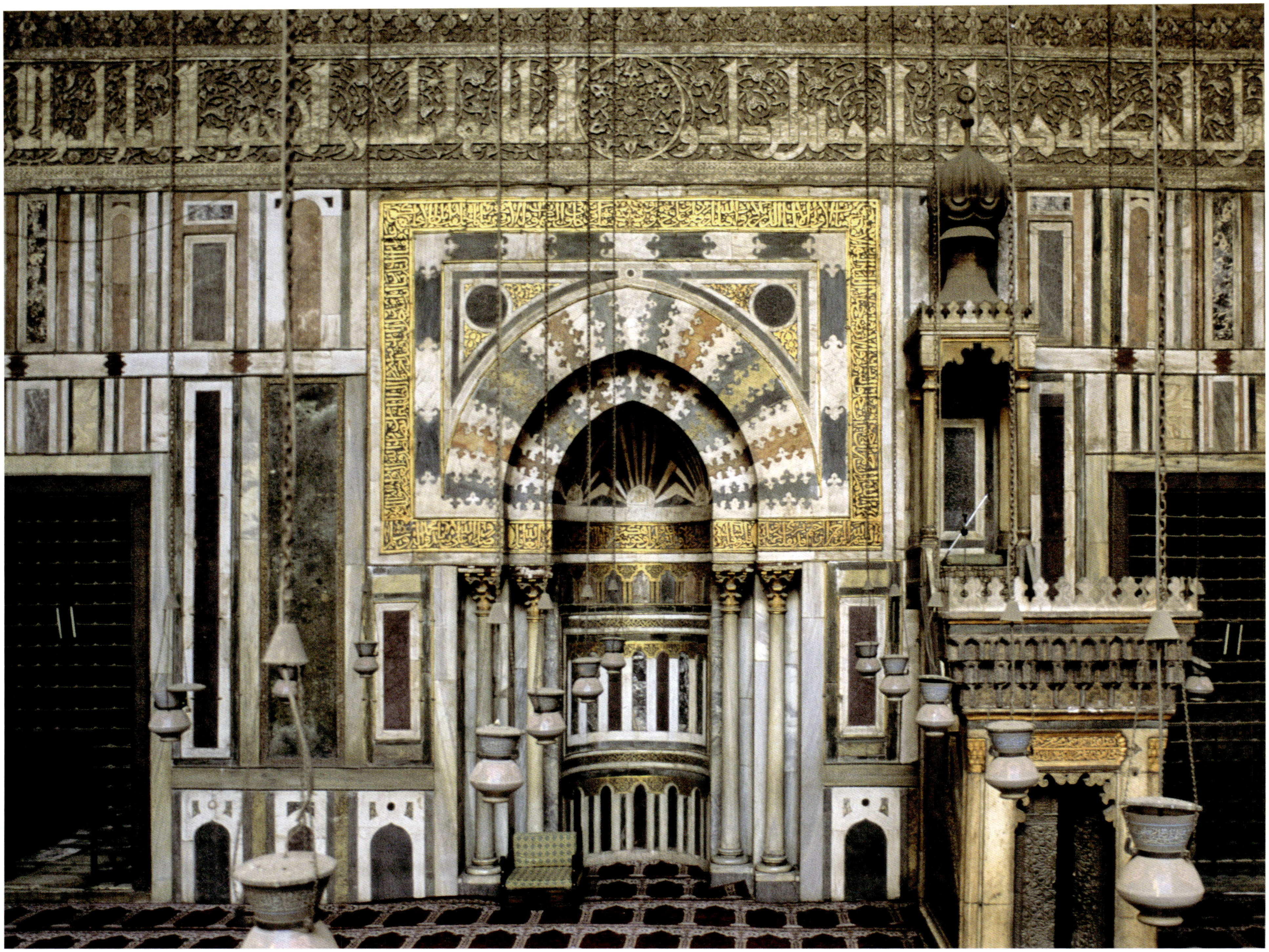

Mosque of Sultan Hasan
Wall of the *qibla* on the main *iwan*
1356–1362
Cairo, Egypt

The *iwan* with the *qibla* wall, unfolding beneath an immense and relatively plain vault in a flamboyant symphony of marble illuminated by the blaze of modern lamps – replicas of originals – is the largest of the Islamic Middle Ages and seems derived from the impressive models of the Byzantine Empire. The monumental marble *minbar,* crowned by an unfortunate carved bulb, is among the biggest and most pretentious of the period. The grille on the left allows access to the mausoleum of the Sultan in line with the *qibla*. The vast stucco inscription in a solemn Kufic script of typically Mamluk taste is encircled by floral motifs and quotes the beginning of the *sura* of Victory (XXIV, 1–3).

Mosque of Sultan Hasan
Mihrab
1356–1362
Cairo, Egypt

The sumptuously decorated *mihrab* is adorned with architectural moulds in white marble in the lower zones and in gold on the upper. At the height of the capitals, probably *spolia* and richly gilded, there unfurls a band of gold showing elegant blind trefoil arches above which runs an inscription in *thulth* characters, a favourite in the Mamluk age for its elegance. Over the niche, the name of Allah is repeated three times, emblazoning the half-dome and illuminating the sultan at his prayers.

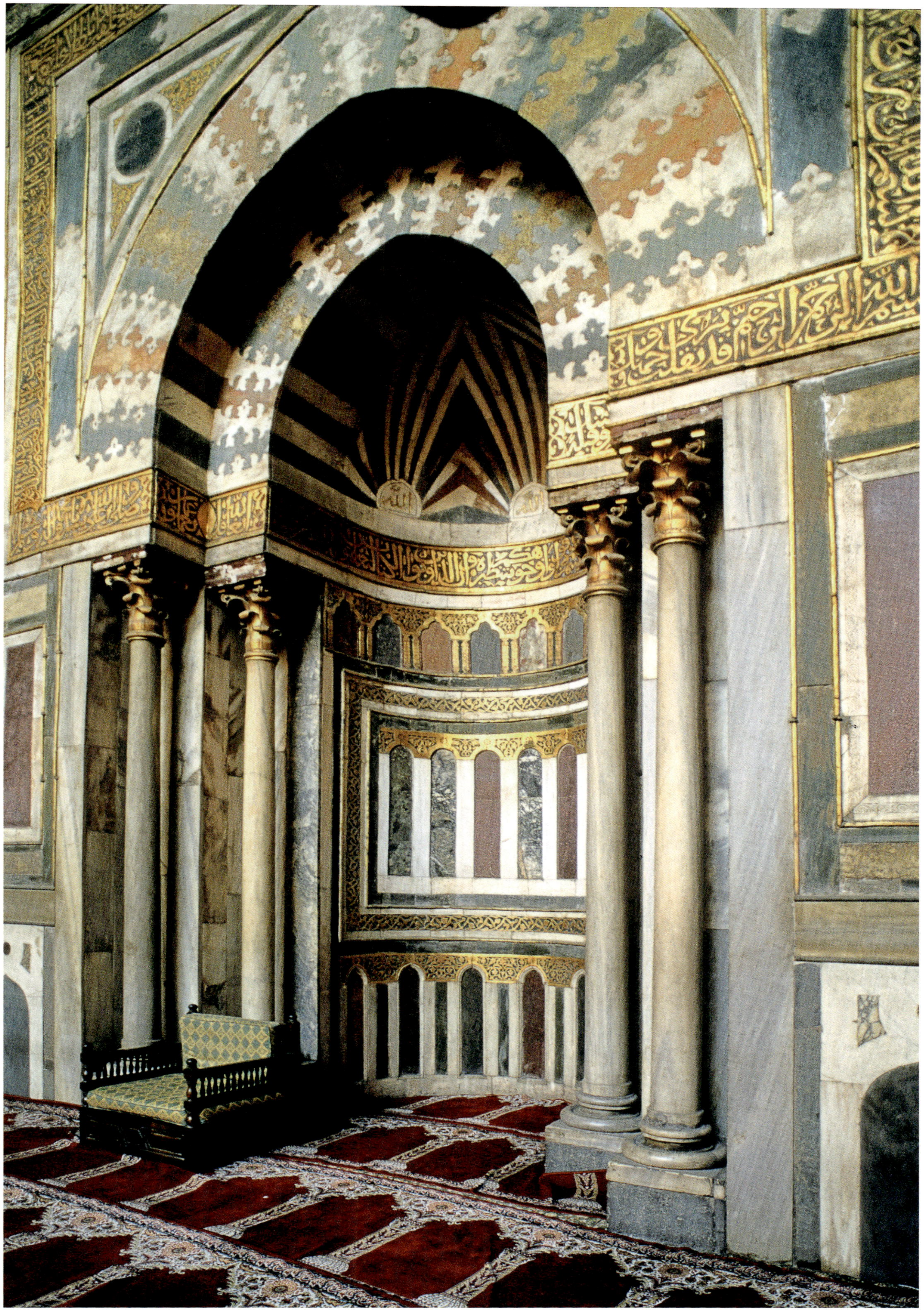

Mausoleum of Sultan Barquq
Khanaqah
1410
Cairo, Egypt

The mausoleum of Sultan Barquq in Cairo is an outsized example of how the Mamluks turned their funerary monuments into an instrument of self-aggrandizement and dynastic propaganda. In the present case, the builder had no hesitation in providing a sizable *khanaqah* – or monastic complex – with a vast façade flanked by two minarets, as well as a suite of lodgings for monks and all requisite facilities. There is also a hypostyle mosque with domes on octagonal pillars and a *minbar* for Friday prayer, and a courtyard with a fountain for ablutions, in addition to the two immense mausoleums on towering cupolas, one dedicated to the sultan and the other to his wife and daughters.

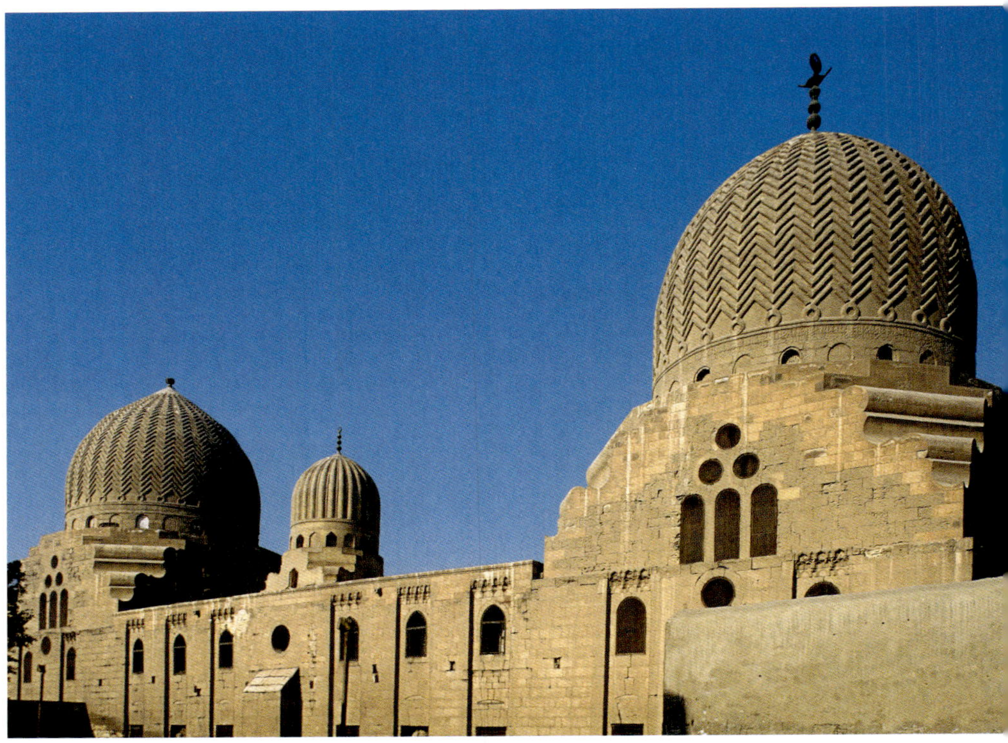

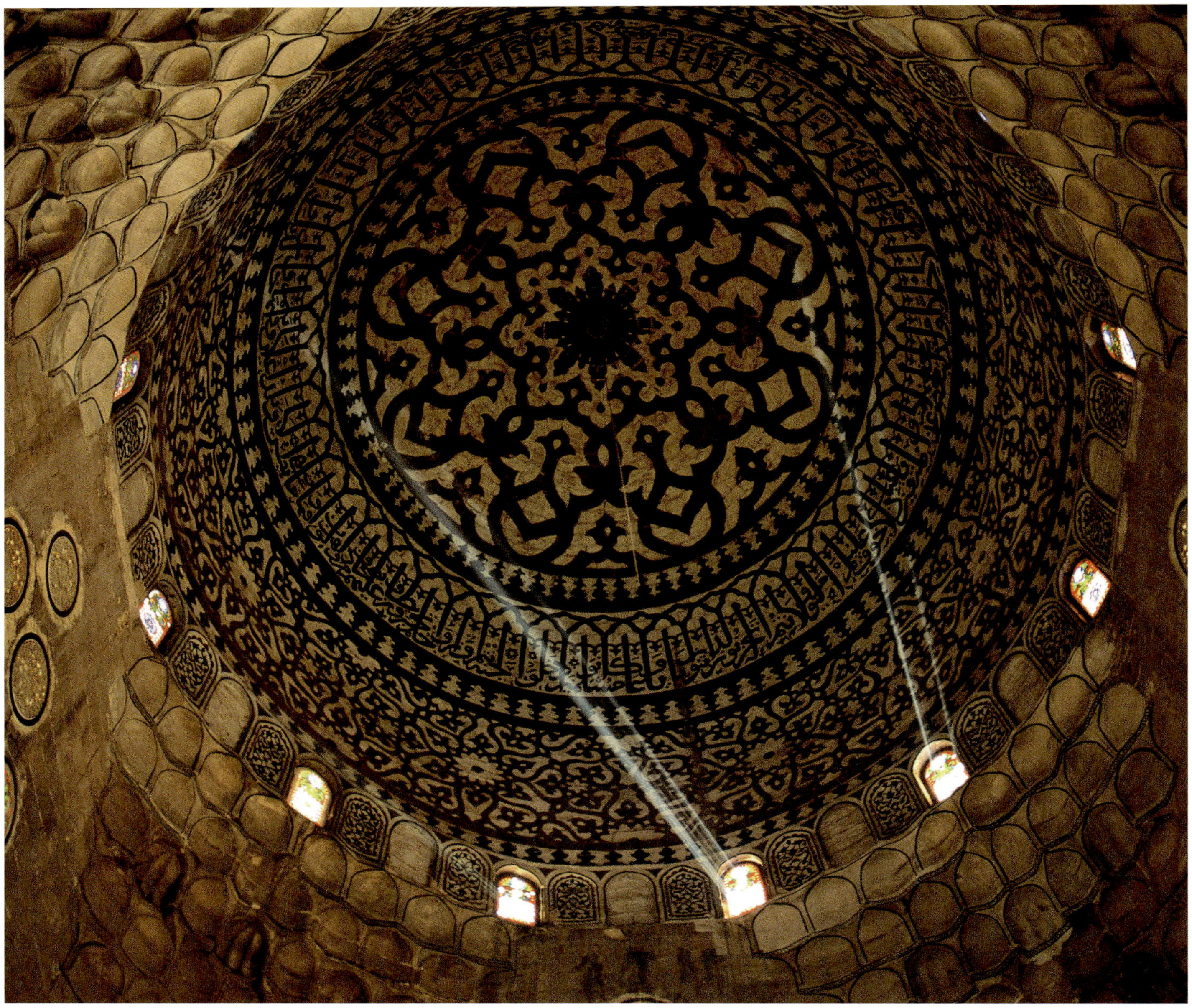

Mausoleum of Sultan Barquq
Dome
1410
Cairo, Egypt

This complex formulates a positive apotheosis of the sultan and his lineage. Their names are recalled forever in the prayers of monks who transformed the burial place into a centre of a cult. Pilgrims would come in droves to earn *baraka,* asking the sultan for favours of every kind and expressing their gratitude with prayers and offerings. The beams of light slicing through the dome exalt the motif of an exploding star in the apex of the cupola in what is an obvious reference to paradise where the spirit of the sultan now dwells.

Necropolis of Amir Azrumuk
Northern mausoleum
1503
Cairo, Egypt

Stone domes were a characteristic of architecture in Mamluk Egypt, without equivalent in other edifices of the Islamic world. The earliest were realized at the beginning of the fourteenth century, the acme in terms of technique and aesthetic being attained towards the end of the fifteenth. With the Ottoman conquest of 1517, this costly architectural custom was abandoned as the new political regime scattered the patron classes. Among the later and most interesting domes is that of the emir Azrumuk, one of thousands of functionaries in the service of Sultan Qansuh Abu Sa'id, remarkable for a splendid decoration of floral motifs between which shimmer droplets of blue majolica, unique of their kind. The original purity of the form, inherited from the Ayyubids and expressed initially with geometric clarity, has been tempered, one might say, Iranized by the delicate transition between rectilinear and curved forms and reaffirmed in the mildly manneristic lyricism of the floral motifs. This emblematic monument, where decorative superstructure plays a role of prime importance, can be said to mark the end of the heyday of Mamluk art.

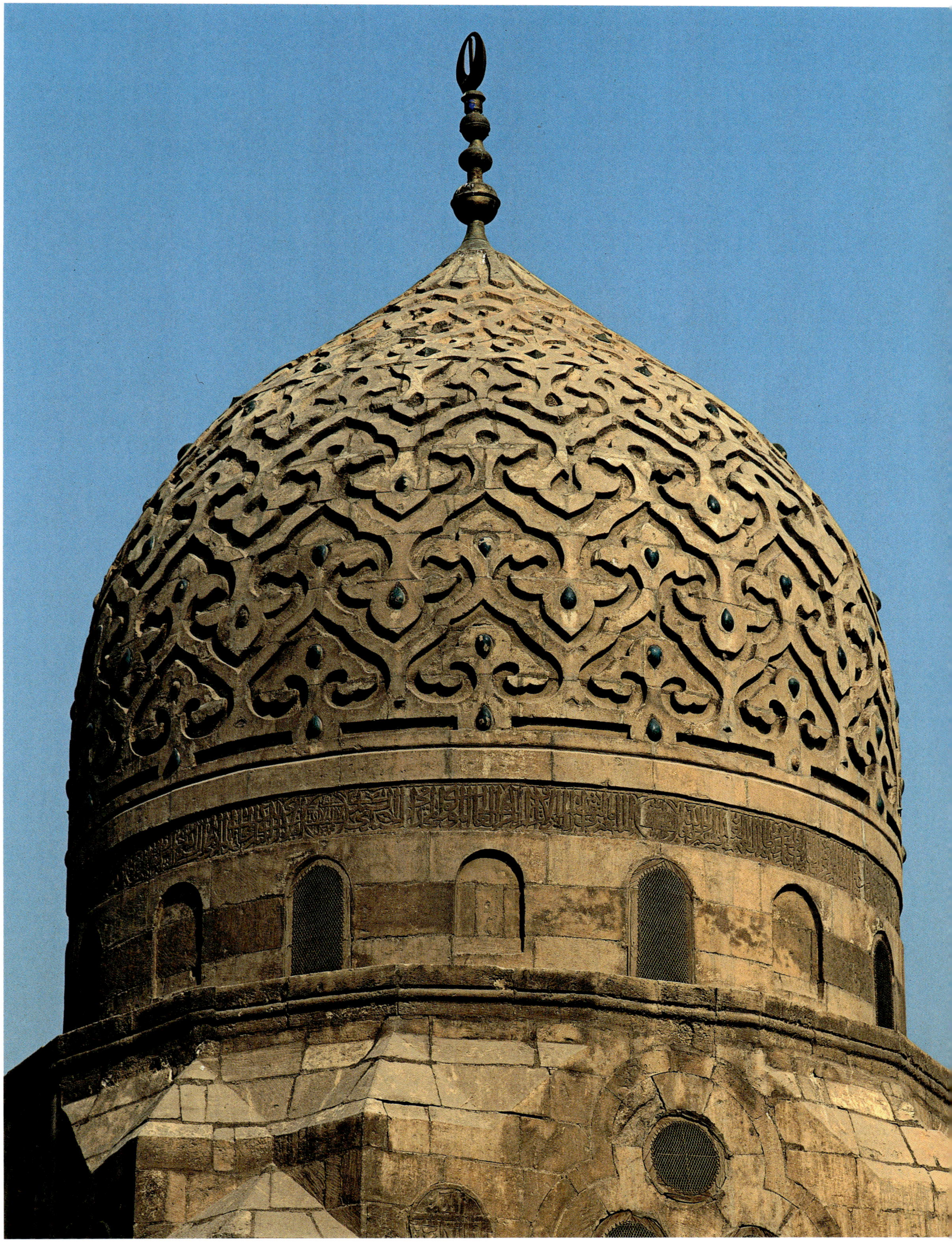

Jug
Late 14th century
Brass inlaid with silver and gold
British Museum, London

The most significant change in metallurgy during the Mamluk era compared to its predecessor lies less in innovations of a technical character than in style and iconography. The exceptionally refined figured decorations made by the craftsmen of Mosul or executed in their style (such as the 'Arenberg Basin') are now replaced by practically non-figurative ornaments dominated by a broad, intricate calligraphy. As in the architecture of the period, epigraphy pandered to the overbearing egocentrism of the nobility, as demonstrated by large-size inscriptions of formidable impact, as well as by embellishments and elaborate variants, such as the almost flamboyant terminations of the letters in *thulth* characters here. Although of small dimensions, the designs in the medallion are of exceptional refinement and employ motifs taken from Chinese imports. The presence of gold and silver in relatively modest quantities indicates that the work was executed in a period of severe inflation.

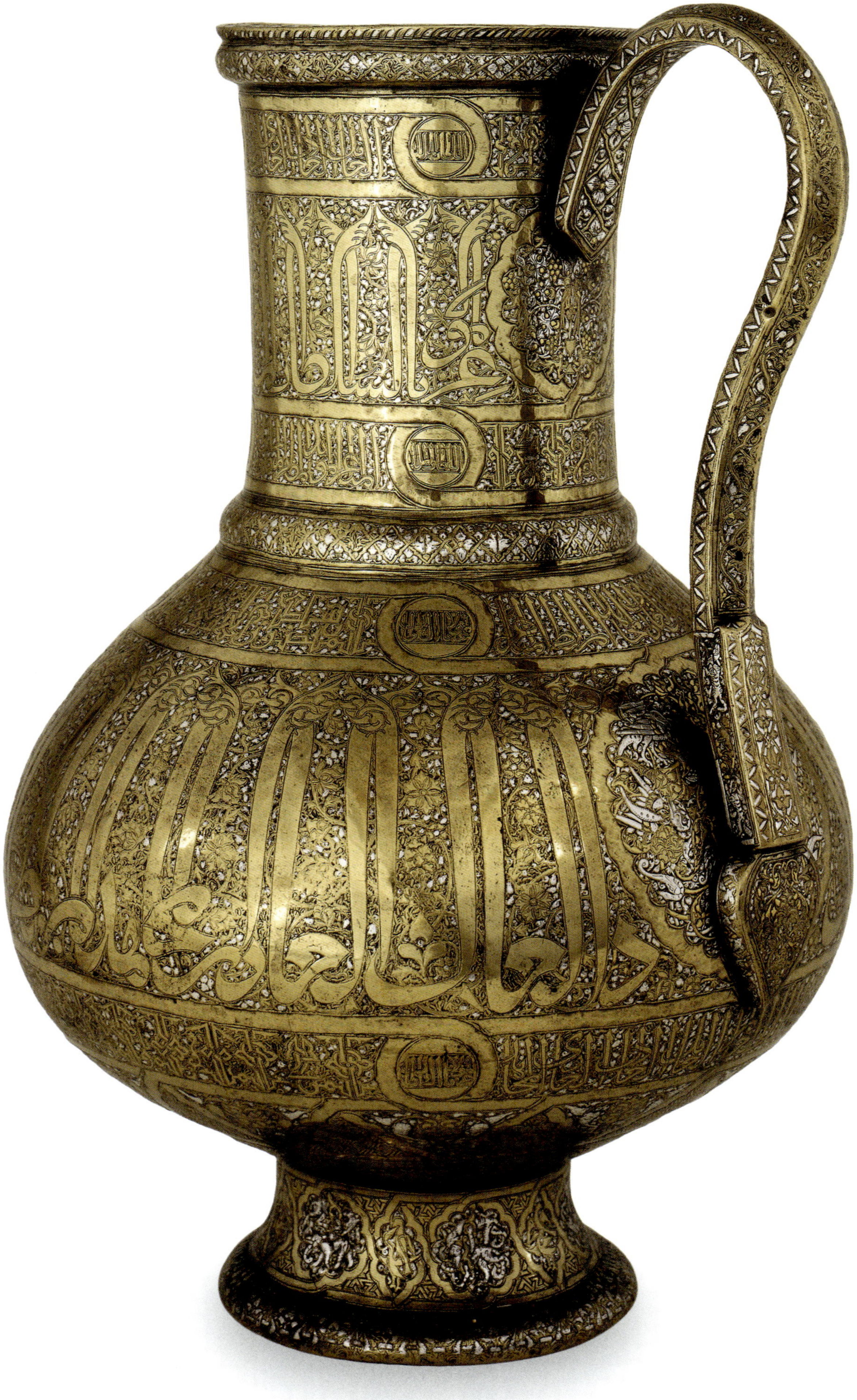

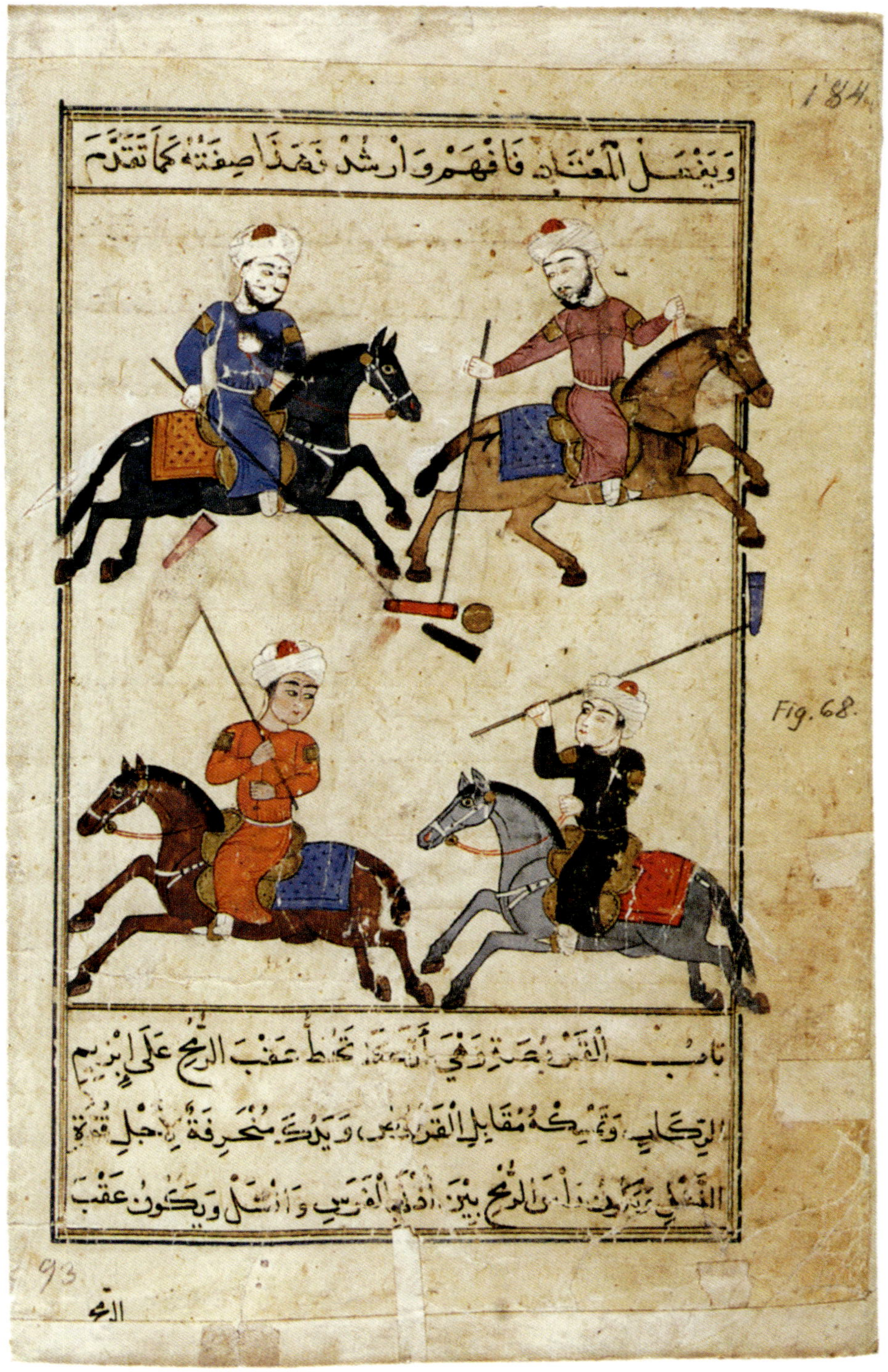

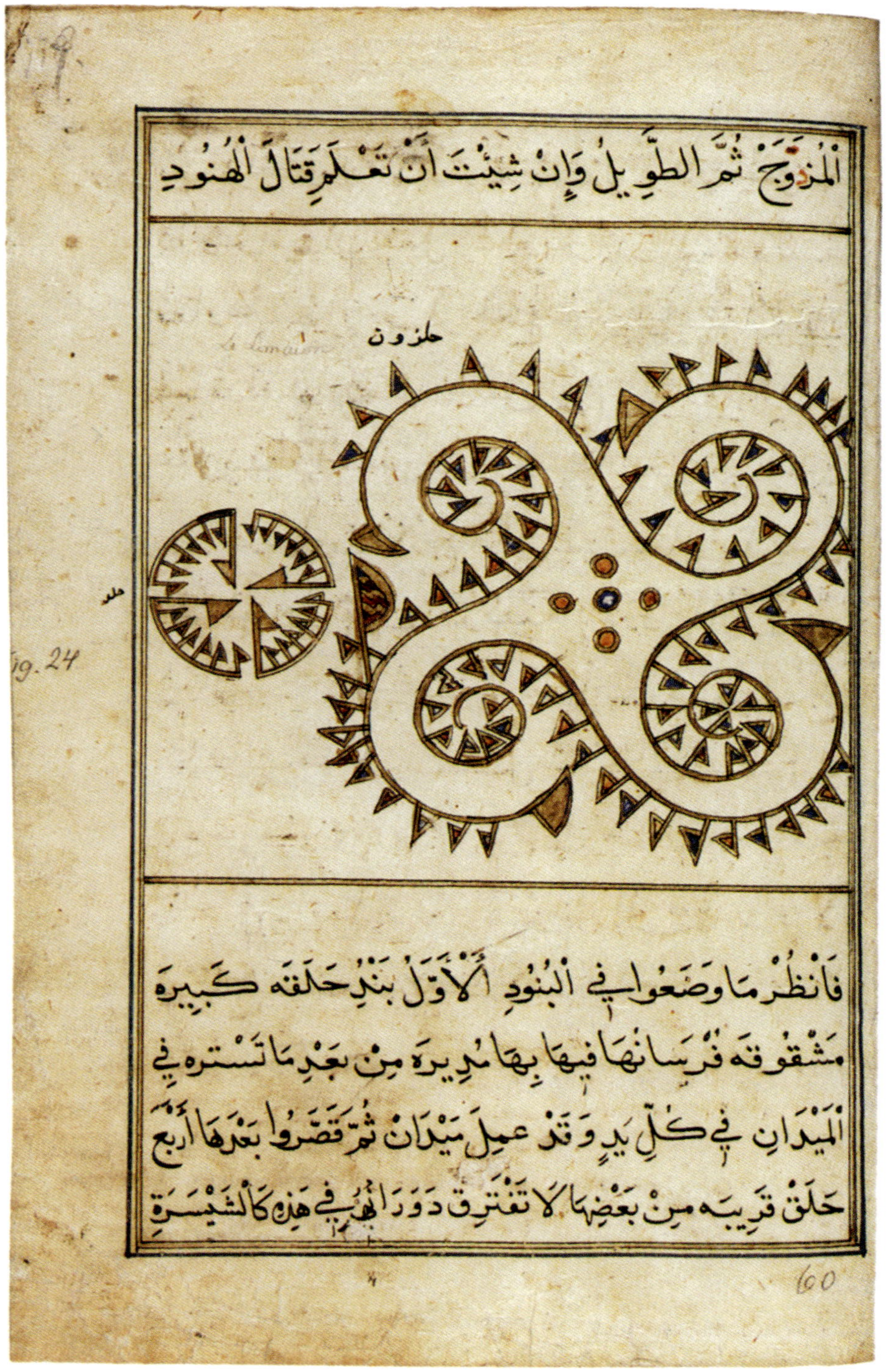

Muhammad ben Yacub Ibn Hazzam al-Huttali (attributed, 14th century)
Leaf from The book of horsemanship
Copied 1474
Russian Academy of Sciences,
St Petersburg

Originating in the Persian domain, this kind of handbook flourished particularly in Syria and Egypt in the ambit of the Crusades, becoming a kind of encyclopaedia. Indispensable for any well-connected important man at the time, it was required reading for the Mamluk élite, who were trained from infancy in special schools of horsemanship. The game of polo, illustrated here, was one of the best-loved sports of the 'young lions' of the time.

Muhammad ben Yacub Ibn Hazzam al-Huttali (attributed, 14th century)
Leaf from The book of horsemanship
Copied 1474
Russian Academy of Sciences,
St Petersburg

The sections dedicated to the art of war proper are illustrated with elaborate diagrams representing various manoeuvres: here, in *naskh* script, it demonstrates how the cavalry should be grouped for battle, at first forming a ring before moving outwards to form a series of hooks so as to crush the adversary.

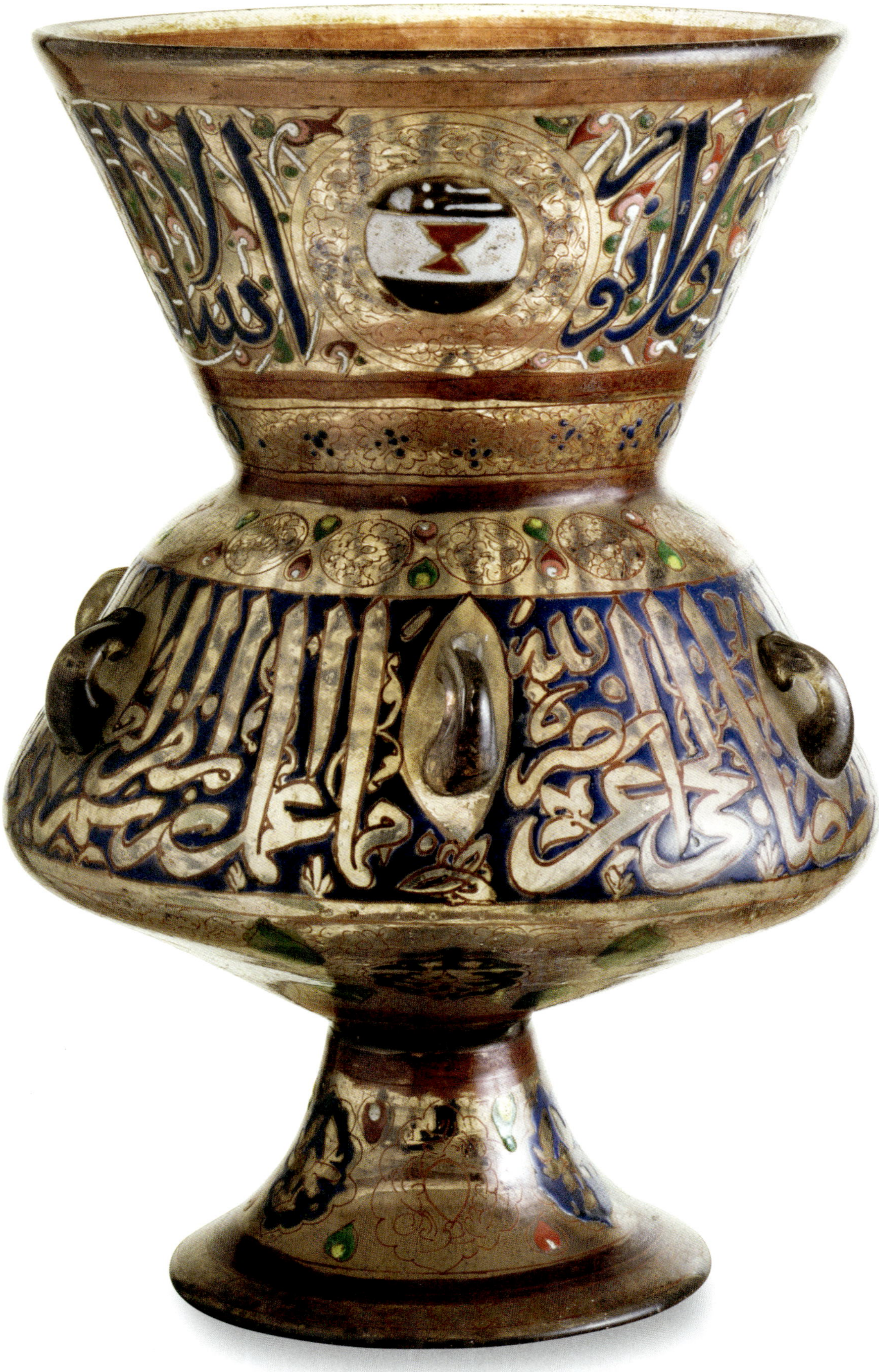

Mosque lamp decorated with the donor's coat-of-arms
14th century
Museo del Bargello, Florence

As far as the art of glass is concerned, the Mamluks inherited the technical expertise of manufactures in Cairo and Syria which, even in the Ayyubid age, had devised lavish chromatic effects that were partially abandoned in favour of innovations obtained from progress in handling enamelling and gilding. Enamel was applied cold, in a manner similar to that in ceramics and metalwork, before being fired at a low temperature. The decorative elements were underscored by red enamel and applied in white, yellow, pink, purple, green and blue to marvellous effect. The signature product was the mosque lamp, the most widespread model standing some forty centimetres high with a swelling body and broad foot, and a wide, markedly evased neck and six rings on the shoulder from which it was suspended by chains. The flame came from a wick inserted into a glass container filled with oil. Besides floral motifs, calligraphy was the most frequent ornamental adjunct, varying elegantly from lamp to lamp and often inscribed with the *sura* of Light which could thus be seen glowing evocatively through the glass.

Twelve-colour carpet
16th century
Silk
Museum für Angewandte Kunst, Vienna

Among the most widespread products of the late Mamluk period are a number of knotted-pile carpets, one group of which is identifiable through a number of specific techniques and designs that can be precisely characterized as 'Mamluk'. Except for a *unicum* in silk, Mamluk rugs were woven in wool of optimum quality, particularly sheer and brilliant, embellished by a rich palette of intense colours: lacquer red, deep blue, green and, to a lesser extent, yellow and ivory. The most common design is based on octagonal geometric elements, generally with the largest motif positioned in the centre and smaller ones gathered in the main field, although these appear on occasion in coloured zones bestowing a lively effect on the surface. The repertoire of motifs includes cartouches, multifoils, octagons, hexagons, triangles and stylized vegetal elements. The border, for the most part relatively broad, may echo the internal pattern or use different shapes and colours. The overall effect is one of strength which is occasionally overplayed.

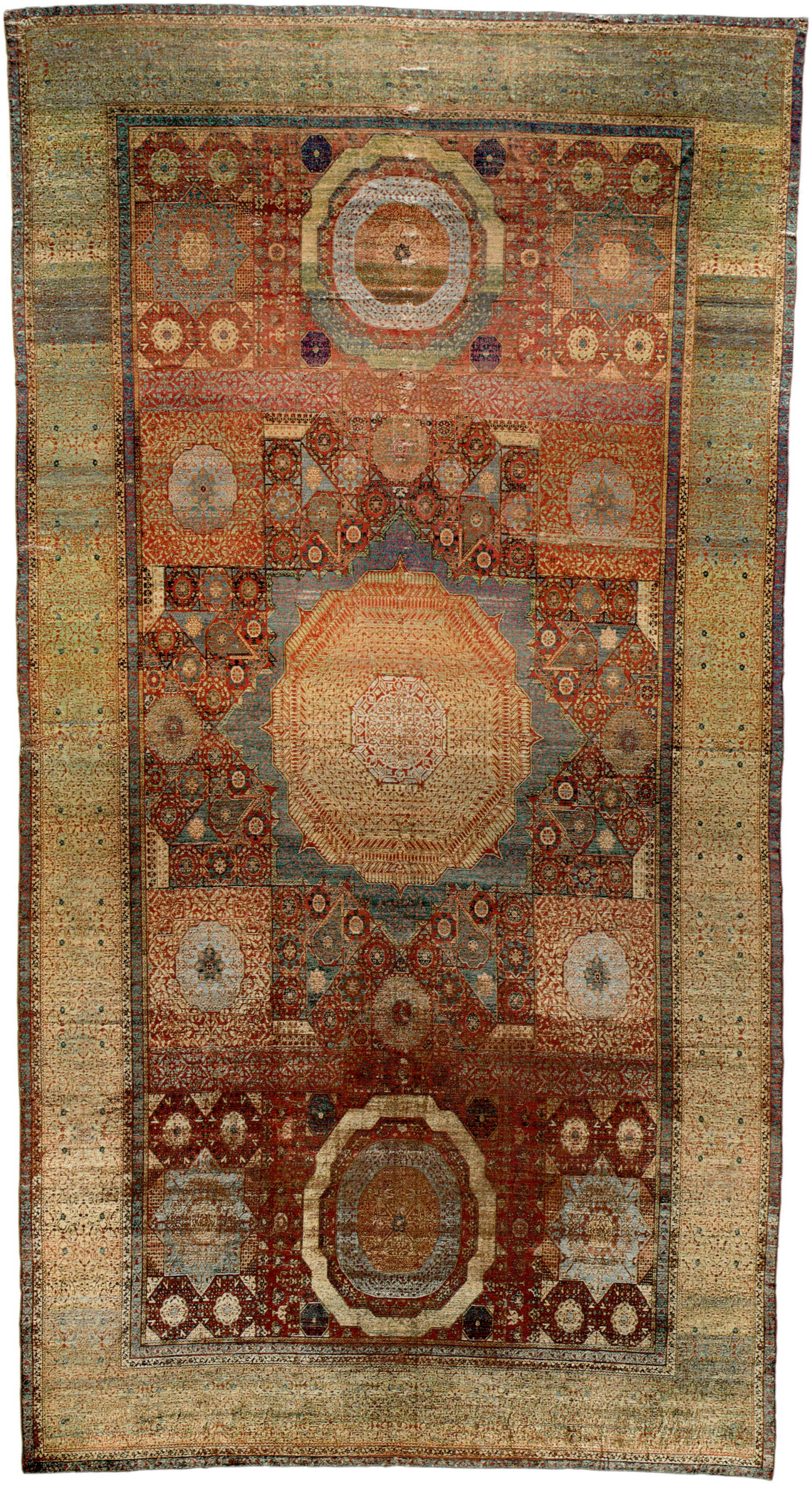

THE SELJUQS

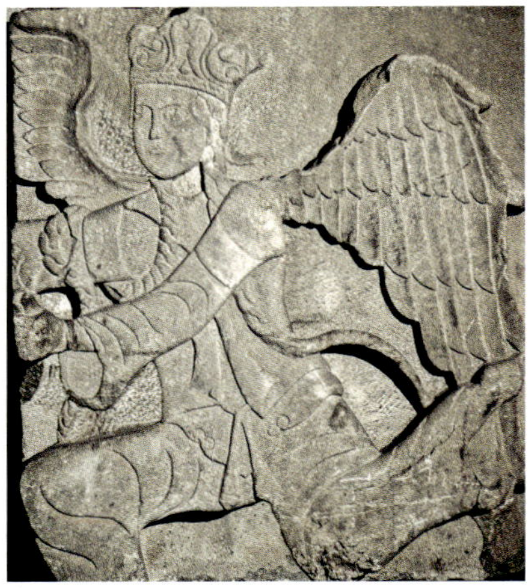

The Seljuqs (Selçuk) were one of the many Turkic clans of Central Asia that migrated progressively westwards. Converted to Sunni Islam from shamanism, they were at first employed as mercenaries in wars between various potentates who were nominally dependent on Baghdad. In 1055, after engaging the Fatimids of Cairo, they freed Baghdad from the Shia Buyids, proclaiming themselves defenders of orthodoxy and receiving from the caliph – though by now lacking any real authority – the title of sultans. In course of the ninth century they coalesced into a formidable ruling class known as the Great Seljuqs who swept from Samarkand down to Iraq, whence they campaigned to wrest Anatolia from Byzantium, so establishing the state of the Seljuqs of Rum.

They ruled over countries and peoples who for the most part shared the Persian language and culture, although they were controlled by a small aristocracy of Turkmen. Towards the end of the eleventh century their kingdom attained its greatest splendour thanks to able administration on the part of Persian and Arabic civil servants who also gave a huge fillip to developments in architecture. Apart from numerous *madrasahs,* needed to inculcate orthodoxy in a mostly Shia country, they erected palaces, mosques, hospitals, hostels, *hammams* and *türbes* (mausoleums). Roads, bridges and caravanserais were built to ensure security and speed for commercial traffic, increasing at the same time the pace of cultural exchange. The wealth thus amassed favoured growth in luxury goods production, while a new open-mindedness in cultural matters fostered anti-conventional philosophy and poetry culminating in the work of Omar Khayyam and Nezami Ganjavi.

By the end of the eleventh century, however, this situation was already being undermined by splinter groups led by warlords or various offshoots of the royal family. The Turkic conception of the state as personal patrimony often set the ruling aristocrats at odds with the demands of a centralized bureaucracy. As the empire fractured into a host of local principalities exposed to Ayyubid expansionism in the south and the shah of the Khorezm in the north, the situation was compounded by penetration from Christians taking part the Crusades.

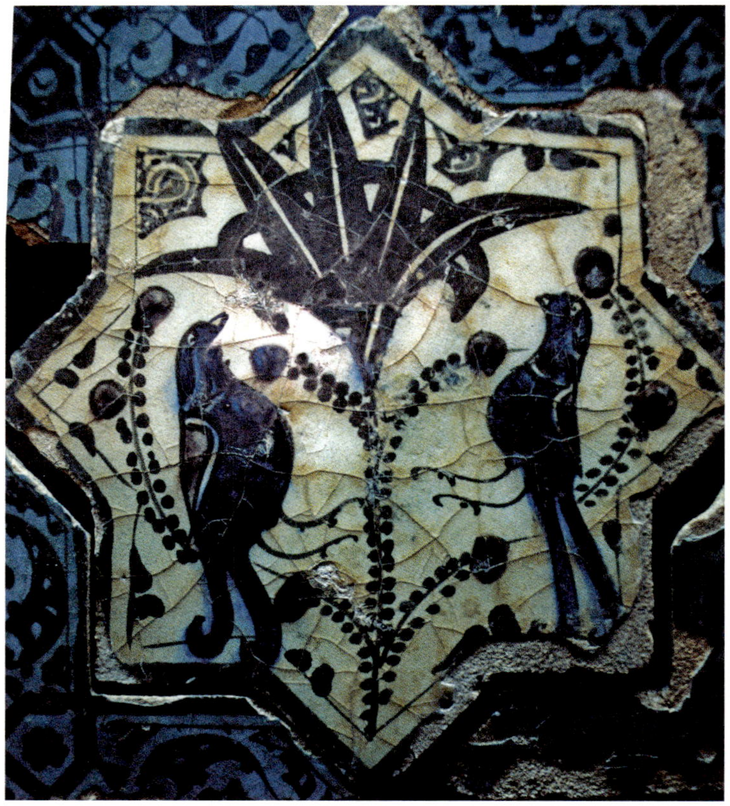

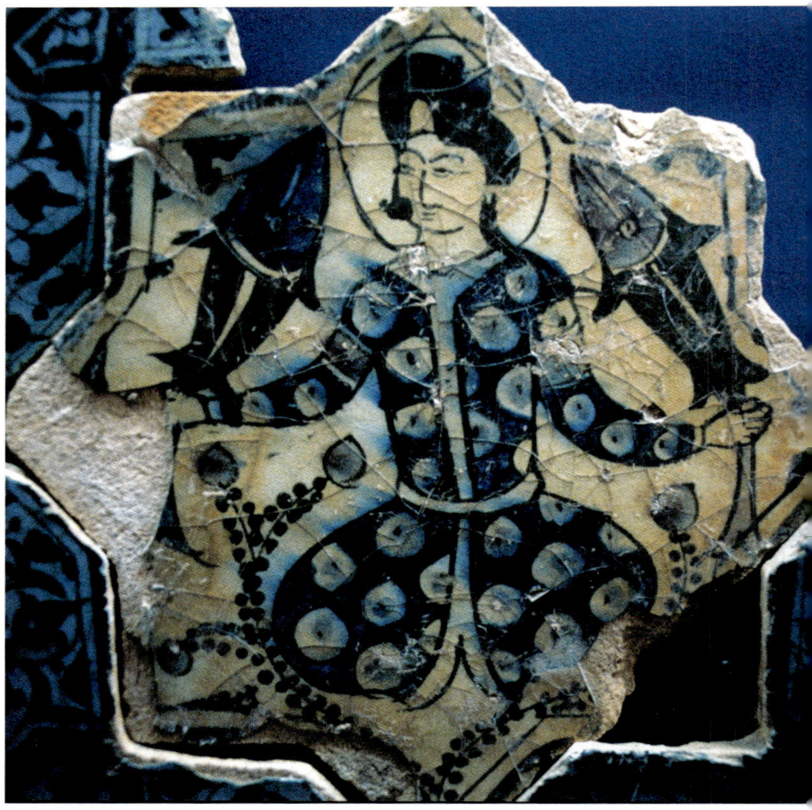

Relief from the Seljuq city walls
c. 1222
Konya, Turkey

Palace of Kubadabad Wall tiles
c. 1227
Karatay Medrese Müzesi, Konya

In spite of a turbulent history, the Seljuq epoch witnessed some extraordinary results in the artistic field in what was a seamless continuum with the 'Abbasid age as pursued by the Buyids, Ghaznavids and Ghorids, since the new rulers inherited a substantial proportion of these kingdoms. Earlier conceptions were assimilated and deployed with exciting grandeur in novel experiments that provided the bases for all later art in Asia: double-shell domes; ribs; bays of unprecedented span; minarets which became ever taller and more slender; *mihrabs* decorated with gloriously exuberant stucco; decorations of unheralded richness and expressive power; and miniatures that couple consummate technical virtuosity with a unique talent for storytelling.
With inexhaustible imagination, architects and craftsmen not only learned how to exploit the characteristics of their materials to the utmost – in particular brick and ceramics deployed with a rationality coupled to inexhaustible creativity – but also acquired the skill and daring required to plug a rigorous, essentially geometric repertory into the intensely symbolic matrix of Persian culture. Surfaces emblazoned with perfect geometrical patterns gave rise to a coherent aesthetic approach, conjoining the virile spirituality and the unquenchable thirst for self-affirmation of the Turkmen with the ancestral sense of measure and harmony tinged with the lyricism of the Iranians. Putting both the resources available and recent technical progress to good use, the Seljuqs oversaw a golden age of architecture and art in Central Asia that can be defined as 'Classical' in a sense analogous to the term as applied to the Athenian artistic experience in the age of Pericles.
In 1071 the Seljuqs began the conquest of Anatolia. When the campaign was concluded, they continued to Constantinople, establishing a capital first at Nicaea and then, after that city fell into the hands of the Crusaders, at Konya, which became the nerve centre of an immense territory (1097). Such fresh conquests entailed the creation of a new state, rich and powerful, known as the Seljuqs of Rum – that is, 'Roman', a word that identified the Byzantines in the Arab-speaking world. It was to adopt its definitive shape over a period of approximately a hundred years. Riven by interminable internecine conflicts and warring Crusaders, Byzantines and other Muslim powers, it had to forge a see-saw of alliances for practical, economic or political – though never religious – reasons. Anatolia ended up as a natural habitat for the Turks, unlike the other regions controlled by the Seljuqs where domination by Turkic-speaking peoples never resulted in the ousting of local ethnic and cultural elements.
Despite the debilitating conflict with the Ayyubids, the brief interlude prior to the Mongol invasion constitutes the zenith of the kingdom. During this time the patronage of the court and of a few dignitaries led to the construction of some of the greatest monuments of the era, providing a springboard for the magnificence of much later Turkish art.
The arrival of the Mongols in 1243 occasioned widespread disruption and pillage, and, from 1246, the sultanate of Rum was relegated to being a vassal state of the Ilkhanids before (in 1308) being relegated to a mere province, without this incurring noteworthy changes in the artistic or architectural fields. Its social structure and wealth were not seriously jeopardized, as demonstrated by the uninterrupted realization of structures of great majesty in all the *beylics* into which the kingdom had been divided which, though weighed down by tribute, benefited from a trading zone stretching from the Mediterranean to China.
Under the formal control of the Ilkhanids, the flowering of Seljuq art in Anatolia produced some gloriously innovative works. This thirty-year period lasting from the conquest of Iran to that of Anatolia corresponds to two generations, a period during which the Turkic arrivals assimilated the culture of the subject country and became, as it were, 'Iranicized'.
In spite of common cultural roots, Anatolian architecture was radically different from Iranian; first and foremost because dressed stone replaced brickwork, allowing the realization of structures of potently rugged stereometric design, but without that ability to transfigure matter through light characteristic of Persian edifices. The classic plan with an open courtyard and four *iwans* typical of Persian and Central Asian architecture was mostly replaced by a covered structure based on a system of domes on pillars, or more rarely by a flat roof on columns. The search for a unified space, particularly in mosques, sanctioned solutions with domes. While the number of supports was reduced, cupolas billowed and the central axes swelled, a course that was later to culminate in the architecture of the Ottomans. This more advanced, sculptural conception, often leading to virtuoso feats of geometric stone-carving, was promoted by Armenian architects and craftsmen, as well as Byzantines, Georgians and Syrians, who contributed that muscular power which is the hallmark of their works. Compared with the more abstract Persian poetics, sustained by an intuition of the lyricism of creation and by a world view informed by the fantastic, Anatolian architecture evinces greater physicality, determined by and analyzed through the solid materiality of stone. It opts for undemonstrative, austere constructions – though with intermittent spates of visionary imagination – that undercut the canonical and rational significance of the Islamic conception of art, infiltrating it with an unexpected and uncontrollable surge of elements originating in an ethnic, ancestral substrate rooted in tribe and totem.

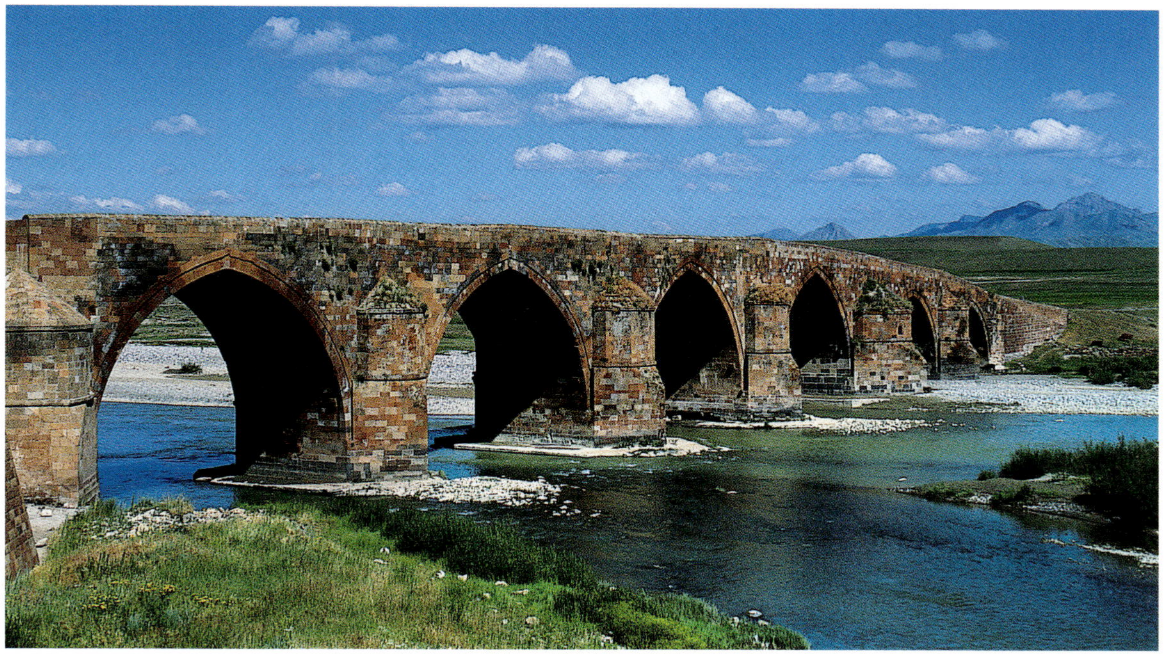

Çobandede Koprüsü
1297–1298
Erzurum, Turkey

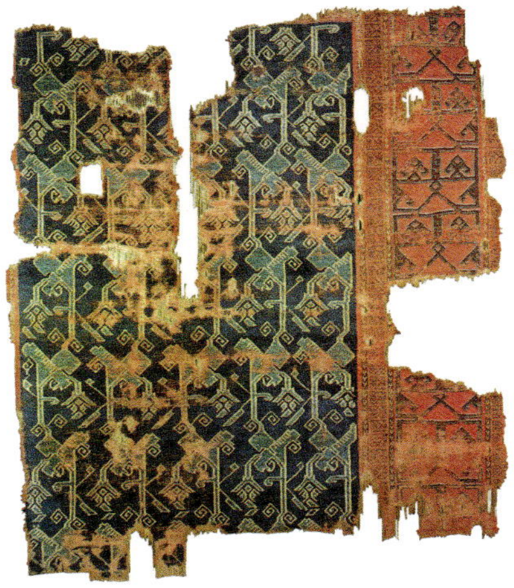

Fragment from a carpet
13th century
From the Eshrefoğlu mosque at Beyshehir
Keir Collection, London

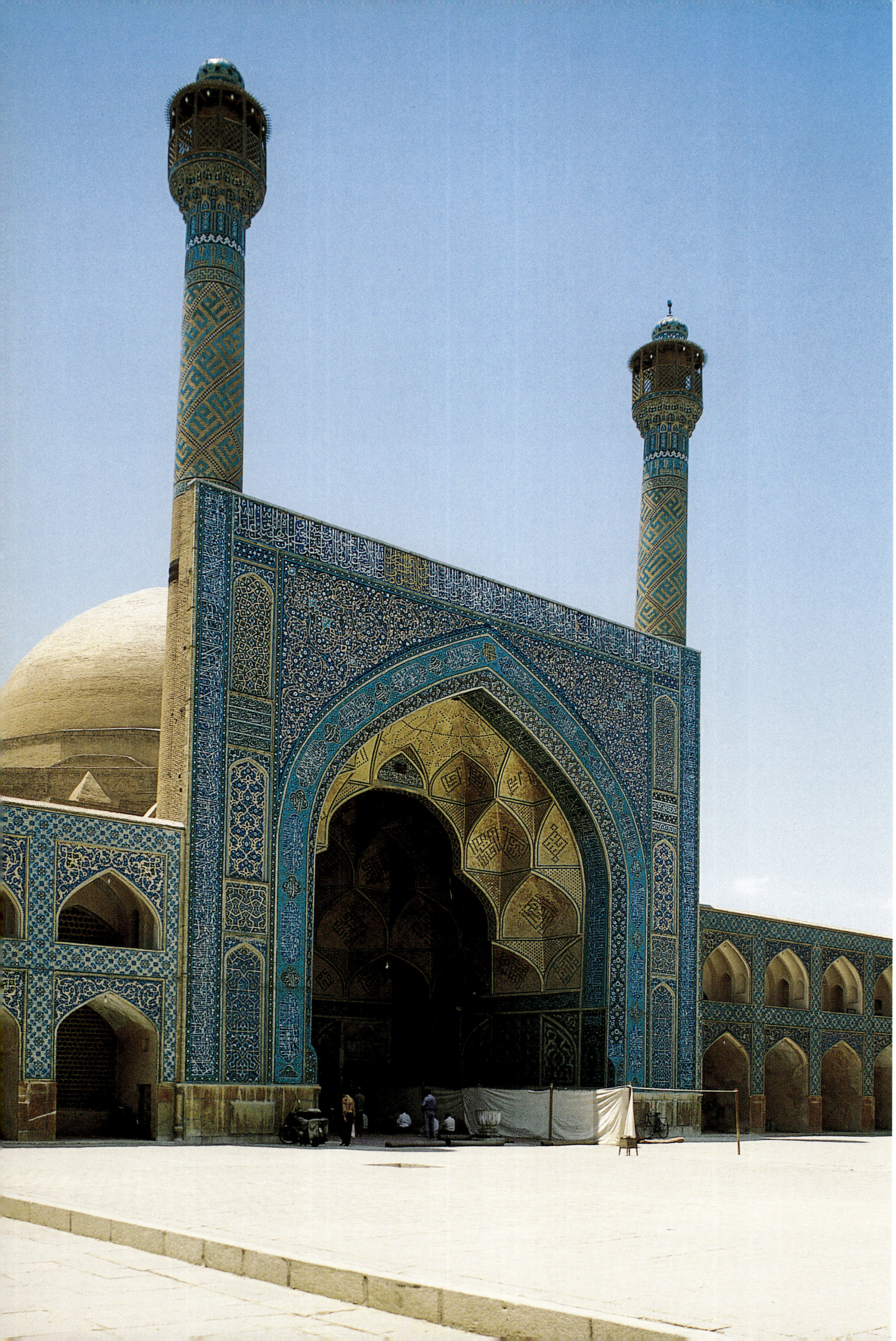

Friday mosque
Southern *iwan*, minarets and ceramic decoration
Isfahan, Iran

The mosque constitutes an impressive example of the sheer power and unadorned, noble solemnity of Seljuq architecture. The original 'Abbasid and Buyid structure was enlarged – and later altered with the addition of new ranges and more importantly with a majolica cladding – but it most clearly bears the Seljuq imprint that characterizes all successive developments in Persian architecture down to the present day.
While from outside the mosque seems absorbed into the bazaar, upon arrival in the vast courtyard the visitor finds himself in another dimension, all hush and grandeur. The huge space is dominated by four colossal *iwans* opening to the centre of the two-tiered archways entirely lined in ceramic mosaics from a later era. The *iwan* (late ninth century) that leads to the hall of the *mihrab* is decorated with ceramics of particular intensity and quality (fifteenth-seventeenth centuries). Above them unfolds the solemn bulk of the brick cupola, spectacularly flanked by two Timurid-type minarets added in the era of the Ak Qoyunlu, at the end of the fifteenth century.

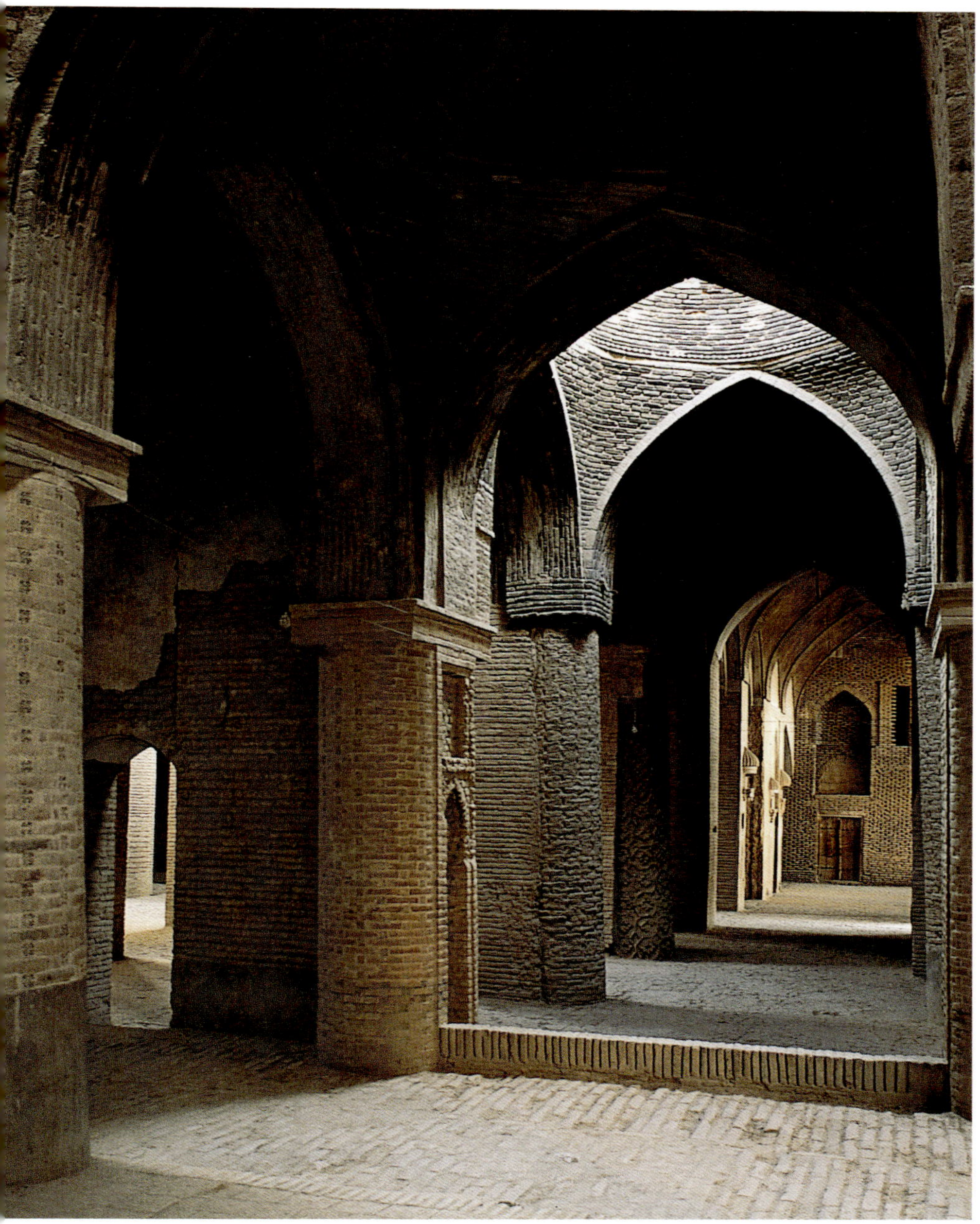

Friday mosque
North dome
1088
Isfahan, Iran

The most significant element in this whole complex is the small but exceptional cupola to the north. Although its function is not at all clear, it was commissioned by Taj al-Mulk, a personal enemy of the minister Nizam al-Mulk, patron of the south dome. The peerless beauty of this structure does not stem from its dimensions but from its style. Every element has been meticulously weighed up; as organic as a musical composition, it has been organized into an absolutely unified ensemble, the formal perfection of which elevates its modest materials. With no concessions to external appearances, it amounts to an austere revelation of the superior order of things, at once rational and poetic, both premise and promise of a later and more authentic state of consciousness.

Friday mosque
Rooms northeast of the hall with the southern cupola
9th–12th centuries
Isfahan Iran

The innovation with respect to the hypostyle hall mosque of the 'Abbasid age (partly recorded from excavations) is abundantly clear: not only are the dimensions decidedly more ample, but the four *iwans* disrupt the simplicity of the original rhythm, breaking with unexpected and dramatically monumental surges over the sides of the *riwaq* and conferring new relevance to the dome in front of a *mihrab* of astonishing proportions. The large southern hall is articulated around the central cupola, set somewhat hesitantly upon massive pillars (perhaps prior to the definitive plan); it is subdivided into small bays roofed by small-sized and individualized cupolas, at times left open to the sky to let daylight into the enormous space. Sober and functional, the deployment of brick is typically Seljuq. Columns and pillars lack both base and capital, while the barrels display trademark motifs impressed by forms applied to the mortar between them. Certain column-cum-pilasters display instead a more 'plastic' decoration created through a special brick course, as can be seen in particular in the rooms to the left of the large covered hall. These architectural elements are most likely to have been taken from the no longer extant 'Abbasid building (the surface of the circular pillars is handled in a way similar to the mosque at Nayn) and redeployed in situ. The endless series of halls is articulated into nearly five hundred bays; those of the Seljuq era in particular are covered with an astonishing and fascinating variety of brick-built cupolas and vaults, often showing innovative technical solutions, at times very similar to certain developments in European Gothic, to the point that some scholars have proposed the possibility of a stylistic influence or relationship.

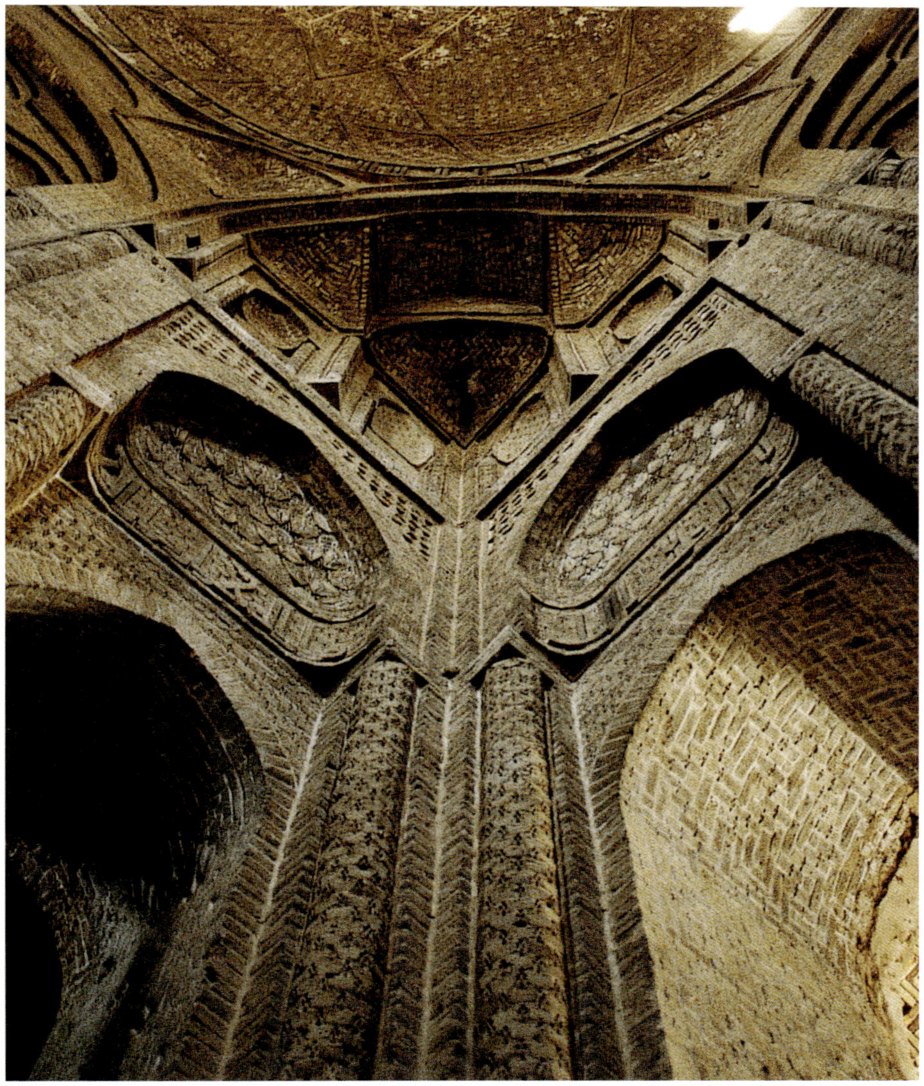

Friday mosque
10th–12th centuries
Ardestan, Iran

One of the purest examples of the classic Seljuq four-*iwan* court is found at Ardestan, where the austerity and asceticism of the unsullied solemnity of Seljuq architecture has not been modified by the later addition of ceramic decoration. The spacious *iwan*, whose gaping void acts as a counterpoint to the minor arches, probably served for instruction, social life, meditation and personal prayer, providing private spaces each suited to an hour, season and temperature. According to the most widely held hypothesis this type of four-*iwan* structure derives from the madrasah, in its turn an adaptation of the traditional Persian dwelling, articulated around a courtyard with four arches and a side entrance. The custom of doming the *mihrab* hall is one of the more typical characteristics of Seljuq architecture and later of Persian architecture in general. Beneath the shady domes, the somewhat severe colour scheme was alleviated by carpets disposed in what was clear allusion to paradise.

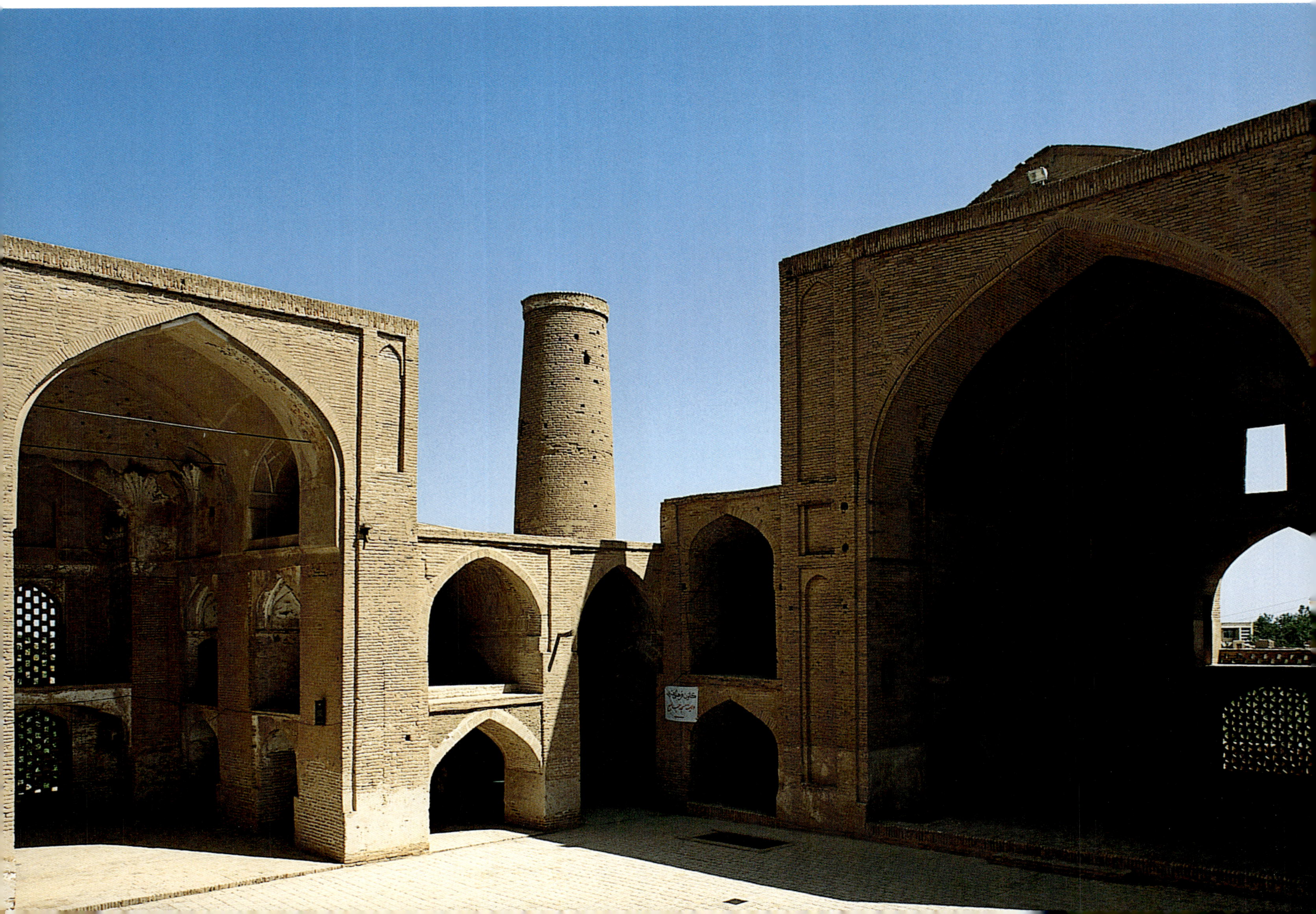

Dome in the *mihrab* hall in the Friday mosque
10th–12th centuries
Ardestan, Iran

The interior decoration of Seljuq mosques remains hypothetical since the original elements have either disappeared or been replaced by more recent decorative schemas. The handful of ragged-looking stucco panels that survive, often painted in vibrant colours, imply that the contrast with the subdued, warm tonality of the brickwork must surely have produced amazing – and in some cases perhaps strident – effects. The cupola preserves the original subdivisions into sixteen sections decorated with a stucco diamond pattern. As the experiment does not appear to have been repeated, perhaps the composition was poorly received.

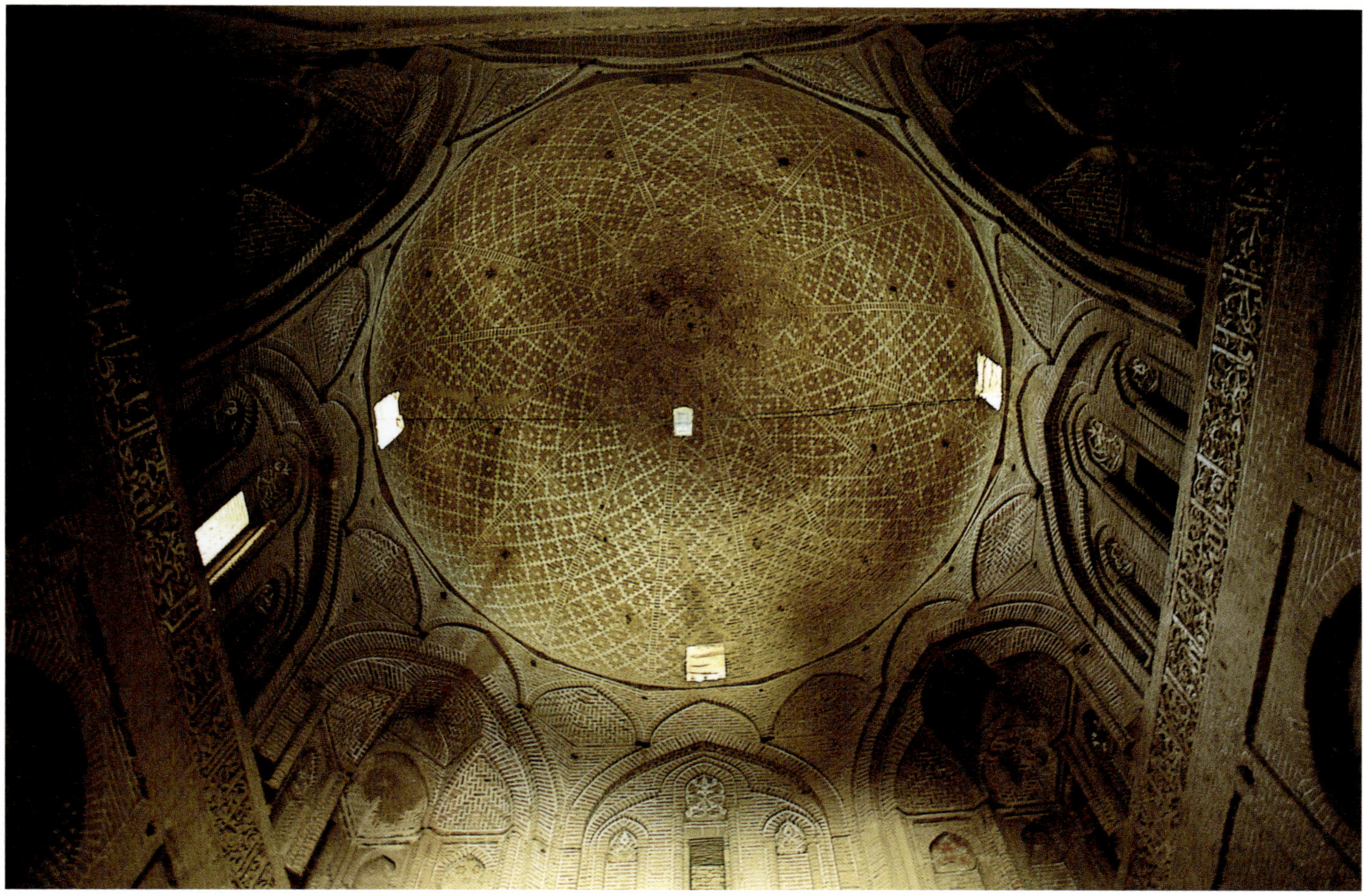

Friday mosque
Mihrab
Late 11th century
Ardestan, Iran

The architectural decoration of the eleventh and twelfth centuries is plentiful and dramatically expressive. It is, however, far from easy to interpret precisely, particularly when the geometry underpinning it proves hard to identify. Over the course of time, the *mihrab* acquired ever greater importance even in architectural contexts, and ended up assimilated into a sort of mock monumental gate. Here the masterful use of stucco attains an overpowering level of expressivity, above all as regards the modest decorative vocabularies of the mosques of the time.
The *mihrab* of the Friday mosque in Ardestan dating to the end of the ninth century is an excellent example of the by then mature harmony between rectilinear and curved elements, together with abstract-plant decoration and script, forming a fascinating agglomeration of inextricable motifs in stucco and brickwork. The exuberant vitality is conjugated therefore with architectural forms and inscriptions which, scarcely distinguishable from the luxuriantly floral forms, celebrate at once the patron and the faith. However, as with other Seljuq creations, it seems as if the architectonic structure, with its inbuilt rationality, has to struggle manfully to keep in check the impetuous and exuberant world within.

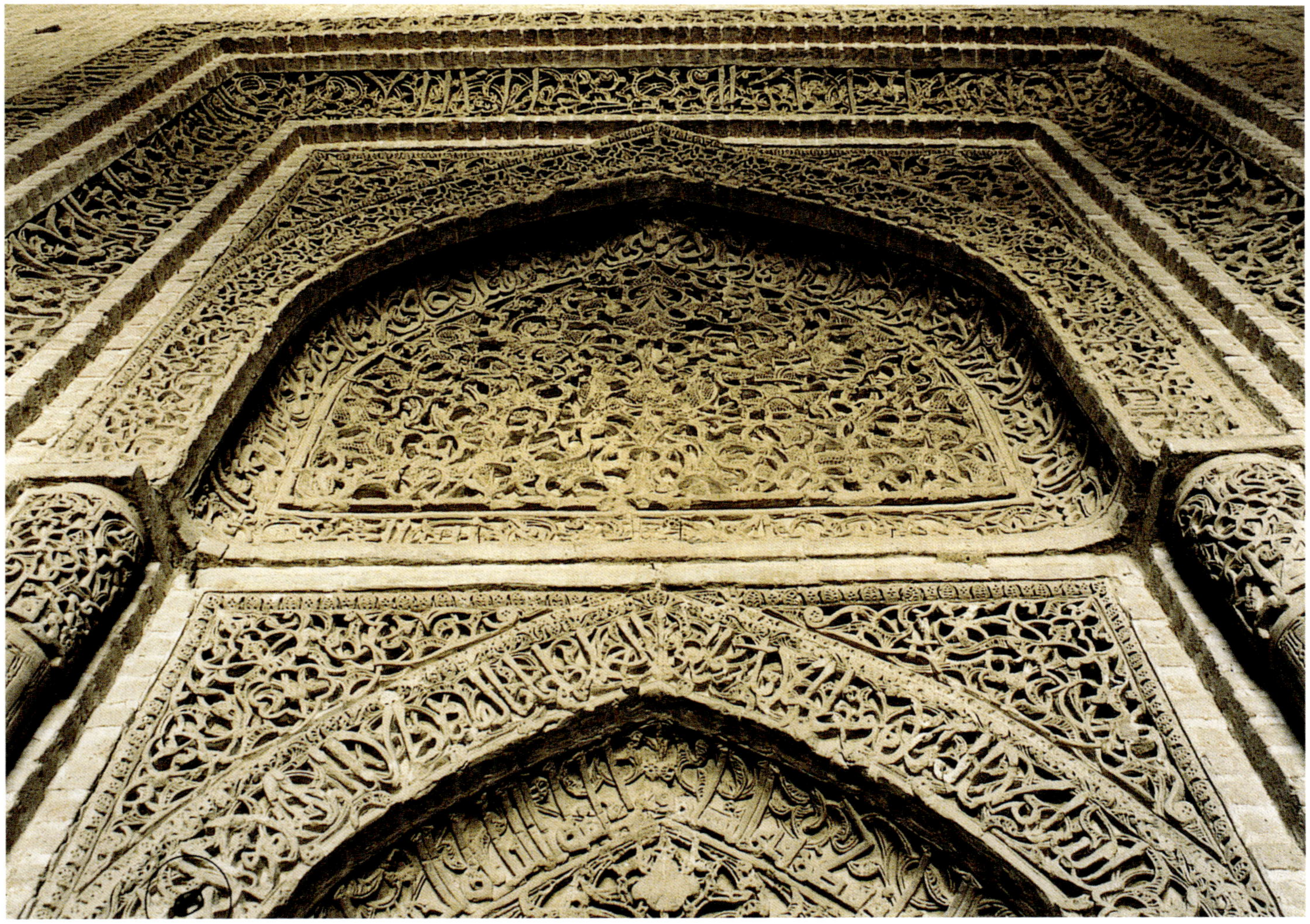

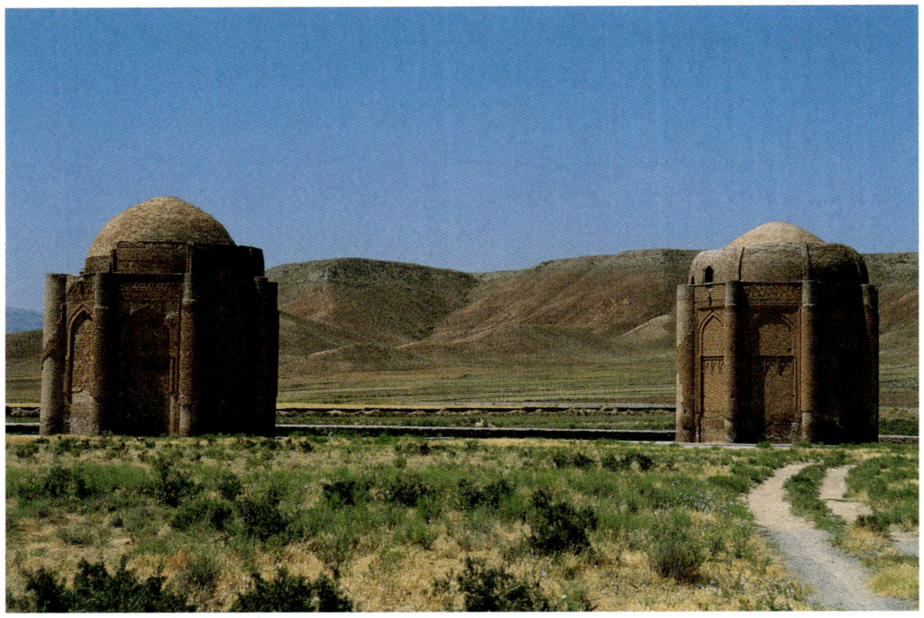

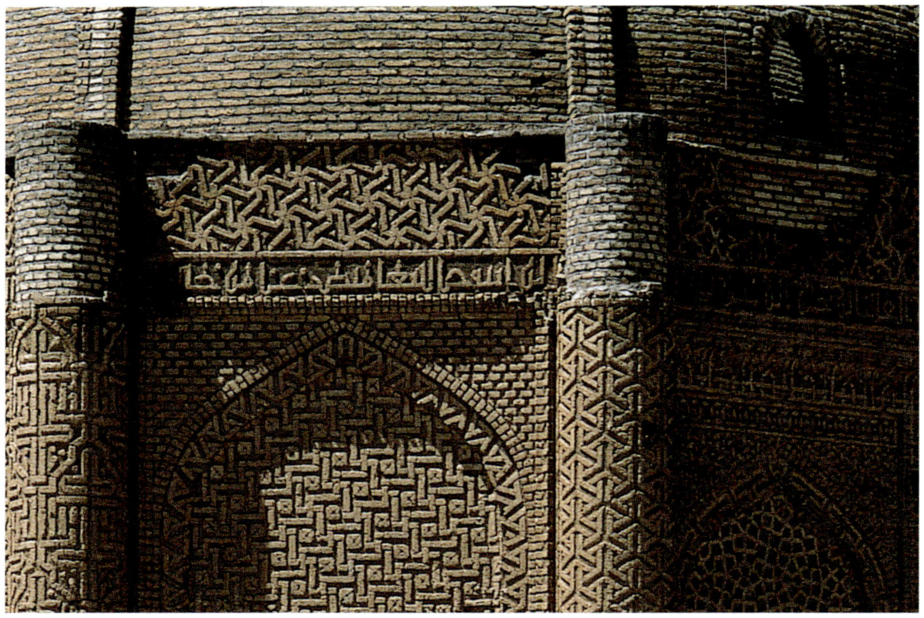

Mausoleums
1068 and 1093
Kharaghan, Iran

The symbolic significance of the burial-place is exemplified by two remarkable mausoleums at Kharaghan, seriously damaged in the earthquake of 2002. The brick structure and the intricate cladding revert to Samanid prototypes, but the accentuation placed on the buttressing and the dome – constructed as a double hull of which only the inner shell survives intact – betrays a more aggressive and sculptural aesthetic which is typically Turkish. The octagonal plan vehicles explicit symbolism to eternal life and paradise conceived as eight gardens entered by eight gateways.

Detail of the mausoleum
1093
Kharaghan, Iran

The decoration of the more recent mausoleums, to the right in illustration, is particularly lavish and of high quality: each of the eight sides with the buttresses is different. Rightly considered as a masterpiece on a par with its neighbour, it stands out even among Seljuq constructions for the singular variety of decorated motifs that deploy an unusually eye-catching and inventive repertory.

Gunbad-e Kabud ('Blue Dome')
1196
Maragheh, Iran

The Gunbad-e Kabud is one of a remarkable group of mausoleums in the city of Maragheh, at the time among the most important in the country. In it can be seen evidence of progressive formal refinement and decorative motifs absent from older examples. The decagonal plan with cylindrical ribs supports the same number of lofty arcades, terminating in *muqarnas* over which the pyramidal top-piece, probably twelve-sided, erupts. The lower section corresponding to the crypt is in dressed stone coursed along a low-lying plinth.

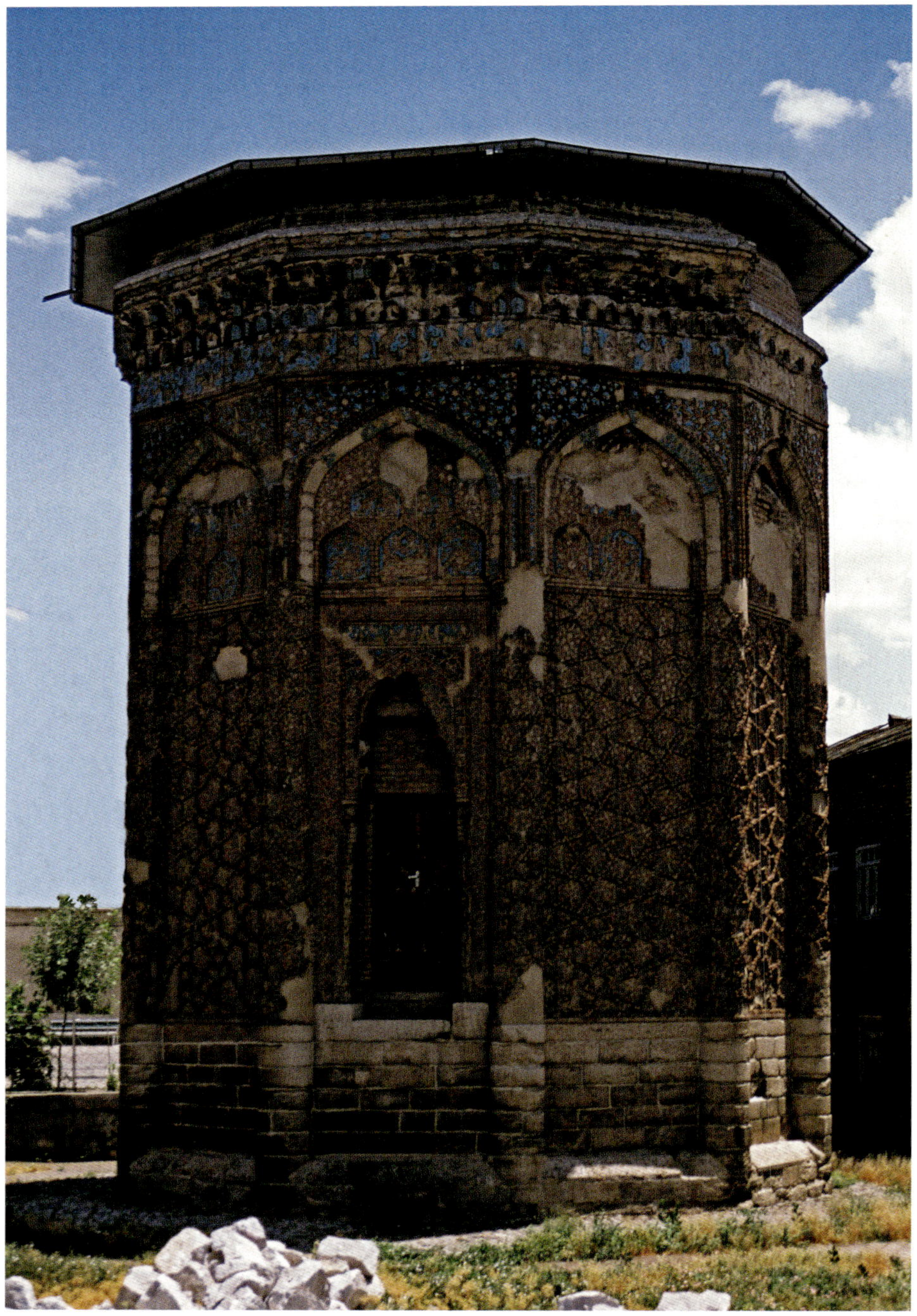

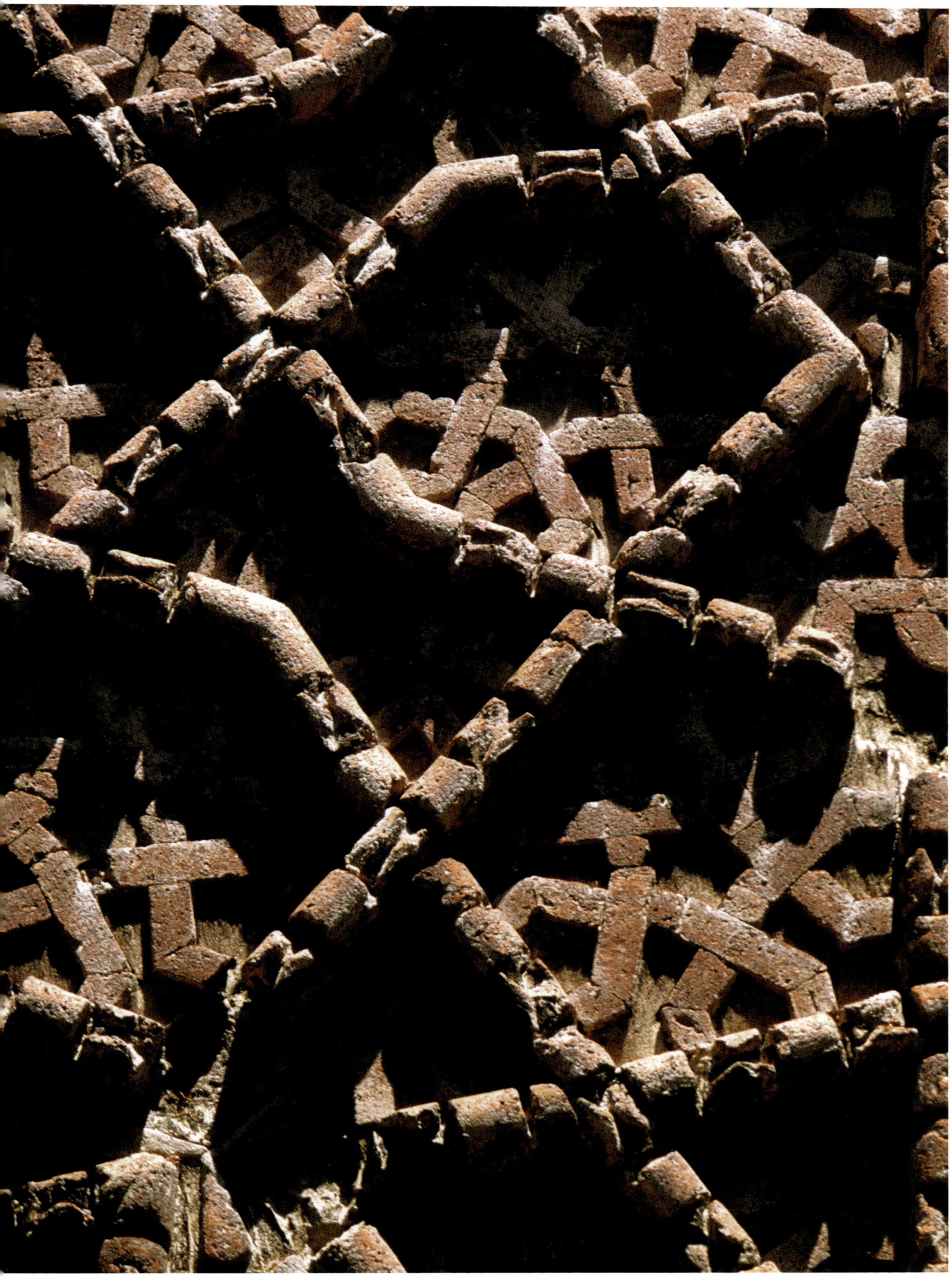

Gunbad-e Kabud ('Blue Dome')
Detail of the decoration
1196
Maragheh, Iran

The decorative 'weave' of the middle zone extends over two levels: in the foreground, in clear relief, whole rounded tile-bricks alternate with grooved ones. Fracturing in the sunlight, they overlay a second, analogous but independent design constructed out of five- and six-pointed stars. This overlay constitutes as it were a ground for the other, which gradually emerges in the light, giving definition to the pattern above and illuminating the shaded zones. The brickwork on the upper surface displays instead a busy geometrical lattice based on a complex pattern generated by the five-pointed star, creating a delicate but never haphazard brick lacework that is set off wonderfully by changes in the incident light.

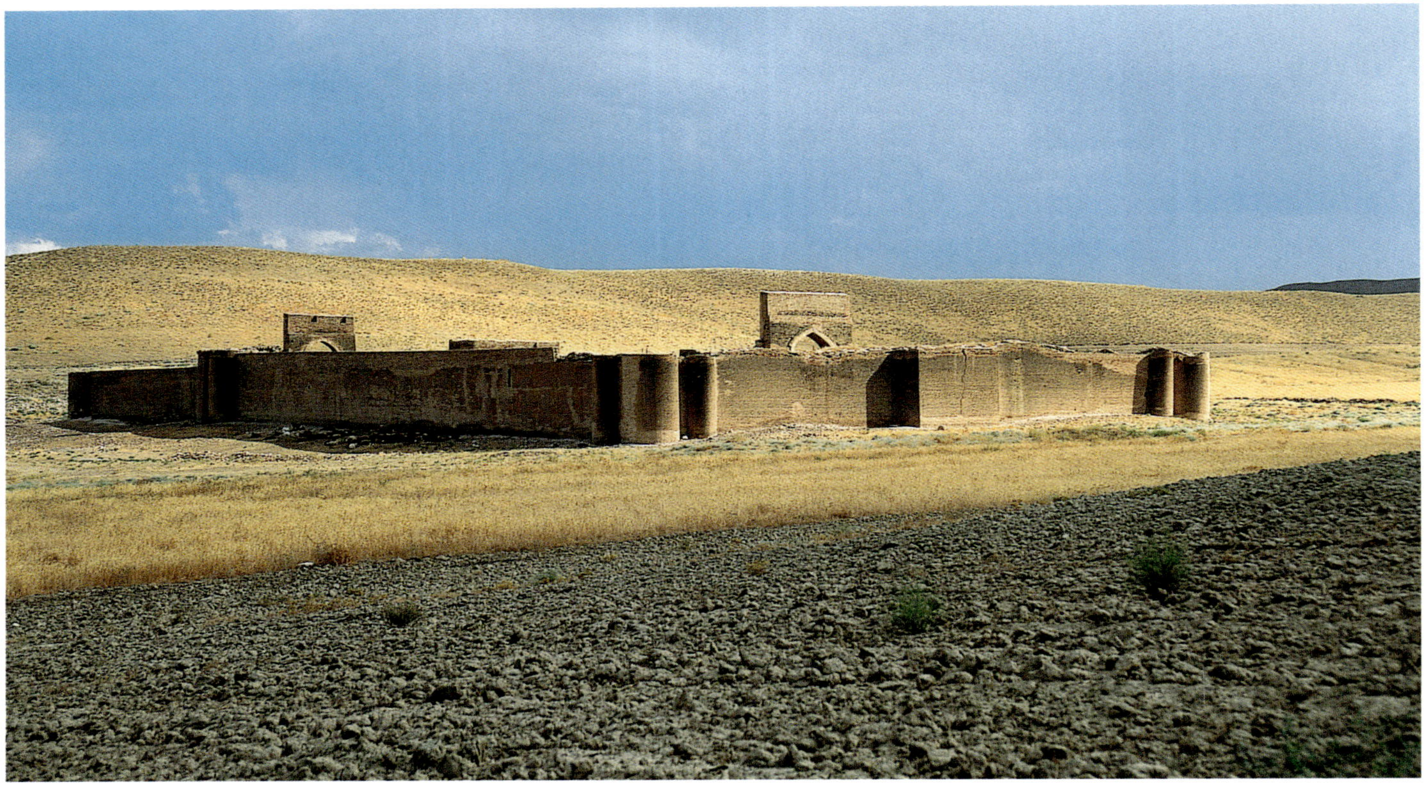

Ribat-e Sharaf
1114, restored in 1154
Sarakhs, Iran

Reduced virtually everywhere to a ruinous state, the only secular buildings surviving from the Seljuq era are a few caravanserais built between the end of the eleventh and early twelfth century. Their imposing dimensions and the brilliance of their execution is a telling indication of the importance allotted to commerce. Located on the caravan route between Merv and the capital Nishapur, the monumental Ribat-e Sharaf is enclosed by a ring of flush walls emboldened by a few projecting towers. Entry is ensured through a magnificent portal with a high *pishtaq* on which part of the splendid brick calligraphy in elegant flourishes of Kufic script traces a delicate decorative web on the walls like an echo of the mausoleum of Isma'il at Bukhara. The number, perfection and arrangement of the spaces articulated around two great squares makes the site reminiscent of a halting-place for a court. Sumptuously decorated, the spaces in the first courtyard are architectonically remarkable, while the second is structured around a typical four-*iwan* plan. The magnificent final space, also comprising a mosque next to the central hall, domed, was probably destined for official receptions. The stucco decoration leading to the reception hall reins in an exuberantly vital style, which – perhaps bequeathed by the ancestral culture of its Turkic forebears that is here reined in by Persian formalism – constantly remerges in the Seljuq aesthetic.

Ribat-e Mahi Caravanserai
Detail of the decor on the entryway
11th–12th centuries
Sarakhs, Iran

Not far from the Ribat-e Sharaf stands another remarkable caravanserai, currently reduced to a heap of ruins, called the Ribat-e Mahi. This should be seen in the context of the city of Sarakhs, an important stopping-place in the ninth century on the then flourishing Silk Road. According to legend, the Ribat-e Mahi was constructed by the great monarch Mahmud of Ghazni on the occasion of an event concerning the epic poet Firdusi. The original structure in all likelihood dates back to the ninth century and was revamped perhaps in 1154, in conjunction with the nearby caravanserai; this might be deduced from the fact that the gates flanking the towers seem to have been altered. Especial attention has been lavished on the entrances. In spite of deterioration over the centuries, the sunlight transfigures their elaborate stucco motifs, enhancing the magnificent graphic articulation of the design, a mix of geometric, floral and calligraphic motifs handled with consummate skill. It is possible that originally the decoration was painted in bright colours.

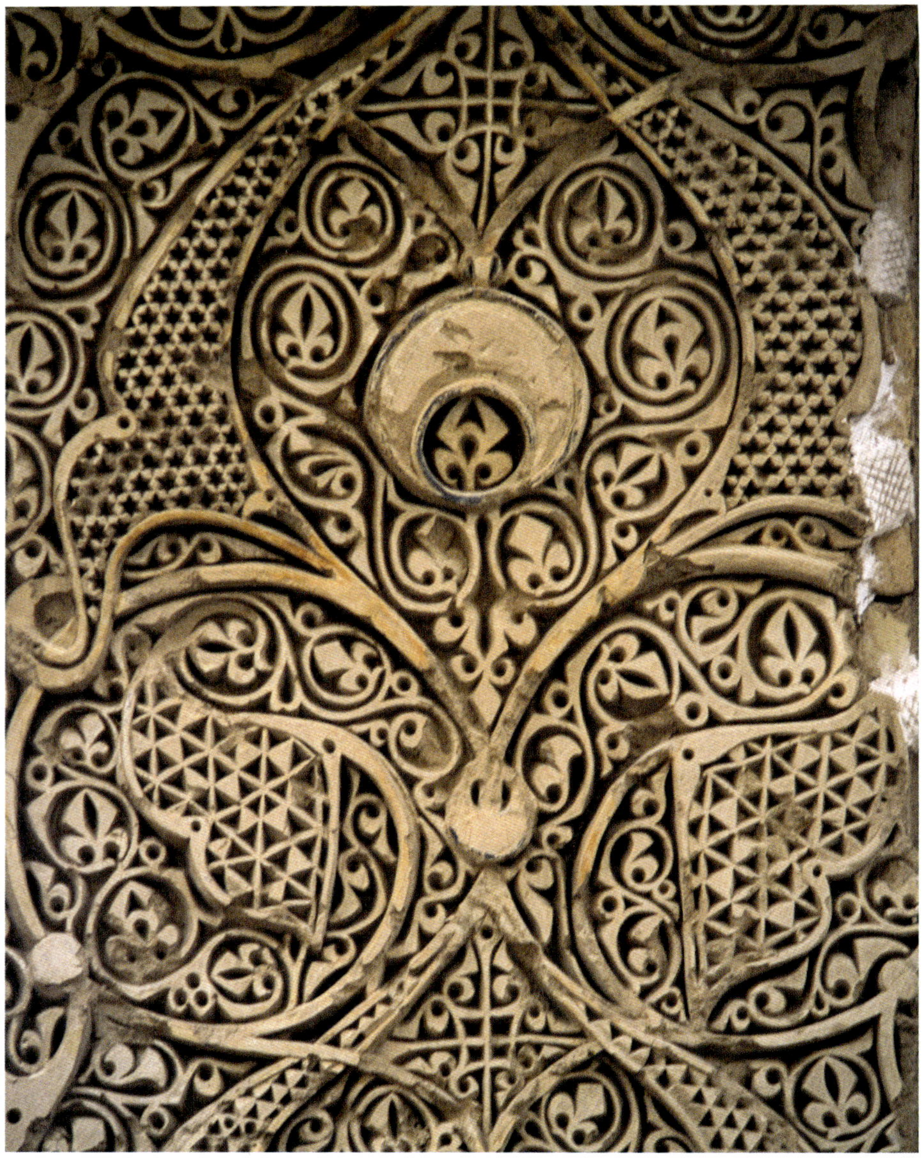

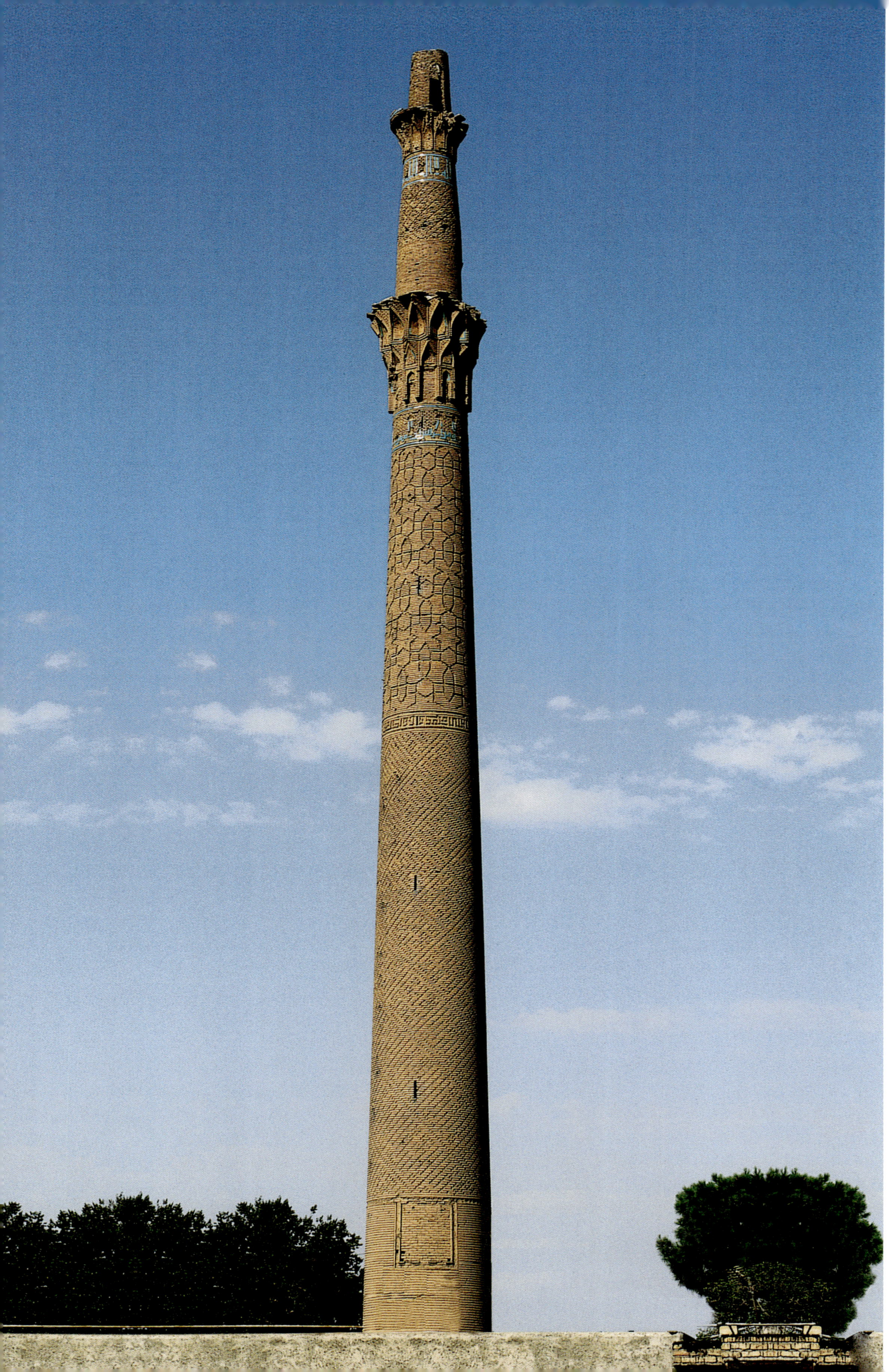

Sareban Minaret
12th–13th centuries
Isfahan, Iran

The product of an immensely talented engineering tradition, Seljuq minarets are of uncommon beauty and technical and structural quality. Thanks to an interior spiral stairway that confers exceptional robustness and elasticity on the structure, minarets have also frequently survived centuries of political upheaval and tremendous earthquakes nearly undamaged, often outliving the mosques next to which they were erected. Constant aesthetic and technical advances conspired to create dizzying and incredibly thin barrels whose intricate weblike patterns in brick seemed to vaporize. These were lined at the time, generally in the topmost reaches, by ceramic tiling of an azure hue that virtually dissolved the summit into the glowing sky above. The Sareban minaret is one of the last to have been erected under Seljuq rule: here the quest for an extreme discrepancy between height and diameter seems designed to be impressive, anticipating the taste for the colossal typical of later Mongol dominance.

Ewer with repoussé decoration
1180–1200
Brass with silver inlay
Persian art of the Khorasan
British Museum, London

This magnificent object was realized for his Seljuq overlords by a craftsman of Persian cultural background. It belongs to a group of water jugs with tall narrow spouts produced in Herat for hand-washing at mealtimes. The lavish astrological decoration shows planets and signs of the zodiac laden with talismanic meanings that might have concerned the maker no less than the owner, as can be gleaned from a poem on a similar vessel that exalts the innovation and beauty of such inlaid brassware: "My most beautiful ewer, harmonious and elegant/who could find an object comparable to you today? ... /Gazing on it a living spirit gushes forth,/that is the water that pours out from it/and every stream of water that slips over our hands/affords us anew unforgettable pleasure." The decorative vocabulary comprises Kufic or *naskh* inscriptions and animals on a ground formed of plant arabesques and culminates in high-relief figures of birds at the point where the vessel's shoulder thickens out abruptly. The incisive language, fluent and exuberant, yet still pervaded with a sense of *horror vacui,* calls to mind Hellenistic pieces reinterpreted through non-Greek eyes.

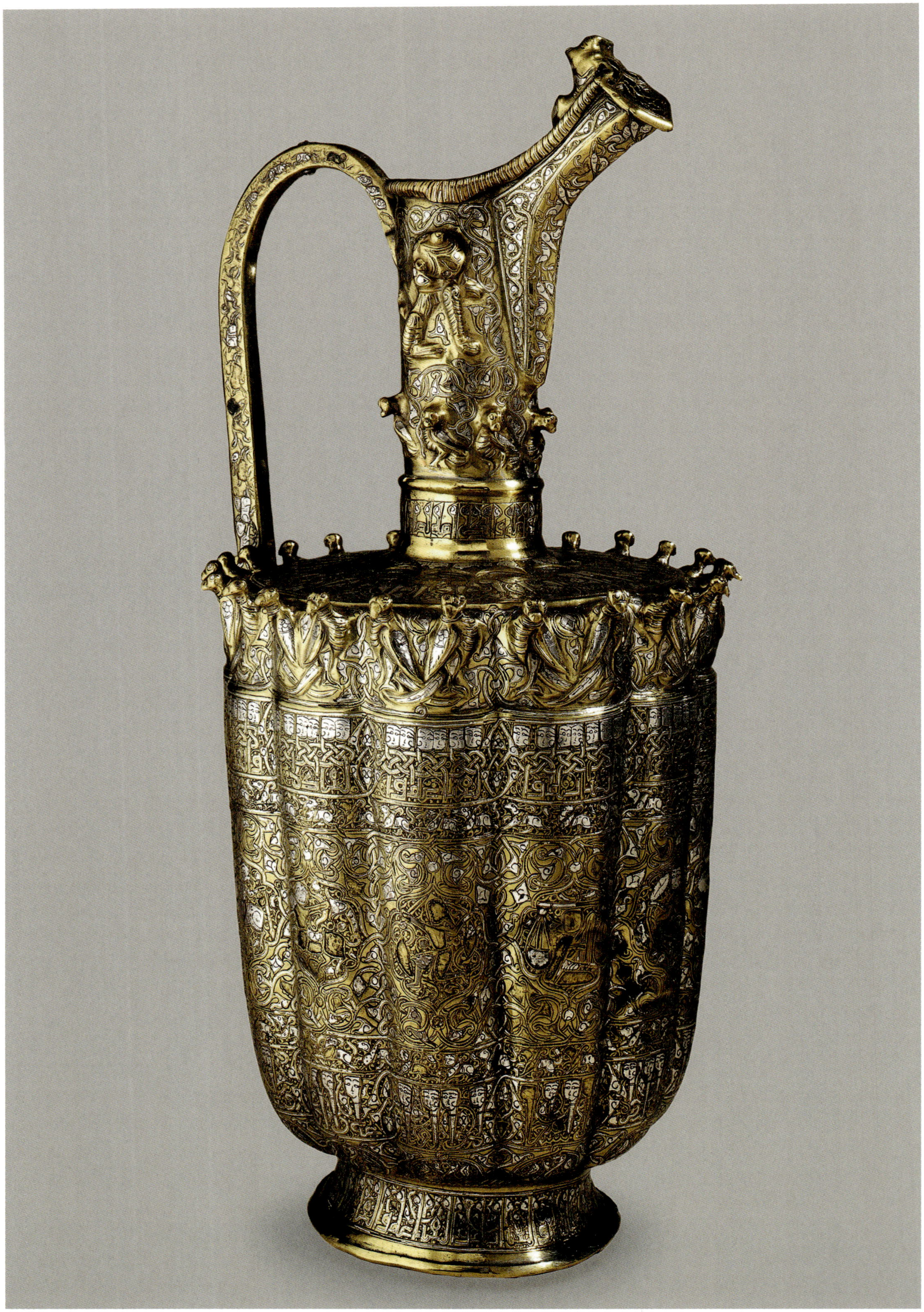

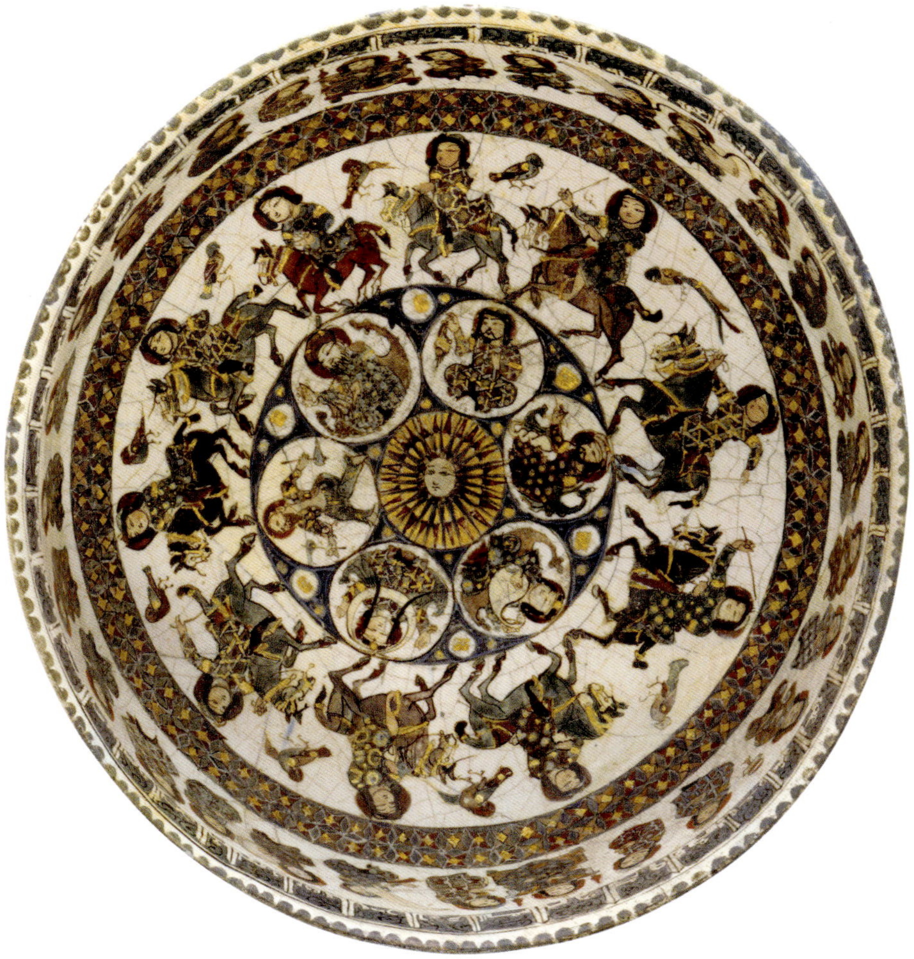

Bowl
Late 12th–early 13th centuries
Vitreous opaque white-glaze fritware with overglaze-painted polychrome and gilding
Metropolitan Museum of Art, New York

Under the Seljuqs, the passion for high-quality ceramics led to experiments with various techniques developed in the centres of greatest importance, such as Rey and Kashan in Iran and at Raqqa in Mesopotamia. The salient characteristic is the use of a new type of white paste that allows the body and glaze to be composed of a single medium, thereby simplifying firing and greatly improving stability. This revival of a process famous from Ancient Egypt consisted in mixing quartz sand with chalk or alabaster so as to obtain a material known as 'frit'. Compact, shiny and transparent (provided it was applied in thin enough layers), it could in its turn be protected beneath a translucent coating of glaze. The glorious sheen obtained could thus compete, superficially at least, with the much sought-after Chinese ceramics, particularly appreciated by the aristocratic classes who had them imported at exorbitant cost. By the end of the twelfth century splendid and elaborate ceramics appeared known as mina'i (enamel), where the glaze is fixed over the enamel by being fired a second time.

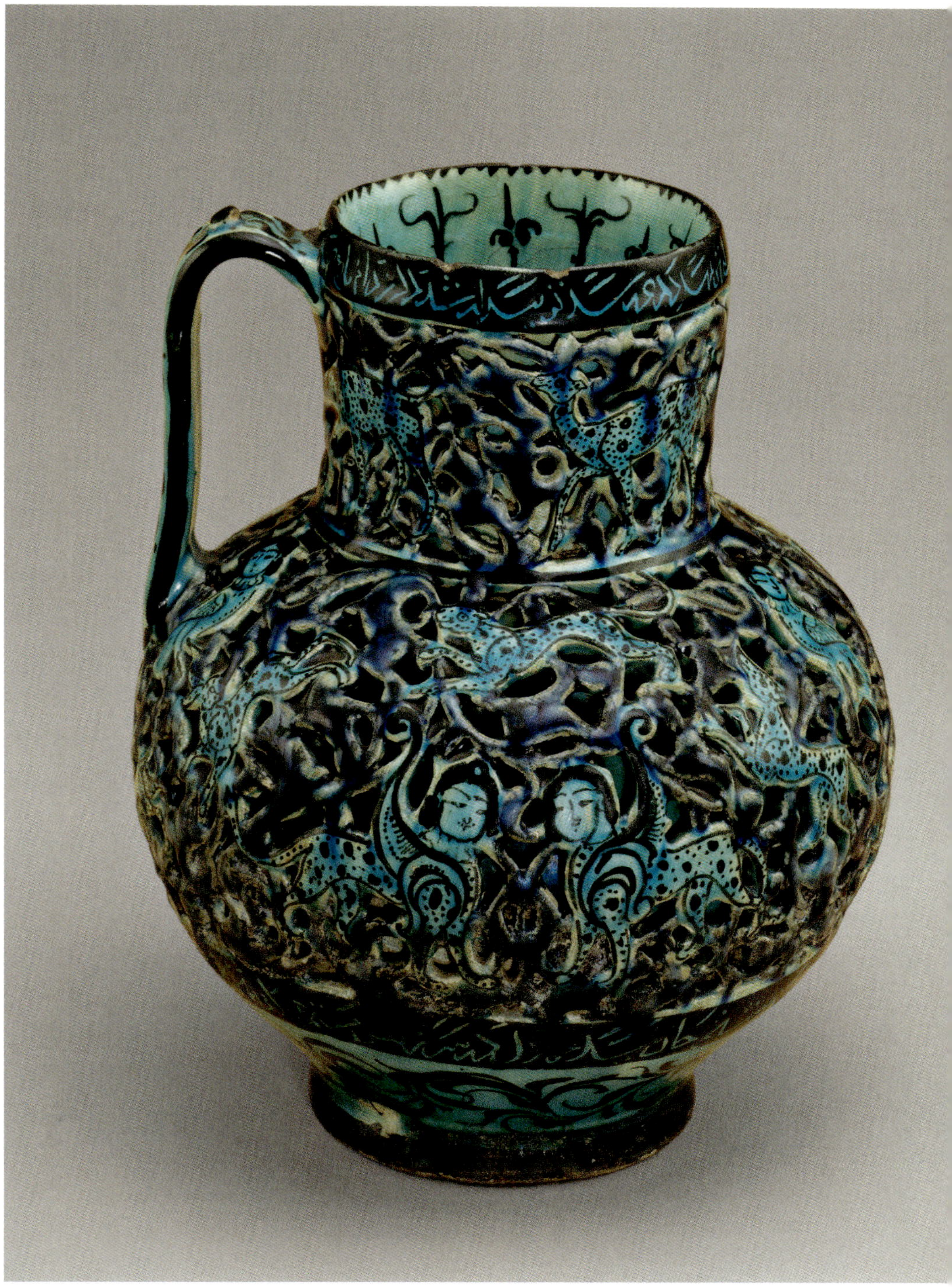

Water jug
1215–1216
Underglaze enamel-painted fritware
Metropolitan Museum of Art, New York

The twelfth century saw the widespread diffusion of lustreware, perhaps of Mesopotamian origin, that attained its absolute acme in manufactures at Rey and Kashan. The addition of tin to the enamel opacifies the paint, while a mix of silver and copper oxides confers the characteristic metallic sheen when fired. The most lavish pieces were decorated with signs of the zodiac, monstrous mythological entities, sphinxes in particular, as well as animal and human figures. In the most intricate pieces, like this water jug, the entire body of the vase is enwrapped in a painted openwork net. In a clear demonstration of the esteem in which the finest craftsmen were held and of the prestige they might obtain through their works, many of the more ambitious vessels were signed.

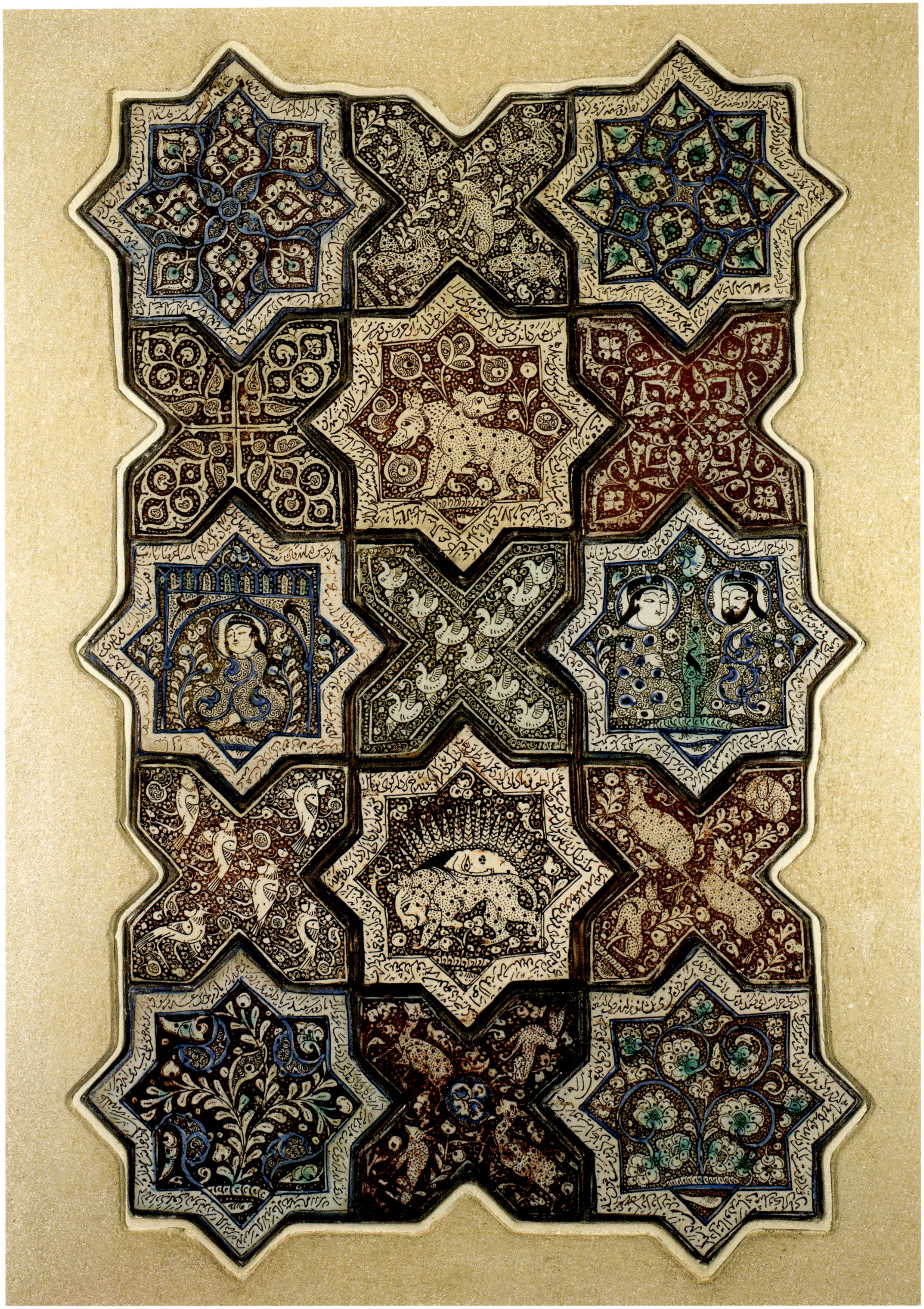

Architectural tiling
13th century
Louvre, Paris

Seljuq palaces have completely disappeared and material providing an idea of the opulence of the various pavilions of which they were probably composed can be recovered solely through excavation. These splendid tiles of alternating eight-pointed stars and crosses in lustre are decorated with floral motifs and real or fantastical beasts, or else scenes of court life with elegantly dressed personages chatting or enjoying some beautiful garden. This system of architectural facing, exceptionally fine and extremely expensive, was destined for the lower section of the walls up to a height of some two metres and could have been afforded only by the court and a few other high-ranking individuals. The figures, plants and animals are all flecked with patches of colour, arabesques and dots that tend to meld into the ground behind, in which the most pronounced elements are faces encircled by a kind of halo inherited from the Sassanid world. The wonderful sense of freshness conferred by the green, sky- and dark blue and gold and white tones must have been particularly welcome during the torrid Iranian summer.

Al-Hassan Ibn al-Arabshah (13th century), *Mihrab* of the Meidan Mosque in Kashan
1226
Glazed and painted lustre ceramics
Staatliche Museen, Berlin

Thanks to unremitting technical progress in matters of colouring and firing, the workshops of Kashan turned out ceramic panels of remarkable size that were produced in various colours but were nonetheless perfectly adapted to the design. Utilized in architecture, particularly in funerary steles and *mihrabs* of exceptional quality and scale, they were also traded throughout Iran, the Caucasus and Central Asia. The most remarkable in terms of quality and dimensions, as well as for its perfect state of conservation, is the *mihrab* signed by al-Hassan Ibn al-Arabshah from Kashan. Comprising several sections, the piece extrapolates the characteristic 'telescoped' trompe-l'oeil perspective motif. The dazzling rectangular cornice along which runs the elegant *naskh* character epigraphy in Persian blue projects markedly as it runs across a dense ground of tendrils. The latter serve to frame three niches of decreasing size with pentagonal insets adorned with calligraphy in an angular Kufic and delimiting panels containing a stylized 'tree of life' in the form of some delicate floral arabesques.

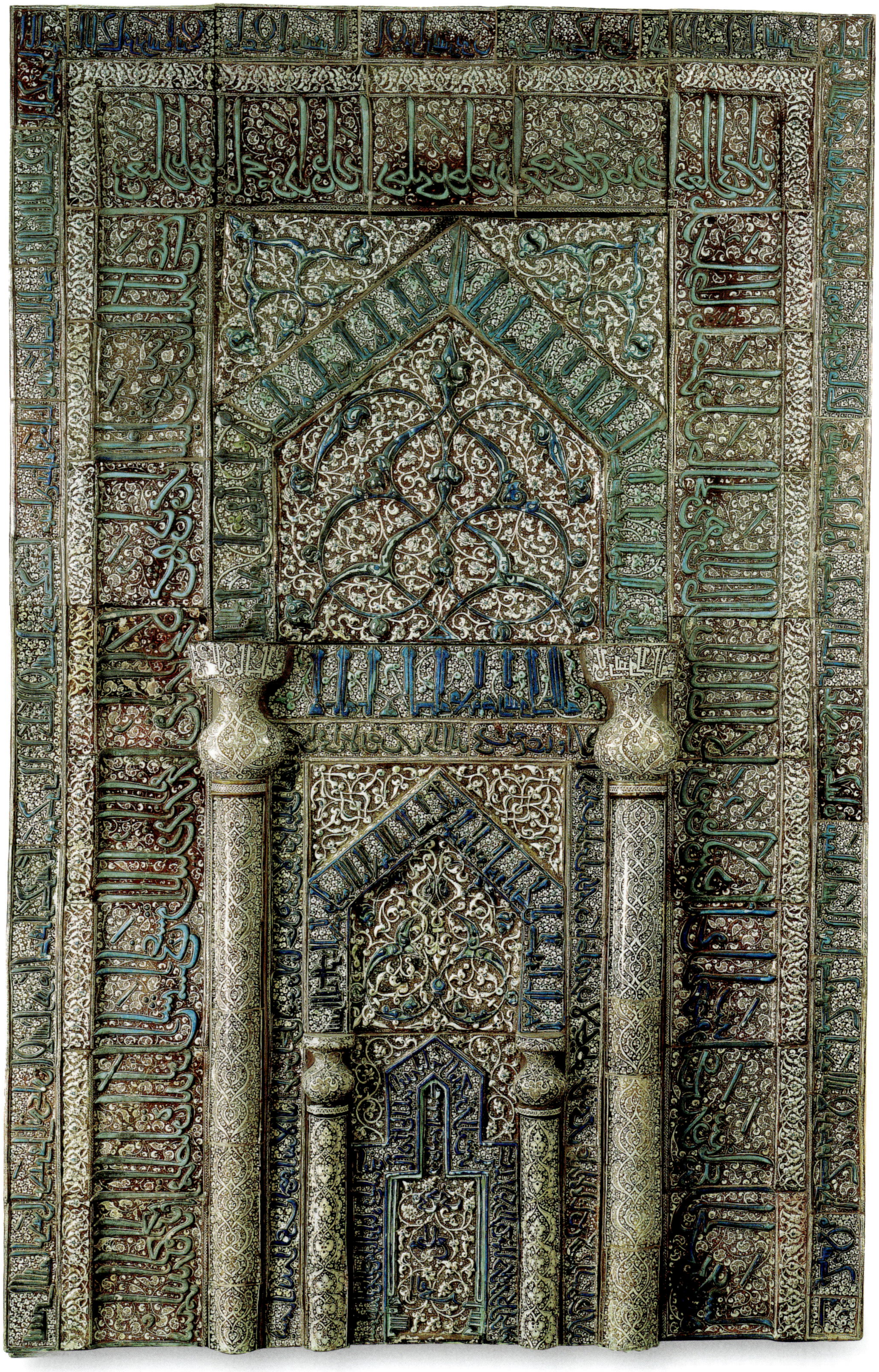

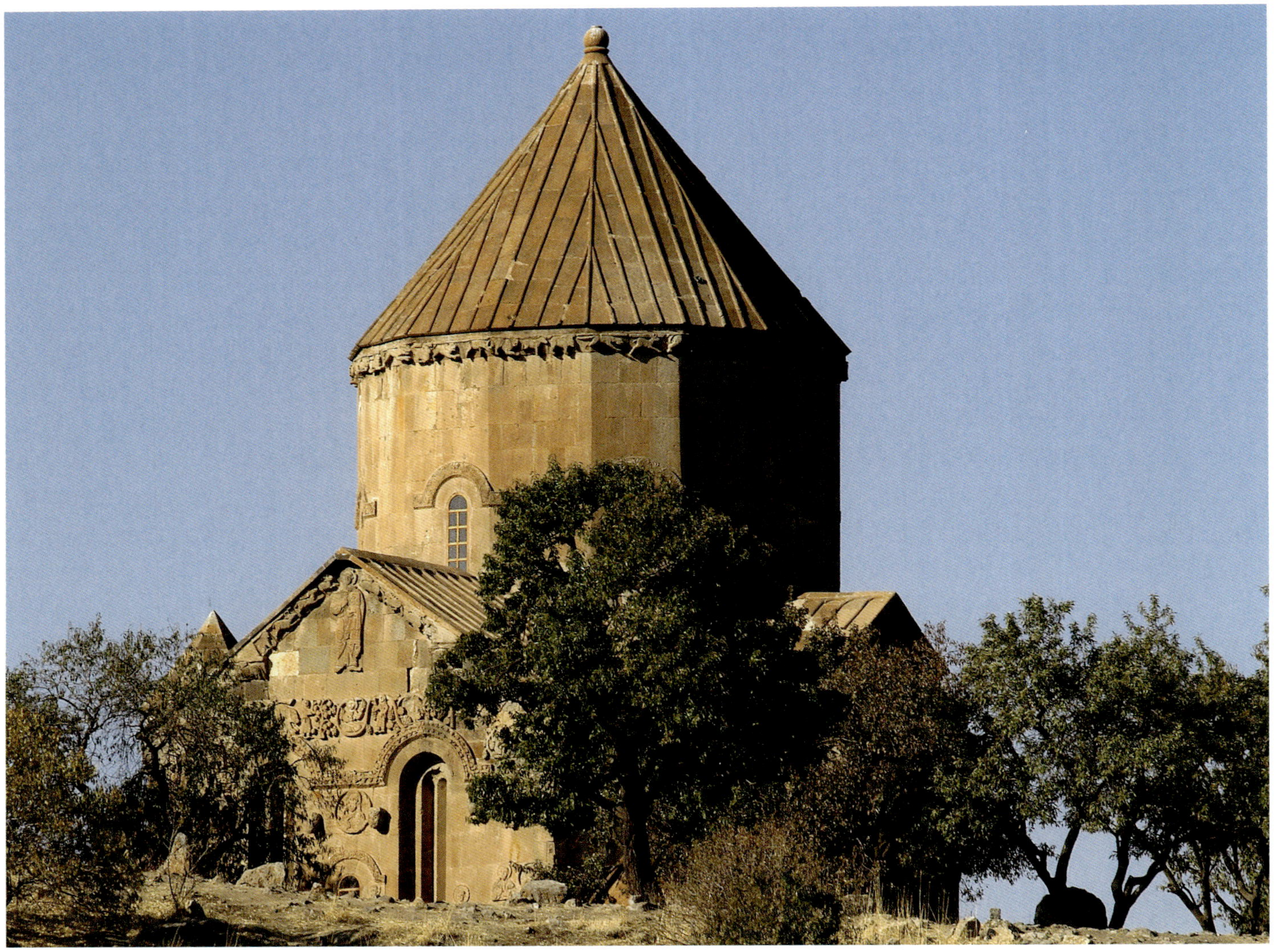

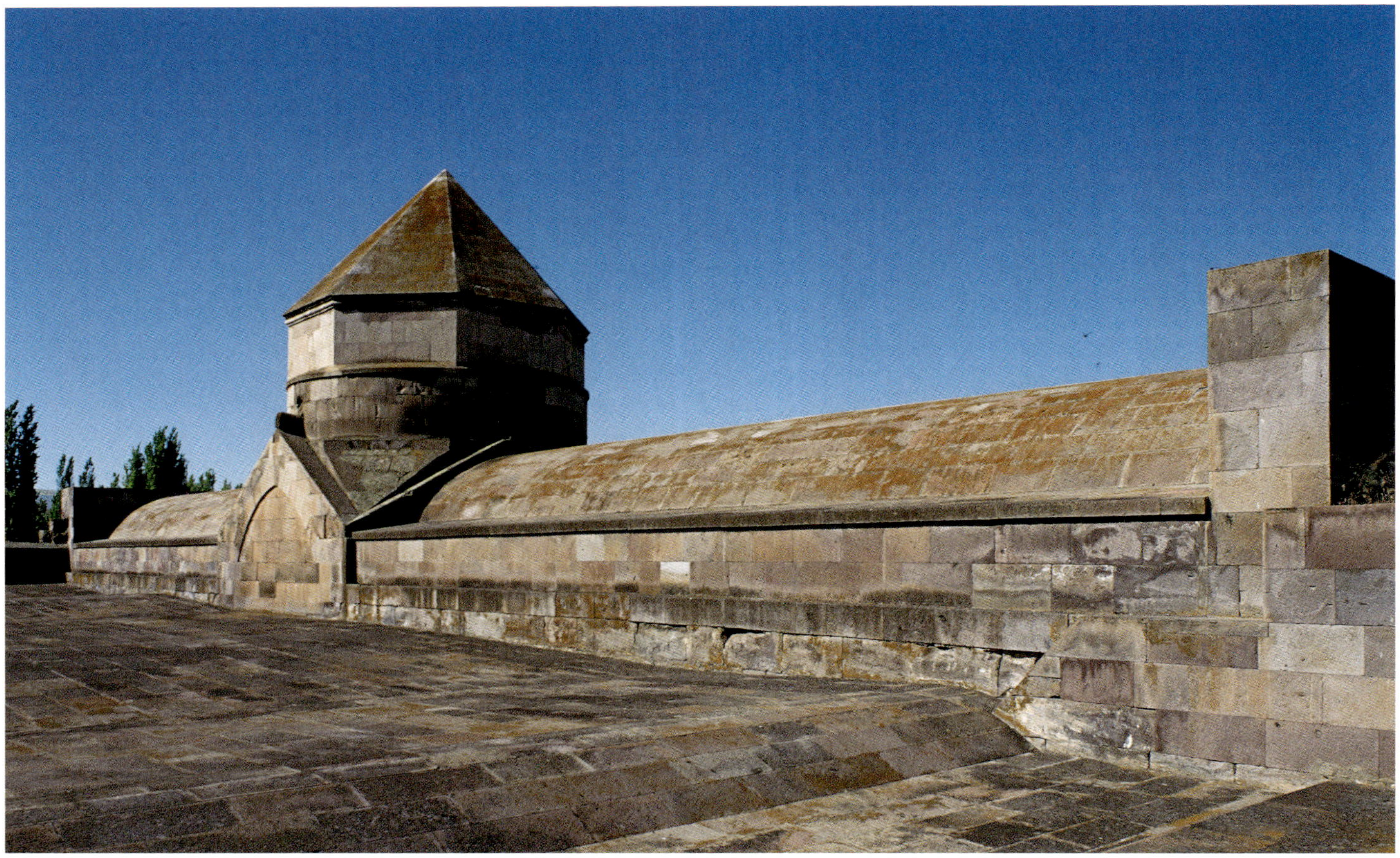

Church on the island of Ahtamar
915–921
Lake Van, Turkey

The architecture of the Seljuqs of Rum differs from that of their Persian 'cousins' by a sculptural conception of stone-cutting. Fostered by Armenian, as well as Byzantine and Syrian architects and craftsmen, this dynamic manifests itself in forms of singularly virile power. The vogue for cuspidate elements, already present in the Iranian ambit and dominant in the Armenian, gives rise in Rum to a novel and still more dramatic sense of form. This is particularly evident in funerary monuments and the drums supporting conical roofs so characteristic of Seljuq architecture. The region around Van was among the first to be conquered: monuments such as the church of Ahtamar bequeathed models particularly consonant with the Turkish sensibility.

Karatay Han
1246
Outskirts of Kayseri, Turkey

In some of the more glamorous Anatolian caravanserai, the conically pitched roof, widely diffused in funerary monuments, as was already the case in Persian regions, was marshalled in novel fashion to crown the covered hall. Numbering among the most impressive realizations of the era, these constructions are in no way inferior to the finest European architecture of the time, even the foremost examples of monastic building. Indeed the comparison has often been made, to the point that some have conjectured that the same craftsmen may have been involved. An impressive example of the four-square idiom of the Seljuqs of Rum, the tight-knit geometry of the masses refracted through the imposing muscular prism of the dome over the main hall conveys an almost telluric sense of power, while the sturdy lantern pierced by slit windows lets a pencil of light filter down into the yawning chasm below. The stark structure of the nave seems to surge up like some colossal submarine from the flat roofs over the side aisles.

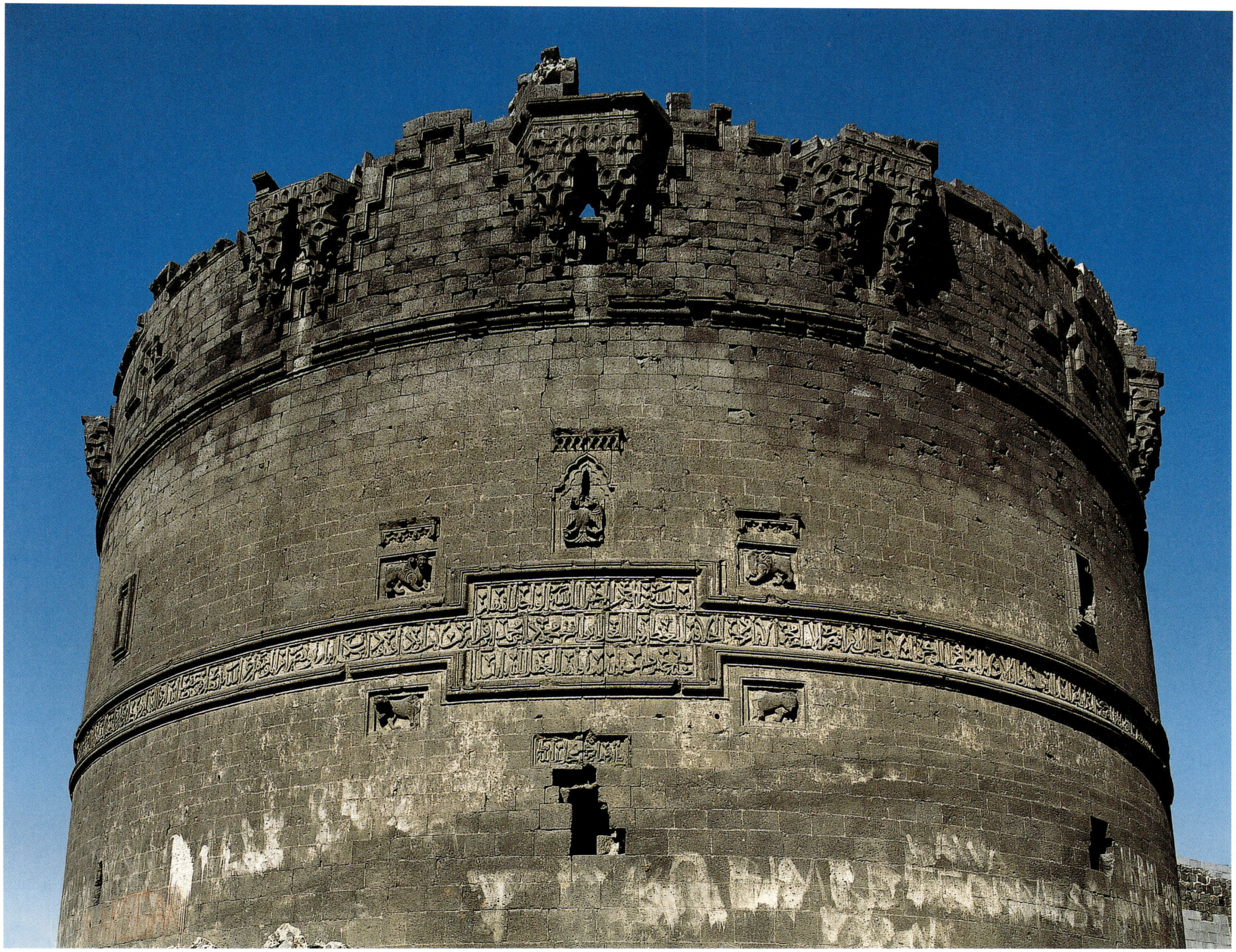

Evli Beden Tower
1208
Diyarbakir, Turkey

The Roman walls of Diyarbakir, rebuilt by the Byzantines, were upgraded in the ninth century by the Arabs, when a source describes them as the greatest fort of the time. The Seljuqs restored them initially, as did the Artuqids and the Ayyubids who took over in 1235. However, the city was overrun by the Mongols in 1259, becoming the capital of the kingdom of the Aq Qoyunlu by the end of the fourteenth century and finally being annexed by the Ottoman Empire in 1515. It is thus extremely hard to provide a precise date for these colossal walls in dark black basalt, pierced by four great gates and defended by gigantic towers on which numerous decorative and apotropaic elements appear, some Byzantine and others of the Seljuq epoch.
The Evli Beden Tower is a formidable example of Artuqid military architecture topped by battlements whose crenels bristle with cascading *muqarnas;* it must have presented a highly effective war machine in the age of the Crusades. A perfect balance between power and rigour also inspires the monumental inscription and the central tablet, surrounded by high reliefs showing animals, symbols of the dynasty with magical powers to protect the structure.

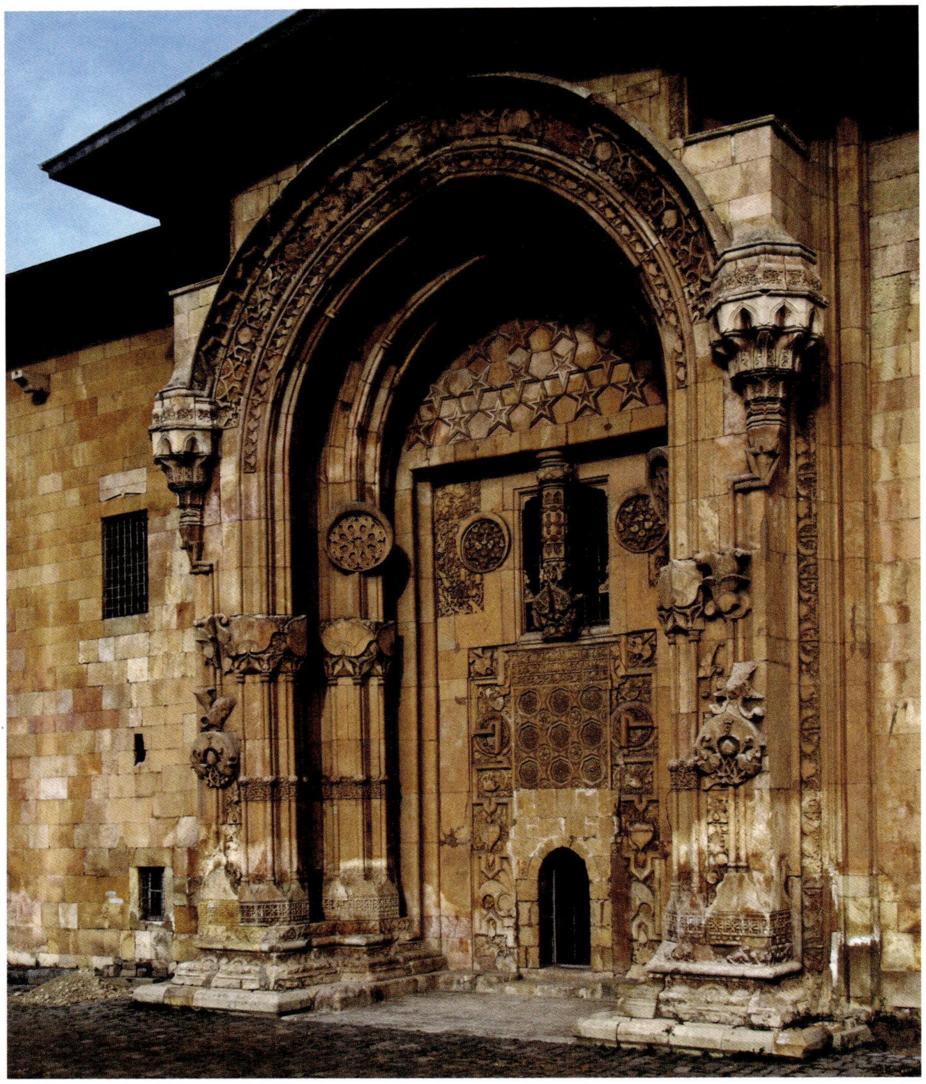

Great Mosque
Northern façade
1228–1229
Divriği, Turkey

It was Ahmad Shah, an emir who recognized Seljuq sovereignty as no more than a formality, who erected this Great Mosque; the nearby hospital was built by his wife. It is probable that both buildings were erected by Armenian craftsmen. The bizarre iconography, whose improbable decorative apparatus attains a *nec plus ultra* of blustering expressionism, makes it the most astonishing complex in all Anatolia. Of the various doorways, decorated with an incredible profusion of low- and high-reliefs and in some cases with sculptures in the round, the most astounding is that to the north. For all its belligerent aspect and the almost insane burgeoning of divers forms, in all likelihood it is supposed to represent the gate to paradise, enwrapped in flowers-cum-trees of unprecedented appearance in an outburst of motifs analogous to a number of stucco experiments in Iranian regions. Here calm Islamic rationalism is overwhelmed by what look like the drug-induced hallucinations of a shaman in petrified form.

Hospital
Façade
1228–1229
Divriği, Turkey

Set on a double arch supported by a cluster of colonnettes over which some impressive and muscular floral motifs clamber, the gateway to the hospital is no less striking although it lacks its upper section. Above it, on a monumental Gothic arch clearly influenced by Christian examples, there scurries a discordant and unlikely proliferation of absurdly disproportioned vegetable forms. The warped and illogical syntax of the architectural vocabulary persists in dissonant variants on traditional geometric repertory.

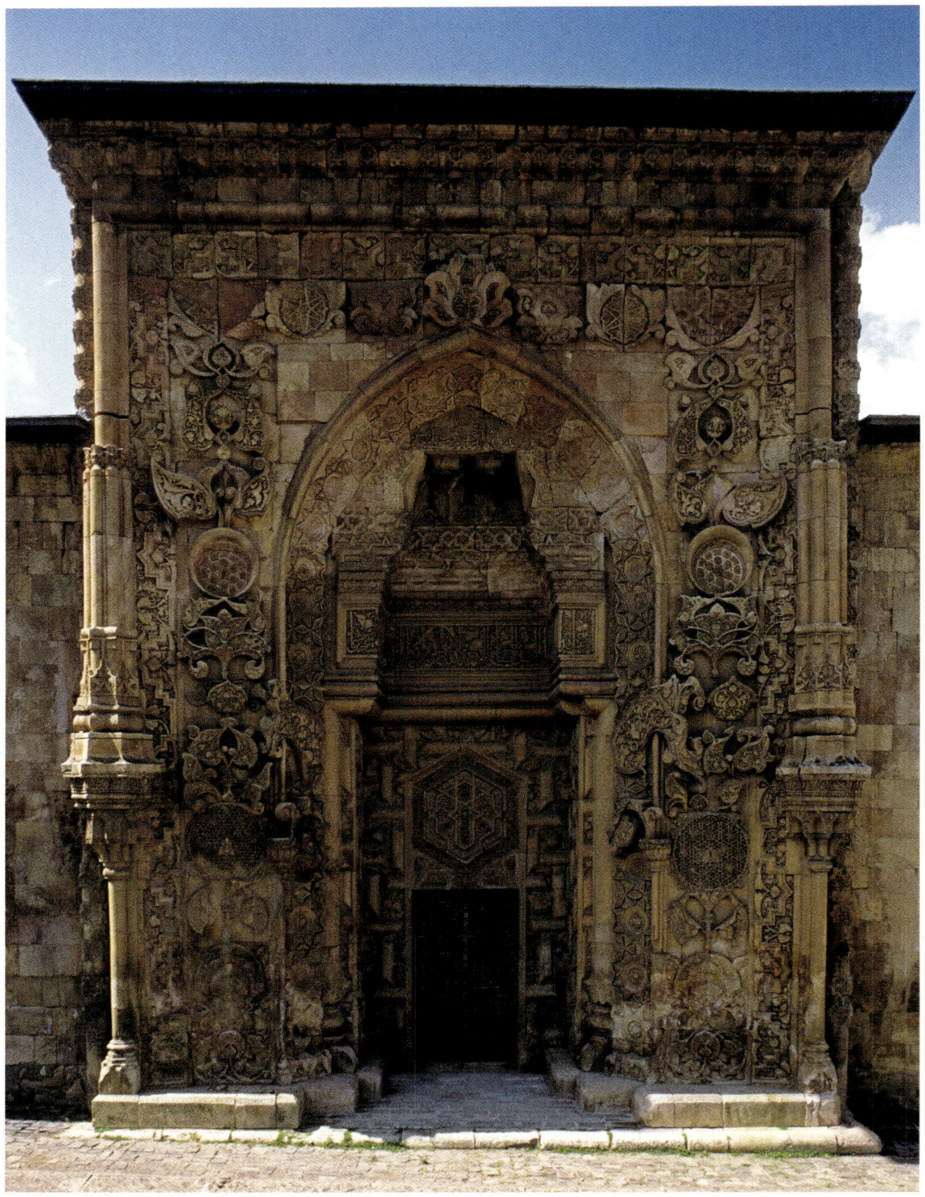

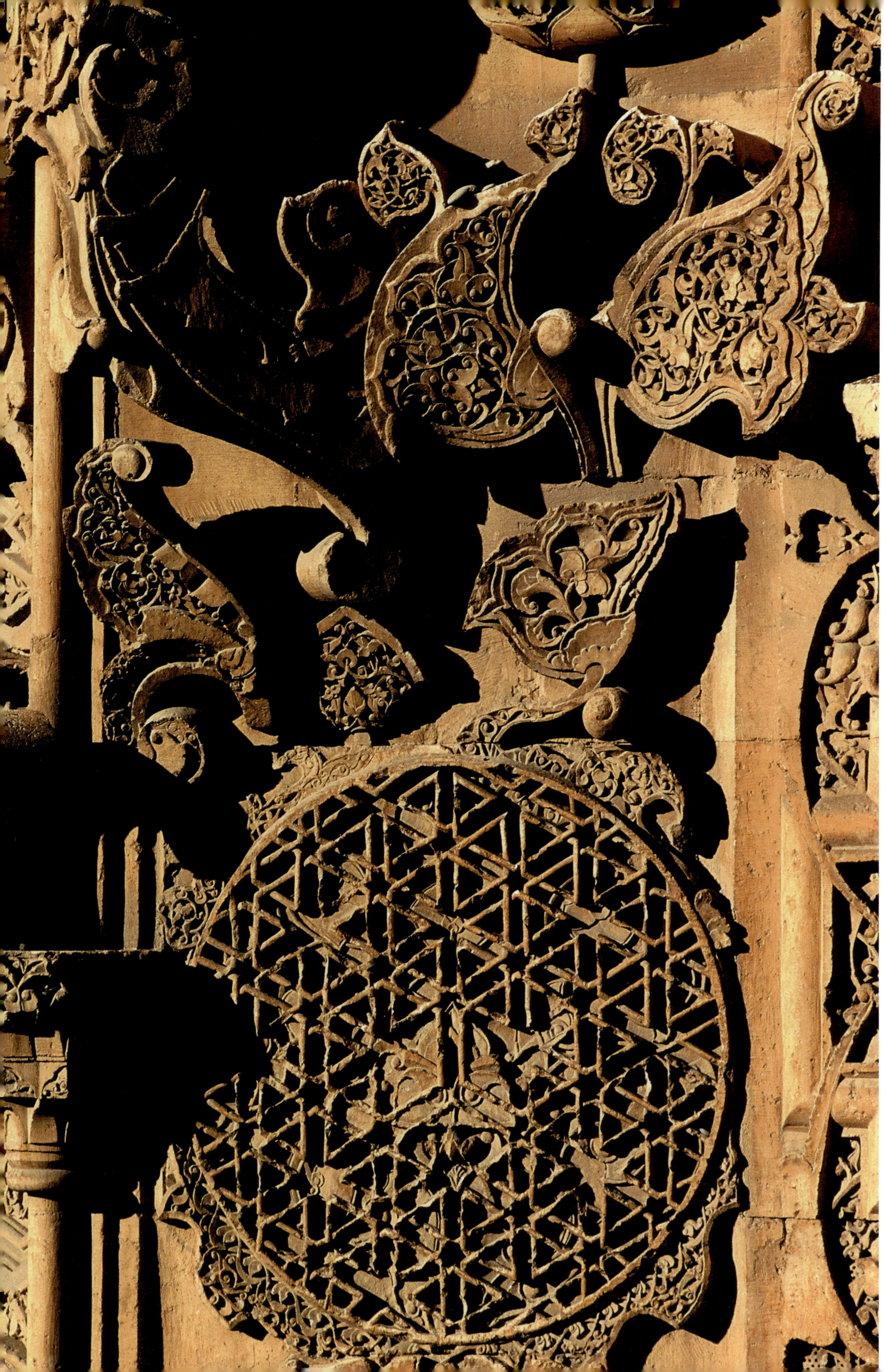

Great Mosque
Detail of the north front
1228–1229
Divriği, Turkey

Around the doorway sprouts an unexpected and abnormal garden, grown thick with threatening sculptural vigour, shooting up from the plane of the façade and climbing in disturbing, even morbid excrescences utterly bereft of any sense of order or harmony.

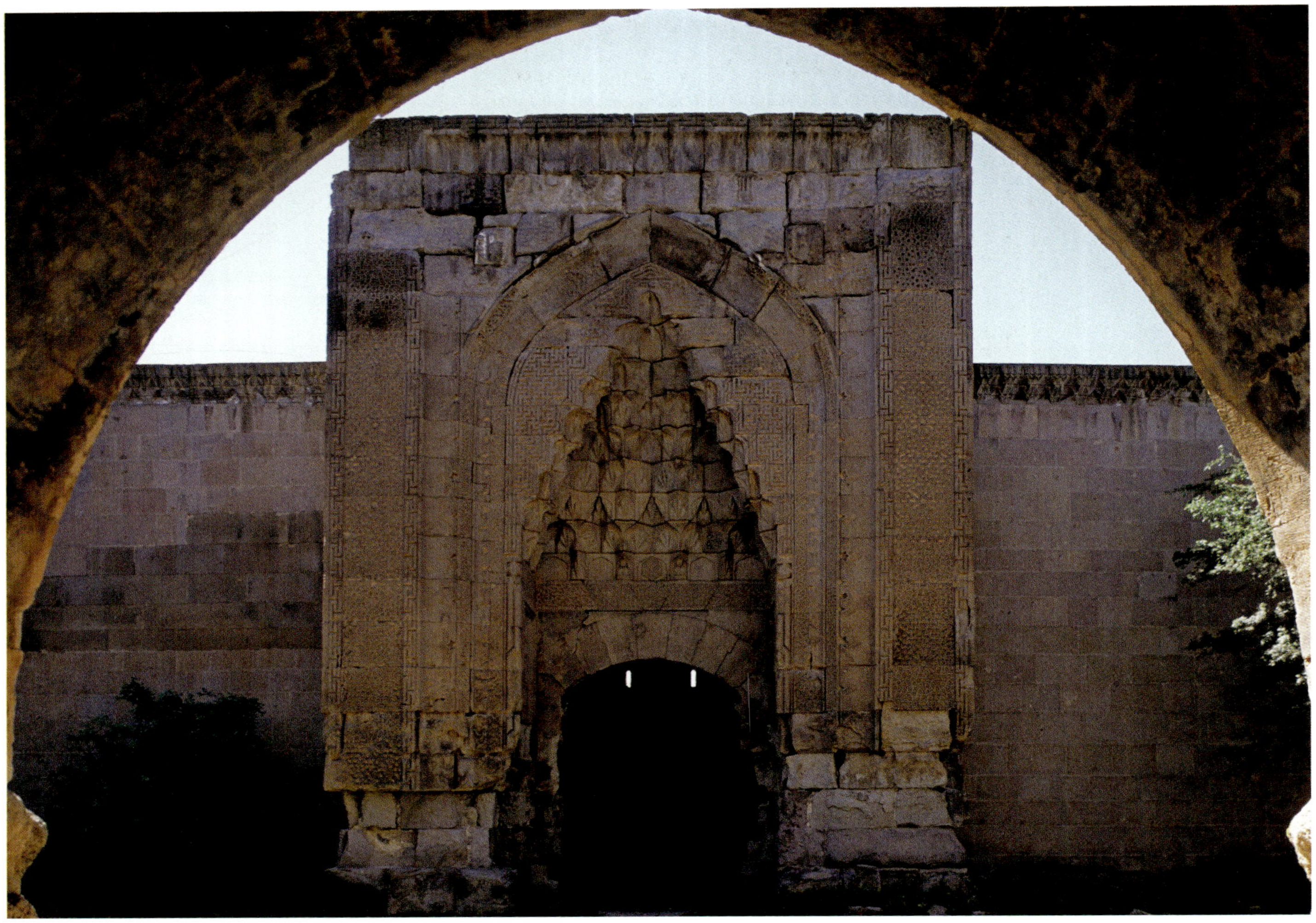

Sultan Han
1232–1236
Outskirts of Kayseri, Turkey

The access to the covered hall is emphasized by an imposing portal in line with the entrance – here framed by the oratory in the middle of the courtyard – very similar to that outside, with a *pishtaq*, a gently pointed arch with a niche filled with *muqarnas*. In both of the recorded caravanserais, as for instance at the Sultan Han, and in numerous others laid out according to the same plan with relatively few variants, the courtyard is flanked by a series of arcades perpendicular to the enceinte walls whose secondary function is to improve the statics of the building. Divided inside into a pair of aisles provided with a series of minor arches, the whole edifice is imbued with the greatest sobriety. In the summer months the men would take shelter here, perhaps with some of their goods from the caravans (the more precious merchandise would be locked away in storerooms, however), while their animals would stand about in the courtyard. The centre of the square contains a small *mescit* ('oratory'), inventively and exuberantly decorated: close up, the elegant decorative pattern resolves into a pair of facing serpents or dragons, an unexpected avatar of the totemic substrate in Seljuq culture on a edifice dedicated to prayer. The fountain would have provided water for the men both for drinking and for ablutions. In line with the entrance and the oratory a second gateway opens up, nearly as spectacular as that without, from which leads a covered winter hall resembling an enormous Cistercian basilica, with five naves, the central one being much higher and capped by a dome on spandrels. Although perhaps not very practical, from the aesthetic point of view it is truly exceptional: the caravanserai is a 'cathedral' dedicated to commerce.

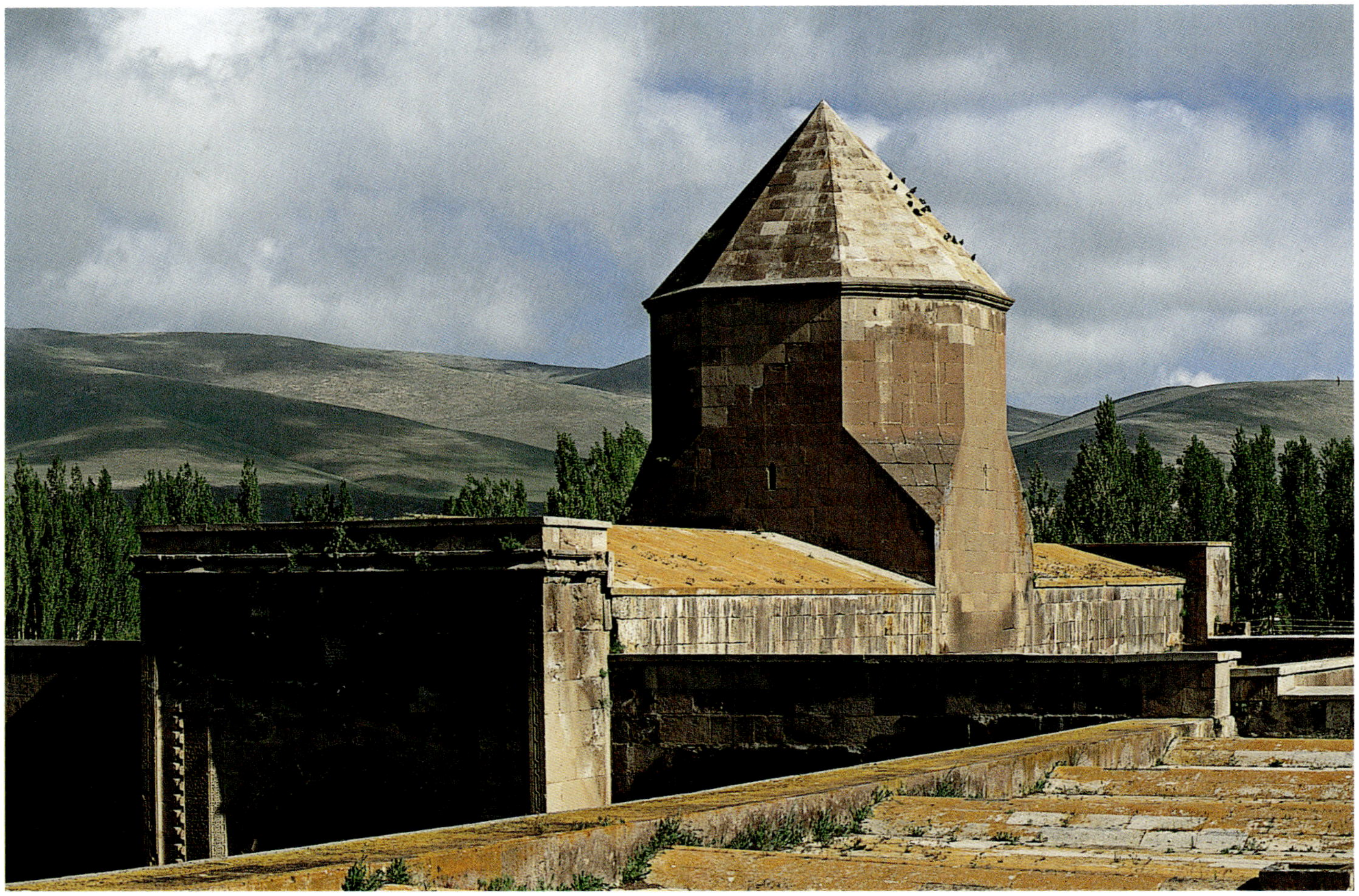

Karatay Han
1246
Outskirts of Kayseri, Turkey

The Seljuqs built hundreds of caravanserais, generally in stone, the largest comprising a great hall, barrel-vaulted on pillars, preceded by an extensive courtyard ringed by spaces open to the air. From outside, they tend to look like fortresses fortified by turrets that function as counterforts, although sometimes of unusual and occasionally outlandish form. The gateway is frequently ensconced within a lofty *pishtaq* presenting a deep niche with stalactites above the entrance proper. To the centre of the courtyard, suspended on four arches shading the watering-place, or on the upper floor at the entrance, there generally stands an oratory, often creatively and intricately embellished.

Sultan Han
Covered hall
1229
Outskirts of Konya, Turkey

In a caravanserai, above all in one financed by the sultan, the covered hall is composed of five aisles of basilica-like disposition. Impressively sedate, it is illumined by tiny slits and culminates in a median nave capped by a central lantern. The organism reveals close technical and formal affinities with the marginally earlier monastic buildings of the French Cistercian order. To explain these remarkable similarities that at times render churches and caravanserais almost indistinguishable, some scholars have hypothesized that, during a period of intense warfare, a number of Armenian or Syrian craftsmen might have taken shelter in Europe, returning in more favourable times having absorbed the technical and formal language of their hosts. In effect, numerous inscriptions document the fact that Armenians, Georgians and Syrians executed and in all probability planned the majority of caravanserais in Anatolia. Since Armenian architects are recorded in Jerusalem and in many other places in Christendom, beyond the nearby kingdom of Lesser Armenia of Cilicia to the south of Konya, it is at least possible that caravanserai builders may have encountered examples of Western architecture in those regions, although the fact that some may have had direct experience of French architecture should not be excluded.

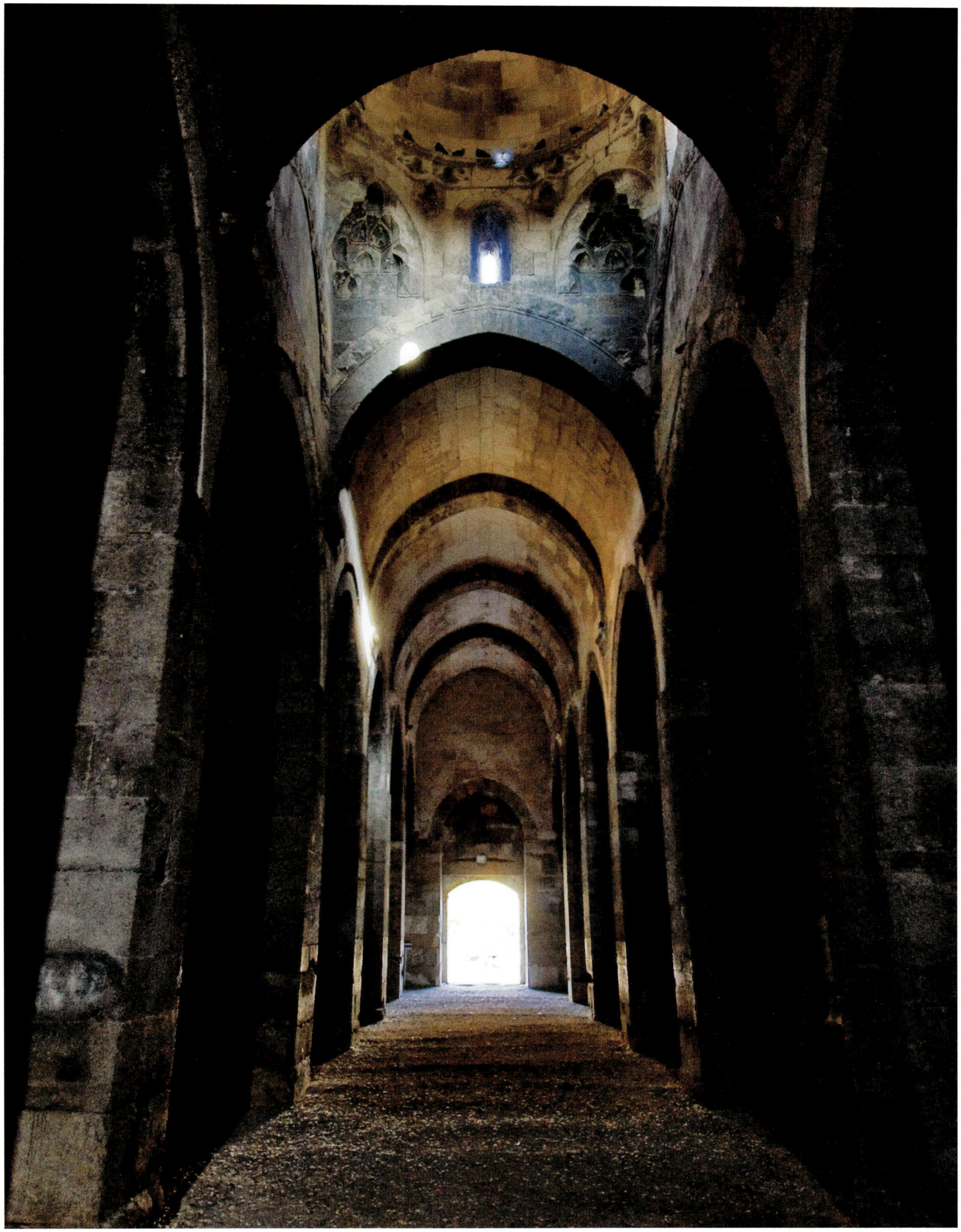

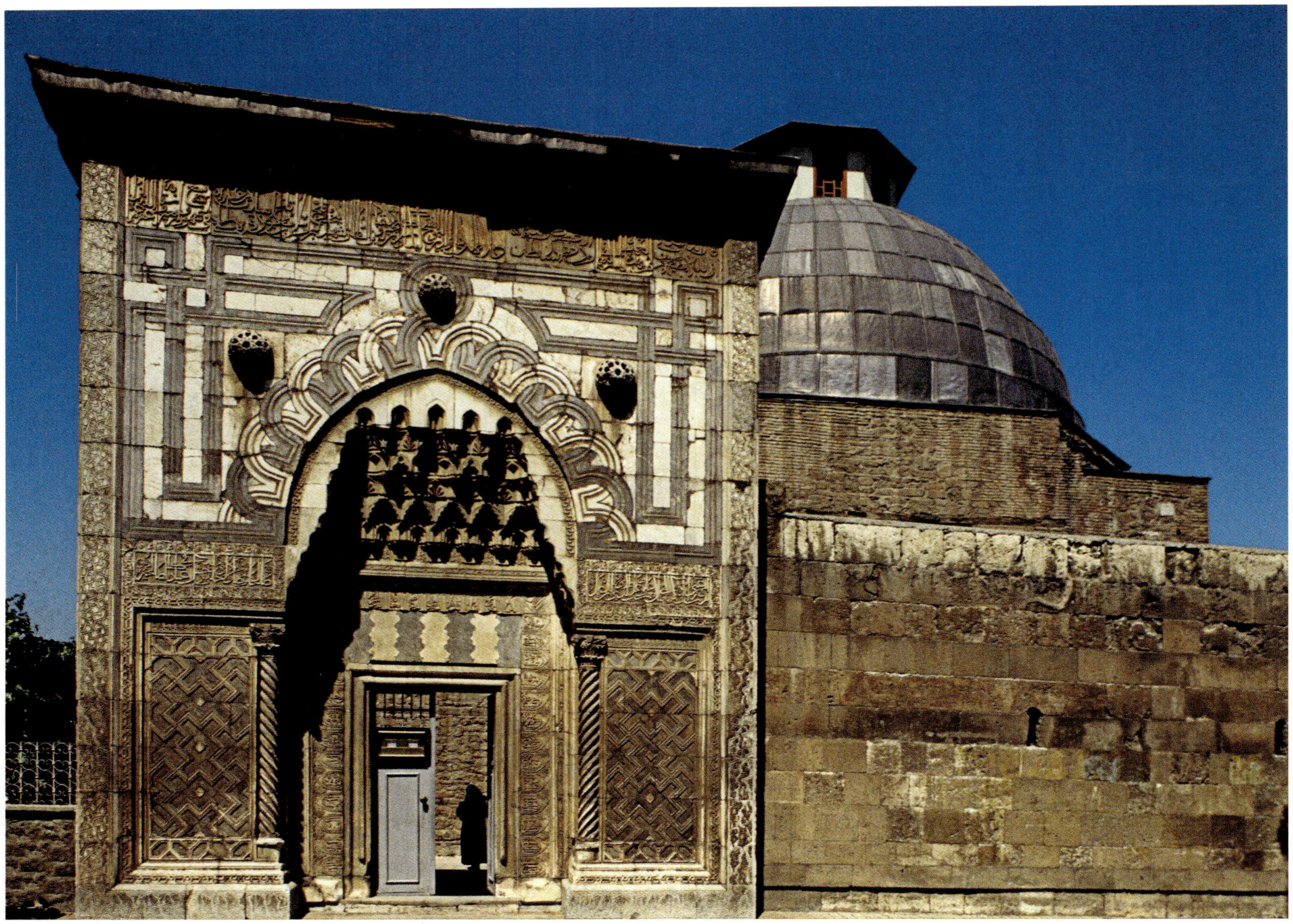

Büyük Karatay Medrese
1251–1252
Konya, Turkey

Self-proclaimed champions of orthodoxy, the Seljuqs also built numerous madrasahs conforming with two basic templates: relatively small constructions, with a single *iwan* around a domed courtyard; and others of larger size planned longitudinally, with a courtyard with three or four *iwans* and a monumental façade appointed with two minarets. The Büyük Karatay is an optimal example of the first type and was constructed by a Syrian architect, as demonstrated by the muscular formulation of a façade crowned by monumental calligraphy, with a two-colour *alfiz* typical of the region around Aleppo, contrasting with *muqarnas* arranged in parallel rows to form a rather shallow niche on an architrave of elegant offset voussoirs.

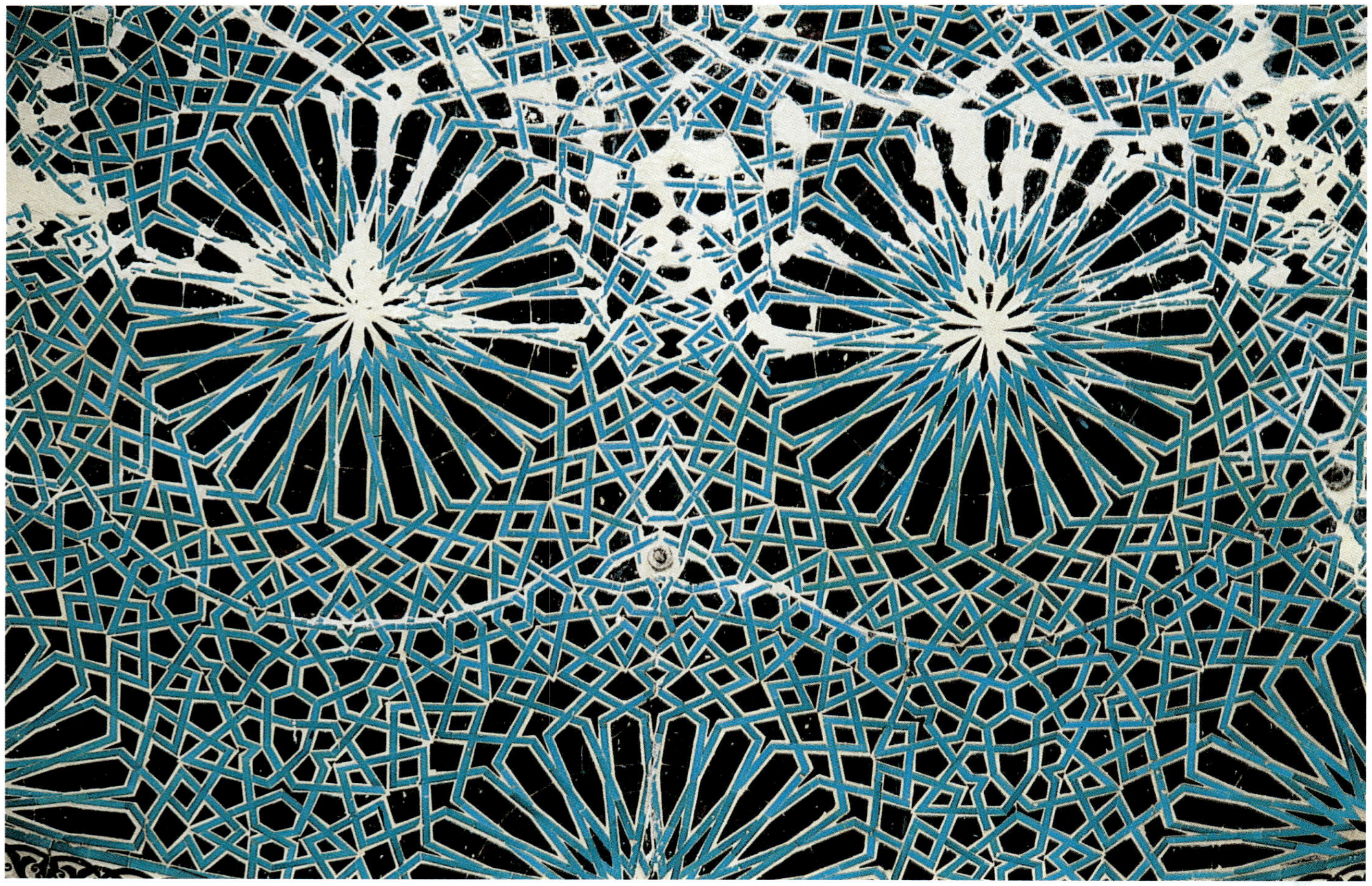

Büyük Karatay Medrese
Detail of the vaulting
1251–1252
Konya, Turkey

The dome is borne on four triangular pendentives emblazoned with the names of the caliphs and the prophets repeated *ad infinitum,* realized with *bannai* ceramics in the heavenly colours of light and cobalt blue. Pulsating with light, the star-strewn universe, immutable in its geometric perfection, ripples out from the intrados, the whole illumined by a central oculus, the sole source of light.

Çifte Minare Medresesi
('Madrasah with the double minaret')
1253
Erzurum, Turkey

The language of symbol veils an archaic and multilayered system of religious thought presented in impressive stylized images that reflect a world of vague perceptions, of gnawing doubts about the origin of life, the essence of the cosmos, the inscrutability of fate and the inevitability of death. Symbols are also the physical representation of the sensations aroused by the mysterious forces of nature and by an intuition of the supernatural world beyond. In passing from totemism to shamanism, the eagle (a key animal in the ancestral heritage of pre-Islamic Turkmen) represents by extension the inapproachability of authority, whereas the tree of life stands for the fulcrum of the cosmos, a linchpin in the shaman's spiritual universe and a symbol deeply rooted in the Assyrian-Mesopotamian imagination. They are often framed by two animals, as here by two dragons or serpents, beasts at once mythical and chthonic. The unexpected presence of this type of figure is an indicator of the ambiguity of Seljuq spirituality, formally orthodox in its adhesion to Islam but profoundly embedded in a substrate of atavistic religion.

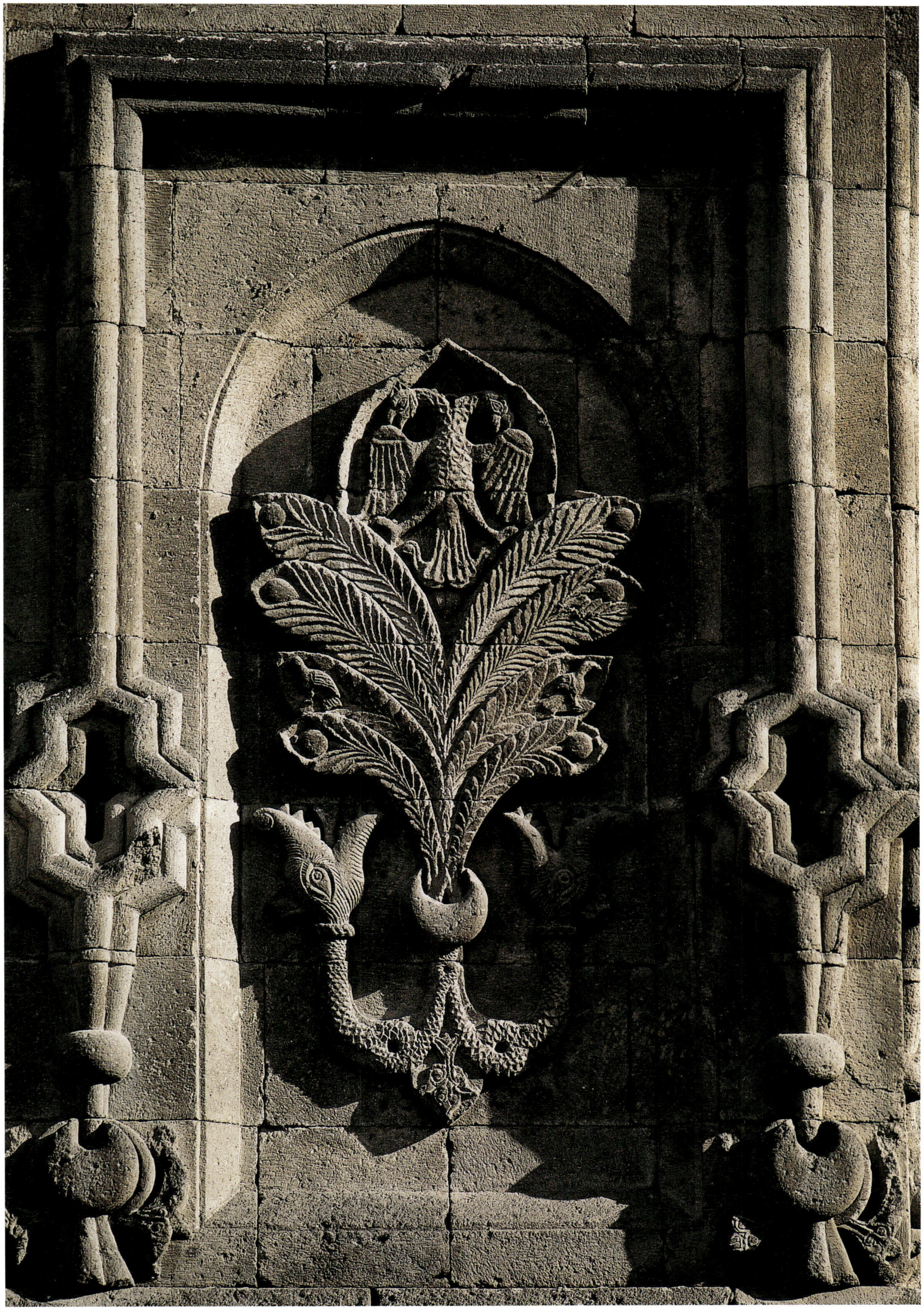

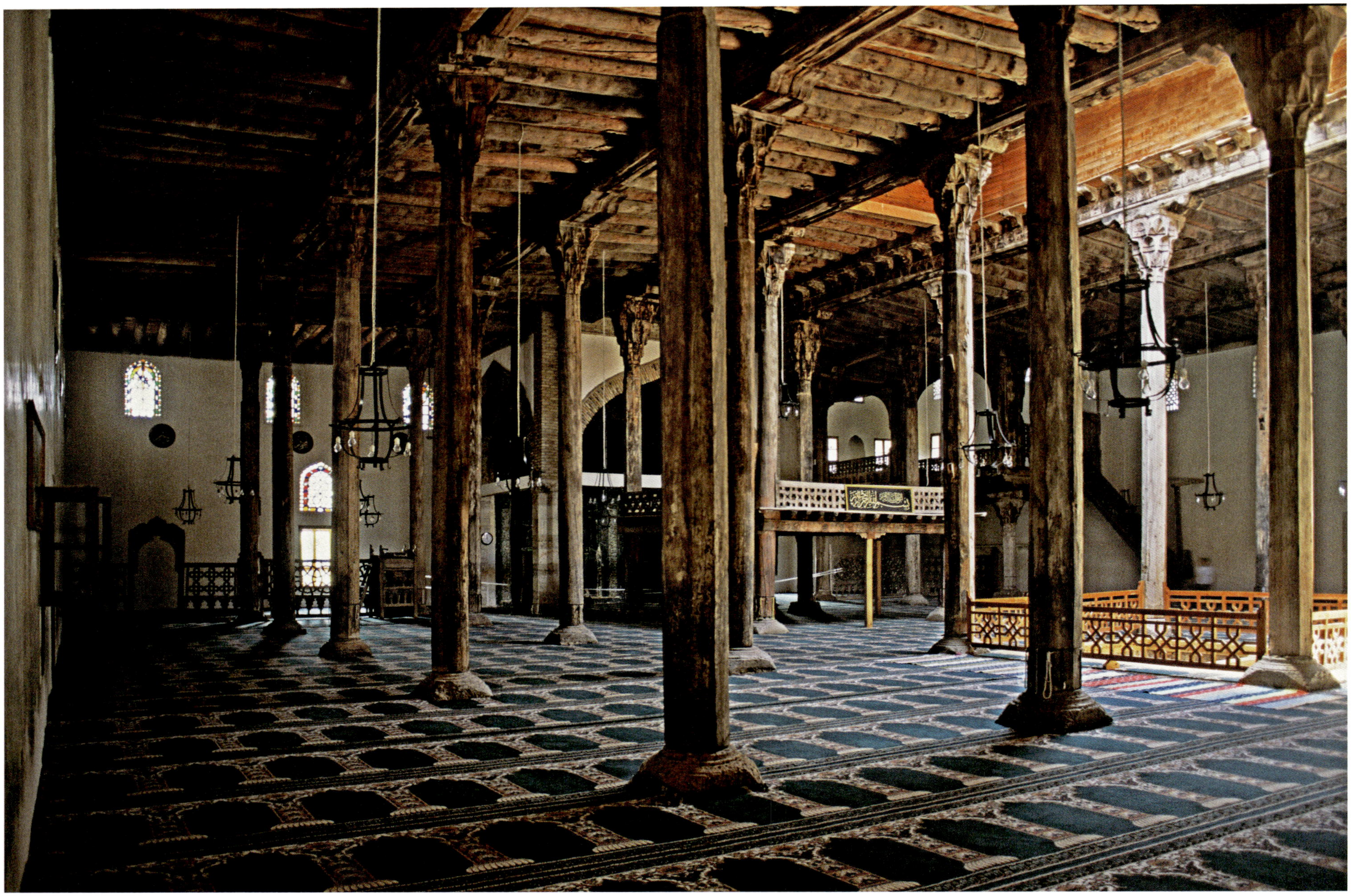

Eshrefoğlu Mosque
Interior
1298
Beyshehir, Turkey

The Eshrefoğlu Cami is perhaps the finest of the very few mosques with hypostyle halls on wooden columns to have survived to the present day. Solemn but airy, the space, structured by slender wooden posts crowned with *muqarnas* capitals, rises apparently effortlessly to support a ceiling with beams bearing rafters running across them. An air- and light-well opens up at the centre. The sober simplicity of the structure is enlivened by the measured use of the chisel and at one time was enriched by colour, scant remnants of which remain visible today. At the rear, shady and refreshing, stands a sort of pavilion lined with enamel tiles that shelters the *mihrab,* the largest in the Konya region. A cascade of stars, it is both a statement of geometry and a haven of poetry. Memories of Achaemenid and Urartian *apadana* seem to come back to life again in this quiet, archaic and noble structure.

Eshrefoğlu Mosque
Detail of the *minbar*
1299
Wood
Beyshehir, Turkey

The magnificent *minbar* in the mosque at Eshrefoğlu was executed by a certain Isa ('Jesus'), by all evidence a Christian, who appended his signature. In severe dark-hued walnut, the piece is perfectly preserved and presents a matchless geometric weft generated by a complex composition of figures of four, five, six or eight sides, arranged according to a potent logic and embellished with tiny floral motifs of visionary power – a silent world of pulsating yet ordered power. Beneath the parapet of the stairway, constructed out of triangular polygons, runs a magnificent inscription in a strongly sculptural and noble Kufic, separated from the geometric universe below by a luxuriant frieze whose plant motifs burgeon disquietingly.

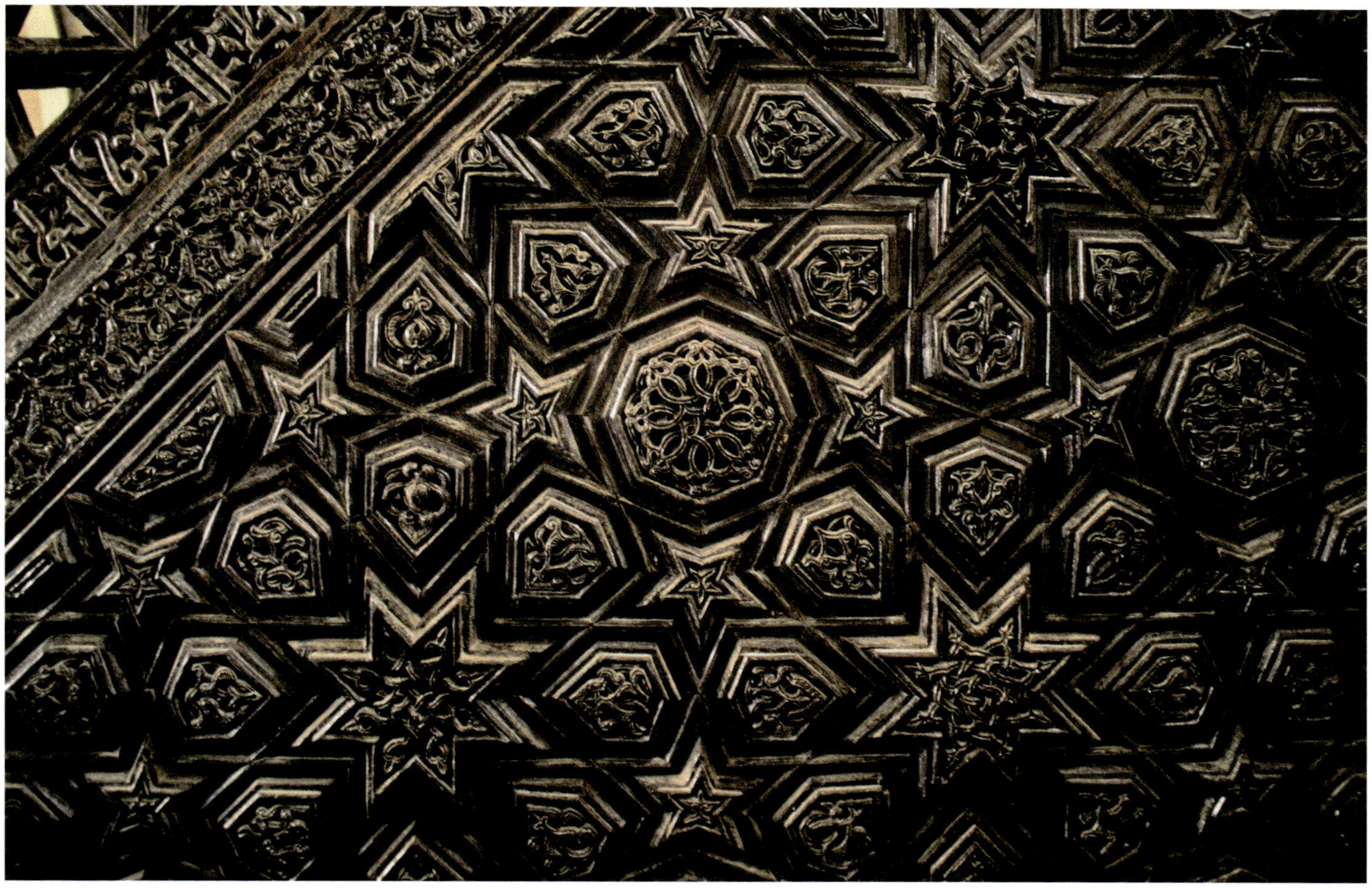

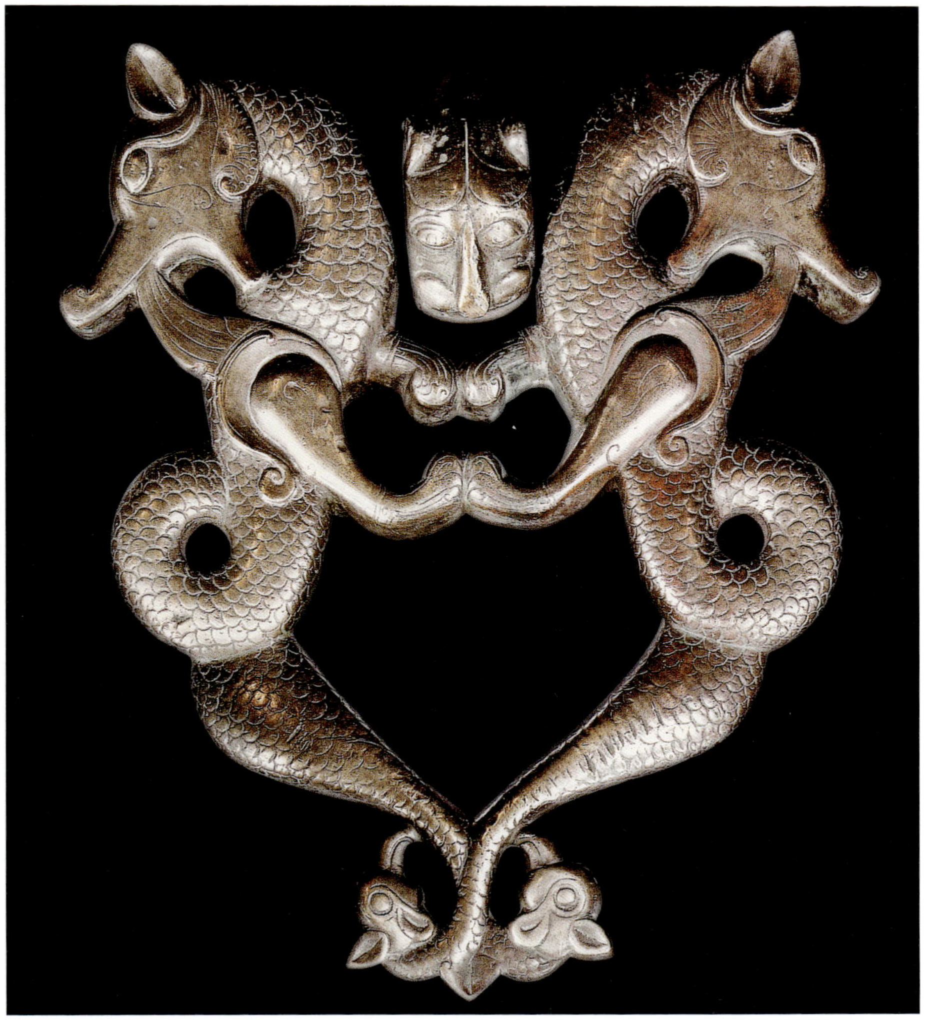

Knocker
c. 1200
Bronze
Museum of Turkish and Islamic Arts, Istanbul

As in numerous examples carved on the façades of buildings, this piece exemplifies the manner in which the atavistic beasts that protected the clan were redeployed in a Muslim context, filtered through the animal art which for centuries had been key to the shared cultural heritage of the people of steppes. Sculptors, craftsmen, and weavers fed the humus of pagan and totemic symbols that nourished the collective imagination, translating it into forms of vibrant and stylized naturalism or muscular graphical abstraction.
Heraldically stylized, these two twisted affronted dragons served as a knocker on the door to the Ulu Cami (mosque) at Cizre. Of breathtaking assuredness of form, this piece – almost a throwback to the animal style that for centuries had constituted the most authentic expression of the inhabitants of the hinterland – once again documents the attachment of the Turkmen to their ancestral myths, as well as the formidable technical and artistic ability of the craftsmen who formed them in stone or bronze.

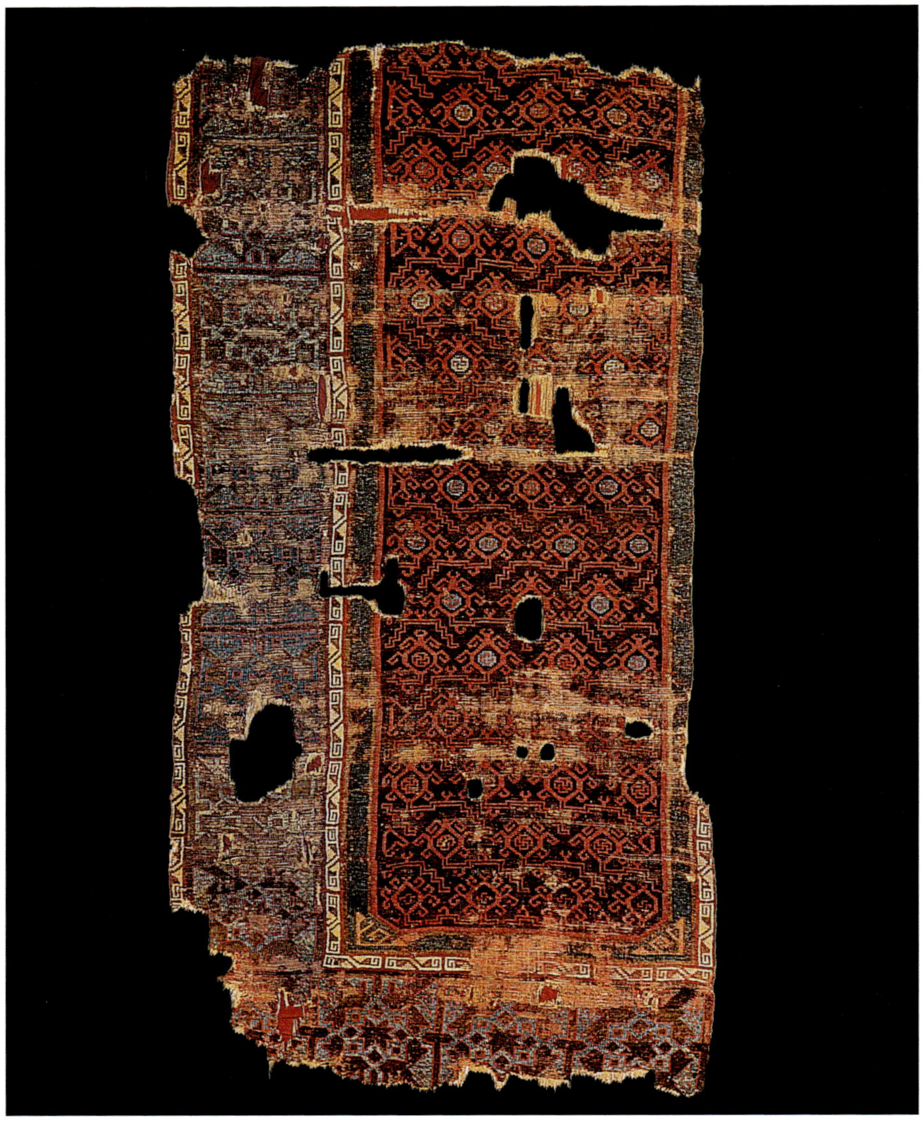

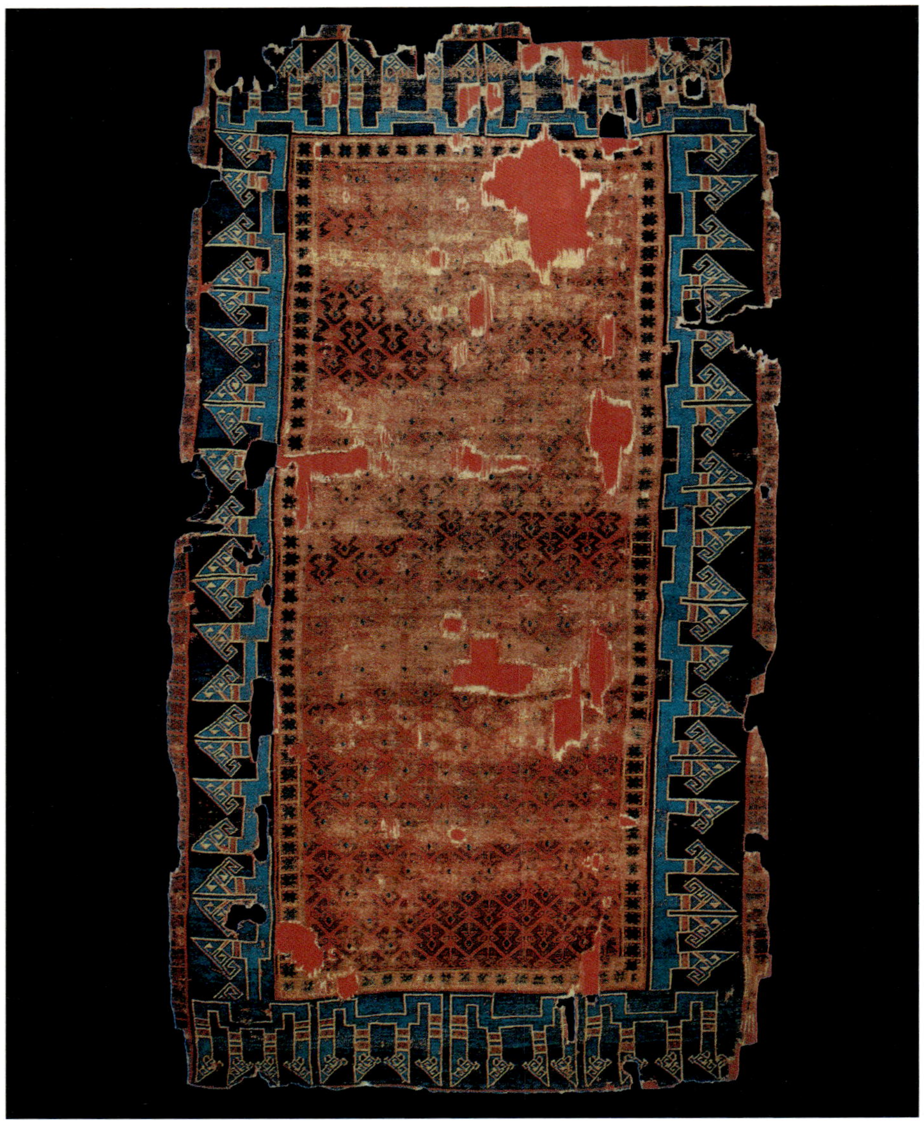

Carpet
13th century
Museum of Turkish and Islamic Arts, Istanbul

Very few examples of Seljuq rugs have survived. Some have been fortuitously recovered, in a precarious state, from the Aladdin Mosque (Alaaddin Cami) at Konya. Owing to their monumental dimensions and extraordinary quality, these were carpets of a ceremonial nature rather than traditional prayer rugs, probably connected in some way with the mausoleum adjacent to the mosque. The chromatic range remains narrow but vigorous and is dominated by a dramatic garnet-coloured ground. Over this is thrown a kind of red net in which can be distinguished a diffuse pattern based on moufflon horns of perhaps apotropaic function arranged into rhomboid motifs containing one final ornament – a lamp with a kind of turquoise gem at the middle. The border is adorned with a sturdy blue pattern rimmed in white with red inserts, whose 'horns' take on a Kufic flavour, the impact on the deep blue ground being powerful indeed.

Carpet
Entire and detail
13th century
Museum of Turkish and Islamic Arts, Istanbul

A chance find in the Aladdin Mosque at Konya led to the discovery of ten or so carpets from the thirteenth century in an optimal state of conservation. Blue, red, white and yellow appear in relatively elementary abstract decorative motifs characterized by impressive visual power and channelled by an unusual sense of hierarchy that does not preclude a certain 'wildness' of unforgettable evocative power. Their vast size, admirable technical control, restricted palette and design testify to a figurative language and an expressiveness analogous to what is found in other artistic disciplines.

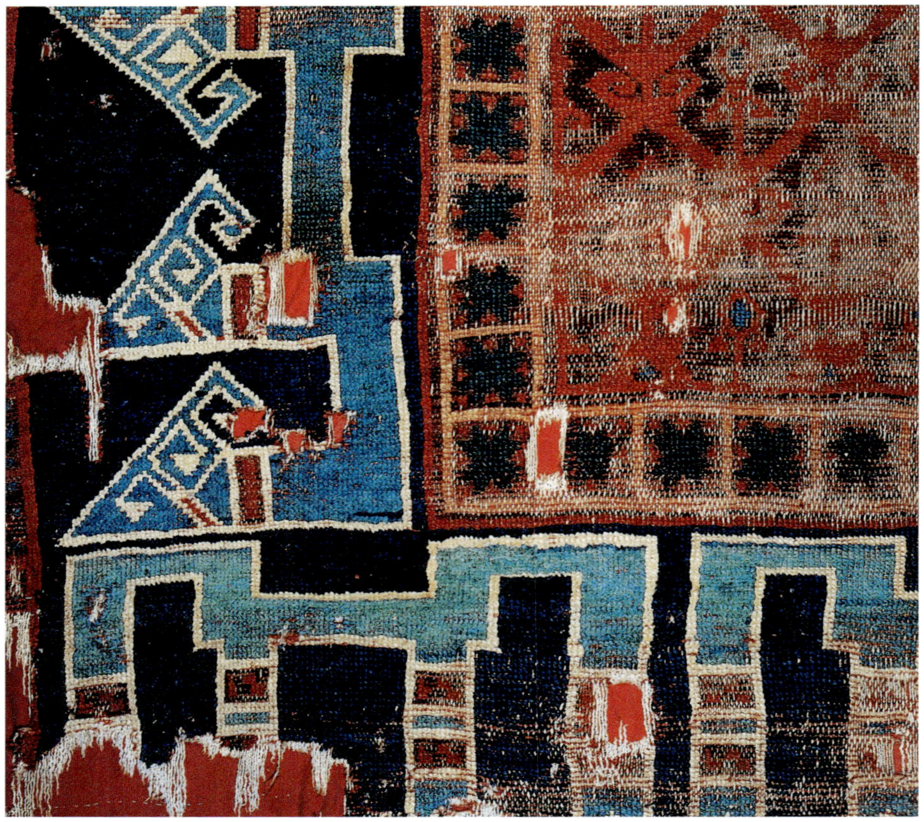

Carpet
13th century
Museum of Turkish and Islamic Arts, Istanbul

Stupendously simple, the irregular iteration on this immense carpet (608 x 246 cm) with an octagonal decorative base in red containing a horn motif repeated four times stands out against a saffron ground. Characterized by an impressive vibrancy that barely reins in an underlying 'savagery' of bubbling imaginative potency, the field is framed by an exiguous border adorned with a pseudo-Kufic motif. Like all others recovered from the same period, this carpet documents the exuberant vitality of an expressive tradition that subsisted unrestrained beneath the veil of Islamic rationalism.

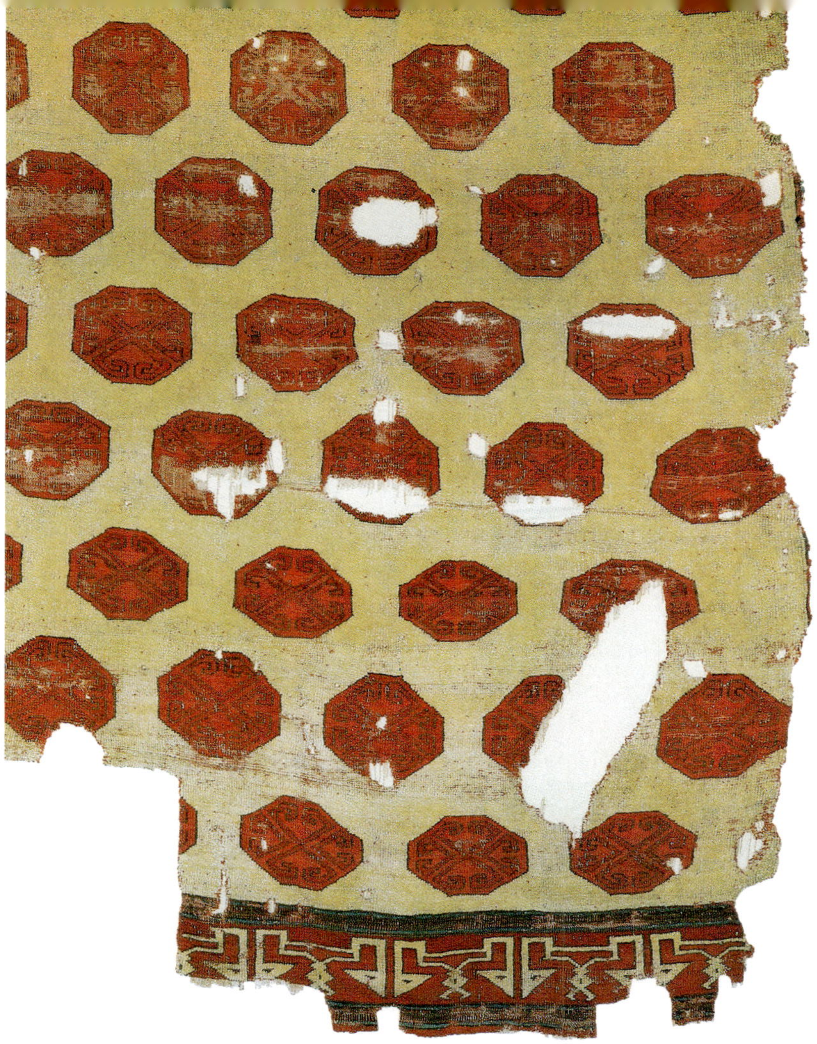

Qur'an stand
Painted wood
13th century
Mevlevi Museum, Konya

Relatively few pieces of handicraft of artistic value produced in Anatolia have survived to the present-day. Wooden Qur'an stands such as this constituted a much sought-after class of object. Made from a thin plank of carved wood hinged in the middle, the two parts open into the characteristic 'X' shape. The lion's share of these lecterns was finely carved with floral motifs and calligraphy. The example from the loggia of the dervishes in the Mevlevi at Konya is particularly rare in that it provides evidence of the pictorial art of the time. At the centre of the stand can be seen a two-headed eagle, a widespread motif in the Seljuq domain, flanked by two prides of eight lions, another animal typical of the time, symmetrically disposed and inextricably intertwined in an essentially floral arabesque.

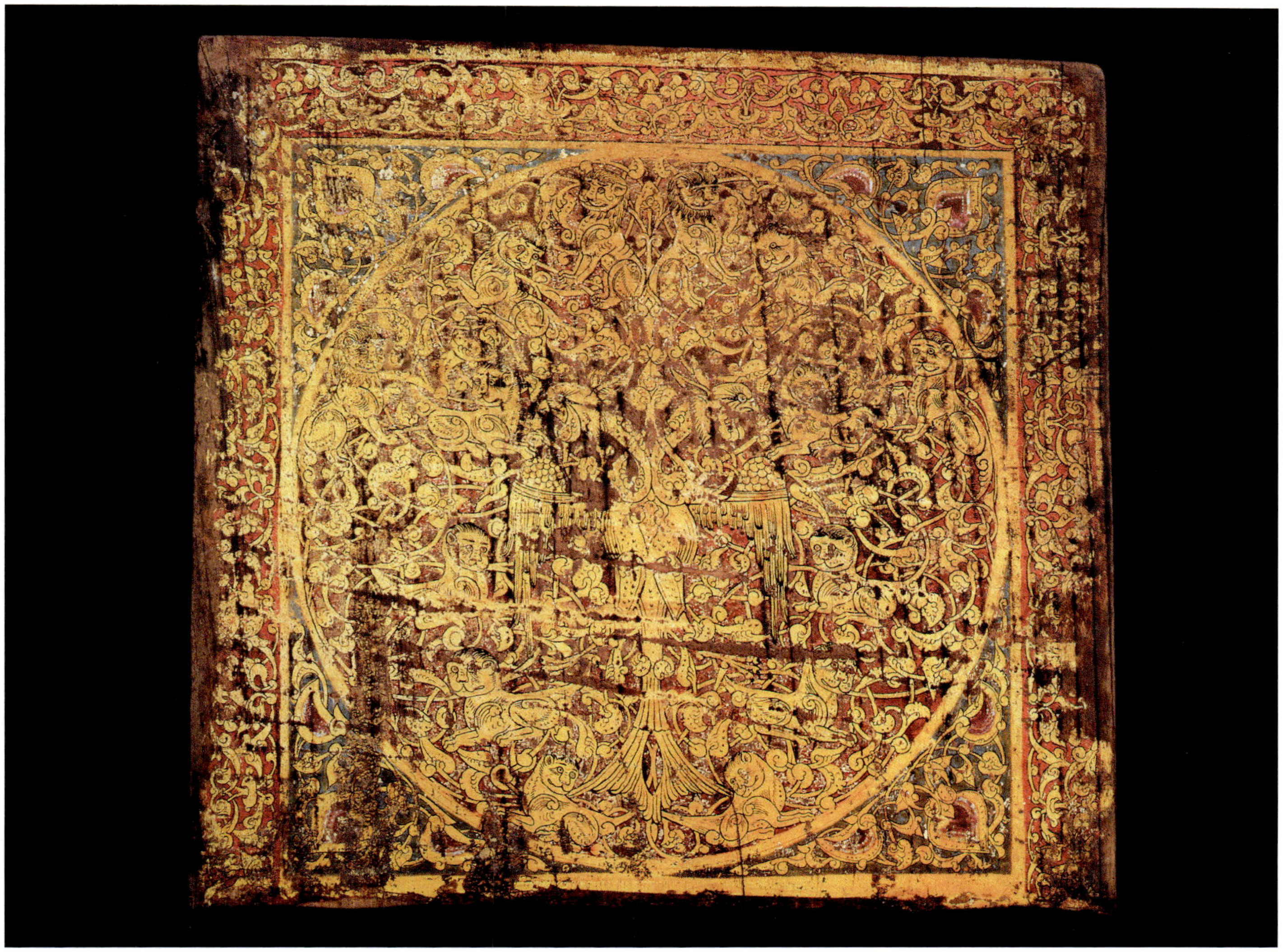

THE ILKHANIDS, THE TIMURIDS AND THE KHANATES

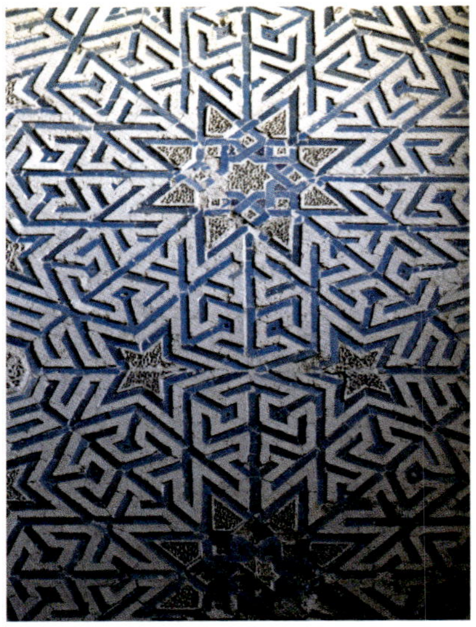

Mongol expansion should be seen in the context of the periodic waves of migration which, setting out from the uncharted Uralo-Altaic region, swept down with irregular frequency and catastrophic effect onto the adjacent lands, at times reaching the shores of the Mediterranean. Led by Genghis Khan (Chinggis Khaan) and brushing aside entire peoples in their wake, the Mongols started by invading the Chinese Empire. Then, in 1219, unwisely provoked by the shah of the Khwarizm (Khorezm), they moved westwards, crushing all resistance and leaving in their wake a trail of death and devastation which has become the stuff of legend. On the death of Genghis Khan in 1227 the empire was split between his sons. They continued his conquests, ousting the Seljuqs in Anatolia and occupying the region of Syria and Mesopotamia, only to be finally halted by the Mamluks in 1260. On the conquest of Baghdad and the demise of the universal caliphate (1258), Iran and Iraq became provinces in an immense Asian empire with a capital (from 1264) located at Khanbaliq (Beijing) and divided in the following manner: the Russian steppes to the Golden Horde (the Jochi khanate); Transoxiana and part of Turkestan to the Chagatai; China to the Great Khan; and Persia and Anatolia to the Ilkhan.

The era of Mongol peace was marked by cultural splendour and coincided with an upsurge in the trade down the various branches of the Silk Road, along which merchandise could now be transported with unprecedented levels of security. This state of affairs also made it possible for adventurous Europeans to travel to the Far East, attracted by a thirst for knowledge, or by the desire to evangelize, to trade or to strengthen alliances against the Turks. The most famous traveller was of course Marco Polo, who left Venice in 1275 and returned in 1292 with an extraordinary storehouse of recollections later compiled into the *Milione.*

After 1256, with the consolidation of the Ilkhanid regime in Persia, there was a return to the pomp of Turkish-Persian civilization; around 1300, the conquerors embraced Islam. The Mongol state was founded on military might piloted by an aristocracy invested with limitless power, to all intents and purposes masters of the world and more than prepared to carve it up among their epigones. The administration however remained in the hands of local notables supported by the urban aristocracy, merchants and the Persian *ulama,* whose role in assuaging the shock incurred by the arrival of new masters often proved decisive.

Relatively few in number and lacking a civilization whose models they might impose, the Mongols thus assimilated Islam and absorbed Persian culture, refreshing it with the cool wind of innovation. Reconstruction in the countries they had subdued progressed apace with spectacular results. Both architectural typology and construction techniques, however, remained stamped by their Persian and Seljuq predecessors since the conquerors, accustomed to living in tents out in the open, possessed no real building tradition of their own. Imbibing the culture of their subject populations, the Mongol princes – with unbounded ambition and disposing of immense financial means – exceeded their forerunners in both grandeur and magnificence. Overwhelming their subjects on their own lands, they expressed their new position in conspicuous statements of dominance. The scale of their edifices was truly gigantic: now centred on the dome, buildings bristled with towers, ceramics covered larger and larger surfaces in ever more dazzling colours, while the façades were

Mausoleum of Oldjetu
Detail of the interior decoration
1313–1316
Painted stucco
Sultaniye, Iran

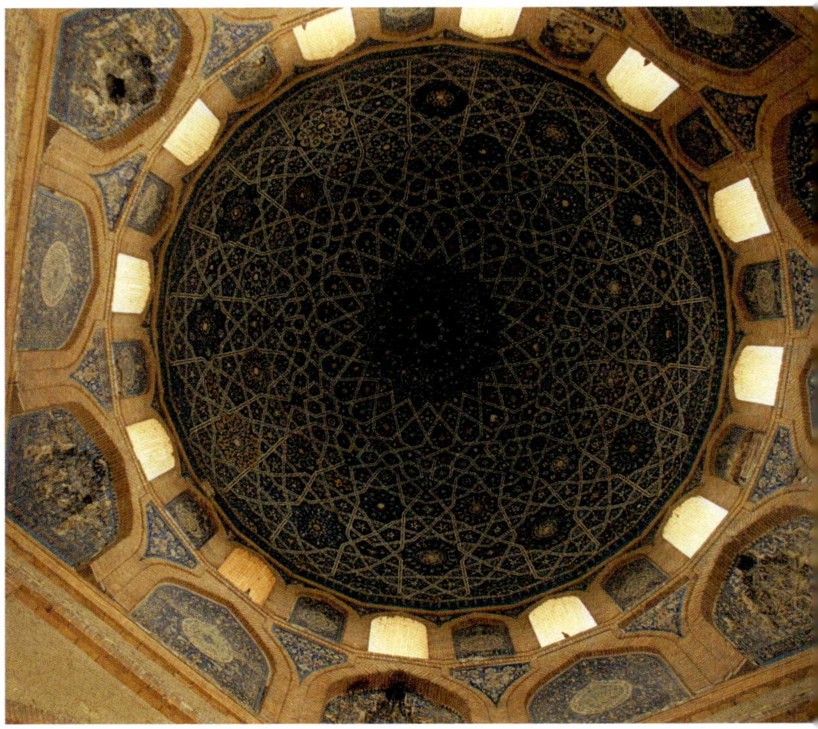

Mausoleum of Turabeg Khanum
Dome
c. 1370
Gurganj (Urgench), Turkmenistan

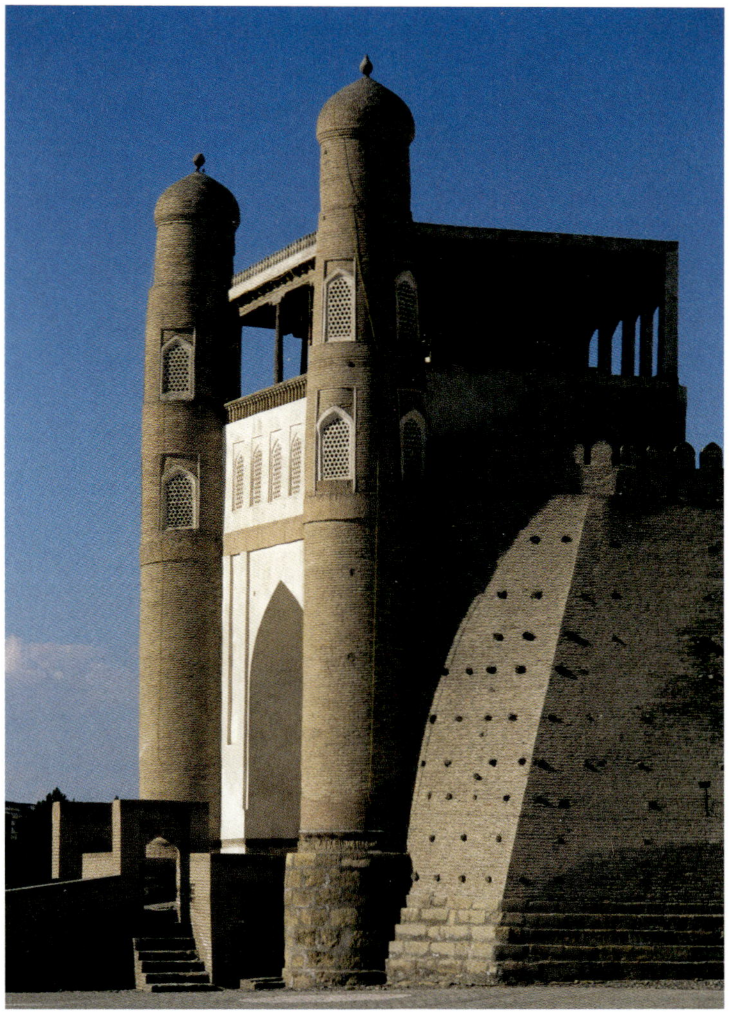

Gate of the Ark ('citadel')
1742
Bukhara, Uzbekistan

enlivened with arched panels of elegant slenderness. Underwritten with a regal indifference to cost, each enterprise was conducted with amazing energy and limitless enthusiasm. The khan Hülagü, who ordered entire cities laid waste in the initial fury of conquest to be rebuilt later, erected a luxury palace and a Buddhist temple in Khoy and, around 1260, financed the celebrated observatory of Maragheh, a veritable hotbed for the science of astronomy. The new city of Sham – founded at the onset of the fourteenth century but completely destroyed today – was celebrated at the time for its variety, planning and magnificence, to the point of being compared with the legendary Persepolis. Yet, incredible though it may seem, even this extraordinary complex, with its monasteries, madrasahs, hospital, library, philosophy academy, administrative buildings, astronomical observatory and imperial residences laid out within a network of elegant arcaded streets and refreshing gardens, was to be outdone just a few years later by the still more splendid university town of Tabriz. Calligraphy, miniatures, products of the loom, goldworking and tableware now attained unheard-of levels of opulence. In 1336, however, the Ilkhanid regime fissured into rival principalities, each pursuing their predecessor's style with spectacular lavishness. But that same year, not far from Samarkand, saw the birth of the Turkmen Mongol Timur Leng (or Lenk; that is, Tamburlaine). Profiting from the anarchy and internal strife between the Mongol khan and the Turkic emirs, Timur was soon taking the lead in a seditious movement that opposed two parties in the form of two ethnic groups, the urbanized and nomadic worlds, Islam and the shamans. Around 1370, he seized Transoxiana and, having established a base at Samarkand, had himself crowned khan. Bolstered by support from the local Muslim élites, the Sufis, as well as both the travelling and settled populations, he began to subject his khanate neighbours to an incessant and terrifyingly bloodthirsty onslaught. Over a murderous campaign lasting some thirty years he seized the entire Chagatai Khanate, and thence Iran, Mesopotamia, Armenia, the Caucasus, eastern Anatolia, the Khanate of the Golden Horde, and Asia Minor. In 1398 came the turn of northern India, with the massacre in Delhi; in 1401, he wrested Syria from the Mamluks, plundered Damascus and put the population of Baghdad to the sword. In 1402, he inflicted a crushing defeat on the Ottoman sultan Bayazid (Bazajet) II, unwittingly, if temporarily, saving Constantinople.

Transoxiana therefore became the heartland of an immense empire. Yet again however, an era drenched in blood was succeeded by an age of splendour for every field of expression and realm of human thought. Obsessed by the desire to bequeath a testimony worthy of his greatness, Timur was devoured by a thirst for the most precious objects and for having the finest artists at his disposal: craftsmen, artists, painters, architects, calligraphers, men of letters and poets from every conquered country were dispatched (sometimes frogmarched) to Samarkand, which became a city of burgeoning, often overbearing domes.

At Timur's death in 1405, his immense kingdom was split between his sons and princes who continued the khan's munificent patronage with less grandiloquence but greater coherence. The dazzling development of Timurid architecture, with its penchant for the colossal, had been nourished by Mongol conceptions and had all but got the better of the measured and serene balance of a previous era founded on an organic approach and equilibrium between structural members. The generations that came in the wake of Timur pruned this exuberance and reverted to a concern with contrasts in proportion; their achievements, particularly in the field of the miniature, are unsurpassed in any age.

In 1500, the Uzbek Shaybanids unseated the Timurids, shaking up the entire fabric of Central Asia. The age now witnessed the birth of local principalities as well as a backlash from Persian nationalism. Under the Shaybanids, Transoxiana experienced a period of notable prosperity and a concomitant artistic flowering (though without much genuine innovation), documented in opulent textiles, remarkable miniatures, and above all in huge architectural monuments inspired by their Timurid forerunners. The Uzbek takeover coincided with a decline in caravan traffic along the Silk Road following the discovery of the sea route to India (1498). Subsequently three noteworthy khanates at Khiva, Bukhara and Kokand were formed: constantly rehashing the glories of their predecessors in a provincial idiom, these hung on, increasingly isolated and ignored by time, until the Russian conquest.

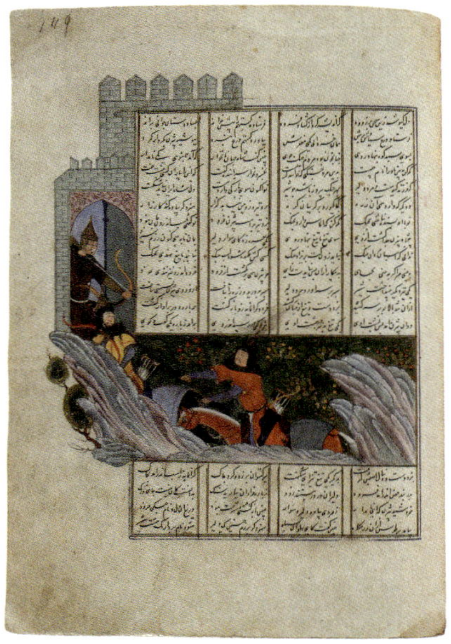

Episode from the Shahnameh (Book of the King) by Firdusi (11th century)
c. 1440–1450
Russian Academy of Sciences, St Petersburg

Funerary complex of Shaykh Abd al-Samad Mausoleum
1307
Natanz, Iran

The complex of Natanz, including a monastery with an inn for pilgrims in an annexe built around the burial-place, has nearly completely vanished, but one of the finest façades in all Persia survives with a well-proportioned minaret counterbalancing the tower tomb of Shaykh Abd al-Samad. Although of undemonstrative dimensions, the mausoleum possesses a strong personality and, thanks to its equilibrium between quietude and dynamism, exudes a serene sense of mystic spirituality. The monument is crowned by an octagonal pyramid dotted about with triangular sections of sky-blue glazed brick arranged in zigzag bands and chevrons, foreshadowed by the lighter coloured pattern in *bannai* characters on the drum: the corporeal, earthy hue of the structure is thus tempered by the blue above, as if accompanying the ascension of the spirit of the deceased as it leaves the body to rise to paradise.
Although here the decorative exuberance typical of the Ilkhanids remains latent, this exquisite transitional work leaves room for a lyrical, if expiring, exhalation.

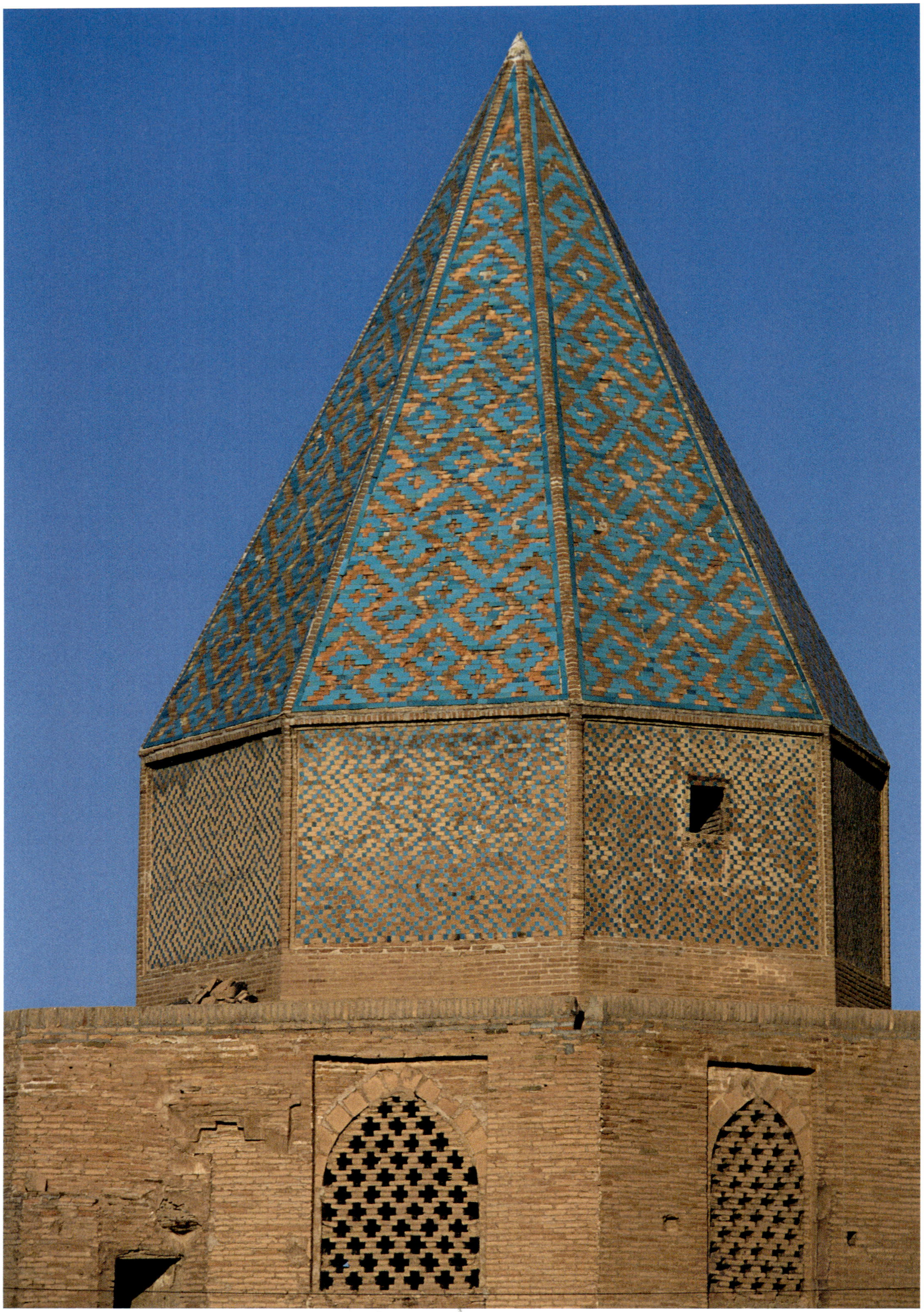

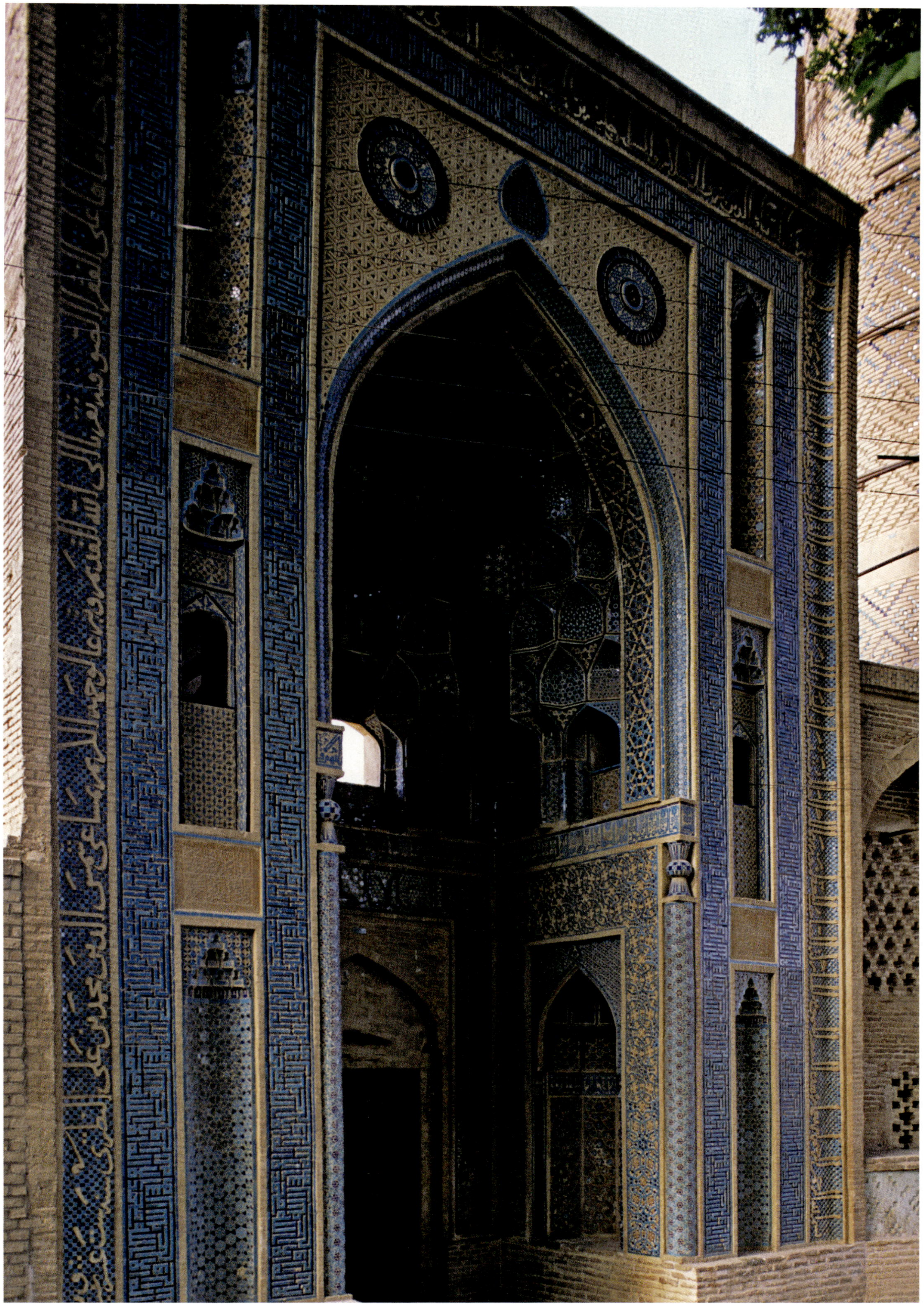

Funerary complex of Shaykh Abd al-Samad Façade with entryway
1307
Natanz, Iran

Within the *iwan,* slender angle colonnettes support an inscription in stucco on which rises a vibrant *muqarnas* vault with sectors decorated in a mosaic of delicate geometry. On an earth-coloured ground, white, sky- and midnight-blue tesserae accompany mouldings arranged in tiers, before plunging into a central rose generated by intersecting hexagons and triangles. This *khanaqah* is one of the finest constructions of the epoch for its energy and the variety of the decorative schemas it deploys in what is a relatively restricted space, as well as for the intensity and the clarity of the deep turquoise of the enamelled ceramics. The arch framing the portal is lofty and gracious, the spandrels adorned with large-sized discs, and the niche closed by *muqarnas* of delicate blue tones conveys a sensation of peace and elevation. The façade is emblazoned with an interlace pattern in place of the more customary floral repertory.

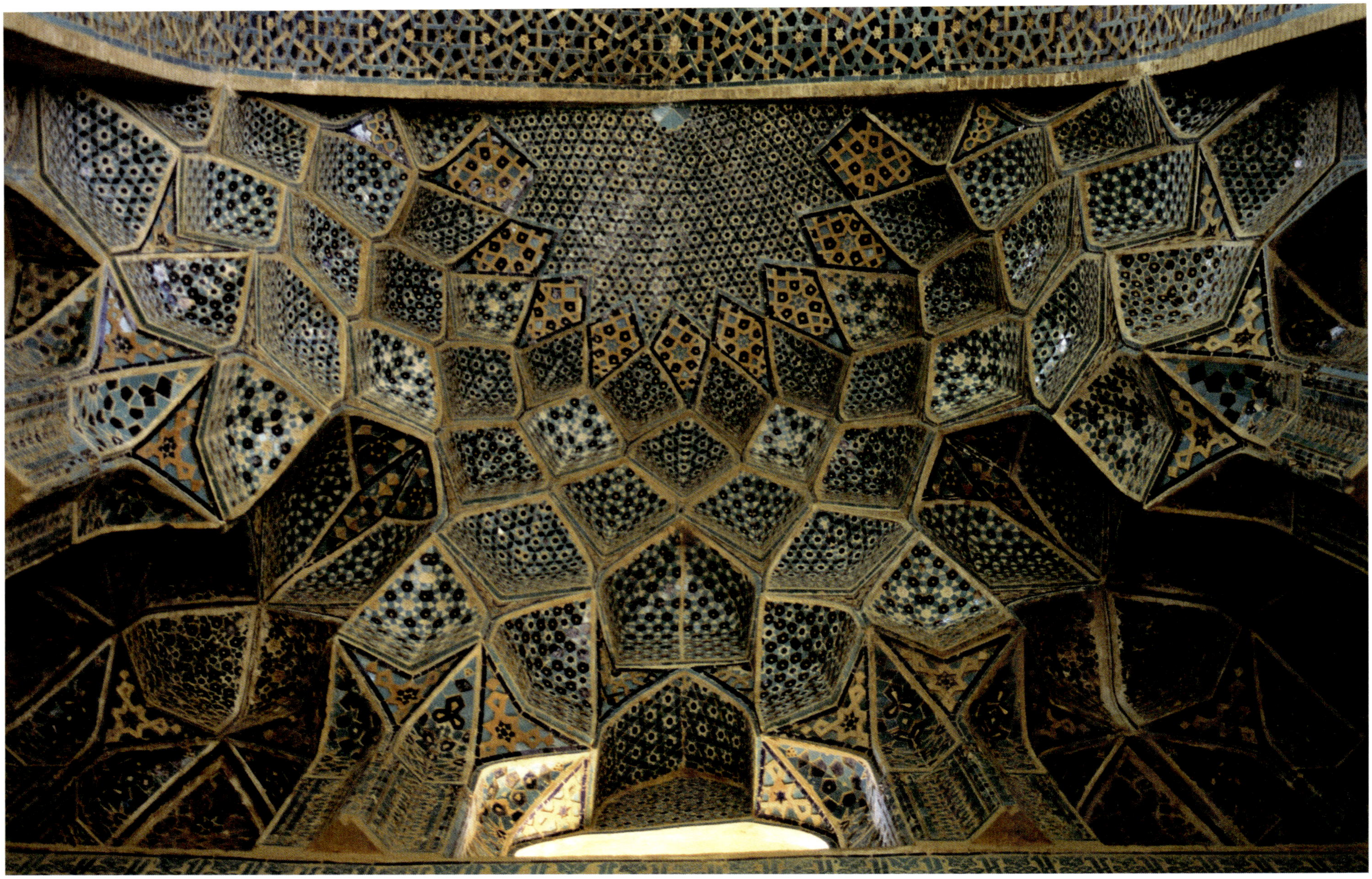

Funerary complex of Shaykh Abd al-Samad
Vault over the entrance
1307
Natanz, Iran

For the delicacy and equilibrium with which the decorative components are arranged, the façade of this *khanaqah* has been justly compared to a leaf of miniatures whose enchanted atmosphere it seems to share. The entrance, added after the other constructions had already been built with the intention of making the composition more harmonious, represents a high-point in a particular episode of Persian architecture and decoration that struck a happy balance between the sinewy statements of the Seljuq period and the sumptuous and at times excessive pomp to the taste of Ilkhanid rulers.
The gate is ensconced into an *iwan* topped by a monumental *pishtaq* far taller than the building's perimeter wall, opening almost to the summit of a towering and broad pointed arch framed by a series of bands in which – in brick and ceramic – stretches of calligraphy alternate with niches in gradations of blue all arranged with steadiness and measure. Once again, the geometrical modules necessary for the realization of the *muqarnas* vaulting are translated into an image of refreshing lyricism.

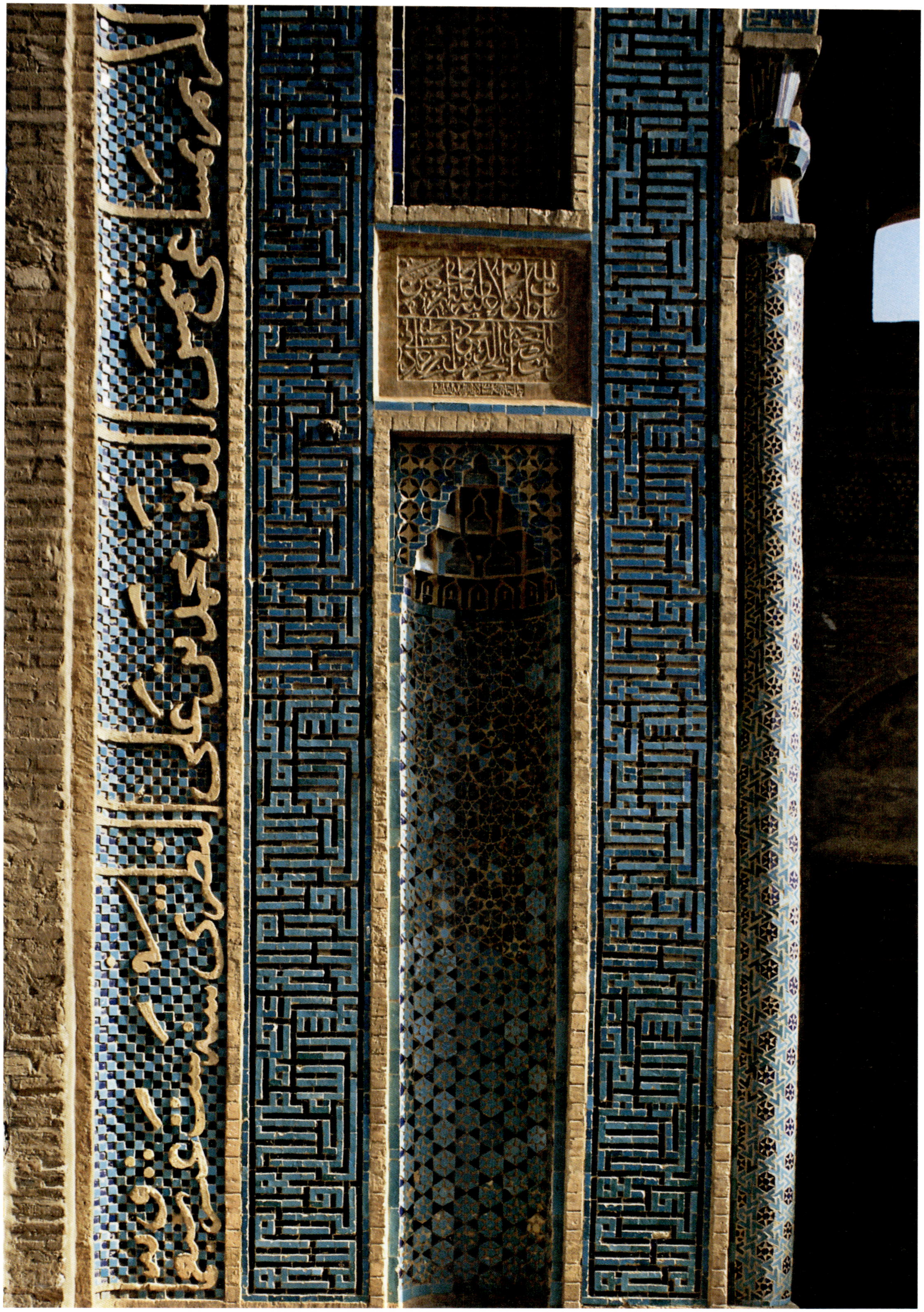

Funerary complex of Shaykh Abd al-Samad Façade with entryway
1307
Natanz, Iran

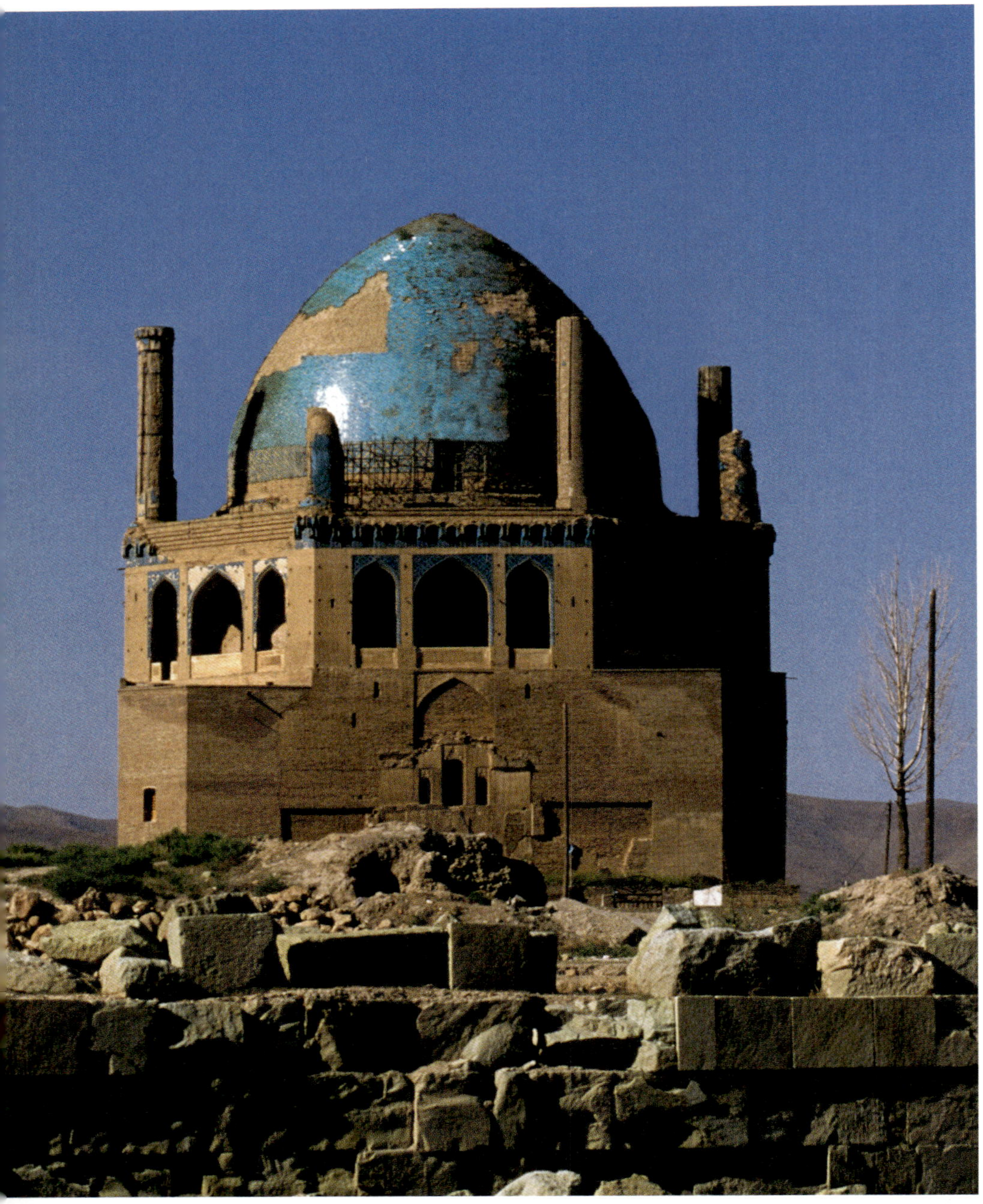

Mausoleum of Oldjetu
External arcade
1305–1313
Sultaniye, Iran

The twenty-four vaults of the gallery outside introduce a wonderfully rich array of motifs in brick and stucco whose lively red, yellow, dark-green and white tonalities present geometrical patterns set with delicate plant motifs and bosses enhanced by some glorious calligraphy. Numerous panels betray close affinities with contemporary miniatures, supporting the hypothesis that the Ilkhanids tended to employ similar models regardless of scale. Armature and ornament here seem inextricably interdependent: the majestic scale, harmonious proportions, richly sparkling colours and painstaking decor fuse into a placid equilibrium, and yet remain sustained by latent inner energy.

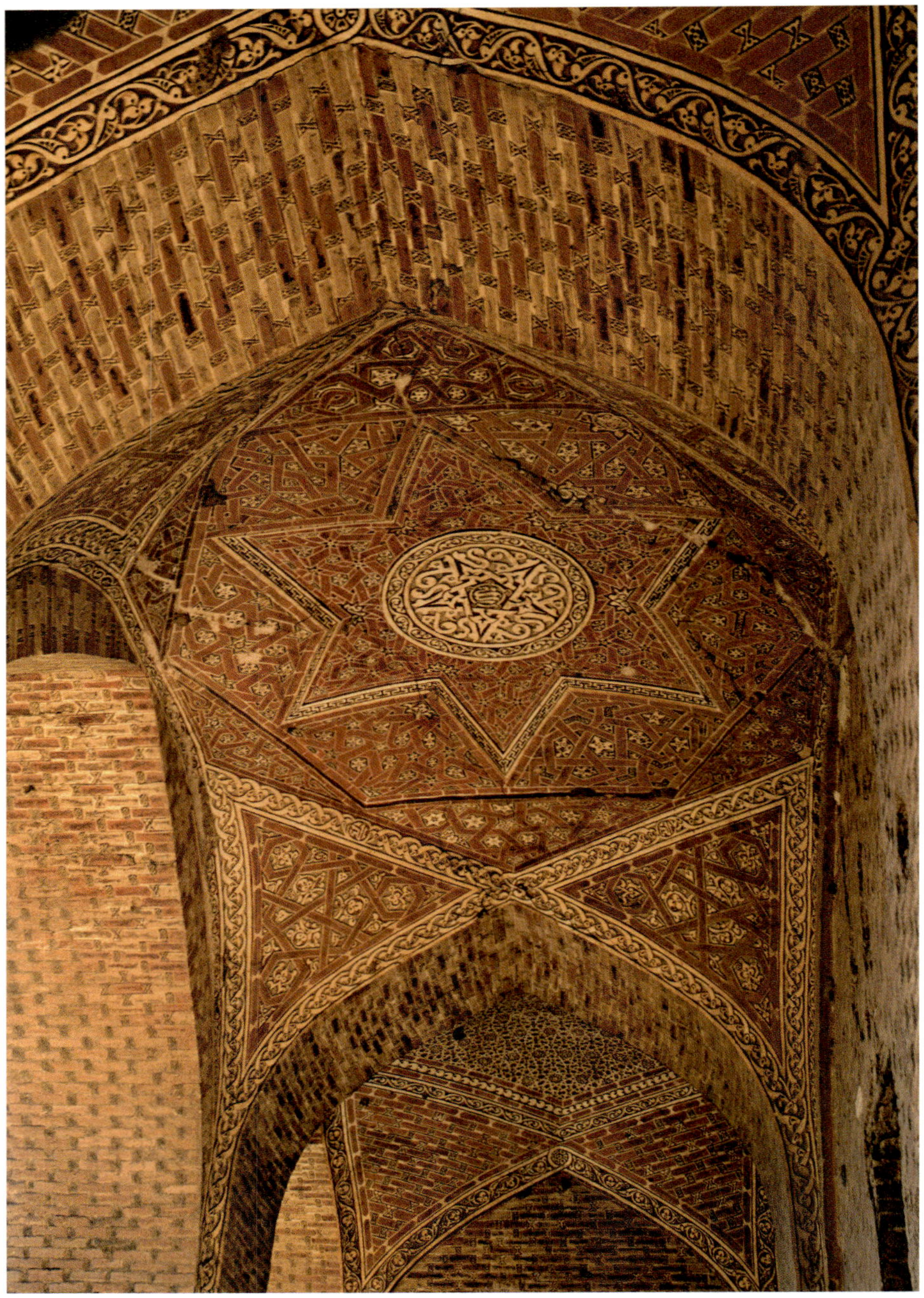

Mausoleum of Oldjetu
1305–1313
Sultaniye, Iran

In 1305 Oldjetu built a third and still more spectacular city as a capital for the empire which has long since crumbled into dust: Sultaniye, dominated by the unruffled but superb celestial grandeur of the dome of his mausoleum. This masterpiece of the Ilkhanid era is quite simply one of most dazzling expressions of architecture in all Persia. The gigantic pile of octagonal plan is capped by a cupola of mildly ogival shape, soaring up more than fifty metres, which blends a sense of universal peace with an expression of man's insatiable appetite for power. The wonderful original tiling (now being replaced by mediocre industrially manufactured pieces) ranged from turquoise to aquamarine. It is no less a masterstroke from the point of view of architectonic structure: mass and thrust are concentrated at a small number of points and the grandiose dome supports itself without the aid of buttressing, banking or pinnacles, the function of the eight small minarets being solely ornamental.

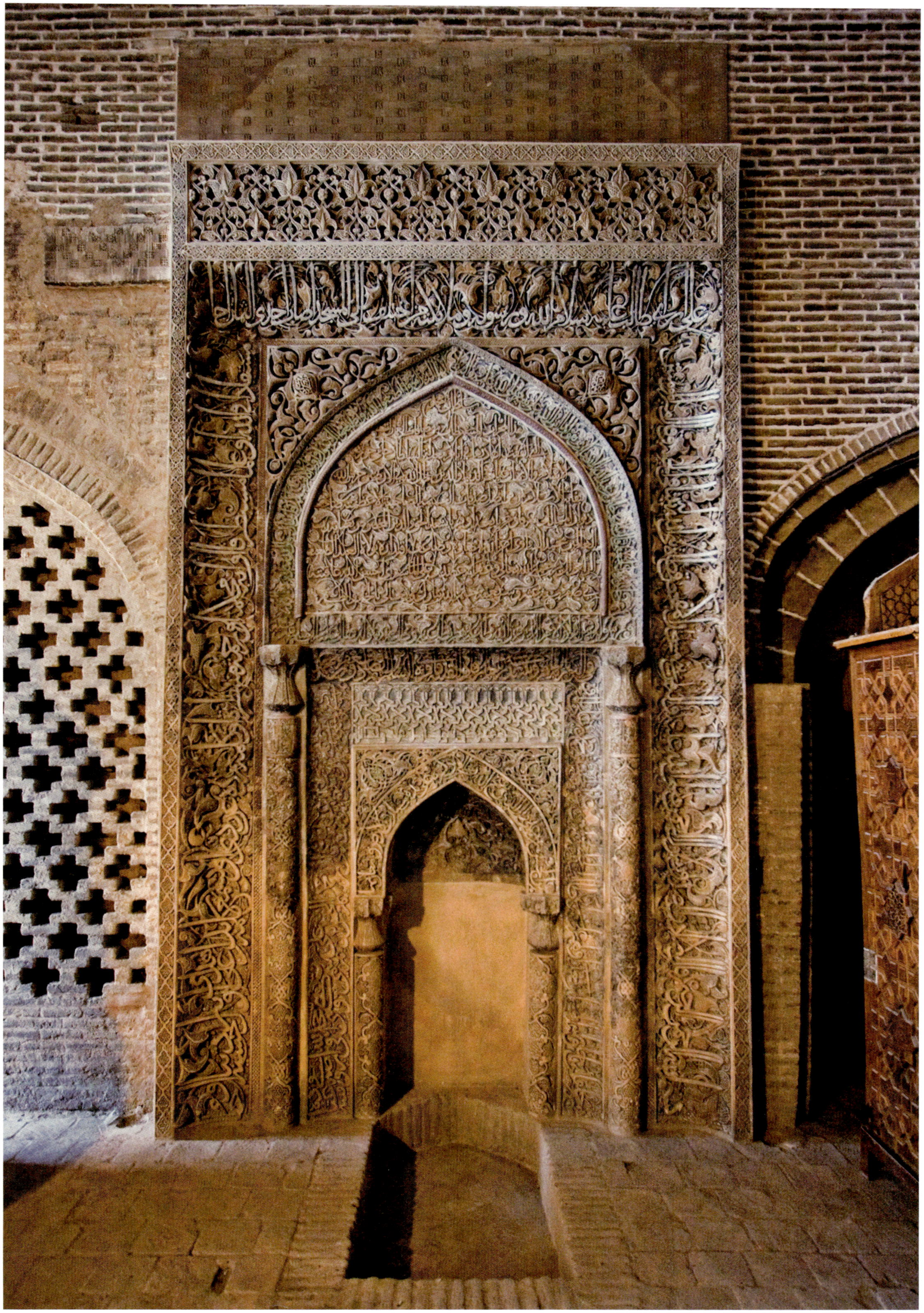

Friday mosque of Oldjetu
Mihrab
1310
Isfahan, Iran

In 1310 Oldjetu added a new prayer hall to the Friday mosque at Isfahan. Based on Seljuq precedents, its *mihrab* intensifies a barely controlled primordial energy here manifested by swirling plant motifs. The usual prototype, a succession of concentric niches set within a rectangular frame, is not dissolved but redeployed in channelling a bubbling formal effusion in which each zone conforms to a distinct decorative design. The spectacular *thulth* inscription in the architrave, in which prayers are addressed to the twelve imams of the Shia tradition, was executed by Haydar, one of the most esteemed calligraphers of the era.

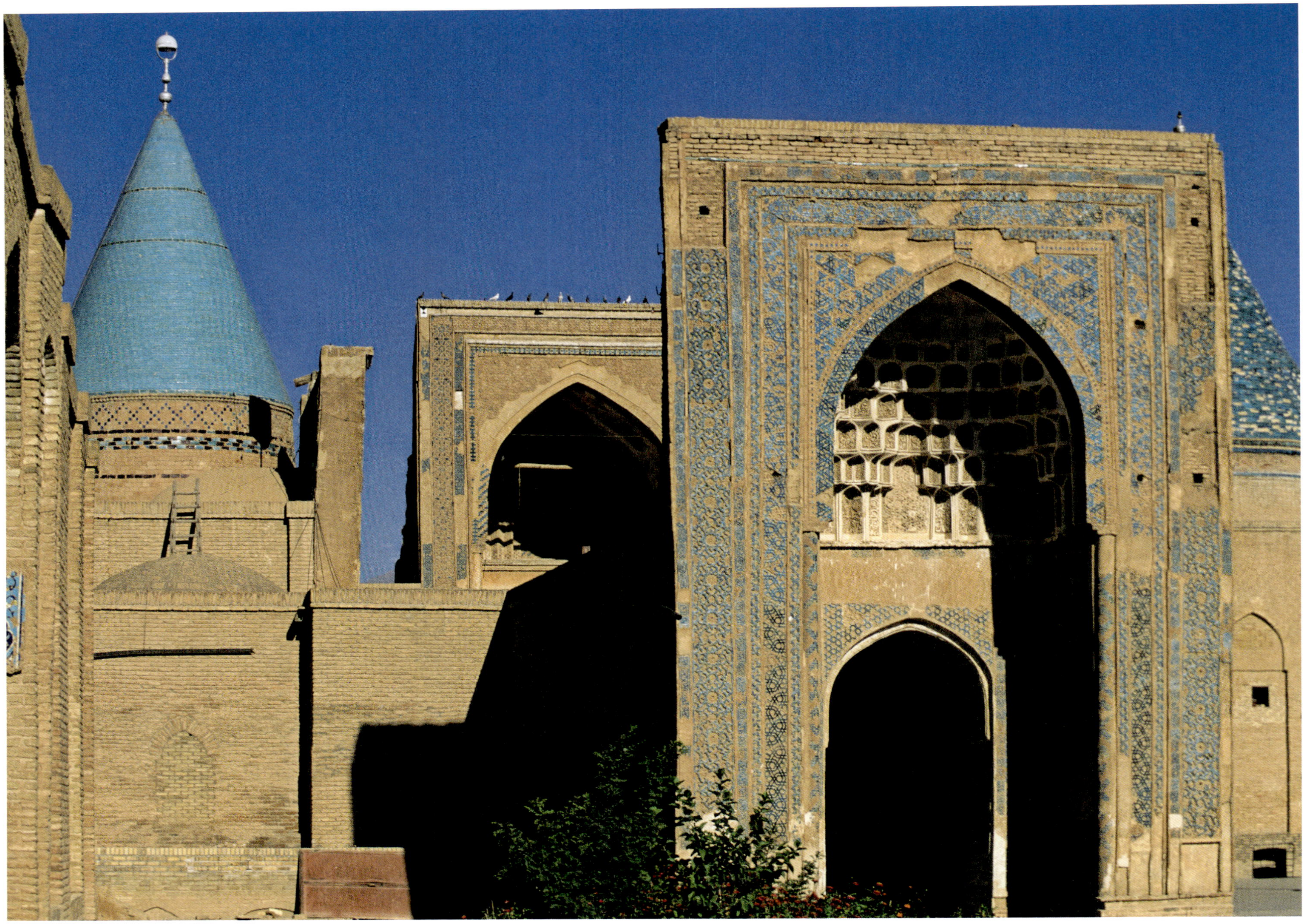

Complex of Shaykh Bayazid
12th–14th centuries
Bastam, Iran

This famous Seljuq sanctuary too was redeveloped by Oldjetu at the beginning of the fourteenth century. Ilkhanid architecture makes use of the formal models and technical solutions adumbrated by the Great Seljuqs, but with, if possible, even greater opulence and with apparently unexampled expressive maturity. The shift between these two idioms occurred however by degrees, like a slow acceleration within identical formal codes. In the absence of documents allowing for firm dating, therefore, stylistic analysis alone is often insufficient to draw definitive conclusions. Thus, in this complex it is possible – but far from established – that the revamped gateways, minarets, and cupolas do date back to the age of Oldjetu. However, the new ceramic decoration can be securely ascribed to him: thanks to some notable technical advances, it dazzles the eye with its extraordinary intensity. The age of vast but rugged volumes of bare brick has come to an end. The gravitas of the Seljuqs, embodied in the conception of the edifice as an 'empty' shell to be infused with spirituality, has slowly been replaced by explosive magnificence.

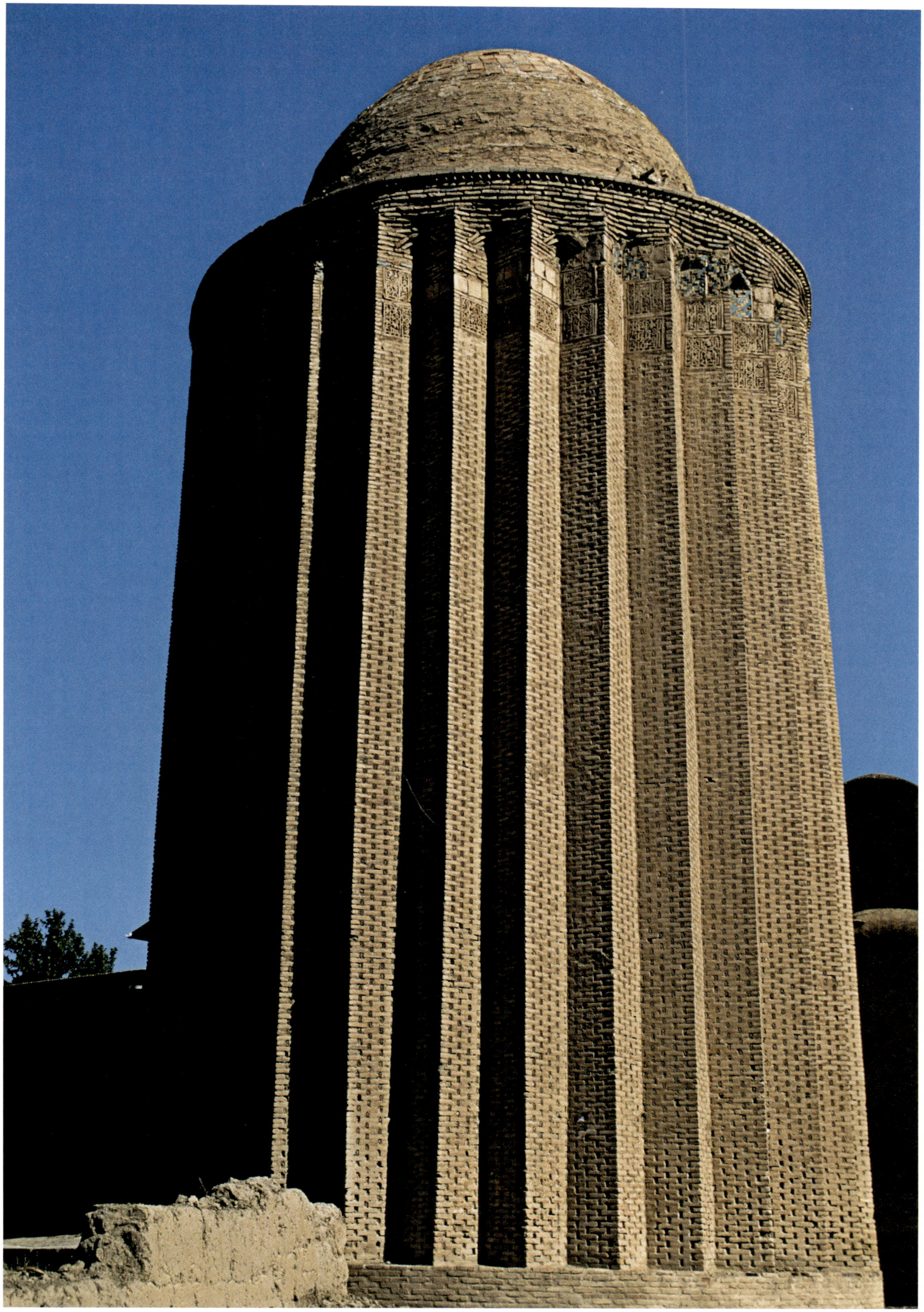

Mausoleum of the Shaykh Bayazid
1313
Bastam, Iran

Ilkhanid architecture also differs from its predecessors in that chiaroscuro effects are often pursued to the detriment of the sense for solid volume which constituted one of its erstwhile ground rules. A masterful example of this tendency can be seen at the tomb tower of Bayazid, dedicated by Oldjetu to his young son, in the glorious complex of Bastam, rebuilt around much the same time. The archetype is clearly identifiable in monuments such as the Gunbad-e Qabus, but here virile, visionary rigour is replaced by a less stereometric and concise solution that diffracts the sunlight over serried ranks of ribs, shimmering over its surface. The original covering, most probably of conical form, has long since been dismantled: the crown of the tower seen today is in fact the shell of the cupola capping the hollow cylinder inside.

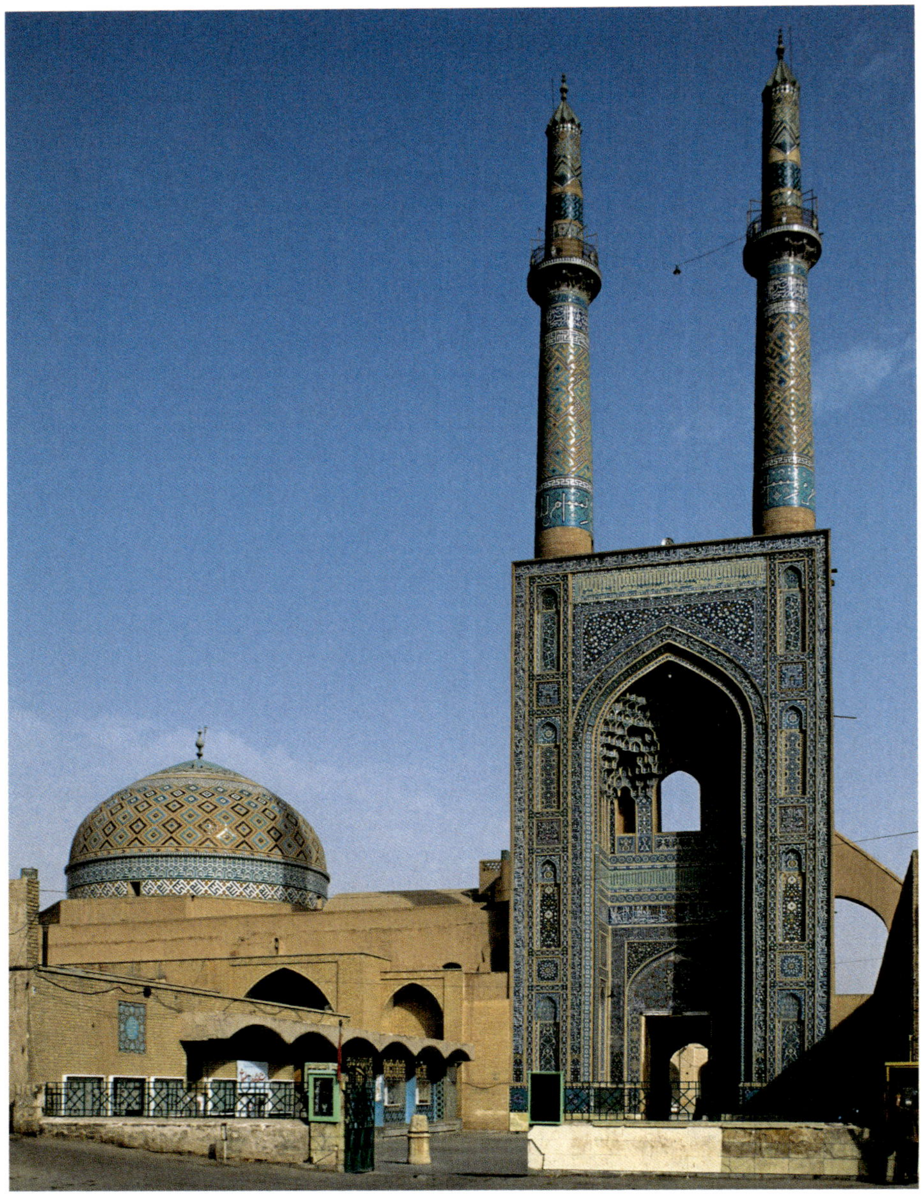

Friday mosque
1325–1365
Yazd, Iran

In the Ilkhanid era, the practice of flanking the *pishtaq* with a duet of minarets – their shafts adorned with twist or lozenge motifs in ceramic and with invocations to Allah, the caliphs or the prophets repeated *ad infinitum* in *bannai* script – became widely accepted for various building typologies. Realized during the Mozaffarid dynasty, the portal of the Friday mosque in Yazd is the most spectacular of its time. The breathtaking and narrow façade is lined entirely with some of the finest ceramic mosaics of the era, while the minarets are simply the tallest in the country. This unheralded emphasis on the vertical of itself constitutes a notable break with tradition.

Friday mosque
Detail of a decorative panel
1325–1365
Yazd, Iran

The Mozaffarids liked to cover vast surfaces using the *mo'arraq* mosaic technique, in which plain colour tiles are cut up, arranged into designs, and then assembled into panels of unequalled chromatic intensity, characterized by crisply delineated and sinuous arabesques accompanied by floral motifs and spirals. The time-honoured palette of turquoise, blue, and black and white is now augmented by new tonalities: green, aubergine, a ruddy black and a golden yellow, allowing for a range of hues closer to those of nature and thus to the topos of a garden covered in plants and flowers. More humane, this colour scheme is less abstractly lyrical compared to its predecessors which were confined to turquoise and blue.

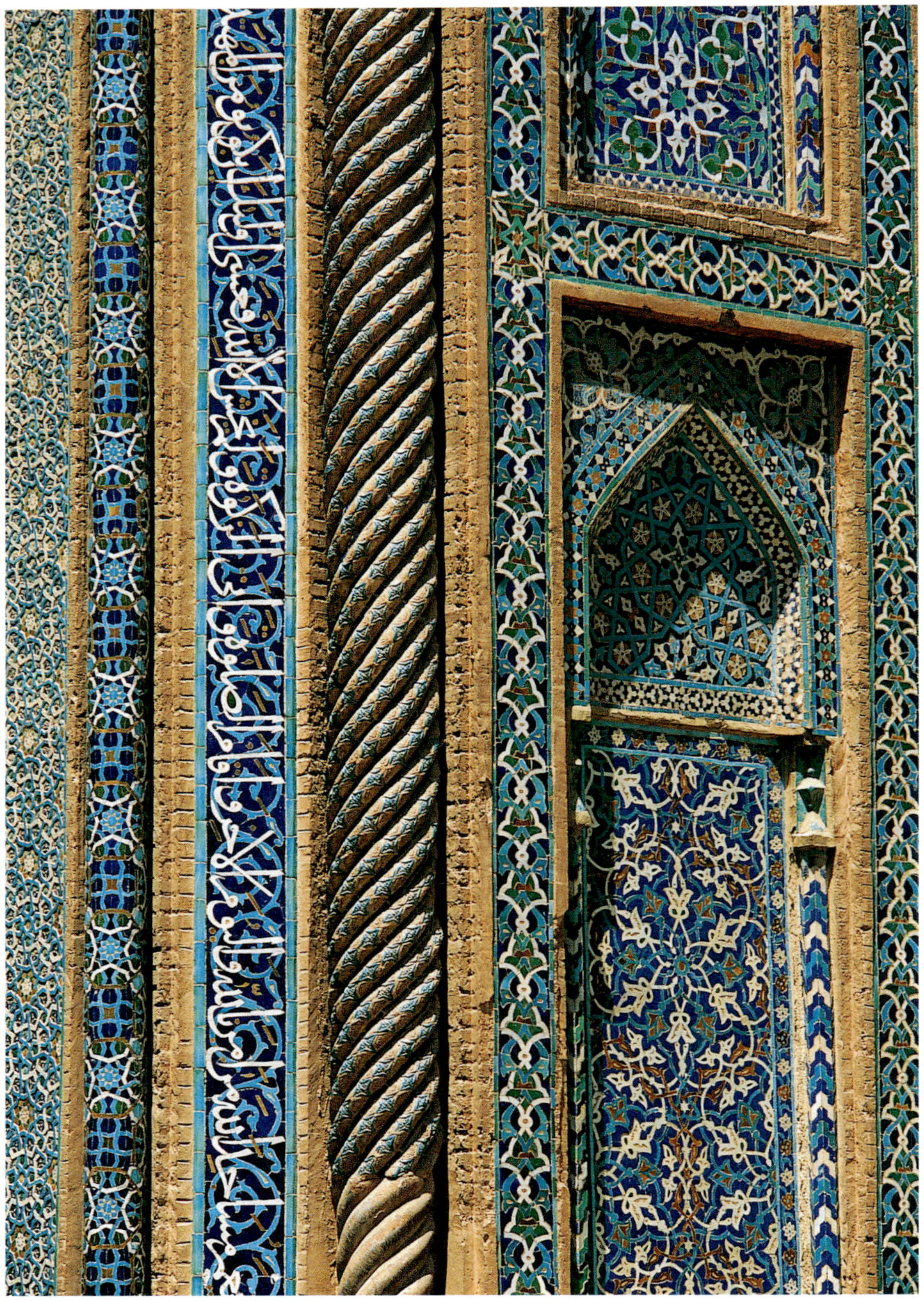

Friday mosque
Detail of the entrance
Begun in 1349
Kerman, Iran

The Ilkhanids adored luxuriance in all its guises and, as well as inflating their structures to vast size, they saturated every inch of surface with ornamental motifs. Overrunning the Seljuq spirit of austerity with a potent, light-filled phantasmagoria shot through with striking chromatic contrasts, their creations betray their unusual receptivity to earthly beauty: this 'intellectual' turning-point is as it were analogous to the marginally earlier shift from Romanesque to Gothic in European art. The more austere artistic expressions of previous centuries, in spite of their undeniable and authentic ability to resonate deeply in the human spirit, can appear disembodied and limited in comparison with the most successful monuments of the fourteenth century. Pageantry and magnificence – worthy and understandable aims in architecture – find their most convincing outlet among the Mongols and their successors. Thanks to their sheer scale and to a fathomless harmony of composition, as well as to insuperable qualities in a decoration that remains formidably inventive, luminous in the use of materials and flawless in execution, their works however never degenerate into the ostentatious reiteration of wealth and power.

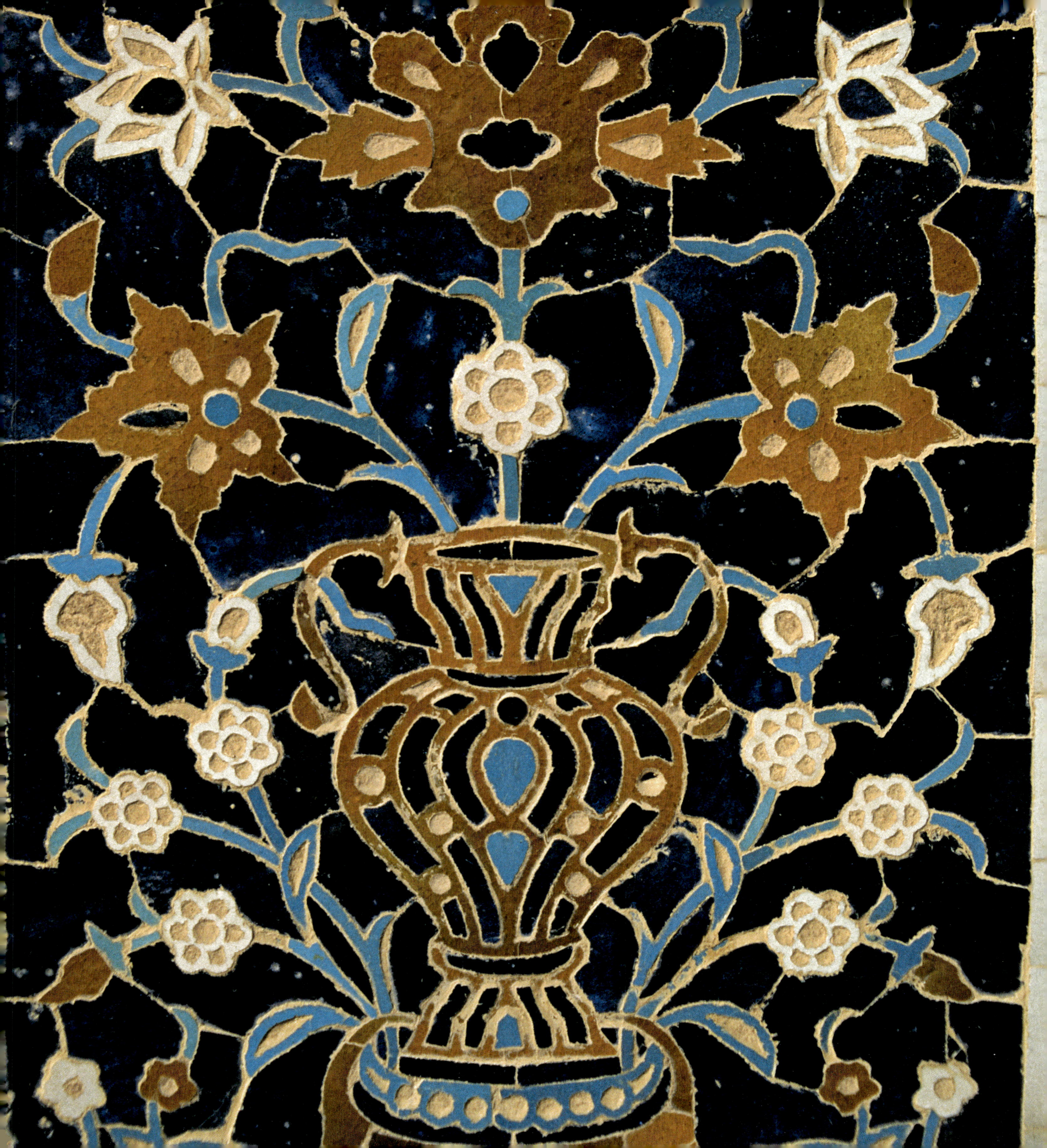

Fragment of a cloth
c. 1250
Cleveland Museum of Art

The handful of surviving scraps of textile from the period offer but a pale reflection of what was surely one of the foremost artistic manifestations of the time – as well as one of the most profitable from the economic point of view. In fact, numerous sources cite 'Tartar cloths' in silk woven with gold thread as possessions of the greatest value. These gold brocade materials were made with the utmost mastery of technique in workshops set up by Genghis Khan in Turkistan and the Khorasan. Field and design are woven as one and the pattern emerges from against the woven silk ground beneath.
The roundels in the Cleveland fragment feature the classic motif of twisting affronted winged lions, while the interstices play host to pairs of gryphons, both typical subjects taken from the Sassanid repertory. The cloud-like motifs in the background and the dragon's heads terminating the manes and tails, however, probably derive from Chinese art. To judge by the peerless quality of this piece it was probably destined for the court.

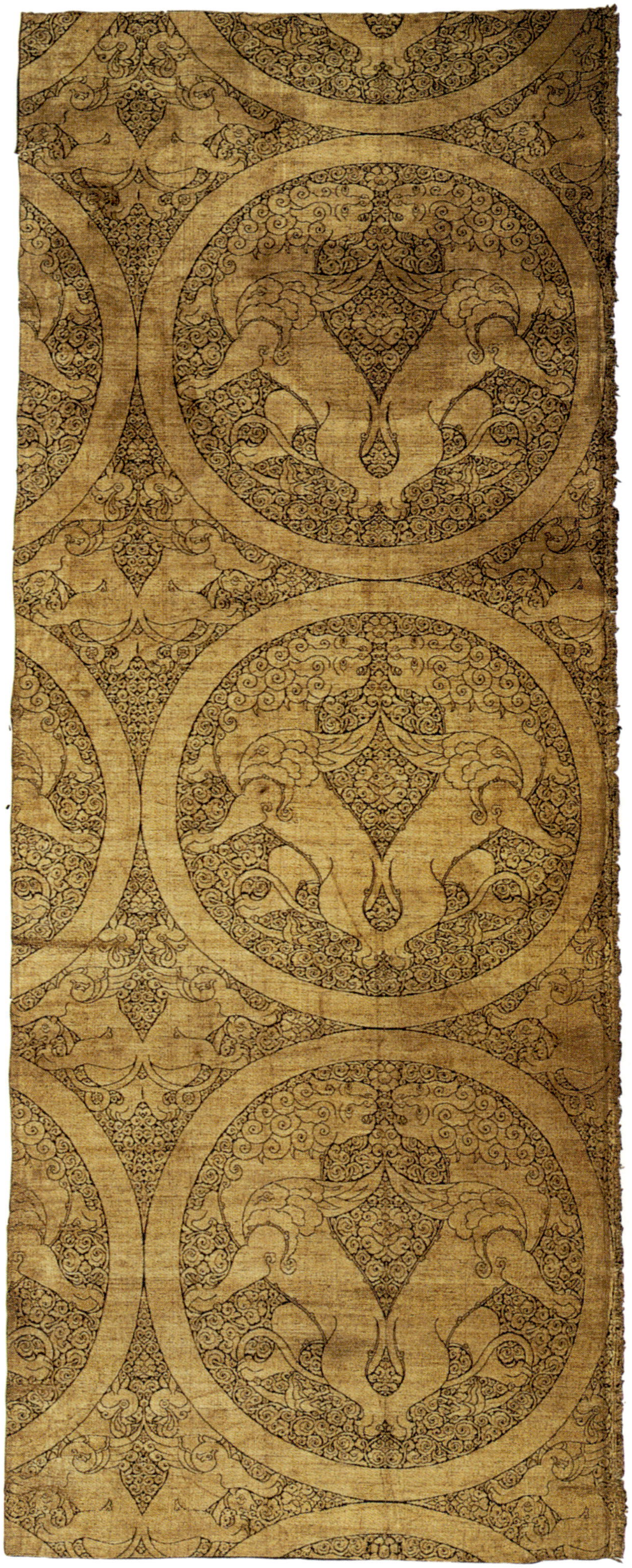

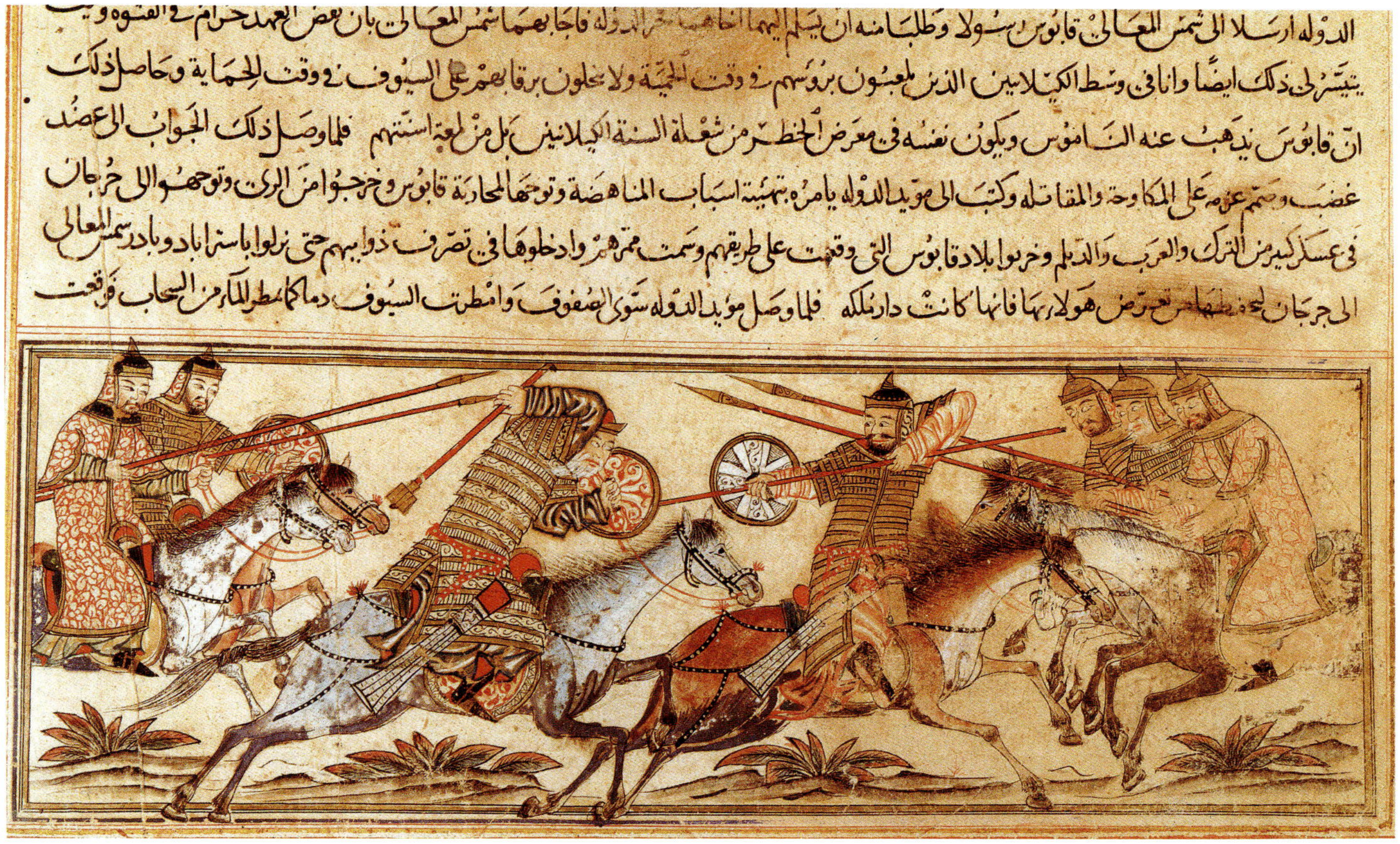

The Mongols Conquer Baghdad
Early 14th century
Staatsbibliothek, Berlin

In the field of the book too the Mongols betrayed their predilection for large dimensions. Each piece was conceived as a complete work of art in every respect: the accuracy of the transcription, the intricacy of the decoration, the wealth of illustration and the quality of the binding. Books treating of contemporary events played a role of prime importance, their production reaching an apogee in the early fifteenth century in parallel with an upsurge in building activity that together celebrated the 'normalization' and integration of the new dominant class.
The illustration shows Mongol forces, some banging a drum and others firing arrows, camped outside the city walls beside a catapult. The city, with its double ring of walls protected by a moat, is depicted in a kind of bird's-eye view. Delineated with calligraphic aplomb, a ship bobs up and down in the water over which a floating bridge has been thrown. Meanwhile two women gaze down from a window. Notwithstanding the theme, the picture resembles a genre scene devoid of drama.

Skirmish between Mongol Horsemen and Seljuqs
Early 14th century
(from the *Jami al-Tawarikh* or 'Compendium of Chronicles', by Rashid to-Din, 1247–1318)
University Library Edinburgh

The Ilkhanids had immense esteem for books. Masterfully penned and illustrated, they were considered priceless objects in themselves and were seen as useful vehicles for publicizing the deeds of the dynasty. The bibliophilic arts thus experienced a meteoric rise that saw the elaboration of six cursive scripts by the great Yaqut al-Mustasimi (died 1298), known as 'the qibla of the scribes', as well as impressive formats, elegant bindings and superb miniatures that all attained a *nec plus ultra. The History of the World Conqueror* by al-Juwayni (1226–1283) and the magnificently illustrated and calligraphied *Compendium of World History* by the vizier of Tabriz, Rashid al-Din (a Persian Jewish convert to Islam, 1247–1318), describes the victories of the Mongols in a perspective presenting them as destined to rule the world – thereby justifying the events of the time in the eyes of their contemporaries and posterity.

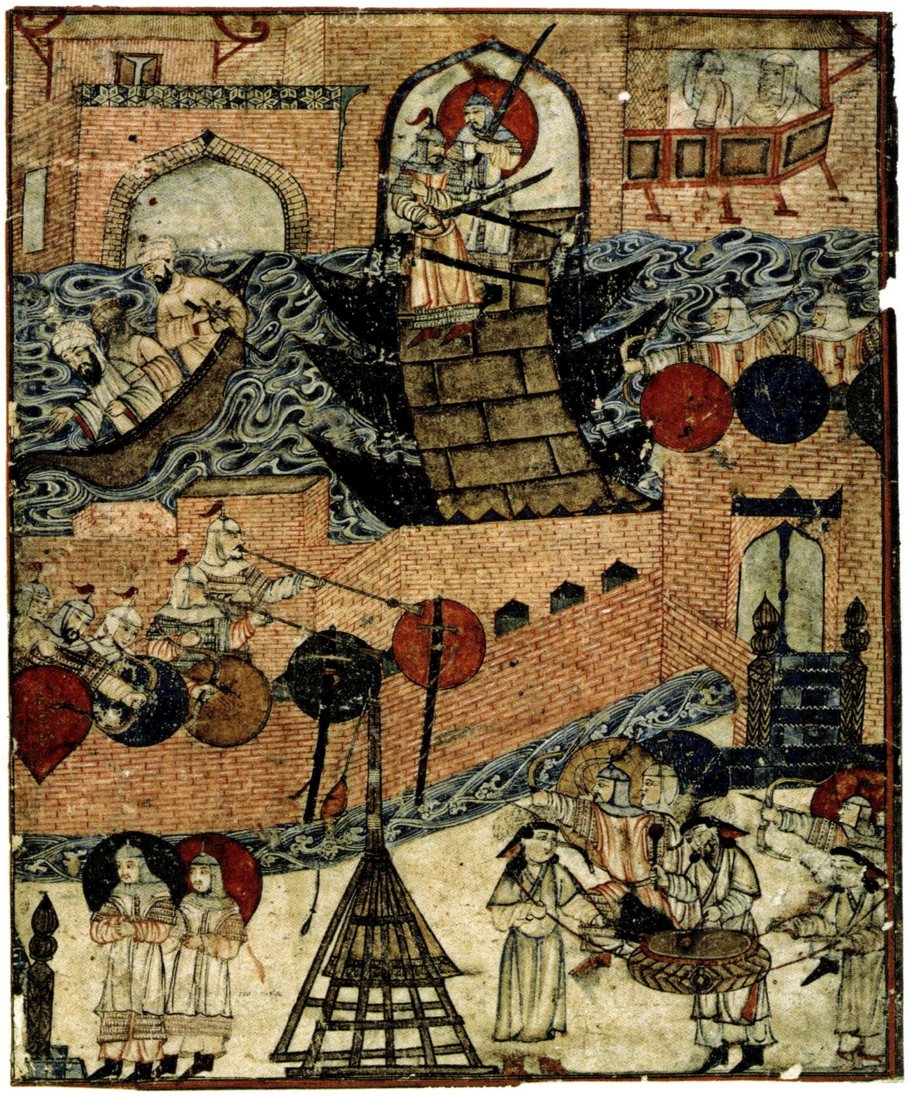

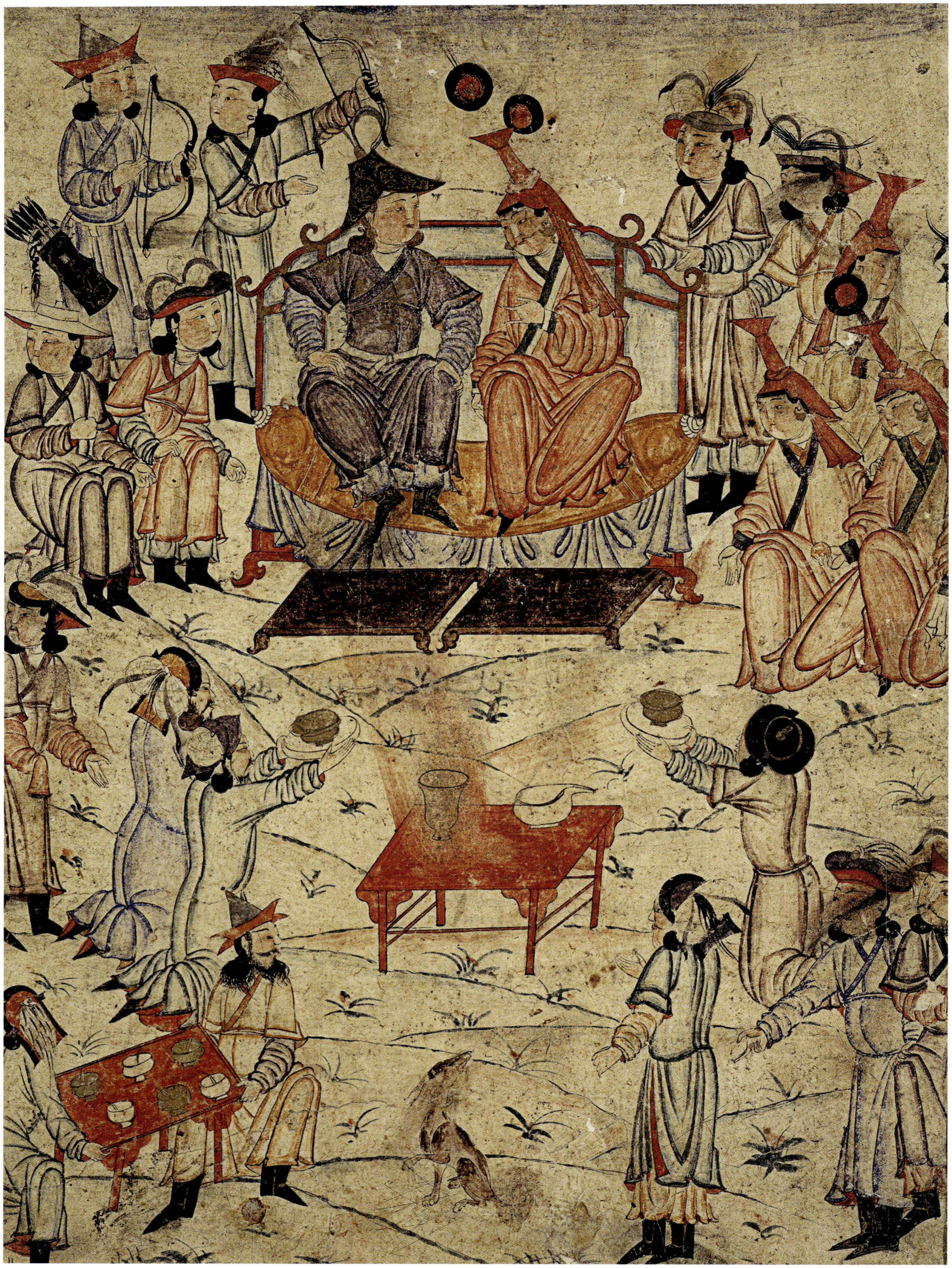

Frontispiece to the Jami al-Tawarikh (Compendium of World History) by Rashid al-Din (1247–1318)
c. 1330
Staatsbibliothek, Berlin

This full-page illuminated miniature is part of a group accurately depicting the customs of an Ilkhanid court regulated by a precise ceremonial that stipulated how each was to behave according to a rigid order of rank. The khan and his wife are shown on a throne in the open air: an interesting detail that documents how, although now the owners of magnificent palaces, Mongol rulers remained wedded to their nomadic origins and continued to follow their traditional lifestyle. The pair is flanked by their children and various dignitaries, while servants prepare drinks. Numerous characteristics in the style demonstrate Chinese influence – in particular the uniformity of the facial features and the stereotyped expressions. Unconcerned with perspective, the scene is nonetheless studiedly and coherently organized.

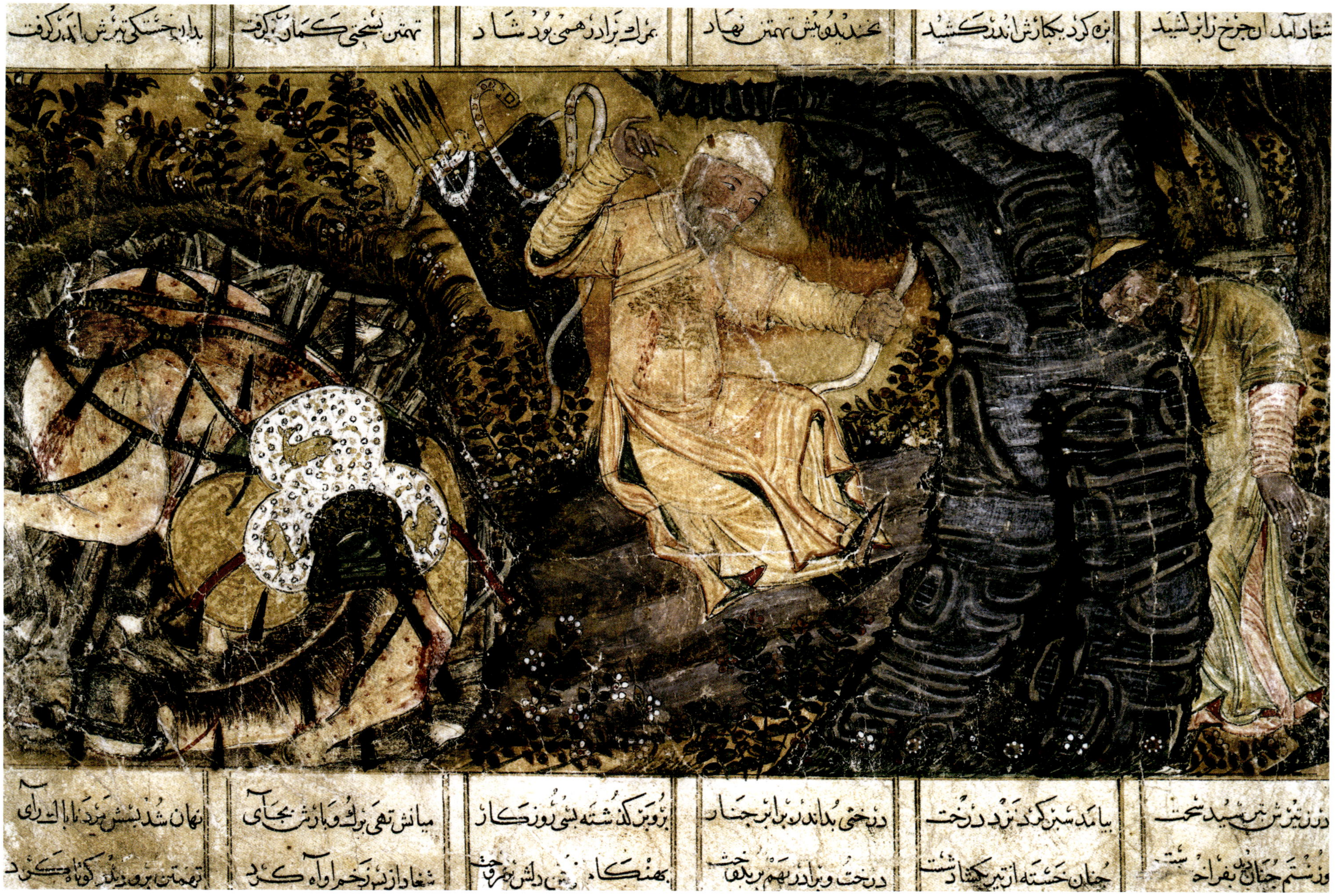

Death of Rustam and His Steed
c. 1335
From the 'Demotte' *Shahnameh* ('Book of the King') by Firdusi (11th century)
British Museum, London

The new rulers claimed to be the legitimate successors of the Ghaznavids, under whose rule the *Shahnameh* ('Book of the King') by Firdusi, the great classic of Persian epic literature was compiled in the early ninth century. The book must have figured among the favourite reading of the Mongol princes. This fascinating text recounts the fabulous adventures of various mythical Persian heroes portrayed as precursors of the Ilkhanids. The dramatic episode shown concludes the grandiloquent legend in tragic fashion.
During a hunt, the hero Rustam and his horse tumble into a trap set by his jealous stepbrother. Coiled up and peppered with spears the faithful steed lies lifeless in the pitfall, while the mortally wounded Rustam looses an arrow through a tree-trunk behind which the traitor cowers, so slaying him. The neat division of the image into three parts prevents the eye being distracted by the details; thus, an evident penchant for naturalism in no way defuses the tension of an episode conveyed with coherence and power. There are plenty of elements taken from Chinese and Italian painting, both known via imported manuscripts.

Necropolis of Shah-e Zinda. Mausoleum of Shadi Mulk Ata
Dome
1372
Samarkand, Uzbekistan

The mausoleum of Shadi Mulk Ata was the first Timurid construction in Samarkand. Dedicated to the beautiful young granddaughter of Timur, who remained deeply affected by her death, an inscription notes: "In this tomb a precious pearl has been lost." The interior is a masterstroke of delicacy and affection, where, in tones of searching harmony and melancholic lyricism, a searing regret for the lost loved one is conveyed through great chromatic sensibility.
The cupola is crowned by an eight-pointed star enclosing a golden circle orbited by half a dozen other discs, the beams framing eight tear-shaped medallions dropping as from the cosmos, each a reiteration of the central motif. Mediating the acceptance of human destiny on the cosmic level and a troubling meditation on death and the inconsolable desolation of those left behind, this intimate and contemplative sepulchre is cleansed of all rhetorical gestures.

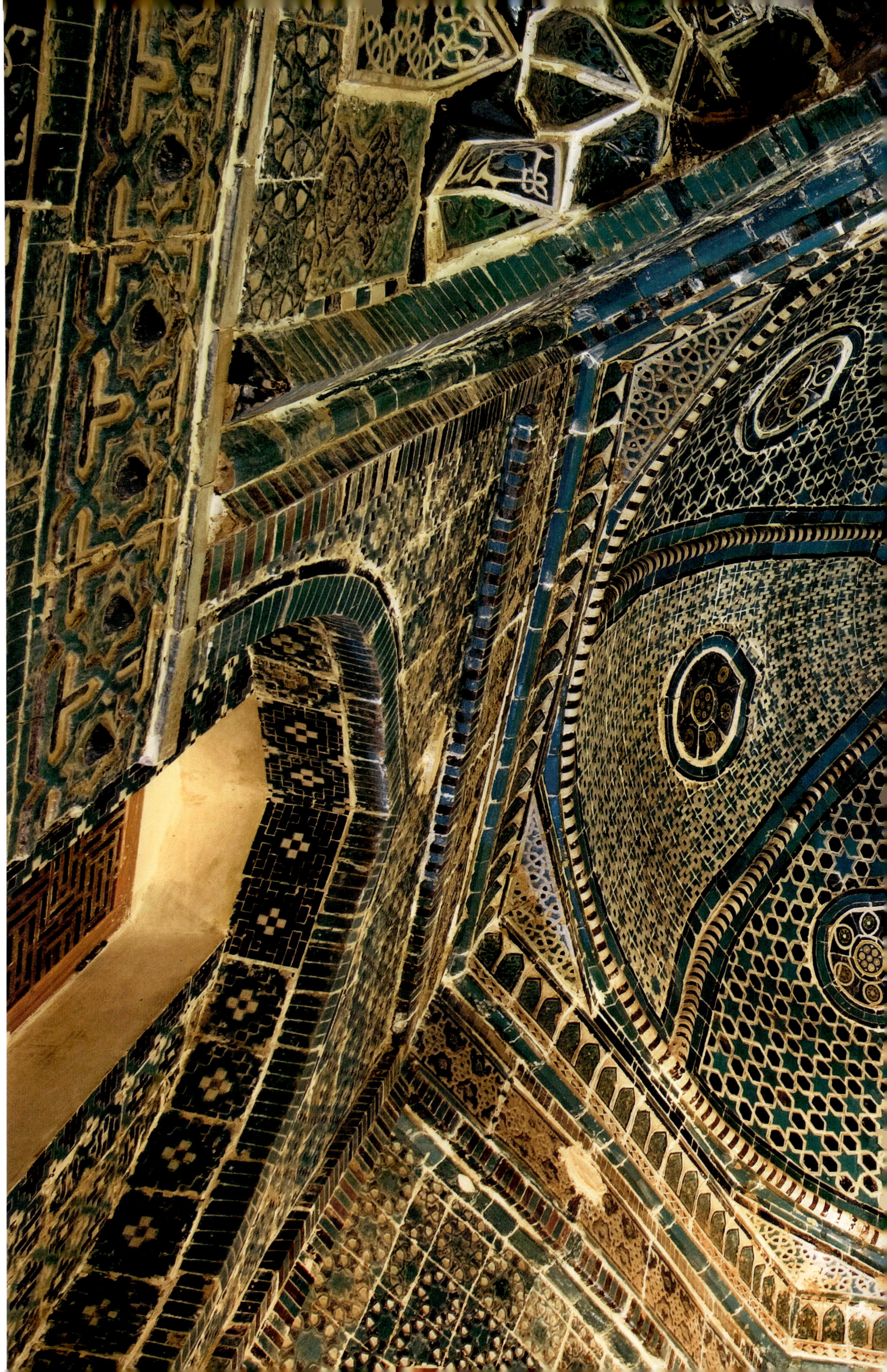

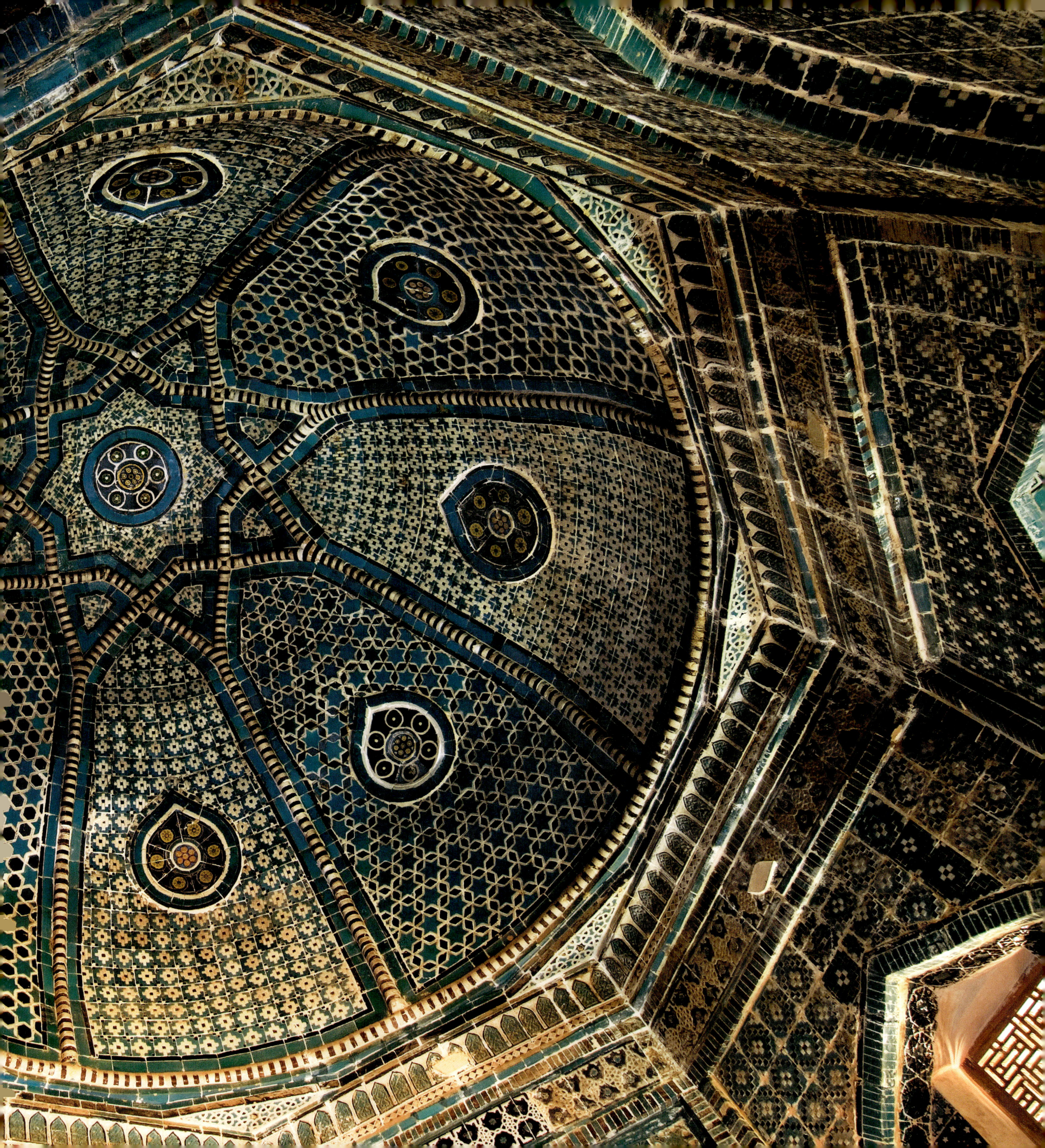

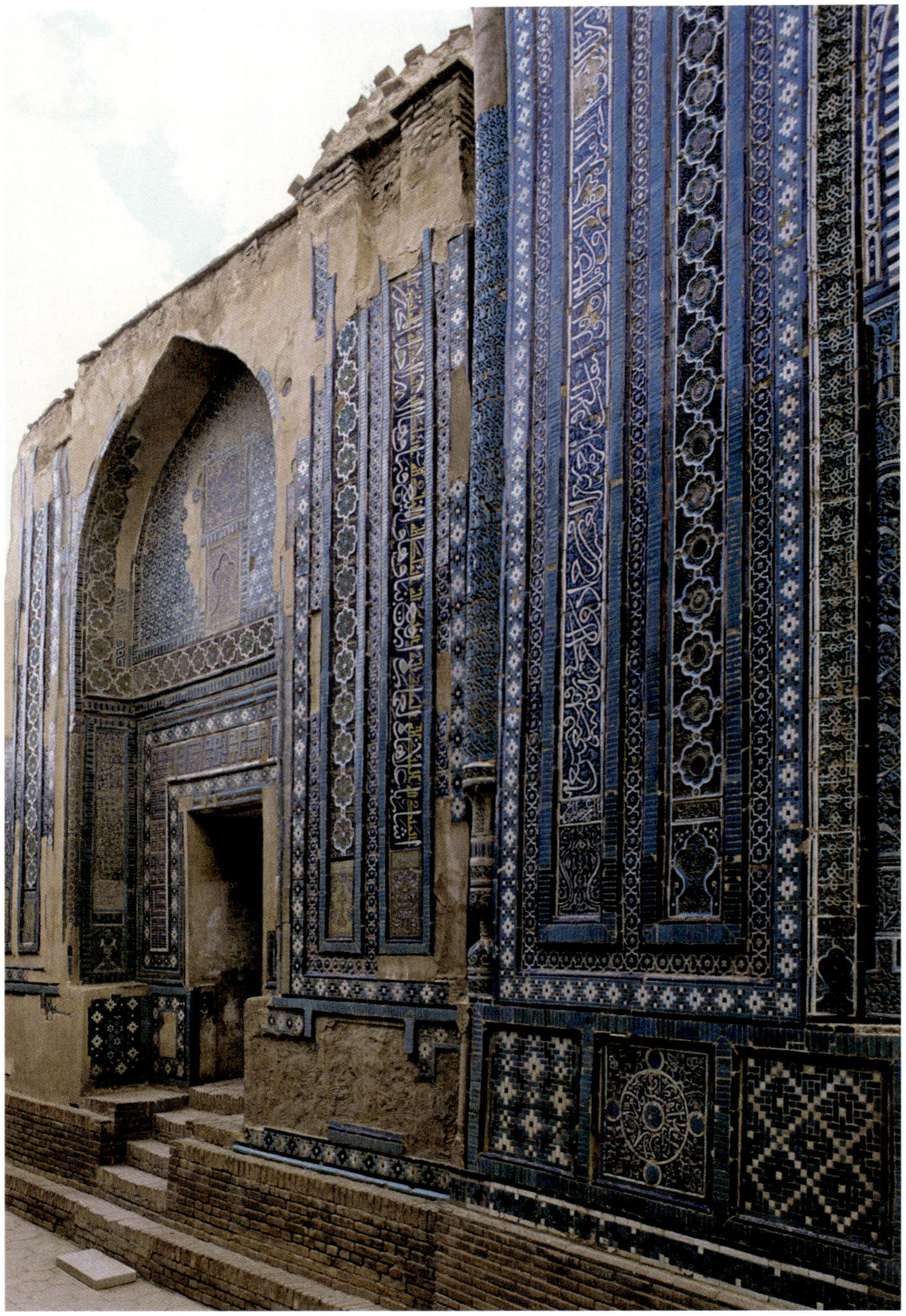

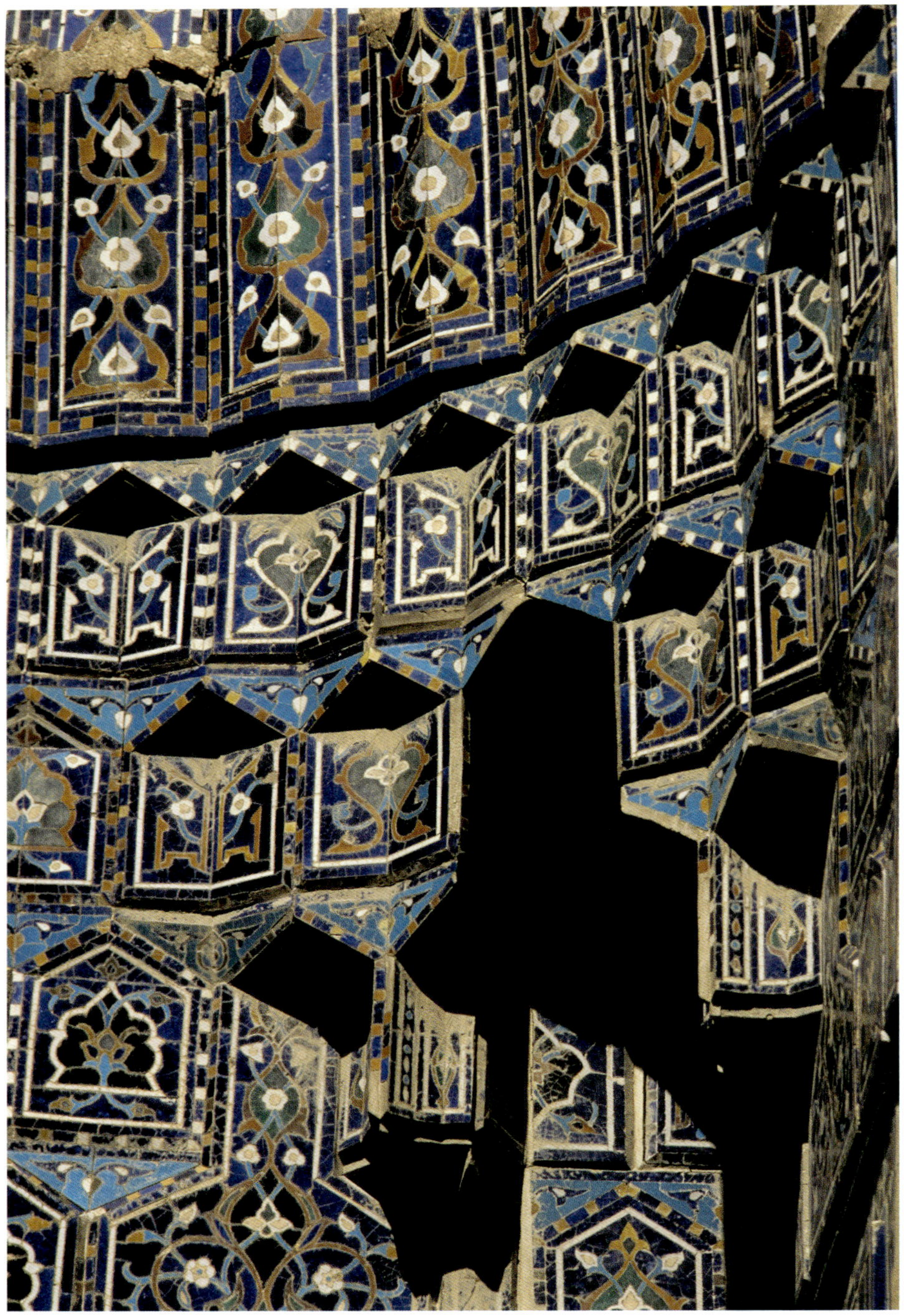

Necropolis of Shah-e Zinda
Mausoleum of Shah-e Mulk Ata
1372
Samarkand, Uzbekistan

The transition to Timurid art occurred seamlessly and the first expressions of the new epoch in architecture are among the most intensely poetic in the entire Central Asian tradition. These mausoleums are arranged in levels resembling a proscenium opening up to heaven along a climb to the necropolis called Shah-e Zinda. There stands an architecture of noble simplicity clad in ceramics of every conceivable shape and shade, from deep or sky blue to turquoise – everywhere predominant – or white, which, like a celestial vault, amounts to the most limpid creation of the age.

Necropolis of Shah-e Zinda
Mausoleum of Shirin Bika Aka
Detail of the *muqarnas* at the entrance
1385
Samarkand, Uzbekistan

Shirin Bika Aka, a sister of Timur's, died in 1385. The decade or more between this mausoleum and the preceding one explains the presence of a technical innovation introduced by craftsmen from Mozaffarid Iran and Azerbaijan: the appearance for the first time in Samarkand of *mo'arraq*. Instead of the classic carved relief combined in shades of a single hue from turquoise to blue, the new technique uses segments of 'pure colour'. The result is increased intensity conveyed by a glittering arsenal of floral forms and colours, dazzling calligraphy, and geometrical elements in compositions limited solely by the creative imagination. Unrecorded in Iran, the 'green of Central Asia' adds vibrations of unparalleled depth to the pearly luminous gleam that responds to the changing angle of the sun's rays and to the warmth or chill of the ambient light.

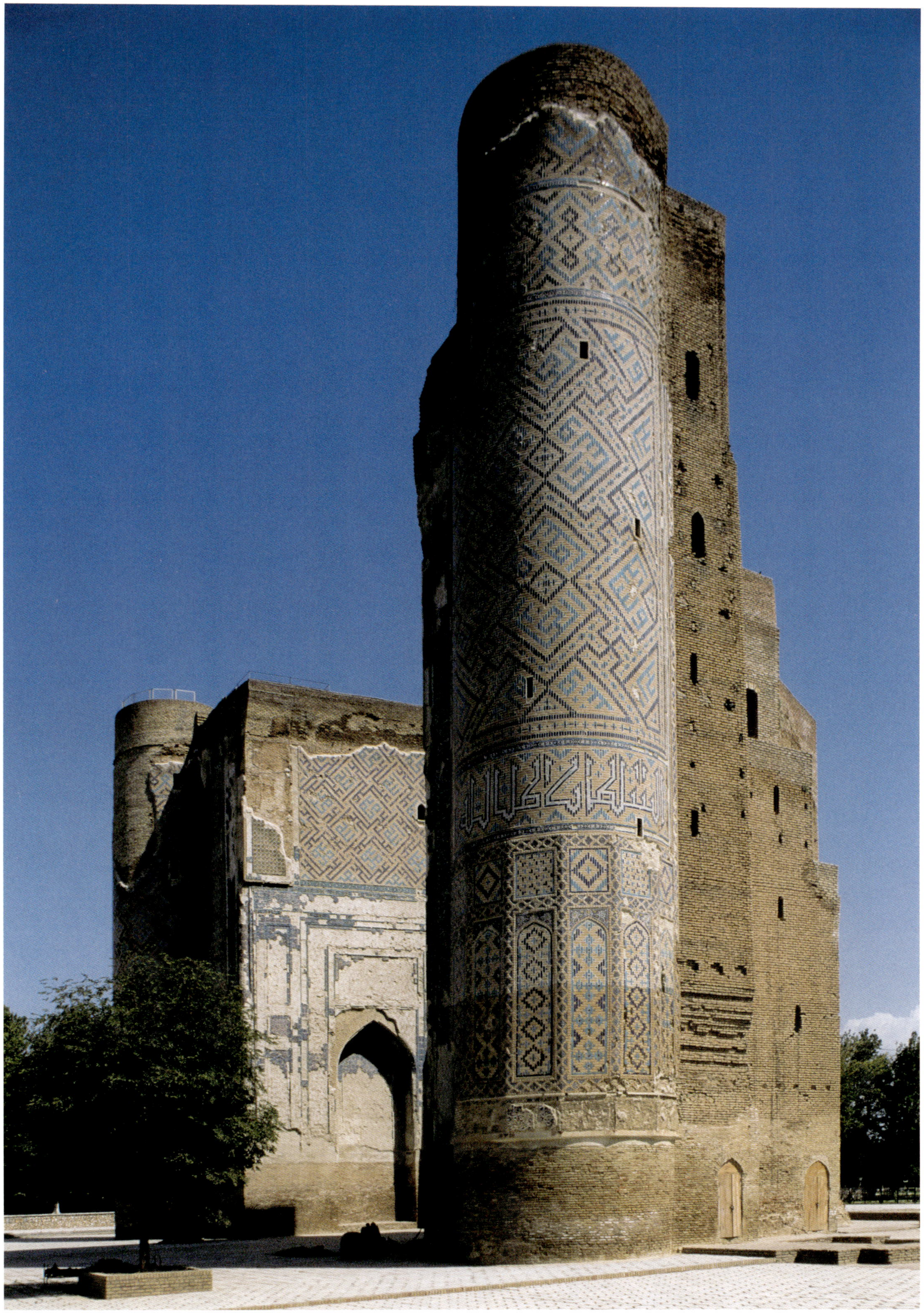

Ak Saray ('White Palace')
1399–1405
Shahr-e Sabz, Uzbekistan

Only vestiges survive of that exemplary expression of insatiable ambition, overweening pride and awe-inspiring power known as the legendary palace of Timur, including this immense arch twenty-two metres wide, fifty high and borne on two minarets, which gives on to the courtyard. Since Timur was obsessed by seeing the job finished, in addition to the lavish but lengthy and laborious technique of *mo'arraq* he ordered the use of another process, called *haft rang* ('seven colours'), in which square tiles are painted before firing. The consequent fall in quality, with runs and blotches, blurred lines and loss of chromatic saturation, was compensated for by an ease of handling and mounting unthinkable with traditional techniques over such vast surfaces.

Bibi Khanum Mosque
Courtyard
1399–1405
Samarkand, Uzbekistan

Although embroidered with legend, one of the most revealing contemporary descriptions of the erection of this colossal ensemble was penned by the Persian court chronicler Sharaf al-Din Ali Yazdi: "The last Sunday in Ramadhan in the year 801 (1399 CE), at an hour and time in favourable conjunction with the stars, skilful architects and expert craftsmen laid the foundation-stone of the building. Five hundred stone carvers from Azerbaijan, Fars, and Hindustan and other places gathered to do the work, together with labourers for hewing the stone from quarries and others for hauling it to the city. Painters and experts in every art, chosen amongst the best each guild could offer, were summoned to the palace from all four corners of the earth. To transport the materials to the site, ninety-five elephants were brought from India which, with the aid of a great number of people, dragged in the enormous blocks. Surrounded by princes and emirs, Timur supervised the work in person. The ceiling of the mosque rests on 480 stone columns, each more than five metres high. The magnificent pavement is executed using artfully squared marble slabs. The height from pavement to ceiling is over seven metres. Were there no sky, the dome would deserve the first place of all, and the same might be asserted for the arch on the *iwan,* were there no Milky Way. Placed along the walls to all four sides stand a like number of minarets, their summits reach up to the sky. The sound of the great metal doors, made from an alloy of seven metals, can be heard by the faithful in every region and calls them to the house of Islam. The walls of the domed hall are lined with calligraphy in stone … When His Highness visited the Great Mosque His Majesty expressed the opinion that the height of the gateway erected during his absence was dishonourably low. He therefore ordered it to be demolished and be replaced by a larger and taller one. Owing to such mistakes committed during construction, the architect Khodja Mahmud Dawud was taken away for interrogation." The ceramic tiles are colour painted using the technique known as *cuerda seca* in imitation of the finest *mo'arraq.* Like all Timur's architectural undertakings, this mosque was realized in record time, but often with poor materials and deficient techniques.

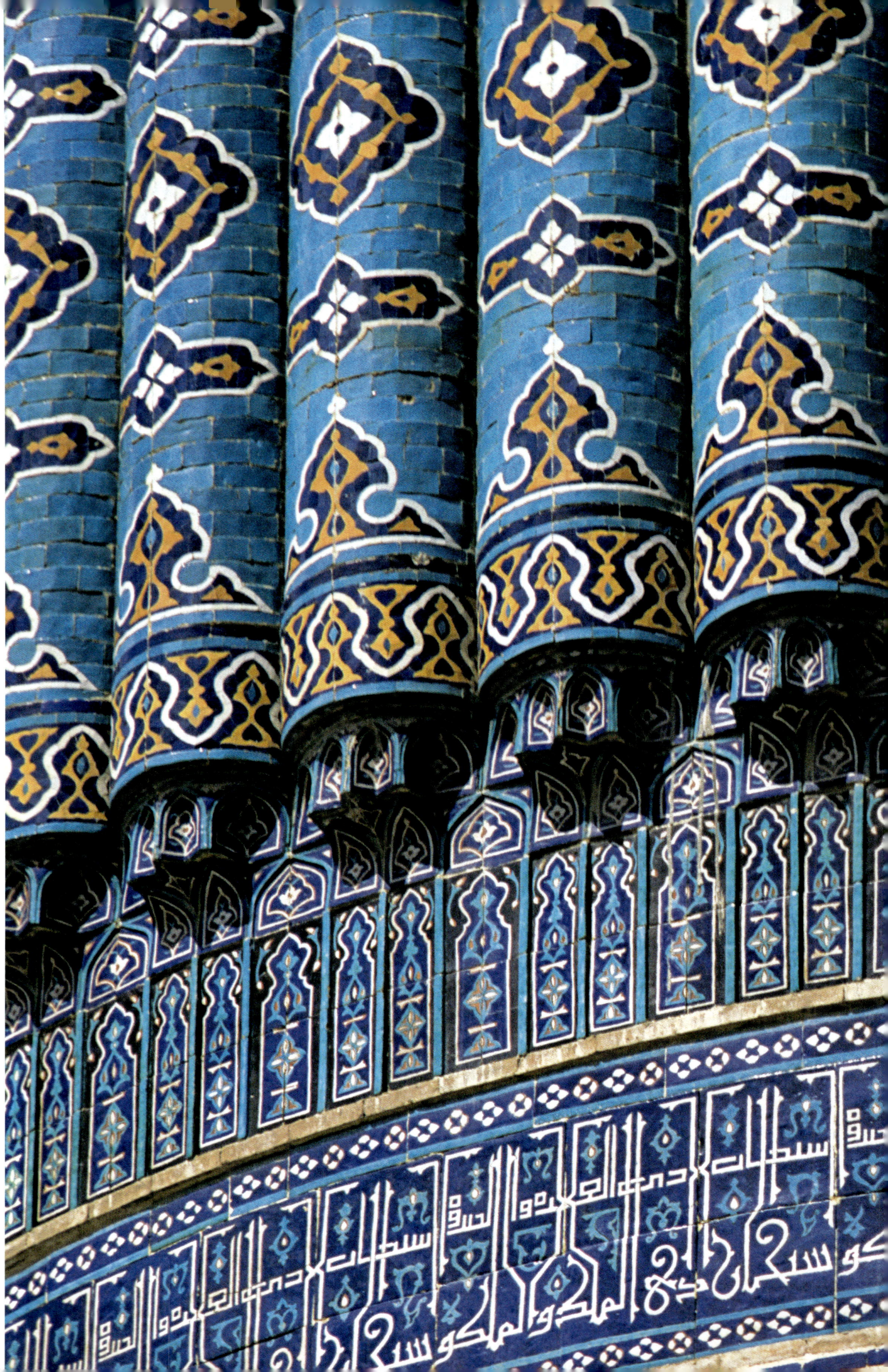

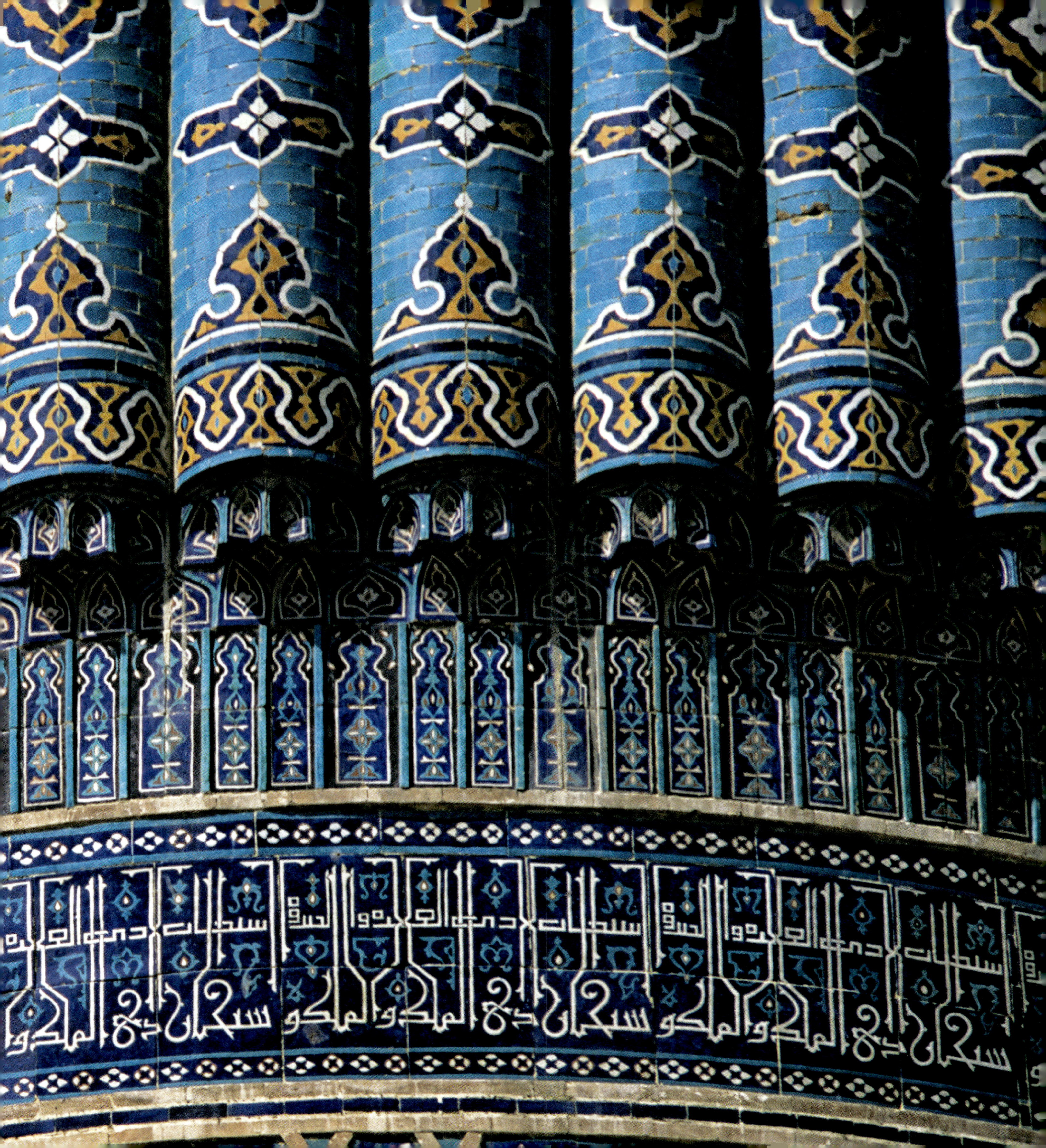

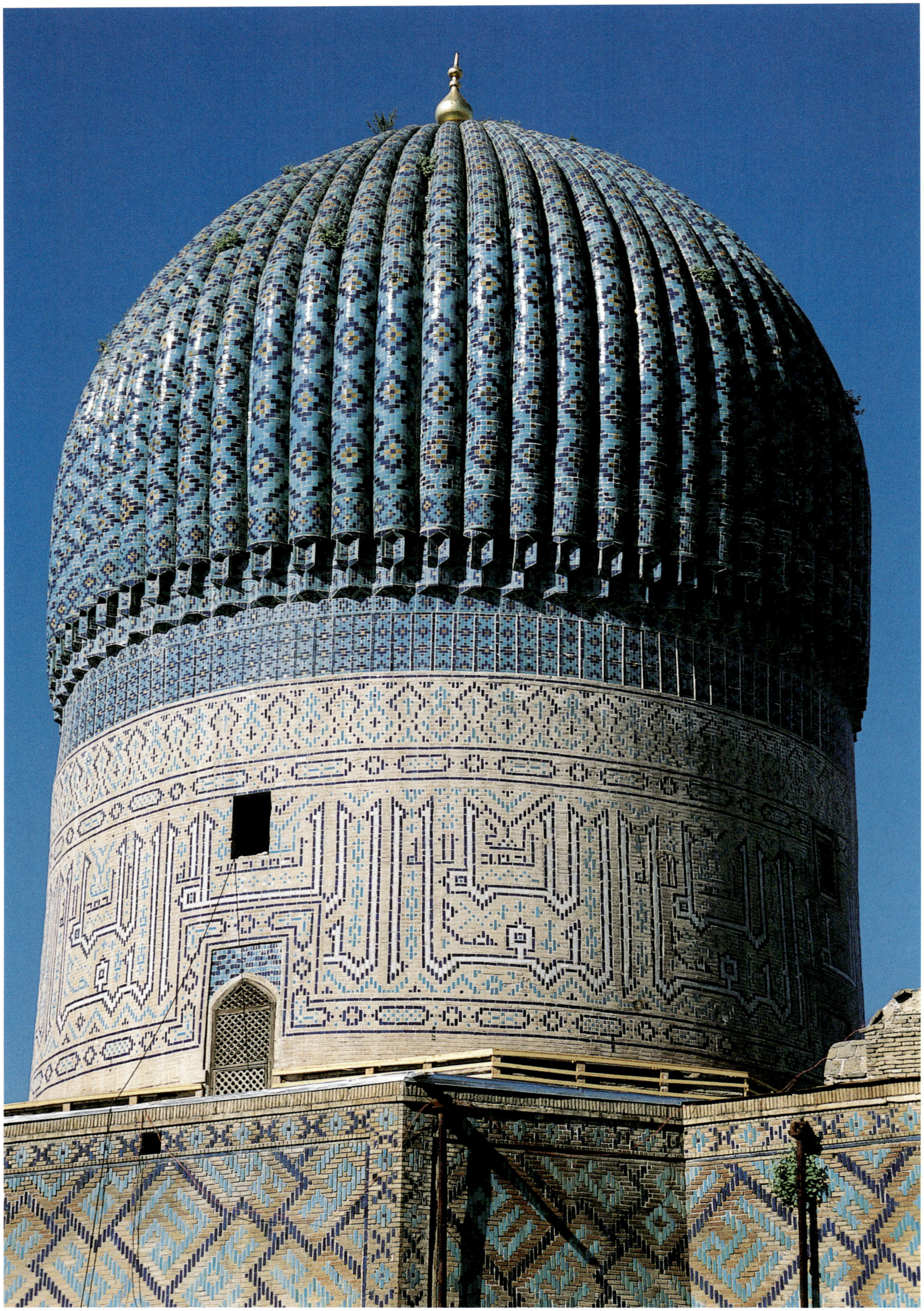

Gur-e Mir ('Tomb of the Emir')
Drum and dome
1404
Samarkand, Uzbekistan

A veritable paradigm for the architecture of its era, Timur's mausoleum – conceived for his successor and grandson, since the tomb intended for himself was never completed – encapsulates like few others the character of an age and the personality of a patron. The magnificent cupola emerges in glory from a tall, narrow cylinder, the eye-catching discrepancy in terms of proportion liberating its pent-up energy. Framed by a madrasah and flanked by a pair of minarets, it makes its point with almost thespian emphasis. Uninterrupted in its abrupt ascension, it hovers, about to burgeon out, seeming to trap the intense blue of the sky in its tubular ribs that quiver with vitality. There is no poetical intuition of a cosmos greater than man here, no meditation on the end of earthly existence; instead, presumptuous self-affirmation, the unmistakable mark of an era of apocalypse.

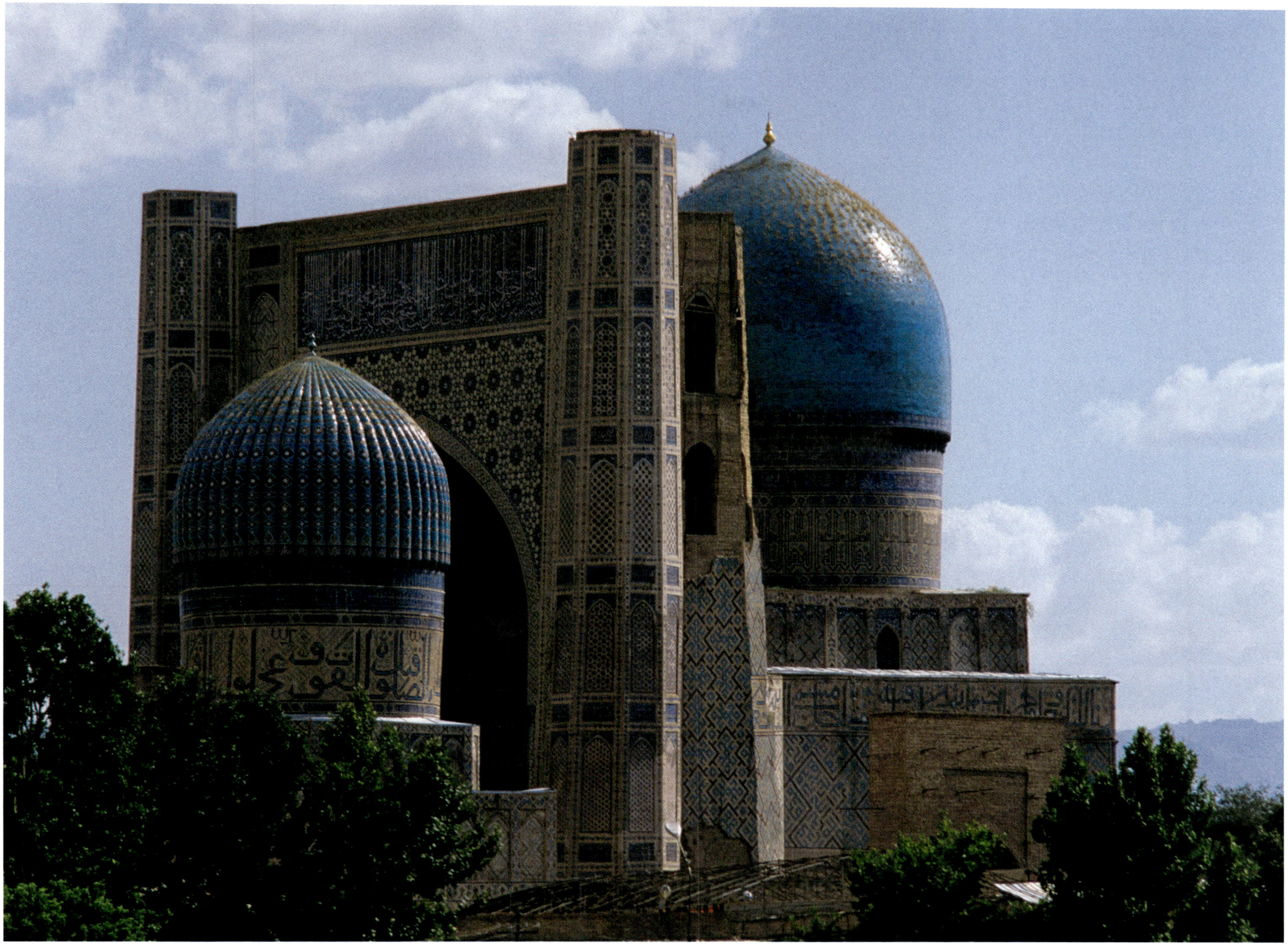

Bibi Khanum Mosque
Smaller northern dome, *iwan* and cupola over the covered hall
1399–1405
Samarkand, Uzbekistan

The Bibi Khanum Mosque adopts the classic Persian four-*iwan* plan, with a gigantic porch corresponding to the entryway, two smaller examples to the sides, complete with thickly ribbed domes, and a last one of unparalleled dimensions over the prayer hall vaulted by a gigantic sky-blue cupola (collapsing almost as soon as it was finished, it has been recently re-erected). The two minarets to either side of the *iwan* absorbing the thrust have also been partially reconstructed. Although enormous – the site boasts more than four hundred smaller domes – it nonetheless fell short of Timur's overwhelming ambition.

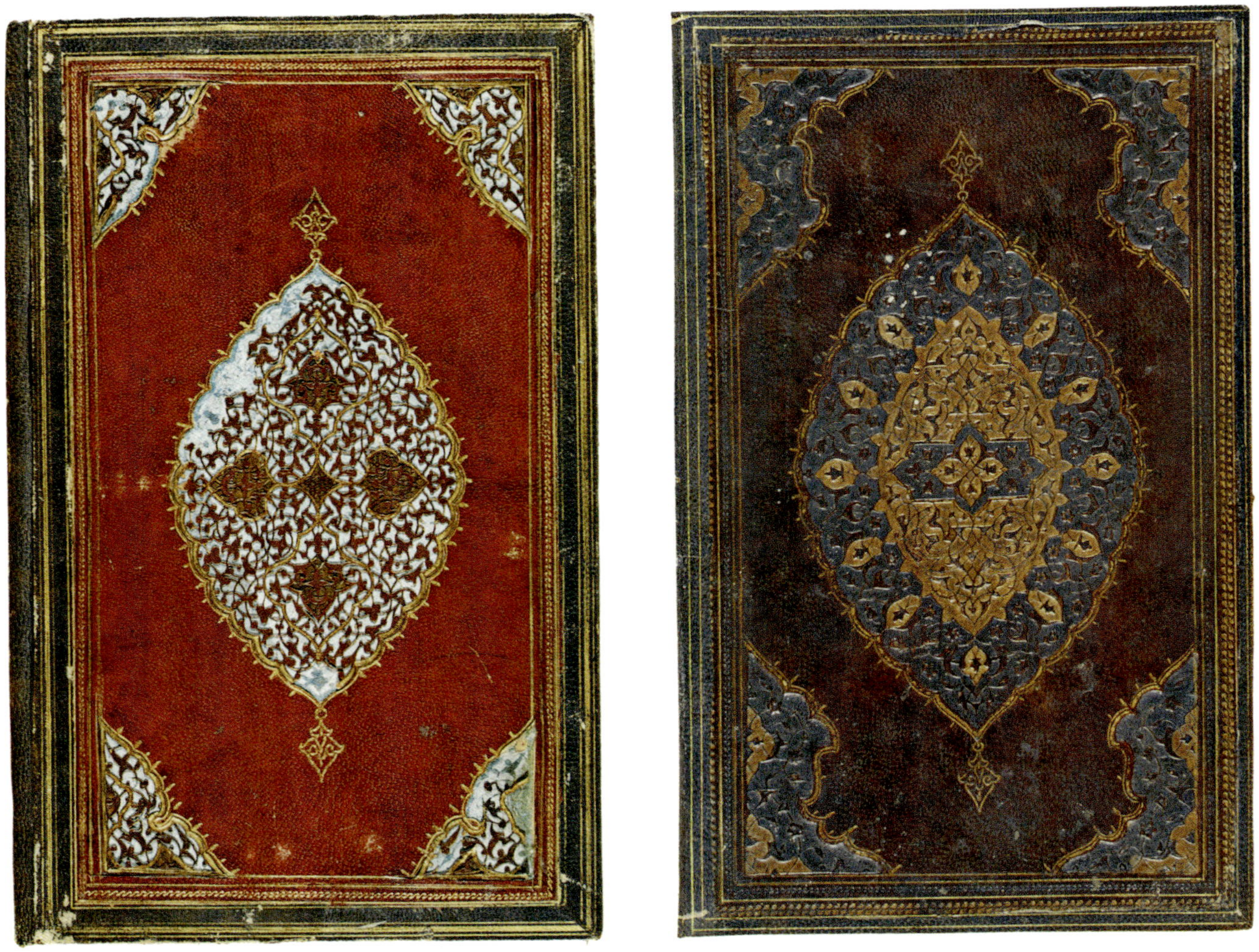

Binding for a book of the poem
Matawi-ye Ma'nawi
by Jalal al-Din Rumi (13th century)
c. 1450
Russian Academy of Sciences,
St Petersburg

The poem Sprirtual Couplets is an important work of mysticism by Rumi, the great Persian poet and founder of the Sufi order of the whirling dervishes who died in Konya in 1273. This remarkable leather binding, deeply tooled with applications in several colours and gold, perfectly balanced in form and colour, is a priceless example of the Timurids' passion for books.

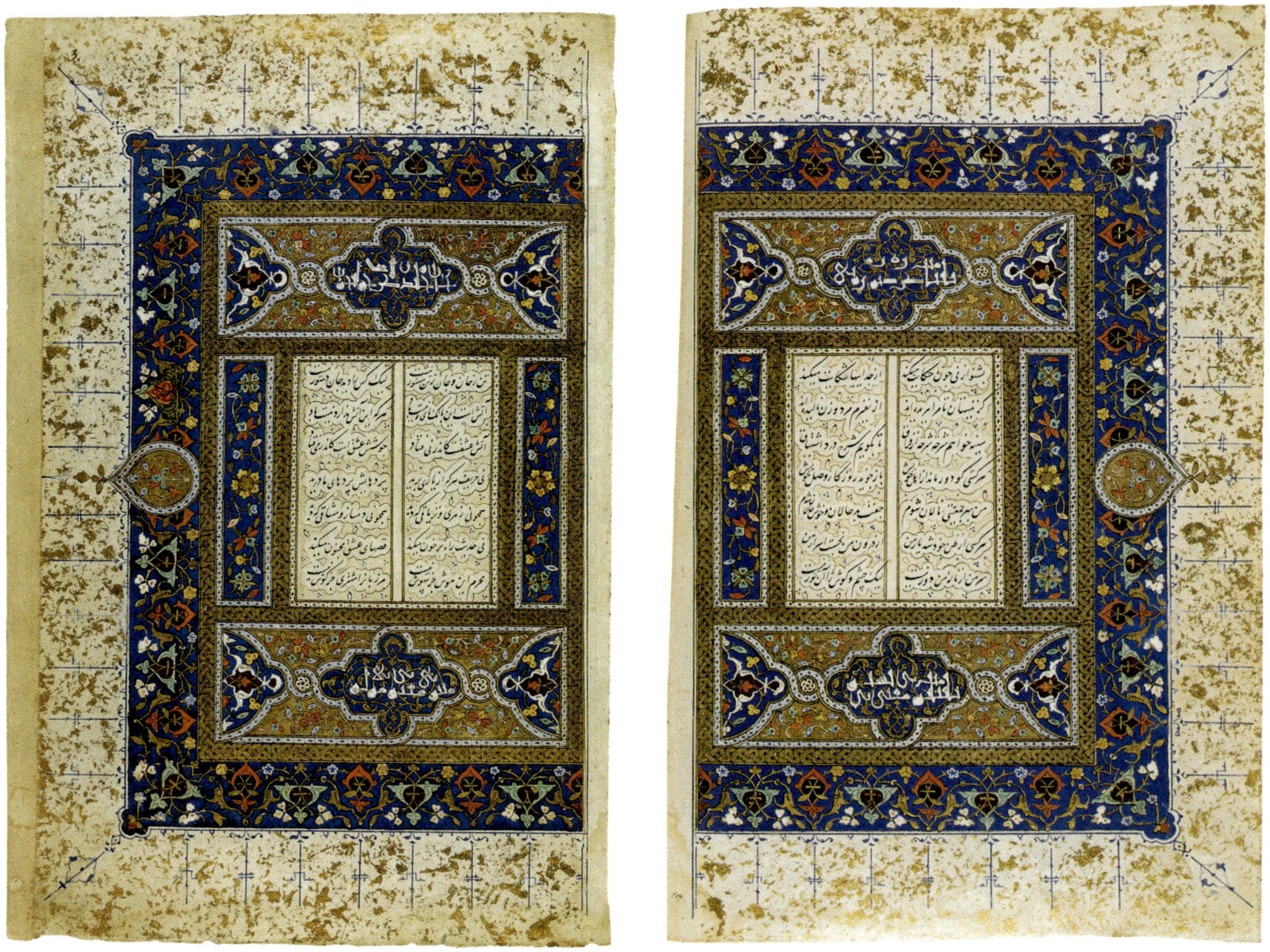

Frontispiece to the poem
Matawi-ye Ma'nawi
by Jalal al-Din Rumi (13th century)
c. 1450
Russian Academy of Sciences,
St Petersburg

Such a wonderful copy was surely produced in the scriptorium-library in the monastery at Konya. The quality of the script, a splendid miniature *nastaliq,* belongs, however, to the most vaunted school of the time to which the best masters deferred: the Timurid school at Herat. The introductory leaves of each of the six volumes are adorned with an exquisite blue frame containing elegant floral motifs and two gold-ground cartouches placed above and beneath the text perfectly in keeping with an ensemble that is at once balanced and elegant.

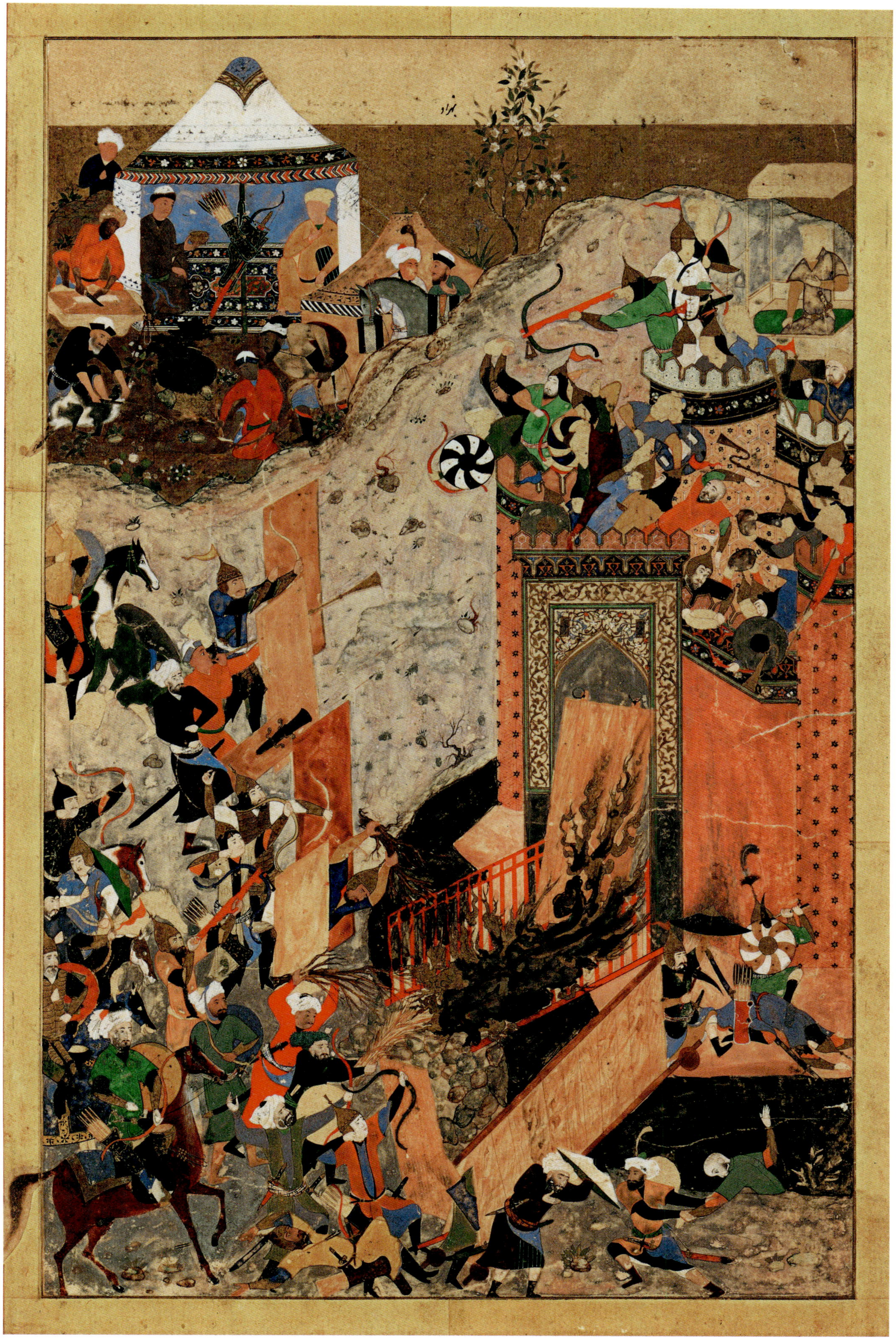

Bihzad (c. 1450–1535)
Onslaught on a Castle
1480–1500
Harvard Art Museum, Cambridge, MA

Bihzad was the most celebrate Persian illuminator, active from approximately 1480 in Herat, where he worked for its cultivated aristocracy and for the sultan, transferring his services to the Shaybanids after the ruler's death. Moving therefore to Tabriz, he then became director of the library of the new Safavid sultanate, organizing a studio of calligraphers, illuminators, gilders and others concerned with the making of books, imposing a unique hallmark on the Persian miniature. The book that best encapsulates his style is perhaps the *Bustan* ('Orchard'), one of the best-loved and best-known poems by the inimitable Persian poet Saadi (1257), made for Husayn Bayqara, where the miniatures are without doubt autograph. The lively figures possess an authentic personality, making the viewer feel involved in their affairs. For the first time perhaps the protagonists are individuals rather than types, while the colours are realistically modulated, and both the verisimilitude of the actions and the 'naturalistic' attention to context are innovative for painting in its time. None of this novelty, however, meant forfeiting that highly charged lyricism which remains the most salient stylistic feature of Bihzad's style as well as of that of the finest Persian miniatures.

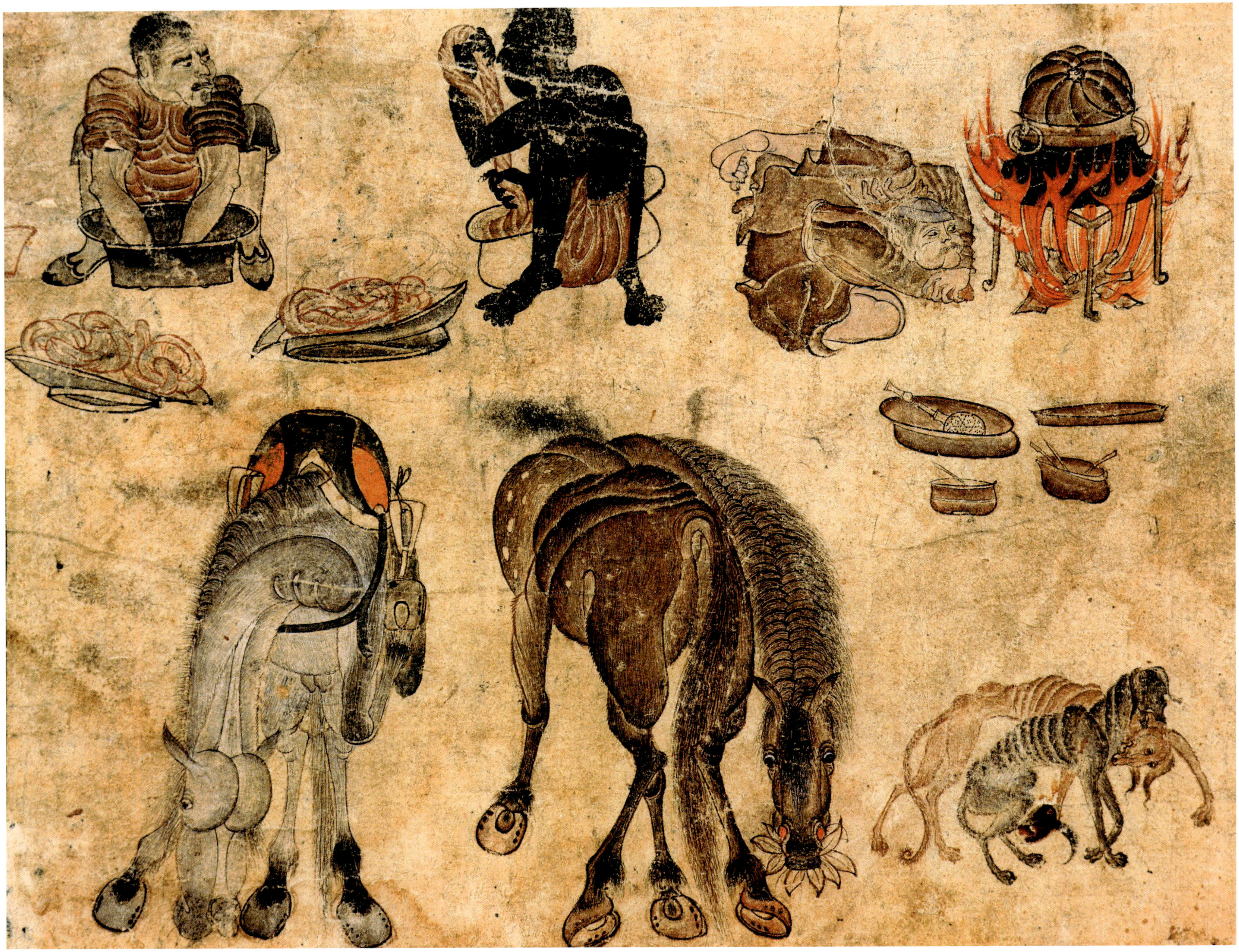

Siyah Qalam (attributed, 1469–1525),
Nomad Encampment
15th century
Museum of the Topkapi Saray, Istanbul

If the classic production of illuminated books followed a well-trodden path and developed in a relatively straightforward fashion – with schools, masters and a public of clients and cognoscenti acting within what was a familiar cultural ambit – the problems posed by the extra-ordinary miniatures contained in an album conserved in Istanbul are far from having been resolved. The sheets are attributed to a master known as Siyah Qalam ('Black Pen') and depict nomads, shamans, dervishes, wayfarers, animals and monstrous figures, with on occasion grotesquely distorted features: with deep roots in the atavistic imagination of Central Asia, this is a conceptual rather than a figurative world that blithely disregards the conventions of Persian painting. The colours are sober, almost 'earthy' and dominated by brownish hues, while each personage is sketched uncompromisingly against the raw, unprepared sheet. Suspended outside all landscape and architecture and adopting poses and expressions on the brink of deformity, the outlines of the figures appear as if convulsed.

Munisak
Late 19th century
The Design Library, New York

The *munisak* was a female outer garment often of Russian manufacture and worn on special occasions, usually embroidered, quilted with a cotton lining and printed with an eye-catching pattern. The term *ikat* ('cloud'), of Indonesian origin, is frequently used to designate cloths or garments knotted and stained with inks, a technique that in ancient Turkestan (and today in Uzbekistan) is called *abrbandi* (similarly, 'clouds'). Technically *ikat* is a dyeing process in which sections of textile are tied as not to absorb the ink into which it is dipped while the areas left exposed are stained, the colours running and blending into one another at the edges of the designs in characteristic fashion. Such tie-dyed weaves were put to various purposes: overcoats, jackets, trousers, blankets, table-cloths, as saddle-cloths, in *suzani* (woven hangings), scarves and so on. It is a tradition that remained unchanged throughout Central Asia until the twentieth century.

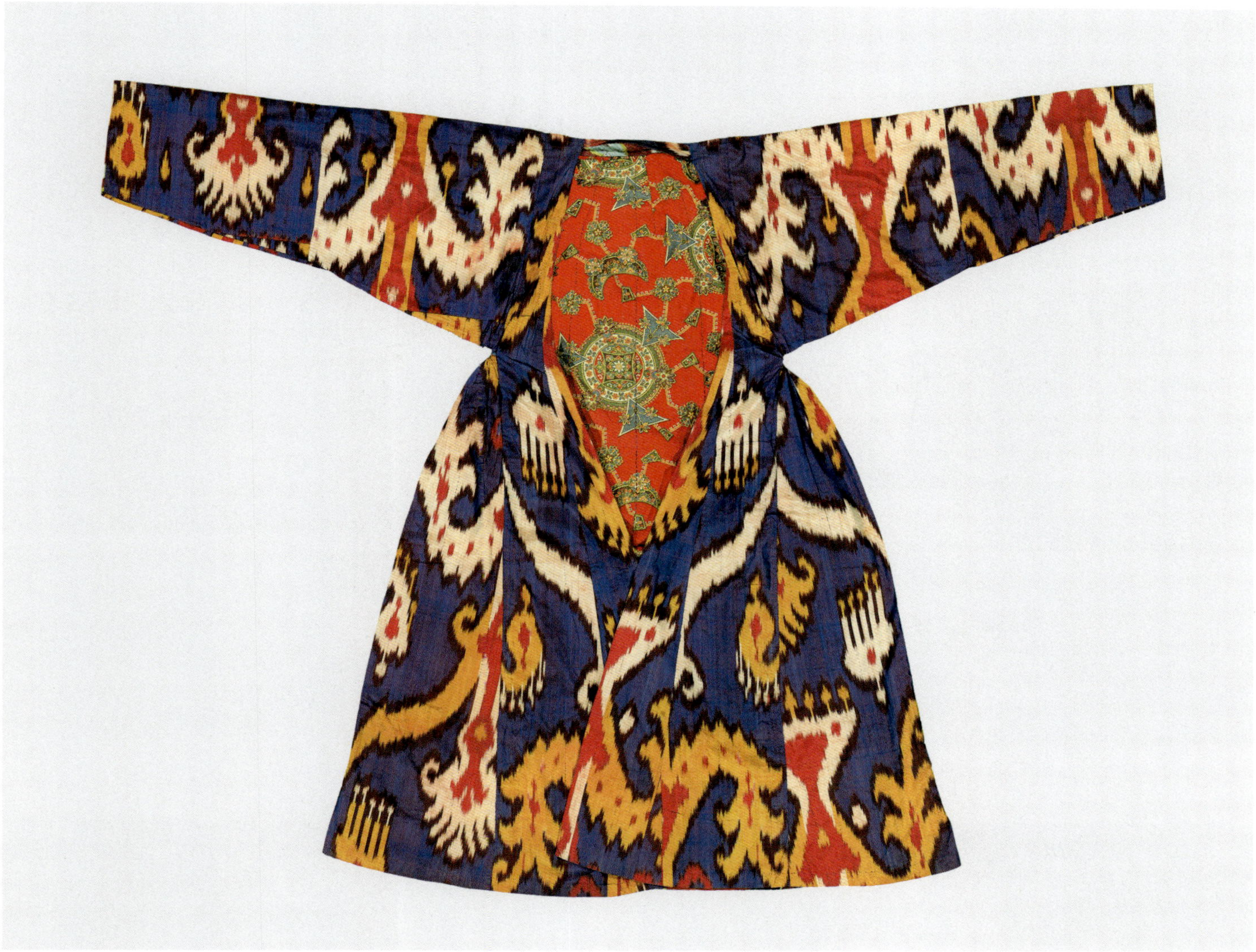

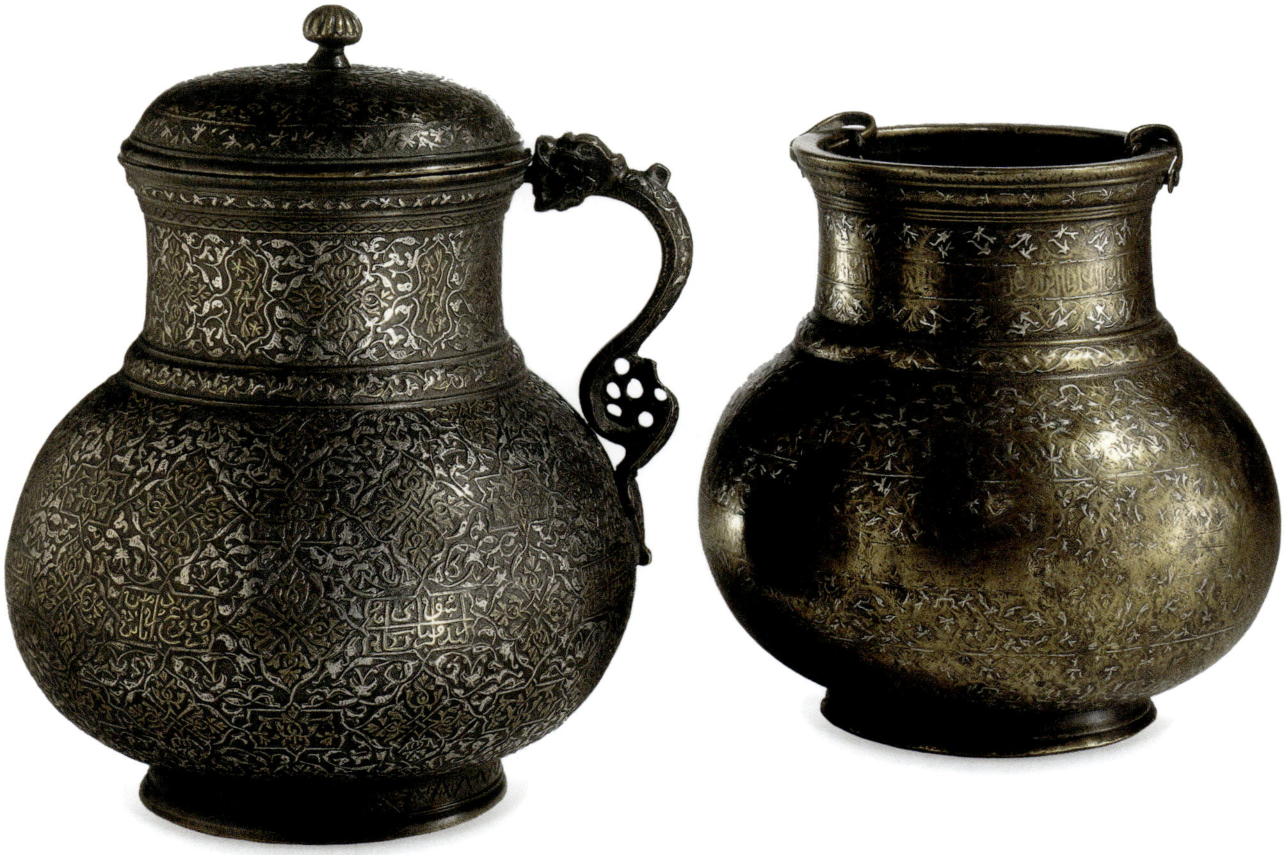

Tankard
1498
Brass inlaid with gold and silver
British Museum, London

The calligraphy around the neck of this vessel mentions a Timurid governor of Herat, Abu al-Ghazi Sultan Husain, a great patron of poetry and the arts. Contemporary accounts recall his sumptuous banquets, complete with music, poetry recitals, literary discussions, and riddle competitions, copiously oiled with interminable libations drunk from tankards such as this one. The Timurids adored partying and revered music and minstrels. Competing in races and mock combats, above all they loved drink which they consumed without moderation, taking in addition quantities of hashish and indulging in unbridled sexuality. Numerous princes died of alcoholism or in accidents occasioned by drunkenness. In spite of the strict moral laws promulgated by Timur, women too enjoyed an extraordinary degree of freedom.

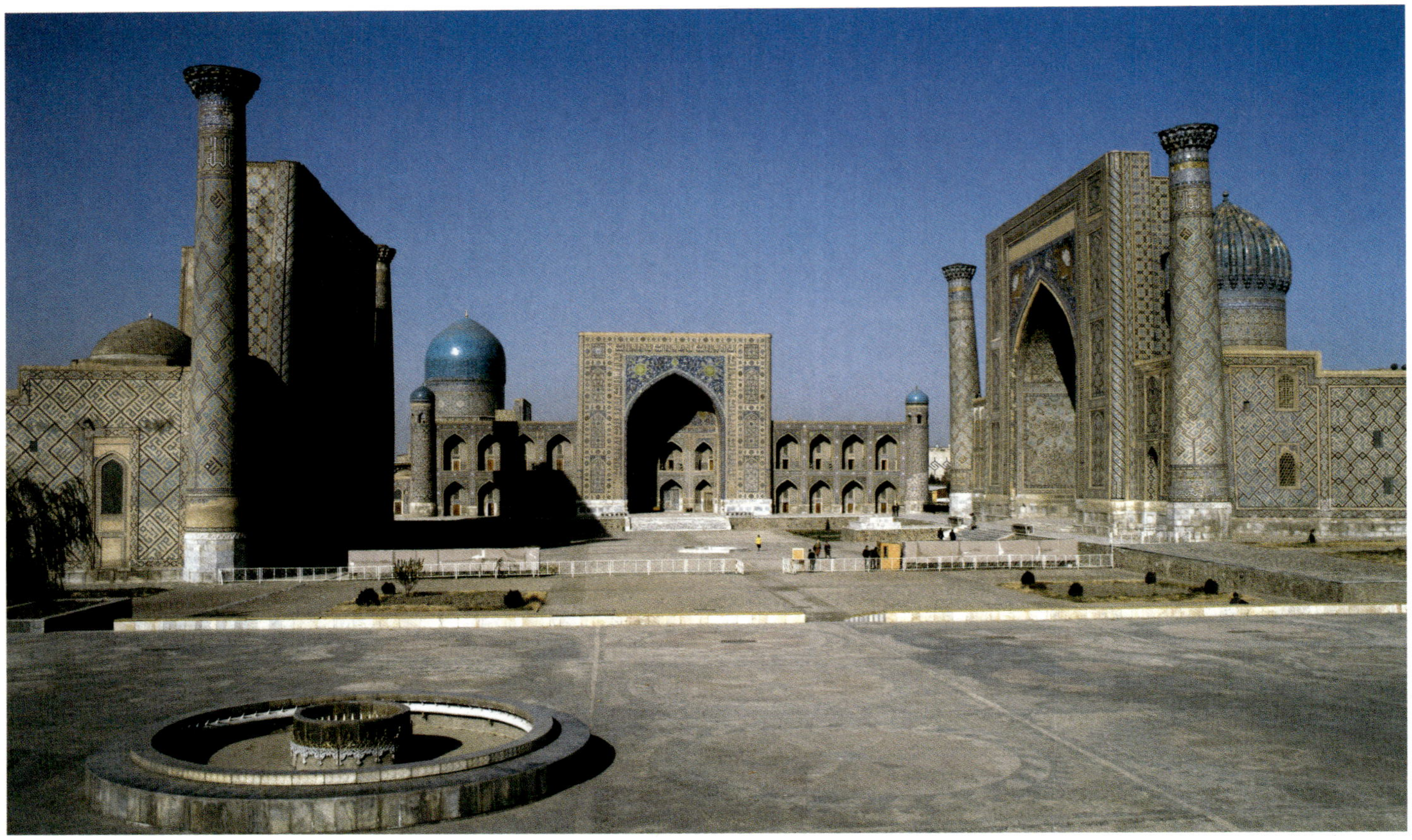

Registan
Madrasas of Ulugh Beg, Tilliya Kar and Shir Dor
1417–1420, 1646–1660, 1619–1663
Samarkand, Uzbekistan

The Registan ('place of sand') lies at the heart of old Samarkand: until the nineteenth century it was the site of popular festivities, the proclamation of the khan's decrees and the carrying out of capital punishments. At the time of Timur there stood a great domed bazaar and it was here that his grandson Ulugh Beg, a talented astronomer and mathematician, constructed his noble madrasah decorated with star motifs in front of which was erected a convent for dervishes, a great *hammam,* a mosque and a *han,* later ruined. In the seventeenth century, to restore this public square to its former uniformity, the governor Yalangtash Bakhadur built two new madrasahs, a group of nearly symmetrical buildings of unprecedented magnificence typical of the theatrical mind of the age. Here two dimensions – the façade's surface and the tapering vertical lines of the minarets – are embellished by globular forms in the shape of a ribbed dome supported on lofty drums. Introducing a dramatic, dynamic element, it terminates in an almost acute angle that shimmers in the changing sunlight.

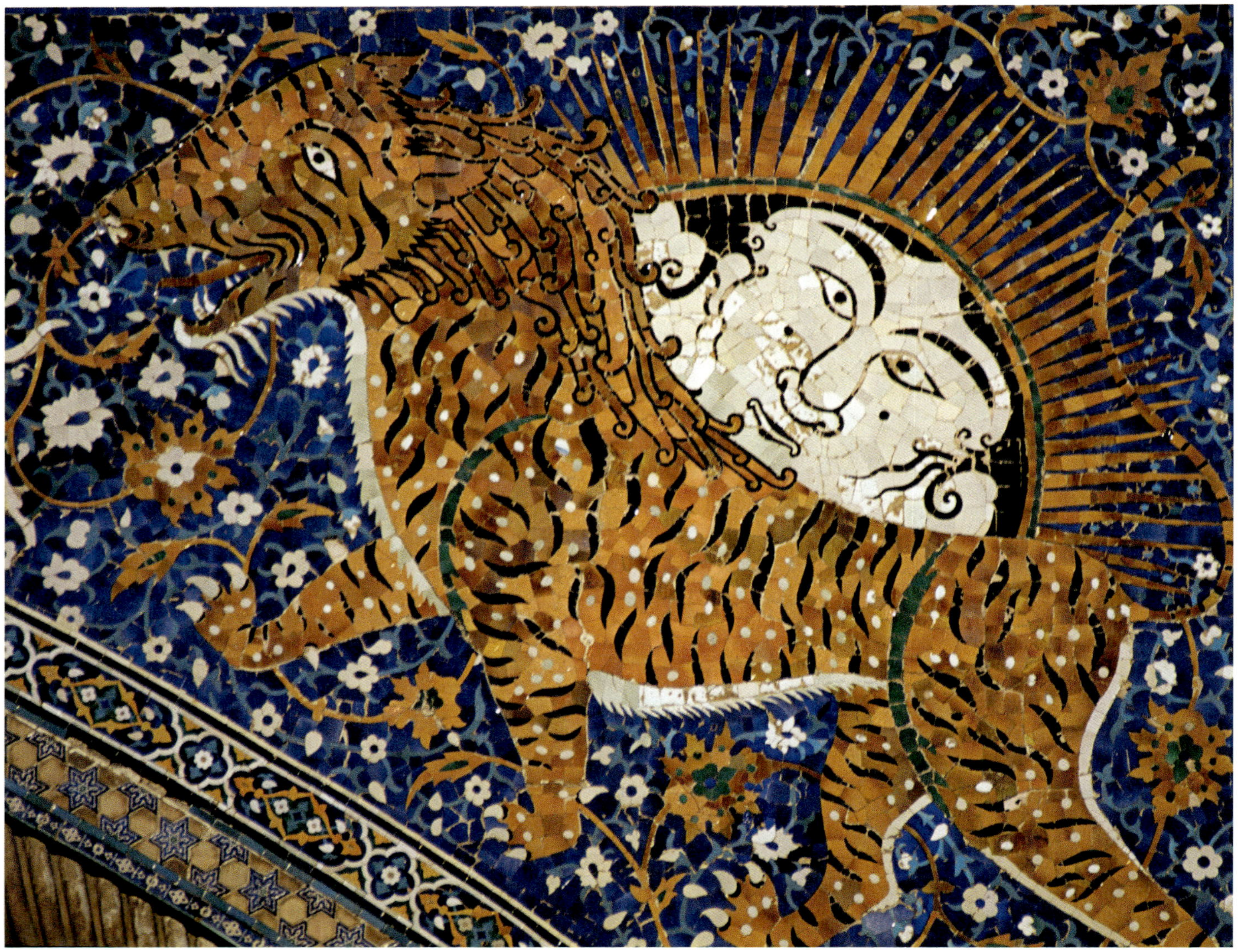

Abd al-Jabbar (17th century)
Shir Dor madrasa
Detail of the decoration on the façade
1619–1663
Samarkand, Uzbekistan

Upon the arch of the façade parade an affronted pair of striped lions, each chasing a gazelle; over their shoulder rises an anthropomorphic sun, in blatant breach of Islamic anti-figuration on a religious building – an infraction which, according to legend, cost the architect his life. The lion, however, could easily stand for the khan himself, illumined by the blazing sun, in accordance with an iconography originating in all probability with the ancient sovereigns of Afrasyab (archaic Samarkand).

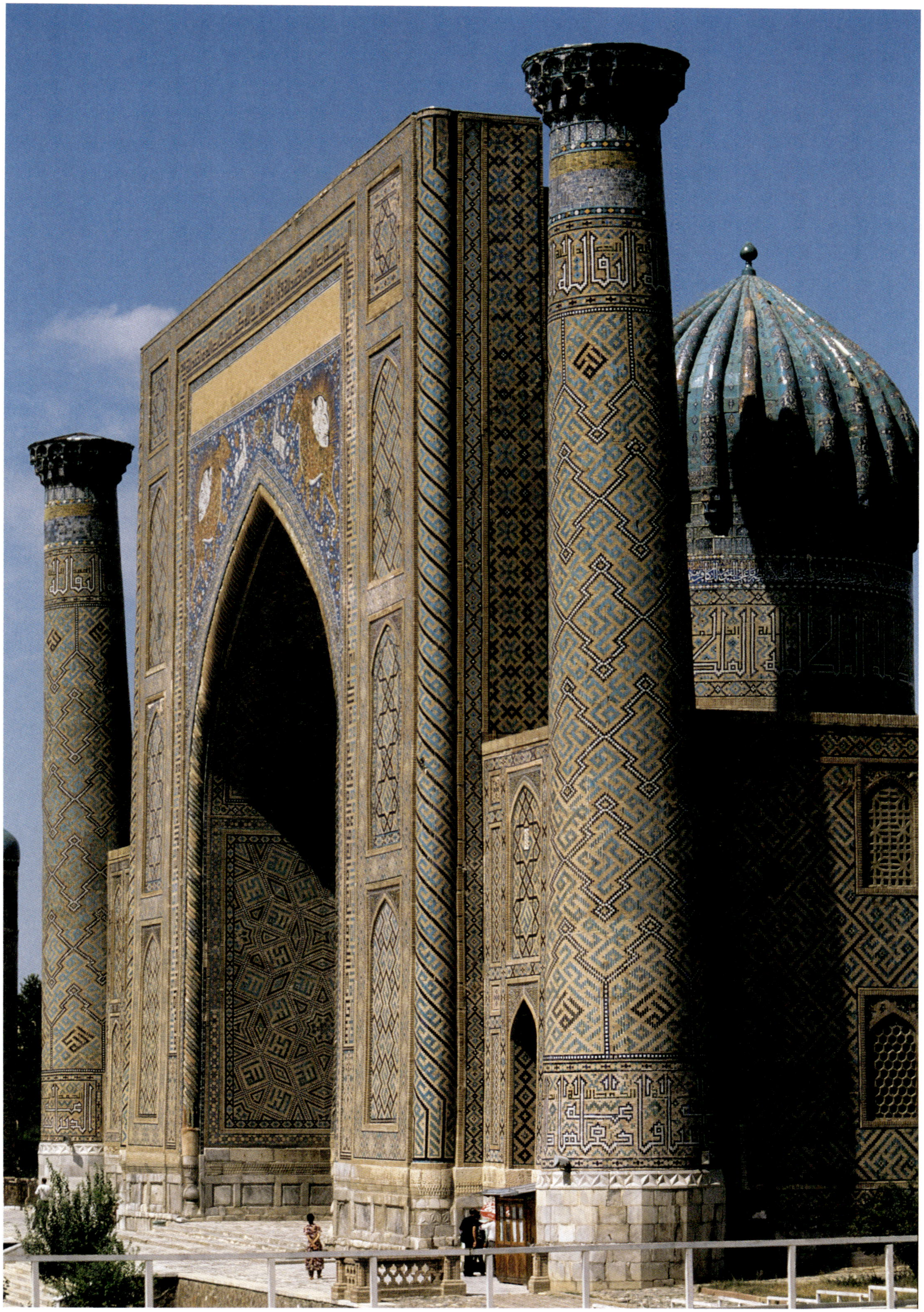

Abd al-Jabbar (17th century)
Shir Dor madrasa
1619–1663
Samarkand, Uzbekistan

An inscription on the madrasah of Yalangtash recalls: "The nimble acrobat of thought climbing along the rope of the imagination will never be able to reach the summit of its inaccessible minarets."
The building enters into a dialogue with the nobility of the madrasah of Ulugh Beg, preferring to the geometric motifs so beloved of the astronomer a more colourful decor that emphasizes a celebratory, evocative colour scheme. The name ('gate of the lions') derives from the carnivores seen on the arch, the culmination of a façade ornamented with especial chromatic vivacity that has recourse to new tones, such as orange and purple, as well as a brilliant yellow and an intense green.

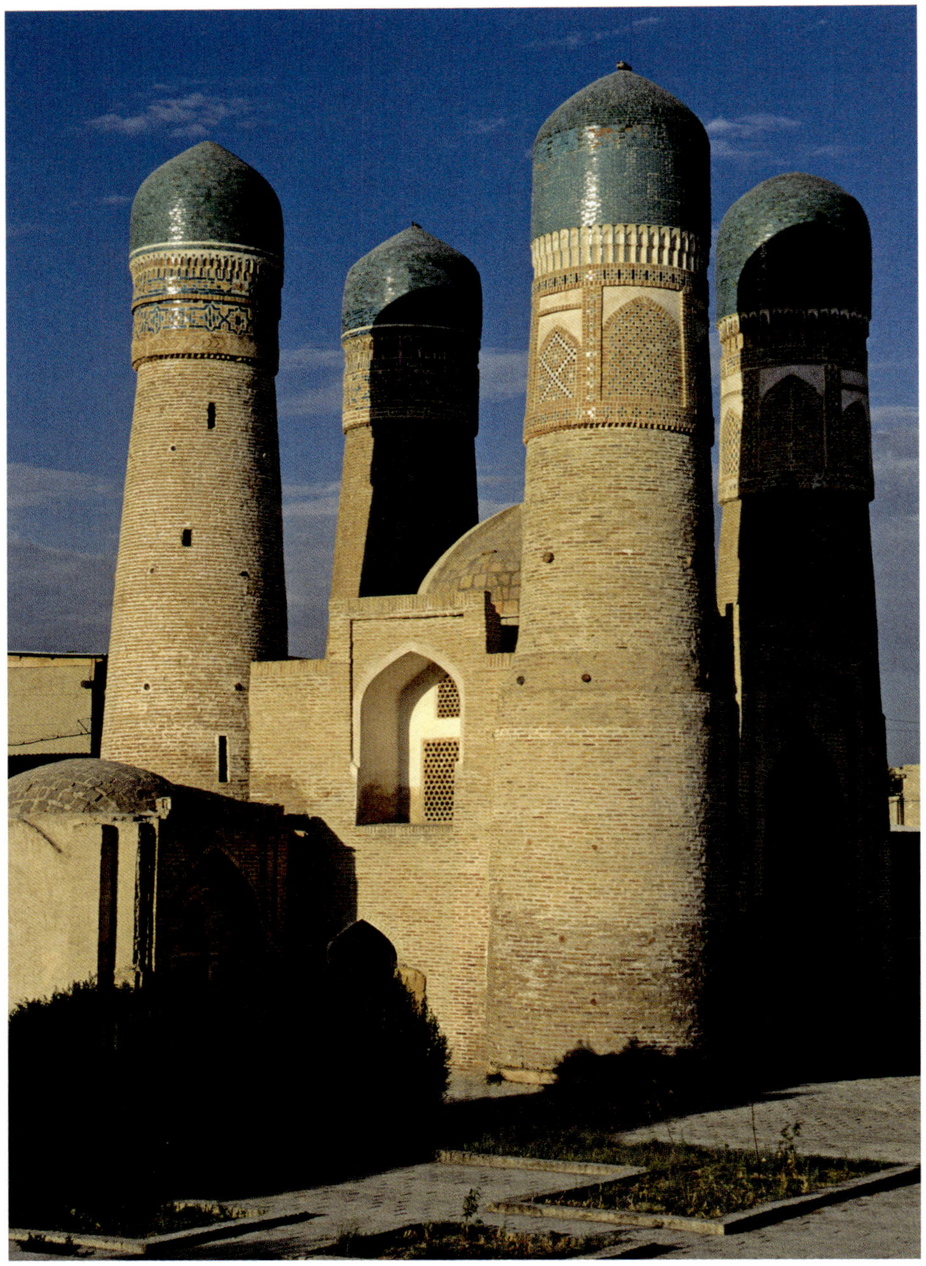

Tash Hauli
Harem courtyard
1831–1841
Khiva, Uzbekistan

In the heart of the despotically governed khanates, the persistence of the Persian tradition could still spawn some remarkably fine examples of architecture. Formally deft and beautifully refined in their decor, seeing them today it is impossible to picture the depths of iniquity and depravity into which the courts in these little enclaves forgotten by the march of history were to sink. Towards 1830 the murderous Khan Allah Quli turned to his court architect Usto Nur Mohammed Tajikhan to build him a new palace. When the plan, articulated around three great courtyards and some 163 rooms, was approved, the Khan promptly ordained that the work be finished in three years. When the hapless architect explained that this was physically impossible, his master had him impaled. The unattractive contract then passed over to the architect Kalender Khivaki, who called upon the services of the famous ceramist Abdullah Jin, in addition to more than a thousand slaves. In the court of the harem, the khan and his four official wives had at their disposition the five glorious southern *iwans,* while the rest of his female entourage was lodged in less lavish apartments. A secret corridor led to the second courtyard, the Ishrat Hauli, used for receptions. In winter, a comfortable *yurt* was erected on a round platform to accommodate Turkmen, Uzbeks and Kazakhs in keeping with their habits. A third courtyard, the Arz Hauli, was dedicated to the administration of justice. Of the two closely guarded exits, one was reserved for the acquitted and the other for the condemned.

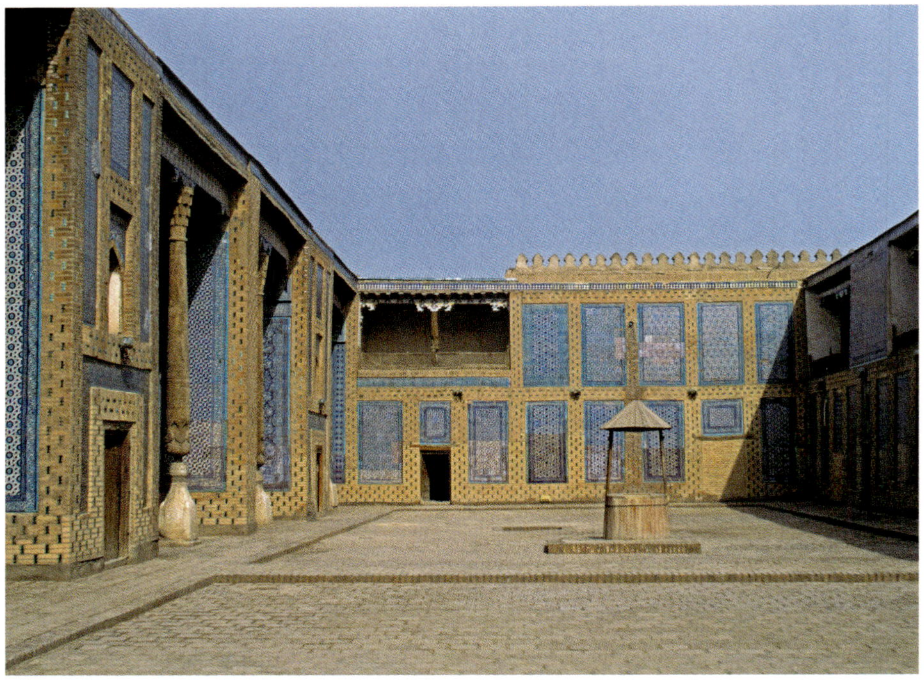

Chor Minar
1807
Bukhara, Uzbekistan

During the darkest days of its history the city of Bukhara was governed by the Manghit dynasty (1753–1920). Characterized by economic stagnation, religious fanaticism and grim viciousness, these autocratic emirs proved either unable to ride out buffetings of history or else fanatic and homicidal in their megalomania. If the great epoch of traditional architecture was by now a thing of the past, a few worthy monuments were erected in a lively if provincial vocabulary, such as the unusual entrance to the madrasah of Calif Niyazkul (since disappeared) known as the Chor Minar ('four minarets').

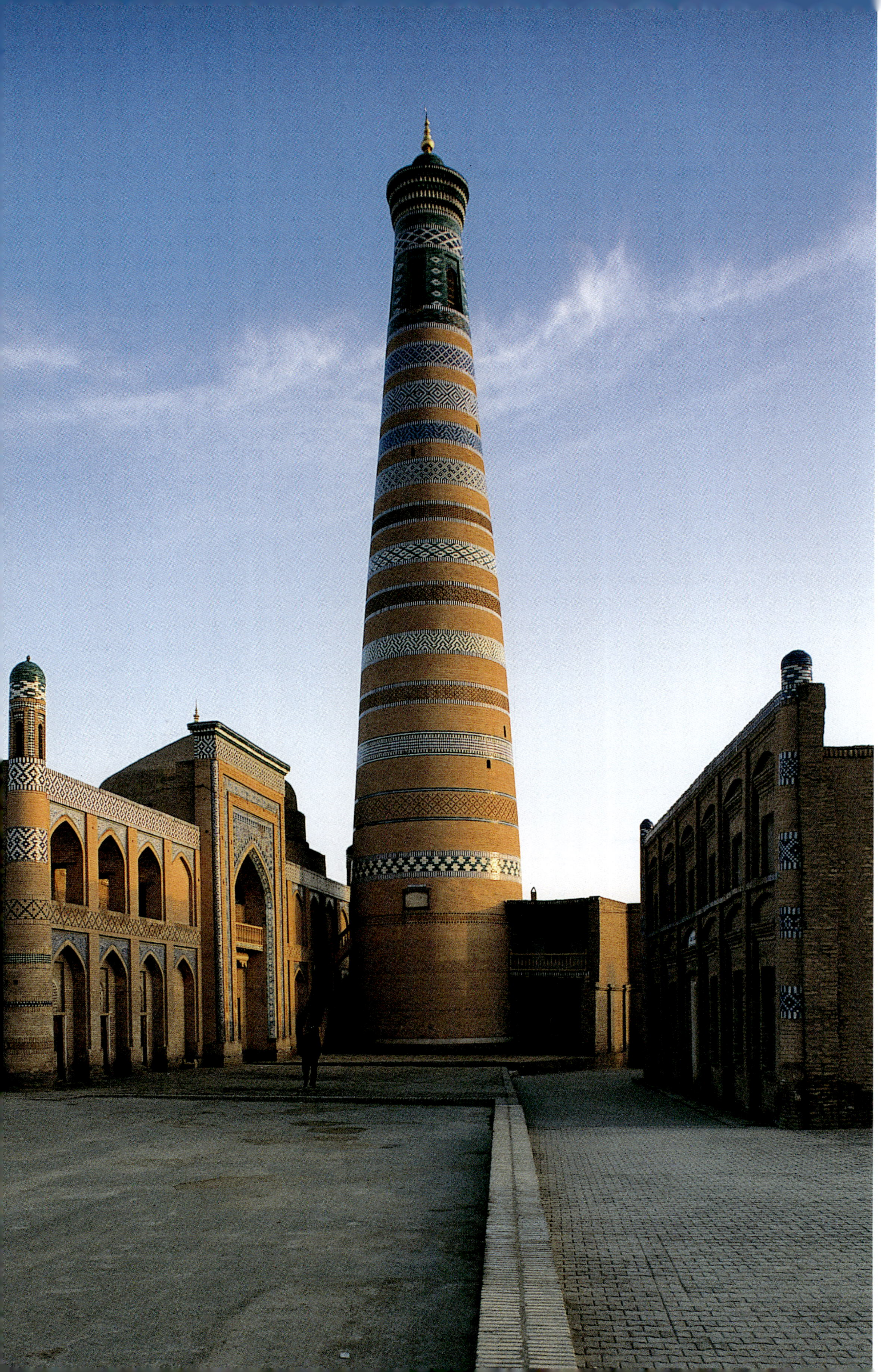

Madrasah and minaret of Islam Khodja (on the left), Soviet school (right)
1908–1910, 1912
Khiva, Uzbekistan

Miraculously intact, Khiva conserves its urban fabric and architecture, as if the clock had stopped in the age of the khans. The present-day surface area corresponds to the seventeenth-century city and is still ringed by the circular beaten earth walls with characteristic bastions of huge size sprouting in heavy and dumpy forms. The modest madrasah of Islam Khodja displays the by now customary solution of the double loggia on the façade, with the inevitable *pishtaq* and slender towerlets at the corners in what is a graceful throwback to the Timurid tradition. Adorned with the usual horizontal ceramic banding, the minaret swells to a width of nine metres at its base and stands approximately forty-five high, although the vertical thrust of the tower is emphasized by its marked taper. The building opposite was the first Soviet school in the city, originally built in 1912 in the local architectural style and thus a relic of a past age. This harmonious ensemble reflects the admittedly embalmed vitality of a thousand-year-old architectural tradition of which the buildings of Khiva remain, in spite of their provincial accents, the very last examples in Central Asia.

THE OTTOMAN EMPIRE

Mehmet Agha (c. 1540–1617)
Sultan Ahmet Mosque
(Blue Mosque)
1609–1617
Istanbul, Turkey

Mimar Sinan (1491–1588)
Mosque of Rüstem Pasha
Interior with the *minbar*
1561–1562
Istanbul, Turkey

The Ottoman beys rose to importance in the region of Iznik (Nicaea) during the decline of Seljuk rule. In 1326 the Ottomans conquered Bursa, making it their capital, and in the following decade took possession of northern Greece, Macedonia and Bulgaria, then of Thrace, where Adrianopolis, renamed Edirne, became their capital on European soil (1366). In 1389, Bayazit I (1389–1402) defeated the Christians in the decisive battle of Kosovo; the Anatolian beyliks still under Ilkhanid rule subsequently fell to him successively. In 1394, the caliph of Cairo conferred on him the title of sultan, which guaranteed his dynasty the right to rule over Islamic countries. In 1402, the seemingly unstoppable Ottoman advance was temporarily halted by Timur, from whom the Anatolian beys had sought protection, in a major battle near Ankara. After a period of disorganization and internal struggles, Bayazit I's expansionist policy resumed, culminating in the triumphal entry of Mehmet II Fatih into Constantinople in 1453. This became the new capital, thus crowning an age-old ambition of the Turks and the Muslims. Anatolia, still for the most part Christian, was islamicized by means of an extensive network of social and charitable institutions and the ubiquitous Sufi missionaries, who took over all the activities hitherto under the control of the Byzantine state and the Orthodox Church. The Ottomans continued the Seljuk policy of supporting religious foundations and lay institutions as a way of controlling them: libraries, mosques, madrasahs, caravanserais, bridges, aqueducts, hospitals and hospices were all built in great numbers, and – at least in the

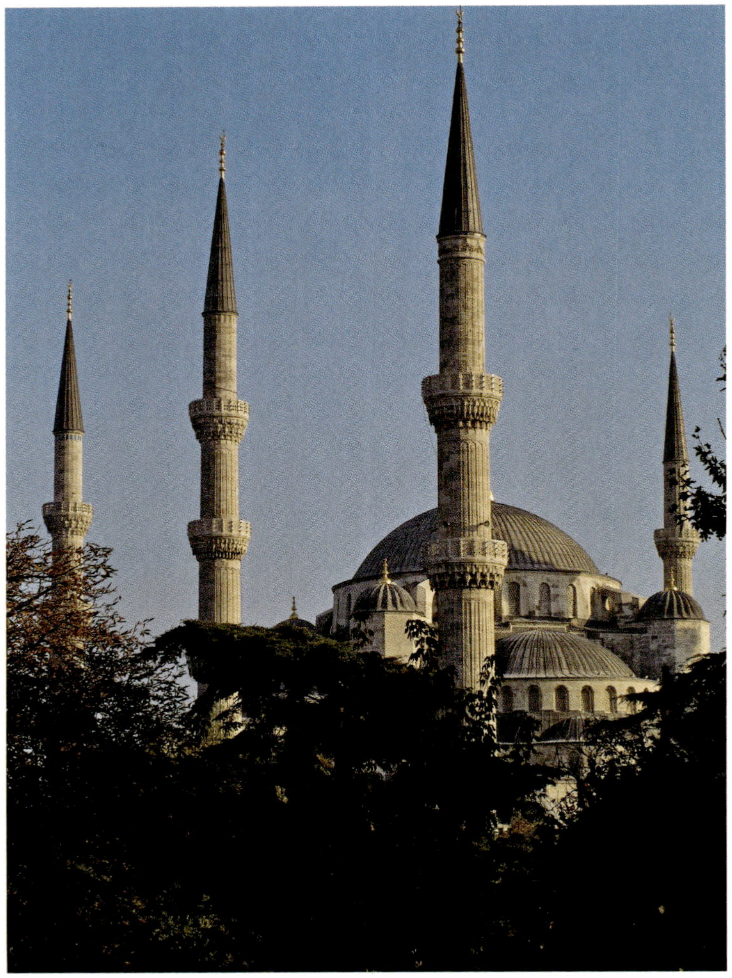

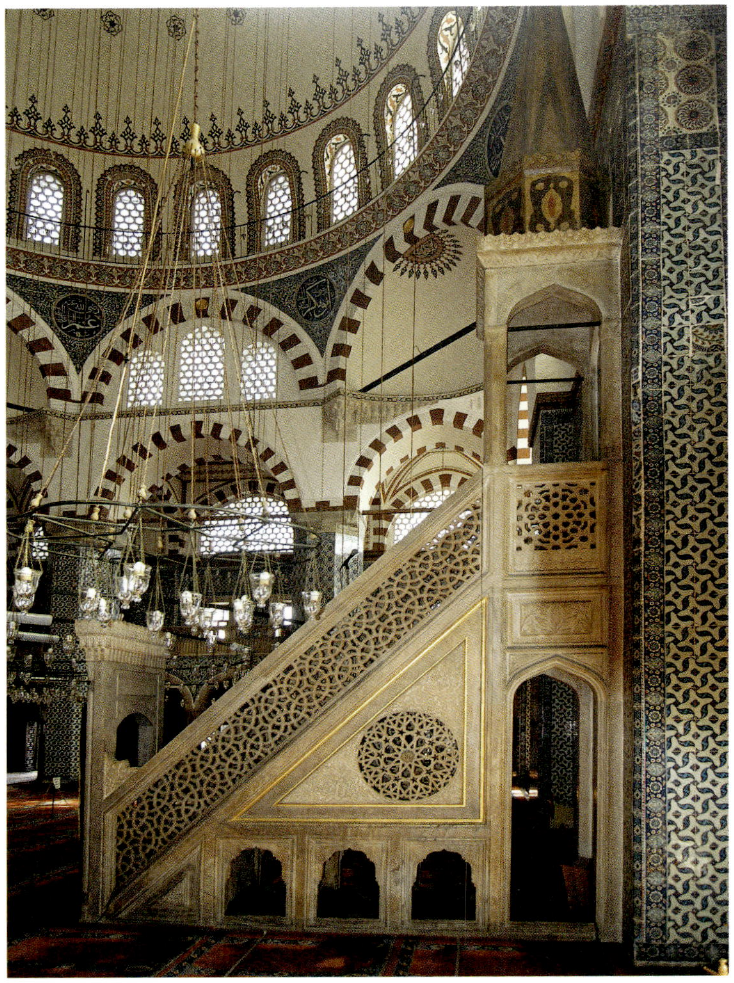

towns – a new entrepreneurial and cosmopolitan urban society involved both the elite groups and the Christian masses in the reconstruction which followed the invasions and the internal strife. With the victory over the Persian Shias at Chaldiran (1514), eastern Anatolia with its trade routes to the Persian Gulf was incorporated into the empire, followed by Syria (1516) and the Mamluk Empire (1517). Under Suleiman I the Lawmaker, known in the West as the Magnificent (1520–1566), the empire reached its zenith in every respect. Suleiman seized Mecca and Medina, setting himself up as their protector, conquered Baghdad (1534) and North Africa except for Morocco (1552), and advanced into Europe as far as Hungary. The cost of these campaigns was extremely high, however, and by around 1580 the capacity of Turkish power to expand further was over. In 1639, after interminable wars, the frontiers with Persia were finally stabilized, conclusively drawing a line between the Turkish and Persian worlds and bringing Turkey closer to Arab and European culture. The last Siege of Vienna (1683) signalled the final waning of the active power of the empire, which thereafter gradually became the object of European interference and eventually broke up in the First World War.

The roots of Ottoman art lie deep in Seljuk Anatolia, whose own inheritance was enriched by its contact with Byzantine art and above all architecture. In a less direct way, it also drew on the architectural and urban legacy of Hellenism, which shaped it like an invisible agency, particularly in architectural matters, and spurred it on in the quest for a major upward leap, to new solutions in vertical development and innovative ideas in town-planning. The earliest examples of Ottoman architecture are found at Iznik, and reflect its progressive assimilation of and then dialogue with Seljuk and Byzantine traditions. From the start, there was a quest for a greater spatial unity using fewer supports in order to cover a larger space with a single dome. The classic Seljuk hypostyle mosque was revived as the *ulu cami* (great mosque), since it could be developed on a grander scale. It was characterized by a flat roof or a dome supported on pillars, as in several religious buildings but more especially in the great covered markets (*bedesten*). The T-plan was developed in Bayazit I's complex of buildings at Bursa from about 1400: in this arrangement several domes are aligned on the same axis, at right angles to a sort of transept matching the façade, whose lateral wings were intended for the fraternities. There were several variations in the ambitious Yesil Cami (1412–1420) and then the Muradiye Cami of 1424–1426, in an only partially successful attempt to unify the interior. The huge doorways with squinches on *muqarnas,* an oculus in one of the domes and rich internal decoration were carried over from Seljuk tradition. After the conquest of Constantinople, direct experience of masterpieces of Byzantine architecture, particularly the Hagia Sophia, allowed the construction of spacious domed halls, opening the way to the great phase of classical Ottoman architecture that culminated in the work of Sinan. Thanks to its Seljuk roots and enriched by its Hellenistic legacy, such architecture could stand comparison with Byzantine masterpieces, assimilating them without being overwhelmed by them and with Sinan himself finally arriving at autonomous solutions of absolute validity that were fully and authentically Ottoman in every detail. The new architectural language was characterized by an inherently imperial propensity for monumentality and a non-iconic, almost puritanical, formal idiom, but with the persistence of Seljuk motifs still confined to established layouts.

Ceramics evolved in a very different way, developing medieval ideas and experiencing continual growth, thanks in particular to the arrival of master ceramicists from Tabriz in the fifteenth and again in the sixteenth centuries. It was a time when a new concept appeared with the introduction of huge panels produced in specialized workshops in Constantinople and intended to cover large areas of interior walls. In a subsequent phase, the manufactories of Iznik proved particularly successful in meeting the ever-growing demand for tiles to cover enormous surfaces and also for luxury tableware.

Iznik's boast was to have combined its industrial-scale production with a quality which, if falling short of the heights of hand-made ceramics, maintained an excellent standard throughout the sixteenth century. Its products were distributed throughout the empire and also successfully exported.

The increase in glazed surfaces in mosques, where polychrome splinters were introduced into mouldings in gesso or stucco, together with the more widespread white glass, gave quite a boost to the art of glass-making. Wall art, particularly if used as a decorative element in the mosques, was part of the Turkish tradition, with geometric motifs, animal forms and stylized vegetation in vivid colours and remarkable calligraphic inserts.

Miniaturists drew on the Turkish heritage from Central Asia rather than Persia, harking back to the Timurid world – at least until, towards the end of the seventeenth century, they began to lose their identity under pressure from Europeanizing fashions.

It was, however, in the carpets of Anatolia that the Turkish spirit emerged with tremendous exuberance, at least up to the sixteenth century, thanks to the development of stepped geometric designs. Their patterns were named after the European painters who reproduced them in their pictures, which is in itself an indication of their extraordinary success and value as status symbols.

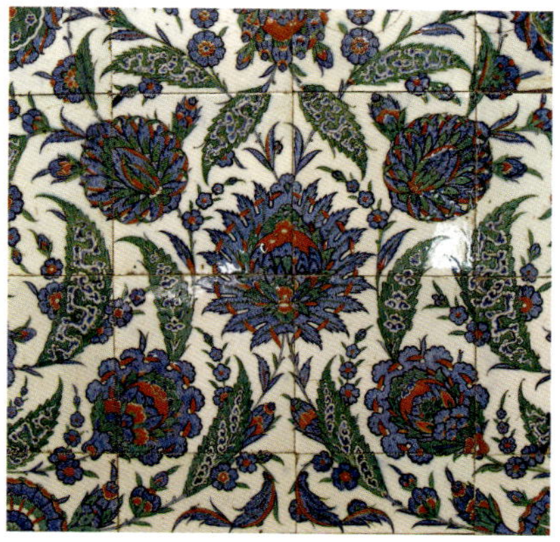

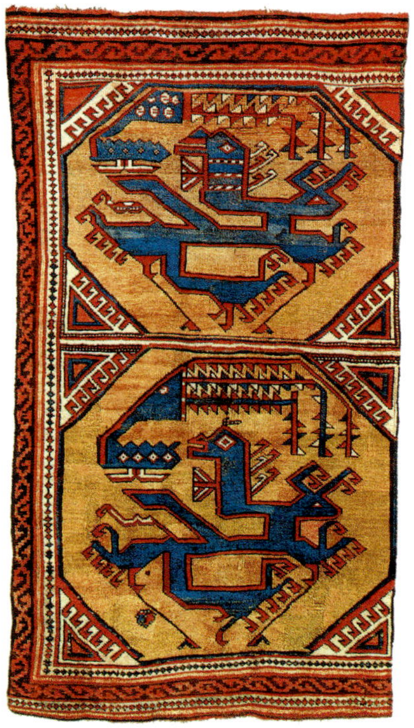

Mosque of Sokullu Mehmet Pasha
Detail of wall covering
1571–1572
Iznik ceramics
Istanbul, Turkey

'Ming' carpet
15th century
Anatolia
Museum für Islamische Kunst, Berlin

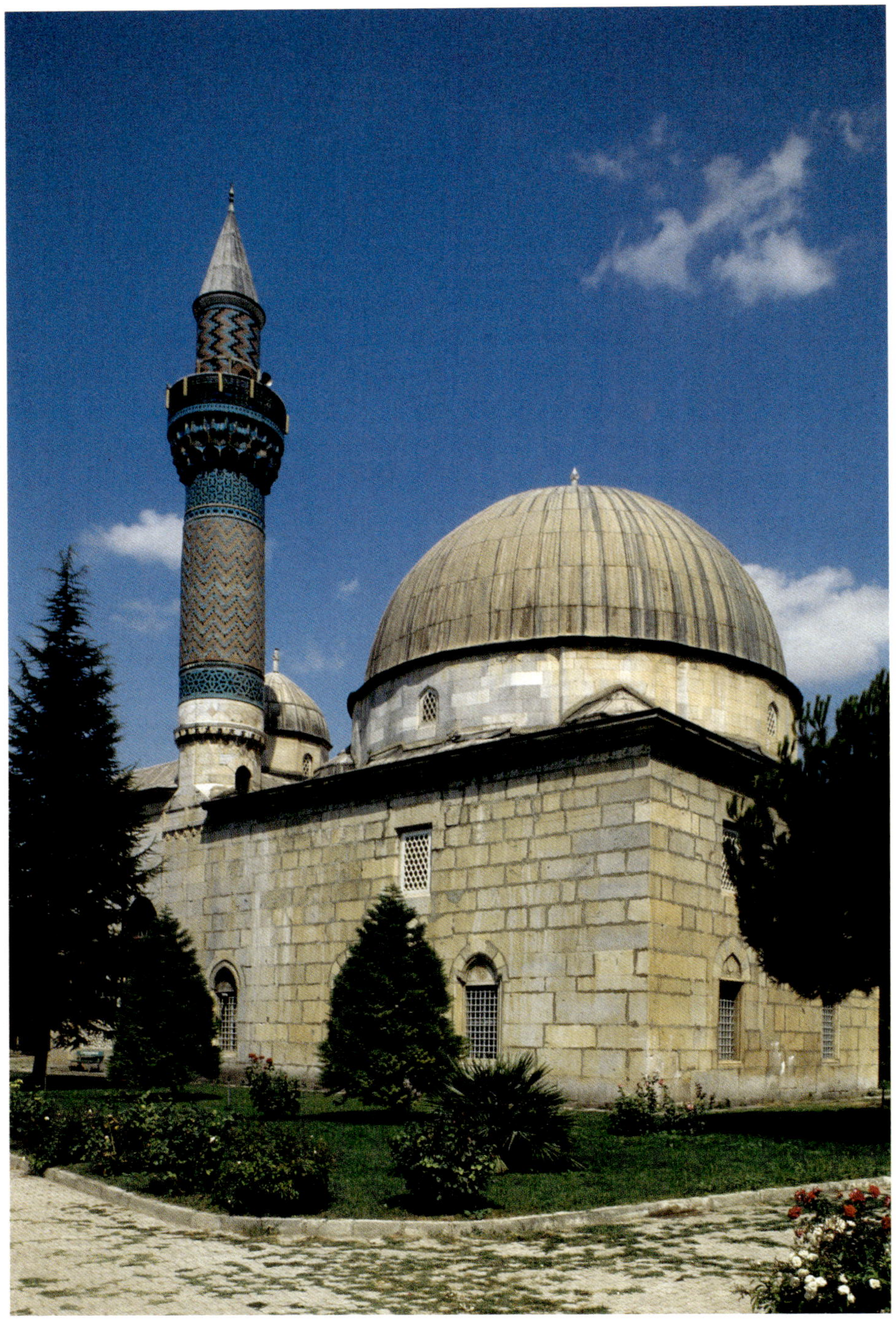

Yesil Cami (Green Mosque)
1378–1391
Iznik, Turkey

Iznik (formerly Nicea) was the first Ottoman capital for some time. Several buildings survive from those years that manifest in embryonic form features that would be developed more authoritatively later on. Even in its borrowings from Seljuk architecture, palpable in the shape and decoration of the restored minaret, there is a search for spatial unity, dominated by the great dome as the principal concern of the new architectural idiom. Marble sourced from classical buildings would be the stone *par excellence* of Ottoman architecture, while the arrangement of windows in several rows shows an explicit interest in improved lighting.

Mosque, Murat II complex
1426–1428
Bursa, Turkey

This complex, known as Muradiye, consists of mosques, madrasahs, an *imaret* (soup kitchen), *sibiyan mektebi* (Qur'anic school for children), *hammam* (hot bath) and twelve mausoleums for members of the Osman family. The mosque adopts the structure of the one built by Bayazit Yldirim twenty years earlier consisting of an inverse T-plan, with a five-arch portico in front leading via a vestibule to a central hall, flanked by two *iwan* at the sides and by a larger *iwan* towards the south that terminates in the niche of the *mihrab*. The central hall and the southern *iwan* are roofed by domes of equal height, supported by a circle of triangular stalactites.
The view from the top of the two aligned domes indicates an attempt to cover the internal space without any supports to interrupt the continuity. In imitating Byzantine models, the structure shows a desire to surpass Seljuk and Arab predecessors, but the side areas (not visible in the photograph) intended for the dervishes are rather unfocused.

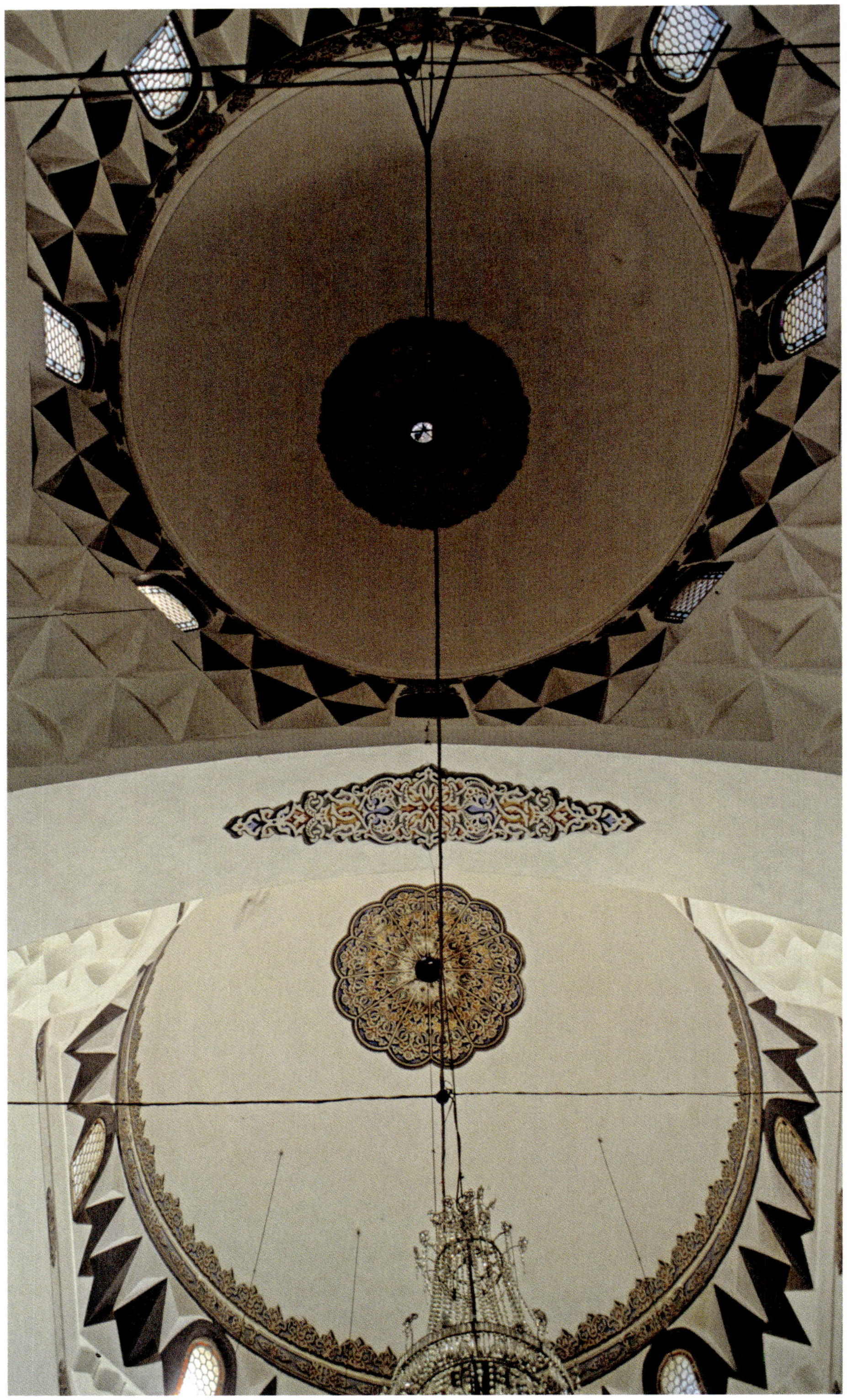

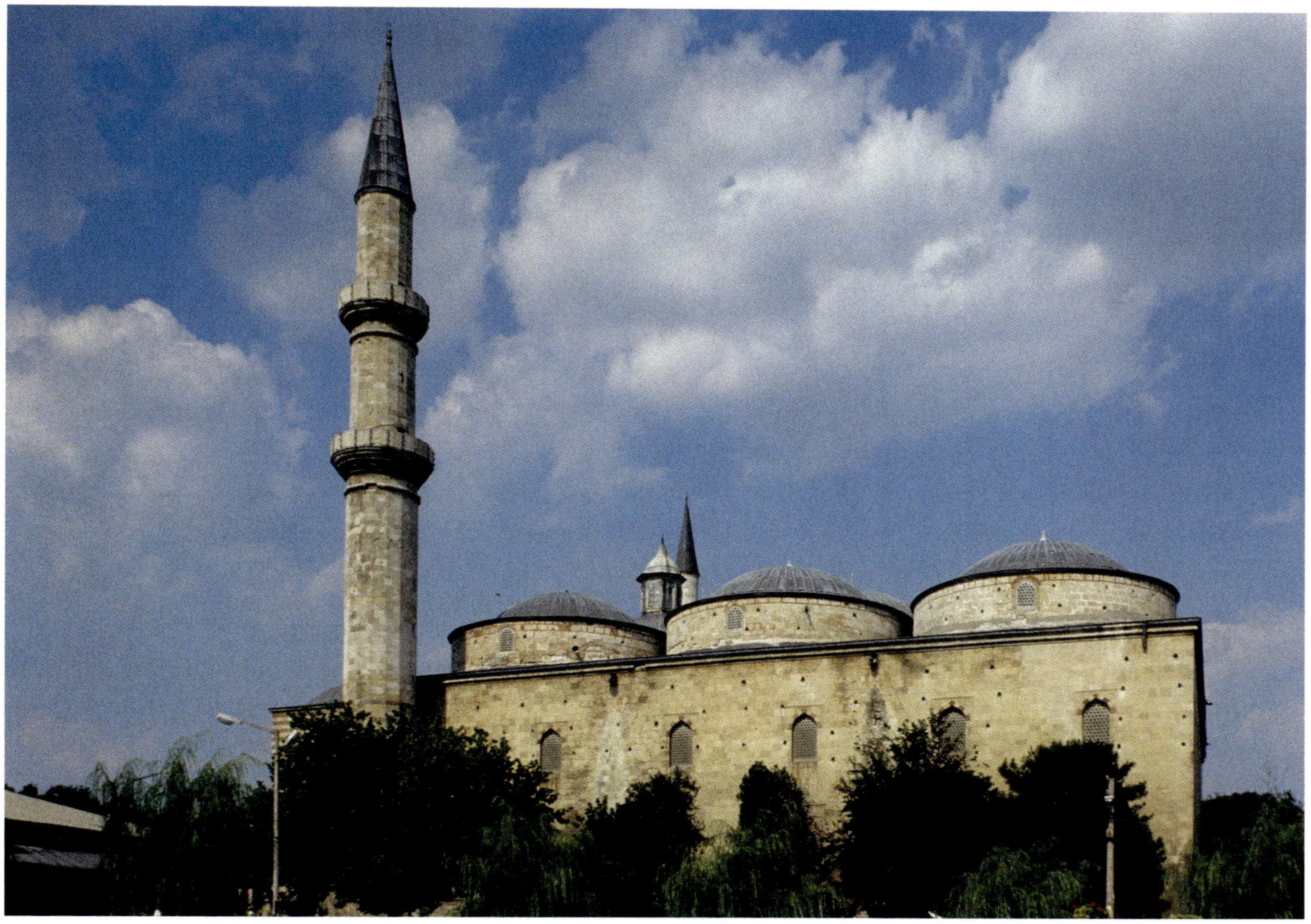

Eski Cami (Old Mosque)
1403–1414
Edirne, Turkey

The Eski Cami is constructed on a square plan with nine domes supported by four sturdy internal pillars. As is clear from the number, position and size of the windows, the lighting is inadequate. Externally it looks like a workaday building, lacking harmony and any clear architectural hierarchy: the three domes of the nave fail to stand out clearly from the others. There is moreover no element to link the rigid polyhedron of the lower part and the domes.

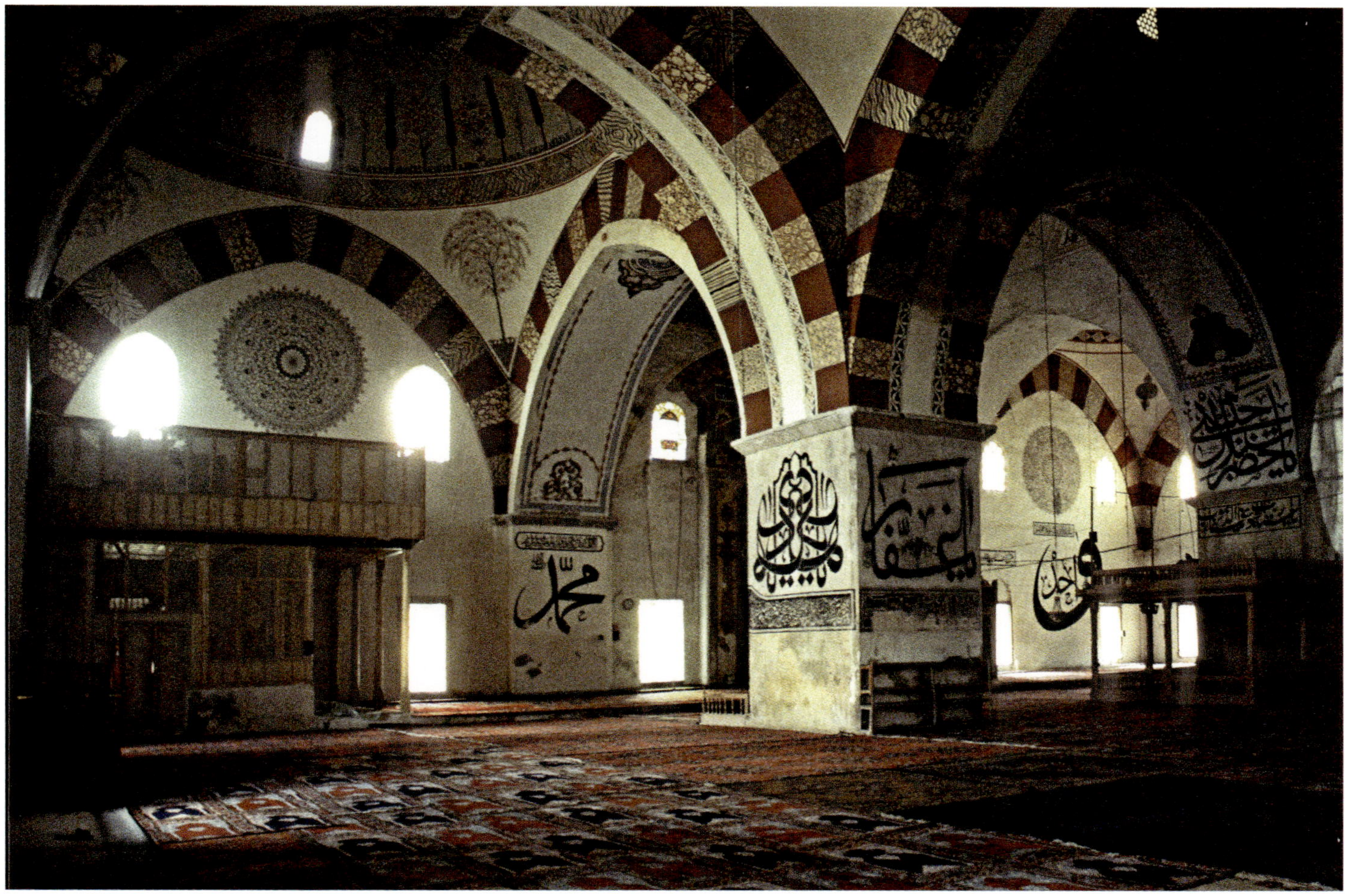

Eski Cami (Old Mosque) interior
1403–1414
Edirne, Turkey

The interior is weighed down by the four dome piers, which break up the spatial continuity and thus mar the centralization of the framework and surrounding areas, which ought to have lent architectural shape to the growing imperial ambitions of the Ottomans. The wonderful inscriptions, several of which repeat the letters in mirror fashion, date from the seventeenth to the eighteenth centuries.

Yesil Medrese (Green Madrasah) Window
1414–1424
Bursa, Turkey

Ottoman architecture offset medieval exuberance with skilfully balanced compositions, handling the relationship between empty and filled spaces and between space and ornament with precision, reducing the scale of details and confining them to inserts that were colourful rather than sculptural and decorative rather than expressive. Small, elegant inlays of Turkish ceramics add a touch of studied artifice to the stately rhythms of the walls.

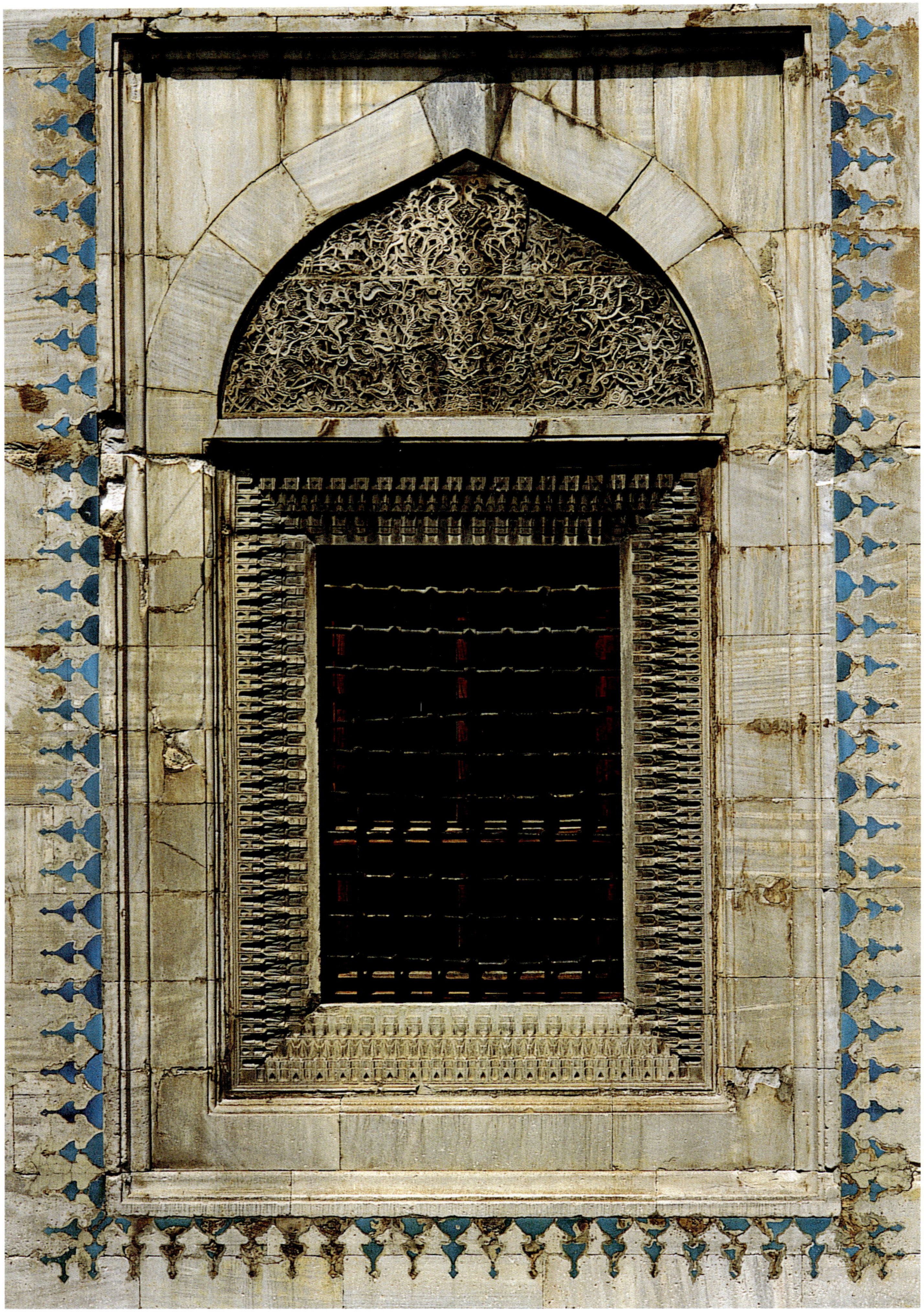

Üç Sherefeli Cami
(Mosque with Three Galleries)
Dome
1438–1447
Edirne, Turkey

The great dome, sumptuously painted with a medallion motif, shows both the aspirations and the limits of achievement among the more important works of the Islamic world at this period: buildings are still squat, heavy and very poorly lit. Construction techniques are unsure, as is shown by the two lateral domes with the relevant cluttered piers, not to mention the position and size of the windows. The more imaginative new development consists in supporting the central dome, as well as its front and back walls, on two free-standing pillars, anticipating the hexagonal plan that Sinan would adopt several times, though with quite different results. On the other hand, although massive, the two pillars do not impede views of the lateral areas reserved for the dervishes, ensuring a degree of spaciousness in the interior. Still evident is the quest for a space more extensive than that available in a mosque with only one dome of modest size, more homogeneous than the experiments with two domes or two vaults tried out in Bursa, and not affected by the dominant feature of depth of the T-plan.

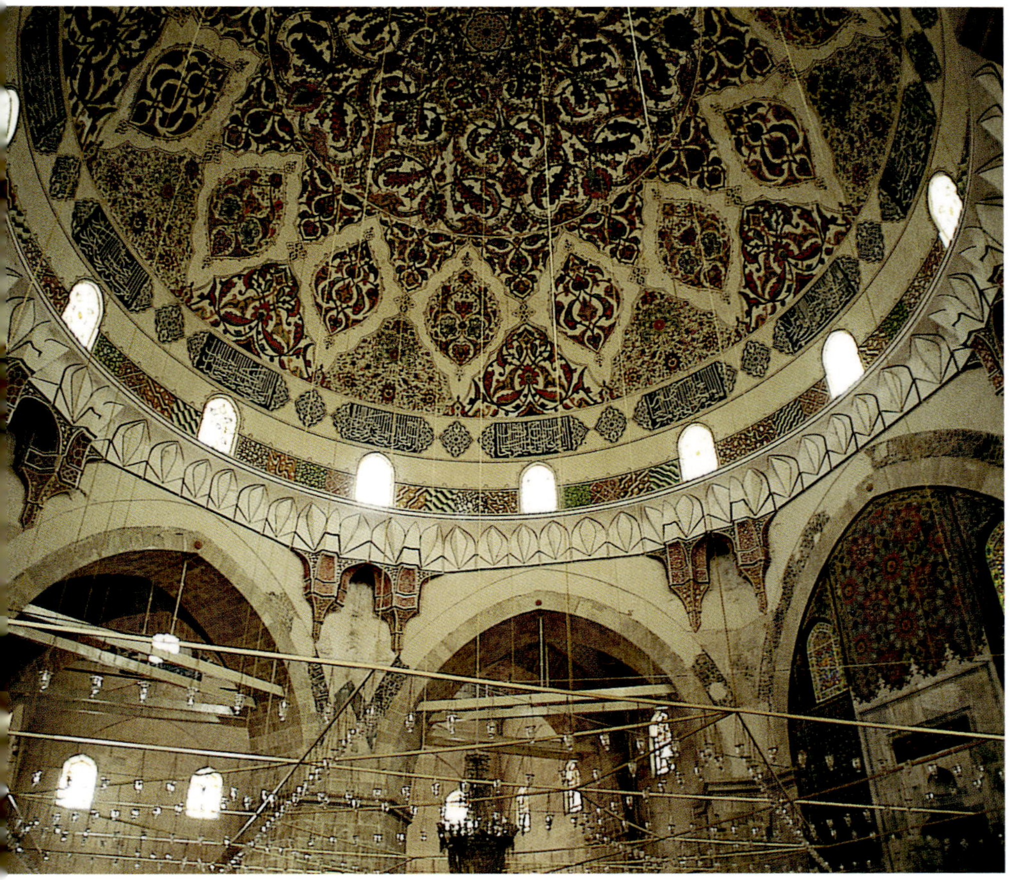

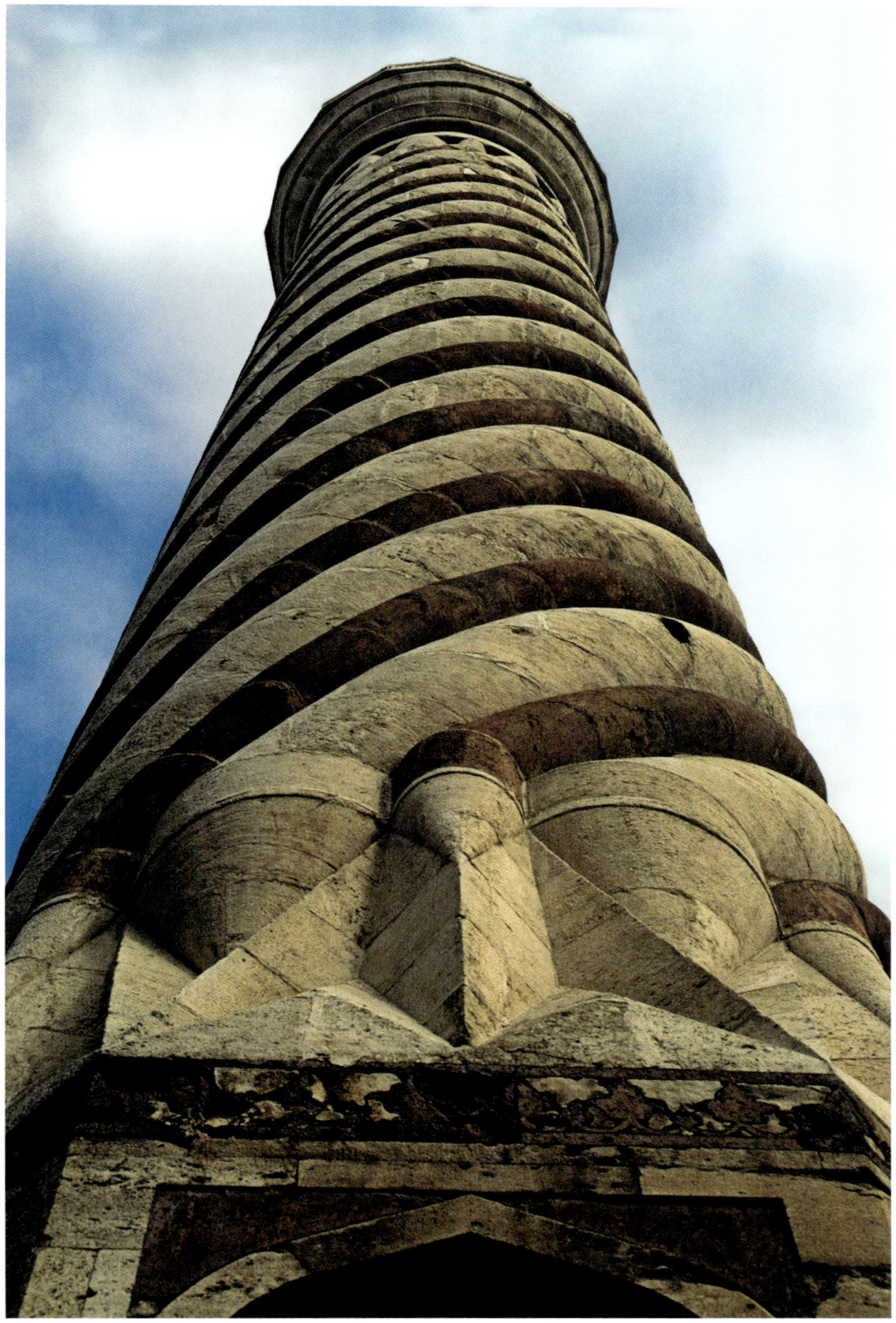

Üç Sherefeli Cami
(Mosque with Three Galleries)
Minaret
1438–1447
Edirne, Turkey

The establishment of the Ottoman architectural style went through a long period of settling in when every element of architectural structure was looked at, from the ground plan down to the smallest detail. Üç Sherefeli Cami is the first mosque to have four minarets, two situated at the very end of the courtyard and two at the point where the courtyard joins the mosque. However, the medieval spirit stands out boldly in the configuration of the minarets and in the decorative display, still strongly linked to Seljuk models, as manifest in the minaret at the southeast corner, which is characterized by a remarkable spiral motif in red stone springing with dramatic force from the octagonal base.

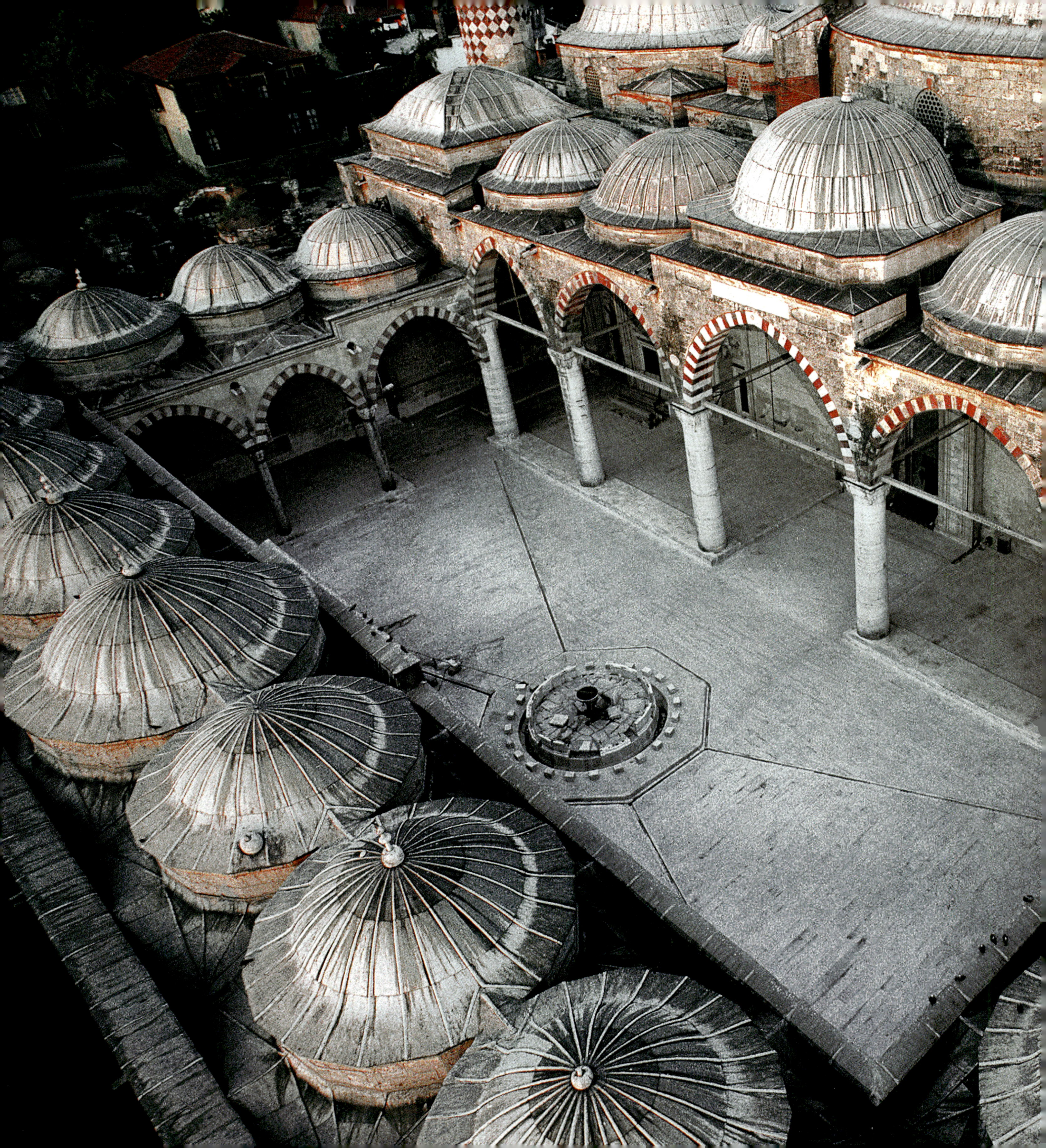

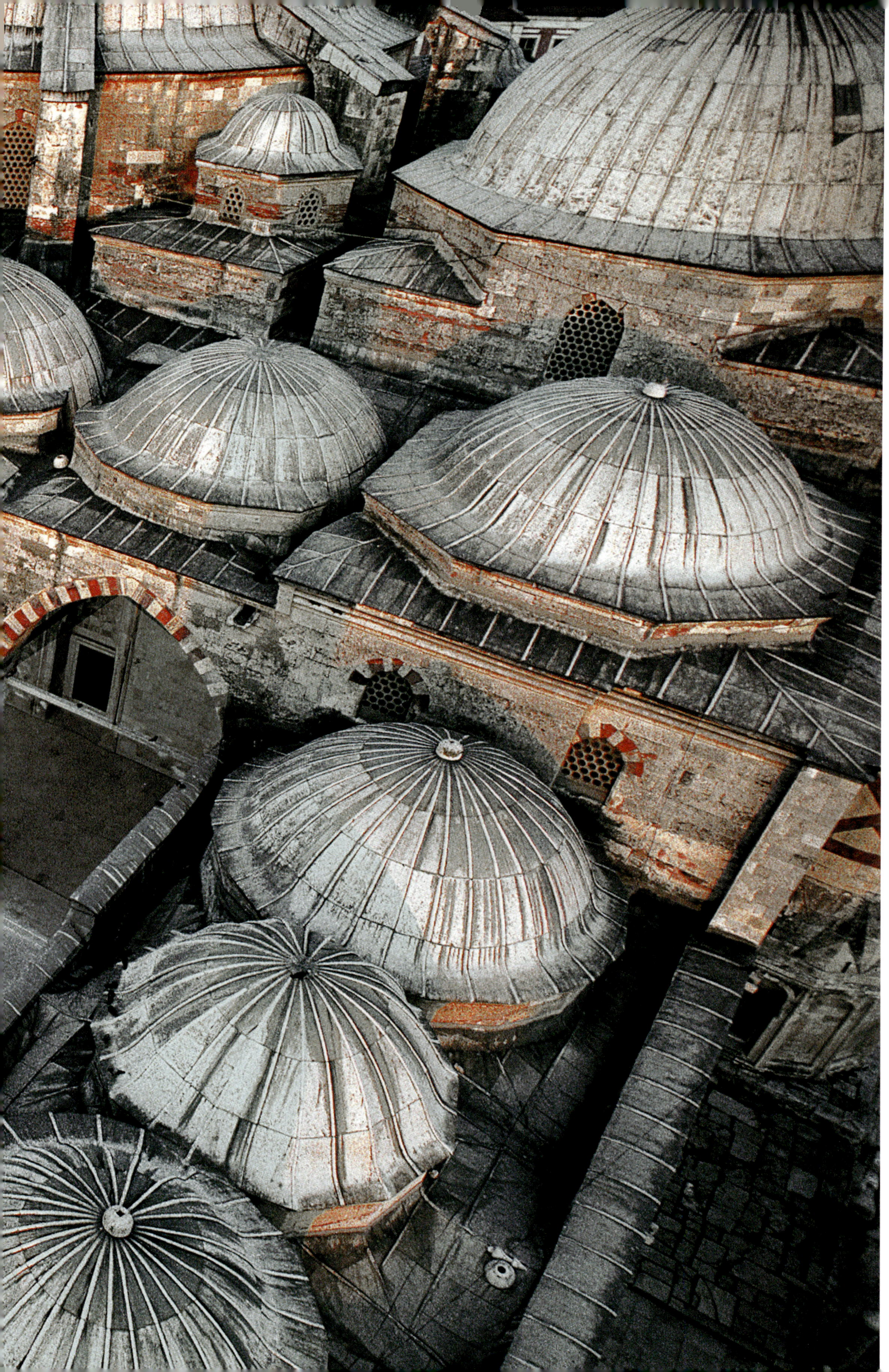

Üç Sherefeli Cami
(Mosque with Three Galleries)
Courtyard
1438–1447
Edirne, Turkey

In the new capital of Edirne, Murat II wanted to build a mosque that fully expressed the imperial ideology, which in the Ottoman era was the principal object of interest in the architecture of mosques. Positioning the courtyard in front of the covered hall was among the first experiments towards a solution that would become magnificently stately in successive implementations. Here, depth is clearly sacrificed, and without sufficient space it was obviously difficult to achieve a sense of majesty in the mosque, which is moreover dissipated between the main dome and the smaller ones beside it. The rhythm of the arches and of the little domes (asymmetrical in shape and number) rising from them is still erratic, even if there was an attempt to create a crescendo culminating in the arch over the entrance. Despite these obvious problems of approach, there is a new sense of clarity and monumentality in comparison with the earlier mosque of Isa Bey at Manisa.

Çinili Kösk (Ceramic Pavilion)
1472–1475
Istanbul, Turkey

Inside his new palace, Mehmet II built a fine pavilion in the area which later would become the complex of the Topkapi, known now as Çinili Kösk and distinguished by an unusual frontage with a long open gallery with columns originally of wood. The inscription in Persian verse indicates that the dome was covered with tiles enamelled green, similar to various mosques in Bursa and Iznik. The *iwan* at the entrance is entirely covered with blue enamel, like the façade, with motifs clearly of Timurid derivation, and it was probably the work of Persian craftsmen or of artists who had trained in Persia.
The interior was similarly splendid, as this inscription records: "Its floor, turquoise with various flowers … evokes the eternal vineyards of paradise."

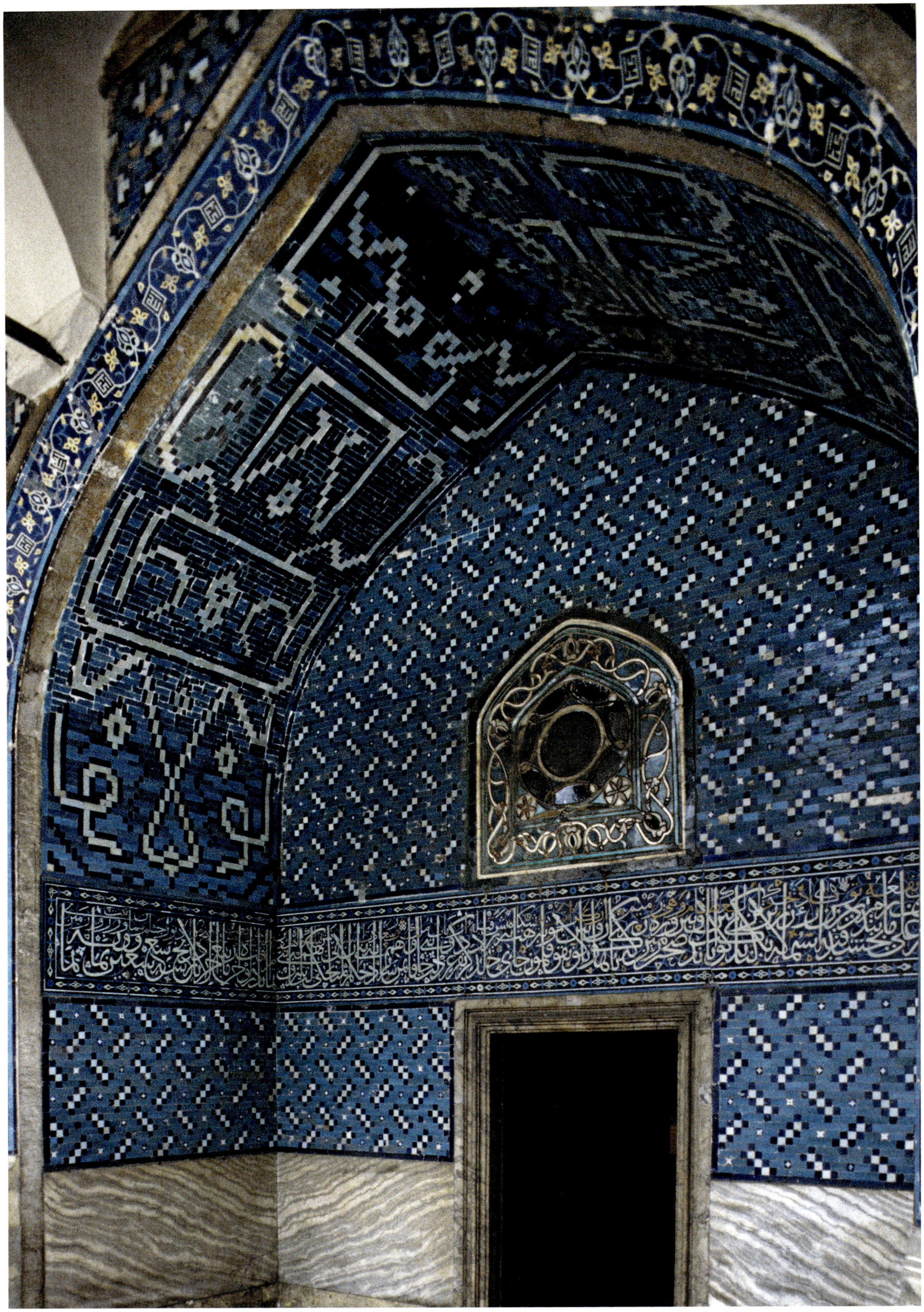

Rumeli Hisar
1452
Istanbul, Turkey

On the point of besieging Constantinople, Mehmet II built the Rumeli Hisar fortress in under four months ("the Rumelian fort," on the Rum [Greek] shore), which, with its counterpart Anadolu Hisar of 1390 on the Asian shore, guaranteed coverage of contacts between the two shores of the Bosphorus). In addition to its military value, the building is an interesting anticipation of the perfect functioning of the administrative machine and coordination of building works that would characterize the next century.

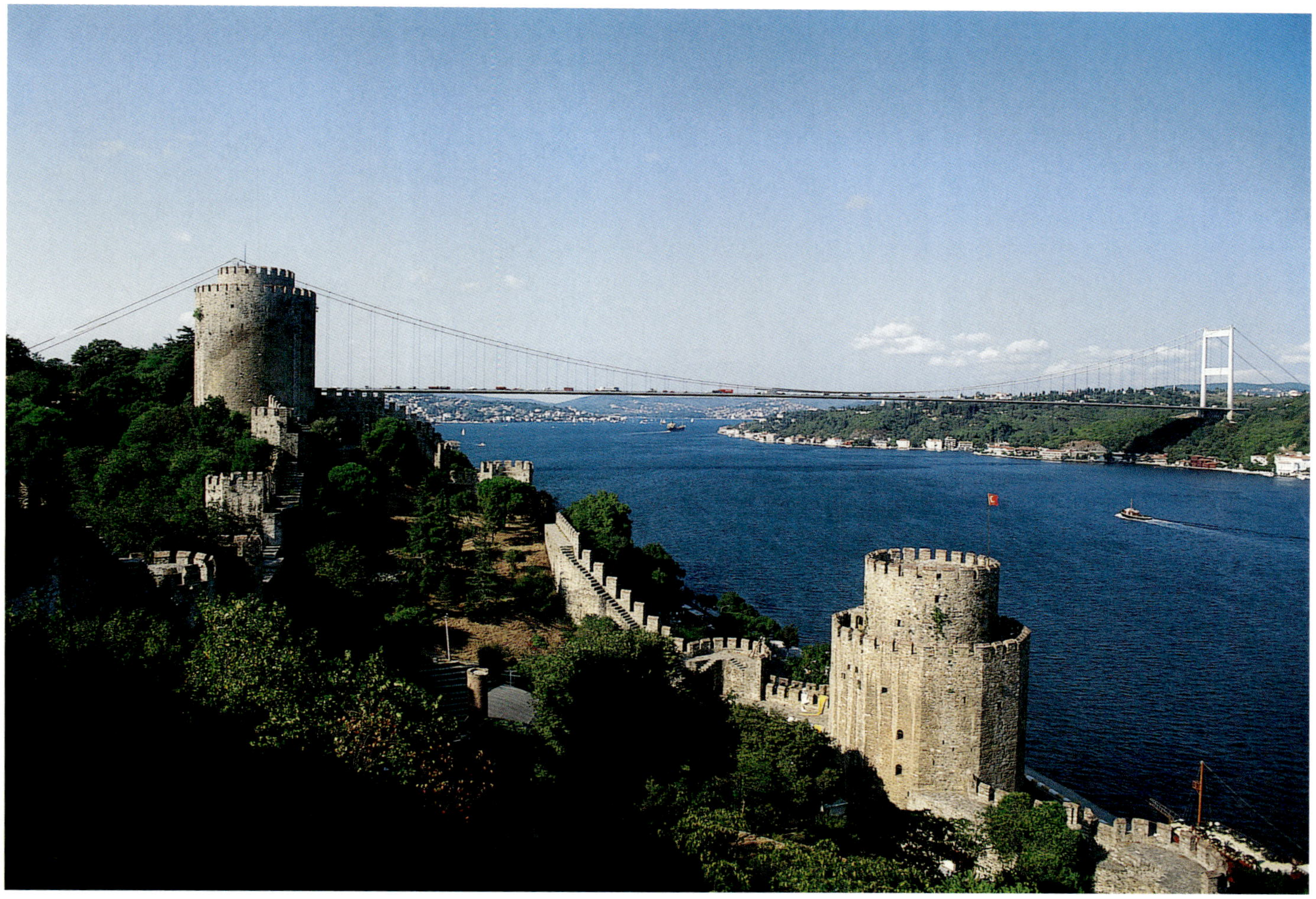

Hayreddin (1442–1512)
***Külliye* of Bayazit II**
1484–1488
Edirne, Turkey

With the *külliye* (a building complex housing charitable functions) at Edirne, built by architect Hayreddin for Bayazit II, Ottoman architecture reached the threshold of its mature form, thanks to the liberal but balanced arrangement of different architectural buildings around an open space. They were unified by an impeccable stylistic consistency, homogeneity of materials, repetition of identical elements and the dynamic crescendo which culminates in the dome of the hexagonal hall of the hospital and its lantern, and is echoed by the grandly austere mass of the mosque framed by its pair of minarets. Other notable features are the relationship between parameters such as surfaces and volumes – horizontal, vertical and curved lines mutate constantly with the angle of perception – and the strong features of the complex. The shape of the mosque is still simple and lacking dynamism: it is just a cube with a sphere inscribed in it, its outline rising in the low arch of the dome without any clear architectural values emerging from this geometrical relationship. The numerous windows along the walls indicate a desire to provide adequate lighting inside.

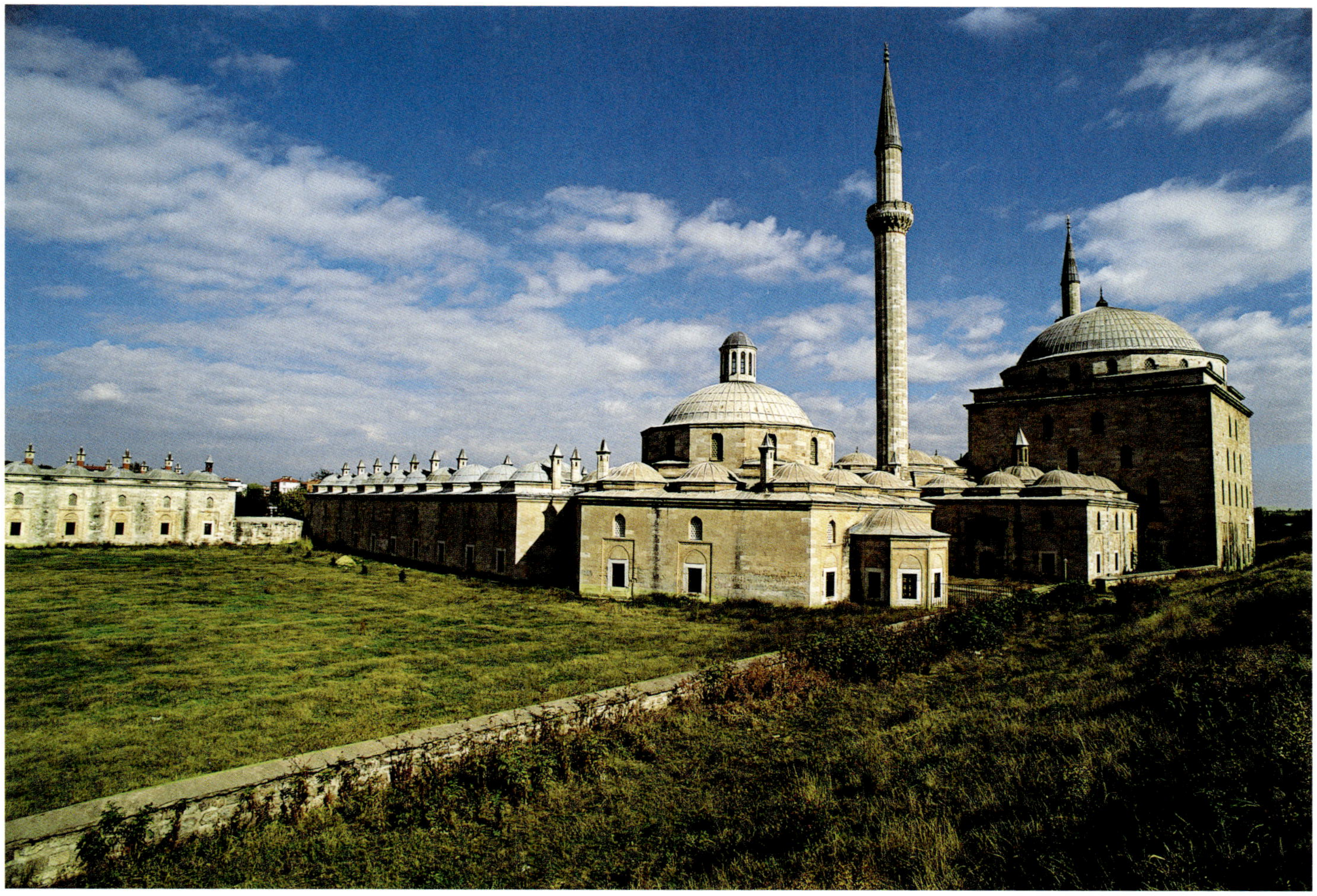

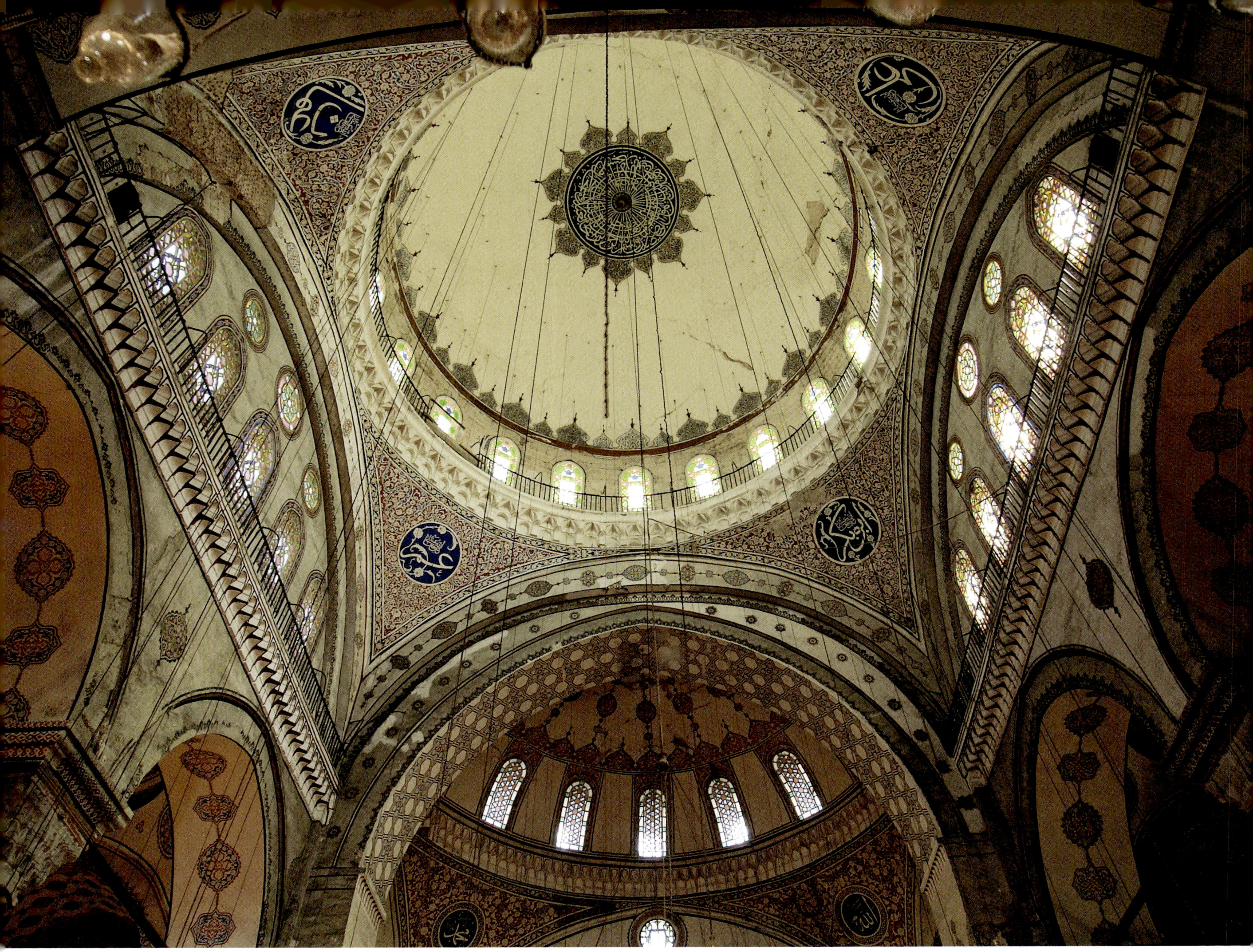

Hayreddin (1442–1512)
Mosque of Bayazit
Dome
1501–1506
Istanbul, Turkey

The construction of the sultan's mosque is probably the work of Hayreddin. It was modelled on Hagia Sophia, although a long way from it in size, or the diameter and height of the dome (31 x 55 metres as opposed to 17.5 x 36 metres in the mosque).
Whereas the use of the half-dome as a support for the principal dome is derived from Hagia Sophia, the mosque differs from it radically by substituting for the galleries a screen with monumental lateral arches supported by a single large pillar. This permits a clearer, more homogeneous space with better light penetration quite distinct from the indeterminate diffuseness of a Byzantine interior, firmly dominated by a dome which, even if its dimensions are relatively modest, does not lack grandeur. After an earthquake destroyed the mosque of Mahomet the Conqueror, the first built in the new capital, the mosque of Bayazit was the first with the authentic imperial look and dimensions.

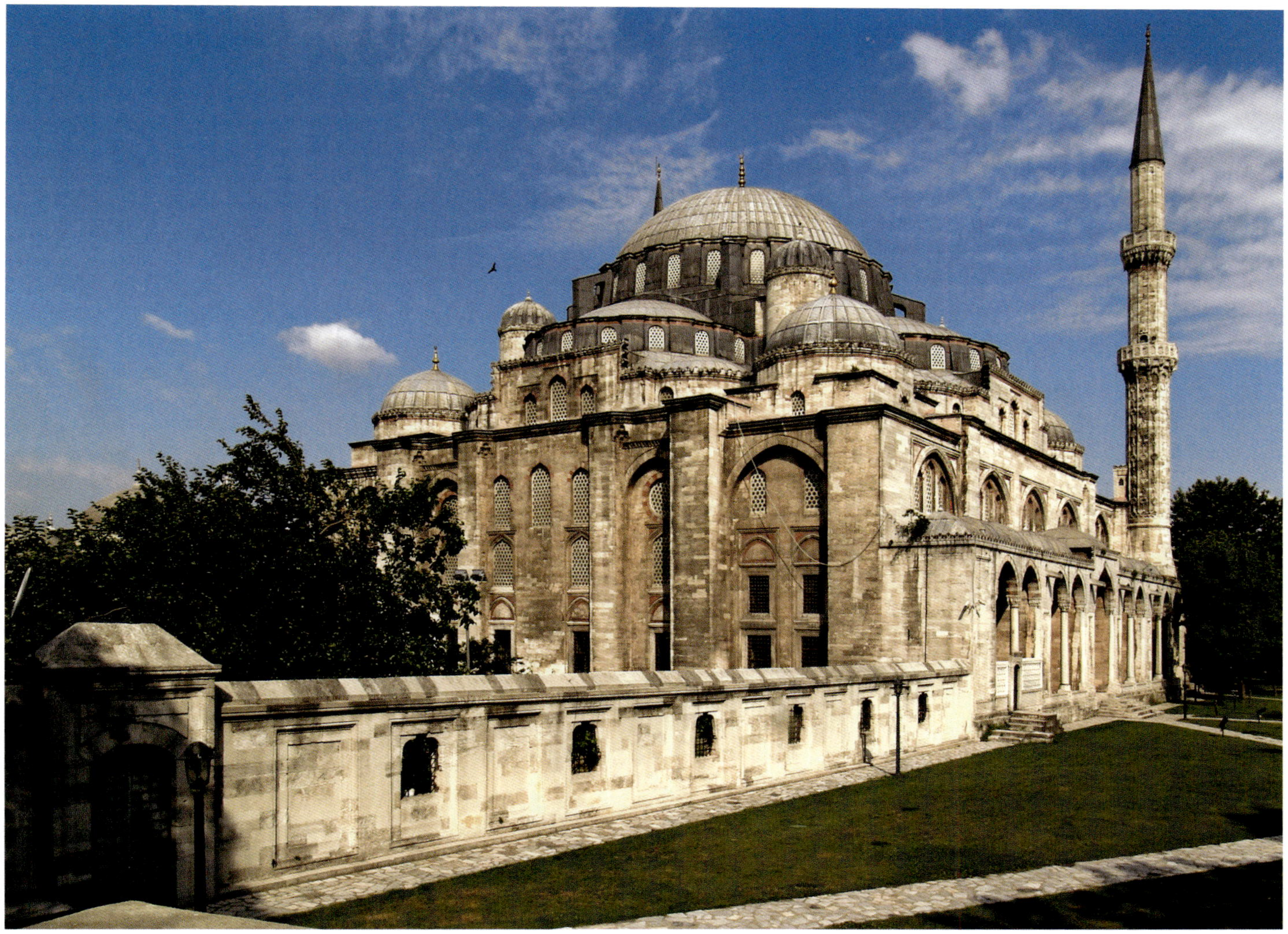

Mimar Sinan (1491–1588)
Sehzade Cami (Prince's Mosque)
1543–1548
Istanbul, Turkey

In 1543, the skyline of Istanbul was enhanced by the silhouette of a new mosque commissioned by Suleiman. It was the first work of Sinan (1491–1588). He was a Christian from central Anatolia, but later educated among the janissary élite as a military engineer, where he acquired extraordinary technical competence. Having become court architect in 1539, Sinan took Ottoman architecture to its peak. The Sehzade Mosque enabled him to put into practice lessons learnt in the course of restoring Hagia Sophia. In order to make the building sounder and create a more coherent space, Sinan added (compared with Hagia Sophia) a half-dome on each side to take the thrust of the central dome carried on four great piers. Thanks to the symmetrical ground plan thus achieved, he simplified to perfection the relationships between the various parts of the building, both inside and outside. The careful arrangement of the four larger half domes and of the smaller ones at the corners also took the weight off the side walls very efficiently, rendering unnecessary the external buttresses added at different times that had darkened the interior of Hagia Sophia.

Hayreddin (1442–1512)
Mosque of Bayazit
1501–1506
Istanbul, Turkey

For the first time, the exterior establishes a monumental (i.e. imperial) iconography, surpassing the Byzantine model in its unparalleled relationship of lines and volumes, conveying a firm hierarchy of the architectural elements in the context of an architecture perceived as something organically coherent. The almost square courtyard anticipates the emergence of the façade from the loggia, while a precise vertical measurement is articulated by the tympanum rising from the central arch. From here the upper volumes seem to develop with great power, even if they are linked together rather hesitantly. Among the weak points which would later be rectified especially in the works of Sinan is the great semicircle of the internal half dome, which is clumsily joined to the square beneath and awkwardly inserted into the end structure. The presence of two side halls for the use of the dervishes is reminiscent of the T-plan, but incompatible with a central building; the two minarets are consequently distanced, being placed right at their extremities so that they remain disconnected and ineffectual at the ends of the setting and sweep of the centrally domed elements.

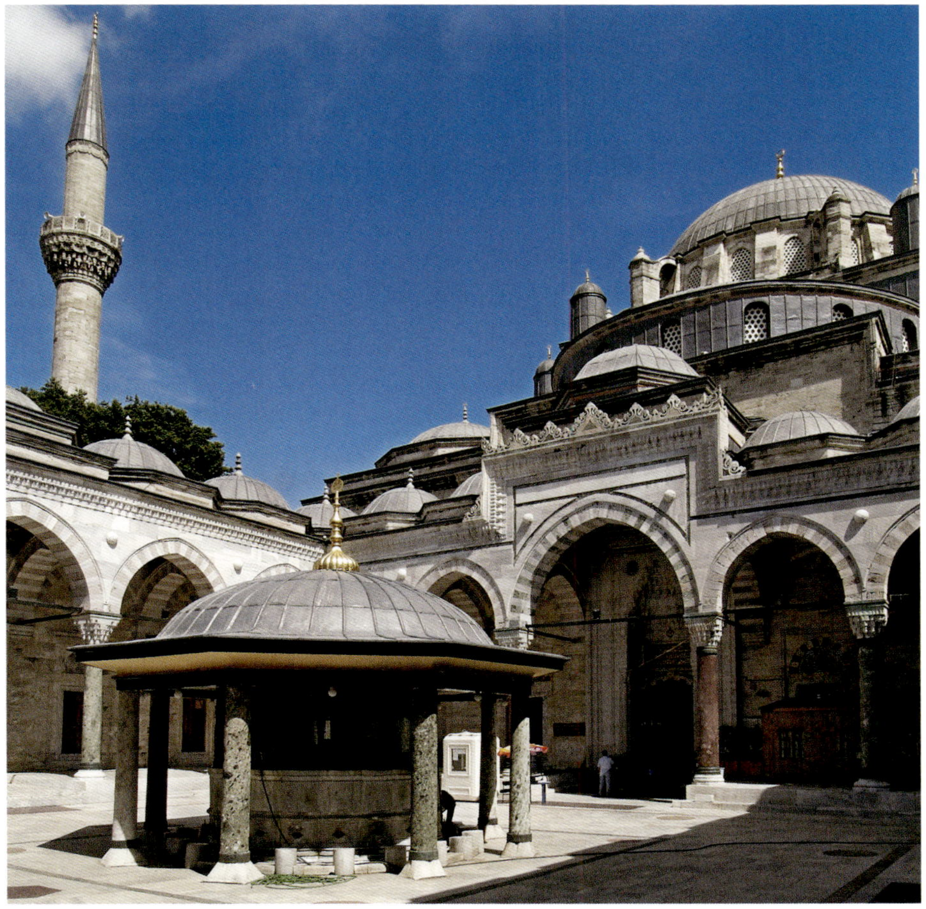

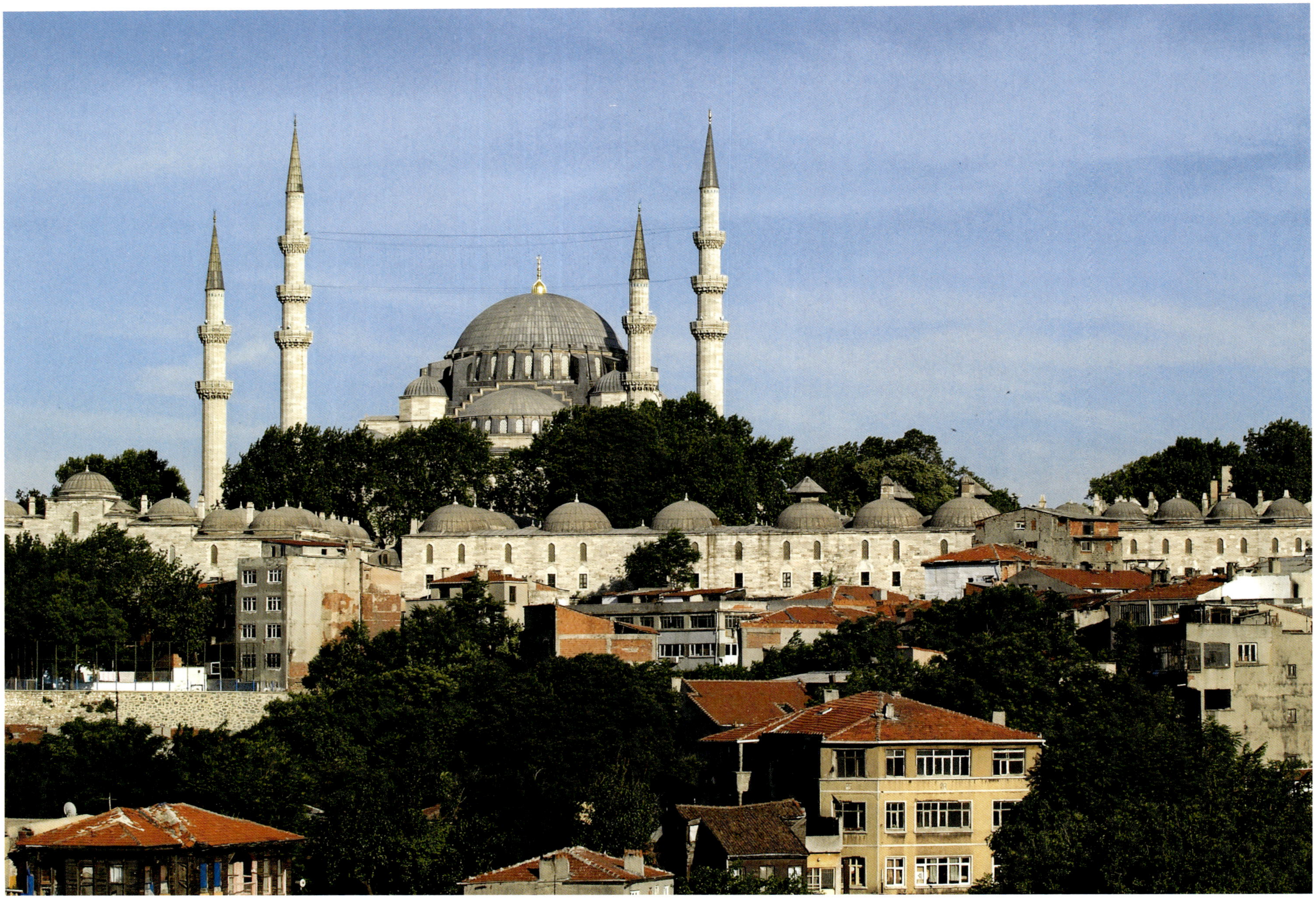

Mimar Sinan (1491–1588)
Süleymaniye Cami (Mosque of Suleiman)
1550–1557
Istanbul, Turkey

A few years after the Sehzade Mosque (named after the deceased prince), Sinan was commissioned to construct an official mosque for Suleiman, which was built in a dominant position, definitively marking the skyline of Constantinople – as the Ottoman capital was still called – in an unequivocally Islamic, Ottoman and imperial way.
Great care was taken over every detail in the Süleymaniye Cami, indicative of a coherence within the overall project that gives Sinan's work an affinity with that of the great Italian Renaissance masters, to such an extent that some scholars have recognized analogies with the theories of Leon Battista Alberti.
Strengthening the feeling of power transmitted by the buildings commissioned by Suleiman was for Sinan not merely a matter of increasing the size. It involved just as importantly defining with extreme precision the relationship between the parts and the whole and the succession of viewpoints in accordance with a town-planning concept which favoured improvised and unexpected glimpses enhanced by staggered positioning on various terraces, unlike the rigid axiality of Italian Renaissance design. The concept of an infinitude of small domes surrounding the central edifice corresponding to the various buildings of the *külliye* symbolizes the way they are organized around the dominating central structure.

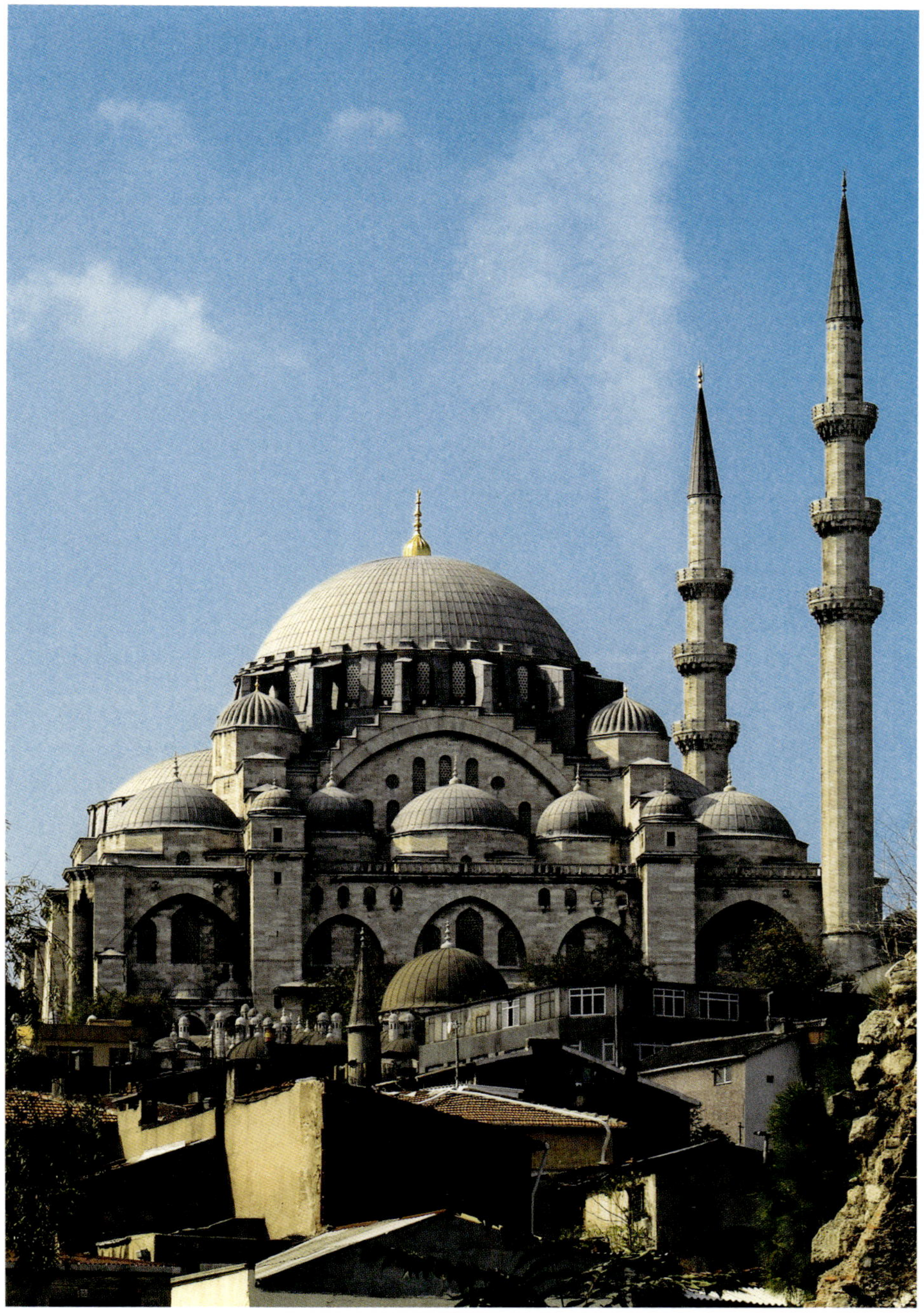

Mimar Sinan (1491–1588)
Süleymaniye Cami (Mosque of Suleiman)
1550–1557
Istanbul, Turkey

The novelty of the design of the Süleymaniye Cami is clearly noticeable from the side view, which is treated with the same precision and consistency as the façade, as if to re-emphasize the centrality of its power from whichever point it is viewed. The serene yet mighty dome, with its classical and unmistakable flattened profile of Byzantine origin, firmly dominates the building beneath. It is supported by the four smaller domes linked to the sturdy buttresses, which descend in steps to form a framework for the structure, corresponding to the four colossal internal arches. The central wall, crowned with its great stepped arch, is lightened by its numerous windows, and falls harmoniously into place over the three domes below. These in turn form a counterpoint with the two corners on them, while the lower wall is divided into five colossal, rhythmically diverse arcades, which make the monumental structure lighter and more dynamic.

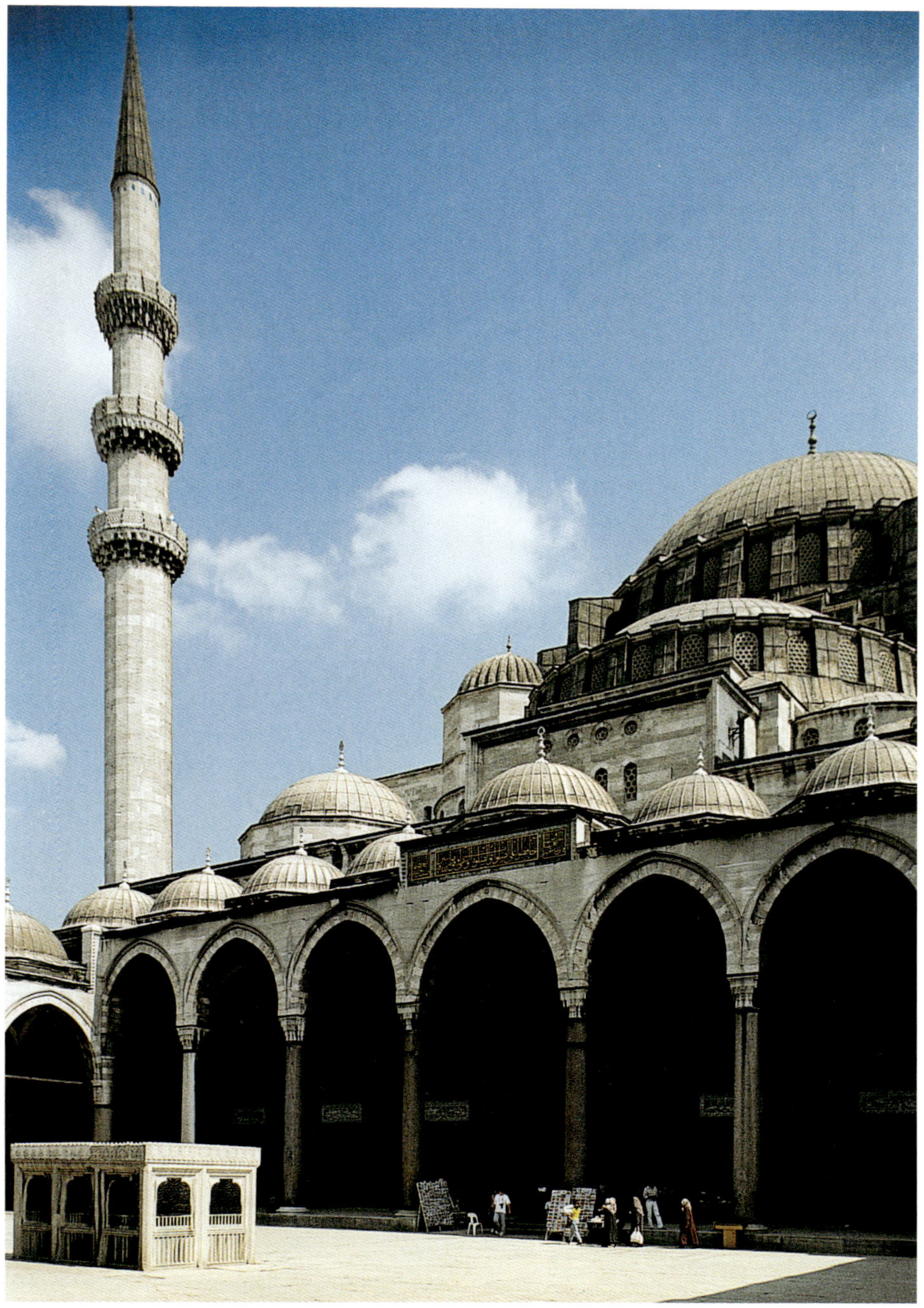

Mimar Sinan (1491–1588)
Süleymaniye Cami (Mosque of Suleiman)
1550–1557
Istanbul, Turkey

The proportions of the courtyard are monumental but harmonious. The material of the columns (marble or granite) was chosen according to the way they fit into the context. The fountain for ablutions is placed outside so that the elegant kiosk at the centre of the courtyard does not interfere with the view of the façade. The portico in front of the mosque is slightly higher than the others, and leads effectively into the majestic enveloping cascade of lines and curves. In a cogent reinterpretation of Byzantine architecture in the light of previous Ottoman experience, Sinan came up with a building composed of masses both powerful and light, austere in the choice of material but ennobled by the light, authoritative and perfectly balanced.

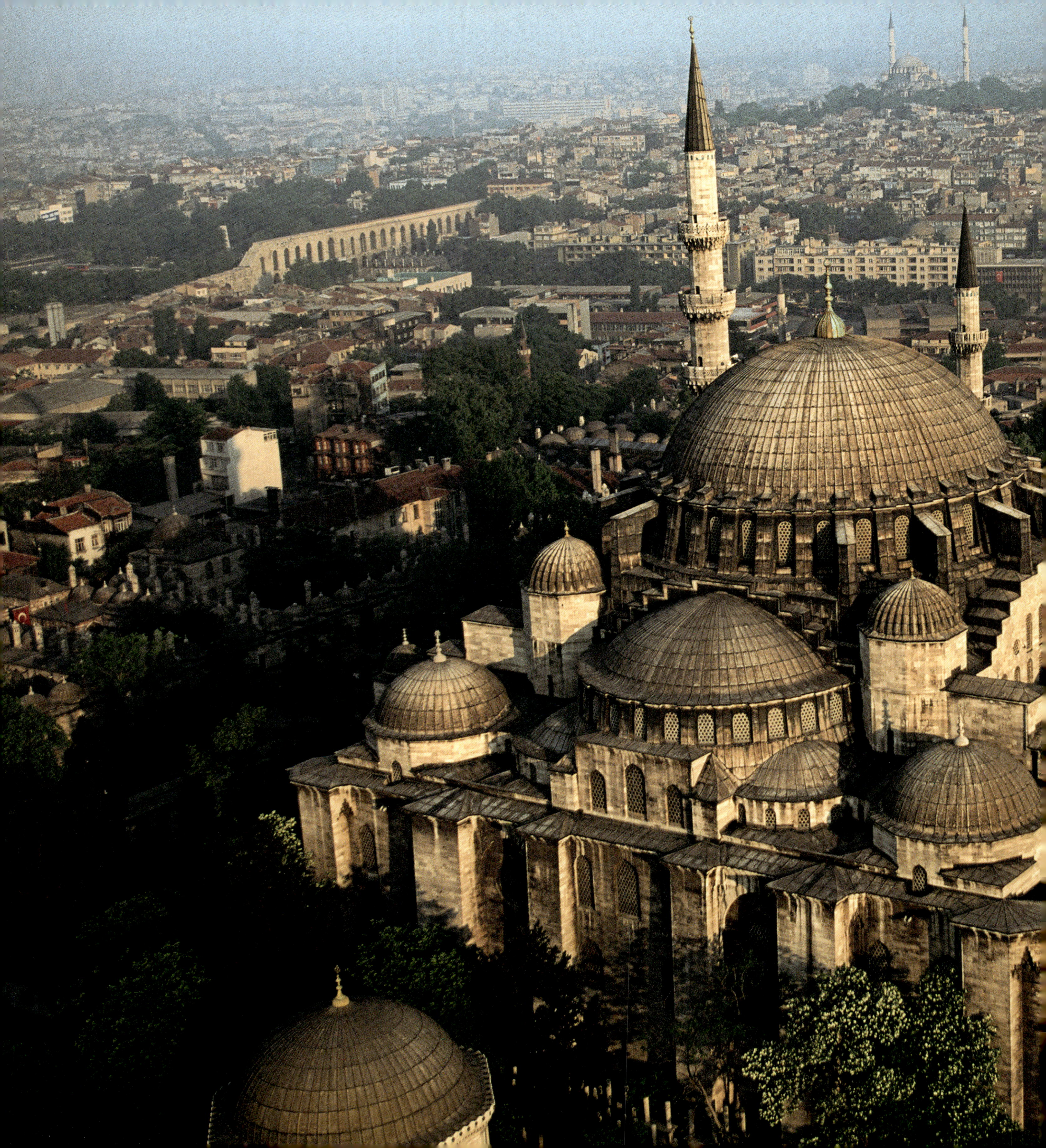

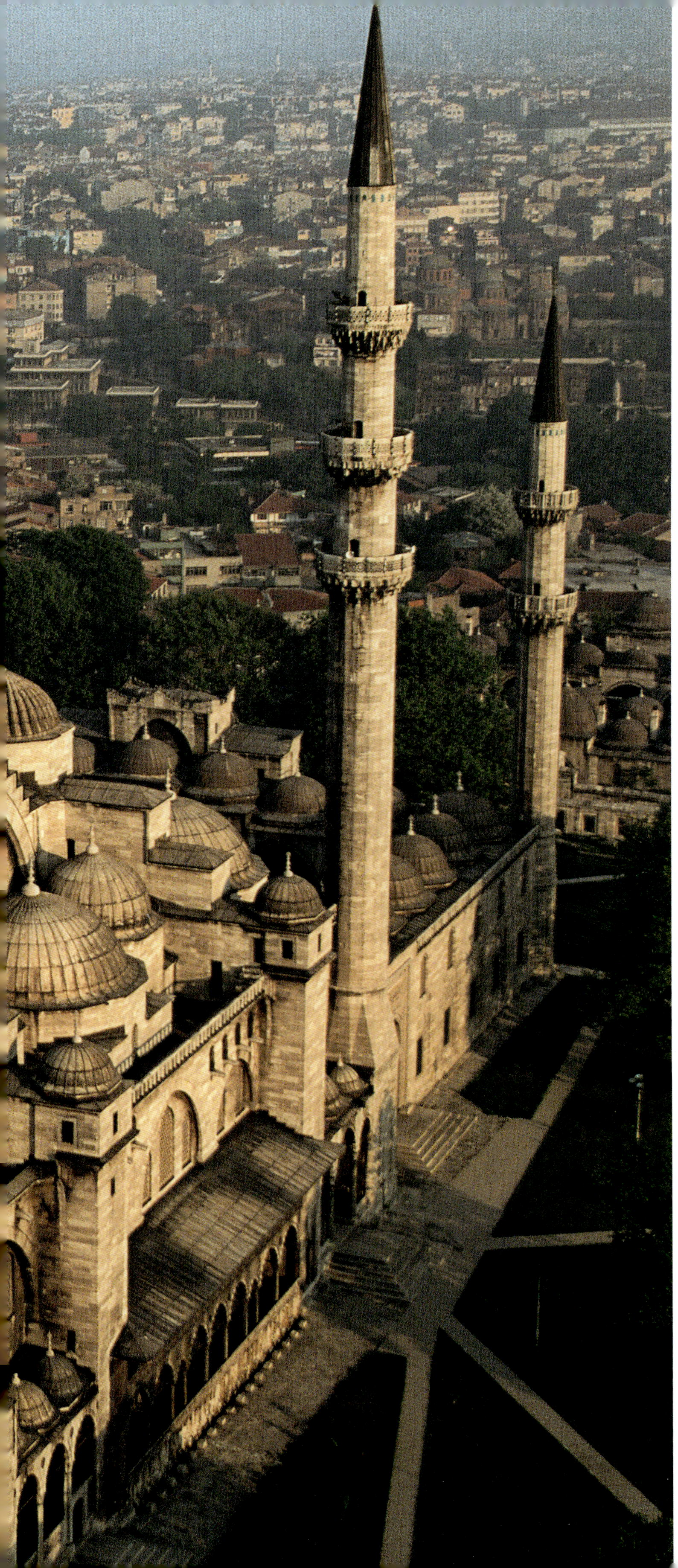

Mimar Sinan (1491–1588)
Süleymaniye Cami (Mosque of Suleiman)
1550–1557
Istanbul, Turkey

The mosque is dominated by the serene volume of the dome, framed by four large cylindrical towers, which are the external endings of the four piers inside. The axis is indicated by the two large half-domes, each flanked by two smaller ones, while the sides are free of infelicitous buttresses because the weight is sufficiently distributed by the extremely wide arch on the longitudinal ones. At the four corners, four domes terminate the broad aisles, drawing together the interplay of the spaces of the half-domes at the front and back and the three domes at the sides (two small ones and one larger dome in the middle). The four minarets, used here for the first time with ascending heights of elegant symmetry, lend an essential vertical element to the huge architectural mass, leaving it suspended between solidity and lightness. A perfect piece of engineering, the structure achieves absolute coherence in the relationship between exterior and interior, and exercises at the same time a fundamental town-planning function. Besides the Great Mosque, the huge *külliye* in which it was placed embraced two elementary schools, four upper schools, a law school, a medical school, a hospital, an *imaret*, a *han*, a library, a public fountain, a *hammam* and of course the sultans' tombs.

Mimar Sinan (1491–1588)
Süleymaniye Cami (Mosque of Suleiman)
Interior
1550–1557
Istanbul, Turkey

The interior is an essay on architecture and its function, with the clear intention of elevating the Ottoman Empire to the status of political and cultural heir of Byzantium. The comparison with Hagia Sophia consists not in the beauty of the decoration, here used with a measure of sobriety, nor in the dimensions – Sinan's dome measures twenty-seven metres in diameter and fifty-four metres in height – but rather in the new organization of architectural space conceived as a vessel containing a pool of light and rationalism, contrasting with the "mysterious" and mystically luminous, unfathomable half-darkness of the Byzantine prototype, pierced by evanescent rays of light reflected by golden mosaics and filtered through the columns of the lateral galleries. Thanks to the perfect centering of the pressures on the buttresses absorbed by the thickness of the walls, domes and walls can be broken up by a great many windows that, besides diminishing the weight and the thrust, guarantee a diffuse brightness within and combine to expand the volume of the majestic stone building without diminishing its physical power and structural clarity.

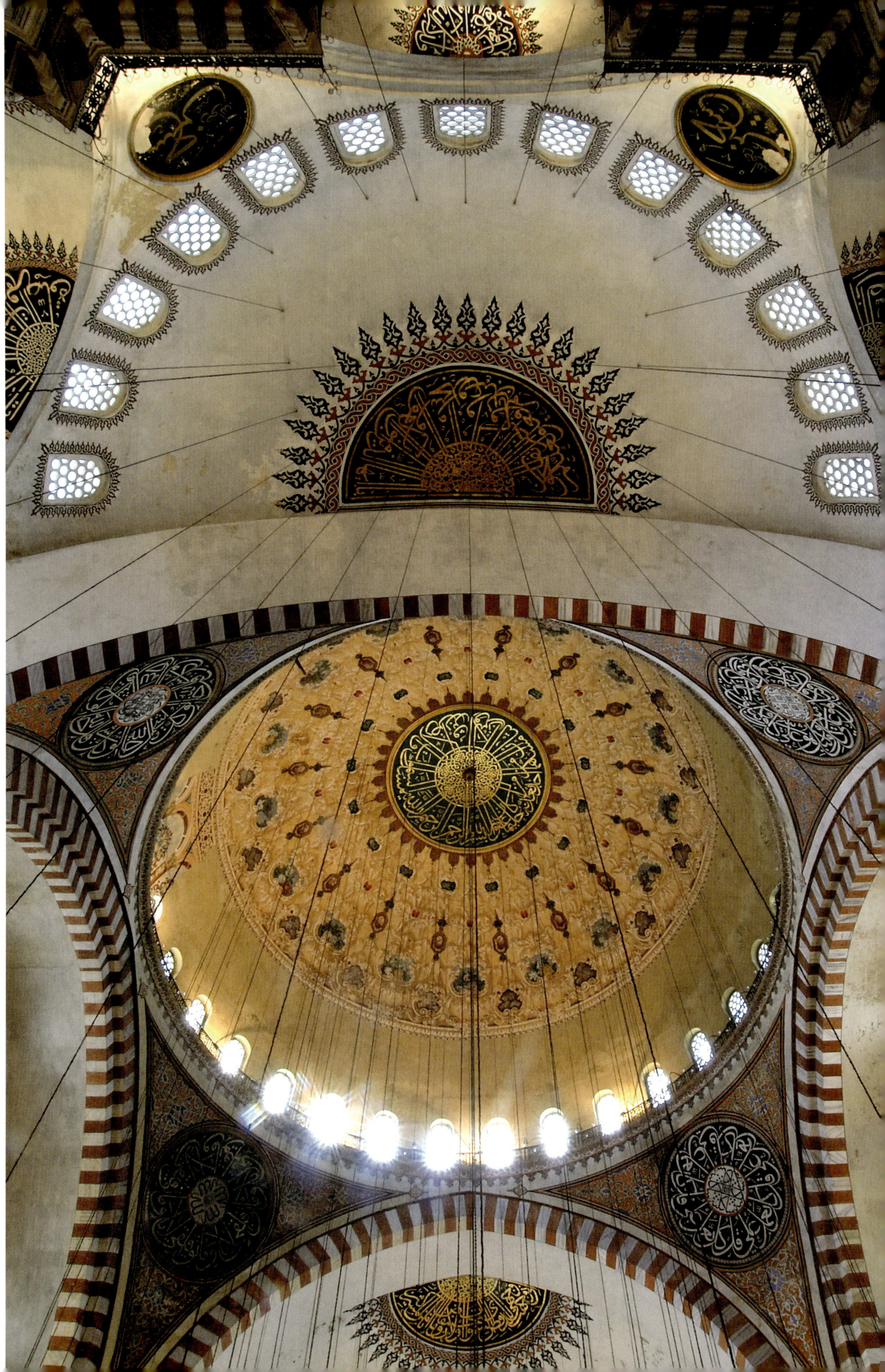

Mosque of Sokullu Mehmet Pasha
Dome
1571–1572
Istanbul, Turkey

In his mature years, despite being busy with the enormous undertaking in Edirne, Sinan achieved results of great quality in several 'lesser' mosques like that commissioned by Grand Vizier Sokullu Mehmet Pasha. The unity of interior space is solved in masterly fashion by linking the basic rectangle to the dome by means of a hexagonal canopy, whose supports are in fact absorbed into the perimeter, and removing the lateral aisles in order to create a firmly unitary space without any dark corners. The brightness of the light was then reinforced by covering the walls with tiles of floral design, in a fresh, dominant blue on a white background – masterpieces of Iznik manufacture, sumptuous but not cheap.

Mosque of Rüstem Pasha
Dome
1561–1562
Istanbul, Turkey

On the death of the Grand Vizier, his wife Mihrimah, daughter of Suleiman, founded a mosque in a narrow site available in the artisan quarter near the Golden Horn. Sinan brilliantly overcame the limitations of the site and built the mosque over the workshops. The interior is among the best organized of those built by the great master in its perfect solution of an octagonal plan and the dazzling wall-covering of high-quality Iznik tiles. These had belonged to Rüstem himself, who had been a dedicated collector of them.

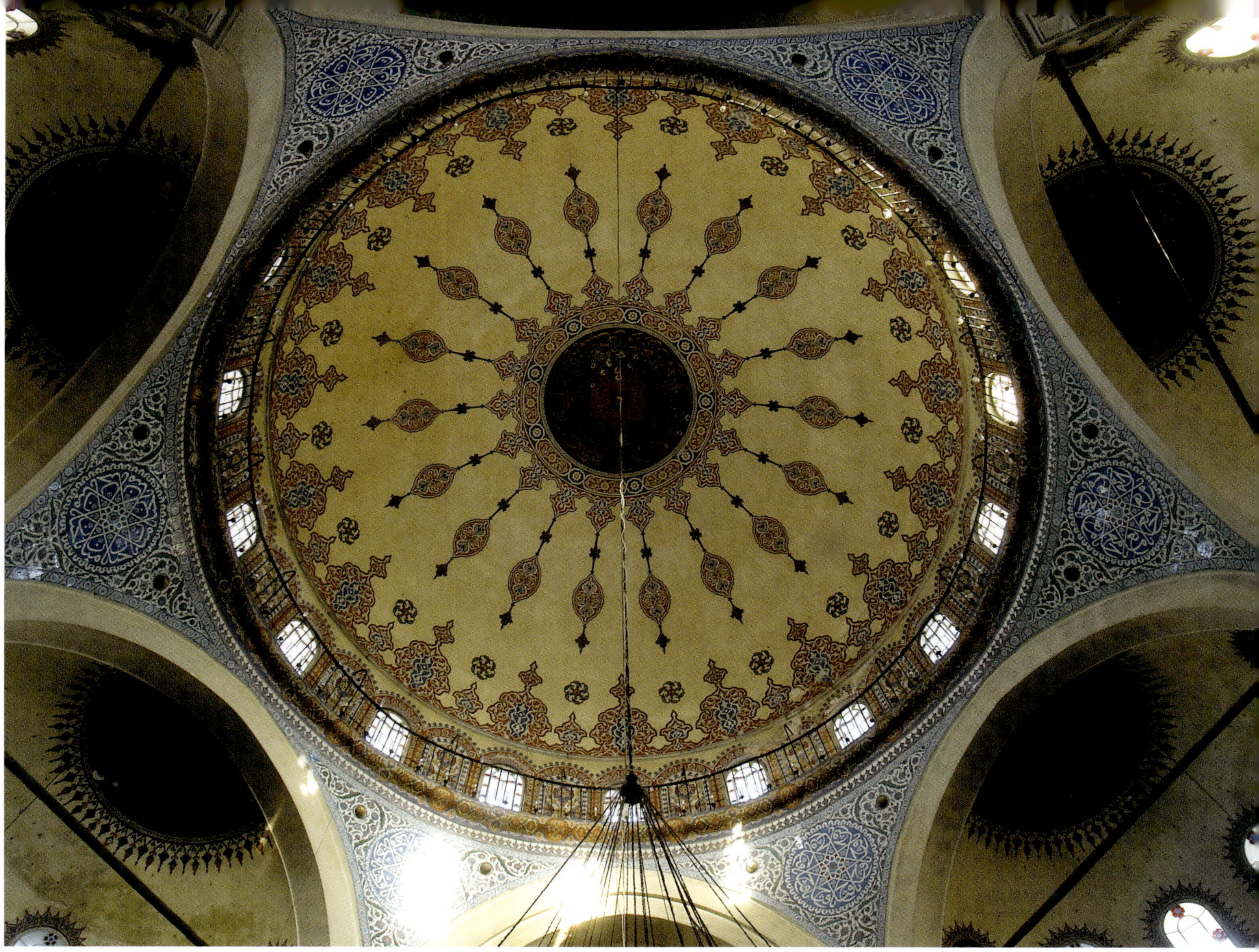

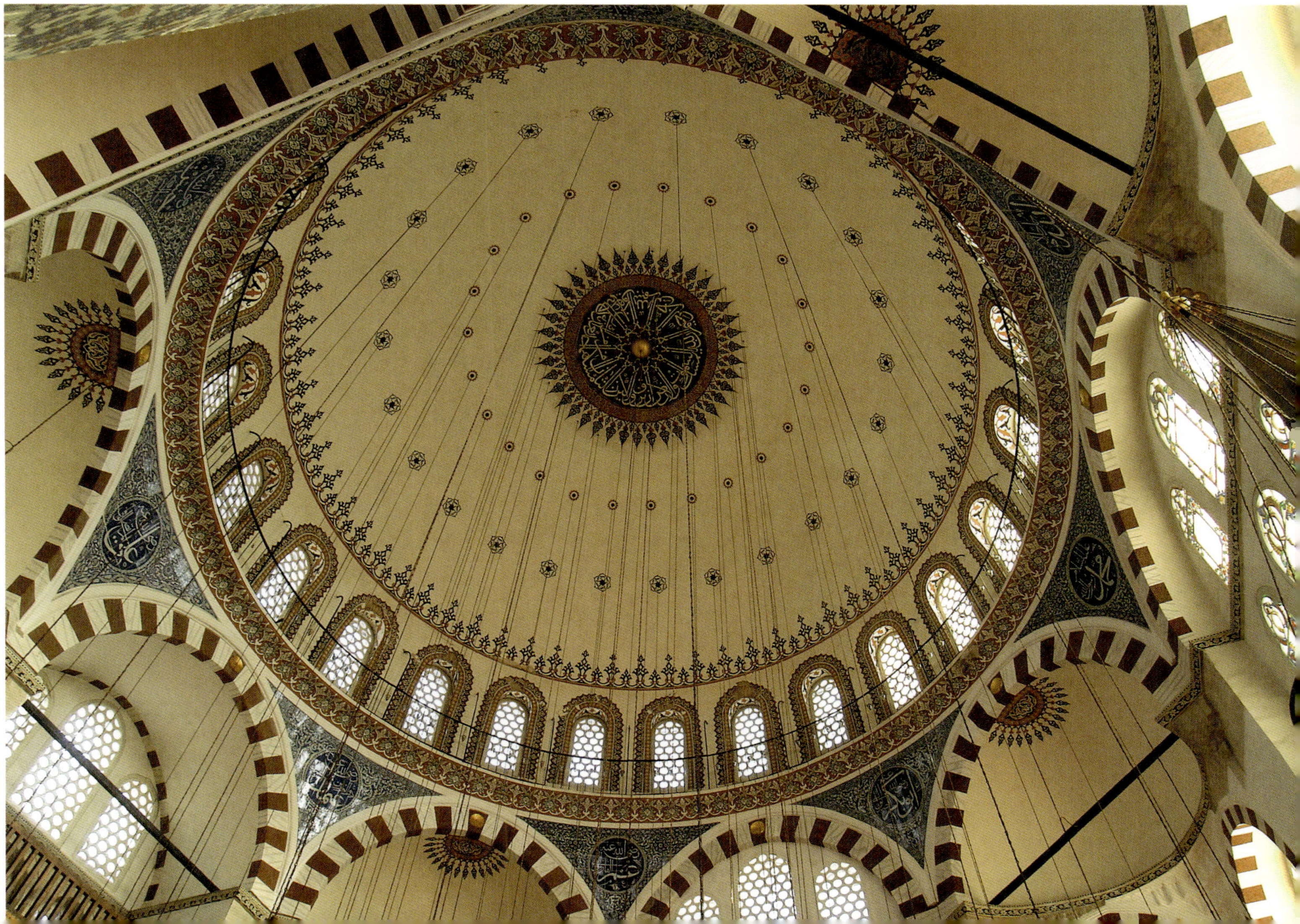

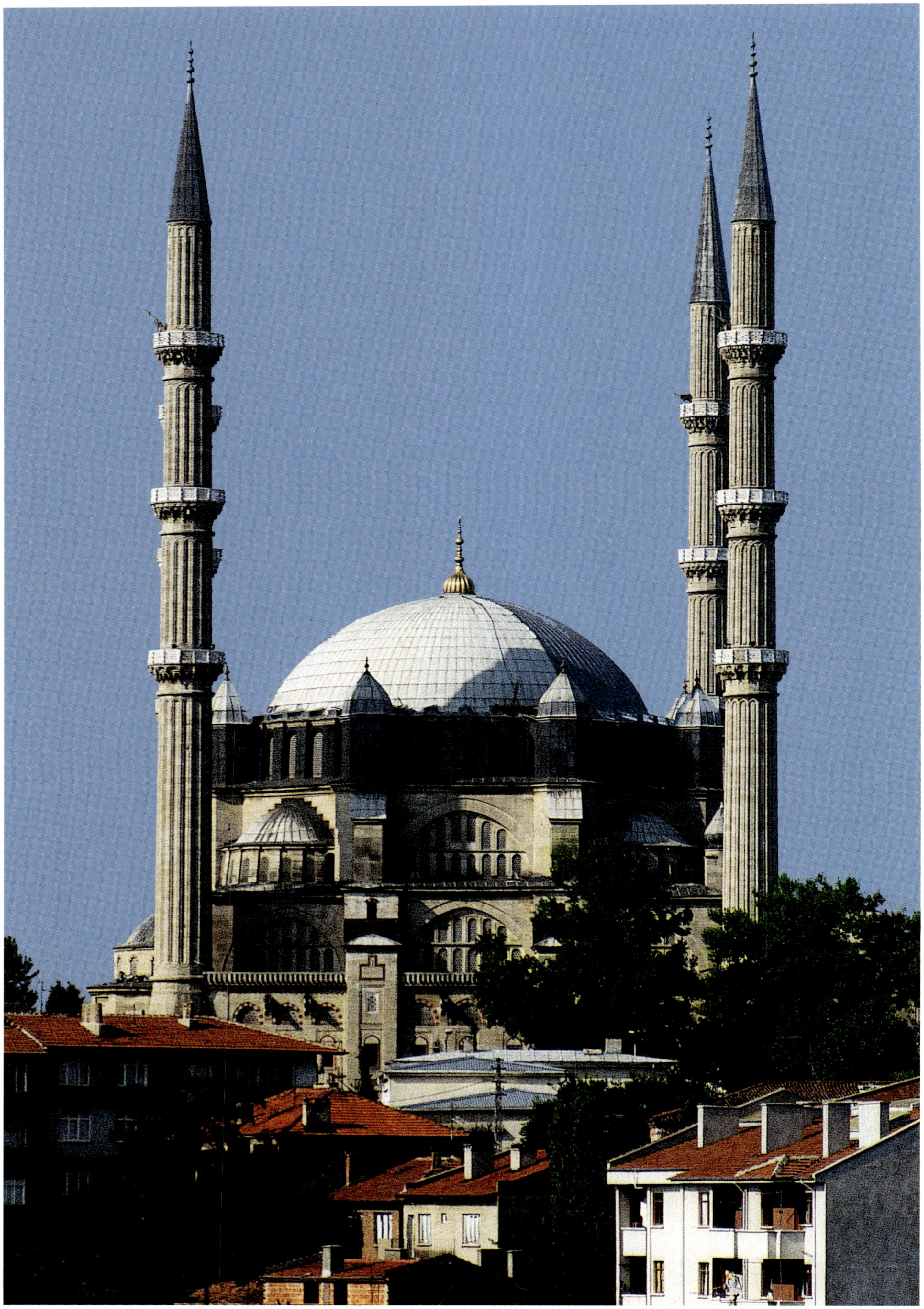

Mimar Sinan (1491–1588)
Selimiye Cami (Mosque of Selim)
1568–1575
Edirne, Turkey

Sinan was almost eighty when he started work on the mosque for Selim II, which he considered his masterpiece. A supreme statement of faith, propaganda (we are at the frontier of Christian Europe) and above all of art, the Selimiye Cami is the apogee of empire, a work of formidable impact in its compact distribution of masses. Pure as a diamond in the clarity of its geometrical structure and perfect in its unitary layout, the mosque terminates in a flattened dome. With serene majesty, this dome crowns the powerful octagonal building, motionless in the presence of the infinite, abutted by four soaring identical eighty-three-metre minarets. The tension between physical mass and verticality, straight lines and curves and above all the massive building and the ambience are achieved with perfect balance. The mosque represented the point at which the tension in Ottoman architecture reached stasis, preventing further development of a story that at one time amounted to a revelation – of the divine, certainly, but also of the empire that represented it on earth.

Mimar Sinan (1494–1588)
Selimiye Cami (Mosque of Selim)
1568–1575
Edirne, Turkey

With a diameter of 31.5 metres, the dome was the first to surpass that of Hagia Sophia, fulfilling a long-standing dream. The compactness of Sinan's design is also visible from above, with all its elements subordinated to the main dome, encircling it with perfect symmetry.

Mimar Sinan (1491–1588)
Selimiye Cami (Mosque of Selim)
Interior
1568–1575
Edirne, Turkey

More than for its noteworthy dimensions, the Selimiye Cami is striking for achieving a previously undreamt-of spatial coherence with its unprecedented fenestration. More than 270 windows make the immense space a welcoming and boundless place. Nothing interrupts the flow of light as it illuminates the shape of the space, because the eight pillars that bear the weight of the dome are virtually part of the walls as internal buttresses, and the partition walls, instead of seeming like boundaries, are conceived as luminous screens. The central plan, based on the square, octagon and the circle inscribed therein, attains here its most complete architectural form.

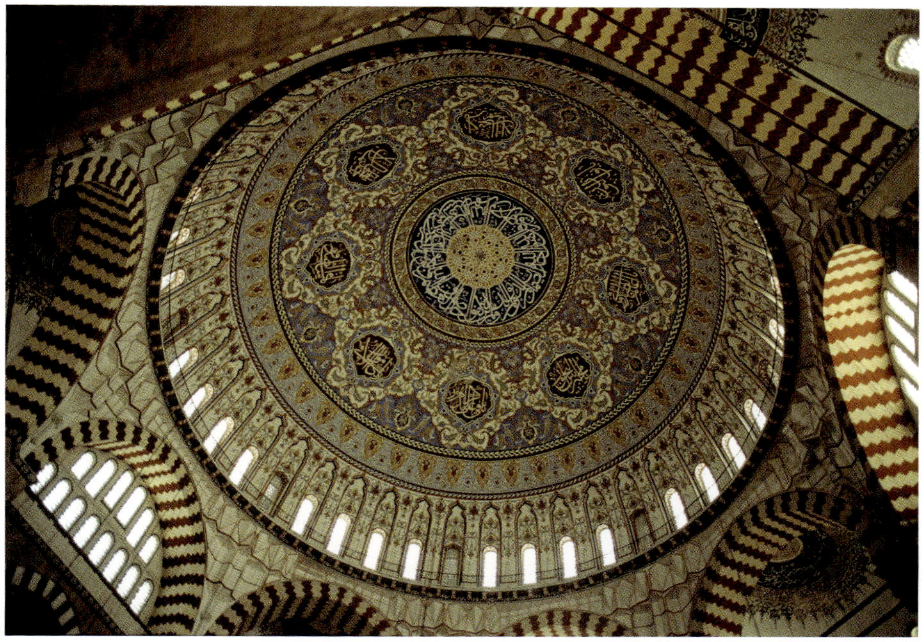

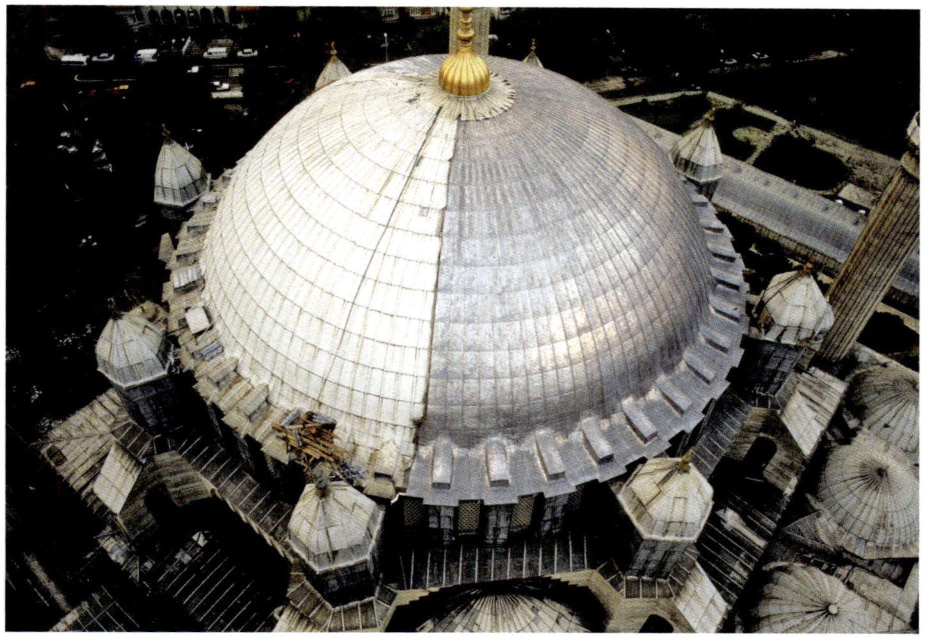

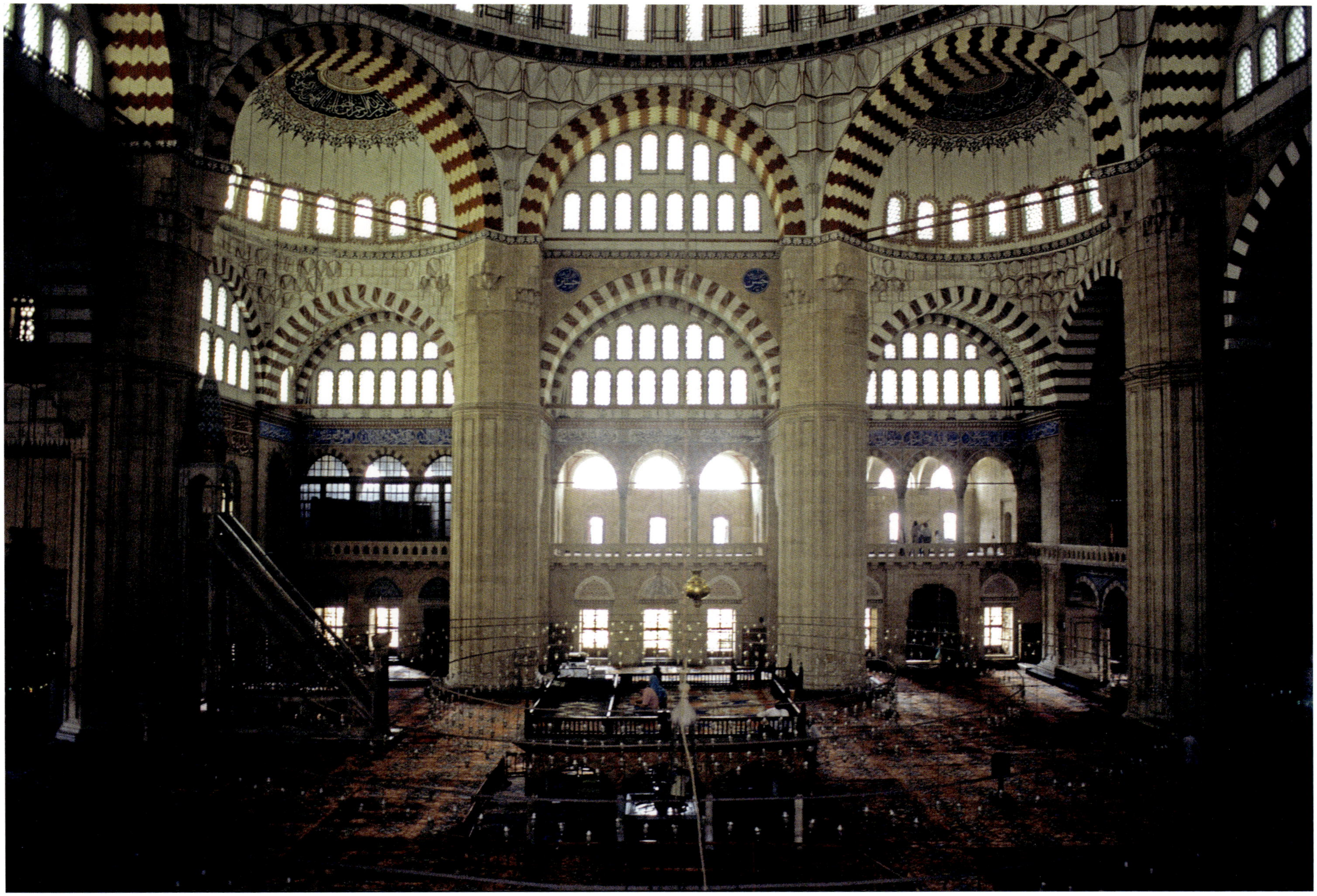

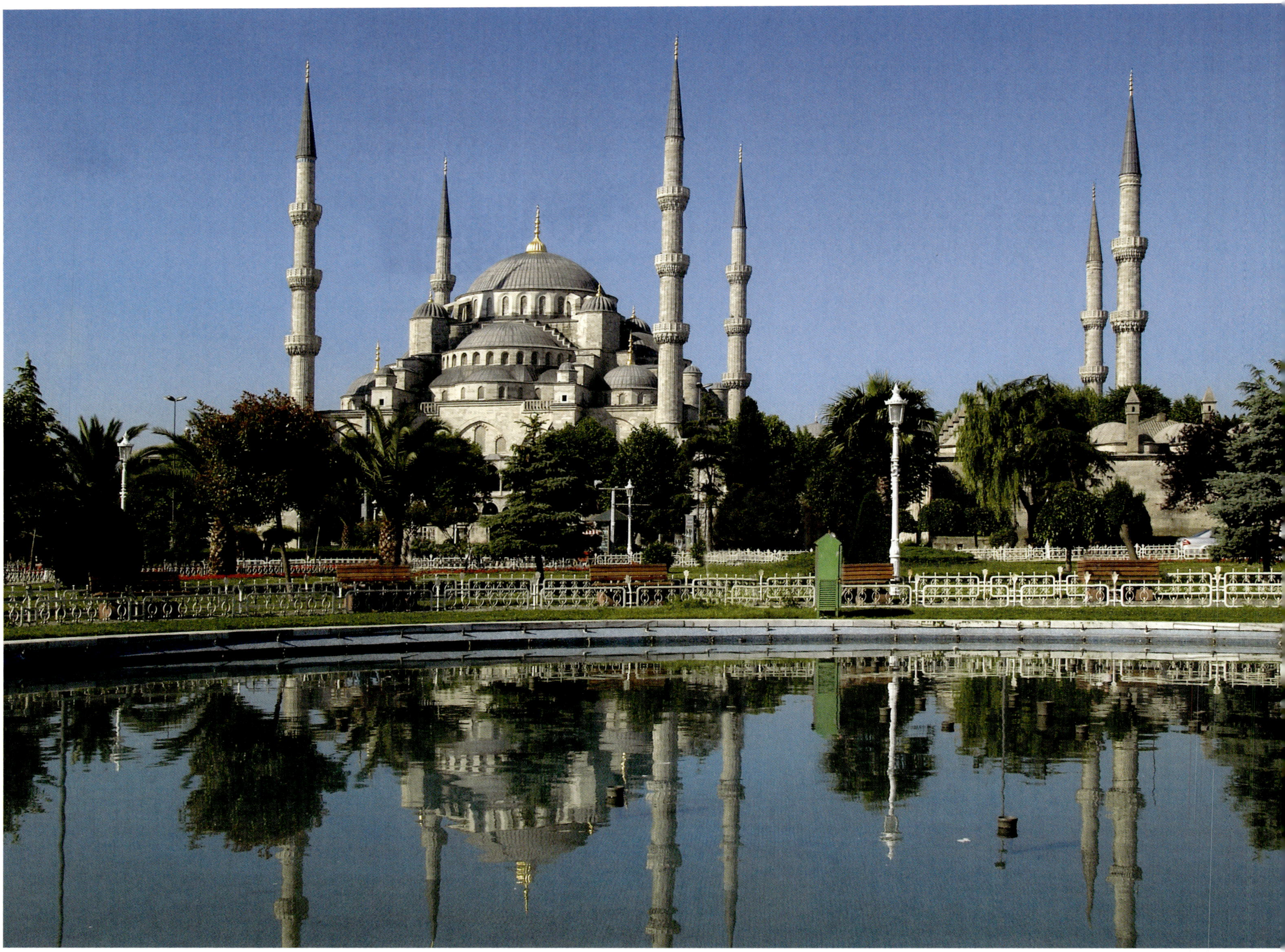

Mehmet Agha (c. 1540–1617)
Mosque of Sultan Ahmet (Blue Mosque)
1609–1617
Istanbul, Turkey

Sinan's death coincided with the progressive contraction (spiritual and geographical) of the Ottoman Empire. The enormous mosque which the ambitious Sultan Ahmet desired so much was built explicitly to rival Hagia Sophia, in a spectacular position on the racecourse, destroying the palaces of Grand Viziers Sokullu Mehmet Pasha and Rüstem Pasha. It is a monument that clearly conveys the start of a period of creative stagnation. It adopts once again the square ground plan with a central dome on enormous pillars and four semi-domes as buttresses that Sinan had experimented with sixty years earlier in the Sehzade Cami, emphasizing the outline with the superb novelty of six minarets (four matching ones at the corners, as at Edirne, and two lower ones on the exterior side of the courtyard) to enhance the silhouette, like those at Süleymaniye. While the interior appears lifeless and redundant, the exterior presents us with one of the most remarkable sights of the city, showing both its good points and its limitations.

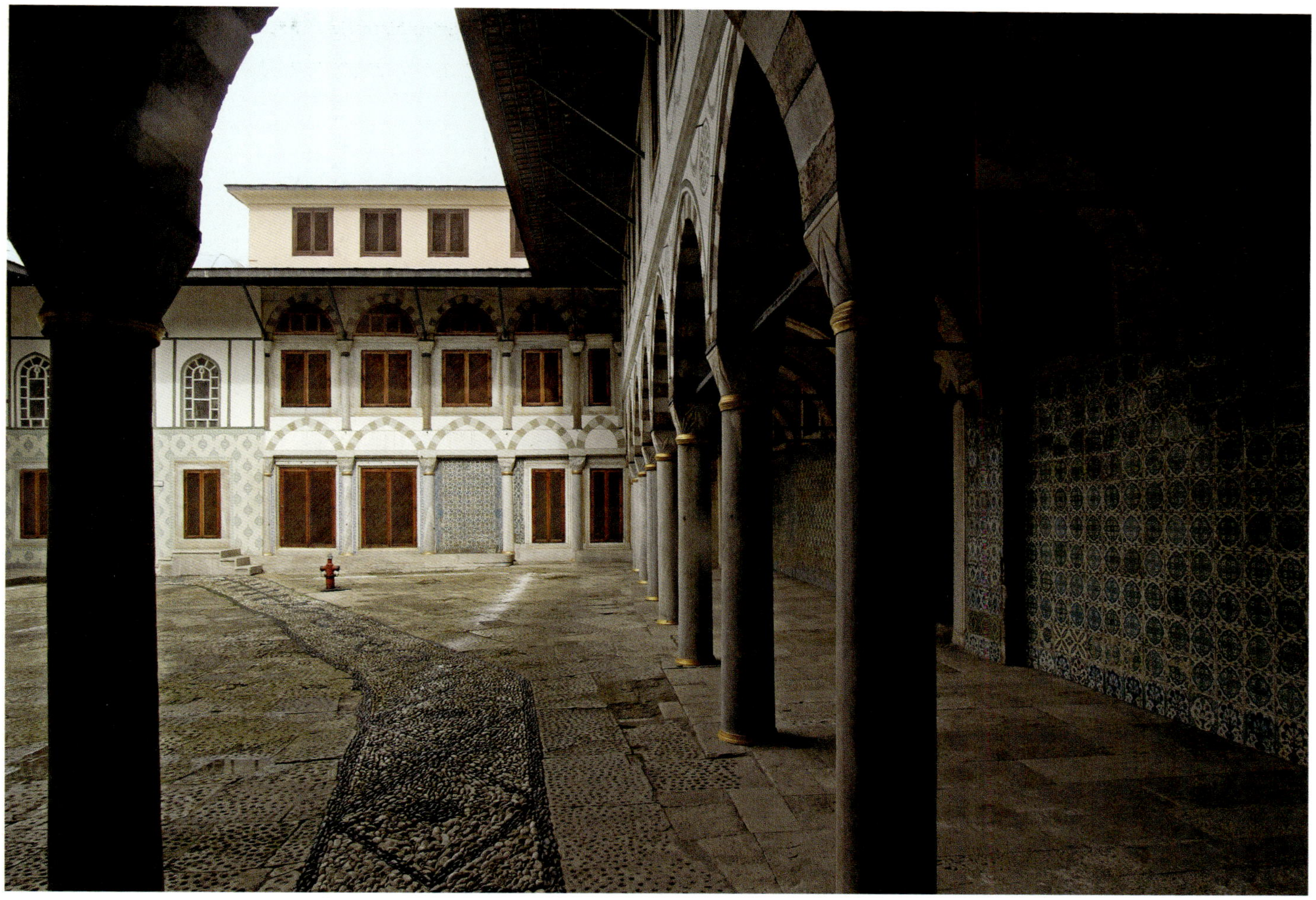

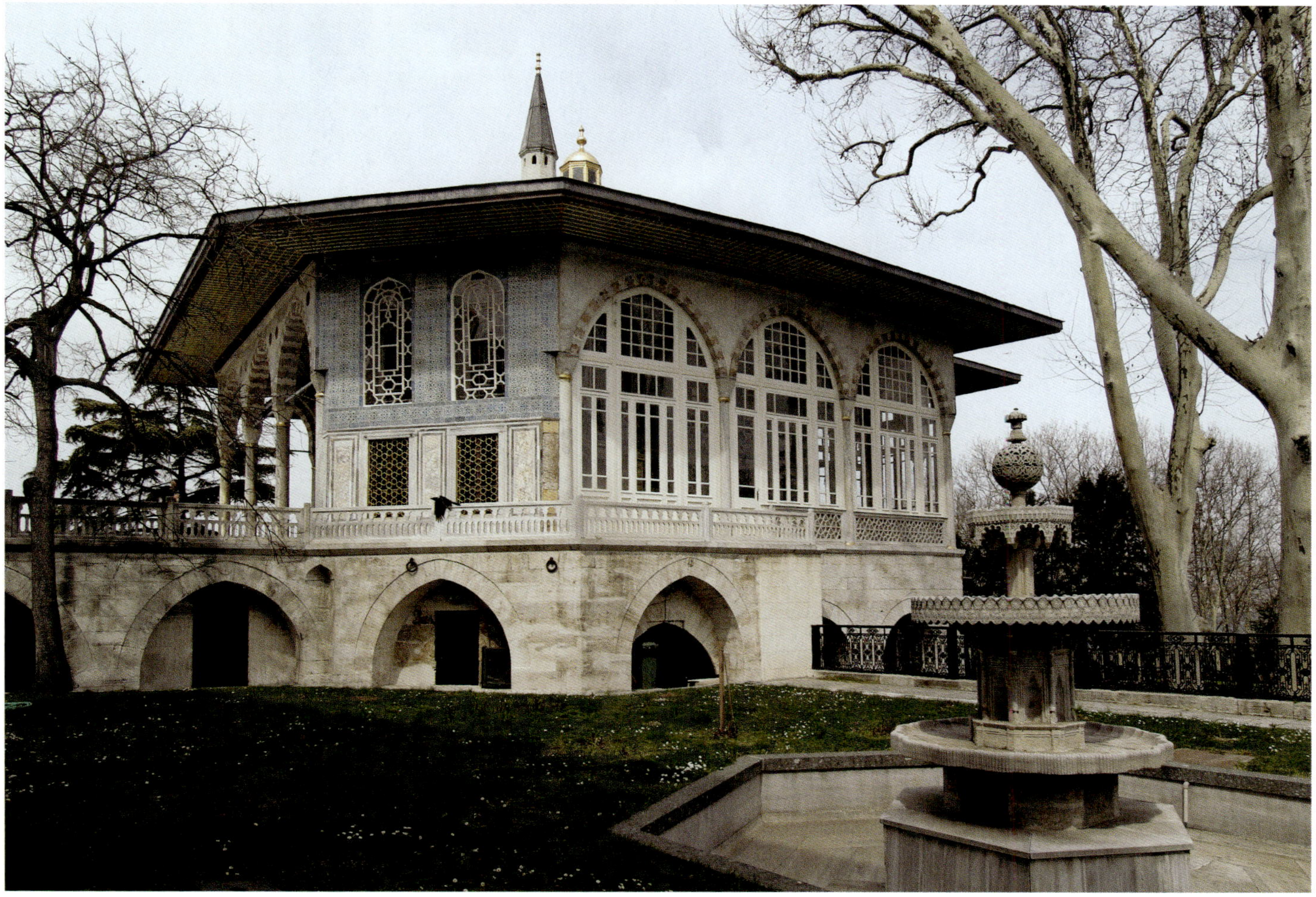

Topkapi Saray
Harem
Courtyard of the Sultan's mother
16th–18th centuries
Istanbul, Turkey

The Topkapi Palace was commissioned by Mehmet II on a magnificent site on the Golden Horn in the area of the Byzantine acropolis, straddling two seas and two continents. The works were begun in 1459 and continued for a decade. Successive restorations, reworkings and additions following fires in 1574 and 1665, and also changes in taste continued until the early nineteenth century, when Topkapi was superseded by the European-style Dolmabahçe Palace on the Bosphorus.

Topkapi Saray
Baghdad Kiosk
1638–1639
Istanbul, Turkey

Despite mixed and overlapping styles and idioms, the Topkapi still reflected the intentions of its founder, and its structure is anything but monumental, being a series of kiosks and pavilions for private and court use, subdivided into fortified enclosures of successive areas of ever greater privacy, and arranged with "hierarchical disorder" into reception rooms, stables, kitchens, pavilions of various forms and dimensions placed in front of reflecting water with fountain displays, as well as the immense and labyrinthine harem.

Topkapi Saray
Baghdad Kiosk
Interior
1638–1639
Istanbul, Turkey

The best features of Ottoman architecture in the seventeenth century are probably to be found in buildings of lesser importance, like the two kiosks erected by Murad IV to commemorate his victories. The interior of the Baghdad Kiosk is cruciform, with a dome and four alcoves with comfortable sofas for enjoying the view of the Golden Horn and the Suleiman Mosque. The walls are completely covered with original sixteenth-century ceramics (and imitations of them, generally mediocre in quality).

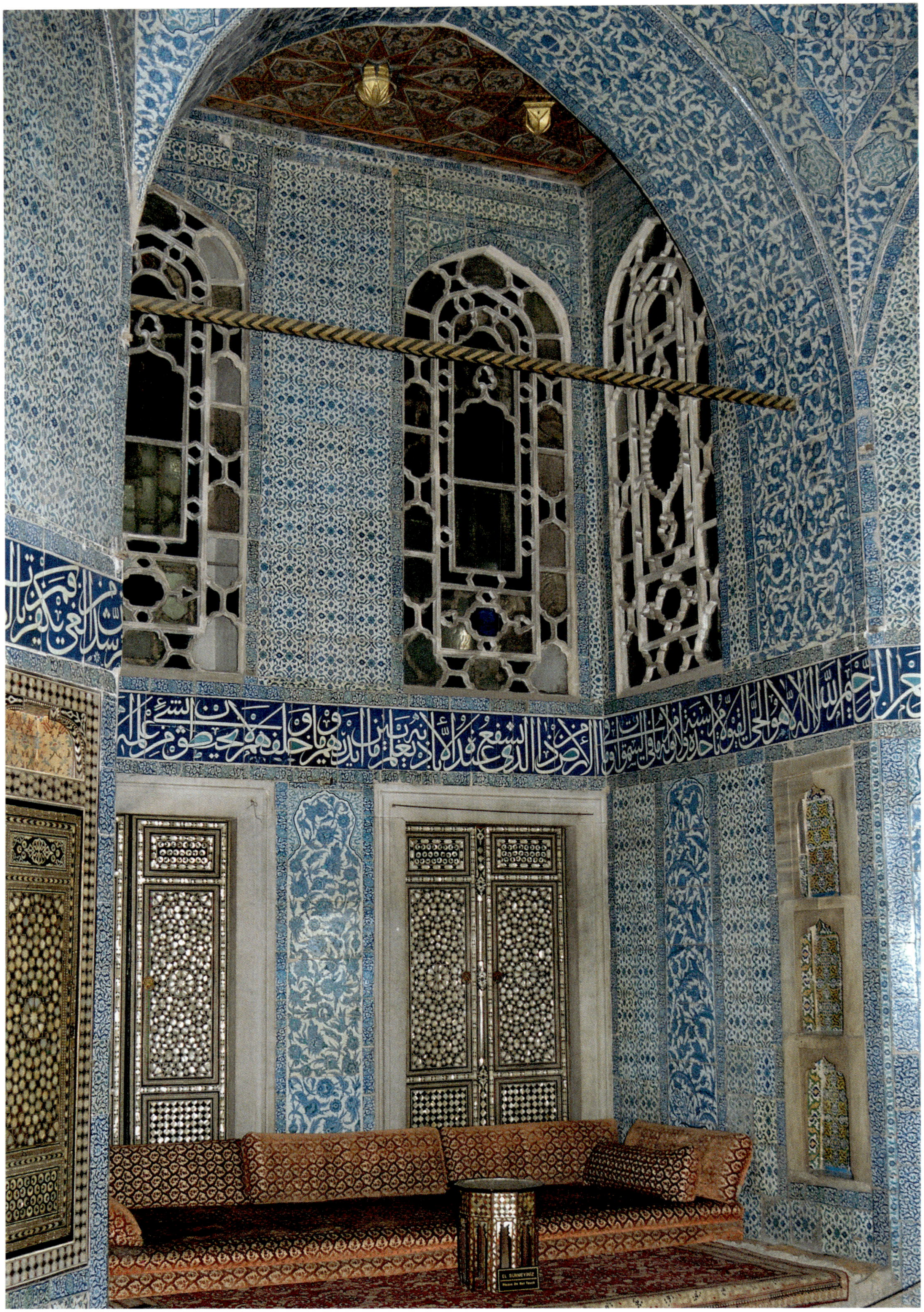

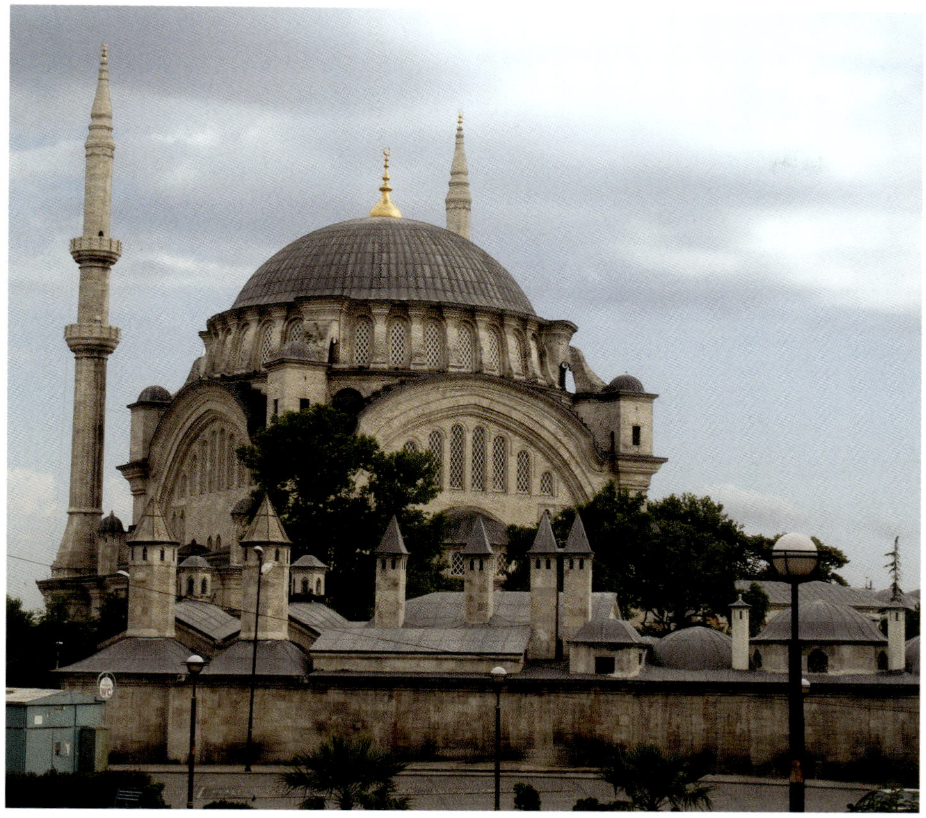

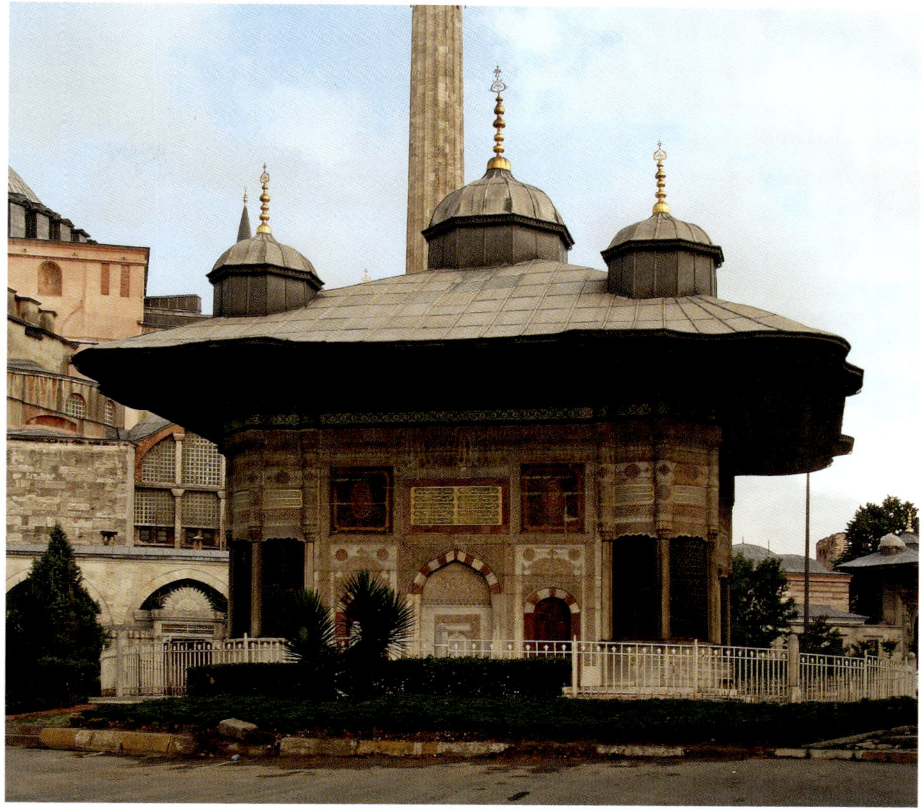

Nuorosmaniye Cami (Light of Osman Mosque)
1748–1755
Istanbul, Turkey

Ottoman architects of the seventeenth and eighteenth centuries drew on the prestigious works of Sinan with ever-decreasing creativity. Towards the mid-eighteenth century, a certain receptivity to Baroque taste is recognizable in the Nuorosmaniye Mosque which, although based on Sinan's Mirimah Cami (a square plan surmounted by a dome) ventured towards daring expansions of idiom in the outline of the arches, heavy cornices, buttresses and finally the very slender minarets terminating in a novel motif. The disposition of mass nevertheless remains serene and perfectly controlled, while the concessions to the Baroque are only superficial.

Ahmet III Fountain
1728
Istanbul, Turkey

The Tulip Age, whose delicate floral style characterized the first decades of the eighteenth century, is well represented in the monumental fountains funded by the munificence of the sultans to please the populace. The Ahmet III Fountain is an elegant square structure enlivened by four projections at the corners – behind whose magnificent grills the water distribution employee stood – and a strongly projecting quincunx roof to keep off the rain and sun. The marble decoration is exquisite, and heavily adorned with calligraphy and floral motifs.

Ortaköy Cami (Ortaköy Mosque)
1856
Istanbul, Turkey

As Europeanizing fashions swept over Turkish society as a whole, tired old ideas were dressed up in elements borrowed from mediocre nineteenth-century Western architecture, relying on a profusion of decoration in a heavy bourgeois taste to perform the impossible task of disguising the empty culture that the Ottoman Empire had become.

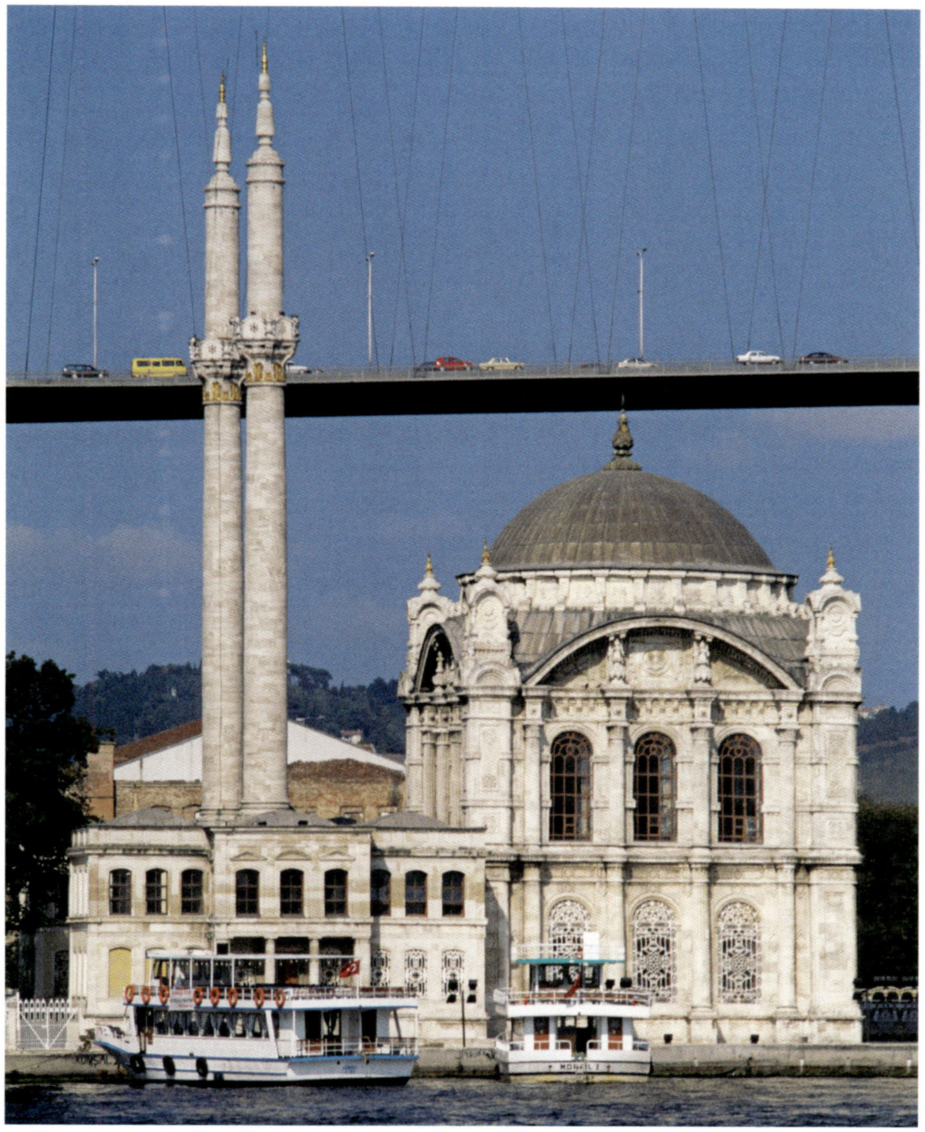

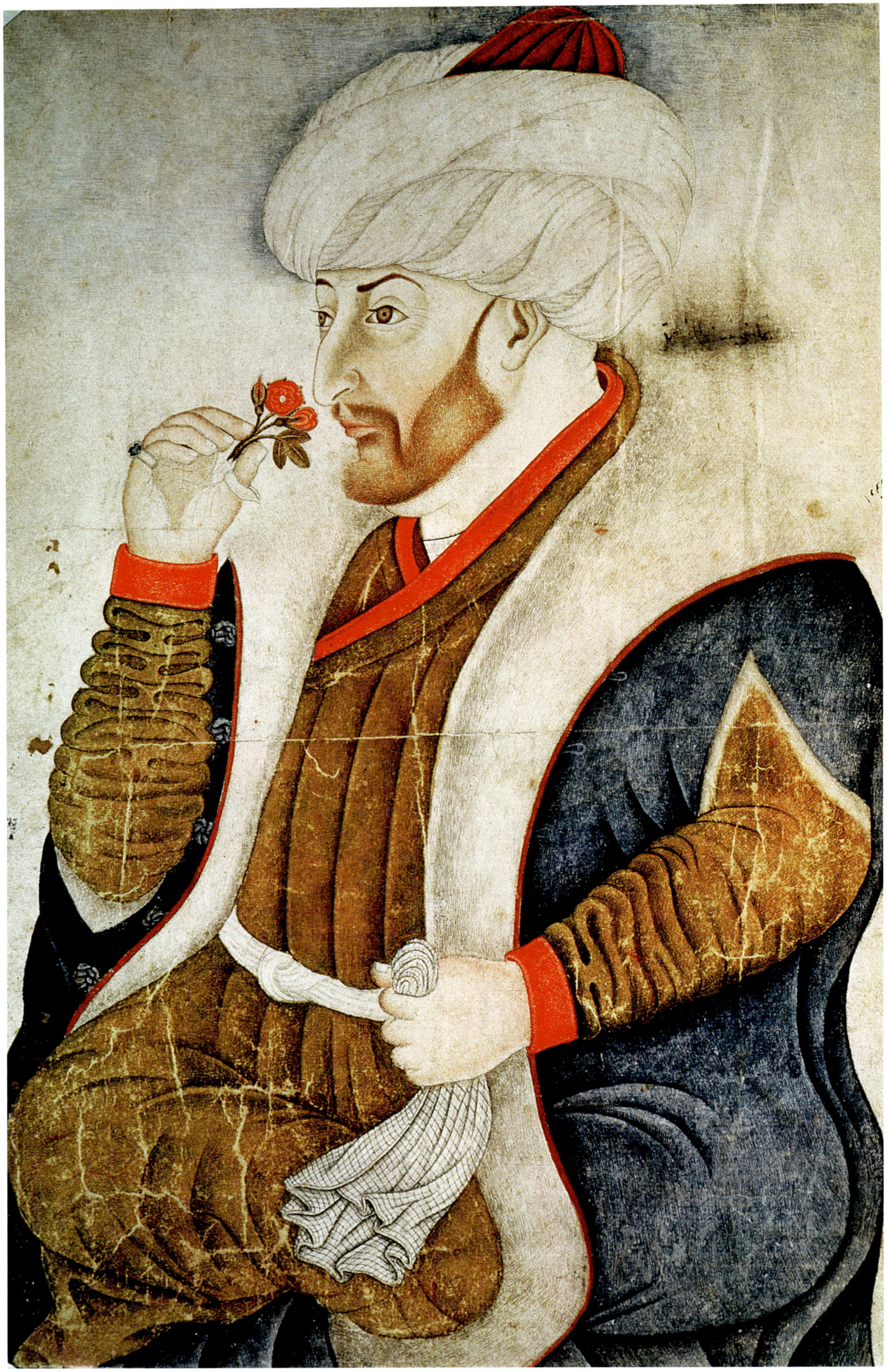

Sinan Bey (15th century)
Portrait of Mehmet II Fatih
1475
Topkapi Saray Museum, Istanbul

Sinan Bey stands out among the leading Turkish painters of the second half of the fifteenth century. He enriched Turkish painting – set in comfortable, anti-naturalistic ways of overtly oriental pattern – with solutions borrowed from the proto-Renaissance art of Venice, and in particular from the paintings of Gentile Bellini, whose works were so appreciated by the great conqueror that he wanted him as a guest in Constantinople. The magnificent portrait hovers between seductive graphic abstractions and penetrating naturalistic observations sketched in with sober, almost three-dimensional brushstrokes and very sparing shading. Carried along by a highly controlled stylistic tension, the painting is a prime example of the moment of transition when Ottoman culture opened up to the Western world. The ample volume of the body conveys a sense of assured superiority, while the gesture of savouring the scent of a flower, contrasting with the look of absorbed determination on his face and the decisiveness with which he clutches the fabric, gives the sultan an air of aloofness.

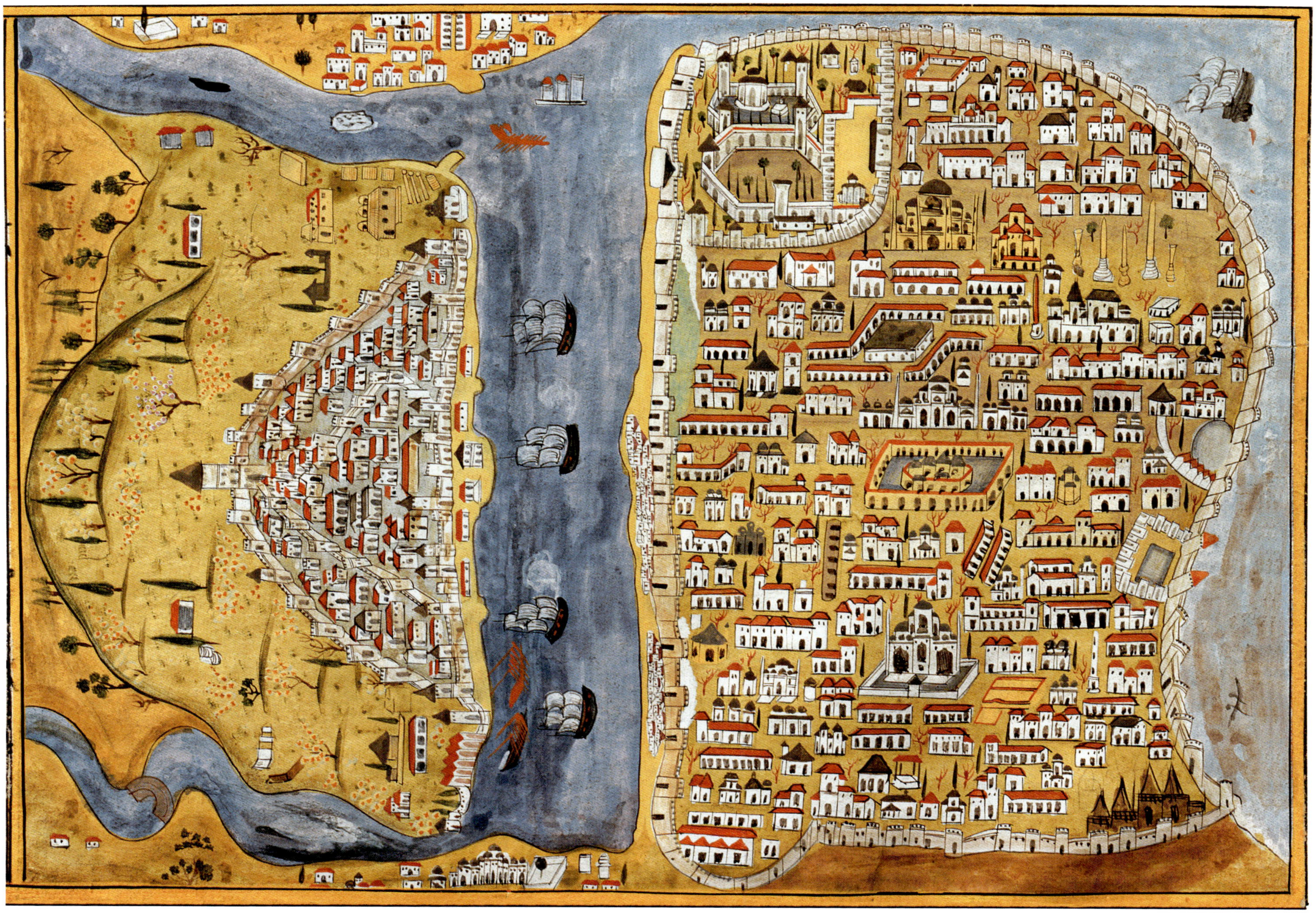

Nasuhü's Silahi Matrakçi (16th century)
Map of Constantinople
1537
From *Beyan-i Menazil-i Sefer-i Irakeyn* (History of the Stages of Campaign in the Two Iraqs)
University Library, Istanbul

In the sixteenth century, Turkish miniatures developed an autonomous style principally in the field of illustrated history, though remaining subject to Persian influences because of the numerous artists who had been transferred to Constantinople after the conquest of Tabriz. The plan of Constantinople defines, although only within the conventions of miniatures, the look of the city prior to the fundamental interventions by Sinan but with Ottoman building works much in evidence. We can recognize the Golden Horn with the suburb of Galata, dominated by the still-extant tower and the more prestigious buildings constructed by the sultans and leading members of the court, interspersed with monumental Roman remains and Byzantine churches. Near the Hippodrome, the monumental outline of Hagia Sophia stands out, transformed into a mosque, as the minarets show, and beside it the Topkapi complex, and the church of St Eirene and its kiosks and stretches of water. Then the Bayazit Mosque with its annexes and the adjacent complex of Eski Saray (Old Palace) and, in a dominant position, the Mehmet Fatih Mosque. The formidable surrounding wall reinforces the appearance of a garden of paradise, with pavilions engulfed in greenery – valuable indications of how the rulers saw their capital.

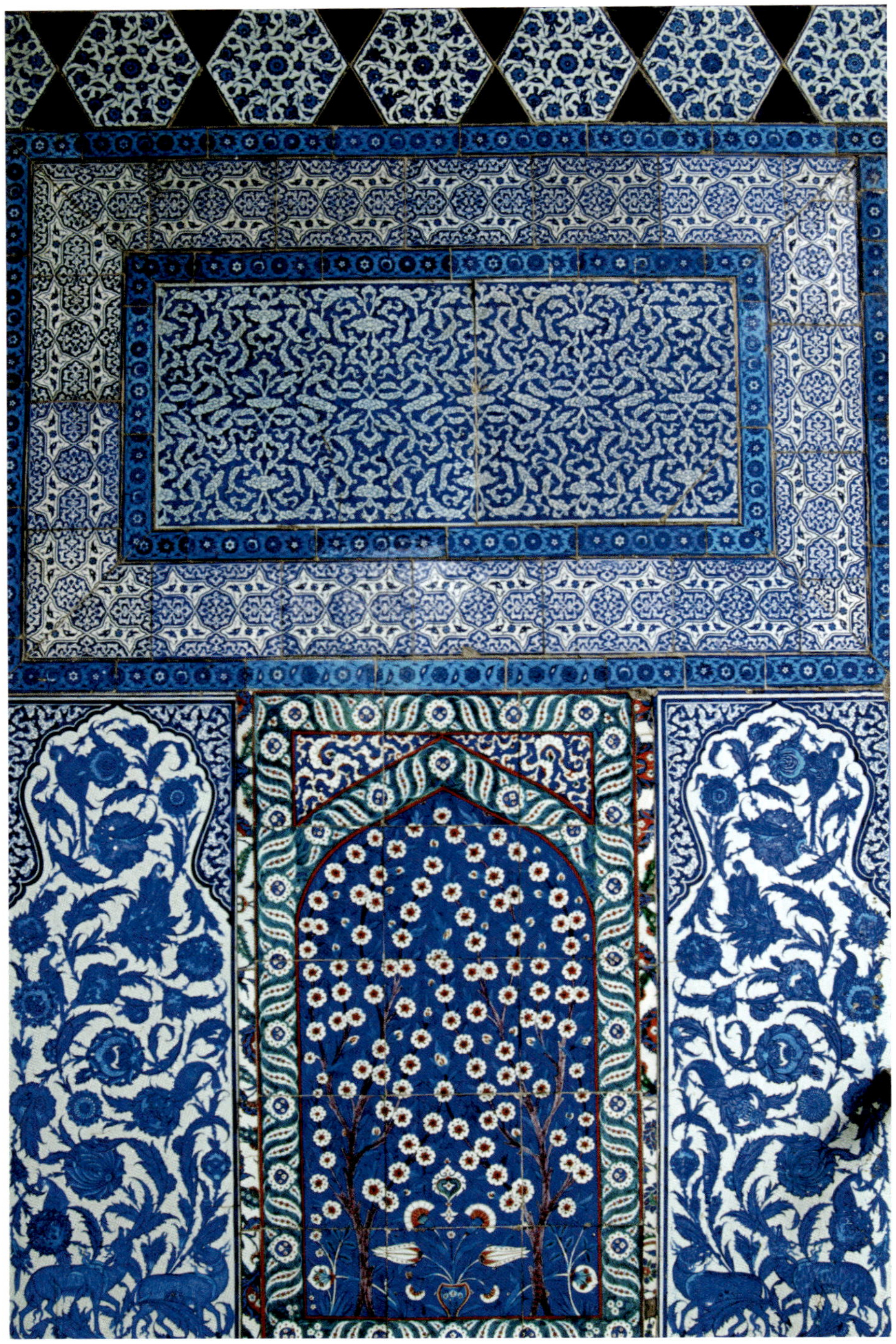

Sünnat Odasi (Circumcision room)
Decorative panels
1526–1528
Topkapi Saray Museum, Istanbul

In 1514, Tabriz fell into the hands of the Ottomans, who transferred miniaturists, musicians, ceramicists, weavers and goldsmiths to Constantinople, increasing the influence of Persian idiom in Ottoman art.
Among the best of these artisans put to work in the imperial workshop in Constantinople was Shah Kulu, in the role of supervisor of twenty-nine artists and twelve apprentices. Considerable sums of money and quality objects came his way, as a mark of the quality of some of his designs. The designs and supervision of the production of five ceramic panels of enormous size were probably by him. They came from a kiosk of Suleiman's destroyed in a fire, and were reused in the seventeenth century on the outside of the Sünnat Odasi. They display exceptional technical and artistic talent in the firing and quality of the glazed blue and turquoise ceramics.

Mosque lamp
1549
Iznik ceramics
British Museum, London

The lamp was produced in Iznik in 1549 and was intended for the Dome of the Rock in Jerusalem, which was restored around that time on Suleiman's orders. The shape is derived from Mamluk examples, but unlike them was executed in opaque material unsuitable for lighting. It must therefore have had a decorative function. Apart from the three blue strips with white calligraphy, the decoration draws on the international Timurid repertoire, coming close – particularly in the strips with the clouds or the delicate black arabesques on a turquoise background and the strips with bunches of tulips in the cartouches – to the *saz* style, which is well represented by a notable group of contemporary bowls. The high quality of the piece was a feature of the pre-industrial phase of Iznik ceramics, when every piece was still unique and appropriately executed for a specific client of high rank.

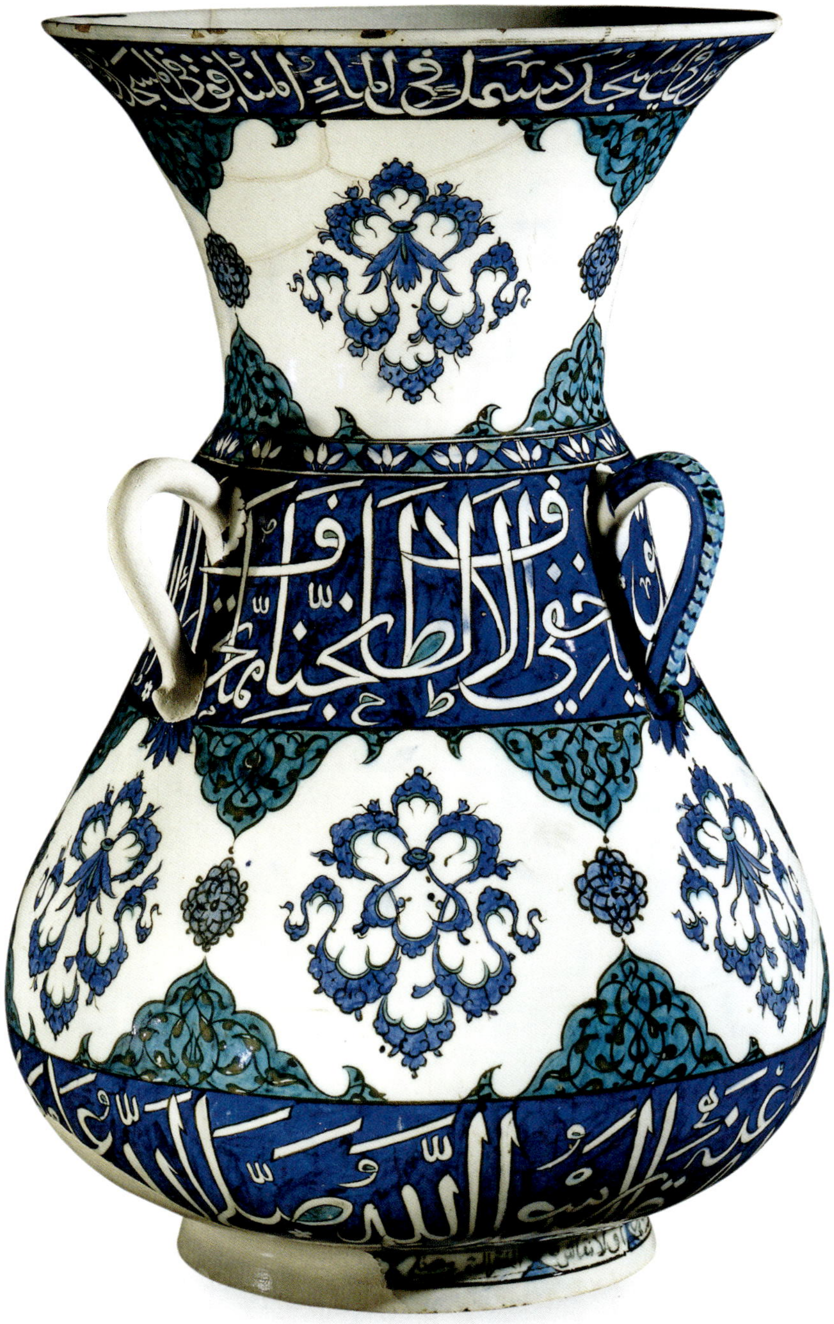

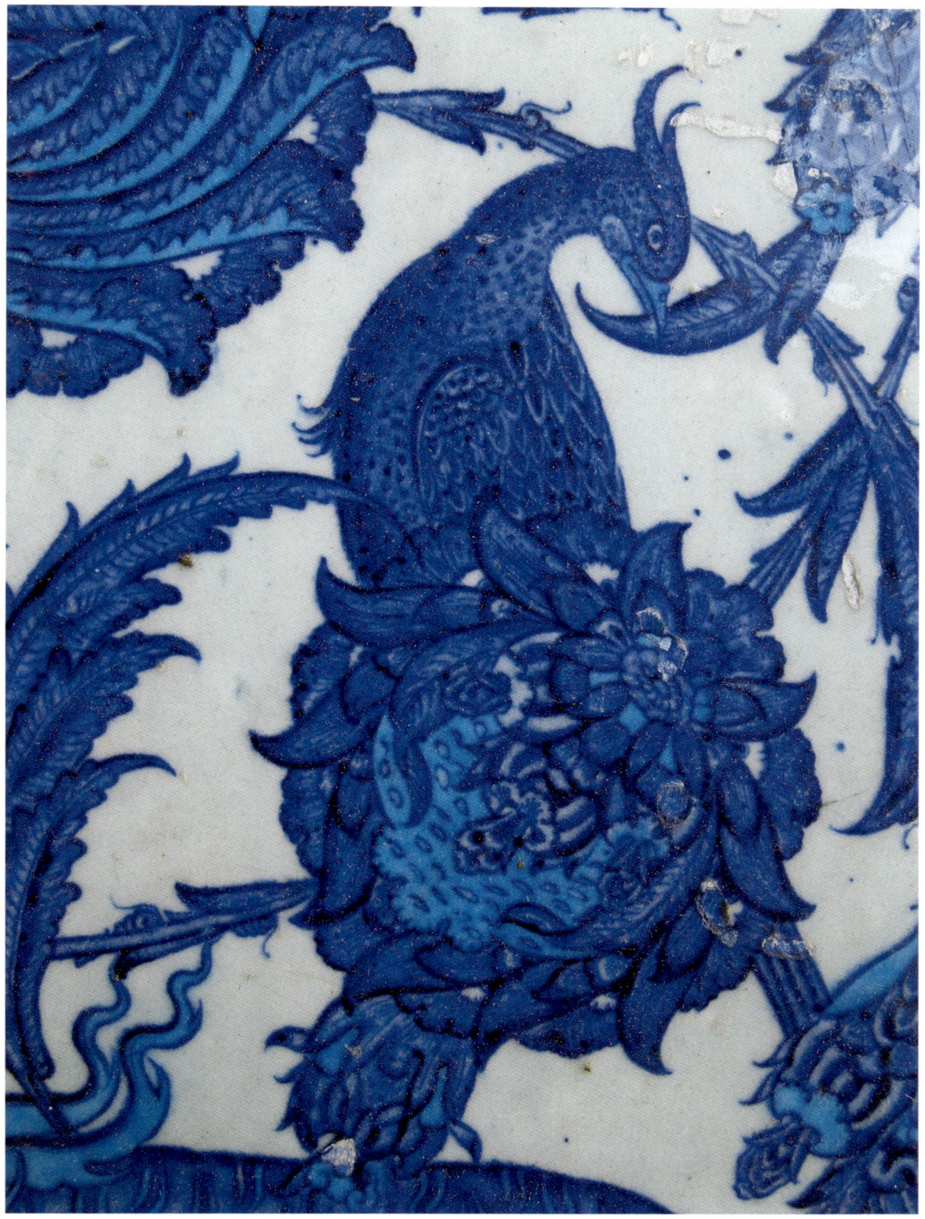

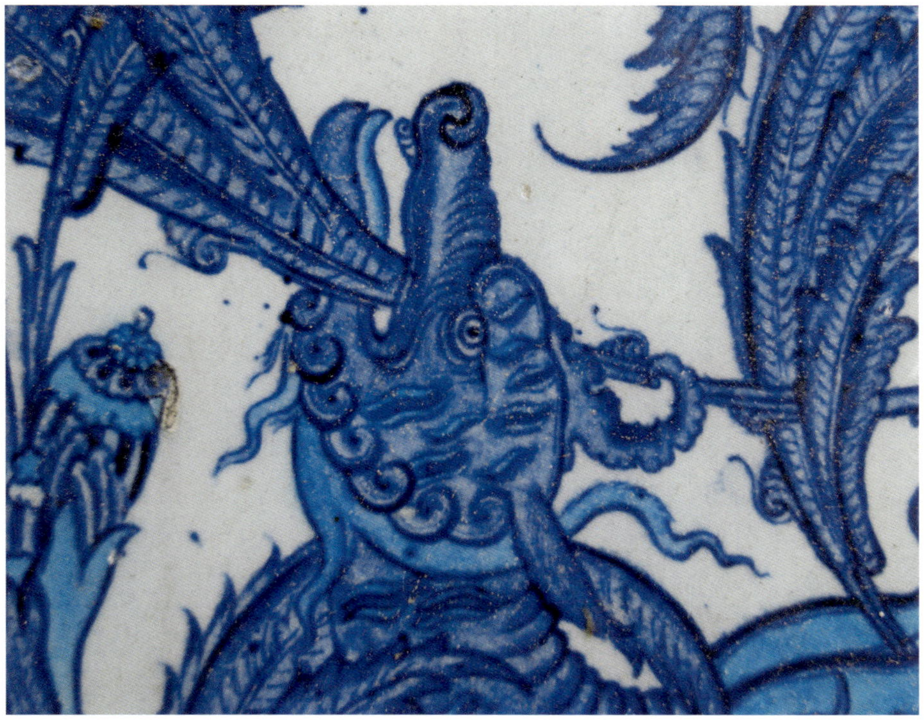

Sünnat Odasi (Circumcision room)
Two details of the decorative panels
c. 1528
Topkapi Saray Museum, Istanbul

The two niche-shaped panels probably represent the peak of quality, both technically and artistically, of Turkish ceramics in the brief period of years when production, carried out directly by Persian craftsmen dedicated to producing a few highly prestigious pieces, was still aiming to achieve ultimate quality. In the following years, needs changed radically, and Iznik switched to industrial production in order to guarantee enormous quantities of good standard. The two panels were composed from the same cartoon so as to achieve a symmetrical image. Animals resembling deer (typical of Chinese tradition) and birds are depicted on the inside of a niche, harmoniously integrated into the highly elegant weave of curving leaves soft as feathers and flowers of delicate and fantastic invention. The tonal harmony of blue and turquoise, then recently introduced, is perfect. This style, called *saz* ('reed', the instrument used for drawing), represents the arrival of the international Timurid style. Only a few years later, it was abandoned in favour of serial production.

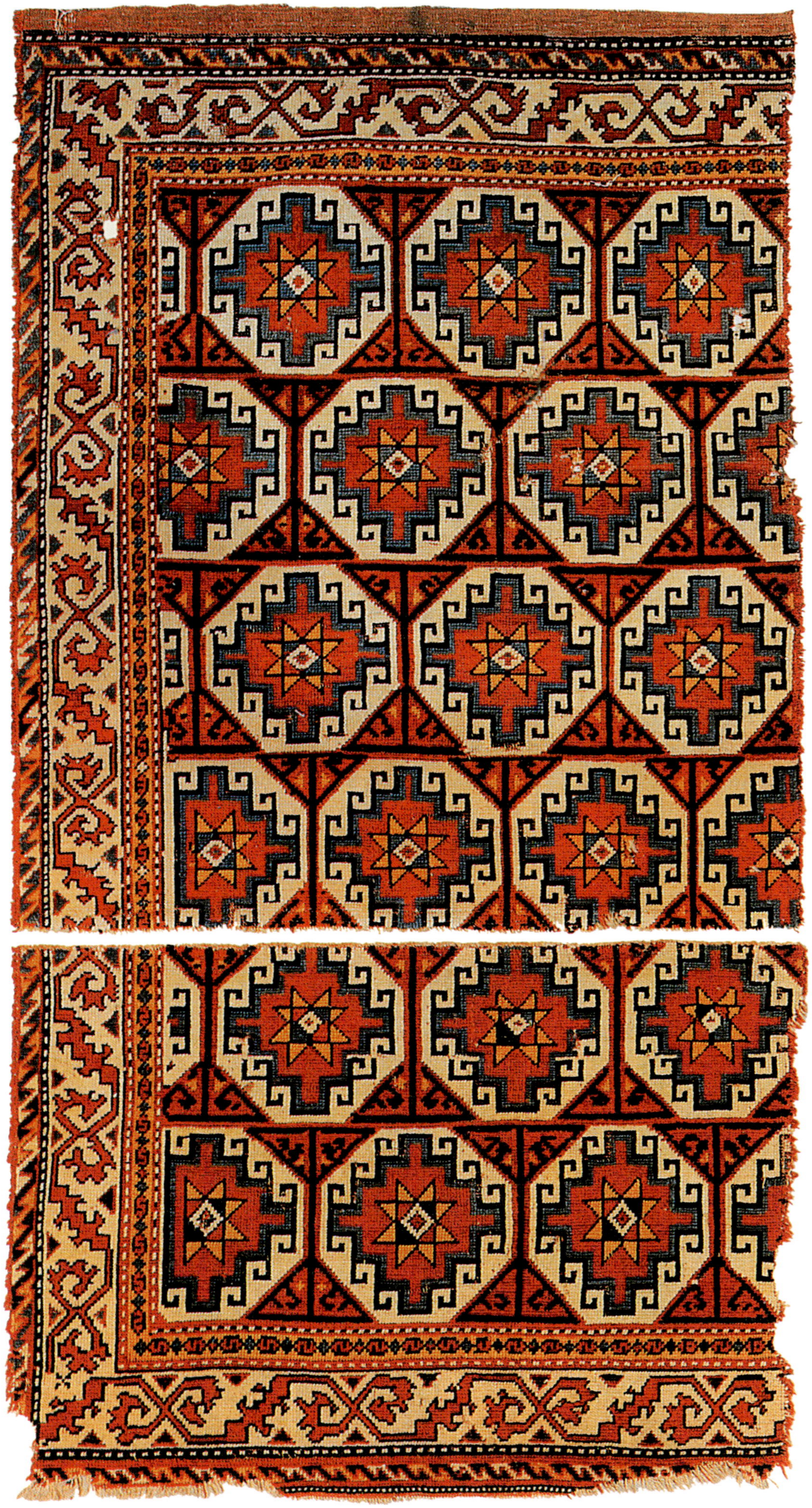

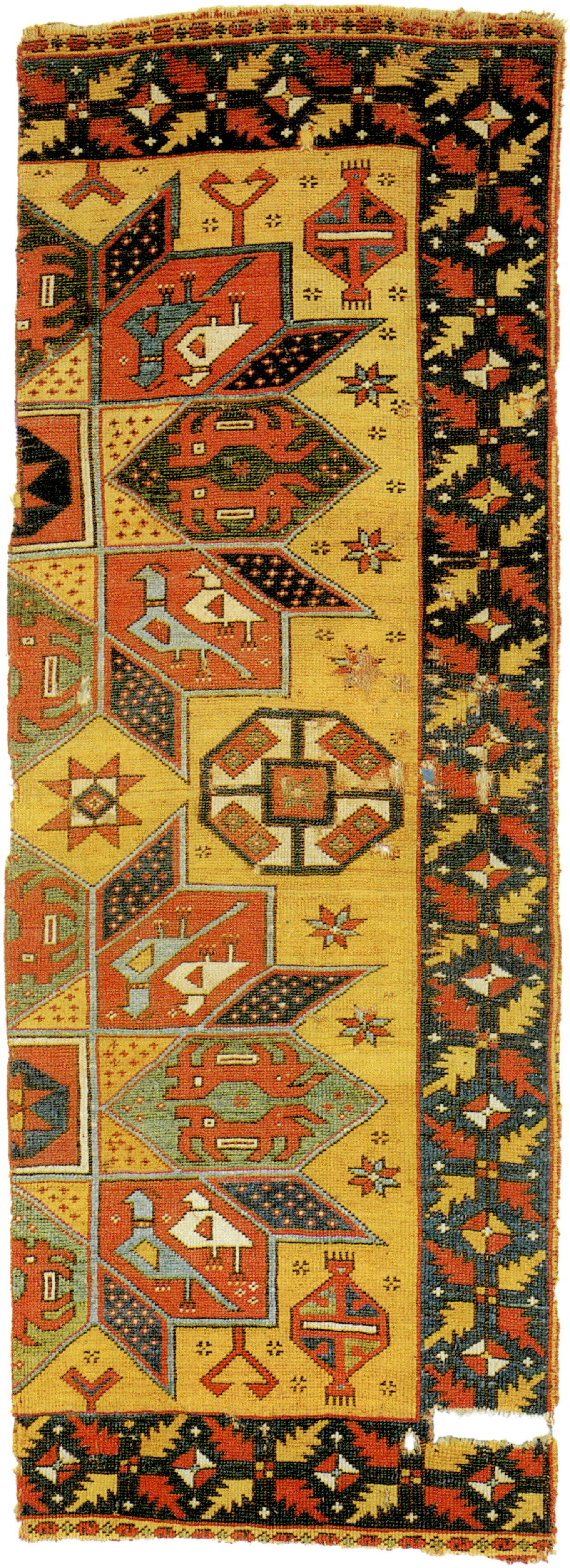

Fragment, Memling carpet
15th century
Anatolia
Iparmüvészeti Múzeum, Budapest

In the second half of the fifteenth century, animal motifs with a mediaeval flavour, well represented by the Ming carpet, began to give way to a new decorative style based on the use of medallions and geometrical lozenges in bright colours that seem to revive the Seljuk spirit in a more disciplined fashion. Memling carpets were a feature of the time. They are notable for their arrays of polygons with inserts of stepped, hook-shaped outlines, which the Flemish painter made famous in many of his paintings.

Fragment of Crivelli carpet
15th century
Anatolia
Iparmüvészeti Múzeum, Budapest

Towards the end of the century, patterns with medallions of more complex shape became popular. They were painted on a background of warm colours, and enlivened by the use of brilliant colours and highly stylized inserts of an animal nature, particularly liked by Venetian painter Crivelli, who found them a perfect foil for his vibrantly sculptural paintings.

Holbein carpet
Mid-16th century
Anatolia
Iparmüvészeti Múzeum, Budapest

Patterns with animal figures in carpets gradually declined during the Ottoman period, an aspect of that general phenomenon in the quest for 'classical' clarity and order that finished up, in every field, in a style that in certain respects is comparable to that of the Italian Renaissance, even if the use of that term obviously has no relevance in a Turkish context. The new idiom did not supersede the feeling of monumental structure in the motifs or impair the overall design or the potency of the medieval colour palette, but was able to revive a number of features that it incorporated into a new formal idiom with numerous variants. Some workshops, while working in this cultural context, kept alive the contact with the medieval world, producing some of the finest carpets of the time. It was the ones known as Holbeins which enjoyed enormous popularity among the European aristocracy. They had in common a decorative style featuring arrays of large medallions with slightly differing formats, patterns and colours so as to enliven an extremely organized and finished whole.

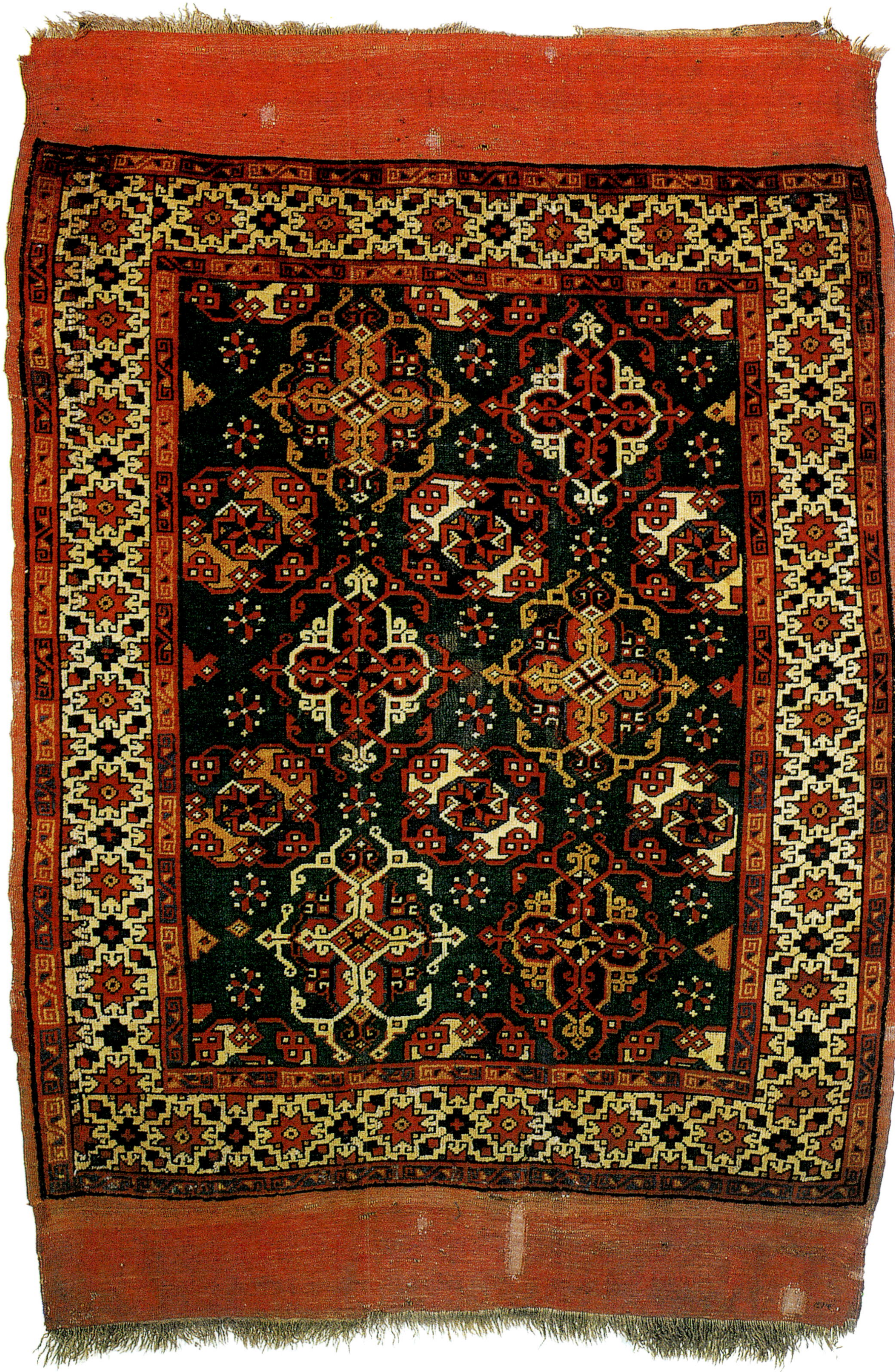

Lotto carpet
16th century
Anatolia
Museum of Art, Philadelphia

The classic Lotto carpet constitutes a happy and elegant variant of the Holbein, documented not only by painting but also in numerous well-preserved examples that have come down to us, many of them decorated with the arms of European aristocratic families and thus demonstrating the importance of the production intended for export. In Lotto carpets, the Holbein medallions seem to unwind to form a complex and flowing weave of signs that, winding along the entire central field strictly in a strong red colour, forms a kind of magnificently saffron grid with hints of gold and enriched with costly blue inserts. The border, particularly in older pieces, which are in general the most beautiful, retains the classic quasi-Kufic motif particularly suited for export inasmuch as it does not contain quotes from the Qu'ran that could be contaminated by non-believers.

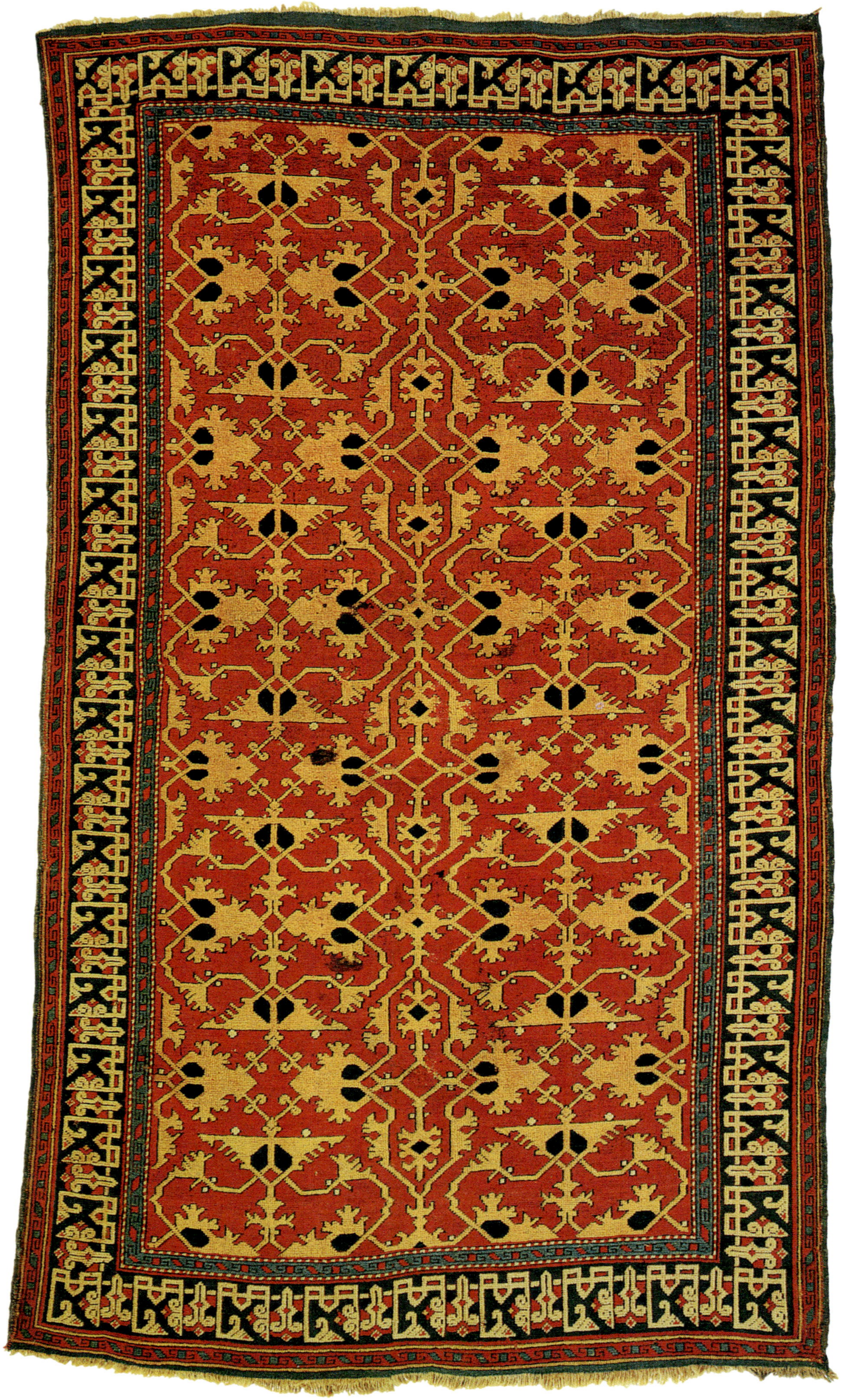

Star-patterned Ushak carpet
16th century
Anatolia
Taher Sabahi Collection, Turin

At the same time as the production of Lottos and Holbeins, the manufactories in Ushak (western central Anatolia) were developing new decorative motifs strongly influenced by Persian ones, which over the course of several decades would be established everywhere as a reference model, making the remaining production obsolete or provincial. The principal novelty consisted of introducing a curvilinear design alien to traditional technique based on the stepped design and requiring the use of a full-size preparatory cartoon.
The most widespread motif was once again the medallion, appearing in a wide variety of shapes and compositions. Generally, an oval medallion was inserted in the field, aligned with other smaller ones along the principal axis and elegantly echoed by some of the motifs unfolding from the sides. The border is decorated with soft floral patterns. Besides these, there were the star-patterned Ushaks, decorated with arrays of stars in highly subdivided patterns, generally blue in colour, alternating with rhomboid or cruciform motifs, but always on a red background.

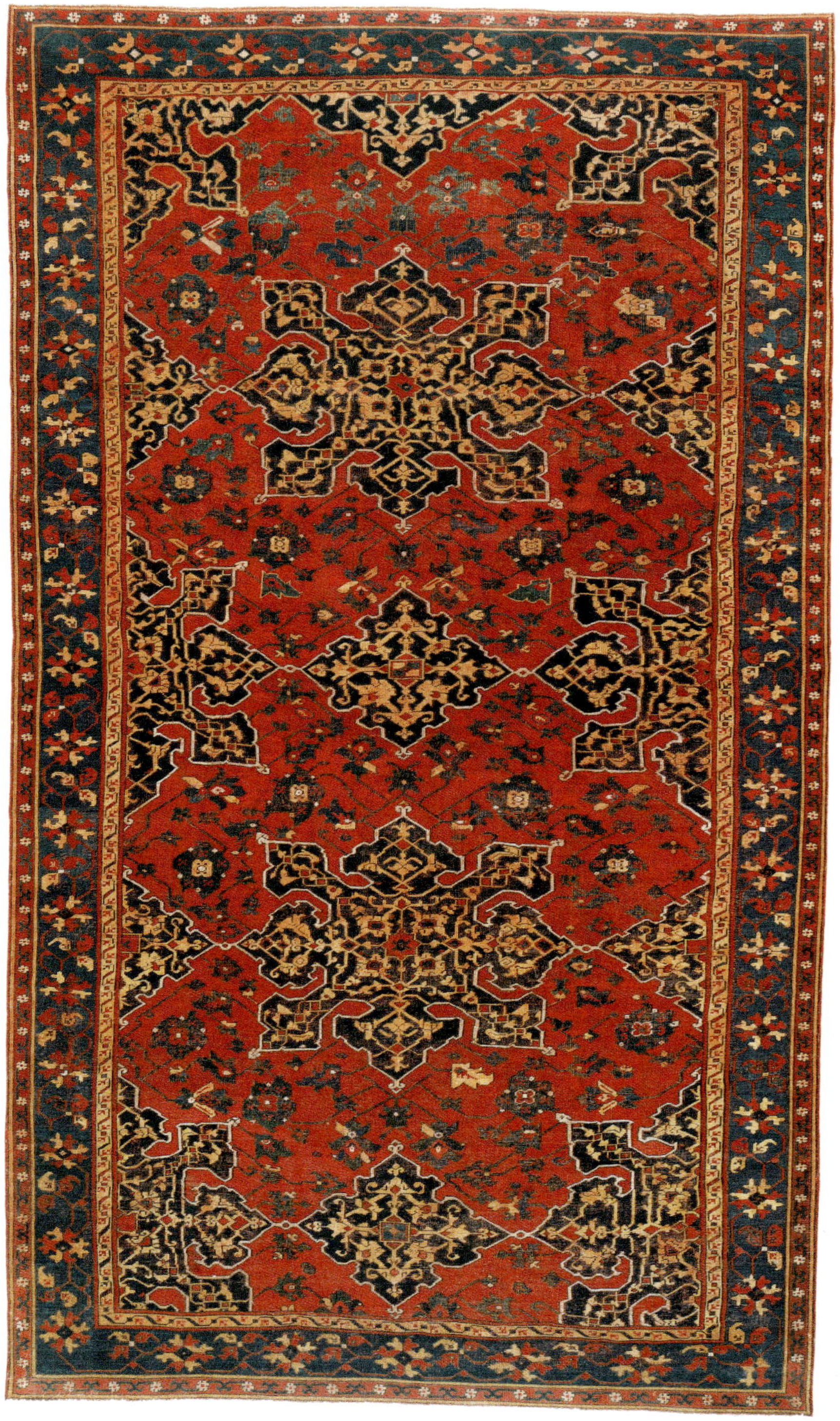

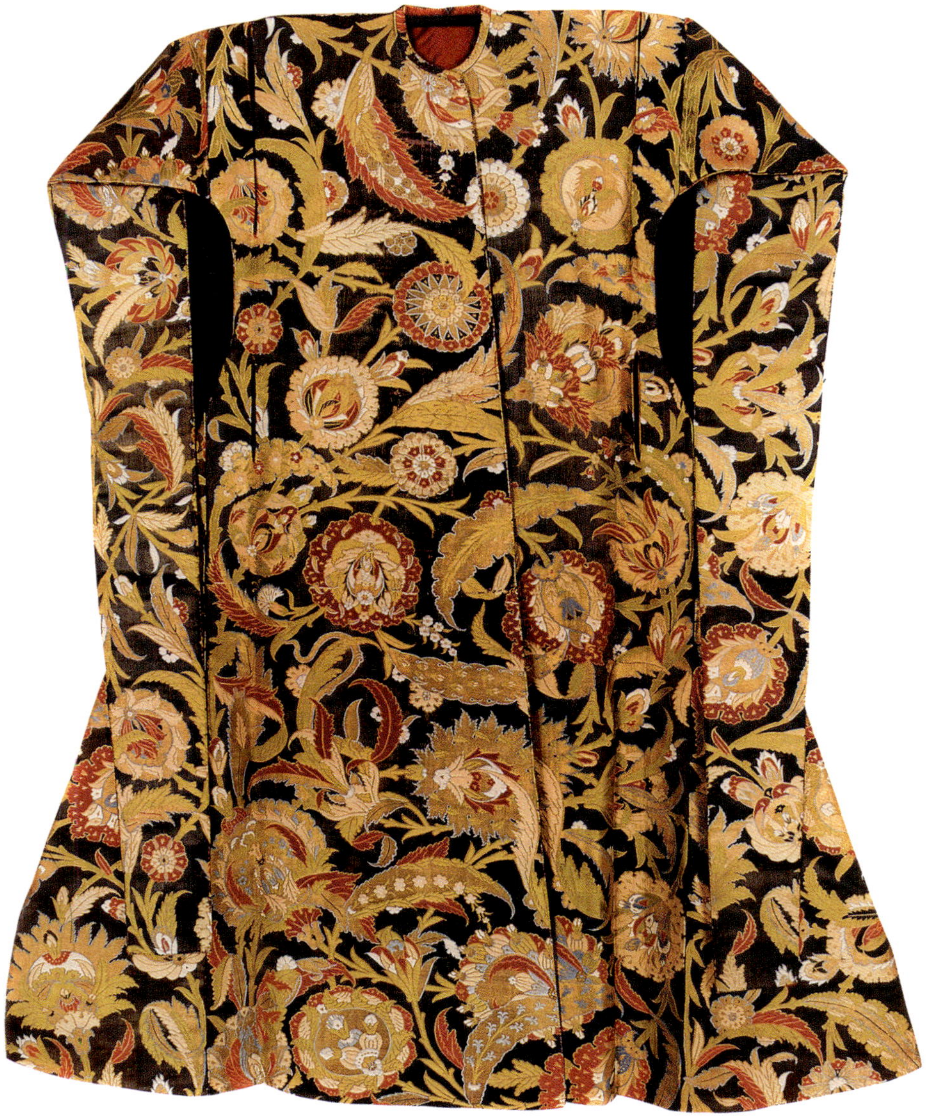

Caftan
c. 1550
Coloured silk and gold thread
Topkapi Saray Museum, Istanbul

Towards the mid-sixteenth century, thanks to the intervention of Rüstem Pasha, the production of luxury textile articles was strongly encouraged and soon attained extraordinary results, well exemplified by this magnificent ceremonial caftan with long ankle-length sleeves and vents for the pockets, in multicoloured silk and gold thread on a dark background. The lavish design is made up of interlacing floral volutes with leaves and flowers in brilliant colours, producing a strongly Chinese look in the *saz* style. Unusually, the pattern does not repeat, confirming the great importance attributed to the piece, which was intended for Bayazit, son of Suleiman. It is perfectly matched by another caftan with a cream background that belonged to his brother Mustafa. As in all other fields, Ottoman art was at its zenith in the luxury garment sector in the mid-sixteenth century.

PERSIA FROM THE SAFAVIDS TO THE QAJAR DYNASTY

Bazaar in the Meydan-e Shah (Shah Maidan) Detail of doorway
c. 1618
Isfahan, Iran

Around 1500, although actually of Turkic origin, the young Isma'il (1487–1524) proclaimed himself a descendant of the revered Shaykh Safi al-Din (hence the term Safavid), as a gesture towards the religious expectations of the Persians. At any rate, he succeeded in getting himself accepted as a descendant of the seventh imam and thus a legitimate wielder of authority, invincible divine messiah and shah. He soon overthrew the Turkmen Ak Koyunlu dynasty that had settled in the northern areas of Iran, eastern Anatolia and Azerbaijan, imposed the Shia faith as the state religion, and within a decade or so had subdued the whole of Persia. The effect was to supply the Persians with a formidable religious cement that is the wellspring of the indestructible feeling of nationhood still flourishing today. The new faith was introduced throughout the country in a form convenient for political power, by way of bequests and property grants to the religious hierarchy bound to the shah, who therewith became a point of reference in matters of faith. Thanks to these policies, a Turkic dynasty established an effective Iranian national dynasty.

The Safavids had to cope constantly with the tendency towards tribal and military divisiveness among the preceding Turkic clans. They therefore reinforced the bureaucracy to counter disruptive forces, relying on the religious establishment and introducing units loyal to the king into the army to keep a balance. However, the weak successors of Isma'il proved incapable of maintaining effective control until Shah Abbas (1588–1629) took a decisive step towards the construction of a modern state. With his arrival, Persia entered a period of extraordinary splendour that notably revived the best Persian (i.e. Seljuk, Ilkhanid, Timurid and Turkmen) traditions in the field of art, especially in architecture and town planning. They produced works of convincing beauty and worth, though tinged with an irrepressible 'courtly' character that became a constant feature of Persian art.

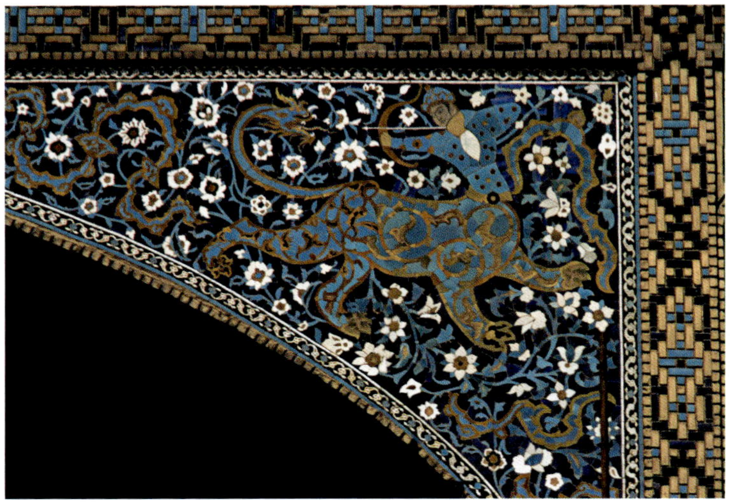

The vulnerability of the frontiers, threatened by the Uzbeks in the northeast and the Ottomans in the West, induced the Safavids to move the capital to Qazwin and then Isfahan, which in a frenzy of urban development was subsequently transformed into an incomparable garden city, with an architectural style directly derived from the Timurids but modified by Turkmen influences and ultimately given a more truly Persian stamp.

The first period of Safavid art is justly famous for the unprecedented boost that the dynasty gave to the art of books, the production of which, particularly in the field of miniatures, was probably the most important in the whole Islamic world. Among the masters, a prime role fell to Bihzad, appointed head of the celebrated school in Tabriz in 1522, where he passed on his supreme skills in the representation of movement, with figures caught in poses and attitudes of great vitality so as to express individuality, along with a keen interest in the landscape and representations of interior architecture, all produced in a rich variety and range of brilliant colours. His successor Sultan Muhammad took the art of miniatures to ultimate perfection, cultivating an imaginative vein so as to depict subjects with greater naturalism without sacrificing a profoundly genuine talent for lyricism and fantasy.

The evolution in pictorial culture also had an effect on architectural decoration, and even revolutionized the production of carpets where, with the introduction of curved lines, repertoires were completely updated, and scenes animated with human and animal figures of unparalleled naturalism and liveliness were introduced, finally bringing the 'medieval' period to an end with a new, elegant delicacy of elaborate draughtsmanship. This lively cultural climate, in which artists were for the first time respected as creators and sought out by collectors, kindled in them a budding awareness of their own worth and expressive individuality, inaugurating a completely new phenomenon in the Islamic world.

In religious architecture, the traditional structures with central plans, along with classic mosques and madrasahs with four-*iwan* courtyards, remained the most common schemes, though the tendency to construct immense *iwans* that blocked the view of the dome at the rear (originating with the Ilkhanids and continued by the Timurids) was tempered by the tradition of western Iran. There, the *iwan* formed a simple vestibule for the domed sanctuary, once again balancing the relationship between the various parts of the monument. However, even there the *muqarnas* in the doorways had lost any functional purpose and proliferated in almost excessive fashion, dispelling the clarity in the execution.

The spread of ceramic panelling to every part of the building continued over the years, eventually culminating in everything – *pishtaq,* minarets, walls, vaults and domes – being entirely covered with a mantle of brightly coloured ceramics that changed in the light according to the different hours of the day and seasons, with new palettes of colours replacing the classic tones of dark and light blue. In this context, the space reserved for architectural calligraphy also increased, following a development begun in Timurid times and evolving into a really individual technique of monumental inscriptions.

In minarets, normally constructed in pairs, taste was tempered by verticalism, with the addition of elegant little wooden balconies resting on a crown of *muqarnas* and terminating in a slender turret with a characteristic little dome. The domes, resting on tall cylindrical drums of Timurid origin, acquired an unmistakable outline – pointed at the top and onion-shaped lower down. This glossy architecture, whose beauty is all on the surface, made no attempt to experiment with formal or structural innovations. The pressing need was to construct a lot in as short a time as possible. The results were convincing in their sheer aggregation, symmetry and above all urban scale, i.e. their capacity to bring to life a truly sumptuous and 'paradisiacal' look to the city, featuring tree-lined avenues connecting groups of pavilions to gardens, bridges conceived as places to stop and enjoy the landscape, and *maidans* as settings for polo games. However, these very characteristics also imposed limits on the concept in imposing urban dimensions on courtly ideals. An inward-looking aristocracy was seduced by the fascination of landscape gardening and large empty spaces intended for its frivolous amusements and idly poetic meditations (indicative of a wholly medieval outlook), and was consequently deaf to the changes that were under way.

In the decoration of Safavid palaces, painting – especially figurative – assumed a new role analogous to that of ceramics, with which it coexisted. Large figurative scenes, for the most part now lost, were probably executed under the influence of European wall painting, although the perspective, monumental and volumetric presuppositions involved were never understood, suggesting that the painters of these works were really miniaturists. The progressive loss of authority by the political power as local potentates increasingly flexed their muscle was exacerbated by growing religious intolerance. This eventually led to the Sunnis rebelling, the Afghan invasion and the fall of the Safavids in 1622. There followed a long period of domination by in part foreign, Afghan (1722–1730), Afshar (1736–1796), Zand (1750–1794) and Qajar (1779–1925) rulers, during which, with the help of European interference, Persia progressively lost its independence. Artistic production documents this unstoppable decline, imitating – albeit in a pathetically provincial dimension – the splendours of the golden age of the Safavids, even recreating with popularizing and banal nationalist taste the legendary glories of the Achemenids and Sassanids. However, despite the general mediocrity of the results, there were nonetheless even in those centuries products of a certain quality that give what was a very long period a distinctive, even if at times decadent, personality.

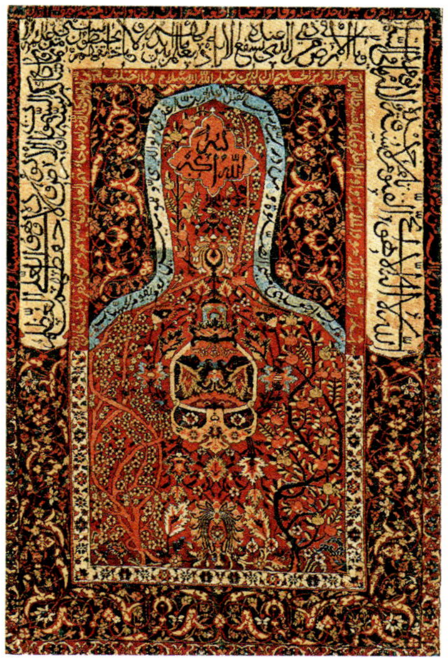

Prayer rug
17th century
Persia
Sanctuary Museum, Mashad

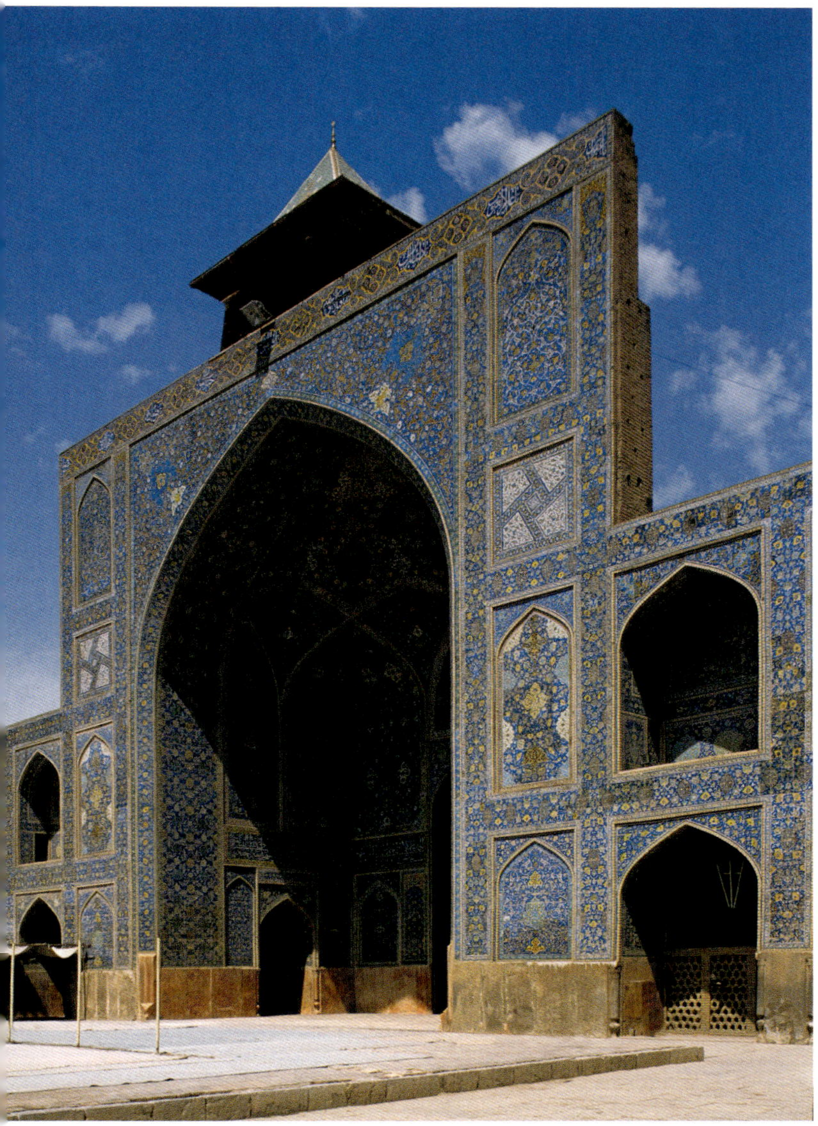

Masjid-e Shah
(Shah Mosque)
Courtyard *iwan*
1612–1638
Isfahan, Iran

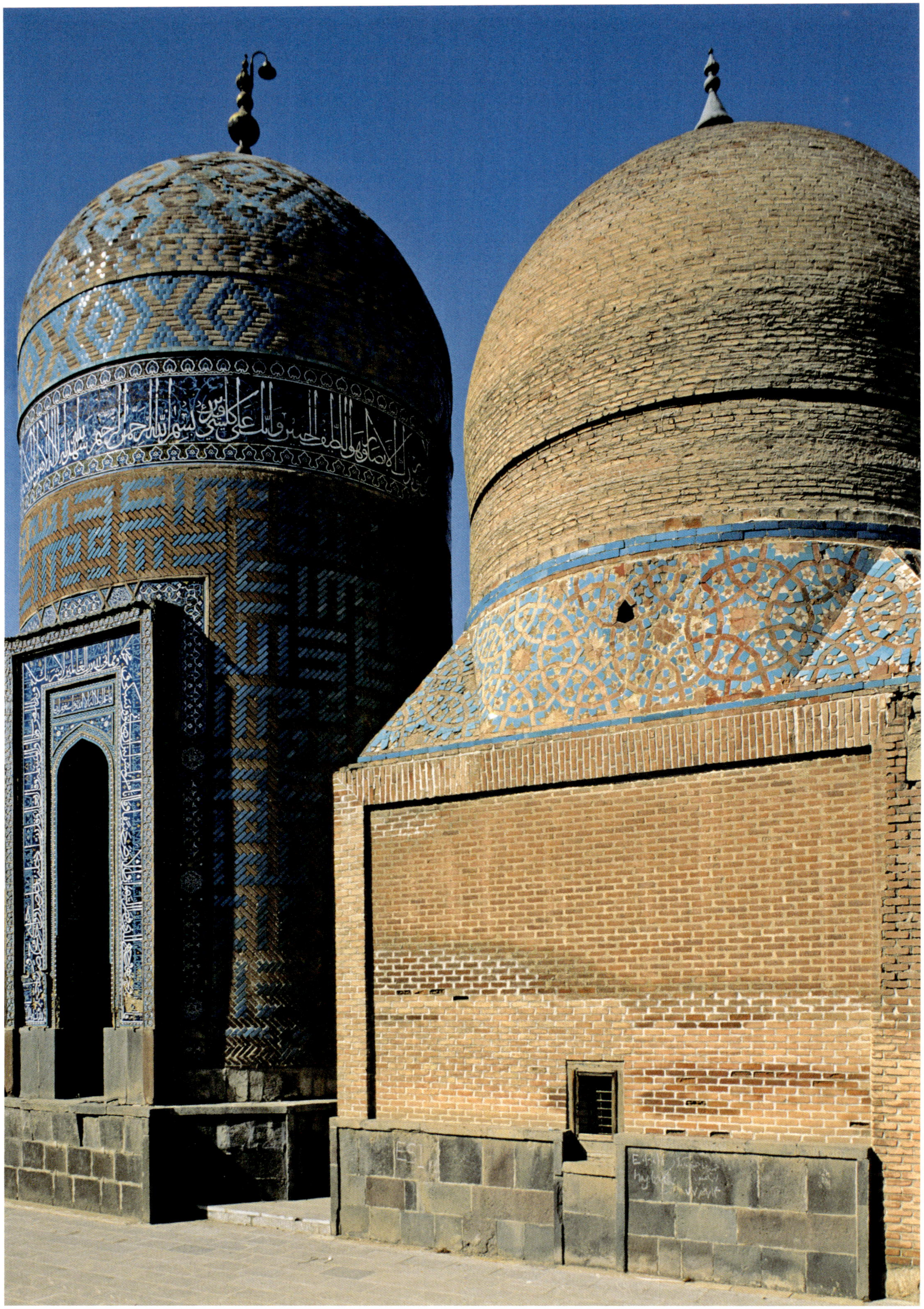

Mausoleums of Shaykh Safi and Shah Isma'il
1345 and c. 1525
Ardebil, Iran

Many Safavids wanted to be buried in the sanctuary at Ardebil near the tomb of Shaykh Safi, a cylindrical tower terminating in a relatively low dome, covered with calligraphy with the name Allah in typically Ilkhanid *bannei* characters and decorative bands of Timurid origin. Beside it, the austere mausoleum of Shah Isma'il seems to express in crudely archaic motifs a kind of virile devoutness. The stupendous turquoise fascia is what remains of a decorative scheme that must have been much richer.

Masjid-i Ali (Ali Mosque)
Detail of the façade
1521
Isfahan, Iran

The Ali Mosque, relatively unassuming and much restored, is the oldest monument of the Safavid period to have survived in Isfahan. What remains of the decoration of the façade belongs in the tradition of the decorative style first seen in the Blue Mosque in Tabriz, though offering a simplified version of it with a precise and serene alternation of parts in brick and parts in ceramics, in a clear, orderly design. The first step was taken here towards a new artistic conception with a distinctive character of elegance rather than grandeur.

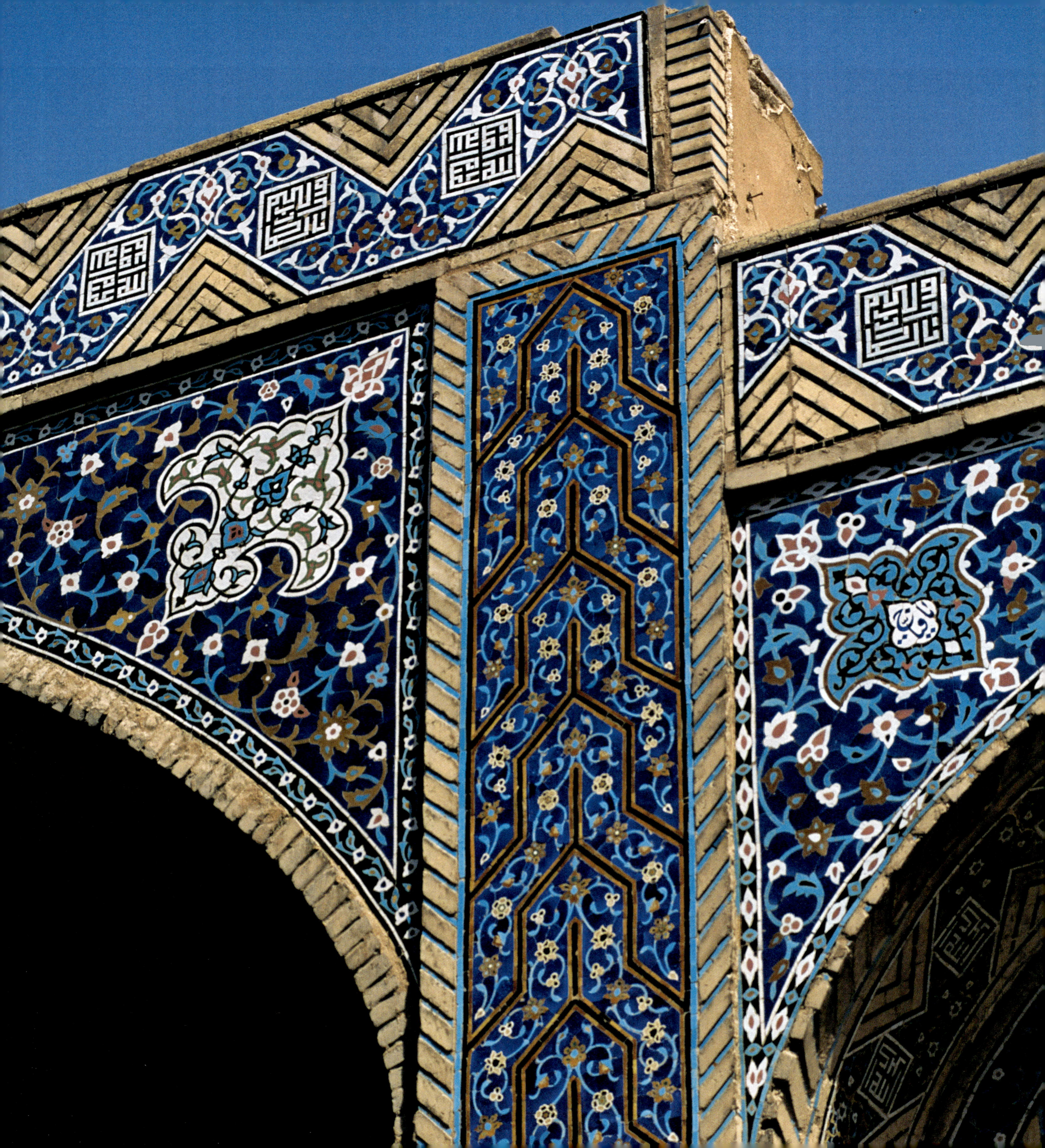

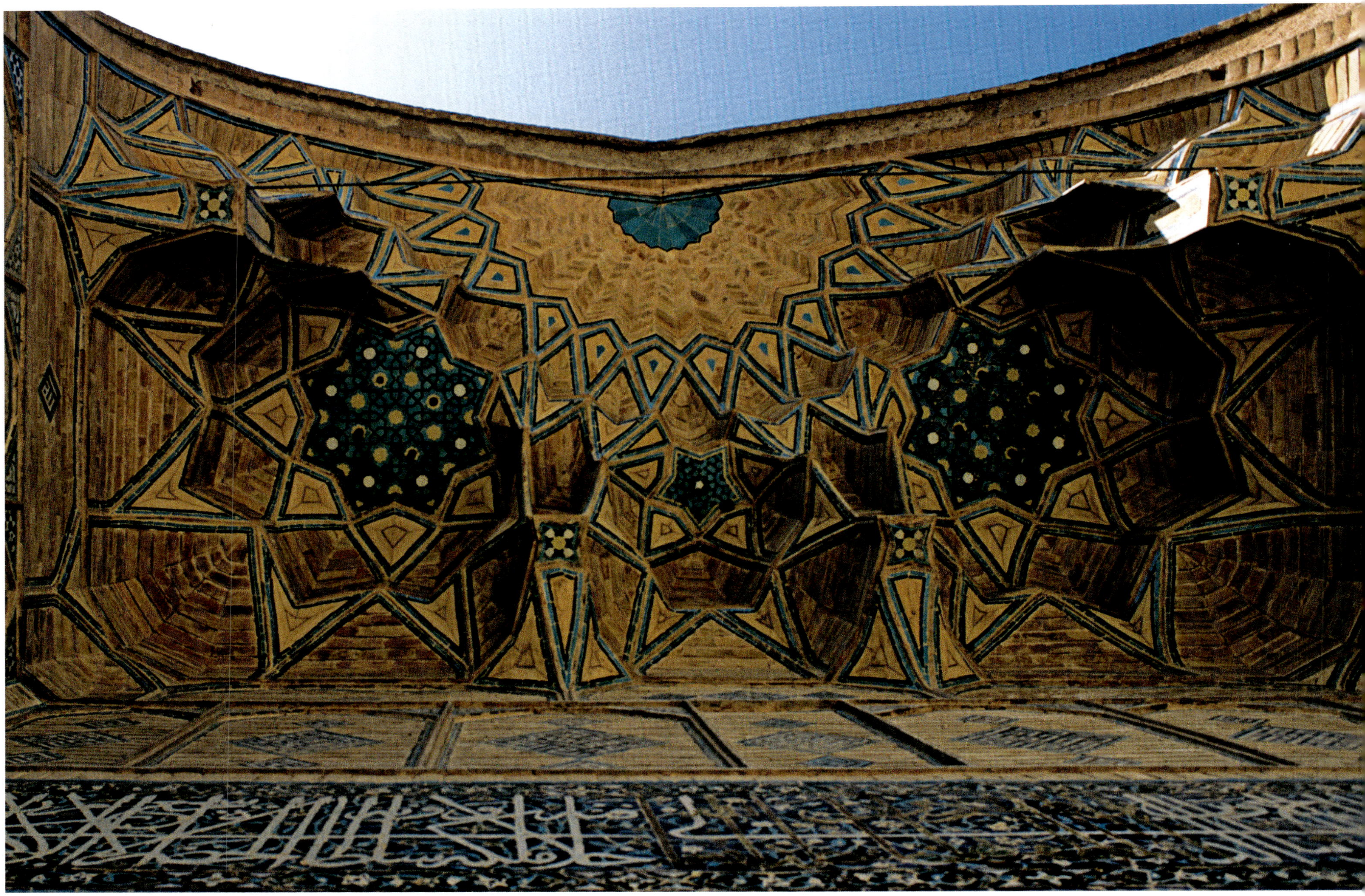

Masjid-i Ali (Mosque of Ali)
Vault over entrance
1522
Isfahan, Iran

The mosque was founded during the Seljuk period, when the still extant spectacular minaret was also constructed. However it was rebuilt under Shah Isma'il, retaining a classic plan of four *iwan* with attached prayer rooms on four sides and a large courtyard terminating in the southern *iwan*, leading on to the domed sanctuary with the *mihrab* and *minbar*. Entrance is effected via an arched doorway, entirely decorated with mosaics and ceramic panels with geometric and floral motifs in typically Timurid turquoise, blue and white tones. An inscription in gilded *thulth* characters, signed by the great Tabriz calligrapher Shams al-Din, records that the mosque was rebuilt by architect Mizra Kamal ad-Din. The *muqarnas* vault with the spectacular cascade of stars was executed in 1522 by master ceramicist Musaddiq, who left his signature in one panel. Blue and turquoise tiles also cover the dome over the sanctuary, embellished with broad floral motifs and wide calligraphic strips in Kufic characters.

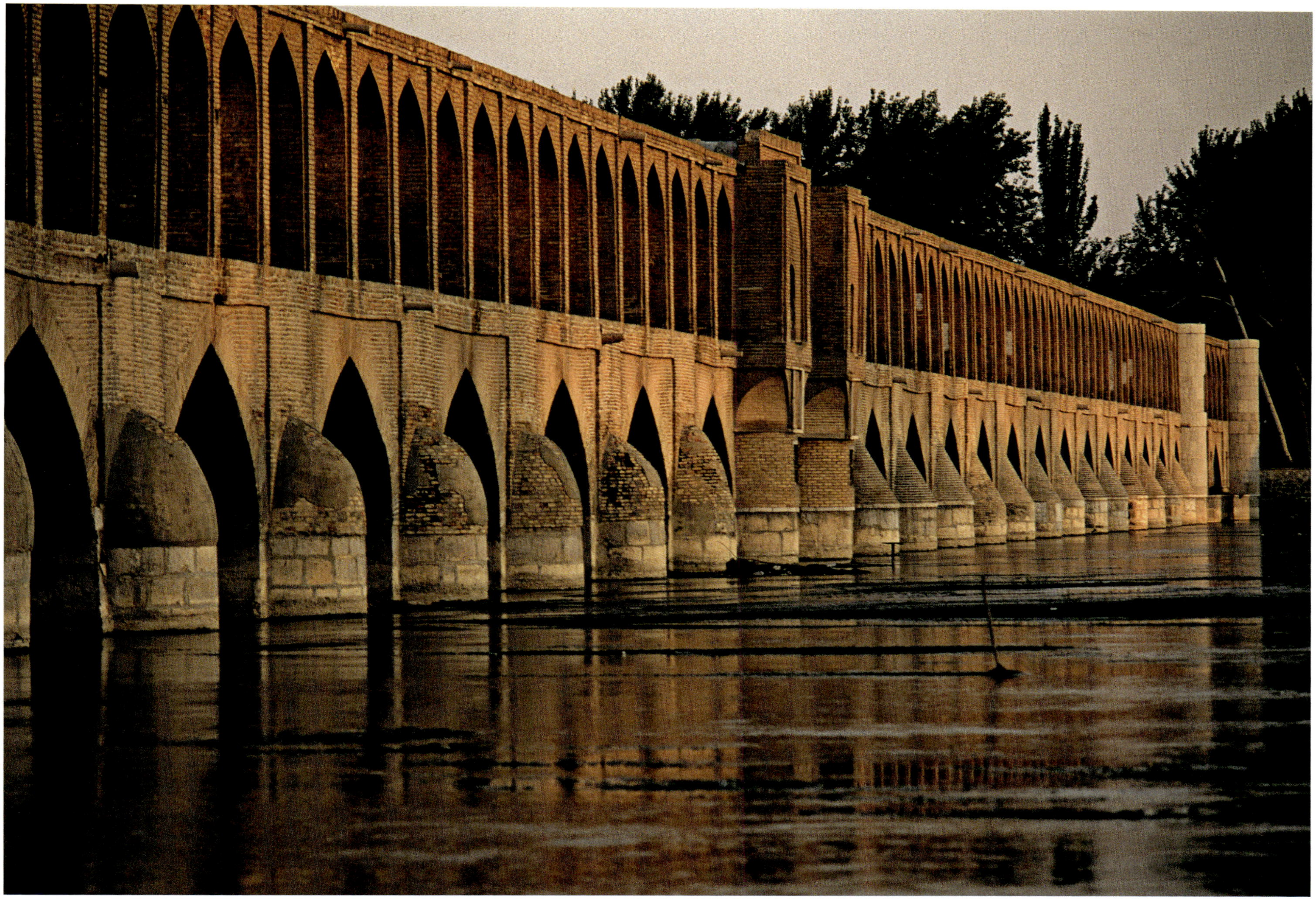

Si-o-seh pol (Thirty-three-arch bridge)
1602
Isfahan, Iran

The classical period of Persian architecture coincided with the greatest achievements neither in the field of architecture nor of miniatures and carpets, but rather with the charmed reign of Shah Abbas I.
Thanks to his patronage, a period began in which richness of details, magnificence of colours and compositional imaginativeness found expression in complex buildings and above all urban development on a huge but serene scale of calm grandeur. In the magnificence of projects, their calibrated emotional impact and the convincing relationship between constructional features and environment, the golden age of Shah Abbas, although not marked by notable technical developments and often mediocre in the quality of materials used, represents the apogee and ultimate expression of Persian Islamic architecture. A perfect example of the decision to make everything that went into the city beautiful are the bridges, conceived as landscape features, dykes to carry water to the gardens, and places of amusement and relaxation for the contemplation of passing time and changing light.

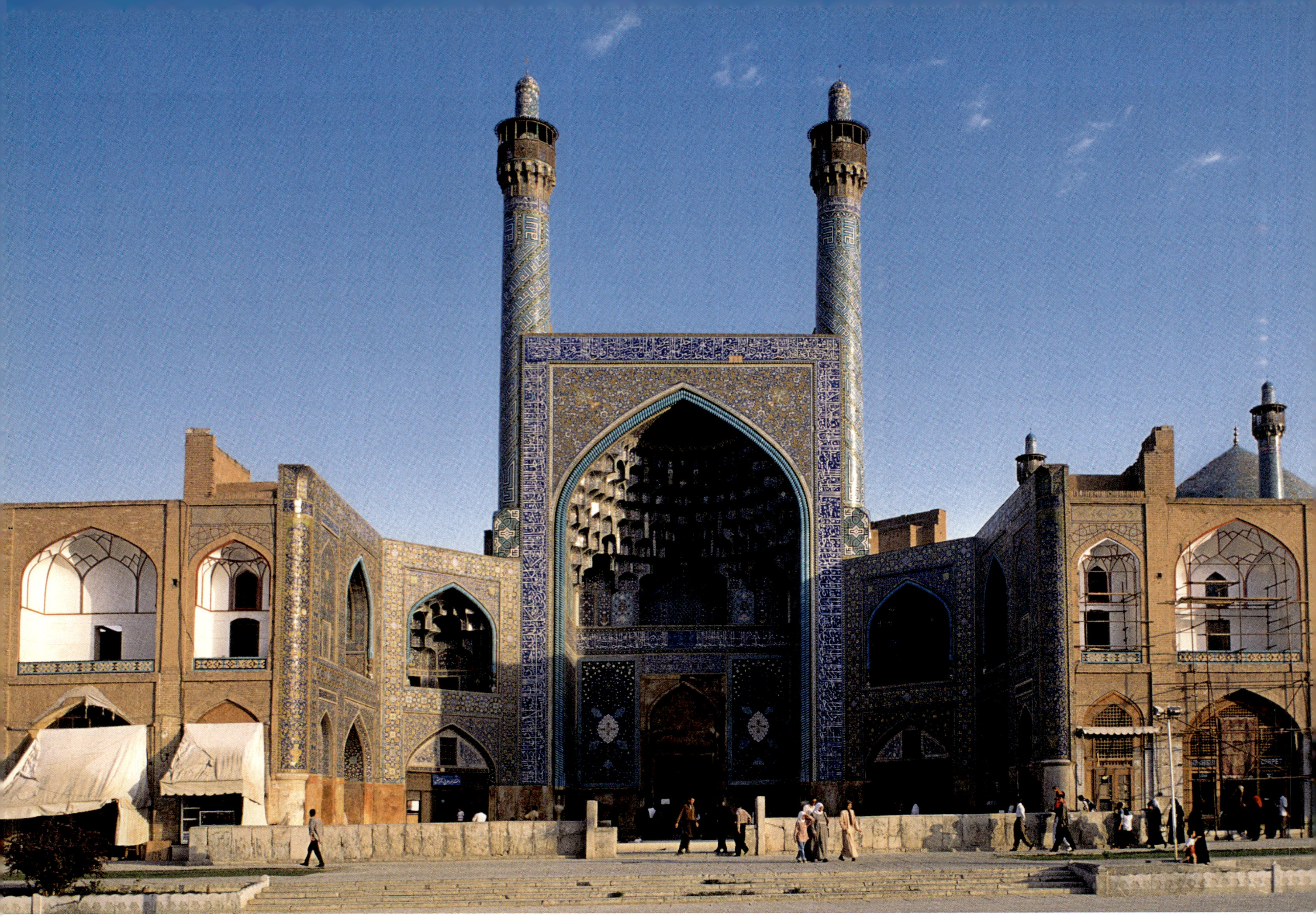

Meydan-e Shah (Shah Maidan)
c. 1617
Isfahan, Iran

The creative nucleus in the urban renovation of Isfahan promoted by Shah Abbas I was the enormous Shah Maidan. It is in this selfsame dimension of horizontal boundlessness, over and beyond its function for parades, processions and above all polo games, that the most fascinating innovation and principal value of this work lies – a space conceived for the entertainment of the aristocracy on their lofty podium outside the Ali Qapu palace seems lost in the infinite dimension of the sky above it. Surrounded by two-storey arcades, the focal point of the *maidan* is the majestic doorway of the Shah Mosque, with that of the bazaar on the opposite side. In the middle of the western side is the Al Qapu, the seat of government and, in front of it the mosque of Sheikh Lutf Allah, the private oratory of Shah Abbas. The repetitive rhythm of the two-storey arcading enhances the feeling of infinite extension, while the architectural elements that mark the four sides are placed so as to break up its uniformity. The stone pillar in front was used for games of polo.

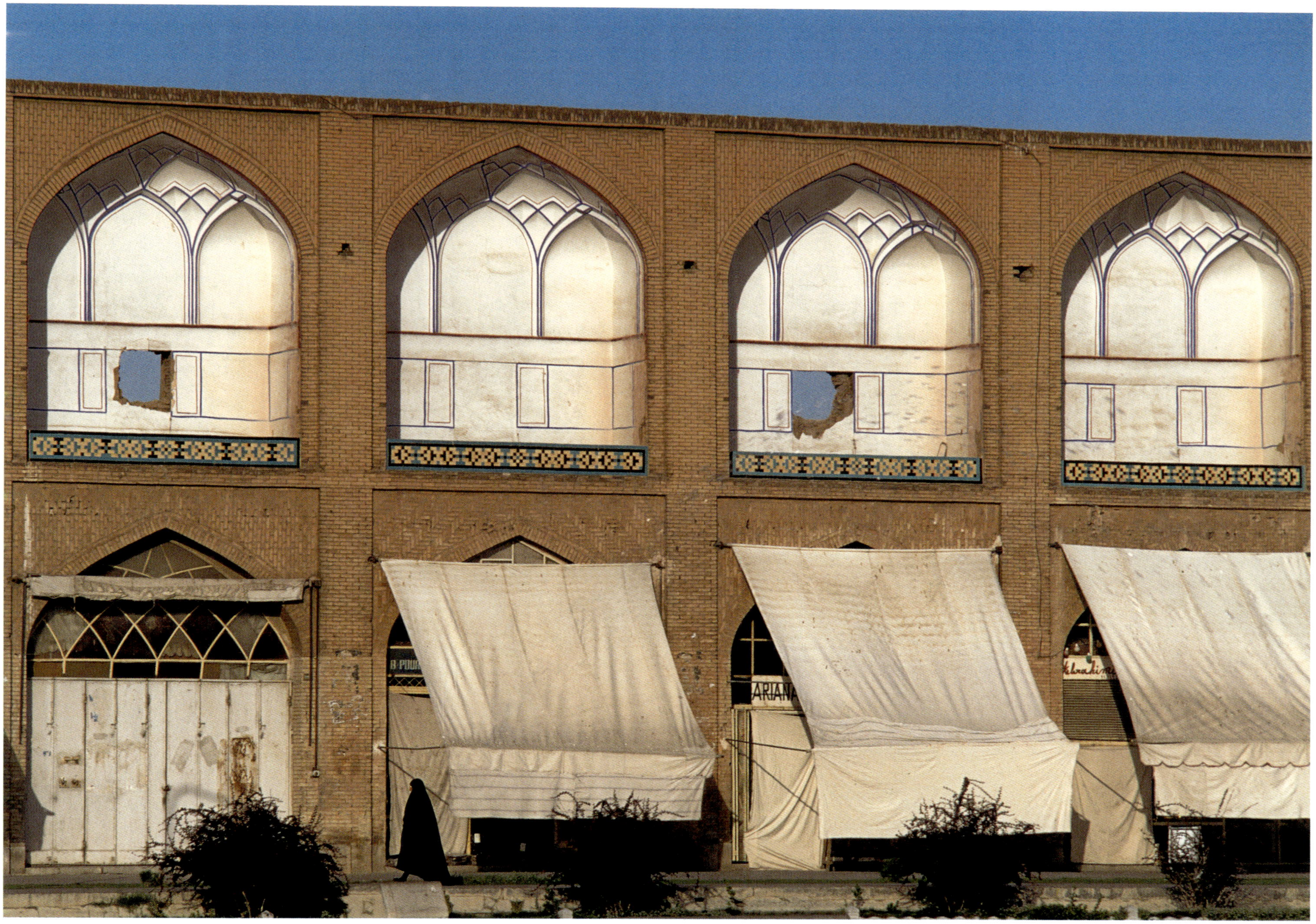

Meydan-e Shah (Shah Maidan)
c. 1618
Isfahan, Iran

The huge frame of arcades that unifies the immense space, originally unpaved, housed shops on the ground floor that faced the *maidan* and opened at the back on to a long gallery that forms a real covered bazaar which continues at random until it joins the existing one, which meanders on as far as the Friday mosque. The arcades of the upper level on the other hand are simply a backdrop and empty at the back, a confirmation of the intrinsically theatrical importance of the architecture of the time.

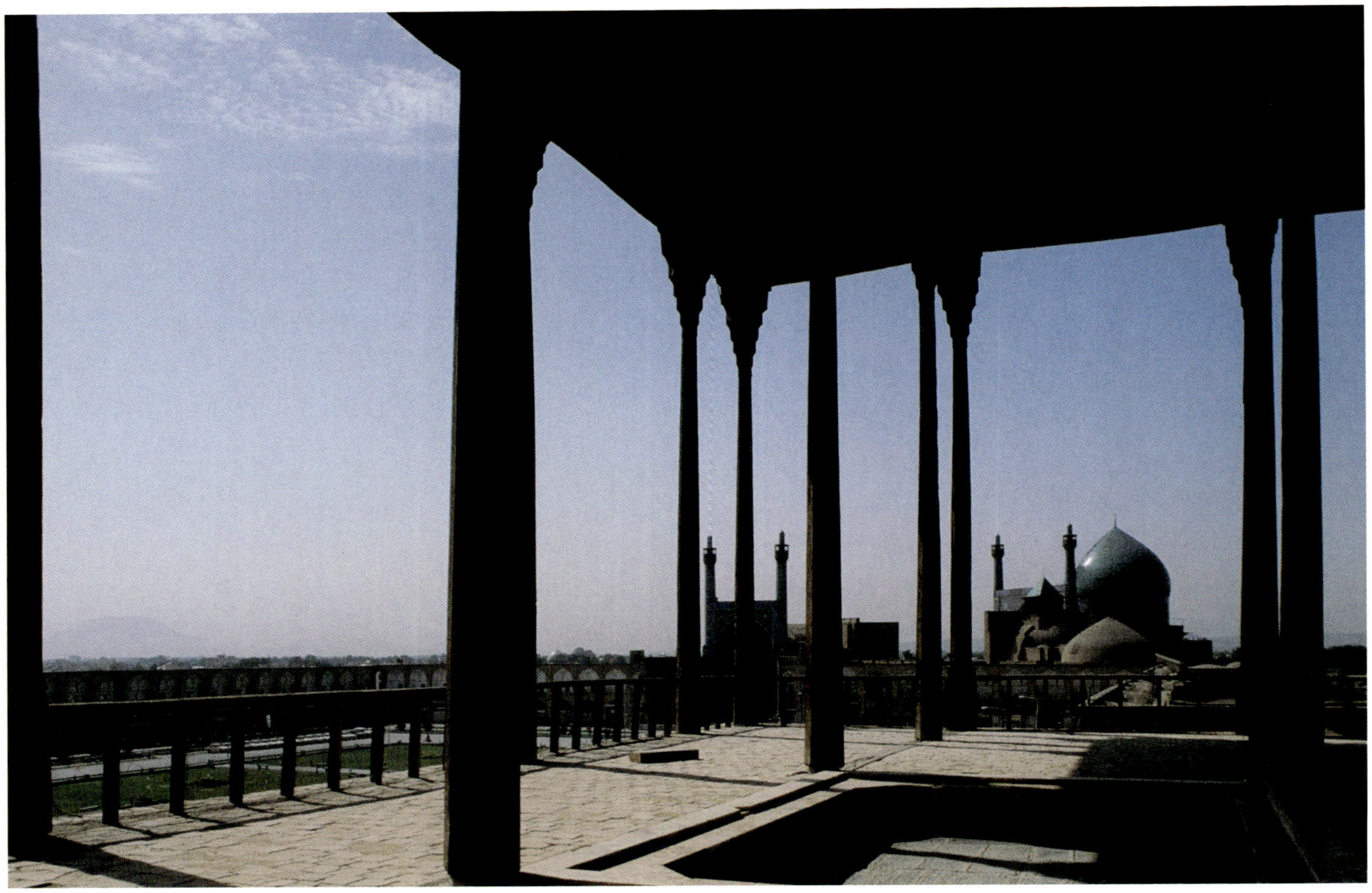

Shah Mosque
from the portico of the Ali Qapu
1612–1638, early 17th century
Isfahan, Iran

From the terrace of the Ali Qapu Palace there is an extraordinary panorama of the Meydan-e Shah and its buildings, including the Shah Mosque and the uninhabited mountain region in the background, at one time the source of the water that ran into the basin on the floor. Each feature of the *maidan* is considered in relation to the others and the immensity of the landscape and the sky; the whole conception of the Safavid city is poised between lyricism and spectacle, between an intuitive sense of the relationship between mankind and the divine and a display of the sophisticated joie-de-vivre enjoyed by an omnipotent and, at least to some extent, literate aristocracy.

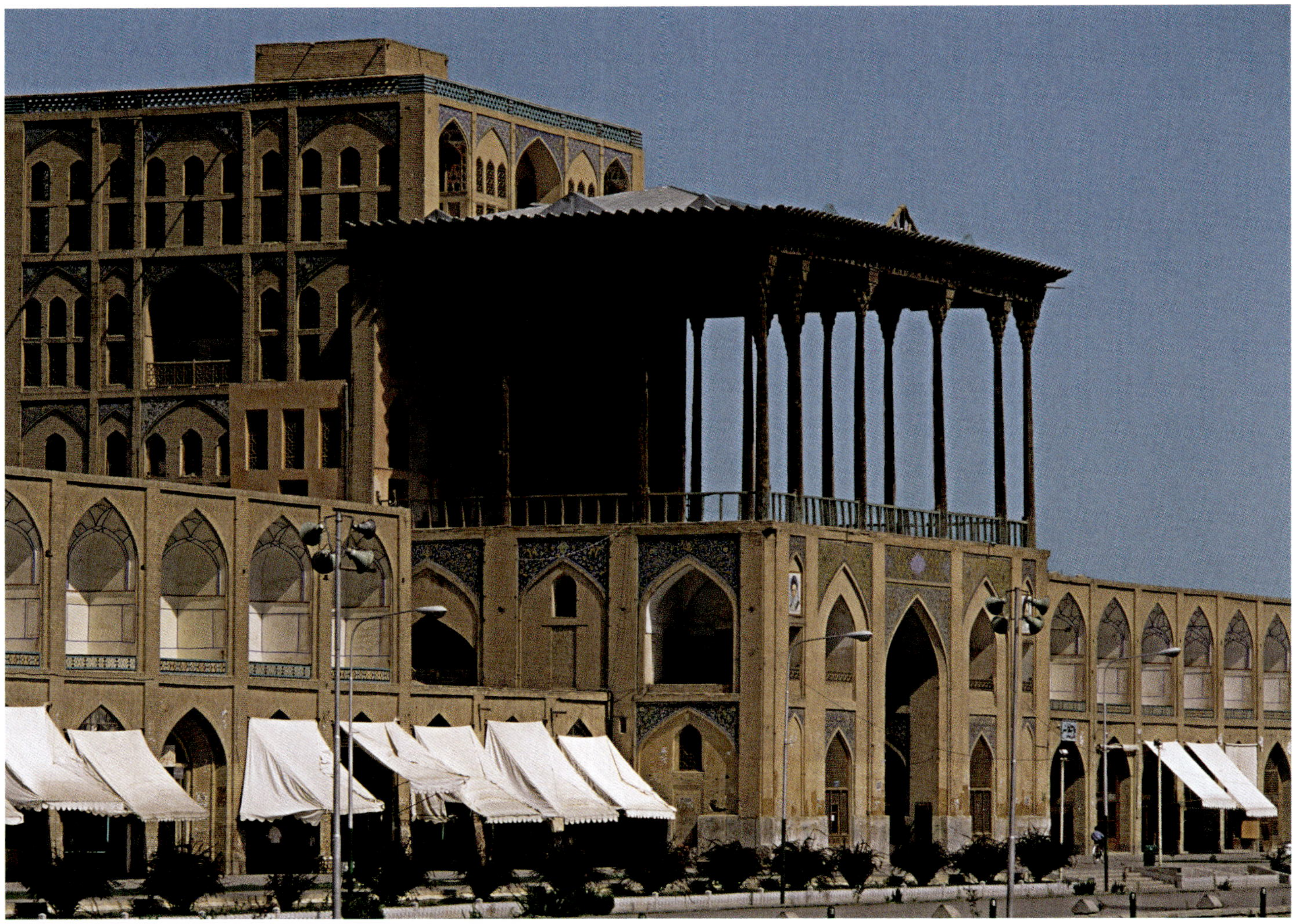

Ali Qapu (Principal Gate)
Early 17th century
Isfahan, Iran

The Ali Qapu Palace was the seat of government. The interior covered seven floors, masked at the front by the graceful *talar* (portico) on the lofty balcony standing on tall, slender columns of wood, a superb product of Central Asian tradition. It was capable of hosting 200 guests. The royal gardens extended alongside the structure, with pavilions surrounded by greenery and a monumental avenue that led across a bridge to the vast gardens on the opposite bank of the river.

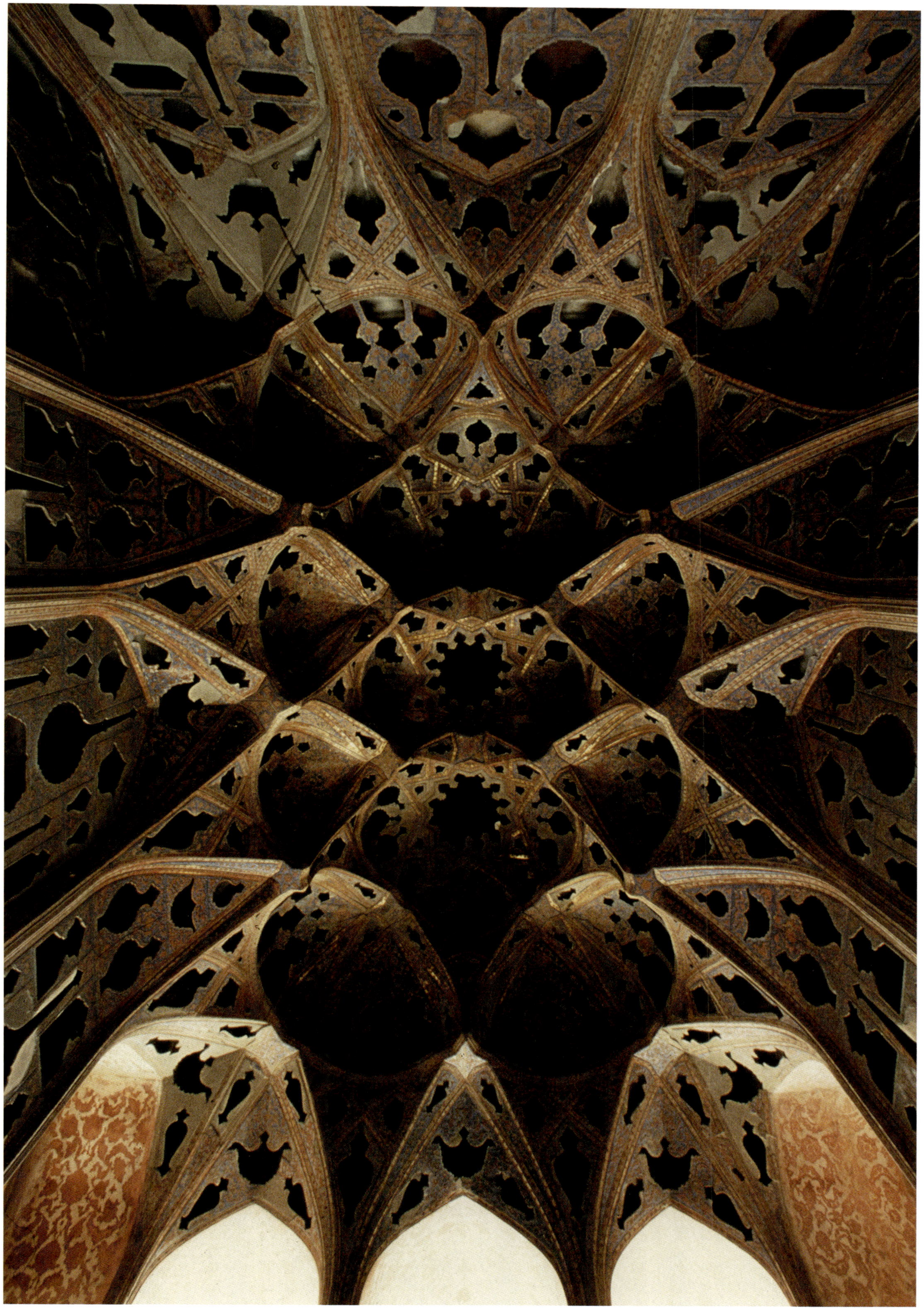

Ali Qapu (Principal Gate)
Detail of the decoration
in the music room
Early 17th century
Isfahan, Iran

Among the decorations of the internal rooms, the particular figures of the music room on the top floor stand out. The hollow outlines of bottles, amphora and pyxes are not used to store precious vessels but rather to act as a sound box during banquets with music, or even better, for simple refined elegance. Around the principal room, almost hidden, are small, private, intimate and sophisticated rooms intended for discreet meetings, in some of which valuable paintings survive with scenes of court love.

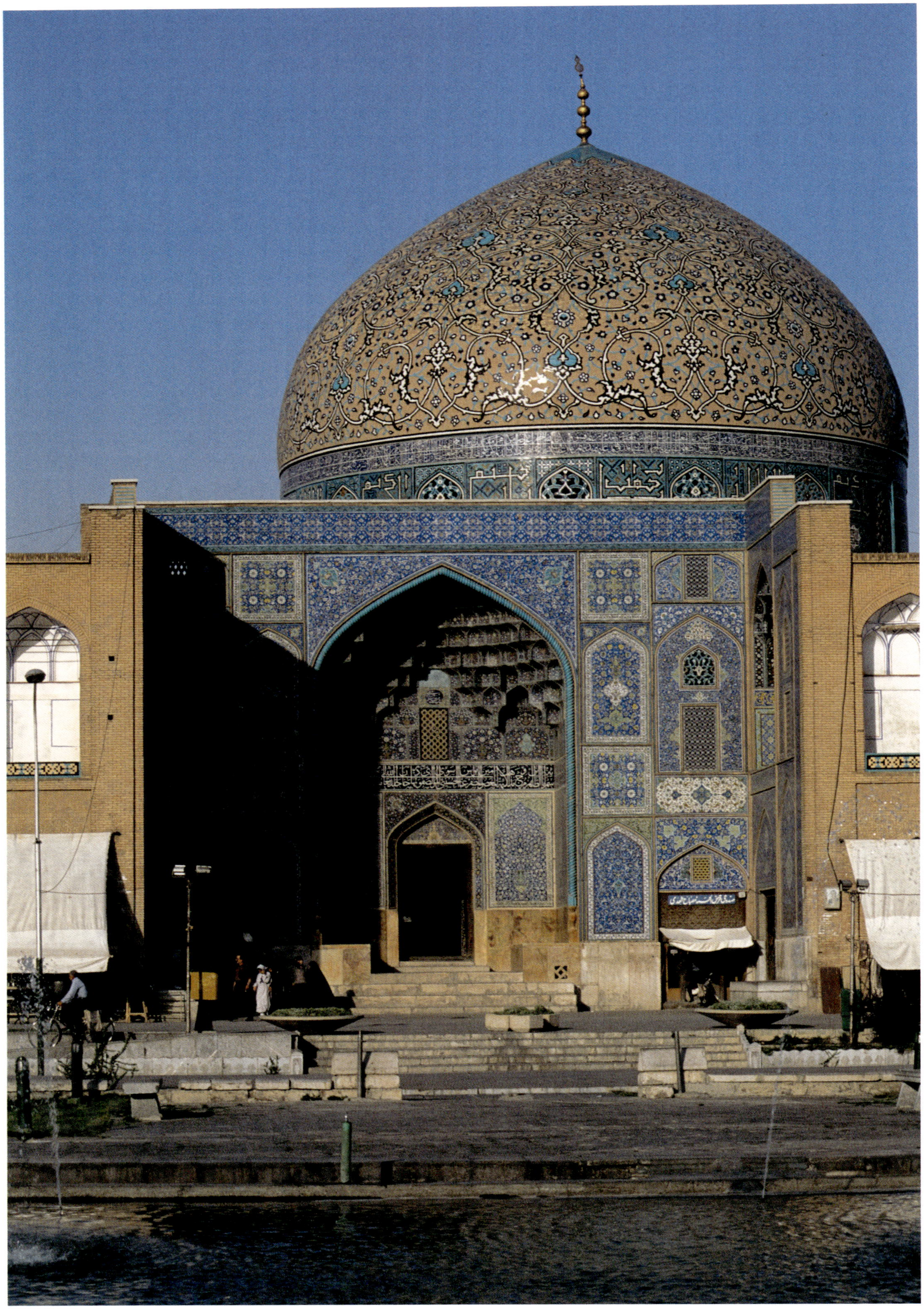

Sheikh Lutf Allah Mosque
1601–1618
Isfahan, Iran

Opposite the Ali Qapu, Shah Abbas constructed an unpretentious mosque of modest dimensions in honour of his devout father-in-law Shaykh Luft Allah that functioned as an oratory for the court. It lacks minarets and *pishtaq*, and has a low-profile dome, and yet it is this same modest dome that dominates the infinite weave of the arches of the portico when its colours warm up delicately in the light of the evening. Its sober essentiality makes this little building one of the lyrical highlights of Persian architecture. From the *maidan*, the profile of the single-shell dome, low and flattened, only fourteen metres in diameter and of solid appearance, lends the structure a sense of absolute repose. White and dark blue arabesques intersect majestically on a milky coffee-coloured background of unglazed bricks that retain the light, while the brilliant doorway with a stalactite vault foreshadows the internal splendour. Like the Shah Mosque, the structure is off axis vis-à-vis the *maidan* in order to line up correctly with the direction of Mecca. Entrance to the interior therefore is via a corridor at right angles, plunged in milky shade as a mystic preparation for revelation.

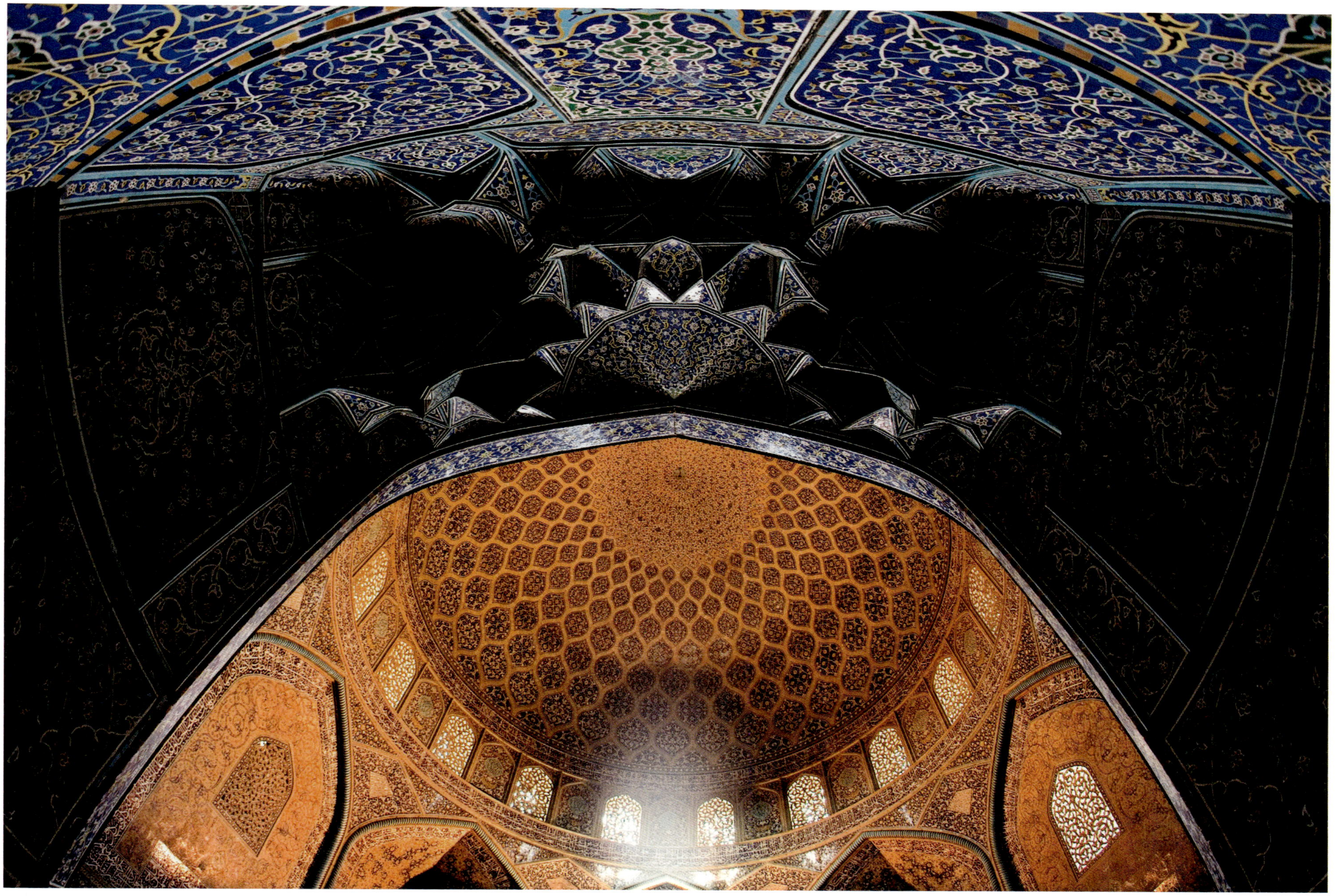

Shaykh Lutf Allah Mosque
Interior of the dome
1601–1618
Isfahan, Iran

Light enters softly from the arabesques of the double grid of plaster, to be reflected from the brilliant surfaces and diffused in space with fresh brightness and without discontinuity. The boundless scale is perfect. The non-figurative decoration is a mirror of divine beauty. It is the lyrical and poetic side of the abstract intellectual rigour that created the northern dome of the Friday mosque more than 150 years earlier.

Shaykh Lutf Allah Mosque
Interior
1601–1618
Isfahan, Iran

The prayer room is crowned by the infinite variations of the dome on a square plan – an essential and infinitely delicate achievement resulting from a progressive refinement of style. The functional but rigid corner squinch, invented in the Parthian age to support the dome, is transformed into an arch that extends majestically to the ground, its shape and dimensions echoing those of the four arches aligned along the walls. With this simple but decisive solution, the base square becomes an octagon projected upwards. The arches are busy with a sturdy spiral moulding in brilliant turquoise, while inside them dazzling white inscriptions unfold on a very dark blue background, the finest work of Ali Reza, the principal calligrapher of the time.

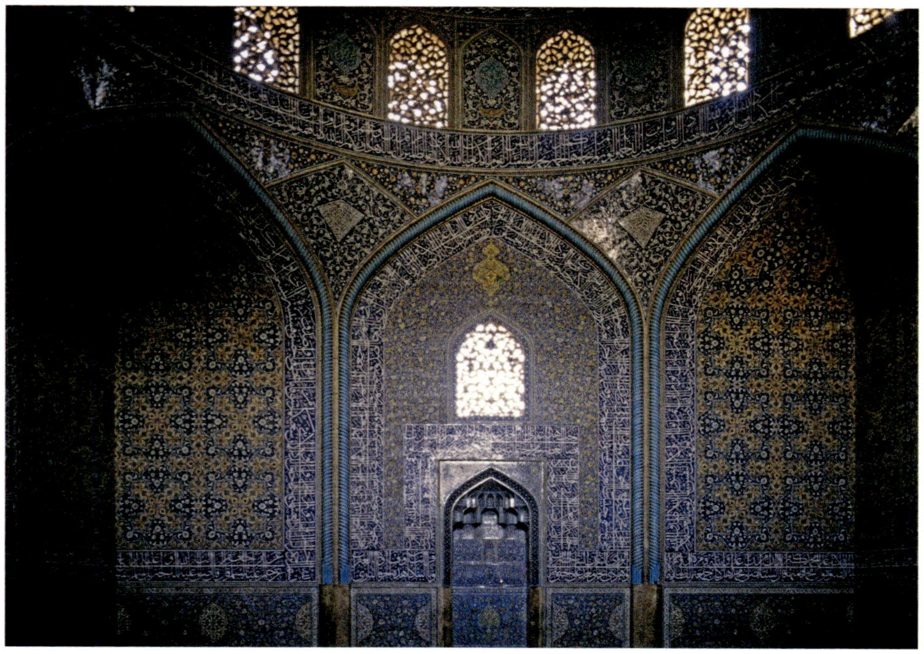

Masjid-e Shah (Shah Mosque)
1612–1638
Isfahan, Iran

The Shah Mosque crowns centuries of Persian building experience in the serene balance of its solemn and majestic splendour. Since the doorway faces north towards the *maidan,* the adjustment towards Mecca required rotation of part of the structure, solved with scenographic efficiency. The cascade of *muqarnas* above the entrance, glittering with stars and marvellous cosmic harmonies, culminates in the punctiform generative motif at the vertex – a divine symbol and universal principle. The fountain in the foreground is modern – originally the *maidan* was unpaved. The two stone posts facing the façade represented the entrance to the polo field.

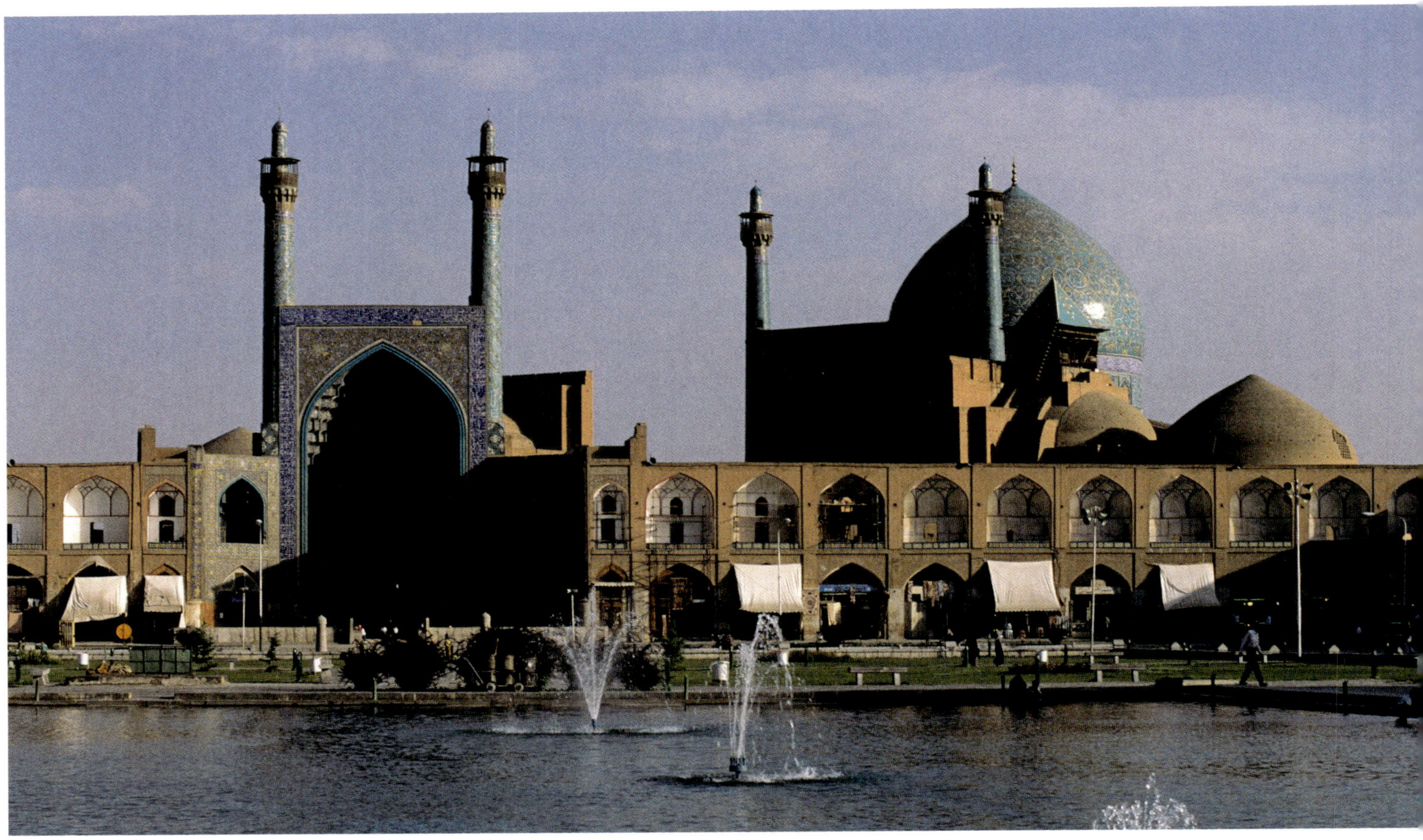

Masjid-e Shah (Shah Mosque)
Courtyard with southern *iwan*
1612–1638
Isfahan, Iran

An octagonal vestibule glimmering with reflections in the mystic half-light forms the perfect axis of the complex, leading to a deceptively Turkish appearance in the majestic courtyard with four *iwan,* a sublime materialization of a universe of superhuman splendour. Every surface proclaims in its magnificence the glory of the shah and Islam, in the certainty that beauty can guarantee a direct experience of transcendence unencumbered by theoretical argumentation and dogma. The deep, lofty vaults and the domes, rationally unfathomable, are a tangible sign of spiritual certainties and incontestable truths. The twin minarets are derived from those added to the Friday mosque in the Turkmen period.

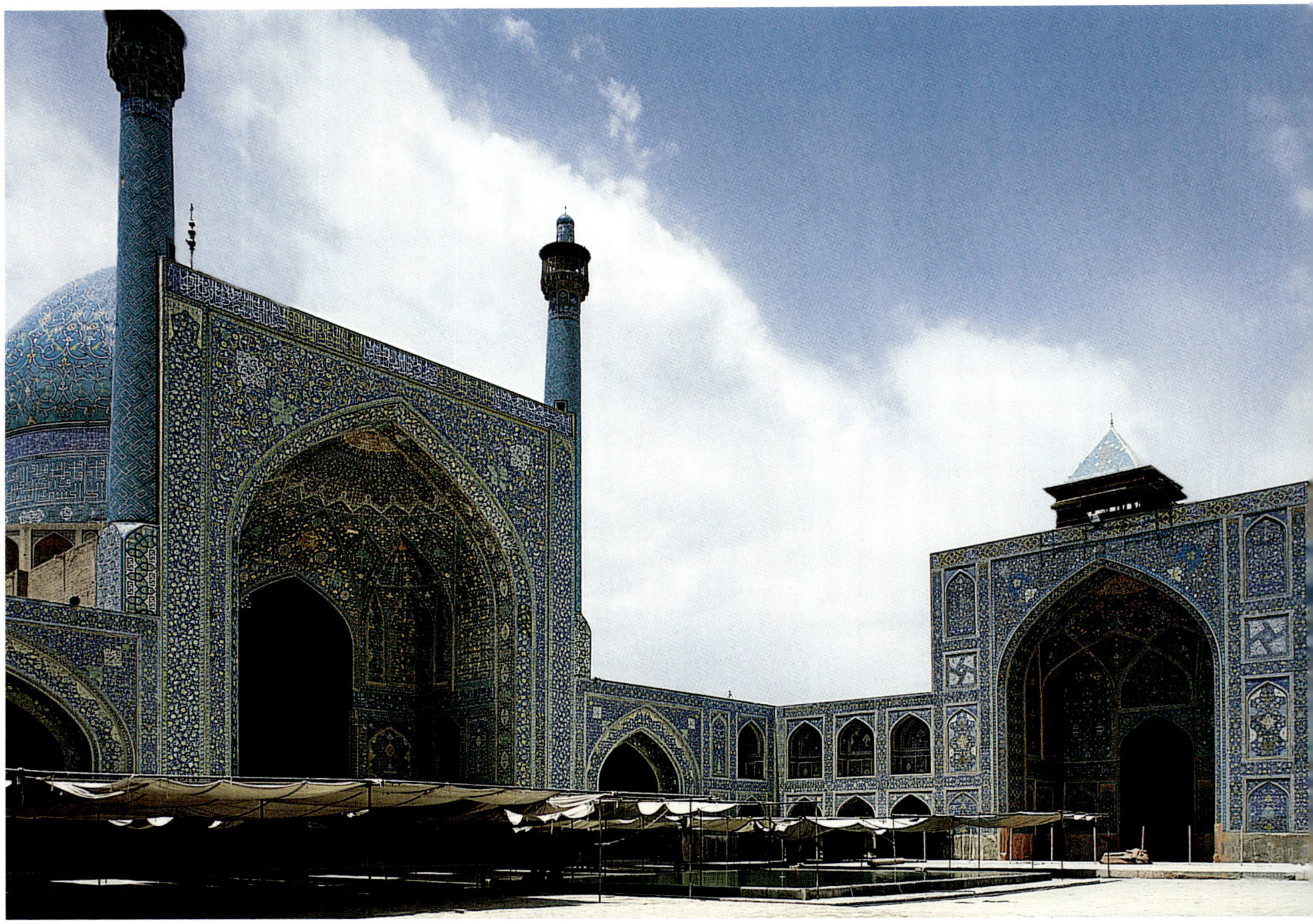

Masjid-e Shah (Shah Mosque)
Detail of the *mihrab* hall
1612–1638
Isfahan, Iran

Shah Abbas wanted to turn his capital in a brief period of years into the most beautiful in the world, and his mosque had to be the most precious flower of his garden city. To achieve this objective and cut the costs and time for carrying it out, the quicker, more economical *haft rang* (seven colours) technique replaced the refined but expensive *mo'arraq* technique. *Haft rang* involved using seven different colours on the same tile, but designed so as to cover huge surfaces within short periods and at limited cost, giving the overall effect preference over the intrinsic beauty of the materials and the details. The rest was there to create light, cunningly exploited. The miracle of the Safavid architects was that they succeeded in this enterprise.

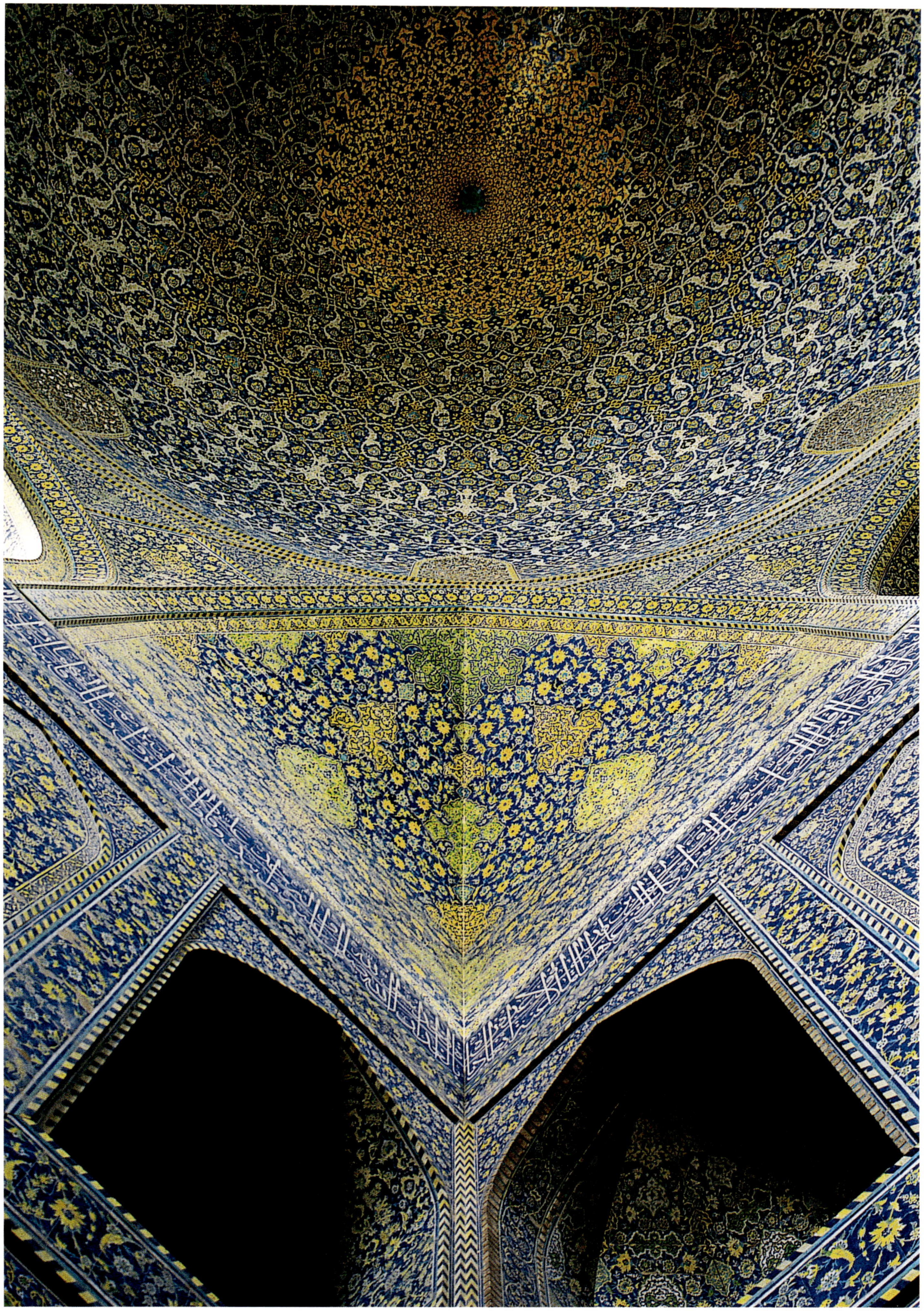

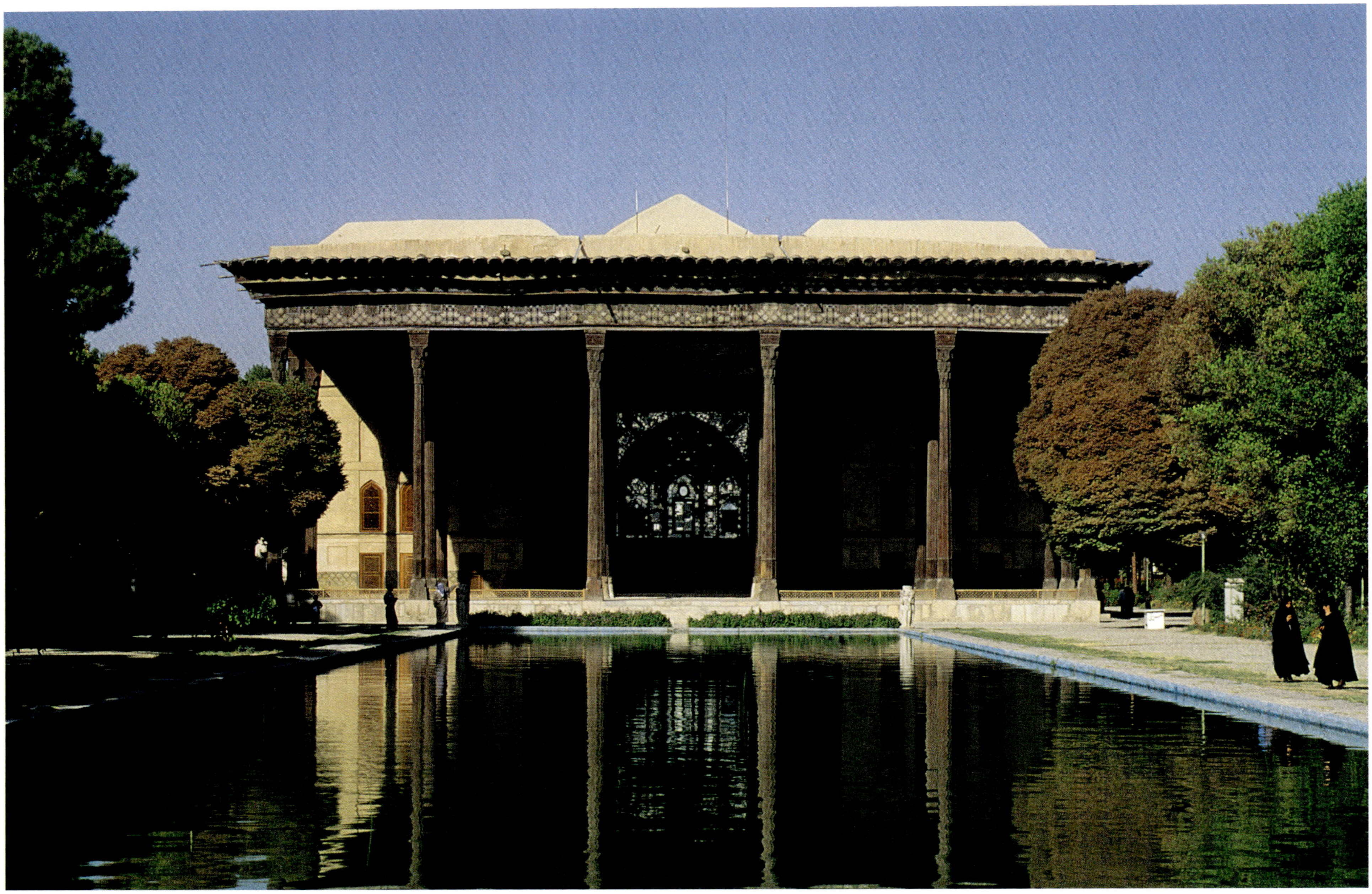

Chihil Sutun (Forty Columns)
Early 17th century
Isfahan, Iran

The palaces of Isfahan, only three of which survive, were sophisticated kiosks inserted into complexes of greater amplitude interposed with gardens, avenues and water channels. The Chihil Sutun was intended to accommodate distinguished guests, welcomed into the shelter of a broad *talar* with twenty very tall wooden columns, enhanced by reflecting surfaces that break up the wall, reflecting the mirror of water outside, which in turn doubles the number of columns.

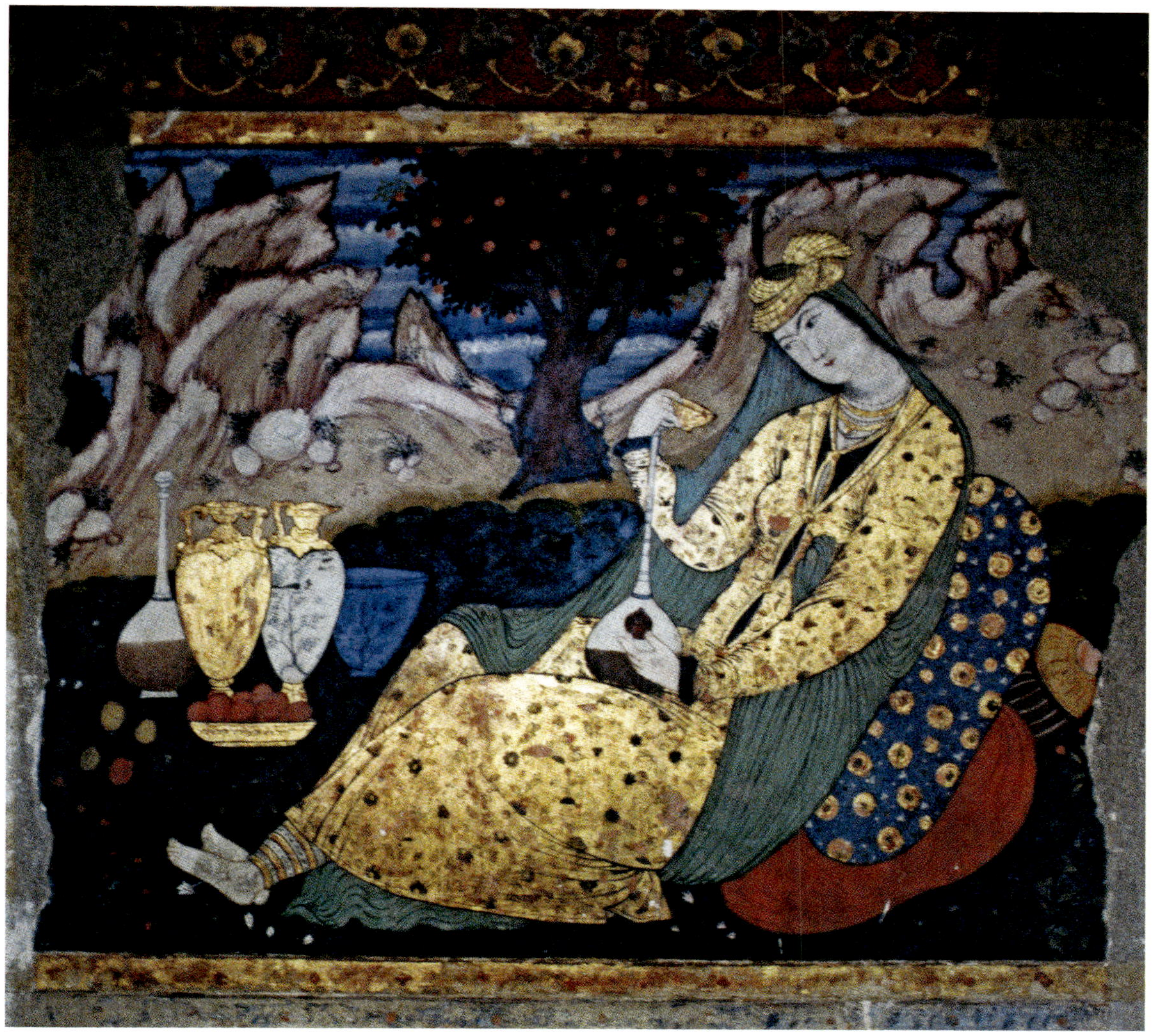

Convivial Scene
c. 1647
Wall painting
Chihil Sutun, Isfahan

The Chihil Sutun contains delightful scenes in an intimate, courtly style placed at eye level. They describe the delights of the vine, music, poetry and love savoured in enchanting scenes that are poetic projections of the gardens in the same apartments, valuable testimony of court customs seen through the eyes of the court itself. All genuine expression is banished. The atmosphere is rarefied, artificial, exquisitely courtly, and the style is that of miniatures.

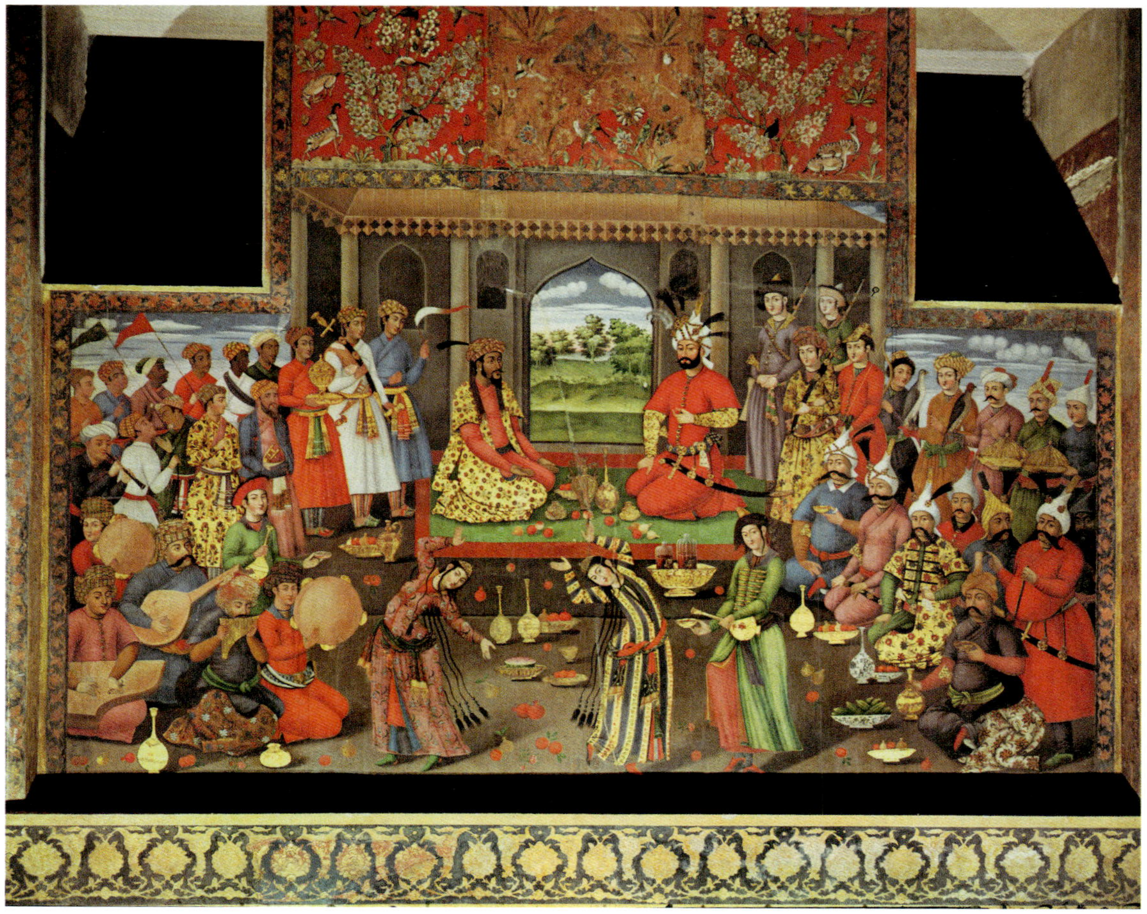

Shah Tahmasp Receiving Great Moghul Humayun in Exile
1665–1670
Wall painting
Chihil Sutun, Isfahan

The Chihil Sutun preserves the principal contemporary series of wall paintings with figurative subjects. The enormous paintings in the principal room, intended to impress distinguished guests, are of a historical and festive nature, and are strongly influenced by European painting, from which they borrow the sculptural feel of the figures and three-dimensionality of space without really assimilating them. The attempt to update the miniaturist Persian idiom with features of Western painting ends up in clumsy and at times comic formal uncertainty.

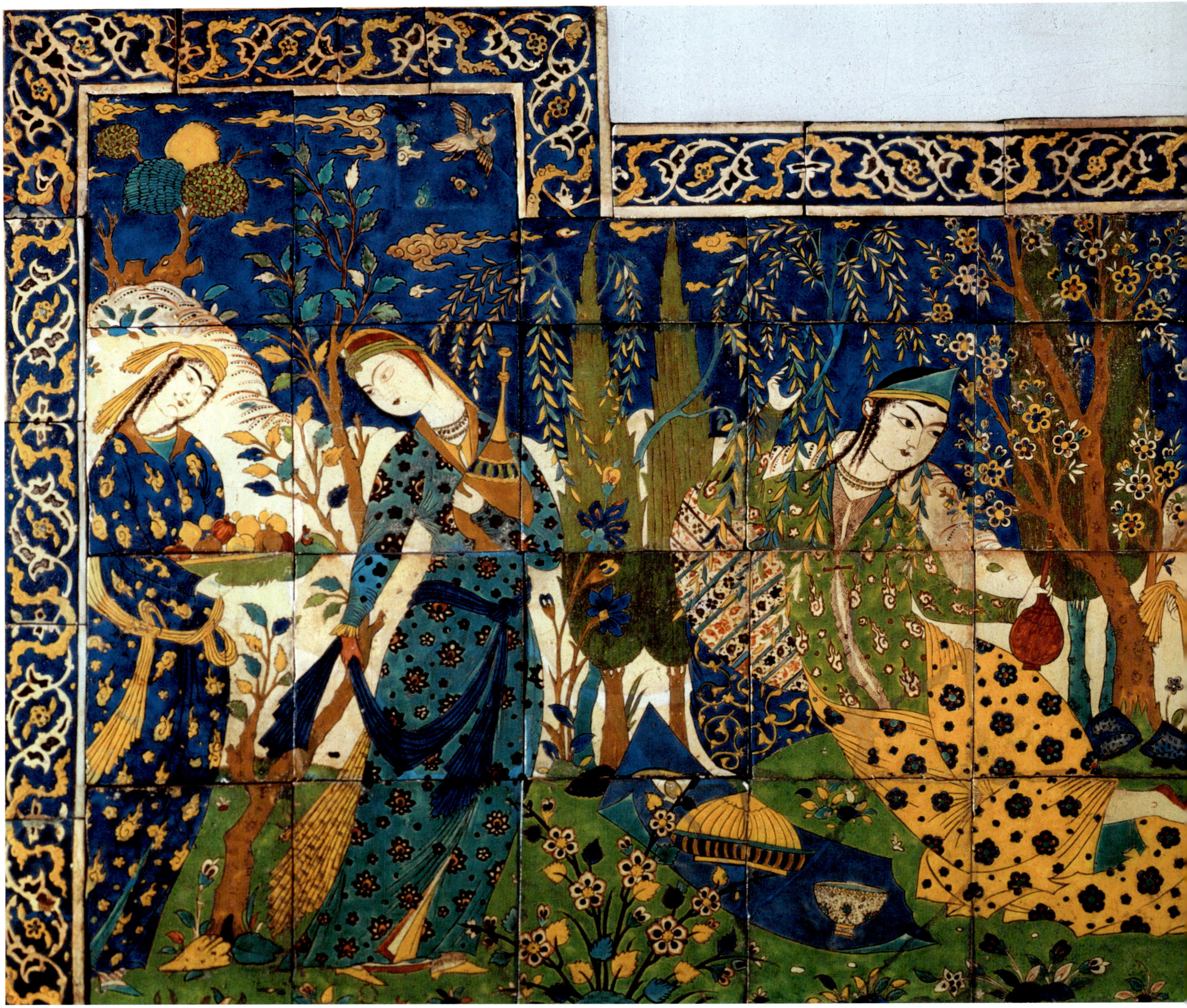

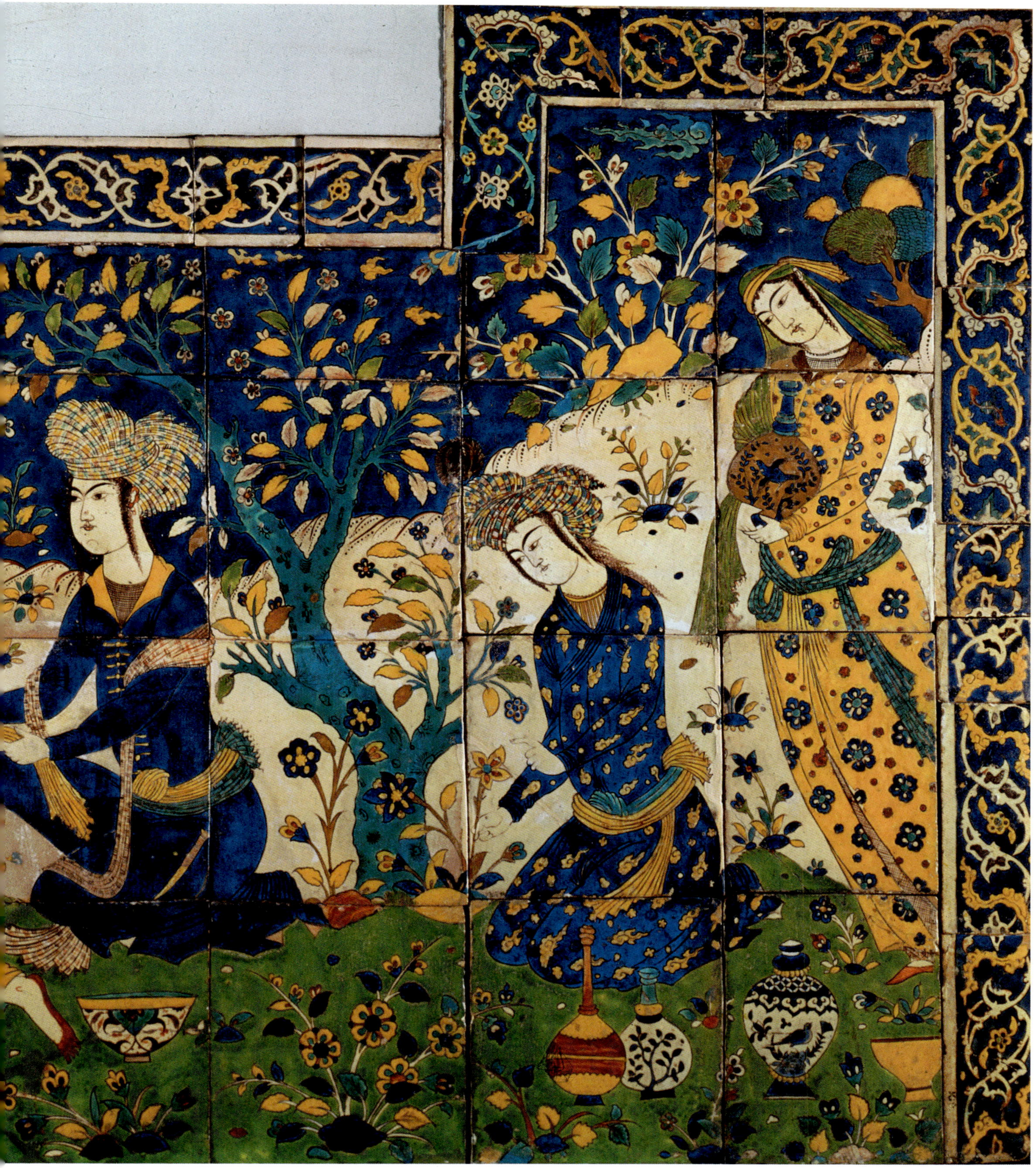

Decorative panel
17th century
Quartz frit painted and glazed
Victoria and Albert Museum, London

In secular architecture, ceramic decoration was used to compose pleasing figurative paintings borrowing subject matter and technique from contemporary miniatures but weighed down by the influence of European painting. Over and beyond the often-cloying execution, these tiles document the passing of a fashion for interpreting architecture as a vehicle of great values. Poses and faces of the figures are extremely artificial and, rather than drawing inspiration from the best miniature painting centres of the time, revive stylistic features of the fifteenth century.

Following double-page spread
Pol-i Khadjou
1641–1666
Isfahan, Iran

Among the many bridges in Isfahan, the Pol-i Khadjou is aesthetically the most elaborate, designed to be crossed for the pleasure rather than the necessity of doing so. The bridge connected the long, tree-lined avenue Chahar Bagh (Four Gardens), which started from the court residential complex, with the royal gardens on the opposite bank of the river. It was constructed as an elegant street suspended over the water thanks to a succession of massive piers furnished with sturdy buttresses with arches slung between them. It is divided into three sections: the centre one is for vehicles, while at the sides are two footways framed by a succession of arches. In the centre, a pentagonal pavilion overhangs, with *iwan* open towards the river intended for relaxation, contemplation and meetings. A further passage is possible between the piers at water level, where various artisan workshops were housed. The ceramic decoration evokes the colour of the river and the sky.

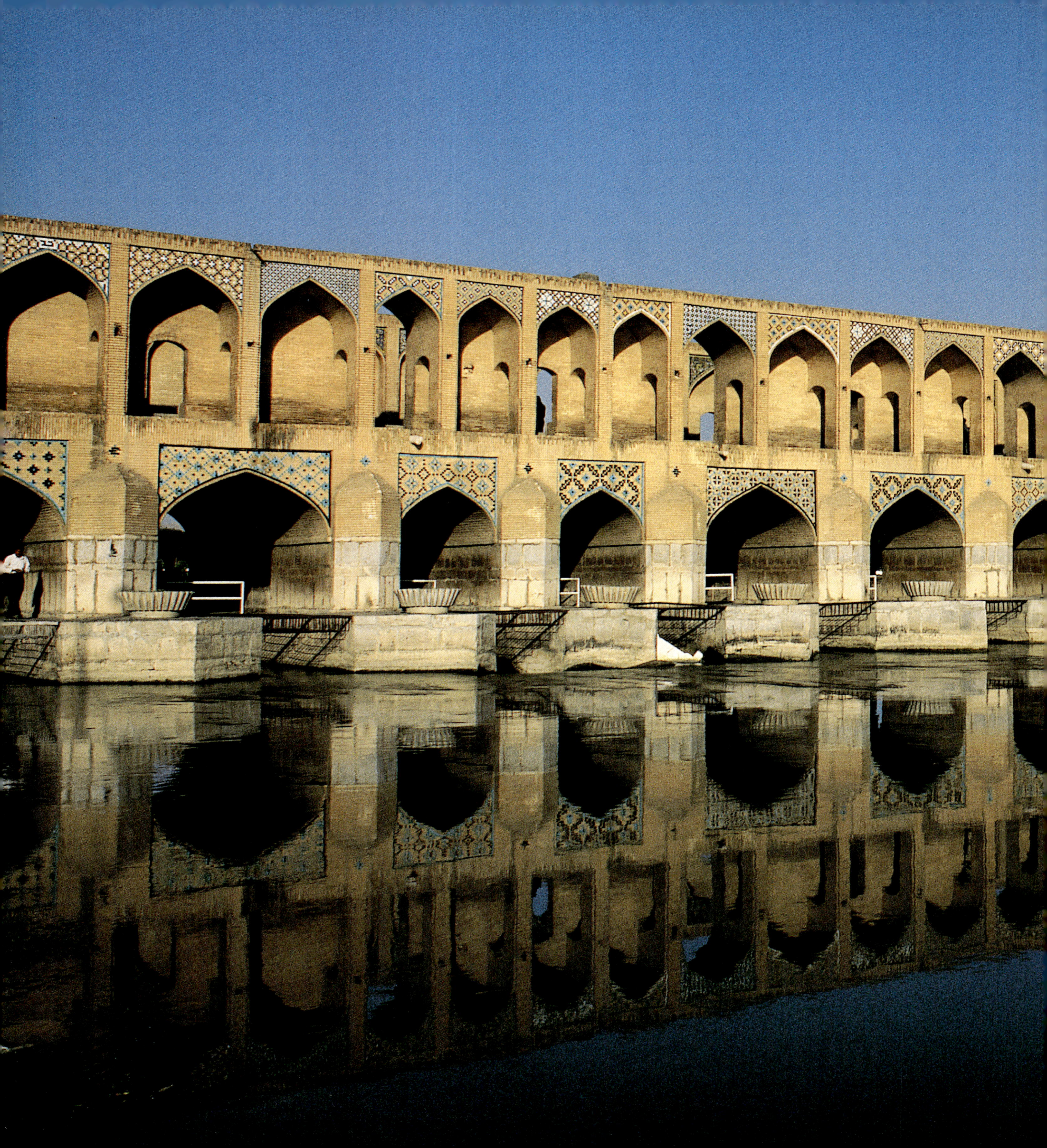

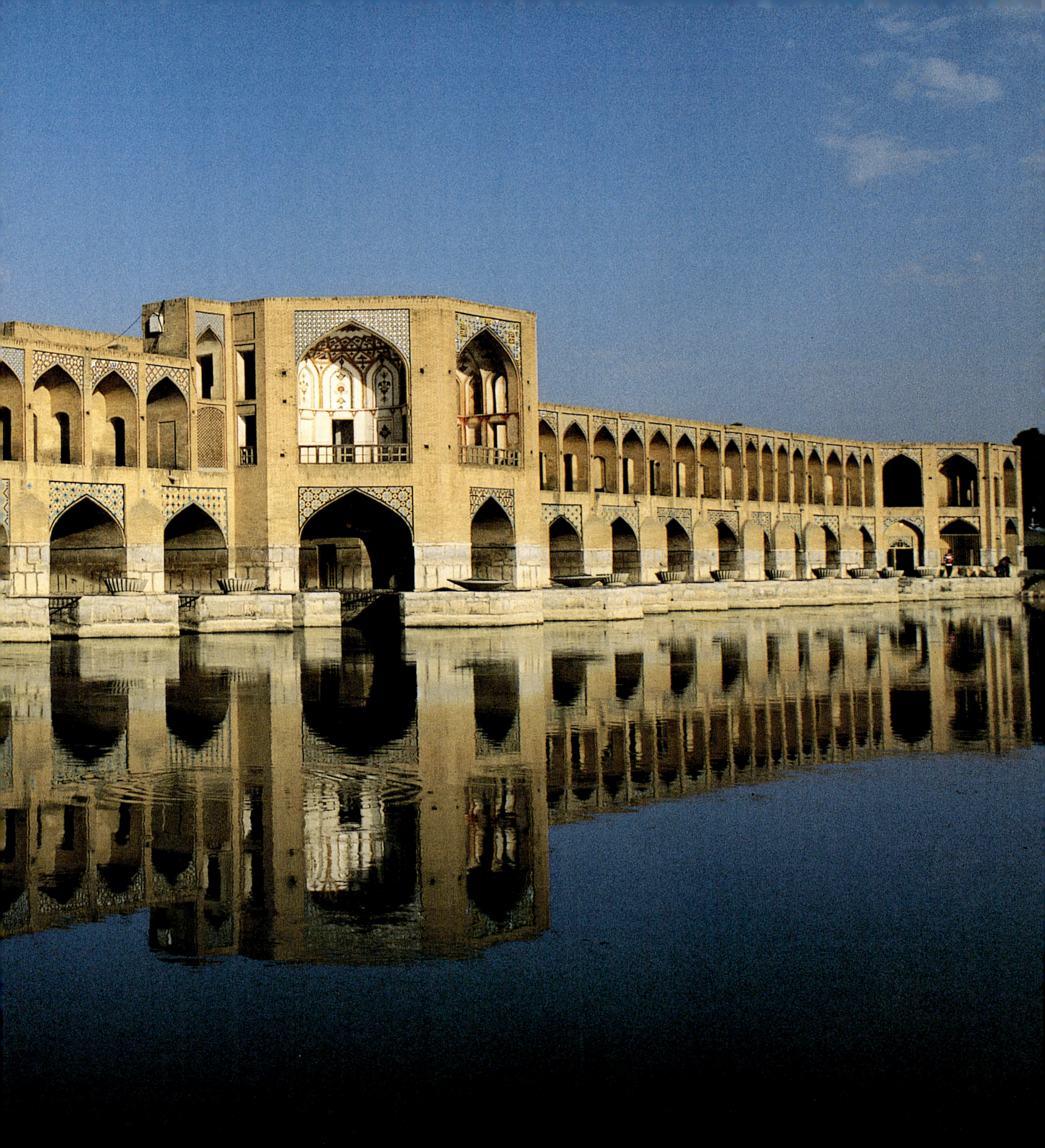

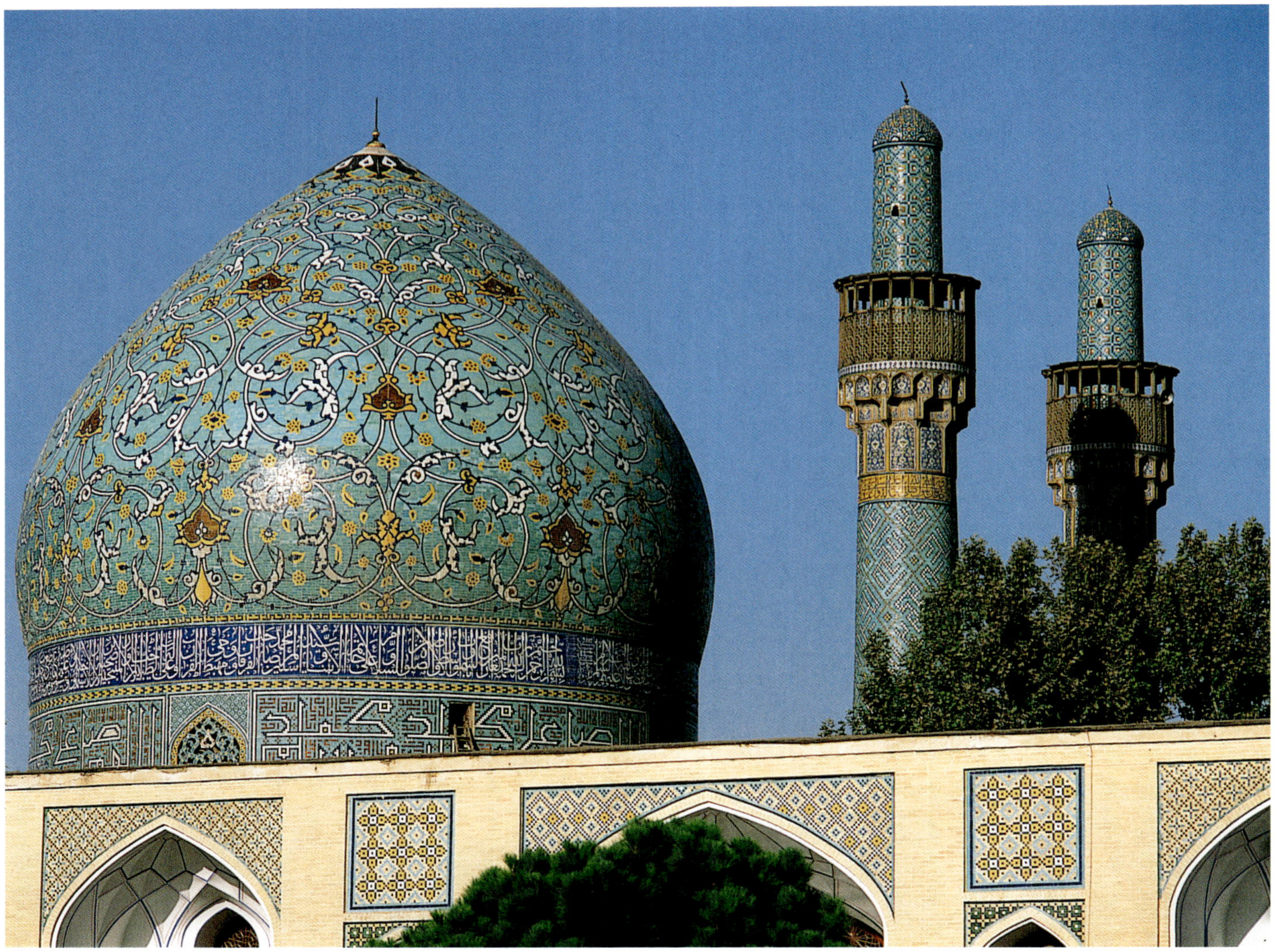

Madrasa-ye Madar-i Shah (Shah's Mother's Madrasah)
1706–1714
Isfahan, Iran

Persian architectural style evolved coherently, step by step and with sustained assurance to reach a peak of brilliance, then began slowly to decline after the death of Shah Abbas I in 1627, although managing to survive periods of political and economic decadence and occasionally producing buildings of quality. The Madrasa-ye Madar-i Shah, an ensemble including a mosque and madrasah constructed by the last of the Safavids, is still a building of noble and well-ordered majesty, superior to anything built at the time elsewhere in the Islamic world. The dome is outlined with elegant assurance against the skyline, brilliantly offset by the pair of sophisticated minarets. The arches on the first floor belong to a contemporary *han,* the profits from which funded the madrasah.

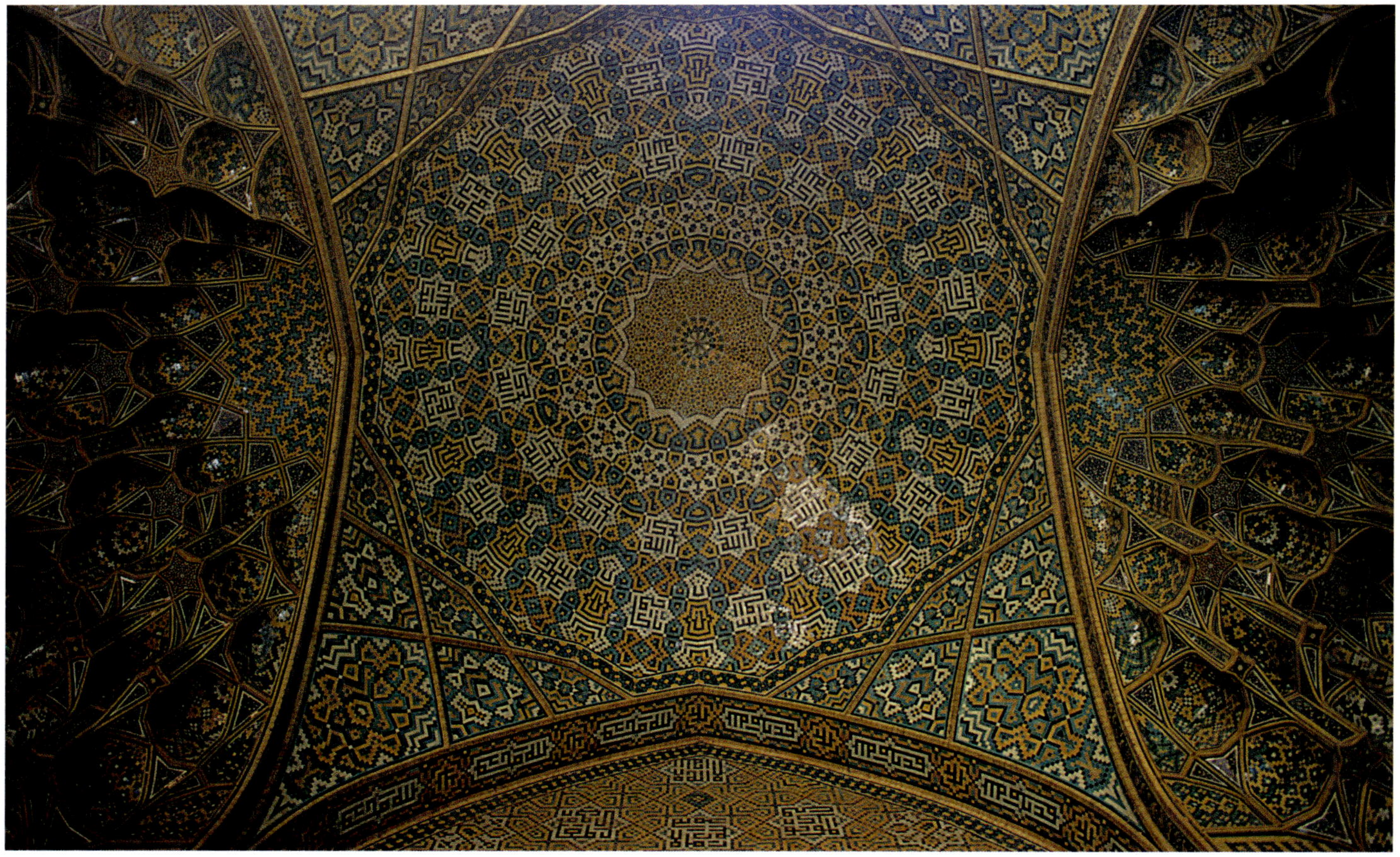

Madrasa-ye Madar-i Shah (Shah's Mother's Madrasah)
Entrance vault
1706–1714
Isfahan, Iran

Commissioned by Husain I in honour of his mother, the complex represents a return to the monumental approach of the days of Abbas I, with the reintroduction of the typical ultra-rigorous and symmetrical axial plan. The madrasah and caravanserai are perfectly aligned with the bazaar and the broad Chahar Bagh avenue. The richly *muqarna*-decorated monumental entrance supporting the flattened central dome opens on to the avenue. The elegant wall coverings mix all shades of gold and green with great skill, adding refined touches of dark blue. This is the last great work of Persian genius.

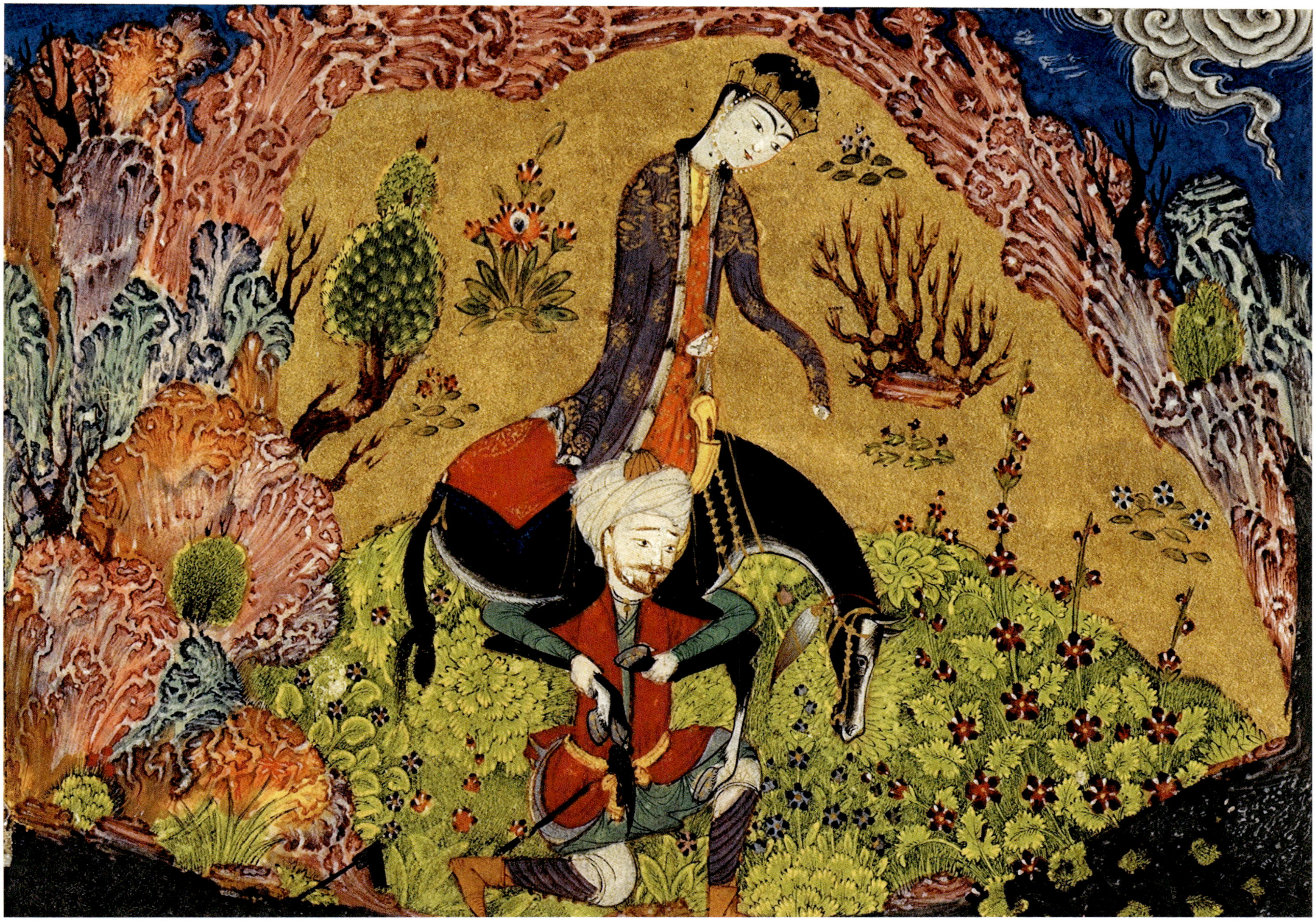

Farhad Carries Princess Shirin and Her Horse on His Shoulders
1505
From *Khamsa* (Five Poems) by Nizami (12th century)

The prestigious manuscript, begun in Herat around the mid-fifteenth century for a Timurid prince, was continued in Tabriz for the Turkmen rulers and finally finished after the conquest of the city (1501) in the first years of the reign of Shah Isma'il. The miniatures of this final phase thus represent the first explicitly Safavid works. In style, however, they are indistinguishable from their immediate predecessors, demonstrating absolute continuity with the Tabriz school of miniatures. It is indeed only a detail of dress that allows us to date it to the Safavid period – the tip of the red headgear that the followers of Isma'il used for winding the fabric of the turban, which was why they were called 'red heads'. The detail is easily recognisable in Farhad's headgear. Note also the remarkable affinity with Chinese painting in the clouds and rocks, represented with very free brushwork.

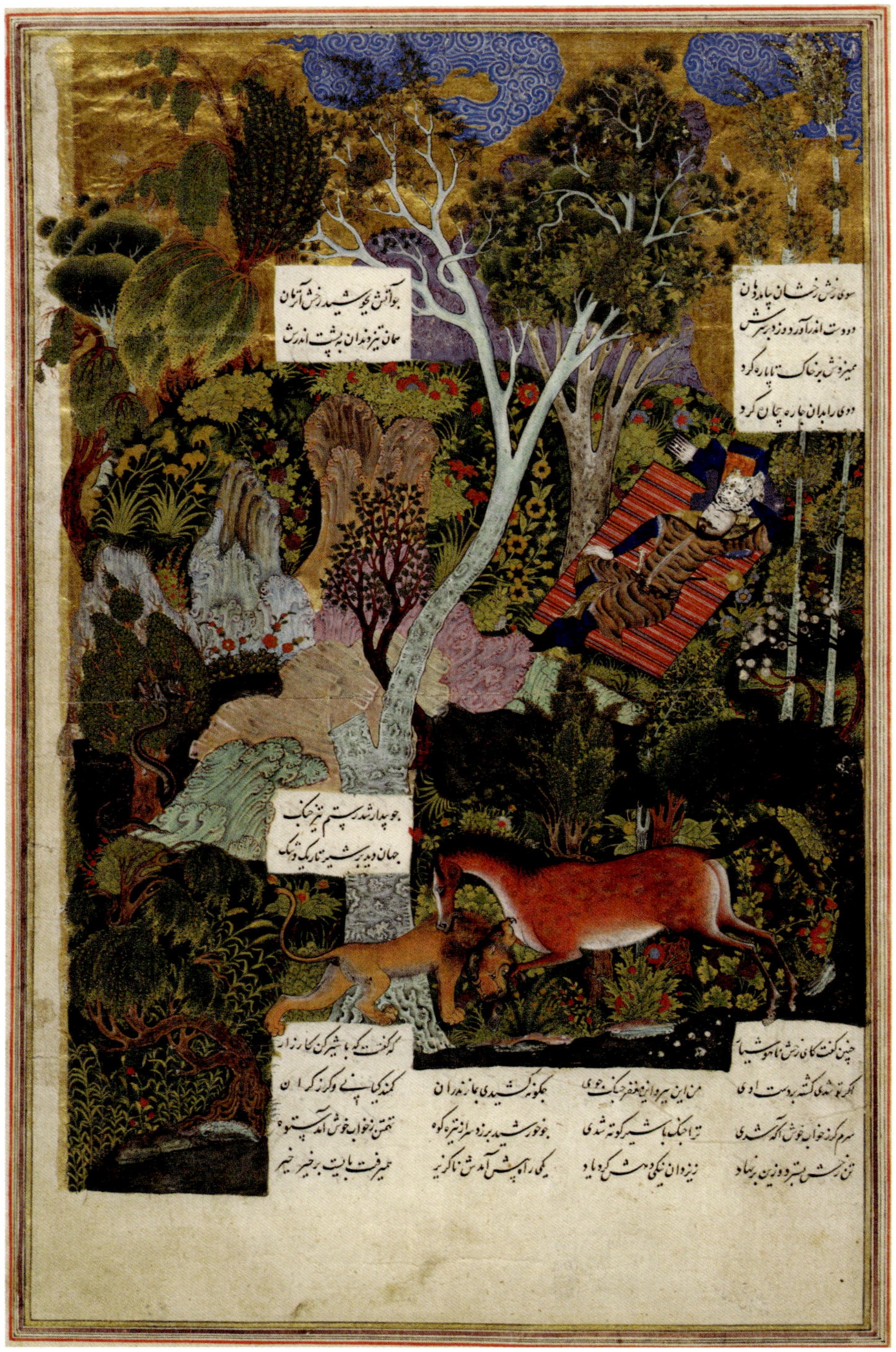

Rustam Sleeps while Rakhsh Battles with a Lion
1515–1522
Gouache on card
From *Shahnameh* (Book of Kings) by Firdusi (11th century)
British Museum, London

The phantasmagorical representation of the vegetation and rocks, painted with a kaleidoscope of brilliant colours and delicate intensity, and the vigorous dynamic that informs the composition, are reliable indications of the Persian style of the Ak Koyunlu Turkmen period in its heyday, concerned with the expression of emotions more than the spatial relationships between the objects or chronological relationships between the narrative circumstances. The sleeping hero appears as if suspended on a flying carpet, embedded in a setting that has the consistency of a dream. It is an essay in poetics, unforgettable in its lyricism. The struggle between Raksh and the lion is transformed into a kind of ballet, devoid of any drama.
The splendid colours, the delicate nuances and the absolute assurance of the pictorial handling and inexhaustible inventive imagination indicate that Shah Isma'il had spared no expense on the work, which remained incomplete. Only this sheet survives.

Riza Abbasi (1565–1635)
Calligrapher
c. 1600
British Museum, London

The second half of the sixteenth century was a difficult time for miniaturists. Shah Tahmasp lost interest in book art, and the best painters emigrated to find work at the Ottoman or Mughal courts. At the same, a new phenomenon began. For want of substantial long-term commissions, miniaturists and calligraphers began to do single sheets to be offered in the market – which implies a picture-loving public – and to think about the aesthetics and contents of their art. The theory was that, while it was sufficient with animals to refer back to the best examples of the past, for people you needed the model in front of you in order to capture their intimate essence. This was the starting point for the patronage of Shah Abbas and the most important painter of his time, Aqa Riza, later called Abbasi since he was the shah's favourite painter. The light of intelligence that shines in the eyes of the figure and the hint of a smile under the beard make this portrait one of the liveliest in Persian art.

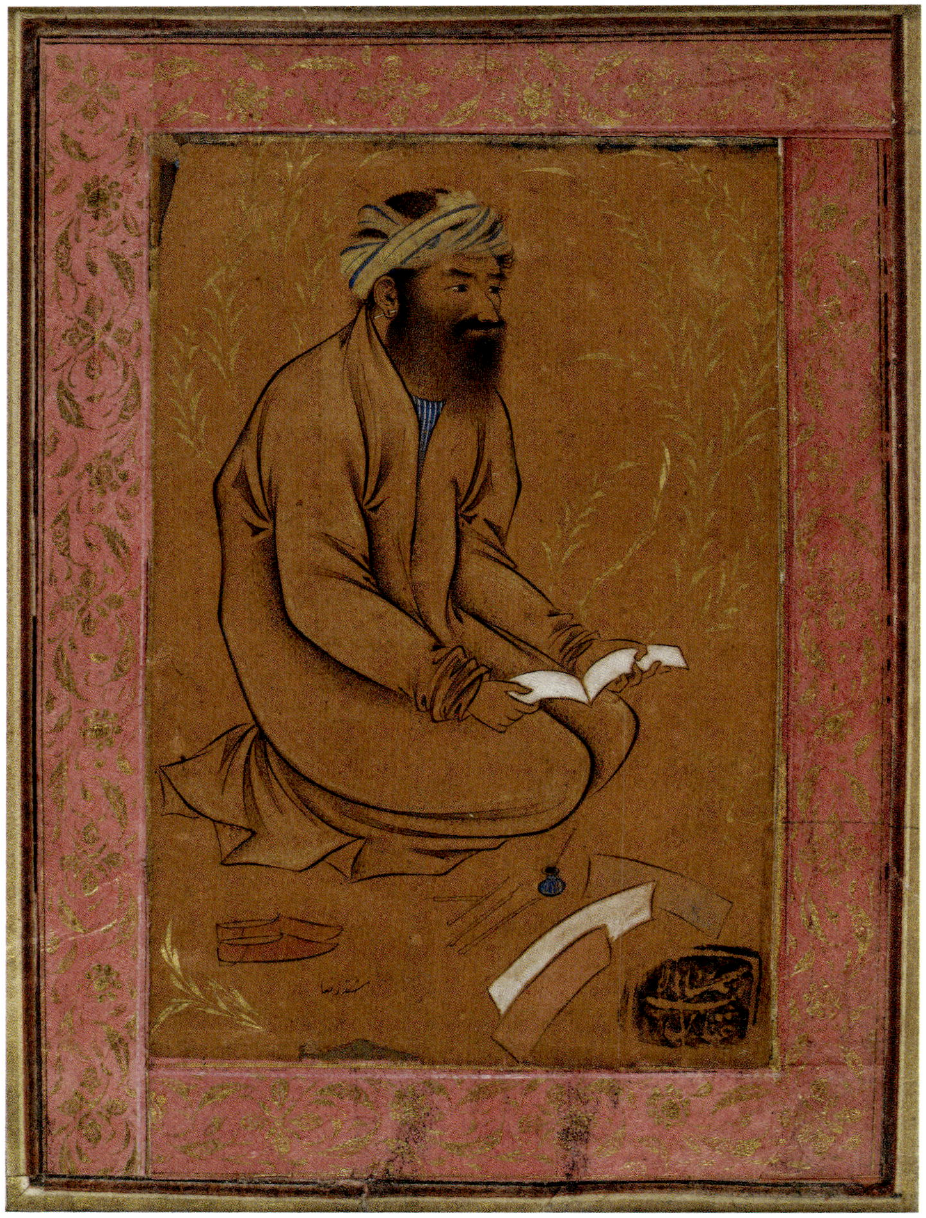

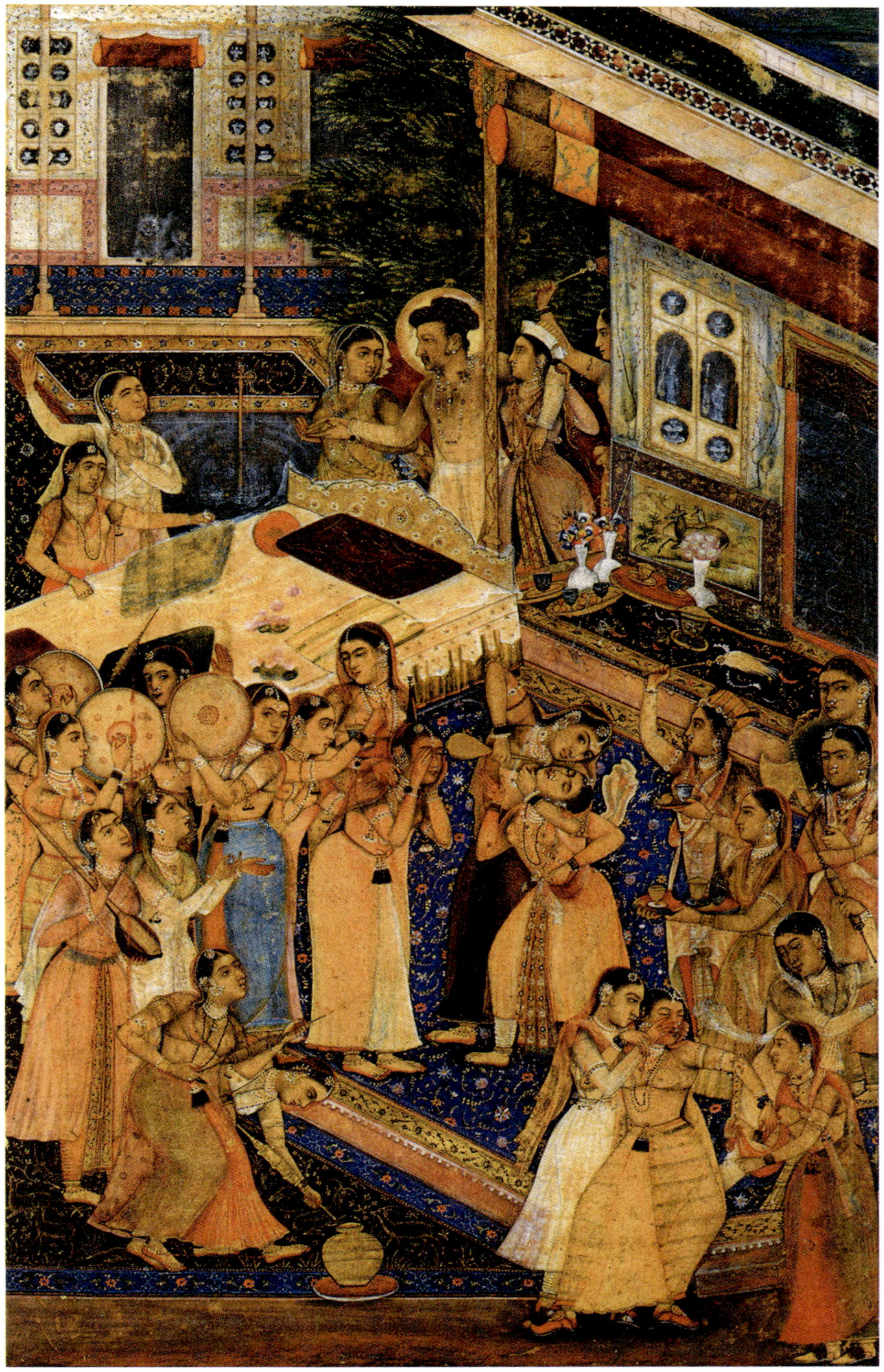

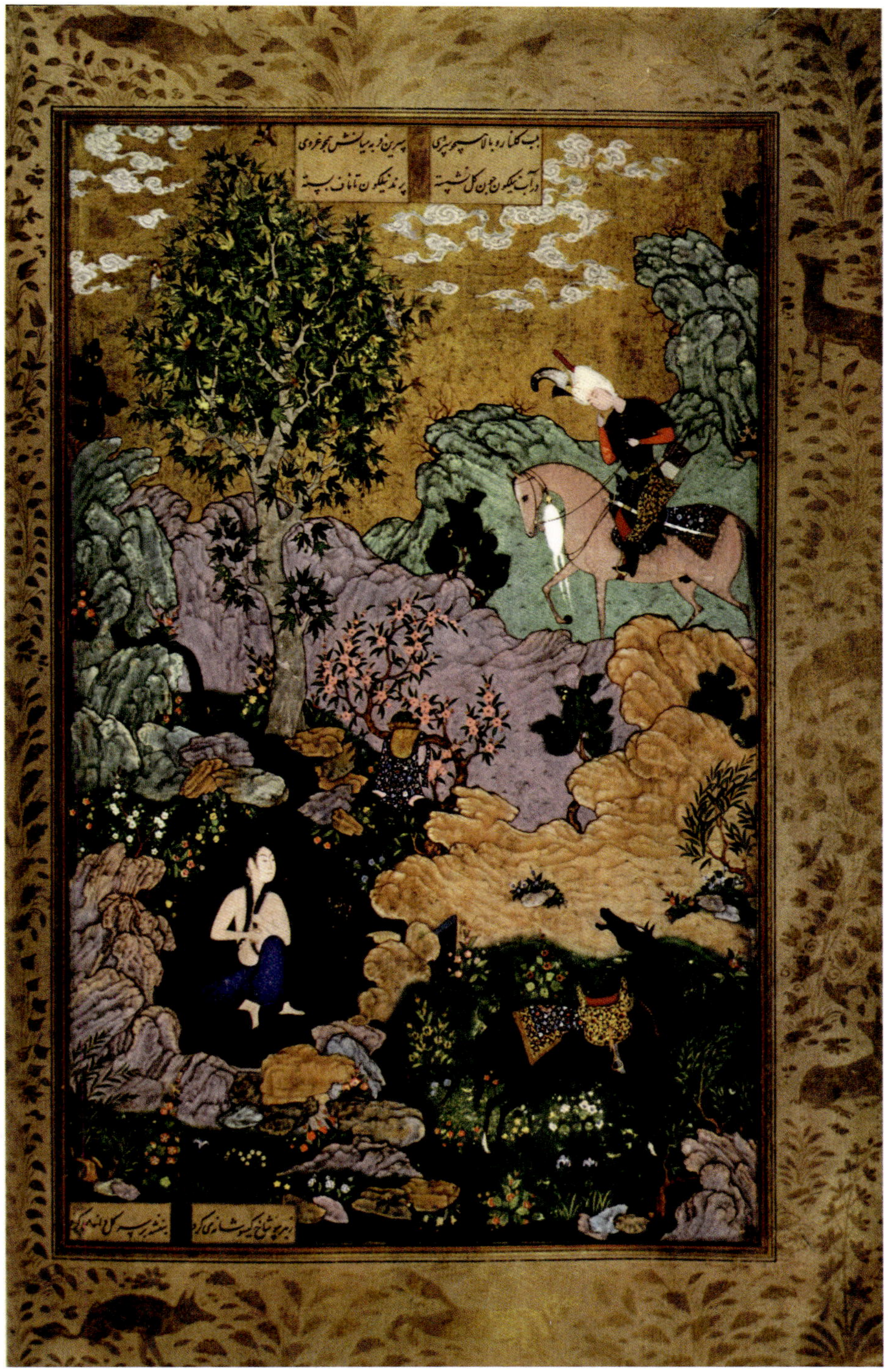

Sultan Muhammad (16th century)
Gayomars's Court
1525–1535
From *Shahnameh* (Book of the Kings) by Firdusi (11th century)
Sadruddin Agha Khan Collection, Geneva

The period in which Safavid miniatures were truly great did not extend beyond the first half of the sixteenth century, after which the technical and poetical level of the great schools working for the Timurid court or the Ak Koyunlu tailed off into a monotonous, repetitive style that came to the fore in the age of Shah Abbas the Great. With the conquest of Tabriz, Isma'il brought several of the best Turkmen workshops into the Safavid orbit, with relevant manuscripts already in production that were continued for the new patron. Illustrated books were held in the greatest esteem and preserved as real treasures. The *Shahnameh,* the compilation of which was directed by Sultan Muhammad, represents the most demanding book undertaking of the century, with 742 pages in an enormous format (47 x 31 cm) and numerous decorations. It was a work avidly coveted by Shah Tahmasp, a sophisticated collector of books and calligraphy of a certain standard. The page presented here is perhaps the finest, a rich display of pictorial virtuosity that does not overwhelm the lyrical narrative features, where men and animals are introduced into a dreamy terrestrial paradise.

Chosroes Sees Shirin Bathing
1539–1545
From Khamsa (Five Poems) by Nizami (12th century)
British Museum, London

In 1539, Shah Tahmasp ordered a luxury edition of the *Khamsa,* a famous collection of five epic poems by the great Persian poet Nizami (1141–1209), reproduced and illustrated innumerable times over the centuries. The text was entrusted to Shah Mahmud of Nishapur, known as Zarim Qalam (Golden Pen), the most celebrated calligrapher of the time, while the illustrations were done by a team of at least four great miniaturists, perhaps under the direction of Sultan Muhammad. The episode in which Chosroes accidentally comes across the young woman bathing in a spring is rendered with delicate discretion, in the cool light of evening and with the gold of the sky to represent the sunset. The landscape is rendered with great care, even if the high-voltage fantasies of earlier years seem to be toned down, perhaps to accommodate the more rigid style being imposed, though the protagonists and their animals still reveal an intimate vitality.

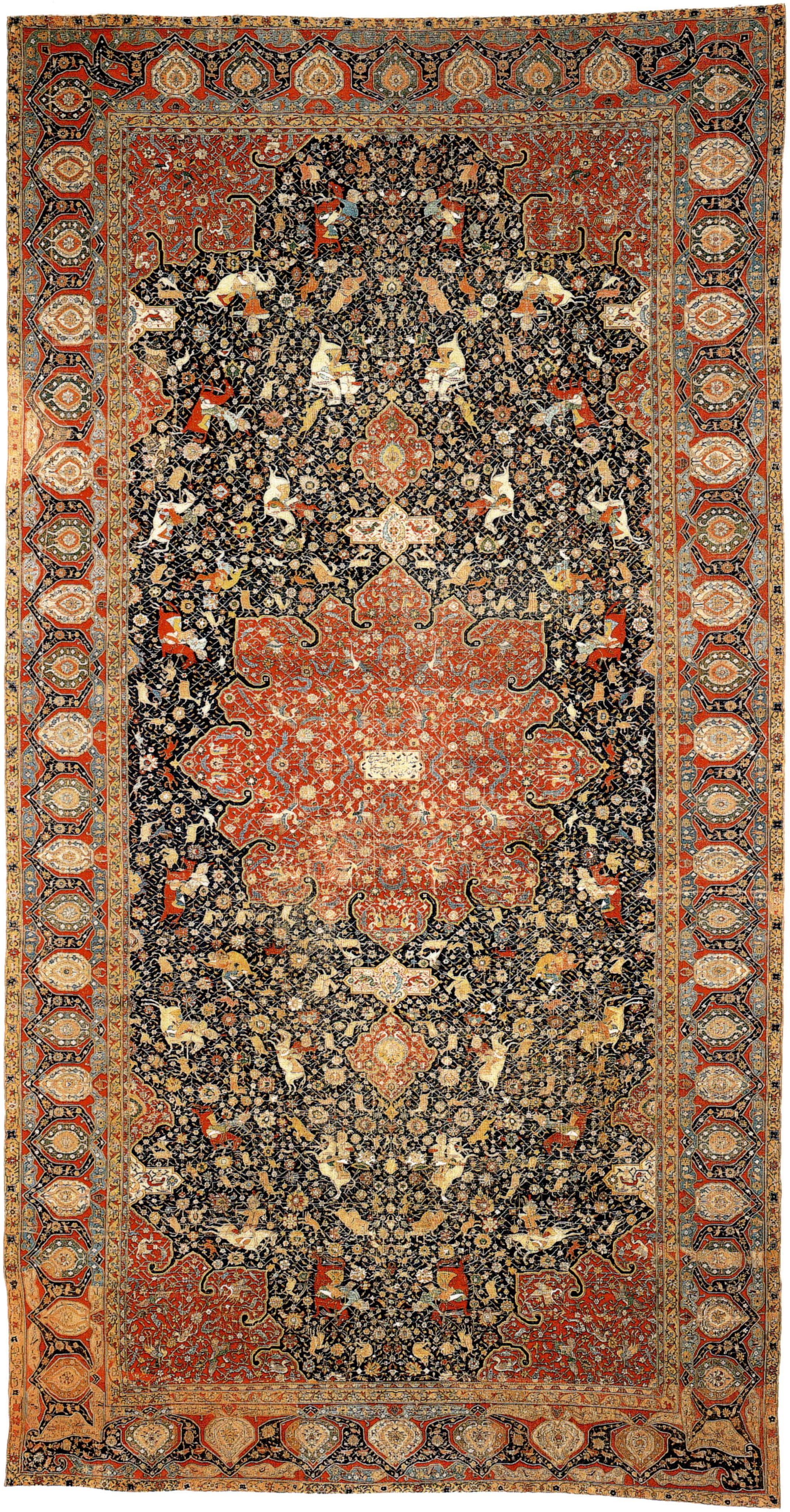

Carpet with hunting scene
Overall and detail
1542–1543
Wool, silk and cotton
Museo Poldi Pezzoli, Milan

The great age of Persian carpets coincided with the establishment of the Safavid dynasty, whose manufactories brought together all the previous skills, whether Seljuk, Mongol or Timurid, though our knowledge of them is limited to a number of fragments and the descriptions in the sources. The curvilinear style was however a Safavid innovation. It necessitated remarkable ability on the part of the weaver, and above all a 1:1 scale drawing, i.e. a cartoon. The court artists, often the same miniaturists, were on hand to provide drawings for the royal manufactories, which by the mid-sixteenth century had attained superb and perhaps unparalleled results. Among the oldest preserved examples are those with hunting scenes, a theme always present in Iranian art. Among these, one signed by Ghyas el-Din Jami stands out. It is dated 1542–1543, and thus contemporary with the most important Persian miniatures, from which it borrows numerous motifs. The superb carpet belongs to the type with a central medallion and four corner areas. The central field is occupied by pictures of mounted hunters and their prey. They are relatively difficult to pick out, being scattered and almost lost among the dense arrangement of floral motifs that fill the background, so that they can only be identified close up. The iconography echoes a number of aesthetic, literary, philosophical and mystic topics of Iranian Islamic tradition – paradise as an enchanted garden, heroes hunting, men and beasts symbolising vices and virtues bound up in a never-ending challenge where there are no victors or vanquished. The imposing dimensions (682 x 356 cm), the finesse of knotting carried out on a warp of silk, and the elegant precision of the design – Ghyas el-Din Jami must have been a miniaturist in Shah Tahmasp's workshop – enable us to appreciate this carpet as a top-quality product earmarked for the court. It was probably given by a shah to a pope, because it was found in very poor condition in the Quirinale Palace in 1870 when that was still the papal residence, and was inappropriately restored using tapestry techniques.

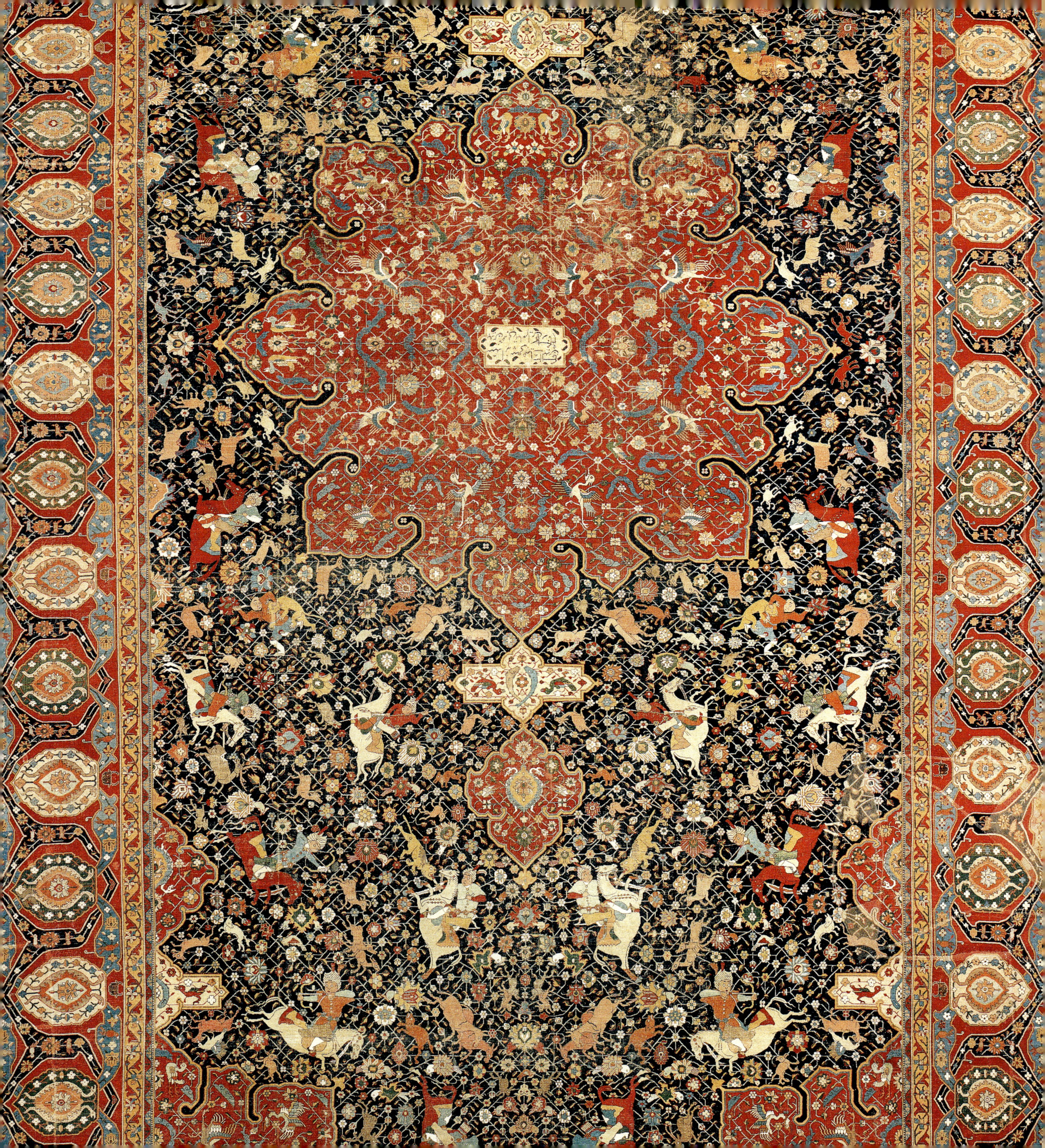

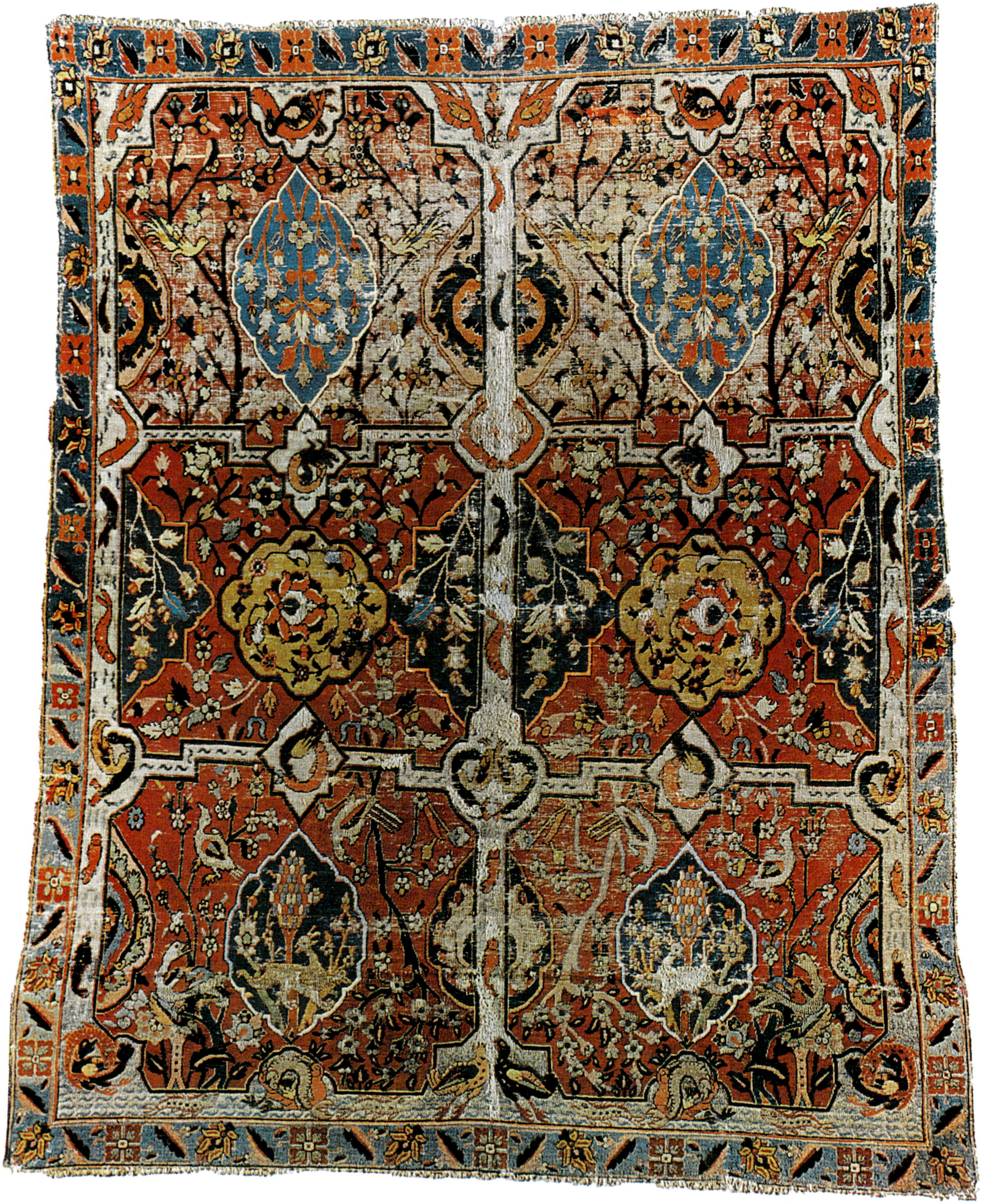

Wagner garden carpet
17th century
Art Gallery Museum, Glasgow

Apart from classic prayer carpets, an important place in Persian production was allocated to the 'garden carpets', the origins of which went directly back to the legendary Baharestan ('Spring') carpet of Persian king Chosroes, made for the audience chamber in the palace at Ctesiphon. It represented an immense garden, but was cut into pieces by the Arab conquerors and divided up as booty. The idea of a portable paradise was too attractive to waste, however, and was adroitly and magnificently taken up again in Persian production. The carpet reproduces the framework of an ideal garden inspired by the model of contemporary Persian gardens seen from above and crossed by a grid of water channels that meet up in a cruciform pool in the centre. The fields in between are pictured as opulent flowerbeds planted with trees, flowers and birds (seen in profile).

The Nasir al-Molk Mosque
Iwan
1876–1887
Shiraz, Iran

The assured sculptural style of classical Persian architecture counterpointed with superficial colour was debased in the Qajar period by shrinking dimensions and a proliferation of multi-linear decorative motifs dominated by an unmistakable yellowy pink tonality. Clarity of form was submerged in a sense of *horror vacui* that reflected the culture of the time – ambitious, superficial and profoundly vacuous. The driving force of Islamic culture, which had sublimated the humble materiality of things in light and thus in spirituality was henceforth a thing of the past. Art was forced to gratify neo-feudal courtly desires and a craving for theatrical spectacle on the part of crude and ignorant spokesmen of the dynasty, men of military and tribal origin interested in ostentation more than the meaning of things.

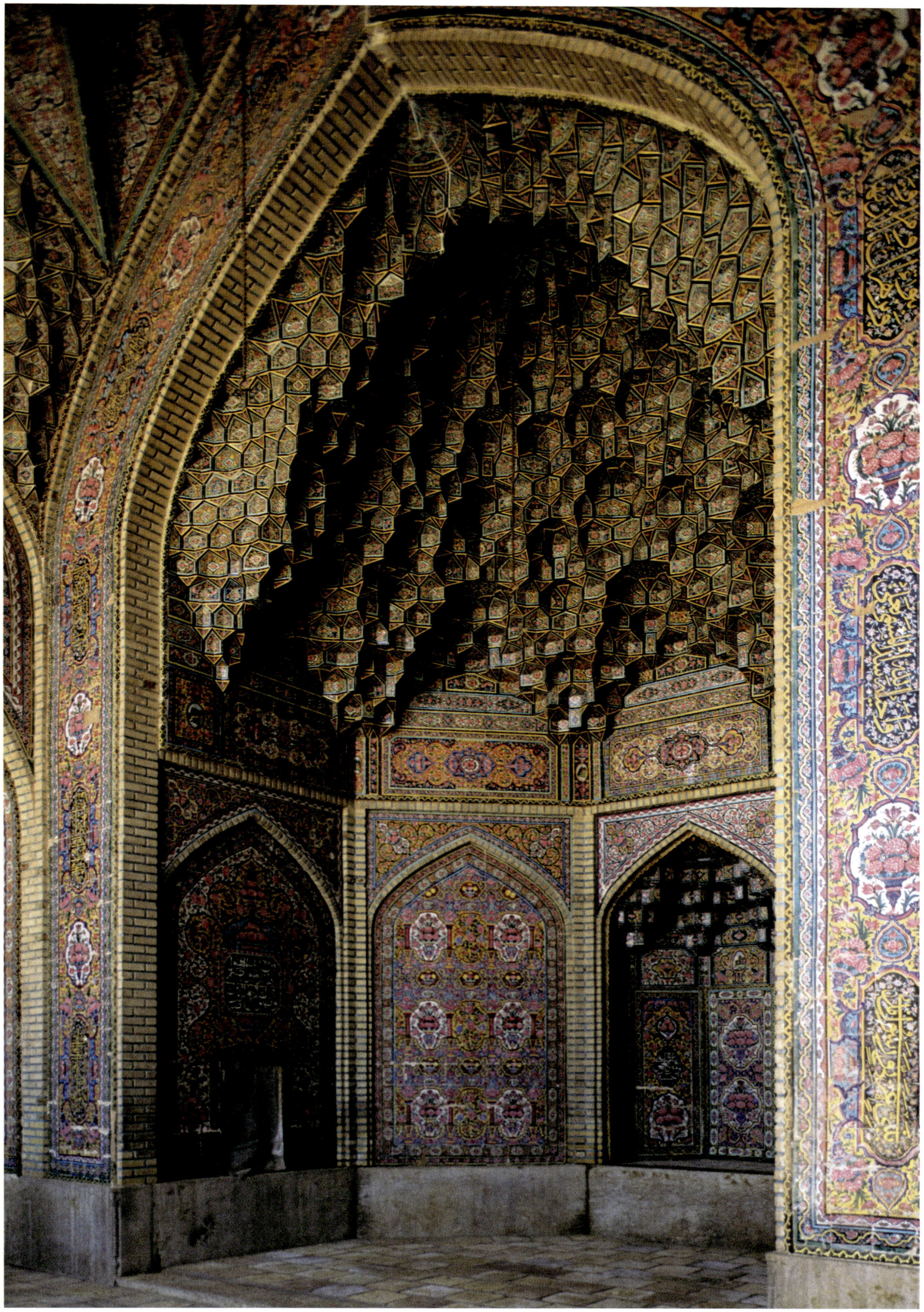

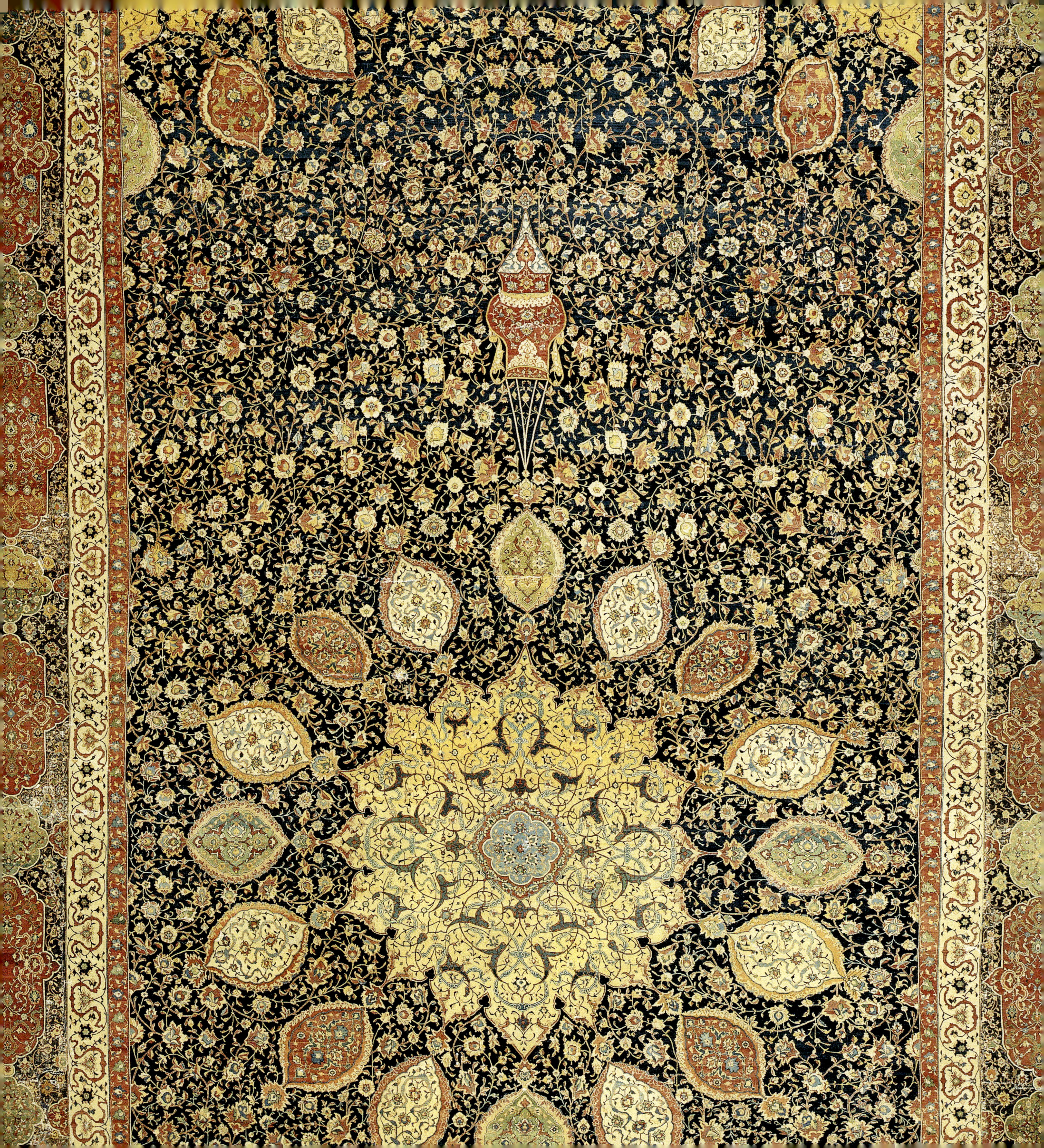

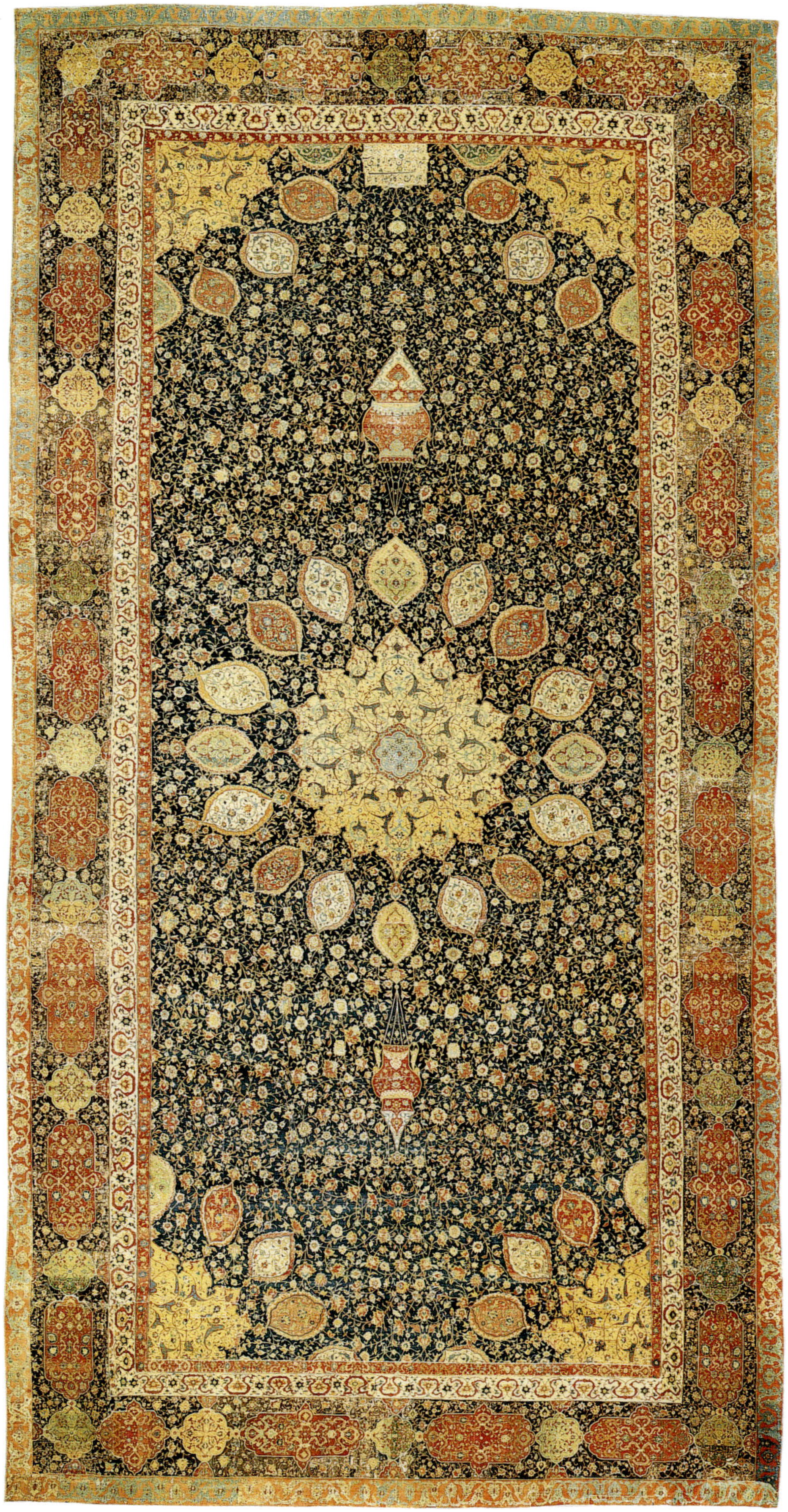

Ardebil medallion carpet
Overall and detail
1539–1540
Wool and silk
Victoria & Albert Museum, London

The most typical Persian carpet product (exported worldwide even today) was the medallion carpet. It is a decorative motif that also occurs in contemporary tiles and on the binding and decoration of books. In this sector as well, the most important pieces go back to the age of Shah Tahmasp. Curvilinear medallions, found in Persian areas only in book art, were probably imported from the Far East and included in a strictly central scheme, with side elements distributed according to a rigid symmetrical double axis. Unlike contemporary Ottoman Ushak carpets deriving from them, this combination of symmetrical rigour and perfect centrality is translated into a static design, well arranged and complete in every element, surrounded and defined by the border – characteristic features of the most dramatic examples from Anatolia. The example found in Ardebil is one of the finest and most monumental of the genre (1152 x 534 cm), even if it is not easy to express a judgement on its state of conservation, because of doubt as to the type and number of restoration attempts it may have undergone. Hanging symmetrically from the central medallion are two mosque lamps silhouetted against the delicate floral frame on a blue background. On one of the short sides of the field there is a cartouche with the date, the signature of Maqsud of Kashan and two famous verses by Hafiz: "There is no place for me in the world if not on your threshold; there is no place for my head elsewhere."

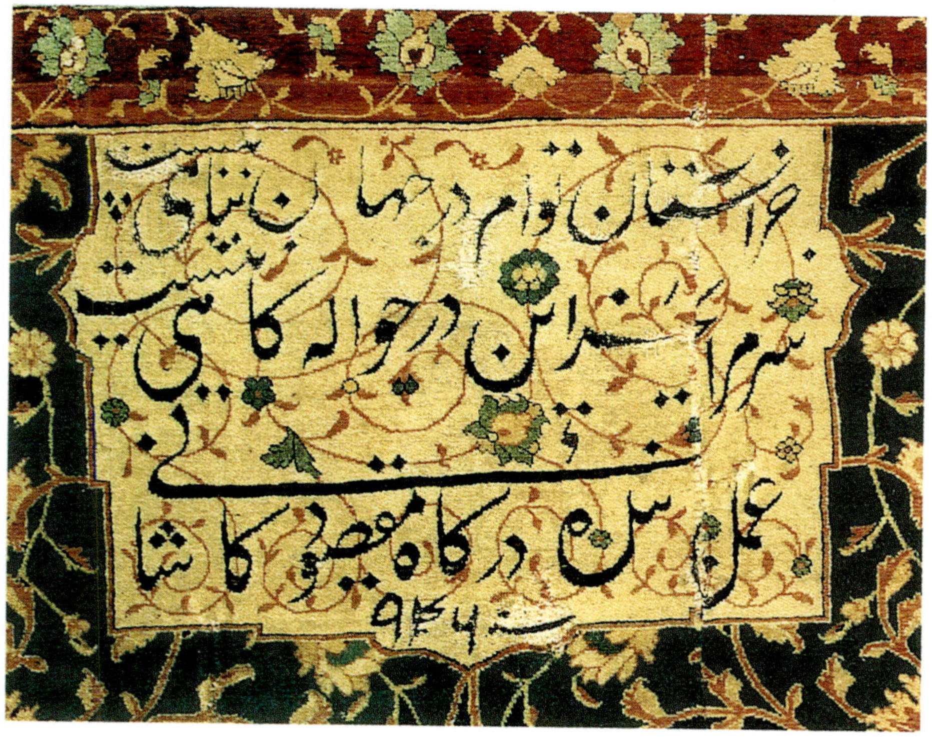

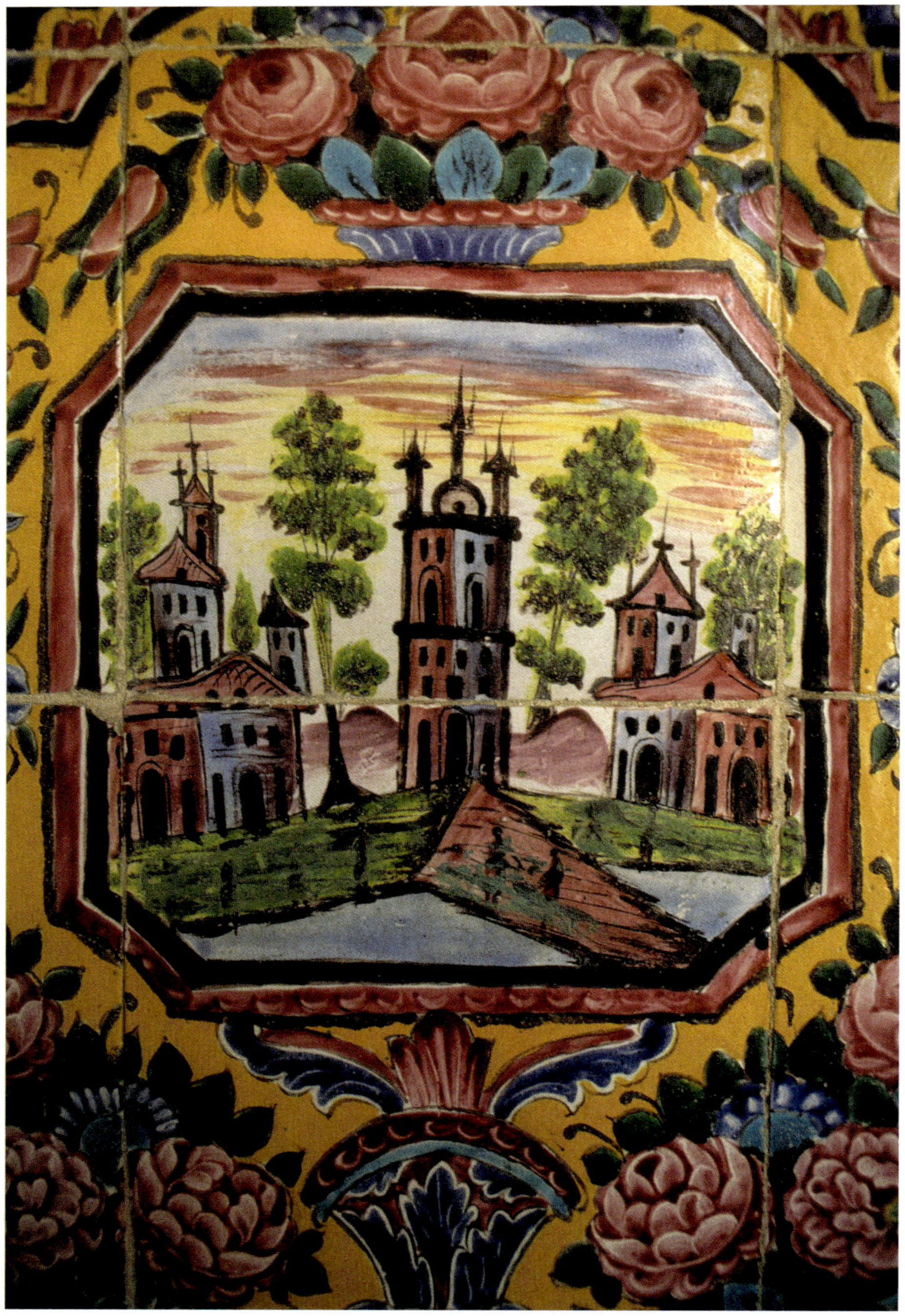

Nasir al-Molk Mosque
Detail of wall covering
1876–1887
Ceramic tiles
Shiraz, Iran

The general tone of the decoration leaves an impression of European petit-bourgeois taste alien to the great Persian tradition, although not displeasing in itself. It is a phenomenon that, beyond surface resemblances, has nothing in common with the universality and profundity of meaning which had constituted the objective of the art and architecture of the past.

Block of flats, Bagh-e Eram
19th century
Shiraz, Iran

Civil architecture in the Qajar period had no great notional values to communicate. It merely reflected aspirations and limits of the taste of the time in a suitable fashion, particularly in a number of well-designed blocks of flats set in pleasing gardens. The elegant, busy façade is enhanced by pleasing decorations in ceramic tiles in the curvilinear pediment. However, these are works that would henceforth belong more to the history of costume than the history of art and ideas.

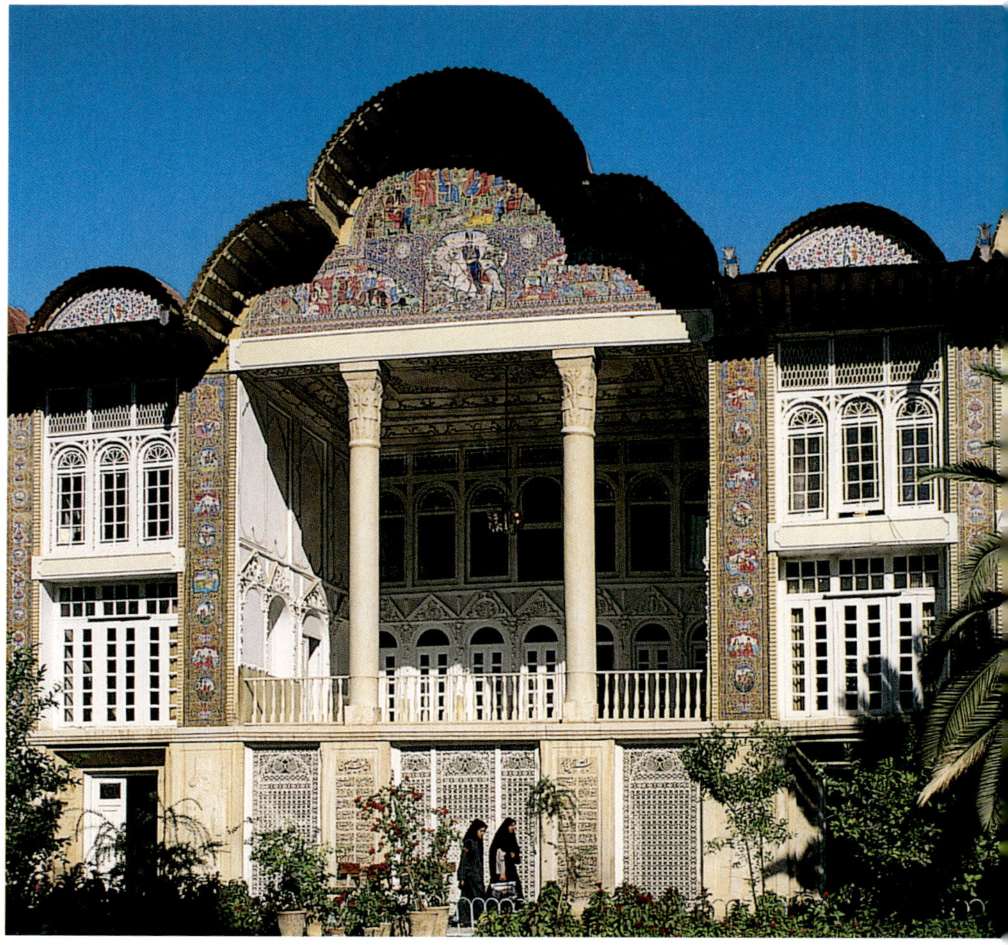

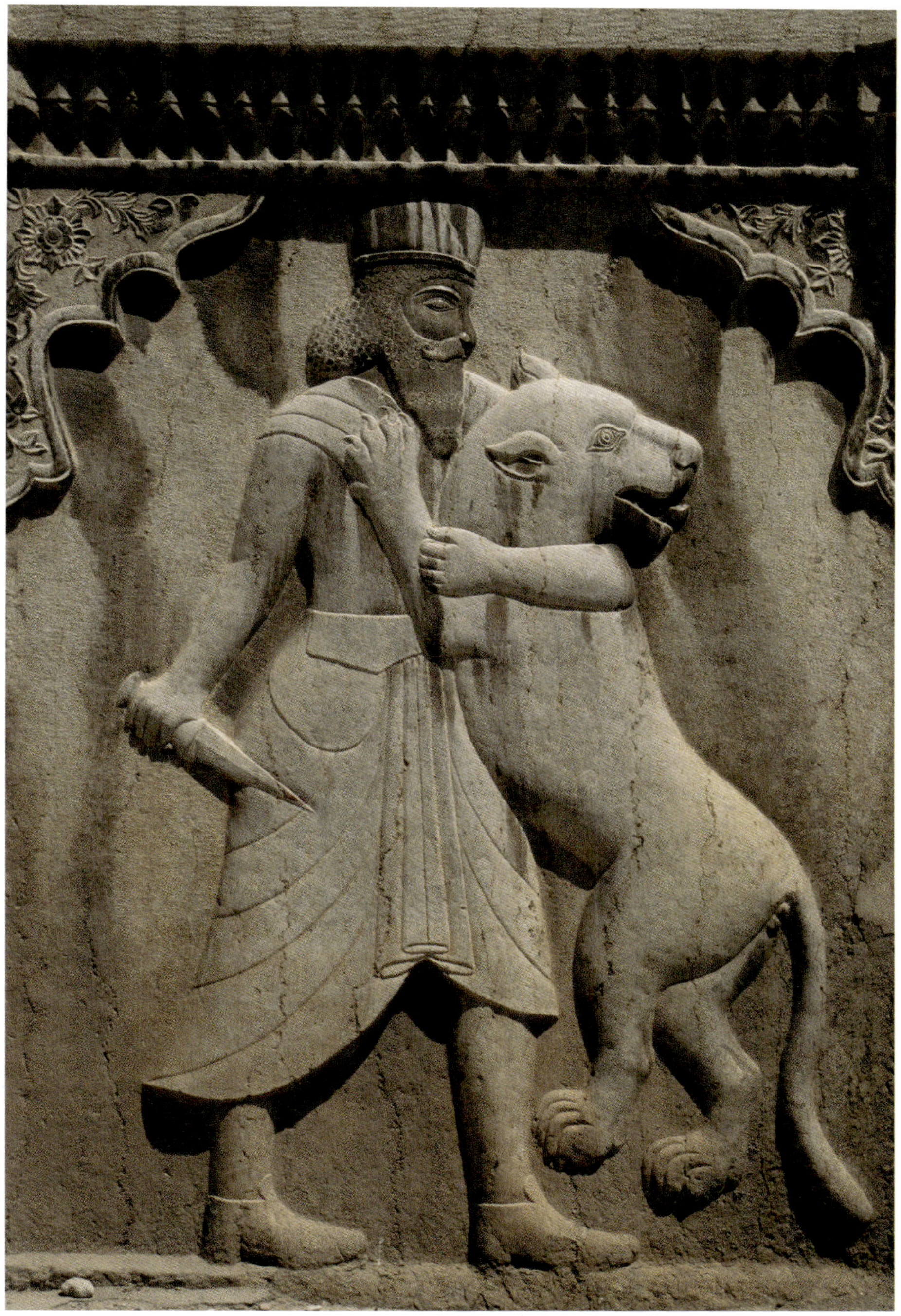

Divankhaneh (Government Palace)
Detail of façade
18th–19th centuries
Shiraz, Iran

The reliefs of Persepolis excited the dull self-importance of the Qajars, who had themselves depicted as latter-day Dariuses in the act of killing lions, personification of the dark forces and chaotic diminutions of the importance of the ruler. Despite the apparent elegance of its shallow stylishness the work lacks real energy. The formidable admonitions of the Achemenid reliefs have been reduced to a decorative motif on a modest urban block rich only in pretentiousness and conceit.

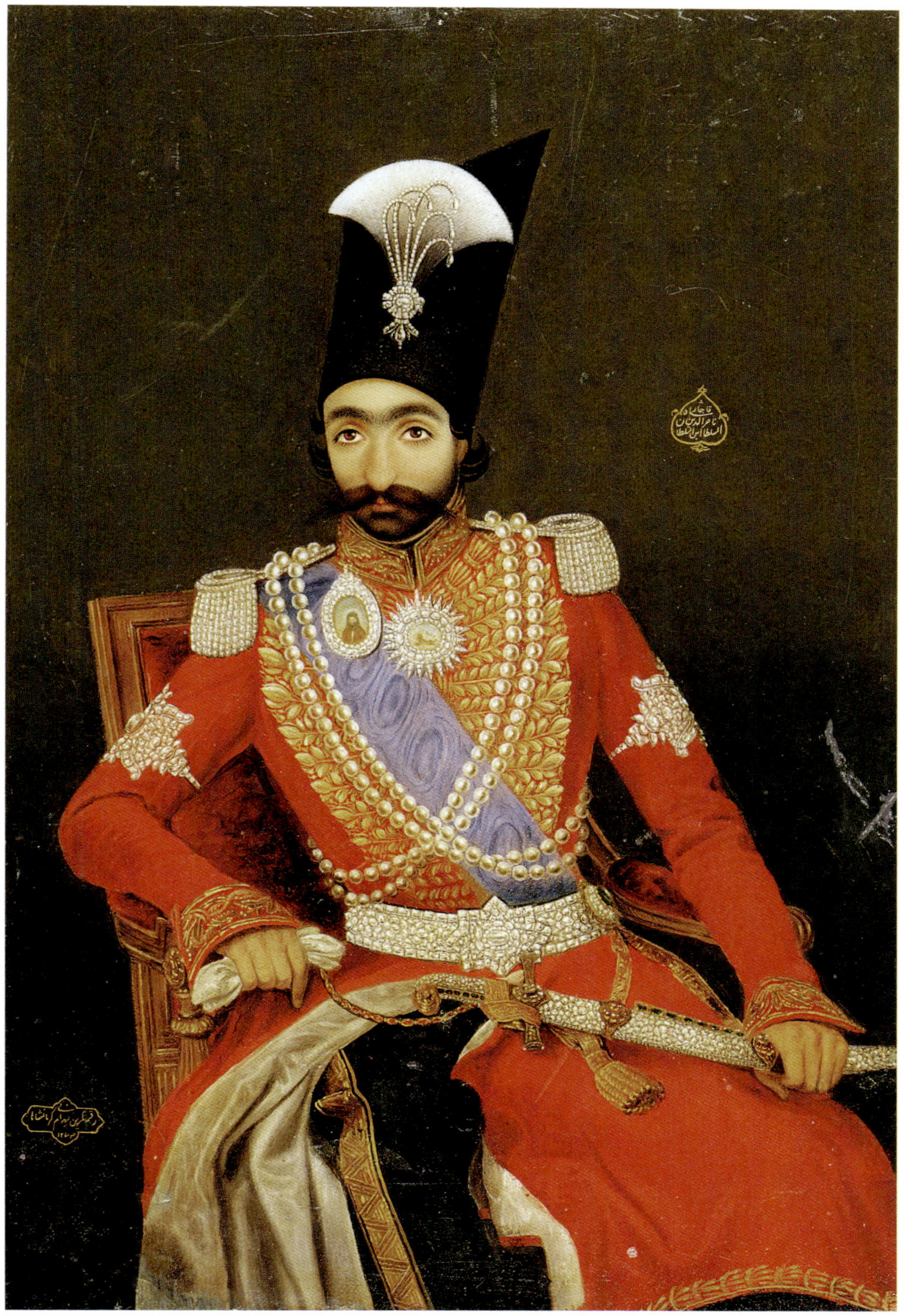

Bahram Kirmanshahi (19th century)
Portrait of King Nasser-al-Din Shah
Louvre, Paris

Under the Qajars, painting and miniatures followed Western models in imitating the new art of photography, and thereby lost the ability to achieve the synthesis of reality, abstraction and lyrical transfiguration that had characterised preceding periods. The introduction of three-dimensionality and misconceived superficial naturalism along with an unsuccessful attempt at psychological insight – both vitiated by a vulgar tendency towards ostentation – is particularly evident in portraits, which ended up in an exoticism of manner alien to Persian culture and unwittingly came close to caricature.

THE INDIAN SUBCONTINENT

Sheikh Salim Mausoleum
1571–1580
Fatehpur Sikri, India

Friday mosque
1571–1580
Fatehpur Sikri, India

In 712, intrepid Arab navigators travelled up a branch of the Indus delta not far from modern Karachi and founded a port there (present-day Bambhore). That is where the foundations of the oldest mosque on the Indian subcontinent, dating to 727, have been uncovered. It was a typical square-plan building identical to contemporary Arab mosques, i.e. a prayer hall with three aisles parallel to the *qibla*, and a porch with two aisles. As with the other surviving Islamic architecture of the early period, only minimal traces of this building remain, though the sources tell of fabulous cities. Outstanding among the latter is al-Mansurah which was compared even to Baghdad.

In the eleventh century, Turco-Persian tribes under the Samanids and Ghaznavids began to make ever more intrusive raids, until the last Ghaznavids, driven out by the Ghorids, retreated to the Punjab, dragging the region into the Islamicized world of Central Asia. The final conquest fell to General Qutb al-Din Aybak, who took Delhi in 1193. On the death of the ruler whose "slave" he had been, he proclaimed himself independent and assumed the title of sultan. Prior to the Mughal period, the sultanate was ruled by five successive Islamic dynasties of Turkish or Afghan origin: the "slave" sultans (1206–1290), followed by the Khalji (1290–1320), Tughluq (1320–1414), Sayyid (1414–1451) and Lodi (1451–1526) dynasties. Later, the Suri dynasty (1540–1555) also wrested power from the Mughals for a brief period.

Although each of these dynasties undertook new campaigns of conquest extending the sultanate at the expense of the neighbouring principalities, their control over the region failed to assume a stable or lasting form. In Delhi, each great ruler left proof of his power by founding his own capital and building monuments of impressive splendour which are still recognizable even today. After the devastating sack of Delhi by Tamerlane (Timur) in 1398, the hegemony of the Delhi Sultanate was weakened, leaving room for many regional potentates to develop their own independent cultures. These were largely rooted in local traditions, and have left behind numerous remarkable monuments.

In 1526, Zahir al-Din Babur took possession of Delhi and, after routing the warlike Rajput princes, established the Mughal Empire. Based on a synthesis of Indian and Persian cultures, the empire was the crowning moment in the history of the Sultanate of Delhi. Babur's successors included princes such as Akbar, notable for great intelligence and a broad-minded, modern outlook. The culture they developed was second to none, able to call on the skills of the best Central Asian practitioners in the field of books and architecture. The arts – especially architecture and miniatures – prospered under them until the mid-seventeenth century, and the fusion of Persian lyricism and Hindu naturalism surpassed the splendid but hybrid results of the early Islamic period, producing works of outstanding value that can rank with the best in all Islamic art.

As happened elsewhere, the Muslim conquerors of India found themselves ruling a very ancient civilization of extreme and multi-faceted complexity that had a long-standing, broad-based religious philosophy and highly sophisticated architecture. It was moreover a civilization that translated its ideas,

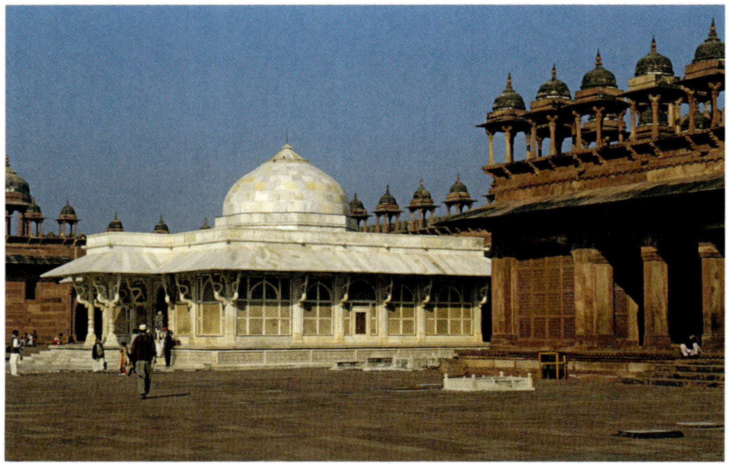

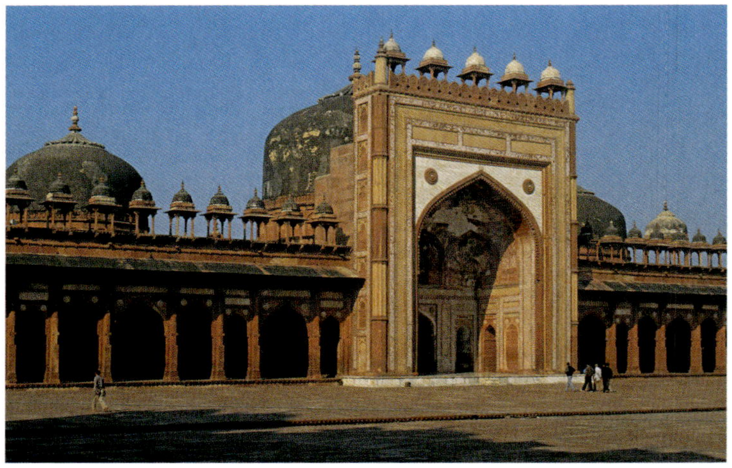

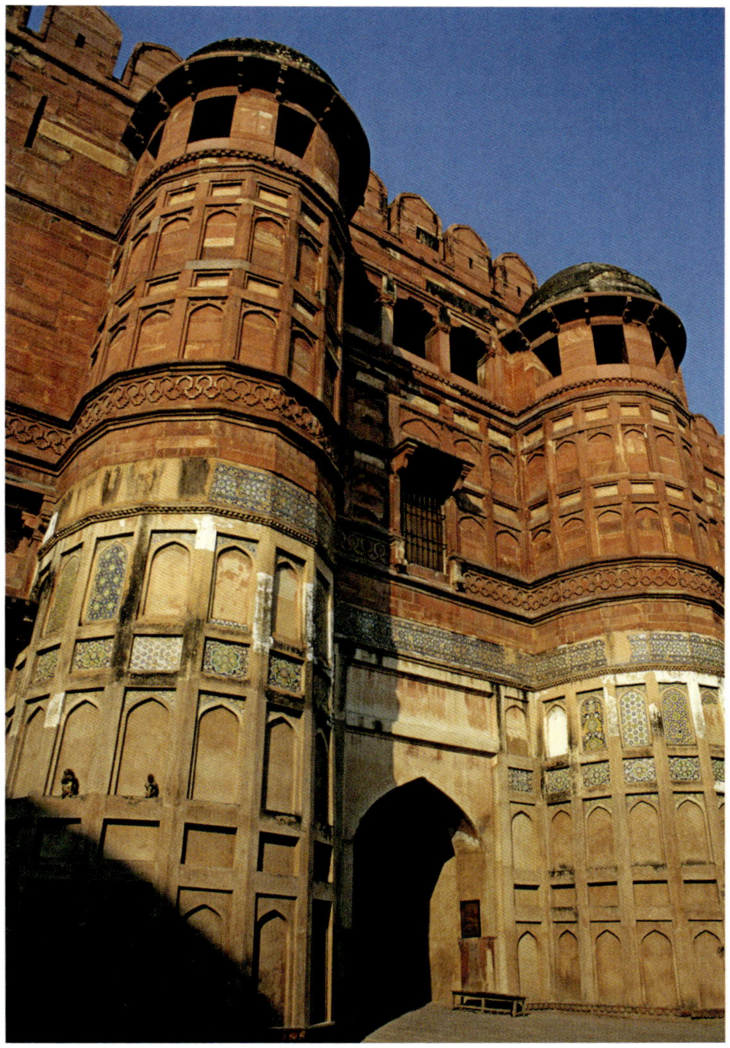

symbols and metaphors into spectacular, gigantic stone structures and sophisticated, seductive images, both carved and painted. Though the Seljuks in Anatolia had encountered a cultural background just as deeply rooted, it should be stressed that Christian architectural culture – whether Armenian, Syrian or Byzantine – had many common roots with the conquerors' Turkish and Islamic culture (which was at that time under profound Persian influence), and their respective religions were similar in being both revealed and monotheistic. In India, religion was far from monotheistic. Its architecture expressed the values of religion, and sought to disseminate its images, perpetuate its mystery and celebrate its rites in all their many shades of diversity. All this was the very antithesis to the victors' Islamic and Turkish spiritual experience, and quite alien to their view of the world. The Indian continent was like a luxuriant and impenetrable jungle, while the world of the Islamicized Turks was like a desert, infinite and commensurate with the greatness of soul of those who ventured there. In rather simplified terms, Indian temples were conceived as the setting for a progressive approach towards an unattainable and mysterious epicentre, situated at the end of a journey involving successive stages, a goal hidden in a small, dark, central place accessible only to initiates. The ultimate shrine would contain an idol placed on the ideal axis of the *shikara* or ritual mountain. This heart of the temple, called *garbha grha* (comparable to a Holy of Holies) was usually preceded by one or more verandahs or protected by a sacred precinct, where there might be cells or a surrounding colonnade. Usually there were vessels for ritual ablutions as well.

Such elements have equivalent forms and functions that a Muslim would understand; but beyond that, what the temple (whether Hindu or Buddhist) expressed was another world, entirely alien to Muslim experience. To begin with, the proliferation of what were often monstrous images, placed on every available surface both inside and outside, delineated a world representing in frenzied fashion (to Muslim eyes) the essences of an abhorrent concept of idolatry and multiplying it to infinity. Conversely, the idea of an abstract and non-representable divinity absolutely beyond conception in anthropomorphic terms was a cardinal tenet of Islam totally alien to the spirituality and the expressive world of India.

The mosque was a functional building conceived as a simple hall for the faithful to gather together, a place of prayer rather than an objective of prayer. It was bare of decoration, spacious and unified for the glorification of collective prayer, and clear and luminous so as to uplift the soul to a spiritual God. That was the complete opposite of an edifice built around mystery. Indian temples were protected by a series of barriers that progressively limited access to an ever-diminishing number of initiates. They swarmed with innumerable deities and subdeities, often grotesquely illustrated with figures depicting the monstrous union of men and animals, with an infinite number of related altars awaiting prayers and laden with devotional offerings.

Yet contact between the two did arise, thanks to the involvement of architects and skilled workmen from Central Asia. The craftsmen had been used to placing countless miniature architectonic items side by side to achieve buildings whose unity came from the sum of an infinitude of identical details. Now they succeeded in building works which, while being undeniably Indian, welded the tone of abstract luminosity of the conquerors' religion on to the ancient legacy of the jungle and its divinities. In the immediate wake of conquest, the invaders were not averse moreover to using plundered material to build the first magnificent mosques, even though the spoil might be crowded with pagan reliefs and symbols. Thus indigenous techniques were used to create buildings of a new type and occasionally novel function commissioned by Muslim patrons. Mosques and tombs were both previously unknown in India.

As far as technique was concerned, the arch appeared alongside the trilith, the cornerstone of Indian architecture. At first, it was an addition to the traditional system. Then it became a structural element of increasing importance, being translated into ever more monumental domes, all in the search for the spatial unity necessary for a congregational mosque.

Unlike developments in architecture, the new faith did not insist on special features for objects in daily use. These continued to be produced in traditional forms, although new alphabets developed over time, especially for the Koran, as did a certain type of figurative painting to illustrate texts. These must have experienced major development, particularly following the import of Timurid features.

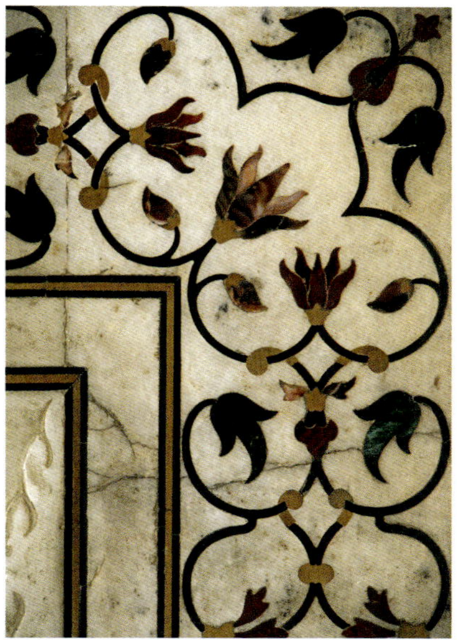

Red Fort: Amar Singh Gate
1644
Agra, India

Taj Mahal
Entrance *iwan*
Detail of bas reliefs of door frame
1632–1654
Agra, India

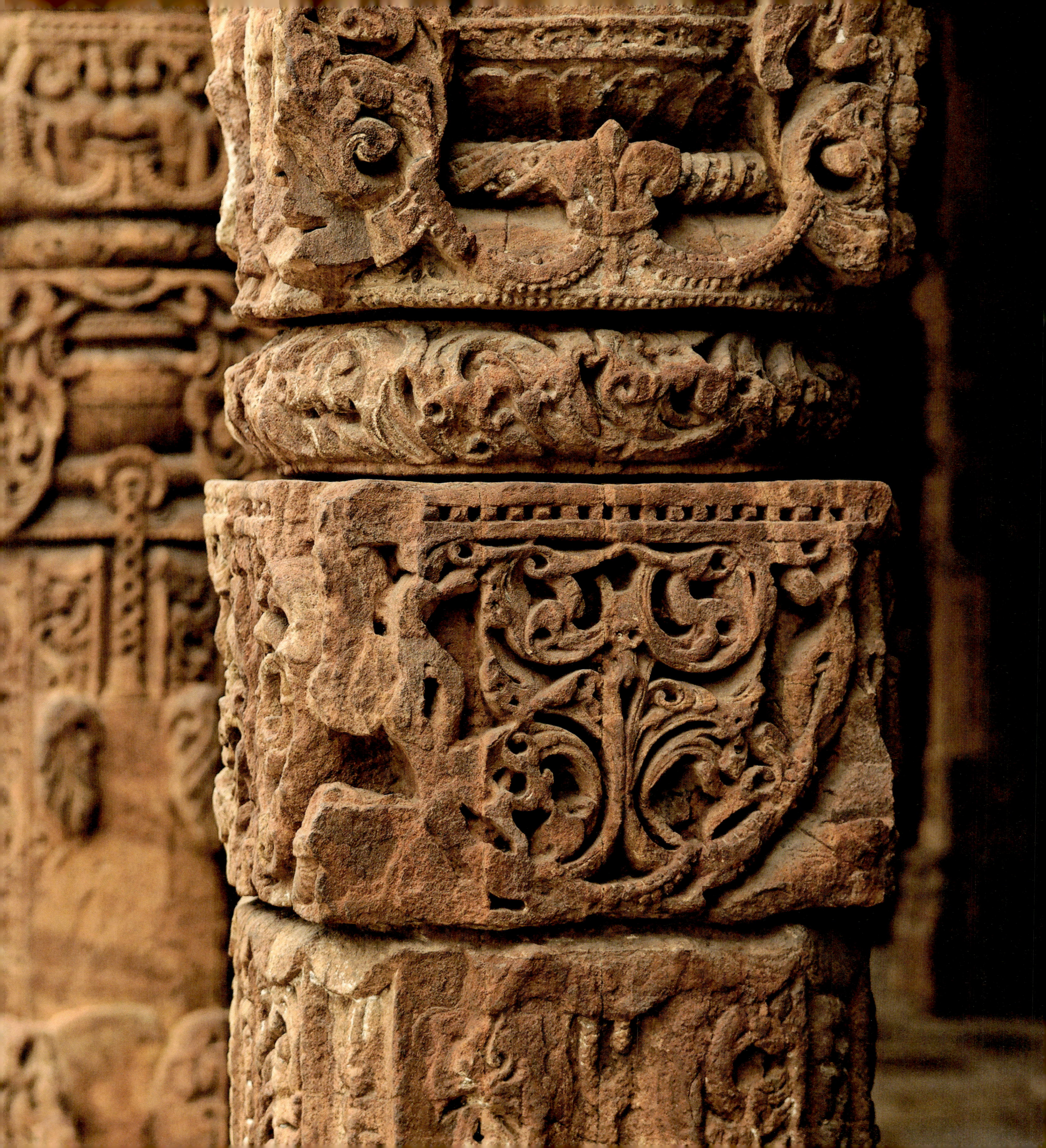

Quwwat al-Islam Mosque
Begun 1193
Delhi, India

The Qutb al-Din Aybak complex consists of a mosque with two minarets (one of them unfinished) surrounded by a series of precincts which doubled and then tripled the extent. They were added over the course of time by Iltutmish and Ala al-Din Khalji to expand the prayer space and bring it into line with the Islamic traditions of Central Asia, as in the case of the partly preserved high screen of pointed arches. Access was effected via four monumental doorways, though only the southern one (Ala i-Darwaza) survives. The first mosque and, to some extent, successive additions were built with materials taken from the twenty-seven Hindu, Buddhist and Jain temples that previously occupied the sacred site. Their columns are perfectly recognizable thanks to the numerous figurative sculptures largely preserved, as well as salvaged blocks used in the architraves and for the roofs.
Apart from the decoration and the shape of the columns, bizarre in an Islamic structure and yet natural enough given the exigencies of the situation, the mosque does not feature any innovative architectural elements. Dedicated to the "power of Islam" (Quwwat al-Islam), it was the first one of its size in the Indian subcontinent, and was deliberately constructed inside the ancient Hindu citadel on the platform of a demolished temple. The first mosque was a simple hall on a hypostyle plan, constructed with columns taken from the demolished Hindu temples. The original bas-reliefs, swarming with figures unacceptable to Muslims, were partly obliterated and the columns, being too low, were placed on top of each other to gain the necessary height.

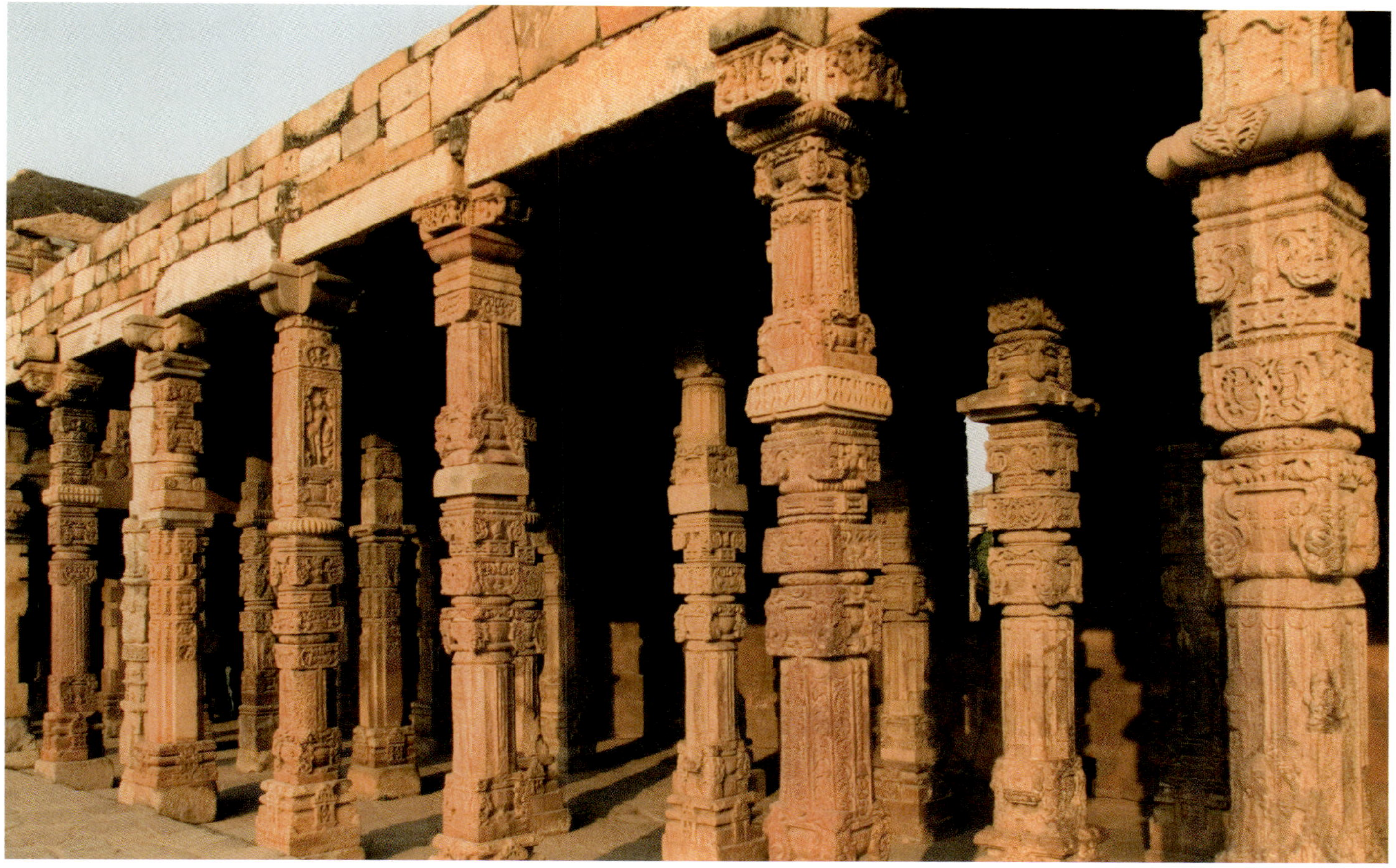

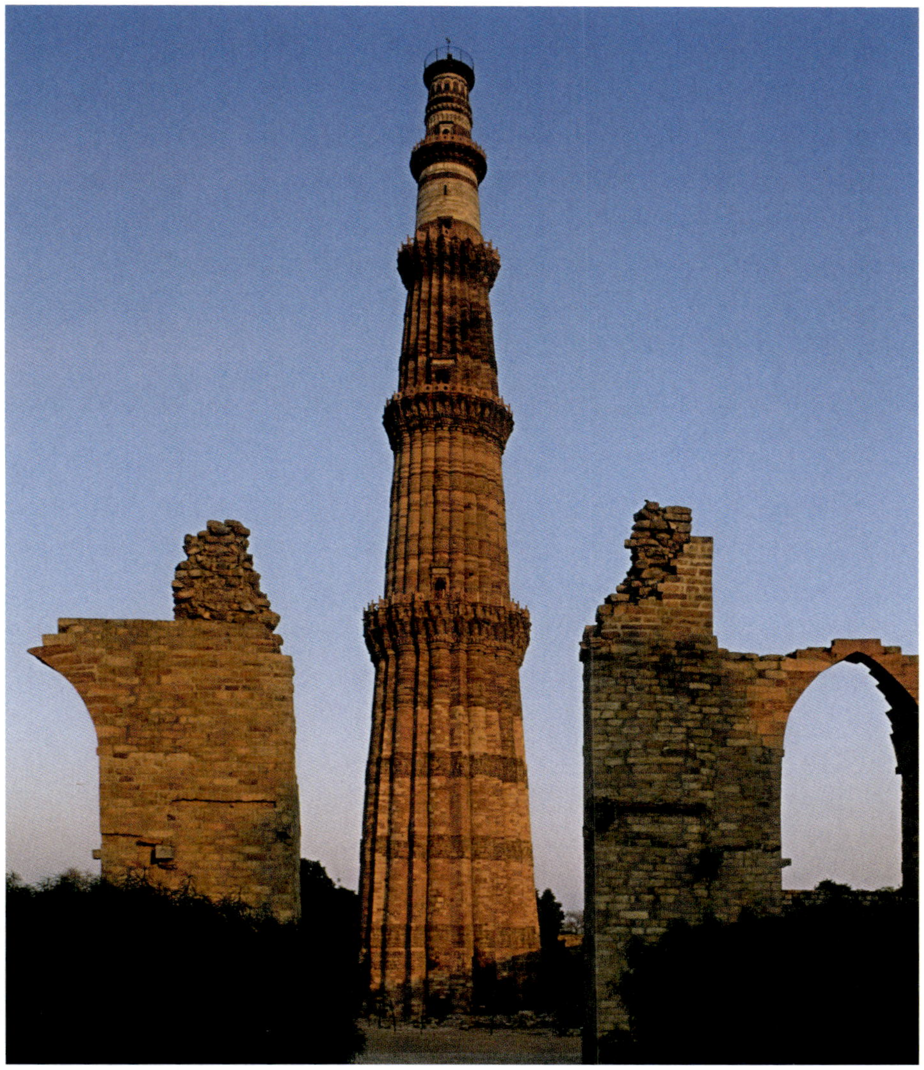

Quwwat al-Islam Mosque
Qutb Minar and screen of arches
Begun 1193
Delhi, India

The gigantic minaret in red sandstone was intended to cast the shadow of God on East and West, as one of its inscriptions proudly declaims. Like similar Afghan and Persian minarets, structurally independent of the mosque, it is an explicit symbol of the triumph of the true faith over the idolatry of the local populations. With a height of seventy-two metres and a diameter of roughly fifteen metres at the base and three metres at the top, it was the tallest minaret of its day. Originally there were four levels. Following lightning damage, the last one was replaced in 1368 by Shah Tughluq with two new levels in a different colour and style. Like the Ghaznavid minarets that preceded it, the Qutb Minar alternates different combinations of circular and triangular ribs, but loads down the supple Central Asian design with the decorative exuberance characteristic of local art. The various levels are separated by monumental *muqarnas* cornices decorated with inscriptions. Around 1199, a stone screen of five ogival arches was erected to emphasize the *qibla* in front of the prayer room. This was an architectural motif unknown to Indian architecture, which used the trilithic system and symbolism of a vegetal nature.

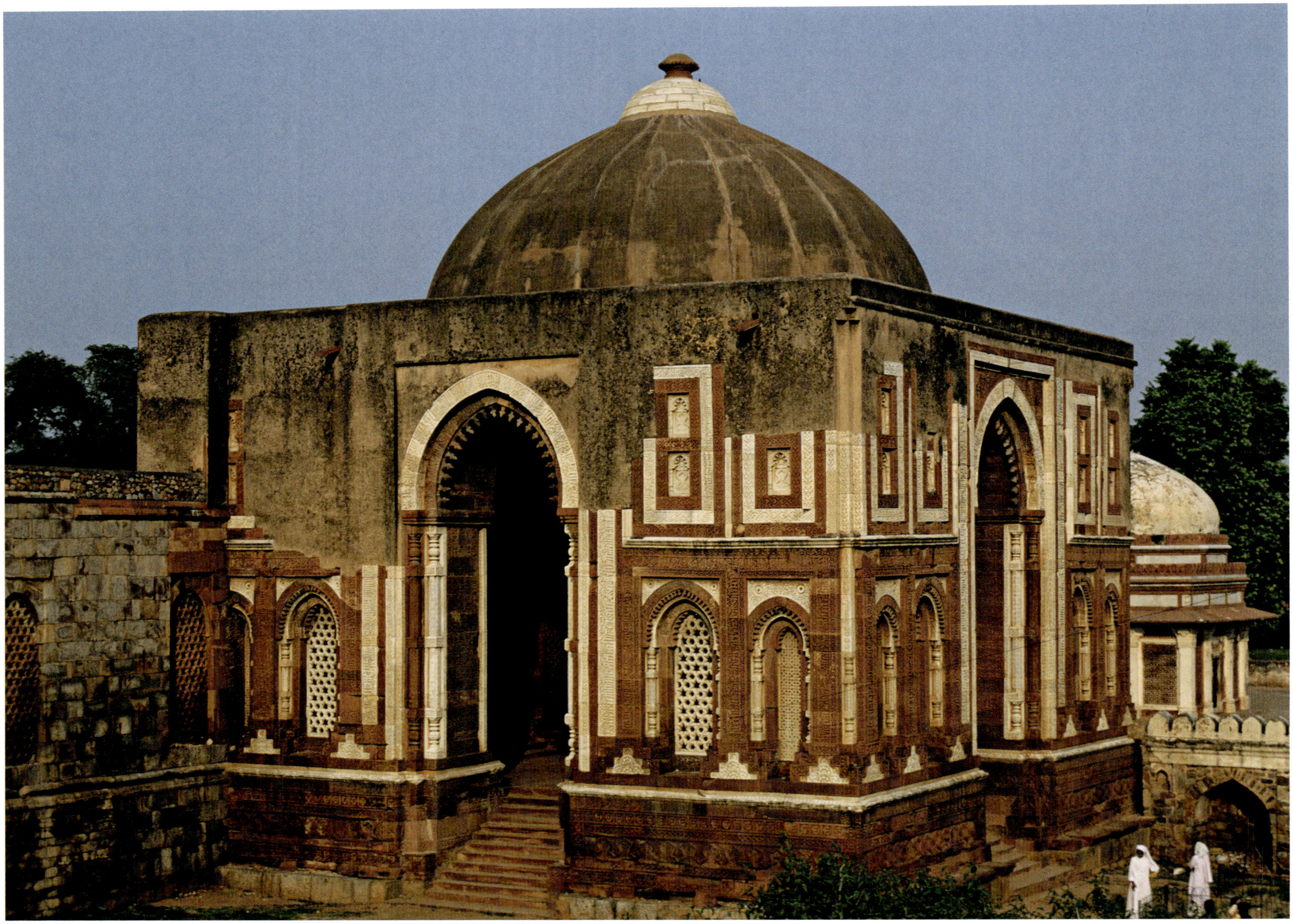

Quwwat al-Islam Mosque
Ala-i Darwaza
1311
Delhi, India

Ala al-Din Khalji, a representative of the new dynasty in power, used the immense plunder he acquired from a brilliant series of victories over neighbouring Indian states for a final enlargement of the congregational mosque. Of this ambitious project, which was left in an embryonic state, the only part completed was the south doorway, the Ala-i Darwaza, notable for its dome, sophisticated two-colour masonry and above all the pierced stone grills, which would become an enduring feature of Indian Islamic architecture.

Quwwat al-Islam Mosque
Mausoleum of Iltutmish
1235
Delhi, India

In 1229, Sultan Shams ad-Din Iltutmish doubled the area of the Quwwat al-Islam Mosque, adding a new screen that also incorporated the giant minaret. A number of years later, he had his own tomb constructed close to the external perimeter of the mosque, where it could benefit from the prayers of the faithful. Though this feature was taken for granted elsewhere in the Islamic world, in India it was an absolute novelty. Buddhists and Hindus practised cremation, so that the idea of burial, particularly of a monumental nature and close to a place of prayer, was absolutely unknown. The tomb consists of a square building with a dome and a crypt beneath, and was clearly constructed by local workmen. However, the opulent proliferation of curvilinear, phytomorphic and figurative designs of the typical Hindu type gave way to an abstract and relatively neat decorative scheme, though with very small motifs.

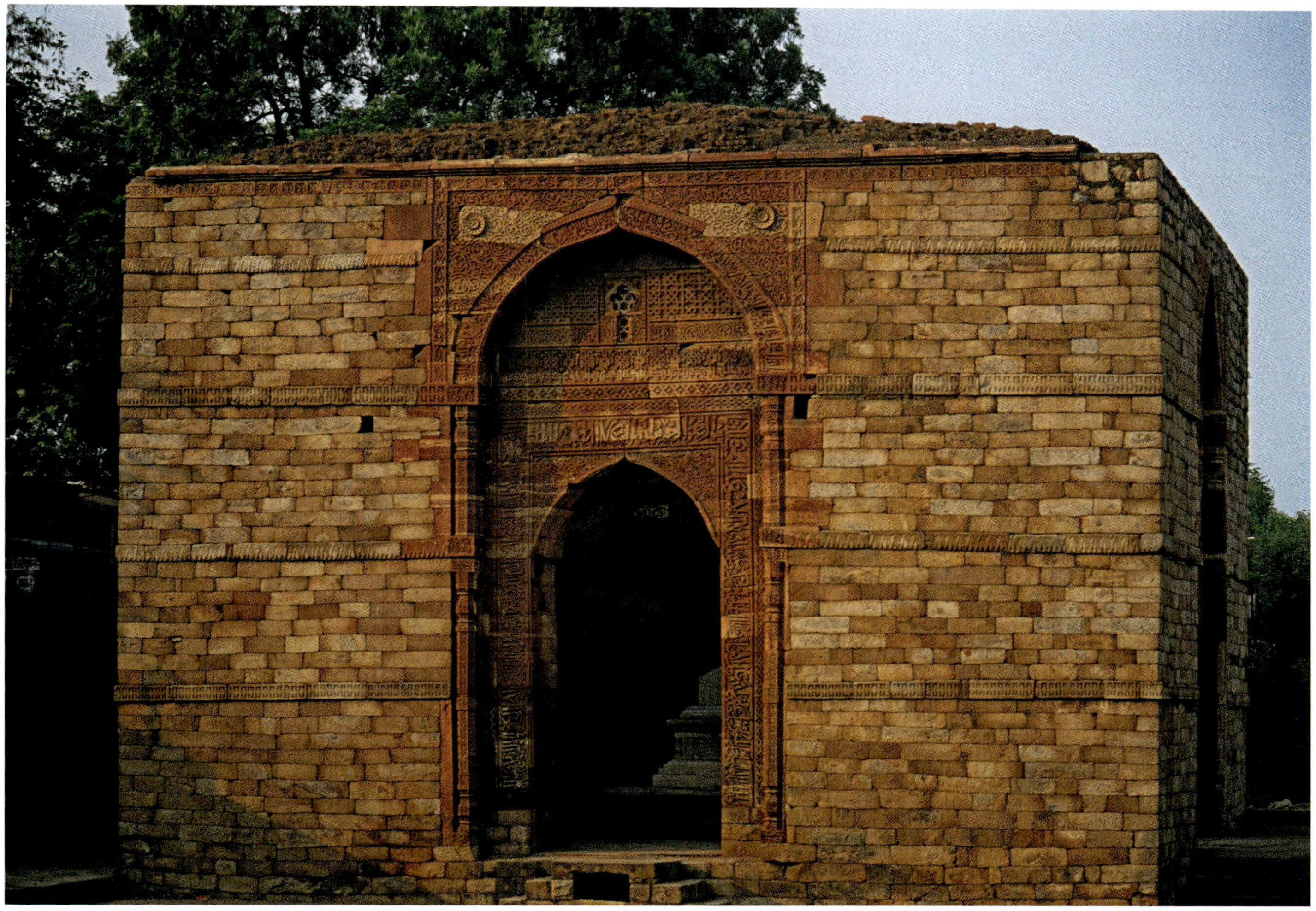

Mausoleum of Ghiyath ad-Din Tughluq
1325
Tughluqabad, Delhi

The death of Ala al-Din Khalji threw the sultanate into chaos, which only came to an end with the installation of Ghiyath ad-Din Tughluq, founder of the dynasty of the same name. He immediately began work on his personal capital, which he called Tughluqabad, a few miles from the previous one. Here, at the centre of a fortified island placed in an artificial lake, he built himself an ambitious tomb. The strange shape – a truncated pyramid with a dome on top – could have been derived from traditional wooden structures in the Punjab, the state the sultan had ruled, and echoes the battered wall and sturdy character of the fortifications that surround it. Apart from this eccentricity, the most significant novelty consists of the great sobriety shown in comparison with previous buildings, with an almost total abandonment of the profuse decoration of Hindu architecture. The white dome is certainly prominent, though not yet onion-shaped, and rises from an octagonal drum that is barely visible. The shape, structure and material constitute a decisive step towards Mughal architecture.

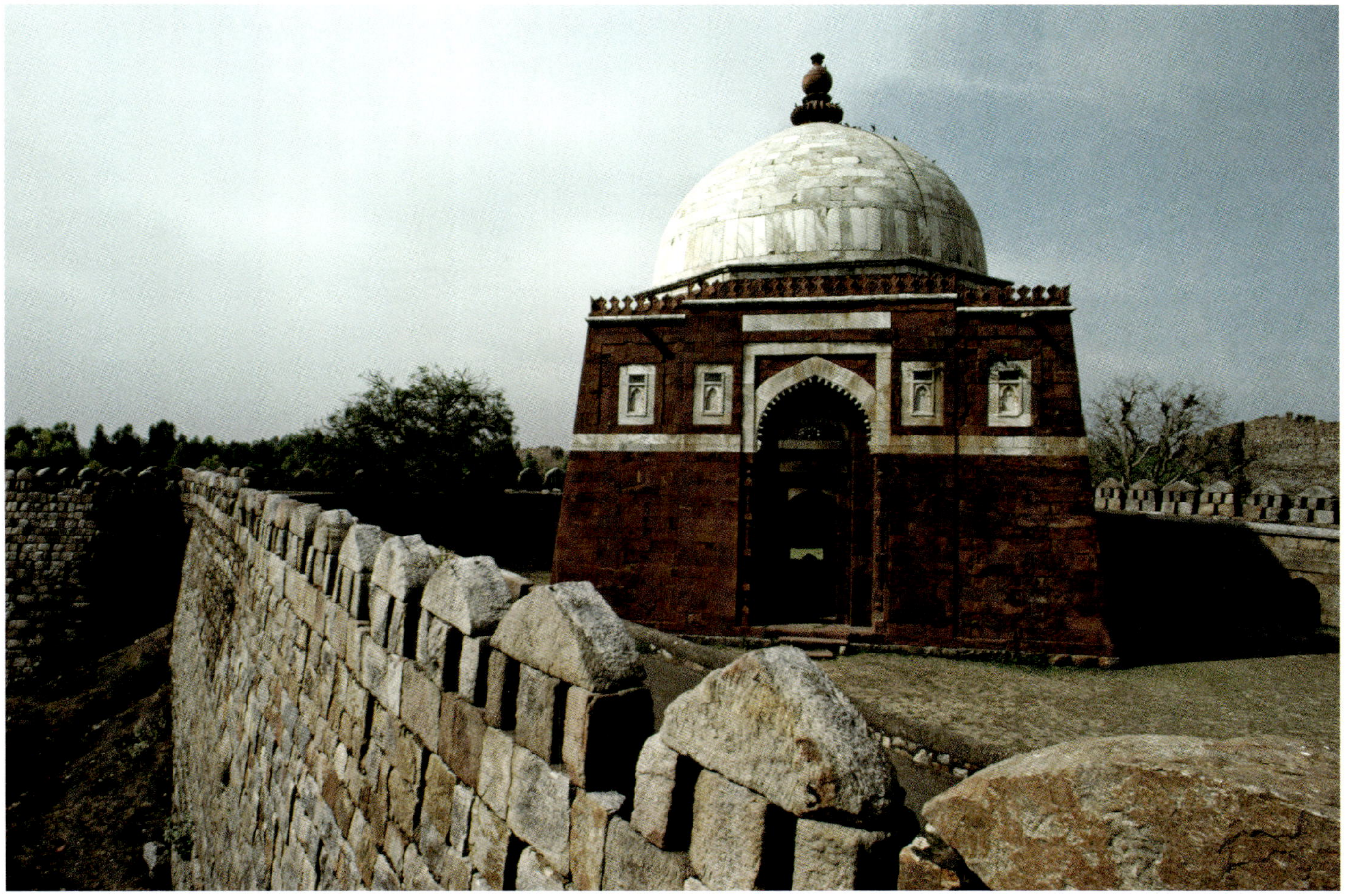

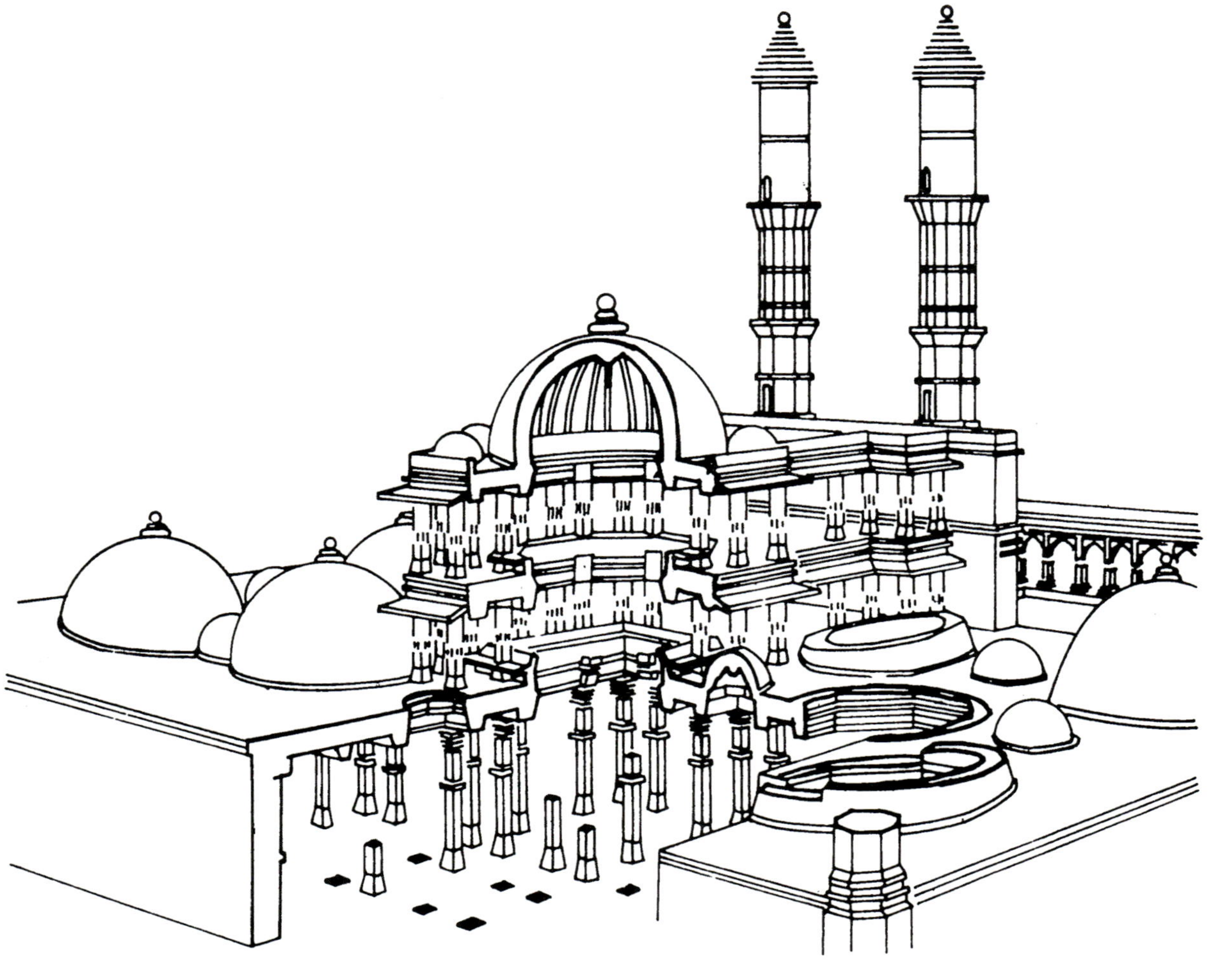

Axonometric section of the Jami Masjid (Friday mosque)
Begun in 1485
Champaner, India

The interior is a trilithic-type structure divided into three levels and crowned by a large dome held up by two orders of columns (a technical solution already adopted in Jain temples), surrounded by other smaller, drumless domes that rise directly from the flat roof, admitting light to the huge interior. The strong presence of traditional Indian elements was due to the proximity of still-flourishing Hindu kingdoms.

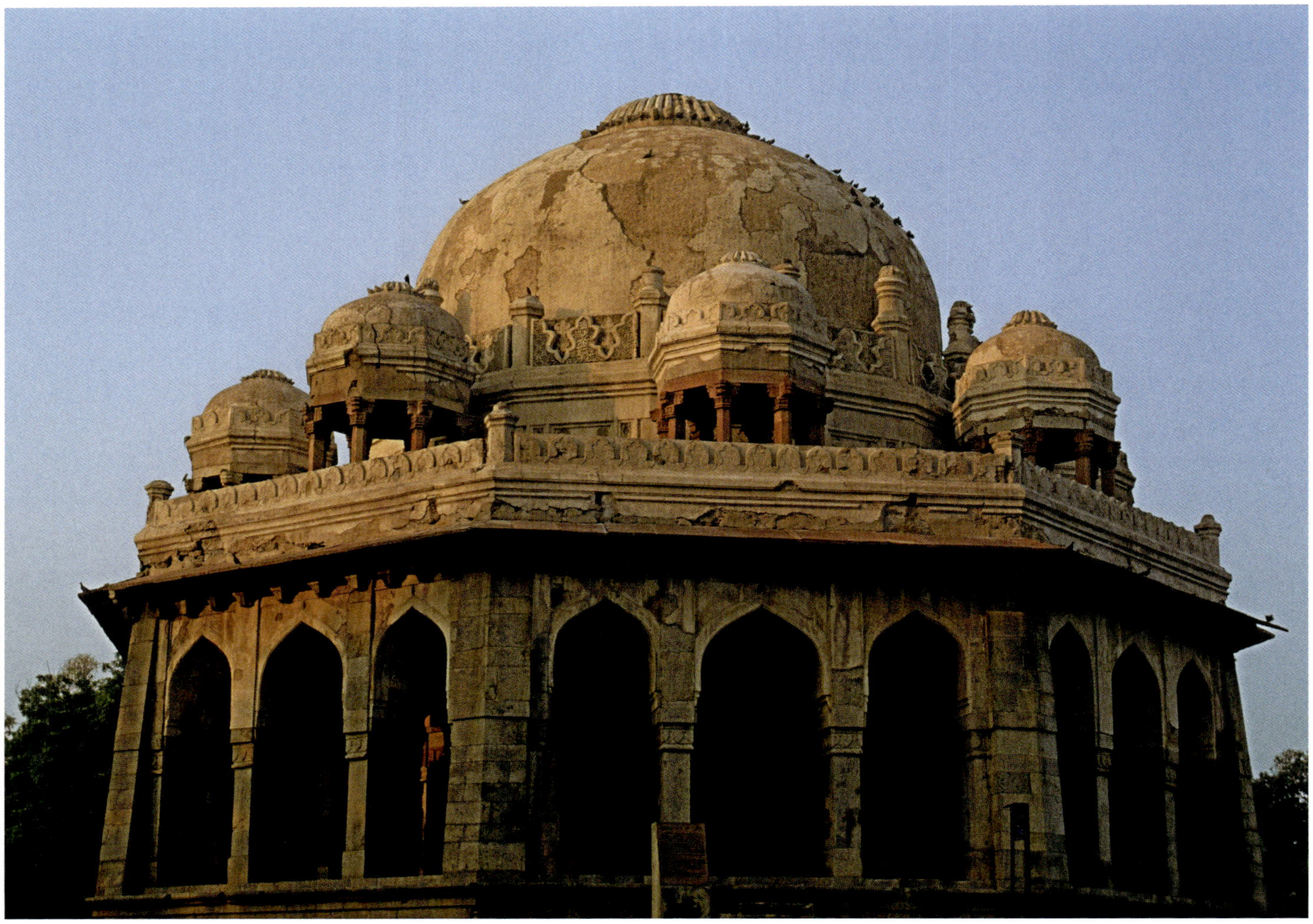

Mausoleum of Shah Sayyid
Mid–15th century
Delhi, India

The Sayyid dynasty introduced the octagonal mausoleum, a type of ground plan familiar in other parts of the Islamic world since the 'Abbasid era. It was arranged around a roofed and domed central feature and was encircled by an ambulatory, in this case open. It is undoubtedly possible that the rite of circumambulation was practised around the monument; however unorthodox it was in strictly religious terms, it was similar to what was happening in the most important sacred places such as the Ka'ba, or the Dome of the Rock in Jerusalem.
On this foundation notable analogies with classic Hindu architecture can be found, particularly in the *chattri* (kiosk domes) around the central dome that bridge the transition from the flat roof of the portico to the curvilinear one above, terminating in a floral motif. Like numerous architectural innovations of the fifteenth century, features of this sort would pass directly into Mughal art.

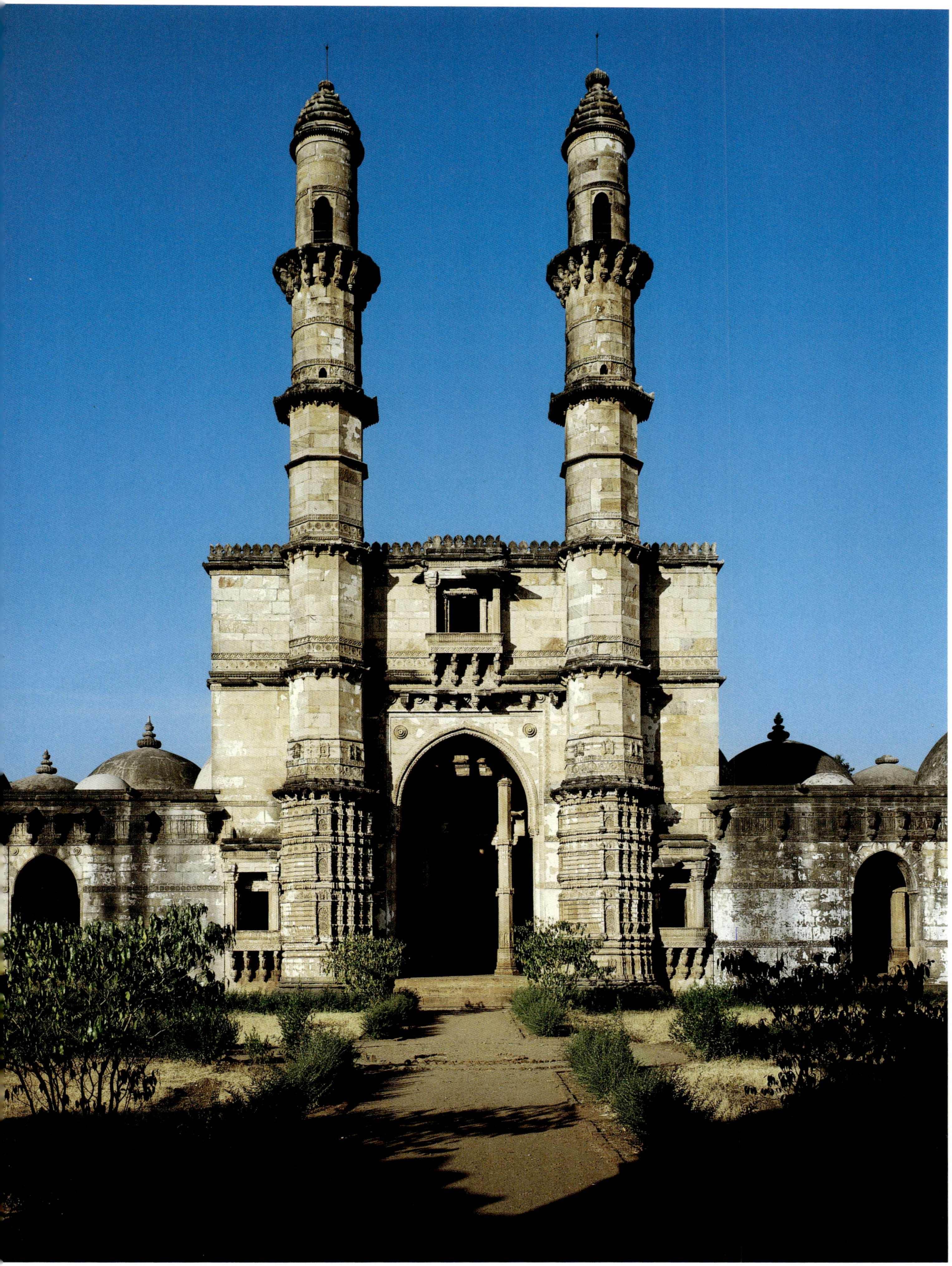

Jami Masjid (Friday mosque)
Façade
Begun in 1485
Champaner, India

Mahmud Begda I transferred the capital of the principality of Gujarat, which had been independent of Delhi from 1407, from Ahmadabad to the Hindu city of Champaner he had just conquered, renaming it Mahmudabad. There he erected a spectacular Friday mosque, funded by the colossal booty he had acquired on his conquests. As in Ajmer, which acted as a partial model, the façade is framed by two very tall, sturdy minarets flanking the huge arch of the entrance to the prayer hall – a solution displaying obvious Timurid influence, even if the verticalism is offset by the force of the horizontal mouldings. The lower part is typically Hindu and still in its original form, whereas the upper part was restored in 1819. The monumental *jarokha* (balcony) on the top floor is, like the narrower ones awkwardly abutting the bases of the minarets, a traditional element of Hindu architecture, as is the busy decoration of the lower part. Distinctive in its imbalances and the use of motifs of diverse origin not yet assimilated into a new and coherent stylistic idiom, the façade indicates that it belongs to a period of transition, and above all to an area on the periphery of the Islamic world. The entrance arch opens without transition into the internal hall, as the tall polygonal columns just inside it indicate in not very aesthetic fashion. They are half in, half out of the arch.

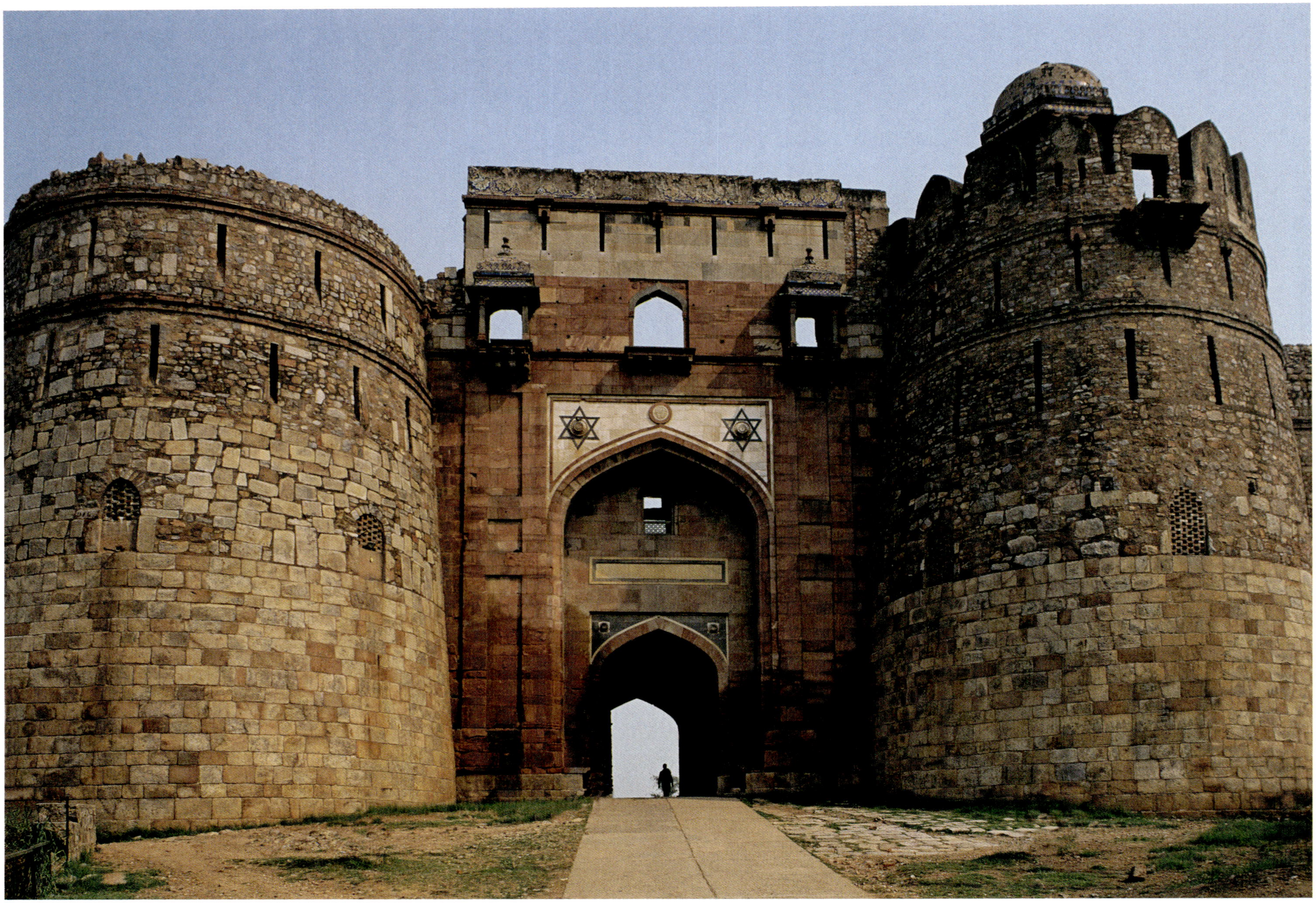

Purana Qila Citadel
Mathura Gate
Begun in 1530
Delhi, India

During the course of his short reign, Babur failed to complete any major architectural works, and the turbulent events of his successor Humayun left no opportunity for any major interventions. The most interesting architectural works of the mid-sixteenth century, forming part of a coherent process of an evolving Islamic architecture that the sultanate had started, therefore all date from the brief intermezzo of the Afghan Suri dynasty. The Purana Qila Citadel, constructed to guard the sixth Islamic capital, is a typical example. Though begun around 1530 by Humayun and called Dinpannah ('Refuge of the Faith'), it was completed by Afghan ruler Sher Shah. The architectural style of those years amounted to a transition between the sultanate, still profoundly influenced by local architecture, and the Persian style – i.e. the Mughal period proper. Evidence of this is the remarkable Mathura Gate. Its classic *jarokhas* for protection from the sun are supported by generous, typically Hindu brackets, while the general sense of orderliness in the red sandstone façade is enhanced by chromatic inserts in other materials, and laid out with exquisitely Persian logic.

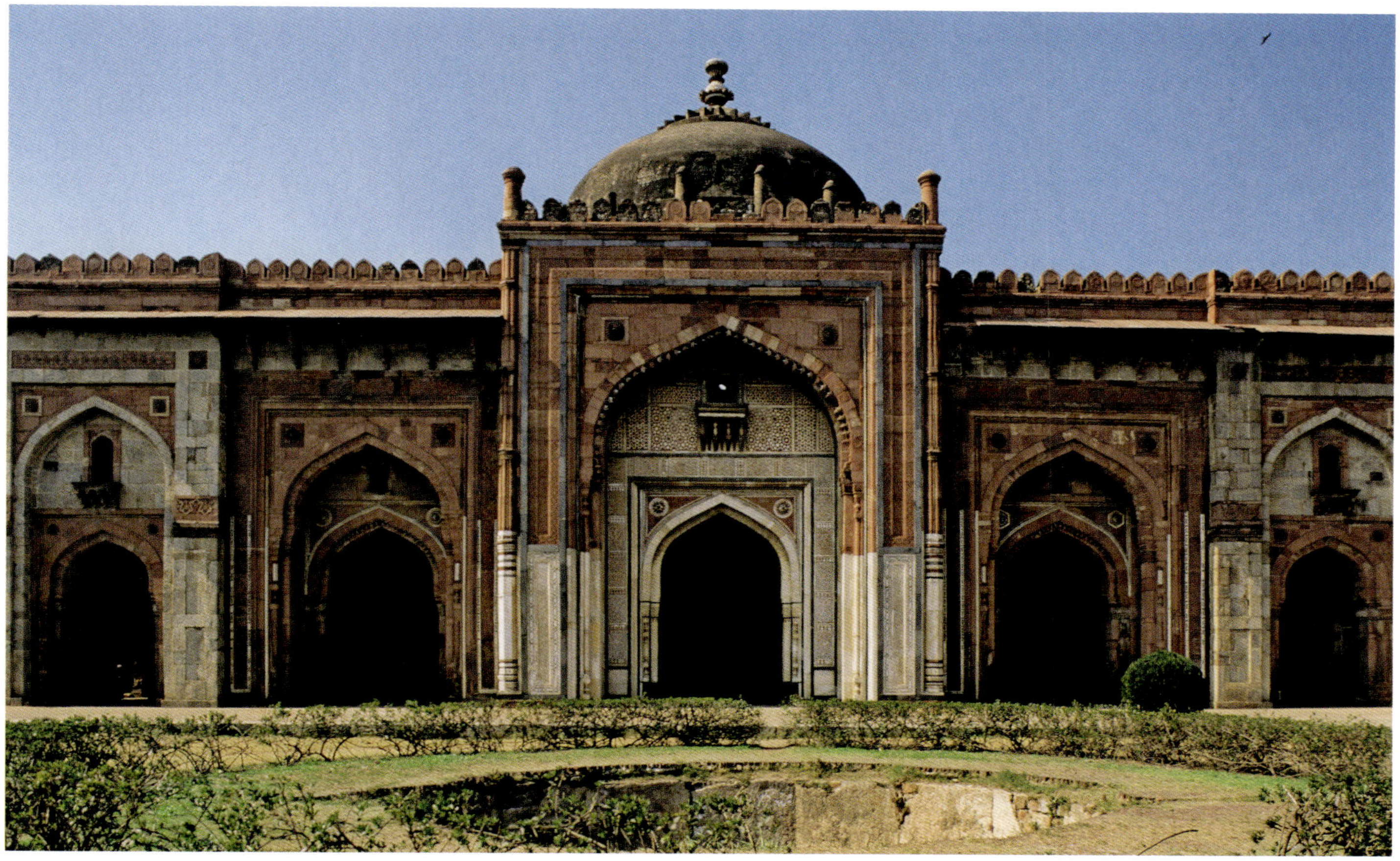

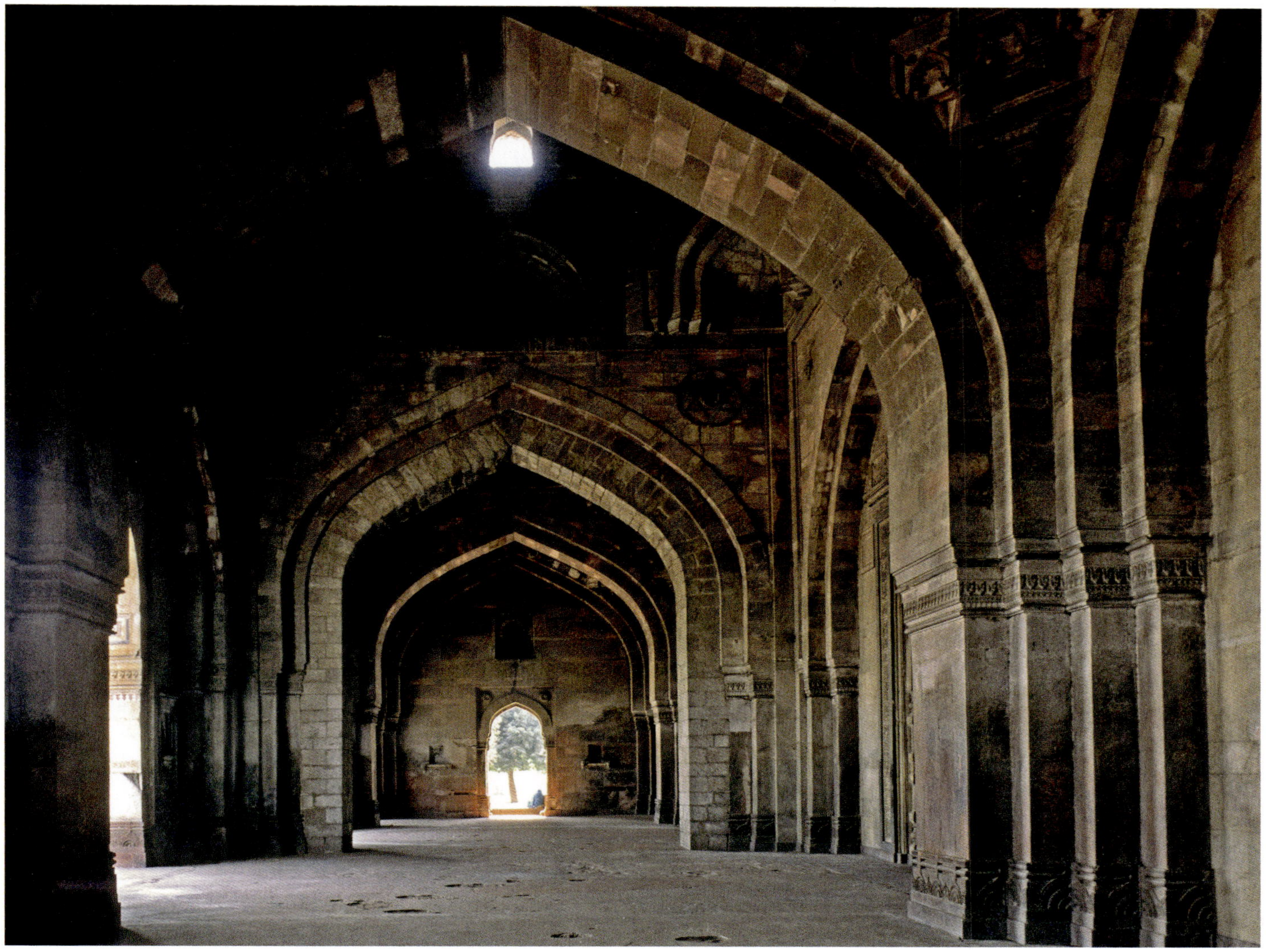

Qala-i Khuna Mosque
Façade
1540–1545
Delhi, India

In the Qala-i Khuna Mosque inside the citadel, the solidity of structure, lucid distribution of the harmoniously proportioned volumes and clear, pure lines all represent innovations relative to what had gone before, and make Sher Shah's buildings the first examples of what would become Mughal art. Particularly important in the façade was the decision to frame each of the tall pointed arches inside another larger arch. The repetition of this motif in different dimensions and chromatic solutions sets up a balanced dynamic rhythm, culminating in the central feature, which is enhanced by geometric decoration and the low dome above. The use of red sandstone with white marble inserts was introduced in the Lodi period, and would become standard.

Qala-i Khuna Mosque
Interior
1540–1545
Delhi, India

The single aisle of the interior parallel to the *qibla*, opening into large arches on the façade and with smaller entrances on the lesser sides, is a feature of the Lodi period. The austere Spartan atmosphere recalls Persian solutions, but the heavy feeling of the material and the massiveness of the structure are typically local.

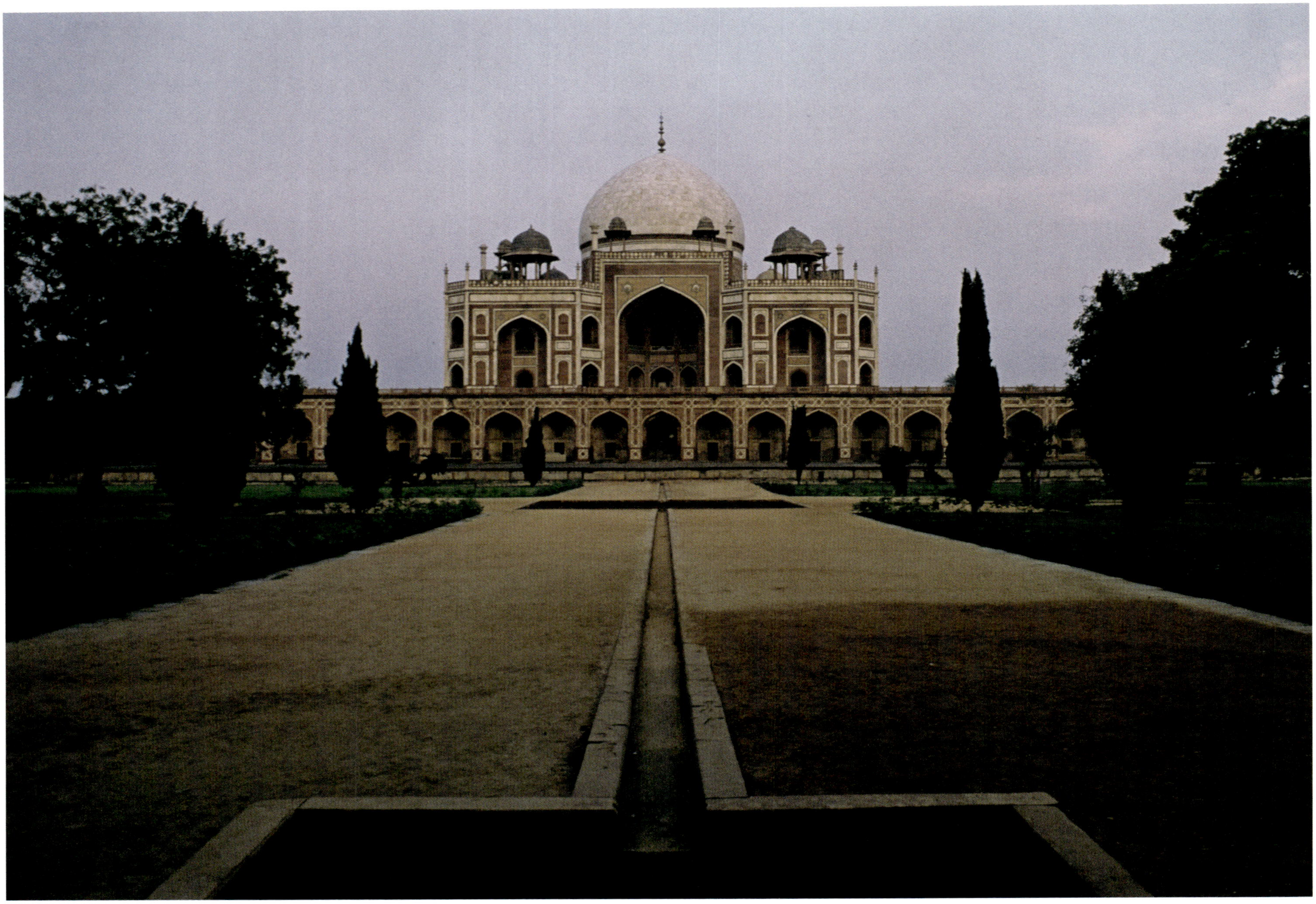

Mausoleum of Humayun
1560–1572
Delhi, India

The mausoleum, which may be considered the first masterpiece of Mughal architecture, was probably constructed by Mirak Mirza Ghiyas, a Persian with a Timurid background, at the behest of Hadji Begum, wife of the deceased emperor. The tomb is surrounded by an immense square garden measuring 365 metres along each side, with three monumental entrances opening into it. The space is subdivided into thirty-six squares by a network of paths with channels and fountains at the junctions of the larger areas, defining the classic garden paradise of Persian tradition (*chahar bagh*). The scheme could also be divided into nine major squares, each formed of four small ones, with the square of the mausoleum at the centre. A monumental entrance on the south side allows access to the crypt and upper terrace via a passage cut into the plinth. The large central room with eight sides terminates in a dome, and is surrounded by four octagonal rooms on two independent levels, uniting the Hindu concept of a closed sanctuary with the Iranian one of a sequence of connected spaces.

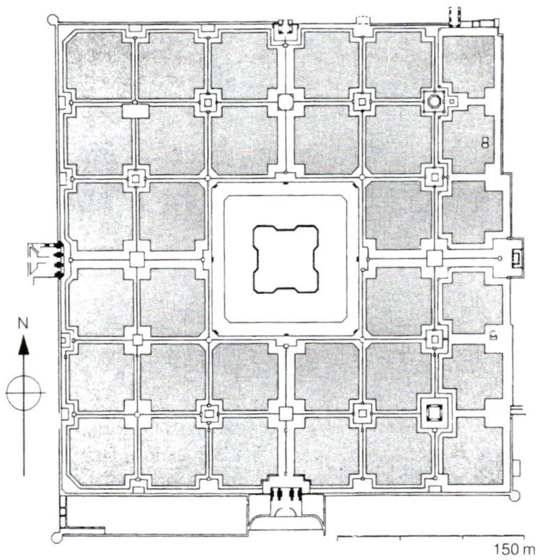

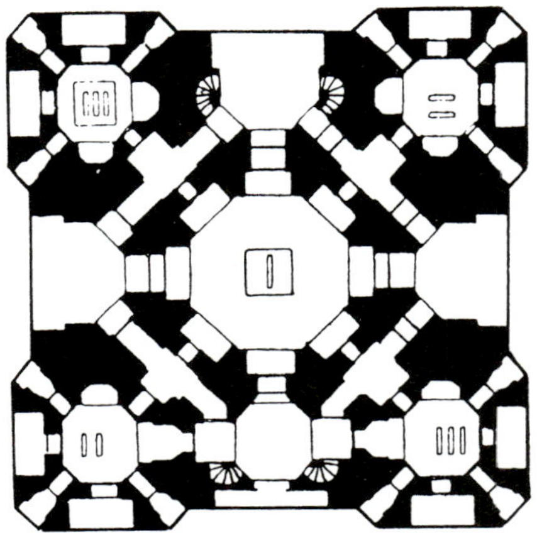

Plan of the Mausoleum of Humayun and the surrounding *chahar bagh*
1560–1572
Delhi, India

Mausoleum of Humayun
Dome
1560–1572
Delhi, India

The marble external shell of the dome enclosing the internal shell was the largest of its day in India, and is framed by four palpably Hindu-style *chattri*. The elevations are well balanced by the sculptural, theatrical distribution of wall masses and volumes by means of arches, blind arcades, pinnacles and kiosks, perfectly held together by the luminous outline of the dome. The masonry of red and yellowish sandstone with inserts of white marble constitutes the Indian equivalent of the Iranian solution of glazed bricks, which are very rare in India. Sculpture as such is completely absent. The simplicity and severity of the cladding belong to the style of monuments of the Lodi and Suri dynasties, while the eight larger finials and sixteen smaller ones have a precedent in the Sher Shah mosque in the Purana Qila, and probably ultimately derive from the Mausoleum of Oldjeitu in Soltaniyeh.

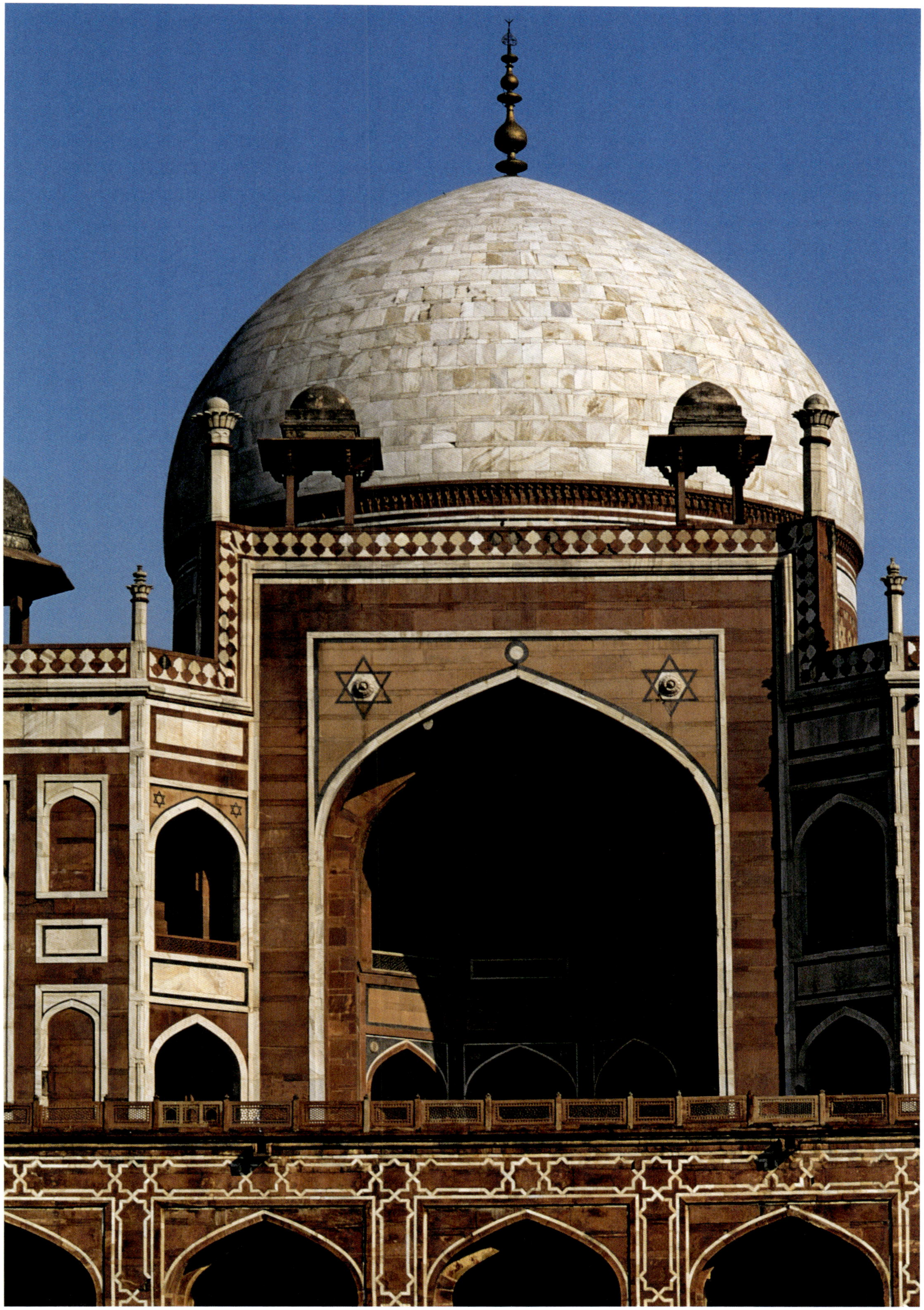

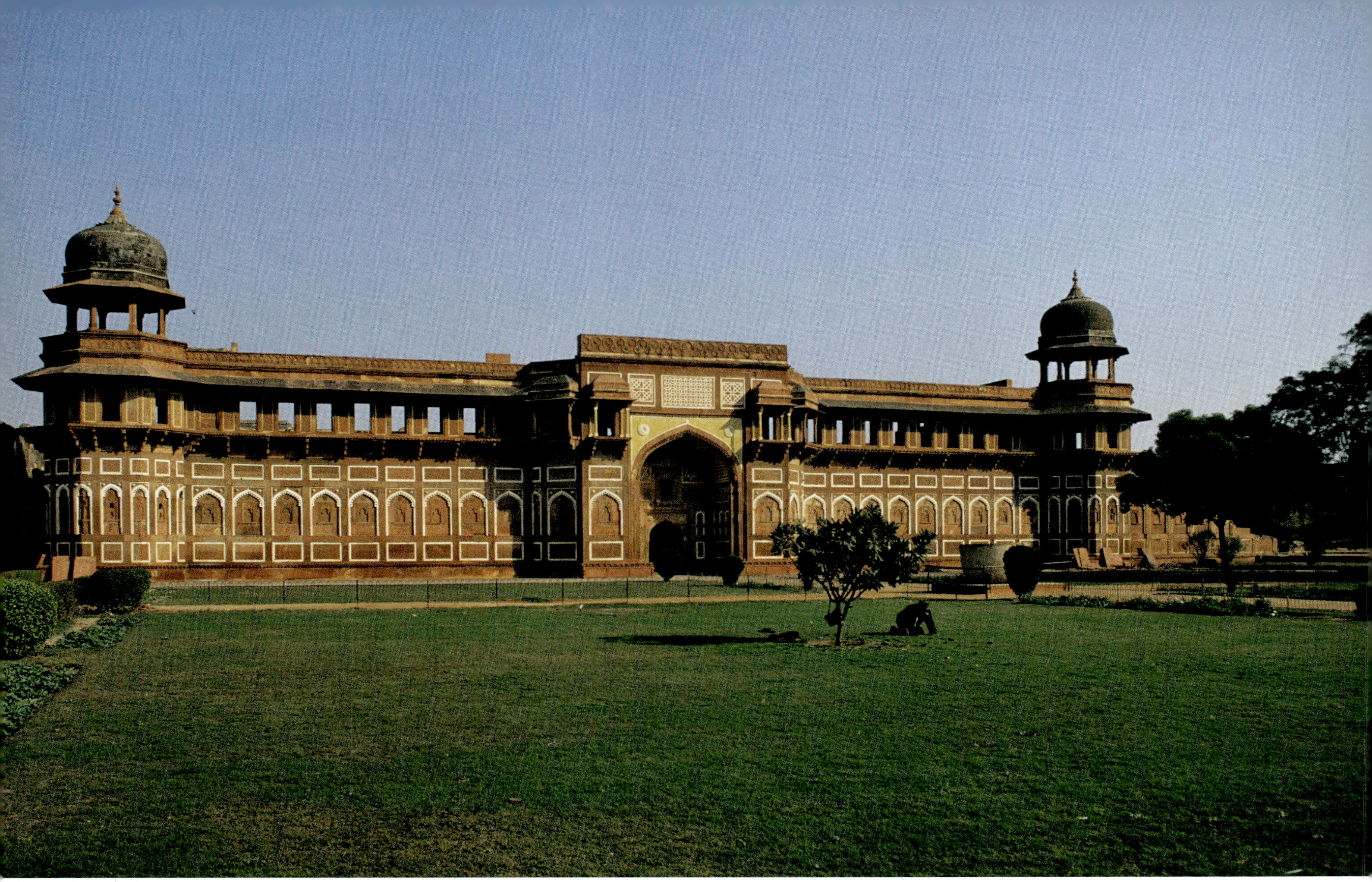

Jahangiri Mahal
1565–1570
Agra, India

In 1565, Akbar undertook reconstruction work on the old Lodi fort in Agra, which had become his capital and the largest city in India, transforming it into the magnificent Red Fort.
Unfortunately, the major works of modernization subsequently undertaken by Shah Jahan obliterated most of his work, but the Jahangiri Mahal, which probably constituted the *zenana*, i.e. the women's quarters, is the most important example of an imperial residence to have come down to us from his time. A broad *iwan* marks the centre of the compact façade, built in beautiful dark red sandstone with highlights of elegantly inlaid, geometrical, mosaic panels. At the ends stand sturdy polygonal towers crowned with large *chattri,* whose domes – of a height proportional with the rest of the façade and standing on slender columns – seem to float in the air. The Hindu features such as the *chajjas* and *jarokhas,* perfectly co-ordinated in the sculptural and atmospheric ordering of the upper part of the façade, are well integrated with the Islamic motifs such as the white marble arches with undercut niches borrowed from the architecture of the sultanate period. They have a remarkable syncretistic feel to them.

Jahangiri Mahal
Courtyard
1560–1570
Agra, India

The internal court is dominated by a profusion of obvious Hindu-style features, which overturns any idea of a balanced fusion of the two cultures such as characterized the façade. There are no chromatic accents in the form of marble inserts, while the sculptured decorations and shapes of the brackets and other architectural features recall Hindu wooden models, from which they are certainly derived. One detail – the crocodile-like creatures with floral volutes unfurling from their jaws – is reminiscent of the Hindu sculptures of Gwalior Palace. Since this was the *zenana* (women's quarters), it is likely that the apertures, in particular those facing outwards, were screened by wooden *jalis*.

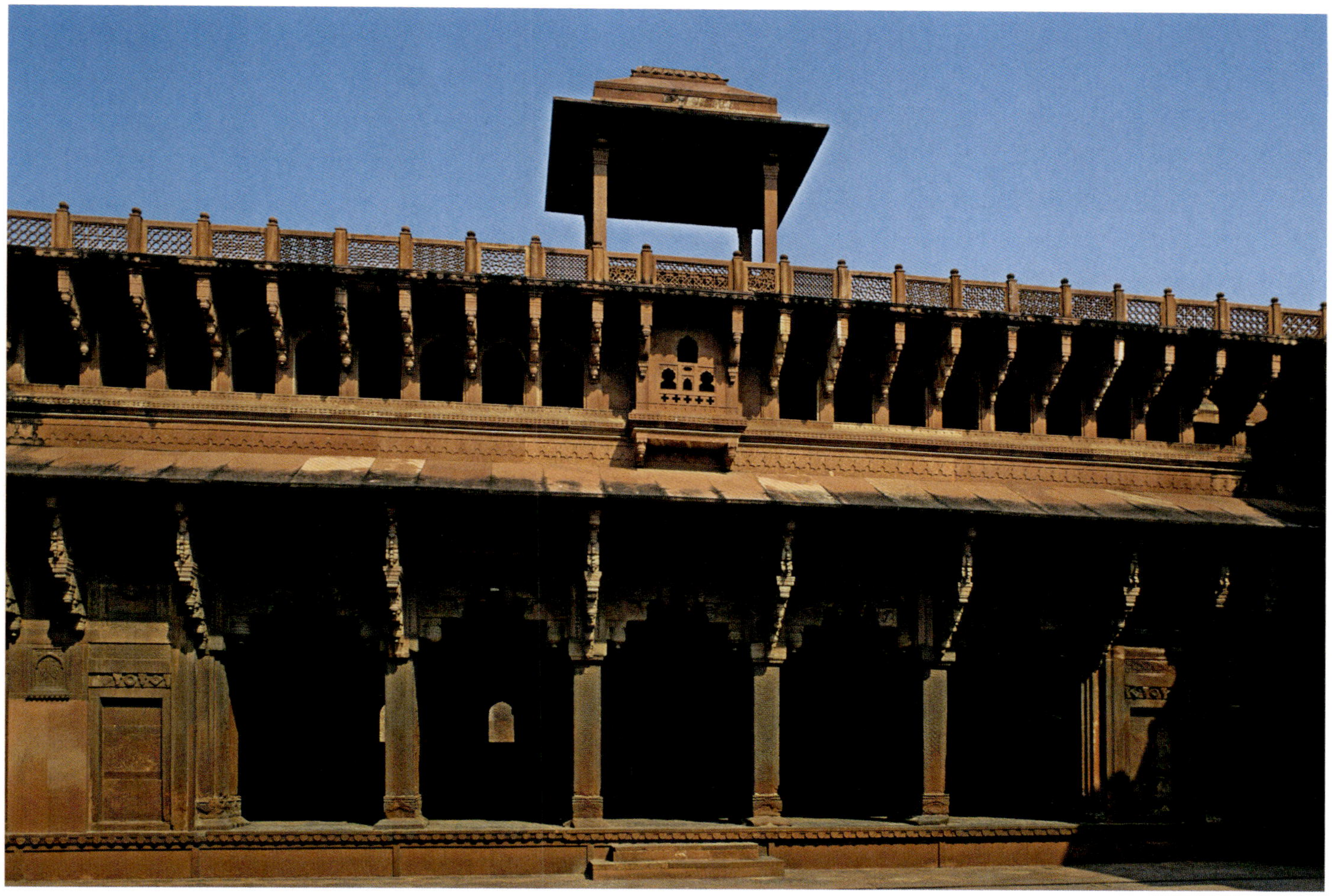

Jahangiri Mahal
Details of the brackets in the courtyard
1565–1570
Agra, India

Arches are replaced by deep brackets and sculpted in detail, repetitions of which support the *chajja* above and, with a profuse richness that becomes almost suffocating, the gallery on the top level. The degree of clarity is restored only by the balustrade at the very top, pierced with geometric motifs and surmounted by the *chattri*. This remarkably simple structure dominates the elegant *jarokha* below, which is pierced by little windows of an orientalizing flavour.

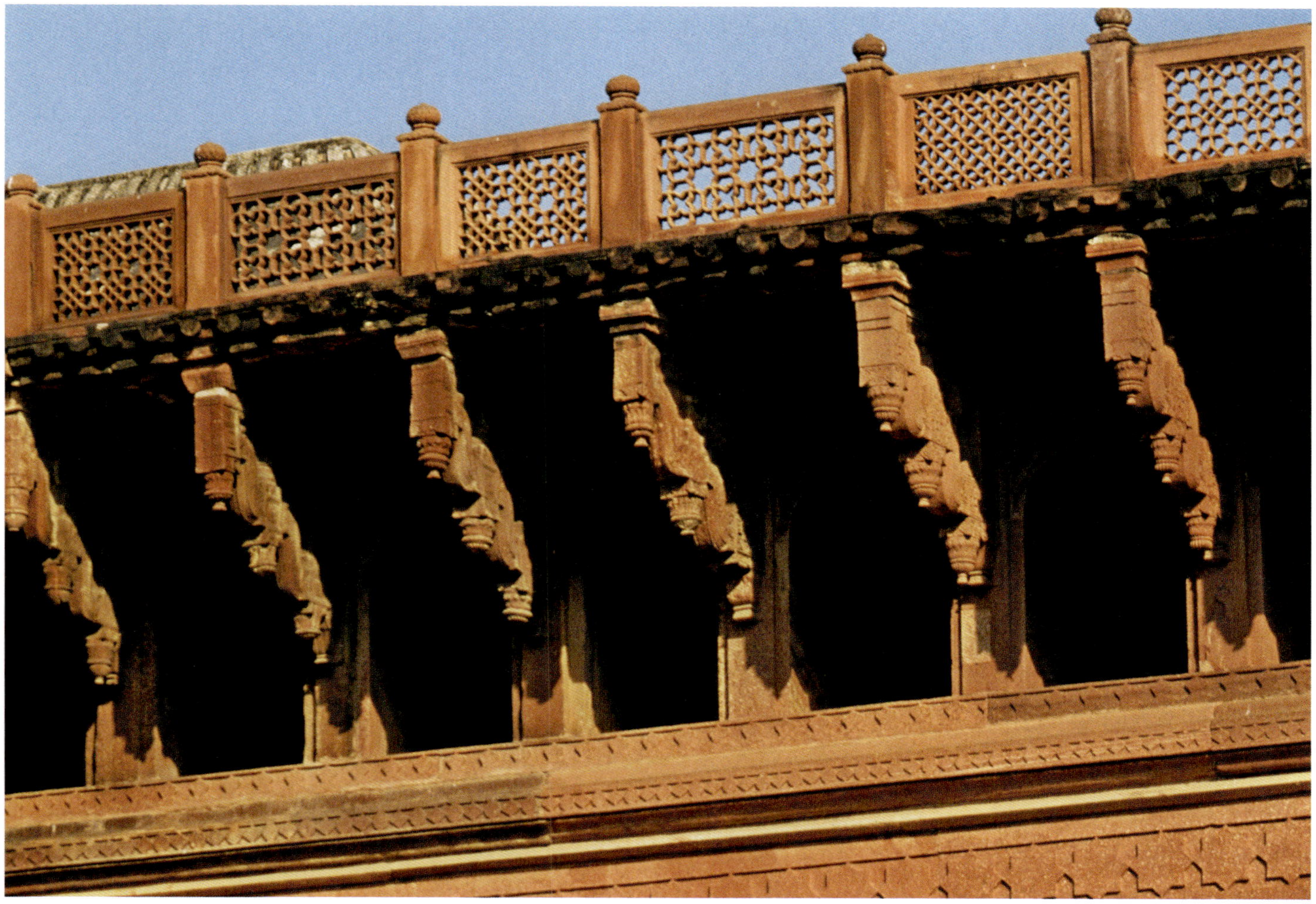

Pancha Mahal
1571
Fatehpur Sikri, India

Emperor Akbar was personally involved in executing the most important architectural projects commissioned by him, the most ambitious of which was the palatial residence at Fatehpur Sikri, which very much bears the stamp of his versatile and complex personality and the discerning culture that he shaped. Created from scratch, the city he built was a splendid and rich thing, but it was already abandoned for Agra in 1585. The beautiful residential complex is constructed of airy buildings spread over vast courtyards, alternating with gardens and water features loosely grouped and oriented towards cardinal points in accordance with precise geometric schemes. It contained low buildings of modest dimensions, often opening along elaborate colonnades and covered by flat roofs crowned with the usual *chattri*. Unique among large capitals, Fatehpur Sikri seems to be the diaphanous materialization of a dream rather than the heart of an immense empire such as, for example, Samarra had been. Suitable curtains stretched from one column to the next to replace walls, providing a screen from sun and wind. The profuse Hindu-style decoration did not obscure the spatial breadth and the simplicity of the different architectural structures, which are almost reminiscent of the provisional simplicity of a camp.

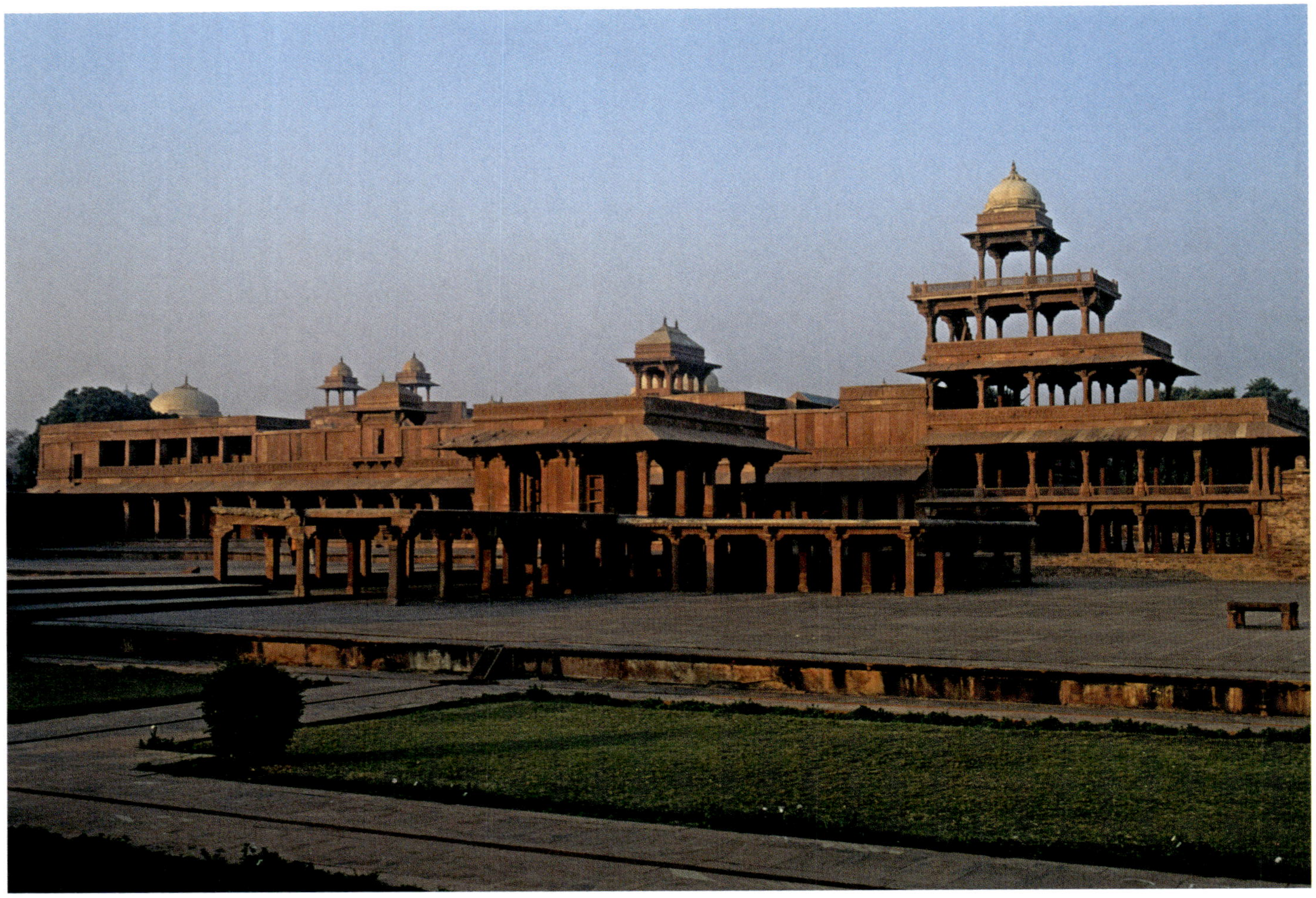

Anup Talao Basin
Panch Mahal (left)
Diwan-i Khas (right background)
Begun in 1571
Fatehpur Sikri, India

In Fatehpur Sikri, the overtly Hindu idiom of Akbar's workmen was subjected to wholly Islamic planimetric control, translating the suggestive garden features into the warm tonality of the local stone, hinted at by the relaxed disposition of the various buildings in the complex. In the foreground is the Anup Talao. In the middle of it is a platform that barely rises above the pool, accessible via four slender walkways suspended above it.

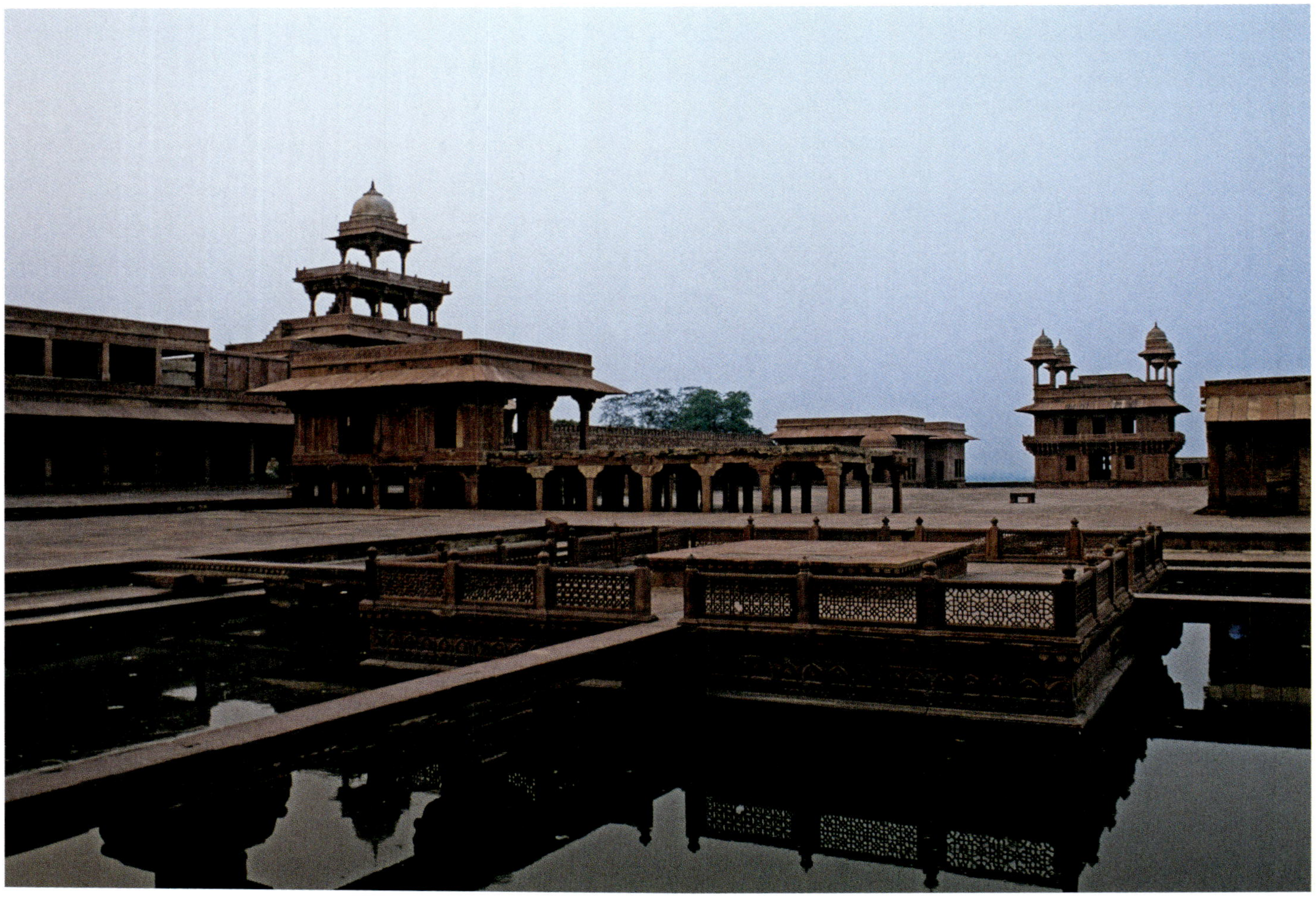

Birbal's Palace
Begun in 1571
Fatehpur Sikri, India

This curious little palace in the women's quarters is noteworthy for its unusual ground plan. It has four square rooms on the ground floor, two of them supporting rooms, the others supporting terraces. This meant one room and one terrace were in the shade throughout the day. The decoration is of excellent quality and distributed with controlled rigour.

Diwan-i Khas
Begun in 1571
Fatehpur Sikri, India

Open-minded and tolerant towards Hinduism but critical of the more conservative aspects of Islam, Akbar liked to know about other faiths, and wanted to be surrounded by representatives of the most important religions. In the end, however, the invective of these scholars made him profoundly sceptical, reinforcing the idea, which he cherished for some time, of his being the repository of superior truths. These he made public with the announcement of a new religion called Din-i tawhid-i-ilahi, which mingled Islam with elements derived from Hinduism, Jainism, Christianity and Zoroastrianism. His role was obviously that of representing God on earth. The Diwan-i Khas, the private audience room, constituted the heart of Fatehpur Sikri. In external appearance, it looks like a modest building on two storeys surrounded by a continuous balcony that accentuates its symmetry, with a *chattri* at every corner of the roof. The inside is made up of a single room, in the middle of which a column terminating in a spectacular and exuberant canopy reaches half way up to the ceiling. Here Akbar received guests, a clear symbol of the axis of the cosmos, represented by the depressed vault above.

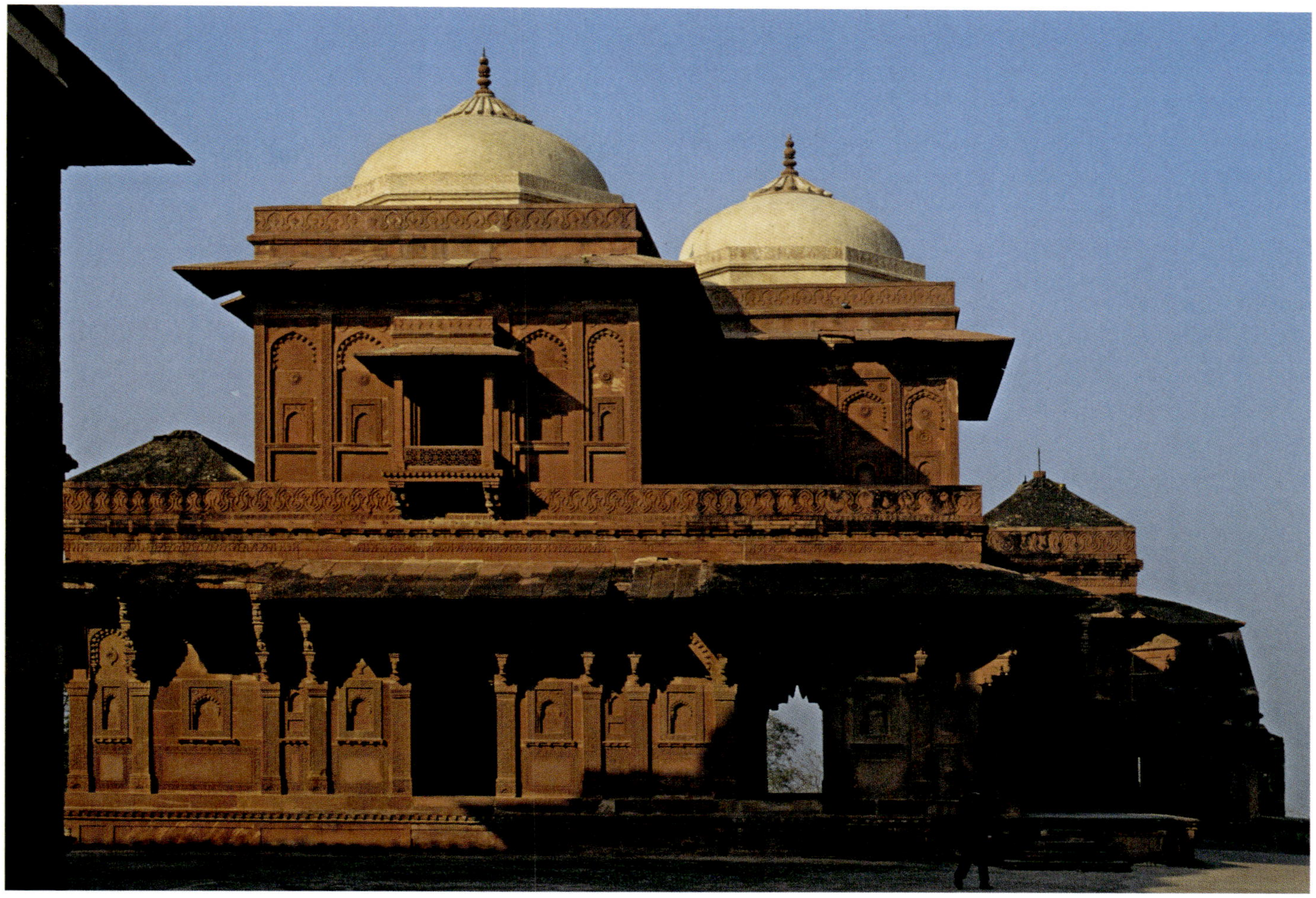

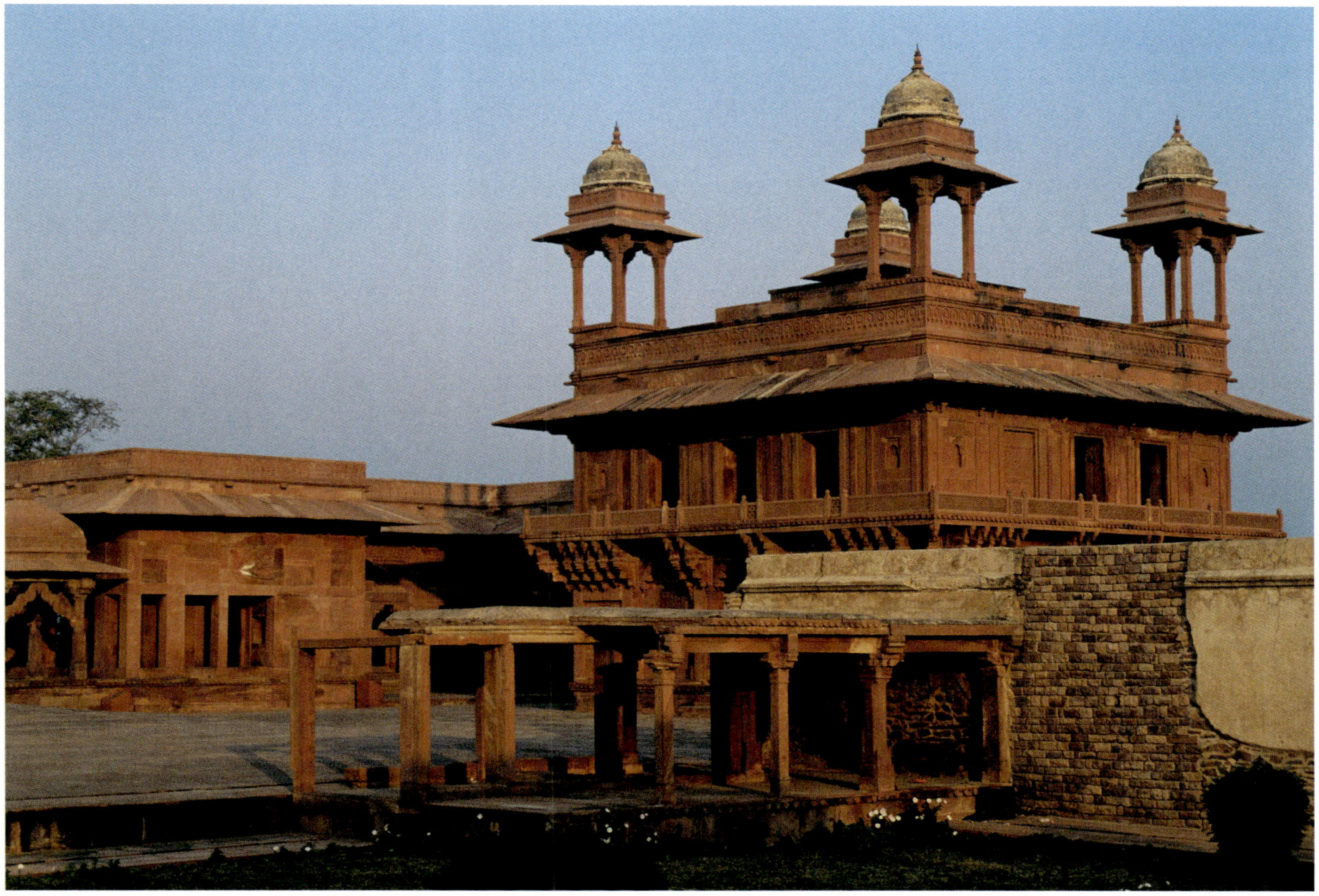

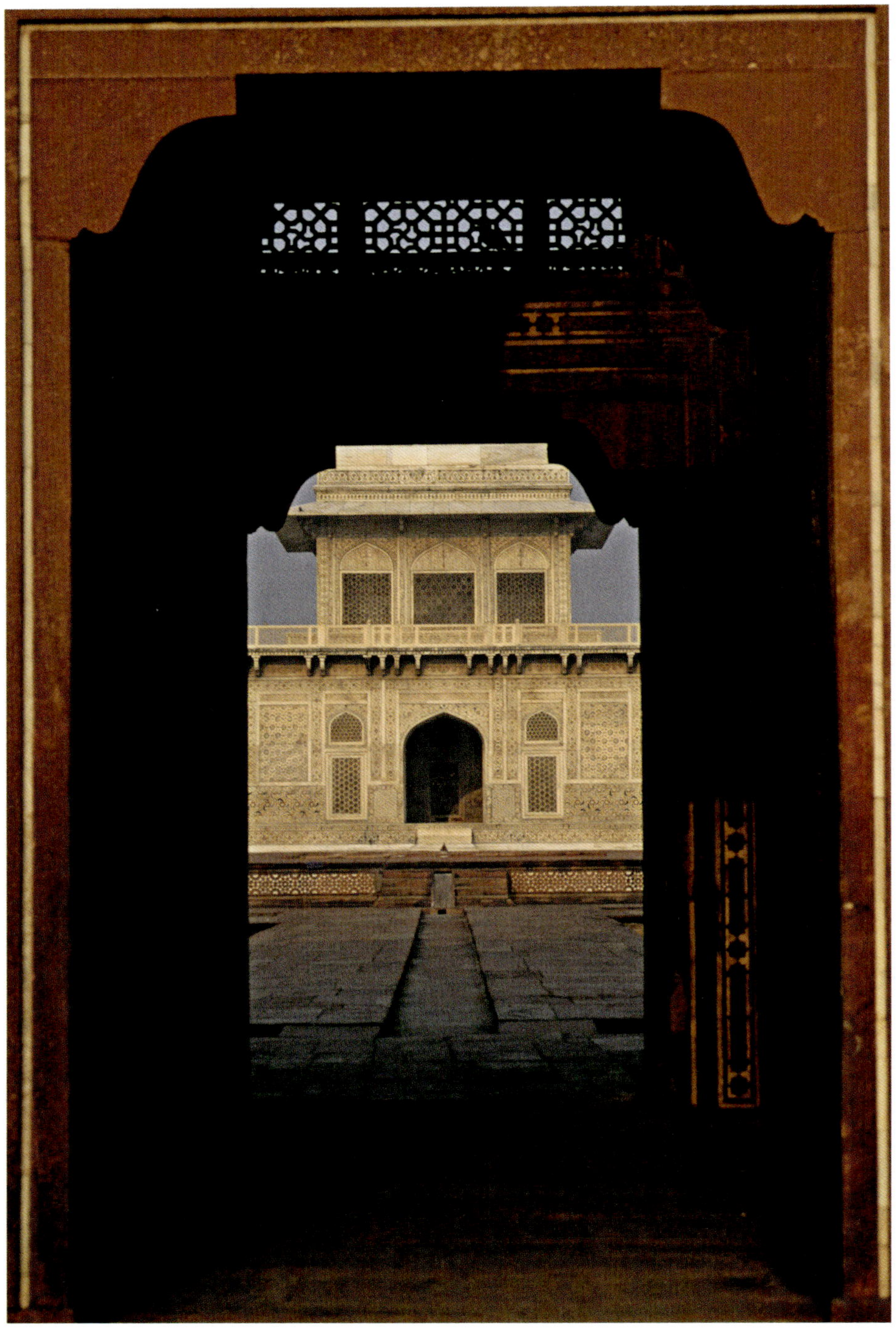

Mausoleum of Itimad ud-Dawla
Entrance doorway
1622–1628
Agra, India

In dimensions, this mausoleum is quite different from the imperial mausolea. It is enhanced by the quality of the decorations and the beauty of the materials. Access to the garden with the sophisticated building in the middle is effected via a monumental doorway in red sandstone. The latter has elegant inserts in marble, perfectly consonant with Persian and Central Asian tradition in the relationship between plain and full, the floral motifs and the luminous delicacy. The tomb was probably constructed under the supervision of Nur Jahan, wife of the emperor Jahangir, to whom the death of her father, an important official in the kingdom, had come as a profound shock. This was the first Indian building in which Jahangir's favourite costly marble replaced the typical red sandstone of Akbar's reign. Cannily, the marble is continued in the doorways and subsidiary buildings in a manner that underlines the hierarchical subsidiarity.

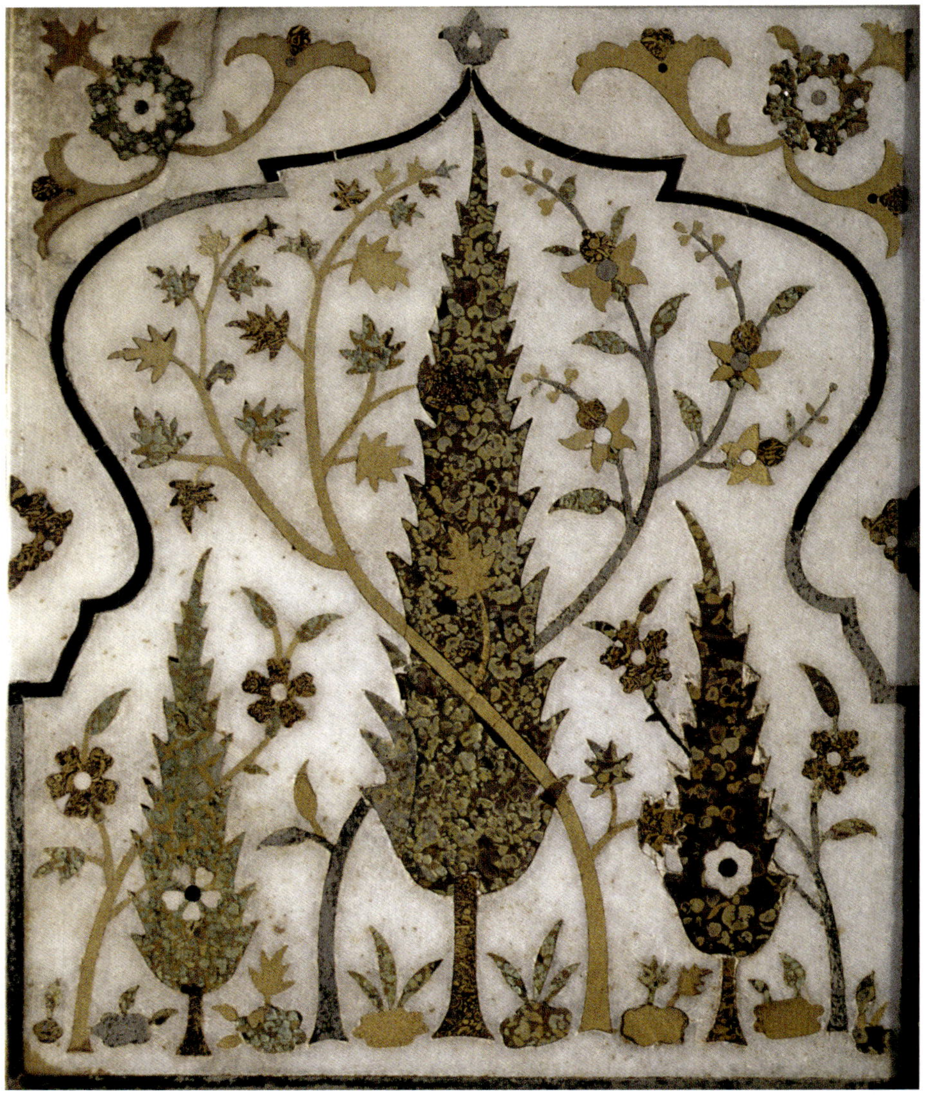

Mausoleum of Itimad ud-Dawla
Decorative panel of the façade
1622–1628
Agra, India

The designs of these brilliantly composed decorative panels represent a notable range of subjects with a very limited palette of colours – black, grey and various tones of ochre and red – that lend the sham niches a sense of sober but sincere nostalgia. They contain vases of various shapes with flowers in them, or containers perhaps full of wine and honey that await believers in paradise. Abstract Persian patterns varied with geometric and floral motifs seem less formal in the flood of light that the transparencies of the marble soak up, its crystal graining reflected like waves of light on the diaphanous designs in *pietra dura.*

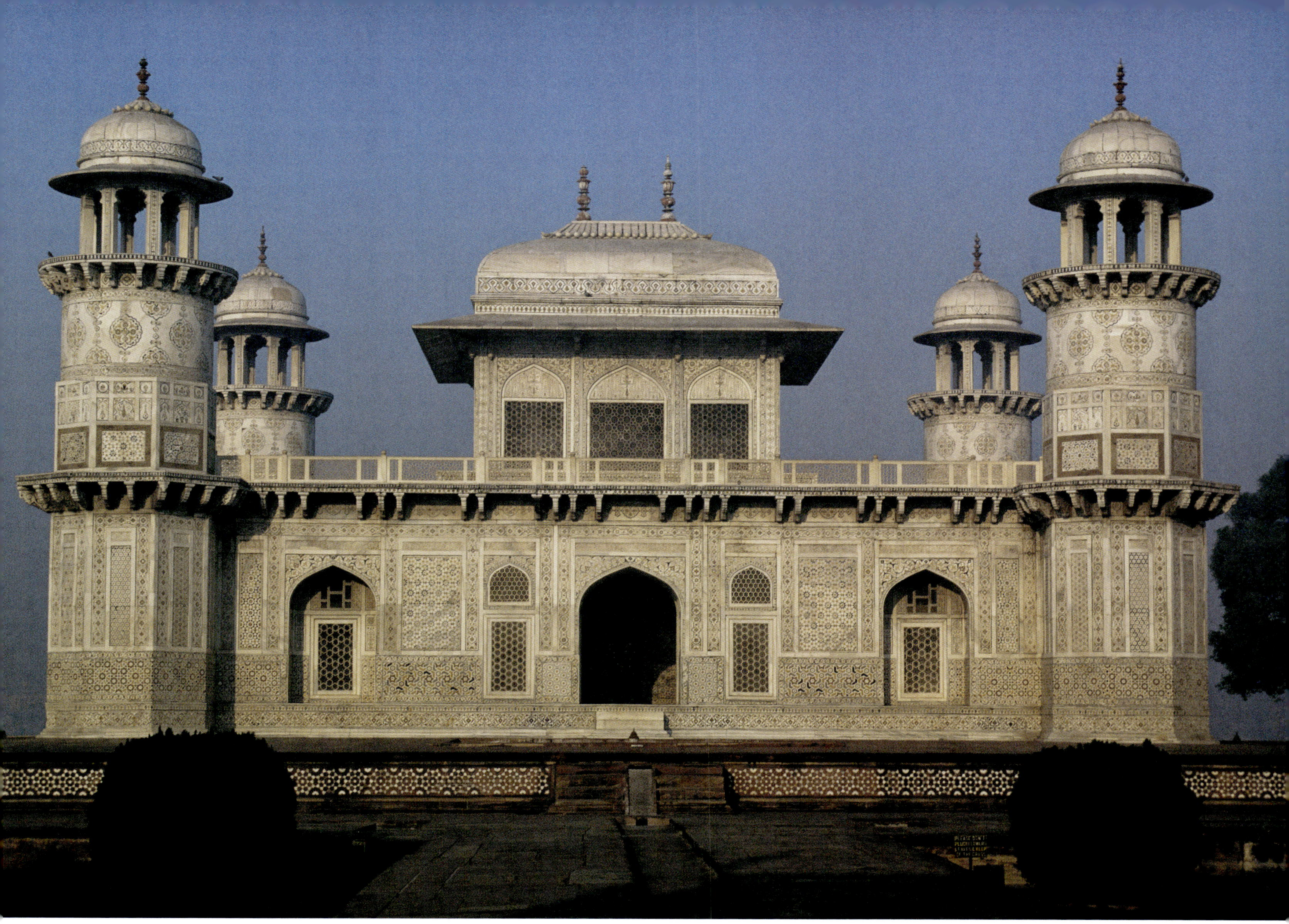

Mausoleum of Itimad ud-Dawla
1622–1628
Agra, India

The tomb rises at the centre of a perfect *chahar bagh* facing the River Yamuna, and gleams like a precious casket of dazzling and melancholy sweetness. It resembles an abode richly fortified with graceful decorations alluding to the delights of paradise. Four octagonal towers that look almost like minarets support an equal number of *chattri*. Although a certain dimensional inadequacy is evident in the relationship between the central feature and the corner ones, the magnificent building is at once both sumptuous and intimate, and inaugurated the best period of Mughal art. Inside, the mausoleum is plastered and painted, whereas the exterior is completely covered with *pietra dura,* composed into panels with geometrical and floral intarsia on a background of dazzling marble whiteness. The decorative scheme is the building's best feature.

Taj Mahal
Cross section and ground plan
1632–1654
Agra, India

The differences with regard to the preceding tradition of Mughal mausolea exceed the numerous points of similarity: the garden is accessed via a doorway that conceals the treasure inside to the last minute; the building stands at the back and not in the centre of the *chahar bagh,* enhancing its outline and multiplying the space in front; the usual podium terminates in minarets; and the internal octagonal room beneath the onion-shaped dome is enclosed by four smaller octagonal rooms on two levels. These are crowned by the associated *chattri,* an explicit borrowing from the Persian *hasht bihist* (eight paradises) model. The actual tomb, with a cenotaph on top, is located in the crypt, but since it remains visible from the upper floor, it also forms part of the domed space and thus of paradise.

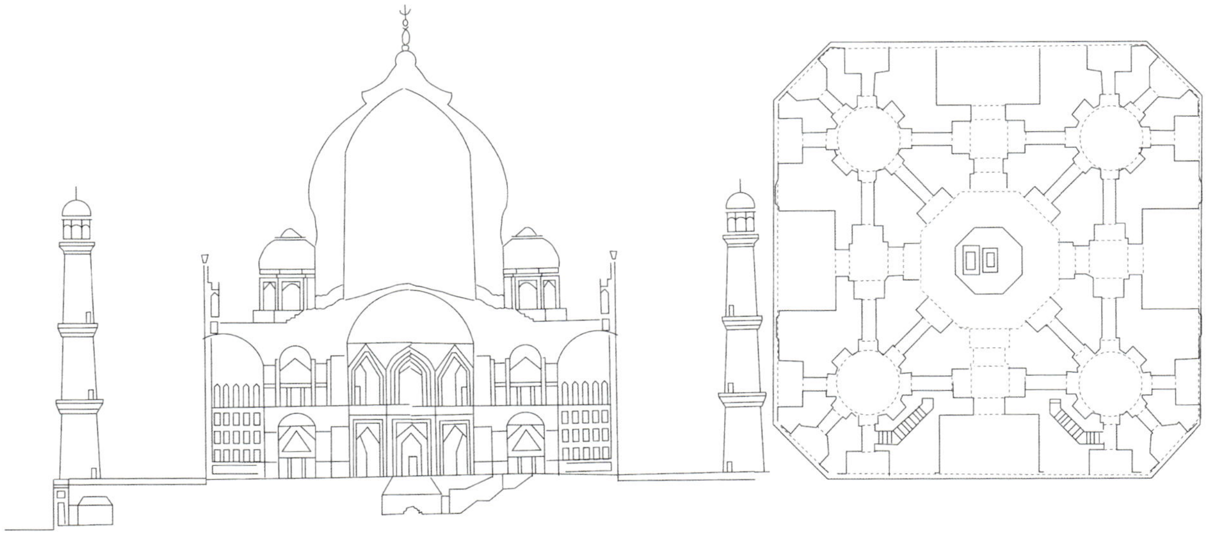

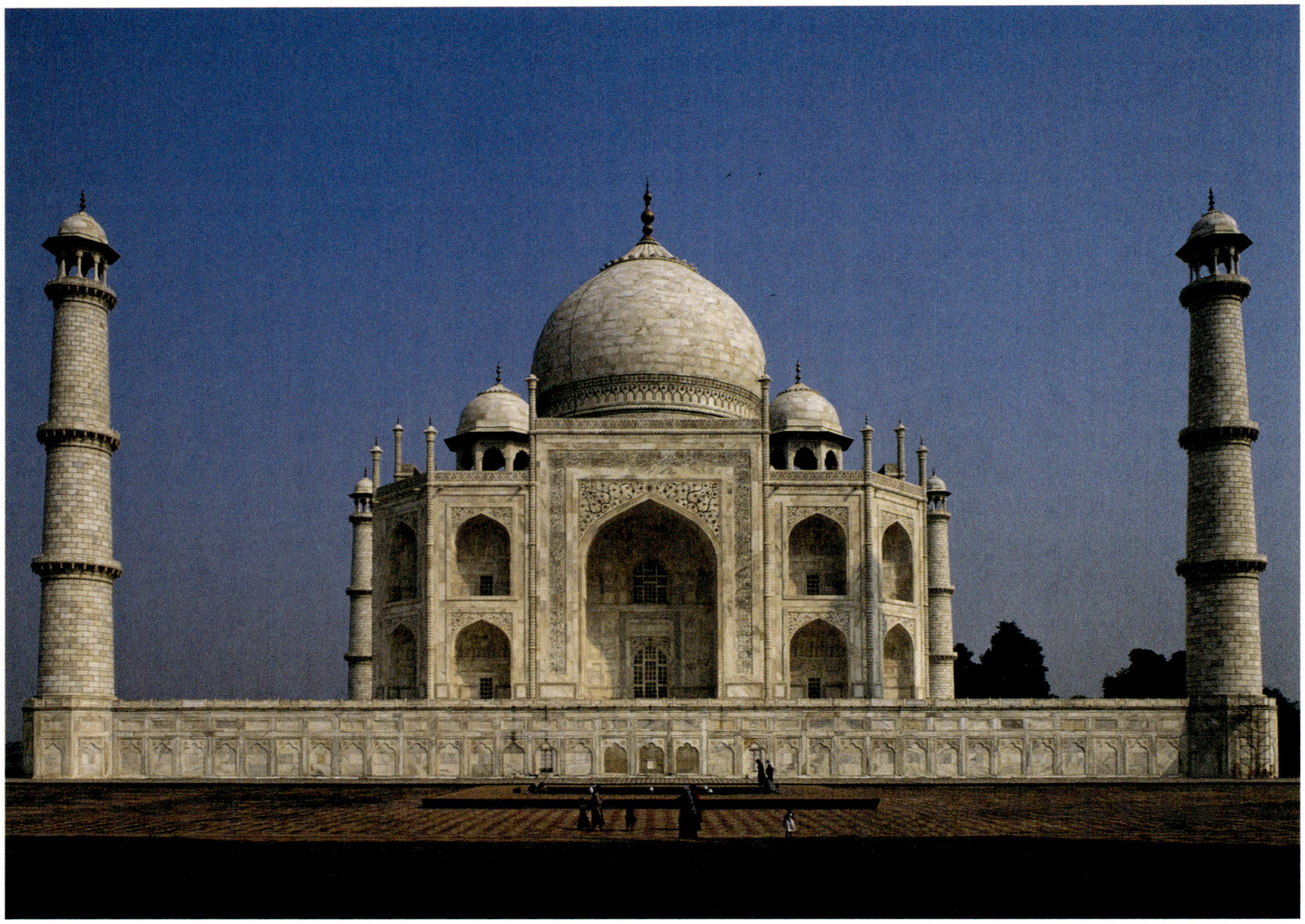

Taj Mahal
1632–1654
Agra, India

The mausoleum called the Taj Mahal ('Palace of the Crown') is, for better or for worse, iconic of the Mughal period. It was built by Shah Jahan for Mumtaz Mahal (the 'Chosen One' of the palace), his preferred wife, who died in childbirth in 1631 having borne him fourteen children. The inconsolable husband wrote: "The sight of this palace provokes sad sighs and brings tears to the eyes of the sun and the moon. This building was erected to show thereby the glory of the creator." The mausoleum rises as if by magic in the middle of a spectacular ensemble, perfectly framed by the four minarets. To emphasize its mirage-like appearance, which he contemplated dejectedly from the loggia of the Anghuri Bagh in his palace on the opposite bank of the river, Shah Jahan had it constructed entirely in white marble, so that the grain of the stone could assume constantly changing hues with variations in the light.

Taj Mahal
Central *iwan*
1632–1654
Agra, India

The central *iwan,* emphasized by the *pishtaq* or vaulted archway, is set slightly back behind the lower side structures, which have smaller openings and rotate to avoid right angles. This confers on the building a sense of infinity and diaphanousness that culminates in the dome. The proportions are sublimely harmonious. The marble that the whole ensemble is built with seems to incarnate the very essence of light, and the elegant but sober decoration introduces delicate vibrations of colour. While not lacking in monumental stature, the mausoleum breathes a unique enchantment, subtly nostalgic and, one would like to think, feminine. The luminousness of the marble, especially under the immense *iwans,* is carried over into luminousness of the shadow, effectively toning down any crude sculptural and therefore "natural" effect. This tends to heighten the intimately atmospheric nature of the whole light-filled building. The decorative richness of even the Mausoleum of Itimad ud-Dawla is surpassed here, thanks to a real understanding of the power of light inherent in the marble when projected into a dimension of unfathomable spirituality.

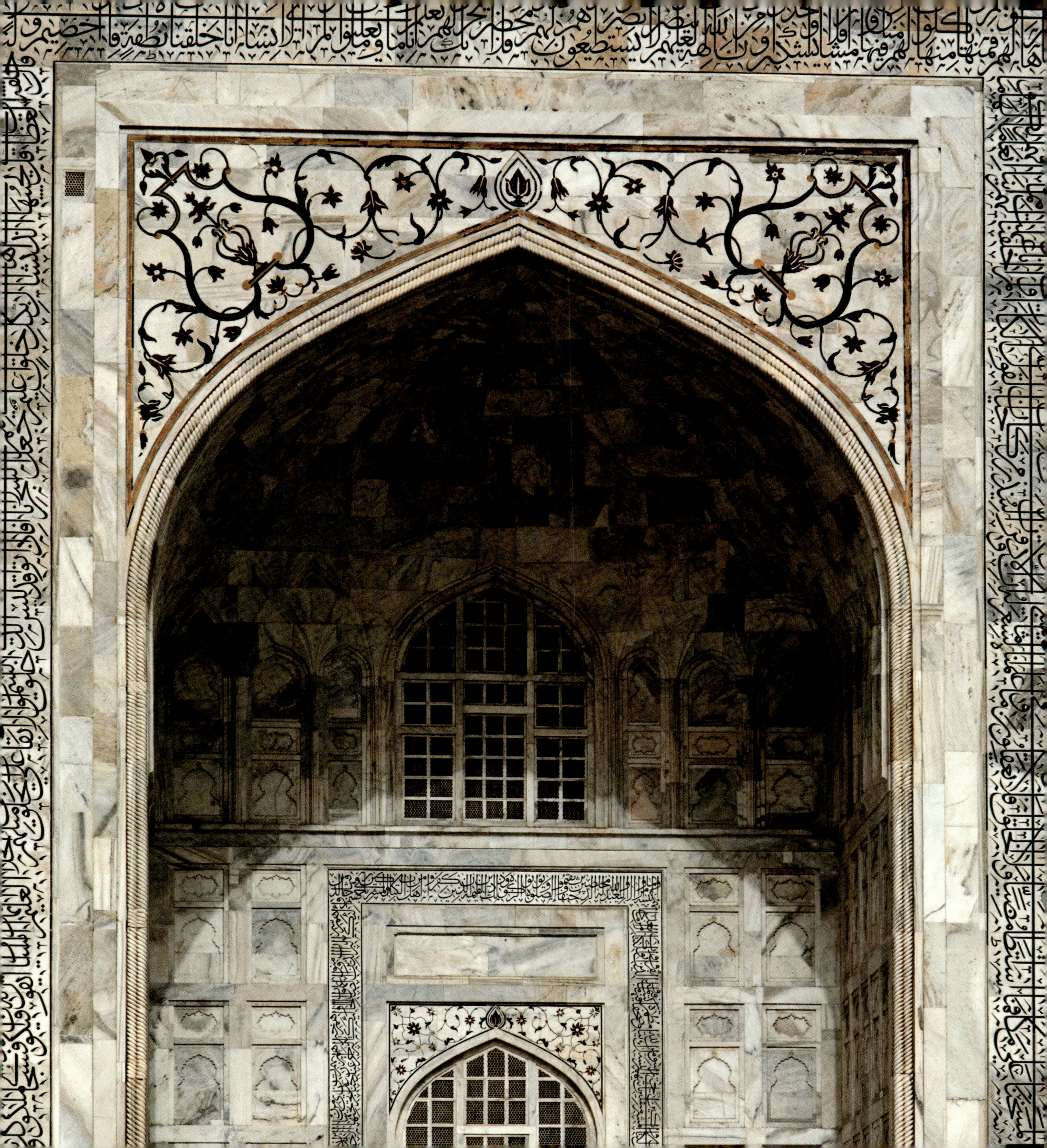

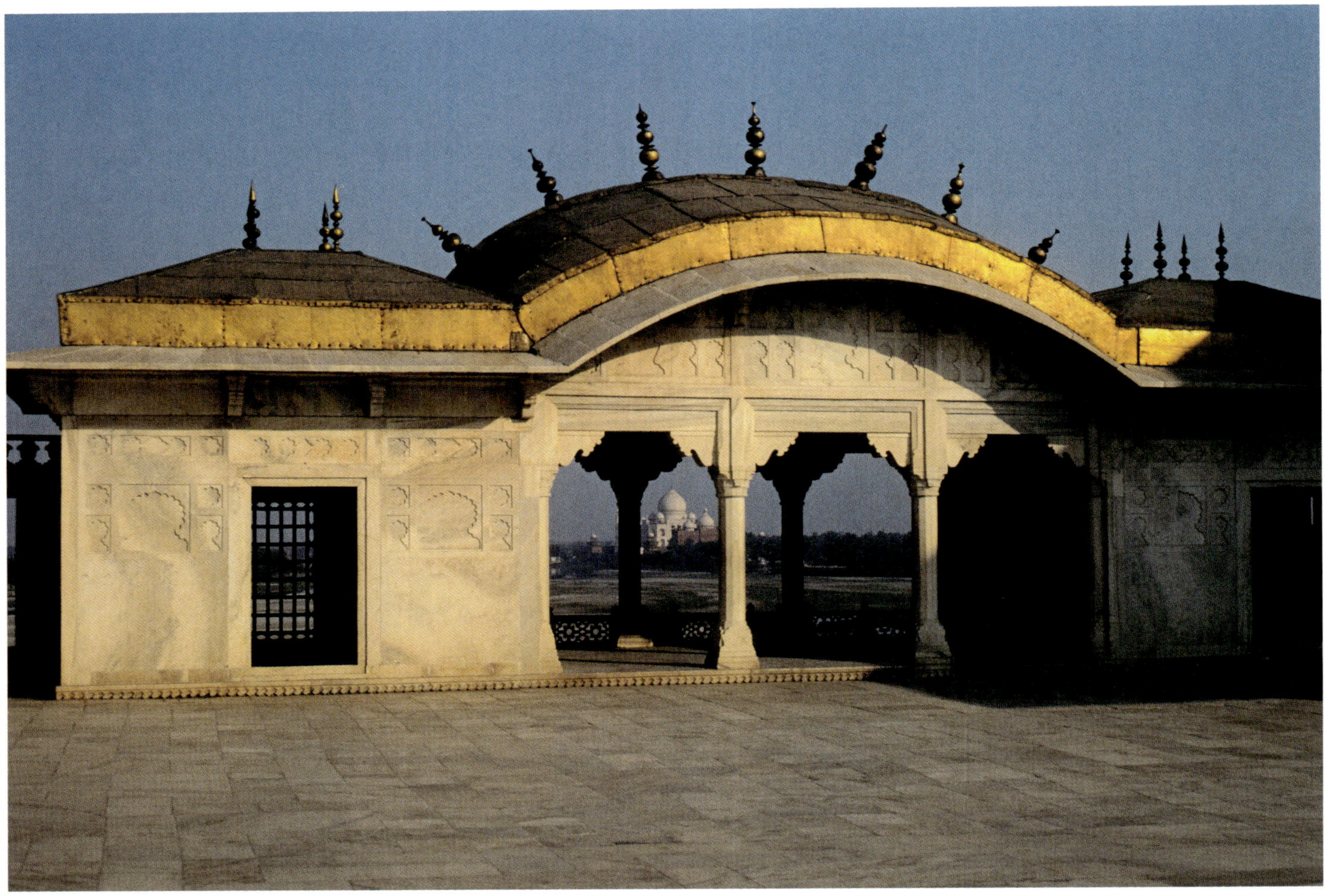

Anghuri Bagh in the Red Fort
1627–1648
Agra, India

The inconsolable Shah Jahan would gaze at the Taj Mahal, where his adored wife rested in death, from the loggia of the Anghuri Bagh. Built with tremendous skill using first-class materials, its formal inventiveness is tempered by a serene sense of proportion. Visible in the balanced blending of Islamic and Hindu motifs, they make this pavilion one of the most significant achievements of Mughal architecture. As in the contemporary Taj Mahal, the eclectic accumulation and combination of heterogeneous elements typical of Akbar's day seems a world away. Here they have been transfigured into an architectural vision of particular clarity and poetic imaginativeness.

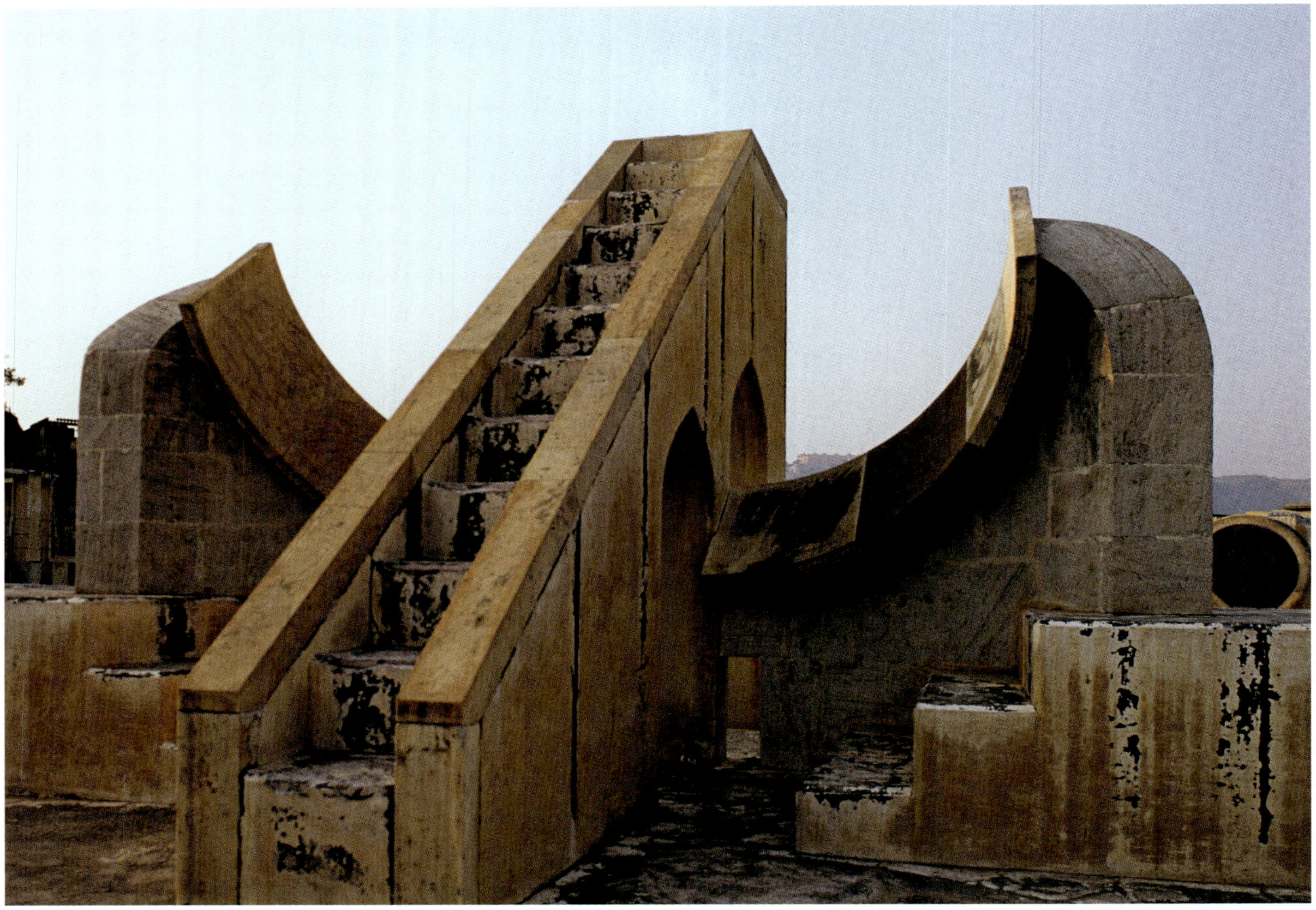

Jantar Mantar
Rashivalaya Yantra
('Calculus of the signs of the Zodiac')
1728
Jaipur, India

The Jantar Mantar is the largest and the most sophisticated of the five colossal astronomical observatories built by Rajah Jai Singh II, a Rajput prince and ally of the Mughal rulers. He was a great connoisseur of the astronomical studies of Ulugh Beg and a scholar of unquestioned authority. The name derives from Sanskrit *yantra mantra*, or "computational tool." Jai Singh II realised that the inaccuracies found in the existing astronomical tables were due to the modest size of the instruments used, and solved the problem by building enormous ones in stone, masonry and marble. The Rashivalaya Yantra ('Calculus of the signs of the Zodiac') was one of a group of twelve instruments, all very similar but with slightly different orientations. They had graduated quadrants on either side whose purpose was probably to determine the exact reckoning of celestial latitude and longitude. The ecliptic pole is not fixed but describes a circle of 23° 27" around the axis. Constructing twelve instruments allowed continuous observation by changing position every two hours or so.

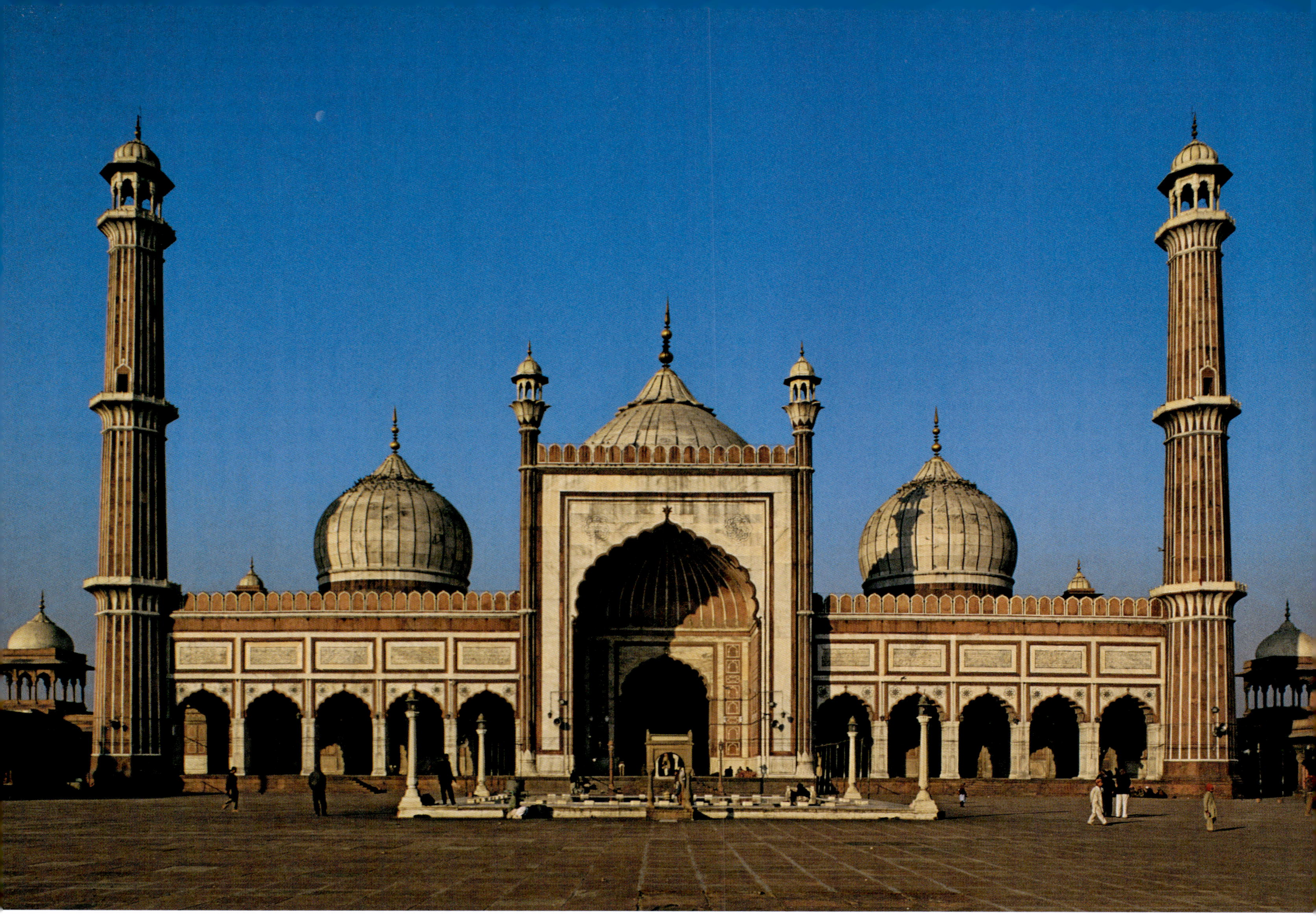

Jami Masjid (Friday mosque)
1650–1656
Delhi, India

In 1638, Shah Jahan abandoned Agra and spent the next twelve years building his new capital of Shahjahanabad, the seventh in the Delhi region. The Jami Masjid, built on a prominence dominating the city, displays a monumental façade towards a very wide arcaded courtyard. It is entered through huge doors crowned by characteristic kiosks at the four corners. The prayer hall is remarkable for its impressive dimensions, enhanced by the panache of the four-step minarets terminating in refined kiosks that echo those at the sides of the *iwan*. The three onion-shaped domes clad in white marble are set slightly back from the ten-arched arcade of the façade, in such a way as to avoid too great a proximity to the *pishtaq*. The broad recess of the latter seems to reflect in its shadow the dazzling light of the silhouette of the main dome, which disappears as it is approached. The restrained decoration sticks to the usual contrast between reddish sandstone and white marble, both externally and internally.

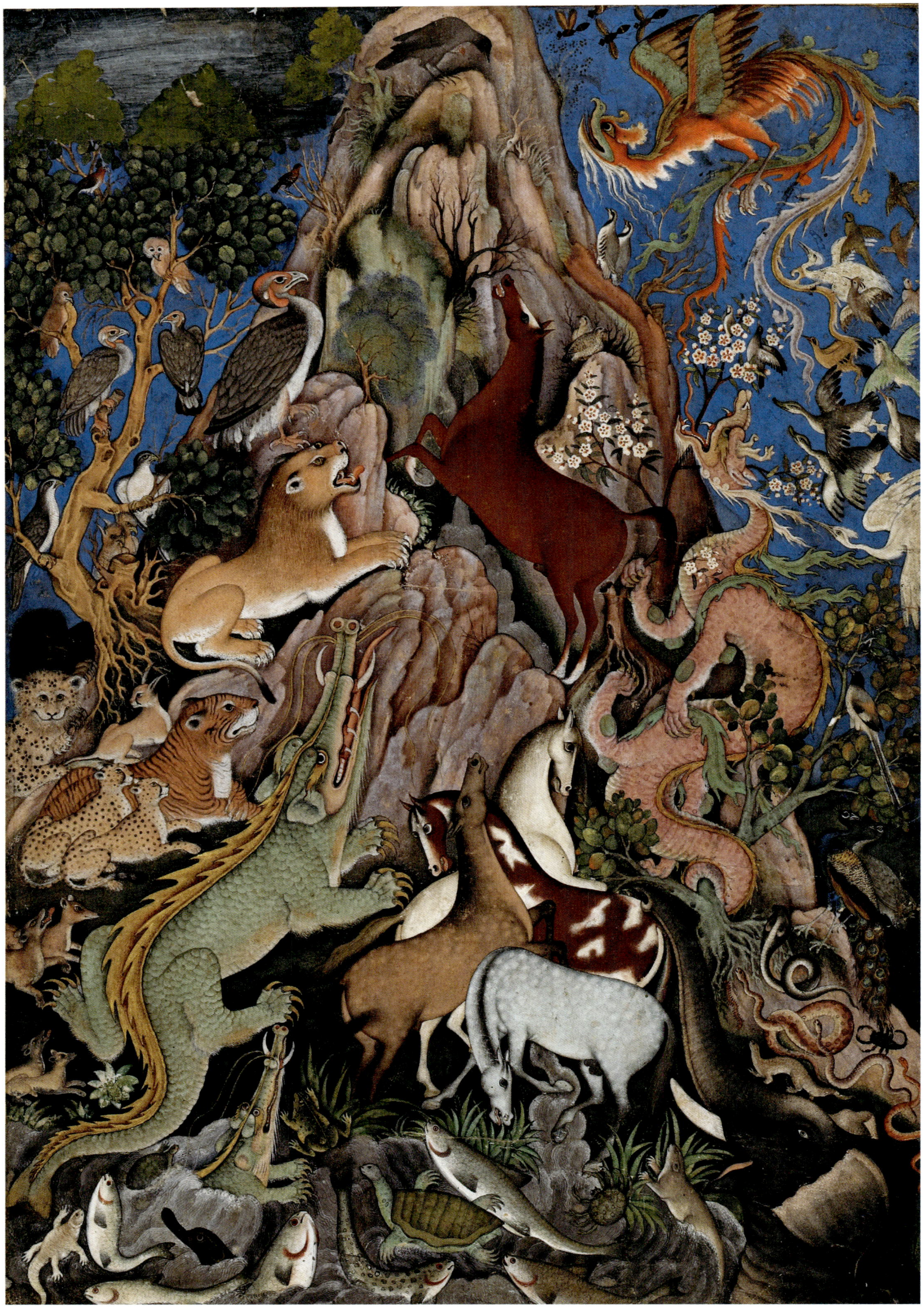

Miskin (attributed, 16th–17th centuries)
The Raven Addresses the Animals
c. 1600
Page of an album
Gouache on paper
British Library, London

The subject, drawn probably from *Sheref ü'l-insan* by Ottoman poet Lami-i Çelebi (d. 1538), illustrates the fable of the animals bewailing, through the voice of the raven, the poor treatment they receive from mankind. Another interpretation is the popular parable of the raven annoyed by the election of an owl as king of the animals. We see examples of a wondrous fauna thronging the steep slopes of a crag, emerging from the waves of the sea, slithering through the grass, crawling along the ground, crouching among the rocky peaks, perching in the trees, climbing up the crevices, clambering along the sheer rock face with the help of protruding branches, climbing the cliffs in a natural way or flying above them. Creatures both real and imaginary co-exist in the enchanted atmosphere: amphibians, fish, frogs, caymans, scorpions, serpents, turtles, peacocks, tigers, leopards, lions, vultures, cobras, mongooses, otters, lynxes, elephants, wolves, magpies, owls, cranes, falcons, quails, partridges, the red dragon with its luxuriant coils, wasps, the legendary *simurgh* with a shooting-star tail, and horses, horses of every colour in fact, with a superb bay neighing and launching itself at the raven at the very top. The emperor Akbar, who loved fables, commissioned a great number of such books for himself and for his son Jahangir. They were sumptuously illustrated by the finest painters in the country.

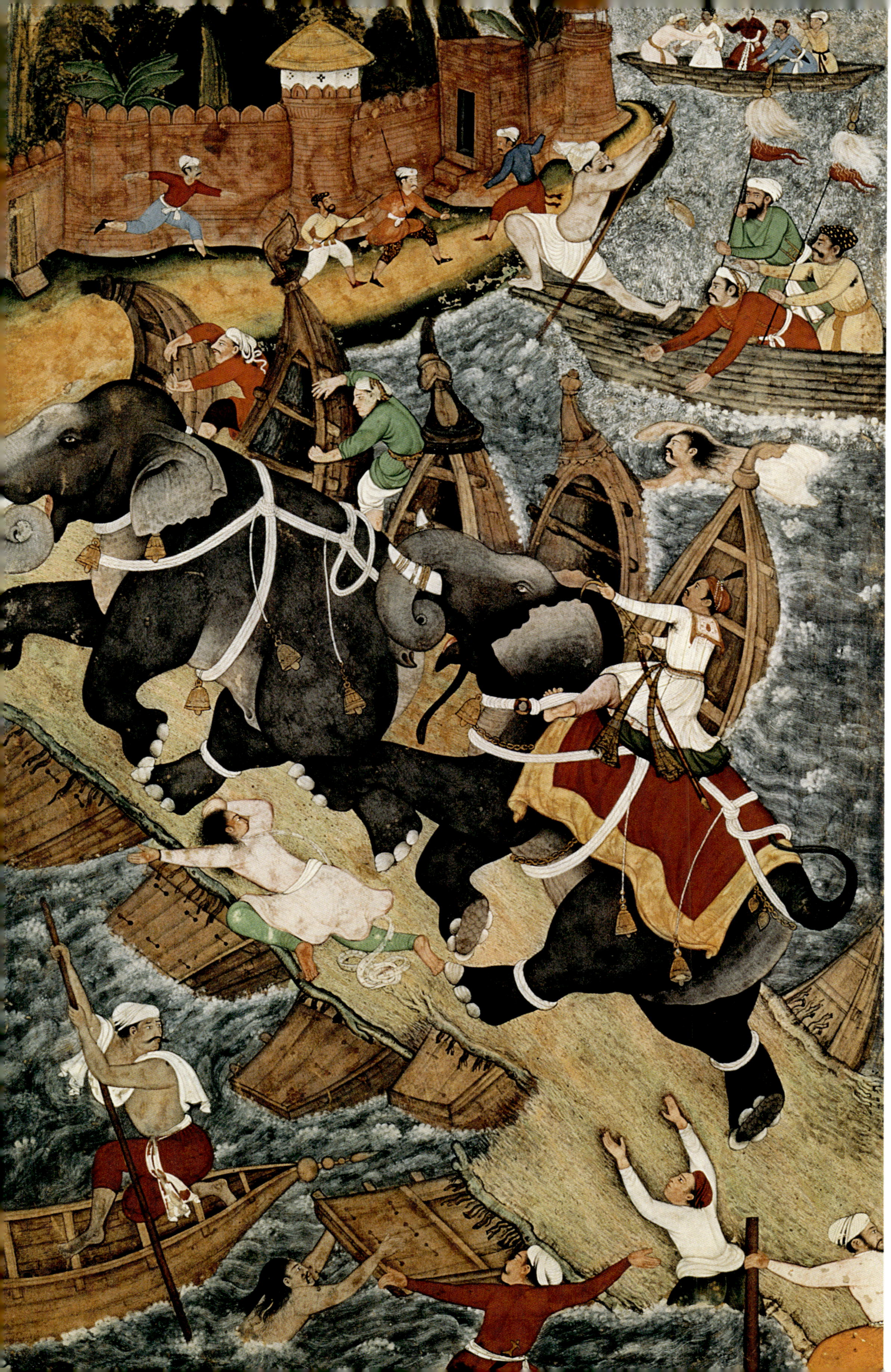

Akbar Tames the Wild Elephant Hawa'l in Front of the Red Fort in Agra
c. 1590
Gouache on paper
From *Akbarnameh* ('Book of Akbar')
by Abul Fazi
British Museum, London

Compared with the autobiographical memoirs written by Babur (*Baburnameh*, or 'Book of Babur'), which is full of personal notes, the *Akbarnameh* ('Book of Akbar') is a panegyric, recreating a fairly reliable picture of the life of the time. Splendidly illustrated with large miniatures of first-rate quality, it has reliable documentary value. Despite the large quantity of Safavid and Timurid manuscripts available to the court and the undeniable attraction which they must have had, and despite the Persian origin of their authors, the miniatures of the text owe very little to the illustrious central Asian pictorial tradition. In fact, they laid the foundations of an authentically Mughal style. Primary colours are used sparingly, a wide range of relatively muted intermediate tones being preferred. Figures are defined with great exactness and naturalism, the landscapes reveal a real grasp of spatial depth, and bodies show unprecedented attention to three-dimensional effects – all clear indications of a fruitful rapport with European painting.

Wine cup of Shah Jahan
1656–1657
White nephrite
Victoria & Albert Museum, London

During his reign, Shah Jahan commissioned works of the highest quality in every field, almost always revealing a happy assimilation of cultural elements from different traditions. Once they had shaken off the eclecticism that in one way or another remained strongly evident in preceding works, objets d'art also reflected the maturing of the Mughal idiom.
This diaphanous and elegant cup bears the date and the emperor's ostentatious title. The exquisite artefact, surely the best of the stone works to come out of the Mughal workshops, stands out for its exceptional assurance of form and impeccable execution. Its shape (a fruit or pumpkin cut in half) shows Chinese influence, the handle ending in the head of a goat, acanthus leaves and protruding base are European-style, and the lotus flower belongs to the Indian repertoire. Nevertheless, the marked naturalism and fusion of disparate elements in a shape of compelling sensitivity are a product of the best Mughal art.

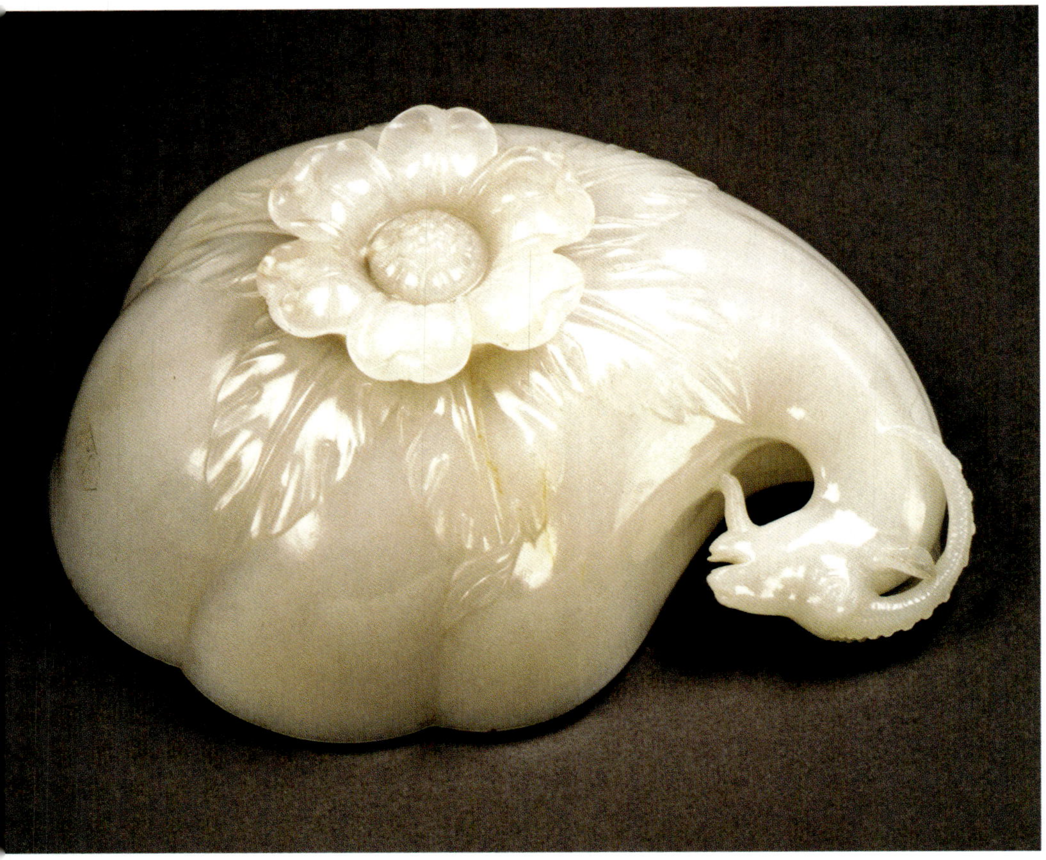

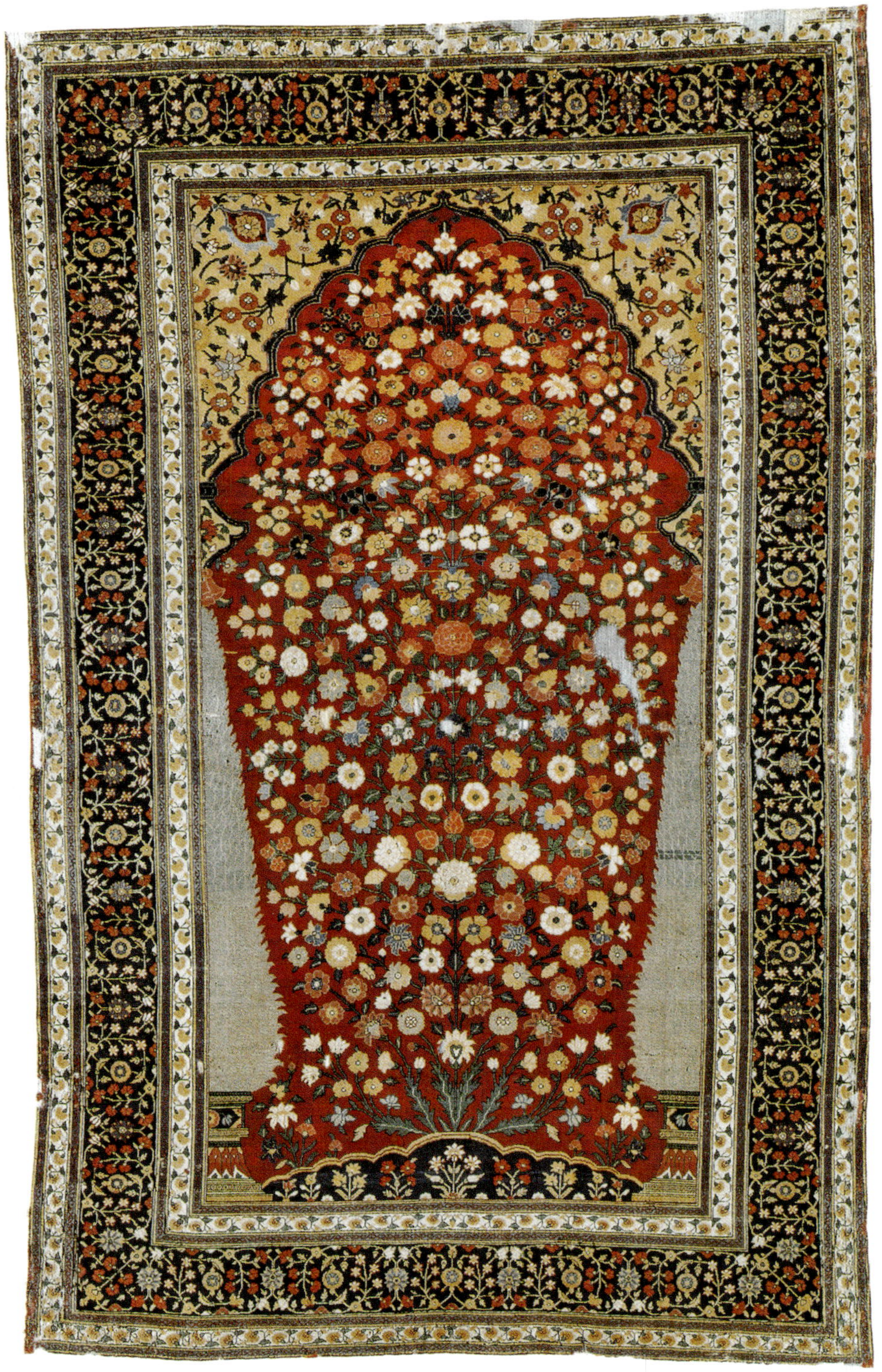

Mille-fleurs carpet
18th century
India
Österreichisches Museum für Angewandte Kunst, Vienna

The creativity of Mughal carpet designs, very different from the "schools" that characterized those produced in other Islamic countries, finds expression in great freedom in the choice of subjects, especially the background composition. The piece illustrated, which belongs to a group of carpets known as "mille-fleurs," has a central area framed by a large shaped niche. This is a type of design that reproduces a traditional arrangement at the sides of doors and is almost a foreshortened image of the architecture of a palace garden. The more central area is adorned by a dense collection of flower petals against a magnificent monochrome background.

Carpet with figures
16th century
Österreichisches Museum für Angewandte Kunst, Vienna

Mughal carpets were characterized by a fondness for reproducing animals and plants, and only rarely show figures. Like classical Persian-style carpets of the chase, these even more exquisitely decorated carpets feature flowers and animals. Real and fantastic beasts (dragons and phoenixes among them) move with a whimsical sense of composition in the main space, while trees and bushes complete the design. This carpet with figures in Vienna represents a paradise garden: though the subject clearly comes from Persian iconography, the way it is elaborated is completely Mughal. The deep rose-coloured central area is entirely occupied by trees with richly flowering foliage, placed at different levels in a fashion unfettered by the rigid criteria of geometrical order. Numerous birds drawn with naturalistic enthusiasm move freely around among them. The remaining spaces are filled with tiny shrubs and flowers, so that no space is left empty. The prominent border on the other hand is divided into concentric elements, unfolding in a majestic though quite regular floral pattern.

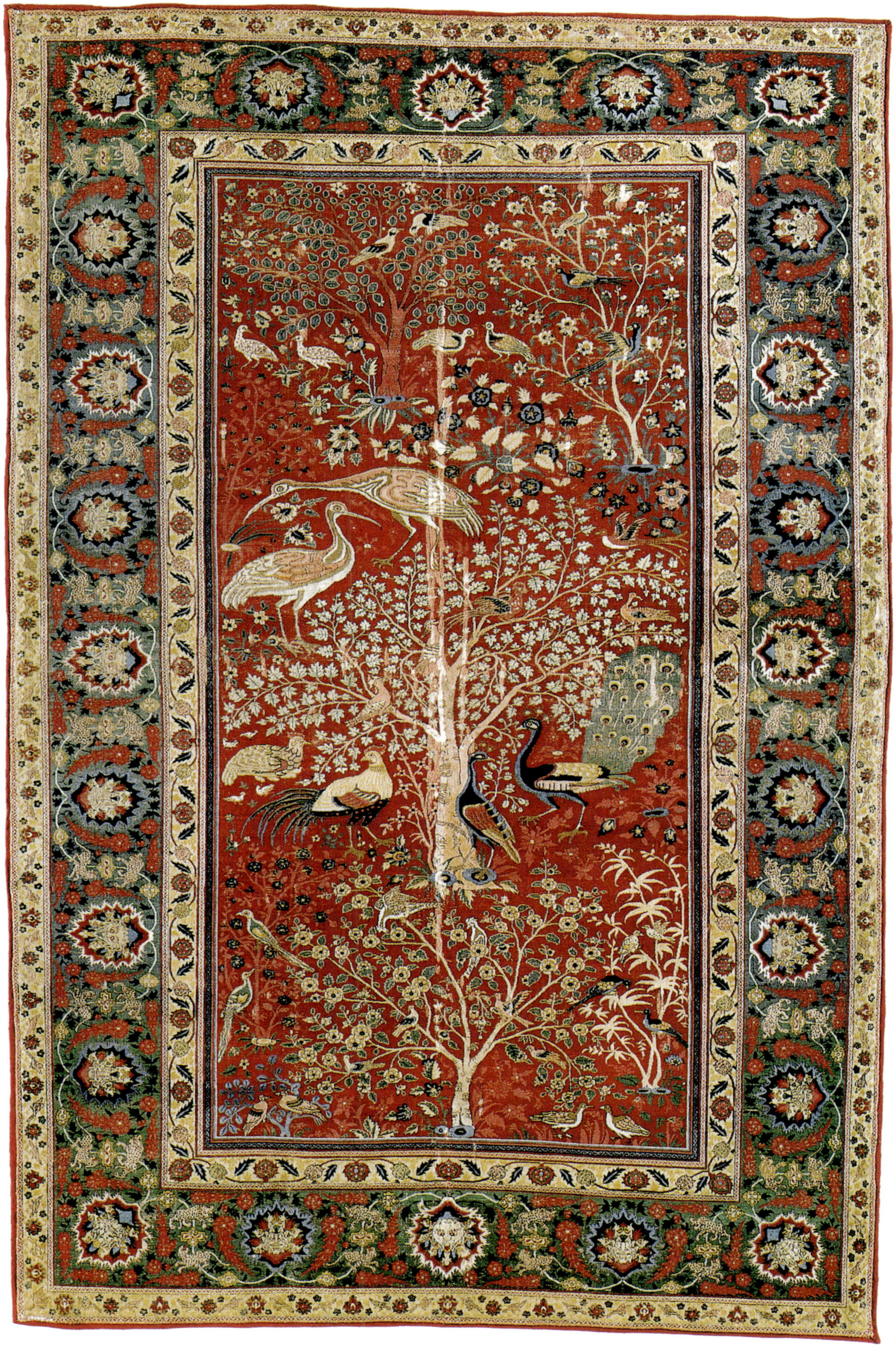

GLOSSARY

A. Arabic
P. Persian
T. Turkish
S. Sanskrit

Abacus Block on a square base constituting the upper member of a capital and supporting the architrave.
Abd (A.) 'Servant', 'slave'. The term often appears at the beginning of composed names of persons where the second part is one of the ninety-nine names of Allah (for example, Abd al-Rahman, 'Servant of the Merciful').
Acropolis (Greek) 'Upper town', elevated, often fortified zone of a city, containing the most important buildings.
Agha (A.) Title borne by officials commanding one or other of the armed forces.
Alcove (from the Arabic *al-qubba*) Blind recess opening into a space.
Alfiz (Spanish, from the Arabic *al-fash*) Rectangular frame round an arch.
Anthropomorphic Of human appearance (of an ornament).
Apodyterium (Greek) Changing-room in a Greek gymnasium; the vestibule constituting the first room in a Roman thermal bath.
Apotropaic Gesture, rite, figure or object designed to ward off bad luck or evil spells.
Apse Generally, a vaulted semicircular or polygonal niche crowned by a half-dome.
Arabesque Repeated ornament of stylized floral or geometric motifs created in the Hellenistic age. Abstract and iterative, it was exceptionally widespread in Islamic decoration, where it was deployed in ordered, geometric patterns.
Arcade A series of arches on columns or pillars. In Umayyad architecture it was called a *riwak* when encircling a *sahn* (qv.) but see *riwak*.
Arch Vaulted structure that supports the weight of an opening in a wall discharging it on to pillars or columns. The summit is closed by a keystone. The curving lower surface is called the intrados, the upper part the extrados. The (curving) triangles between the arch and the adjacent surfaces are known as spandrels. The shape of an arch is generated by a semicircle or by segments of a circle composing it. The round or semicircular arch is borne on a semicircle. The horseshoe arch is composed of a segment of a three-quarter circle supported over a rectangular base. The keel-arch starts out as a circular segment with the centre inside, before the curve turns in the opposite direction, i.e. with a centre to the outside, thereby forming a kind of 'S'; it culminates in a tip. The drop arch is formed of two circular segments, lowered and ending in a point. The ogive or ogival (Gothic) arch tapers inwards towards the apex, its outline being determined by two intersecting equilateral semicircular segments. A multifoil or polybate arch is composed of the intersection of a number of (small) semicircular segments.
Architrave Lower section of the entablature immediately above the capitals on the columns. It supports the structure (often a pediment) above.
Archivolt Arch functioning as an architrave round an opening.
Arg (P.) Citadel, fortress (in Turkish, *ark*).
Arianism Christian doctrine professed by the Alexandrian prelate Arian (256–336) and condemned as heretical at a synod in Alexandria in 320, and again at the Council of Nicaea in 325. It denies the consubstantiality of the Father, Son and Holy Ghost as God, and in consequence rejects the notion of the perfectly divine nature of Jesus Christ.
Atabeg, atabey (T.) Aristocratic title in Turkic lands.
Atrium In Palaeo-Christian churches, the court preceding the narthex (qv.).
Azulejo (Spanish, from the Arabic *az-zuallij*). Tin-enamelled ceramic tile.

Bagh (P.) Garden.
Baradari (P.) From twelve doors; pavilion with tripartite archway or colonnade to each side; summerhouse.
Baraka Benediction, good fortune, favourable destiny emanating from a sacred place or from near the tomb of an important personage. One of the major benefits sought by pilgrims.
Bazaar (P.) Economic district of a city.
Bedesten (T.) Covered market characteristic of Turkish architecture and urban planning. Used for selling valuable merchandise, its gates would be shut at night.
Berber Collective term for various peoples in North Africa of probable Mediterranean origin who all speak the Berber language.
Betyl Sacred stone considered by the Semites as a dwelling-place of God or worshipped as an idol.
Bey (T.) Turkish title meaning 'gentleman'. From old Turkish, *beg*, synonym of the Arabic 'emir'.
Beylicate (T.) Sovereign jurisdiction of a *bey*.
Beyt Dwelling or apartment in a palace.

Cadi Judge, magistrate whose function it is to apply religious edicts (v. Shari'a).
Calidarium The warmest room in Roman *thermae* intended for hot baths.
Caliph (A.) From *al-Khalifa*, meaning 'successor', 'representative'. According to the Sunnites this is the successor of the Prophet, but already in the Umayyad era caliphs considered themselves the "shadow of God on earth." The problem of the succession of the Prophet, who left no stipulations on the subject, has created deep splits in the Islamic world, principally between Shias and Sunnis (qv.). The first four are called the Rightly Guided Caliphs (qv. in the section on Islamic Dynasties)
Calligraphy Writing in any of the various scripts codified and invented over the course of time is considered the supreme art, almost on a par with prayer in that it endows the divine word revealed in the Qur'an with a perfect form. The main scripts are the Kufic (qv.), *naskh* (qv.) and *thuluth* (qv.).
Cami (pronounced 'jami') (T.) Mosque.
Capital Upper section of a column or pillar that acts as a transition between the barrel and the architrave.
Caravanserai Term of Persian origin designating an inn. Caravanserais are stopping-places along routes taken by camel trains placed at regular intervals of one day's march. In cities, these buildings can possess additional, commercial functions. Organized around a central courtyard, the ground floor is divided into warehouses, while the upper storey provides lodgings for the merchants, usually outsiders, who stay over while selling their goods.
Cenotaph Funerary monument containing no corpse.
Chaharbagh (P.) 'Four-fold garden', a garden subdivided in four (or more) parts by water channels.
Chahartaq (P.) Structure of square plan with four arches to the sides, vaulted by a central dome.
Chajja (S.) Projecting stone eaves.
Chattri (S.) Domed kiosk.
Church (types of plan) The two most frequent plan types in the Palaeo-Christian era were the basilican and the central, both adopted by the Byzantines and adapted to the requirements of their liturgy. The basilican plan results in a church of vast proportions, preceded by an entrance hall and narthex, with three or five aisles and a longitudinal axis leading the eye to the apse. The central plan generates a church covered at the centre by a vast masonry cupola, thus emphasising the building's vertical thrust. Liturgical demands soon led to the addition of an apse at the east. The domed basilica arose from the combination of these two types and predominated from the 6th to 10th centuries. A third type, the Greek cross, was born in the 9th century and became characteristic of the Byzantine age. The plan possesses four arms of equal length, with a dome rising on a polygonal drum at the crossing.
Citadel Fortification constructed in the best protected quarter of a city comprising buildings such as the most important residences and services ringed by a wall erected within the one encircling the city.
Coptic (from the Arabic-Egyptian *qubt*, adaptation of the word 'Copt' – language spoken in Egypt until the 16th century – that is, *gyptios*, from the Greek *aighyptios*, 'Egyptian') Term designating the Monophysite Christians of Egypt and Ethiopia and the art they produce.
Cuerda seca (Spanish, 'dry yarn') Technique for enamelling ceramics, in which various parts of the multicoloured design are separated by lines of powdered manganese dioxide mixed with a greasy adhesive. On firing, these lines remain blackish in hue.

Dar al-Imara Princely palace or government building.
Darusshifa (T.) Hospital.
Dervish (P.) Mendicant, Sufi. The term designates adepts of Islamic confraternities (*tariqa*) that live in poverty under the guide of a *shaykh* and who strive, through spiritual discipline, to reduce their dependence on the body and so free the spirit. During mystical ceremonies, the adepts of some orders indulge in special practices with music and dance, falling into a trance and entering into communication with the irrational.
Diwan, divan A collection of poems; also the muster roll registry listing the members of the army at the beginning of the Islamic period. Hall, particularly one with administrative or governmental functions.

Emir Commander, governor. *De facto* caliph or monarch.

Firman (T.) Word of Persian derivation that designates a decree promulgated by the Ottoman sultan.
Foggara Underground draining conduit with a regular slope, with holes for inspecting and cleaning the culvert. It corresponds to the Persian *khanat*.
Fresco Wall-painting applied to a ground that is still moist.
Frieze In architecture, a continuous decorative band, made in any of various materials, generally affixed to a wall.
Frigidarium The cool room in Roman bathhouse.
Funduq Inn.

Ghazi Warrior who combats the infidel.
Gunbad (P.) Dome and, by extension, tomb.

Hadith Story, narrative incorporating sayings or deeds of Muhammad (qv.), the Sunnah, transmitted orally by the Companions of the Prophet and written down after his death. They possess legal value.
Hajj (A.) Pilgrimage to Mecca. Pilgrimage, not just to Mecca, is one of the five duties of Islam and the *hajj* is obligatory at least once in the lifetime of every Muslim who is financially and physically able to do so. It can be made at any time of the year, but is considered of greater value when performed in the allotted month. A pilgrimage can last anything from ten to twenty days, during the course of which the pilgrim, wearing an *ihram*, a garment lacking seams, walks seven times around the Ka'ba (qv.), kissing or touching the black stone, taking part in processions and completing a series of ritual visits to holy sites in Mecca (qv.) and Medina (qv.). A *Hâjj* is someone who has completed the pilgrimage to Mecca.
Hammam (from A., 'to heat') Public or private bathhouse typical of the Islamic world and based on Hellenistic-Roman *thermae*.
Han, khan (P.) Caravanserai, typical Turkish inn for travellers and merchants with storehouses and quarters for spending the night.
Harem (from the Arabic *harim* 'inviolable place') In the Islamic world, it designates the room(s) in the house reserved for women and children; the only males who can enter are members of the same family.

Hegira (from the Arabic *hijra* 'emigration') On 16 July 622, Muhammad (qv.), faced with hostility to his preaching in Mecca, left the city with his followers and took shelter at the oasis of Yatrib, the future Medina (qv.). This date marks the beginning of the Islamic era.
Hutba Predication delivered in the mosque during Friday prayers.
Hypostyle Edifice, or space therein, supported on columns.

Iconoclasm Doctrine opposed to the cult of religious imagery (in the Byzantine tradition, icons reflected the glory of the divine being and were not simply an aid to prayer or an intermediary). It resulted in the emperors of Constantinople entering into direct conflict with the Church of Rome, that rejected the interdicts against them. The controversy, which was sparked in 726, concluded in 843 when Empress Theodora reinstituted their veneration.
Ijma (A.) 'Consent' of the community of believers called to deliberate on an issue that cannot be resolved by recourse to the Qur'an (qv.) or *ahadith* (v. *hadith*).
Imam (A.) Broadly speaking, he who guides, in various ways, believers in Islam in the ways of Allah. The term is also used to designate those who, well-acquainted with the Qur'an in the madrasah (qv.), lead collective prayers in the mosque. For the Shias, he is also head of the community.
Imaret (A.) Hostel catering for the poor. One of a number of devout foundations surrounding some mosques.
Islam is based on five fundamental duties or obligations, known as 'Pillars': the profession of faith, which consists in declaiming a formula (qv. *shahada*) in various circumstances (conversion to Islam, prayer, dying words); prayer (v. *salat*); fasting (*sawn*) in the month of Ramadhan (qv.); obligatory almsgiving (v. *zakat*); the pilgrimage (qv. *hajj*) to Mecca (qv.). The prescriptions of the religion are taken from the Qur'an and other sources. Interdicts include lending at interest (usury), apostasy, murder, theft, insulting the Prophet, adultery, gambling, fornication, acts against nature, slander, drinking alcoholic beverages and eating pork (and also horse and ass meat), as well as the practice of black magic. Although the punishments in the Qur'an for theft and murder were those of the *lex talionis*, the same source also advocates forgiveness. As many as four spouses can be legally wedded and, although repudiation is permitted. it is discouraged. Other traditional customs were not explicitly formulated in the Qur'an, such as circumcision and, for women, seclusion in the *harem* and wearing the veil.
Islamic calendar Employed for religious purposes, it is based on a lunar year of 354 or 355 days: each year starts ten or eleven days before the Gregorian. The month begins on the appearance of the first crescent moon and the twelve months vary in length between twenty-nine and thirty days. The Islamic lunar cycle is completed in thirty years, with nineteen of 354 and eleven of 355 days. The duration of the day is reckoned from one sunset to the next and is uniformly divided into two halves of twelve hours. The day is then subdivided into five unequal parts, each occasioning a ritual prayer. The Islamic calendar as a whole started with the Hegira (qv.).
Isma'ilis Branch of Shiism (qv.).
Iwan or ***ivan*** (also ***liwan***) (P.) Vaulted space opening onto a courtyard. If lofty and jutting beyond the height of the wall, it is known as a *pishtaq* (qv.).

Jali (S.) Fretted, openwork stone grating.
Jami (A.) Meaning 'Friday'. *Masjid-i jami:* a mosque where daily and Friday prayers are held.
Janissaries Special body of Ottoman infantry commanded directly by the sultan instituted in the 14th century. Later becoming a kind of Praetorian Guard, they were brutally suppressed in 1826.
Jarokha (S.) Small overhanging covered balcony.
Jihad Inner personal battle or physical combat with the aim of attaining moral perfection. Hence, holy war against the infidel.

Ka'ba Pre-Islamic sanctuary of cubic shape situated at Mecca (qv.) that is thought to have been founded by Abraham. As well as the meteorite known as the 'black stone' numerous idols were once venerated there that Muhammad destroyed. For more than a millennium it has constituted the chief destination for Islamic pilgrimage (qv. *hajj*), during which believers must walk round the construction seven times.
Kasbah (A.) Citadel, fortified building in the cities of the Maghreb.
Khan (T.) Nobiliary title.
Khanah (P.) House, room.
Khanaqah (P.) Monastery for Islamic mystics located in an isolated spot and usually combined with a mosque.
Khanate (T.) Territory governed by a khan.
Kharijites (from the Arabic, 'those who turned away') Political-religious movement born in the aftermath of the arbitration on Ali's position. Considering his abdication as degrading to the dignity of the office (657), their followers believed that the caliph should be elected by part of the community. Entering into open rebellion, they were defeated by Ali in 658, but their ideas continue to inform some politically egalitarian stands of Islam.
Khorasan (also **Horasan** and **Khurasan**) Region in northwest Iran and the adjacent areas of what is today Afghanistan, Uzbekistan, Turkmenistan and Tajikistan.
Kosh (P.) Two connected foreparts in a structure.
Kösk (T.) Kiosk, small aedicule or pavilion often erected at the centre of a garden, generally with a domed roof supported on columns.
Kufic The most ancient type of Arabic calligraphy, originating in the city of Kufa in Iraq. It employs straight, angular characters which, depending on the variant, are enriched with geometric or vegetal interlace (knotted or floral Kufic).
Külliye (T.) Ensemble of buildings constituting a sacred complex around a mosque: madrasah, *imaret*, hammam, *türbe*, *shifahane* (qv.).
Kümbet (T.) Mausoleum typical of Central Asian cultures, made up of a crypt in which the body of the deceased is placed, and an element above, cylindrical or polygonal in form, terminating in a conical or pyramidal roof.

Lantern Open structure placed at the summit of a cupola to allow in the light.
Lesene Vertical ornamental strip on a wall.

Madrasah Public establishment originally for all types of education but later concentrating mainly on Islamic theology and law. Hence, centre for advanced education in Islam.
Mahal (P.) Palace.
Mahdi Messianic figure in the Islamic religion, taken up especially among the Shias; a member of the Prophet's family (for example, Ali, or one of his sons) who did not die, but remains hidden and destined to return to earth to impose justice.
Majolica Type of porous ceramic coated with a tin-based white glaze.
Mamluk Originally, slave or manumitted slave employed in the army.
Maqsura Area of the mosque reserved for high-ranking personages, usually cordoned off by a grille or a curtain, and occasionally covered by a dome.
Mardana (P.) Quarters in a palace solely for males.
Maristan (A.) Hospital forming part of a complex of devout foundations associated with the larger mosques.
Martyrion (Greek) In religious architecture, Byzantine crypt containing the remains or relics of a saint, over which a mausoleum-cum-church may be erected.
Masjid (A.) Mosque in which prayers are celebrated every day.
Mazdaism Religion founded by Zoroaster (Zarathustra; Balkh?, 7th century BCE?). The name derives from the supreme beneficial divinity, Ahura Mazda ('Wise Lord'), whose opposite number is Ahriman ('Evil Spirit'). Based on a sacred text, the *Avesta,* Mazdaism remained dominant throughout the Persian region from the Achaemenid to the Sassanid period, when it was elevated to the status of a state religion. Following the Arab invasions it almost vanished.
Mecca City in western Saudi Arabia, an important trading centre and a stopover on the caravan route connecting Yemen to Syria. It is considered the first holy city in Islam, since the Prophet was born and lived there before moving to Medina. It is the site of the Ka'ba (qv.). All mosques in the Islamic world are oriented towards Mecca and worshippers must face it when at worship.
Medina (in Arabic, *madina*, 'city') The second holy city in Islam, after Mecca (qv.). Prior to the Islamic period, it was a small Arab oasis called Yatrib (today in Saudi Arabia); later it became Madinat al-Nabi, 'the City of the Prophet', when the latter moved there after encountering difficulties in Mecca.
Mesçit (T.) Small mosque (from the Arabic, *masjid*).
Mihrab (A.) In a mosque, a niche set in the direction of Mecca, the *qibla* (qv.), towards which Muslims face in order to pray.
Minaret Tower standing next to a mosque from which the muezzin (qv.) calls the faithful to prayer.
Minbar (A.) In a mosque, pulpit composed of a staircase surmounted by a throne, from the summit of which the *hutba* (qv.) is pronounced.
Mo'arraq (A.) Mosaic technique consisting in cutting up glazed ceramic tiles, each of a single colour, arranging them in patterns and then often assembling them in panels. The term probably derives from the word for vine-shoot.
Monophysitism Heterodox Christian doctrine that arose in the 5th century. It recognizes solely the divine nature of Christ, denying His humanity.
***Moriscos,* Moors** Term designating the Muslims who were forcibly converted to Christianity following the Reconquista (though in secret they often kept their former religion) and the artistic style they adopted.
Mosaic Decorative cladding composed of fragments of marble or stone *tesserae* in various colours (subsequently replaced by glass paste) cemented to a base to form a pavement or, above all in the Byzantine period, a panel of wall decoration. The oldest Greek mosaics (5th–4th centuries BCE) were composed out of pebbles and the use of true *tesserae* appears only in the Hellenistic period. Mosaics became extremely popular in the Roman imperial era and reached their acme in the Byzantine period.
Mosque (from the Arabic *masjid* 'place of prostration') Generic name for a place of prayer composed essentially of a prayer hall containing a *mihrab* (qv.) and *minbar* (qv.). The congregational type is called a *masjid-i jam*. The Arab mosque was originally a simple hypostyle hall, while in Persia it conformed to a cruciform system with four *iwans* placed around a courtyard. The Seljuq mosque combines these two typologies while the Ottoman variant was a single hall roofed by a great dome and preceded by an open court ringed by porticoes.
Mozarab, Mozarabic (from the Arabic *mustarib*, 'Arabised') Term designating the Christians of Visigoth Spain who kept their faith and language following the Islamic conquest.
Mudejar (Spanish, from the Arabic *mudaggian*, 'tamed') Muslims who, after the Reconquista, remained in Spain, paying a tribute. Adjectively, it refers to the art these populations provided for Christian monuments.
Muezzin The Muslim assigned to call the faithful to prayer (*ezan*) from the top of the minaret (qv.) or from a terrace.
Mufti Scholar authorized by Islamic law to issue edicts in theological and legal matters.
Mughal (A.) From 'Mongol', the name of a dynasty of Turkmen-Mongol origin that ruled over India.
Mullah (P.) Title designating a religious scholar.
Muqarnas, mukarnas (A.) An arched niche subdivided over several levels into small spandrels or niches forming a honeycomb structure whose function is decorative as against load-bearing. The stalactite vault is one variant of this form.
Musalla (A.) Space for communal prayer.
Muslim One who is devoted or who submits to God.
Mu'tazilism Current of Islamic thought holding that religious dogma, including Qur'anic revelation, can be understood, explained and justified by reasoning and rationality, rather than be simply accepted literally and dogmatically. Mu'tazilism became state doctrine at the 'Abbasid court in the 9th century.

Namazgah (A.) 'Place of prayer'. Wall with *mihrab* (qv.) indicating the *qibla* (qv.) and perhaps a *minbar* (qv.), sometimes cordoned off. This is the basic shape of a Great Mosque for collective prayer, often constructed before the city so as to ensure that religious observances are performed correctly.
Narthex Vestibule or covered porch closed on the external side that in Byzantine and Palaeo-Christian churches precedes the nave being reserved for catechumens and penitents.
Naskh (A.) Term deriving from an Arabic root meaning 'to copy'. A cursive script of roundish form that appeared around the 12th century, becoming quickly widespread in Arabic calligraphy in conjunction with Kufic (qv.).
Necropolis Cemetery of large size situated outside of the city fortifications.

Nestorianism Christological doctrine advocated by Nestorius (c. 380–451), patriarch of Constantinople, according to which the union of the two natures in Christ amounts to a mere 'conjunction'. Condemned as heretical at the Council of Ephesus in 430, Nestorius was sent into exile to Egypt.
Nimbus Luminous disc (halo) around or behind the head of a venerated personage in an image, probably inspired by Sassanid iconography.

Oxiana Ancient name of the region neighbouring the river known to classical Antiquity as the Oxus, today as Amu Darya, that forms the border between Afghanistan and Tajikistan as well as between Uzbekistan and Turkmenistan, before disgorging into the Aral Sea.

Palmette Ornamental motif inspired by the palm-leaf, composed of a central triangular element from which sprouts a number of small leaves.
Pasha (P.) Title attributed to provincial governors and to the highest ranks in the army under the Ottomans.
Patio Open-air internal courtyard.
Pediment Front to a façade, generally triangular in shape, surmounting the entablature in large-scale buildings.
Pendentive Transitional surface in the shape of a triangle projected onto a sphere linking the piers below to a dome erected above a space of square or polygonal plan.
Peristyle Courtyard encircled by porticoes, and, by extension, a porch with colonnade.
Pisé A cost-effective, rapid but extremely durable construction technique in which clay or earth is compacted between planks of wood fixed with crosspieces the gaps in which, after mounting, allow the wall to breathe.
Pishtaq (P.) Monumental gateway composed of a huge frame around an arch opening on to an *iwan* (qv.).
Protoma Figure of the forepart of an animal or human figure applied as decoration to a wall.
Pulvin, pulvinus Element in a column, typical of Byzantine architecture, of the shape of an upside-down truncated pyramid placed between a capital and an arch impost.
Purification Prior to their prayer, Muslims must complete a ritual ablution of their hands, mouth, face, arms, ears and feet. In the case of serious impurity, the entire body must be cleansed. In the absence of water, the worshipper may perform the ablution symbolically by rubbing sand or earth over his body.

Qal'a (T.) Citadel.
Qasr (***kasr, ksar***) (A.) Palace, pavilion, castle; from the Latin *castrum*.
Qibla The direction of Mecca indicated in the mosque by the *mihrab* (qv.) towards which all prayers must be addressed.
Qiyas (A.) The third source of Islamic thought and law, after the Qur'an (qv.) and *ahadith* (v. *hadith*). This 'judgment by analogy' allows problems to be solved that are not clarified in the two primary texts, the solution being extrapolated from circumstances similar to those of the matter in hand.
Qubba (A.) Pavilion, domed kiosk, tomb.
Quincunx Arrangement resembling the five dots on the face of a die.
Qur'an (Arabic, *qur'an*, 'to read', 'to recite') The term initially referred to recitation of sections of the revelation that the Prophet brought back to his followers. It then came to mean the reciting by the entire Islamic community, in which the cornerstone of education is constituted by the commitment to memory and correct recitation of the Qur'an. For Muslims the Qur'an is the word of God, transmitted through the Prophet as physical intermediary. Perfect and unique (unlike other revealed books), it confers absolute supremacy on the Arabic language. Its verses number more than 6,200 and are organized into 114 'chapters' (*suras*, qv.), arranged in order of decreasing length. In Islamic countries, the Qur'an constitutes the primary source of morality, law and even governance (qv. *Sharia*). Islamic law is however also based on other sources, three of which are fundamental: the *ahadith* (qv.), the *qiyas* (qv.) and the *igma* (qv.).

Rajiput (S.) Member of northern Indian warrior caste.
Ramadhan The ninth month of the Islamic lunar year given over to the observance of the ritual fast (*sawm, sawn*). During this month, all Muslims of age must abstain from eating, drinking, smoking, quarrelling and sexual relations from sunrise to sunset. Children, the sick, the very old, pregnant and nursing women, travellers and those involved in heavy work are exempted (in exchange for some form of compensation, such as additional almsgiving). The end of the month is celebrated by a major festival, the 'id-al Saghir (or 'id al-Fitr).
Ribat (A.) Fortification on a frontier occupied by Islamic 'warrior monks' who divided their lives between prayer and Holy War.
Riwaq (***riwak***) (A.) Porch, archway on columns or pillars, bordering the courtyard of a mosque, or *sahn*.
Rustication Treatment of a stone that disengages a channel in the masonry, the surface often being left raw or rough-dressed.

Sahn (A.) Internal court of a mosque.
Salat Ritual prayer, the Muslim's visible sign of submission to Allah and one of the five obligations of Islam. It is composed of fixed Qur'anic formulae and pre-established gestures and is performed at five specific times of day, though in any place or situation and in a group or individually. The hour of prayer is announced by the muezzin's (qv.) call and the ritual can only be completed after the body is carefully purified (qv.), wearing clean clothes and in an unsullied place. It is performed five times a day: at dawn, at noon, three hours after noon, at sunset and approximately two hours after sunset. The faithful turns in the direction of Mecca and recites a fixed number of ritual formulae in a series of rigidly codified positions: standing, with the hands held open at the height of the shoulders, he pronounces the formula of consecration ('God is great'); lowering the hands, he recites the *fatiha*, the first *sura* in the Qur'an; bowing forward with hands on the knees; prostrate; squatting on the heels before prostrating himself a second time. This series of movements, apart from the first, constitutes a *rak'a*; an entire prayer requires the completion of a *rak'a* from two to four times depending on the hour of day. Finally, once again kneeling, the worshipper recites the *shahada* (qv.), as well as a prayer for the Prophet before a concluding formula. No entreaties are made. On Friday, the faithful must recite the noon *salat*, divided according to sex, in an appropriate mosque (called for this reason Friday or Congregational mosques), distinct from those in which everyday prayers are recited. Prayers are led by the *imam* while the *khatib* is responsible for the predication; holders of both these offices are designated by the community.
Saray (P.) Palace.
Satrap Governor of a province under the Achaemenids.
Sawm, sawn (A.) see Ramadhan.
Sebil (A.) Public watering-place supplied by paid water-carriers.
Sebka (A.) Brick decor typical of Almohad art consisting in a repeated motif of lobate arches forming a diamond lattice pattern.
Shadirvan (P.) Fountain or pool for ritual ablution set up in the courtyard of a mosque.
Shahada The profession of faith in Islam recited with the phrases, *La ilaha illa Allah* ('There is no God but God [Allah]') and *Muhammad rasul Allah* ('Muhammad is the Messenger of God [His Messenger]'), pronounced before witnesses.
Shari'a (A.) Canonical law of Islam, derived primarily from the Qur'an (qv.). It establishes the rules of the religion and the prescriptions relative to conduct in social and legal matters.
Sharif Honorary title that in the Islamic period designates a descendant of the family of Muhammad.
Shaykh, sheikh (A.) Islamic holy man.
Shi'at (A.) Party, faction (v. Shiism).
Shifahane Hospital.
Shiism (strictly 'Shi'ism', from the Arabic *shi'at* 'party') Islamic denomination comprising seven branches, among them those who recognize Muhammad's son-in-law, Ali (qv.), and his descendants as the Prophet's sole heirs. The only country where Shias or Shiites constitute the majority of the population is Iran, while in Iraq Shias comprise almost half the Islamic community. Overall, Shias number slightly more than ten per cent of all Muslims.
Squinch Type of spandrel in which the connection between the polygonal base and the impost of the dome is obtained by means of the curved surface of conic section , rather than spherical, as in the normal pendentive.
Sufism Type of Islamic mysticism that arose around the 7th century consisting in a search for a spiritual path to God. In general, Sufis consider the 'inner path' more important than the observance of religious tenets. For this reason they were frequently condemned as heretical, or at the least suspicious, by orthodox Sunni.
Sultan In use from the 10th century, this title adopted by Islamic sovereigns designates monarchs independent from the caliph.
Sunnah (A.) Literally, custom, habit; the collection of actions and sayings concerning the Prophet contained in the *ahadith* (v. *hadith*), used as a reference in cases for which the Qur'an lacks conclusive information.
Sunnites, Sunni Name covering orthodox Muslims, in contrast to the Shias, considered as schismatic early on. Historically, the Sunnites descend from those Muslims who, at the dawn of Islam, came to the defence of al-Muawiyya against Ali. Today they represent nearly ninety per cent of all Muslims.
Suq, souk (A.) Market.
Sura Name given to each of the 114 verses into which the Qur'an is divided.

T-plan Type of mosque plan in which the aisle perpendicular to the *qibla* (qv.) is of greater length than the others and forms with the nave of the *qibla* a shape like a 'T', so emphasizing the area of the *mihrab*.
Taifa 'Faction', name of certain Spanish kingdoms that arose on the dissolution of the caliphate.
Talar (P.) Open hypostyle hall.
Tariqa (A.) Confraternity, brotherhood.
Tekke (T.) Dervish (qv.) monastery sometimes also used as accommodation for travelling Muslims.
Thermae Public bathhouses often of vast proportions that became extremely widespread in the Roman period. They were composed of a vestibule and of several other rooms of various temperatures. In the Byzantine, and above all in the Islamic era, their popularity was immense.
Thuluth One of the six main styles of Arabic cursive script, used abundantly in e.g. Ottoman inscriptions.
Transoxiana Ancient name of the region between a river known in classic antiquity as the Oxus (the Amu Darya) and the northernmost Syr Darya (the ancient Jaxartes), corresponding to present-day Uzbekistan, Tajikistan and the southern part of Kyrgyzstan and Kazakhstan.
Truss Triangular timber that relieves the stresses at work in a roof.
Türbe (T.) Turkish funerary monument, Islamic variant on the *kümbet*, originally from Central Asia. As the practice of mummification fell out of favour and the corpse had to be placed directly in the ground, crypts too began to fall into disuse.

Ulama Plural of *alim* ('sage'), designating those who have attained a specific level of theological-juridical knowledge. *Muftis*, *shaykhs*, *hatib*, *imams* and teachers at Qur'anic schools are all recruited from the *ulama*.
Ulus (Mongol) Specific country or territory and its inhabitants, khanate.
Umma (A.) Community of believers.

Vizier Administrative office, minister.

Waqf (A.) Bequest of land or real estate whose revenues are assigned to religious foundations or the public good.

Yamur (A.) Gilded ornament of globular form placed on the top of mosques and minarets.

Zakat (A.) Legally enforced almsgiving. A fundamental obligation in Islam, they amount to the tenth part. The redistribution of this tax to those in need expunges the sin of possessing worldly goods that are considered impure. Originally it was also payable in kind.
Zawiya, zaouia (A.) Sanctuary. The term n general designates a small Sufi convent.
Zellij (A.) Enamelled ceramic tile of small dimensions disposed in geometric patterns in paving or as wall covering.
Zenana (P.) Women's quarters.
Ziyada (A.) The space between the mosque and the outside world provided as a mark of respect and protected by a high wall.
Zoomorphic Of animal-like appearance; in general decorative.
Zoroastrianism see Mazdaism.

PRINCIPAL DYNASTIES AND FIGURES OF THE ISLAMIC WORLD

'Abbasids
750–1258
The second dynasty of the Arab caliphs who succeeded the Umayyads. Their capital was Baghdad from 762 to 1258 and then Samarra (Iraq) from 836 to 892. The 'Abbasids belonged to the Arabic tribe (Banu) al-Abbas who, as descendants of Muhammad's uncle, considered themselves the most legitimate heirs to the Umayyad caliphate. Forging an alliance with Shia groups, they overturned the Umayyad dynasty in 750 and from the outset placed the emphasis on the theological aspects of their power. This approach was probably influenced by Persian ideas of the divine origin of regal authority going back to the Sassanids and, prior to them, to the Achaemenids. They were later promoted by Abu Muslim, whose revolt in Khorasan (747) was decisive in assuring the eventual victory of the 'Abbasids. The first caliph, Abu al-Abbas (750–754), assumed power at Kufa, but maintained links with the Khorasan region whence the forces that had brought him to power came. This is demonstrated by the construction of an imposing edifice at Merv, characterized by a hall covered by a lofty dome and with four doors that give out onto as many *iwans* leading to four square *sahns*. Of essentially symbolic import, architectural elements like these were to form the basis for the radial plan of Baghdad and for numerous palaces of the later capital at Samarra. The cultural and political zenith of the dynasty was reached under Harun al-Rashid (786–809), whose kingdom is bathed in an aura of legendary splendour. Thanks to this caliph and his son al-Mamun (813–833) Baghdad became a scientific centre of the first rank, where Mutazilite rationalism (which held that religious dogma could be understood and explained through rational argument), was elevated to the status of an official doctrine. In these same years, however, the unity of the empire was compromised by the progressive independence of many provinces, where local dynasties that theoretically recognized the authority of the caliphate gradually asserted themselves. Following the murder of al-Mutawakkil (847–861), the situation degenerated and military dynasties grew up, above all Persian and Turkic ones. They confined the authority of the caliph to the religious sphere, and even that was soon contested by the proclamation of rival potentates. In 945 the Buyids occupied Baghdad, relegating the caliphate to the level of a protectorate. Thus ended the unity of the Islamic world and the successors of those dubbed the Great 'Abbasids possessed little more than nominal authority. In 1258 the Mongols swept away all that lingered of 'Abbasid rule, by now moreover controlled by the Seljuqs (who in 1055 had ousted the Buyids). The caliphate was removed by the Mamluks to Cairo (1260–1517) and thence to Istanbul by the Ottomans (1517–1924).

Aghlabids
800–909
Arab dynasty in Ifriqiya (the name in Arabic for eastern Algeria, Tunisia and western Libya), Malta, part of southern Italy and Sicily, with their capital at Kairouan (Tunisia). The son of an 'Abbasid general called Ibrahim Ibn Aghlab (800–812) became governor of Ifriqiya in 787. In 800, making the most of the troubles besetting the authority of the caliphate in the East, he declared independence despite confirming formal acceptance of the caliphate at the foundation of al-Abbasiya (801), near Kairouan. The subsequent governments of Abdallah (812–827) and Ziyadat Allah (827–838) were characterized by the gradual assertion of the state; the emirs devoted themselves to erecting magnificent buildings and planning great towns. In 827 there began the conquest of Sicily; by 841 Bari had been taken, and in 846 even Rome was plundered. Malta was occupied in 868, thereby consolidating Aghlabid supremacy over the coastal towns of Italy and forcing them to pay tributes. The end of the ninth century marked the onset of a decline, hammered home by constant Berber revolts, Byzantine counter-attacks in southern Italy and clashes with the Tulunids of Cairo. In 909, the Aghlabids were deposed in the course of the Fatimid insurrection.

Alawids
Dynasty of *sharifs* that reigned in Morocco from 1666 with a capital at Fez, then at Meknes (1672–1727), and finally at Rabat from 1912. Descendants of a grandson of Muhammad, the Alawids reached Morocco in the thirteenth century, establishing themselves in the region of Tafilalet to the south of the High Atlas. In 1666 Mulai al-Rashid (1664–1672) conquered Fez and usurped the sultanate. The reign of his son Mulai Isma'il (1672–1727) marked the zenith of the kingdom and it was he who recovered the cities in Morocco lost to the Europeans. By the dawn of the nineteenth century, however, increasing interference from European powers accelerated the country's decline, to the point that in 1912 it was reduced to a French and Spanish protectorate. In 1956, however, Sultan Sidi Muhammad (1927–1961) proclaimed independence, assuming the title of King Muhammad V.

Ali (**Ali Ibn Abu Talib**)
Mecca, 602–Kufa, 661
Cousin and son-in-law of the Prophet (as husband of his daughter, Fatima), he was father of Muhammad's sole male descendants, Hasan and Husayn. Caliph from 656 to 661. According to a proportion of the Muslim community at the time, he should have succeeded Muhammad directly. In fact, Ali only became caliph after the murder of the third incumbent, 'Uthman. This fourth successor of the Prophet found himself in a difficult situation: a relative of 'Uthman's, Muawiyya (Muawiyah), governor of Syria, believed Ali to be implicated in the murder and organized a rebellion of the opposition known as 'revenge for the blood of 'Uthman'. This division broke out into armed conflict which was finally resolved by arbitration. The decision went against the party of Ali, who himself was in the end assassinated in the great mosque at Kufa, his capital, in 661. From these vicissitudes arose the chief Islamic schism between the Shias, that is the partisans of Ali and his descendants, the Kharijites, who rejected arbitration, and the Sunnites, the successors of the supporters of Muawiyya.

Almohads
1130–1269
Berber dynasty of North Africa (Morocco, Algeria, Tunisia, Libya), with a capital at Marrakesh (Morocco), and of Spain, with a capital at Seville. The Almohad dynasty sprang from those Berber tribes who resisted Arab dominion, coalescing into a political party around Ibn Tumart (1080–1130), an intransigent reformer who sparked a vast movement of rigorous renewal against the decadence of the Almoravid regime. The name of the dynasty derives from the Arabic *al-Muwahhidun* 'that believes in the unity of God'. The struggle against the Almoravids was begun in 1124 by Ibn Tumart, who established a capital at Tinmal. It continued under Abd al-Mumin (1130–1163), who, having seized Marrakesh in 1147, succeeded in wresting control of all Morocco and conquered over the following years not only the northern coast of Africa as far as Libya but also from 1146, Islamic Spain. The end of the twelfth century coincides with the Almohad empire's period of greatest magnificence under Abu Yacub Yusuf (1163–1184) and Yusuf Yacub al-Mansur (1184–99). It was under the latter that Averroes (Ibn Rushd, 1126–1198), philosopher and doctor, a major Aristotelian scholar and supporter of an allegorical-philosophical interpretation of the Qur'an, lived in Cordoba. In 1212, led by an-Nasir (1199–1213), they suffered a crushing victory at the hands of the Christians at Las Navas de Tolosa. The Almohads were thus driven from Spain and, over the following years, from Tunisia and Algeria as well. From 1244 on, the advance of the Merinids undermined their sovereignty even in Morocco until their definitive overthrow in 1269.

Almoravids
1056–1147
Berber dynasty of Morocco, Mauritania, western Algeria and Spain, with capitals first at Fez and then, from 1086, at Marrakesh (Morocco). The name *al-Murabitun*, rather than meaning 'men of the *ribat*', probably derives from the Qur'anic root '*r-b-t*', signifying 'fighting in serried ranks', 'in close formation'. Originating in the region of the Sahara, where they patrolled the caravan routes, they conquered Ghana, subsequently moving on to North Africa, where they imposed a determined policy of reform that fused religious elements to ideas of markedly ethnic and anti-Arab character. In 1062 they founded Marrakesh and over the next few decades led a campaign to take al-Andalus, whose Taifa kingdoms they saw as the epitome of decadence (1089–1094). At the beginning of the twelfth century, under pressure from the Reconquista in al-Andalus, they began to retreat in Morocco as well, harassed by the Almohads, who in 1147 grabbed Marrakesh, thereby ending the dynasty.

Aq Qoyunlu (or **Ak Koyunlu**)
14th century, 1467–1502
A federation of Turkmen tribes known, owing to their totemic animal, as the White Sheep, which extended its dominion over eastern Anatolia, Azerbaijan, Turkestan, Persia, Afghanistan and Iraq. From 1468, their capital was at Tabriz (Iran). The Aq Qoyunlu appeared in the west towards the mid-fourteenth century, with raids at the expense of the Byzantines and the Ilkhanid principalities in Syria, Mesopotamia and Kurdistan. They reached their greatest splendour during the reign of Qara Yülük 'Uthman (1389–1435), emir of Diyarbakir and ally of Timur Leng (Tamerlane). Around 1435 the Aq Qoyunlu began to cede terrain to a powerful rival federation, the Qara Qoyunlu, but in 1467 they were defeated in turn and their territories annexed by Uzun Hasan (1453–1478). The Aq Qoyunlu now reached their apogee and became one of the foremost Islamic powers of the period. Within a short space of time, they conquered part of Georgia (1459) and the region of Hasankeyef (1462), until their advance into Anatolia was halted by the Ottomans in 1473. Around 1490, the power of the Safavids was on the ascendant to the East and in 1501 the Aq Qoyunlu lost Tabriz. The final representative of the dynasty was chased out of Mardin in 1507.

Artuqids
1098–1232/1408
Turkic dynasty of Kurdistan. Penetrating westwards as allies of the Seljuqs, in 1086 they became governors of Jerusalem in their name. Chased out by the Fatimids in 1091, they took possession of the rugged region of Kurdistan, which they divided into various entities: Diyarbakir and Hasankeyef (1098–1232), Mardin (1104–1408) and Harput (1185–1233). One-time vassals of the Seljuqs, of the Zangids and the shah of the Khwarizm, they enjoyed a substantial degree of autonomy during the upheaval occasioned by the Crusades, until they were unseated by the Ayyubids in 1233 and further by the Qara Qoyunlu in 1408.

Ayyubids
1171–1250/1260
Kurdish dynasty centred on Egypt, Syria, Iraq, with capitals at Damascus and Cairo. The father of the line was Ayyub, a brilliant military leader who became governor of Damascus for the Zangids. His brother Shirkuh (Shir Kuh) and his grandson Salah al-Din (Saladin, 1138–1393) entered the service of the Fatimids of Cairo. A masterful general, skilled politician and a man of culture and moral rectitude, Saladin was able to play a key role in the wars against the Crusaders as a result of the position he had gained in Egypt. He became grand vizier of Cairo in 1169 and overturned the Fatimids in 1171. Extending his dominion over Syria and Palestine, he was officially recognized as caliph of Baghdad. In 1187 he resoundingly crushed the Crusaders at Hattin, thereby taking Jerusalem.

His offspring, however, failed to maintain the unity of a kingdom that then split into the sultanate of Cairo and various principalities in Syria. In 1250 the Mamluks assassinated the last Ayyubid sultan; shortly afterwards the principalities of Syria fell into the hands of the Ilkhanids.

Buyids
932/945–1056/1062
Iranian dynasty from the region of Dailam that governed eastern Iran and Mesopotamia and claimed descent from ancient Sassanid sovereigns. Initially in the service of the Samanids, they conquered Fars, Iraq and eastern Iran. In 945 Ahmad Muizz ad-Dawla (932–967) occupied Baghdad and offered the caliph his 'protection', thereby putting an end to the power of the 'Abbasids and henceforth giving a Persian flavour to the Islamic world in the Orient. This flourishing kingdom, racked by internecine struggles between pretenders to the throne, was swept up by the advent of Turkic peoples, who went on to inherit their advanced Persian culture: in 1023 the Ghaznavids seized Rey, while in 1056 the Seljuqs took Kerman.

Delhi, Sultanates of
1206–1555
Islamic dynasties in India, heirs to the Ghaznavids and the Ghurids (Ghori). The first dynasty, known as the 'Slave Sultans', was founded by the Turkic general, Qutb ad-Din Aybak (1206–1210), Ghurid governor of Delhi, who made a successful bid for independence at the death of his monarch. His successor Iltutmish (1210–1236) consolidated this position, going on to conquer a good part of northern India. In the wake of the tidal wave whipped up by the Mongol invasion, the following dynasties succeeded: the Khaljis (1290–1320), who liberated the country from the Mongols and entered the Deccan; the Tughluqs (1320–1414), under whom many independent sultanates gradually emerged, disrupted by the sack of Delhi by Timur Leng (1398); the Sayyds (1414–1451) who recognized Timurid overlordship; the Afghan Lodi (1451–1526), defeated by Babur, founder of the Mughal dynasty; and the Suri (1540–1555), also Afghans, who drove out the Mughal Humayun, who subsequently succeeded in retaking the country.

Fatimids
909–1171
Shia caliphate opposed to that of Baghdad and ruled over Tunisia, Egypt, Syria, for a time extending its dominion to the entire northern coast of Africa, as well as the Arabian Peninsula. The first capital was Kairouan (Tunisia), then from 920 Mahdia (Tunisia), and from 973 Cairo (Egypt). The Fatimids supported the descendants of Isma'il – the last *imam* of the 'Sevener' Shia schism – and therefore of Muhammad's daughter, Fatima. The founder of the dynasty, Ubaydallah (909–934), known as Mahdi, exploiting the crisis affecting Sunnism that coincided with uncertainty around the caliphate, deposed the Aghlabids and in a few short years seized Tunisia, eastern Algeria, Libya and Sicily. In 969 al-Muizz (953–975) conquered Egypt and founded Cairo in the vicinity the ancient capital of al-Fustat, transferring the capital in 973 to tighten the dynasty's grip on its interests in the east. It was between the end of the tenth and the eleventh century, with figures such as al-Aziz (975–996), al-Hakim (996–1021) and al-Mustansir (1036–1094), that the caliphate reached the apogee of its economic power and cultural flowering, extending its influence over the Holy Sites. In the twelfth century, religious cleavages, combined with problems arising from the extreme youth of a number of the caliphs, resulted in a progressive decline, of which the military took full advantage. In 1171 the Ayyubid Saladin restored the Sunnites and suppressed the Fatimids.

Genghiskhanids
Name conventionally given to the Mongol empires that formed on the death of Genghis Khan (1227), when his vast conquests were divided between his four sons. Jöchi (died 1227) received the regions to the west of the Volga and to the north of Oxiana, corresponding to the *ulus* of the Golden Horde; Chagatai (died 1242) inherited an equivalent *ulus*, comprising Oxiana, part of Afghanistan and of eastern Turkestan; Ögödei (or Ogodai; died 1241), Great Khan from 1229, ruled Mongolia, the cradle of the line; and Tolui (died 1232), acted as regent between 1227–1229. Tolui was the father of the next Great Khan Mönkge (1251–1259); of Khubilai (Kublai Khan; 1260–1294), conqueror of China and founder of the Chinese dynasty of the Yuan; and finally of the Ilkhan Hülägü (1253–1265), who in 1256 subdued Transoxiana and then Persia. In 1257 he went on to seize Baghdad, where he unseated the last caliph and founded the kingdom of the Ilkhanids of Persia (1258), who converted to Islam in 1295. This example was followed in 1313 when Jöchi's *ulus* also converted and again in 1326 with the *ulus* of Chagatai.

Ghaznavids
977–1150
Turkic dynasty of Afghanistan, Khorasan (northeast Persia), northern India, also in the Punjab until 1186; with capitals at Ghazna (Afghanistan) and from 1156 in Lahore (Pakistan). In 962 the Turkish mercenary Alptegin (Alptekin) had conquered Ghazna on behalf of the Samanids. De facto independent, his successor Subütegin (977–997) extended and consolidated the sphere of influence to the west. In 999 his son in turn, the great Mahmud of Ghazni (997–1030), overthrew Samanid dominance and made short work of the Khorasan, eastern Persia, the Khwarizm, Afghanistan and part of northern India, whose conversion to Islam he instigated. Mahmud thus founded the dynasty of the Ghaznavids, successively waging war against the Qarakhanids to the north and the Shiite Buyids in Persia. His son Masud I (1030–1040) was, however, defeated at Dandanaqan by the Seljuqs (1040), who went on to annex the Khorasan. In the twelfth century, the kingdom found itself reduced to Afghanistan and the Punjab. In 1161 the Ghurids took Ghazni and in 1186 Lahore, thereby overthrowing the Ghaznavids.

Ghurids
1150–1212
Afghan dynasty in Afghanistan and northern India, with their capital at Firuzkuh (Afghanistan). In 1099 the Ghurids, a tribe from central Afghanistan, were made governors of Ghazna in that region on behalf of the Ghaznavids. Becoming independent in Firuzkuh in 1146, they then plundered Ghazna (1150); later, under the leadership of 'Ala ad-Din Husayn (1149–1161), they seized all the Afghan regions at that time under Ghaznavid control. After a series of campaigns in India, they conquered Lahore in 1186, thus extinguishing the Ghaznavids and inheriting the eastern sector of their empire, which they expanded in 1193 with the conquest of Delhi. The kingdom was divided between two siblings: Ghiyath ad-Din (1163–1203) and Muizz ad-Din (1173–1206), who headed a dazzling succession of military excursions. With the murder of Muizz ad-Din, the kingdom descended into chaos, being split between the shah of Khwarizm, who annexed Afghanistan, and the Turkic general Aybak, already the Ghurid governor of Delhi, who proclaimed independence and went on to found the sultanate of Delhi.

Husayn
One of the two sons of Ali and Fatima, and thus grandson of the Prophet, who in 680 attempted to overthrow the Umayyad dynasty and had himself proclaimed caliph, only to be defeated and killed at the battle of Kerbela.

Idrisids
788–974
Arab dynasty of Morocco with its capital at Fez. In 786 Idris Ibn Abdallah (788–793), escaping the slaughter of his family by the 'Abbasids, sought shelter in Morocco, where he was well received by the Berbers who proclaimed him *imam*. He assumed the title of Idris in 788. After he was poisoned, perhaps on the orders of Harun al-Rashid, he was venerated as a saint and hailed as the founder of Morocco, on which he had imposed political unity for the first time. His son, Idris II (793–828), continued and consolidated his efforts, transferring the capital to Fez. Under his descendants, the kingdom gradually disintegrated due to internal dissension. In 917 the country was overrun by the Fatimids and, from 932, by the Umayyads from Andalusia, who controlled it until the capture of the last Idrissid in 974.

Ilkhanids (**Il-Khanids**)
1252–1335
Mongol dynasty that ruled over Persia and Iraq, part of Syria, eastern Anatolia and the Caucasus, with capitals at Tabriz and Soltaniye (Iran). Essentially, the kingdom was founded by Hülagü Khan (c. 1217–1265), grandson of Genghis Khan, who completed the conquest of Persia begun under Ögedei, as well as of the 'Abbasid Empire with the conquest of Baghdad and the deposition of its last caliph (1258). The whole enterprise was concluded with Hülagü as general to his brother, the great khan Möngke, whose supremacy he recognized, assuming the title of *il-khan* ('subordinate khan'). Though seemingly irresistible, the advance towards Egypt was halted by the Mamluk sultan Baybars in 1260; the efforts of his son Abaqa (1265–1282) to retake it proved fruitless. The empire reached its acme with Ghazan Khan (1295–1304), who embraced Islam, elevating it to the status of a state religion, and his brother Oldjetu (1304–1316), who between them erected the most impressive architectural complexes of the age. Abu Said (1316–1335), who restored the control of the Seljuq lords of Anatolia, was the last great representative of the dynasty. After his death, the empire dissolved into numerous turbulent statelets.

Khans of Khiva
1511–1919
Uzbek dynasty of the Khwarizm, with capitals at Gurganj (Turkmenistan) and Khiva (Uzbekistan). Heirs to the Khanate of the Golden Horde, the princes of Khiva, khan from the nineteenth century, were often at odds with the khanate of Bukhara, whose subjects they were to become on more than one occasion. In 1873 the khanate was occupied by the Russians.

Khwarizm-Shah (**Khwarezm-** or **Khorezm-**)
1077–1231
Turkic dynasty of Transoxiana. At the time of its maximum expansion it held sway over Turkestan, Afghanistan, Iran and part of Iraq. Its capitals were Khiva and, from 1212, Samarkand (Uzbekistan). The founder of the dynasty, Anustegin (1077–1097), a Turkish slave of the Ghaznavids, was named governor of the Khwarizm after its conquest by the Seljuqs. In the twelfth century, the region became an independent kingdom and was soon engaged in conflict with the neighbouring Seljuqs, from whom Il-Arslan (1156–1172) wrested vast tracts of territory in 1157. On the collapse of the empire of the Great Seljuqs, the Khwarezm-Shah occupied the Khorasan in 1187, eventually imposing their protection on the caliphate. In 1206, the ambitious and adroit 'Ala ad-Din Muhammad (1200–1220) ousted the Ghurids from Afghanistan and, once the Qarakhanids had been chased out of Samarkand, adopted the city as his capital (1212). Six years later, he committed the fatal error of allowing the extermination of a caravan of Mongol merchants and sending a haughty reply to a demand for damages dispatched by Genghis Khan, who promptly made the most of this pretext to unleash his hordes to the west.

Mamluks
1250–1517
Dynasty of military slaves of Turkish origin. They governed Egypt, Syria and Iraq, with their capital at Cairo. The name derives from the Arabic *al-mamluk* 'slave'. The Mamluks were a military caste comprised of slaves and mercenaries originally in the service of the Ayyubids, exceptionally well-trained and faithful, and kept strictly separate from the civilian population lest they become embroiled in political intrigue. In 1250, on the murder of the Ayyubid sultan al-Muazzam, they arrogated power, which they subsequently exercised with efficiency and ruthlessness. They were threatened by the Mongols, who until then had remained undefeated, and even succeeded in inflicting a severe defeat on them in 1260 under the banner of Sultan Baybars (1260–1277). In the same year, they removed the heir to the 'Abbasid caliphate – which by now was devoid of its erstwhile charisma – to Cairo, where he was relegated to the condition of a puppet. Boasting a highly effective army, in 1291 they wrestled St John Acre (Akko), the last Christian bastion in the Holy Land, back from the Crusaders. Under their governance, commerce prospered and the whole state, Cairo particularly, enjoyed a period of exceptional splendour. The danger of a Timurid invasion that had already devastated Syria was defused by the skilful strategy of Sultan Barquq (1382–1399). Naturally enough in a state whose life depended on the smooth functioning of the military machine, the decline coincided with a lack of modernization in the army compared with the new technologies which their Ottoman neighbours cultivated so assiduously. By 1517 it thus became possible for Selim I to chase out the Mamluks and annex the territories they controlled to the Ottoman Empire.

Merinids
1244–1465
A Berber dynasty of Morocco with its capital at Fez. In the twelfth century, the tribe of the Banu

Merin from the eastern Sahara had progressively penetrated those regions of Morocco adjacent to Algeria. They increasingly entered into open conflict with the Almohads who, from 1212, were trying to come to terms with the repercussions of the disaster at Las Navas de Tolosa. In 1244 the Merinids seized Meknes, followed by Fez and finally Marrakesh (1269), eradicating the last Almohad stronghold. A firm hand in the governing of the state and remarkable military prowess made possible numerous incursions into al-Andalus and the conquest of Algeria. The kingdom reached its highpoint towards the mid-fourteenth century: Abu al-Hasan (1331–1351) and Abu Inan Faris (1351–1358) promoted a successful cultural policy, sponsoring the construction of numerous splendid madrasahs, as well as managing, albeit only for a short period, to occupy Tunisia. After this chapter of triumph, the dynasty decayed rapidly: lacking adult heirs, the regency was assumed by the Wattasid Berbers. It was then taken over for twenty years or so by the Nasrids of Granada (1374–1393), before returning under the tutelage of the Wattasid until 1472, when the latter took power definitively with the seizure of Fez.

Mozaffarids
1318–1393
Arabic dynasty of southern Iran and Kurdistan, which for a short period gained sway over nearly all Persia, with their capital at Yazd (Iran). In 1318 Mubariz ad-Din Muhammad (1314–1358), son of Mozaffar, Ilkhanid governor of Maibod near Isfahan, annexed Yazd, becoming its authoritarian governor. With the collapse of the Ilkhans in 1335, he proclaimed his independence, taking over up the important cities in Fars (central Iran). With the seizure of Tabriz (1357) the Mozaffarids became the greatest power in the region, even contesting control of the Iraq borderlands with the Jalayrids. The immense riches of the kingdom allowed Shah Shuja (1358–1384) to finance some exceptional architecture that developed certain Ilkhanid features and on occasion anticipated the Timurid idiom. After his death, struggles between pretenders to the throne rendered the kingdom easy prey to an army dispatched by Timur Leng in 1393.

Mughals
1526–1857
Timurid (Turco-Mongol) dynasty that replaced the Sultanate of Delhi in India, establishing its capital at Agra. In 1504, Babur, heir to the principality of Fergana (1494) and overlord of Samarkand (1497), took Kabul. In 1526, having lost hope of recovering Samarkand – which had fallen into the hands of the Uzbeks – he marched into India and defeated the Lodis and later the regional Rajiputs to become emperor (1526–1530). His son Humayun (1530–1556), defeated by Sher Shah of Sur, had to escape to Afghanistan, managing to retake Delhi only in 1555. The following reign, that of Akbar (1556–1605), witnessed the apogee of the dynasty, particularly in terms of religious tolerance and the farsighted handling of the many adversaries waiting in the wings. Through such policies, Akbar managed to turn potential enemies into faithful allies of the empire, associating them closely with the destiny of the Mughal dynasty and appealing their common interests. Jahangir (1605–1627) and Shah Jahan (1627–1658) continued this approach and widened the borders of the dynasty. As well as extending and consolidating trading conditions, they presided over an unprecedented era of artistic greatness. With Aurangzeb (1658–1707) these open-minded policies came to an abrupt halt and the country was stifled by religious obscurantism. Meanwhile, interference in commerce by the Portuguese and above all by the English was increasingly damaging, threatening the integrity of the whole empire. To promote their aims, these new powers made much play of internal rivalries fuelled by Aurangzeb's misguided attitude. The eighteenth century witnessed a drop in the quality of its sovereigns and the monarchy forfeited its power forever. In 1739, the Turko-Afghan warlord Nadir Shah, who had seized the throne of Persia, even plundered Delhi; by 1803, however, the city was occupied by the British. Over the following decades, the British grip increased, exhausting the country and creating conditions for the violent outburst known as the Sepoy (Indian) Mutiny of 1857. After the repression of the revolt and the arrest of the last Mughal, Queen Victoria became empress of India.

Muhammad (Abu al-Qasim Muhammad ibn Abd Allah, called **Muhammad**, the 'Glorified' or 'Praiseworthy')
Founder of Islam and, for Muslims, the last prophet after Abraham, Noah, Moses and Jesus. He is the Messenger of Allah, who received the revelation of the Qur'an. Born in Mecca between 562 and 572 (according to tradition) in a noble but far from wealthy family (belonging perhaps to the tribe of the Quraysh, Meccan aristocrats), he was brought up by his uncle Abu Talib, together with his cousin Ali. In his youth he accompanied caravans to Syria – where he would surely have had the opportunity of familiarizing himself with Christianity – on the behalf of a rich widow called Khadija, whom he later wed. From this union was born a daughter, Fatima (Fatma). He received his first revelation in around 610, beginning shortly afterwards to preach and acquiring followers among the inhabitants of Mecca. He encountered hostility on the part of the Quraysh, who were afraid lest his new ideas affect their privileges. The central theme of his preaching was the oneness of the creator God, as against the dominant polytheism, and the announcement of the universal judgment to come. In 615 Muhammad and his adepts repaired for the first time to Abyssinia. 621 saw his ascension and miraculous journey through the sky to Jerusalem, known as the *mi'raj*. In 622, the hostility of the ruling classes in Mecca forced him to emigrate, together with his first band of followers, to the oasis of Yatrib (Hegira). The following years saw a confused situation with skirmishes and raids during which the lives of Muhammad and those close to him were often in jeopardy. The final outcome was favourable to the Muslims, however, and in 630, they entered Mecca, removing the idols from the Ka'ba, but keeping the 'black stone'. Henceforth the pilgrimage to Mecca became the preserve of Muslims alone. Finally, in 631, after dogged resistance, the pagan tribes were overcome. After completing the *hajj* Muhammad died in Medina on June 8, 632, shortly before the entire Arabian Peninsula was converted to Islam.

Nasrids
1232–1492
Arab-Andalusian dynasty of Granada that emerged from the ruins of the Almohad state, when Muhammad ibn Nasr proclaimed himself sultan under the name Muhammad I (1232–1273) and annexed vast stretches of Andalusia. His son Muhammad II (1273–1302) consolidated the state with a shrewd plan based on alliances and negotiations with the Castilians and the Merinids. The kingdom attained its economic and cultural apogee in the reigns of Yusuf I (1333–1354) and Muhammad V (1354–1359 and 1362–1391), which saw the construction of the palace of the Alhambra. Succeeding sultans, preoccupied with internecine conflicts and pressed hard by unremitting attacks from the Christians, became less and less independent from Castile. Following one final flowering at the end of the fifteenth century but faced with the utter intransigence of their Most Catholic Majesties, they were forced to capitulate in 1492.

Ottomans
1280–1922
Turkish dynasty that ruled an immense empire comprising the Balkans, Anatolia, Azerbaijan, Armenia, Kurdistan, Syria, Iraq, Palestine, the Holy Land, Egypt, Libya, Tunisia and Algeria. They instituted numerous capitals that changed as their borders extended: 1280 at Yenisehir, 1326 at Bursa, 1366 at Edirne, and 1453 at Istanbul. In the thirteenth century, with other Oguz (Oghuz) Turks, they had been pushed westwards by the Mongols, who had invaded their ancestral lands in Central Asia. Around 1237 they had formed a military emirate in Bithynia (Turkey), whence they marched out to do battle with the Byzantines and the Seljuqs. The founder of the dynasty Osman (1280/1300–1324) and his successors implemented an aggressive policy waged at the expense above all of the Byzantines, who had to cede much of their territory. The institution of the elite body of the Janissaries supplied the Ottomans with a formidable war machine, with which they swallowed up the Balkans and inflicted crushing defeats on many major European armies (Kosovo, 1389, and Nicopolis, 1396). The conquest of Constantinople was however forestalled when the supposedly invincible Bayazit I (1389–1402) was checked near Ankara and taken prisoner by Timur Leng. Such a setback would have signalled the end of a less solid empire, but after a decade of disorder, Mehmet I (1413–1428) and Murat II (1428–1451) succeeded in reorganizing the state and resuming its expansionistic policies. Finally, in 1453, Mehmet (Mehmed) II Fatih 'The Conqueror' (reigned 1444–1446 and 1451–1481) made his triumphant entry into Constantinople. The Ottoman power was the greatest of the period and its expansion continued unabated under Selim I (1512–1520), who, in 1514, defeated his Persian rival, the Shia Shah Isma'il at the battle of Chaldiran, taking eastern Anatolia, together with its trade routes to the Persian Gulf. The following years saw the conquest of Syria (1516) and the Mamluk Empire (1517), and Selim assumed the title of caliph. Suleiman II Kanuni (the 'Lawmaker', known in the West as the 'Magnificent', 1520–1566) brought the empire to its apogee in every domain. Seizing Mecca and Medina, he imposed himself as protector of the Holy Sites, conquering Baghdad (1534), extending his sovereignty all along the North African coast to Morocco (1552), and conquering the Balkans to Hungary. After his death, however, the international balance of power began to shift. The great European empires, thanks to the influx of wealth from the New World, came to the fore, while the neglect of the land trade routes with India and therefore of the Mediterranean ports sidelined the Ottomans. Their plight was compounded by the ineptitude of the majority of the sultans, too often caught up in court intrigue and undermined by the wiles of omnipotent viziers. Gradually the empire descended into a spiral of debilitating corruption and inadequate governance. By the eighteenth century, the perennial enemy, the Hapsburg Empire, had seized the initiative. The Ottomans, forced inexorably onto the defensive, were buffeted by international events, including the awakening of national consciousness, manipulated by the European powers to stir up rebellions in once-Christian nations. Faced with the dissolution of the empire, new ideologies of European origin were taken up by the elites and, in 1908, the party of the Young Turks assumed power, depriving the sultan of any effective authority. Joining the central powers in World War I, on its defeat the Ottoman Empire was dismembered at the Treaty of Sèvres in 1920. In 1922 Mustafa Kemal Atatürk abolished the sultanate and in 1924 the caliphate. Turkey had become a republic.

Qajars
1779–1925
Turkmen dynasty of the shahs of Persia, founded in 1786, with its capital at Tehran. Descendants of Turkmen nomads, the Qajars had governed Astarabad (Iranian Azerbaijan) from 1750. Their chief Agha Muhammad Khan (1779–1797), having massacred the Zands at Kerman in 1794 and the Afsharids at Mashad in 1796, held the reins of power over all Persia and proclaimed himself shah. Shortly afterwards, Persia was one of the theatres of the clash between the Russians, who occupied the northern regions, and the British, who invaded the south, thereby obtaining a series of monopolies that delivered the lion's share of the country's resources into their hands. A sequence of putsches attempted to deflect the policy of faint-hearted shahs concerned solely with their personal comfort, leaving the country to be picked over by foreign powers. Finally it fell to Reza Khan Pahlavi to depose the last Qajar – whose power was anyway by then a fiction – in 1925.

Qarakhanids (Kara-Khanids)
840–1212
Turkic dynasty of Transoxiana and eastern Turkestan with a capital at Kara Ordu (China), and then Kashgar (China), from 992 at Bukhara and from 1042 at Samarkand (Uzbekistan). Around the eighth century the Qarluq tribe settled in Kashgaria (Chinese Turkestan). They were members of the federation of the Uyghur Turkic tribes of Mongolia, who had developed a remarkable civilization. Some time around the tenth century the Qarluq abandoned Buddhism and Nestorianism and adopted Islam, which had probably been introduced by merchants. Expanding westwards, they conquered the kingdom of the Samanids in 999, inheriting their sophisticated civilization. Over the following decades they clashed with the Ghaznavids and the Seljuqs, and in 1041, the kaghanate (the Mongol equivalent of khanate) was then split into eastern and western halves. The western kaghanate experienced an age of extraordinary splendour in the eleventh century, before being draw into in the Seljuq orbit, while the eastern sector had to contend with the Mongol Kara-Khitai. Between 1210 and 1212 both were absorbed by the Shah of the Khwarizm.

Qara Qoyunlu (or **Kara Koyunlu**)
1380–1469
Turkmen tribal federation that ruled over eastern Anatolia, Azerbaijan, the Caucasus and parts

of Iran and Iraq, with their capital at Tabriz (Iran) and, from 1411, at Baghdad (Iraq); they were known as the Black Sheep from their totemic animal. Setting out from the territory they had settled around Lake Van (Turkey), they seized Armenia and Azerbaijan to the north with the support of the Jalayrids, from whom Qara Yusuf (1390–1420) later succeeded in asserting independence, and subsequently even occupied their capital Tabriz (1391). Having clashed on more than one occasion with Timur Leng, after the latter's death Qara Yusuf managed to get the better of the situation (1405). He annexed territories to the south of his dominions from the Jalayrids and went on to occupy Baghdad in 1411 and Diyarbakir in 1419. The zenith of the power of this warlike kingdom was attained under Jahanshah (1435–1467), who in 1447 was finally victorious in the interminable conflict with the Timurids in the impassable regions of Kurdistan and southern Caucasus; he seized central Persia with Isfahan in 1452 and reached Herat in 1458. Their decline coincided with the rise to power of the rival Aq Qoyunlu clan, which in 1469 crushed the last representative of the Qara Qoyunlu. Taking refuge in India in 1478, the survivors managed to found the dynasty of the Qutb Shah at Golconda, where they were to reign until 1687, when Aurangzeb annexed the Deccan to the Mughal Empire.

Rightly Guided Caliphs
In Arabic '*al-Khalifa*' designates a 'successor' or 'representative'. According to the Sunni, the caliph was the successor of the Prophet. But even in the Umayyad period, the caliphs considered themselves as the "shadow of God on earth." The problem of the succession of the Prophet, who left no specific instructions on the subject, has occasioned deep splits in the Muslim community – not least that between the Shias and the Sunni. The first four caliphs are known as the 'Rightly Guided' Caliphs. Abu Bakr (632–634), father-in-law and close friend of Muhammad, was one of his first followers and was constantly by his side. When the Prophet was ill it was he who led prayers in Muhammad's house and his choice as caliph was accepted by all. 'Umar Ibn al-Khattab (634–644) was also a companion and was for a long time his most confidential advisor. He was elected caliph unanimously. This choice was an inspired one: thanks to his humanity and military qualities, 'Umar is considered the true founder of the Islamic Empire. 'Uthman Ibn Affan (644–656) was Muhammad's son-in-law. Probably elected due to his undeniable piety, it soon transpired that he was unable to wield political power and was an inept commander. Ignoring murmurings from the community, he was assassinated as an old man bent over the Qur'an he was reading. He was probably responsible for a codification of the Qur'an, fruit of his long studies on the various partial versions of the text then in circulation. He was succeeded by Ali ibn Abu-Talib (656–661), husband of Fatima, daughter of Muhammad (v. Ali).

Safavids (Safavi)
1501–1722
Turkmen dynasty of the shahs of Persia, with its capital at Tabriz, from 1548, Qazvin until 1598 and then Isfahan (Iran). Towards 1300, a Turkmen Shaykh Safi ad-Din Ishaq (1252–1334) founded a Sufi movement in Ardebil (Iran), in the Azeri region to the west of the Caspian Sea. Around the mid-fifteenth century the Safavid movement adhered to Shiism, constituting by the end of the century a powerful regional force forged into a solid political structure whose military arm was made up of *kizilbash* (*kizilbas*, 'red heads', from the colour of their headgear). The reins of the movement were taken up by the young Isma'il, then around thirteen (1501–1524), who engaged in a merciless propaganda and military campaign against the Aq Qoyunlu, gaining Tabriz. Declaring himself the descendant of the seventh *imam* and therefore the invincible messiah and intermediary of divine authority summoned to exercise temporal power, he was made shah. Isma'il's victories came thick and fast and in a few short years he had conquered Persia and Iraq (1507). In the political arena, thanks to the glue of religion, he managed to couple a Turkish military system with a Persian bureaucracy. His sweeping victories, routing even the Uzbeks in 1510, were abruptly curtailed in 1514 by the crushing defeat at Chaldiran, where his army was decimated by the muskets of the Ottoman Selim. Abandoning expansionistic policies, his successors expended their efforts in keeping at arm's length both the Ottomans in the west and the Uzbeks to the northeast. After a difficult transitional period, under Shah Abbas I (the 1587–1629) the state reached the apex of its power and extension, documented in extraordinary manifestations of patronage that made Isfahan one of the most beautiful cities in the world. In a few years Shah Abbas bolstered Persian presence in the gulf, opening up a highly profitable route to the Orient, and succeeded in defeating the Ottomans, conquering Armenia and Georgia, grabbing the western quarter of Afghanistan and, finally, annexing Kurdistan and Iraq. After a final flourish during the reign of Shah Abbas II (1642–1666), this splendid political construct gradually gave way under pressure following repeated bids for autonomy on the part of local tribes combined with the ineptitude of his successors, who undersold basic resources to the Europeans and often displayed intolerance in the religious sphere. When Sultan Husayn (1694–1722) tried to force the entire population to adopt the Shiite doctrine, a rebellion broke out led by the Afghans, who entered Isfahan in 1722, overthrowing the sultan. Though the Safavid monarch continued to reign in name, true power now lay in the hands of the Afghan Afshars.

Samanids
819–999
Iranian dynasty. Governors from 819 on behalf of the Tahirids of Samarkand, Ferghana, Shash and Herat, independent, under the nominal sovereignty of Baghdad, after the collapse of their suzerains in 874. Towards 900 Isma'il (892–907) brought down the empire of the Saffarids and took possession of Afghanistan and a large part of Persia. A few years later, under Nasir II (914–943), the empire attained its apogee, controlling Baghdad, Persia, Mazandaran (the Persian Gulf) and extending to the borders of India. In 945 the Samanids were gradually worn down by the Buyids, who harried them as far as Transoxiana and Khorasan. Notwithstanding these setbacks, in the second half of the tenth century, the court became the cynosure of cultural life for the entire Persian region. By the end of the century, however, the kingdom was submerged beneath the progressive advance of the Ghaznavids and Qarakhanids.

Seljuqs (also, **Seljuks**)
1038–1157
A Turkic dynasty that reigned over western Turkestan, Persia, Afghanistan, eastern Anatolia, Iraq, Syria, and the Arabian Peninsula, with capitals at Merv (Turkmenistan) and Isfahan (Iran). Originating in Central Asia, between Lake Balhash and the Altai Mountains, the Seljuqs were a clan of the Turkmen federation of Oguz. By the beginning of the tenth century, they were being employed as mercenaries to hold back the advance of Islamic forces. But, around 960, they too converted to Islam and offered their services to the Samanids, settling in the area surrounding Samarkand. When the Samanids were swept aside by the Qarakhanids they joined them against the Ghaznavids. In 1026, when Mahmud of Ghazni in turn defeated the Qarakhanids, Tughril (1038–1063) and Chagri (1038–1060) divided up the territory with their respective capitals at Merv and Isfahan. In 1040 Tughril defeated the Ghaznavids at the great battles of Dandanaqan and briefly extended his possessions into Persia and Kurdistan. Seizing Baghdad from the last of the Buyids (1055) they usurped their predecessor's role as protectors of the caliph and champions of Sunnism, thus legitimizing their power in the eyes of the Islamic world. Under successive masters such as Alp Arslan (1060–1072) and Malik Shah (1072–1092), and thanks to their grand vizier Nizam al-Mulk (1060–1092), the kingdom of the Great Seljuqs (as distinct from the Seljuqs of Rum) flourished and enjoyed marked successes in every field. Conquests came thick and fast: Armenia in 1064, the Holy Sites in 1070, until an overwhelming victory over the Byzantines at Manzikert (1071) brought them to the gates of Anatolia. The dramatic deaths of Malik Shah and Nizam al-Mulk dealt severe blows, however, giving rise to a struggle for the succession and fanning the flames of the inextinguishable tribal autonomy of the Turks. The western part of the kingdom entered a downward spiral, though the eastern branch enjoyed a new period of splendour under Sultan Sanjar (1118–1157). On his death the kingdom fell into the hands of the shahs of the Khwarizm, who, in 1194, also grabbed the western kingdom. Some secondary offshoots of the Seljuqs lingered on such as those in Kerman (1041–1187) and Syria (1094–1117), in addition to the Seljuqs of Rum.

Seljuqs of Rum
1077–1308
Turkic dynasty of Anatolia. Their first capital was at Iznik and, from 1116, at Konya. After the triumph at Manzikert (1071), Qutalmish, a relative of the Great Seljuqs Toghril (Tugrul) and Chagri, founded a new dynasty whose history was to be completely independent from that of the Persian branch, thanks to the increasing role it played in the conflict with the Crusaders. After a century of incessant conflict, their first period of splendour occurred at a relatively late stage under Kilij (Qilich) Arslan II (r. 1156–1192), who kept a firm hold on the kingdom and promoted huge architecture projects and city planning. The state prospered further under Ghiyat ad-Din Keykhosrow (r. 1204–1211), Izz ad-Din (Izzeddin) Keykavus (r. 1211–1219) and Ali ad-Din Kaykobad (r. 1219–1237), after which it began to crumble. In 1243 the Seljuqs confronted the Mongols at Köse Dag (Kose Dagh) near Ankara and suffered a crushing defeat, becoming subordinate to the Persian Ilkhans from 1279 and losing all remnants of independence by 1308.

Shaybanids
1500–1599
An Uzbek dynasty that reigned over Transoxiana and Afghanistan with its capital at Samarkand. The khanate of Transoxiana was founded by Muhammad Shayban (Shiban) Khan (1500–1510), a descendant of Genghis Khan, who governed Turkestan in 1487, terminating the rule of the Timurids by seizing Samarkand in 1497 and continuing to vie for its possession with Babur until 1501. Proceeding to annex Tashkent, Herat and Urgench (Gurganj), he fell in battle against the Safavid Shah Isma'il. Under Abdallah II (1556–1598), khan of Bukhara, the khanate enjoyed a period of glory, but his demise kindled an era of internecine strife and the kingdom fell in the hands of the Jalayrids.

Taifas (kingdoms of)
1031–1110
Designation that covers a number of modestly proportioned Spanish kingdoms of dazzling wealth and rich culture that came to prominence after the breakup of the Andalusian caliphate. The most important were the Abbadids of Seville, the Hudids of Zaragoza, the Zirids of Granada, the Hammudids of Malaga and Algeciras, the Amirids of Valencia and the Aftasids of Badajoz. Their internal squabbles played into the hands of the Christian Reconquista. In 1090 they were eliminated by the Almoravids.

Timurids
1363–1506
Turkic dynasty that reigned over Transoxiana, the Khwarizm, Afghanistan and, until 1405, Iran, Iraq, Syria, eastern Anatolia, part of Transcaucasia and northern India, with a capital at Samarkand and, after 1405, at Herat. The fortune of the dynasty was founded by Timur Leng (or Lenk, known in the West as Tamerlane; 1336–1405), thanks to a resourceful approach that blended military might and opportune alliances. Emir of Kesh from 1360, he seized Samarkand in 1366 and shortly afterwards was recognized as overlord of Transoxiana by the Mongol *ulus* of Chagatai, under whose aegis he undertook a series of campaigns that gained him the Khwarizm. In 1382, making the most of the chaos that ensured after the dissolution of the Ilkhanid Empire, he embarked on the conquest of Persia, defeating the Mozaffarids (1387) and, on reaching Baghdad, overthrowing the Jalayrids in 1393. Over the course of these years, from 1382 he embarked on a series of hard-won campaigns against Tokhtamysh, potentate of the Golden Horde, obtaining a sequence of victories. In 1398 he penetrated as far as India, perpetrating the infamous Sack of Delhi. In 1400 he went on to overrun Syria, retaking Baghdad in 1401 and razing it to the ground. In 1402, near Ankara, he decimated the Ottoman army. The immense wealth amassed during his endless wars attracted some of the finest artists and architects of the time to Samarkand, where they were put to work realizing his enormous projects to despotically tight deadlines. In 1405, shortly after launching a tough winter campaign against China, Timur died. From his capital at Herat Timur's son Shah Rukh (1405–1447) nonetheless managed to maintain part of the state under his sway. Thanks to the patronage of a principal wife, Gohar Shad, the city had become one of the greatest artistic centres of the age. The regions to the west of Afghanistan, however, were to be snatched from the kingdom by the Qara Qoyunlu. Ulugh Beg (1409–1449), grandson of Timur,

governed Samarkand and promoted scholarship, in particular in the field of astronomy. In the second half of the century, the Uzbeks stepped up their depredations and, by 1497, Samarkand fell. There was a final Timurid flourish in Herat, which, under the great Husayn Baiqara (1469–1506), resembled the glorious age of Shah Rukh. The last Timurid, Babur, failed in his attempt to recover Samarkand, going on instead to establish an empire in India, founding the Mughal dynasty.

Tulunids
868–905
Turkish dynasty that reigned over Egypt, Syria and Palestine, with its capital at al-Fustat (Egypt). It was founded by Ibn Tulun, a Turkish slave at the 'Abbasid court who rose to become bodyguard to the caliph. His son Ahmad (868–884), was named governor of Egypt and gained his independence, later also occupying Syria and Palestine. Although relations with the 'Abbasid Empire had improved, eventually, in 905, the Tulunids, exhausted by the revolt of the Qarmatians, were overrun by the caliphate.

Umayyads
661–750
The first dynasty of the Arab caliphs, with their capital at Damascus. Their founder was Muawiya ibn Abu Sufayn (661–680), descendant of Umayya, a member of the tribe of Muhammad, governor of Syria. Defeated by Ali in the election to the caliphate (657), he gained power after the latter's murder (661), in which he was accused of having played a part; he turned the post into a hereditary one, against both Islamic custom and law. Under successive caliphs and in spite of incessant skirmishes with dissident Arab tribes, the state was organized on a solid and enduring basis, in particular by Abd al-Malik (685–705) and al-Walid I (705–715), who advanced to conquer Spain and Oxiana. It is to them that we owe the two most important monuments of early Islam, the Dome of the Rock in Jerusalem and the Great Mosque at Damascus. The empire was subsequently shaken by religious crises and rebellions that gnawed away the prestige of the dynasty and laid the groundwork for the 'Abbasid coup d'état, which ended with the slaughter of the Umayyad family in 750. The only member to survive managed to make his way to al-Andalus where, in 756, he founded the Umayyad kingdom of Spain (al-Andalus).

Umayyads of al-Andalus
756–1031
Caliphs from 929. An Arab dynasty in Spain, with its capital at Cordoba. The dynasty was founded by Abd al-Rahman I (756–788), the only Umayyad of Damascus to escape the massacre perpetrated by the 'Abbasids in 750. Taking shelter in Andalusia, he exploited his prestige and seized power, managing the new position with finesse and insight. The same power politics were adroitly played by his successors Hisham I (788–796) and al-Hakam (796–822), who forged Andalusia (al-Andalus) into a single unified state. This flourishing society played a key role in international trade and remained more than capable of keeping at bay Christian kingdoms in the north and internal dissension at home. The ascension of Abd al-Rahman II (822–852) signalled an exceptional period on the cultural plane that witnessed al-Andalus becoming the heart of Islam in the West. Following an interlude of feebleness at the centre of power, Abd al-Rahman III (912–961) brought the territory to the summit of its development, confirming its independence in 929 by assuming the title of caliph, in open competition with Baghdad, whose prestige was in free-fall. After a series of campaigns extending into Africa, the Umayyads defeated the Fatimids, who at that time were masters in Morocco. Abd al-Rahman III's son al-Hakam II (961–976) consolidated the position of the state, which then suffered a period of stagnation under the inexperienced Hisham (976–1013), though the reins of the state were actually held by the adroit minister, al-Mansur (978–1002). Succeeding years saw the country wracked by dynastic disputes and, in 1031, with the abdication of the last caliph, the great kingdom shattered into a plethora of independent factional principalities, known as the kingdoms of Taifa.

Zangids
1127–1174/1262
Turkic dynasty of Syria and Iraq, with capitals at Aleppo and Damascus. It was founded by Imam ad-Din Zangi (1127–1146), son of an enslaved soldier in the service of the Seljuqs, governor of Iraq from 1127, who rapidly overran Baghdad and Aleppo and earned an honourable reputation thanks to his victories over the Crusaders. The dynasty reached its acme under his son, the great Nur ad-Din (1146–1174), who occupied Damascus. The wealth of the dynasty financed grandiose projects of patronage. In 1174, Saladin, who had trained as a general with the Zangids, expelled the Fatimids from Cairo and then turned on his former masters, undermining their power base. Reigning in Mosul the last branch of the dynasty was decimated by the Mongols in 1262.

Zirids of the Maghreb
971–1152
Berber dynasty of Tunisia and northern Algeria, with a capital at al-Mansuriya, and then at Kairouan and finally Mahdia (Tunisia). A powerful Berber tribe of the region of Algeria, the Banu Ziri were vassals of the Fatimids of Ifriqiya. In 971 Buluggin Ibn Manad, who had managed to become an almost independent governor, extended control from Morocco to Tunisia and founded the dynasty proper. Most noteworthy among his successors were the Zirids of Granada, the future kings of Taifa (1012–1090) and the Hammadids of Algeria (1007–1152).

BIBLIOGRAPHY

The following bibliography contains suggestions for further reading designed for readers approaching this topic for the first time and wishing to explore it more deeply. Unless of special interest, hard-to-obtain and out-of-print works have been omitted, as have articles in specialized journals.

Texts of general character: architecture, the arts and crafts

Blair S. S. and J. M. Bloom, *The Art and Architecture of Islam. 1250–1800*, New Haven – London 1994 (new ed. 1995). Substantial, complete and up-to-date, with a bibliography. Adequately illustrated with photographs.
Burckhardt T., *The Art of Islam: Language and Meaning*, Bloomington [1985] 2002. Stimulating.
Cassanelli R. (ed.), *Il Mediterraneo e l'arte nel Medioevo*, Milan 2000. Well-illustrated, with a comprehensive bibliography.
Critchlow K., *Islamic Patterns. An Analytical and Cosmological Approach*, London 1992. Fascinating and enthralling, with a wealth of explanatory drawings.
Daneshvari A., *Medieval Tomb Towers of Iran. An Iconographical Study*, Lexington 1986. Fundamental critical study on the symbolism of Islamic burial places, with an excellent bibliography.
Enciclopedia universale dell'arte, Venice – Rome, 1958–1967. Contains all the relevant entries. Dated, but important; one of the best works in Italian.
The Encyclopedia of Islam, Leiden 1960 et sq. Fundamental reference work.
Ettinghausen, R., O. Grabar, and M. Jenkins-Madina, *The Art and Architecture of Islam. 650–1250*, New Haven – London 1987 (new ed. 2001). Well-researched; complete and up-to-date, with bibliography. Adequately illustrated with photographs.
Grabar O., *The Mediation of Ornament*, Princeton 1992. Intelligent and penetrating.
Hattstein M. and P. Delius (eds.), *Islam. Art and architecture*, Cologne 2001. Vast but readable synthesis of the highest order, with excellent illustrations and a thorough bibliography.
Hillenbrand R., *Islamic Architecture*, New York 1994. Splendid. Organized by typology rather than by region or timeframe.
Hillenbrand R., *Islamic Art and Architecture*, London 1988. Excellent overview.
Hoag John D., *Islamic Architecture*, London 2004. A handbook.
Khatibi A., and M. Sijelmassi, *The Splendor of Islamic Calligraphy*, London 1976. Enthralling and well illustrated, with specialized bibliography.
Mandel Khan G., *Arabic Script*, New York 2006. Good illustrated introduction, with a bibliography.
Michell G. (ed.), *Architecture of the Islamic World*, London 1978. Interesting thematically arranged introduction with a gazetteer of the chief monuments.
Mozzati L., *Islam*, Milan 2002. An introductory text with many new photographs.
O'Kane B. (ed.), *The Iconography of Islamic Art: Studies in Honour of Robert Hillenbrand*, Edinburgh 2005. Important, with recent research.
Petersen A., *Dictionary of Islamic Architecture*, London 1999. Useful and up-to-date.
Petrucciolі A., *Gardens in the Time of the Great Muslim Empires,* Leiden 1997. Groundbreaking, multifaceted approach to the topic, with a first-rate bibliography.
Pope A. U. and P. Ackermann (eds.), *A Survey of Persian Art from Prehistoric Times to the Present*, 12 vols., London – New York 1938–1939 et sq. Partly superseded, but a key source of reference.
Porter V., *Islamic Tiles*, London 1995. Succinct and well illustrated.
Ward R., *Islamic Metalwork*, London 1993. A concise introduction to metallurgy.

Texts of general character: history and religion

Bausani A. (ed.), *Il Qur'an*, Milan 1988. Possibly the best Italian edition, with a critical introduction, numerous comments and a basic bibliography.
The Cambridge History of Iran, Cambridge 1968. Important reference work.
The Cambridge History of Islam, Cambridge 1970 et seq. Reference work.
Campanini M. (ed.), *Dizionario dell'Islam*, Milan 2005. Practical and up-to-date.
Clifford E. B., *The New Islamic Dynasties. A Chronological and Genealogical Manual*, Edinburgh 1996. Reference work.
Crespi G., *The Arabs in Europe*, New York 1986. Good in every respect: text, pictures, bibliography.
Di Nola A. M., *Muhammad*, Rome 1996. Excellent and concise critical biography with interesting bibliography on pre-Islamic Arabia.
Enciclopedia delle religioni, Milan 1993. Useful.
The Encyclopaedia of Islam, Leiden 1960. Fundamental reference work.
Lapidus I., *History of Islamic Societies*, Cambridge 2002. Exhaustive introduction providing a key to the understanding of the subject up to the present-day; with an extensive bibliography.
Mandel Khan G., *Islam*, Milan 2006. Illustrated introduction.
Mozzati L., *Islam*, Milan 2008. Introduction with illustrations.
Roux J. P., *Histoire des turcs*, Paris 2000 (new ed.). The best summary of Turkish history from the origins to today.
Runciman S., *History of the Crusades* 3 vols., Harmondsworth 1993 (new ed.). Essential.

Formative period: 'Umayyads, 'Abbasids

Creswell K. A. C., *A Short Account of Early Islamic Architecture*, Baltimore 1958, Cairo 1989. Well-documented overview revised with essential and otherwise unavailable studies by the author. With a bibliography.
Curatola G. (ed.), *Iraq. The Art and Architecture of Mesopotamia*, New York 2007.
Gabrieli F. et al., *Carlo Magno e Muhammad*, Milan 1986. Fine all-round study in terms of text, illustrative material and bibliography.
Grabar O., *The Formation of Islamic Art* [1972], London 2002. A remarkable if involved analysis. With a bibliography.
Hawting G. D. *The First Dynasty of Islam: The Umayyad Caliphate 661–750 AD.*
Gli Omayyadi, Milan 2000. Carefully illustrated guide with relevant introductory text.
Stierlin H., *Islam. From Baghdad to Cordoba*, Cologne 2009. Readable, adequate text with wonderful photos.

Spain

L'arte mudejar, Milan 2001. Well-illustrated guide.
Barrucand M., and A. Bednorz, *Moorish Architecture*, Cologne 1999. The best popular synthesis, with excellent illustrations and extensive bibliography.
Goodwin G., *Islamic Spain*, New York 1990. A good guide to the architecture.
Hintzen-Bohlen B., *Andalusia Art and Architecture*, Cologne 2000. Delightful synthesis, with fine illustrations.
Leroy B., *L'Espagne au moyen-âge*, Paris 1988. Good historical portrait, with bibliography.
Schreiber H., *Gli arabi in Spagna*, Milan 1982. Revealing.

Maghreb

Hill D., L. Golvin, and R. Hillebrand., *Islamic Architecture in North Africa*, London 1976. A brilliant reference, with bibliography.
Ifriqiya, London 2002. Reasonably illustrated guide with a succinct introduction.
Mezzine, M. *Andalusian Morocco,* London 2001. Adequately illustrated guide with a concise introduction.
Il Medioevo arabo e islamico dell'Africa del Nord, Milan 1991. Exellent and with fine illustrations and a bibliography.

Iran

Curatola G., and G. Scarcia, *Iran. Art and architecture of Persia*, New York 2007. Interesting and well illustrated.
Hillenbrand R., *Persian Painting: from the Mongols to the Qajars*, 2001. Important.
Pope A. U., and P. Ackermann (eds.), *A Survey of Persian Art from Prehistoric Times to the Present*, 12 vols., London – New York 1938–1939 et sq.. Monumental and exceptional library reference work.

Central Asia

Boulnois L., *Silk Road*, Hong Kong 2003. An approachable classic.
Giammanco R., *La più lunga frontiera dell'Islam*, Bari 1983. Fascinating and penetrating, Central Asia from unusual angle.
Roux J. P., *L'Asie centrale*, Paris 1997. Panoramic fresco, with important bibliography.
Uhlig H., *La via della seta*, Milan 1991. Quality popular approach.

Egypt

Allen T., *Ayyubid Architecture*, California 1996–1999. Extremely exhaustive, with bibliography.
El-Banessi S. A. (ed.) *Mamluk Art*, Brussels 2001. Reasonably illustrated guidebook.
Behrens-Abouseif D., *Islamic Architecture in Cairo. An Introduction*, Cairo 1989. Excellent and clear synthesis with bibliography.
Williams C., *Islamic Monuments in Cairo. A Practical Guide*, Cairo 1985. Easy to read and concise.

Seljuks

Ertugh A. (ed.), *The Seljuks*, Istanbul 1991. Brief text exceptionally illustrated.
Mirfendereski F. N. and M. A., and A. F. Zonuzi, *Ceramica nell'architettura in Persia*, Florence 1992. Fine text, splendid photographs, with bibliography.
Pope A. U., *Persian Architecture*, London 1965. Succinct and illuminating.
Pope A. U., and P. Ackermann (gen. eds.), *A Survey of Persian Art from Prehistoric Times to the Present*, 12 vols., London – New York 1938–1939 et sq. Monumental and exceptional library reference.
Roux J. P., *La religion des turcs et des mongoles*, Paris 1984. Sometimes tough going, but important.
Sözen M., *The Evolution of Turkish Art and Architecture*, Istanbul 1987. Modest introduction, if at times tendentious; well illustrated.
Stierlin H. and A., *Turkey. Art and Architecture*, Cologne 1998. Splendid introduction, with first-rate illustrations.

Mongols

Phillips E. D., *The Mongols*, London 1969. Interesting historical approach.
Pope A. U., and P. Ackermann (gen. eds.), *A Survey of Persian Art from Prehistoric Times to the Present*, 12 vols., London – New York

1938–1939 et sq. Monumental and exceptional library reference.
Roux J. P., *Histoire de l'empire mongol*, Paris 1993. Fundamental and enthralling; with a detailed bibliography.
Roux J. P., *La religion des turcs et des mongoles*, Paris 1984. Not always easy to read, but important; with bibliography.

Timurids

Ashrafi M., *The Samarkand Miniature Paintings of the XV Century*, Tashkent 1996. Good text on the finest works of Islamic miniature.
Canby S. R., *Persian Painting*, London 1993. Concise, clear and well illustratated.
Golombek L., and D. Wilber, *The Timurid Architecture of Iran and Turan*, 2 vols., Princeton 1988. Monumental specialist inventory of excellent quality.
Jackson P., and L. Lockart (eds.), *The Timurid and Safavid Periods. The Cambridge History of Iran*, 6 vols., Cambridge 1986. A reference.
Mirfenderesky F. N. and M. A., and A. F. Zonuzi, *Ceramica nell'architettura in Persia*, Florence 1992. Fine text, glorious pictures.
Pavaloi K., *Uzbekistan*, London 1997. Splendid all-round historical and cultural synthesis with fine photographs and bibliography.
Pope A. U., *Persian Architecture*, London 1965. Succinct and enlightening.
Pope A. U., and P. Ackermann (eds.), *A Survey of Persian Art from Prehistoric Times to the Present*, 12 vols., London – New York 1938–1939 et sq. Monumental and exceptional library reference.
Roux J. P., *Tamerlane*, Paris 1991. The best biography written by one of the foremost specialists in Central Asia, with bibliography.

Ottomans

Babinger F., *Mehmet the Conqueror and his Time*, Berkeley [1954], 1992. Still essential.
Bartoli L., E. Galdieri, and F. Gurrieri, *Mimar Sinan. Architettura tra Oriente e Occidente*, Florence 1992. The best work on Sinan in Italian.
Bombali S. J. Shaw, *The History of the Ottoman Empire and Modern Turkey*, 2 vols., Cambridge 1977.
Clot A., *Suleiman the Magnificent*, London 2005. Worthwhile popular study.
Ducellier A., *Le drame de Byzance*, Paris 1986. Exhaustive and thorough, with bibliography.
Gennaro P., *Istanbul: l'opera di Sinan*, Milan 1992. Skilful inventory with concise text and a wealth of plans and photographs.
Goodwin G., *A History of Ottoman Architecture*, Baltimore – London 1971. Essential; an excellent and complete analysis, though the dearth of illustration is a drawback.
Goodwin G., *Sinan, Ottoman Architecture and its Values Today*, London 2001 (new ed.). First-rate.
Inalcic H., *The Ottoman Empire. The Classical Age 1300–1600*, London 1973. High-quality historical synthesis.
Kuran A., *Sinan, the Grand Old Master of Ottoman Architecture*, Washington – Istanbul 1987. Perhaps the finest study on Sinan.
Necipoglu, N. *The Age of Sinan*, London, 2005.
Runciman S., *Fall of Constantinople 1453*, London 1963. Reference.
Sözen M., *The Evolution of Turkish Art and Architecture*, Istanbul 1987. Reasonable introduction, well illustrated, occasionally arguable.
Stierlin H., *Turkey*, Cologne 1999. Excellent introduction richly illustrated.
Vellmans T. (ed.), *Bisanzio, Costantinopoli, Istanbul*, Milan 2008. Good and up-to-date.

Safavids

Canby S. R., *The Golden Age of Persian Art. 1501–1722*, London 1999. Good text by one of today's best scholars.
Canby S. R., *Persian Painting*, London 1993. Concise and well illustrated.
Jackson P., and L. Lockart (gen. eds.), *The Timurid and Safavid Periods. The Cambridge History of Iran*, 6 vols., Cambridge 1986. Reference work.
Mirfenderesky F. N. and M. A., and A. F. Zonuzi, *Ceramica nell'architettura in Persia*, Florence 1992. Good text, splendid pictures.
Pope A. U., *Persian Architecture*, London 1965. Succinct and enlightening.
Pope A. U., and P. Ackermann (gen. eds.), *A Survey of Persian Art from Prehistoric Times to the Present*, 12 vols., London – New York 1938–1939 et sq. Monumental and exceptional library reference.

Medieval and Mughal India

Asher C. B., *The New Cambridge History of India. Architecture of Mughal India*, Cambridge 1992. First-rate, profound, up-to-date, with a bibliography.
Behr H. G., *Moghul imperatori dell'India*, Milan 1985. Very readable introduction with a good bibliography for memoirs and travellers' accounts.
Brown P., *Indian Architecture. The Islamic Period* (6th ed.), Mumbai 1975. A classic of research with fine plans, let down by decidedly mediocre photos.
Koch E., *Mughal Architecture. An Outline of its History and Development. 1526–1858*, Munich 1991. Solid work.
Michell G., and M. Zebrowsky, *The New Cambridge History of India. Architecture and Art of the Deccan Sultanates*, Cambridge 1999. Recent and thorough, the best on the subject, with a bibliography.
Nabi Khan Ahmad, *Islamic Architecture in South Asia*, Oxford 2003. Excellent and up-to-date.
Okada A., *Indian Miniatures of the Mughal Court*, New York 1992. Splendid and well-illustrated synthesis, with bibliography.
Tillotson G.H.R., *India Moghul*, Milan 1992. Excellent, concise guide.

Memoirs and travellers' accounts, poets and writers

Anon., *Storia segreta dei mongoli*, Milan 1995. Genghis Khan before he became Genghis Khan. A lively picture of Mongol society written by a contemporary of the events.
Babur, *Babur-nama*, English translation, New Delhi 1970. The colourful and fascinating memoirs of the Mughal emperor Babur compiled in the 16th century.
The Baburnama: Memoirs of Babur, Prince and Emperor (tr. Wheeler M. Thackston), New Juvayni, Ala al-Din Ata Malik [1226–1283], *Genghis Khan: The History of the World-Conqueror* (tr. John Andrew Boyle), Seattle 1997 York 2002.
Bombaci A., *La letteratura turca, con un profilo della letteratura mongola*, Milan 1969. Good introduction with an anthology of texts.
Brandi C., *Persia mirabile*, in *Viaggi in Oriente*, Rome 1993. A poetical interpretation by a major art critic.
Byron R., *La via per l'Oxiana*, Milan 1993. Classic of English travel literature describing his journey in 1933. Unique, unmissable.
Clavijo Ruy Gonzalez de, *Viaggio a Samarcanda 1403–1406*, Rome 1999. A Spanish ambassador at the court of Tamerlane. Extremely interesting.
Damiani, Anita. *Enlightened Observers: British Travellers to the Near East 1715–1855*, Beirut, 1979.
Gabrieli F., Vacca V. (ed.), *Antologia della letteratura araba*, Milan 1976. Important selection of tests with a brief introduction.
Harvey, W. and N. J. Dawood (eds.), *Tales from the Arabian Nights*), Penguin, London, 2004. A modern translation.
Ibn Battuta, *Rihla*, superb Italian translation of selected passages ed. Gabrieli F., in *Poesia e avventura nel mondo arabo*, Florence 1988 (for a complete French ed., see *Voyages, La Decouverte*, Paris 1982). An early 14th-century Marco Polo from the Maghreb.
Ibn Battuta, *Travels in Asia and Africa 1325–1354* (tr. and ed. H. A. R. Gibb), London 1929.
Inea Bushnaq, *Favole del mondo arabo*, Milan1987. Instructive.
Istanbul, Viaggi d'autore, Antologia di testi, Milan 1996.
Khayyam O., *Quartine* (ed. A. Bausani), Einaudi 1956. The finest translation of the Persian poet most loved in the West.
Maillart E., *Vagabonda nel Turkestan*, Turin 1995. A woman alone in Turkestan in the Stalin years; extraordinary.
Maillart E., *La via crudele*, Turin 1993. Two women drive from Europe to Kabul in 1939. Astonishing.
Marco Polo, *Il Milione*, Milan 1975. Probably the best edition.
Le mille e una notte (*Alf laila wa laila*), anthology probably compiled in Iran in the 9th century from a collection of tales of probably Indian origin, and perhaps dating from the precious century. The most famous anthology of Arab and Islamic tales.
Nezami, *Il libro della fortuna di Alessandro*, Milan 1997. A romanticised Alexander seen from a 12th-century Islamic point of view.
Persia, Viaggi d'autore, Antologia di testi, Milan 1997.
Rumi, *Poesie mistiche* (ed. A. Bausani 1st ed.) Milan 1980. First-rate introduction.
Searight, Sarah. *The British in the Middle East*, London, 1969
Shepherd, Naomi. *The Zealous Intruders. From Napoleon to the Dawn of Zionism – the Explorers, Artists, Tourists, Pilgrims, and Visionaries who opened Palestine to the West*, San Francisco, 1987
Starkey, Paul, and Janet Starkey (ed.), *Travellers to Egypt*, London – New York, 1998.
Vambery A., *Un falso derviscio a Samarcanda*, Milan 1997. Travelling in disguise through the Turkmen steppes and the fierce Khanates of 1870. Exceptional.

Front cover: Mimar Sinan, roof of the Sehzade mosque, Istanbul, Turkey, detail, see page 34
Pages 2–3: Ulu Cami ('Great Mosque'), detail of minaret, 12th century, Artuqid dynasty Hasankeyf, Turkey.
Pages 4–5: Mudjur carpet, detail, 20th century, Ziya Bozoglu Collection, Perugia.
Pages 6–7: Mausoleum of Humayun, 1560, Mughal period, Delhi, India

Prestel Verlag, Munich
A Member of Verlagsgruppe Random House GmbH

Prestel Verlag
Königinstrasse 9
80539 Munich
Tel. +49 (0)89 24 29 08-300
Fax +49 (0)89 24 29 08-335

Prestel Publishing Ltd.
4 Bloomsbury Place
London WC1A 2QA
Tel. +44 (0)20 7323-5004
Fax +44 (0)20 7636-8004

Prestel Publishing
900 Broadway, Suite 603
New York, NY 10003
Tel. +1 (212) 995-2720
Fax +1 (212) 995-2733

www.prestel.com

Library of Congress Control Number: 2009942605

British Library Cataloguing-in-Publication Data: a catalogue record for this book is available from the British Library;
Deutsche Nationalbibliothek holds a record of this publication in the Deutsche Nationalbibliografie; detailed bibliographical data can be found under: http://dnb.d-nb.de

Prestel books are available worldwide. Please contact your nearest bookseller or one of the above addresses for information concerning your local distributor.

Translation from the Italian: D. Radzinowicz (pp. 13–219, 310–320), Paul Aston, Sliema, and Tessa Frank, Ludlow (pp. 220–309)
Editorial direction: Curt Holtz
Copyediting: Jane Michael, Munich
Layout and page design: Giorgia Dalla Pietà
Production: Büro für Lektorat & Producing, Dr. Doris Hansmann, Cologne
Typesetting: ce redaktionsbüro, Heinsberg
Printing and binding: Passavia Druckservice GmbH, Passau

FSC
Mixed Sources
Product group from well-managed forests and other controlled sources
Cert no. SGS-COC-003859
www.fsc.org
© 1996 Forest Stewardship Council

Verlagsgruppe Random House FSC-DEU-0100
The FSC-certified paper *EuroBulk* is produced by mill Sappi, Biberist, Switzerland.

Printed in Germany

ISBN 978-3-7913-4455-3

Photo credits

Russian Academy of Sciences of St Petersburg: pp. 14 left, 54, 91, 159, 189 left, 212 Akg-Images, Berlin: / Bildarchiv Steffens, pp. 52, 83 right, 84, 87 below, 95 left; / British Library, pp. 17, 48; / British Museum, p. 275 right; / Gérard Degeorge, pp. 88, 142, 179, 261; / Werner Forman, pp. 22 left, 147; / Philippe Maillard, pp. 60, 81 below; / Russian Picture Service, p. 216 above © Alamy / Granataimages, Milan: / Charles Bowman, p. 68 above; / Allen Brown, p. 195; / Eddie Gerald, pp. 98, 99; / Edinburgh University Library, p. 201 above; / GM Photo Images, pp. 204-205; / Israel Images, p. 68 below; / Betty Johnson, p. 181; / Nick Ledger, p. 138 right; / Bill Lyons, p. 72 above; / Navin Mistry, p. 286; / B. O'Kane, p. 64; / Pearlimage, p. 287 above; / Pep Roig, p. 303; / Jane Sweeney, p. 129 Archivio Mondadori Electa, Milan / Paolo Manusardi: pp. 276, 277 Archivo Oronoz, Madrid: pp. 55, 113, 118, 120, 121 below, 140 Art Gallery and Museum, Glasgow: p. 278 Biblioteca Apostolica Vaticana, Roma: p. 141 / Yann Arthus-Bertrand, pp. 106, 234-235; / Paul H. Kuiper, p. 246 left; / Abilio Lope, p. 86; / Olivier Martel, p. 111 above; / Boris Roessler/dpa, p. 263 above; / Hans Georg Roth, p. 40; / Smithsonian Institution, Washington DC p. 150; / Frédéric Soltan/ Sygma, p. 70; / Arthur Thévenart, p. 193; / Ruggero Vanni, p. 242; / Sandro Vannini, p. 102; / Nik Wheeler, p. 87 above; / Adam Woolfitt, p. 289 below, Davids Samling, Copenhagen: p. 51 © Foto Scala, Florence: p. 79; / BPK, Bildagentur Museen zu Berlin, pp. 83 above, 175, 201 below, 202; / V&A Images/Victoria and Albert Museum, London, pp. 280, 281, 308 below; / 2009 The Metropolitan Museum of Art, New York / Art Resource, p. 173 Iparmüveszeti Muzesi, Budapest: pp. 248, 249 Andrea Jemolo, Rome: p. 29 Leemage, Paris: / Aisa, pp. 105, 133 above; / Jean Bernard, p. 119; / Heritage Images, pp. 50, 273; / Marthelot, p. 85 Lessing / Archivio Contrasto, Milan: pp. 69, 101, 104 above, 109, 110, 115, 130 below, 136, 146, 161, 174, 283 right Luca Mozzati, Milan: pp. 2-3, 6-7, 14 right, 15, 18, 19, 22 right, 23, 26, 27, 28, 30, 31, 32, 33, 34, 35, 36, 37, 38, 39, 42, 43, 44, 45, 46, 47 above, 49, 53, 56, 57, 58, 59, 61 below, 62, 66, 67, 71, 73, 74, 78, 79, 77 above, 78, 80, 82, 94, 95 above, 96, 97, 103, 107, 108, 111 below, 112, 114, 121 above, 122, 123, 124, 125, 126, 127, 129, 132, 133 below, 134, 138 left, 139, 143, 144, 145, 148, 149, 153, 154, 155, 156, 157, 162, 163 above, 164, 165, 166, 167, 168, 169, 170, 171, 172, 176, 177, 178, 180, 182, 183, 184, 185 above, 188, 189 left, 190, 191, 192, 194, 196, 197, 198, 199, 206, 207, 208-209, 210, 211, 216 below, 217, 218, 219, 220, 221 above, 222, 223, 224, 225, 226-227, 228, 229, 230, 231, 232, 233, 236, 237, 238, 239, 240, 241, 243, 247, 252, 253 left, 254, 255, 256, 257, 258, 259, 260, 262, 263 below, 264, 265, 266, 267 above, 270-271, 272, 279, 282, 283 left, 284, 285, 287 below, 288, 289 above, 291, 292, 293, 294, 295, 296, 297, 298, 299, 300, 301, 302, 304, 305 State Hermitage Museum, St Petersburg: p. 131 Mevlevi Museum, Konya: p. 187 below Museum of Art, Philadelphia: p. 250 Österreichisches Museum für angewandte Kunst, Vienna: pp. 308 above, 309 The Art Archive, London/ Bibliothèque Nationale de France, Paris, p. 161/ British Library, London, p. 12/ Gianni Dagli Orti, pp. 89, 152/ Musée du Louvre, Paris / Gianni Dagli Orti, pp. 63, 117, 130 above/ Museum of Islamic Art, Cairo / Gianni Dagli Orti, p. 95 right/ Palazzo Pitti, Florence / Alfredo Dagli Orti, p. 104 below/ Topkapi Saray Müzesi, Istanbul / Gianni Dagli Orti, p. 215 / Turkish and Islamic Art Museum, Istanbul / Gianni Dagli Orti, p. 61 above / University Library, Istanbul / Gianni Dagli Orti, p. 245/ The Bridgeman Art Library, London: pp. 20, 41, 47 below, 77 below, 81 above, 90, 100, 135, 137, 160, 213, 215 above, 221 below, 244, 267 below, 268-269, 307 / The British Museum, London: pp. 83 left, 92, 93, 158, 203, 215 below, 246 right, 274, 306/ The Cleveland Museum of Art, Cleveland: p. 200 / Topkapi Saray Müzesi, Istanbul: p. 251 right / Türk ve Islam Eserleri Müzesi, Istanbul: pp. 185, 186, 187 above

We have made every effort to identify the copyright holders. If there are any omissions, please contact the publisher.